INTERNATIONAL RELATIONS
IN PERSPECTIVE

INTERNATIONAL RELATIONS IN PERSPECTIVE

A Reader

Henry R. Nau, Editor
George Washington University

CQ PRESS

A Division of SAGE
Washington, D.C.

CQ Press
2300 N Street, NW, Suite 800
Washington, DC 20037

Phone: 202-729-1900; toll-free, 1-866-4CQ-PRESS (1-866-427-7737)

Web: www.cqpress.com

Cover design: Naylor Design Inc.
Cover photos: iStock
Typesetting: C&M Digitals (P) Ltd.

⊗ The paper used in this publication exceeds the requirements of the American National Standard for Information Sciences—Permanence of Paper for Printed Library Materials, ANSI Z39.48-1992.

Printed and bound in the United States of America

18 19 20   6 7 8

Library of Congress Cataloging-in-Publication Data

International relations in perspective : a reader / Henry R. Nau, editor.
    p. cm.
Includes bibliographical references.
ISBN 978-1-60426-993-2 (pbk. : alk. paper) 1. International relations. 2. World politics—20th century. 3. World politics—21st century. I. Nau, Henry R. II. Title.

JZ1305.I5644 2009
327—dc22

                                                        2009042274

To Norman J. Padelford, professor at M.I.T.,
who first sparked my interest in international affairs

CONTENTS

PREFACE

Collections of scholarly and contemporary essays (readers) in the field of international affairs generally seek to achieve two objectives. First, they introduce students to the seminal articles in the field that lay out the most important concepts of international relations. Second, they offer supplementary readings, often to a related textbook, that illuminate persisting debates in the field.

This reader, *International Relations in Perspective,* which accompanies the textbook *Perspectives on International Relations: Power, Institutions, and Ideas,* accomplishes these two objectives and adds a third. It illustrates more systematically and consistently than other readers how each of these articles, seminal and contemporary, uses and emphasizes the various theoretical perspectives and levels of analysis for understanding international relations. The reader thus extends the unique contribution of the textbook, which integrates theory and events seamlessly to show that all students of international affairs, even the most famous and popular, have to use perspectives and levels of analysis to make any sense of an infinitely complex world.

The reader is organized following the table of contents of *Perspectives on International Relations,* making it easy to pair the essays with corresponding chapters in the textbook dealing with security, international political economy, and global issues. Each article is introduced by a headnote that not only highlights the contribution of the article but also indicates the theoretical perspective and level of analysis that the article illustrates. Sometimes, the headnotes also raise questions that lead students to ask critical questions about the articles.

The essays are appropriate for an undergraduate audience and, in the aggregate, represent the range of alternative opinion about important issues. They have been carefully edited to preserve the complexity of the scholarship but also to capture the heart of an argument. Instructors will find that the book not only complements *Perspectives on International Relations* but also stands on its own as a book of readings for just about any course focusing on international relations.

As always, many colleagues and coworkers have contributed to putting this reader together. CQ Press solicited suggestions from many quarters and assembled an advisory committee whose help was indispensable. My thanks go out to all of them:

Victor Asal, SUNY Albany
Alice Ba, University of Delaware
Daniel Braaten, University of Nebraska–Lincoln
Gitika Commuri, California State University–Bakersfield
Kathleen Hancock, University of Texas–San Antonio (Downtown)
Paul Hensel, University of North Texas
Katia Levintova, University of Wisconsin–Green Bay
Timothy Lim, California State University–Los Angeles
Mary Manjikian, Regent University
Todd Myers, Grossmont College
Jennifer Ramos, Loyola Marymount University
Maria Post Rublee, University of Texas
Cameron D. Theis, University of Missouri
Patricia Weitsman, Ohio University
Andrew Yeo, Catholic University

My greatest debt, as with the textbook, goes to Elise Frasier, the acquisitions and development editor at CQ Press who has shepherded these publications since the beginning. I am grateful not only to her but also to Brenda Carter, Charisse Kiino, and others at CQ Press who kept the team in place and ensured the continuity that makes it not only productive but fun to work with this press. Special thanks, too, goes to Gwenda Larsen, who did the production work on the reader as well as the textbook and often worked late hours to meet deadlines and move the books to market. Similarly, Kate Davey, in the face of very tight deadlines, did exceptional legwork to secure and negotiate permissions for the pieces in this volume. Once again Julie Nemer, who has copyedited all of my books over the past ten years, did her usual magic to catch wayward errors of syntax and turn them into artful expressions of clarity.

I dedicate the reader to Norman J. Padelford, my professor at M.I.T., who first ignited my interest in international affairs as an undergraduate student. He and his wife, Helen, befriended not only me but also my sweetheart at the time and now my wife, Marion (Micki), during the crucial year in which we decided to spend the rest of our lives together. One of the Padelford's daughters, Margaret (Peggy) Karns, remains a friend and colleague in the field of international relations, most recently at the University of Dayton.

Introduction

WHY WE DISAGREE ABOUT INTERNATIONAL RELATIONS

I.1

THE DILEMMA OF SCIENTIFIC MAN

Hans J. Morgenthau

> Hans J. Morgenthau, known in American political science as the father of classical realism, attacks the philosophy of liberalism, which holds that the social world can be understood in the same rational terms as the natural world. Because this liberal faith repeatedly fails, humankind is subject to antiliberal reactions such as fascism. It is better, according to Morgenthau, to make "the assumption that power politics, rooted in the lust for power which is common to all men, is for this reason inseparable from social life itself." We apply reason to politics (notice his commitment to rationalist perspectives and methodologies, not critical theory or constructivist methodologies), but reason never supplies a definitive answer independent of the material circumstances of individual human beings, including scholars. For Morgenthau, power conditions the pursuit of reason, while philosophy (ideas) remains the elusive object of that pursuit. Can you see why he is first and foremost a realist, although as a classical realist he is also interested in the pursuit of ideas/values?

The Modern Temper

Two moods determine the attitude of our civilization to the social world: confidence in the power of reason, as represented by modern science, to solve the social problems of our age and despair at the ever renewed failure of scientific reason to solve them. That mood of despair is not new to our civilization, nor is it peculiar to it. The intellectual and moral history of mankind is the story of

Source: Hans J. Morgenthau, "The Dilemma of Scientific Man," in *Scientific Man vs. Power Politics* (Chicago: University of Chicago Press, 1946), 1–10.

inner insecurity, of the anticipation of impending doom, of metaphysical anxieties. These are rooted in the situation of man as a creature which, being conscious of itself, has lost its animal innocence and security and is now forever striving to recapture this innocence and security in religious, moral, and social worlds of its own. What is new in the present situation is not the existence of these anxieties in popular feeling but their strength and confusion, on the one hand, and their absence in the main currents of philosophy and political thought, on the other.

* * *

Yet the very crisis of our civilization reveals itself in the tenacity with which it clings to its assumptions in the face of ever more potent signs that its rationalist philosophy cannot give meaning to the experiences of the mid-twentieth century. Our civilization assumes that the social world is susceptible to rational control conceived after the model of the natural sciences, while the experiences, domestic and international, of the age contradict this assumption. However, instead of asking itself whether an assumption such as this is in need of revision, the age defends its assumptions to the utmost and, by doing so, involves itself still deeper in the contradictions between its philosophy and its experience. In the end, the ever widening gap between philosophy and experience paralyzes both thought and action. The age becomes unable to accept either its invalid philosophy (for its experience contradicts it) or a more valid alternative (for its insecure philosophy cannot admit of change); it can no longer face either its unsolved problems or their solutions. It becomes an age, first, of uneasy confusion, then, of cynical despair; and, finally, it risks being overwhelmed by the enemies from within and from without.

The Crisis of Philosophy

When speaking of philosophy we are referring to the largely unconscious intellectual assumptions by which the age lives, its basic convictions as to the nature of man and society, which give meaning to thought and action. The main characteristic of this philosophy is the reliance on reason to find through a series of logical deductions from either postulated or empirical premises the truths of philosophy, ethics, and politics alike, and through its own inner force to re-create reality in the image of these truths. This philosophy has found its classical realization in the rationalism of the seventeenth and eighteenth centuries. Yet its influence extends beyond these centuries and, as a mode of thought apart from any particular school of philosophy, dominates the modern mind. While rationalism in the classical sense derives its postulates from a priori premises, since the latter part of the eighteenth century, philosophy has tended to seek its foundation in experience and to become a science. Aside from the continuing influence which the original rationalistic philosophy exerts in our civilization under the guise of scientific terminologies, seventeenth- and eighteenth-century rationalism and the mode of thought prevailing in the nineteenth and twentieth centuries have, however, two qualities in common, both of which are rooted in rationalistic assumptions: the conception of the social and the physical world as being intelligible through the same rational processes, however these processes are to be defined, and the conviction that understanding in terms of these rational processes is all that is needed for the rational control of the social and the physical world. From the seventeenth century to the present, rationalism has maintained the unity under reason of the social and the physical world and the ability of the human mind to mold both worlds through the application of the same rational principles.[1]

In the nineteenth and twentieth centuries, the belief in science has been the main manifestation of this mode of thought. This belief in science is the one intellectual trait which sets our age apart from preceding periods of history. Whatever different philosophic, economic, and political beliefs people may hold, they are united in the conviction that science is able, at least potentially, to solve all the problems of man. In this view, the problems of society and nature are essentially identical and the solution of social problems depends upon the quantitative extension of the method of the natural sciences to the social sphere....

On the political scene this mode of thought is most typically represented by the political philosophy of liberalism. Yet it is not limited to the adherents of liberal political principles but permeates nonliberal thought as well and has thus become typical of the political thinking of the age. Whatever else may separate the White House from the Kremlin, liberals from conservatives, all share the belief that if not now, at least ultimately, politics can be replaced by science, however differently defined.

The rationalist mode of thought has remained virtually unchanged since the turn of the eighteenth century, while conditions of life in the same period have undergone the most profound changes in recorded history. We think in terms of the outgoing eighteenth century and live in terms of the mid-twentieth. If the philosophical and political ideas of the eighteenth century would represent eternal verities under the conditions of a particular time and place, they would be able to guide the thought and action of our time as well as of any other. There have been philosophies which were at least partly of this kind, such as the political philosophies of Plato and Aristotle, but the philosophy of the eighteenth century is not among them. It is, on the contrary, a philosophical structure which gives the appearance of eternal verities to certain anthropological, social, and political assumptions which are true, if at all, only under the conditions of a particular historic experience. The historic experience of the Industrial Revolution and the rise of the middle classes has given way to different historic configurations, but the philosophy of the epoch still dominates the Western mind as though its tenets were not subject to the revising processes of history.

The philosophy of rationalism has misunderstood the nature of man, the nature of the social world, and the nature of reason itself. It does not see that man's nature has three dimensions: biological, rational, and spiritual. By neglecting the biological impulses and spiritual aspirations of man, it misconstrues the function reason fulfils within the whole of human existence; it distorts the problem of ethics, especially in the political field; and it perverts the natural sciences into an instrument of social salvation for which neither their own nature nor the nature of the social world fits them.

As a political philosophy, rationalism has misconstrued the nature of politics and of political action altogether. The period between the two world wars, which saw its triumph in theory and in practice, witnessed also its intellectual, moral, and political bankruptcy. History, it is true, has its accidents.... Yet the political and military catastrophes of the thirties and early forties and the political crises of the mid-forties bear too uniform a pattern to be attributed to accidents or to the shortcomings of individuals alone. They are but the outward manifestations of an intellectual, moral, and political disease which has its roots in the basic philosophic assumptions of the age.

The Challenge of Fascism

It would be tempting yet rash to take it for granted that those who believe in these assumptions were victorious in war because they believe in them. Military victory proves only what it actually signifies: that militarily one group of men is superior to another. Those men may also excel in philosophic insight, moral wisdom, and statecraft; but if they do, they do so by virtue of their excellence in these respective fields and not because they have shown themselves to be adept in the art of warfare. The monopoly of the atomic bomb may coincide with a monopoly in virtue; but no necessity makes the latter an attribute of the former. The fact alone that Western civilization could completely misunderstand the intellectual, moral, and political challenge of fascism and be brought to the brink of disaster by those very forces it had defeated on the battlefield but twenty years before should raise doubts in the soundness of its philosophy, morality, and statecraft.

The very appearance of fascism not only in Germany and Italy but in our own midst ought to have convinced us that the age of reason, of progress, and of peace, as we understood it from the teachings of the eighteenth and nineteenth centuries, had become a reminiscence of the past. Fascism is not, as we prefer to believe, a mere temporary retrogression into irrationality, an atavistic revival of autocratic and barbaric rule. In its mastery of the technological attainments and potentialities of the age, it is truly progressive—were not the propaganda machine of Goebbels and the gas chambers of Himmler models of technical rationality?—and in its denial of the ethics of Western civilization it reaps the harvest of a philosophy which clings to the tenets of Western civilization without understanding its foundations. In a sense it is, like all real revolutions, but the receiver of the bankrupt age that preceded it.

The Answer

Not only the condition of Western civilization but also the task of its defender can be learned from the experience of fascism. For the gap between the conditions of life and the official philosophies, which today threatens to swallow Western civilization, preceded the triumph of fascism in Europe. Man, even the most "practical" … cannot live without a philosophy which gives meaning to his existence, by explaining it in terms of causality, rationalizing it in terms of philosophy proper, and justifying it in terms of ethics. A philosophy as a system of intellectual assumptions is static; life is in constant flux. Life is always in a "period of transition," by which standard phrase the age reveals its embarrassment at its intellectual inability to cope with the experience of modern life. In the face of this contradiction between philosophy and experience, it is the easiest thing in the world to stick to one's philosophic guns and, pointing to the intellectual and moral excellence of one's philosophy, to substitute for the creative revisions and revolutions of true philosophy the sterile incantations of a self-sufficient dogmatism.

Intellectual victories, however, are not won that way. The dominance of a philosophy over its age and its fecundity for the future are not determined by the standards of a seminar in logic or metaphysics but by its relation to the life experiences of the common man. That philosophy wins out in the competition of the market place, which, with greater faithfulness than any other, makes explicit and meaningful what the man in the street but dimly perceives yet strongly feels.

Man may continue to live for a while with a philosophy which falls short of this standard. He may still believe in its assumptions, listen to it exhortations, and wonder in confusion what is true and false, good and evil, right and wrong in this conflict between the known dogmas of the old philosophy and the felt experiences of the new life. Yet man will not forever accept a philosophy which is patently at odds with his experience. He will not forever listen to "appeals to reason" when he experiences the power of irrational forces over his own life and the lives of his fellow-men. He will not forever believe in "progress" when the comparison between his own moral and social experience and those of his ancestors shows him that there is no such thing. He will not forever cherish the redeeming powers of science which demonstrates through its results its moral ambiguity in its own sphere and its scientific ambiguity in the social world. He will not forever accept as true the essentially harmonious constitution of human existence when his inner and outer life bears the marks of constant conflict and strife.

Man will not live without answers to his questions, and when the answers are not forthcoming from the traditional custodians of Western thought, he will look for them elsewhere. He will turn to any philosophy which seems to be less at variance with his experience than the one in which he can no longer believe. So the Germans rejected, with rationalism and liberalism, the whole Western tradition and embraced in fascism a philosophy which promised to reinterpret their experiences, to guide their actions, and to create a new society. Fascism failed as a practical philosophy because it did not understand the nature of man, who is not only an object of political manipulation but also a moral person endowed with resources which do not yield to manipulation. The failure of fascism and its defeat in battle have given Western civilization another chance to re-examine its own philosophy, to revise its own assumptions, and to reconcile its traditions with the experiences and exigencies of modern life.

Such a task is not extraordinary but is a familiar one to all creative ages. All philosophies tend to elevate their truths into suppositions of absolute validity, based upon the authority of reason and claiming the objectivity of what the modern age calls science. It is for each succeeding age to examine this claim in the light of its own experiences and to reject it where a truth, qualified by the conditions of time and place, tries to perpetuate itself in a new epoch. Thus, the scientia of ancient civilization was superseded by Christian philosophy, which introduced a new inner experience into the consciousness of the Western world. This new philosophy calcified into the pseudo-scientific dogmatism of some of the medieval schools, which in turn were overcome by a new philosophy born of the experience of experimental science. The ability of an age to perform such a task of rejuvenation, which is also a task of destruction, is the measure of its intellectual vitality.

The failure of the dogmatic scientism of our age to explain the social and, more particularly, political problems of this age and to give guidance for successful action calls for a re-examination of these problems in the light of the prerationalist Western tradition. This re-examination must start with the assumption that power politics, rooted in the lust for power which is common to all men, is for this reason inseparable from social life itself. In order to eliminate from the political sphere not power politics—which is beyond the ability of any political philosophy or system—but the destructiveness of power politics, rational faculties are needed which are different from, and superior to, the reason of the scientific age.

Politics must be understood through reason, yet it is not in reason that it finds its model. The principles of scientific reason are always simple, consistent, and abstract; the social world is always complicated, incongruous, and concrete. To apply the former to the latter is either futile, in that the social reality remains impervious to the attack of that "one-eyed reason, deficient in its vision of depth";[2] or it is fatal, in that it will bring about results destructive of the intended purpose. Politics is an art and not a science, and what is required for its mastery is not the rationality of the engineer but the wisdom and the moral strength of the statesman. The social world, deaf to the appeal to reason pure and simple, yields only to that intricate combination of moral and material pressures which the art of the statesman creates and maintains.

Contemptuous of power politics and incapable of the statesmanship which alone is able to master it, the age has tried to make politics a science. By doing so, it has demonstrated its intellectual confusion, moral blindness, and political decay. A book such as this can picture the disease but cannot cure it. More especially, it must leave the production of neat and rational solutions to those who believe in the philosophy against which this book is written. It must deprive the reader of that exhilaration which the rational solution of an oversimplified problem, from the single tax to the outlawry of war, so easily imparts. Yet, if it might lift the veil of oblivion from a truth once known, it would do for the theory and, in the long run, for the practice of politics all that a book can do.

Notes

1. See, with regard to the relations between rationalism and scientism, George H. Sabine, *History of Political Theory* (New York: Henry Holt & Co., 1937), p. 573: "Yet this empiricism had, so to speak, all the bias of rationalism; it had the foible of omniscience and the itch for simplicity. It appealed to the fact but it insisted that facts should speak a predetermined language. Even the new ethics of utility and the new economics, which were the chief additions made to social theory, were logically incoherent for precisely this reason. They professed to rest on an empirical theory of human motives but they assumed a harmony of nature for which no scientific proof could ever have been given. Thus the popular thought of the eighteenth century reiterated a philosophy which in effect it only half practiced."
2. Alfred North Whitehead, *Science and the Modern World* (New York: Macmillan Co., 1926), p. 86.

JAPAN, ASIAN-PACIFIC SECURITY, AND THE CASE FOR ANALYTICAL ECLECTICISM

Peter J. Katzenstein and Nobuo Okawara

In their essay, Peter J. Katzenstein and Nobuo Okawara make the case for thinking about international affairs in terms of alternative theories, applied in this case to the Asian-Pacific region. Notice that the theories they identify coincide with the three mainstream perspectives—realist, liberal, and constructivist (or what we call identity)—developed in *Perspectives on International Relations*. Notice also that each perspective includes many variations such as, in the case of the liberal perspective, classical liberalism (which takes democracy into account) and neoliberalism (which focuses more exclusively on institutions). Initially, Katzenstein and Okawara describe some of the bilateral and multilateral facts related to Japan and Asian-Pacific security. But are they applying perspectives already to select the facts? Then, they combine various perspectives to elucidate the underlying causes of the facts. But which combination of perspectives explains more? If all perspectives matter, then none matters, and we have what scholars call an overdetermined outcome.

In recent years *International Security* has published a large number of articles and exchanges articulating the advantages and shortcomings of different analytical perspectives in international relations.[1] Controversies about the merits of neoliberalism, constructivism, rationalism, and realism have become an accepted part of both scholarly debate and graduate teaching.

* * *

Given the substantial proportion of pages that *International Security* has devoted to grand debates in the last decade, it is our sense that the intellectual returns from these exchanges are diminishing sharply. Extolling, in the abstract, the virtues of a specific analytical perspective to the exclusion of others is intellectually less important than making sense of empirical anomalies and stripping notions of what is "natural" of their intuitive plausibility. With specific reference to Japanese and Asian-Pacific security affairs, this article argues against the

Source: Peter J. Katzenstein and Nobuo Okawara, "Japan, Asian-Pacific Security, and the Case for Analytical Eclecticism," *International Security* 26, no. 3 (2001–2002): 153–185.

privileging of parsimony that has become the hallmark of paradigmatic debates. The complex links between power, interest, and norms defy analytical capture by any one paradigm. They are made more intelligible by drawing selectively on different paradigms—that is, by analytical eclecticism, not parsimony.

We illustrate this general point with specific reference to Asia-Pacific, an area central to security affairs since the end of the Cold War....

* * *

Bilateralism and Multilateralism in Japanese and Asian-Pacific Security

Analytical eclecticism is particularly well suited to capture the complexities of the fluid security environment in Asia-Pacific. Japan's security policy, and Asian-Pacific security affairs more generally, rest on a firm foundation of formal and informal bilateral agreements, supplemented by a variety of embryonic multilateral arrangements.[2]

Bilateralism

In the early years of the Clinton administration, growing bilateral trade conflicts, Japanese uncertainty about U.S. strategy in Asia-Pacific, and an increasing emphasis on Asia-Pacific in Japanese foreign policy all pointed to the possibility of a loosening of bilateral ties between Japan and the United States. Despite these potential signals, a series of reevaluations of strategic options in both Tokyo and Washington culminated in the April 1996 signing of the Japan-U.S. Joint Declaration on Security and the September 1997 Revised Guidelines for Japan-U.S. Defense Cooperation. The joint declaration calls for a review of the 1978 Guidelines for Japan-U.S. Defense Cooperation, and the revised guidelines spell out the roles of the U.S. military and Japan's Self-Defense Forces (SDF) in the event of a crisis. The latter refers specifically to "situations in areas surrounding Japan that will have an important influence on Japan's peace and security" as the context in which the two governments could provide each other with supplies and services.[3]

In the context of modern warfare, the expanded regional scope of the new Japanese-U.S. defense cooperation arrangements has somewhat diluted Japan's traditional postwar policy against the use of force in the absence of a direct attack. SDF operations, for example, will no longer focus solely on the defense of the Japanese home islands.[4] In a future crisis, this may make it difficult for the Maritime Self-Defense Force to delineate Japan's defense perimeter.[5] The 1995 revised National Defense Program Outline (which calls for the SDF's acquiring the capability to cope with situations in areas surrounding Japan that could adversely affect its peace and security) and the Defense Cooperation Guidelines have effectively broadened the mission of the SDF. The mission of Japan's military is no longer simply the defense of the home islands against a direct attack, thus securing Japan's position in a global anticommunist alliance. In the eyes of the proponents of the revised mission of the SDF, Japan's military is also committed to enhancing regional stability in Asia-Pacific and thus, indirectly, Japan's own security.

The importance of bilateralism is not restricted to Japan's security relations with the United States. As an example, senior Japan Defense Agency (JDA) officials met annually between 1993 and 1997 and again in 1999 with their Chinese counterparts to discuss a variety of issues of mutual concern. (The 1998 hiatus was most likely occasioned by the adoption of the revised U.S.-Japan guidelines.[6]) In addition, Japan has initiated regular bilateral security talks with Australia (since 1996), Singapore (since 1997), Indonesia (since 1997), Canada (since 1997), and Malaysia (since 1999).[7] In brief, the JDA is increasingly engaging Asia-Pacific in a broad range of bilateral security contacts.[8]

Informal bilateralism has been Japan's most important response to transnational crime. Combating problems such as illegal immigration, organized crime, money laundering, the distribution of illegal narcotics, and terrorism remain almost without exception under the exclusive prerogative of national governments. Nevertheless, Japan's National Policy Agency (NPA) has begun systematic cultivation of contacts with law enforcement agencies in other Asian-Pacific countries in an effort to increase trust among police professionals throughout the region. In so doing, the NPA hopes to create a climate in which Japan's police will be able to cooperate more easily with foreign police forces on an ad hoc basis.[9]

The NPA seeks this cooperation primarily by encouraging the systematic exchange of information through the development of personal relationships with law enforcement officials from other countries. This is especially true of Japan's bilateral contacts with Burma, Cambodia, China, Laos, Taiwan, Thailand, and Vietnam. In the view of the NPA, bilateral police relations are good or excellent with the members of the Association of Southeast Asian Nations (ASEAN), Hong Kong, South Korea, and the United States. High-level police contacts with law enforcement authorities in Taiwan are good, but Taiwan's ambiguous diplomatic status severely constrains cooperation at lower levels.

Japan's relations with China are difficult because of the strong central control that China's vast Public Security Department bureaucracy exercises over its localities, such as Fujian Province, where drugs are produced and shipped to Japan. The department's insistence on strict observance of its rules and procedures seriously undermines bilateral police cooperation.[10] The NPA remains nonetheless eager to strengthen its contacts with police officials from Fujian.[11] For example, the NPA funds projects that send Japanese researchers to northeast China. These researchers investigate the local conditions that permit China's crime syndicates to operate in Japan. They also develop closer ties with provincial police forces.[12] Even more significant are recent joint operations between the Japanese and Chinese police. For instance, in 1997 the NPA helped Japan's prefectural police departments in contacting the police in Hong Kong, Canton, and Shanghai. International police cooperation resulted in several arrests in 1997–98.[13] In addition, NPA officials met with their Shanghai and Cantonese counterparts, having already established ties with the Hong Kong police before 1997.[14]

Multilateralism

The 1990s also witnessed the gradual emergence of a variety of Asian-Pacific multilateral security arrangements involving track-one (government to government), track-two (semigovernmental think tanks), and track-three (private institutions) dialogues.[15] Differences in the institutional affiliation of national research organizations participating in track-two activities, however, confound efforts to draw a sharp distinction among different tracks. They vary from being integral to the ministries of foreign affairs (the two Koreas, China, and Laos), to being totally (Vietnam) or partly (Japan) funded and largely (Vietnam) or moderately (Japan) staffed by the ministry of foreign affairs, to having very close proximity to the prime minister (Malaysia), to exhibiting high degrees of independence (Thailand and Indonesia).[16] For most Japanese officials, whatever the precise character of these dialogues, they involve semi-official or private contacts that are useful to the extent that they facilitate government-to-government talks; however, they have no value in and of themselves.[17]

The trend toward security multilateralism in Asia-Pacific is reflected in several track-two dialogues. Since 1993, for example, Japan, seeking to enhance mutual confidence on security, economic, and environmental issues, has participated with China, Russia, South Korea, and the United States in the Northeast Asia Cooperation Dialogue (NEACD). In addition, since 1994 a Japanese research organization (the Japan Institute of International Affairs) has cosponsored with its American and Russian counterparts (the Center for Strategic and International Studies and the Institute of World Economy and International Relations, respectively) the Trilateral Forum on North Pacific Security, which is regularly attended by senior government officials from all three countries. Furthermore, since 1998 Japan has conducted semiofficial trilateral security talks with China and the United States.[18]

Important track-two talks arguably occur in the Council for Security Cooperation in the Asia Pacific (CSCAP),[19] whose predecessor was the ASEAN-affiliated Institutes for Strategic and International Studies. In the early 1990s, the institutes played a crucial role in encouraging ASEAN to commence systematic security dialogues. And with the establishment of the track-one ASEAN Regional Forum (ARF) in 1994, the track-two activities of these institutes have grown in significance. For example, they prepare studies that may be too sensitive for governments to conduct, and they organize meetings on topics that for political reasons governments may be unwilling or unable to host.

Track-two activities shape the climate of opinion in national settings in which security affairs are conducted. They can also help decisionmakers in articulating new ideas. Over time, they may socialize elites either directly or indirectly to different norms and identities. They may also build transnational coalitions of elites with considerable domestic influence. In brief, they have become an important feature of Asian-Pacific security affairs.

An embryonic multilateralism is also evident on issues of internal security. Since 1989 the NPA has hosted annual three-day meetings on how to combat organized crime. Funded by Japan's foreign aid program, these meetings are designed to strengthen cooperative police relationships.[20] Also, confronting its third wave of stimulant abuse since 1945, Japan convened an Asian Drug Law Enforcement Conference in Tokyo in the winter of 1999.[21] Ironically, at that meeting the director of the United Nations Drug Control Program chastised the Japanese government for its limited commitment to multilateral efforts to curtail regional trafficking in methamphetamines.[22] The NPA attended as an observer a May 1999 meeting in which the five Southeast Asian-Pacific countries (Burma, Cambodia, Laos, Thailand, and Vietnam) and China formally approved a policy strategy to deal with international drug trafficking.[23] And in January 2000, the NPA organized a conference, attended by officials from thirty-seven countries, to discuss how police cooperation could stem the spread of narcotics.[24]

Because terrorism is a direct threat to the state, it has been an item on the internal security agenda of the multilateral Group of Seven/Eight meetings since the mid-1970s. More recent summit meetings in Ottawa (December 1995), Sharm al-Sheikh (March 1996), Paris (July 1996), Denver (June 1997), and Cologne (1999) reflect the concerns that this threat continues to generate. Since the September 11 attacks on the World Trade Center and the Pentagon, these concerns have catapulted to the top of the security agenda of the United States and the G-7/8. Over the last few years, Japan has sought to create similar regional collaborations in Asia-Pacific.[25] Generally speaking, however, on the issue of internal security the absence of multilateral regional institutions in Asia-Pacific remains striking. A recent inventory of transnational crimes lists several global institutional fora in which these concerns are addressed but, besides CSCAP's working group on transnational crime for Asia-Pacific, there is only one other regional forum: the ASEAN ministry on drugs.[26]

Bilateralism and Multilateralism

Asia-Pacific's entrenched bilateralism and incipient multilateralism need not conflict.[27] Amitav Acharya speaks of an interlocking "spider web" form of bilateralism that compensates in part for the absence of multilateral security cooperation in Asia-Pacific.[28] In the 1960s and 1970s, for example, a commitment to anticommunism provided the rationale for joint police operations and cross-border "hot pursuits" of communist guerrillas (e.g., between Malaysia and Indonesia and between Malaysia and Thailand). And as Michael Stankiewicz observes, efforts in the 1990s to deal with the North Korean nuclear crisis illustrated "the increasing complementarity between bilateral and multilateral diplomatic efforts in Northeast Asia."[29] Equally interesting, improvements in bilateral relations in Asia-Pacific, occasioned by the conflict on the Korean

Peninsula, are fostering a gradual strengthening of multilateral security arrangements such as the NEACD and the Korean Peninsula Energy Development Organization. Thus the potential for a flash point crisis between North Korea and its neighbors has been a source for strengthening nascent multilateral security arrangements in Northeast Asia. The April 1999 creation of the Trilateral Coordination and Oversight Group by Japan, South Korea, and the United States to orchestrate policy toward North Korea is but the most recent example of this trend.[30]

Japanese diplomacy thus is beginning to make new connections between bilateral and multilateral security dialogues.[31] This policy accords with the argument of the Advisory Group on Defense Issues in its report to the prime minister that "the Japan-U.S. relationship of cooperation in the area of security must be considered not only from the bilateral viewpoint but, at the same time, also from the broader perspective of security in the entire Asia/Pacific region."[32] According to one member of that advisory group, Akio Watanabe: "I don't feel it's a question of choosing one framework or the other. From my standpoint, the issue is the necessity of redefining the Japan-U.S. security relationship within the new international conditions of the post–cold-war era."[33] Takashi Inoguchi agrees when he writes that "the Japan-U.S. relationship could develop into an arrangement having multilateral aspects."[34]

Japan's government takes a pragmatic approach: It views multilateralism as a complement rather than as a substitute for bilateralism. The informal exchange of information on a range of difficult issues around the edges of official talks enhances predictability and helps to build trust. Although multilateral dialogues do not solve problems, they can make the underlying system of bilateral security arrangements in Asia-Pacific operate more smoothly.[35] Given this sense of pragmatism, it is not surprising that, as Paul Midford[36] notes, Foreign Minister Taro Nakayama's July 1991 proposal for a new multilateral security dialogue in Asia-Pacific did not resemble the European-style multilateralism that John Ruggie[37] has analyzed: Nakayama's proposal excluded socialist states such as the Soviet Union; it was implicitly discriminatory by according the United States and Japan special status as major powers; and it did not advocate diffuse reciprocity but recognized instead the role of the United States as a security provider in Asia-Pacific and the circumstances of Japan as operating under domestic legal restrictions.

With Japan's active support, Asia-Pacific in the 1990s began to develop an embryonic set of multilateral security institutions and practices. But compared with the scope and strength of both its formal and informal bilateral arrangements, Asia-Pacific's achievements in multilateralism remain limited at best. Even ASEAN's long-standing and relatively successful multilateralism has encountered serious setbacks since Asia's 1997 financial crisis. The multilateralism that Japan has traditionally supported has been modest. In sum, formal and informal bilateral approaches, supplemented by nascent forms of multilateralism, are defining both Japanese security policies and Asian-Pacific security relations. As we show in the next section, analytical eclecticism is particularly well suited to the task of analyzing the fluid politics of Japanese and Asian-Pacific security.

Analytical Eclecticism in the Analysis of Japanese and Asian-Pacific Security

* * *

Disadvantages of Parsimonious Explanations

Strict formulations of realism, liberalism, and constructivism sacrifice explanatory power in the interest of analytical purity. Yet in understanding political problems, we typically need to weigh the causal importance of different types of factors, for example, material and ideal, international and domestic. Eclectic theorizing, not the insistence on received paradigms, helps us understand inherently complex social and political processes.

Realism. Realist theory has various guises. Drawing on an increasingly rich literature, Robert Jervis,[38] for example, operates with a twofold distinction (between offensive and defensive realism). Alastair Johnston[39] favors a more complex fourfold categorization (balance of power, power maximization, balance of threat, and identity realism). Although they formulate their analyses somewhat differently, they and other realists share many insights—the most important being the effects of the security dilemma on state behavior. Realists such as Kenneth Waltz underline the brevity of the uni-polar moment that the United States has enjoyed since the end of the Cold War and the disintegration of the Soviet Union.[40] For them, however, the magnitude of current U.S. capabilities is less important than the policy follies—such as interventions in areas of the world not directly tied to the national interests of the United States—that squander it. Hence "the all-but-inevitable movement from unipolarity to multipolarity is taking place not in Europe but in Asia.... Theory enables one to say that a new balance of power will form but not to say how long it will take."[41] Though distinctively his own in style of argumentation, Waltz's analysis is in broad agreement with other types of realist analysis that consider factors besides the international distribution of capabilities, such as absolute security needs and threats. Japan and China are rising great powers in Asia-Pacific. In view of a large number of potential military flash points, the security dilemma confronting Asian-Pacific states is serious. Between 1950 and 1990, one study reports 129 territorial disputes worldwide, with Asia accounting for the largest number. Of the 54 borders disputed in 1990, the highest ratio of unresolved disputes as a fraction of total contested borders was located in East and Southeast Asia.[42] In this view, Asia-Pacific may well be "ripe for rivalry."[43] For realists, balancing against the United States as the only superpower, currently by China and in the near future by Japan, is the most important prediction that the theory generates.[44]

Realist theory, however, is indeterminate. It cannot say whether Japan will balance with China against the United States as the preeminent threat or whether it will balance with the United States against China as the rising regional power in East Asia.[45] Balance-of-power theory predicts that a withdrawal of U.S. forces from East Asia would leave Japan no choice but to rearm. Alternatively, balancing theory can also support a very different line of reasoning in which Japan, though wary of China, might recognize China's central position in Asia-Pacific and stop far short of adopting a policy of full-fledged remilitarization.[46] To infer anything about the direction of balancing requires auxiliary assumptions that typically invoke interest, threat, or prestige—all variables that require liberal or constructivist styles of analysis. Moreover, it is unclear whether a united Korea will balance against Japan (with its powerful navy that might ultimately control the sea-lanes on which Korean trade depends so heavily) or against China (with the strongest ground forces in Asia and with whom Korea shares a common border).[47] Thus realist theory points to omnipresent balancing behavior but tells us little about the direction of that balancing.

Nor do military expenditures alone yield a clear picture of the geostrategic situation in Asia-Pacific. Asia's 1997 financial crisis slowed Asian-Pacific arms rivalries and lowered military spending.[48] Thus instead of worrying about escalating arms rivalries, some defense experts began to express greater concern over potential risks created by possible imbalances in military modernization and financial strength. After 1997 countries less affected by the financial crisis—such as China, Japan, Korea, Singapore, and Taiwan—appeared to be much better positioned to harness sophisticated technologies to enhance their military strength.[49]

Liberalism. On its own, liberal theory also encounters serious difficulties. Some analysts have suggested that the U.S.-Japan alliance can last only if it articulates common values. Mike Mochizuki and Michael O'Hanlon, for example, have advocated that the alliance should become as "close, balanced and principle-based as the U.S.-U.K. special relationship." Not a common military threat but common interests derived from shared democratic values, Mochizuki and O'Hanlon argue, are the best guarantor for sustaining the U.S.-Japan alliance.[50]

What would happen, however, if the United States or Japan were no longer a member of the "free world"? Liberal analysis is hindered by the theory's underlying assumption that identities are unchanging. Do liberal values really constitute both the United States and Japan as actors? This is implausible. The promotion of democracy as a positive value, for example, is handled very differently by the U.S. and Japanese governments. The philosophical assumption informing U.S. policy is that democracy and human rights should proceed hand in hand with economic development. In contrast, Japanese policy assumes that economic development is conducive to the building of democratic institutions. This difference in philosophy leads to an equally noticeable difference in method. The United States operates with legal briefs, economic sanctions, and "sticks." Japan prefers constructive engagement through dialogue, economic assistance, and "carrots."[51] Such systematic differences in approach undercut a liberal redefinition of the U.S.-Japan alliance. To Japan they make the United States appear high-handed and evangelical, while to the United States Japan seems opportunistic and parochial. These differences point to the importance of collective identities not shared rather than of democratic institutions that are shared.

An alternative neoliberal analysis of the U.S.-Japan alliance focuses not on shared values but on efficiency.[52] For example, after the 1993–94 missile crisis on the Korean Peninsula, policymakers in Japan and the United States became convinced that their bilateral defense guidelines needed to be revised to enhance the efficiency of defense cooperation. The 1960 Mutual Cooperation and Security Treaty and the 1978 Guidelines for Japan-U.S. Defense Cooperation had left unclear the role to be played by Japan in regional crises. Specifically, they left undefined both the extent to which Japan would provide logistical support and whether the U.S. military would have access to Japan's SDF and civilian facilities. The 1997 revised defense guidelines reduce these ambiguities and thus help to prepare Japan for potential participation in both possible U.S. and UN operations undertaken, in the eyes of the proponents of the revised guidelines, in the interest of regional peace and security. This is an instance of government policies seeking to lower transaction costs and enhance efficiencies through institutionalized cooperation.[53]

The revision of the defense guidelines was, however, a central feature of Japanese security policy in the last decade that eludes neoliberal explanations. It extends the scope of the U.S.-Japan security arrangement under the provisions of the treaty for the maintenance of peace and security in "the Far East" to include "situations in areas surrounding Japan." The operative understanding of "the Far East" in Article 6 of the security treaty was geographically defined by the Japanese government in 1960 as "primarily the region north of the Philippines, as well as Japan and its surrounding area," including South Korea and Taiwan. The revised guidelines explicitly state that the phrase "situations in areas surrounding Japan" (short for "situations in areas surrounding Japan that will have an important influence on Japan's peace and security") is conceptual and has no geographic connotations. In situations when rear-area support may be required, these areas are not necessarily limited to East Asia.[54]

This ambiguity has given rise to much debate in Japan and beyond. Under the revised guidelines, U.S.-Japanese cooperation in combat is obligatory only in situations involving the defense of Japan's home islands. In the view of revision advocates, problems may emerge in a crisis not involving an attack on Japan—including any that arise in the Asia-Pacific region—but that would require general defense cooperation with the United States in the interest of regional stability and security. For some the revised defense guidelines free Japan to provide logistical and other forms of support to the United States, falling short of military combat, as long as the crisis is politically construed as constituting a serious security threat to Japan.[55] Adopting a less flexible approach, the ministry of foreign affairs director of the North American

Affairs Bureau stated in May 1998, before the Lower House Foreign Affairs Committee, that "situations in areas surrounding Japan" were restricted to those occurring in the Far East and its surrounding areas.[56]

In the future, the clash between more or less flexible interpretations of the scope of U.S.-Japan defense cooperation will be shaped by changing international and domestic political conditions. The ambiguity that lurks behind conflicting viewpoints and temporary victories of one side or the other is central to how Japanese officials adapt security policy to change. According to the government's official interpretation, it is the specific security threat at a specific time that in the judgment of the cabinet and the Diet will determine whether that threat will be covered by the ambiguous wording of the revised guidelines. Thus the scope of the areas surrounding Japan is variable and depends on a functional and conceptual, rather than a geographic and objective, construction of Japan's changing security environment.

Neoliberal explanations of the U.S.-Japan alliance cannot explain the deliberate ambiguity in the definition of the term "surrounding area" in the revised defense guidelines. This ambiguity undercuts efficiency because it leaves unspecified the contingencies under which the Japanese government might choose to participate in regional security cooperation measures. Yet for the guidelines' advocates, ambiguity, by deflecting criticism in Japan, may well increase U.S.-Japanese defense cooperation. In seeking to create flexibility in policy through a politics of interpretation and reinterpretation of text, ambiguity is a defining characteristic of Japan's security policy.[57]

Constructivism. Parsimonious constructivist analysis of Japanese and Asian-Pacific security also lacks plausibility. Contrary to claims by neoliberals, multilateral institutions do more than facilitate the exchange of information. ASEAN processes of trust building, for example, appear to be well under way.[58] The ARF is more than an intraorganizational balancing of threats and capabilities. Yuen Foong Khong writes that it is the only "mechanism for defusing the conflictual by-products of power balancing practices" in Asia-Pacific.[59] It is thus understandable why governments are eager to adjust regional security institutions to new conditions rather than to abandon them altogether. Exclusive reliance on balancing strategies of the kind favored by realists appears to Asian-Pacific governments to be fraught with risk.[60]

In three carefully researched case studies dealing with relations between Malaysia and the Philippines between the 1960s and 1990s, ASEAN's policies after Vietnam's 1978 invasion of Cambodia, and the period of strategic uncertainty after the end of the Cold War, Nikolas Busse has shown that ASEAN norms have noticeably influenced government policy.[61] In the 1990s, specifically, ASEAN members did not balance against the destabilizing possibilities of U.S. disengagement, Japanese reassertion, and Chinese expansion. Instead member states sought to export the ASEAN way of intensive consultation to East Asia through the ARF and the Workshops on Managing Potential Conflicts in the South China Sea that Indonesia has convened since 1990. More recently, the ASEAN plus Three meetings have provided a forum for discussion of security issues involving ASEAN members, Japan, South Korea, and China.[62] And in 2000, the ARF officially accepted North Korea as a member. Busse's research points to the importance of the legitimacy, success, and prominence of norms of informal consultations; consensus building; and nonintervention for Asian-Pacific security. In brief, ASEAN's strategy made China, the United States, and Japan part of ongoing security dialogues that replicate three important ASEAN norms: informal diplomacy, personal contacts, and respect for the principle of nonintervention.

The redefinition of collective identities, however, is a process measured in decades, not years. The accomplishments of various track-one and track-two security dialogues in Asia-Pacific remain limited. Bilateralism and multilateralism, as Acharya has pointed out, are less threat and more uncertainty oriented.[63] Collective identity is therefore less directly at stake than are trust and reputation. Skeptics have joked that the bark of the ARF is worse than its bite. The ARF has sidestepped the most pressing security issues in Asia: conflicts on the Korean Peninsula, across the Taiwan Strait, and in the South China Sea. North Korea's nuclear and missile programs have become a major source of instability in Asia-Pacific.[64] Hoping to defuse this crisis, the United States, Japan, China, and South Korea are all engaged in complicated, interlinked diplomatic initiatives that exclude both ASEAN and the ARF. The same is true of the smoldering Taiwan Strait crisis. With China declaring the status of Taiwan a domestic matter, the ASEAN norm of nonintervention has prevented the ARF from playing a mediating role in this crisis.[65] Finally, in the South China Sea the ARF has been slightly more engaged while still falling well short of seeking the role of active mediator between clashing state interests.[66]

The restricted scope of ARF activity is reflected in its minuscule organizational resources. Since its first meeting in 1994, the ARF has modeled itself after ASEAN. It has "participants" rather than "members," thus signaling the premium that it places on a lack of permanency and formality. ARF has no headquarters or secretariat, and it is unlikely that either will be established.[67] Although there are a number of intersessional working groups, the ARF itself meets annually for one day only.[68]

The ARF has been weakened further by three developments in the late 1990s. First, Asia's financial crisis has put new strains on relations among several ASEAN members (including Malaysia and Singapore) and has illustrated, in the words of former Prime Minister of Singapore Lee Kuan Yew, that "we can't help each other."[69] Second, the ARF was unable to act in a politically meaningful way in the 1999 crisis in East Timor. The United Nations, not the ARF, was the central international arena and actor to which Indonesia turned. Third; there are some indications that, according to Michael Leifer, the accession of Cambodia, Laos, and Vietnam to ASEAN is leading to "revisionary fragmentation," with the three governments meeting separately at times from the older ASEAN members.[70] In addition, the United States is putting increasing emphasis on bilateral diplomatic and military relationships. Since 1996, for example, it has strengthened its links with Japan and Australia and has expanded its military access to ASEAN members such as Singapore, Malaysia, Indonesia, Thailand, and the Philippines.[71]

* * *

Advantages of Eclectic Explanations

Compelling analyses of empirical puzzles can be built through combining realist, liberal, and constructivist modes of explanation. Realism and liberalism together, for example, can generate powerful insights into the mixture of balance-of-power and multilateral politics. A soft form of balance-of-power theorizing, for example, informs the 1995 Nye report that provides a rationale for continued U.S. military engagement in East Asia.[72] At one level the report is about increasing trust, communication, transparency, and reliability in a U.S.-Japan relationship marked by complex interdependence, thus seeking to stabilize the alliance and enhance predictability and stability in the region. But it is also about maintaining U.S. primacy. The 1997 Revised Guidelines for Japan-U.S. Defense Cooperation spell out the operations that Japan would be expected to carry out in a regional crisis, and thus ensure that in such a crisis potentially hostile states could not drive a wedge between the United States and Japan; Japan's support of U.S. forces would be sufficiently robust to prevent a backlash in the U.S. Congress against either the alliance or the forward deployment of U.S. forces in Asia-Pacific; Japan's defense posture would continue to be guided by alliance planning; and finally, the United States would be able to win decisively in a possible military conflict with North Korea without shouldering excessive costs.[73]

In this realist-liberal perspective, the United States remains militarily and economically fully engaged in Asia-Pacific, thus reassuring Asian-Pacific states against the threat posed by Japan's present economic preponderance and potential military rearmament. Japan emerges as a potential economic and political leader contained within well-defined political boundaries. This double-barreled U.S. approach is rounded out by hopes for a unified and peaceful Korea and an economically prospering China increasingly engaged with the West, Japan, and the rest of Asia-Pacific.[74]

Japan's China policy also reflects a mixture of realist and liberal elements.[75] Just as Germany avoids at all cost having to choose between the United States and France, Japan avoids having to choose between the United States and China. Without risking its primary security relationship with the United States, Japan since the 1970s has consistently sought to engage China diplomatically. This entails an element of balancing as Japan seeks to constrain China, a potential opponent, through a policy of engagement. From Japan's perspective, countering China is possible only through alignment with the United States. Because China's military does not currently pose a serious threat to the region, and because military modernization is a costly and prolonged process measured in decades rather than years, the military aspects of the Japan-China relationship are relatively unimportant. Instead Japan's diplomacy aims at a slow, steady, and prolonged process of encouraging China to contribute more to regional stability and prosperity. On several issues—such as China's growing involvement in the ARF, an officially unacknowledged but nonetheless evident policy of seeking to enhance stability on the Korean Peninsula, and the somewhat greater flexibility with which the leadership in Beijing has addressed encroachments on China's sovereignty on issues of political authority and economic independence (as opposed to those involving territorial integrity and jurisdictional monopoly)—Japanese patience is being rewarded.[76] The settlement of virtually all of China's border conflicts, its acceptance into the World Trade Organization (WTO), and its far-reaching domestic reforms all point to a general political climate conducive to Japan's policy of engagement.[77]

A combination of realist and constructivist styles of analysis also has considerable heuristic power, as David Spiro and Alastair Johnston have argued.[78] The volatile issue of Taiwan, potentially the most serious trouble spot in Asia-Pacific, illustrates this analytical possibility.[79] The use of the term "surrounding areas" rather than "Far East" in the revised guidelines creates ambiguities, but they have been acceptable to both U.S. and Japanese defense officials for instrumental reasons. The United States has an interest in enhancing the deterrent effect of its alliance with Japan against China; Japanese officials have an interest in leaving undefined Japan's response to a possible crisis over Taiwan. The advantages of ambiguity on Taiwan are widely acknowledged inside the Japanese government,[80] as are the risks.[81] In the 1979 Taiwan Relations Act, the United States combined its diplomatic recognition of the People's Republic of China with a commitment to Taiwan's military defense. Japan, however, has kept its stance on Taiwan as ambiguous as possible. Japanese insistence on the domestic nature of the conflict between Beijing and Taipei, however, may not suffice in future crises. More than any other issue, Taiwan's status potentially confronts Japan and the United States with serious difficulties in defense cooperation should China seek to resolve this issue through military means.[82]

A combination of constructivism and realism also offers historical insights. John Fairbank, for example, has offered a broad interpretation of East Asian international relations.[83] For many centuries, Asian international relations were institutionalized as a suzerain, rather than as a sovereign, system of states in which the central power did not seek to subordinate or intervene unduly in the affairs of lesser powers within its ambit.[84] China was the center of a system of tributary trade in which polities emulated and aligned with the central power. Focusing on systems with a preponderant source of power, Randall Schweller speaks of "bandwagoning for profit."[85] Less material objects than profits narrowly construed were involved, however. In Asia tribute was not only trade. It was also an institutional transmission belt for collective norms and identities in Chinese culture. Power, trade, and culture were central in defining the political relationships between the Middle Kingdom and its neighbors.

The Sinocentric world order was anarchic and organized around the principle of self-help. Power and geographic location mattered, just as realism leads us to expect. Yet Chinese diplomatic practices also facilitated cultural emulation, thus yielding a system with a distinctive mixture of hierarchy and equality. In this Sinocentric world, discrepancies between norms and practice were common, as is true of the Westphalian system of sovereign states. But as Michel Oksenberg has observed, the nature of the misfit was different, so that certain ambiguous solutions of the past concerning territorial disputes over Taiwan, Tibet, and Hong Kong are today rendered more intractable.[86] Amending his own published work, Robert Jervis usefully underlines a theoretical point that many realists and neoliberals discount unduly: the dynamic and unanticipated consequences that institutions can have for preferences over outcomes, especially by affecting through domestic politics "deeper changes in what the actors want and how they conceive of their interests."[87]

Liberalism and constructivism can also be combined to good effect. This decade, for example, has witnessed the growth of formal and informal multilateral security arrangements in Asia-Pacific. "Cooperative" approaches focus on military and nonmilitary dimensions of security, seek to prevent the emergence of manifest security threats, and are inclusive in their membership. Dialogues and various confidence-building measures are crucial to the creation of mutual trust.[88] These seek to lower the costs of making political contacts, facilitate the exchange of information, enhance transparency, and strengthen trust between governments.[89]

Multilateral security institutions can enhance efficiencies and over time alter underlying preferences and thus redefine interests.[90] The analytical difference between these two effects is mirrored in the attitudes of Japanese officials between a more skeptical and "realistic" stance on Asian security institutions on the one hand and a more enthusiastic and "pacifist" one on the other.[91]

Over longer periods, multilateral security institutions can do more than create efficiencies in the relations between governments. They can redefine identities and acceptable standards of behavior and thus reduce or enhance fear and hostility or the collective pursuit of economic prosperity and political cooperation. Scholars who have written on the ARF, for example, have made a strong case for the importance of informal and formal dialogues as ways of creating not only more transparency but also arenas of persuasion and a partial change in preferences and interests.[92]

Analytical eclecticism offers distinct advantages. Whether they stress materialist or ideational factors, rationalist analytical perspectives such as realism and liberalism are enriched when employed in tandem. They are also enriched by the incorporation of constructivist elements. When realists and liberals in their empirically informed theoretical and policy writings slight norms and identities, they undermine the contribution to knowledge and policy advice they seek to make.[93]

Conclusion

The paradigmatic clashes in international relations theory and the field of security studies are part of a broader set of disagreements in political science and the social sciences. Theoretical debates between proponents of rationalist, culturalist, and historical-institutional approaches appear these days in various guises and combinations in virtually all fields of social inquiry. These debates reveal differences in problem focus, acceptable analytic methods, and substantive hypotheses. More important, they point to deep divides about unverifiable, underlying assumptions concerning the possibilities, character, and purpose of social knowledge; the different routes we take to gain that knowledge; and the ontological status and epistemological significance of the relations between agents and structures and of the material and ideal aspects of social life.[94]

* * *

Instead of approach-driven analysis, we advocate problem-driven research. The insistence on parsimony clashes with the complexity of social processes occurring within specific contexts of both time and space.[95] As this article has illustrated, and with no claim to originality, international relations analysis can build on the identification of empirical anomalies for any one analytical perspective. A problem-driven approach to research has one big advantage. It sidesteps often bitter, repetitive, and inherently inconclusive paradigmatic debates. Such debates detract scholars and graduate students from the primary task at hand: recognizing interesting questions and testing alternative explanations.

* * *

This is not to argue that analytical eclecticism is cost-free. This approach may be too flexible to define by itself a research program capable of mobilizing strong political preferences and enduring professional ties. The advantages of eclecticism, however, may well outweigh these costs. Scholars and policy-makers try to gain analytical leverage over multilayered and complex connections between power, interest, and norms. Analytical eclecticism highlights different layers and connections that parsimonious explanations conceal. And it is attuned to empirical anomalies that analytical parsimony slights. Eclecticism protects us from taking as natural paradigmatic assumptions about the world. It regards with discomfort the certainties that derive from relying solely on a single paradigm. And it protects us, imperfectly to be sure, from the inevitable failings of any one paradigm, unfounded expectations of what is natural, and the adoption of flawed policies that embody those very expectations. Theory and policy are both served better by eclecticism, not parsimony.

Notes

1. On neoliberalism, see John J. Mearsheimer, "The False Promise of International Institutions," *International Security,* Vol. 19, No. 3 (Winter 1994/95), pp. 5–49; Robert O. Keohane and Lisa L. Martin, "The Promise of Institutionalist Theory," *International Security,* Vol. 20, No. 1 (Summer 1995), pp. 39–51; Charles A. Kupchan and Clifford A. Kupchan, "The Promise of Collective Security," ibid., pp. 52–61; John Gerard Ruggie, "The False Premise of Realism," ibid., pp. 62–70; Alexander Wendt, "Constructing International Politics," ibid., pp. 71–81; and John J. Mearsheimer, "A Realist

Reply," ibid., pp. 82–93. On constructivism, see Michael C. Desch, "Culture Clash: Assessing the Importance of Ideas in Security Studies," *International Security,* Vol. 23, No. 1 (Summer 1998), pp. 141–170; Ted Hopf, "The Promise of Constructivism in International Relations Theory," ibid., pp. 171–200; and John S. Duffield, Theo Farrell, Richard Price, and Michael C. Desch, "Correspondence: Isms and Schisms: Culturalism versus Realism in Security Studies," *International Security,* Vol. 24, No. 1 (Summer 1999), pp. 156–180. On rationalism, see Stephen M. Walt, "Rigor or Rigor Mortis? Rational Choice and Security Studies," *International Security,* Vol. 23, No. 4 (Spring 1999), pp. 5–48; Bruce Bueno de Mesquita and James D. Morrow, "Sorting through the Wealth of Notions," *International Security,* Vol. 24, No. 2 (Fall 1999), pp. 56–73; Lisa L. Martin, "The Contributions of Rational Choice: A Defense of Pluralism," ibid., pp. 74–83; Emerson M.S. Niou and Peter C. Ordeshook, "Return of the Luddites," ibid., pp. 84–96; Robert Powell, "The Modeling Enterprise and Security Studies," ibid., pp. 97–106; Frank C. Zagare, "All Mortis, No Rigor," ibid., pp. 107–114; and Stephen M. Walt, "A Model Disagreement," ibid., pp. 115–130. On realism, see Jeffrey W. Legro and Andrew Moravcsik, "Is Anybody Still a Realist?" *International Security,* Vol. 24, No. 2 (Fall 1999), pp. 5–55; Peter D. Feaver, Gunther Hellmann, Randall L. Schweller, Jeffrey W. Taliaferro, William C. Wohlforth, and Jeffrey W. Legro and Andrew Moravcsik, "Correspondence: Brother, Can You Spare a Paradigm? (Or Was Anybody Ever a Realist?)," *International Security,* Vol. 25, No. 1 (Summer 2000), pp. 165–193.

2. This section draws on more extensive evidence reported in Nobuo Okawara and Peter J. Katzenstein, "Japan and Asian-Pacific Security: Regionalization, Entrenched Bilateralism, and Incipient Multilateralism," *Pacific Review,* Vol. 14, No. 2 (2001), pp. 165–194.

3. *Gaiko Forum* [Foreign affairs forum], special issue, November 1999, pp. 134–135, 141; and Defense Agency, *Defense of Japan, 1999* (Tokyo: Japan Times, 2000), p. 236.

4. Interview 03-99, Tokyo, January 12, 1999.

5. Interviews 12-99 and 13-99, Tokyo, January 14, 1999.

6. Interview 13-00, Tokyo, January 14, 2000.

7. Boeicho (Defense Agency), *Boei Hakusho* [Defense white paper] (Tokyo: Okurasho Insatsu-kyoku, 2000), p. 187.

8. Interviews 10-00 and 13-00, Tokyo, January 14, 2000. With the tightening of U.S.-Japan security relations after 1994, Japan has become more self-conscious in developing a broad set of bilateral defense talks and exchanges that both complement its persistent dependence on the United States and cement the U.S. presence in the region. By 1999 Japan had committed to about ten regular bi-lateral talks, too many for the two officials assigned by the JDA to this task. India, for example, was interested in commencing bilateral defense consultations, but Japan stalled, not for reasons of policy but simply because of resource constraints. Interview 13-00, Tokyo, January 14, 2000.

9. This intensification of bilateral contacts builds on a small foundation of transnational police links that Japan's NPA had developed before the 1990s. For example, the NPA has organized short-term training courses for small numbers of police officials from other Asian-Pacific states dealing with drug offenses (since 1962), criminal investigations (since 1975), organized crime (since 1988), police administration

(since 1989), and community policing (since 1989). National Police Agency, International Cooperation Division, International Affairs Department, *Police of Japan, '98* (Tokyo: National Police Agency, 1998), p. 62. Japan also runs regular international seminars dealing with criminal justice issues. Finally, Japanese experts travel to various countries in Asia-Pacific to train local law-enforcement personnel. These seminars and visits help to enhance the capacity of Asian-Pacific police forces, by spreading information and establishing contacts that might be useful in subsequent, ad hoc coordination of police work across national borders. Keisatsucho (National Policy Agency), *Keisatsu Hakusho, 1997* [White paper on police, 1997] (Tokyo: Okurasho Insatsu-kyoku, 1997), pp. 95–99; Jack Donnelly, "International Human Rights: A Regime Analysis," *International Organization*, Vol. 40, No. 3 (Summer 1986), p. 628; and Katzenstein, *Cultural Norms and National Security*, pp. 68–71.

10. Interview 06-99, Tokyo, January 13, 1999.

11. Interviews 09-99 and 10-99, Tokyo, January 13, 1999.

12. Interviews 04-00, Tokyo, January 12, 2000.

13. Interviews 08-99 and 10-99, Tokyo, January 13, 1999; and Kazuharu Hirano, "Hito no Mitsuyu? Kokusai Soshiki Hanzai no Genjo to Gaiji Keisatsu no Taio" [Alien smuggling? Current state of transnational organized crime and police countermeasures], *Keisatsu-gaku Ronshu* [Journal of police science], Vol. 51, No. 9 (September 1998), pp. 45–46.

14. Interview 10-99, Tokyo, January 13, 1999.

15. Diane Stone, "Networks, Second Track Diplomacy, and Regional Cooperation: The Role of Southeast Asian Think Tanks," paper presented at the Thirty-eighth Annual International Studies Association Convention, Toronto, Canada, March 22–26, 1997; and Jun Wada, "Applying Track Two to China-Japan-U.S. Relations," in Ryosei Kokubun, ed., *Challenges for China-Japan-U.S. Cooperation* (Tokyo: Japan Center for International Exchange, 1998), pp. 154–183.

16. Interview 04-00, Tokyo, January 12, 2000.

17. Interview 01-00, Tokyo, January 11, 2000. Track-two institutions thus tend to support rather than undermine the state. There are instances when we should think of them not as nongovernmental organizations (NGOs) but as governmentally organized NGOs. In many states in Asia-Pacific, the divide between public and private is easily bridged. Prominent businesspeople and scholars, nominally in the private sector, are often linked informally to politicians and bureaucrats whose attendance at track-two meetings in their "private" capacity is polite fiction. Hence the choice between the multilateralism of different tracks can be a matter of political convenience for governments. Diane Stone, *Capturing the Political Imagination: Think Tanks and the Policy Process* (London: Frank Cass, 1996), pp. 9–25. But both the nature of private-sector participants and the pattern of influence between such participants and their governments vary widely.

18. "Nichi-Bei-Chu no Anpo Taiwa Shido" [Japan-U.S.-China security dialogue starts], *Asahi Shimbun,* July 16, 1998, 14th ed.; Yosuke Naito, "Private-Sector Northeast Asia Security Forum Upbeat," *Japan Times,* September 28, 1999; Akiko Fukushima, "Japan's Emerging View of Security Multilateralism in Asia," University of California Institute on Global Conflict and Cooperation, Policy Paper 51 (June 1999), p. 36; and Yoshitaka Sasaki, "Asian Trilateral Security Talks Debut," *Asahi Evening News,* November 7, 1997.

19. Interview 04-00; Sheldon W. Simon, "Security Prospects in Southeast Asia: Collaborative Efforts and the ASEAN Regional Forum," *Pacific Review,* Vol. 11, No. 2 (1998), pp. 207–209; Stone, "Networks, Second Track Diplomacy, and Regional Cooperation," pp. 21–25; Wada, "Applying Track Two to China-Japan-U.S. Relations," pp. 162–165; and Brian L. Job, "Non-Governmental Regional Institutions in the Evolving Asia Pacific Security Order," paper prepared for the Second Workshop on Security Order in the Asia Pacific, Bali, Indonesia, May 30–June 2, 2000.

20. Since 1996 the NPA, in an effort to build more cooperative international police relations to suppress the smuggling of narcotics and after consultations with the U.S. Drug Enforcement Agency, has begun to host two annual meetings in Tokyo. Each gathering involves forty to fifty high-level police officials: one with representatives from China in attendance; the other with representatives from Taiwan. Each lasts four days, but the official part of the program consists of only a one-day plenary session. The rest of the time is spent on group tours of Japanese police facilities, sightseeing, and socializing. Interview 06-99, Tokyo, January 13, 1999.

21. The meeting was attended by representatives from five Southeast Asian-Pacific countries (Burma, Cambodia, Laos, Thailand, and Vietnam) and China, as well as by officials from the United Nations and observers from eight countries and the European Union. Jiro Haraguchi, "Yakubutsu Taisaku no Genjo to Kadai" [Current state of and problems concerning drug control], *Keisatsu-gaku Ronshu* [Journal of political science], Vol. 52, No. 7 (July 1999), pp. 30, 36–37; Toshio Jo, "Tokyo Pledges to Finance U.N. Anti-Drug Plan," *Asahi Evening News,* February 3, 1999; and Hisane Masaki, "Seven Nations to Gang Up against Illegal Stimulant Use," *Japan Times,* December 6, 1998.

22. H. Richard Friman, "International Drug Control Policies: Variations and Effectiveness," Department of Political Science, Marquette University, 1999.

23. Haraguchi, "Yakubutsu Taisaku no Genjo to Kadai," pp. 36–37.

24. "Asia-Pacific States Vow to Combat Drugs," *Asahi Evening News,* January 28, 2000.

25. In June 1997, for example, the NPA was instrumental in helping to create the Japan and ASEAN Anti-Terrorism Network, which seeks to strengthen ties among national police agencies, streamline information gathering, and coordinate investigations when acts of terrorism occur. Following up on an initiative taken by Prime Minister Ryutaro Hashimoto during his travels through Southeast Asia in January 1997, the NPA and the ministry of foreign affairs jointly hosted in October 1997 a Japan-ASEAN Conference on Counterterrorism for senior police and foreign affairs officials from nine ASEAN countries. National Police Agency, *Police of Japan, '98,* p. 53. Interview 07-99, Tokyo, January 13, 1999. And in October 1998, the NPA and foreign ministry cohosted a joint Asian Pacific–Latin American conference on counterterrorism. Based on findings from the 1996–97 Peruvian hostage crisis—in which a Peruvian antigovernment group, demanding that President Alberto Fujimori order the release of all of its members from prison, occupied the Japanese ambassador's official residence in Lima for 127 days—the NPA sought to strengthen international cooperation on antiterrorist measures. Gaimusho (Ministry of Foreign Affairs), *Gaiko Seisho, 1999* [Foreign affairs blue book, 1999] (Tokyo: Okurasho Insatsu-kyoku, 1999), Vol. 1, pp. 103–104; Hishinuma, Takao, "Japan to Propose

Antiterrorism Meeting at G-7 Summit," *Daily Yomiuri,* May 9, 1997; and Keisatsu-cho (National Policy Agency), *Keisatsu Hakusho, 1999* [Police white paper, 1999] (Tokyo: Okurasho Insatsu-kyoku, 1999), p. 231.

26. James Shinn, "American Stakes in Asian Problems," in Shinn, ed., *Fires across the Water: Transnational Problems in Asia* (New York: Council on Foreign Relations, 1998), pp. 170–171.

27. David H. Capie, Paul M. Evans, and Akiko Fukushima, "Speaking Asian Pacific Security: A Lexicon of English Terms with Chinese and Japanese Translations and a Note on the Japanese Translation," Working Paper (Toronto: Joint Centre for Asia Pacific Studies, University of Toronto-York University, 1998), pp. 7–8, 16–17, 60–63, IV/3–4, 7.

28. Amitav Acharya, *A Survey of Military Cooperation among the ASEAN States: Bilateralism or Alliance?* Occasional Paper No. 14 (Toronto: Centre for International and Strategic Studies, 1990); and Amitav Acharya, "Regional Institutions and Security Order in Asia," paper prepared for the Second Workshop on Security Order in the Asia-Pacific, Bali, Indonesia, May 30–June 2, 2000, p. 18. In early 2001 Dennis C. Blair, the commander in chief of the U.S. Pacific Command at the time, also spoke of forming a "web of regional relationships and capabilities" on the basis of bilateral security relationships in the Asia-Pacific. See Dennis C. Blair and John T. Hanley Jr., "From Wheels to Webs: Reconstructing Asia-Pacific Security Arrangements," *Washington Quarterly,* Vol. 24, No. 1 (Winter 2001), pp. 7–17.

29. Michael Stankiewicz, "Preface: The Bilateral-Multilateral Context in Northeast Asian Security," *Korean Peninsula Security and the U.S.-Japan Defense Guidelines,* 1GCC (Institute on Global Conflict and Cooperation) Policy Paper No. 45 (San Diego, Calif.: Northeast Asia Cooperation Dialogue VII, October 1998), p. 2.

30. The group decided to meet at least once every three months. Takaaki Mizuno, "Nichi-Bei-Kan ga Chosei Group" [Japan, U.S., and South Korea Form Coordinating Group on North Korea], *Asahi Shimbun,* April 26, 1999, evening, 4th ed.; Masato Tainaka, "Nations Renew N. Korea Efforts," *Asahi Evening News,* March 31, 2000; and interviews 02-99 and 05-99, Tokyo, January 11–12, 1999.

31. Interviews 02-99 and 05-99, Tokyo, January 11–12, 1999.

32. Advisory Group on Defense Issues, *The Modality of the Security and Defense Capability of Japan: The Outlook for the 21st Century* (Tokyo: Advisory Group on Defense Issues, 1994), p. 16.

33. Takeshi Igarashi and Akio Watanabe, "Beyond the Defense Guidelines," *Japan Echo,* December 1997, p. 36.

34. Takashi Inoguchi, "The New Security Setup and Japan's Options," *Japan Echo,* Autumn 1996, p. 37. A similar "twin-track" stance also characterizes Japan's trade policy since the WTO debacle in Seattle. See Gillian Tett, "Tokyo Shifts Trade Policy," *Financial Times,* May 12, 2000, p. 1; and more generally Muthia Alagappa, "Asia-Pacific Regional Security Order: Introduction and Analytical Framework," paper prepared for the Second Workshop on Security Order in the Asia-Pacific, Bali, Indonesia, May 30–June 2, 2000, pp. 6–7.

35. Interviews 01-00, 02-00, 03-00, and 04-00, Tokyo, January 11–12, 2000.

36. Paul Midford, "From Reactive State to Cautious Leader: The Nakayama Proposal, the Miyazawa Doctrine, and Japan's Role in Promoting the Creation of the ASEAN Regional Forum," paper prepared for the annual conference of the International Studies Association, Minneapolis, Minnesota, March 17–21, 1998.

37. John Gerard Ruggie, "Multilateralism: The Anatomy of an Institution," in Ruggie, ed., *Multilateralism Matters: The Theory and Praxis of an Institutional Form* (New York: Columbia University Press, 1993), pp. 3–47.

38. Robert Jervis, "Realism, Neoliberalism, and Cooperation: Understanding the Debate," *International Security,* Vol. 24, No. 1 (Summer 1999), pp. 42–43.

39. Alastair Iain Johnston, "Realism(s) and Chinese Security Policy in the Post–Cold War Period," in Ethan B. Kapstein and Michael Mastanduno, eds., *Unipolar Politics: Realism and State Strategies after the Cold War* (New York: Columbia University Press, 1999), pp. 261–318.

40. Kenneth N. Waltz, "Realism after the Cold War," Institute of War and Peace Studies, Columbia University, December 1998.

41. Ibid., pp. 30, 19.

42. Paul K. Huth, *Standing Your Ground: Territorial Disputes and International Conflict* (Ann Arbor: University of Michigan Press, 1996), p. 32.

43. Aaron L. Friedberg, "Ripe for Rivalry: Prospects for Peace in a Multipolar Asia," *International Security,* Vol. 18, No. 3 (Winter 1993/94), pp. 5–33; and Richard K. Betts, "Wealth, Power, and Instability: East Asia and the United States after the Cold War," ibid., pp. 34–77.

44. Mike M. Mochizuki, "American and Japanese Strategic Debates: The Need for a New Synthesis," in Mochizuki, ed., *Toward a True Alliance: Restructuring U.S.-Japan Security Relations* (Washington, D.C.: Brookings, 1997), pp. 43–82.

45. This limitation is not restricted to realist analysis of Asian-Pacific security affairs. In strict analogy, realism was unable to specify whether at the end of the Cold War European states would balance with Germany against the United States as the remaining superpower or with the United States against a united Germany as a potential regional hegemon.

46. The astonishing reticence on, and lack of contact with, Taiwan that characterizes the Japanese bureaucracy provides some evidence for this view. See interview 04-00, Tokyo, January 12, 2000.

47. Victor D. Cha, "Abandonment, Entrapment, and Neoclassical Realism in Asia: The United States, Japan, and Korea," *International Studies Quarterly,* Vol. 44, No. 2 (June 2000), pp. 261–291.

48. Taking account of weakening currency values, defense spending (measured in U.S. dollars, 1997 prices) was cut in 1998 by 39 percent in Thailand, 35 percent in South Korea, 32 percent in the Philippines, 26 percent in Vietnam, and 10 percent in Japan—if measured in yen, this represents the first reduction since 1955. Asagumo Shimbun-sha, *Boei Hando Bukku* [Defense handbook] (Tokyo: Asagumo Shimbun-sha, 1998), pp. 263–267; and Tim Huxley and Susan Willett, *Arming East Asia,* Adelphi Paper 329 (Oxford: International Institute for Strategic Studies [IISS], 1999). Many analysts expect that these reductions will continue for several years. Michael Richardson, "Asian Crisis Stills Appetite for Arms," *International Herald Tribune,* April 23, 1998; and National Institute for Defense Studies, *East Asian Strategic Review, 1998–1999* (Tokyo: National Institute for Defense Studies, 1999), pp. 33–35. Only China, Taiwan, and Indonesia have avoided cuts in military expenditures. Huxley and Willett, *Arming East Asia,* p. 16. See also Frank Umbach, "Military Balance in the Asia Pacific: Trends and Implications," pp. 12–17, and Desmond Ball, "Military Balance in the Asia Pacific: Trends and Implications,"

papers prepared for the Fourteenth Asia-Pacific Roundtable, Kuala Lumpur, Malaysia, June 3–7, 2000. Since the end of the Cold War, Japanese defense expenditures show rates of increase that are much smaller than those of China. Between 1990 and 1997, while China's defense spending increased 45 percent from $25.1 billion to $36.5 billion, Japan's defense budget increased only 18 percent from $34.3 billion to $40.8 billion (1997 exchange rates). Asagumo Shimbun-sha, *Boei Hando Bukku,* p. 267; and Koro Bessho, *Identities and Security in East Asia,* Adelphi Paper 325 (Oxford: IISS, 1999), p. 35. Differences in China's and Japan's inflation rates overstate, however, the real increases in Chinese expenditures in the first half of the 1990s.

49. Michael Richardson, "Asia's Widening Arms Gap: Uneven Spread of New Weapons Systems May Jeopardize Balance of Power in East," *International Herald Tribune,* January 7, 2000.

50. Mike M. Mochizuki and Michael O'Hanlon, "A Liberal Vision for the U.S.-Japan Alliance," *Survival,* Vol. 40, No. 2 (Summer 1998), p. 127.

51. Yasuhiro Takeda, "Democracy Promotion Policies: Overcoming Japan-U.S. Discord," in Ralph A. Cossa, ed., *Restructuring the U.S.-Japan Alliance: Toward a More Equal Partnership* (Washington, D.C.: CSIS [Center for Strategic and International Studies] Press, 1997), pp. 50–62.

52. Miles Kahler, *International Institutions and the Political Economy of Integration* (Washington, D.C.: Brookings, 1995), pp. 80–81, 107–116; and Takashi Inoguchi and Grant B. Stillman, eds., *North-East Asian Regional Security: The Role of International Institutions* (Tokyo: United Nations University Press, 1997).

53. Council on Foreign Relations Independent Study Group, *The Tests of War and the Strains of Peace: The U.S.-Japan Security Relationship* (New York: Council on Foreign Relations, 1998), pp. 20–26.

54. The political leadership has denied, however, that "situations in areas surrounding Japan" involve no geographic element whatsoever. Prime Minister Keizo Obuchi claimed before the lower house budget committee that the "Middle East, the Indian Ocean, and the other side of the globe" cannot be conceived of as being covered by the new guidelines. According to this interpretation, even though an interruption of oil supplies from the Middle East would constitute a potentially serious threat to Japan, that threat, insofar as it is located in the Middle East or the Indian Ocean, would not be covered by the guidelines. "Shuhen Jitai; Chiriteki Yoso Fukumu" [Situation in areas surrounding Japan includes geographical factor], *Asahi Shimbun,* January 27, 1999, 14th ed.; and interview 01-99, January 11, 1999.

55. Interview 03-99, Tokyo, January 12, 1999.

56. "Shuhen Jitai no Chiriteki Han'i; Kyokuto to sono Shuhen" [Geographical scope of situation in areas surrounding Japan is Far East and its surrounding areas], *Asahi Shimbun,* May 23, 1998, 14th ed. Because the statement ran afoul of the government's wariness of Chinese criticism of the revised guidelines, the official was removed from his post. "Seifu Hokubei Kyokucho wo Kotetsu" [Government removes director of North American Affairs Bureau from post], *Asahi Shimbun,* July 7, 1998, evening, 4th ed.; and "Shuhen Jitai ni Aimaisa" [Situation in areas surrounding Japan is ambiguous], *Asahi Shimbun,* July 8, 1998, 14th ed.

57. Katzenstein, *Cultural Norms and National Security,* pp. 59–130.

58. Simon, "Security Prospects in Southeast Asia"; Amitav Acharya, *Constructing a Security Community: ASEAN and the Problem of Regional Order* (London: Routledge, 2000); Acharya, "Regional Institutions and Security Order in Asia"; Amitav Acharya, "Institutionalism and Balancing in the Asia Pacific Region: ASEAN, U.S. Strategic Frameworks, and the ASEAN Regional Forum" (Toronto: Department of Political Science, York University; and Singapore: Institute of Defense and Strategic Studies, Nanyang Technological University, 1999); Amitav Acharya, "Collective Identity and Conflict Management in Southeast Asia," in Emanuel Adler and Michael Barnett, eds., *Security Communities* (Cambridge: Cambridge University Press, 1998), pp. 198–227; Amitav Acharya, "A Regional Security Community in Southeast Asia?" *Journal of Strategic Studies,* Vol. 18, No. 3 (September 1995), pp. 181–182; Amitav Acharya, "The Association of Southeast Asian Nations: 'Security Community' or 'Defense Community'"? *Pacific Affairs,* Vol. 64, No. 2 (Summer 1991), pp. 159–177; Yuen Foong Khong, "Making Bricks without Straw in the Asia Pacific?" *Pacific Review,* Vol. 10, No. 2 (1997), pp. 289–300; and Yuen Foong Khong, "ASEAN's Collective Identity: Sources, Shifts, and Security Consequences," paper prepared for the annual meeting of the American Political Science Association, Boston, Massachusetts, September 3–6, 1998.

59. Khong, "Making Bricks without Straw in the Asia Pacific?" p. 296.

60. Acharya, "Institutionalism and Balancing in the Asia Pacific Region."

61. Nikolas Busse, *Die Entstehung von kollektiven Identitäten: Das Beispiel der ASEAN-Staaten* [The rise of collective identity: The example of the ASEAN states] (Baden-Baden: Nomos, 2000); and Nikolas Busse, "Constructivism and Southeast Asian Security," *Pacific Review,* Vol. 12, No. 1 (1999), pp. 39–60.

62. Interview 01-00, Singapore, June 7, 2000. South Korea used to be wary of ASEAN-led multilateral consultations, which it saw as being focused primarily on South China Sea issues. See Hideya Kurata, "Multilateralism and the Korean Problem with Respect to the Asia-Pacific Region," *Journal of Pacific Asia,* Vol. 3 (1996), pp. 132–138.

63. Acharya, "Regional Institutions and Security Order in Asia," p. 18.

64. Christopher W. Hughes, "The North Korean Nuclear Crisis and Japanese Security," *Survival,* Vol. 38, No. 2 (Summer 1996), pp. 79–103.

65. This is not an exception. All Asian states either voted against or abstained from voting on the September 27, 1999, United Nations High Commissioner for Refugees resolution calling on the UN secretary-general to establish an international commission of inquiry into violations of international law in East Timor. Rosemary Foot, "Global Institutions and the Management of Regional Security in the Asia Pacific," paper prepared for the Second Workshop on Security Order in the Asia-Pacific, Bali, Indonesia, May 30–June 2, 2000, p. 20.

66. Interviews 08-98, 01-00, and 07-00, Beijing, June 21, 1998, June 13, 2000, and June 15, 2000.

67. Interview 07-00, Tokyo, January 13, 2000.

68. In 1996, for example, Japan cochaired the ARF working group on confidence- and security-building measures. Boeicho (Defense Agency), *Boei Hakusho* [Defense white paper] (Tokyo: Okurasho Insatsu-kyoku, 1999), p. 187; Gaimusho, *Gaiko Seisho,* 1998, p. 31; and Hisane Masaki, "Japan to Co-chair Peacekeeping Group," *Japan Times,* July 17, 1998.

69. Quoted in "ASEAN's Failure: The Limits of Politeness," *Economist,* February 28, 1994, p. 44; Acharya, "Institutionalism and Balancing in the Asia Pacific Region," pp. 3, 26; and Jürgen Rüland, "ASEAN and the Asian Crisis: Theoretical Implications and Practical Consequences for Southeast Asian Regionalism," *Pacific Review,* Vol. 13, No. 3 (2000), p. 439.

70. Michael Leifer, "Regionalism Compared: The Perils and Benefits of Expansion," paper prepared for the Fourteenth Asia-Pacific Roundtable, Kuala Lumpur, Malaysia, June 3–7, 2000, p. 4.

71. Acharya, "Institutionalism and Balancing in the Asia Pacific Region," p. 2.

72. Doug Bandow, "Old Wine in New Bottles: The Pentagon's East Asia Security Strategy Report," *Policy Analysis,* No. 344, CATO Institute, May 18, 1999; Council on Foreign Relations Independent Study Group, *The Tests of War and the Strains of Peace;* and Joseph S. Nye, "The 'Nye Report': Six Years Later," *International Relations of the Asia-Pacific,* Vol. 1, No. 1 (2001), pp. 95–104.

73. We would like to thank Michael Green for clarifying this point for us.

74. James E. Auer, "A Win-Win Alliance for Asia," *Japan Times,* August 8, 1998.

75. Interview 03-00, Tokyo, January 11, 1999.

76. Interviews 01-98, 04-98, 05-98, 07-98, and 09-98, Beijing, June 15, 16, 19, 20, and 22, 1998; and Allen M. Carlson, "The Lock on China's Door: Chinese Foreign Policy and the Sovereignty Norm," Ph.D. dissertation, Yale University, 2000. See also the cautious notes of optimism in Christensen, "China, the U.S.-Japan Alliance, and the Security Dilemma in East Asia," pp. 69–80.

77. A mixture of realist and liberal categories is also better than either alone to capture the combination of balancing and engagement characteristic of the diplomatic strategies of many Asian-Pacific states. Interview 02-00, Tokyo, January 11, 1999. Even though some Southeast Asian states (such as Indonesia, the Philippines, and Vietnam) are wary of China because of past or current territorial disputes, they nevertheless seek to engage it in multilateral institutions such as the ARF. And even though Japan is the overwhelming power in Southeast Asia, its relations with states in the region have been good and are getting better in the wake of the Asian financial crisis.

78. David E. Spiro, *The Hidden Hand of American Hegemony: Petrodollar Recycling and International Markets* (Ithaca, N.Y.: Cornell University Press, 1999); and Alastair Iain Johnston, *Cultural Realism: Strategic Culture and Grand Strategy in Chinese History* (Princeton, N.J.: Princeton University Press, 1995).

79. Christensen, "China, the U.S.-Japan Alliance, and the Security Dilemma in East Asia," pp. 62–69.

80. Interviews 02-99, 05-99, 11-99, and 13-99, Tokyo, January 11–12 and 14, 1999.

81. Interview 03-99, Tokyo, January 12, 1999.

82. Interviews 02-99 and 13-99, Tokyo, January 11 and 14, 1999.

83. John King Fairbank, ed., *The Chinese World Order: Traditional China's Foreign Relations* (Cambridge, Mass.: Harvard University Press, 1968).

84. David C. Kang, "Asian Nations Bandwagon," in G. John Ikenberry and Michael Mastanduno, eds., *The Emerging International Relations of the Asia Pacific Region* (New York: Columbia University Press, forthcoming), pp. 14–16 (ms.); and Susanne Feske, "Japan und die USA: Zivilmächte im asiatisch-pazifischen Raum?" [Japan and the U.S.A.: Civilian Powers in Asia-Pacific?] Trier Arbeitspapiere zum

DFG-Forschungsprojekt "Zivilmächte in der internationalen Politik" [Trier working papers for the DFG research project "Civilian powers in international politics"] Trier, Germany, July 1997, pp. 18–19.

85. Randall L. Schweller, "Bandwagoning for Profit: Bringing the Revisionist State Back In," *International Security,* Vol. 19, No. 1 (Summer 1994), pp. 72–107.

86. Michel Oksenberg, "The Issue of Sovereignty in the Asian Historical Context," in Stephen D. Krasner, ed., *Problematic Sovereignty: Contested Rules and Political Possibilities* (New York: Columbia University Press, 2001), pp. 83–104. See also Stephen D. Krasner, "Organized Hypocrisy in 19th Century East Asia," *International Relations of the Asia-Pacific,* Vol. 1, No. 2 (2001), pp. 173–197. Fairbank has been criticized often for taking the self-interested descriptions of Chinese court literati as unproblematic data describing how the system of tributary trade was actually working. For follow-up research that investigates how this system of trade may have operated in practice, see, for example, Morris Rossabi, ed., *China among Equals: The Middle Kingdom and Its Neighbors, 10th–14th Centuries* (Berkeley: University of California Press, 1983); John E. Wills, Jr., *Embassies and Illusions: Dutch and Portuguese Envoys to K'ang-hsi, 1666–1687* (Cambridge, Mass.: Harvard University Press, 1984); and James L. Hevia, *Cherishing Men from Afar: Qing Guest Ritual and the Macartney Embassy of 1793* (Durham, N.C.: Duke University Press, 1995). Fairbank's failing is not uncommon. It is shared by realists who rely on Thucydides as an unquestioned historical source for the Peloponnesian War.

87. Jervis, "Realism, Neoliberalism, and Cooperation," pp. 61–62.

88. Matake Kamiya, "The U.S.-Japan Alliance and Regional Security Cooperation: Toward a Double-Layered Security System," in Cossa, *Restructuring the U.S.-Japan Alliance,* pp. 21–22.

89. Interview 13-99, Tokyo, January 14, 1999.

90. Peter Alexis Gourevitch, "The Governance Problem in International Relations," in David A. Lake and Robert Powell, eds., *Strategic Choice and International Relations* (Princeton, N.J.: Princeton University Press, 1999), p. 137; and Jervis, "Realism, Neoliberalism, and Cooperation," pp. 58–63.

91. Interview 04-00, Tokyo, January 12, 2000.

92. Acharya, "Institutionalism and Balancing in the Asia Pacific Region"; Amitav Acharya, "Regionalism and the Emerging (Intrusive) World Order: Sovereignty, Autonomy, Identity," paper presented at the CSGR (Centre for the Study of Globalisation and Regionalisation) Third Annual Conference, After the Global Crisis What Next for Regionalism? Scarman House, University of Warwick, September 16–18, 1999; Acharya, "Collective Identity"; Acharya, "A Regional Security Community"; Busse, *Die Entstehung von kollektiven Identitäten;* Busse, "Constructivism and Southeast Asian Security"; Joseph Y. S. Cheng, "China's ASEAN Policy in the 1990s: Pushing for Multipolarity in the Regional Context," Contemporary China Centre, City University of Hong Kong, n.d.; Alastair Iain Johnston, "The Myth of the ASEAN Way? Explaining the Evolution of the ASEAN Regional Forum," in Helga Haftendorn, Robert O. Keohane, and Celeste A. Wallander, eds., *Imperfect Unions: Security Institutions over Time and Space* (Oxford: Oxford University Press, 1999), pp. 287–324; Khong, "ASEAN's Collective Identity"; and Simon, "Security Prospects for Southeast Asia."

93. To the extent that recent analyses of Japanese and Asian-Pacific security have chosen to simply ignore or misinterpret sociology or constructivism, they have unnecessarily weakened the contribution they make by misconstruing sociological analyses as inherently optimistic (Robert M. Uriu, "Domestic-International Interactions and Japanese Security Studies," *Journal of Asian and African Studies*, Vol. 33, No. 1 [1998], pp. 76–93) and ahistorical (Robert M. Uriu, "Domestic-International Inter-actions and Japanese Security Studies," in James Sperling, Yogendra Malik, and David Louscher, eds., *Zones of Amity, Zones of Enmity: The Prospects for Economic and Military Security in Asia* [Leiden: Brill, 1998], pp. 85–86); failing to address explicitly the relevance of collective identities, while appealing obliquely to regional security communities that presuppose the existence of such identities (Mochizuki and O'Hanlon, "A Liberal Vision"); offering a misleadingly partial analysis of mercantilism that both neglects the ideological component of that intriguing concept and misinterprets a sociological explanation of Japanese foreign policy as dealing merely with an exceptional case in a realist world (Eric Hegin-botham and Richard J. Samuels, "Mercantile Realism and Japanese Foreign Policy," *International Security*, Vol. 22, No. 4 [Spring 1998], pp. 171–203), in sharp con-trast to the much richer and more compelling argument proposed by Richard J. Samuels in his book *Rich Nation, Strong Army: National Security and the Techno-logical Transformation of Japan* (Ithaca, N.Y.: Cornell University Press, 1994); wavering between a cultural and a materialist presentation of realist theory (Michael J. Green, "State of the Field Report: Research on Japanese Security Policy," *Access Asia Review*, Vol. 2, No. 1 [September 1998], pp. 13, 15, 37); neglecting that, in the case of Japanese security, sociological analyses focus their attention not on specific variants of realism but on rationalist explanations more generally, and that they explain not merely national security narrowly construed but also internal and economic security more broadly understood, issues that elude realist theorizing (Tsuyoshi Kawasaki, "Postclassical Realism and Japanese Security Policy," paper prepared for the annual meeting of the American Political Science Association, Atlanta, Georgia, September 2–5, 1999); and by overlooking how norms that constitute Japan's collective identity as a "non-threatening, peace-loving, state" are nested in underlying and more fundamental norms of Japan as a nonmajoritarian political community (Daniel Okimoto, "The Japan-America Security Alliance: Prospects for the Twenty-First Century," Stanford University, Institute for Interna-tional Studies, Asia/Pacific Research Center, 1998, pp. 28–29).

94. Rudra Sil, "The Foundations of Eclecticism: The Epistemological Status of Agency, Culture, and Structure in Social Theory," *Journal of Theoretical Politics*, Vol. 12, No. 3 (2000), pp. 353, 387.

95. Robert Jervis, *System Effects: Complexity in Political and Social Life* (Princeton, N.J.: Princeton University Press, 1997).

Chapter 1

HOW TO THINK ABOUT INTERNATIONAL RELATIONS: PERSPECTIVES AND LEVELS OF ANALYSIS

1.1

THE REALIST CRITIQUE

E. H. Carr

In this seminal essay written before World War II, E. H. Carr attacks the idealist or utopian view of world affairs. His "realist critique" is that all theory, thought, and ideas are a product of material circumstances and serve the interests and power of the people and societies that propound them. There are no universal principles or propositions that rise above historical circumstances. The one reality is the dispersion of power, which begets in turn the dispersion of principles. Notice that material factors (realist) cause ideational ones (identity). Ideas are "epiphenomenal." All thinking is relative to the purpose and interests of powerful leaders, groups, or societies. These groups, because their self-interest dominates the common interest, "come easily to believe that arrangements agreeable to themselves are beneficial to others." But the common interests of "laissez-faire" in the nineteenth century and of "international order" and "international solidarity" in the twentieth century were nothing more than the national interests of Great Britain and the United States and the Soviet Union, the preeminent powers of those times.

... [R]ealism enters the field far behind utopianism and by way of reaction from it. The thesis that "justice is the right of the stronger" was, indeed, familiar in the Hellenic world. But it never represented anything more than the protest of an uninfluential minority, puzzled by the divergence between political

Source: E. H. Carr and Michael Cox, "The Realist Critique," in *The Twenty Years' Crisis, 1919–1939: An Introduction to the Study of International Relations* (Basingstoke, UK: Palgrave, 2001 [1940]), 62–83.

theory and political practice. Under the supremacy of the Roman Empire, and later of the Catholic Church, the problem could hardly arise; for the political good, first of the empire, then of the church, could be regarded as identical with moral good. It was only with the break-up of the mediaeval system that the divergence between political theory and political practice became acute and challenging. Machiavelli is the first important political realist.

Machiavelli's starting-point is a revolt against the utopianism of current political thought:

> It being my intention to write a thing which shall be useful to him who appre-hends it, it appears to me more appropriate to follow up the real truth of a matter than the imagination of it; for many have pictured republics and prin-cipalities which in fact have never been seen and known, because how one lives is so far distant from how one ought to live that he who neglects what is done for what ought to be done sooner effects his ruin than his preservation.

The three essential tenets implicit in Machiavelli's doctrine are the foundation-stones of the realist philosophy. In the first place, history is a sequence of cause and effect, whose course can be analyzed and understood by intellectual effort, but not (as the utopians believe) directed by "imagination." Secondly, theory does not (as the utopians assume) create practice, but practice theory. In Machiavelli's words, "good counsels, whencesoever they come, are born of the wisdom of the prince, and not the wisdom of the prince from good counsels." Thirdly, politics are not (as the utopians pretend) a function of ethics, but ethics of politics. Men "are kept honest by constraint." Machiavelli recognized the importance of morality, but thought that there could be no effective morality where there was no effective authority. Morality is the product of power.[1]

* * *

Modern realism differs, however, in one important respect from that of the sixteenth and seventeenth centuries. Both utopianism and realism accepted and incorporated in their philosophies the eighteenth-century belief in progress, with the curious and somewhat paradoxical result that realism became in appearance more "progressive" than utopianism. Utopianism grafted its belief in progress on to its belief in an absolute ethical standard, which remained *ex hypothesi* static. Realism, having no such sheet-anchor, became more and more dynamic and relativist. Progress became part of the inner essence of the historical process; and mankind was moving forward towards a goal which was left undefined, or was differently defined by different philosophers. The "his-torical school" of realists had its home in Germany, and its development is traced through the great names of Hegel and Marx. But no country in Western Europe, and no branch of thought, was immune from its influence in the middle and later years of the nineteenth century; and this development, while it has freed realism from the pessimistic coloring imparted to it by thinkers like Machiavelli and Hobbes, has thrown its determinist character into stronger relief.

* * *

The Relativity of Thought

The outstanding achievement of modern realism, however, has been to reveal, not merely the determinist aspects of the historical process, but the relative and pragmatic character of thought itself. In the last fifty years, thanks mainly though not wholly to the influence of Marx, the principles of the historical school have been applied to the analysis of thought; and the foundations of a new science have been laid, principally by German thinkers under the name of the "sociology of knowledge." The realist has thus been enabled to demonstrate that the intellectual theories and ethical standards of utopianism, far from being the expression of absolute and *a priori* principles, are historically conditioned, being both products of circumstances and interests and weapons framed for the furtherance of interests. "Ethical notions," as Mr. Bertrand Russell has remarked, "are very seldom a cause, but almost always an effect, a means of claiming universal legislative authority for our own preferences, not, as we fondly imagine, the actual ground of those preferences."[2] This is by far the most formidable attack which utopianism has to face; for here the very foundations of its belief are undermined by the realist critique.

* * *

The principle has an extremely wide field of application. It has become a commonplace to say that theories do not mould the course of events, but are invented to explain them. "Empire precedes imperialism."[3] Eighteenth-century England "put into practice the policy of *laissez-faire* before it found a justification, or even an apparent justification, in the new doctrine";[4] and "the virtual break-up of *laissez-faire* as a body of doctrine ... has followed, and not preceded, the decline of *laissez-faire* in the real world."[5] The theory of "socialism in a single country" promulgated in Soviet Russia in 1924 was manifestly a product of the failure of Soviet regimes to establish themselves in other countries.

* * *

The Adjustment of Thought to Purpose

Thought is not merely relative to the circumstances and interests of the thinker: it is also pragmatic in the sense that it is directed to the fulfillment of his purposes. For the realist, as a witty writer has put it, truth is "no more than the perception of discordant experience pragmatically adjusted for a particular purpose and for the time being."[6] The purposeful character of thought has been discussed in a previous chapter; and a few examples will suffice here to illustrate the importance of this phenomenon in international politics.

Theories designed to discredit an enemy or potential enemy are one of the commonest forms of purposeful thinking. To depict one's enemies or one's prospective victims as inferior beings in the sight of God has been a familiar technique at any rate since the days of the Old Testament. Racial theories, ancient and modern, belong to this category; for the rule of one people or class over another is always justified by a belief in the mental and moral inferiority of the ruled. In such theories, sexual abnormality and sexual offenses are commonly imputed to the discredited race or group. Sexual depravity is imputed by the white American to the Negro; by the white South African to the Kaffir; by the Anglo-Indian to the Hindu; and by the Nazi German to the Jew. The most popular and most absurd of the charges leveled against the Bolsheviks in the early days of the Russian revolution was that they advocated sexual promiscuity. Atrocity stories, among which offenses of a sexual character predominate, are the familiar product of war. On the eve of their invasion of Abyssinia, the Italians issued an official Green Book of Abyssinian atrocities. "The Italian Government", as the Abyssinian delegate at Geneva correctly observed, "having resolved to conquer and destroy Ethiopia, begins by giving Ethiopia a bad name."[7]

*   *   *

The converse of this propagation of theories designed to throw moral discredit on an enemy is the propagation of theories reflecting moral credit on oneself and one's own policies. Bismarck records the remark made to him by Walewski, the French Foreign Minister, in 1857, that it was the business of a diplomat to cloak the interests of his country in the language of universal justice. More recently, Mr. Churchill told the House of Commons that "there must be a moral basis for British rearmament and foreign policy."[8] It is rare, however, for modern statesmen to express themselves with this frankness; and in contemporary British and American politics, the most powerful influence has been wielded by those more utopian statesmen who are sincerely convinced that policy is deduced from ethical principles, not ethical principles from policy. The realist is nevertheless obliged to uncover the hollowness of this conviction. "The right," said Woodrow Wilson to the United States Congress in 1917, "is more precious than peace."[9] "Peace comes before all," said Briand ten years later to the League of Nations Assembly, "peace comes even before justice."[10] Considered as ethical principles, both these contradictory pronouncements are tenable and could muster respectable support. Are we therefore to believe that we are dealing with a clash of ethical standards, and that if Wilson's and Briand's policies differed it was because they deduced them from opposite principles? No serious student of politics will entertain this belief. The most cursory examination shows that the principles were deduced from the policies, not the policies from the principles. In 1917, Wilson had decided on the policy of war with Germany, and he proceeded to clothe that policy in the appropriate garment of righteousness. In 1928 Briand was fearful of attempts made in the name of justice to disturb a peace settlement favorable to France; and he had no more difficulty than Wilson in finding the moral phraseology which fitted his policy. It would be irrelevant to discuss this supposed difference of principles on ethical grounds. The principles merely reflected different national policies framed to meet different conditions.

* * *

National Interest and the Universal Good

The realist should not, however, linger over the infliction of these pin-pricks through chinks in the utopian defenses. His task is to bring down the whole cardboard structure of utopian thought by exposing the hollowness of the material out of which it is built. The weapon of the relativity of thought must be used to demolish the utopian concept of a fixed and absolute standard by which policies and actions can be judged. If theories are revealed as a reflection of practice and principles of political needs, this discovery will apply to the fundamental theories and principles of the utopian creed, and not least to the doctrine of the harmony of interests which is its essential postulate.

It will not be difficult to show that the Utopian, when he preaches the doctrine of the harmony of interests, is innocently and unconsciously adopting Walewski's maxim, and clothing his own interest in the guise of a universal interest for the purpose of imposing it on the rest of the world. "Men come easily to believe that arrangements agreeable to themselves are beneficial to others," as Dicey observed;[11] and theories of the public good, which turn out on inspection to be an elegant disguise for some particular interest, are as common in international as in national affairs. The utopian, however eager he may be to establish an absolute standard, does not argue that it is the duty of his country, in conformity with that standard, to put the interest of the world at large before its own interest; for that would be contrary to his theory that the interest of all coincides with the interest of each. He argues that what is best for the world is best for his country, and then reverses the argument to read that what is best for his country is best for the world, the two propositions being, from the utopian standpoint, identical; and this unconscious cynicism of the contemporary utopian has proved a far more effective diplomatic weapon than the deliberate and self-conscious cynicism of a Walewski or a Bismarck. British writers of the past half-century have been particularly eloquent supporters of the theory that the maintenance of British supremacy is the performance of a duty to mankind. "If Great Britain has turned itself into a coal-shed and blacksmith's forge," remarked *The Times* ingenuously in 1885, "it is for the behoof of mankind as well as its own."[12] The following extract is typical of a dozen which might be culled from memoirs of public men of the period:

I have but one great object in this world, and that is to maintain the greatness of the Empire. But apart from my John Bull sentiment upon the point, I firmly believe that in doing so I work in the cause of Christianity, of peace, of civilization, and the happiness of the human race generally.[13]

"I contend that we are the first race in the world," wrote Cecil Rhodes, "and that the more of the world we inhabit the better it is for the human race."[14] In 1891, the most popular and brilliant journalist of the day, W. T. Stead, founded the *Review of Reviews*. "We believe in God, in England and in Humanity," ran the editorial manifesto in its opening number. "The English-speaking race is one of the chief of God's chosen agents for executing coming improvements in the lot of mankind."[15] An Oxford professor was convinced in 1912 that the secret of Britain's history was that "in fighting for her own independence she has been fighting for the freedom of Europe, and that the service thus rendered to Europe and to mankind has carried with it the possibility of that larger service to which we give the name Empire."[16]

*   *   *

In recent times, the same phenomenon has become endemic in the United States. The story how McKinley prayed for divine guidance and decided to annex the Philippines is a classic of modern American history; and this annexation was the occasion of a popular outburst of moral self-approval hitherto more familiar in the foreign policy of Great Britain, than of the United States. Theodore Roosevelt, who believed more firmly than any previous American President in the doctrine *L'etat, c'est moi,* carried the process a step further. The following curious dialogue occurred in his cross-examination during a libel action brought against him in 1915 by a Tammany leader:

Query: How did you know that substantial justice was done?

Roosevelt: Because I did it, because … I was doing my best.

Query: You mean to say that, when you do a thing, thereby substantial justice is done.

Roosevelt: I do. When I do a thing, I do it so as to do substantial justice. I mean just that.[17]

Woodrow Wilson was less naively egotistical, but more profoundly confident of the identity of American policy and universal justice. After the bombardment of Vera Cruz in 1914, he assured the world that "the United States had gone down to Mexico to serve mankind."[18] During the first world war, he advised American naval cadets "not only always to think first of America, but Always, also, to think, first of humanity"—a feat rendered slightly less difficult by his explanation that the United States had been "founded for the benefit of humanity."[19] Shortly before the entry of the United States into the war, in an address to the Senate on war aims, he stated the identification still more categorically: "These are American principles American Policies.... They are the principles of mankind and must prevail."[20]

* * *

... Theories of social morality are always the product of a dominant group which identifies itself with the community as a whole, and which possesses facilities denied to subordinate groups or individuals for imposing its view of life on the community. Theories of international morality are, for the same reason and in virtue of the same process, the product of dominant nations or groups of nations. For the past hundred years, and more especially since 1918, the English-speaking peoples have formed the dominant group in the world; and current theories of international morality have been designed to perpetuate their supremacy and expressed in the idiom peculiar to them. France, retaining something of her eighteenth-century tradition and restored to a position of dominance for a short period after 1918, has played a minor part in the creation of current international morality, mainly through her insistence on the role of law in the moral order. Germany, never a dominant Power and reduced to helplessness after 1918, has remained for these reasons outside the charmed circle of creators of international morality. Both the view that the English-speaking peoples are monopolists of international morality and the view that they are consummate international hypocrites may be reduced to the plain fact that the current canons of international virtue have, by a natural and inevitable process, been mainly created by them.

The Realist Critique of the Harmony of Interests

The doctrine of the harmony of interests yields readily to analysis in terms of this principle. It is the natural assumption of a prosperous and privileged class, whose members have a dominant voice in the community and are therefore naturally prone to identify its interest with their own. In virtue of this identification, any assailant of the interests of the dominant group is made to incur the odium of assailing the alleged common interest of the whole community, and is told that in making this assault he is attacking his own higher interests. The doctrine of the harmony of interests thus serves as an ingenious moral device invoked, in perfect sincerity, by privileged groups in order to justify and maintain their dominant position. But a further point requires notice. The supremacy within the community of the privileged group may be, and often is, so overwhelming that there is, in fact, a sense in which its interests are those of the community, since its well-being necessarily carries with it some measure of well-being for other members of the community, and its collapse would entail the collapse of the community as a whole. In so far, therefore, as the alleged natural harmony of interests has any reality, it is created by the overwhelming power of the privileged group, and is an excellent illustration of the Machiavellian maxim that morality is the product of Power. A few examples will make this analysis of the doctrine of the harmony of interests clear.

In the nineteenth century, the British manufacturer or merchant, having discovered that *Laissez-faire* promoted his own prosperity, was sincerely convinced that it also promoted British prosperity as a whole. Nor was this alleged harmony of interests between himself and the community entirely fictitious. The predominance of the manufacturer and the merchant was so overwhelming that there was a sense in which an identity between their prosperity and British prosperity as a whole could be correctly asserted. From this it was only a short step to argue that a worker on strike, in damaging the prosperity of the British manufacturer, was damaging British prosperity as a whole, and thereby damaging his own, so that he could be plausibly denounced by the predecessors of Professor Toynbee as immoral and by the predecessors of Professor Zimmern as muddle-headed. Moreover, there was a sense in which this argument was perfectly correct. Nevertheless, the doctrine of the harmony of interests and of solidarity between the classes must have seemed a bitter mockery to the underprivileged worker, whose inferior status and insignificant stake in "British prosperity" were consecrated by it; and presently he was strong enough to force the abandonment of *laissez-faire* and the substitution for it of the "social service state," which implicitly denies the natural harmony of interests and sets out to create a new harmony by artificial means.

The same analysis may be applied in international relations. British nineteenth-century statesmen, having discovered that free trade promoted British prosperity, were sincerely convinced that, in doing so, it also promoted the prosperity of the world as a whole. British predominance in world trade was at that time so overwhelming that there was a certain undeniable harmony between British interests and the interests of the world. British prosperity flowed over into other countries, and a British economic collapse would have meant world-wide ruin. British free traders could and did argue that protectionist Countries were not only egotistically damaging the prosperity of the world as a whole, but were stupidly damaging their own, so that their behavior was both immoral and muddle headed. In British eyes, it was irrefutably proved that international trade was a single whole, and flourished or slumped to ether. Nevertheless, this alleged international harmony of interests seemed a mockery to those under-privileged nations whose inferior status and insignificant stake in international trade were consecrated by it. The revolt against it destroyed that overwhelming British preponderance which had provided: a plausible basis for the theory. Economically, Great Britain in the nineteenth century was dominant enough to make a bold bid to impose on the world her own conception of international economic morality. When competition of all against all replaced the domination of the world market by a single Power, conceptions of international economic morality necessarily became chaotic.

*   *   *

The Realist Critique of Internationalism

The concept of internationalism is a special form of the doctrine of the harmony of interests. It yields to the same analysis; and there are the same difficulties about regarding it as an absolute standard independent of the interests and policies of those who promulgate it. "Cosmopolitanism," wrote Sun Yat-sen, "is the same thing as China's theory of world empire two thousand years ago.... China once wanted to be sovereign lord of the earth and to stand above every other nation, so she espoused cosmopolitanism."[21] In the Egypt of the Eighteenth Dynasty, according to Freud, "imperialism was reflected in religion as universality and monotheism."[22] The doctrine of a single world-state, propagated by the Roman Empire and later by the Catholic Church, was the symbol of a claim to universal dominion. Modern internationalism has its genesis in seventeenth- and eighteenth-century France, during which French hegemony in Europe was at its height. This was the period which produced Sully's *Grand Dessin* and the Abbè Saint-Pierre's *Projet de Paix Perpetuelle* (both plans to perpetuate an international *status quo* favorable to the French monarchy), which saw the birth of the humanitarian and cosmopolitan doctrines of the Enlightenment, and which established French as the universal language of educated people. In the next century, the leadership passed to Great Britain, which became the home of internationalism. On the eve of the Great Exhibition of 1851 which, more than any other single event, established Great Britain's title to world supremacy, the Prince Consort spoke movingly of "that great end to which ... all history points—the realization of the unity of mankind";[23] and Tennyson hymned "the parliament of man, the federation of the world." France chose the moment of her greatest supremacy in the nineteen-twenties to launch a plan of European Union"; and Japan shortly afterwards developed an ambition to proclaim herself the leader of a united Asia. It was symptomatic of the growing international predominance of the United States when widespread popularity was enjoyed in the late nineteen-thirties by the book of an American journalist advocating a world union of democracies, in which the United States would play the predominant role.[24]

Just as pleas for "national solidarity" in domestic politics always come from a dominant group which can use this solidarity to strengthen its own control over the nation as a whole, so pleas for international solidarity and world union come from those dominant nations which may hope to exercise control over a unified world. Countries which are struggling to force their way into the dominant group naturally tend to invoke nationalism against the internationalism of the controlling Powers. In the sixteenth century, England opposed her nascent nationalism to the internationalism of the Papacy and the Empire. In the past century and a half Germany opposed her nascent nationalism to the internationalism first of France, then of Great Britain. This circumstance made her impervious to those universalist and humanitarian doctrines which were popular in eighteenth-century France and nineteenth-century Britain; and her hostility to internationalism was further aggravated after 1919, when Great Britain and

France endeavored to create a new "international order" as a bulwark of their own predominance. "By 'international'," wrote a German correspondent in *The Times,* "we have come to understand a conception that places other nations at an advantage over our own."[25] Nevertheless, there was little doubt that Germany, if she became supreme in Europe, would adopt international slogans and establish some kind of international organization to bolster up her power. A British Labor ex-Minister at one moment advocated the suppression of Article 16 of the Covenant of the League of Nations on the unexpected ground that the totalitarian states might some day capture the League and invoke that article to justify the use of force by themselves.[26] It seemed more likely that they would seek to develop the Anti-Comintern Pact into some form of international organization. "The Anti-Comintern Pact," said Hitler in the Reichstag on January 30, 1939, "will perhaps one day become the crystallization point of a group of Powers whose ultimate aim is none other than to eliminate the menace to the peace and culture of the world instigated by a satanic apparition." "Either Europe must achieve solidarity," remarked an Italian journal about the same time, "or the 'axis' will impose it."[27] "Europe in its entirety," said Goebbels, "is adopting a new order and a new orientation under the intellectual leadership of National Socialist Germany and Fascist Italy."[28] These were symptoms not of a change of heart, but of the fact that Germany and Italy felt themselves to be approaching the time when they might become strong enough to espouse internationalism. "International order" and "international solidarity" will always be slogans of those who feel strong enough to impose them on others.

* * *

Notes

1. Machiavelli, *The Prince,* chs. 15 and 23 (Engl. Transl., Everyman's Library, pp. 121, 193).
2. *Proceedings of the Aristotelian Society,* 1915–16, p. 302.
3. J. A. Hobson, *Free Thought in the Social Sciences,* p. 190.
4. Elie Halevy, *The Growth of Philosophic Radicalism* (Engl. transl.), p. 104.
5. M. Dobb, *Political Economy and Capitalism,* p. 188.
6. Carl Becker, *Yale Review,* xxvii, p. 461.
7. *League of Nations: Official Journal,* November 1935, p. 1140.
8. House of Commons, March 14, 1938: *Official Report,* cols. 95–9.
9. *The Public Papers of Woodrow Wilson: War and Peace,* ed. R. S. Baker, i. p. 16.
10. *League of Nations: Ninth Assembly,* p. 83.
11. A. V. Dicey, *Law and Opinion in England* (2nd ed.), pp. 14–5.
12. *The Times,* August 27, 1885.
13. Sir Frederick Maurice and Sir George Arthur, *The Life of Lord Wolseley,* p. 314.
14. W. T. Stead, *The Last Will and Testament of Cecil J. Rhodes,* p. 58.
15. *Review of Reviews,* January 15, 1891.
16. Spencer Wilkinson, *Government and the War,* p. 116.

17. Quoted in H. F. Pringle, *Theodore Roosevelt,* p. 318.
18. *Public Papers of Woodrow Wilson: The New Democracy,* ed. R. S. Baker, i. p. 104.
19. Ibid., p. 318–19.
20. Ibid., ii. p. 414.
21. Sun Yat-sen, *San Min Chu I* (Engl. transl.), pp. 68–9.
22. Sigmund Freud, *Moses and Monotheism,* p. 36.
23. T. Martin, *Life of the Prince Consort,* iii. p. 247.
24. Clarence Streit, *Union Now.*
25. *The Times,* November 5, 1938.
26. Lord Marley in the House of Lords, November 30, 1938: *Official Report,* col. 258.
27. *Relazioni Internazionali,* quoted in *The Times,* December 5, 1938.
28. *Volkischer Beobachter,* April 1, 1939.

1.2

REALISM AND COMPLEX INTERDEPENDENCE

Robert O. Keohane and Joseph S. Nye

> In this early article, Robert O. Keohane and Joseph S. Nye outline an alternative liberal perspective on international relations, one they call "complex interdependence." Notice that they shift the focus persistently away from factors emphasized by realist perspectives to factors emphasized by liberal perspectives: from state to nonstate actors, from security (self-help) to economics (collective goods), from force and war to interdependence and international organizations, and from hierarchy to multiple issue areas that make the vertical linkage of issues more difficult and horizontal bargaining more reciprocal. As they say, complex interdependence does not replace the balance of military power; "military power can still be useful politically." But they are confident that modernization is changing the world in a way that devalues the use of force. They give the emphasis, in other words, to liberal versus realist perspectives.

One's assumptions about world politics profoundly affect what one sees and how one constructs theories to explain events. We believe that the assumptions of political realists, whose theories dominated the postwar period, are often an inadequate basis for analyzing the politics of interdependence. The realist assumptions about world politics can be seen as defining an extreme set of conditions or *ideal type*. One could also imagine very different conditions. In this chapter, we shall construct another ideal type, the opposite of realism. We call it *complex interdependence*. After establishing the differences between realism and complex interdependence, we shall argue that complex interdependence sometimes comes closer to reality than does realism. When it does, traditional explanations of change in international regimes become questionable and the search for new explanatory models becomes more urgent.

For political realists, international politics, like all other politics, is a struggle for power but, unlike domestic politics, a struggle dominated by organized violence. In the words of the most influential postwar textbook, "All history shows that nations active in international politics are continuously preparing for,

Source: Robert O. Keohane and Joseph S. Nye, "Realism and Complex Interdependence," in *Power and Interdependence: World Politics in Transition* (Boston: Little, Brown, 1977), 23–37.

actively involved in, or recovering from organized violence in the form of war."[1]
Three assumptions are integral to the realist vision. First, states as coherent
units are the dominant actors in world politics. This is a double assumption:
states are predominant; and they act as coherent units. Second, realists assume
that force is a usable and effective instrument of policy. Other instruments may
also be employed, but using or threatening force is the most effective means of
wielding power. Third, partly because of their second assumption, realists
assume a hierarchy of issues in world politics, headed by questions of military
security: the "high politics" of military security dominates the "low politics" of
economic and social affairs.

These realist assumptions define an ideal type of world politics. They allow
us to imagine a world in which politics is continually characterized by active or
potential conflict among states, with the use of force possible at any time. Each
state attempts to defend its territory and interests from real or perceived threats.
Political integration among states is slight and lasts only as long as it serves the
national interests of the most powerful states. Transnational actors either do
not exist or are politically unimportant. Only the adept exercise of force or the
threat of force permits states to survive, and only while statesmen succeed in
adjusting their interests, as in a well-functioning balance of power, is the system
stable.

Each of the realist assumptions can be challenged. If we challenge them
all simultaneously, we can imagine a world in which actors other than states
participate directly in world politics, in which a clear hierarchy of issues does
not exist, and in which force is an ineffective instrument of policy. Under these
conditions—which we call the characteristics of complex interdependence—one
would expect world politics to be very different than under realist conditions.

We will explore these differences in the next section of this chapter. We do
not argue, however, that complex interdependence faithfully reflects world
political reality. Quite the contrary: both it and the realist portrait are ideal
types. Most situations will fall somewhere between these two extremes. Sometimes, realist assumptions will be accurate, or largely accurate, but frequently
complex interdependence will provide a better portrayal of reality. Before one
decides what explanatory model to apply to a situation or problem, one will
need to understand the degree to which realist or complex interdependence
assumptions correspond to the situation.

The Characteristics of Complex Interdependence

Complex interdependence has three main characteristics:

1. *Multiple channels* connect societies, including: informal ties between
governmental elites as well as formal foreign office arrangements; informal ties
among nongovernmental elites (face-to-face and through telecommunications);
and transnational organizations (such as multinational banks or corporations).
These channels can be summarized as interstate, transgovernmental, and transnational relations. *Interstate* relations are the normal channels assumed by realists.

Transgovernmental applies when we relax the realist assumption that states act coherently as units; *transnational* applies when we relax the assumption that states are the only units.

2. The agenda of interstate relationships consists of multiple issues that are not arranged in a clear or consistent hierarchy. This *absence of hierarchy among issues* means, among other things, that military security does not consistently dominate the agenda. Many issues arise from what used to be considered domestic policy, and the distinction between domestic and foreign issues becomes blurred. These issues are considered in several government departments (not just foreign offices), and at several levels. Inadequate policy coordination on these issues involves significant costs. Different issues generate different coalitions, both within governments and across them, and involve different degrees of conflict. Politics does not stop at the waters' edge.

3. Military force is not used by governments toward other governments within the region, or on the issues, when complex interdependence prevails. It may, however, be important in these governments' relations with governments outside that region, or on other issues. Military force could, for instance, be irrelevant to resolving disagreements on economic issues among members of an alliance, yet at the same time be very important for that alliance's political and military relations with a rival bloc. For the former relationships this condition of complex interdependence would be met; for the latter, it would not.

* * *

Multiple Channels

A visit to any major airport is a dramatic way to confirm the existence of multiple channels of contact among advanced industrial countries; there is a voluminous literature to prove it.[2] Bureaucrats from different countries deal directly with one another at meetings and on the telephone as well as in writing. Similarly, nongovernmental elites frequently get together in the normal course of business, in organizations such as the Trilateral Commission, and in conferences sponsored by private foundations.

In addition, multinational firms and banks affect both domestic and interstate relations. The limits on private firms, or the closeness of ties between government and business, vary considerably from one society to another; but the participation of large and dynamic organizations, not controlled entirely by governments, has become a normal part of foreign as well as domestic relations.

These actors are important not only because of their activities in pursuit of their own interests, but also because they act as transmission belts, making government policies in various countries more sensitive to one another. As the scope of governments' domestic activities has broadened, and as corporations, banks, and (to a lesser extent) trade unions have made decisions that transcend national boundaries, the domestic policies of different countries impinge on one another more and more. Transnational communications reinforce these effects. Thus, foreign economic policies touch more domestic economic activity than in the past, blurring the lines between domestic and foreign policy and increasing the number of issues relevant to foreign policy. Parallel developments in issues of environmental regulation and control over technology reinforce this trend.

Absence of Hierarchy among Issues

Foreign affairs agendas—that is, sets of issues relevant to foreign policy with which governments are concerned—have become larger and more diverse. No longer can all issues be subordinated to military security. As Secretary of State Kissinger described the situation in 1975:

> progress in dealing with the traditional agenda is no longer enough. A new and unprecedented kind of issue has emerged. The problems of energy, resources, environment, population, the uses of space and the seas now rank with questions of military security, ideology and territorial rivalry which have traditionally made up the diplomatic agenda.[3]

Kissinger's list, which could be expanded, illustrates how governments' policies, even those previously considered merely domestic, impinge on one another. The extensive consultative arrangements developed by the OECD, as well as the GATT, IMF, and the European Community, indicate how characteristic the overlap of domestic and foreign policy is among developed pluralist countries. The organization within nine major departments of the United States government (Agriculture, Commerce, Defense, Health, Education and Welfare, Interior, Justice, Labor, State, and Treasury) and many other agencies reflects their extensive international commitments. The multiple, overlapping issues that result make a nightmare of governmental organization.[4]

When there are multiple issues on the agenda, many of which threaten the interests of domestic groups but do not clearly threaten the nation as a whole, the problems of formulating a coherent and consistent foreign policy increase. In 1975 energy was a foreign policy problem, but specific remedies, such as a tax on gasoline and automobiles, involved domestic legislation opposed by auto workers and companies alike. As one commentator observed, "virtually every time Congress has set a national policy that changed the way people live ... the action came after a consensus had developed, bit by bit, over the years, that a problem existed and that there was one best way to solve it."[5] Opportunities for delay, for special protection, for inconsistency and incoherence abound when international politics requires aligning the domestic policies of pluralist democratic countries.

Minor Role of Military Force

Political scientists have traditionally emphasized the role of military force in international politics. As we saw in the first chapter, force dominates other means of power: *if* there are no constraints on one's choice of instruments (a hypothetical situation that has only been approximated in the two world wars), the state with superior military force will prevail. If the security dilemma for all states were extremely acute, military force, supported by economic and other resources, would clearly be the dominant source of power. Survival is the primary goal of all states, and in the worst situations, force is ultimately necessary to guarantee survival. Thus military force is always a central component of national power.

Yet particularly among industrialized, pluralist countries, the perceived margin of safety has widened: fears of attack in general have declined, and fears of attacks *by one another* are virtually nonexistent. France has abandoned the *tous azimuts* (defense in all directions) strategy that President de Gaulle advocated (it was not taken entirely seriously even at the time). Canada's last war plans for fighting the United States were abandoned half a century ago. Britain and Germany no longer feel threatened by each other. Intense relationships of mutual influence exist between these countries, but in most of them force is irrelevant or unimportant as an instrument of policy.

Moreover, force is often not an appropriate way of achieving other goals (such as economic and ecological welfare) that are becoming more important. It is not impossible to imagine dramatic conflict or revolutionary change in which the use or threat of military force over an economic issue or among advanced industrial countries might become plausible. Then realist assumptions would again be a reliable guide to events. But in most situations, the effects of military force are both costly and uncertain.[6]

Even when the direct use of force is barred among a group of countries, however, military power can still be used politically. Each superpower continues to use the threat of force to deter attacks by other superpowers on itself or its allies; its deterrence ability thus serves an indirect, protective role, which it can use in bargaining on other issues with its allies. This bargaining tool is particularly important for the United States, whose allies are concerned about potential Soviet threats and which has fewer other means of influence over its allies than does the Soviet Union over its Eastern European partners. The United States has, accordingly, taken advantage of the Europeans' (particularly the Germans') desire for its protection and linked the issue of troop levels in Europe to trade and monetary negotiations. Thus, although the first-order effect of deterrent force is essentially negative—to deny effective offensive power to a superpower opponent—a state can use that force positively—to gain political influence.

Thus, even for countries whose relations approximate complex interdependence, two serious qualifications remain: (1) drastic social and political change could cause force again to become an important direct instrument of policy; and (2) even when elites' interests are complementary, a country that uses military force to protect another may have significant political influence over the other country.

* * *

The Political Processes of Complex Interdependence

The three main characteristics of complex interdependence give rise to distinctive political processes, which translate power resources into power as control of outcomes. As we argued earlier, something is usually lost or added in the translation. Under conditions of complex interdependence the translation will be different than under realist conditions, and our predictions about outcomes will need to be adjusted accordingly.

In the realist world, military security will be the dominant goal of states. It will even affect issues that are not directly involved with military power or territorial defense. Nonmilitary problems will not only be subordinated to military ones; they will be studied for their politico-military implications. Balance of payments issues, for instance, will be considered at least as much in the light of their implications for world power generally as for their purely financial ramifications. McGeorge Bundy conformed to realist expectations when he argued in 1964 that devaluation of the dollar should be seriously considered if necessary to fight the war in Vietnam.[7] To some extent, so did former Treasury Secretary Henry Fowler when he contended in 1971 that the United States needed a trade surplus of $4 billion to $6 billion in order to lead in Western defense.[8]

In a world of complex interdependence, however, one expects some officials, particularly at lower levels, to emphasize the *variety* of state goals that must be pursued. In the absence of a clear hierarchy of issues, goals will vary by issue, and may not be closely related. Each bureaucracy will pursue its own concerns; and although several agencies may reach compromises on issues that affect them all, they will find that a consistent pattern of policy is difficult to maintain. Moreover, transnational actors will introduce different goals into various groups of issues.

Linkage Strategies

Goals will therefore vary by issue area under complex interdependence, but so will the distribution of power and the typical political processes. Traditional analysis focuses on *the* international system, and leads us to anticipate similar political processes on a variety of issues. Militarily and economically strong states will dominate a variety of organizations and a variety of issues, by linking their own policies on some issues to other states' policies on other issues. By using their overall dominance to prevail on their weak issues, the strongest states will, in the traditional model, ensure a congruence between the overall structure of military and economic power and the pattern of outcomes on any one issue area. Thus world politics can be treated as a seamless web.

Under complex interdependence, such congruence is less likely to occur. As military force is devalued, militarily strong states will find it more difficult to use their overall dominance to control outcomes on issues in which they are weak. And since the distribution of power resources in trade, shipping, or oil, for example, may be quite different, patterns of outcomes and distinctive political processes are likely to vary from one set of issues to another. If force were readily applicable, and military security were the highest foreign policy goal, these variations in the issue structures of power would not matter very much. The linkages drawn from them to military issues would ensure consistent dominance by the overall strongest states. But when military force is largely immobilized, strong states will find that linkage is less effective. They may still attempt such links, but in the absence of a hierarchy of issues, their success will be problematic.

* * *

Agenda Setting

Our second assumption of complex interdependence, the lack of clear hierarchy among multiple issues, leads us to expect that the politics of agenda formation and control will become more important. Traditional analyses lead statesmen to focus on politico-military issues and to pay little attention to the broader politics of agenda formation. Statesmen assume that the agenda will be set by shifts in the balance of power, actual or anticipated, and by perceived threats to the security of states. Other issues will only be very important when they seem to affect security and military power. In these cases, agendas will be influenced strongly by considerations of the overall balance of power.

Yet, today, some nonmilitary issues are emphasized in interstate relations at one time, whereas others of seemingly equal importance are neglected or quietly handled at a technical level. International monetary politics, problems of commodity terms of trade, oil, food, and multinational corporations have all been important during the last decade; but not all have been high on interstate agendas throughout that period.

Traditional analysts of international politics have paid little attention to agenda formation: to how issues come to receive sustained attention by high officials. The traditional orientation toward military and security affairs implies that the crucial problems of foreign policy are imposed on states by the actions or threats of other states. These are high politics as opposed to the low politics of economic affairs. Yet, as the complexity of actors and issues in world politics increases, the utility of force declines and the line between domestic policy and foreign policy becomes blurred: as the conditions of complex interdependence are more closely approximated, the politics of agenda formation becomes more subtle and differentiated.

* * *

Transnational and Transgovernmental Relations

Our third condition of complex interdependence, multiple channels of contact among societies, further blurs the distinction between domestic and international politics. The availability of partners in political coalitions is not necessarily limited by national boundaries as traditional analysis assumes. The nearer a situation is to complex interdependence, the more we expect the outcomes of political bargaining to be affected by transnational relations. Multinational corporations may be significant both as independent actors and as instruments manipulated by governments. The attitudes and policy stands of domestic groups are likely to be affected by communications, organized or not, between them and their counterparts abroad.

Thus the existence of multiple channels of contact leads us to expect limits, beyond those normally found in domestic politics, on the ability of statesmen to calculate the manipulation of interdependence or follow a consistent strategy of linkage. Statesmen must consider differential as well as aggregate effects of interdependence strategies and their likely implications for politicization and agenda control. Transactions among societies—economic and social transactions more than security ones—affect groups differently. Opportunities and costs from increased transnational ties may be greater for certain groups—for instance, American workers in the textile or shoe industries—than for others. Some organizations or groups may interact directly with actors in other societies or with other governments to increase their benefits from a network of interaction. Some actors may therefore be less vulnerable as well as less sensitive to changes elsewhere in the network than are others, and this will affect patterns of political action.

The multiple channels of contact found in complex interdependence are not limited to nongovernmental actors. Contacts between governmental bureaucracies charged with similar tasks may not only alter their perspectives but lead to transgovernmental coalitions on particular policy questions. To improve their chances of success, government agencies attempt to bring actors from other governments into their own decision-making processes as allies. Agencies of powerful states such as the United States have used such coalitions to penetrate weaker governments in such countries as Turkey and Chile. They have also been used to help agencies of other governments penetrate the United States bureaucracy.[9] ...

* * *

Role of International Organizations

Finally, the existence of multiple channels leads one to predict a different and significant role for international organizations in world politics. Realists in the tradition of Hans J. Morgenthau have portrayed a world in which states, acting from self-interest, struggle for "power and peace." Security issues are dominant; war threatens. In such a world, one may assume that international institutions will have a minor role, limited by the rare congruence of such interests. International organizations are then clearly peripheral to world politics. But in a world of multiple issues imperfectly linked, in which coalitions are formed transnationally and transgovernmentally, the potential role of international institutions in political bargaining is greatly increased. In particular, they help set the international agenda, and act as catalysts for coalition-formation and as arenas for political initiatives and linkage by weak states.

Governments must organize themselves to cope with the flow of business generated by international organizations. By defining the salient issues, and deciding which issues can be grouped together, organizations may help to determine governmental priorities and the nature of interdepartmental committees and other arrangements within governments. The 1972 Stockholm Environment Conference strengthened the position of environmental agencies in various governments. The 1974 World Food Conference focused the attention of important parts of the United States government on prevention of food shortages. The September 1975 United Nations special session on proposals for a New International Economic Order generated an intragovernmental debate about policies toward the Third World in general. The International Monetary Fund and the General Agreement on Tariffs and Trade have focused governmental activity on money and trade instead of on private direct investment, which has no comparable international organization.

By bringing officials together, international organizations help to activate potential coalitions in world politics. It is quite obvious that international organizations have been very important in bringing together representatives of less developed countries, most of which do not maintain embassies in one another's capitals. Third World strategies of solidarity among poor countries have been developed in and for a series of international conferences, mostly under the auspices of the United Nations.[10] International organizations also allow agencies of governments, which might not otherwise come into contact, to turn potential or tacit coalitions into explicit transgovernmental coalitions characterized by direct communications. In some cases, international secretariats deliberately promote this process by forming coalitions with groups of governments, or with units of governments, as well as with nongovernmental organizations having similar interests.[11]

International organizations are frequently congenial institutions for weak states. The one-state-one-vote norm of the United Nations system favors coalitions of the small and powerless. Secretariats are often responsive to Third World demands. Furthermore, the substantive norms of most international organizations, as they have developed over the years, stress social and economic equity as well as the equality of states. Past resolutions expressing Third World positions, sometimes agreed to with reservations by industrialized countries, are used to legitimize other demands. These agreements are rarely binding, but up to a point the norms of the institution make opposition look more harshly self-interested and less defensible.

International organizations also allow small and weak states to pursue linkage strategies. In the discussions on a New International Economic Order, Third World states insisted on linking oil price and availability to other questions on which they had traditionally been unable to achieve their objectives.... [S]mall and weak states have also followed a strategy of linkage in the series of Law of the Sea conferences sponsored by the United Nations.

Complex interdependence therefore yields different political patterns than does the realist conception of the world.... Thus, one would expect traditional theories to fail to explain international regime change in situations of complex interdependence. But, for a situation that approximates realist conditions, traditional theories should be appropriate....

Notes

1. Hans J. Morgenthau, *Politics Among Nations: The Struggle for Power and Peace,* 4th ed. (New York: Knopf, 1967), p. 36.
2. See the material referred to in footnotes 9 and 13, Chapter 1; also see Edward L. Morse, "Transnational Economic Processes," in Robert O. Keohane and Joseph S. Nye, Jr. (eds.), *Transnational Relations and World Politics* (Cambridge, Mass.: Harvard University Press, 1972).
3. Henry A. Kissinger, "A New National Partnership," *Department of State Bulletin,* February 17, 1975, p. 199.
4. See the report of the Commission on the Organization of the Government for the Conduct of Foreign Policy (Murphy Commission) (Washington, D.C.: U.S. Government Printing Office, 1975), and the studies prepared for that report. See also Raymond Hopkins, "The International Role of 'Domestic' Bureaucracy," *International Organization* 30, no. 3 (Summer 1976).
5. *New York Times,* May 22, 1975.
6. For a valuable discussion, see Klaus Knorr, *The Power of Nations: The Political Economy of International Relations* (New York: Basic Books, 1975).
7. Henry Brandon, *The Retreat of American Power* (New York: Doubleday, 1974), p. 218.
8. *International Implications of the New Economic Policy,* U.S. Congress, House of Representatives, Committee on Foreign Affairs, Subcommittee on Foreign Economic Policy, Hearings, September 16, 1971.
9. For a more detailed discussion, see Robert O. Keohane and Joseph S. Nye, Jr., "Transgovernmental Relations and International Organizations," *World Politics* 27, no. 1 (October 1974): 39–62.
10. Branislav Gosovic and John Gerard Ruggie, "On the Creation of a New International Economic Order: Issue Linkage and the Seventh Special Session of the UN General Assembly," *International Organization* 30, no. 2 (Spring 1976); 309–46.
11. Robert W. Cox, "The Executive Head," *International Organization* 23, no. 2 (Spring 1969): 205–30.

1.3

ANARCHY IS WHAT STATES MAKE OF IT: THE SOCIAL CONSTRUCTION OF POWER POLITICS

Alexander Wendt

In this seminal article, Alexander Wendt defines the constructivist approach to the study of international relations. While both realism and liberalism accept anarchy as the basic condition of states and use rationalist methodologies to study state behavior, not state identities and interests (which are taken as given), constructivism explores the "structure of identities and interests" or "the distribution of knowledge" by which states "construct" identities and "interpret" the distribution of power. From this perspective, "anarchy is what states make of it." It may be warlike, as it is among predator states; competitive, as it is among sovereign states; cooperative, as it might be in the European Union; or peaceful, as it is within a single state or among democratic states. What matters is how states see themselves and one another through a repetitive process of social interactions and substantive communications that define the community they share. Are they enemies, rivals, partners, or friends? Shared images and ideas (identity) define these outcomes more than the distribution of power (realist) or the role of institutions (liberal). Notice that all three perspectives are involved but that the identity perspective matters most. And notice too that the constructivist methodology addresses facts as social and embedded, not as separate and isolated, as in rationalist methodologies.

The debate between realists and liberals has reemerged as an axis of contention in international relations theory.[1] Revolving in the past around competing theories of human nature, the debate is more concerned today with the extent to which state action is influenced by "structure" (anarchy and the distribution of power) versus "process" (interaction and learning) and institutions. Does the absence of centralized political authority force states to play competitive power politics? Can international regimes overcome this logic, and under what conditions? What in anarchy is given and immutable, and what is amenable to change?

Source: Alexander Wendt, "Anarchy Is What States Make of It: The Social Construction of Power Politics," *International Organization* 46, no. 2 (1992): 391–425.

The debate between "neorealists" and "neoliberals" has been based on a shared commitment to "rationalism."[2] Like all social theories, rational choice directs us to ask some questions and not others, treating the identities and interests of agents as exogenously given and focusing on how the behavior of agents generates outcomes. As such, rationalism offers a fundamentally behavioral conception of both process and institutions: they change behavior but not identities and interests.[3] In addition to this way of framing research problems, neorealists and neoliberals share generally similar assumptions about agents: states are the dominant actors in the system, and they define security in "self-interested" terms. Neorealists and neoliberals may disagree about the extent to which states are motivated by relative versus absolute gains, but both groups take the self-interested state as the starting point for theory.

This starting point makes substantive sense for neorealists, since they believe anarchies are necessarily "self-help" systems, systems in which both central authority and collective security are absent. The self-help corollary to anarchy does enormous work in neorealism, generating the inherently competitive dynamics of the security dilemma and collective action problem. Self-help is not seen as an "institution" and as such occupies a privileged explanatory role vis-à-vis process, setting the terms for, and unaffected by, interaction. Since states failing to conform to the logic of self-help will be driven from the system, only simple learning or behavioral adaptation is possible; the complex learning involved in redefinitions of identity and interest is not.[4] Questions about identity- and interest-formation are therefore not important to students of international relations. A rationalist problématique, which reduces process to dynamics of behavioral interaction among exogenously constituted actors, defines the scope of systemic theory.

By adopting such reasoning, liberals concede to neorealists the causal powers of anarchic structure, but they gain the rhetorically powerful argument that process can generate cooperative behavior, even in an exogenously given, self-help system. Some liberals may believe that anarchy does, in fact, constitute states with self-interested identities exogenous to practice. Such "weak" liberals concede the causal powers of anarchy both rhetorically and substantively and accept rationalism's limited, behavioral conception of the causal powers of institutions. They are realists before liberals (we might call them "weak real-ists"), since only if international institutions can change powers and interests do they go beyond the "limits" of realism.[5]

Yet some liberals want more. When Joseph Nye speaks of "complex learn-ing," or Robert Jervis of "changing conceptions of self and interest," or Robert Keohane of "sociological" conceptions of interest, each is asserting an impor-tant role for transformations of identity and interest in the liberal research program and, by extension, a potentially much stronger conception of process and institutions in world politics.[6] "Strong" liberals should be troubled by the dichotomous privileging of structure over process, since transformations of identity and interest through process are transformations of structure.

*   *   *

... [C]onstructivism might contribute significantly to the strong liberal interest in identity- and interest-formation and thereby perhaps itself be enriched with liberal insights about learning and cognition which it has neglected.

My strategy ... will be to argue against the neorealist claim that self-help is given by anarchic structure exogenously to process.... [S]elf-help and power politics do not follow either logically or causally from anarchy and that if today we find ourselves in a self-help world, this is due to process, not structure. There is no "logic" of anarchy apart from the practices that create and instantiate one structure of identities and interests rather than another; structure has no existence or causal powers apart from process. Self-help and power politics are institutions, not essential features of anarchy. *Anarchy is what states make of it.*

*   *   *

Anarchy and Power Politics

*   *   *

Anarchy, Self-help, and Intersubjective Knowledge

[Kenneth] Waltz defines political structure on three dimensions: ordering principles (in this case, anarchy), principles of differentiation (which here drop out), and the distribution of capabilities.[7] By itself, this definition predicts little about state behavior. It does not predict whether two states will be friends or foes, will recognize each other's sovereignty, will have dynastic ties, will be revisionist or status quo powers, and so on. These factors, which are fundamentally intersubjective, affect states' security interests and thus the character of their interaction under anarchy. In an important revision of Waltz's theory, Stephen Walt implies as much when he argues that the "balance of threats," rather than the balance of power, determines state action, threats being socially constructed.[8] Put more generally, without assumptions about the structure of identities and interests in the system, Waltz's definition of structure cannot predict the content or dynamics of anarchy. Self-help is one such intersubjective structure and, as such, does the decisive explanatory work in the theory. The question is whether self-help is a logical or contingent feature of anarchy. In this section, I develop the concept of a "structure of identity and interest" and show that no particular one follows logically from anarchy.

A fundamental principle of constructivist social theory is that people act toward objects, including other actors, on the basis of the meanings that the objects have for them.[9] States act differently toward enemies than they do toward friends because enemies are threatening and friends are not. Anarchy and the distribution of power are insufficient to tell us which is which. U.S. military power has a different significance for Canada than for Cuba, despite their similar "structural" positions, just as British missiles have a different significance for the United States than do Soviet missiles. The distribution of power may always affect states' calculations, but how it does so depends on the intersubjective understandings and expectations, on the "distribution of knowledge," that constitute their conceptions of self and other.[10] If society "forgets" what a university is, the powers and practices of professor and student cease to exist; if the United States and Soviet Union decide that they are no longer enemies, "the cold war is over." It is collective meanings that constitute the structures which organize our actions.

Actors acquire identities—relatively stable, role-specific understandings and expectations about self—by participating in such collective meanings.[11] Identities are inherently relational: "Identity, with its appropriate attachments of psychological reality, is always identity within a specific, socially constructed world," Peter Berger argues.[12] Each person has many identities linked to institutional roles, such as brother, son, teacher, and citizen. Similarly, a state may have multiple identities as "sovereign," "leader of the free world," "imperial power," and so on.[13] The commitment to and the salience of particular identities vary, but each identity is an inherently social definition of the actor grounded in the theories which actors collectively hold about themselves and one another and which constitute the structure of the social world.

Identities are the basis of interests. Actors do not have a "portfolio" of interests that they carry around independent of social context; instead, they define their interests in the process of defining situations.[14] As Nelson Foote puts it: "Motivation ... refer[s] to the degree to which a human being, as a participant in the ongoing social process in which he necessarily finds himself, defines a problematic situation as calling for the performance of a particular act, with more or less anticipated consummations and consequences, and thereby his organism releases the energy appropriate to performing it."[15] Sometimes situations are unprecedented in our experience, and in these cases we have to construct their meaning, and thus our interests, by analogy or invent them de novo. More often they have routine qualities in which we assign meanings on the basis of institutionally defined roles. When we say that professors have an "interest" in teaching, research, or going on leave, we are saying that to function in the role identity of "professor," they have to define certain situations as calling for certain actions. This does not mean that they will necessarily do so (expectations and competence do not equal performance), but if they do not, they will not get tenure. The absence or failure of roles makes defining situations and interests more difficult, and identity confusion may result. This seems to be happening today in the United States and the former Soviet Union: without the cold war's mutual attributions of threat and hostility to define their identities, these states seem unsure of what their "interests" should be.

An institution is a relatively stable set or "structure" of identities and interests. Such structures are often codified in formal rules and norms, but these have motivational force only in virtue of actors' socialization to and participation in collective knowledge. Institutions are fundamentally cognitive entities that do not exist apart from actors' ideas about how the world works.[16] This does not mean that institutions are not real or objective, that they are "nothing but" beliefs. As collective knowledge, they are experienced as having an existence "over and above the individuals who happen to embody them at the moment."[17] In this way, institutions come to confront individuals as more or less coercive social facts, but they are still a function of what actors collectively "know." Identities and such collective cognitions do not exist apart from each other; they are "mutually constitutive."[18] On this view, institutionalization is a process of internalizing new identities and interests, not something occurring outside them and affecting only behavior; socialization is a cognitive process, not just a behavioral one. Conceived in this way, institutions may be cooperative or conflictual, a point sometimes lost in scholarship on international regimes, which tends to equate institutions with cooperation. There are important differences between conflictual and cooperative institutions to be sure, but all relatively stable self-other relations—even those of "enemies"—are defined intersubjectively.

Self-help is an institution, one of various structures of identity and interest that may exist under anarchy. Processes of identity-formation under anarchy are concerned first and foremost with preservation or "security" of the self. Concepts of security therefore differ in the extent to which and the manner in which the self is identified cognitively with the other,[19] and, I want to suggest, it is upon this cognitive variation that the meaning of anarchy and the distribution of power depends. Let me illustrate with a standard continuum of security systems.[20]

At one end is the "competitive" security system, in which states identify negatively with each other's security so that ego's gain is seen as alter's loss. Negative identification under anarchy constitutes systems of "realist" power politics: risk-averse actors that infer intentions from capabilities and worry about relative gains and losses. At the limit—in the Hobbesian war of all against all—collective action is nearly impossible in such a system because each actor must constantly fear being stabbed in the back.

In the middle is the "individualistic" security system, in which states are indifferent to the relationship between their own and others' security. This constitutes "neoliberal" systems: states are still self-regarding about their security but are concerned primarily with absolute gains rather than relative gains. One's position in the distribution of power is less important, and collective action is more possible (though still subject to free riding because states continue to be "egoists").

Competitive and individualistic systems are both "self-help" forms of anarchy in the sense that states do not positively identify the security of self with that of others but instead treat security as the individual responsibility of each. Given the lack of a positive cognitive identification on the basis of which to build security regimes, power politics within such systems will necessarily consist of efforts to manipulate others to satisfy self-regarding interests.

This contrasts with the "cooperative" security system, in which states identify positively with one another so that the security of each is perceived as the responsibility of all. This is not self-help in any interesting sense, since the "self" in terms of which interests are defined is the community; national interests are international interests.[21] In practice, of course, the extent to which states' identification with the community varies, from the limited form found in "concerts" to the full-blown form seen in "collective security" arrangements.[22] Depending on how well developed the collective self is, it will produce security practices that are in varying degrees altruistic or prosocial. This makes collective action less dependent on the presence of active threats and less prone to free riding.[23] Moreover, it restructures efforts to advance one's objectives, or "power politics," in terms of shared norms rather than relative power.[24]

On this view, the tendency in international relations scholarship to view power and institutions as two opposing explanations of foreign policy is therefore misleading, since anarchy and the distribution of power only have meaning for state action in virtue of the understandings and expectations that constitute institutional identities and interests. Self-help is one such institution, constituting one kind of anarchy but not the only kind. Waltz's three-part definition of structure therefore seems underspecified. In order to go from structure to action, we need to add a fourth: the intersubjectively constituted structure of identities and interests in the system.

* * *

Institutional Transformations of Power Politics

* * *

In the remainder of this article, I examine three institutional transformations of identity and security interest through which states might escape a Hobbesian world of their own making. In so doing, I seek to clarify what it means to say that "institutions transform identities and interests," emphasizing that the key to such transformations is relatively stable practice.

Sovereignty, Recognition, and Security

In a Hobbesian state of nature, states are individuated by the domestic processes that constitute them as states and by their material capacity to deter threats from other states. In this world, even if free momentarily from the predations of others, state security does not have any basis in social recognition—in intersubjective understandings or norms that a state has a right to its existence, territory, and subjects. Security is a matter of national power, nothing more.

The principle of sovereignty transforms this situation by providing a social basis for the individuality and security of states. Sovereignty is an institution, and so it exists only in virtue of certain intersubjective understandings and expectations; there is no sovereignty without an other. These understandings and expectations not only constitute a particular kind of state—the "sovereign" state—but also constitute a particular form of community, since identities are relational.

The essence of this community is a mutual recognition of one another's right to exercise exclusive political authority within territorial limits. These reciprocal "permissions"[25] constitute a spatially rather than functionally differentiated world—a world in which fields of practice constitute and are organized around "domestic" and "international" spaces rather than around the performance of particular activities.[26] The location of the boundaries between these spaces is of course sometimes contested, war being one practice through which states negotiate the terms of their individuality. But this does not change the fact that it is only in virtue of mutual recognition that states have "territorial property rights."[27] This recognition functions as a form of "social closure" that disempowers non-state actors and empowers and helps stabilize interaction among states.[28]

Sovereignty norms are now so taken for granted, so natural, that it is easy to overlook the extent to which they are both presupposed by and an ongoing artifact of practice. When states tax "their" "citizens" and not others, when they "protect" their markets against foreign "imports," when they kill thousands of Iraqis in one kind of war and then refuse to "intervene" to kill even one person in another kind, a "civil" war, and when they fight a global war against a regime that sought to destroy the institution of sovereignty and then give Germany back to the Germans, they are acting against the background of, and thereby reproducing, shared norms about what it means to be a sovereign state.

If states stopped acting on those norms, their identity as "sovereigns" (if not necessarily as "states") would disappear. The sovereign state is an ongoing accomplishment of practice, not a once-and-for-all creation of norms that somehow exist apart from practice.[29] Thus, saying that "the institution of sovereignty transforms identities" is shorthand for saying that "regular practices produce mutually constituting sovereign identities (agents) and their associated institutional norms (structures)." Practice is the core of constructivist resolutions of the agent-structure problem. This ongoing process may not be politically problematic in particular historical contexts and, indeed, once a community of mutual recognition is constituted, its members—even the disadvantaged ones[30]—may have a vested interest in reproducing it. In fact, this is part of what having an identity means. But this identity and institution remain dependent on what actors do: removing those practices will remove their intersubjective conditions of existence.

This may tell us something about how institutions of sovereign states are reproduced through social interaction, but it does not tell us why such a structure of identity and interest would arise in the first place. Two conditions would seem necessary for this to happen: (1) the density and regularity of interactions must be sufficiently high and (2) actors must be dissatisfied with preexisting forms of identity and interaction. Given these conditions, a norm of mutual recognition is relatively undemanding in terms of social trust, having the form of an assurance game in which a player will acknowledge the sovereignty of the others as long as they will in turn acknowledge that player's own sovereignty. Articulating international legal principles such as those embodied in the Peace of Augsburg (1555) and the Peace of Westphalia (1648) may also help by establishing explicit criteria for determining violations of the nascent social consensus.[31] But whether such a consensus holds depends on what states do. If they treat each other as if they were sovereign, then over time they will institutionalize that mode of subjectivity; if they do not, then that mode will not become the norm.

Practices of sovereignty will transform understandings of security and power politics in at least three ways. First, states will come to define their (and our) security in terms of preserving their "property rights" over particular territories. We now see this as natural, but the preservation of territorial frontiers is not, in fact, equivalent to the survival of the state or its people. Indeed, some states would probably be more secure if they would relinquish certain territories— the "Soviet Union" of some minority republics, "Yugoslavia" of Croatia and Slovenia, Israel of the West Bank, and so on. The fact that sovereignty practices have historically been oriented toward producing distinct territorial spaces, in other words, affects states' conceptualization of what they must "secure" to function in that identity, a process that may help account for the "hardening" of territorial boundaries over the centuries.[32]

Second, to the extent that states successfully internalize sovereignty norms, they will be more respectful toward the territorial rights of others.[33] This restraint is *not* primarily because of the costs of violating sovereignty norms, although when violators do get punished (as in the Gulf War) it reminds everyone of what these costs can be, but because part of what it means to be a "sovereign" state is that one does not violate the territorial rights of others without "just cause." A clear example of such an institutional effect, convincingly argued by David Strang, is the markedly different treatment that weak states receive within and outside communities of mutual recognition.[34] What keeps the United States from conquering the Bahamas, or Nigeria from seizing Togo, or Australia from occupying Vanuatu? Clearly, power is not the issue, and in these cases even the cost of sanctions would probably be negligible. One might argue that great powers simply have no "interest" in these conquests, and this might be so, but this lack of interest can only be understood in terms of their recognition of weak states' sovereignty. I have no interest in exploiting my friends, not because of the relative costs and benefits of such action but because they are my friends. The absence of recognition, in turn, helps explain the Western states' practices of territorial conquest, enslavement, and genocide against Native American and African peoples. It is in *that* world that only power matters, not the world of today.

Finally, to the extent that their ongoing socialization teaches states that their sovereignty depends on recognition by other states, they can afford to rely more on the institutional fabric of international society and less on individual national means—especially military power—to protect their security. The intersubjective understandings embodied in the institution of sovereignty, in other words, may redefine the meaning of others' power for the security of the self. In policy terms, this means that states can be less worried about short-term survival and relative power and can thus shift their resources accordingly. Ironically, it is the great powers, the states with the greatest national means, that may have the hardest time learning this lesson; small powers do not have the luxury of relying on national means and may therefore learn faster that collective recognition is a cornerstone of security.

None of this is to say that power becomes irrelevant in a community of sovereign states. Sometimes states *are* threatened by others that do not recognize their existence or particular territorial claims, that resent the externalities from their economic policies, and so on. But most of the time, these threats are played out within the terms of the sovereignty game. The fates of Napoleon and Hitler show what happens when they are not.

Cooperation among Egoists and Transformations of Identity

We began this section with a Hobbesian state of nature. Cooperation for joint gain is extremely difficult in this context, since trust is lacking, time horizons are short, and relative power concerns are high. Life is "nasty, brutish, and short." Sovereignty transforms this system into a Lockean world of (mostly) mutually recognized property rights and (mostly) egoistic rather than competitive conceptions of security, reducing the fear that what states already have will be seized at any moment by potential collaborators, thereby enabling them to contemplate more direct forms of cooperation. A necessary condition for such cooperation is that outcomes be positively interdependent in the sense that potential gains exist which cannot be realized by unilateral action. States such as Brazil and Botswana may recognize each other's sovereignty, but they need further incentives to engage in joint action. One important source of incentives is the growing "dynamic density" of interaction among states in a world with new communications technology, nuclear weapons, externalities from industrial development, and so on.[35] Unfortunately, growing dynamic density does not ensure that states will in fact realize joint gains; interdependence also entails vulnerability and the risk of being "the sucker," which if exploited will become a source of conflict rather than cooperation.

This is the rationale for the familiar assumption that egoistic states will often find themselves facing prisoners' dilemma, a game in which the dominant strategy, if played only once, is to defect. As Michael Taylor and Robert Axelrod have shown, however, given iteration and a sufficient shadow of the future, egoists using a tit-for-tat strategy can escape this result and build cooperative institutions.[36] The story they tell about this process on the surface seems quite similar to George Herbert Mead's constructivist analysis of interaction, part of which is also told in terms of "games."[37] Cooperation is a gesture indicating ego's willingness to cooperate; if alter defects, ego does likewise, signaling its unwillingness to be exploited; over time and through reciprocal play, each learns to form relatively stable expectations about the other's behavior, and through these, habits of cooperation (or defection) form. Despite similar concerns with communication, learning, and habit-formation, however, there is an important difference between the game-theoretic and constructivist analysis of interaction that bears on how we conceptualize the causal powers of institutions.

In the traditional game-theoretic analysis of cooperation, even an iterated one, the structure of the game—of identities and interests—is exogenous to interaction and, as such, does not change.[38] A "black box" is put around identity- and interest-formation, and analysis focuses instead on the relationship between expectations and behavior. The norms that evolve from interaction are treated as rules and behavioral regularities which are external to the actors and which resist change because of the transaction costs of creating new ones. The game-theoretic analysis of cooperation among egoists is at base behavioral.

A constructivist analysis of cooperation, in contrast, would concentrate on how the expectations produced by behavior affect identities and interests. The process of creating institutions is one of internalizing new understandings of self and other, of acquiring new role identities, not just of creating external constraints on the behavior of exogenously constituted actors.[39] Even if not intended as such, in other words, the process by which egoists learn to cooperate is at the same time a process of reconstructing their interests in terms of shared commitments to social norms. Over time, this will tend to transform a positive interdependence of *outcomes* into a positive interdependence of *utilities* or collective interest organized around the norms in question. These norms will resist change because they are tied to actors' commitments to their identities and interests, not merely because of transaction costs. A constructivist analysis of "the cooperation problem," in other words, is at base cognitive rather than behavioral, since it treats the intersubjective knowledge that defines the structure of identities and interests, of the "game," as endogenous to and instantiated by interaction itself.

The debate over the future of collective security in Western Europe may illustrate the significance of this difference. A weak liberal or rationalist analysis would assume that the European states' "portfolio" of interests has not fundamentally changed and that the emergence of new factors, such as the collapse of the Soviet threat and the rise of Germany, would alter their cost-benefit ratios for pursuing current arrangements, thereby causing existing institutions to break down. The European states formed collaborative institutions for good, exogenously constituted egoistic reasons, and the same reasons may lead them to reject those institutions; the game of European power politics has not changed. A strong liberal or constructivist analysis of this problem would suggest that four decades of cooperation may have transformed a positive interdependence of outcomes into a collective "European identity" in terms of which states increasingly define their "self"-interests.[40] Even if egoistic reasons were its starting point, the process of cooperating tends to redefine those reasons by reconstituting identities and interests in terms of new intersubjective understandings and commitments. Changes in the distribution of power during the late twentieth century are undoubtedly a challenge to these new understandings, but it is not as if West European states have some inherent, exogenously given interest in abandoning collective security if the price is right. Their identities and security interests are continuously in process, and if collective identities become "embedded," they will be as resistant to change as egoistic ones.[41] Through participation in new forms of social knowledge, in other words, the European states of 1990 might no longer be the states of 1950.

Critical Strategic Theory and Collective Security

The transformation of identity and interest through an "evolution of cooperation" faces two important constraints. The first is that the process is incremental and slow. Actors' objectives in such a process are typically to realize joint gains within what they take to be a relatively stable context, and they are therefore unlikely to engage in substantial reflection about how to change the parameters of that context (including the structure of identities and interests) and unlikely to pursue policies specifically designed to bring about such changes. Learning to cooperate may change those parameters, but this occurs as an unintended consequence of policies pursued for other reasons rather than as a result of intentional efforts to transcend existing institutions.

A second, more fundamental, constraint is that the evolution of cooperation story presupposes that actors do not identify negatively with one another. Actors must be concerned primarily with absolute gains; to the extent that antipathy and distrust lead them to define their security in relativistic terms, it will be hard to accept the vulnerabilities that attend cooperation.[42] This is important because it is precisely the "central balance" in the state system that seems to be so often afflicted with such competitive thinking, and realists can therefore argue that the possibility of cooperation within one "pole" (for example, the West) is parasitic on the dominance of competition between poles (the East-West conflict). Relations between the poles may be amenable to some positive reciprocity in areas such as arms control, but the atmosphere of distrust leaves little room for such cooperation and its transformative consequences.[43] The conditions of negative identification that make an "evolution of cooperation" most needed work precisely against such a logic.

This seemingly intractable situation may nevertheless be amenable to quite a different logic of transformation, one driven more by self-conscious efforts to change structures of identity and interest than by unintended consequences. Such voluntarism may seem to contradict the spirit of constructivism, since would-be revolutionaries are presumably themselves effects of socialization to structures of identity and interest. How can they think about changing that to which they owe their identity? The possibility lies in the distinction between the social determination of the self and the personal determination of choice, between what Mead called the "me" and the "I."[44] The "me" is that part of subjectivity which is defined in terms of others; the character and behavioral expectations of a person's role identity as "professor," or of the United States as "leader of the alliance," for example, are socially constituted. Roles are not played in mechanical fashion according to precise scripts, however, but are "taken" and adapted in idiosyncratic ways by each actor.[45] Even in the most constrained situations, role performance involves a choice by the actor. The "I" is the part of subjectivity in which this appropriation and reaction to roles and its corresponding existential freedom lie.

The fact that roles are "taken" means that, in principle, actors always have a capacity for "character planning"—for engaging in critical self-reflection and choices designed to bring about changes in their lives.[46] But when or under what conditions can this creative capacity be exercised? Clearly, much of the time it cannot: if actors were constantly reinventing their identities, social order would be impossible, and the relative stability of identities and interests in the real world is indicative of our propensity for habitual rather than creative action. The exceptional, conscious choosing to transform or transcend roles has at least two preconditions. First, there must be a reason to think of oneself in novel terms. This would most likely stem from the presence of new social situations that cannot be managed in terms of preexisting self-conceptions. Second, the expected costs of intentional role change—the sanctions imposed by others with whom one interacted in previous roles—cannot be greater than its rewards.

When these conditions are present, actors can engage in self-reflection and practice specifically designed to transform their identities and interests and thus to "change the games" in which they are embedded. Such "critical" strategic theory and practice has not received the attention it merits from students of world politics (another legacy of exogenously given interests perhaps), particularly given that one of the most important phenomena in contemporary world politics, Mikhail Gorbachev's policy of "New Thinking," is arguably precisely that.[47] Let me therefore use this policy as an example of how states might transform a competitive security system into a cooperative one, dividing the transformative process into four stages.

The first stage in intentional transformation is the breakdown of consensus about identity commitments. In the Soviet case, identity commitments centered on the Leninist theory of imperialism, with its belief that relations between capitalist and socialist states are inherently conflictual, and on the alliance patterns that this belief engendered. In the 1980s, the consensus within the Soviet Union over the Leninist theory broke down for a variety of reasons, principal among which seem to have been the state's inability to meet the economic-technological-military challenge from the West, the government's decline of political legitimacy at home, and the reassurance from the West that it did not intend to invade the Soviet Union, a reassurance that reduced the external costs of role change.[48] These factors paved the way for a radical leadership transition and for a subsequent "unfreezing of conflict schemas" concerning relations with the West.[49]

The breakdown of consensus makes possible a second stage of critical examination of old ideas about self and other and, by extension, of the structures of interaction by which the ideas have been sustained. In periods of relatively stable role identities, ideas and structures may become reified and thus treated as things that exist independently of social action. If so, the second stage is one of denaturalization, of identifying the practices that reproduce seemingly inevitable ideas about self and other; to that extent, it is a form of "critical" rather than "problem-solving" theory.[50] The result of such a critique should be an identification of new "possible selves" and aspirations.[51] New Thinking embodies such critical theorizing. Gorbachev wants to free the Soviet Union from the coercive social logic of the cold war and engage the West in far-reaching cooperation. Toward this end, he has rejected the Leninist belief in the inherent conflict of interest between socialist and capitalist states and, perhaps more important, has recognized the crucial role that Soviet aggressive practices played in sustaining that conflict.

Such rethinking paves the way for a third stage of new practice. In most cases, it is not enough to rethink one's own ideas about self and other, since old identities have been sustained by systems of interaction with *other actors,* the practices of which remain a social fact for the transformative agent. In order to change the self, then, it is often necessary to change the identities and interests of the others that help sustain those systems of interaction. The vehicle for inducing such change is one's own practice and, in particular, the practice of "altercasting"—a technique of interactor control in which ego uses tactics of self-presentation and stage management in an attempt to frame alter's definitions of social situations in ways that create the role which ego desires alter to play.[52] In effect, in altercasting ego tries to induce alter to take on a new identity (and thereby enlist alter in ego's effort to change itself) by treating alter *as if* it already had that identity. The logic of this follows directly from the mirror theory of identity-formation, in which alter's identity is a reflection of ego's practices; change those practices and ego begins to change alter's conception of itself.

What these practices should consist of depends on the logic by which the preexisting identities were sustained. Competitive security systems are sustained by practices that create insecurity and distrust. In this case, transformative practices should attempt to teach other states that one's own state can be trusted and should not be viewed as a threat to their security. The fastest way to do this is to make unilateral initiatives and self-binding commitments of sufficient significance that another state is faced with "an offer it cannot refuse."[53] Gorbachev has tried to do this by withdrawing from Afghanistan and Eastern Europe, implementing asymmetric cuts in nuclear and conventional forces, calling for "defensive defense," and so on. In addition, he has skillfully cast the West in the role of being morally required to give aid and comfort to the Soviet Union, has emphasized the bonds of common fate between the Soviet Union and the West, and has indicated that further progress in East-West relations is contingent upon the West assuming the identity being projected onto it. These actions are all dimensions of altercasting, the intention of which is to take away the Western "excuse" for distrusting the Soviet Union, which, in Gorbachev's view, has helped sustain competitive identities in the past.

Yet by themselves such practices cannot transform a competitive security system, since if they are not reciprocated by alter, they will expose ego to a "sucker" payoff and quickly wither on the vine. In order for critical strategic practice to transform competitive identities, it must be "rewarded" by alter, which will encourage more such practice by ego, and so on.[54] Over time, this will institutionalize a positive rather than a negative identification between the security of self and other and will thereby provide a firm intersubjective basis for what were initially tentative commitments to new identities and interests.[55]

Notwithstanding today's rhetoric about the end of the cold war, skeptics may still doubt whether Gorbachev (or some future leader) will succeed in building an intersubjective basis for a new Soviet (or Russian) role identity. There are important domestic, bureaucratic, and cognitive-ideological sources of resistance in both East and West to such a change, not the least of which is the shakiness of the democratic forces' domestic position. But if my argument about the role of intersubjective knowledge in creating competitive structures of identity and interest is right, then at least New Thinking shows a greater appreciation—conscious or not—for the deep structure of power politics than we are accustomed to in international relations practice.

* * *

Notes

1. See, for example, Joseph Grieco, "Anarchy and the Limits of Cooperation: A Realist Critique of the Newest Liberal Institutionalism," *International Organization* 42 (Summer 1988), pp. 485–507; Joseph Nye, "Neorealism and Neoliberalism," *World Politics* 40 (January 1988), pp. 235–51; Robert Keohane, "Neoliberal Institutionalism: A Perspective on World Politics," in his collection of essays entitled *International Institutions and State Power* (Boulder, Colo.: Westview Press, 1989), pp. 1–20; John Mearsheimer, "Back to the Future: Instability in Europe After the Cold War," *International Security* 13 (Summer 1990), pp. 5–56, along with subsequent published correspondence regarding Mearsheimer's article; and Emerson Niou and Peter Ordeshook, "Realism Versus Neoliberalism: A Formulation," *American Journal of Political Science* 35 (May 1991), pp. 481–511.

2. See Robert Keohane, "International Institutions: Two Approaches," *International Studies Quarterly* 32 (December 1988), pp. 379–96.

3. Behavioral and rationalist models of man and institutions share a common intellectual heritage in the materialist individualism of Hobbes, Locke, and Bentham. On the relationship between the two models, see Jonathan Turner, *A Theory of Social Interaction* (Stanford, Calif.: Stanford University Press, 1988), pp. 24–31; and George Homans, "Rational Choice Theory and Behavioral Psychology," in Craig Calhoun et al., eds., *Structures of Power and Constraint* (Cambridge: Cambridge University Press, 1991), pp. 77–89.

4. On neorealist conceptions of learning, see Philip Tetlock, "Learning in U.S. and Soviet Foreign Policy," in George Breslauer and Philip Tetlock, eds., *Learning in U.S. and Soviet Foreign Policy* (Boulder, Colo.: Westview Press, 1991), pp. 24–27. On the difference between behavioral and cognitive learning, see ibid., pp. 20–61; Joseph Nye, "Nuclear Learning and U.S.-Soviet Security Regimes," *International Organization* 41 (Summer 1987), pp. 371–402; and Ernst Haas, *When Knowledge Is Power* (Berkeley: University of California Press, 1990), pp. 17–49.

5. See Stephen Krasner, "Regimes and the Limits of Realism: Regimes as Autonomous Variables," in Stephen Krasner, ed., *International Regimes* (Ithaca, N.Y.: Cornell University Press, 1983), pp. 355–68.

6. See Nye, "Nuclear Learning and U.S.-Soviet Security Regimes"; Robert Jervis, "Realism, Game Theory, and Cooperation," *World Politics* 40 (April 1988), pp. 340–44; and Robert Keohane, "International Liberalism Reconsidered," in John Dunn, ed., *The Economic Limits to Modern Politics* (Cambridge: Cambridge University Press, 1990), pp. 183.

7. Kenneth Waltz, *Theory of International Politics* (Boston: Addison-Wesley, 1979), pp. 79–101.

8. Stephen Walt, *The Origins of Alliances* (Ithaca, N.Y.: Cornell University Press, 1987).

9. See, for example, Herbert Blumer, "The Methodological Position of Symbolic Interactionism," in his *Symbolic Interactionism: Perspective and Method* (Englewood Cliffs, N.J.: Prentice-Hall, 1969), p. 2. Throughout this article, I assume that a theoretically productive analogy can be made between individuals and states. There are at least two justifications for this anthropomorphism. Rhetorically, the analogy is an accepted practice in mainstream international relations discourse, and since this article is an immanent rather than external critique, it should follow the practice. Substantively, states are collectivities of individuals that through their practices constitute each other as "persons" having interests, fears, and so on. A full theory of state identity- and interest-formation would nevertheless need to draw insights from the social psychology of groups and organizational theory, and for that reason my anthropomorphism is merely suggestive.

10. The phrase "distribution of knowledge" is Barry Barnes's, as discussed in his work *The Nature of Power* (Cambridge: Polity Press, 1988); see also Peter Berger and Thomas Luckmann, *The Social Construction of Reality* (New York: Anchor Books, 1966). The concern of recent international relations scholarship on "epistemic communities" with the cause-and-effect understandings of the world held by scientists, experts, and policymakers is an important aspect of the role of knowledge in world politics; see Peter Haas, "Do Regimes Matter? Epistemic Communities and Mediterranean Pollution Control," *International Organization* 43 (Summer 1989), pp. 377–404; and Ernst Haas, *When Knowledge Is Power*. My constructivist approach would merely add to this an equal emphasis on how such knowledge also *constitutes* the structures and subjects of social life.

11. For an excellent short statement of how collective meanings constitute identities, see Peter Berger, "Identity as a Problem in the Sociology of Knowledge," *European Journal of Sociology,* vol. 7, no. 1, 1966, pp. 32–40. See also David Morgan and Michael Schwalbe, "Mind and Self in Society: Linking Social Structure and Social Cognition," *Social Psychology Quarterly* 53 (June 1990), pp. 148–64. In my discussion, I draw on the following interactionist texts: George Herbert Mead, *Mind, Self, and Society* (Chicago: University of Chicago Press, 1934); Berger and Luckmann, *The Social Construction of Reality;* Sheldon Stryker, *Symbolic Interactionism: A Social Structural Version* (Menlo Park, Calif.: Benjamin/Cummings, 1980); R. S. Perinbanayagam, *Signifying Acts: Structure and Meaning in Everyday Life* (Carbondale: Southern Illinois University Press, 1985); John Hewitt, *Self and Society: A Symbolic Interactionist Social Psychology* (Boston: Allyn & Bacon, 1988); and Turner, *A Theory of Social Interaction*. Despite some differences, much the same points are made by structurationists such as Bhaskar and Giddens. See Roy Bhaskar, *The Possibility of Naturalism* (Atlantic Highlands, N.J.: Humanities Press, 1979); and Anthony Giddens, *Central Problems in Social Theory* (Berkeley: University of California Press, 1979).

12. Berger, "Identity as a Problem in the Sociology of Knowledge," p. 111.

13. While not normally cast in such terms, foreign policy scholarship on national role conceptions could be adapted to such identity language. See Kal Holsti, "National

Role Conceptions in the Study of Foreign Policy," *International Studies Quarterly* 14 (September 1970), pp. 233–309; and Stephen Walker, ed., *Role Theory and Foreign Policy Analysis* (Durham, N.C.: Duke University Press, 1987). For an important effort to do so, see Stephen Walker, "Symbolic Interactionism and International Politics: Role Theory's Contribution to International Organization," in C. Shih and Martha Cottam, eds., *Contending Dramas: A Cognitive Approach to Post-War International Organizational Processes* (New York: Praeger, forthcoming).

14. On the "portfolio" conception of interests, see Barry Hindess, *Political Choice and Social Structure* (Aldershot, U.K.: Edward Elgar, 1989), pp. 2–3. The "definition of the situation" is a central concept in interactionist theory.

15. Nelson Foote, "Identification as the Basis for a Theory of Motivation," *American Sociological Review* 16 (February 1951), p. 15. Such strongly sociological conceptions of interest have been criticized, with some justice, for being "oversocialized"; see Dennis Wrong, "The Oversocialized Conception of Man in Modern Sociology," *American Sociological Review* 26 (April 1961), pp. 183–93. For useful correctives, which focus on the activation of presocial but nondetermining human needs within social contexts, see Turner, *A Theory of Social Interaction,* pp. 23–69; and Viktor Gecas, "The Self-Concept as a Basis for a Theory of Motivation," in Judith Howard and Peter Callero, eds., *The Self-Society Dynamic* (Cambridge: Cambridge University Press, 1991), pp. 171–87.

16. In neo-Durkheimian parlance, institutions are "social representations." See Serge Moscovici, "The Phenomenon of Social Representations," in Rob Farr and Serge Moscovici, eds., *Social Representations* (Cambridge: Cambridge University Press, 1984), pp. 3–69. See also Barnes, *The Nature of Power.* Note that this is a considerably more socialized cognitivism than that found in much of the recent scholarship on the role of "ideas" in world politics, which tends to treat ideas as commodities that are held by individuals and intervene between the distribution of power and outcomes. For a form of cognitivism closer to my own, see Emanuel Adler, "Cognitive Evolution: A Dynamic Approach for the Study of International Relations and Their Progress," in Emanuel Adler and Beverly Crawford, eds., *Progress in Postwar International Relations* (New York: Columbia University Press, 1991), pp. 43–88.

17. Berger and Luckmann, *The Social Construction of Reality,* p. 58.

18. See Giddens, *Central Problems in Social Theory;* and Alexander Wendt and Raymond Duvall, "Institutions and International Order," in Ernst-Otto Czempiel and James Rosenau, eds., *Global Changes and Theoretical Challenges* (Lexington, Mass.: Lexington Books, 1989), pp. 51–74.

19. Proponents of choice theory might put this in terms of "interdependent utilities." For a useful overview of relevant choice-theoretic discourse, most of which has focused on the specific case of altruism, see Harold Hochman and Shmuel Nitzan, "Concepts of Extended Preference," *Journal of Economic Behavior and Organization* 6 (June 1985), pp. 161–76. The literature on choice theory usually does not link behavior to issues of identity. For an exception, see Amartya Sen, "Goals, Commitment, and Identity," *Journal of Law, Economics, and Organization* 1 (Fall 1985), pp. 341–55; and Robert Higgs, "Identity and Cooperation: A Comment on Sen's Alternative Program," *Journal of Law, Economics, and Organization* 3 (Spring 1987), pp. 140–42.

20. Security systems might also vary in the extent to which there is a functional differentiation or a hierarchical relationship between patron and client, with the patron playing a hegemonic role within its sphere of influence in defining the security interests of its clients. I do not examine this dimension here; for preliminary discussion, see Alexander Wendt, "The States System and Global Militarization," Ph.D. diss., University of Minnesota, Minneapolis, 1989; and Alexander Wendt and Michael Barnett, "The International System and Third World Militarization," unpublished manuscript, 1991.

21. This amounts to an "internationalization of the state." For a discussion of this subject, see Raymond Duvall and Alexander Wendt, "The International Capital Regime and the Internationalization of the State," unpublished manuscript, 1987. See also R. B. J. Walker, "Sovereignty, Identity, Community: Reflections on the Horizons of Contemporary Political Practice," in R. B. J. Walker and Saul Mendlovitz, eds., *Contending Sovereignties* (Boulder, Colo.: Lynne Rienner, 1990), pp. 159–85.

22. On the spectrum of cooperative security arrangements, see Charles Kupchan and Clifford Kupchan, "Concerts, Collective Security, and the Future of Europe," *International Security* 16 (Summer 1991), pp. 114–61; and Richard Smoke, "A Theory of Mutual Security," in Richard Smoke and Andrei Kortunov, eds., *Mutual Security* (New York: St. Martin's Press, 1991), pp. 59–111. These may be usefully set alongside Christopher Jencks' "Varieties of Altruism," in Jane Mansbridge, ed., *Beyond Self-Interest* (Chicago: University of Chicago Press, 1990), pp. 53–67.

23. On the role of collective identity in reducing collective action problems, see Bruce Fireman and William Gamson, "Utilitarian Logic in the Resource Mobilization Perspective," in Mayer Zald and John McCarthy, eds., *The Dynamics of Social Movements* (Cambridge, Mass.: Winthrop, 1979), pp. 8–44; Robyn Dawes et al., "Cooperation for the Benefit of Us—Not Me, or My Conscience," in Mansbridge, *Beyond Self-Interest,* pp. 97–110; and Craig Calhoun, "The Problem of Identity in Collective Action," in Joan Huber, ed., *Macro-Micro Linkages in Sociology* (Beverly Hills, Calif.: Sage, 1991), pp. 51–75.

24. See Thomas Risse-Kappen, "Are Democratic Alliances Special?" unpublished manuscript, Yale University, New Haven, Conn., 1991. This line of argument could be expanded usefully in feminist terms. For a useful overview of the relational nature of feminist conceptions of self, see Paula England and Barbara Stanek Kilbourne, "Feminist Critiques of the Separative Model of Self: Implications for Rational Choice Theory," *Rationality and Society* 2 (April 1990), pp. 156–71. On feminist conceptualizations of power, see Ann Tickner, "Hans Morgenthau's Principles of Political Realism: A Feminist Reformulation," *Millennium* 17 (Winter 1988), pp. 429–40; and Thomas Wartenberg, "The Concept of Power in Feminist Theory," *Praxis International* 8 (October 1988), pp. 301–16.

25. Haskell Fain, *Normative Politics and the Community of Nations* (Philadelphia: Temple University Press, 1987).

26. This is the intersubjective basis for the principle of functional nondifferentiation among states, which "drops out" of Waltz's definition of structure because the latter has no explicit intersubjective basis. In international relations scholarship, the social production of territorial space has been emphasized primarily by poststructuralists. See, for example, Richard Ashley, "The Geopolitics of Geopolitical Space: Toward

a Critical Social Theory of International Politics," *Alternatives* 12 (October 1987), pp. 403–34; and Simon Dalby, *Creating the Second Cold War* (London: Pinter, 1990). But the idea of space as both product and constituent of practice is also prominent in structurationist discourse. See Giddens, *Central Problems in Social Theory*; and Derek Gregory and John Urry, eds., *Social Relations and Spatial Structures* (London: Macmillan, 1985).

27. See John Ruggie, "Continuity and Transformation in the World Polity: Toward a Neorealist Synthesis," *World Politics* 35 (January 1983), pp. 261–85. In *Mind, Self, and Society,* p. 161, Mead offers the following argument: "If we say 'this is my property, I shall control it,' that affirmation calls out a certain set of responses which must be the same in any community in which property exists. It involves an organized attitude with reference to property which is common to all members of the community. One must have a definite attitude of control of his own property and respect for the property of others. Those attitudes (as organized sets of responses) must be there on the part of all, so that when one says such a thing he calls out in himself the response of the others. That which makes society possible is such common responses."

28. For a definition and discussion of "social closure," see Raymond Murphy, *Social Closure* (Oxford: Clarendon Press, 1988).

29. See Richard Ashley, "Untying the Sovereign State: A Double Reading of the Anarchy Problematique," *Millennium* 17 (Summer 1988), pp. 227–62. Those with more modernist sensibilities will find an equally practice-centric view of institutions in Blumer's observation on p. 19 of "The Methodological Position of Symbolic Interactionism": "A gratuitous acceptance of the concepts of norms, values, social rules and the like should not blind the social scientist to the fact that any one of them is subtended by a process of social interaction—a process that is necessary not only for their change but equally well for their retention in a fixed form. It is the social process in group life that creates and upholds the rules, not the rules that create and uphold group life."

30. See, for example, Mohammed Ayoob, "The Third World in the System of States: Acute Schizophrenia or Growing Pains?" *International Studies Quarterly* 33 (March 1989), pp. 67–80.

31. See William Coplin, "International Law and Assumptions About the State System," *World Politics* 17 (July 1965), pp. 615–34.

32. See Anthony Smith, "States and Homelands: The Social and Geopolitical Implications of National Territory," *Millennium* 10 (Autumn 1981), pp. 187–202.

33. This assumes that there are no other, competing, principles that organize political space and identity in the international system and coexist with traditional notions of sovereignty; in fact, of course, there are. On "spheres of influence" and "informal empires," see Jan Triska, ed., *Dominant Powers and Subordinate States* (Durham, N.C.: Duke University Press, 1986); and Ronald Robinson, "The Excentric Idea of Imperialism, With or Without Empire," in Wolfgang Mommsen and Jurgen Osterhammel, eds., *Imperialism and After: Continuities and Discontinuities* (London: Allen & Unwin, 1986), pp. 267–89. On Arab conceptions of sovereignty, see Michael Barnett, "Sovereignty, Institutions, and Identity: From Pan-Arabism to the Arab State System," unpublished manuscript, University of Wisconsin, Madison, 1991.

34. David Strang, "Anomaly and Commonplace in European Expansion: Realist and Institutional Accounts," *International Organization* 45 (Spring 1991), pp. 143–62.

35. On "dynamic density," see Ruggie, "Continuity and Transformation in the World Polity"; and Waltz, "Reflections on *Theory of International Politics*." The role of interdependence in conditioning the speed and depth of social learning is much greater than the attention to which I have paid it. On the consequences of interdependence under anarchy, see Helen Milner, "The Assumption of Anarchy in International Relations Theory: A Critique," *Review of International Studies* 17 (January 1991), pp. 67–85.

36. See Michael Taylor, *Anarchy and Cooperation* (New York: Wiley, 1976); and Robert Axelrod, *The Evolution of Cooperation* (New York: Basic Books, 1984).

37. Mead, *Mind, Self, and Society.*

38. Strictly speaking, this is not true, since in iterated games the addition of future benefits to current ones changes the payoff structure of the game at T1, in this case from prisoners' dilemma to an assurance game. This transformation of interest takes place entirely within the actor, however, and as such is not a function of interaction with the other.

39. In fairness to Axelrod, he does point out that internalization of norms is a real possibility that may increase the resilience of institutions. My point is that this important idea cannot be derived from an approach to theory that takes identities and interests as exogenously given.

40. On "European identity," see Barry Buzan et al., eds., *The European Security Order Recast* (London: Pinter, 1990), pp. 45–63.

41. On "embeddedness," see John Ruggie, "International Regimes, Transactions, and Change: Embedded Liberalism in a Postwar Economic Order," in Krasner, *International Regimes,* pp. 195–232.

42. See Grieco, "Anarchy and the Limits of Cooperation."

43. On the difficulties of creating cooperative security regimes given competitive interests, see Robert Jervis, "Security Regimes," in Krasner, *International Regimes,* pp. 173–94; and Charles Lipson, "International Cooperation in Economic and Security Affairs," *World Politics* 37 (October 1984), pp. 1–23.

44. See Mead, *Mind, Self, and Society.* For useful discussions of this distinction and its implications for notions of creativity in social systems, see George Cronk, *The Philosophical Anthropology of George Herbert Mead* (New York: Peter Lang, 1987), pp. 36–40; and Howard, "From Changing Selves Toward Changing Society."

45. Ralph Turner, "Role-Taking: Process Versus Conformity," in Arnold Rose, ed., *Human Behavior and Social Processes* (Boston: Houghton Mifflin, 1962).

46. On "character planning," see Jon Elster, *Sour Grapes: Studies in the Subversion of Rationality* (Cambridge: Cambridge University Press, 1983), p. 117. For other approaches to the problem of self-initiated change, see Harry Frankfurt, "Freedom of the Will and the Concept of a Person," *Journal of Philosophy* 68 (January 1971), pp. 5–20; Amartya Sen, "Rational Fools: A Critique of the Behavioral Foundations of Economic Theory," *Philosophy and Public Affairs* 6 (Summer 1977), pp. 317–44; and Thomas Schelling, "The Intimate Contest for Self-Command," *The Public Interest* 60 (Summer 1980), pp. 94–118.

47. For useful overviews of New Thinking, see Mikhail Gorbachev, *Perestroika: New Thinking for Our Country and the World* (New York: Harper & Row, 1987); Vendulka Kubalkova and Albert Cruickshank, *Thinking New About Soviet "New Thinking"* (Berkeley: Institute of International Studies, 1989); and Allen Lynch, *Gorbachev's International Outlook: Intellectual Origins and Political Consequences* (New York: Institute for East-West Security Studies, 1989). It is not clear to what extent New Thinking is a conscious policy as opposed to an ad hoc policy. The intense theoretical and policy debate within the Soviet Union over New Thinking and the frequently stated idea of taking away the Western "excuse" for fearing the Soviet Union both suggest the former, but I will remain agnostic here and simply assume that it can be fruitfully interpreted "as if" it had the form that I describe.

48. For useful overviews of these factors, see Jack Snyder, "The Gorbachev Revolution: A Waning of Soviet Expansionism?" *World Politics* 12 (Winter 1987–88), pp. 93–121; and Stephen Meyer, "The Sources and Prospects of Gorbachev's New Political Thinking on Security," *International Security* 13 (Fall 1988), pp. 124–63.

49. See Daniel Bar-Tal et al., "Conflict Termination: An Epistemological Analysis of International Cases," *Political Psychology* 10 (June 1989), pp. 233–55. For an unrelated but interesting illustration of how changing cognitions in turn make possible organizational change, see Jean Bartunek, "Changing Interpretive Schemes and Organizational Restructuring: The Example of a Religious Order," *Administrative Science Quarterly* 29 (September 1984), pp. 355–72.

50. See Robert Cox, "Social Forces, States and World Orders: Beyond International Relations Theory," in Keohane, *Neorealism and Its Critics,* pp. 204–55. See also Brian Fay, *Critical Social Science* (Ithaca, N.Y.: Cornell University Press, 1987).

51. Hazel Markus and Paula Nurius, "Possible Selves," *American Psychologist* 41 (September 1986), pp. 954–69.

52. See Erving Goffman, *The Presentation of Self in Everyday Life* (New York: Doubleday, 1959); Eugene Weinstein and Paul Deutschberger, "Some Dimensions of Altercasting," *Sociometry* 26 (December 1963), pp. 454–66; and Walter Earle, "International Relations and the Psychology of Control: Alternative Control Strategies and Their Consequences," *Political Psychology* 7 (June 1986), pp. 369–75.

53. See Volker Boge and Peter Wilke, "Peace Movements and Unilateral Disarmament: Old Concepts in a New Light," *Arms Control* 7 (September 1986), pp. 156–70; Zeev Maoz and Daniel Felsenthal, "Self-Binding Commitments, the Inducement of Trust, Social Choice, and the Theory of International Cooperation," *International Studies Quarterly* 31 (June 1987), pp. 177–200; and V. Sakamoto, "Unilateral Initiative as an Alternative Strategy," *World Futures,* vol. 24, nos. 1–4, 1987, pp. 107–34.

54. On rewards, see Thomas Milburn and Daniel Christie, "Rewarding in International Politics," *Political Psychology* 10 (December 1989), pp. 625–45.

55. The importance of reciprocity in completing the process of structural transformation makes the logic in this stage similar to that in the "evolution of cooperation." The difference is one of prerequisites and objective: in the former, ego's tentative redefinition of self enables it to try and change alter by acting "as if" both were already playing a new game; in the latter, ego acts only on the basis of given interests and prior experience, with transformation emerging only as an unintended consequence.

1.4

KARL MARX

Milja Kurki

> Karl Marx is a prototypical critical theorist who sees people and history embedded in a holistic context from which individual variables, such as nations and foreign policy actors, cannot be isolated and manipulated (there is no disaggregated sequence of cause and effect). Although, as Milja Kurki points out, Marx believed in progress, that progress was "programmed" into the "laws" of historical materialism in which the driving forces were ultimately economic (modes of production), not ideational, as Hegel argued. To what extent class consciousness (a product of economic forces) and alienation (a product of the dialectical conflict between classes) persist today (for example, in developing countries marginalized by globalization) and whether revolution is necessary to emancipate oppressed peoples—these questions constitute Marx's enduring legacy in the contemporary international relations debate.

Karl Marx's philosophical, sociological, economic and political writings have had a deep impact on the practice of politics and international politics during the past two centuries. They have also had far-reaching influence on critical social theorising: Marx's thought has served as both the bedrock and the primary focus of theoretical challenge for most twentieth century 'critical theorists'. Yet, while the influential nature of Marx's thought is in no doubt, the precise nature of his legacy has remained contested. Various contrasting interpretations—from sympathetic 'humanist' readings to various 'deterministic' readings—have been advanced, each interpretation carrying with it important theoretical, rhetorical and political ramifications. Because of the difficult interpretational problems associated with Marx's writings, it would be impossible to provide a definitive interpretation of Marx's ideas here. The focus here, rather modestly, is on, first, giving a brief account of the context of Marx's writings before proceeding to outline some of the key concepts associated with his work. I conclude by reflecting briefly on the legacy of Marx for twentieth century critical social theory.

Source: Milja Kurki, "Karl Marx," in *Critical Theorists and International Relations,* ed. Jenny Edkins and Nick Vaughan-Williams (London and New York: Routledge, 2009), 246–250.

Life, Core Writings and Influences

Karl Marx was born in Trier in Prussia in 1818. He studied initially at the University of Bonn and later at the *Friedrich-Willhelm Universität* in Berlin. Having completed his doctoral study on classical philosophy, he resided in Paris, Brussels, and latterly in London, his movements often dictated by the constraints levelled on his residence owing to his association with various revolutionary movements and journals. For most of his life, especially during his years spent in London, Marx lived in relative poverty and was often financially reliant on his friend and supporter Friedrich Engels, who was also, following Marx's death in 1883, responsible for editing and publishing some of his posthumous work, notably the last two volumes of *Capital*.

As with any author that wrote during a long time-span, it is difficult to pin down Marx's thought to an entirely coherent set of views: some of his arguments, and his explanatory interests, shifted significantly over the years. Marx's early works tend to be philosophical in nature and are focused on dealing with the controversies that surrounded the debate between Hegelian philosophers and the so-called 'Young Hegelians' associated with Ludwig Feuerbach (upon whose works Marx drew heavily). In his early works, such as *On the Jewish Question* (1843), *Contribution to a Critique of Hegel's Philosophy of Right* (1943), *Economic and Philosophical Manuscripts* (1944), *Theses on Feuerbach* (1845) and *German Ideology* (1846), he dealt with many of the philosophical issues that formed the cornerstone of his historically materialist conception of human nature, philosophy and reality. He set out a critique of liberal conceptions of emancipation, a critique of religion as a derivative of material exploitation, a concept of alienation and a dialectical materialist position against Hegel.

His later works, on the other hand, focused more explicitly on issues of political economy and engaged with and critiqued the writings of so-called 'classical political economists', most notably Adam Smith and David Ricardo. In these later writings, notably in the *Grundrisse* (1857), *The Preface to the Contribution to a Critique of Political Economy* (1859), *Theories of Surplus Value* (1862) and *Capital* (vol. 1 published in 1865, later volumes published posthumously in 1885 and 1894), he set out his famous interpretation of the labour theory of value and the capitalist mode of production. As Marx attempted to understand the laws and contradictions characteristic of the capitalist system, these later works took on a distinctly 'scientific' (and some say 'deterministic') tone.

Besides his contributions to philosophical, social theoretical and political economic theories, it should also be noted that Marx was also closely associated with various revolutionary movements, perhaps most notably with the International Working Men's Association (or the so-called First International). Marx and Engels' *Communist Manifesto* (1948) with its call for 'working men of all countries to unite' certainly came to play an important role in nineteenth and twentieth century socialist movements and revolutions. Indeed, it is important to note that Marx was not only a philosopher but also an active participant in the political struggles of his time. His *Theses on Feuerbach* summarises the 'practical' sentiment of his approach well: 'philosophers have only *interpreted* the world, in various ways; the point, however, is to *change* it' (Marx 1970: 30).

Key Concepts

The philosophical underpinnings of Marx's social and economic theories revolved around two core ideas: a *contextual view of human nature,* and a *dialectical* and *historical materialist conception of history.* Liberal thinkers have classically taken as their starting point the notion that human beings should be conceived of as autonomous rational individuals who should be allowed to exercise their judgement free of unnecessary constraints so as to enable them to best follow and fulfil their interests. Marx took exception with the liberal idea of human nature: for Marx, individuals must be understood not as 'abstract individuals' but as fundamentally social beings, tied to their natural and social environment. Human beings for Marx are socially and historically engendered actors that exist in multiple sets of social relations with each other that condition their actions and beliefs—although human beings are also capable of transforming their social situations (not as they please, but as conditions allow). Marx built on this idea by accepting the basic premise of Hegel's dialectical view of history, the view that history develops out of the process of negotiation of contrasting forms of consciousness. However, against Hegel, the driving forces of history for Marx were material, not 'ideational', in nature. For Marx, human beings exist in historically specific forms of material reality and it is their material social context that conditions their 'consciousness'. This, notably, does not entail that 'brute' material forces in history 'determine' our actions (in a 'when A, then B' manner), but simply that social relations are always materially embedded and that they constrain and condition our thoughts and capabilities for societal interaction and transformation. For Marx, crucially, if we analyse people in relation to their social and historical material context, we can come to discern the role of various structural forces and oppressions inherent within the modern system of capitalist economics and in the 'bourgeois democratic' governance attached to it.

The key aspects of the material context of individuals, for Marx, were the 'forces of' and 'relations of' production (the former denoting the technology and resources of production, and the latter the relations of people in production). These together constituted a *mode of production.* Marx famously argued that a shift had taken place in the mode of production underlying societal life—from a feudal system to a capitalist mode of production. He predicted a further shift towards a communist mode of production and society, arising from the contradictions inherent in the capitalist system. The key driving force of this change was the *class antagonism* existing within the capitalist mode of production. In the capitalist system, this manifested itself in the exploitation of workers (the proletariat) by capitalists. While workers earned a wage which facilitated a minimal existence, capitalists by virtue of their power position in the mode of production extracted *surplus value* from the products of the worker's labour, which they appropriated as 'profit'.

One of the key aspects of the capitalist mode of production was the specific forms of *alienation* to which it subjected the proletariat: in the capitalist mode of production workers became alienated from the products of their labour, the process of labour, their 'species-being' and their fellow workers. This alienation was supported by a system of ideology that the capitalist society propagated: through the law, the state and the semblance of democracy, the proletariat was pacified to live under a *false consciousness* which legitimised the state of their oppression and hid away the underlying economic exploitation of the proletariat. It followed that the development of *class consciousness* was necessary among the workers: it was important that they realise that their 'real interests' lay not in competing with each other for jobs but in challenging the system of capitalist exploitation. Equipped with a realisation of the 'deep running' nature of class conflict, they would come to understand that any revolutionary change would need to entail a holistic challenge to the material/productive and ideational/superstructural forces in society.

It would also be necessary to reflect on the consequences of the capitalist drive for profit on an international scale: as later Marxists (especially Lenin) argued, the profit-motive could also be seen to be a key driver of *imperialism* by capitalist states. Capitalism for Marxists is not a domestic phenomenon but a global one.

Many contentions have been made about whether Marx assumed that there would be an inevitable shift in the capitalist mode of production towards communism or whether social actors should take an active role in bringing about the end of the capitalist mode of exploitation. Marx's frequent references to the laws inherent in political economy structures seemed to imply an inexorable logic of development, although arguably the emphasis on laws (and a positivist idea of science) was a consequence of Engels' particular posthumous interpretation of Marx's work. Because of the unclear nature of Marx's view on political action, as the twentieth century unfolded so did complex debates about what constitutes legitimate proletarian political action (e.g. in Soviet and Chinese contexts) and about how change can be achieved in countries where the working classes are reluctant to take action against capitalist elites and states (e.g. Western Europe and the US). Much of twentieth century Marxist tradition and critical theory thought has focused on dealing with the tensions and unanswered questions that arose out of Marx's thinking on the logic of the capitalist system, the super-structural forces attached to it and the question of revolutionary social change. Certainly, Gramsci, the Frankfurt School and post-Marxists, such as Laclau and Mouffe, have all in their own ways sought to negotiate new interpretations of Marx's ideas for the purposes of devising emancipatory political action in their specific contexts.

Indeed, although most twentieth century critical theorists seek to go beyond Marx's categories—many of them especially expanding the analysis of ideological or cultural forms of oppression and domination—these analyses could be seen, to a significant extent, as derivatives of, although also to a significant extent as novel elaborations on, Marx's initial analysis of alienation and false consciousness within capitalist industrial society. Also, many critical theorists' emphasis on philosophy and theory as a reflection of social conditions, and on theory as closely tied to the practice of politics, also have affinities with Marx's ideas.

Of course the great confidence Marx had in the proletariat as an agent of emancipatory change, and the reductionist and deterministic aspects characteristic of his thought, have been legitimate targets of attack by later critical theorists. Marx was very much an Enlightenment figure and a believer in progressive change in society, something that is distinctly unpopular in the current era of social theory where ideas of progress, emancipation and grand political projects are in doubt. Yet, it seems fair to say that Marx still constitutes an important reference point for contemporary debates and it should not be forgotten that in dealing with world political issues such as globalisation, some theorists still consider it important to defend Marxism, especially in its 'humanist' forms. It seems then that Marx's thought is still not 'irrelevant' despite the many proclamations to that effect in the post-Cold War era: the legacy of Marx is still very much alive, and as contested as ever.

1.5

THOROUGHLY MODERN MARX: LIGHTS. CAMERA. ACTION. *DAS KAPITAL.* NOW.

Leo Panitch

> If you think that Karl Marx, who died in 1883, has no relevance for today's world economy, you might think again after reading this piece. As Leo Panitch shows, Marx would not have been surprised by the financial crisis that beset the world in 2008–2009. He would have argued that the debt and derivative debacle that brought the system down represented another "death lurch" on the part of capitalism as it struggled to create enough demand to absorb its products. He would have decried "Band-Aid" proposals to fix the system by nationalizing banks or controlling carbon emissions and called for more radical steps to mobilize the consciousness of the passive masses and break completely with the logic of capitalism. Marx may be dead, but his ideas live on to inspire revolutionary proposals such as the recent one that Panitch mentions by Englishman Willem Buiter to convert the world's entire financial system (banks, investment houses, insurance companies, and so on) into a "public utility" run by the state on the basis of costs not profits. Marx, who called for "the centralization of credit" in *Das Kapital,* would have said, "Right on."

The economic crisis has spawned a resurgence of interest in Karl Marx. Worldwide sales of *Das Kapital* have shot up (one lone German publisher sold thousands of copies in 2008, compared with 100 the year before), a measure of a crisis so broad in scope and devastation that it has global capitalism—and its high priests—in an ideological tailspin.

Yet even as faith in neoliberal orthodoxies has imploded, why resurrect Marx? To start, Marx was far ahead of his time in predicting the successful capitalist globalization of recent decades. He accurately foresaw many of the fateful factors that would give rise to today's global economic crisis: what he called the "contradictions" inherent in a world comprised of competitive markets, commodity production, and financial speculation.

Penning his most famous works in an era when the French and American revolutions were less than a hundred years old, Marx had premonitions of AIG

Source: Leo Panitch, "Thoroughly Modern Marx: Lights. Camera. Action. *Das Kapital.* Now," *Foreign Policy* no. 172 (May–June 2009): 140–145.

and Bear Stearns trembling a century and a half later. He was singularly cognizant of what he called the "most revolutionary part" played in human history by the bourgeoisie—those forerunners of today's Wall Street bankers and corporate executives. As Marx put it in *The Communist Manifesto,* "The bourgeoisie cannot exist without constantly revolutionizing the instruments of production, and thereby relations of production, and with them the whole relations of society.... In one word, it creates a world after its own image."

But Marx was no booster of capitalist globalization in his time or ours. Instead, he understood that "the need for a constantly expanding market for its products chases the bourgeoisie over the whole surface of the globe," foreseeing that the development of capitalism would inevitably be "paving the way for more extensive and exhaustive crises." Marx identified how disastrous speculation could trigger and exacerbate crises in the whole economy. And he saw through the political illusions of those who would argue that such crises could be permanently prevented through incremental reform.

Like every revolutionary, Marx wanted to see the old order overthrown in his lifetime. But capitalism had plenty of life left in it, and he could only glimpse, however perceptively, the mistakes and wrong turns that future generations would commit. Those of us now cracking open Marx will find he had much to say that is relevant today, at least for those looking to "recover the spirit of the revolution," not merely to "set its ghost walking again."

If he were observing the current downturn, Marx would certainly relish pointing out how flaws inherent in capitalism led to the current crisis. He would see how modern developments in finance, such as securitization and derivatives, have allowed markets to spread the risks of global economic integration. Without these innovations, capital accumulation over the previous decades would have been significantly lower. And so would it have been if finance had not penetrated more and more deeply into society. The result has been that consumer demand (and hence, prosperity) in recent years has depended more and more on credit cards and mortgage debt at the same time that the weakened power of trade unions and cutbacks in social welfare have made people more vulnerable to market shocks.

This leveraged, volatile global financial system contributed to overall economic growth in recent decades. But it also produced a series of inevitable financial bubbles, the most dangerous of which emerged in the U.S. housing sector. That bubble's subsequent bursting had such a profound impact around the globe precisely because of its centrality to sustaining both U.S. consumer demand and international financial markets. Marx would no doubt point to this crisis as a perfect instance of when capitalism looks like "the sorcerer who is no longer able to control the powers of the netherworld whom he has called up by his spells."

Despite the depth of our current predicament, Marx would have no illusions that economic catastrophe would itself bring about change. He knew very well that capitalism, by its nature, breeds and fosters social isolation. Such a system, he wrote, "leaves no other nexus between man and man than naked self-interest, than callous 'cash payment.'" Indeed, capitalism leaves societies mired "in the icy water of egotistical calculation." The resulting social isolation creates passivity in the face of personal crises, from factory layoffs to home foreclosures. So, too, does this isolation impede communities of active, informed citizens from coming together to take up radical alternatives to capitalism.

Marx would ask first and foremost how to overcome this all-consuming social passivity. He thought that unions and workers' parties developing in his time were a step forward. Thus in *Das Kapital* he wrote that the "immediate aim" was "the organization of the proletarians into a class" whose "first task" would be "to win the battle for democracy." Today, he would encourage the formation of new collective identities, associations, and institutions within which people could resist the capitalist status quo and begin deciding how to better fulfill their needs.

No such ambitious vision for enacting change has arisen from the crisis so far, and it is this void that Marx would find most troubling of all. In the United States, some recent attention-getting proposals have been derided as "socialist," but only appear to be radical because they go beyond what the left of the Democratic Party is now prepared to advocate. Dean Baker, codirector of the Center for Economic and Policy Research, for example, has called for a $2 million cap on certain Wall Street salaries and the enactment of a financial transactions tax, which would impose an incremental fee on the sale or transfer of stocks, bonds, and other financial assets. Marx would view this proposal as a perfect case of thinking inside the box, because it explicitly endorses (even while limiting) the very thing that is now popularly identified as the problem: a culture of risk disassociated from consequence. Marx would be no less derisive toward those who think that bank nationalizations—such as those that took place in Sweden and Japan during their financial crises in the 1990s—would amount to real change.

Ironically, one of the most radical proposals making the rounds today has come from an economist at the London School of Economics, Willem Buiter, a former member of the Bank of England's Monetary Policy Committee and certainly no Marxist. Buiter has proposed that the whole financial sector be turned into a public utility. Because banks in the contemporary world cannot exist without public deposit insurance and public central banks that act as lenders of last resort, there is no case, he argues, for their continuing existence as privately owned, profit-seeking institutions. Instead they should be publicly owned and run as public services. This proposal echoes the demand for "centralization of credit in the banks of the state" that Marx himself made in the *Manifesto*. To him, a financial-system overhaul would reinforce the importance of the working classes' winning "the battle of democracy" to radically change the state from an organ imposed upon society to one that responds to it.

"From financialisation of the economy to the socialisation of finance," Buiter wrote, is "a small step for the lawyers, a huge step for mankind." Clearly, you don't need to be a Marxist to have radical aspirations. You do, however, have to be some sort of Marxist to recognize that even at a time like the present, when the capitalist class is on its heels, demoralized and confused, radical change is not likely to start in the form of "a small step for the lawyers" (presumably after getting all the "stakeholders" to sit down together in a room to sign a document or two). Marx would tell you that, without the development of popular forces through radical new movements and parties, the socialization of finance will fall on infertile ground. Notably, during the economic crisis of the 1970s, radical forces inside many of Europe's social democratic parties put forward similar suggestions, but they were unable to get the leaders of those parties to go along with proposals they derided as old-fashioned.

Attempts to talk seriously about the need to democratize our economies in such radical ways were largely shunted aside by parties of all stripes for the next several decades, and we are still paying the price for marginalizing those ideas. The irrationality built into the basic logic of capitalist markets—and so deftly analyzed by Marx—is once again evident. Trying just to stay afloat, each factory and firm lays off workers and tries to pay less to those kept on. Undermining job security has the effect of undercutting demand throughout the economy. As Marx knew, microrational behavior has the worst macroeconomic outcomes. We now can see where ignoring Marx while trusting in Adam Smith's "invisible hand" gets you.

The financial crisis today also exposes irrationalities in realms beyond finance. One example is U.S. President Barack Obama's call for trading in carbon credits as a solution to the climate crisis. In that supposedly progressive proposal, corporations that meet emissions standards sell credits to others that fail to meet their own targets. The Kyoto Protocol called for a similar system swapped across states. Fatefully however, both plans depend on the same volatile derivatives markets that are inherently open to manipulation and credit crashes. Marx would insist that, to find solutions to global problems such as climate change, we need to break with the logic of capitalist markets rather than use state institutions to reinforce them. Likewise, he would call for international economic solidarity rather than competition among states. As he put it in the *Manifesto,* "United action, of the leading ... countries, at least, is the first condition for the emancipation of the proletariat."

Yet the work of building new institutions and movements for change must begin at home. Although he made the call "Workers of the world, unite!" Marx still insisted that workers in each country "first of all settle things with their own bourgeoisie." The measures required to transform existing economic, political, and legal institutions would "of course be different in different countries." But in every case, Marx would insist that the way to bring about radical change is first to get people to think ambitiously again.

How likely is that to happen? Even at a moment when the financial crisis is bleeding dry a vast swath of the world's people, when collective anxiety shakes every age, religious, and racial group, and when, as always, the deprivations and burdens are falling most heavily on ordinary working people, the prognosis is uncertain. If he were alive today, Marx would not look to pinpoint exactly when or how the current crisis would end. Rather, he would perhaps note that such crises are part and parcel of capitalism's continued dynamic existence. Reformist politicians who think they can do away with the inherent class inequalities and recurrent crises of capitalist society are the real romantics of our day, themselves clinging to a naive utopian vision of what the world might be. If the current crisis has demonstrated one thing, it is that Marx was the greater realist.

1.6

THE LEVEL-OF-ANALYSIS PROBLEM IN INTERNATIONAL RELATIONS

J. David Singer

> In a seminal article written early in the development of contemporary
> international relations, J. David Singer describes the advantages and
> disadvantages of the four major levels of analysis—the systemic,
> nation-state, and (within the latter) individual actor and foreign pol-
> icy levels. As he points out, no one level is necessarily the best, and
> some levels of analysis may be better suited for the use of some per-
> spectives than for the use of others. Studies operating at the systemic
> level of analysis, for example, find it difficult to apply perspectives
> that emphasize psychological or goal-seeking motives and behavior
> by individual actors. These are better dealt with through what Singer
> calls "phenomenological" approaches at the individual and foreign
> policy levels of analysis.

In any area of scholarly inquiry, there are always several ways in which the
phenomena under study may be sorted and arranged for purposes of systemic
analysis. Whether in the physical or social sciences, the observer may choose
to focus upon the parts or upon the whole, upon the components or upon
the system. He may, for example, choose between the flowers or the garden, the
rocks or the quarry, the trees or the forest, the houses or the neighborhood, the
cars or the traffic jam, the delinquents or the gang, the legislators or the legislative, and so on.[1] Whether he selects the micro- or macro-level of analysis is
ostensibly a mere matter of methodological or conceptual convenience. Yet the
choice often turns out to be quite difficult, and may well become a central issue
within the discipline concerned. The complexity and significance of these level-
of-analysis decisions are readily suggested by the long-standing controversies
between social psychology and sociology, personality-oriented and culture-
oriented anthropology, or micro- and macro-economics, to mention but a few.
In the vernacular of general systems theory, the observer is always confronted
with a system, its sub-systems, and their respective environments, and while he
may choose as his system any cluster of phenomena from the most minute
organism to the universe itself, such choice cannot be merely a function of whim

Source: J. David Singer, "The Level-of-Analysis Problem in International Relations," *The International System: Theoretical Essays,* special issue of *World Politics* 14, no. 1 (1961): 77–92.

or caprice, habit or familiarity.[2] The responsible scholar must be prepared to evaluate the relative utility—conceptual and methodological—of the various alternatives open to him, and to appraise the manifold implications of the level of analysis finally selected. So it is with international relations.

But whereas the pros and cons of the various possible levels of analysis have been debated exhaustively in many of the social sciences, the issue has scarcely been raised among students of our emerging discipline.[3] Such tranquillity may be seen by some as a reassuring indication that the issue is not germane to our field, and by others as evidence that it has already been resolved, but this writer perceives the quietude with a measure of concern. He is quite persuaded of its relevance and certain that it has yet to be resolved. Rather, it is contended that the issue has been ignored by scholars still steeped in the intuitive and artistic tradition of the humanities or enmeshed in the web of "practical" policy. We have, in our texts and elsewhere, roamed up and down the ladder of organizational complexity with remarkable abandon, focusing upon the total system, international organizations, regions, coalitions, extra-national associations, nations, domestic pressure groups, social classes, elites, and individuals as the needs of the moment required. And though most of us have tended to settle upon the nation as our most comfortable resting place, we have retained our propensity for vertical drift, failing to appreciate the value of a stable point of focus.[4] Whether this lack of concern is a function of the relative infancy of the discipline or the nature of the intellectual traditions from whence it springs, it nevertheless remains a significant variable in the general sluggishness which characterizes the development of theory in the study of relations among nations. It is the purpose of this paper to raise the issue, articulate the alternatives, and examine the theoretical implications and consequences of two of the more widely employed levels of analysis: the international system and the national sub-systems.

I. The Requirements of an Analytical Model

Prior to an examination of the theoretical implications of the level of analysis or orientation employed in our model, it might be worthwhile to discuss the uses to which any such model might be put, and the requirements which such uses might expect of it.

Obviously, we would demand that it offer a highly accurate *description* of the phenomena under consideration. Therefore the scheme must present as complete and undistorted a picture of these phenomena as is possible; it must correlate with objective reality and coincide with our empirical referents to the highest possible degree. Yet we know that such accurate representation of a complex and wide-ranging body of phenomena is extremely difficult. Perhaps a useful illustration may be borrowed from cartography; the oblate spheroid which the planet earth most closely represents is not transferable to the two-dimensional surface of a map without *some* distortion. Thus, the Mercator projection exaggerates distance and distorts direction at an increasing rate as we move north or south *from* the equator, while the polar gnomonic projection suffers from these same debilities as we move *toward* the equator. Neither offers therefore a wholly accurate presentation, yet each is true enough to reality to be quite useful for certain specific purposes. The same sort of tolerance is necessary in evaluating any analytical model for the study of international relations; if we must sacrifice total representational accuracy, the problem is to decide where distortion is least dysfunctional and where such accuracy is absolutely essential.

These decisions are, in turn, a function of the second requirement of any such model—a capacity to *explain* the relationships among the phenomena under investigation. Here our concern is not so much with accuracy of description as with validity of explanation. Our model must have such analytical capabilities as to treat the causal relationships in a fashion which is not only valid and thorough, but parsimonious; this latter requirement is often overlooked, yet its implications for research strategy are not inconsequential.[5] It should be asserted here that the primary purpose of theory is to explain, and when descriptive and explanatory requirements are in conflict, the latter ought to be given priority, even at the cost of some representational inaccuracy.

Finally, we may legitimately demand that any analytical model offer the promise of reliable *prediction*. In mentioning this requirement last, there is no implication that it is the most demanding or difficult of the three. Despite the popular belief to the contrary, prediction demands less of one's model than does explanation or even description. For example, any informed layman can predict that pressure on the accelerator of a slowly moving car will increase its speed; that more or less of the moon will be visible tonight than last night; or that the normal human will flinch when confronted with an impending blow. These *predictions* do not require a particularly elegant or sophisticated model of the universe, but their *explanation* demands far more than most of us carry around in our minds. Likewise, we can predict with impressive reliability that any nation will respond to military attack in kind, but a description and understanding of the processes and factors leading to such a response are considerably more elusive, despite the gross simplicity of the acts themselves.

Having articulated rather briefly the requirements of an adequate analytical model, we might turn now to a consideration of the ways in which one's choice of analytical focus impinges upon such a model and affects its descriptive, explanatory, and predictive adequacy.

II. The International System as Level of Analysis

Beginning with the systemic level of analysis, we find in the total international system a partially familiar and highly promising point of focus. First of all, it is the most comprehensive of the levels available, encompassing the totality of interactions which take place within the system and its environment. By focusing on the system, we are enabled to study the patterns of interaction which the system reveals, and to generalize about such phenomena as the creation and dissolution of coalitions, the frequency and duration of specific power configurations, modifications in its stability, its responsiveness to changes in formal political institutions, and the norms and folklore which it manifests as a societal system. In other words, the systemic level of analysis, and only this level, permits us to examine international relations in the whole, with a comprehensiveness that is of necessity lost when our focus is shifted to a lower, and more partial, level. For descriptive purposes, then, it offers both advantages and disadvantages; the former flow from its comprehensiveness, and the latter from the necessary dearth of detail.

As to explanatory capability, the system-oriented model poses some genuine difficulties. In the first place, it tends to lead the observer into a position which exaggerates the impact of the system upon the national actors and, conversely, discounts the impact of the actors on the system. This is, of course, by no means inevitable; one could conceivably look upon the system as a rather passive environment in which dynamic states act out their relationships rather than as a socio-political entity with a dynamic of its own. But there is a natural tendency to endow that upon which we focus our attention with somewhat greater potential than it might normally be expected to have. Thus, we tend to move, in a system-oriented model, away from notions implying much national autonomy and independence of choice and toward a more deterministic orientation.

Secondly, this particular level of analysis almost inevitably requires that we postulate a high degree of uniformity in the foreign policy operational codes of our national actors. By definition, we allow little room for divergence in the behavior of our parts when we focus upon the whole. It is no coincidence that our most prominent theoretician—and one of the very few text writers focusing upon the international system—should "assume that [all] statesmen think and act in terms of interest defined as power."[6] If this single-minded behavior be interpreted literally and narrowly, we have a simplistic image comparable to economic man or sexual man, and if it be defined broadly, we are no better off than the psychologist whose human model pursues "self-realization" or "maximization of gain"; all such gross models suffer from the same fatal weakness as the utilitarian's "pleasure-pain" principle. Just as individuals differ widely in what they deem to be pleasure and pain, or gain and loss, nations may differ widely in what they consider to be the national interest, and we end up having to break down and refine the larger category. Moreover, Professor Morgenthau finds himself compelled to go still further and disavow the relevance of both motives and ideological preferences in national behavior, and these represent two of the more useful dimensions in differentiating among the several nations in our international system. By eschewing any empirical concern with the domestic and internal variations within the separate nations, the system-oriented approach tends to produce a sort of "black box" or "billiard ball" concept of the national actors.[7] By discounting—or denying—the differences among nations, or by positing the near-impossibility of observing many of these differences at work within them,[8] one concludes with a highly homogenized image of our nations in the international system. And though this may be an inadequate foundation upon which to base any *causal* statements, it offers a reasonably adequate basis for *correlative* statements. More specifically, it permits us to observe and measure correlations between certain forces or stimuli which seem to impinge upon the nation and the behavior patterns which are the apparent consequence of these stimuli. But one must stress the limitations implied in the word "apparent"; what is thought to be the consequence of a given stimulus may only be a coincidence or artifact, and until one investigates the major elements in the causal link—no matter how persuasive the deductive logic—one may speak only of correlation, not of consequence.

Moreover, by avoiding the multitudinous pitfalls of intra-nation observation, one emerges with a singularly manageable model, requiring as it does little of the methodological sophistication or onerous empiricism called for when one probes beneath the behavioral externalities of the actor. Finally, as has already been suggested in the introduction, the systemic orientation should prove to be reasonably satisfactory as a basis for prediction, even if such prediction is to extend beyond the characteristics of the system and attempt anticipatory statements regarding the actors themselves; this assumes, of course, that the actors are characterized and their behavior predicted in relatively gross and general terms.

These, then, are some of the more significant implications of a model which focuses upon the international system as a whole. Let us turn now to the more familiar of our two orientations, the national state itself.

III. The National State as Level of Analysis

The other level of analysis to be considered in this paper is the national state—our primary actor in international relations. This is clearly the traditional focus among Western students, and is the one which dominates almost all of the texts employed in English-speaking colleges and universities.

Its most obvious advantage is that it permits significant differentiation among our actors in the international system. Because it does not require the attribution of great similarity to the national actors, it encourages the observer to examine them in greater detail. The favorable results of such intensive analysis cannot be overlooked, as it is only when the actors are studied in some depth that we are able to make really valid generalizations of a comparative nature. And though the systemic model does not necessarily preclude comparison and contrast among the national sub-systems, it usually eventuates in rather gross comparisons based on relatively crude dimensions and characteristics. On the other hand, there is no assurance that the nation-oriented approach will produce a sophisticated model for the comparative study of foreign policy; with perhaps the exception of the Haas and Whiting study,[9] none of our major texts makes a serious and successful effort to describe and explain national behavior in terms of most of the significant variables by which such behavior might be comparatively analyzed. But this would seem to be a function, not of the level of analysis employed, but of our general unfamiliarity with the other social sciences (in which comparison is a major preoccupation) and of the retarded state of comparative government and politics, a field in which most international relations specialists are likely to have had some experience.

But just as the nation-as-actor focus permits us to avoid the inaccurate homogenization which often flows from the systemic focus, it also may lead us into the opposite type of distortion—a marked exaggeration of the differences among our sub-systemic actors. While it is evident that neither of these extremes is conducive to the development of a sophisticated comparison of foreign policies, and such comparison requires a balanced preoccupation with both similarity and difference, the danger seems to be greatest when we succumb to the tendency to overdifferentiate; comparison and contrast can proceed only from observed uniformities.[10]

One of the additional liabilities which flow in turn from the pressure to overdifferentiate is that of Ptolemaic parochialism. Thus, in overemphasizing the differences among the many national states, the observer is prone to attribute many of what he conceives to be virtues to his own nation and the vices to others, especially the adversaries of the moment. That this ethnocentrism is by no means an idle fear is borne out by perusal of the major international relations texts published in the United States since 1945. Not only is the world often perceived through the prism of the American national interest, but an inordinate degree of attention (if not spleen) is directed toward the Soviet Union; it would hardly be amiss to observe that most of these might qualify equally well as studies in American foreign policy. The scientific inadequacies of this sort of "we-they" orientation hardly require elaboration, yet they remain a potent danger in any utilization of the national actor model.

Another significant implication of the sub-systemic orientation is that it is only within its particular framework that we can expect any useful application of the decision-making approach.[11] Not all of us, of course, will find its inapplicability a major loss; considering the criticism which has been leveled at the decision-making approach, and the failure of most of us to attempt its application, one might conclude that it is no loss at all. But the important thing to note here is that a system-oriented model would not offer a hospitable framework for such a detailed and comparative approach to the study of international relations, no matter what our appraisal of the decision-making approach might be.

Another and perhaps more subtle implication of selecting the nation as our focus or level of analysis is that it raises the entire question of goals, motivation, and purpose in national policy.[12] Though it may well be a peculiarity of the Western philosophical tradition, we seem to exhibit, when confronted with the need to explain individual or collective behavior, a strong proclivity for a goal-seeking approach. The question of whether national behavior is purposive or not seems to require discussion in two distinct (but not always exclusive) dimensions.

Firstly, there is the more obvious issue of whether those who act on behalf of the nation in formulating and executing foreign policy consciously pursue rather concrete goals. And it would be difficult to deny, for example, that these role-fulfilling individuals envisage certain specific outcomes which they hope to realize by pursuing a particular strategy. In this sense, then, nations may be said to be goal-seeking organisms which exhibit purposive behavior.

However, purposiveness may be viewed in a somewhat different light, by asking whether it is not merely an intellectual construct that man imputes to himself by reason of his vain addiction to the free-will doctrine as he searches for characteristics which distinguish him from physical matter and the lower animals. And having attributed this conscious goal-pursuing behavior to himself as an individual, it may be argued that man then proceeds to project this attribute to the social organizations of which he is a member. The question would seem to distill down to whether man and his societies pursue goals of their own choosing or are moved toward those imposed upon them by forces which are primarily beyond their control.[13] Another way of stating the dilemma would be to ask whether we are concerned with the ends which men and nations strive for or the ends toward which they are impelled by the past and present characteristics of their social and physical milieu. Obviously, we are using the terms "ends," "goals," and "purpose" in two rather distinct ways; one refers to those which are consciously envisaged and more or less rationally pursued, and the other to those of which the actor has little knowledge but toward which he is nevertheless propelled.

Taking a middle ground in what is essentially a specific case of the free will vs. determinism debate, one can agree that nations move toward outcomes of which they have little knowledge and over which they have less control, but that they nevertheless do prefer, and therefore select, particular outcomes and *attempt* to realize them by conscious formulation of strategies.

Also involved in the goal-seeking problem when we employ the nation-oriented model is the question of how and why certain nations pursue specific sorts of goals. While the question may be ignored in the system-oriented model or resolved by attributing identical goals to all national actors, the nation-as-actor approach demands that we investigate the processes by which national goals are selected, the internal and external factors that impinge on those processes, and the institutional framework from which they emerge. It is worthy of note that despite the strong predilection for the nation-oriented model in most of our texts, empirical or even deductive analyses of these processes are conspicuously few.[14] Again, one might attribute these lacunae to the methodological and conceptual inadequacies of the graduate training which international relations specialists traditionally receive.[15] But in any event, goals and motivations are both dependent and independent variables, and if we intend to explain a nation's foreign policy, we cannot settle for the mere postulation of these goals; we are compelled to go back a step and inquire into their genesis and the process by which they become the crucial variables that they seem to be in the behavior of nations.

There is still another dilemma involved in our selection of the nation-as-actor model, and that concerns the phenomenological issue: do we examine our actor's behavior in terms of the objective factors which allegedly influence that behavior, or do we do so in terms of the actor's *perception* of these "objective factors"? Though these two approaches are not completely exclusive of one another, they proceed from greatly different and often incompatible assumptions, and produce markedly divergent models of national behavior.[16]

The first of these assumptions concerns the broad question of social causation. One view holds that individuals and groups respond in a quasi-deterministic fashion to the realities of physical environment, the acts or power of other individuals or groups, and similar "objective" and "real" forces or stimuli. An opposite view holds that individuals and groups are not influenced in their behavior by such objective forces, but by the fashion in which these forces are perceived and evaluated, however distorted or incomplete such perceptions may be. For adherents of this position, the only reality is the phenomenal—that which is discerned by the human senses; forces that are not discerned do not exist for that actor, and those that do exist do so only in the fashion in which they are perceived. Though it is difficult to accept the position that an individual, a group, or a nation is affected by such forces as climate, distance, or a neighbor's physical power only insofar as they are recognized and appraised, one must concede that perceptions will certainly affect the manner in which such forces are responded to. As has often been pointed out, an individual will fall to the ground when he steps out of a tenth-story window regardless of his perception of gravitational forces, but on the other hand such perception is a major factor in whether or not he steps out of the window in the first place.[17] The point here is that if we embrace a phenomenological view of causation, we will tend to utilize a phenomenological model for explanatory purposes.

The second assumption which bears on one's predilection for the phenomenological approach is more restricted, and is primarily a methodological one. Thus, it may be argued that any description of national behavior in a given international situation would be highly incomplete were it to ignore the link between the external forces at work upon the nation and its general foreign policy behavior. Furthermore, if our concern extends beyond the mere description of "what happens" to the realm of explanation, it could be contended that such omission of the cognitive and the perceptual linkage would be ontologically disastrous. How, it might be asked, can one speak of "causes" of a nation's policies when one has ignored the media by which external conditions and factors are translated into a policy decision? We may observe correlations between all sorts of forces in the international system and the behavior of nations, but their causal relationship must remain strictly deductive and hypothetical in the absence of empirical investigation into the causal chain which allegedly links the two. Therefore, even if we are satisfied with the less-than-complete descriptive capabilities of a non-phenomenological model, we are still drawn to it if we are to make any progress in explanation.

The contrary view would hold that the above argument proceeds from an erroneous comprehension of the nature of explanation in social science. One is by no means required to trace every perception, transmission, and receipt between stimulus and response or input and output in order to explain the behavior of the nation or any other human group. Furthermore, who is to say that empirical observation—subject as it is to a host of errors—is any better a basis of explanation than informed deduction, inference, or analogy? Isn't an explanation which flows logically from a coherent theoretical model just as reliable as one based upon a misleading and elusive body of data, most of which is susceptible to analysis only by techniques and concepts foreign to political science and history?

This leads, in turn, to the third of the premises relevant to one's stand on the phenomenological issue: are the dimensions and characteristics of the policy-makers' phenomenal field empirically discernible? Or, more accurately, even if we are convinced that their perceptions and beliefs constitute a crucial variable in the explanation of a nation's foreign policy, can they be observed in an accurate and systematic fashion?[18] Furthermore, are we not required by the phenomenological model to go beyond a classification and description of such variables, and be drawn into the tangled web of relationships out of which they emerge? If we believe that these phenomenal variables are systematically observable, are explainable, and can be fitted into our explanation of a nation's behavior in the international system, then there is a further tendency to embrace the phenomenological approach. If not, or if we are convinced that the gathering of such data is inefficient or uneconomical, we will tend to shy clear of it.

The fourth issue in the phenomenological dispute concerns the very nature of the nation as an actor in international relations. Who or what is it that we study? Is it a distinct social entity with well-defined boundaries—a unity unto itself? Or is it an agglomeration of individuals, institutions, customs, and procedures? It should be quite evident that those who view the nation or the state as an integral social unit could not attach much utility to the phenomenological approach, particularly if they are prone to concretize or reify the abstraction. Such abstractions are incapable of perception, cognition, or anticipation (unless, of course, the reification goes so far as to anthropomorphize and assign to the abstraction such attributes as will, mind, or personality). On the other hand, if the nation or state is seen as a group of individuals operating within an institutional framework, then it makes perfect sense to focus on the phenomenal field of those individuals who participate in the policy-making process. In other words, *people* are capable of experiences, images, and expectations, while institutional abstractions are not, except in the metaphorical sense. Thus, if our actor cannot even have a phenomenal field, there is little point in employing a phenomenological approach.[19]

These, then, are some of the questions around which the phenomenological issue would seem to revolve. Those of us who think of social forces as operative regardless of the actor's awareness, who believe that explanation need not include all of the steps in a causal chain, who are dubious of the practicality of gathering phenomenal data, or who visualize the nation as a distinct entity apart from its individual members, will tend to reject the phenomenological approach.[20] Logically, only those who disagree with each of the above four assumptions would be *compelled* to adopt the approach. Disagreement with any one would be *sufficient* grounds for so doing.

The above represent some of the more significant implications and fascinating problems raised by the adoption of our second model. They seem to indicate that this sub-systemic orientation is likely to produce richer description and more satisfactory (from the empiricist's point of view) explanation of international relations, though its predictive power would appear no greater than the systemic orientation. But the descriptive and explanatory advantages are achieved only at the price of considerable methodological complexity.

IV. Conclusion

Having discussed some of the descriptive, explanatory, and predictive capabilities of these two possible levels of analysis, it might now be useful to assess the relative utility of the two and attempt some general statement as to their prospective contributions to greater theoretical growth in the study of international relations.

In terms of description, we find that the systemic level produces a more comprehensive and total picture of international relations than does the national or sub-systemic level. On the other hand, the atomized and less coherent image produced by the lower level of analysis is somewhat balanced by its richer detail, greater depth, and more intensive portrayal.[21] As to explanation, there seems little doubt that the sub-systemic or actor orientation is considerably more fruitful, permitting as it does a more thorough investigation of the processes by which foreign policies are made. Here we are enabled to go beyond the limitations imposed by the systemic level and to replace mere correlation with the more significant causation. And in terms of prediction, both orientations seem to offer a similar degree of promise. Here the issue is a function of what we seek to predict. Thus the policy-maker will tend to prefer predictions about the way in which nation x or y will react to a contemplated move on his own nation's part, while the scholar will probably prefer either generalized predictions regarding the behavior of a given class of nations or those regarding the system itself.

Does this summary add up to an overriding case for one or another of the two models? It would seem not. For a staggering variety of reasons the scholar may be more interested in one level than another at any given time and will undoubtedly shift his orientation according to his research needs. So the problem is really not one of deciding which level is most valuable to the discipline as a whole and then demanding that it be adhered to from now unto eternity.[22] Rather, it is one of realizing that there *is* this preliminary conceptual issue and that it must be temporarily resolved prior to any given research undertaking. And it must also be stressed that we have dealt here only with two of the more common orientations, and that many others are available and perhaps even more fruitful potentially than either of those selected here. Moreover, the international system gives many indications of prospective change, and it may well be that existing institutional forms will take on new characteristics or that new ones will appear to take their place. As a matter of fact, if incapacity to perform its functions leads to the transformation or decay of an institution, we may expect a steady deterioration and even ultimate disappearance of the national state as a significant actor in the world political system.

However, even if the case for one or another of the possible levels of analysis cannot be made with any certainty, one must nevertheless maintain a continuing awareness as to their use. We may utilize one level here and another there, but we cannot afford to shift our orientation in the midst of a study. And when we do in fact make an original selection or replace one with another at appropriate times, we must do so with a full awareness of the descriptive, explanatory, and predictive implications of such choice.

A final point remains to be discussed. Despite this lengthy exegesis, one might still be prone to inquire whether this is not merely a sterile exercise in verbal gymnastics. What, it might be asked, is the difference between the two levels of analysis if the empirical referents remain essentially the same? Or, to put it another way, is there any difference between international relations and comparative foreign policy? Perhaps a few illustrations will illuminate the subtle but important differences which emerge when one's level of analysis shifts. One might, for example, postulate that when the international system is characterized by political conflict between two of its most powerful actors, there is a strong tendency for the system to bipolarize. This is a systemic-oriented proposition. A sub-systemic proposition, dealing with the same general empirical referents, would state that when a powerful actor finds itself in political conflict with another of approximate parity, it will tend to exert pressure on its weaker neighbors to join its coalition. Each proposition, assuming it is true, is theoretically useful by itself, but each is verified by a different intellectual operation. Moreover—and this is the crucial thing for theoretical development—one could not add these two kinds of statements together to achieve a cumulative growth of empirical generalizations.

To illustrate further, one could, at the systemic level, postulate that when the distribution of power in the international system is highly diffused, it is more stable than when the discernible clustering of well-defined coalitions occurs. And at the sub-systemic or national level, the same empirical phenomena would produce this sort of proposition: when a nation's decision-makers find it difficult to categorize other nations readily as friend or foe, they tend to behave toward all in a more uniform and moderate fashion. Now, taking these two sets of propositions, how much cumulative usefulness would arise from attempting to merge and codify the systemic proposition from the first illustration with the sub-systemic proposition from the second, or vice versa? Representing different levels of analysis and couched in different frames of reference, they would defy theoretical integration; one may well be a corollary of the other, but they are not immediately combinable. A prior translation from one level to another must take place.

This, it is submitted, is quite crucial for the theoretical development of our discipline. With all of the current emphasis on the need for more empirical and data-gathering research as a prerequisite to theory-building, one finds little concern with the relationship among these separate and discrete data-gathering activities. Even if we were to declare a moratorium on deductive and speculative research for the next decade, and all of us were to labor diligently in the vineyards of historical and contemporary data, the state of international relations theory would probably be no more advanced at that time than it is now, unless such empirical activity becomes far more systematic. And "systematic" is used here to indicate the cumulative growth of inductive and deductive generalizations into an impressive array of statements conceptually related to one another and flowing from some common frame of reference. What that frame of reference should be, or will be, cannot be said with much certainty, but it does seem clear that it must exist. As long as we evade some of these crucial *a priori* decisions, our empiricism will amount to little more than an ever-growing potpourri of discrete, disparate, non-comparable, and isolated bits of information or extremely low-level generalizations. And, as such, they will make little contribution to the growth of a theory of international relations.

Notes

1. As Kurt Lewin observed in his classic contribution to the social sciences: "The first prerequisite of a successful observation in any science is a definite understanding about what size of unit one is going to observe at a given time." *Field Theory in Social Science,* New York, 1951, p. 157.

2. For a useful introductory statement on the definitional and taxonomic problems in a general systems approach, see the papers by Ludwig von Bertalanffy, "General System Theory," and Kenneth Boulding, "General System Theory: The Skeleton of Science," in Society for the Advancement of General Systems Theory, *General Systems,* Ann Arbor, Mich., 1956, 1, part 1.

3. An important pioneering attempt to deal with some of the implications of one's level of analysis, however, is Kenneth N. Waltz, *Man, the State, and War,* New York, 1959. But Waltz restricts himself to a consideration of these implications as they impinge on the question of the causes of war. See also this writer's review of Waltz, "International Conflict: Three Levels of Analysis," *World Politics,* XII (April 1960), pp. 453–61.

4. Even during the debate between "realism" and "idealism" the analytical implications of the various levels of analysis received only the scantiest attention; rather the emphasis seems to have been at the two extremes of pragmatic policy and speculative metaphysics.

5. For example, one critic of the decision-making model formulated by Richard C. Snyder, H. W. Bruck, and Burton Sapin, in *Decision-Making as an Approach to the Study of International Politics* (Princeton, N.J., 1954), points out that no single researcher could deal with all the variables in that model and expect to complete more than a very few comparative studies in his lifetime. See Herbert McClosky, "Concerning Strategies for a Science of International Politics," *World Politics,* VIII (January 1956), pp. 281–95. In defense, however, one might call attention to the relative ease with which many of Snyder's categories could be collapsed into more inclusive ones, as was apparently done in the subsequent case study (see note 11 below). Perhaps a more telling criticism of the monograph is McClosky's comment that "Until a greater measure of theory is introduced into the proposal and the relations among variables are specified more concretely, it is likely to remain little more than a setting-out of categories and, like any taxonomy, fairly limited in its utility" (p. 291).

6. Hans J. Morgenthau, *Politics Among Nations,* 3rd ed., New York, 1960, pp. 5–7. Obviously, his model does not preclude the use of power as a dimension for the differentiation of nations.

7. The "black box" figure comes from some of the simpler versions of S-R psychology, in which the observer more or less ignores what goes on within the individual and

concentrates upon the correlation between stimulus and response; these are viewed as empirically verifiable, whereas cognition, perception, and other mental processes have to be imputed to the individual with a heavy reliance on these assumed "intervening variables." The "billiard ball" figure seems to carry the same sort of connotation, and is best employed by Arnold Wolfers in "The Actors in International Politics" in William T. R. Fox, ed., *Theoretical Aspects of International Relations,* Notre Dame, Ind., 1959, pp. 83–106. See also, in this context, Richard C. Snyder, "International Relations Theory—Continued," *World Politics,* XIII (January 1961), pp. 300–12; and J. David Singer, "Theorizing About Theory in International Politics," *Journal of Conflict Resolution,* IV (December 1960), pp. 431–42. Both are review articles dealing with the Fox anthology.

8. Morgenthau observes, for example, that it is "futile" to search for motives because they are "the most illusive of psychological data, distorted as they are, frequently beyond recognition, by the interests and emotions of actor and observer alike" (*op. cit.,* p. 6).

9. Ernst B. Haas and Allen S. Whiting, *Dynamics of International Relations,* New York, 1956.

10. A frequent by-product of this tendency to overdifferentiate is what Waltz calls the "second-image fallacy," in which one explains the peaceful or bellicose nature of a nation's foreign policy exclusively in terms of its domestic economic, political, or social characteristics (*op. cit.,* chs. 4 and 5).

11. Its most well-known and successful statement is found in Snyder *et al. op. cit.* Much of this model is utilized in the text which Snyder wrote with Edgar S. Furniss, Jr., *American Foreign Policy: Formulation, Principles, and Programs,* New York, 1954. A more specific application is found in Snyder and Glenn D. Paige, "The United States Decision to Resist Aggression in Korea: The Application of an Analytical Scheme," *Administrative Science Quarterly,* III (December 1958), pp. 341–78. For those interested in this approach, very useful is Paul Wasserman and Fred S. Silander, *Decision-Making: An Annotated Bibliography,* Ithaca, N.Y., 1958.

12. And if the decision-making version of this model is employed, the issue is unavoidable. See the discussion of motivation in Snyder, Bruck, and Sapin, *op. cit.,* pp. 92–117; note that 25 of the 49 pages on "The Major Determinants of Action" are devoted to motives.

13. A highly suggestive, but more abstract treatment of this teleological question is in Talcott Parsons, *The Structure of Social Action,* 2nd ed., Glencoe, Ill., 1949, especially in his analysis of Durkheim and Weber. It is interesting to note that for Parsons an act implies, *inter alia,* "a future state of affairs toward which the process of action is oriented," and he therefore comments that "in this sense and this sense only, the schema of action is inherently teleological" (p. 44).

14. Among the exceptions are Haas and Whiting, *op. cit.,* chs. 2 and 3; and some of the chapters in Roy C. Macridis, ed., *Foreign Policy in World Politics,* Englewood Cliffs, N.J., 1958, especially that on West Germany by Karl Deutsch and Lewis Edinger.

15. As early as 1934, Edith E. Ware noted that "... the study of international relations is no longer entirely a subject for political science or law, but that economics, history, sociology, geography—all the social sciences—are called upon to contribute

towards the understanding ... of the international system." See *The Study of International Relations in the United States,* New York, 1934, p. 172. For some contemporary suggestions, see Karl Deutsch, "The Place of Behavioral Sciences in Graduate Training in International Relations," *Behavioral Science,* III (July 1958), pp. 278–84; and J. David Singer, "The Relevance of the Behavioral Sciences to the Study of International Relations," *ibid.,* VI (October 1961), pp. 324–35.

16. The father of phenomenological philosophy is generally acknowledged to be Edmund Husserl (1859–1938), author of *Ideas: General Introduction to Pure Phenomenology,* New York, 1931, trans. by W. R. Boyce Gibson; the original was published in 1913 under the title *Ideen zu einer reinen Phänomenologie und Phänomenologischen Philosophie.* Application of this approach to social psychology has come primarily through the work of Koffka and Lewin.

17. This issue has been raised from time to time in all of the social sciences, but for an excellent discussion of it in terms of the present problem, see Harold and Margaret Sprout, *Man-Milieu Relationship Hypotheses in the Context of International Politics,* Princeton University, Center of International Studies, 1956, pp. 63–71.

18. This is another of the criticisms leveled at the decision-making approach which, almost by definition, seems compelled to adopt some form of the phenomenological model. For a comprehensive treatment of the elements involved in human perception, see Karl Zener *et al.,* eds., "Inter-relationships Between Perception and Personality: A Symposium," *Journal of Personality,* XVIII (1949), pp. 1–266.

19. Many of these issues are raised in the ongoing debate over "methodological individualism," and are discussed cogently in Ernest Nagel, *The Structure of Science,* New York, 1961, pp. 535–46.

20. Parenthetically, holders of these specific views should also be less inclined to adopt the national or sub-systemic model in the first place.

21. In a review article dealing with two of the more recent and provocative efforts toward theory (Morton A. Kaplan, *System and Process in International Politics,* New York, 1957, and George Liska, *International Equilibrium,* Cambridge, Mass., 1957), Charles P. Kindleberger adds a further—if not altogether persuasive—argument in favor of the lower, sub-systemic level of analysis: "The total system is infinitely complex with everything interacting. One can discuss it intelligently, therefore, only bit by bit." "Scientific International Politics," *World Politics,* XI (October 1958), p. 86.

22. It should also be kept in mind that one could conceivably develop a theoretical model which successfully embraces both of these levels of analysis without sacrificing conceptual clarity and internal consistency. In this writer's view, such has not been done to date, though Kaplan's *System and Process in International Politics* seems to come fairly close.

Chapter 2

PERSPECTIVES ON WORLD HISTORY: CHANGE AND CONTINUITY

2.1

HISTORICAL REALITY VS. NEO-REALIST THEORY

Paul Schroeder

Paul Schroeder, like many historians, is skeptical of general theories of international relations. In this essay, he attacks two principal arguments of realism: that states always resort to self-help to balance or be balanced and that states do not play different roles in the system other than those determined by their relative power. He reviews a series of historical cases from the beginning of the Westphalian state system in 1648 through World War II, when realism should best apply, and finds that, instead of balancing and imitating one another, states pursued a variety of nonbalancing behaviors (hiding, transcending, and bandwagoning) as well as specialized roles not necessarily determined by their power position (leading, guardian, buffer, political, or neutral roles). Notice that the nonbalancing behaviors and specialized roles that he emphasizes bring into play liberal factors, such as "transcending" behavior (which "attempt[s] to surmount international anarchy ... through some institutional arrangement"), or ignore possible identity factors causing "hiding" behavior, such as U.S. exceptionalism leading to isolationism after World War I or Denmark's and Norway's pacifism leading to their refusal to arm before World War II. Theory slips into his account even as he critiques theory. Historians can't tell us all the facts, so they too have to rely on perspectives to select the most important ones.

Source: Paul Schroeder, "Historical Reality vs. Neo-realist Theory," *International Security* 19, no. 1 (1994): 108–148.

Realism has been for some time the reigning tradition in international theory and remains a major current in it.[1] The neo-realism or structural realism developed in Kenneth N. Waltz's *Theory of International Politics* is generally considered a major advance on the classical version of Hans Morgenthau and others. The central argument is that the broad outcomes of international politics derive more from the structural constraints of the states system than from unit behavior. The theory proceeds in a series of logical inferences from the fundamental postulate of a states system in which all units are autonomous, so that the system is structured by anarchy rather than hierarchy; to the primacy of survival, security, and independence for each unit wishing to remain part of the system; to the mandate of self-help this need imposes upon each unit; and to a resultant competition between units which produces a recurrent pattern of various balances of power....

Much current debate over neo-realism centers on what implications the end of the Cold War might have for realist theory, in terms of its ability both to explain this particular outcome and to prescribe future policy.[2] This essay will not, however, discuss how neo-realist theory fits recent and current history. Instead it takes up a question seldom if ever discussed, yet clearly important for international historians and arguably also for international relations theorists, namely, whether neo-realist theory is adequate and useful as an explanatory framework for the history of international politics in general, over the whole Westphalian era from 1648 to 1945, the period in which the validity of a realist paradigm of some sort is widely accepted even by non-realists.[3]

* * *

The Neo-realist Historical World

Two main assertions concerning international politics over history are made by Waltz in various forms and contexts throughout his work, especially in his *Theory of International Politics*: first, he asserts that the conduct of states in international politics has always been basically the same: all states are guided by structural constraints and imperatives of anarchy, self-help, and balance of power, and must be if they hope to survive and prosper.[4]

Second, states are not functionally differentiated within the structure of international politics. Their common, primary function, structurally determined, is to survive and remain independent through self-help. What differentiates states is instead their position within the system, i.e., their power relative to others. Domestic society, structured by hierarchy and heteronomy, enforces upon its units the mandate of specialization in order to survive. International society, structured by autonomy and anarchy, imposes on its units the mandate not to specialize but to concentrate their resources first and foremost on security. Only after that requirement is at least minimally met dare they pursue their particular aims. States ignoring this rule suffer serious consequences.[5]

Both historical generalizations are asserted as self-evident, something every-one knows, rather than based on much evidence or on inductive as opposed to deductive argument. In *Theory of International Politics,* Waltz uses historical evidence, drawn mainly from the recent past, primarily for purposes of instan-tiation and to back up certain other particular theses, e.g., that a bipolar balance is superior to a multipolar one, or that force has not declined in utility in the recent past. His most extended historical discussion of how structure shapes outcomes in international politics draws on material from domestic rather than international politics, arguing that the different British and American political systems have historically produced different kinds of leaders. Other broad his-torical assertions accompany and support his two main ones, for example, the contentions that "states prefer to join the weaker of two coalitions" and that "secondary states, if they are free to choose, flock to the weaker side; for it is the stronger side that threatens them," likewise without adducing historical evidence or argument.[6]

Yet both of Waltz's central assertions concerning the conduct of international politics throughout history are vital to neo-realist theory, for according to Waltz, the broad outcomes of international politics over the ages and its same-ness and repetitive character can be explained only by the structure of interna-tional politics as he presents it. The theory also purports to predict and explain the persistent strong tendency toward balance in the system,[7] and to account for the absence of functional differentiation among units and their differentiation solely by their position (i.e., relative power and capability) within it. Waltz also argues elsewhere that the placement of countries within the system by their relative power is the main determinant of their behavior within it, and this time cites historical examples as proof.[8]

A Historian's View of the Neo-realist Historical World

Some facts in the history of international politics seem to hold broadly for the model European states system through much of its existence and thus give the Waltzian picture a *prima facie* plausibility. It is generally true, though not at all uniformly so, that states in the modern era, regardless of their ideology, domes-tic structure, individual aims, etc., have claimed exclusive sovereignty over their territory and the sole right to the legitimate use of force within it, have set a high value on their independence and security, have upheld their right to use force in self-defense, have tried to provide means for their defense, and have conducted foreign policy with an eye to maintaining their security and independence. This is obvious and familiar. Nevertheless, the more one examines Waltz's historical generalizations about the conduct of international politics throughout history with the aid of the historian's knowledge of the actual course of history, the more doubtful—in fact, strange—these generalizations become.

Self-Help: Theory Confronts Practice

Do all states, or virtually all, or all that really count, actually resort to self-help in the face of threats to their security and independence? Though Waltz does not clearly define self-help or describe its practice, one may reasonably infer, given the link frequently drawn between self-help and the balance of power, and given Waltz's insistence on the primacy of power and the structural role of the potential and actual use of force in international politics, that self-help means, at least generally and primarily, the potential or actual use of a state's own power along with that of other units for the purposes of compellence, deterrence, and other modes of controlling the actions of one's opponents. By Waltz's rules for testing theories, neo-realist theory should correctly predict or confirm this kind of conduct in international politics throughout history, and Waltz clearly believes it does so.... [S]o do (and to some extent must) other realists.

I do not. I cannot construct a history of the European states system from 1648 to 1945 based on the generalization that most unit actors within that system responded to crucial threats to their security and independence by resorting to self-help, as defined above. In the majority of instances this just did not happen. In each major period in these three centuries, most unit actors tried if they possibly could to protect their vital interests in other ways. (This includes great powers as well as smaller ones, undermining the neo-realist argument that weaker states are more inclined to bandwagon than stronger ones, as discussed below.) The reasons are clear. For one thing, most states, most of the time, could not afford a strategy of self-help of this kind. They were like landowners with valuable property which they knew they could not possibly insure, first because insurance premiums were ruinously expensive, second because against the most devastating dangers no insurance policy was available at any price, and third because the very attempt on their part to take out an insurance policy would encourage robbers to attack them.[9] Hence the insurance policies they took out and maintained in the form of armed forces, alliances, and diplomacy were mostly intended to protect against minor risks and to deter casual attacks or vandalism, with the full knowledge that if something more serious threatened, another recourse would be necessary.

Other strategies were available and often tried. One commonly employed was *hiding* from threats. This could take various forms: simply ignoring the threat or declaring neutrality in a general crisis, possibly approaching other states on one or both sides of a quarrel to get them to guarantee one's safety; trying to withdraw into isolation; assuming a purely defensive position in the hope that the storm would blow over; or, usually as a later or last resort, seeking protection from some other power or powers in exchange for diplomatic services, friendship, or non-military support, without joining that power or powers as an ally or committing itself to any use of force on its part.[10] A strategy less common, but far from unusual or unknown, was *transcending*, i.e., attempting to surmount international anarchy and go beyond the normal limits of conflictual politics: to solve the problem, end the threat, and prevent its recurrence through some institutional arrangement involving an international consensus or formal agreement on norms, rules, and procedures for these purposes. Efforts of this kind were made in every era of these centuries.

Another strategy was *bandwagoning,* i.e., joining the stronger side for the sake of protection and payoffs, even if this meant insecurity *vis-à-vis* the protecting power and a certain sacrifice of independence. Against the views of some, such as Waltz and Stephen M. Walt,[11] I see bandwagoning as historically more common than balancing, particularly by smaller powers. Finally comes the strategy which, according to Waltz and others, is dominant and structural in international politics: *self-help* in the form of balancing against an actual or potential hegemon. Once again, contrary to the view of many scholars including historians, I see this as having been relatively rare, and often a fallback policy or last resort.[12]

A concrete example illustrating these different strategies in practice is the crisis in Germany (the Holy Roman Empire or Reich) caused by the Austrian Emperor Joseph II's attempt in 1785 to carry through the exchange of the Austrian Netherlands (Belgium) for Bavaria.[13] Almost all German states and principalities saw this move as a threat to the German "balance"—by which they meant not simply the balance of power between the German great powers, Austria and Prussia, and their respective clients, but even more importantly for some states, the balance provided by the Reich constitution between the sovereign powers of Germany's various states and the limits to individual state power and guarantees of corporate "liberties" (i.e., privileges) within those states. The reason the proposed move would threaten the independence and security of the Reich and its members was not just that it would strengthen Austria, but also and mainly that it would damage the Reich as a legal order guaranteeing the liberties of all its members (another indication of the ways in which a purely power-political view of international politics is too crude to capture vital elements of the process).[14] Many units hid from the threat, i.e., simply ignored the issue or remained neutral, even though they knew the outcome might affect them critically. Some balanced against it. Prussia and Hanover, old rivals, joined to exploit an idea already current, that of forming a Protestant League of Princes to check the Catholic Emperor and his ecclesiastical princely clients.[15] Some began by hiding out, then saw that Emperor Joseph would lose his nerve, and bandwagoned to the winning Prussian side. But some also tried to transcend; that is, certain lesser princes attempted to form a union of smaller states not to stop Prussia or Austria by force (which they knew was beyond their resources) or to balance with either great power or against both, but to rise above the quarrel, reviving and reforming the institutions and constitution of the Empire so as to provide guarantees for everyone's territorial rights, and a machinery for the arbitration of future disputes.[16]

This kind of scenario, in which different states perceiving the same threat or similar ones adopted differing strategies to meet them, is seen in almost every major crisis throughout the centuries in question. For this reason alone, neorealist theory cannot accommodate the history of international politics as I know it; too many facts and insights vital for explaining broad developments and results do not pass through its prism.

To be sure, this assertion has been supported here only by example rather than by proof; even after a thorough historical elaboration it would still remain controversial, given the debates over historical interpretation and the notorious difficulties of deciding which motives and strategies guided historical actors. Yet the problem of divergent strategies here indicated is not unknown to theorists. Stephen Walt proposes to meet it with an argument that states balance against threats rather than simply against power. This does not, however, really help answer the question of which of the four strategies—hiding, transcending, bandwagoning, or self-help—or which combination of them, prevailed in each instance. Walt's thesis, designed to help neo-realist theory explain why states so often join overwhelmingly powerful coalitions, actually makes it virtually impossible to distinguish between "balancing" and "bandwagoning" or to determine the real motives of actors, since any bandwagoning state is likely to claim that it is actually "balancing" against a threatening enemy. The argument thus begs the very question it is supposed to answer, namely, whether weaker states tend to balance or to bandwagon in the face of threats from more powerful states.[17] Besides, states seldom choose a strategy unconditionally or without mixed motives, and in particular they consider what strategy will yield the greatest side payments (territorial gains, future alliances, political concessions, prestige, etc.).[18]

Even if no ironclad case can be made from history, I can back the assertion that neorealism is incorrect in its claims for the repetitiveness of strategy and the prevalence of balancing in international politics, with brief examples of how the various competing strategies were used in the face of threat in four major periods of war: the French revolutionary and Napoleonic wars (1792–1815), the Crimean War (1853–56), the First World War (1914–18), and the Second World War (1939–45). These make a *prima facie* case against Waltz's generalizations.

French Revolutionary and Napoleonic Wars. The French revolutionary and Napoleonic wars are often considered a classic case of balancing, with allied coalitions repeatedly being formed to defeat France's bid for hegemony and restore the balance of power. However, this view will not stand examination. The First Coalition (1792–97) was formed against France at a time when, though it provoked the coalition into being and started the war by its aggressive behavior and ideology, France was militarily extremely weak and vulnerable and had lost all its allies and political influence in Europe. Austria and Prussia (or at least most of their leaders) expected to win the war easily; the smaller states, if they could not hide from the conflict, gravitated toward the apparently overwhelmingly superior allied coalition, which included Spain, Piedmont, Tuscany, Naples, and various German states, soon joined in early 1793 by Great Britain. Once France's real revolutionary power became apparent from late 1793 on, states began hiding by leaving the coalition (Prussia, Tuscany, and some German states) or bandwagoning by joining France, as Spain did.[19] The same thing happened to the Second Coalition (1798–1801): states hid or bandwagoned to the allied side so long as it was winning, to mid-1799, and then bandwagoned to France's side from late 1799 on. Even Russia, a main founder of the Second Coalition, did so.[20] In every succeeding war from late 1799 to mid-1813, despite the fact that France under Napoleon had become by far both the most powerful Continental state and the most ambitious and insatiable one, the French-led coalition was always larger and stronger than its counterpart; more states always bandwagoned than balanced. In several instances Napoleon was able to organize most of Europe for war against a single isolated foe (Britain in 1803 and 1807, Prussia in 1806, Spain in 1808, Austria in 1809, Russia in 1812). In short, the main response to Napoleonic hegemony and imperialism by European states, large and small alike, was not balancing but either hiding or bandwagoning. (There were also attempts to transcend, mainly in the form of trying to transform French conquest and domination into a new federal order for Germany and Europe, but these proved futile in the face of Napoleon's militarism.) Besides the smaller, weaker states who bandwagoned as Napoleon's satellites, many of them willingly and profitably, every major power in Europe except Great Britain—Prussia, Austria, Russia, Spain—bandwagoned as France's active ally for a considerable period. Wars continued to break out mainly not because European states tried to balance against France as a hegemonic power, but because Napoleon's ambition and lawless conduct frustrated their repeated efforts to hide or bandwagon. This happened to Prussia from 1795 to 1806 and from 1807 to 1810, Spain from 1795 to 1808, Austria in 1806–08 and 1809–13, and Russia in 1807–12.[21] Even after Napoleon's disastrous defeat in Russia in 1812, the Continental coalition that Russia and Prussia formed in early 1813 to "balance" against France was smaller than the coalition Napoleon re-formed from his allies and satellites, and was initially defeated by it. Only after the failure of Austria's attempt to transcend the crisis, by mediating a negotiated peace in the summer of 1813, did Austria join the coalition (for purposes of controlling and ending rather than winning the war), and only after the decisive defeat of Napoleon's army at Leipzig in October 1813 did his coalition break up, with smaller states bandwagoning to the winning allied side.[22]

The Crimean War. The Crimean War, originally seen by most Britons and still viewed by some historians as a case of "balancing" against Russian domination of Europe, actually began with a clearly superior allied coalition (Britain, France, and the Ottoman Empire) facing a Russia diplomatically isolated, politically and militarily threatened, aware of its peril, and looking for an honorable retreat. No neutral state in Europe therefore considered Russia a military threat at that time. Even Austria, which had a general fear of Russian domination of the Balkans, recognized that this danger was for the moment allayed, and tried hard to prevent the war. Most German states, including Prussia, considered the Anglo-French coalition a greater military and political threat to their security and interests. Yet Sardinia-Piedmont joined the dominant coalition militarily, Austria did so politically, and even Prussia and the German Confederation, although sympathetic to Russia and wanting only to hide from the conflict, were dragged into helping force Russia to admit defeat and accept an imposed settlement. In short, some states, great and small, bandwagoned; others tried to hide and then bandwagoned; still others, like Sweden, Denmark, and the Low Countries, remained in hiding; none balanced against Anglo-French domination. Once again, moreover, there was a major effort to transcend: Austria's attempt to stop the war short of victory by a negotiated settlement intended to produce a new concert and a permanent solution to the Eastern question.[23]

The First World War. The distinction between balancing and bandwagoning becomes especially difficult to draw in the First World War. It is possible, though far from clear, that initially both sides were balancing against the other's threat rather than bidding for hegemony. However, the distinction between aiming for balance or hegemony, always problematic, becomes virtually meaningless here, since, once engaged in war, both sides could envision security only through clear military supremacy, and both fought for imperialist goals designed to insure it.[24] Moreover, other states plainly preferred either to hide (Spain, Holland, Denmark, Sweden, Switzerland) or to bandwagon with the victor so as to defeat their particular enemies and make gains at their expense (Turkey, Bulgaria, Italy, Rumania, Greece, Japan, and China). As things turned out, only two powers joined the smaller and putatively weaker Central Powers (Bulgaria and Turkey, both under a degree of duress); more joined the larger allied one (Italy, Rumania, Greece, Japan, China, the United States, and all the British Dominions). Certain of these, especially Italy and Rumania, explicitly tried to bandwagon with the victorious side at the right moment to share the spoils. Moreover, one cannot overlook attempts by neutrals (the Papal State, Sweden, Switzerland, the United States) and even certain belligerents (Austria-Hungary and the Russian Provisional Government in 1917) to transcend the conflict by promoting a negotiated peace.[25]

World War Two. The pattern is a bit clearer in World War Two in Europe. Even before the war, Germany's growing power and political success promoted extensive hiding and bandwagoning in Western and Eastern Europe. Belgium dropped its ties to France in 1936 and reverted to neutrality; Holland, Denmark, and Norway not only remained ostentatiously neutral but declined even to arm for self-defense before they were overrun. Chamberlain's appeasement policy was certainly not balancing, but an attempt at a British partnership with Germany for peace; Daladier's abandonment of Czechoslovakia can be seen as France's attempt to avoid war by hiding. The Little Entente of Czechoslovakia, Rumania, and Yugoslavia, a potential instrument for balancing against Germany, fell apart even before Munich; the French-Czech-Russian alliance collapsed at Munich; and Poland and Hungary joined with Germany in despoiling Czechoslovakia. Italy, despite Mussolini's and Ciano's fears of Germany, moved decisively to Hitler's side in May 1939, and the Soviet Union followed in August. The Poles, although standing firm against German demands and accepting a British guarantee, steadfastly refused to join a balancing alliance with Russia against Germany and essentially pinned their hopes of salvation on hiding in independent neutrality. After France's defeat, the Vichy regime tried to bandwagon with Hitler's Germany. Hungary, Bulgaria, and Rumania joined his camp, while Yugoslavia's apparent reversal of its decision to do so in March 1941 was actually a purely domestic political coup. Even neutrals (Sweden, Turkey, Switzerland, Spain) leaned toward Germany so long as the tide of war was going Hitler's way. Once the tide of battle turned in 1941–42, however, states began bandwagoning with Hitler's enemies, many joining the "United Nations." Even Franco's Spain and Peron's Argentina finally leaned toward the Allies (although Spain felt a threat from Britain and Argentina from the United States), while Fascist Italy did an eighteenth-century *volte-face* and joined them as a co-belligerent.

Even if one allows considerable room for differences of interpretation of these well-known developments, neo-realist generalizations about the repetitiveness of strategy and the prevalence of balancing in international politics do not withstand historical scrutiny.

The neo-realist answer is likely to be that regardless of all the supposed variations in unit behavior, neo-realism still explains and predicts the broad patterns of behavior and overall outcomes of international history. Hiding, transcending, and bandwagoning are all just different forms and strategies of self-help; and in the last analysis, bids for hegemony are defeated, and new balances of power do emerge. The historian's preliminary reply would be, first, to ask what serious content remains to the concept of self-help if it includes strategies so diverse and even contradictory as these. Indeed, what becomes of the structural constraints of anarchy if they are elastic enough to allow some of the behaviors involved in transcending? Second, it is far from obvious (as discussed below) that in the long run bids for hegemony always fail and new balances emerge. Finally, if these central generalizations of neo-realist theory do not hold, what use is it to the historian? What does it really explain and predict?

The Fact of Functional Differentiation

Waltz's second generalization is that states are differentiated in the international system not by their functions but only by their power position within it. In fact, however, during every period of the Westphalian era, states of various sizes defined their place and role within the system, and were accorded status and recognition by other states, not simply according to their positions of power, even relative to other adjacent units, but also, and often mainly, on the basis of their specific functions within the system. My claim is not that the functional differentiation here alluded to, within the international system, is equivalent to what Waltz or other neo-realists mean by functional differentiation within hierarchical systems, e.g., between various offices within a domestic government, or between firms in a domestic economy. Obviously the two are not the same, in either kind or degree. Nor is this merely a general complaint that more functional differentiation of some sort has been involved in the history of international politics than neo-realism recognizes.[26] Even if true, that might be unimportant as an objection to the theory.

The issue involved is again the central one of this essay: does neo-realism adequately explain the broad outcomes and general pattern of international history? The question of functional differentiation is raised here to address this point, first, by showing that Waltz's argument—that "the domestic imperative is 'specialize!'" and "the international imperative is 'take care of yourself!'" so that "what each state does for itself is much like what all of the others are doing"[27]—is unsound even as a broad historical generalization; and second and still more important, by arguing that major outcomes and overall patterns in international history cannot be explained adequately unless one recognizes and allows for a great amount of functional differentiation of a particular kind.

To be specific: throughout the Westphalian era states both great and small, aware of their vulnerability and threats, sought survival in the international arena not only by means of strategies other than balancing (by bandwagoning, hiding, and transcending) but also, precisely, by specializing. They claimed, that is, an ability to perform certain important international functions or fill particular vital roles within the system that no other unit could do or do as well, and expected other powers to recognize these functions, to give them support or assistance, and even to accept their leadership on these functional grounds. These claims, far from being regularly dismissed as propaganda or window-dressing, were often discussed and debated. Questions of how functions and roles were assigned to individual actors within the international system, whether these roles were necessary and justified, and how well the actors were fulfilling them, became major issues in international politics (and still are), and formed the basis for many decisions and actions. Most important, they affected broad outcomes. The survival of states could depend on them: states that successfully specialized within the international system could continue to exist and prosper long after they were unable or unwilling to defend themselves, while states that failed to specialize or whose specialty lost its international relevance might be destroyed. In other words, the international imperative was not just "Take care of yourself!" but also, in a real sense, "Specialize!"; failure to specialize in the international system could equally well be punished. Furthermore, the durability, stability, and peaceful or bellicose character of the system of international politics in different eras could and did depend to a major degree upon whether this kind of functional differentiation between states was allowed and promoted, or was discouraged and destroyed.

To prove these assertions in detail would spring the bounds of this article, but a list of examples drawn from the first half of the nineteenth century (1815–48) will illustrate the functional differentiation posited here:

Britain, for example, claimed during this period and others to be the special holder of the European balance, protecting small states, promoting constitutional liberty, encouraging commerce, and preserving peace.

Russia claimed to be the guardian of the monarchical order in Europe, defender of all states against revolution, and protector especially of smaller states against threats or domination by other great powers.

The United Netherlands after 1815 claimed special treatment, and after 1830 Belgium claimed guaranteed neutrality, because the Low Countries served Britain and others as a barrier against French expansion, and served Austria, Prussia, and the lesser German states as a vital economic and political link connecting Britain to the Continent and Central Europe, curbing its drift toward isolation and preoccupation with its empire.

Switzerland had special functions as a neutral state under joint European guarantee, which were both strategic—to keep the passes between Germany and Italy out of any one great power's control—and broadly political—to make France, Austria, and Germany jointly responsible for a crucial area.

Denmark and Sweden undertook roles as neutrals guarding the entrance to the Baltic, thus serving everyone's commercial interests and preventing the constant struggles over the region from 1558 to 1815 from flaring up again.

The Papal State functioned as the political base for the Pope's independent reign as head of the Catholic church, which was considered vital by many states, including Protestant ones, to prevent international struggles over control of the church and religion.

The Ottoman Empire played roles both strategic—keeping the Turkish Straits and other vital areas out of great-power hands—and political—buffering against possible Austro-Russian clashes over influence in the Balkans, or Anglo-Russian conflict over the routes to India.

The smaller German powers played roles as independent states in forestalling struggles between Austria or Prussia for control of Germany, or attempts by France or Russia to dominate it from the flanks; as well as buffers and decompression zones between the absolutist East and the liberal-constitutionalist West.

Many special international functions were assigned to the German Confederation from 1815 on: regulating and controlling conflicts between individual German states, between estates and princes within individual states, between the Confederation and the individual states, between Protestants and Catholics, and between the great powers Austria and Prussia, former bitter rivals for supremacy in Germany and now required to work together to manage the Confederation.

Any historian knowledgeable in this area could extend this list. It is hard to conceive an international history of this period or any other which did not explicitly or implicitly deal with the different roles and functions filled by various units within the international system, and their effects. It is no answer to say that many of these special international functions were related to questions of security, and therefore can be considered as aspects of the states' relative power position within the structure. Of course they were often (but not always) *related* to questions of power and security. That is almost axiomatic in an international system. But this does not mean that these roles can be *reduced* to security factors and considered solely for their effects on security and the balance of power. Moreover, one can easily show in many instances that these functions and roles modified the behavior of states, including great powers, and significantly changed their purposes and methods in using power. For example, one reason Russia's conduct toward the Ottoman Empire in this period differed so strikingly from that in the previous half-century was the Russian Tsars' new self-conception as guardians of the European order and peace.[28] Britain's continental policy was powerfully influenced by its self-imposed role of advancing liberalism and constitutionalism.[29] Finally, to reduce or subordinate functional differentiation as here described to purposes of security and balance of power would stand its meaning, purposes, and effects in international history on their heads. The basic point of making these functional claims and of differentiating roles in all eras, but above all in 1815–48, is that states and their leaders, seeing that certain problems if left unmanaged would lead to dangerous security issues and balance of power confrontations, used the device of functional differentiation to remove problem areas and states from power politics and balance of power competition by recognizing and sanctioning particular roles and functions for particular states. Every example of functional differentiation in the Vienna system noted above illustrates this rule. They were all, in other words, instances not of balancing but of transcending, often in a collective, consensual way.[30]

The ideal example to show that the role of a state within the international system cannot be reduced to its power position, but must include its wider systemic functions, is the Habsburg Monarchy. Since its emergence as a great power in the late seventeenth century, the Monarchy had vital security interests to protect and strategic roles to play. In the Vienna system from 1815 on it was supposed to control Italy, help check Russia and France, help preserve the Ottoman Empire, and share in the organization and leadership of the German Confederation with Prussia, all in the interests of a peaceful, independent, defensively-oriented central Europe. But besides these security-related functions, which, if one were determined to do so, could all somehow be subsumed under the protean category of "balance of power," Austria also had other roles and functions, widely recognized (though not in formal treaties) and at least as indispensable for European peace and stability as its strategic-security ones, especially as the century wore on. It was fated by its own history, geography, and ethnic composition to be an arena where the two largest ethnic groups in Europe, Germans and Slavs, met and interpenetrated, along with other peoples neither German nor Slav. Within the Monarchy, as elsewhere in Eastern Europe, different cultures, religions, and nationalities crossed, clashed, and mingled with each other, making Austria, like it or not, the main seed-bed and nursery for one of the most important developments in nineteenth-century international history: the awakening of the peoples of east-central Europe to a consciousness of their nationality and a desire for political autonomy, if not independence. Only Austria conceivably had a chance to manage that process within and without its own borders in the interest of international stability; only if Austria continued to exist as an independent state, moreover, could Europe seriously hope to avoid an eventual struggle between Teuton and Slav for control of this area, and with it the mastery of Europe. It is therefore critical to an understanding of the nineteenth-century international system and of its two most important power-political problems—the emergence of nationalities and national states, and the potential struggle between Teuton and Slav for mastery in east-central Europe—to see that the system's functioning in a real sense depended upon Austria-Hungary's filling certain special, vital functions and roles, whether it wanted to or not. The character of international politics generally, and the survival of the system, would depend very heavily on both whether Austria proved able and willing to carry out these tasks, and whether the prevailing systemic rules and principles of international conduct in various periods allowed and encouraged this functional differentiation, or instead discouraged, punished, and ultimately destroyed it. Much of nineteenth-century European international history—indeed, the heart of it—must be seen in these terms. Otherwise one cannot really understand or explain either the remarkable peacefulness of the system in 1815–48 (the real "Long Peace" of international history, in most respects far superior to the much-celebrated "Long Peace" since 1945), the wars and strains of the mid-century, or the final degeneration and collapse by 1914.[31] A theory that holds that states are differentiated within the system solely by their relative power position cannot possibly deal successfully with this history or its outcome, any more than Newtonian physics can work for quantum mechanics. This neo-realist assumption, like its view of the unchanging, repetitive nature of balance-of-power politics and outcomes throughout the ages, may make its theory of international politics simple, parsimonious, and elegant; they also make it, for the historian at least, unhistorical, unusable, and wrong.

* * *

Notes

1. The central work is Kenneth N. Waltz, *Theory of International Politics* (Reading, Mass.: Addison-Wesley, 1979). Other expositions by Waltz of his position are his *Man, the State, and War: a Theoretical Analysis* (New York: Columbia University Press, 1959); "The Origins of War in Neo-realist Theory," in Robert I. Rotberg and Theodore K. Rabb, eds., *The Origin and Prevention of Major Wars* (Cambridge: Cambridge University Press, 1989), pp. 39–52; and "The Stability of a Bipolar World," *Daedalus,* Vol. 93, No. 3 (1964), pp. 881–909. Robert J. Art and Kenneth N. Waltz, eds., *The Use of Force: Military Power and International Politics,* 4th ed. (Lanham, Md.: University Press of America, 1993) contains many articles exemplifying neo-realist arguments and assumptions, including three by Waltz. Other versions and applications of realist theory may be found in Stephen M. Walt, *The Origins of Alliances* (Ithaca, N.Y.: Cornell University Press, 1987); Barry R. Posen, *The Sources of Military Doctrine: France, Britain, and Germany Between the World Wars*

(Ithaca, N.Y.: Cornell University Press, 1984); Robert Gilpin, *War and Change in World Politics* (Cambridge: Cambridge University Press, 1981); and John Mearsheimer, *Conventional Deterrence* (Ithaca, N.Y: Cornell University Press, 1983). For a good introduction to realism and its chief current rival, idealism, see Joseph S. Nye, Jr., *Understanding International Conflicts: An Introduction to Theory and History* (London: HarperCollins, 1993). The classic work of the older realism, emphasizing the state's natural drive for power rather than structural constraints as the chief source of power politics and conflict, is Hans Morgenthau, *Politics Among Nations: The Struggle for Power and Peace* (New York: Knopf, 1948).

2. For current neo-realist arguments, see John Mearsheimer, "Back to the Future: Instability in Europe After the Cold War," *International Security,* Vol. 15, No. 1 (Summer 1990), pp. 5–55; Christopher Layne, "The Unipolar Illusion: Why New Great Powers Will Rise," *International Security,* Vol. 17, No. 4 (Spring 1993), pp. 5–51; and Kenneth N. Waltz, "The Emerging Structure of International Politics," *International Security,* Vol. 18, No. 2 (Fall 1993), pp. 44–79.... For divergent views, see Robert Jervis, "International Primacy: Is the Game Worth the Candle?" *International Security,* Vol. 17, No. 4 (Spring 1993), pp. 52–67; Jervis, "A Usable Past for the Future," in Michael J. Hogan, ed., *The End of the Cold War: Its Meaning and Implications* (Cambridge: Cambridge University Press, 1992), pp. 257–268; and John Mueller, "Quiet Cataclysm: Some Afterthoughts on World War II," in Hogan, *The End of the Cold War,* pp. 39–52. See also Kenneth A. Oye, Robert J. Lieber, and Donald Rothchild, *Eagle in a New World: American Grand Strategy in the Post-Cold War Era* (London: HarperCollins, 1992); Mark Bowker and Robin Brown, eds., *From Cold War to Collapse: Theory and World Politics in the 1980s* (Cambridge: Cambridge University Press, 1993); Geir Lundestad and Odd Arne Westad, eds., *Beyond the Cold War: Future Dimensions in International Relations* (Oxford: Oxford University Press, 1993); and Stanley Hoffmann, Robert O. Keohane, and Joseph S. Nye, Jr., eds., *After the Cold War: International Institutions and State Strategies in Europe, 1989–91* (Cambridge, Mass.: Harvard University Press, 1993).

3. It is striking, for example, that a strong opponent of realism, Bruce Russett, seems to accept the validity of the realist paradigm for this period in writing: "It may be possible in part to supersede the 'realist' principles (anarchy, the security dilemma of states) that have dominated practice to the exclusion of 'liberal' or 'idealist' ones since at least the seventeenth century." Russett, *Grasping the Democratic Peace* (Princeton, N.J.: Princeton University Press, 1993), p. 24.

4. "The daily presence of force and recurrent reliance on it mark the affairs of nations. Since Thucydides in Greece and Kautilya in India, the use of force and the possibility of controlling it have been the preoccupations of international-political studies." Waltz, *Theory of International Politics,* p. 186. "Balance-of-power politics in much the form that we know it has been practiced over the millennia by many different types of political units, from ancient China and India, to the Greek and Italian city states, and unto our own day." Waltz, "A Response to My Critics," in Keohane, ed., *Neo-Realism,* p. 341. "Over the centuries states have changed in many ways, but the

quality of international life has remained much the same." Waltz, *Theory of International Politics,* p. 110. More such statements could be cited.

5. Waltz, *Theory of International Politics,* pp. 97–99, 107, 126, and *passim.* It is worth noting that these generalizations are not solely Waltz's but are widely shared by neo-realists, and constitutive of the theory. For example, another eminent realist, Robert Gilpin, shares them in both *War and Change* and *Political Economy,* and these general premises form the specific bases of the arguments of Mearsheimer, "Back to the Future"; and Layne "The Unipolar Illusion."

6. Waltz, *Theory of International Politics,* pp. 126–127.

7. Ibid., pp. 124, 128,

8. In Waltz, "America as a Model for World? A Foreign Policy Perspective," *PS: Political Science and Politics* (December 1991), pp. 667–70, Waltz contends that because the United States and the Soviet Union were similarly placed since 1945 by their power, their behavior was also similar, and he explains the "arbitrary and arrogant behavior" of such past rulers as Charles V, Louis XIV, Napoleon, and Kaiser Wilhelm II chiefly by their "surplus of power" (p. 669).

9. A classic example of this can be seen in the origins of the War of the Austrian Succession in 1740. The Habsburg monarch and German Emperor Charles VI had devoted years of costly diplomacy to trying to insure the rights of his daughter Maria Theresa to inherit his Austrian lands against any challenge to the succession on his death, by getting all interested powers including Prussia formally to endorse the so-called Pragmatic Sanction of her title. Frederick II of Prussia, seeing Charles rely on this insurance policy, and knowing that others were likely also to disregard their obligations under it, immediately seized Austrian Silesia when he and Maria Theresa acceded to their thrones in 1740, and France and Bavaria quickly joined in the attack on Austria. For the historical details, see on the French and European side especially Paul Vaucher, *Robert Walpole et la politique de Fleury (1731–1742)* (Paris: Plon-Nourrit, 1924); on the Austrian, Max Braubach, *Versailles und Wien von Ludwig XIV bis Kaunitz* (Bonn: L. Röhrschild, 1952).

10. What I here call "hiding" may be related to "buckpassing"; see Thomas J. Christensen and Jack Snyder, "Chain Gangs and Passed Bucks: Predicting Alliance Patterns in Multipolarity," *International Organization,* Vol. 44, No. 2 (Spring 1990), pp. 137–168. Hiding, however, would seem to be broader in scope, often involving not just an effort to pass the costs of international politics to someone else, or to avoid any active participation in it, but a search for some method of handling the threat apart from being drawn into the power-political fray, often by a very active foreign policy. "Hiding" may therefore be somewhat misleading as a blanket term for all these forms of conduct, but I can think of no more satisfactory one.

11. Walt, *Origins of Alliances.*

12. This list of the ways states have reacted to international crises and threats or tried to use them is not proposed as exhaustive. It was common, for example, to try to exploit threats, i.e., use them to gain some particular advantage for one's own state, often at the expense of another state than the one posing the threat. This strategy, however, seems impossible to characterize as a particular response to threats, since it always or almost always plays into attempts to balance or bandwagon, and frequently is involved in attempts to hide and transcend as well. Thus it would seem

characteristic of competitive power politics in general, and not a particular mode of response to threats within it.

13. Good discussions are in K. O. von Aretin, *Heiliges Römisches Reich 1776–1806,* 2 vols. (Wiesbaden: F. Steiner, 1967); and Max Braubach, *Maria Theresias jüngster Sohn Max Franz, letzter Kurfürst von Köln* (Vienna: Herold, 1961).

14. Aretin, *Heiliges Römisches Reich,* repeatedly stresses this theme, but it is also generally recognized by students of the constitutional history of the Empire. See for example John C. Gagliardo, *Reich and Nation: The Holy Roman Empire as Idea and Reality, 1763–1806* (Bloomington: Indiana University Press, 1980); Jean-François Noël, *Le Saint Empire* (Paris: Presses Universitaires de France, 1976). This tension between balance of power and balance of rights, *Machtordnung* and *Rechtsordnung,* prominent especially in the old regime but important in all eras, tends to be blurred or erased by the neo-realist approach.

15. T. C. W. Blanning, "George III and the Fürstenbund," *Historical Journal,* Vol. 20, No. 2 (June 1977), pp. 311–344.

16. For evidence that this kind of transcending was not an uncommon occurrence, but a frequent feature of Imperial politics, see K. O. von Aretin, ed., *Der Kürfurst von Mainz und die Kreisassoziationen 1648–1746* (Wiesbaden: F. Steiner, 1975).

17. An example: when Japan and China declared war on Germany during the First World War, they were plainly bandwagoning—Japan in order to seize German possessions in Asia, China to escape isolation and gain British and French protection against Japan and Imperial Russia. Yet both Japan and China claimed to be balancing against German imperialism. Or in 1939–40, when various states in southeastern Europe (Hungary, Rumania, Bulgaria, and momentarily Yugoslavia) allied with Germany, they were plainly bandwagoning—but also, perhaps genuinely, balancing against the threat from the USSR.

18. A good example is the conduct of Piedmont-Savoy under King Victor Amadeus II before and during the War of the Spanish Succession (1702–14). He always bandwagoned with the stronger side, shifting alliances to do so; he always exacted the highest possible price for doing so; and he always claimed (and conceivably to some extent believed) that he was balancing against the greatest threat to his state and Europe. For his policy, see Geoffrey Symcox, *Victor Amadeus II* (Berkeley: University of California Press, 1983), chaps. 8, 10, and 12.

19. I draw here on the account in my [book] *The Transformation of European Politics, 1763–1848* (Oxford: Clarendon Press, 1994), chap. 3; but see also T. C. W. Blanning, *The Origins of the French Revolutionary Wars* (London: Longman's, 1986).

20. Paul W. Schroeder, "The Collapse of the Second Coalition," *Journal of Modern History,* Vol. 59, No. 2 (June 1987), pp. 244–290.

21. For a brief survey of the evidence, see Paul W. Schroeder, "Napoleon's Foreign Policy: A Criminal Enterprise," *Journal of Military History,* Vol. 54, No. 2 (April 1990), pp. 147–162.

22. Again, this is shown in detail in my *Transformation of European Politics,* chaps. 5–8, 10–12.

23. See Paul W. Schroeder, *Austria, Great Britain and the Crimean War* (Ithaca, N.Y.: Cornell University Press, 1972); Winfried Baumgart, *Der Frieden von Paris 1856* (Wiesbaden: F. Steiner, 1972); Ann Pottinger Saab, *Origins of the Crimean Alliance*

(Charlottesville: University of Virginia Press, 1977); and Norman Rich, *Why the Crimean War?* (Hanover, N.H.: University Press of New England, 1985).

24. A brilliant recent study proving this with massive evidence, especially for the Allied side, is G.-H. Soutou, *L'Or et le Sang: les buts de guerre économiaues de la Premiere Guerre mondiale* (Paris: Fayard, 1989).

25. The literature here is too massive to summarize; a good recent overview is David Stevenson, *The First World War and International Politics* (Oxford: Clarendon, 1988).

26. See Buzan, Jones, and Little, *Logic of Anarchy,* pp. 131, 146, and 238–239.

27. Waltz, *Theory of International Politics,* pp. 106–107.

28. See, for example, Barbara Jelavich, *Russia's Balkan Entanglements 1806–1914* (New York: Cambridge University Press, 1991).

29. Anselm Doering-Manteuffel, *Von Wiener Kongress zur Pariser Konferenz. England, die deutsche Frage und das Mächtesystem 1815–1856* (Göttingen: Vandenhoeck & Ruprecht, 1991).

30. Though this principle applies especially to 1815–48, it was never absent from other periods. For example, the long sixteenth-seventeenth century contest between Habsburg Spain and France, often seen as a straightforward struggle for hegemony, has been shown also to have been a struggle over which power was better fitted and entitled to fill the vital European functions of leading Christendom and guaranteeing peace. See, *inter alia,* Eberhard Straub, *Pax et Imperium; Spaniens Kampfum seine Friedensordnung in Europa zwischen 1617 und 1635* (Paderborn: Schöningh, 1980).

31. For an elaboration of this thesis, see Paul W. Schroeder, "World War I as Galloping Gertie: A Reply to Joachim Remak," *Journal of Modern History,* Vol. 44, No. 3 (September 1972), pp. 319–344; for Austrian foreign policy, see above all F. R. Bridge, *The Habsburg Monarchy among the Great Powers, 1815–1918* (New York: Berg, 1991). For another instance of the major effects of eliminating small states and their special functions in the system, see Paul W. Schroeder, "The Lost Intermediaries: The Impact of 1870 on the European System," *International History Review,* Vol. 6, No. 1 (February 1984), pp. 1–27.

2.2

THE FRAGMENTATION AND CONSOLIDATION OF INTERNATIONAL SYSTEMS

Stuart J. Kaufman

Stuart J. Kaufman shows how history, even ancient history, can be studied to understand contemporary international affairs. Working at the systemic level of analysis, he contrasts power transition realist theories (Morton Kaplan) that predict consolidation in the international system with power-balancing neorealist theories (Kenneth Waltz) that predict fragmentation. He then asks: What explains the cycling between fragmentation (anarchy) and consolidation (empire)? He adds additional variables to his model from liberal and identity perspectives—economic interdependence, unit identity, and administrative technology—and tests this less parsimonious model against the pendulum swings between anarchy and empire in the ancient Middle East. He finds that the model, although not proven, explains transitions between anarchy and empire better than realism alone does. Applying the model to contemporary trends in international affairs, he concludes that forces of fragmentation—nationalism reinforcing sovereignty (identity), economic integration making small states viable (liberal), and military technologies favoring small actors (realist)—appear to conspire to limit forces of consolidation. By including too many variables, however, has he produced an overdetermined outcome?

* * *

In this article, I sketch out a theory suggesting a way to conceptualize and explain the ongoing transformation of the international system. I begin by broadening the concept of the distribution of power into a concept of system consolidation. Systems vary not just from multi- to bi- or perhaps unipolar but from extreme consolidation (imperial hegemony), through balance-of-power systems (with varying numbers of "poles"), to extreme fragmentation (splintering into many units with no poles at all), with many possible gradations in

Source: Stuart J. Kaufman, "The Fragmentation and Consolidation of International Systems," *International Organization* 51, no. 2 (1997): 173–208.

between.[1] Differing degrees of system consolidation promote different dynamics in the international system, including different kinds and degrees of international order.

Four main forces, I argue, drive system consolidation and fragmentation. First is the "self-help" behavior promoted by anarchy, which encourages not stability but consolidation, as states are motivated to annex their neighbors when they can. The second force is economic interdependence, which also tends to promote state expansion and thus system consolidation. The third force, principles of unit identity, usually pushes in the opposite direction, tending to destabilize empires and promote system fragmentation. The fourth factor is administrative capability, or "social technology," which acts as a limiting factor: system consolidation depends on the existence of social technologies adequate for administering large units. My argument is that when all of these factors favor a specific degree of system consolidation, the system is likely to stabilize at that level. Highly consolidated systems may be destabilized, however, if any of the four factors strongly favors fragmentation.[2]

Since my topic is the nature of the international system, the system itself is the unit of analysis; studying it therefore requires surveying very broad sweeps of history.[3] The four centuries before 1990 are defined by only two systems—a multipolar balance among empires until 1945, and the bipolar Cold War—so attention to other periods of history is essential to find other examples of international systems. The history of the ancient Middle East, which provides examples of many different types of international systems over two millenia, is fertile ground for such study. While any article-length study of such a broad sweep of history can only be suggestive, it does show the empirical plausibility of the theory of system transformation I propose. Studying ancient history also shows the durability of the issues I consider: these factors have been influencing international politics literally since the beginning of recorded history.[4]

* * *

The Spectrum of System Consolidation

We can best understand the degree of system consolidation as a range from a single hegemonic empire, through polar balances of power, to fragmented international systems. At one end of the spectrum are fragmented systems, which may consist of hundreds of tribes or city-states. Next come polar balances of power, which vary not only according to the number of poles but in the degree to which the poles jointly dominate the system. A large degree of such domination defines systems of dual or multiple hegemony. Hegemonic systems, at the other end of the spectrum, vary according to how much of the system is subject to direct imperial control or suzerainty, and how much only to informal hegemonic influence....

This view represents something of a middle ground between the two existing concepts of international structure. At one extreme is the view of Kenneth

Waltz that because there has never been a world empire, the international system has always been anarchic and polar. At the other extreme is Adam Watson's argument that the international system has followed a pendulum pattern between anarchy at one end and empire at the other, with intermediate degrees of hegemony the historic norm.[5] ...

* * *

Neorealism, Structural Realism, and System Transformation

The Balance of Power and System Consolidation

Properly understood, the logic of neorealism generates the prediction not of the preservation of a balance of power, but of its collapse.[6] The central claim of the theory is that anarchy forces states to engage in a particular kind of self-help, which in a multipolar system requires that they coalesce against any would-be hegemon in order to prevent hegemony and retain their own autonomy.[7] The maintenance of the European balance-of-power system in the three centuries after the Peace of Westphalia is commonly adduced as evidence for this view. This conclusion, however, is supported neither by the logic of the theory nor by the historical evidence.

The logical problem is summarized in Morton Kaplan's discussion of a multipolar balance of power.[8] Kaplan, like later neorealists, assumes that states are driven to seek power relative to one another. It therefore follows that after wars, losing powers great and small should be annexed by the winners: the winners should calculate that the certain power gain from annexation is preferable to the hope of aligning with the losing states later. Strictly followed, then, the logic of neorealism should predict a reduction in the number of great powers over time, at least to two, the allegedly most stable configuration. Recognizing the problem, Kaplan asserts that system maintenance also requires a rule that essential actors be preserved.[9] Kaplan's critics were correct that such behavior was neither deducible from realist logic nor fully compatible with the historical record, but such criticisms simply reinforce the dilemma: unless states make this sacrifice to maintain the system, multipolar systems will be subject to erosion in their membership.

Balancing, furthermore, is not the only behavior compatible with neorealist logic.[10] Statesmen may calculate that they can safely "hide" from an aggressor, "passing the buck" to force some other state to take the risks of balancing. Alternatively, they may choose to "bandwagon" with the aggressor, seizing the chance for opportunistic expansion while turning the aggressor's attention elsewhere.[11] The trouble with these alternatives from the point of view of neorealism is that they do not contribute to the prevention of hegemony. Indeed, if such tactics do not lead to hegemony, the reason must lie in factors other than balancing behavior—factors neorealism leaves implicit.

* * *

... Arguing that Waltz's approach is "unnecessarily narrow, static, and ... ahistorical," Barry Buzan and his colleagues have suggested that the functional differentiation of units, the distribution of attributes other than power, and systemic interaction capacity are also important systemic variables.[12] By this logic, we can consider the other key causes of systems change I identify— economic interdependence, principles of unit legitimacy, and administrative technology—as systemic variables.[13] I explain further below.

Economic Interdependence. Increasing economic interdependence is a strong factor promoting system consolidation, for several reasons. First, as Waltz notes, states can decrease their interdependence, and therefore their vulnerability, by growing larger (implicitly, by annexing trading partners).[14] Second, states that control entire trade routes may more easily tax the trade, and thus deprive others of its economic benefits, if they so choose.[15] This argument is, of course, the core argument of hegemonic stability theory: interdependence promotes imperial expansion and therefore system consolidation.[16] Even if trade is carried out privately such expansion can be economically as well as politically rational, as the imperial state can provide protection against bandits, a single set of rules, a single currency, and no more than one taxing authority.[17] When states cannot gain control over needed resources, hegemonic stability theory suggests that they should logically fall back on the establishment of trade regimes to limit any exploitation of their dependence.[18]

The converse of this hypothesis is not necessarily true: low international economic interdependence need not lead to system fragmentation. Obviously, unsophisticated societies that engage in little trade tend to have less sophisticated political economies, rendering them less capable of building or sustaining empires. Large mercantilist empires, however, may carry on most of their trade internally, and in so doing define a relatively stable consolidated system with low economic interdependence. What causes system disintegration is the disruption of vital trade routes in a system of interdependent states, usually as a result of the interposition of hostile actors.

I argue that economic interdependence is actually a component of system structure, because it is an expression of the functional differentiation of units.[19] Since reasonably sophisticated economies must be specialized (differentiated), they inherently depend on trade. Some of the trade is typically international, meaning that states are interdependent economically. The degree of this economic interdependence varies, but it is in any case built into the structure of the international system.

*   *   *

Principles of Unit Identity. International systems are defined largely by the principles of legitimacy on which their component units are based.[20] Historians note this point when they use terms such as the "age of imperialism" or the "age of nationalism." More rigorously, the degree of system consolidation is determined by the nature of the units in the system—Gilpin's distinction between empires, nation-states, and city-states is a good starting point. The nature of the units in the system is, in the long run, determined by the sort of unit the people consider legitimate. The question of where principles of legitimacy come from, and why particular ones are accepted at particular times, is an important question that deserves further research, but I cannot examine it here.

My argument begins with the point that the nature and distribution of these principles is part of the structure of the international system. This can be so because the system itself is "socially constructed":[21] while material realities powerfully influence international interactions, international relations are in essence social relations structured by ideas and attitudes. The constituent units of the system, states, are themselves merely social constructions—systems of relationships among people. The international system, then, is a social construction created by people acting on behalf of social constructions: diplomats negotiating, soldiers following orders to shoot, officials taxing goods when they cross imaginary lines on a map. The defining principles of the states, then, govern its interactions. These principles determine to whom diplomats are loyal, where the lines on the map are drawn, and whose orders soldiers follow. Thus, the principles according to which its member states are organized define the system, meaning that the states' legitimizing principles are part of the system's ordering principles.[22]

One of the principles on which state legitimacy is based is the principle of unit identity. If the dominant units identify themselves as empires, for example, international norms and practices must recognize not only anarchy (among empires) but also hierarchy (between empires and their various dominions, protectorates, and the like). In the contemporary system based on national identity, in contrast, states insist on international norms and practices that recognize no such hierarchies, because such norms and practices help preserve their identity and sovereignty as nation-states.[23] Principles of *government* legitimacy, such as democracy, may also help to define the international system—thus the democratic peace phenomenon may be partly a systemic phenomenon—but I will not pursue that issue here.[24]

A simple scheme for distinguishing among principles of unit identity would recognize three basic types: personalism, nationalism, and imperialism. "Personalist" principles define the legitimate political unit as one consisting of people who can all in principle be personally acquainted. Such units include clans, tribes, or ancient city-states. Thus an age characterized by city-states and nomadic tribes, with few if any larger political units, is a personalist age. Larger units based on personalist principles are possible—agglomerations of tribes, for example, may be welded together by charismatic personalities, and lord-vassal relations can create "groups of groups"—but such units are typically unstable.[25]

A more inclusive concept of identity is ethnicity, which is based on a common name, history, culture, territorial association, and myth of common descent.[26] According to Ernst Haas, if an ethnic or other group is mobilized by modern technology, and "striv[es] to create or maintain [its] own state," it is a "nation" and its principle of identity is nationalism.[27] Most theorists do not consider premodern groups to have been nations—the nation, in this view, is uniquely the product of modern communications technology.[28] Anthony Smith points out, however, that premodern ethnic groups did exist and that some shared many characteristics of modern nations, including a degree of mobilization in pursuit of political independence.[29] I use the awkward but suggestive label "protonationalism" to identify the principle of identity of such groups.

Imperialism is a political principle that justifies the formation and maintenance of empires incorporating many nations and groups. Imperialism is commonly justified by assertion of religious principles, such as the claim of a divinely granted right to rule, or the desire to unite all believers in one state. Ideologies such as Communism can be viewed as secular religions that legitimize their actions on similar principles. Nonreligious justifications for empire can include national chauvinism or "hyper-nationalism," of which racism is a variant. In more stable empires, the imperial principle is accepted not only by rulers but also by the ruled, who consider subordination to empire to be inevitable or even appropriate.[30]

The degree of system consolidation is influenced by the nature and distribution of these principles of identity.[31] Empires or nation-states can be reasonably stable only when and where both rulers and ruled accept the imperialist or nationalist idea. Maintaining illegitimate rule requires more effort than if rule is legitimate, because it drains the state of resources needed for other purposes—thereby creating an advantage for more legitimate units.[32] Thus, personalistically oriented peoples such as tribes or city-states may be easy to conquer, but because they are notoriously difficult to rule, imperial rule over them should be unstable. Self-conscious nations are more capable of defending themselves and are even more difficult for aliens to rule. When present, therefore, personalism and nationalism should sap the strength of empires, leading to frequent revolts by discontented nations, tribes, and city-states. While empires can be kept together by brute force for a time, the cost of doing so is likely to be ruinous, leading eventually to the collapse of such empires into more legitimate local or national units.

If anti-imperial principles come to be encoded in international law or international norms, they can also create external pressures on empires. If imperial expansion violates accepted principles, for example, states are more likely to perceive it as the sort of threat that justifies forming a balancing coalition. Similarly, the pressure of systemically accepted principles promoted twentieth-century decolonization: the norms of national self-determination—useful for legitimizing leading states' independence—became so ingrained in international practice after World War II that even in cases where both colony and metropole might have preferred to maintain their relationships, the tide of decolonization often could not be stemmed.[33]

* * *

Administrative Technology. Technology does not refer to physical machines only; some key effects on the international system come from *social technology*— the capabilities and sophistication of social institutions, especially technologies for state administration. Obviously, units can last only if appropriate administrative mechanisms are invented. If an empire cannot be administered, it dies with its creator (like Alexander's), if not before. More broadly, all states contemplating expansion face the eventual problem of diminishing marginal returns; administrative technologies help determine at what point further expansion produces more costs than benefits—and therefore define the largest stable unit size.[34] Furthermore, the kind of social technology is important: states based on a system of governance akin to feudalism, in which most functions of government are delegated to vassals, interact differently from those administered by centralized bureaucracies. In medieval Europe, for example, kings often had to stop fighting after the traditional forty days of feudal service had been rendered.

Social technology for state administration is a systemic variable because it defines a kind of functional differentiation of states. Bureaucratic states take on functions that feudal kingdoms do not, for example, while tribal units take on fewer functions still. Since some administrative technologies, like the invention of bureaucratic government, may make a critical contribution to state power, we can assume (for good neorealist reasons) that such inventions will tend to diffuse across the system relatively quickly. As a result, they will come to characterize all of the leading states in the system and therefore the period as a whole. However, since not all states have a social structure that can support such administrative technologies—bureaucracy, for example, requires an adequate pool of literate people acceptant of discipline in a hierarchy—administrative technologies are likely to vary, resulting in some states being functionally different from others. Those capable of supporting the most effective technologies, of course, will as a result become the leading states.

* * *

The Logic of International Systems Change

The argument so far has maintained that the causes of system transformation are systemic ones; it has not, however, made a systematic case for why these are the crucial causes. My core reason is inductive: all four of these forces seem necessary to explain patterns in international system transformation. The pressures of anarchy and economic interdependence, the favorites of current theory, are undeniably important, but both usually push in the direction of system consolidation. The mediating impact of military technology is not alone sufficient to explain system fragmentation. The effects of administrative technology and principles of unit identity are therefore necessary to explain why, and when, system fragmentation occurs. In short, deductive parsimony on this matter does not work, so I have fallen back on a more inclusive inductive approach.

* * *

The relationships among these variables are inherently recursive and col-linear—that is, the "effects" rebound to affect the "causes," and the causes are not independent but influence one another, ... A simple case of recursion is that while more inclusive principles of identity promote increased system consolida-tion (i.e., the emergence of larger units), that consolidation can create pressures encouraging acceptance of more inclusive identity principles elsewhere, in order to legitimize the creation of larger states that can better protect themselves. Similarly, while economic interdependence may promote system consolidation, that consolidation can either reduce interdependence (by including whole trade routes in one empire) or increase it (by reducing trade disruptions). Anarchy may also spur imperial expansion (and system consolidation) as a form of self-help, but that expansion can result in the emergence of a hegemon, altering the basic systemic ordering principle from anarchy to hierarchy. Finally, while adequate administrative technologies are necessary to maintain empires, the existence of empire may itself spur the invention and diffusion of appropriate administrative technologies.

All of the causal variables also affect one another. Principles of unit identity (for example, personalistic lord-vassal principles) may determine which social technology is considered appropriate (feudalism), but a more effective social technology (royal bureaucracy) may promote acceptance of a different identity principle (dynastic imperialism). Interdependence, for its part, may aid in the creation of social technologies, as trading skills are applied to governance; and it may promote the emergence of imperial identity principles to justify eco-nomically motivated expansion. Conversely, effective social technologies can stabilize the empires that keep trade routes open, promoting more interdepen-dence, while narrow nationalist identity principles may promote protectionism and therefore decrease interdependence.

Even anarchy and its effects are subject to such influence. Thus while anarchy may provoke states to decrease their economic interdependence, interdepen-dence may prompt them to amalgamate into larger units, replacing anarchy with hierarchy. Similarly, while groups may be influenced by the self-help imperative to accept broader principles of identity, anti-imperial legitimizing principles can also reduce the "fight or die" self-help imperative, mitigating the impact of anarchy. Finally, while self-help may prompt states to adopt more effective social technologies, those technologies (i.e., institutions) may make possible forms of coordination or hierarchy that transform anarchy.

These phenomena of recursion and collinearity would be barriers to analysis if I were attempting to determine the specific weights of these variables in affect-ing systems change. The purpose of this article, however, is to argue only that these variables do affect systems change, so recursion and collinearity are not a problem for this analysis.

International Relations in the Ancient Middle East

The following study of Middle Eastern history between about 2400 B.C. and 100 B.C. illustrates the ability of [our hypotheses about anarchy and its effects] to explain system transformation. I focus on this period because international systems lasted, on average, only about a century; the period therefore provides examples of twenty or more different systems, and of the transitions from each to the next. It is particularly interesting because it provides examples of systems defined by all three types of legitimizing principles—personalism, (proto-) nationalism, and imperialism.

* * *

Early Dynastic Period (circa 2900–2400 B.C.)

This period is backdrop for rather than the focus of this study. Sumerian civilization reached its peak in the mid-third millenium B.C. and was centered around a number of city-states in the lower Tigris and Euphrates valleys.

Akkadian to Old Babylonian Periods (circa 2400–1500 B.C.)

This era saw several periods of hegemony by single empires. Although they were mostly short-lived ones based in the old Sumerian heartland, they at times dominated most of modern Iraq, southwestern Iran, and parts of northern Syria.[35] The periods of imperial hegemony were those under the Sargonid or Akkadian Empire (circa 2334–2193 B.C.), ... the Third Dynasty of Ur, or Ur III Empire (circa 2112–2004), the first Assyrian Empire under Shamshi-Adad (circa 1813–1780), and the Old Babylonian Empire of Hammurabi (circa 1760–1730). All four empires broke down, due to external pressure and internal rebellion, into blocs of city-states, which engaged for some time in multipolar balance-of-power politics before eventually succumbing to another empire.

Amarna Period (circa 1500–1082 B.C.)

This period was characterized by two balance-of-power systems.[36] For roughly the first century, the system was a bipolar one in which the empires of Egypt and Mitanni were the superpowers, dividing Syria between them. The 1300s and 1200s ... represented a multipolar balance of power among proto-nation-states, as the Hittite and Assyrian states supplanted imperial Mitanni, and Babylonia under Kassite rule joined Egypt to form a quadripolar system with a highly developed diplomatic apparatus. The system ended around 1200 B.C., when the Hittite state was destroyed, and the Egyptians pushed back into Egypt, by a tide of tribal attackers. A remnant Assyrian-Babylonian-Elamite balance-of-power system in Mesopotamia collapsed a century later as Assyria and Babylonia were nearly destroyed by a wave of tribal Aramaean invaders.

Early Biblical Period (circa 1200–900 B.C.)

This period in the Levant (beginning a century later in Mesopotamia) was a primarily tribal system. This is the time described in the biblical books of Judges and Samuel, which continued to about 1020. In the Judges period, the Hebrews like most of their neighbors were organized on a loose tribal basis. There were no major states among which a balance of power could form. The small Hebrew kingdom under David and Solomon was able to dominate much of the Levant in the next century (circa 1000–930) because it grew essentially in a vacuum; that is, there were no more powerful states to check its growth. Further east, the Babylonian king in the mid-900s did not have firm control even over the immediate vicinity of his own capital.[37]

Later Biblical Period (circa 900–500 B.C.)

By about 900 B.C., a new balance-of-power system had emerged, … Assyria was the leading state in the Fertile Crescent but was checked by a number of neighbors of comparable power, including Urartu to the north, Babylonia to the east, Phrygia to the west, and Damascus to the south, with Egypt further away (Israel, divided by civil war, was subject to Damascus). By 729, however, Assyria had annexed Damascus and taken control of Babylonia; tribal Cimmerians had destroyed Phrygia and reduced Urartu soon after. Thus Assyria was left as hegemon, roughly from 729 to 612, even holding Egypt for a few decades.[38]

Assyria's fall was sudden, as it succumbed to a combined assault by a new Median empire, rebelling Babylonians, and tribal Scythians in 612. The resulting system, from 612–539, was quadripolar, with Media, Babylonia, Egypt, and (in western Anatolia) Lydia in relatively peaceful equilibrium. That system again collapsed suddenly, however, after Cyrus the Persian took control of the Median Empire and transformed it into the Persian Empire. Between 549 and 539, Cyrus conquered both Lydia and Babylonia (his son added Egypt a bit later), establishing Persia's hegemonic control over the Fertile Crescent for two centuries.[39]

Classical Period (circa 500–100 B.C.)

This period encompasses several political systems. After Xerxes' defeat at Salamis and Plataea (480), Persia never again invaded Greece, leaving the multipolar Greek city-state system autonomous from the Persian-dominated Middle East. A bipolar subsystem led by Athens and Sparta soon emerged there and quickly degenerated into the Peloponnesian War (449–404).[40] As a result of that war, all of the Greek city-states were so weakened that they succumbed to conquest from the north, first by Thebes and later by Macedonia. Alexander the Great (336–323) briefly extended Macedonian hegemony over the entire Persian Empire, but his successors divided his empire into several parts, creating the Hellenistic period balance-of-power system, which lasted for about two centuries (circa 300–100), until the advent of Roman rule.

In the Western Mediterranean, the bipolar system dominated by Rome and Carthage quickly degenerated into the first two Punic Wars (264–201), resulting in Carthage's submission and anticlimactic destruction decades later. During the next century, Rome established its dominance over the Hellenistic states of the Levant as well.

Consolidation and Distintegration in Ancient International Systems

The above discussion outlines what international systems changes occurred in the period under study; I turn now to explaining why they occurred. I have hypothesized that four main factors should explain those changes: unstable balance of power dynamics, principles of unit identity, economic interdependence, and administrative technologies. I consider each factor below.[41]

The Rise and Fall of Balances of Power

Balance-of-power systems are one natural outcome of international politics, and they did repeatedly emerge in the ancient world. In some cases, these were longstanding multipolar balances among city-states, as in Babylonia in Hammurabi's time or Greece early in the fifth century B.C. After the effective domestication of the horse, multipolar balances of power could form among proto–nation-states (the Amarna period) or empires (the later biblical period). In other periods, the system resolved into bipolar standoffs: Egypt and Mitanni, Sparta and Athens, Rome and Carthage.

... [B]alances of power were not necessarily stable. Sargon, Ur-Nammu (founder of the Ur III dynasty), and Hammurabi each overcame competing city-states not only to unite their own Sumerian-Akkadian cultural area but also to conquer (at least in part) neighboring cultures like the Elamites of southwestern Iran. Similarly, Assyria eventually defeated all of its rivals to achieve hegemony in the 700s B.C., and Persia conquered three other great powers in the 500s.

Each of these consolidations occurred for theoretically definable reasons. Hammurabi's rise to hegemony, for example, occurred because one of his key rivals chose to bandwagon rather than to balance. A diplomat of the time described the system as a multipolar balance of power, with Babylon one among five to seven comparable great powers.[42] By 1763 B.C., however, Hammurabi had amassed enough power to defeat a coalition of three rivals— Assyria, Elam, and Eshnunna—apparently in a defensive battle. At this point Eshnunna decided to bandwagon, joining Hammurabi in destroying their mutual rival, Larsa. The following year, however, Hammurabi turned on his partner, conquering Eshnunna and its ally Assyria. By the time of his death in 1749 B.C., Hammurabi had consolidated a multipolar balance of power into Babylonian hegemony.[43]

In the case of Assyria's rise during the biblical period, the key enabling factors were annexation and a sort of bandwagoning. The bandwagoning came from peripheral actors, the Cimmerian tribes, who defeated two of Assyria's great power rivals, Phrygia and Urartu, in order to settle the latter's territory. Assyria was then freed to eliminate the rest of its opponents—most importantly Egypt and Babylonia—either by annexing them or turning them into satellites.[44]

Assyria's later fall can be understood as the result of balancing and bandwagoning; its replacement by Persia was caused by "hiding." When the Median Empire emerged as a new great power in the seventh century B.C., it balanced with a rebelling Babylonia to end Assyrian hegemony. When the Scythians bandwagoned with the coalition, Assyria was destroyed (612) and a new multipolar balance of power resulted. Later, when Cyrus the Persian took control of Media and attacked Lydia (546), Nabonidus of Babylonia, apparently intimidated, chose to hide—that is, to appease Cyrus—instead of aiding his Lydian ally.[45] When Babylonia's turn came in 539, Egypt, the other remaining power, also chose to hide (behind the Sinai desert). They were therefore conquered one at a time, resulting in two centuries of Persian hegemony.

When balance-of-power systems were bipolar, they usually decayed rapidly, ... Thus the Athens-Sparta system lasted only forty-five years, and the Rome-Carthage system lasted sixty-four years, both collapsing after a systemic war. The result of the Peloponnesian War was to pave the way for outside hegemons such as Macedonia; the Punic Wars, of course, led to enduring Roman hegemony. The Amarna period Mitanni-Egypt standoff was an exception to the rule, lasting a full century and remaining peaceful for most of that time; but the peace may well be attributable to internal weaknesses in both states, more than to any system-level stability.[46]

... [C]hanges in military technology played an important mediating role in these processes. In each case, it was the invention not just of new weapons but also of suitable tactics and organizations for their use that had the largest effect. The most dramatic example was the invention of effective war chariots by tribal invaders of the seventeenth century B.C.—Hittites, Hurrians, Kassites, and others who were then able to sweep away the remnants of Hammurabi's empire and (in the guise of the Hyksos) conquer northern Egypt.[47] After a period of fragmentation, the result was the chariot-based empires of the Amarna period. This period marks a watershed: the first effective employment of horses dramatically improved the mobility and communications of imperial armies, leading to longer-lasting and more stable empires than were possible in earlier periods. The example also shows that the stability of ages of empire depended not only on the nature of military technology but also on what was done with that technology. Chariot-driving tribesmen destroyed the empires they found, but their descendants became chariot-driving aristocrats who built and maintained even better empires.

Other military innovations had different, sometimes equally profound, effects. Thus, new infantry tactics that gave tribal invaders the advantage over imperial charioteers apparently contributed to the collapse of the Amarana period empires after 1200 B.C.[48] Similarly, the evolution of the highly sophisticated Assyrian combined-arms tactics, which returned the advantage to aggressive imperial armies, was largely responsible for transforming the fragmented system of the early biblical period into the imperial system of the late biblical period.[49]

Principles of Unit Identity

... [S]ystems should reflect, or be transformed to reflect, the accepted principles of unit legitimacy. That did occur repeatedly. When tribally (i.e., personalistically) organized groups—Amorites around 2000 B.C., and Aramaeans after 1100 B.C.—overran parts of the Middle East, their ability to unite militarily against powerful empires was not translated into the creation of new empires. Instead, they formed systems of many independent tribal and city-state units that resisted all efforts to form larger units for centuries. The Amorites, for example, never reunited the Babylonian region into a stable unit: Hammurabi's state split up during the reign of his successor, and Babylonia was not reunified again until Kassite times.

Peoples with entrenched city-state identities behaved similarly. In Early Dynastic (pre-Sargonid) Sumer, for example, the theology held that each city existed primarily to serve a particular god, with each city-state's ruler considered the delegate of his city's god.[50] Although a concept of overall kingship did exist, it legitimized only a loose and tenuous suzerainty, rather than any real imperial control.[51] Therefore, when Sargon united the Sumerian city-states by force, his empire was not considered legitimate, especially by the powerful priests.[52] Partly as a result, every Sargonid ruler faced repeated rebellions as the Sumerian cities repeatedly tried to regain their traditional, and religiously sanctioned, independence.[53] The Greek cities of the classical age also held strong principles of city-state identity, and they too resisted unification: neither Sparta, Thebes, nor Macedonia was able to establish lasting control over the fractious Hellenic cities.

When larger units remained stable, that stability was supported by broader principles of identity. The kernel of the Ur III empire, for example, was established by a leader who explicitly appealed to Sumerian patriotism, producing inscriptions denouncing foreign occupiers as "enemy of the gods, who ... filled Sumer with evil," and praising his own work because it "restored the kingship of Sumer into its own hand."[54] His successors acted to strengthen Sumerian identity further, promoting myths that emphasized Sumer's common cultural identity and glorified the Sargonid precedent of unity. Ur III kings also gained priestly sanction for their rule by piously carrying out religious ceremonies and building lavish temples for the priests.[55] These patriotic appeals, combined with improved social technology, seem to have worked: Ur III kings apparently faced few revolts in the Sumerian heartland, though the culturally distinctive Elamites were much less submissive.[56] Later Kassite kings followed the same formula of religious ceremony, temple-building projects, and deference to tradition with even more success: they controlled Babylonia for some three centuries, apparently with few attempts at revolt.[57]

During the Amarna period, in fact, proto-national identity became the norm systemwide, not only in Kassite Babylonia.[58] The period began when the Egyptians, out of protonationalist pride, revolted against the rule of the Hyksos, "despised Asiatic barbarians," and established an empire in Canaan and Syria.[59] In northern Syria, they met the Mitannian empire, which was built around ethnic Hurrians.[60] The Assyrians, divided between Mitanni and Kassite Babylonia, reacted by developing for the first time a concept of "the Land of Assur"—that is, Assyria—rallying together to assert their independence from both rival empires.[61] Similarly, the Hittites, harking back in one text to "ancient times [when] the Land of Hatti [the Hittite country] ... used to rage against the surrounding countries like a lion," re-established their own state.[62] Eventually, the Hittites and Assyrians divided Mitanni between them.

All five Armarna period empires were based on ethnic groups distinguished from their neighbors by the same factors that differentiate ethnic groups today: language, religion, traditional homeland, political and legal norms, and other cultural traits. Like modern ethnic distinctions, ancient ones were not always neat: the Hittites, for example, used two different written languages and were ethnically related to the Arzawans, their neighbors to the west. Nevertheless, where it existed, a sense of ethnocultural unity often provided part of the glue that held ancient states together.

Conversely, ethnic identity was sometimes an obstacle when states tried to control lands inhabited by alien groups. For example, Mesopotamian empires repeatedly tried to control ethnically separate Elam, but Elam repeatedly rebelled, destroying the Ur III dynasty and weakening its successors. Similarly, the last Assyrian empire collapsed in 612 due largely to rebellions by the main proto-nations subordinated in it, Babylonia and Egypt. The Hittites faced similar problems ruling Hurrians, who, in O. R. Gurney's words, did not "take kindly to government by barbarian Anatolians."[63]

In most of these cases, the result was the reestablishment of earlier, more legitimate units. Elam repeatedly reestablished its independence after each Babylonian conquest, for example, and Babylonia and Egypt reestablished their independence after the later Assyrian collapse. Alexander the Great's multiethnic empire broke up even more quickly into more legitimate units, with Egypt, Macedonia, and several fractious Greek states splitting off from the core of the previous Persian empire, now under Seleucid rule. The Hittite example shows how exceptions could be made: they managed to hold onto Hurrian regions by governing through native vassals to reduce local resentment.

One reason why Persia's hegemony lasted twice as long as Assyria's was that the Persians were more sensitive to such issues of legitimacy. As Mario Liverani describes, biblical period Assyrian elites interpreted their religious beliefs to hold that "the Assyrian kingship is the only one to legitimately exercise universal dominion, the Assyrian king 'has no equal.' "[64] Thus while Assyrian kings were able to reduce Babylonian discontent by carrying out certain religious rituals, most reflected the arrogance of their ideology and ruled by repression instead. As a result, they faced repeated Babylonian uprisings that eventually led to their undoing.[65] The Persians, in contrast, improved the lot of most conquered peoples, practicing religious toleration, allowing people exiled by Assyria (such as the Hebrews) to return home, and granting autonomy to subject peoples. Hence, Persia survived as hegemon for two centuries, collapsing only due to attack from the outside.

In sum, the structure of the international system was shaped by the cultural identities of major groups, and it changed only when those identities were extinguished by genocide or assimilation. Assyria, Babylonia, Egypt, and Elam were key actors in one period after another because even when they were conquered, they either assimilated their conquerors, or else built a new state on the old identity when the conquerors weakened. Lasting hegemonic rule in the region was only made possible by massive cultural shifts: first Assyria broke the resistance of the fractious Aramaeans to imperial rule, then it virtually annihilated the Elamites in a military campaign during Assyria's final decline. The Medes and Persians later broke Assyrian and Babylonian power, opening the way for both groups to be assimilated to the Aramaic language, whose alphabetic script was easier to transmit than the Babylonians' clumsy cuneiform writing.[66] Only then was the way opened for the succession of empires—Persian, Hellenistic, and Roman—that dominated the area for the next millennium.

The reader might protest, but for whom did state legitimacy, in any ancient period, matter? Surely the mass of illiterate peasant farmers could have little known or cared which king ruled them? The answer is complex. Certainly each age held politically relevant classes whose aid, or at least acquiescence, was necessary for imperial rule. Disloyal scribes could conceal important information from rulers; recalcitrant landowners could withhold foodstuffs; and resentful priests could promote opposition among all classes. In the Amarna age, the chariot-driving military aristocracy was also the landed gentry, and kings could not move without their consent. In cities, even the masses could be important, as their attitude could determine whether an urban revolt would have any staying power: even a small dissenting minority would be able to open the city gates to besieging imperial armies.

Economic Interdependence

Throughout the period under study, international trade was economically vital. Babylonia, especially, had little native timber or metal, so it always was forced to trade, usually exporting foodstuffs in exchange for other goods.... [D]esire to control that trade seems to explain much of the imperialist impulse shown by the prominent leaders of the time. In some cases, when a sufficiently expansive empire was infeasible, rulers fell back on the establishment of institutionalized trade regimes. When trade was disrupted ... , trading states collapsed and agricultural states were weakened.

The evidence that economic motives were typical for empire builders is fairly strong. Ancient texts describing Sargon's conquests as including "the Cedar

Forest" (in Lebanon) and "the Silver Mountains" (the Amanus and Taurus ranges) strongly suggest his objectives for his wood- and metal-poor empire.[67] Indeed, control of land routes across the Fertile Crescent generated enough business to interest even distant trading partners in the accumulated riches: seagoing trade in the Sargonic and Ur III periods reached as far as the Indus valley.[68] Similarly, Hittite expansionism to the west in the 1300s B.C. apparently was motivated by desire to control the trade routes to tin and copper mines (whose products defined the Bronze Age) in Bohemia and elsewhere.[69] Assyria's rivalry with Urartu in the 800s and 700s B.C. largely was centered around competition for control over similar routes; Cyrus of Persia conquered Lydia and Babylonia partly for the same reason.[70]

The Amarna period presents a somewhat different picture. In a period when several great powers—mutually agreed to be equal in status—coexisted for a long time, leaders apparently accepted that none was capable of conquering the others, so they had to find an alternative to imperial expansion. The expedient they hit upon ... was state-sponsored international trade in the form of "gifts" among sovereigns.[71] For Egypt, the system approximated cash trade, as Pharaohs sent large quantities of gold in exchange for the horses bred in Assyria and Babylonia but needed as much by Pharaoh's chariot armies as by his neighbors'.

Furthermore, empires could be seriously undermined when their trade routes were cut off, ... For example, the collapse of the Hittites after 1200 B.C. is largely due to the severing of the western trade routes by migrating tribes. The resulting economic decline made it possible for the Hittites' local enemies to overwhelm them.[72] A few centuries later, Assyria strangled its rival Urartu by severing its trade lifeline.[73] The evidence is everywhere—from the Ur III period to the final Babylonian collapse of 539 B.C. and beyond—that imperial collapse was often preceded by disruptions of trade, inflation, famine, and a resulting administrative, military and ideological collapse.

The cutoff of imperial trade often happened because key international trade routes extended beyond the military reach of any of the empires dependent on them—and therefore beyond the boundaries of the international political-military system.[74] The Amarna period's dependence on central European tin is one example. The trade routes apparently emerged in response to market forces, and trade continued as long as intermediaries chose to profit from it rather than disrupt it. During the interregnum after the fall of the Ur III dynasty, a similar situation occurred, as the seagoing Persian Gulf trade continued to provide such goods as gold, copper ore, ivory, and precious woods to the port at Ur.[75] Only when migrating tribes destroyed the Sumerians' trading partners in the Indus Valley, and others chose to rob the Hittite-bound caravans instead of taxing them, did the trade routes—and eventually the markets they served—collapse.

Administrative Technology

... [E]mpires' staying power depended largely on the quality of their administrative technologies. Sargon created the first known system of direct imperial administration, but it was only moderately effective, plagued by repeated rebellions by fractious city-states. The first really effective system came under the Ur III dynasty, which built one of the most impressive systems of political administration of ancient times. Administration and military command were carried out by different officials, who were circulated among forty districts to prevent their adoption of local loyalties. The economy was mostly state-owned, run by a huge system of royal bureaucrats reporting either to the crown or to the priestly establishment. The judicial system, too, was separated from the bureaucracy.[76] The effectiveness of this administrative system was probably an important reason why the Ur III empire did not suffer from the endemic uprisings that its Sargonid predecessor had faced. Its like was not seen again until the Assyrian empire was approaching its peak over a millenium later.

During the Amarna period, with aristocratic charioteers dominant on the battlefield, state organization was more feudal than bureaucratic.[77] In this context, the highly developed diplomacy of the era was simultaneously an administrative tool, as great power control was asserted by varying forms of suzerainty codified in carefully worded international treaties. The improved communications permitted by domesticated horses also aided administration, helping to tie together the loose empires of the period.

* * *

Summary: The Empirical Record

The survey of ancient history presented here provides some supporting evidence for each of the hypotheses about causes of system consolidation. Balancing "failures" did repeatedly cause multipolar systems to collapse into hegemonic ones, ... The clearest examples were the failure of Mesopotamian city-states to balance against Hammurabi and the failure of Babylonia and Egypt to balance against Persia. Two out of three bipolar systems (Athens and Sparta, Rome and Carthage) collapsed quickly into systemic war and then hegemony, ... Further, ages of empire were typically distinguished by the superior military forms they developed—for example, the chariot-based armies of the Amarna period, Alexander's phalanx, and Rome's legion.... Conversely, shifts in military technology sometimes explained imperial collapse, as at the end of the Amarna period.

Principles of unit identity typically acted ... to destabilize empires and promote the establishment of smaller units among which balances of power could emerge. Thus when Sargon or Alexander tried to unite cities with strong city-state identities, they faced repeated rebellions, eventually ending in the independence of the city-states. Similarly, the efforts of imperial Assyria to swallow proto-national Babylonia also met with repeated rebellions and the eventual reemergence of an independent Babylonia. More legitimate units, in contrast, tended to create more stable systems. Thus balances of power among city-states could last for centuries, and re-form even after conquests by a Sargon or

Alexander; the Sumerian city-states coalesced into a stable Babylonian state only after their identity principles changed. Similarly, the later Amarna age empires, based on proto-nations such as Egypt, Babylonia, and Assyria, remained a stable balance of power for centuries.

Economic interdependence also affected systems.... Conquerors from Sargon to the Hittites and Assyrians were motivated largely by the desire to control key trade routes or sources of raw materials—such as Sargon's "Silver Mountains" and "Cedar Forest".... When conquest was infeasible, some states, such as the Amarna period great powers, fell back on establishment of norms of interstate trade. The risk in the latter course ... is that when trade—whether within the system or with partners outside it—was cut off, trading empires declined and sometimes even collapsed.

Finally, I find some evidence ... that the longevity of empires depends partly on the development of adequate social technologies for imperial administration. Thus, empires that were based purely on individual genius—Hammurabi's or Alexander's—hardly outlasted their founders, while those that developed sophisticated systems of administration, such as Ur III's, Assyria's, and to a greater extent Persia's and Rome's, tended to last for centuries.

Obviously, this evidence by no means constitutes proof of these hypotheses. It does, however, show the importance of dynamics that neorealism narrowly construed ignores. Taken together, these examples also suggest a broader pattern: entropy—the tendency for disorder to increase—does operate in international systems. In general, only one factor favoring fragmentation was sufficient to destabilize highly consolidated systems (for example, lack of legitimacy in Assyria's empire), while several favorable factors typically had to be in place to lead to system consolidation.

Implications for the Modern International System

* * *

This theory of system consolidation is useful for explaining modern as well as ancient international politics. The sixteenth through nineteenth centuries, for example, saw increasing system consolidation because all major factors promoted it. European states were able to build large empires because they possessed superior military and administrative technologies; because both rulers and ruled accepted imperial principles of legitimacy; and because inter-European efforts at balancing and at economic competition spurred competitive expansion. By one criterion, system consolidation proceeded even further in the early twentieth century, as the pressures of power balancing led to the elimination of major actors.... Specifically, the multipolar Westphalian system collapsed into bipolarity as great powers were systematically eliminated or reduced—the Austrian and Ottoman Empires in World War I; and the British, French, German, Japanese, and others after World War II.

In other ways, however, the twentieth century showed a pattern of increasing system fragmentation. The rise of modern nationalism as the dominant principle of unit identity so delegitimized empires—even the empires of the winners of the world wars—that all of them collapsed: colonized areas asserted the right of national self-determination, and imperial powers lost the confidence and will to retain them by force.[78] At the same time, the imperialists' military advantage was eroded (as the French learned, to their cost), and the social technologies of imperialism (colonial administrations) were turned into instruments of separatism. The Soviet empire, with the most sophisticated alternative to nationalism as an identity principle, was the last to fall. However, the bipolar cold war rivalry, leading both superpowers to overreact to each other's moves, exhausted the Soviet Union in a few decades, occasioning its 1991 breakup along nationalist lines.

In the post–cold war world, national self-determination remains the overwhelmingly dominant principle of unit legitimacy, shaping the international system in several ways.[79] First, states legitimized in this way have a mutual interest in promoting acceptance of a norm of mutual recognition of sovereign equality: such a norm, by delegitimizing annexation, improves the security of all recognized states and therefore mitigates the security dilemma imperative of "fight or die."[80] In fact, the principle of national self-determination has been so successfully embedded in international law, norms, and practice that it largely muzzles the "balance-of-power" push toward system consolidation: conquests are typically sources of weakness rather than strength, and they harm the conqueror's strategic position—as Saddam Hussein learned to his cost in 1991—by creating large hostile coalitions opposing the conqueror.

With annexations impractical in a system defined by so-called national self-determination (a term left ambiguous enough to legitimize most existing states), great powers or regional powers must resort to lesser degrees of political control, such as reducing clients to satellites. Even these lesser forms of control are difficult to sustain against national assertiveness, however, as the Soviet Union learned in Eastern Europe and Afghanistan. Indeed, the U.S. experience in places such as Bosnia, Liberia, and Somalia in the early 1980s shows that great powers have difficulty imposing their will even on much smaller states. As a result, great power spheres of influence are, generally, shrinking in the post–cold war world.

In a global system with almost two hundred often fractious "nation-states," this shrinking military-political reach of great powers means that unipolarity cannot easily be equated with hegemony. The would-be hegemon lacks the ability to enforce its will simultaneously against large numbers of dissenting states; it therefore lacks the ability to impose its leadership. In fact, rather than hegemony, the current system may be more likely to devolve into regionalization, as regional subsystems become increasingly autonomous from global forces.[81] Some regional subsystems, such as that in Northeast Asia or perhaps East Asia more generally, might develop into regional balances of power. Other regions, such as parts of Africa, may be characterized by further fragmentation and disorder.

Principles of legitimacy are, in fact, promoting such fragmentation. As state breakup from Ethiopia to Yugoslavia is now making clear, the principles of legitimacy people accept are increasingly narrow ones, rather than the broader syncretic nationalisms that drove decolonization. Thus Yugoslav nationalism yielded to Serbian, Croatian, and Slovenian nationalism; while Somali solidarity seems to have been replaced by sub-clan loyalties. Among other things, this trend suggests that most future wars are, like most recent ones, likely to be internal wars, especially ethnonationalist wars for secession or domination, rather than interstate wars as in the Iraq-Kuwait example. Furthermore, since even many of the larger states are to varying degrees threatened by breakup, as reviving Scottish and Quebecois nationalisms exemplify, the prospects for the emergence even of stable regional orders are problematic.

In a system marked by nationalism, forces that can cause identity change—such as migration, which may cause the assimilation of one nation by another—become politically important. Consequently, the forces that may spur such migration, such as environmental change and economic disruption, may also have systemic effects. Today, the rate of international migration is higher than it's been in fifty years, and environmental trends (for example, overpopulation leading to desertification) threaten to push millions more across borders. Populations are intuitively aware of the possibility that migration might lead to their group's assimilation by another, pushing issues of immigration high onto the agenda of states worldwide. This concern justifies the recent theoretical attention to the idea of "societal security": if people fear that the greatest threat to their nation's existence is immigration leading to assimilation, immigration becomes a "national security" issue.[82] The threat is often exaggerated, but governments must address it nonetheless.

... International economic integration and modern communications technologies are increasingly combining to make the state too small a unit of economic organization. Since ideas about identity are tending to reduce the size of states rather than facilitate empire building, the only alternative is the creation of international economic regimes among relatively small political units, in a system like the one among the post-Ur III city-states. Hence international and supranational organizations from the European Union to the new World Trade Organization are becoming increasingly important, at the expense of the state. However, the continuing power of nationalism makes consensus in supranational units hard to achieve, as is evident in the oft-noted lament that Europe is an economic giant but a political dwarf.

... [A]s system fragmentation shrinks the effective political-military reach of major states, even the international economic system becomes increasingly susceptible to disruption. One reason is that trade outside the great powers' political-military reach is subject to disruption due to political-military instability: thus post-Ur III trade collapsed when the Sumerians' trade routes were disrupted by migrating tribes. The modern system could be similarly affected by domestic political instability in the Middle East leading to disruption of oil supplies. U.S.

impotence in the face of the oil shock of 1979, occasioned by the Iranian revolution, illustrates the limited control of great powers over such disruptions.

If the system is decreasingly hegemonic, maintenance of the international economic system will increasingly depend on reaching voluntary consensus on rules of behavior. The effects of nationalism, however, are likely to make such consensus harder to reach, for three reasons. First, increasingly narrow nationalisms are increasing the number of states in the system, and the more states that have to reach agreement, the more difficult it is to find solutions that all will accept. Second, nationalists tend to guard jealously their national autonomy: China and Russia wish to join the World Trade Organization, for example, but not to submit to all its rules. Third, reaching consensus on rules typically depends on some agreement about underlying principles, but rising nationalism may tend to undercut that consensus. The current world trade system is built on liberal internationalist principles, but "economic nationalism" leads to neomercantilist policies that contradict those principles. Additionally, the costs of economic interdependence (for example, those imposed on workers and firms harmed by foreign competition) promote just such economic nationalist thinking. In sum, the combination of relatively declining great powers, rising political nationalism, and ideological dissensus on economic principles means that the problems of cooperation "after hegemony" are more serious than hegemonic stability theory might suggest.

... [A]dministrative technology generates interesting questions, if not clear answers, about the contemporary system. For example, are existing social technologies adequate for administering the modern state? Formal bureaucracy was an astonishing innovation for the Ur III empire in the twenty-first century B.C; but scholars, journalists, and politicians increasingly sense its limitations for the twenty-first century A.D Similarly, Mancur Olson casts doubt on the ability of modern democracy to avoid dirigiste collusion among special interests at the cost of the general interest.[83] Indeed, given the rise of narrowly defined nationalisms, the task of reinventing government to make it more responsive and efficient, and less bureaucratic, is likely to be a critical factor in determining the fate of many existing states. The northern Italian movement toward secession, driven by disgust with corruption in Rome, illustrates the possibilities in both directions.

... [T]he effects of military technology, also generates interesting questions. On the surface, the Persian Gulf War would seem to have demonstrated the superiority of great power military capabilities over even the most formidable middle-power challengers, implying a powerful force for system consolidation. However, the political results of that conflict—namely, Saddam Hussein's continued defiance, justified by reference to nationalism, of foreigners' demands regarding Iraq's weapons programs and Kurdish policy—show that great power military technology is not easily translated into political influence.

Furthermore, as the average state decreases in size, while sophisticated weaponry becomes less and less expensive, the relative influence of nonstate actors is likely to rise. Thus technology may increasingly favor terrorists over states. The reappearance of corporate-controlled mercenaries (as in the old British East

India Company) might not be far behind, if states cannot protect vital corporate interests. Already, private contractors provide paramilitary services, including the training of armies, provision of security guards, and logistical support for the military operations of states and international governmental organizations.

Nuclear weapons, whether used or not, may provide further impetus for system fragmentation. Nuclear deterrence, on the one hand, leads nuclear powers to avoid direct confrontation with one another and therefore deters the great power wars that can promote system consolidation. Thus any reconsolidation in the eastern half of Europe, for example, will have to come about by slower economic and political rather than military means, if it happens at all. If nuclear weapons were to be used on any significant scale, of course, they would likely devastate the attacked states' economic and administrative structures, leading to the breakup of those states.

Structural realism must pay attention to such variables if it is to remain relevant. Working from his narrow neorealist perspective, Waltz is able to say little more about the post–cold war system than that new great powers will arise to compete with the United States, because "hegemony leads to balance," and has done so "through all of the centuries we can contemplate."[84] As I have tried to show, this argument is dubious historically; it is also misleading for the current, more fragmented age. Furthermore, Waltz's approach does not address such critical issues as the breakup of the Soviet Union, the importance of internal ethnic conflicts elsewhere, the prospects for further European integration, whether great power competition will imperil economic cooperation, or anything at all about the future of the Third World, including the geopolitically pivotal Middle East.

* * *

Notes

1. For discussion of this distinction in some detail, see Watson 1992; Buzan, Jones, and Little 1993; and Buzan and Little 1994. Compare Doyle 1986; Ferguson and Mansbach 1996; and Wallerstein 1974 and 1991.

2. For a discussion of economic motives in particular, see Doyle 1986; Gilpin 1981; and Wallerstein 1991. On the importance of all four factors, see McNeill 1963, 51–52 and *passim*. For other attempts to integrate some of these ideas, see Ferguson and Mansbach 1996; Mayall 1990; McNeill 1963; and Watson 1992.

3. Here I follow the suggestion of Holsti 1995, chap. 2.

4. On the need for works from historical and cross-cultural perspectives, see Cox 1986, 208–9; and Ferguson and Mansbach 1991, 367–68. For examples of such work, see Cioffi-Revilla 1996; Ferguson and Mansbach 1996; Midlarsky 1995; and Watson 1992.

5. Buzan and Little 1994, 248–49, quoting Watson 1992. For a similar typology of types of hegemonic control, see Doyle 1986.

6. For a logical argument supporting this view, see Cederman 1994; and for an empirical one, see Watson 1992.

7. For a classic expression of this view, see Morgenthau 1967. For other versions, see, for example, Kaplan 1957; and Gulick 1955.
8. Kaplan 1957.
9. For another discussion of this problem, see Morgenthau 1967.
10. David 1991.
11. See Schroeder 1994; and Christensen and Snyder 1990. I thank W. Alexander Vacca and James Schlicht for the insight that bandwagoning behavior may be compatible with realist logic.
12. Buzan, Jones, and Little 1993. For a creative attempt to apply these variables, differently defined, to explain international politics, see Collins 1986.
13. For a different approach to including these factors, see Ferguson and Mansbach 1996.
14. Waltz 1979, 144–45.
15. Friedman 1977.
16. See, especially, Gilpin 1981. Others making similar arguments include Bean 1973; Friedman 1977; McNeill 1963; and Spruyt 1994.
17. For an argument regarding the economic benefits of state governance in early modern Europe, see Spruyt 1994.
18. The seminal argument that hegemons establish such regimes is found in Gilpin 1981. For an argument that "collective hegemons" can do so, see Snidal 1985. The classic functionalist argument for international integration is Mitrany 1933.
19. Buzan, Jones, and Little 1993, 44. For another suggestion that interdependence might be a systemic variable, see Milner 1993.
20. This point is suggested by Jackson 1990; Mayall 1990; and Walker 1984 and 1993.
21. The inspiration for this argument comes from Wendt 1987, 1992.
22. For a somewhat similar logic, see Buzan, Jones, and Little 1993.
23. For amplification, see Jackson 1990. Compare Mayall 1990; Walker 1984; and Walker 1993.
24. See Doyle 1983; Russett and Maoz 1993; and Owen 1994.
25. Armstrong 1982, 27–37.
26. Smith 1986, 22–28.
27. The quotation is drawn from Haas 1986, 726.
28. See Gellner 1983; Hobsbawm 1990; and Anderson 1983.
29. Smith 1986, 11.
30. For some evocative nineteenth-century examples, see Jackson 1990.
31. See, for example, Franck 1990; Jackson 1990; and Watson 1992.
32. Jackman 1993, chap. 5.
33. See especially Jackson 1990.
34. Bean 1975.
35. For two good sources on this period, see Oates 1986; and Saggs 1995.
36. For a good, though dated, source on the period, see Edwards et al. 1975.
37. Saggs 1995, 131–32.
38. McEvedy 1967, 42–47.
39. This history is nicely summarized in McEvedy 1967, 50.
40. Thucydides 1951.
41. For a broadly compatible recent treatment of the period, see Ferguson and Mansbach 1996.
42. Oates 1986.

43. See Oates 1986, 60–67; and Hinz 1973, 264.
44. For a brief summary of this period, see McEvedy 1967, 44. See also Saggs 1965.
45. Lloyd 1973, 100–102.
46. See Goetze 1975, 5; and Wilhelm 1989, 28–30.
47. McNeill 1971.
48. Drews 1993.
49. Breasted 1953, 198.
50. Saggs 1962.
51. Westenholz 1979. For a different interpretation, see Watson 1992.
52. For evidence of priestly opposition to the Sargonids, see Saggs 1995, 72–75.
53. See ibid., 73; and Oates 1986, 34–37.
54. The quotations, attributed to the Sumerian leader Utu-Khegal, are from Gadd 1971, 462.
55. Oates 1986, 45–49.
56. Saggs 1995, 85–90.
57. See, for example, Saggs 1962, 79; Oates 1986, 86–89; and Saggs 1995, 116–21.
58. For a detailed discussion, see Smith 1986.
59. This characterization is from McNeill 1963, 82.
60. Wilhelm 1989, 49–76.
61. See Larsen 1979, 82; and Postgate 1992, 247.
62. Gurney 1979, 154.
63. Ibid., 157.
64. Liverani 1979, 310.
65. Porter 1993, chap. 5. Compare Oates 1986, 116–21.
66. Smith 1986.
67. The quotation and interpretation are from Oates 1986, 38.
68. Saggs 1962, 272–75.
69. Macqueen 1986, 37–41.
70. Saggs 1962, 285–86.
71. Saggs 1995, 117–21.
72. Macqueen 1986, 50–51.
73. Saggs 1962, 91 and 283–85.
74. For the suggestion that the international political system and the international economic system should be distinguished, see Buzan, Jones, and Little 1993.
75. Woolley 1928, 116.
76. Oates 1986, 43.
77. See McNeill 1971, 52; and Oates 1986, 101.
78. See, for example, Organski 1968; and Strang 1991.
79. Mayall 1990.
80. For a seminal work on international society, see Bull 1977. The criterion for defining international society is from Buzan, Jones, and Little 1993.
81. Friedberg 1993–94.
82. Waever et al. 1993. See also Weiner 1995.
83. Olson 1982.
84. Waltz 1993, 77.

References

Anderson, Benedict. 1983. *Imagined communities: Reflections on the origin and spread of nationalism.* London; Verso Editions and NLB.

Armstrong, John. 1982. *Nations before nationalism.* Chapel Hill: University of North Carolina Press.

Bean, Richard. 1973. War and the birth of the nation state. *Journal of Economic History* 33: 203–21.

Breasted, James. 1953. *Ancient times: A history of the early world.* Boston: Ginn and Company.

Bull, Hedley. 1977. *The anarchical society: A study of order in world politics.* New York: Columbia University Press.

Buzan, Barry, Charles Jones, and Richard Little. 1993. *The logic of anarchy: Neorealism to structural realism.* New York: Columbia University Press.

Buzan, Barry, and Richard Little. 1994. The idea of "international system": Theory meets reality. *International Political Science Review* 15: 231–55.

Cederman, Lars-Erik. 1994. Emergent polarity: Analyzing state-formation and power politics. *International Studies Quarterly* 38: 501–34.

Christensen, Thomas J., and Jack Snyder. 1990. Chain gangs and passed bucks: Predicting alliance patterns in multipolarity. *International Organization* 44: 137–68.

Cioffi-Revilla, Claudio. 1996. Origins and evolution of war and politics. *International Studies Quarterly* 40: 1–22.

Collins, Randall. 1986. *Weberian sociological theory.* Cambridge: Cambridge University Press.

Cox, Robert W. 1986. Social forces, states, and world orders: Beyond international relations theory. In *Neorealism and its critics,* edited by Robert O. Keohane, 204–54. New York: Columbia University Press.

David, Steven R. 1991. *Choosing sides: Alignment and realignment in the Third World.* Baltimore, Md.: Johns Hopkins University Press.

Doyle, Michael W. 1983. Kant, liberal legacies, and foreign affairs. Part 1. *Philosophy and Public Affairs* 12(3): 205–35.

———. 1986. *Empires.* Ithaca, N.Y.: Cornell University Press.

Drews, Robert. 1993. *The end of the Bronze Age: Changes in warfare and the catastrophe circa 1200 B.C.* Princeton, N.J.: Princeton University Press.

Edwards, I. E. S., C. J. Gadd, N. G. L. Hammond, and E. Sollberger, eds. 1975. *The Cambridge ancient history.* 3d ed., vol. 2, part 2. *History of the Middle East and the Aegean region circa 1380–1000 B.C.* Cambridge: Cambridge University Press.

Ferguson, Yale H., and Richard W. Mansbach. 1991. Between celebration and despair: Constructive suggestions for future international theory. *International Studies Quarterly* 35: 363–86.

———. 1996. *Polities: Authority, identities, and change.* Columbia: University of South Carolina Press.

Franck, Thomas M. 1990. *The power of legitimacy among nations.* Oxford: Oxford University Press.

Friedberg, Aaron L. 1993–94. Ripe for rivalry: Prospects for peace in a multipolar Asia. *International Security* 18(3): 5–33.

Friedman, David. 1977. A theory of the size and shape of nations. *Journal of Political Economy* 85: 59–77.

Gadd, C. J. 1971. The dynasty of Agade and the Gutian invasion. In *The Cambridge ancient history,* 3d ed., vol. 1, part 2. *Early history of the Middle East,* edited by I. E. S. Edwards, C. J. Gadd, and N. G. L. Hammond, 417–63. Cambridge: Cambridge University Press.

Goetze, A. 1975. The struggle for the domination of Syria. In Edwards et al. 1975, 1–20.

Gellner, Ernest. 1983. *Nations and nationalism.* Ithaca, N.Y.: Cornell University Press.

Gilpin, Robert. 1981. *War and change in world politics.* Cambridge: Cambridge University Press.

Gulick, Edward Vose. 1955. *Europe's classical balance of power.* New York: W. W. Norton.

Gurney, O. R. 1979. The Hittite empire. In *Power and propaganda: A symposium on ancient empires,* edited by Mogens Trolle Larsen. 151–66. Vol. 7 of Mesopotamia: Copenhagen Studies in Assyriology, Copenhagen: Akademisk Forlag.

Haas, Ernst. 1986. What is nationalism and why should we study it? *International Organization,* 40: 707–44.

Hinz, Walther. 1973. Persia circa 1800–1550 B.C. In *The Cambridge ancient history.* 3d ed., vol. 2, part 1. *History of the Middle East and Aegean region circa 1800–1380 B.C.,* edited by I. E. S. Edwards, C. J. Gadd, H. G. L. Hammond, and E. Solberger, 256–88. Cambridge: Cambridge University Press.

Hobsbawm, E. J. 1990. *Nations and nationalism since 1780: Programme, myth, reality.* Cambridge: Cambridge University Press.

Holsti, K. J. 1995. *International politics: A framework for analysis.* 7th ed. Englewood Cliffs, N.J.: Prentice Hall.

Jackman, Robert W. 1993. *Power without force.* Ann Arbor: University of Michigan Press.

Jackson, Robert H. 1990. *Quasi-states: Sovereignty, international relations, and the third world.* Cambridge: Cambridge University Press.

Kaplan, Morton. 1957. *System and process in international politics.* New York: Wiley.

Larsen, Mogens Trolle. 1979. The tradition of empire in Mesopotamia. In *Power and propaganda: A symposium on ancient empires,* edited by Mogens Trolle Larsen. 75–103. Vol. 7 of Mesopotamia: Copenhagen studies in Assyriology. Copenhagen: Akademisk Forlag.

Liverani, Mario. 1979. The ideology of the Assyrian Empire. In *Power and propaganda: A symposium on ancient empires,* edited by Mogens Trolle Larsen. 297–318. Vol. 7 of Mesopotamia: Copenhagen Studies in Assyriology, Copenhagen: Akademisk Porlag.

Lloyd, Alan. 1973. *Marathon: The story of civilizations on a collision course.* New York: Random House.

Macqueen, J. G. 1986. *The Hittites.* London: Thames and Hudson.

Mayall, James. 1990. *Nationalism and international society.* Cambridge: Cambridge University Press.

McEvedy, Colin. 1967. *The Penguin atlas of ancient history.* Harmondsworth: Penguin Books.

McNeill, William H. 1963. *The rise of the West: A history of the human community.* Chicago: University of Chicago Press.

——. 1971. *A world history.* 2d ed. New York: Oxford University Press.

Midlarsky, Manus I. 1995. Environmental influences on democracy: Aridity, warfare, and a reversal of the causal arrow. *Journal of Conflict Resolution* 39: 224–62.

Milner, Helen. 1993. The assumption of anarchy in international relations theory: A critique. In *Neorealism and neoliberalism: The contemporary debate,* edited by David A. Baldwin, 143–69. New York: Columbia University Press.

Mitrany, David. 1933. *The progress of international government.* New Haven, Conn.: Yale University Press.

Morgenthau, Hans J. 1967. *Politics among nations: The struggle for power and peace.* New York: Knopf.

Oates, Joan. 1986. *Babylon.* London: Thames and Hudson.

Olson, Mancur. 1982. *The rise and decline of nations.* New Haven, Conn.: Yale University Press.

Organski, A. F. K. 1968. *World politics.* New York: Alfred A. Knopf.

Owen, David M. 1994. How liberalism produces the democratic peace. *International Security* 19(2): 87–125.

Porter, Barbara Nevling. 1993. *Images, power, and politics: Figurative aspects of Esarhaddon's Babylonian policy.* Philadelphia: American Philosophical Society.

Postgate, J. N. 1992. The Land of Assur and the yoke of Assur. *World Archaeology* 23: 247–63.

Russett, Bruce, and Zeev Maoz. 1993. Normative and structural causes of democratic peace. *American Political Science Review* 87: 624–38.

Saggs, H. W. F. 1962. *The greatness that was Babylon.* New York: Praeger.

——. 1965. *Everyday life in Babylonia and Assyria.* London: Batsford Press.

——. 1995. *Babylonians.* London: British Museum Press.

Schroeder, Paul. 1994. Historical reality versus neorealist theory. *International Security* 19(1): 108–48.

Smith, Anthony D. 1986. *The ethnic origins of nations.* Oxford: Basil Blackwell.

Snidal, Duncan. 1985. The limits of hegemonic stability theory. *International Organization* 39: 579–614.

Spruyt, Hendrick, 1994. *The sovereign state and its competitors.* Princeton, N.J.: Princeton University Press.

Strang, David. 1991. Global patterns of decolonization, 1500–1987. *International Studies Quarterly* 35: 429–454.

Thucydides. 1951. *The Peloponnesian War.* Translated by John H. Finley. New York: Random House.

Waever, Ole, Barry Buzan, Morten Kelsttup, and Pierre Lemaitre. 1993. *Identity, migration, and the new security agenda in Europe.* New York: St. Martin's.

Walker, R. B. J. 1984. East wind, west wind: Civilizations, hegemonies, and world orders. In *Culture, ideology and world order,* edited by R. B. J. Walker, 2–23. Boulder, Colo.: Westview Press.

——. 1993. *Inside/outside: International relations as political theory.* New York: Cambridge University Press, 1993.

Wallerstein, Immanuel. 1974. *The modern world-system.* New York: Academic Press.

———. 1991. *Geopolitics and geoculture: Essays on the changing world-system.* Cambridge: Cambridge University Press.

Waltz, Kenneth N. 1979. *Theory of international politics.* Reading, Mass.: Addison-Wesley.

———. 1993. The emerging structure of international politics. *International Security* 18(2): 44–79.

Watson, Adam. 1992. *The evolution of international society.* London: Routledge.

Weiner, Myron. 1995. *The global migration crisis.* New York: HarperCollins.

Wendt, Alexander. 1987. The agent-structure problem in international relations theory. *International Organization* 41: 335–70.

———. 1992. Anarchy is what states make of it: The social construction of power politics. *International Organization* 46: 391–425.

Westenholz, Aage. 1979. The Old Akkadian Empire in contemporary opinion. In *Power and propaganda: A symposium on ancient empires,* edited by Mogens Trolle Larsen, 107–24. Vol. 7 of Mesopotamia: Copenhagen Studies in Assyriology, Copenhagen: Akademisk Forlag.

Wilhelm, Gemot. 1989. *The Hurrians.* Warminster, England: Aris and Phillips.

Woolley, C. Leonard. 1928. *The Sumerians.* Oxford: Clarendon Press.

2.3

INTERVENTION AND INTERNATIONAL ORDER

Martha Finnemore

Martha Finnemore offers a constructivist interpretation of the balance of power across four historical periods. She hypothesizes that, in each period, shared norms (identity) gave different meanings to the rules of international order (liberal) and the practices of military intervention (realist). She then shows that relative material capabilities changed less across these four periods than the norms governing the rules and practices for using these capabilities. Identity factors clearly shaped liberal and realist ones. She excludes the international orders from 1850 to 1945 because, she argues, these orders were less coherent. However, realists might want to include this later century because it involved more significant material power shifts and catastrophic wars, which could provide evidence that the role of norms in defining international orders is more limited or, alternately, that the norms that exist in international orders more often reflect rather than limit competition and warfare, as the realist perspective expects.

* * *

Concepts of Order and Mechanisms for Maintaining It

What made 1815 a concert and 1950 a cold war was not the material distribution of capabilities but the shared meanings and interpretations participants imposed on those capabilities. Castlereigh, Canning, and Palmerston did not stand in radically different material positions, vis-à-vis the Russians, than did Dulles or Acheson; but they did have a radically different view of desirable and legitimate international political order—one their Russian counterparts largely shared. These understandings of the international order, in turn, shaped much of the intervention behavior we see. A spheres-of-influence understanding of the world prescribes and justifies different kinds of intervention behavior than does a balance-of-power system or a hegemony. A concert interpretation of a multipolar balance, such as that which prevailed after the Napoleonic wars, supports

---

Source: Martha Finnemore, "Intervention and International Order," in *The Purpose of Intervention: Changing Beliefs About the Use of Force* (Ithaca and London: Cornell University Press, 2003), 85–140.

143

different behavior than the foregoing understandings of the balance in the eighteenth century. Material capabilities do matter in constructing these orders. They set boundary conditions on the types of orders that participants are likely to consider. Few would seriously consider organizing contemporary politics in a way that excluded the United States. Similarly, although it may be unclear why the Vienna settlement created a concert rather than bipolarity or why the Concert recognized Prussia as a great power, material capabilities give us a fairly good understanding of why no one seriously considered letting Luxemburg run the continent's affairs in 1815. Material conditions thus set basic constraints on what kinds of political orders are possible. Within that range, however, we can only understand why one order emerges rather than another by examining the ideas, culture, and social purpose of the actors involved.

This section contrasts the shared understandings underpinning four different types of order in the West since 1713: balance of power, concert, spheres of influence, and the current order. These were chosen because each embodies well-articulated rules and principles that participants broadly understood. Further, these rules and principles differ significantly across these orders, providing some comparative perspective and allowing discussion of social change. The period omitted by this sample, roughly 1850–1945, is certainly interesting and saw a great deal of military intervention; however, it is weak on these two criteria, which makes it difficult to draw out useful connections between intervention and widely held notions about international order. The second half of the nineteenth century was less coherent as an order than the first half and was not sufficiently distinct as an order to merit separate analysis in this limited space. The period from 1914 to 1945 is one in which there was no clear "order" at all. Indeed, the large wars of this period have often been viewed as wars fought to determine the kind of order that should prevail.

* * *

Balance of Power

* * *

From the seventeenth through the nineteenth centuries, European interstate politics was shaped by a shared notion of a balance of power. Europeans believed that such a balance should, could, and often did exist; they valued the benefits it brought, and they shaped policies according to its dictates. The balance worked, indeed it existed, only because Europeans believed it did and acted accordingly.[1] It was a social construction. Nothing in the material fact of multipolarity made balancing obvious or inevitable. In many instances, bandwagoning would have served material aggrandizement better than balancing.[2] Further, balance-of-power behavior continued even through periods when the distribution of material capabilities was not multipolar, as it did after 1815. Maintaining a balance-of-power arrangement required a lot of shared social and cultural baggage. The balance of power existed only because Europeans shared a number of beliefs about what was necessary and good in politics.[3]

Central to these beliefs was the notion that hegemony or empire was the chief evil to be avoided in international affairs. There is nothing obvious or necessary about this conclusion. Contemporary scholars have spilt much ink praising the benefits of hegemony and worrying about how to maintain the collective goods hegemons supply in the face of hegemonic decline.[4] Policy makers of earlier eras, however, were much less sanguine about the benefits of hegemony and, for centuries, made its prevention the cornerstone of their collective foreign policies. Hegemons may (or may not) provide collective goods, but a balance of power was the condition of international freedom in their view. The normative justification for a balance-of-power order was a direct analog to the justifications used for domestic constitutions: Absolute power corrupts, and only with a distribution of power among states of the European community can respect for the rights and freedoms of its members be insured.[5]

Although this fundamental orientation dominated balance-of-power thinking throughout the period during which it prevailed in Europe (roughly the seventeenth through nineteenth centuries), notions about how, exactly, the balance should work in this mission to prevent empire evolved over that period. The Concert of Europe, in particular, marked a significant shift in balance-of-power thinking and self-consciously operated according to different rules than its eighteenth-century predecessor had. Although notions of order in both periods were structured around balancing, understandings about when military force was legitimate or effective for any purpose—and, specifically, the role of military force in maintaining the balance—changed significantly between the two periods in ways that altered what we would now call "military intervention" and, in fact, gave rise to the whole notion of intervention as a commonly understood practice.

The Eighteenth-Century Balance[6]

In the second half of the seventeenth century, European writing about the balance of power is very much focused on the utility of countervailing alliances to deter threats and advance state interests.[7] Balancing of this type was viewed as a policy prescription for wise and ambitious statesmen, not as a description of the prevailing order. Counterpoised alliances were viewed as useful, even essential, to the success of rulers, but they were not understood to be natural, inevitable, or even expected. Duke Henry de Rohan thus laments the fact that rulers often do not perceive their "true interests"; if they did, many of the smaller states could exploit the bipolar "counterpoise" between the Houses of Bourbon and Hapsburg that dominated politics of his time in order to increase security.[8] Indeed, much of the "balance" writing of this period refers not to a system of balancing but to the strategic advantage to a particular state of "holding the balance of power," as Henry VIII was understood to have done.[9]

The normative orientation that such balancing created a natural or desirable systemic order, as opposed to being simply an advantageous strategy for the ambitious, was not clearly articulated until the beginning of the eighteenth century. One important component of this shift in thinking was the growing perception of "Europe" as a system or community with identity and interests as a whole. This was new, and comment on it was widespread. William III frequently spoke and wrote about the "general interests of all Europe"; Vattel described Europe as a "sort of republic"; the Abbé de Pradt portrayed it as a "single social body which one might rightly call a European Republic"; Voltaire depicted Europe as "a kind of great republic divided into several states"; and Vogt, a well-known writer about international affairs, entitled his book, *About the European Republic.*[10]

Protecting and promoting the balance of power became a major objective of interstate politics and an explicit goal of major treaties beginning with Utrecht (1713), and had been visible in the writings of publicists and diplomats for some years earlier.[11] It is starkly apparent in Fénelon's defense of the balance of power based on natural law principles (c. 1700).[12]

> Therefore every nation is obliged, for its proper security, to watch against, and by all means restrain, the excessive increase of greatness in any of its neighbours. Nor is this injustice: 'tis to preserve itself and its neighbours from servitude; 'tis to contend for the liberty, tranquility, and happiness of all in general: For the over-increase of power in any one influences the general system of all the surrounding nations.

Similarly,

> This care to maintain a kind of equality and balance among neighbouring nations, is that which secures the common repose; and in this respect such nations, being joined together by commerce, compose, as it were one great body and a kind of community. Christendom, for example, makes a sort of general republic which has its interests, its dangers, and its policy. All the members of this great body owe to one another for the common good, and to themselves for their particular security, that they oppose the progress of any one member, which may destroy the balance, and tend to the inevitable ruin of the other members.[13]

Fénelon portrays Europe as a community with common interests, liberty being foremost among these, which can only be protected through preservation of the balance. This understanding has at least two corollaries for behavior that were not clear in the seventeenth century. First, it creates duties: States have a duty or obligation, in Fénelon's view, to uphold the balance for the collective good. That this duty also serves a conception of self-interest does not make it less of a duty, according to Fénelon. Second, it requires restraint. This, too, was absent in earlier writings but is a frequent topic in the eighteenth century. Fénelon emphasizes that when balancing against a rising power, "such bounds must be set to it as it may not entirely destroy that power which it was formed only to limit and moderate."[14] Daniel Defoe, writing from another state, one that was attempting to balance Fénelon's France, shared this view of the necessity of restraint: "All the pretensions Declarations and Claims of the confederacy are to reduce *not France,* but the *exorbitant Power of France;* all the professed Intention of the Nation in this War is to restore a lasting Peace to *Europe,* and bring *France* to Reason.[15]

Neither a duty to balance nor a duty to be restrained flows obviously from simple realpolitik strategizing about self-interest. Bandwagoning may be an equally effective way to serve self-interest, as might devastation or outright annexation of an enemy in war. Claims that balancing and restraint are logical ways to serve self-interest are compelling only when made in a context of shared perception of threats and shared goals in politics—in this case, that hegemony is a threat to liberty and the overriding evil in interstate politics.

Supporting this basic normative structure was a set of widely understood rules about how, exactly, the balance was to be maintained and restraint exercised. Participants understood these rules clearly and talked about them explicitly in diplomatic correspondence, negotiations, and treaties.[16] One of these concerned compensations: States expected to be compensated for gains made by important neighbors in order to preserve the balance. Such claims were made even by states that had lost those territories in war. Maria Theresa was persistent, for example, in her claims that Austria must be compensated for Frederick's annexation of Silesia, and, when France seized Lorraine, the Duke of that territory was given Tuscany in compensation. Philip V of Spain was offered a variety of Italian territories to appease his loss of Spain itself at the end of the War of the Spanish Succession. Settlements of major conflicts always involved protracted haggling over territorial redistribution; the Congress of Vienna went so far as to set up a "statistical" committee to calculate comparisons and ensure an equitable distribution of territories among participants.[17]

Alliances, too, were enmeshed in a detailed set of quid pro quo expectations about compensation and indemnification for services rendered or losses suffered. Alliances were not open-ended pacts of enduring friendship but business arrangements for particular conflicts that commonly specified the number and types of armed forces that allies were to provide (or some equivalent amount in monetary payment so that mercenaries could be hired) as well as the division of spoils anticipated from the venture.[18]

Perhaps most important, however, was the role of notions about honor, glory, and status in the eighteenth-century system. The purpose of political action in this system was to advance the interests of the state, which then, as now, included power, security, and wealth but also, and perhaps especially, the monarch's honor and prestige among other rulers. In Louis XIV's view, "The virtue of the good ruler is always aiming at ... the greatness and the glory of his state." Frederick the Great similarly "made it a point of honor to have contributed more than anyone to the aggrandisement of my House."[19] States have always wanted to be respected internationally but the eighteenth-century concern about glory is different from contemporary concerns about credibility or reputation. Credibility is about trust and keeping promises, not preeminence. Reputations can be of many types and still be sought after. Canada, for example, values its reputation as an honest broker in world politics and would actively object to the notion that it is seeking glory in the self-aggrandizing eighteenth-century sense. And so would may other states. Glory and honor, in the eighteenth-century sense, were about status and precedence; rulers wanted to be *more* glorious than others, and the surest way to glory was through success in war. Louis XIV admitted that he always preferred conquering states to acquiring them through negotiations because war "was undoubtedly the most brilliant way to acquire glory." To be prevented from conquest by arms was an "injustice," according to Louis.[20] This emphasis on glory and honor created a different normative valuation on the use of force than currently prevails in the discourse of leaders of dominant states. Force and war were not necessary evils, reluctantly employed. They were positive goods, and opportunities to make use of them were to be quickly seized. This emphasis on honor and glory also created a different meaning for a state's pursuit of security and wealth in the eighteenth-century system than we have now. In contemporary politics, security and wealth are viewed as means to another end—for example, the welfare of citizens—by all the major powers of the system. However, in the eighteenth century, although enlightened monarchs might act to promote the welfare of subjects, this was not the primary goal of the state or its foreign policy; the welfare of subjects was a reflection of the power and glory of the state, not the reverse.[21] Thus, although states have always wanted to be well regarded internationally, what constitutes being "well regarded" has changed.

This set of goals and rules had important implications for the way force was used among states and the pattern of what we would now call military intervention behavior. War, even aggressive war, was a legitimate tool of foreign policy in pursuit of state power, and success at arms was by far the best means of achieving the honor and glory that were central to state goals. Rulers could and often did justify wars by claiming that the glory of their state demanded it—a justification that is unthinkable in contemporary politics. The result was the rather rapacious politics for which the eighteenth century is famous, although shared notions about the balance and its associated rules shaped the rapaciousness in patterned ways. Belief in, and normative valuation of, the balance prescribed balancing even when bandwagoning might be more materially advantageous. It prescribed military action early and, if necessary, often to maintain the balance. Lord Bolingbroke, architect of the Peace of Utrecht, wrote "If the scales can be brought back by a war nearly, though not exactly to the point where they were at before this great deviation from it, the rest may be left to accidents, and to the use that good policy is able to make of them."[22] Military action could be unilateral or multilateral; there was no clear normative preference. The prevailing rules allowed the acquisition of territory as a goal of military action and allowed territory to be traded freely among participants with relatively few restrictions as a means of redrawing the balance under changing conditions.

Like any intellectual framework, this set of normative orientations about what was desirable and how best to achieve those things enabled certain kinds of action and discouraged others. It did so not so much by making rules against otherwise desirable action but by connecting certain kinds of means to some desired ends rather than others and by making some kinds of action imaginable and others unimaginable. This system recognized war as the preeminent means to international prestige rather than, for example, the welfare of subjects or rising GNP per capita, and participants' actions reflect this. Conversely, the system did not provide intellectual connections that would seem obvious and natural in subsequent frameworks of thinking. For example, apart from dynastic affiliation, the internal structure of states was not a matter of much concern to eighteenth-century diplomats in calculating power or threats. Although there was some recognition that "good government" could increase a state's power (and this recognition increased over the eighteenth century), neither diplomats nor statesmen, before the French Revolution, perceived the internal organization or government of states to be a threat or grounds for military intervention.[23]

* * *

The Nineteenth-Century Concert

Although the post-Napoleonic system continued to operate within the broad parameters of a balance of power, underpinned by consensus that empire of hegemony was the principal evil to be avoided, shared expectations about the nature of the balance and how it would be maintained differed in significant ways from those prevailing in the eighteenth century.[24] The most obvious change was the expectation that serious problems would be resolved through consultation and negotiation among the Great Powers rather than immediate resort to arms. Certainly there was diplomacy in the eighteenth century to resolve crises, but there was nothing analogous to the nineteenth-century Congress system in which an oligarchy of Great Powers expected to (and was expected to) settle disputes among states.

Participants in the politics of this era well understood the radical shift in political rules they had engineered at Vienna. Friedrich von Gentz, a Prussian diplomat, publicist, intimate councillor of Metternich, and Secretary-General of the Vienna Congress, describes it this way:

> The political system existing in Europe since 1814 and 1815 is a phenomenon without precedent in the world's history. In place of the principle of ... counterweights formed by separate alliances, the principle that has governed and too often has also troubled and bloodied Europe for three centuries, there has succeeded a principle of general union, uniting all the states collectively with a federative bond, under the guidance of the five principal Powers, four of which have equal shares in that guidance, while the fifth at this time is still subject to a kind of tutelage, from which it will soon emerge to place itself upon a par with its custodians.[25]

Gentz's succinct description highlights several important changes in the Vienna system. First, the eighteenth-century balance had been what Little has called an "adversarial" one; it functioned by deterrence. The dominant logic that was to prevent hegemony was countervailing force and bloody war. The nineteenth-century balance was more "associative," in Little's terms (governed by a "principle of general union," in Gentz's) and involved as much assurance as deterrence.[26] An associative balance achieved, at least in part, through assurance implies both a shift in political ends as well as political means.

As Schroeder discusses at some length, the goal sought by participants at the Vienna Congress was not balance of power but "political equilibrium."[27] The two are related but not identical, since political equilibrium encompassed the countervailing force of a balance of power but within a larger political, social, and moral context. A stable political equilibrium was one in which all the major states felt reasonably secure that their existence, status, and core rights would not be threatened. The balance, as the Vienna participants understood it, was designed to protect both "the independence [and] the essential rights" of the various states.[28] The goal of the settlement, according to Kissinger, was "to create an order in which change could be brought about through a sense of obligation, instead of through an assertion of power."[29] The new settlement thus was a balance of duties and rights (*équilibre des droits*) as much as a balance of power.[30] The deterrent effect of a balance of material power may be self-enforcing, but a balance of rights requires some external assurance to be convincing and effective. In the nineteenth-century system, this assurance came from an institutionalized system of treaties and positive international law backed up by the "general guarantee" of the Great Powers and collective consultation among them. The Great Power guarantee provided some assurance to smaller states that borders would be respected; the collective consultation provided reassurance to the Great Powers, themselves, that they would be part of any decision to rearrange the peace.

Negotiators at Vienna, whose understandings of political goals and legitimate means to those goals had been altered by twenty years of revolution and continental conquest, consciously constructed these systemic changes. The notion that the Great Powers would collectively guarantee and manage the Vienna settlement was clearly new. Treaty guarantees themselves were not new. It was not unusual for a strong power to act as outside guarantor of a treaty between smaller states. What was new was "applying a guarantee to the whole of Europe and making the Powers subscribe to it."[31] The arrangement had its origins in correspondence between Pitt and the Russian tsar as early as 1792–93.[32] In 1805 Alexander made a proposal to "form at the restoration of peace a general agreement and guarantee for the mutual protection and security of different Powers, and for reestablishing a general system of public law in Europe."[33] The European peace was to be guaranteed by a league of Great Powers who would draw up a code of international law that would bind them to unite against any violator. It was a remarkable and innovative proposal. Equally remarkable is that Pitt accepted it, replying:

It seems necessary at the period of a general pacification, to form a Treaty to which all the principal Powers of Europe should be parties, by which their respective rights and possessions, as they shall then have been established, shall be fixed and recognized. And they should all bind themselves mutually to protect and support each other, against any attempt to infringe them—it should re-establish a general and comprehensive system of public law in Europe, and provide, as far as possible, for repressing future attempts to disturb the general tranquility; and above all, for restraining any projects of aggrandizement and ambition similar to those which have produced all the calamities inflicted on Europe since the disastrous era of the French Revolution.[34]

Negotiations to bring about the "general pacification" that would allow execution of these ideas in 1805, of course, collapsed, since Napoleon had no intention of agreeing to the territorial settlements the British and Russians then proposed. Ten years later, however, Castlereagh, who had assisted Pitt in drafting the 1805 reply to Alexander's original proposal, returned to these notions in designing his settlement and tried to put them into practice.[35] The result was Article VI of the Quadruple Alliance, which states:

The High Contracting Parties have agreed to renew their meetings at fixed periods, either under the immediate auspices of the Sovereigns themselves, or by their respective Ministers, for the purpose of consulting upon their common interests, and for the consideration of the measures which at each of those periods shall be considered the most salutary for the repose and prosperity of Nations and for the maintenance of the peace in Europe.

This clause was the basis for the Congress system of meetings among the Great Powers through which they managed European affairs in subsequent decades. Alexander had initially wanted the congresses to deal only with matters arising out of the treaty itself, but Castlereagh rewrote the language so that the congresses could be (and were) used to deal with any problem of interest to the Great Powers.[36]

Underlying the novelty of the Congress system was a more general change in diplomatic practice. Face-to-face meetings among principals, preferably in some neutral setting, are now a standard diplomatic tool for reaching agreement and building confidence among parties that agreements will be honored. Contemporary diplomats take Nitze's and Kvitsinsky's famous "walk in the woods" at Geneva and the meetings at Oslo and Camp David as testaments to the efficacy of intimacy and isolation in promoting understanding. But this was not standard diplomatic practice before Vienna. The Treaties of Münster and Osnabrück, for example, were negotiated largely in writing, by diplomatic notes.[37] Written interaction had important advantages in diplomacy, particularly in high-stakes peace negotiations, which practitioners at the time commented on. Written notes allowed precision and care in their crafting. They passed through several drafts and so were less prone to verbal slips of the tongue or incautious language that might be regretted later. They were always on record, and all parties involved could refer to them if necessary. Altogether, written interaction gave negotiators much more control and precision than face-to-face verbal communication.[38] Contemporary preferences for personal verbal and informal diplomacy are therefore not at all "obvious" or natural but require explanation.[39]

The practice of face-to-face personal meetings as a means of interstate diplomacy emerged from largely unintended and unexpected experiences at Vienna. Negotiators at Vienna spent almost two years in one another's company during the negotiations, some even sharing board and lodgings. This was owing in part to the complexity of the negotiations, but the return of Napoleon and his ensuing Hundred Days also stretched things out greatly. The result was that Alexander, Metternich, Castlereagh, Hardenberg, Tallyrand, and others experienced this political roller coaster of events together and got to know one another and one another's views well.[40] The experience had a particularly strong effect on Castlereagh. It made him by far the most "European" in outlook of the British statesmen of this period, a feature both contemporaries and historians commented on. It also convinced him of the utility of personal diplomacy and the need for frequent face-to-face meetings among decision makers to overcome the kind of intrigue and opportunism that had undermined previous peace agreements. Earl Ripon, who accompanied Castlereagh in his journey to the Continent in 1814, recounts the following conversation:

> He stated to me that one of the great difficulties which he expected to encounter in the approaching negotiations would arise from the want of an habitual confidential and free intercourse between the Ministers of the Great Powers *as a body*; and that many pretensions might be modified, asperities removed, and causes of irritation anticipated and met, by bringing the respective parties into unrestricted communication common to them all, and embracing in confidential and united discussion all the great points in which they were severally interested.[41]

The Congress system was an explicit attempt to create this kind of "habitual confidential and free intercourse" among ministers and so change the diplomatic dynamics among them. Certainly the congresses were no panacea; they did not breed universal friendship nor did Castlereagh expect them to. But they did create a different political dynamic, one sufficiently different to be discernable, even remarkable, to both participants of the time and historians subsequently.[42]

In the years immediately following Vienna, Castlereagh also made it an explicit mission to change the diplomatic culture beyond the Five Powers from one of intrigue and suspicion to one of assurance, in which treaty adherence was the expectation. Writing to Vaughan, the Secretary of Embassy at Madrid, he was clear in his instructions to foster a different diplomatic practice in that capital:

> It is unfortunately too much the diplomatic practice in such governments as that of Spain to work and to intrigue for influence upon the parties that from

day to day distract the public councils. In return, a feeble Government uneasy at being excluded from what it holds to be its due share of influence in the greater politics of Europe is not unlikely to endeavour to ferment disunion amongst the Powers whose existing connection diminishes its influence. You will hold these observations in view, and although it is always the duty of a Foreign Minister to be vigilant and to keep his Court informed, you will be cautious in giving any ostensible credit to jealousies, which, although resting on private channels of information, have yet received no countenance, either from the public acts of the Powers whom they affect, or from the correspondence of your own Government.... [I]n the meantime, it will be the province of the Ministers of this Court abroad to inculcate in all quarters the importance of union, to the preservation of that peace for which the Powers have so long and so gloriously contended, and to keep down as far as possible to spirit of local intrigue which has so often proved no less fatal to the repose of States than the personal ambition of Sovereigns.[43]

He gave similar instructions to his representative at Naples, Sir William A'Court.[44] This is a very different view of the kinds of diplomatic activity useful to the state (in this case Britain) than prevailed in the eighteenth century.

This incorporation of assurance, achieved through Great Power consultation and respect for treaty law, into the balance of the nineteenth century had implications for perceptions about effective and desirable uses of force in interstate relations. The new equilibrist understanding of order in Europe, secured by law and treaty, normatively devalued war as a tool of foreign policy. War was no longer a routine or "good" means of achieving political ends. Rather, military force was increasingly viewed as a tool of last resort, to be used only when accepted means of achieving ends (treaty, diplomacy) failed.[45] This change cannot simply be attributed to the devastation of Europe caused by the Napoleonic wars, since the level of material carnage in earlier wars was higher. The Thirty Years War, for example, was much bloodier. Frederick the Great estimated that one in nine of the Prussian population died during the Seven Years War—a much higher proportion than died in twentieth-century wars.[46] Along with this change went changes in notions about honor that had been so important in driving eighteenth-century politics. Glorious achievements in war and aggrandizement, even through duplicity and cunning, were less valued means to honor than they had been. Honor in the nineteenth century became more connected to trustworthiness and moral rectitude, which meant honoring commitments (for example, in treaties) and upholding the general European equilibrium. Changes in such international values were also deeply intertwined with normative changes in the domestic politics of these states. Absolutist states did not fear liberalism without cause. These governments were deeply fearful that launching a major war could open the door to revolution at home. Nor did liberal bourgeois sentiment in Britain, and to a lesser extent in France, favor the kinds of adventurist military policies popular in the eighteenth century. Domestic political concerns, created by liberal values, thus shaped, in important ways, the purposes decision makers pursued.[47]

These new interpretations of political ends (an equilibrium of rights via respect for law and treaties) by no means eliminated power-seeking and self-interested behavior among participants in the nineteenth-century system, but they did redirect behavior in patterned ways by creating new tools for action and eliminating old ones. Bismarck's goals involved a major reconfiguration of the European balance, but he achieved these ends largely through the tools available to him under the nineteenth-century system—astute negotiation, treaties, and recognition of the new Germany by the Great Powers. Under eighteenth-century rules, such German unification could not have happened without major continental wars; the prevailing norms about compensations, indemnification, and honor would not have permitted it. Those rules provided no basis on which other powers could accept such drastic changes (certainly not peacefully) or understand them to be legitimate. Similarly, France's annexation of Nice and Savoy in the 1860s was accomplished not by military conquest but "legally" via treaties, negotiated by Cavour, designed to unify northern Italy, and sanctioned by both Prussia and Russia.[48]

The new ends and means of the nineteenth-century system of order thus enabled some kinds of political action that had not been possible previously. They also made certain actions difficult that had previously been routine, among them self-aggrandizing warfare and territorial conquest within Europe, discussed above. The collective character of the Vienna guarantee now made territorial expansion a collective concern, to be managed by the Great Powers and requiring their consent, since any change in boundaries now automatically involved the whole of Europe.

The Napoleonic experience also changed the way participants in the nineteenth century viewed threats. The eighteenth century had been an unusual period in which, apart from dynastic affiliation (which was a threat not so much because of its internal consequences but because it determined alliance behavior, discussed below), states were not much concerned with their neighbors' internal organization and did not perceive the form of government in other states to be a threat.[49] The French Revolution and Napoleon had made it abundantly clear to the dynastic powers (Russia, Prussia, and Austria) that the internal organization of states was, perhaps, the premier threat in international politics—one that must be dealt with firmly, even ruthlessly. This perception, that some of the most important threats lay in the internal politics of other states, coupled with the increased difficulty of annexing or conquering them (since this would disturb the carefully constructed territorial balance), enabled the construction of "intervention" as a category of military behavior distinct from war and made such a distinction intelligible and useful. The old eighteenth-century solution to such threats—conquest and annexation—ran afoul of other central norms of the nineteenth century system, such as collective boundary guarantees and normative skepticism about aggressive war. Military intervention to influence or alter domestic governing arrangements, leaving boundaries intact, provided a potential solution to the problem of internal threats and still respected the fundamental rules and norms of the systemic order.

If the new perception that threat was rooted in domestic politics created a functional need for this new behavior called "intervention," international law provided much of the language and ideology that made the concept intelligible and persuasive. It provided the intellectual and cultural "toolkit" policy makers would use to contest intervention's meaning and was an essential part of the normative "frame" in which claims about it had to resonate.[50] Participants in the concert strongly believed that the new Vienna order was a form of "law," as distinct from mere convenience or convention. All decision makers of the age consistently spoke of the treaty as law and, more important, of attempts to change or revise it by force as "illegal." One corollary of this was that, for the dynastic powers, revolution was not simply undesirable or threatening, it was an "illegal" mode of political change. Metternich is very clear on this point. Revolutionaries were not political opponents or enemies in a war; they were outlaws and "brigands," and suppression of their actions was a form of policing ("gendarmerie").[51] Understanding revolutions as illegal (rather than as acts of self-determination, national liberation, or simple self-aggrandizement) made suppression of revolution by intervention not only permissible but normatively necessary for these powers. The British, particularly Whigs, were less quick to condemn these violent revolutions, but they, too, couched their opposing arguments in legal terms, relying on natural-law principles to make arguments about the conditions under which intervention might be justified within the legal Vienna settlement. The Glorious Revolution had created a stronger notion in Britain of the duties sovereigns owed subjects to govern well; it also created much more sympathy with the notion that bad rulers could forfeit their legal and moral right to rule, thereby justifying revolution or intervention.[52] For all parties, however, there was a clear understanding that the use of force under debate was something different than war and that it was different because of the practice's standing in law.[53]

That participants in the nineteenth-century system all understood the meaning and purpose of this new class of military behavior, armed intervention, by no means meant that they all agreed on the rules concerning it. In fact, debates over intervention were some of the most contentious and most salient foreign policy struggles of the post–Napoleonic period. Arguments between British statesmen (first Castlereagh, then Canning and Palmerston) and Metternich, in particular, were dominated by this question when revolutions appeared, first in the Iberian Peninsula, then in Italy and Greece. Throughout the period there was sharp disagreement about when it was legitimate to intervene in these states.[54]

Scholarly focus on these very public disagreements has often obscured what the Great Powers did *not* fight about, because they all agreed, namely, that eighteenth-century options for the use of force in these weaker states were no longer available. Powers argued hard about intervention rules precisely because they could no longer legitimately exercise other military options. They could no longer simply conquer and annex these places, nor could they shuffle these territories to friendly clients or allies. The Great Powers agreed, above all, that the Vienna treaties had to be respected. All the quarreling of this period about intervention is couched in alternative interpretations of the major Vienna treaties. Positions lacking plausible support in those treaties were not advanced or were given no hearing. Thus Austria, Russia, and Prussia argued that, as a settlement of rights designed to ensure security of major states, the settlement justified intervention to deal with threats to those states. The Napoleonic experience gave these states good reason to believe that liberalism was expansionist and aggressive, and presented clear threats to the legitimate international order and legitimate rights of these dynastic states guaranteed by the Vienna accords. Revolution justified military intervention because it was an "illegal" method of changing government and posed dangers to the existing system of rights guaranteed by international law.[55]

Castlereagh and Canning countered with their own interpretation of the treaty. They argued that the Quadruple Alliance obligated states to intervene only in France in case of a Bonapartist return. Other interventions were not part of the intent or the text of the treaties and therefore were not legally required. The security the treaties guaranteed was territorial security, and Britain could intervene when "the Territorial Balance of Europe is disturbed." However, intervention to suppress popular revolutions was contrary to Whig principles set down in 1688 with the accession of the House of Hanover (that monarchs who abuse power must forfeit it) and, generally, was bad policy because it was not likely to succeed.[56]

These debates were never resolved in the Vienna system, but their terms and scope defined the possibilities for and limits on intervention. The cardinal rule was that military interventions could not upset the delicate territorial settlement of Vienna. If territory shifted, the Great Powers all had to agree to the change that would be formalized legally, by treaty. Potential interventions were always aired as a collective problem, but it was perceived that unilateral intervention was often less destabilizing than a multilateral intervention would be. Britain, for example, gave Austria permission to intervene unilaterally in Naples in 1820. Unlike the Spanish case of a popular uprising against a bad king, Britain viewed the Naples case as an unwarranted coup against a benign government, which (again unlike the Spanish case) created clear contagion problems in neighboring states. The British were concerned that any collective intervention by all the Powers would undermine Britain's overall nonintervention interpretation of the Vienna accords and feed arguments that the settlement contained a positive obligation to intervene to support the status quo.[57] Unilateral intervention also kept military activity by the Great Powers contained geographically. Although the British decried French intervention in Spain, French unilateral intervention was far preferable to the threatened collective intervention that would bring Russian and Hapsburg troops marching westward across Europe and onto the Iberian Peninsula.

In sum, intervention became an important tool of foreign policy when major states began to perceive serious threats in the domestic politics of other states and when specific characteristics of the Vienna settlement (normative devaluation of aggressive war, boundary changes only by collective agreement and treaty) made eighteenth-century–style conquest of these places illegitimate or politically very costly. All Powers agreed that intervention was legitimate if the target sought to change territorial boundaries (i.e., threaten the "territorial balance"). Territorial changes were only possible if all Powers agreed. The Powers also agreed that any intervention was a legitimate concern of all Great Powers collectively, even when they did not agree on whether intervention was the right policy. There was recognition that each of the Great Powers had areas of vital and lesser interest, and this often (but not always) determined which Power's view would prevail, but everywhere in Europe was now the business of all the Great Powers. Finally, there was no great normative preference in this period between unilateral and multilateral intervention. Both were used; both were recognized as legitimate.

* * *

Spheres of Influence

Unlike the Vienna system, the spheres-of-influence system that prevailed during the cold war was not the result of conscious negotiation. Conscious negotiation certainly took place, but the visions states were propounding in talks during World War II had little in common with the system that ultimately prevailed. That system evolved through a series of events in the late 1940s and 1950s that have been described elsewhere in great detail.[58] My concern here, in general, is with the kinds of rules that eventually developed and became accepted by states, especially the superpowers, during the cold war, and, specifically, with the implications of those rules for military intervention.

As relations between the Soviet Union and the Western powers deteriorated in the late 1940s, a bipolar system emerged. The system was the result of, as Melvyn Leffler put it, a "fusion of ideological competition with geostrategic threat."[59] Ideology alone was not sufficient to create a cold war spheres-of-influence system. After all, the Soviet state and its ideology had been around for decades; the cold war only began when Soviet material power expanded and Soviet armies were in a position to influence the politics of postwar Europe and Asia. Conversely, material power could not be sufficient, since, as discussed, roughly analogous distributions of power at other periods (for example, in 1815 between Russia and Britain) did not result in a cold war. What made the Soviet Union a threat, indeed a mortal danger, was its ideology and social purpose which ran directly counter to the most fundamental principles of the U.S. polity.

From the 1950s on, each of the two superpowers worked hard to consolidate a global network of alliances under its control. Although some analysts have written about the "balance of power" between the two sides, this was clearly not a balance-of-power system in its classic European meaning. Neither side in the cold war viewed the other as a good or necessary part of a system to prevent hegemony; both sides would have preferred hegemony, with themselves as hegemon.[60] Restraint in this system came not from any normative conviction that shared power among states was good or was the "condition of international freedom."[61] Restraint came from terror of thermonuclear weapons. Most obviously, ideological conflict drove this system in a way it had not permeated European politics since the wars of religion in the sixteenth and seventeenth centuries. The European balance of power had always been explicitly nonideological; that alliances in those balance systems crossed religious lines (and later absolutist/liberal lines) was a feature that distinguished balance politics from previous eras. During the cold war, by contrast, the "condition of international freedom" for both sides was one that could be secured only by eliminating the other—a view that made restraint difficult and cross-camp alliances almost impossible. It is hard to imagine any U.S. (or Soviet) leader adopting the eighteenth-century distinction articulated by Defoe, above, that it was only preponderant power they objected to, not the state itself. Rather than feeling "part of a common republic," each of these states objected to the very existence of the other as illegitimate and threatening.

Ideological bipolarity thus divided the world into two "spheres of influence" in which each superpower could organize political and economic life according to its ideology. States in the Western sphere were organized into a transnational capitalist economy underpinned by American economic resources and run largely according to American rules. States in the Soviet sphere were analogously organized into command economies linked to a Soviet center. Neither side was as particular about the domestic political niceties of liberal democracy or socialism in their Third World clients as they were about external economic and military behavior. Both tolerated a wide range of authoritarian regimes in weak client states as long as those governments adhered to the rules of external alliance and economic behavior of the network.[62]

Spheres provided one important context for intervention behavior in this period. The other critical feature of the system was the nature of sovereignty under the spheres system. Sovereignty in this system was strongly tied to territory. Rather than the ruler being the state, as in the eighteenth century ("*l'etat, c'est moi*"), the territory was the state. Although there were occasional border changes during the process of decolonization, once statehood was achieved, borders were generally fixed. Governments could rise and fall, ethnic compositions could shift with migration, but territorial boundaries were no longer subject to change by force. The only way borders could legitimately be changed in this system was by mutual consent. Jackson and Zacher provide extensive evidence of this normative shift, showing how it was endorsed both in declarative terms, in state discourse, and in state behavior. All the major multilateral agreements since 1945 have endorsements of territorial integrity as foundational normative principles. The UN Charter states that members "shall refrain in their international relations from the threat or use of force against the territorial integrity or political independence of any state." The Conference on Security and Cooperation in Europe (CSCE) (and later the OSCE) reiterated similar support for the principle in the Helsinki Final Act, which states that "frontiers can [only] be changed, in accordance with international law, by peaceful means and by agreement." The Organization of African Unity espoused similar principles. State behavior largely conformed to these declarations of principle. There was a huge drop in territorial boundary changes accomplished by force after 1945. Between 1648 and 1945, the percentage of conflicts in which territory was redistributed is consistently between 77 percent and 82 percent; between 1945 and 1996, it is 23 percent.[63]

Other sovereignty norms exerted power but were much more contested and less absolute. Notions about ethnic nationalities as the basis of the state had normative power and provided the basis for mobilizing people in wars of liberation, but the correspondence between nations and states continued (and continues) to be weak. Related notions about self-determination were also powerful in speeding the decolonization process and creating new sovereignties where none had existed previously by making it politically costly for colonizers to hold on to colonies.[64] But the "self" that got to do the determining in this period was a territorial self. The political autonomy of many of these newer "selfs" and the independence of their self-determination processes was highly questionable. Superpowers sometimes exercised enormous control over the political structure of client states. Thus, although both nationalism and self-determination were powerful and were used extensively to mobilize support for and to justify policies, they were not essential for the recognized exercise of sovereignty in this system, and many, perhaps most, of the governments of newly created states in this system were not representative of either an ethnic nation or a popular will.[65]

Similarly, self-determination norms created prescriptions that intervention should only take place by invitation or consent of the government in the target state (for example, to put down insurgency, protect it from external aggression, or restore order). Both superpowers publicly accepted this rule, yet its practical effect at channeling intervention behavior was minimal or mixed, since its effects hinged entirely on which government the superpowers recognized as the legitimate one, competent to issue invitations.[66]

Maintaining order in this system meant maintaining the spheres of influence and the ideologies that underpinned them. Challenges within states to the dominant ideology of the sphere were the most common kind of threat and, in the view of the superpowers, justified intervention.[67] Soviet interventions in Hungary and Czechoslovakia, and American interventions in Central America and the Caribbean, were all aimed at preventing political change in the target state that would undermine ideological principles or switch the state into the enemy sphere altogether. Unlike the Vienna system, however, interventions to deal with ideological revolutions were not a matter for collective consultation during the cold war. Superpowers were entitled under the rules of this system to intervene unilaterally to put down revolutions inside their sphere. Cross-sphere intervention was extremely threatening in this system, and while each super-power had spies and covert operations in the other's sphere, the United States and the USSR both well understood that overt intervention by the United States in Eastern Europe or by the USSR in Western Europe or the Americas would be seen as grossly illegitimate and cause for major war.[68]

Areas of the world that were not firmly anchored in one or the other sphere—Africa, south and southeast Asia, the Middle East—were prizes to be gained, and much of the cold war was a struggle for the allegiance of these states. Intervention was an important tool in this struggle, since one way to secure allegiance was to put your allies in power. Sometimes the intervention was overt, as in Vietnam or Korea, but much more often superpowers went to great lengths to disguise and deny their role in destabilizing these governments, since, under prevailing self-determination norms, governments imposed from outside were often plagued by challenges to their legitimacy. This tension between perceived ideological threats (justifying intervention) and self-determination norms (undermining its result) shaped much of the intervention behavior of the superpowers and other intervening states during the cold war. It created incentives for covert intervention, intervention by proxy or client states, and indirect intervention of many kinds (such as training and equipping indigenous troops in the target state rather than sending one's own troops) that would allow both interveners and their allies in target states to publicly deny the intervention when necessary to protect legitimacy claims.[69] This kind of secret intervention was much less common during the nineteenth century concert when normative incentives to states were different. The Holy Alliance was not concerned about adhering to the forms of self-determination as a basis of legitimacy, but Britain, too, saw no particular reason for secrecy about these operations out of concern for the legitimacy of the governments they helped.[70] Without the kind of self-determination norms prevailing in the mid-twentieth century, there was no particular reason to hide assistance from powerful friends. In fact, one would usually advertise such assistance, not disguise it, as a means of deterring challenges to one's power....

* * *

The Current System

The nature of international order after the cold war is still emerging, but it is already clear that the pattern of intervention behavior in this system will be very different from the cold war. Communism has largely disappeared as a threat to the reigning capitalist liberal-democratic consensus, and ideological blocs and spheres of influence, in the cold war sense, have disappeared with it. Three kinds of threats now seem capable of provoking intervention: violations of territorial borders (Iraq's actions in Kuwait), civil conflicts involving massive humanitarian disasters (Somalia, Bosnia, Haiti), and massive terrorist attacks (Afghanistan). A fourth, proliferation of weapons of mass destruction (WMD), may also be emerging.

The perception that border violations and attempts to annex territory are threatening is hardly surprising or new. These have provoked armed responses in all eras. Similarly, although massive attacks on civilians like those on September 11, 2001, do not have a good analog in history, there is every reason to think such action would have provoked a military response in any era. Two changes in military responses are worth noting, however. First, there is an increasing reluctance to declare war in these cases. Invasion, attack, and forcible border changes have always been sufficient justification for war, not just intervention, yet major military responses, even to the most consensually obvious violations of basic sovereignty, are being termed "interventions," or "operations," or some other code word for war. Although in common parlance the public speaks of the Korean War, the Vietnam War, the Gulf War, and the war on terrorism, there were no declarations of war in any of these instances. We thus appear to have reversed the eighteenth-century relationship between war and intervention. In the eighteenth-century war was glorious, and the notion of "intervention" had little utility; now intervention is normatively preferable, and war is shunned. No major power has declared war since 1945, and very few minor powers have. Second, even in cases of territorial violation and attack, where states have a clear *causus belli,* they will go to great lengths to make their response multilateral. I noted this dynamic in the case of humanitarian intervention, but in that situation states had (and have) reason to be concerned that other states will not recognize the legitimacy of military deployments that violate sovereignty for humanitarian purposes if done unilaterally (as, indeed, they did not for India in 1971). Multilateralism there provided political cover for military operations whose legitimacy was contested internationally. Saddam's invasion of Kuwait, however, was as blatant a violation of international rules as one could ask for and should have justified immediate unilateral response by any Kuwaiti ally if anything could justify unilateral action. That the United States felt the political need to invest significant resources in coalition building and working through the UN, even in such a clear case of aggression when provocations were apparent and violations uncontested, points to an even greater importance for multilateralism norms.[71]

Such strong multilateralism norms are not what one would expect from a distribution of material capabilities so overwhelmingly unipolar. Certainly they are not norms that have been strong in other eras of relative unipolarity (e.g., Britain in the mid- to late nineteenth century). Ruggie and his colleagues have traced the history of these norms to show that they reflect particular U.S. notions about political legitimacy: What matters, they argue, is not overwhelming concentration of power but the fact that that power was American.[72] It is the peculiar social purpose of *American* power, and the success of Americans at both exporting these notions to other powerful states (notably Western Europe and Japan) and institutionalizing them in international organizations and treaties, that has been important for establishing these multilateralism norms that now shape contemporary world politics and intervention behavior. Indeed, it is precisely the successful export of multilateral norms that made George W. Bush's unilateral assertions so controversial and politically costly.

... During the cold war, the spheres-of-influence system was underpinned as a modus vivendi in large part by a willingness of strong states to decouple certain aspects of the internal behavior of states from assessments of the external threat they posed. The internal organization of states mattered greatly on a capitalist-communist dimension, since it determined alliance behavior and allegiance in the grand world struggle. Once states were situated within a sphere, however, there was relatively strong agreement that the way they treated their citizens was a domestic matter and that interference from other states was a significant violation of sovereignty. The prevailing understanding was that a state's ability to be a reliable ally maintaining peaceful relations with other states could be decoupled from its internal behavior toward its own citizens.... [I]nterventions against even the most egregious human rights violators during this period, for example Idi Amin and Pol Pot, met with skepticism or condemnation. Reactions from other states, particularly what were then called Third World states, all emphasized the threat posed to sovereignty by these interventions and made clear that sovereignty trumped human rights concerns.

The view has changed. States no longer decouple external and internal assessments of violent behavior to the degree they did during the cold war. States now explicitly and openly use assessments of internal aggressive behavior as an indicator of external policy.[73] States that abuse citizens in massive or systematic ways are now viewed as security threats both because the flows of refugees and social tensions that such policies create are destabilizing to neighbors and because aggressive behavior internally is seen as an indicator of the capacity to behave aggressively externally. This shift in perceptions has historical roots in the anti-apartheid campaign, during which opponents of apartheid were able to frame human rights abuses as threats to regional peace and security.[74] This link became institutionalized in international institutions by the 1990s, especially in the UN, and in the foreign policies of a variety of powerful states such that, by the 1990s, security could not be said to exist internationally without human rights protections.[75]

This coupling of security with human rights has implications for intervention behavior. What used to be simple atrocities are now understood as threats to international peace and order in ways that were not true during previous eras.

Consequently, intervention in these places now occurs not simply with the aim of stopping killing, as was true in the 1860s in Lebanon but instead has the mission of reconstructing entire states and societies in ways that did not occur in previous periods of history. Interventions in failed states are no longer simply military affairs in which killers are disarmed and, if necessary, replaced in government by a new set of rulers. These interventions now involve a wide range of nonmilitary components involving reconstruction and social services, mostly provided by international organizations, aimed at overhauling war-torn societies and remaking them in accordance with the normatively preferred liberal democratic model.

Intervention is thus becoming difficult (if not impossible) to separate from nation building in contemporary politics; one cannot do the first without the second. Even governments skeptical about the efficacy of nation building, for example, the second Bush administration at this writing, find themselves hip-deep in it once they intervene. They engage in nation building not out of altruism or sympathy for their targets (although they may well have such motives). They do so because they understand it to be useful and necessary. They understand their own security to be best secured by the creation of a polity in the target nation that has not just a certain kind of government but a certain kind of society with very particular connections to that government. Simply handing over the reins of government to a new group is relatively easy, and intervenors have been doing this for centuries. Insuring broad social reorganization is much harder.

One of the most interesting features of contemporary nation building is that most of it is being done by international organizations. Individual states cannot legitimately do this alone. That would be colonialism. Instead, the same multilateral norms are strongly at work here, just as they are in the military side of intervention. The UN, the OSCE, the World Bank, and other internationally recognized multilateral organizations are the actors who can legitimately remake states—organizing and monitoring elections, overseeing transitions, coordinating reconstruction, and development assistance. Only multilateral bodies can carry out these tasks in ways that have the appearance of serving the community's interests as opposed to the particularistic interests of self-seeking states. Whether these interventions and subsequent attempts to rebuild will ultimately succeed in producing lasting peace remains to be seen, but that the effort is being made, and being made in many places around the globe, is unprecedented. Understanding why intervenors are behaving in this way, intervening in these places and with these diversified post-conflict rebuilding efforts, makes sense only in light of the concept of security and order that has developed in recent years and, particularly, its coupling with human rights protections.

* * *

Notes

1. There was disagreement among writers throughout the balance period about whether the balance was something that occurred naturally or needed to be consciously constructed by wise statesmen. Rousseau is the most well known proponent of the former view, but this was, by far, a minority position. The latter was the more common position (M. S. Anderson, "Eighteenth-Century Theories of the Balance of Power," in *Studies in Diplomatic History: Essays in Memory of David Bayne Horn,* ed. Ragnhild Hatton and M. S. Anderson (Hamden, Conn.: Archon, 1970), 189–90).

2. Cromwell was criticized for bandwagoning with preponderant France, rather than balancing against it by allying with Spain. In his analysis of these events, Viscount Henry St. John Bolingbroke (architect of the Utrecht settlement in 1713) can only explain these actions as the result of stupidity on Cromwell's part or that he was "induced by reasons of private interest to act against the general interests of Europe" ("Letters on the Study and Use of History, Letter VII," in *The Works of Lord Bolingbroke* [Philadelphia: Carey and Hart, 1841], 257). Slingsby Bethel, writing in 1668, similarly faults Cromwell as the man who "broke the balance between the two Crowns of Spain and France" (quoted in Michael Sheehan, *Balance of Power: History and Theory* [New York: Routledge, 1996], 39). Similarly, Prussia's failure to balance and join the Third Coalition against Napoleon in the first decade of the nineteenth century was a source of much vexation for the Allies (and much short-term profit for Prussia) (*Cambridge History of British Foreign Policy,* 1:342–48).

3. Note that mere balancing behavior is not the same as a balance-of-power system. Countervailing alliances happen all the time in all kinds of places without being understood as a basis of international order or the guiding principle of foreign policy. Mere balancing is not a balance of power. A balance of power requires the institutionalized expectation of balancing behavior and consistent behavior accordingly.

4. Steve Krasner, *International Regimes* (Ithaca, N.Y.: Cornell University Press, 1983); Robert O. Keohane, *After Hegemony: Cooperation and Discord in the World Political Economy* (Princeton, N.J.: Princeton University Press, 1984).

5. Martin Wight, "The Balance of Power and International Order," in *The Bases of International Order: Essays in Honor of W. A. W. Manning,* ed. Alan James (London: Oxford University Press, 1973), 85–115. Fénelon expresses this view explicitly as did Palmerston, 150 years later, as the quotations in Wight and elsewhere make clear (see Wight, "The Balance of Power and International Order," 100–101). Wight also notes that it is no accident that the pioneers of balance-of-power theory were often Dutch, English, and German—states where the constitutional arguments about these matters had been most fully aired (96).

6. What follows is a radical generalization about historical practices and ideas. Evan Luard's *The Balance of Power: The System of International Relations, 1648–1815* (New York: St. Martin's, 1992) provides a book-length treatment of this period that is particularly useful for political scientists. Also useful are Anderson, "Eighteenth-Century Theories," 183–98; Paul Schroeder, *The Transformation of European Politics: 1763–1848* (New York: Oxford University Press, 1994); and the writings

of this period collected in Moorhead Wright, *Theory and Practice of the Balance of Power* (Totowa, N.J.: Rowman and Littlefield, 1975).

7. The degree to which this thinking followed directly from Italian writing of the fifteenth and sixteenth centuries is a matter of debate. Some writers trace a clear intellectual lineage, whereas others claim little trans-Alpine influence. Francesco Guicciardini's *History of Italy* (1561), which was widely read north of the Alps, was particularly influential in articulating the logic and benefits of countervailing alliances among the Italian city-states before the French invasion of 1494. It is worth noting that although the idealized picture Guicciardini paints of pre-invasion Italian politics that he attributes to Lorenzo de'Medici's wise diplomacy did much to advance the popularity of this kind of foreign policy, Lorenzo's own letters reveal different motives and understandings than those Guicciardini attributed to him. See Wright, *Theory and Practice of the Balance of Power,* 1–12 (Lorrenzo de'Medici, "Two Letters on Florentine Diplomacy" and an extract from Francesco Guicciardini, *History of Italy*). Guicciardini, like Lorenzo, was a participant in these politics. He served as Florentine ambassador to the court of Ferdinand of Spain and later (disastrously) as governor of several of the Papal States.

8. Duke Henri de Rohan, *A Treatise of the Interest of the Princes and States of Christendome,* trans. H. H. (Paris, 1640), 1–3, 18–21, 24–25; quoted in Wright, *Theory and Practice of the Balance of Power,* 35–38. Rohan (1579–1638) was a diplomat in the service of Henry IV and later led the Huguenots during the religious wars. He subsequently regained Richelieu's confidence and became ambassador to Switzerland (Wright, *Theory and Practice of the Balance of Power,* 35).

9. Francis Bacon publicized this view of Henry VIII's policy, but observers outside England, such as Giovanni Botero, shared the interpretation. For Bacon's discussion, see Wright, *Theory and Practice of the Balance of Power,* xvi; Botero's "Of the Counterpoise of Princes' Forces" is also excerpted in Wright's work (19–23).

10. All quoted in Luard, *The Balance of Power,* 339.

11. The French also invoked protection of the balance in their guarantee of the Pragmatic Sanction in 1735 (Anderson, "Eighteenth-Century Theories," 184).

12. Fénelon was Archbishop of Cambrai and an adviser to Louis XIV.

13. François de Salignac de la Mothe Fénelon, "On the Necessity of Forming Alliances, Both Offensive and Defensive, against a Foreign Power Which Manifestly Aspires to Universal Monarchy," in "Two Essays on the Balance of Power in Europe ... Printed in the Year 1720," *A Collection of Scarce and Valuable Tracts (Lord Somers Tracts),* xiii, 2d ed. (1815), 766–70. Reprinted in Wright, *Theory and Practice of the Balance of Power,* 39–45; quotes from 40, 41.

14. Reprinted in Wright, *Theory and Practice of the Balance of Power,* 41.

15. Daniel Defoe, *A Review of the State of the English Nation* 3, no. 65 (really 66) (June 1, 1706): 261–63. Reprinted in Wright, *Theory and Practice of the Balance of Power,* 45–49; quote at 47. In addition to his literary career, Defoe was an active pamphleteer and supporter of William of Orange, whose diplomacy, in Defoe's view, exemplified balance-of-power principles. The *Review* in which this appeared was a main government organ from 1704 to 1713; the war he refers to is what we now call the War of the Spanish Succession (Wright, *Theory and Practice of the Balance of Power,* 45–46). On restraint, or what he calls "moderation," see also

Edward Vose Gulick, *Europe's Classical Balance of Power* (New York: Norton, 1955), 72–77.

16. See Luard, *The Balance of Power*; Anderson, "Eighteenth-Century Theories," 183–98; and Schroeder, *The Transformation of European Politics*.

17. Schroeder, *The Transformation of European Politics*, 6–7; Luard, *The Balance of Power*, 76, 201–3; Gulick, *Europe's Classical Balance of Power*, 70–72, chap. 9. Gulick provides examples of the statistical calculations at Vienna in his analysis of the resolution of the Saxon question there (248–51).

18. Schroeder, *The Transformation of European Politics*, 7.

19. Both quotes are in Luard, *The Balance of Power*, 129. Luard also provides an extended discussion of the manifestations of this concern with honor and status in diplomatic dealings and the obsession in this age with precedence, ceremonial protocol, titles, and related issues (*The Balance of Power*, chap. 5).

20. From Louis XIV, *Mémoires*, as quoted in Luard, *Balance of Power*, 132. Kalevi Holsti discusses the influence of glory on military politics of the period in his *Peace and War: Armed Conflicts and International Order, 1648–1989* (New York: Cambridge University Press, 1991), 65–68.

21. Schroeder, *The Transformation of European Politics*, 8.

22. Bolingbroke, "Letters on the Study and Use of History, Letter VII," 291. See also the discussion on how preservation of the balance required military intervention, in Robert E. Osgood and Robert W. Tucker, *Force, Order, and Justice* (Baltimore: The Johns Hopkins University Press, 1967), 96–104.

23. Anderson, "Eighteenth-Century Theories," 191; Luard, *Balance of Power*, 334.

24. Distinguishing the rules and practices of the nineteenth-century system from the eighteenth-century system has been a major focus of Paul Schroeder's work, which I draw on here. See the following works by Schroeder: *The Transformation of European Politics*; "The 19th-Century International System: Changes in the Structure," *World Politics* 39, no. 1 (October 1986): 1–26; "The Nineteenth-Century System: Balance of Power or Political Equilibrium?" *Review of International Studies* 15 (1989): 135–53; and "Did the Vienna Settlement Rest on a Balance of Power?" *American Historical Review* 97, no. 3 (June 1992): 683–706.

25. Friedrich von Gentz, "Considerations on the Political System Now Existing in Europe," report written to the rulers of Wallachia probably in early 1818, as reprinted in Mack Walker, ed., *Metternich's Europe, 1813–1848* (New York: Harper and Row, 1968), 71–72. See also Gentz's *Fragments upon the Present State of the Political Balance in Europe* (London: Peltier, 1806); and the biographical information on von Gentz in Wright, *Theory and Practice of the Balance of Power*, 94. The fifth power referred to here is France, which was quickly incorporated into the concert in 1818 at the Congress at Aix-la-Chappelle. For a similar quotation by Metternich about the distinctive "associative" character of the Vienna peace, see Gordon Craig and Alexander George, *Force and Statecraft* (New York: Oxford University Press, 1983), 29.

26. Richard Little, "Deconstructing the Balance of Power," *Review of International Studies* 15, no. 2 (April 1989): 87–100. Schroeder thanks Edward Kolodziej for pointing out to him the deterrence/assurance distinction between these two eras (Schroeder, "Did the Vienna Settlement Rest on a Balance of Power?" 697 n. 31).

That distinction has a long history in the political science literature. For seminal discussions, see Thomas Schelling, *Arms and Influence* (New Haven: Yale University Press, 1966), 74–78; and, on "inducement theory," Alexander L. George and Richard Smoke, *Deterrence in American Foreign Policy: Theory and Practice* (New York: Columbia University Press, 1974), 606–10.

27. "Just equilibrium" was the phrase Castlereagh repeatedly used (*Cambridge History of British Foreign Policy,* 1:465). For an extended discussion of "political equilibrium" and its relationship to earlier balance-of-power notions, see Schroeder, "The Nineteenth-Century System: Balance of Power or Political Equilibrium?" 135–53; and Schroeder, "Did the Vienna Settlement Rest on a Balance of Power?" 683–706. Kissinger, like Schroeder, talks about the quest for a "legitimate equilibrium" in his analysis, distinguishing it from previous balance-of-power arrangements (*A World Restored,* e.g., 184).

28. Gentz, *Fragments,* 55.

29. Kissinger, *A World Restored,* 172. Kissinger's argument that participants in the settlement were concerned above all that the new order be seen as "legitimate" because "it is the legitimizing principle which established the relative 'justice' of competing claims and the mode of their adjustment" fits with both Schroeder's analysis of political equilibrium and Little's analysis of the associative character of this balance (*A World Restored,* chap. 9, quote from 145).

30. Schroeder, "Did the Vienna Settlement Rest on a Balance of Power?" 683–706, esp. 698.

31. Harold Temperley and Lillian Penson, *Foundations of British Foreign Policy from Pitt (1792) to Salisbury (1902)*; or, *Documents, Old and New, Selected and Edited, with Historical Introductions* (Cambridge: Cambridge University Press, 1938), 28; Luard, *The Balance of Power,* 285–90.

32. Temperley and Penson, *Foundations of British Foreign Policy,* 9.

33. *Cambridge History of British Foreign Policy,* 1:325; Kissinger, *A World Restored,* 27–40. H. G. Schenk provides some intellectual history for this proposal and describes how it was that embodying Enlightenment thinking came to surface in proposals from "Europe's most backward social milieu." See H. G. Schenk, *The Aftermath of the Napoleonic Wars: The Concert of Europe—An Experiment* (New York: Oxford University Press, 1947), esp. chap. 2.

34. "Pitt's Memorandum on the Deliverance and Security of Europe, 19 January 1805." Reprinted in Temperley and Penson, *Foundations of British Foreign Policy,* 18.

35. *Cambridge History of British Foreign Policy,* 1:491, 464.

36. Charles K. Webster, *The Foreign Policy of Castlereagh, 1815–1822* (London: Bell, 1925), 55–56; quote on 55.

37. R. B. Mowat, *Diplomacy and Peace* (New York: Robert M. McBride, 1936), 50.

38. Ibid., 52.

39. Another feature of modern diplomacy that appears natural to us is the "conference" style of negotiation where all participants sit together around a table and are party to discussions. "Congresses" of the concert were gatherings to facilitate intensive one-on-one meetings and small-group negotiations. They were not boardroom-style "meetings" of all participants around a table. That kind of openness and inclusiveness would have been viewed as damaging to clear understandings

between representatives, since it would prevent them from tailoring their messages to particular audiences (Mowat, *Diplomacy and Peace*, 71–72).

40. Webster, *The Foreign Policy of Castlereagh*, 64; R. W. Seton-Watson, *Britain in Europe, 1789 to 1914* (New York: Macmillan, 1937), 49; Arthur May, *The Age of Metternich, 1814–1848* (New York: Henry Hold, 1933), 8–11; Roy Bridge, "Allied Diplomacy in Peacetime: The Failure of the Congress 'System,' 1815–23," in *Europe's Balance of Power: 1815–1848*, ed. Alan Sked (New York: Harper and Row, 1979), 34–53.

41. The Earl of Ripon to the Marquess of Londonderry, as quoted in Webster, *The Foreign Policy of Castlereagh*, 56, italics original.

42. Kissinger, perhaps predictably, thinks that Castlereagh's logic was misguided, and argues that Castlereagh mistakenly "considered confidential relationships not the expression, but the cause, of harmony" (*A World Restored*, 186). Less important here is whether Kissinger or Castlereagh is right about cause and effect than that Castlereagh, not Kissinger, was designing the Vienna peace and used his ideas to shape behavior in that period.

43. Quoted in Webster, *The Foreign Policy of Castlereagh*, 65–66.

44. Ibid., 66.

45. One common imputed cause of this changed attitude toward force in the nineteenth century and the anomalous peace of that century in general is war-weariness. The Napoleonic wars had been so terrible, the argument goes, that leaders had "learned" that war was bad and changed their normative frameworks. Schroeder offers a detailed refutation of this thesis that begins with the question, why would war-weariness have this transforming effect in 1815 but not after other arguably worse conflicts at other points in history, for example, the Thirty Years' War, which had many more battle deaths ("The 19th-Century International System," 1–26 at 4).

46. Ibid.; Luard, *Balance of Power*, 336. Holsti cites estimates that one-third of Germany's entire population died in the Thirty Years War and that Germany's total population declined from thirteen million to four million, or by 69 percent (*Peace and War*, 28–29).

47. Osgood and Tucker make this argument in *Force, Order, and Justice*, 79. I am grateful to Steve Walt for bringing it to my attention.

48. Schroeder, "The Nineteenth-Century System: Balance of Power or Political Equilibrium," 135–53; Seton-Watson, *Britain in Europe*, 381. I do not mean to imply here that Italian unification was bloodless, only that nineteenth-century rules created new "legal" means of expansion that had not existed previously.

49. This was unusual in European history. Before 1648, religions established inside states were considered threatening and cause for war. After 1815, dynastic monarchs perceived liberalism as a threat. After 1945, communist and capitalist states felt threatened by each other's organizing principles.

50. On normative and cultural "toolkits," see Ann Swidler, "Culture in Action: Symbols and Strategies," *American Sociological Review* 51 (1986): 273–86; on framing, see Erving Goffman, *Frame Analysis: An Essay on the Organization of Experience* (Cambridge, Mass.: Harvard University Press, 1974); David Snow, E. Burke Rochford, Steven K. Worden, and Robert D. Benford, "Frame Alignment Processes, Micromobilization, and Movement Participation," *American Sociological Review* 51 (1986): 464–81; David Snow, "Master Frames and Cycles of

Protest," in *Frontiers in Social Movement Theory,* ed. Aldon Morris and Carol McClurg Mueller (New Haven: Yale University Press, 1992), 133–55; Sidney Tarrow, *Power in Movement: Social Movements, Collective Action, and Politics* (New York: Cambridge University Press, 1994), esp. chap. 7.

51. "Ce sont les brigands qui récusent la gendarmerie, et les incendiares qui protestent contre les pompiers.... [N]ous nous reconnaîtrons ... toujours le droit de nous rendre à l'appel que nous adressera une autorité légale en faveur de sa defense, tout comme nous nous reconnaissons celui d'aller éteindre le feu dans la maison du voisin, pour empêcher qu'il ne gagne la nôtre" [These are brigands who resist the police and arsonists who obstruct firefighters. We always recognize our right to appeal to a legal authority for defense just as we recognize our duty to put out a fire in our neighbor's house to prevent it from burning our own] (Metternich, *Mémoires,* 3:505, as quoted in Carsten Holbraad, *The Concert of Europe: A Study in German and British International Theory, 1815–1914* [London: Longman, 1970], 32). Gentz articulates similar views in *Fragments,* 112.

52. Lord John Russell justified his Italian policy by appealing to "the doctrines of the Revolution of 1688," arguing that "all power held by Sovereigns may be forfeited by misconduct" (Lord John Russell to Queen Victoria, January 11, 1860, cited in Seton-Watson, *Britain in Europe,* 404). This common history of 1688 did not prevent great disagreement within Britain about what, exactly, constituted a ruler's misconduct.

53. For more on the many facets of these debates in Britain and on the Continent, and their relation to both natural and positive international law, see Holbraad, *The Concert of Europe;* R. J. Vincent, *Nonintervention and International Order* (Princeton, N.J.: Princeton University Press, 1974), esp. chaps. 2–4; and Winfield, "The History of Intervention in International Law," 130–49. Note that international law writings at this point in the nineteenth century lie in the realm of philosophy and morals.... [I]nternational law does not become a profession with extensive practical applications until later in that century.

54. For more on these debates, see Vincent, *Nonintervention and International Order,* 64–103; Seton-Watson, *Britain in Europe,* chaps. 1–5; Temperley and Penson, *Foundations of British Foreign Policy,* 47–63, 82–116; and Kissinger, *A World Restored,* 11–16.

55. Seton-Watson, *Britain in Europe,* 57–8. For excellent discussions of the different parties' positions in these debates over intervention, see Vincent, *Nonintervention and International Order,* 70–102; Temperley and Penson, *Foundations of British Foreign Policy,* esp. 47–67 (Castlereagh's State Paper of May 5, 1820, 81–87; Canning's Doctrine of Guarantee and his views on constitutions, 88–136; assorted documents by Palmerston, including debates with Metternich).

56. Castlereagh's State Paper of May 20, 1805, is the clearest statement of the British position, and later British statesmen appeal to it. It is reprinted in Temperley and Penson, *Foundations of British Foreign Policy,* 48–63; quote on 62. The "principles of 1688" argument was not only or even principally a foreign policy argument. As Castlereagh makes clear, parliamentary opposition to most of the Holy Alliance's opposed interventions would have been huge, in part because many Britons favored the reforms of the revolutionaries.

57. Webster, *Foreign Policy of Castlereagh,* 259–64; Vincent, *Nonintervention and World Order,* 78–9, 83; Seton-Watson, *Britain in Europe,* 56.

58. See Walter LaFeber, *America, Russia, and the Cold War, 1945–1975,* 3d ed. (New York: Wiley, 1976); John Lewis Gaddis, *Russia, the Soviet Union, and the United States: An Interpretive History,* 2d ed. (New York: McGraw-Hill, 1990): Deborah Welch Larson, *Origins of Containment: A Psychological Explanation* (Princeton, N.J.: Princeton University Press, 1985); Ernest R. May, ed., *American Cold War Strategy: Interpreting NSC 68* (Boston: Bedford Books, 1993); John Lewis Gaddis, *We Now Know: Rethinking Cold War History* (New York: Oxford University Press, 1992): Vladislav Zubok and Constantine Pleshakov, *Inside the Kremlin's Cold War* (Cambridge, Mass.: Harvard University Press, 1996).

59. Melvyn P. Leffler, *The Specter of Communism: The United States and the Origins of the Cold War, 1917–1953* (New York: Hill and Wang, 1994), vii.

60. Ronald Reagan's description of the Soviet Union as an "evil empire," for example, contrasts sharply with the way nineteenth-century statesmen spoke about one another and about other states in the system. Castlereagh and Metternich certainly did not view each other or each other's states as "evil."

61. The Americans did value multilateralism within their sphere and actively tried to build up both Europe and Japan as centers of power, but their aim was power sharing within their sphere only. They had no interest in aiding or protecting Soviet states as a systemic good.

62. For a related view of intervention in this period written during the cold war, see Philip Windsor, "Superpower Intervention," in *Intervention in World Politics,* ed. Hedley Bull (New York: Oxford University Press, 1984), 45–65.

63. Robert H. Jackson and Mark W. Zacher, "The Territorial Covenant: International Security and the Stabilization of Boundaries" (Vancouver: Institute of International Relations, Working Paper No. 5, University of British Columbia, July 1997).

64. Michael Barnett, "The New United Nations and the Politics of Peace: From Juridical to Empirical Sovereignty," *Global Governance* 1, no. 1 (winter 1995): 79–97.

65. One testament to the power of these norms is the lengths to which states, including superpowers, went to preserve the forms and rituals of self-determination by resident nations in the state. Elaborate demonstrations of "the will of the people" (elections, rallies) were manufactured and advertised internationally by governments where they had no relation to political decision making or control. For theoretical discussions of why it is to important for states to maintain the appearance of conforming to these norms, even or especially when they violate them, see Robert Jackson, *Quasi-States: Sovereignty, International Relations, and the Third World* (Cambridge: Cambridge University Press, 1990); and John W. Meyer and Brian Rowan, "Institutionalized Organizations: Formal Structure as Myth and Ceremony," *American Journal of Sociology* 83 (1977): 340–63.

66. Neil Matheson, *The "Rules of the Game" of Superpower Military Intervention in the Third World, 1975–1980* (New York: University Press of America, 1982), 19–24.

67. Small states often tried to use self-determination norms to justify these changes, especially when the changes were broadly popular, but superpowers usually rejected these justifications.

68. Matheson provides an extended discussion of this in his *"Rules of the Game,"* chap. 5.

69. Ibid., chap. 6.

70. Obviously there might be other reasons for secrecy about one's involvement in the affairs of other states. My point is only that the legitimacy of the target government was not one of these reasons.

71. For an alternative view of the role of multilateral norms in U.S. foreign policy, see David Lake, *Entangling Relations: American Foreign Policy in Its Century* (Princeton, N.J.: Princeton University Press, 1999), esp. chap. 6. Note that the non-state status of the September 11 attackers made appropriate legal response for the United States in that instance less clear than in the case of Kuwait.

72. Ruggie, *Multilateralism Matters.* Slaughter's essay in Ruggie's edited volume traces multilateral norms established in international politics after 1945 to U.S. domestic legal norms, but see Christian Reus-Smit's argument, in *The Moral Purpose of the State: Culture, Social Identity, and Institutional Rationality in International Relations* (Princeton, N.J.: Princeton University Press, 1999), chap. 6, that American "moral purpose" was necessary but not sufficient for the emergency of contemporary multilateral norms.

73. Barnett, "The New United Nations and the Politics of Peace," 79–97.

74. Audie Klotz, *Protesting Prejudice: Apartheid and the Politics of Norms in International Relations* (Ithaca, N.Y.: Cornell University Press, 1995).

75. Michael Barnett and Martha Finnemore, "The Politics, Power, and Pathologies of International Organizations," *International Organization* 53, no. 4 (1999): 699–732 at 712.

Chapter 3

WORLD WAR I: WORLD ON FIRE

3.1

THE COMING OF THE FIRST WORLD WAR: A REASSESSMENT

Marc Trachtenberg

These excerpts from a much longer chapter in Marc Trachtenberg's book *History and Strategy* (which you should read if you get interested) illustrate an explanation of World War I that falls between a liberal perspective that the war was accidental (caused by path dependence and unintended consequences) and an offensive realist perspective that the war was intentional (caused by expansionist aims). Working at a domestic and foreign policy level of analysis, Trachtenberg counters arguments that the war was caused primarily by rigid military plans, military strategies based on the "cult of the offensive," or misunderstandings about what mobilization meant. Rather, he argues, leaders, although not intending to cause a war, nevertheless were ready to accept it and did not do enough to avoid it. They later cultivated explanations that the war occurred because of factors beyond their control to deflect responsibility for their decisions.

The idea that a great war need not be the product of deliberate decision—that it can come because statesmen "lose control" of events—is one of the most basic and most common notions in contemporary American strategic thought. A crisis, it is widely assumed, might unleash forces of an essentially military nature that overwhelm the political process and bring on a war that nobody wants. Many important conclusions, about the risk of nuclear war and thus about the political meaning of nuclear forces, rest on this fundamental idea.[1]

Source: Marc Trachtenberg, "The Coming of the First World War: A Reassessment," in *History and Strategy* (Princeton, N.J.: Princeton University Press, 1991), 47–99.

This theory of "inadvertent war" is in turn rooted, to a quite extraordinary degree, in a specific interpretation of a single historical episode: the coming of the First World War during the July Crisis in 1914.[2] It is often taken for granted that the sort of military system that existed in Europe at the time, a system of interlocking mobilizations and of war plans that placed a great emphasis on rapid offensive action, directly led to a conflict that might otherwise have been avoided. "The war systems of the day," Paul Bracken says, "stimulated each other into a frenzy. Political leaders lost control of the tremendous momentum built up when their armies went on alert."[3] It was as though an enormous, uncontrollable machine had begun to move. There was, Thomas Schelling writes, "a great starting of engines, a clutching and gearing and releasing of brakes and gathering momentum until the machines were on collision course."[4] "Armies," says Michael Howard, "were juggernauts which even their own generals could hardly control."[5]

* * *

The main purpose of this article is to examine the idea that World War I was in this sense an inadvertent war. Before this analysis can begin, however, there is one major issue that first has to be cleared up. It is necessary at the outset to examine the claim that Germany deliberately set out from the very start of the crisis to provoke a European conflict. For if World War I were in essence a war of German aggression, one could hardly claim that it came about because a political process, which might otherwise have brought about a peaceful settlement, had been swamped by forces from within the military sphere. It turns out that the argument that Germany contrived throughout the crisis to bring on a great war is quite weak, but this in itself does not mean that the European nations simply stumbled into the conflict. A positive case has to be made if the "inadvertent war" thesis is to be accepted. To test this theory, the specific arguments on which it rests therefore have to be examined, and the most important of these arguments will be analyzed here: claims about the rigidity of military plans, about the "cult of the offensive," and, most importantly, about preemption and interlocking mobilizations. What this analysis will show is that this theory, broadly speaking, is not supported by the evidence. The war did not break out in 1914 because events had "slipped out of control"—because statesmen had been overwhelmed by forces that brought on a conflict that all the governments had been trying to avoid.

* * *

The Rigidity of Military Plans

The argument that the German government consciously and systematically engineered a European war in 1914 is quite weak. If the war, however, cannot be attributed simply to German aggression, it does not automatically follow from this that it came about because statesmen "lost control" of events, and were overwhelmed by forces of a military nature. A positive argument has to be made, and indeed the "inadvertent war" theory rests on a series of claims which purport to lay out what those forces are—that is, what these mechanisms were that led to a war that otherwise might well have been avoided. To test the theory, these claims therefore need to be examined systematically.

The first of these arguments focuses on the nature of military planning in the period before 1914. It is often alleged that the "inflexibility" of operational thinking and the "rigidity" of war and mobilization plans played a very important role in bringing on the war.[6] The war plans themselves, it is said, had a momentum of their own which statesmen were in the end powerless to resist.

In support of this claim, one story is told over and over again. At the very last minute, on August 1, with the storm in its full fury about to break, the German government was told by its ambassador in London that Britain might remain neutral, and might even guarantee French neutrality, if Germany did not attack France and conducted the war only in the east. The emperor was jubilant and wanted to take the British up on this offer and march only against Russia. But General Helmuth von Moltke, the chief of the general staff, explained that Germany had only one war plan—what has come to be called the "Schlieffen Plan" after its architect, General Alfred von Schlieffen, head of the general staff from 1891 to 1905—and this provided only for a massive initial attack on France to be followed after France's defeat by a campaign against Russia. It was too late now, he said, to change that strategy; the plan would have to be carried out. The chancellor and the emperor, Gordon Craig writes—and this is characteristic of the way this story appears in many accounts—"had no answer for this and gave way."[7] It soon turned out that British views had been misunderstood, but Bernard Brodie's comment on the affair is typical of the way this story is interpreted: "The falsity of the initial report saved that particular episode from being utterly grotesque; but the whole situation of which it formed a part reveals a rigidity and a habit of pleading 'military necessity' that made it impossible after a certain point to prevent a war which no one wanted and which was to prove infinitely disastrous to all the nations concerned."[8]

This is certainly a wonderful story. The only problem with it is that it happens to be wrong on the most important point. On the issue of whether the attack on France had to proceed as planned, it was the Kaiser and not Moltke who won. This should have been clear from the most important source on the incident, Moltke's memoirs, written in November 1914 and published posthumously in 1922; Moltke's account is confirmed by a number of other sources, extracts from which appear in the sections on the episode in Albertini's book.[9] It is true that there was a violent argument on August 1 between Moltke and the political leadership about whether to accept what appears to be the British proposal. Although Moltke succeeded in convincing the emperor that for technical reasons the concentration in the west would have to "be carried out as planned," and that only after it was completed could troops be transferred to the east, a basic decision was made to accept the "offer." "In the course of this scene," Moltke wrote, "I nearly fell into despair." Bethmann then pointed out how important it was, in connection with this British proposal, that the plan for the occupation of neutral Luxemburg be suspended. "As I stood there the Kaiser, without asking me," Moltke went on, "turned to the aide-de-camp on duty and commanded him to telegraph immediate instructions to the 16th Division at Trier not to march into Luxemburg. I thought my heart would break." Moltke again pleaded that the very complicated mobilization plan, "which has to be worked out down to the smallest details," could not be changed without disastrous results. It was essential, he said, for Germany to secure control over the Luxemburg railroads. "I was snubbed with the remark that I should use other railroads instead. The order must stand. Therewith I was dismissed. It is impossible to describe the state of mind in which I returned home. I was absolutely broken and shed tears of despair."[10]

This story is of interest not only in itself, but also because it bears on the general issue of the relationship between strategy and policy in pre-war Europe. It is commonly argued that at least in Germany, and perhaps in Europe as a whole, there was an almost hermetic separation between military and political concerns. The war plans had been based mainly on technical military considerations; political considerations had been essentially ignored. The plans could not be adjusted to changing political conditions. Governments, on the other hand, had not been able to adjust their foreign policies to these immutable strategic realities, because the military authorities had kept the political leadership in the dark: the civilians were not familiar with the plans, and were thus overwhelmed during the crisis by military imperatives that they had not been able to anticipate.[11]

Had the plans been worked out essentially on the basis of technical military considerations—that is, had political considerations been largely ignored? Germany is held up as the principal case in point: the Schlieffen Plan, according to Gerhard Ritter, was rooted not "in political considerations, but exclusively in military-technical ones."[12] There is, however, a certain basis for skepticism on this issue. The German military leadership was not sealed off from its political counterpart: Schlieffen and Friedrich von Holstein, the leading figure at the Foreign Office in Schlieffen's day, were on particularly intimate terms.[13] The military leadership, as Ritter himself shows, had strong political convictions. The elder Moltke, chief of staff during the Bismarckian period, had, according to Gerhard Ritter, been very much against "territorial conquests in Russia or anywhere else." It is hard to believe that such a view was unrelated to the very conservative military strategy he had opted for.[14] The opposition of his nephew, the younger Moltke, on August 1, 1914, to any change in the German war plan, was based not just on narrow, military considerations, but on his skepticism that France would really keep out of a Russo-German war—that is, on what turned out be a perfectly realistic *political* judgment.[15]

* * *

The "Cult of the Offensive"

In Europe before 1914, there was a great bias in favor of offensive as opposed to defensive military operations; the attack was glorified, and highly offensive strategies were assumed to be the best way to conduct a war. This "cult of the offensive," it has been argued in recent years, was a root cause of a wide range of dangers that played an important role in bringing on the war.[16]

* * *

Stephen Van Evera in his influential article, "The Cult of the Offensive and the Origins of the First World War," identifies a series of dangers "which helped pull the world to war," and discusses how those dangers were linked to the emphasis on offensive military action.[17] Germany's expansionist policy, first of all, was rooted in a belief that the offense had the advantage. It was this, he says, that "made empire appear both feasible and necessary."[18] The "cult of the offensive," moreover, "magnified the incentive to preempt": the first strike or first mobilization advantage is more valuable in a world where small shifts in force ratios between states lead to major shifts "in their relative capacity to conquer territory." Furthermore, it was this belief in offense-dominance that caused people to be so concerned with impending shifts in the military balance: Germany's "window of opportunity" opened wider, and the "window of vulnerability" which German statesmen saw opening a few years down the road was taken more seriously than it would have been if German leaders had understood that it was the defense that really had the upper hand in land warfare at the time.[19] Indeed, the "cult" was based on an extraordinary misconception: if the military realities of 1914 had been understood, if the actual power of the defense had been recognized, the whole system would have been much more stable, and "in all likelihood, the Austro-Serbian conflict would have been a minor and soon-forgotten disturbance on the periphery of European politics."[20]

What is to be made of these arguments? That a "cult" existed, in the sense of a set of military practices considerably more extreme than what the objective situation truly warranted, seems to me beyond question. Scott Sagan, in criticizing the "cult of the offense" theorists, argued that it was the political need to support allies and relieve military pressure on them that led states to adopt offense strategies. Alliance considerations were of course important, but these strategies went well beyond what was needed for such purposes. Sagan, for example, in arguing that the French opted for a more offensive strategy because they were "haunted" by the prospect that if they stayed on the defensive, Germany would be able to defeat her opponents piecemeal, quotes General Joffre, the French chief of staff, as saying that the French increased the emphasis they placed on offensive action in part because they were afraid the Germans might return to the strategy of the elder Moltke for a campaign focusing on the east. It might have been necessary, of course, for France to prepare for offensive action against Germany as soon as there were indications that Germany was returning to the old Moltke strategy. But until she showed signs of doing so, a defensive strategy would have made more sense for the first phase of the war, since, as Sagan himself points out, "it has been generally recognized since Clausewitz that defense is almost always 'easier' in land warfare because of the advantages of cover and the capability to choose and prepare terrain and fortify positions."[21] Joffre's preference for offense at the beginning of the war, before France's allies had a chance to fully generate their own forces, can therefore scarcely be rationalized in terms of alliance considerations.[22]

It is one thing, however, to recognize the existence of a certain degree of irrationality in this area. It is quite another to show that it was in major ways responsible for the coming of the war. How well do the specific arguments about the relationship between the "cult" and the outbreak of the war hold up in the light of the evidence? The weakest claim relates to the alleged connection between German expansionism and the belief in offense-dominance. When one looks at such a broadly based phenomenon as German imperialism, it is difficult to see a technical judgment about the balance between offense and defense on the battlefield as a major driving force. Indeed, if such a judgment were the key factor, and physical security against land attack were the fundamental goal, one would expect German expansionism to have focused on adjoining areas in Europe. Instead, the interests Germany most actively pursued lay in Africa and the Near East. In an offense-dominant world, where security is (in Van Evera's term) a "scarce asset,"[23] one would expect a continental power like Germany to concentrate on building a strong land army; instead, resources were diverted into the construction of a great navy. The purpose of the navy was to help Germany acquire an empire. But even if she succeeded in acquiring colonies, this would hardly improve her security position: as the most clear-sighted Entente statesmen occasionally pointed out, German colonies would be hostage to Anglo-French naval power.[24] Whether this policy was successful or not, the whole effort was bound to have an unfavorable effect on Germany's security position: the policy in fact drove Britain onto the side of her enemies, thereby strengthening France and Russia and thus enabling them to pursue more aggressive anti-German policies, first in Morocco and then, with the formation of the Balkan League in 1912, in southeastern Europe as well.[25] Germany's position had been weakened by the policy; but she continued to pursue it, even when it became clear that she was paying such a price, and indeed was taking on Britain, France, and Russia all at the same time. This was hardly a world in which for Germany "security was scarce." Germany was not driven to expand because, in Jervis's phrase, "there seemed no way for [her] merely to retain and safeguard her existing position."[26] If that had been her basic goal, her foreign policy problems would have been quite manageable. As Kiderlen-Wächter, then foreign secretary, pointed out in 1910 in a passage quoted by Van Evera, the British and the French were too committed to peace to ever cause a war, so if Germany did not provoke one, "no one else certainly will do so."[27]

The "cult of the offensive" theorists are on firm ground when they turn to factors more purely military in nature. The various war plans, and above all the Schlieffen Plan, placed an extraordinary emphasis on offensive military operations: if a war was to be fought, total victory had to be the goal, and the only way to achieve it was by overwhelming the enemy as quickly as possible, and destroying his power to resist. But while these plans certainly reflected a belief that a heavy emphasis on offense was *necessary,* they did not reflect a belief that offense would be *easy.* The point of departure for the German strategy was Schlieffen's realization that French defenses on the border with Germany made direct attack out of the question, and indeed the chief of staff was fully aware of the defender's advantages: "We shall find the experience of all earlier conquerors confirmed, that a war of aggression calls for much strength, and also consumes much, that this strength dwindles constantly as the defender's increases, and all this particularly in a country with fortresses."[28]

A strategy of this sort led to a certain interest in preemption. A swift seizure of the Belgian city of Liège became an important part of the German war plan in 1911. The Liège fortress system, Moltke wrote, had to be neutralized at the very beginning of the war: "everything depends on meticulous preparation and surprise."[29] It is not altogether clear, however, what role such considerations played in bringing on the war; the "cult of the offensive" theorists are in any case quite moderate in their claims about preemption.[30] But whatever interest there was in preemption in 1914, it is important to note that it was not rooted in a belief that conquest would be easy. It was because conquest was viewed as so difficult that small advantages, which if seized might just swing the balance, could count for so much on the margin—that is, as long as one was absolutely committed to total victory. Nor is it clear that preemption would have been less likely if the Germans had not opted for the Schlieffen strategy. If they *had* been able to see what the war was going to be like, and had chosen to stay on the defensive in the west and fought the war mainly in the east—that is, the more rational strategy that Van Evera assumes they would have adopted if no "cult of the offensive" had existed[31]—the slowness of the Russian mobilization might still have given the Germans a great incentive to act quickly and attack the Russians before their preparations were complete. Indeed, the elder Moltke's final plan, worked out in 1888, provided for "the encirclement of the main Russian force behind Warsaw and a surprise attack while it was deploying."[32]

Van Evera's strongest argument relates to "windows" and preventive war. In 1914, victory was still possible; but the balance was moving against Germany, and it is certainly true that many influential people thought that Germany should take advantage of what we would now call this "window of opportunity" before it closed and perhaps deliberately bring about a war.[33] The preventive war argument in its pure form was particularly strong in the army. The views of the political leadership were less extreme. From its point of view, given the way things were moving, there was a good chance that Germany would eventually find herself at war with the Entente; this was especially true if Russia was determined to tighten the noose around the Central Powers; if such a war was inevitable, it was better for Germany that it come sooner rather than later; and the test of its inevitability, the test of Russian intentions, was whether the Russians would now tolerate a tough Austrian policy against Serbia. A policy of annihilating Serbia as an independent factor in European politics was thus for Germany, as Naumann put it at the time, "the touchstone whether Russia meant war or not."[34]

This assessment of how the balance was shifting—this sense that Germany's "window of opportunity" was closing rapidly—was in turn rooted in the sort of strategy that Germany had adopted, the highly offense-oriented strategy embodied in the Schlieffen Plan. This plan depended on the existence of a tactical "window": Germany would be able to attack France with the great mass of her army because the slowness of Russian mobilization meant that Germany's eastern border would not have to be heavily defended during the initial phase of the war. But with the construction of Russian strategic railroads and other measures, this tactical "window" was disappearing—indeed, the central purpose of these measures was to close it[35]—and this meant that the Schlieffen Plan would soon become unworkable. In other words, the disappearance of the tactical window meant that Germany's strategy window was also closing.[36] With a more defensive strategy, the "preventive war" arguments would have carried much less weight.

This does not in itself mean, however, that "window" thinking was an important cause of the war. The reason is that these "window" arguments should have had opposite effects on the two sides: Germany's "window of opportunity" was the Entente's "window of vulnerability," and although Germany had an extra incentive to act, Russia and France had an extra incentive to be cautious and put off the conflict if they could. It seems in fact that Russian leaders understood the situation in these terms.[37] Why did the two effects not cancel each other out? If they did not neutralize each other, other factors must have intervened, in which case they, and not the "window" arguments, were the crucial factors as far as the war origins question is concerned. And certainly some of these factors were not military in nature—for example, the astonishing irrationality of the Russian leadership at the time, in the sense of its willingness to plunge into a venture that it knew was beyond Russia's strength.[38]

* * *

Mobilization Plans and Preemption

"World War I," says George Quester, "broke out as a spasm of pre-emptive mobilization schedules."[39] It was this system of interlocking mobilization plans, Paul Bracken writes, that "swamped the political process in 1914."[40] Statesmen tried to draw back on the eve of the war, according to Barbara Tuchman, "but the pull of military schedule dragged them forward."[41] A. J. P. Taylor agrees: in

1914, Schlieffen's "dead hand automatically pulled the trigger."[42] Arguments of this sort are extremely common and form the heart of the "inadvertent war" thesis. Given how important and how widespread they are, it is amazing how little critical analysis such arguments have received.[43]...

It is not that the conventional wisdom is wrong in assuming that there was a system of interlocking mobilization plans in 1914. A system of this sort certainly did exist, with the Schlieffen Plan as its linchpin. That strategy proposed to take advantage of the relative slowness of Russian mobilization: the idea was that Germany, by mobilizing rapidly and then attacking in the west with the great mass of her army, would be able to defeat France before having to face Russia. The Germans could not therefore allow a Russian general mobilization to run its course without ordering their own mobilization and in fact attacking France. Russian mobilization would lead to German mobilization, and under the German war plan mobilization meant war.

A mechanism of this sort clearly existed, but was it actually a *cause* of the war? It is important to think through what is implied by the claim that this mechanism of interlocking mobilization plans helped bring on the cataclysm. One can begin with a simple analogy. Suppose it takes me thirty minutes to get home when the traffic is light, but a full hour during the rush hour. I promise to be home by 6:00, but I choose to leave at 5:30 and arrive a half-hour late: "I'm sorry about the delay, but it's not my fault. It was because the traffic was so bad." The rush hour traffic, however, could hardly be said to be a *cause* of the delay, since I had chosen to leave at 5:30, knowing full well what the situation was. Knowledge of the situation had been factored into the original decision. On the other hand, if the heavy traffic had been caused by something that had not been anticipated—by an accident, for example—then it would make more sense to blame it for the delay.

Similarly, if in 1914 everyone understood the system and knew, for example, that a Russian general mobilization would lead to war, the existence of the system of interlocking mobilization plans could hardly be said in itself to have been a cause of war—assuming, that is, that the political authorities were free agents and that their hands had not been forced by military imperatives. Some people argue that the mobilization system was a "cause" of war because once it was set off the time for negotiation was cut short. But if the working of the system was understood in advance, a decision for general mobilization was a decision for war; statesmen would in that case be opting for war with their eyes open. To argue that the system was a "cause" of the war would be like arguing that any military operation that marked the effective beginning of hostilities—the crossing of borders, for example, or an initial attack on enemy forces—was a real cause of an armed conflict, simply because it foreclosed the possibility of a negotiated settlement. Such operations are in no real sense a "cause" of war, because their implications are universally understood in advance. Similarly, assuming everyone understood how the system worked, the mobilization process could not be viewed as a cause of the war, but should instead be seen simply as its opening phase.

* * *

Conclusion

* * *

Did the war come because statesmen in 1914 were overwhelmed by forces they could not control, and, for the most part, scarcely even understood? Was Europe carried into war by the rigidity of its military plans and by the premium they placed on preemption? Was the problem rooted in the fact that military planning had taken place in a political vacuum, that the soldiers were apolitical technicians, that the political leadership had been kept in the dark? During the crisis, were the political leaders stampeded into war by the generals and by the system the military had created? Did the political authorities surrender to the generals, who eventually took control of policy and made the crucial decisions that led to the war?

The answer in every case is essentially no. The military plans were not based on purely technical considerations; the generals had strong political views of their own, which were certainly reflected in the strategies they adopted. The political leaders were well aware of the basic thrust of the war plans, and they understood what they meant—not to the last detail of course, but they did understand the basic logic of the situation that these plans had created. There was, moreover, no "capitulation" to the generals; the military had in no real sense taken control of policy.

The First World War did not come about because statesmen had "lost control" of events; preemption was not nearly as important in 1914 as is commonly assumed. Instead of generals "pounding the table for the signal to move," one finds Falkenhayn saying on the 29th that it would not matter much if Germany mobilized two or three days after Russia, and Moltke that same day not even supporting the proclamation of the "Kriegsgefahrzustand." On the afternoon of the 30th, Moltke did begin to press for military measures, but this was very probably in reaction to what the Russians were doing in this area. As long as German policy was reactive, it can hardly be considered a source of "instability" in the contemporary sense of the term.

The Russian generals, on the other hand, did press for early mobilization. But this was only because they thought that war was unavoidable, a view that the civilian government also shared. A decision for general mobilization was a decision for war: it was not that Sazonov and the political leadership as a whole were trying desperately to preserve the peace, but were drawn into the abyss by the "pull of military schedules." It hardly make sense, therefore, to see the Russian decision to seize the military advantages of the first mobilization as proof that "control had been lost" or that war had come "inadvertently." In 1941, the Japanese government attacked American forces at Pearl Harbor and in the Philippines after becoming convinced that war with the United States could not be avoided. Even if this judgment had been mistaken—even if one assumes that President Roosevelt could not have taken the country into war if the Japanese had avoided contact with American forces and limited their attack to the Dutch East Indies—no one would say that the fact that the Japanese chose to seize the first strike advantage by launching a surprise attack against vulnerable American forces means that the War in the Pacific was essentially an "inadvertent" conflict. The same point, however, applies to 1914.

The idea that the First World War came about because statesmen were overwhelmed by military imperatives and thus "lost control" of the situation came to be accepted for essentially political reasons, and not because it was the product of careful and disinterested historical analysis. It was hardly an accident that the first to propagate this idea were the statesmen whose policies in 1914 had led directly to the conflict—that is, the very people who had the greatest interest in avoiding responsibility for the catastrophe. On the very eve of the disaster—on July 31, 1914—Bethmann was already arguing along these lines.[44]

After the war, it became apparent that the Germans would never accept a peace settlement based on the notion that they had been responsible for the conflict. If a true peace of reconciliation was to take shape, it was important to move toward a new theory of the origins of the war, and the easiest thing was to assume that no one had really been responsible for it. The conflict could be readily blamed on great impersonal forces—on the alliance system, on the arms race and on the military system that had evolved before 1914. On their uncomplaining shoulders the burden of guilt could be safely placed. For many people, it thus became an article of faith that military factors, and especially the arms competition, had led directly to the catastrophe. "Great armaments," Grey, for example, wrote in his memoirs, "lead inevitably to war." This, he said, was the obvious moral to be drawn from a study of the pre-1914 period.[45]

* * *

Notes

1. For a penetrating analysis of the question of "loss of control," see Robert Powell, "The Theoretical Foundations of Strategic Nuclear Deterrence," *Political Science Quarterly,* vol. 100, no. 1 (Spring 1985), esp. pp. 83–92.
2. See, for example: Thomas Schelling, *Arms and Influence* (New Haven, Conn., 1966), pp. 221–25; Graham Allison, Albert Carnesale, and Joseph Nye, eds., *Hawks, Doves, and Owls: An Agenda for Avoiding Nuclear War* (New York, 1985), pp. 17–18, 30, 43, 210, 217; Richard Ned Lebow, *Nuclear Crisis Management: A Dangerous Illusion* (Ithaca, N.Y., 1987), pp. 24–26, 32–35, 59–60, 109–13, 122–23. Note also the rather extreme argument in Paul Bracken's *The Command and Control of Nuclear Forces* (New Haven, Conn., 1983). This book is

laced with references to the July Crisis; see esp. p. 65 where Bracken admits that his argument about how a nuclear war could begin might sound a bit extreme "were it not for the history of the outbreak of World War I." A certain interpretation of the Cuban Missile Crisis is also frequently used to support the inadvertent war theory. For an analysis of that interpretation, see Marc Trachtenberg, "New Light on the Cuban Missile Crisis?" *Diplomatic History,* vol. 14, no. 2 (Spring 1990).

3. Bracken, *Command and Control,* p. 53.

4. Schelling, *Arms and Influence,* p. 221.

5. Michael Howard, "Lest We Forget," *Encounter* (January 1964), p. 65.

6. See, for example: Bernard Brodie, "Unlimited Weapons and Limited War," *The Reporter,* November 18, 1954, p. 21; Howard, "Lest We Forget," p. 65; Gordon Craig, *The Politics of the Prussian Army* (New York, 1964), p. 295. For the most influential account: Barbara Tuchman, *The Guns of August* (New York, 1962), esp. pp. 72, 79, 169. These are, of course, all old, and—from the point of view of many contemporary historians—outdated sources. But they played an important role in shaping beliefs about the meaning of the July crisis in what remain the classic works in the strategic studies literature, and are still frequently cited in that literature. Since the present aim is not simply to report contemporary historical opinion, but rather to examine certain traditional views, these older works will be taken seriously here—not because of their intrinsic merit, but simply because they provided the basis for what are still strongly held beliefs about the coming of the war, beliefs which have an important bearing on how the fundamental problem of war and peace is approached today.

7. Craig, *Politics of the Prussian Army,* p. 294. See also Fritz Fischer, *Germany's Aims in the First World War* (New York, 1967), p. 86; Barry Posen (citing Craig), "Inadvertent Nuclear War? Escalation and NATO's Northern Flank," *International Security,* vol. 7, no. 2 (Fall 1982), p. 32; Brodie, "Unlimited Weapons and Limited War," p. 21.

8. Brodie, "Unlimited Weapons and Limited War," p. 21.

9. Helmuth von Moltke, *Erinnerungen—Briefe—Dokumente,* 1877–1916 (Stuttgart, 1922); extracts appeared in translation in *Living Age,* January 20, 1923, pp. 131–34. Luigi Albertini, *The Origins of the War of 1914* (London, 1952–57), vol. 3, pp. 171–81, 380–85. See also Harry Young, "The Misunderstanding of August 1, 1914," *Journal of Modern History,* vol. 48, no. 4 (December 1976), pp. 644–65.

10. Quoted in Albertini, *Origins,* vol. 3, pp. 172–76. It is sometimes argued that despite the Kaiser's order, the Luxemburg frontier was violated, and that this shows that the plans had a momentum of their own, which the political leadership was unable to control. In fact, an infantry company had moved into Luxemburg before the Kaiser's order had been received, but a little later a second detachment arrived and ordered it out (in accordance, one assumes, with the Kaiser's instructions). This episode thus scarcely proves that central control over military operations had been lost. The story has been clear since the publication of the Kautsky documents in 1919, the source Tuchman relies on for her accurate account in *Guns of August,* p. 82. Note also the story about the revocation of the Russian general mobilization order by the Tsar after he had agreed to it the first time on July 29. According to one account, when the Chief of Staff told him "that it was not possible to stop mobilization, Nicholas had replied: 'Stop it all the same,'" and of course this order was respected. Albertini,

Origins, vol. 2, p. 560. See also the excellent analysis and refutation of Conrad's claim that technical military requirements prevented him from adjusting his strategy to the new situation created by Russian mobilization in N. Stone, "Moltke and Conrad: Relations between the Austro-Hungarian and German General Staffs, 1909–1914," in Paul Kennedy, ed., *The War Plans of the Great Powers, 1880–1914* (London, 1979), pp. 235–412; see also Stone's chapter on Austria–Hungary in Ernest May, ed., *Knowing One's Enemies: Intelligence Assessment before the Two World Wars* (Princeton, 1984).

11. See, for example, Craig, *Politics of the Prussian Army,* p. 25; Howard, "Lest We Forget," p. 65; Albertini, *Origins,* vol. 2, pp. 479–83, 579; and, for a more contemporary example, Richard Ned Lebow, "The Soviet Offensive in Europe: The Schlieffen Plan Revisited?" *International Security* (Spring 1985), p. 69. Some other examples are cited and then criticized in L. C. F. Turner, "The Role of the General Staffs in July 1914," *Australian Journal of Politics and History,* vol. 11, no. 3 (December 1965).

12. Gerhard Ritter, *The Schlieffen Plan: Critique of a Myth* (London, 1958), p. 97. Note also Fischer's comment on the plan to violate the neutrality of the Low Countries: "The military technician Schlieffen had taken no account of the political implications of such violations of neutrality and it was not really for him to do so." Fritz Fischer, *War of Illusions: German Policies from 1911 to 1914* (New York, 1975), p. 391.

13. Norman Rich, *Friedrich von Holstein: Politics and Diplomacy in the Era of Bismarck and William II,* vol. 3 (Cambridge, Mass., 1965), p. 698.

14. Ritter, *Schlieffen Plan,* p. 18.

15. See the extracts from Moltke's memoirs quoted in Albertini, *Origins,* vol. 3, pp. 173–74. On these issues in general, see M. Messerschmidt, *Militar und Politik in der Bismarckzeit und in Wilhelminischen Deutschland* (Darmstadt, 1975).

16. Stephen Van Evera, "The Cult of the Offensive and the Origins of the First World War," *International Security,* vol. 9, no. 1 (Summer 1984), esp. pp. 58, 105; see also Jack Snyder, "Civil-Military Relations and the Cult of the Offensive, 1914 and 1984," *International Security,* vol. 9, no. 1 (Summer 1984). Note also Steven Miller's introduction to the issue of *International Security* in which these articles appeared: "The Great War and the Nuclear Age: Sarajevo after Seventy Years," pp. 3–5. The whole issue was republished as Steven Miller, ed., *Military Strategy and the Origins of the First World War* (Princeton, 1985). Note also in this context the section "Deterrence and World War II; Spiral Model and World War I," in Robert Jervis, *Perception and Misperception in International Politics* (Princeton, 1976), pp. 94ff.

17. Van Evera, "Cult of the Offensive"; the quotation is on p. 105.

18. Ibid., p. 68.

19. Ibid., pp. 64–65, 79ff.

20. Ibid., p. 105. See also Jervis, "Cooperation under the Security Dilemma," *World Politics,* vol. 30, no. 2 (January 1978), pp. 191–214.

21. Scott Sagan, "1914 Revisited: Allies, Offense and Instability," *International Security,* vol. 11, no. 2 (Fall 1986), pp. 161, 164. See also the correspondence between Sagan and Snyder in *International Security,* vol. 11, no. 3 (Winter 1986–87).

22. The German emphasis on offense reflects a similar degree of irrationality. In his famous memorandum of December 1905, Schlieffen had outlined a strategy for a one-front war, but even this he thought was "an enterprise for which we are too weak." Over the next decade, Russia recovered her strength, and it became clear that Britain would probably intervene with a sizable expeditionary force. Schlieffen himself, in his writings after his retirement, ignored these factors; he suppressed his own skepticism about the "theory of a decisive battle" in the west; this, he had said in 1905, was "not the way of wars today." One answer was to increase the size of the force the Germans would be able to deploy when the war began; but although there were significant increases in the army budget before the war, the measures taken were by no means adequate to deal with the problem. A massive expansion was resisted in large part because it would have altered the social composition of the officer corps and thus might in the long run have reduced the power of the old Junker elite. But the plans were never adequately adjusted to all these realties. See Ritter, *Schlieffen Plan*, pp. 53, 66–67, 73–74, 77, and Jack Snyder, *The Ideology of the Offensive: Military Decision Making and the Disasters of 1914* (Ithaca, N.Y., 1984), pp. 139, 141–45, 153. For a similar point about Austria, see Samuel Williamson, "Military Dimensions of Habsburg-Romanov Relations during the Era of the Balkan Wars," in Bela Kiraly and Dimitrije Djordjevic, eds. *East Central European and the Balkan Wars* (Boulder, Colo., 1987), esp. pp. 330–31.
23. Van Evera, "Cult of the Offensive," p. 64.
24. See especially the remarkable analysis by Jules Cambon, French ambassador in Berlin: Cambon to Pichon, July 8, 1913, *Documents diplomatiques français,* series 3, vol. 7, no. 317, esp. p. 352.
25. When Poincaré, then prime minister, was shown the text of the basic treaty setting up the Balkan League, he remarked that "it contained the seeds not only of a war against Turkey, but of a war against Austria as well." Quoted in Pierre Renouvin, *La Crise européenne et la première guerre mondiale* (Paris, 1962), p. 173.
26. Jervis, "Security Dilemma," p. 173.
27. Quoted in Van Evera, "Cult of the Offensive," p. 69.
28. Quoted in Turner, "Schlieffen Plan," p. 50.
29. Moltke memorandum, in Ritter, *Schlieffen Plan,* p. 166.
30. Van Evera, "Cult of the Offensive," p. 79, says that the war was "in some modest measure preemptive." Snyder does not see preemption as a decisive factor for either Germany or Russia: "Civil-Military Relations," pp. 113–14.
31. Van Evera, "Cult of the Offensive," p. 90.
32. Ritter, *Schlieffen Plan,* p. 20.
33. On preventive war thinking in Germany before the war, see especially Walter Kloster, *Der deutsche Generalstab und deer Präventivkriegsgedanke* (Stuttgart, 1932); Adolf Gasser, "Deutschlands Entschluss zum Präventivkrieg 1913/14." In Marc Sieber, ed., *Discordia concors: Festgabe für Edgar Bonjour,* vol. 1 (Basel, 1968); and Albrecht Moritz, *Das Problem des Präventivkrieges in der deutschen Politik während der ersten Marokkokrise* (Frankfurt, 1974).
34. Geiss, *July 1914,* p. 66. Some of these considerations are reflected in other documents; see for example Szögyény to Berchtold, July 12, 1914, and Jagow to Lichnowsky, July

18, 1914, both in Geiss, *July 1914*, pp. 110, 123, and also Mérey's comments quoted in Albertini, vol. 2, p. 383. Note also an important letter from Count Hoyos describing his mission to Berlin at the beginning of the crisis (during which the famous "blank check" was issued). The Austrians wanted to know, Hoyos said, how the Germans felt about an Austrian move against Serbia, and in particular, "whether, from a political and a military point of view, it judged the moment as favorable." The chancellor and a top foreign office official replied that "if war should break out, we [that is, the Germans] think that it is better that it should happen now than in one or two years when the Entente will have become stronger." Hoyos to Mérey, July 20, 1917, *Revue d'histoire de la guerre mondiale*, vol. 10, no. 1 (January 1932), pp. 110–11.

35. This emphasis on the construction of strategic railroads thus reflects a basic understanding of the logic of the Schlieffen Plan by the French and Russian military leadership. The French were especially eager for the construction of these railroads, and made Russian cooperation in this area a condition for the issuance of new loans to Russia. This was thus not a subject that the military could keep to themselves; the civil authorities had to be brought in. Much of the story can be followed in *Documents diplomatiques français,* series 3, vols. 7–9; see also René Girault, *Emprunts russes et investissements français en Russie, 1887–1914* (Paris, 1973), pp. 561–68.

36. For an exceptionally well informed discussion of this issue, see Norman Stone, *The Eastern Front 1914–1917* (New York, 1975), pp. 39–43.

37. See, for example, I. V. Bestuzhev, "Russian Foreign Policy, February–June 1914," in Walter Laqueur and George Mosse, eds. *1914: The Coming of the First World War* (New York, 1966), p. 91, and also the testimony of General Yanushkevich, in 1914 the Chief of Staff, quoted in Albertini, *Origins*, vol. 2, p. 559.

38. In 1909, Russia had given in during the Bosnian Crisis after General Roediger, the war minister, had stated that the army could not even wage a defensive war against Germany and Austria. But the war minister in 1914, Sukhomlinov, while admitting in private, as Albertini says, that "Russia was throwing herself unprepared into a venture beyond her strength," and even warning Sazonov through an intermediary that Russia was not fully prepared for war, was unwilling to come out openly and tell the Council of Ministers what the real situation was. The minister of the interior, Maklakov, when asked to sign the mobilization *ukaze,* spoke about how war would bring revolution; but "sitting at a table laden with ikons and religious lamps," crossed himself, saying "we cannot escape our fate," and then signed the document. Albertini, *Origins,* vol. 2, p. 546; Lieven, *Russia and the Origins of the First World War,* pp. 108–9, 115.

39. George Quester, *Deterrence Before Hiroshima* (New York, 1966), p. 17.

40. Paul Bracken, *Command and Control,* p. 2.

41. Tuchman, *Guns of August,* p. 72.

42. A. J. P. Taylor, *Illustrated History of the First World War* (New York, 1964), p. 15.

43. The best discussion is in Van Evera, "Cult of the Offensive," pp. 71–79.

44. Albertini, *Origins,* vol. 3, pp. 15–17.

45. Viscount Grey of Fallodon, *Twenty-Five Years* (New York, 1925), vol. 1, pp. 89–90. Arguments of this sort rarely take cognizance of even the basic figures on the defense burden, which in fact throw a very different light on this whole issue. In Germany, for example, defense spending as a proportion of national income had been somewhat

higher at the end of the Bismarckian period in 1889 and 1890 than it was on the eve of the war. Indeed, for most of the immediate prewar period, defense spending as a percent of GNP had been in decline, going from 2.98 percent in 1901 down to 2.46 percent in 1912, before rising back to 3.02 percent in 1913. (The corresponding figure for 1890 had been 3.47 percent.) If this was a race, Germany obviously was not running very hard: these figures are of course quite low by contemporary standards. The percentages were computed from the national income figures in B. R. Mitchell, *European Historical Statistics 1750–1970,* abridged edition (New York, 1978), table J1, and from the figures for defense spending in W. G. Hoffman, *Das Wachstum der deutschen Wirtschaft seit der Mitt des 19. Jahrhunderts* (Berlin, 1965), table 199, col. 6. Contemporary equivalents are conveniently summarized in the statistical tables in United States Arms Control and Disarmament Agency, *World Military Expenditures and Arms Transfers,* an annual publication available from ACDA's defense Program and Analysis Division.

3.2

THE JULY CRISIS AND THE OUTBREAK OF WORLD WAR I

Dale C. Copeland

If you like suspense, you'll love this account by Dale C. Copeland of the diplomacy of July 1914 that led to World War I. Here is a blow-by-blow, hour-by-hour drama that in the end cost 15 million people their lives. What went wrong? In contrast to Marc Trachtenberg's account in the previous selection, Copeland concludes that the war was fully intentional, not a consequence of interactive factors that led to war accidentally (liberal) or by resignation. Germany wanted war from the outset not because it was innately aggressive (offensive realism) but because Russia would become stronger in the future (defensive realism applied to the future). The solution was a "preventive war" (against a future, not presently visible threat) as long as Germany could blame that war on Russia and secure solid domestic support. Germany was not surprised by Britain's involvement, as Trachtenberg argues. Although Copeland examines diplomacy at the foreign policy level in excruciating detail, his account is systemic structural because the causes of war come ultimately from concerns of policymakers about the future structure of the balance of power, not from domestic pressures to avert a civil war or from the path-dependent, diplomatic dueling during the month of July. (The German chancellor, referred to in this excerpt as Bethmann, is Theodore von Bethmann Hollweg.)

* * *

Preference Orderings for the Key Actors

Each interpretation of the cause(s) of World War I depends heavily on an author's implicit or explicit views regarding the preferences of the actors for four main outcomes: localized war between Austria and Serbia; continental war of the great powers excluding Britain; world war which would include Britain; and a negotiated peace between the actors representing a maintenance to some

---

Source: Dale C. Copeland, "The July Crisis and the Outbreak of World War I," in *The Origins of Major War* (Ithaca: Cornell University Press, 2000), 79–117. Bracketed editorial insertions are present in the original except where identified as a volume editor's note.

degree of the status quo.[1] The inadvertent war thesis has to assume that German leaders, while they might have desired a localized war above all else, certainly preferred a negotiated peace to either a continental war or world war. Otherwise, major war would have been something Germany sought, instead of something it did not want but was unable to prevent. The "Fischer Controversy" was sparked exactly by Fischer's assertion that Berlin preferred continental war to a return to the status quo; Germany, Fischer asserts, wanted war, although not a world war with Britain included.

The problem with this debate, as will become clearer, is that it too narrowly circumscribes the nature of the possible outcomes seen by leaders in Germany. The four options listed above had subtle variants that were crucial to ultimate decision-making. Attached to the outcomes of continental war or world war were two possibilities: either the German public supports the war or it does not; and either Austria supports Germany militarily on the eastern front, or it does not.[2] Attached to the outcome of world war was the question of whether Britain might delay its involvement long enough to help Germany defeat France, or whether Britain would enter immediately. The negotiated peace outcome was also far more subtle than is commonly believed: there were at least eight different diplomatic solutions discussed at the critical stages of the crisis, ranging from one extreme—giving Austria essentially what it wanted, namely, the destruction of Serbia—to the other, where Russia would secure a return to the status quo.[3]

The essence of my argument is that German leaders, as Fischer suggests, saw continental war with domestic and Austrian support as their best option, and certainly preferred that option to a return to the status quo. More important, however, they saw a world war that had domestic and Austrian support as better not only than the status quo, but also than a negotiated peace that gave Austria a diplomatic victory almost equal to victory in a localized war (that is, one where Serbia would be effectively destroyed). If, however, domestic and Austrian support could not be secured, then Berlin preferred a negotiated peace.[4] As I show, Bethmann's strategy throughout July was thus to achieve the domestic and Austrian support required to fight either a continental or a world war and, once that was achieved, to cut off all possibility of a negotiated settlement.

Early July: Setting the Stage for Preventive World War

Archduke Ferdinand, heir to the Austrian throne, was assassinated on Sunday, 28 June. On 4 July Count Alexander Hoyos, the Foreign Ministry's chief of cabinet, was sent to Berlin to inform the Austrian ambassador, Szögyény, of Vienna's desire for action against Serbia. Szögyény met with Kaiser Wilhelm at Potsdam the next day. In the first meeting, about midday, the kaiser told Szögyény that he could not give a definite answer until he had consulted the chancellor, noting the risk of grave complications in Europe.[5] In the afternoon, however, the kaiser, after talks with Bethmann, assured Szögyény of

Germany's full support in whatever strong measures Austria chose to pursue. Austria had its "blank check."

Why did Germany press Austria to take such a hard-line stance, when in previous Balkan crises it had restrained its ally whenever Serbia was involved? There are three possible explanations: Berlin falsely assumed that Russia would not intervene (consistent with the inadvertent war thesis); Berlin expected and hoped that the conflict would remain localized but accepted the possibility of continental war (the notion of "calculated risk"); Berlin, seeking preventive war, expected and hoped that Russia *would* intervene so it could blame Russia for the general war to follow. The evidence supports the third interpretation.

Recall that Bethmann, in February 1913, had noted that it was impossible for Russia to be an inactive spectator should Austria attack Serbia. To uphold the inadvertent war or calculated risk theses, one has to argue that Bethmann and his associates had somehow forgotten the chancellor's own counsel a year and a half later. They had not. Foreign Office Undersecretary Zimmermann had let slip in conversations with Hoyos that an Austrian attack on Serbia would lead "with a probability of 90 percent to a European war."[6]

On 2 July, the Saxon minister in Berlin reported to his capital that should an Austro-Serbian war occur, the top officials in the Foreign Office believed that "Russia would mobilize and world war could no longer be prevented." He added that the military favored "allowing [this] thing to drift to war while Russia is still unprepared," although the kaiser might prevent this.[7] The Saxon plenipotentiary the next day communicated that Count Georg Waldersee, quarter-master general in the German General Staff, felt that everything depended on Russia's reaction: "I had the impression that they would regard it with favour [in Supreme Headquarters] if war were to come about now. Conditions and prospects would never become better for us."[8] Thus we see that of the key participants, only the kaiser was worried about the prospects of general war. The chancellor, his Foreign Office, and the military all viewed general war as a necessary evil to deal with the rise of Russia.

Perhaps the most telling evidence on the preference for general war comes in the diaries of Kurt Riezler, Bethmann's personal secretary and confidant. The diaries show that Bethmann, faced with the choice between German decline or fighting while Germany still had a chance, reluctantly put Germany on the path to war. On 6 July, the day after the blank check, the chancellor had a long talk with Riezler. Bethmann's secret news, Riezler recorded, "gives me a unnerving picture." Anglo-Russian naval negotiations were the last link in the chain.

> Russia's military power [is] growing rapidly; with the strategic extension [of Russian railways] into Poland the situation is intolerable. Austria increasingly weaker and immobile....
>
>   ... An action against Serbia can lead to a world war [*Weltkrieg*]. From a war, regardless of the outcome, the chancellor expects a revolution of

everything that exists.... Heydebrand said a war would lead to a strengthening of the patriarchal order.... The chancellor is furious about such
nonsense. Generally, delusion all around, a thick fog over the people.... The
future belongs to Russia, which grows and grows, and thrusts on us a heavier
and heavier nightmare.[9]

This passage highlights three points. First and most important is the clear
statement that general war is critical owing to Russia's growth. Second, Bethmann is not pushing Germany toward war to solve a domestic crisis. Instead, he
expects that war, regardless of whether Germany wins or loses, will only
increase the likelihood of social revolution at home. Third, Bethmann is aware
even by 6 July that any great power war will likely be a world war, not a continental war; that is, Britain will be involved.

These revelations align with his thinking up to July. Bethmann had written
to Lichnowsky in June that "not only the extremists, but even level-headed
politicians are worried at the increase in Russian strength.[10] On 20 July, three
days before Austria's ultimatum to Serbia, Riezler writes of another talk with
Bethmann. The feeling was that Russia, with its "tremendous dynamic power"
could "no longer be contained within a few years, especially if the present European constellation continues."[11] Bethmann's subordinates thought similarly.
On 25 July, Foreign Minister Jagow smiled as he confidentially told Theodore
Wolff, editor of the *Berlin Tageblatt,* that war would certainly occur soon if
things continued on as they were, "and in two years' time Russia would be
stronger than it is now." Wolff heard this logic reiterated later that day in conversations with Wilhelm von Stumm, political director of the Foreign Office.[12]

Three years later, Bethmann acknowledged to Wolff that preventive war had
dominated his thinking. Since the visit of Russian Foreign Minister Sazonov and
Russian Finance Minister K. N. Kokovtsov to Berlin in January 1914, "I had
the fear that war was becoming inevitable." The Russians had just received 500
million francs from Paris "under the familiar conditions," namely, that the
money would go to building strategic railways in Poland. Kokovstov "did not
want [war]." But "I sensed from him that he himself feared that this would set
a war in motion." To Wolff's statement that a diplomatic arrangement with
Russia might have been possible, the chancellor shot back: "Who can say? But
if war had come about later, Russia would have been in a better position. Where
would we have been then?"[13]

Bethmann's deep concern that war would lead to revolution is shown by his
comments in June to Lerchenfeld, the Bavarian minister to Berlin. Some still
thought that war might improve internal conditions, he noted. But he thought
"that the effects would be the exact opposite; a world war, with its incalculable
consequences, would greatly increase the power of Social Democracy, because
it had preached peace, and would bring down many a throne."[14] While this
quotation is Fischer's, it and the Riezler passage put the final nail in the coffin
of the argument that war was driven by domestic politics. Given Bethmann's

recognition that war only increased the chances of revolution, Germany's internal tensions should have inclined him toward peace. Yet systemic trends pushed him to war.

Bethmann's point to Riezler that the war would be a "world war" is consistent with his view in 1912 that Britain would act to uphold the balance of power. He never relinquished this view. On 5 June 1914, Bethmann told the leader of the National Liberal Party that "if there is a war with France, every last Englishman will march against us."[15] The day before, the chancellor noted to Lerchenfeld that through history, "British power had stood against the strongest power on the continent," and now would oppose Germany.[16] That the chancellor knew that world war, not continental war, was very likely should Russia react has great significance: it helps explode the myth that he scrambled to avoid war on 29 July.

Reinforcing the argument that Bethmann sought general war is a revealing entry in Riezler's diaries from 8 July:

> Message delivered by Hoyos to Franz Joseph.... The chancellor thinks that perhaps the old kaiser [i.e., Franz Joseph] will in the end decide against it. If the war comes from the East, so that we go to war for Austria and not Austria for us, then we have the prospect of winning it. If the war does not come because the czar does not want it or because an alarmed France counsels peace, then we still have the prospect [*so haben wir doch noch Aussicht*] of maneuvering the Entente apart over this matter.[17]

This passage not only expresses the expectation that general war is more likely than a localized war, but it strongly implies that the former is *preferable* to the latter. If war "comes from the East"—that is, if Russia is seen to be the initiator—then the Austrians will likely fall into line, and victory is possible. Yet if war is averted, Germany will "still" have the prospect of splitting the Entente. The "still" is critical since it indicates that localized war is seen as the second-best outcome (as in: "if we can't get A, then we can still get B"). Moreover, note that general war might be avoided not because Germany did not desire it, but because Russia, possibly restrained by France, might decide against intervention.

This discussion makes clear that by early July Berlin was seeking to bring on a preventive war, even a preventive world war, before it was too late.

Executing the Plan for General War

Between 8 and 23 July, there was what Imanuel Geiss calls the "lull before the storm."[18] Yet Bethmann and his associates were hardly relaxing. Although they had convinced Wilhelm and military leaders to go ahead with the planned holidays so as not to create suspicion abroad, behind the scenes they were actively preparing for the coming war. German public opinion had to be shaped to accept Russia as the aggressor; an Austrian ultimatum to Serbia had to be designed to preclude a negotiated settlement; Italy had to be convinced to join the German side through whatever means, including territorial concessions from Vienna; and as many secret military measures as possible had to be taken to facilitate immediate mobilization once it was announced.

A key concern was keeping Austria on the course to war against Serbia, so as to draw Russia in. The fear was that Vienna would get cold feet once Russia intervened. On 5 July, Minister of War Erich von Falkenhayn wrote to Moltke that Bethmann had "as little faith as I do that [Vienna] is really earnest," even if its language seemed resolute.[19] On July 9, Zimmermann told H. von Schoen, the Bavarian chargé d'affaires in Berlin, that he doubted that Vienna would really move against Serbia. These feelings were apparently shared by all German leaders.[20]

Berlin had the means to influence Vienna's behavior. Heinrich von Tschirschky, German ambassador in Vienna, was in constant contact with Austrian leaders and even attended many of their most important conferences. Berlin also wielded the ultimate weapon: the implied threat that Germany would abandon Austria to its enemies. On 8 July, Berchtold remarked to Hungarian Prime Minister Stephan von Tisza, after Tschirschky told him "most emphatically" that Berlin expected action, that it would see any Austrian-Serbian deal as a sign of weakness, "which must have repercussions on our position in the Triple Alliance and on Germany's future policy."[21]

The Austrian ultimatum to Serbia, delivered on 23 July, was designed to avoid any diplomatic solution, and German complicity here is beyond doubt. On 8 July, Tschirschky informed Berlin that Berchtold would make the demands impossible to accept.[22] Vienna, aware that Berlin was expecting such a stand, had Tschirschky relay Austria's position that "the note is being composed so that the possibility of its acceptance is *practically excluded.*"[23] The essential contents of the ultimatum were known by Berlin as early as 12 July, with the full text communicated 22 July, the evening before the ultimatum was to be delivered.[24] This gave German leaders almost a full day to reject the harshness of the demands if indeed they wanted to avoid a confrontation. They did not do this, and for good reason, since they were pressing Austria to be as harsh as possible.

Integral to the plan was the creation of the facade that Germany had no responsibility for the events that were to follow. From Riezler's diary on 14 July:

> Yesterday and today, [we] worked a little on an old web of lies [*Gespinsten*]. The countryside is wrapped up in it.... If war should come and the veil [*Schleier*] then should fall, the whole nation will follow, driven by need and danger. Victory is liberation. The chancellor thinks that I am too young not to succumb to the lure of the unknown, the new, the great movement. For him this action is a leap in the dark and a most serious duty. Kiderlen [foreign minister until 1912] had always said we must fight.[25]

Italy wanted as a price for its participation the Austrian-occupied territory of Trentino, Riezler continued. However, "one cannot talk to them beforehand; it would give away everything in Petersburg." If war came, "England [will] immediately march." Italy, however, would join in only if Germany's victory seemed assured.[26]

The chancellor was evidently setting the stage, however reluctantly, for a successful general war. This is also shown by the secret military measures taken even before the ultimatum was delivered. On 6 July, the navy had been quietly mobilized.[27] On 18 July, important preparations for mobilization were initiated in the key ministries in Berlin.[28] By the next morning, General Waldersee, who was in charge as Moltke remained on holiday, could tell Jagow that he was "ready to jump"; the General Staff was "all prepared."[29]

In conferences between 18 and 20 July, Bethmann met with Interior Ministry officials to discuss actions to ensure popular support for the war. The chancellor worried that all-out mobilization, despite its military benefits, "would not compensate for the damage which it would do in the political and ideological spheres."[30] Of particular concern was the reaction of the workers. On 23 July, Riezler records that if war came, Bethmann would "ensure himself [of the Social Democrats' support] by personally negotiating with them," and by offering guarantees against "red-baiters" in the military. Reflecting preparations taken, Riezler notes: "mobilization of transportation; secret war-defenses emphasized."[31] Two days later, and still before any word on Russian military measures, Riezler writes that Bethmann was constantly on the phone with the military. "Merchant marine has been warned. Havenstein [prepares] financial mobilization." Still, "at present, nothing may be done out in the open."[32]

The Austrian ultimatum was delivered at 6:00 P.M. on Thursday, 23 July. Only forty-eight hours were given for the Serbian reply. On 24 July, the Russians held a top level meeting to discuss the ultimatum. Given Russia's slow mobilization schedules, it was decided to start military preparations as a first step to either partial or general mobilization.[33]

To avert a diplomatic solution, Berlin meanwhile was pushing Austria to declare war on Serbia as soon as possible after the ultimatum deadline at 6:00 P.M., 25 July. Vienna, however, wanted to declare war only after mobilization was complete, and this was communicated to Berlin on 24 July. Since the Austrians required sixteen days to mobilize properly, Berlin immediately rejected this timetable. Austrian ambassador Szögyény telegraphed from Berlin on 25 July that Germany's position was that once Serbia rejected the demands, Austria's declaration of war should follow immediately. Any delay in war operations "is regarded as signifying the danger.... that foreign powers might interfere."[34] Yet the German fear was not that powers like Russia might intervene militarily; as we have seen, war with Russia was desired. Rather, Berlin was concerned that Russia might pressure Serbia to concede to avert general war. In addition, German leaders worried that without a declaration of war, another state might find a diplomatic way out: *Austria*. These dual fears are revealed in Schoen's report on 18 July of a conversation with Zimmermann. German leaders wanted Austria to act, he wrote, but Jagow and Zimmermann were doubtful. Vienna

> [did] not seem to have expected such an unconditional support ... and Mr. Zimmermann has the impression that it is almost embarrassing to the always timid and undecided authorities at Vienna not to be admonished by Germany to caution and self-restraint.... So it would have been liked even better here if [the Austrians] had not waited so long with their action against Serbia, and the Serbian Government had not been given time to make an offer of satisfaction on its own account, perhaps acting under Russo-French pressure.[35]

Ironically, it was the head of the Austrian army, Conrad, the man in Austria who had most supported preventive war over the previous five years who now resisted German pressure to declare war immediately. Berlin wanted the declaration by 28 July at the latest; Conrad argued internally for 12 August. On Monday afternoon, 27 July, Berchtold overruled Conrad and agreed to the German request. At 3:20 P.M, Tschirschky relayed to Berlin, "They have decided here to send out the declaration of war tomorrow, or the day after tomorrow at the latest, chiefly to frustrate any attempt at intervention."[36] Berchtold's report to Franz Joseph that evening shows his understanding of Berlin's logic: the Triple Entente "might make another attempt to achieve a peaceful settlement of the conflict unless a clear situation is created by the declaration of war."[37]

The reasons for German maneuvering here help to make sense of that great mystery on 1 August: Germany's surprise declaration of war on Russia. As we will see, the only plausible explanation for this action is the same as that for the declaration of war on 28 July, namely, Berlin's desire to forestall any last-minute diplomatic solution.

This takes us to the most critical seven days of the crisis, Sunday, 26 July to Saturday, 1 August. Interpretations of this week have been driven by the universally accepted belief that German civilian leaders—specifically Bethmann Hollweg—got cold feet on the night of 29–30 July and then tried but failed to keep Austria from pulling the system into war. This notion—critical to almost every explanation of the war[38]—grows out of two crucial telegrams, sent at 2:55 A.M and 3:00 A.M on July 30. The telegrams seem to show a German chancellor, worried that world war is about to occur, pleading with Austria to reach an agreement with Russia to keep the peace.[39]

Yet if one puts these telegrams within the context of everything happening that night, the previous two nights, and the next day, a very different picture emerges. As I discuss, these telegrams represent only one thing: Bethmann's effort to get the Austrians to moderate their position as it appears to the world, so that Russia would still be blamed for the general war to follow. Pinning responsibility on Russia, as noted, was essential to build domestic support, to ensure that Austria fought, and, it was hoped, to delay British intervention. Yet to achieve this, Russia had to be perceived as being poised to attack the

German homeland. Austria also had to be convinced not to back out through a negotiated solution with Russia. Finally, the world, and the German people in particular, had to believe that Russia mobilized while Germany and Austria were still seeking a peaceful outcome to the dispute. If any of these elements failed, the preventive war could not be successfully waged.

The German plan for achieving these ends consisted of seven carefully coordinated steps. First, Russia had to be provoked into at least partial mobilization against Austria—that is, a mobilization similar to the one in 1912–13. This was achieved not only by having Austria declare war on and then immediately attack Serbia, but also by falsely promising Petersburg that partial mobilization would not lead to general war. Second, Germany had to position itself as the honest broker, appearing to know little about Austria's tough stand, but desiring the localization of conflict. Third, Germany had to scare Russia into proceeding to a general mobilization that would direct Russian forces against Germany. At the same time, the public had to believe that fixed mobilization schedules meant that Germany was not to blame if, for security reasons, it felt it must preempt the enemy's attack.

Fourth, once Russian general mobilization was a given, Berlin had to ensure that the Russians did not get cold feet. This required softening German diplomatic rhetoric, to convince Petersburg that mobilization on both sides could proceed without automatically bringing on war. Fifth, the world had to believe that German and Austrian leaders were pursuing a negotiated solution until the end, but that Russian general mobilization had precluded a diplomatic solution. To this end, Austria had to appear to be negotiating seriously with Russia, and Germany had to appear to be actively mediating on behalf of peace. Sixth, Austrian leaders had to be prevented from negotiating a last-minute agreement with Russia. These last two steps worked against each other, since the more Vienna appeared to be negotiating by actually making concrete offers, the greater the chance that either Austria or Russia would find an acceptable negotiated solution. Austria thus would have to be pressed to present the appearance of negotiating, while actually keeping its demands extreme enough that Russia could not agree to them.

The seventh step was the most ingenious. Berlin would send Moscow an ultimatum, stating that Germany would have to go to mobilization in twelve hours, but giving no indication that mobilization would mean war. Then, as soon as the twelve-hour limit was up, Germany would surprise Russia with a declaration of war. As with the declaration of war on Serbia, this would preclude any last-minute negotiated solution. Germany thus would have its major war under the "favorable conditions" being sought for the previous two years.

Although this view seems to attribute supreme Machiavellian dexterity to German officials more often disparaged as incompetent bumblers, the following shows that it is the only consistent explanation for the events of the last week of the crisis. In fact, convincing the world that they were not in control of events was all part of the German plan. They were so successful that even eighty years later, the conflict is still seen as the archetype of a major war that no state wanted.

The Fateful Week: July 26 to August 1

In drawing Russia into a war, German leaders faced a possible dilemma: while they knew that Russia would not remain an inactive spectator should Austria attack Serbia, they also knew Moscow had no desire for war, if only because Russia was still rearming. Hence, even though a hard-line Austrian stance would probably push Russia to mobilize against Austria, as it had in 1912–13, the Russians might back down in the crunch if they knew the war would be general.

The evidence that Berlin knew that the Russians had status-quo intentions is overwhelming. On 16 June, Bethmann wrote Lichnowsky that while Russia now had more resolve to defend its interests in the Balkans, "I do not believe that Russia is planning an early war against us."[40] A month later, on 18 July, Jagow wrote Lichnowsky that "Russia is not ready to strike at present.... According to all competent observation, Russia will be prepared to fight in a few years. Then she will crush us by the number of her soldiers.... In Russia this is well known, and they are therefore determined to have peace for a few years yet."[41] A week later, Jagow confirmed to Wolff that "neither Russia, nor France, nor England wanted war."[42]

Even *after* word that Russia had started military preparations, Berlin knew that the Russians sought peace. On 30 July, in a session of the Prussian Ministry of State in which Bethmann said that "it was of the greatest importance to put Russia in the position of the guilty party," he also acknowledged: "Although Russia had proclaimed mobilization its mobilization measures could not be compared with those of the West European [powers]. Russian troops could remain standing in the state of mobilization for many weeks. Russia did not want a war, it had been forced by Austria to take this step."[43]

This evidence calls into question a critical element of the inadvertent war explanation, namely, that the Germans launched a preemptive war on the assumption that Russian mobilization signaled aggressive Russian intentions. Indeed, Bethmann's statement confirms that he knew that Russian mobilization did not in any way mean Russia had to attack Germany, and that many weeks for negotiations remained.

German leaders knew Petersburg did not want war, but they also knew that it would resist any Austrian attack on Serbia. On 25 July, Friedrich von Pourtalès, German ambassador in Petersburg, sent a telegram recording Sazonov's stern warning: "If Austria-Hungary devours Serbia, we will go to war with her."[44] The next day, Pourtalès relayed word that "Grand Headquarters are in the throes of great excitement over Austria's procedure. I have the impression that all preparations are being made for mobilization against Austria."[45] So by Sunday, 26 July, three days before the Russian partial mobilization, Berlin was perfectly aware of Russian resolve. Nor should this have been a surprise, since the Russians had done the same thing in 1912–13.[46]

The key now was to provoke Russia into partial mobilization without scaring it into capitulation. In the afternoon on 26 July, Bethmann received word that Russia had implemented preparatory measures, a stage below partial mobilization. At 7:15 P.M. that evening, he wired Pourtalès that he should tell Sazonov that such measures would force Germany to mobilize its army, and "mobilization ... would mean war" against both Russia and France. Yet if at the same time Russia took a "waiting attitude" toward the Austria-Serbian dispute, Berlin would act to preserve Serbia's integrity, with agreement still possible "at a further stage of the affair."[47] The phrase that mobilization would mean war—used here for the first time—is one with great significance. As we shall see, the chancellor used it selectively during the next week whenever he wanted to goad an adversary into *speeding up* its mobilization effort, as he did with the French on 31 July.

The even more Machiavellian element of this telegram is its suggestion that Germany would accept Russian partial mobilization as long as Russia took a "waiting attitude." This was designed to assure Russia that, as in 1912–13, it could mobilize against Austria without bringing on general war. The next day, Jagow bolstered this belief by letting it be widely known that Germany would not respond to a Russian partial mobilization. This was pure deception: Bethmann and Jagow were already planning to use Russian partial mobilization as the *casus foederis* needed to unleash war—if indeed they could not get Russia to go all the way to general mobilization.[48]

I now turn to evidence showing that German leaders did nothing in the last week of the crisis to help achieve a negotiated peace, even though it was clear that a world war was almost certain. Many diplomatic solutions were offered up from 26 July to 31 July; none was seriously pursued. Moreover, as it became clear that Petersburg was desperately seeking a way out, Berlin sought to forestall any agreement, while still giving the appearance that it desired peace.

In the early morning of Monday, 27 July, three telegrams arrived. At 12:07 A.M., a note from Lichnowsky arrived noting London's view that Foreign Secretary Edward Grey's proposal to hold a European-wide ("*à quatre*") conference was "the only possibility of avoiding a general war." The tone was very serious. The English position was that Austria must not cross into Serbia, or "everything would be at an end, as no Russian Government would be able to tolerate this." Then, "world war would be inevitable."[49]

At 12:45 A.M., a message arrived from Petersburg stating that Sazonov was "looking for a way out" of the crisis. Pourtalès had taken the unauthorized step of proposing direct talks between Russia and Austria with a third party (implying Germany) acting as mediator, a step which pleased Sazonov.[50] Also at 12:45 A.M., information was received that Italy "would not dare to intervene actively."[51] Three more telegrams were received between 4:37 and 8:40 P.M., reinforcing that London saw it in Berlin's hands to stop the war, and that if Berlin did not, Britain would actively oppose Germany.[52]

By Monday evening, then, it was apparent that an Austro-Serbian conflict could not be contained to even a continental war, and that Italy would not support Germany. Some scholars argue that German leaders discounted this evidence, since they were convinced that war would remain localized. This view is critical to sustaining the idea that it was only on Wednesday night that they woke up to the reality and then tried to avert a general war.[53] Riezler's diary for Monday, however, shows that Berlin was perfectly aware of Britain's new stand: "The reports all point to war.... England's language has changed. Obviously London has suddenly realized that a rift will develop in the Entente if it is too lukewarm [in its support] of Russia."[54] Since Riezler, given his position, could only have gathered this information through the chancellor, Bethmann was clearly aware by Monday that if things continued as they were, a world war would result.

That night Bethmann wrote to Tschirschky, stating that since Berlin had already rejected Grey's proposal for a European conference, it could not now ignore the new English suggestion that Germany act as mediator. He went on: "By refusing every proposition for mediation, we should be held responsible for the conflagration by the whole world, and be set forth as the original instigators of the war. That would also make our position impossible in our own country, where we must appear as having been forced into the war."[55] This passage is revealing. Bethmann is not only seeking to shift the blame; he is assuming war as a given, despite the fact that Austria had not yet declared war on Serbia, nor had Russia moved to even partial mobilization. Moreover, the issue of blame is critical not because of any need for British neutrality, but simply to ensure domestic support for the war.[56]

Back in Berlin, the German Foreign Office and the chancellor were playing an elaborate game to prevent the kaiser from wrecking the plan for war. The text of the Serbian reply arrived in the afternoon of 27 July. Wilhelm, against Bethmann's advice, had returned from his cruise that same afternoon. This created the possibility that Wilhelm, after seeing Serbia's conciliatory position, would try to get Austria to cancel the declaration of war set for 28 July. The Serbian reply was thus delivered to him only the next morning. Yet, as feared, the mercurial kaiser got cold feet. He wrote to Jagow that the reply was a "capitulation of the most humiliating kind, and as a result, every cause for war falls to the ground." Although Austria should still act, it could be "so arranged that Austria would receive a hostage (Belgrade), as a guaranty for the enforcement and carrying out of the promises."[57]

This is the kaiser's famous "Halt in Belgrade" proposal. It was actually an ingenious diplomatic measure, since it would allow Austria to ensure Serbian compliance, while giving Russia a face-saving way out, since Serbia would not be completely destroyed.[58] Yet Bethmann and the Foreign Office immediately acted to subvert its potential value, even while appearing to be upholding its spirit.

Wilhelm ends his note by instructing Jagow to "submit a proposal to me along the lines sketched out, which shall be communicated to Vienna." Although these instructions were received at 10:00 A.M. on 28 July, Bethmann and Jagow waited until 10:15 that evening to send a message to Vienna, that is, until after word was received confirming the Austrian declaration of war. This ensured that a reluctant Vienna was given no excuse to delay the declaration.

More important, the proposal was significantly altered. Wilhelm's formula consisted of a halt in Belgrade alone; negotiations were to follow, implying European-wide negotiations. In a telegram Tuesday night, Bethmann instructed Tschirschky to tell the Austrians to consider halting in Belgrade *plus* "other places." Moreover, there was no hint of negotiations, let alone the European conference desired by England. This telegram is perhaps the single most revealing document of the crisis, and deserves to be quoted at length.

The telegram begins by emphasizing the need for more information on Austria's military and diplomatic plans. Serbia's conciliatory reply to the ultimatum was a problem, since "in case of a completely uncompromising attitude on the part of [Vienna], it will become necessary to reckon upon the gradual defection from its cause of public opinion throughout all Europe."

The next paragraph focuses on the need to blame Russia for the war to come. As with the telegram the previous night, this had nothing to do with keeping Britain neutral; war with Britain is assumed as a given.

> According to the statements of the Austrian General Staff, an active military movement against Serbia will not be possible before the 12th of August. As a result, [Germany] is placed in the extraordinarily difficult position of being exposed in the meantime to the mediation and conference proposals of the other Cabinets, and if it continues to maintain its previous aloofness in the face of such proposals, it will incur the odium of having been responsible for a world war [*Weltkrieg*], even, finally, among the German people themselves. A successful war on three fronts cannot be commenced and carried on on any such basis. It is imperative that the responsibility for the eventual extension of the war among those nations not originally immediately concerned should, under all circumstances, fall on Russia.

Having established the importance of blaming Russia, the chancellor turned to the problem at hand: how Austria is perceived by others. Since Sazonov had conceded that Serbia would have to be punished, Vienna should tell Petersburg that it had no territorial aims, and that

> her military preparations are solely for the purpose of a temporary occupation of Belgrade and certain other localities on Serbian territory in order to force the Serbian Government to the complete fulfillment of her demands.... An occupation like the German occupation of French territory after the Peace of Frankfort, for the purpose of securing compliance with the demands for war indemnity, is suggested.

Here is the chancellor's Halt proposal. Far from recommending Wilhelm's "Halt plus negotiations," Bethmann is suggesting a peace equivalent to that imposed on France after the Franco-Prussian war! He could hardly have believed Russia would accept such a proposal. It seems clear that Bethmann's only goal was to so alter the original Halt formula as to placate Wilhelm while shifting world and German public opinion against Russia. As he notes, should Petersburg fail to see the justice of this position, "it would have against it the public opinion of all Europe, which is now in the process of turning away from Austria. As a result, the general diplomatic, and probably the military, situation would undergo material alteration in favor of Austria-Hungary and her allies [i.e., Germany]."[59]

Thus by Tuesday night, the groundwork in the campaign to blame Russia was being laid. Much more was to come. At 1:45 A.M. the next day, the kaiser sent a letter to the czar, written by the Foreign Office, providing a moral justification for Austria's tough stance. The letter indicated that Wilhelm had already started mediation efforts, which was false, since he had had no contact with Vienna, nor was he ever to have.[60] This first of the Kaiser's telegrams to the czar seems to suggest that Berlin now sought a peaceful solution. Yet the message went out more than two days after word was received that the Russians felt that a telegram from Wilhelm to Nicholas "would prove the surest means of maintaining peace."[61] Had Bethmann really wanted peace, why wait so long to open such a dialogue? As will become clear, Bethmann encouraged the "Willy-Nicky" correspondence only to provide evidence of Russia's responsibility for the war.

At 6:15 A.M. on 29 July, Berlin was informed that Sazonov was again earnestly seeking German mediation to avoid war.[62] For Bethmann, this message, plus the fact that Russian partial mobilization had not yet been confirmed,[63] posed a problem: if Russia did not go to at least partial mobilization, it could not be blamed for the war. Hence, Bethmann sent out two telegrams that, when contrasted with his actions on 31 July, provide a key piece of evidence that Germany sought war. On 29 July, Bethmann was very threatening with the Russians, yet reassuring with the French. On 31 July, he was the exact opposite: reassuring to Russia but threatening to France.

The best explanation for this bizarre behavior is the following (see also the discussion below for 31 July). On 29 July, Russia had not mobilized and Bethmann needed them to, so he was deliberately provocative. Yet since the French were faster mobilizers, he needed them to postpone mobilization until Germany had a reason to mobilize, that is, until after Russia had done so. By 31 July, Russia had gone to general mobilization, and thus Germany could act. But because Bethmann feared that the Russians would get cold feet, he needed to assure them that negotiations could continue while both sides mobilized. With the French, he now needed a justification for attacking them first. Thus he wanted to provoke them into mobilization.

Bethmann's one-sentence telegram to Pourtalès at 12:50 P.M. on 29 July stated:

> Kindly call Mr. Sazonov's serious attention to the fact that further continuation of Russian mobilization measures [*Massnahmen*] *would* force us to mobilize, and in that case a European war could scarcely be prevented.

His telegram to Paris, sent at exactly the same time, read as follows:

> Reports of French preparations for war are becoming more frequent. Kindly take up the matter with the French Government and call its attention to the fact that such measures [*Massnahmen*] would force us to take actions for our self-protection. We should have to proclaim a state of "risk of war" which, although it would not yet mean mobilization or the calling in of any reserves to the colors, would nevertheless increase the tension. We continue to hope for the preservation of peace).[64]

Note that these telegrams are in response to military "preparations"/"measures" by both France and Russia, steps much less serious than mobilization, as all governments understood (and as indeed the second telegram reiterates). Yet while Russia is told that its measures will force Germany to mobilize, such that war could not be prevented, France is told that its measures would not even lead to German mobilization, let alone war. If Bethmann had been truly seeking peace, and perhaps thought that threats would deter Germany's adversaries from going further, the tone of the telegrams should have been the opposite. France, as the much faster mobilizer, should have been the one to receive the strong threat; Russia, since its forces would not be up to full strength for many weeks, should have been sent the much weaker and more hopeful telegram.

Given that the German threat to mobilize in response to mere Russian preparations was so disproportional—and the opposite behavior from 1912–13—Berlin evidently expected that Moscow would view this telegram as a sign that Germany was looking for a pretext for war. This is exactly how the Russians saw it. Coupled with Vienna's refusal to engage in direct talks and the bombardment of Belgrade on the morning of 29 July, Sazonov could only conclude that Germany wanted war. General mobilization by Russia would have to be called.[65]

Two hours after the dispatch of these two telegrams, the first confirmation that Russia had ordered partial mobilization was received.[66] Although part of Bethmann's objective had been achieved, this was still not the optimal scenario: Germany could go to war over partial mobilization, but to truly blame Russia, Berlin needed a Russian general mobilization. In a conference later that afternoon, Bethmann was able to convince the military to delay even public "risk of war" preparations until word of Russian general mobilization. Without this Russian action, he argued, "we would not have public opinion on our side."[67] Moltke supported Bethmann, which is not surprising considering his point in

February 1913 that the aggression must be seen to come from Russia. They knew that they did not have long to wait. Signs were growing that the Russians would soon go to general mobilization. In Petersburg, the necessity of general mobilization had been discussed on the night of 28 July; the next morning, the czar signed two orders, one for partial and one for general mobilization, the latter to be implemented only on his command.

The night of 29–30 July, most historians would agree, is probably the most pivotal of the crisis. It is generally interpreted as the night German civilian leaders confirmed British opposition, got cold feet, and hurriedly scrambled to find a last-minute solution. This interpretation is based on two key telegrams sent to Vienna in the early morning of Thursday, July 30 that seem to show Bethmann desperately seeking to rein in Austria to prevent world war. Nothing could be further from the truth. As with Bethmann's policy over the two previous nights, he was only attempting in the face of Austrian intransigence to push Germany's ally to appear more conciliatory. Thrusting blame onto Russia remained his prime objective.

A 5:07 P.M. telegram from London noted Grey's agreement that direct talks between Russia and Austria were the most likely way to peace. Yet the British were "firmly convinced" that "unless Austria is willing to enter upon a discussion of the Serbian question, a world war is inevitable."[68] The term "world war" (*Weltkrieg*) reinforced what had been known since Monday—that the British would oppose Germany. Thus twelve hours before the world-on-fire telegrams, it was evident that the only choices left were negotiated peace or all-out world war. Berlin still did nothing.

At 8:29 P.M., a telegram was received from Petersburg. Sazonov had been notified that Vienna had refused direct Austro-Russian talks, and had replied that there was now nothing left but to return to British proposals for conversations *à quatre*. Sazonov made clear that he was not expecting Austria "to submit to a sort of European court of arbitration," but that "he was only looking for a way out of the present difficulties, and that in doing so he was grasping at every straw."[69] Bethmann now had to be careful. He had heard nothing from Vienna regarding his instructions the previous night, and he needed Austria to appear to be negotiating with Russia. But in Sazonov's desperate state of mind, he might accept an Austrian offer if it allowed him to save face. Thus, at 10:18 and then again at 10:30 P.M., Bethmann sent two one-sentence messages to Vienna. The first asked if the 28 July instructions—the long telegram detailing his version of the Halt proposal—had arrived; the second said simply that he "expect[ed] immediate carrying out" of these instructions. His urgency is shown by the fact that the first message went out uncoded, to speed up transmission.[70]

Four telegrams arrived between 8:29 P.M. and 10:14 P.M. strongly suggesting that Russia would soon move from partial to general mobilization.[71] Bethmann had provoked Russia into a total military response. It was now time to shift to a softer position to lead Petersburg to believe that, as in 1912–13, Germany would tolerate Russian mobilization as long as Austria was not attacked. At 11:05 P.M., Bethmann sent a telegram to Petersburg containing none of the previous threats. Instead, he stated that although things were starting to get out of hand, Berlin was still seeking a negotiated solution.[72]

I now turn to the two world-on-fire telegrams sent to Vienna at 2:50 and 3:00 A.M. It is typically argued that they reflect the chancellor's realization that Britain would indeed fight, based on a Lichnowsky telegram arriving at 9:12 P.M. and on a meeting with the English ambassador at 10:00 P.M. Yet this view cannot explain why Bethmann's telegrams to Vienna for the six hours between 9:00 P.M. and 3:00 A.M. show no signs of nervousness about Germany's situation. Instead, they show Berlin pressing Austria to appear to be negotiating with Petersburg in order to blame Russia for war. At the same time, they are carefully manipulated to mislead Vienna as to Russian resolve, and thus the real possibility of world war. In behavior perfectly consistent with the previous two nights, Bethmann sought to avoid the appearance of responsibility while simultaneously ensuring that Austria did not back out for fear of general war.

Bethmann sent a message to Tschirschky at 12:10 A.M. providing information on the kaiser-czar correspondence. The full texts of the kaiser's two letters to the czar are included, emphasizing that Russia could remain a spectator of any Austro-Serbian conflict and that an understanding between Petersburg and Vienna was desirable.[73] Significantly, however, Bethmann does not give the text of the czar's letter, but says of it only that the czar "made an appeal for the mediation of His Majesty [the kaiser]." Nicholas had indeed made such an appeal. But the czar's missing text is conspicuous in its absence:

> The *indignation* in Russia [regarding the Austrian declaration of war], *shared fully by me, is enormous.* I foresee that very soon I shall be *overwhelmed* by the *pressure* brought upon me, and be *forced* to take extreme measures which will *lead to war.* To try and avoid such a calamity as a European war, I beg you in the name of our old friendship to do what you can *to stop* your *allies* from *going too far.*[74]

That this was a deliberate effort on Bethmann's part to downplay the likelihood of war is clear: in an almost identical telegram to the ambassador in Petersburg less than an hour later, he reproduces the kaiser's letters and then provides the complete text of the czar's response.[75]

At 12:30 A.M., the chancellor sent another message to Vienna. Instead of communicating the text of Lichnowsky's telegram from 9:12 P.M.—the clearest statement that England would fight with France—Bethmann sent only selective parts of the Lichnowsky telegram that had arrived at 5:07 P.M. Since he had been completely informed of the 9:12 P.M. telegram, this move was again designed to avoid scaring Vienna unless it was absolutely necessary. Of the 5:07 P.M. telegram, Bethmann relayed only two small parts: that Russia was aware that Vienna had refused direct talks; and that Grey was forwarding a proposal suggesting Serbia might accept the harsher demands if Austria agreed to it.[76] Conveniently, Bethmann left out the part where Grey warned that Russia "could not and would not stand by quietly" while Serbia was destroyed.[77] The chancellor instructed Tschirschky to inform the Austrian leaders that Berlin considered compliance to the proposal "an appropriate basis for negotiations, if founded on an occupation of a portion of Serbian territory as a hostage."[78] Bethmann had still heard no word on whether Vienna would agree to appear to negotiate with Russia. He thus reiterated his watered-down Halt proposal.

At the same moment, 12:30 A.M., Bethmann sent another message to Vienna relaying Pourtalès's message that Russia had gone to partial mobilization. This telegram nicely demonstrates Bethmann's technique of relaying the text from other ambassadors either word-for-word or with his own paraphrasing, depending on the desired impact. Here, instead of quoting Pourtalès's text, he simply states that "Russian mobilization, however, is far from meaning war, as in western Europe; the Russian army might be a long time under arms without crossing a frontier; relations with Vienna not broken off, and Russia wants to avoid war, if in any way possible."[79] These lines are actually Sazonov's, but Bethmann presents them as *Berlin's* opinion of the situation! The chancellor was obviously trying to convince Vienna not to be too worried by Russian partial mobilization.[80] The chancellor ends the telegram saying that "Russia complains that ... the conferences [have not] made any headway. Hence we must urgently request, in order to prevent a general catastrophe, or at least to put Russia in the wrong, that Vienna inaugurate and continue with the conference according to telegram 174.[81]

Telegram 174 was the one that went the previous night with the modified Halt proposal (*DD*: doc. 323). So here we have the German chancellor, more than three hours after final confirmation of British opposition, telling Tschirschky to carry out instructions that he knew had little chance of success, in order to "at least put Russia in the wrong."[82] Where are the cold feet that Bethmann should have had at this time? Is it at all conceivable, since the world-on-fire telegrams did not go out until 3:00 A.M., that the information from Britain somehow had a delayed psychological effect on him, enough to then prompt a change of mind? Of course not. If it had not hit him by 12:30 A.M. that his policy was leading to world war, there is no reason why it would hit him two and a half hours later, especially since no new troubling information was received during that time. Indeed, the very fact that Bethmann would stay up until the small hours of the morning indicates that he was waiting for some other piece of crucial information.

So what information did arrive that led to the world-on-fire telegrams? Finally, at 1:30 A.M., after sending three telegrams that evening seeking information on Vienna's response to the Halt proposal,[83] Bethmann received the following message from Tschirschky:

> Count Berchtold's thanks for the suggestion. Minister is ready to repeat declaration concerning territorial disinterestedness which he has already made at Petersburg.... So far as the further declaration with reference to military measures is concerned, Count Berchtold says that he is not in a position to give me a reply at once.

In spite of my representations as to the urgency of the matter, I have up to this evening received no further communication.[84]

This telegram could not have pleased the chancellor. That Austria continued to show resolve was heartening. But Vienna had not implemented his modified Halt proposal. As Bethmann had stated on Tuesday night, such an uncompromising attitude from Austria would make it impossible to carry out a successful war on three fronts.

The chancellor was thus in a bind: now that he had pushed Vienna into a hard-line posture, Austria was so convinced it could destroy Serbia—or that Berlin would accept nothing less—that it would not even go through the motions of appearing willing to compromise. To shift responsibility, Berlin had to be seen to favor the English proposals for a mediated solution. This was especially so now that Russia, after Austria's intransigence, had turned to England and its idea of European-wide conversations.[85]

Yet here was the dilemma. If Bethmann suggested that Austria accept the idea of European-wide mediation, as had occurred in December 1912, Austria would likely refuse, and the odium for world war would fall on Germany's shoulders. Even worse, Austria, fearing general war, might *accept* the idea. Russia would then agree, and preventive war would have to be postponed. Berlin therefore needed something to satisfy the British request, make Austria appear to want peace, and at the same time ensure that no diplomatic solution could ever be achieved. The solution: direct Austrian-Russia talks around an unacceptable Halt proposal, with Germany playing the role of mediator.

It is this objective that led to the two world-on-fire telegrams, sent to Vienna at 2:55 and 3:00 A.M. The first began by providing the first three paragraphs of the Lichnowsky telegram that had arrived at 9:12 P.M. on Wednesday (the last two paragraphs being studiously left off). The first two paragraphs concerned Sazonov's request that Grey again take up mediation efforts. Grey saw two possibilities: mediation either *à quatre* (European-wide) or by Bethmann himself. It would be a suitable basis for mediation, Grey said, if Austria, after occupying Belgrade or other places, should announce its conditions. The third paragraph contained Grey's warning that if Germany and France were to become involved, Britain could not stand aside, and the resulting war would be the greatest catastrophe ever experienced.[86] After the presentation of Lichnowsky's message, Bethmann writes that if Austria continued to refuse all mediation, Austria and Germany would stand alone against all other great powers including England. Austria could satisfy its honor and claims against Serbia by the occupation of Belgrade or of other places.

Under these circumstances we must urgently and impressively suggest to the consideration of the Vienna Cabinet the acceptance of mediation on the above-mentioned honorable conditions. The responsibility for the consequences that would otherwise follow would be an uncommonly heavy one both for Austria and for us.[87]

This grim picture of an impending world war, with a suggestion for a diplomatic way out, seems to demonstrate a sudden desire for peace on the part of the chancellor. Yet note that Vienna is not asked to accept a Halt, but only *"mediation on the above-mentioned conditions,"* that is, negotiations with the Halt as a potential point of discussion. The beginning of such negotiations would deflect blame from Germany while ensuring that no solution was quickly found.[88] And what kind of mediation is Berlin pushing for here? This message is vague as to whether Vienna should accept mediation *à quatre* or only through Germany. The second telegram to Tschirchsky at 3:00 A.M. resolves this ambiguity: Austria should choose the second.

This telegram starts off by reproducing most of the Pourtalès telegram that had arrived in Berlin at 8:29 P.M. on 29 July. Sazonov had told Pourtalès of Vienna's categorical refusal to enter into direct negotiations, and that therefore it seemed necessary to return to British proposals for conversations *à quatre*.[89] Bethmann told Tschirschky that this did not agree with Tschirschky's previous reports indicating that Count Berchtold and the Russian ambassador in Vienna had begun discussions (i.e., bilaterally, not *à quatre*).

> [Vienna's] refusal to hold any exchange of opinions with Petersburg ... [is] a serious error, as it would be [a] direct provocation of Russia's armed interference, which Austria-Hungary is beyond all else interested to prevent.
>   We are, of course, ready to fulfill the obligations of our alliance, but must decline to be drawn wantonly into a world conflagration by Vienna, without having any regard paid to our counsel.[90]

Berlin was clearly pushing Austria to accept direct Russian-Austrian talks with German mediation, as opposed to European-wide intervention. Yet this proposal did not represent any real change from what Berlin had been suggesting since Monday evening. By controlling the mediation process, Germany could not only appear as the honest broker; it could also ensure that any Austrian offer to "halt" remained harsh enough to preclude Russian agreement.

If any doubt remains that the chancellor and the Foreign Office conspired to unleash general war under favorable conditions, it is dispelled by their other actions from 29 July to 1 August. The trick was to maneuver Germany and German public opinion into position so that as soon as Russian general mobilization was announced, war could be instantly initiated. As Admiral Müller nicely summarized on 27 July, the "tendency of our policy [is] to keep quiet, letting Russia put itself in the wrong, but then not shying away from war."[91]

On 29 July, as noted, Bethmann had secured the military's agreement to delay even the announcement of "risk of war" preparations until after Russian general mobilization. That same day, in meetings with the top officials of the Social Democratic Party, he secured their support for a general war against the Slavic threat.[92] By the next day, Bethmann could tell his colleagues that the "general public feeling was good in Germany," with "[nothing] particular to fear from Social Democracy or from the leadership of the Social Democratic Party."[93]

Riezler had noted on 27 July that the chancellor was going to "work the Social Democrats from all sides."[94] The strategy was evidently paying off.

One potential obstacle remained: the kaiser. Since his signature was needed to wage war, he had to be convinced that Russian actions would necessitate German mobilization without scaring him into a compromise. At 11:15 A.M. on 30 July, the chancellor sent two telegrams to Wilhelm. In the first, Bethmann confirmed England's determination to fight and then noted that while he had carried out Wilhelm's instructions regarding mediation, he had heard no word yet from Vienna. Needless to say, Bethmann did not explain that he had altered the kaiser's instructions without authorization. His next lines are revealing as to his intentions:

> I instructed [Tschirschky] ... to demand an immediate explanation from Count Berchtold, in order that this episode may be closed in one way or another. I also called his attention to the fact that every declaration by Vienna to Petersburg concerning the purpose and extent of Austria's action against Serbia would only emphasize and openly label Russia's responsibility before the entire world.[95]

This language is hard to reconcile with the view that the chancellor sought peace when he sent the world-on-fire telegrams. Here he is, a mere eight hours later, talking again about thrusting blame onto Russia.

In the second 11:15 message, we see the chancellor using the kaiser to advance his plan. Bethmann suggests that Wilhelm send a message to the czar stating that if Russia continues with partial mobilization, "then the role of mediator which I [the kaiser] took upon myself at your request will be endangered, if not made impossible. Yours alone is for the moment the responsibility of deciding." Bethmann ends his telegram with the following:

> As this telegram will be a particularly important document historically, I would most humbly advise that Your Majesty do not—as long as Vienna's decision is still outstanding—express in it the fact that Your Majesty's role as mediator is ended.[96]

Why would Bethmann say such an odd thing just when he should have been seeking a negotiated solution? The answer, of course, is that he wanted no such solution. Hence, he was already planning ahead to the time when the German people would be given documented evidence on Russian aggression. It is no coincidence that the German White Book—titled "Germany's Reasons for War with Russia"—was published just three days later on 2 August [97] and then presented to the Reichstag the next day (before hostilities with France began). Considering simple publishing logistics, the book must have been in preparation all through the previous week, when Berlin was supposedly seeking a mediated solution. It is also not by accident that Exhibit 23 of the White Book is Wilhelm's very telegram to the czar that Bethmann notes will be a "particularly important document historically."

The machinations do not end there. In the White Book, the telegram's time of sending is given as 1 A.M., 30 July. But it was actually sent at 3:30 P.M. Berlin time that day, and only arrived in St. Petersburg at 5:30 P.M. The final version of the telegram, and the one appearing in the White Book, ends: "the whole weight of the decision lies solely on your [the czar's] shoulders now, who have to bear the responsibility for peace or war."[98] Given that Russian general mobilization was not ordered until 5:00 P.M., an earlier dispatch time had to be put on the published document to make it appear that the Russians, despite being given plenty of forewarning, had still aggressively moved to mobilization against Germany. A "particularly important document historically" indeed![99]

During the day on 30 July, reports showed that Russia was gearing up for general mobilization.[100] The night before, it had been ordered by the czar at around 8:00 Moscow time. Just after 10:00, however, Nicholas received a letter from Wilhelm which frightened him enough that he canceled the order. On the morning of 30 July, Sazonov and the military, distressed by this change, agreed on the need to reinstate general mobilization. At around 3:00 P.M. Moscow time, Nicholas and Sazonov met, and after about an hour, the reluctant czar agreed to move once again to general mobilization. By 5:00, the order was sent out, with a starting date of 31 July.[101]

The need to sustain Russian mobilization gave Bethmann and his colleagues still one more scheme to execute. The chancellor had already secured the military's agreement to delay public military moves until after Russian general mobilization. The next part of the plan went as follows. As soon as word was received from Petersburg confirming this mobilization, Berlin would send Russia an ultimatum giving it only twelve hours to recall it or face German general mobilization. Meanwhile, all energy would be directed to averting any last-minute diplomatic solution. This required a coordinated three-pronged effort.

First, Russia would be told that rejecting the ultimatum would lead only to German mobilization, with any hint that mobilization meant war now removed. Petersburg would thus believe that mobilization could continue while both sides negotiated an agreement. Yet upon the Russian rejection, Berlin would surprise Russia by declaring war. This move, as with the declaration of war on Serbia, would prevent all possible diplomatic settlements. Second, Austria would be instructed to cease all negotiations and move immediately to war against Russia. If the Austrian leaders were getting cold feet, this tactic would forestall an Austrian-Russian agreement. Moreover, it would ensure that Austria redirected the bulk of its troops against Russia rather than concentrating on its main goal, the destruction of Serbia.

Third, Britain, the power most able to play the honest broker, had to be prevented from convincing Russia to capitulate. London therefore had to be told that Russian-Austrian talks had begun and that Berlin was actively mediating. It was also important that London not know that Germany was preparing to jump immediately to war, since it might then press the czar to accept Austrian terms, and war would be off. With France, Berlin had an ironic and self-caused dilemma: France had not proceeded far enough in its mobilization to allow Berlin to blame France for the blow to come. Hence, on 31 July, the same technique previously used to provoke Russia was now to be employed against the French: Paris would be told that its military measures inevitably meant war. In short, German diplomacy toward Russia and France would be reversed from just two days before. On 29 July, Russia had been provoked and France assuaged; now, Russia would be assured that negotiations could continue, while France was told that nothing more could be done.[102]

Up until Russian general mobilization was confirmed, Berlin still needed Austrian agreement to open talks with Petersburg along the instructed lines. Hence, all through Thursday, 30 July, Bethmann continued to press for word from Vienna. At 5:20 P.M., a report from Tschirschky arrived stating that Austria had instructed its ambassador in Russia to begin conversations with Sazonov. This, although overdue, was encouraging. Yet the telegram also indicated that Austria was unwilling to halt on Serbian territory, and would pull back only after peace was concluded to "compel [Serbia] to the complete fulfillment of [Austrian] demands." Of equal concern was word that despite Vienna's partial mobilization against Serbia, the Austrians were uncertain as to whether general mobilization was necessary.[103] In short, it seemed by late Thursday that Austria might not only fail to appear conciliatory, but also that it would not fight Russia in the critical first days of war.

As they had done in February 1913, Bethmann and Moltke worked together to whip Austria into line. At 9:00 on Thursday night, Bethmann wrote to Tschirschky, noting that should Vienna decline to make concessions, "it [would] hardly be possible any longer to place the guilt of the outbreak of a European conflagration on Russia's shoulders." Austria's stand in the face of English diplomacy "would place us, in the eyes of our own people, in an untenable situation. Thus we can only urgently advise that Austria accept the [British] proposal."[104] Once again, Bethmann's goal was not to save the peace, but to shift blame to Russia. That afternoon, Moltke spoke with Austria's military attaché, who reported to Vienna at 5:30 P.M. that Berlin desired Austria's immediate mobilization against Russia. Moltke also promised that this move would invoke German alliance obligations, a promise Vienna had been anxious to hear.[105]

Late in the evening, Bethmann met with Moltke and Falkenhayn to discuss the military situation. The military now revealed that Russian general mobilization was truly impending.[106] The significance was clear: Germany could now blame Russia for the war. Yet Bethmann now had to *stop* Austria from acting on Berlin's demand that it offer Russia a halt in Serbia (a demand Bethmann had reiterated just two hours before). At 11:20 P.M., Bethmann sent uncoded (to speed transmission) the one-line message "Please do not carry out instructions number 200 [the 9:00 P.M. telegram] for the present." The reason for this sudden cancellation was written up but never sent, probably because it revealed too well Berlin's plan to await Russian mobilization and then compel Austria to fight:

I [Bethmann] cancelled the order of instruction in No. 200, as the General Staff just informs me that the military preparations of our neighbors, especially in the east, will force us to a speedy decision, unless we do not wish to expose ourselves to the danger of surprise. General Staff earnestly desires to be informed definitely and immediately as to Vienna's decisions, particularly those of a military nature.

Instead, at 2:45 A.M. on 31 July Berlin forwarded a spurious explanation stating that the cancellation was a result of a letter from the king of England.[107]

The situation was now primed for war. On the morning of Friday, 31 July, the chancellor and the military gathered to wait for word of Russian general mobilization. At 11:40 A.M., confirmation was received.[108] General Karl von Wenninger recorded the reaction at the German War Ministry: "Everywhere beaming faces, people shaking hands in the corridors, congratulating one another on having cleared the hurdle."[109] The hurdle here is obviously the risk that Russia would *not* go to general mobilization, thus preventing Germany from blaming Russia for the war.

Now Bethmann could execute the final diplomatic instruments to ensure Russian responsibility. An ultimatum with a twelve-hour deadline was prepared for dispatch to Petersburg, telling the Russians to back down or face German mobilization. The wording of this ultimatum, and the way other embassies were informed, constitute perhaps Bethmann's most subtle manipulation in the crisis, so subtle that it has been missed by almost every historical account.[110] Between 1:45 P.M. and 3:30 P.M. on 31 July, five telegrams were sent to the five key capitals. All but the one to Vienna paint a similar picture: that Berlin was being forced by circumstances to present an ultimatum to Russia. The telegram to Russia containing the ultimatum was written by the chancellor himself. The other four were written by Jagow but carefully altered by Bethmann before being forwarded.[111] This allowed Bethmann to tell each capital a slightly different story, tailored to his objectives for each situation.

The ultimatum to Petersburg, sent at 3:30 P.M., stated:

In spite of the still pending negotiations for mediation and although we ourselves have up to the present hour taken no mobilization measures of any kind, Russia has mobilized her entire army and navy, thus against us also. For the security of the Empire, we have been compelled by these Russian measures to declare a state of threatening danger of war, which does not yet mean mobilization. Mobilization must follow, however, in case Russia does not suspend every war measure against Austria-Hungary and ourselves within twelve hours and make us a distinct declaration to that effect.[112]

The first sentence is deliberately deceptive. Negotiations were not "still pending"; Berlin had asked Tschirschky to cease pursuing them the previous night. And while Germany had not yet gone to mobilization, it had secretly taken all measures needed to achieve it within days (indeed it was able to cross into Luxembourg on 2 August).

The critical aspect of this telegram, however, lies in what it does not say. There is no mention that Berlin was preparing to follow a Russian rejection of the ultimatum with a declaration of war, as was already planned as the ultimatum was being drawn up. Moreover, even though on 26 and 29 July Berlin had threatened war in response to mere preparations, there was now not even a hint that German mobilization would lead to war.

This was no oversight. The telegram to Paris, sent at the same time, begins with the same line about "still pending negotiations" and Russian mobilization. But it continues:

> As a result we have declared a state of threatening danger of war, which must be followed by mobilization in case Russia does not suspend every war measure against Austria and ourselves within twelve hours. *Mobilization will inevitably mean war.* Please ask the French Government if it intends to remain neutral in a Russo-German war. Answer must be given within eighteen hours.[113]

"Mobilization will inevitably mean war"?! If Berlin had truly wanted to warn the Russians, it should have included this line in the Russian draft. Yet this line, absent from Jagow's original draft, was added by Bethmann just before it went out.[114] Since Berlin had been telling Paris that a negotiated peace was still possible, the reason for the switch is clear: having used the "mobilization means war" phrase to provoke Russia, it was now time to push France into mobilization to blame the French for Germany's attack in the west.[115]

Thus while the ultimatum to Petersburg was designed to prevent Russia from capitulating, the note to Paris was designed to force the French to go instantly to general mobilization (as they did). The telegrams to Britain and Italy were equally manipulative. Each begins by protesting Russia's mobilization. The dispatch to Rome notes that Germany would move to mobilization if Russia did not "suspend every war measure against Austria and ourselves within twelve hours." It continues:

> Mobilization will mean war. We have put the question to France whether she will remain neutral.... If France's reply should be in the negative, as we certainly expect, war between France and ourselves will also have to be declared at once.
>
> We are counting with assurance upon the fact that Italy will live up to the obligations she has assumed.[116]

Drawing Italy into war was clearly the goal. Since the Triple Alliance invoked support only if an ally was attacked, Bethmann moderated the blunt tone of Jagow's original draft. Jagow had used the phrase: "mobilization will inevitably mean war." Bethmann, clearly realizing that the word "inevitably" might signal that Germany was seeking a pretext for war, deleted it from the final draft, and added the phrase suggesting that Russia could prevent war by canceling its war measures.[117]

With London, the objective was to keep the British off the scent long enough to prevent them from intervening at Petersburg. Hence, Bethmann had to minimize suspicions that Germany wanted war, and instead convince London that a diplomatic solution was still possible. In the opening line about "still pending negotiations" common to all four telegrams, it is only in the message to Britain that the words "and apparently not hopeless mediation" are included, words that would have helped buoy British hopes. The phrase in both French and Italian telegrams—that Germany would mobilize if Russia did not cancel its war measures—is also in the British. Yet there is no subsequent line that "mobilization will mean war," as the Italians were told, or that it will "inevitably mean war," as the French were informed. In Jagow's draft, we see that he thought Bethmann would want at least to hint at the possibility of war, since after stating that Russian rejection of the demand would be followed by German mobilization, Jagow wrote: "it looks as if war with Russia were hardly to be avoided." The chancellor in the final draft crossed out this line.[118] As restrained as Jagow's draft is, Bethmann's final version communicates a very different message: it eliminates any linkage between mobilization and war, while implying that Germany is willing, for the sake of peace, to give Russia more time. Read independently, this telegram is only a low-key warning that tensions are rising. The reality—that Berlin planned to declare war on Russia within a day, and then invade Luxembourg hours after that—is nicely hidden.

These four telegrams clearly confound the argument that Bethmann lost control over the process after 30 July. Yet where is the telegram to Austria? In fact, no parallel message ever went out to inform Austria of the ultimatum to Russia and the twelve-hour limit. Instead, about two hours before, at 1:45 P.M., Bethmann sent a short dispatch to Vienna:

> Since the Russian mobilization we have declared threatening danger of war, which will presumably be followed within forty-eight hours by mobilization. This inevitably means war. We expect from Austria immediate ACTIVE participation in the war with Russia.[119]

The incredible nature of this telegram, from a state supposedly seeking peace or at least the localization of conflict, might not be evident at first glance. Not only is Vienna the only capital not informed of the ultimatum, but Bethmann tells the Austrians that the declaration of threatening danger of war will *"presumably* be followed within *forty-eight hours* by *mobilization."* It was not "presumably," it was for certain; it was not "forty-eight hours," but something less than twenty-four (considering transmission time of the ultimatum and the twelve-hour limit); it was not to be mobilization, but a declaration of war ending all negotiations. One might think that if any state should have been told the truth of the matter, it should have been Germany's last true ally.

Combined with the telegram the night before canceling the instruction that Austria offer Russia a halt in Serbia, there seems only one explanation for this deception: Berlin wanted Vienna to know that the time for diplomacy had ended, and that it must move immediately to a war footing against Russia, not Serbia. To have told the Austrians of the ultimatum, let alone of the real plan, would have alerted them to the urgency of concluding an agreement with Russia, something Berlin did not want.

All this is shown by the chancellor's words "This inevitably means war. We expect from Austria immediate ACTIVE participation in the war with Russia." The phrase "inevitably means war" suspiciously arises again. The reason is evident: if war is a given, then diplomacy, by definition, is at an end. There is also a simple explanation for the phrase that Berlin "expects" from Austria immediate and active participation in the war against Russia. That Vienna's goal was to destroy Serbia, not to fight the superior Russians, was well known. Moreover, for the previous few days, Conrad had been hinting that even if Germany pulled Austria into general war, the bulk of the Austrian forces would still be deployed south against Serbia. Moltke had tried to persuade Conrad that it was in Austria's own interest to fight a general war, but Conrad remained unconvinced.[120] Hence, Berlin was now not "requesting" or "suggesting" that Austria "consider" waging war against Russia—the kind of language used on previous nights with regard to the Halt proposals; rather, it was "expecting" it. In diplomatic terms, given Germany's preponderant position in the alliance, this was essentially a demand.

Moreover, the expectation was for "immediate ACTIVE" participation, with Bethmann's emphasis on the active. To make the Schlieffen Plan work, Berlin needed Austria not only to concentrate troops against Russia, but also to go on the offensive to divert Russian forces away from Germany. For obvious reasons, Austria was reluctant to sacrifice its troops just so Germany could dispose of France. Berlin had already employed the implicit threat of leaving Austria to the full onslaught of the Russians, the Austrians' single greatest fear.[121] This short telegram thus could have had only one meaning to the Austrians: do not presume that you can focus on Serbia or use diplomacy to keep the Russians out; general war is a given, so all effort must go against Russia.

Only one possible hitch remained: Russia might back out by capitulating to Austrian demands. There was one sure way to prevent this, namely, a declaration of war on Russia. Germany's premature declaration of war on 1 August provides the final proof that by the end of July, world war was preferred over all possible negotiated solutions, even one giving Austria everything it wanted. Through Bethmann's diplomacy, German workers were ready to fight a war of self-defense against the Slavic aggressors, and with Austrian help. Such favorable conditions, with Germany at the peak of its military power, would be hard ever to recreate.

Thus we have the puzzle that confounds other theories: Why would German civilian leaders plan for a declaration of war on Russia as soon as the twelve-hour ultimatum was up, and yet not warn anyone, including the Russians? Military strategy would argue against declaring war until one's forces were ready to attack. Recognizing this, the civilian leaders kept the decision to declare war secret from all the top military leaders (except one) until after it was a fait accompli. It also makes no sense to argue, as Bethmann tried with his outraged military, that Germany was compelled to follow international law, which required declarations of war before an attack commenced. Considering Germany's unannounced plunge into neutral Belgium three days later, this argument is clearly absurd. Moreover, Berlin deliberately held back the declaration of war against France, even though France was to be attacked weeks before Russia. Nor can it be argued that the declaration of war had a diplomatic or political value. If anything, the declaration hurt Bethmann's own efforts to blame Russia for the war.

The argument that the leaders acted irrationally, without thinking through the implications, also cannot stand. Against this view, we have the careful planning that went into the declaration and the moves to keep it secret from the military. We also have the evidence that Germany pushed Austria to declare war on 28 July solely to preclude a diplomatic solution. One has to wonder how German leaders could have put less thought into a declaration guaranteeing general war than one merely ensuring an Austro-Serbian war. Moreover, it seems odd that the reasoning behind the premature declaration on 28 July could have been forgotten less than a week later.

Finally, we have two important pieces of direct evidence. A senior official in the German Foreign Office made a slip on 31 July. He admitted to a representative of a neutral power who then told George Buchanan, British ambassador in Petersburg, that "the only thing which [the German] Government fears was that Russia would, at the eleventh hour, climb down and accept [the ultimatum]."[122] Even more damaging is a comment by Army Chief of Staff Moltke, the only individual in the military informed of the plan to declare war on Russia. On 1 August, just after the kaiser had signed the mobilization order, Moltke was recalled and told of an English promise to keep France neutral. Wilhelm, overjoyed with the idea that France would stay out of the war, called for an immediate halt to deployment in the west. Admiral Müller's diary records Moltke's emotional response:

> This we cannot do; the whole army would fall into disarray and we would end all chances of winning. Besides, our patrols have already invaded Luxembourg and the division from Trier is immediately following up. All we need now is for Russia to back off as well [*Jetzt fehlte nur noch, doss auch Russland abschnappt*].[123]

Far from fearing Russian attack, Moltke is worried that Russia might also want peace! The fact that Moltke could say this in the presence of Germany's most important civilian and military leaders, and that Müller records no reaction, suggests either that his opinion was already well known or that they agreed with it. Either way, combined with the evidence presented below, it is clear that the biggest fear in Berlin in the last days of peace was not that war might occur, but that it might not.

We have seen that the German ultimatum to Russia mentioned only that mobilization would follow its rejection, not war. One might suppose that on the afternoon of 31 July when the ultimatum was sent, Berlin still sought peace, and therefore worried that stronger threats might make Russia hostile to negotiation. Yet the very same day the ultimatum was sent, a telegram that would be used to instruct Pourtalès to hand over a declaration of war rather than the promised word of German mobilization was being drafted in the Foreign Office.[124] In short, it was not as though on 1 August, due to the emotions of the moment, the civilian leaders panicked and declared war. They had already decided *the day before* to surprise Russia with the declaration of war immediately after the deadline.

Berlin also made sure that the peace-inclined Pourtalès would not hint to Sazonov that refusing the ultimatum would lead to a surprise declaration, thus providing Sazonov a last-second chance to back down. Pourtalès was instructed not to hand over the declaration of war until Sazonov gave him official word that Russia was rejecting the German demands.[125] As it was, Pourtalès, when he met with Sazonov at 7:00 P.M. on 1 August, asked him three times whether he could accept the ultimatum; following the negative reply, he reluctantly handed over the declaration of war. Thus every diplomatic detail was organized to guarantee Russia's refusal of the ultimatum.

The telegram with the declaration of war went out at 12:52 P.M. on 1 August. It again pinned all blame on Russia, stating that Germany would have to declare war for purely defensive reasons. So that Russia did not try to prolong negotiations by simply not responding to the ultimatum (as opposed to an outright refusal), the declaration of war had written into it both possibilities, neither of which could change the outcome.[126] Bethmann and his cohorts also carefully planned the timing of its hand-over to prevent any intervention by Wilhelm and the German military, both of whom were kept in the dark regarding the impending declaration. Hence, while the original telegram said that Pourtalès should present the declaration "immediately upon the expiration of the respite, at the latest, however, this afternoon at five o'clock," Jagow and Bethmann crossed this out and substituted the much more precise statement: "at 5 o'clock this afternoon, according to Central European time,"[127] or five hours after the actual deadline. It is surely not coincidental that this was the exact time military and civilian leaders were to meet with Wilhelm to get his signature on the order for general mobilization. The civilians were making it physically impossible for either the kaiser or the military to stop the declaration of war from being presented, even if they somehow got wind of it at this meeting.

The meeting at 5:00 P.M. is also of interest because of the news presented to Wilhelm of an apparent British offer, received by the Foreign Office at 4:23 P.M., that "in case [Germany] did not attack France, England would remain neutral and would guarantee France's neutrality."[128] Sometime after the meeting started, just after Wilhelm had signed the mobilization order, Jagow announced that a "very important dispatch" had arrived and would be brought in shortly. Despite this news, Moltke and Falkenhayn left the meeting to send the order to the troops. As Albertini suggests, they almost certainly did this to avoid the chance that the dispatch might avert war.[129]

As noted, the kaiser, delighted by the English offer, recalled Moltke to tell him that Germany could now focus on the east. Bethmann and Jagow expressed joy over the English message, but it seems certain that this was just an act to placate Wilhelm's fears. Behind the scenes, they did everything to ensure war proceeded. Jagow's announcement of this "very important dispatch" ten minutes before it was brought into the meeting is suspicious. How could he have known it was very important unless he had already read at least parts of it? Yet he provided the group with no details, nor did he try to restrain Moltke and Falkenhayn before they ran off to implement mobilization.[130] It thus seems likely that his announcement was simply a cue to the military to leave as soon as possible.

The evening of 1 August was a nerve-racking one for Moltke, as the kaiser had put the Schlieffen Plan on hold as Berlin awaited the English response. Around 11:00 P.M., word was received that the English proposals were a misunderstanding.[131] Wilhelm recalled Moltke, telling him, "now you can do as you will."[132] The Schlieffen Plan was thus back on, with the invasion of Luxembourg to take place early the next morning.

The view that after 30 July the civilians gave up control to the military and their mobilization schedules—a myth Bethmann helped foster, and one accepted not only by inadvertent war scholars, but even by Albertini and Fischer—has been severely shaken by the above evidence. It is now time to put it in its final resting place. Far from the military's controlling the process, only one military leader—Army Chief of Staff Moltke—knew of the plan that would have a much greater effect on military actions than on civilian operations: the surprise declaration of war on Russia. When Tirpitz found out in the late evening of 1 August, he was outraged. Aside from the obvious military reasons for not declaring war until Germany was ready to attack Russia, Tirpitz felt that the move would undermine efforts to blame German adversaries for the war.[133] Minister of War Falkenhayn was also up in arms. To smooth ruffled feathers, at 2:30 A.M. on 2 August Bethmann met with Tirpitz and the generals to discuss the issue, as well as the timing of the declaration of war on France.

From records of the meeting, it is clear that many in the military were still wondering whether the declaration of war on Russia had actually been served. Bethmann admitted that the telegram containing the declaration had already been sent. But by failing to mention that it was to be delivered to Sazonov at 5:00 P.M. the previous day, he evidently sought to keep them confused on this point. In yet another example of Bethmann and Moltke's insidious collaboration, Moltke informed the group that Russia had fired shots across the border. Tirpitz then records Bethmann's response: "then, of course, the case is clear, that means the Russians have been the first to start and I shall have the declaration of war handed over the frontier by the nearest General." The military left the meeting still believing that the declaration of war was in the *process* of being delivered, even though the Russians had received it more than eight hours before. Thus Falkenhayn grabbed Jagow just after the meeting, pleading with him "to prevent the foolish and premature declaration of war on Russia." Jagow's reply: it was now too late.[134]

It is surely revealing that Moltke knew the whole time of the plan to declare war, yet said nothing to his colleagues. As with the chancellor, Moltke's key objective over the previous two days was to ensure that Austria kept on the road to war with Russia. On 30 July, Moltke had sent messages to Conrad instructing him to turn his forces against Russia. By the evening of 31 July–1 August, however, Berlin had received no confirmation of Austrian military plans, and the signs were unfavorable. On the afternoon of 31 July, Conrad hinted to Moltke that Austria would focus on Serbia and would stay on the defensive against Russia. Moltke immediately replied that Germany would soon be at war with Russia, but like Bethmann's message to Vienna that same afternoon, he said nothing about an ultimatum to Russia, nor of an impending declaration of war. Instead, he asked pointedly: "will Austria leave [us] in the lurch?"[135]

At 9:30 that evening, Conrad wrote back to say that Austria had already proved its willingness to wage war, and that it was only holding back to shift the blame by letting Russia declare war first, as per Berlin's "desire." He then said the words Moltke did not want to hear: that he thought he could "count on finishing off [the] war against Serbia before [the] move against Russia [is] necessary." Conrad asked for clarification on German intentions, pleading that only on 31 July had he received information "mak[ing] known Germany's intention to begin war against France and Russia."[136] Bethmann and Moltke's communications to Vienna had gotten them into a bind. Since neither could admit how quickly war was to come without scaring Austria off, they had said nothing to their Austrian counterparts about the twelve-hour ultimatum to Russia, let alone the plan to declare war. Conrad was thus under the impression he still had time to destroy Serbia.

For Berlin, this was worrisome. Despite Bethmann's 1:35 P.M. dispatch demanding Austria's immediate participation in the war with Russia, it now seemed that Austria was concentrating its troops in the south, not the east. This fear was reinforced by another telegram received from Conrad at 10:30 P.M. on 31 July:

> I beg His Excellency von Moltke for a definite statement whether it is now necessary to reckon with waging a major war against Russia immediately and unconditionally, that, in other words, there is no likelihood of our desisting from the war against Serbia without coming to grips with Russia. This definite statement is indispensable and urgent for our own decision.[137]

A moment of decision had arrived. If Berlin now revealed the plan against Russia, it would not only show that Bethmann had withheld information; it might push Austria into a peace with Russia, the very fear that had led to the withholding of information. But the revelation of Berlin's plan now seemed necessary if Austria was to play its designated role in the Schlieffen Plan. Hence, at 11:20 P.M., Moltke revealed that indeed there was an ultimatum.[138] Then at 2:20 A.M. on 1 August, knowing that Conrad had to decide that day whether to concentrate troops against Serbia or Russia, Moltke finally let him know the truth. Germany had demanded Russia's suspension of all military measures.

> If Russia rejects this demand, German declaration of war follows immediately. Russian reply demanded with twelve-hour time limit. Thus decision must be taken tomorrow. I regard acceptance of German demands by Russia as impossible.[139]

Conrad now knew that localized war against Serbia was out, and that he had to concentrate forces against the Russian masses.

This interchange reveals much about Moltke's role in the last days of the crisis. With Moltke the only military leader privy to the plan to declare war on Russia, there is little doubt that he conspired with the civilian leaders—Bethmann, Jagow, and the others in the Foreign Office—to bring on war while minimizing last-minute interference from either the kaiser *or* the German military. The declaration of war on Russia was a brilliant stroke, as Moltke surely understood: as with the Austrian declaration of war against Serbia, it would end any possibility of diplomatic intervention. Preventive war could then proceed. It is not surprising therefore that Moltke would confide to a friend a year later, just after being dismissed: "It is dreadful to be condemned to inactivity in this war which I prepared and initiated."[140]

The final piece of evidence showing the German leadership's guilt is its efforts to blame the French for the German attack on Belgium and France. By telling Paris on 31 July that Germany would mobilize after Russian rejection of the ultimatum, and that mobilization inevitably means war, Germany had successfully provoked France into mobilization. This mobilization was confirmed on the evening of 1 August. After heated discussions the next morning, it was agreed that the declaration of war against France should be delayed until Monday night at 7:00 P.M.

Why the delay, when the military now knew of the declaration of war on Russia and also understood that France had to be attacked first? Bethmann Hollweg provides the answer. At 9:00 A.M. on 2 August, just a few hours after meeting with the military, the chancellor sent a telegram to the kaiser. He informed Wilhelm of reports of Russian border crossings, as well as his requests to Vienna that it fulfill its alliance obligations. He continued: "In accordance with understanding with Ministry of War and General Staff, presentation of declaration of war to France not necessary today for any MILITARY reasons.

Consequently it will not be done, in the hope that the French will attack us."[141] Berlin was holding off a declaration of war in the hope that the French would attack? Perhaps no single line better demolishes the argument, critical to the preemptive-war thesis, that Germany went to war because it feared it would be attacked first, given the supposed advantage of the offensive. Here, instead of a French invasion feared, that invasion is actually desired. Undoubtedly Bethmann was hoping, as he had with the Russians, to thrust the blame for war onto French shoulders.

The argument that Germany was forced by mobilization schedules into war collapses completely when one sees that the real fear was not that France would get the jump on Germany, but that the French would not mobilize *enough*. Despite confirmation of French mobilization, by 2 August there was still worry that France had not mobilized extensively enough to give Germany the pretext to launch the Schlieffen Plan. Moltke's memo to the Foreign Office on the military situation, delivered that afternoon, noted: "I do not consider it necessary yet to deliver the declaration of war to France; [rather] I am counting on the likelihood that, if it is held back for the present, France, on her part, will be forced by public opinion to organize warlike measures against Germany." Moltke expressed the hope that France would move into Belgium once it heard of the harsh German ultimatum to Brussels (written by Moltke). Thus a crossing into France would be avoided "until activities on the part of France render it necessary."[142] It would be hard to find a clearer statement of the coordinated machinations of Moltke and Bethmann's Foreign Office in the final days of peace. By delaying the move against France, German leaders hoped France would increase its military readiness and even enter Belgium. Germany could then justify its full-scale attack.

For the next two days, until the declaration of war against France was delivered at 7:00 P.M. on 3 August, Berlin did its utmost to convince the world—especially Britain, which still might delay its involvement—that Germany was only responding to French provocations. French violations and atrocities were fabricated and communicated to London as truths.[143] French leaders, however, refused to fall into the German trap. They wisely mobilized, but the troops were ordered to move back ten kilometers from the border to prevent even an accidental clash that could be interpreted as French aggression. By Monday it was evident that France would not go into Belgium first. Although France took these precautionary measures to ensure British support, the measures made it difficult for Berlin to blame the French for the war.

By Monday afternoon, German leaders could wait no longer for evidence of French hostility. Hence, they simply pretended that it existed, and proceeded anyway. Paris was told that even though German troops had obeyed orders to respect the French frontier, French troops, in spite of the assurance of the ten-kilometer zone, had already crossed over the German frontier. Accordingly, "France has forced us into a state of war."[144]

On 4 August, as German troops crossed into Belgium, London sent an ultimatum to abstain or face a British declaration of war. It was ignored. The intricate maneuverings of the chancellor, the Foreign Office, and Moltke had delivered a war under favorable conditions: with Russia taking the blame, the German public supported a war for the survival of the fatherland; and Vienna had been cornered not only into fulfilling its alliance obligations, but into concentrating its troops on the Russian, rather than Serbian, border. English neutrality was not secured, but no one including Bethmann had ever thought it was likely in the first place. Yet by stringing London along, Berlin had at least delayed by a few days the deployment of the British Expeditionary Forces.[145] It is no wonder that Admiral Müller would write in his diary on 1 August: "The morning papers carry the speeches of the Emperor and of the Reich Chancellor to the enthusiastic crowd assembled outside the Palace and the Chancellor's Palais respectively. The mood is brilliant. The government has managed brilliantly to make us appear the attacked."[146] Bethmann and his cohorts had indeed succeeded in the difficult task of making others seem responsible for a war only Germany wanted. Their activities were so effective that eighty years later we still debate who or what caused the First World War.

*   *   *

Notes

1. Jack S. Levy, "Preferences, Constraints, and Choices in July 1914," *International Security* 15 (winter 1990–91): 153–63.
2. In actual fact, of course, German leaders thought in terms of *degrees* of support for both possibilities, from low to high, but for simplicity we can think in terms of a dichotomy.
3. Most of the options revolved around variations of the "Halt in Belgrade" proposal suggested by the kaiser on 28 July. The core debate between Austria and Russia was over the degree to which Serbia, Russia's ally, would be destroyed by a negotiated settlement: Austria wanted a higher degree, and Russia a lesser degree. Also of significance was how the settlement would appear to other states, especially Russia's Balkan and French allies. Russia could not be seen to be giving away the farm, even if, as its proposals in the final days indicate, it was willing to do so. Finally, the means to a settlement was important. Russia preferred a European-wide conference, since this would bring to bear the weight of other powers. Austria wanted at most German mediation. Both, however, were somewhat amenable to direct Austro-Russian talks, perhaps mediated by Germany.

   All of this led to eight possible outcomes that were heatedly discussed in the final days. From Austria's to Russia's most preferred, they were: (1) Austro-Serbian localized war; (2) temporary occupation of Serbia to force compliance to Austrian demands (*DD*: docs. 380, 433; 29 and 30 July) [VOLUME EDITOR'S NOTE: *DD* is *Die Deutschen Dokumente zum Kriegsausbruch*; Karl Kautsky, Max Montgelas, and Walther Schücking, eds., *The Outbreak of the World War: German Documents,* trans. Carnegie Endowment for International Peace. New York: Oxford University Press, 1924.]; (3) a Halt in Belgrade and "other places" to force Serbian compliance to Austrian demands (*DD*: doc. 323; 28 July); (4) a Halt in Belgrade and "other places" plus German mediation (*DD*: docs. 395, 396; 30 July); (5) a Halt in Belgrade and "other places," overseen by all the great powers (*DD*: doc. 460; 30 July); (6) Austrian military operations, but Austrian willingness to accept some modifications on its demands and to state that it is a European affair (Sazonov's "formula," *DD*: doc. 421; 30 July); (7) a negotiated peace through a four-power conference (*"à quatre"*) (*DD*: docs. 236, 248; 26 and 27 July); (8) an Austrian capitulation and return to status quo. I shall show how Berlin used these proposals so that it appeared to want peace, while ensuring that Austria and Russia would never reach a peaceful solution.

4. The purely-localized-war outcome was slightly higher in ranking to this negotiated peace. But since German leaders knew that it was unlikely from the beginning of July and next to impossible by its end, it cannot count as a serious possibility. Even so, statements by Bethmann discussed below indicate that general war with domestic and Austrian support was preferred to localized war. While the debate between Fischer and his critics now seems to revolve around whether Germany preferred localized war to continental war (with Fischer now arguing that continental war was preferred; Langdon, *July 1914,* chaps. 4–5), the real debate between the camps concerns whether Germany preferred negotiated peace to continental war. The calculated risk notion of the critics makes little sense unless one assumes that Berlin preferred a negotiated peace to continental war but risked the possibility of things getting out of hand (continental war or worse) to achieve the best option of a localized war.

5. Imanuel Geiss, ed., *July 1914* (New York: Scribner's, 1967), 70.

6. Quoted in Hartmut Pogge von Strandmann, "Germany," in R. J. W. Evans and Strandmann, eds., *The Coming of the First World War* (Oxford: Clarendon, 1988), 115. Bethmann also told Hoyos that "if [general] war was to become inevitable, the present moment would be more favorable than a later one." Quoted in Fritz Fellner, "Die 'Mission Hoyos,'" in Wilhelm Alff, ed., *Deutschlands Sonderung von Europa, 1862–1945* (Frankfurt: Lang, 1984), 295; see also *ÖA,* vol. 8, doc. 10076.

7. Geiss, *July 1914,* doc. 4.

8. Ibid., doc. 5. The military's pessimism was reinforced by two reports received on 5 July from the general staff, titled "The Completion of the Russian Railway Network" and "The Growing Power of Russia" (Konrad H. Jarausch, *The Enigmatic Chancellor* [New Haven: Yale University Press, 1973], 468, n. 9).

9. Kurt Riezler, *Tagebücher, Aufsätze, Dokumente,* ed. Karl D. Erdmann (Göttingen: Vandenhoeck und Ruprecht, 1972), 182–83 (except for minor changes, my translation here follows Wayne C. Thompson, *In the Eye of the Storm* [Iowa City: University of Iowa Press, 1980], 74–75).

10. Quoted in Norman Stone, *The Eastern Front, 1914–1917* (New York: Scribner's, 1975), 42.

11. Riezler, *Tagebücher,* 187.

12. Theodor Wolff, *Tagebücher 1914–1919,* ed. Bernd Sösemann (Boppard: Harald Boldt, 1984), 64. On 17 February 1915, Stumm told Wolff that in July 1914 "we

were not bluffing"; "We were reconciled to the fact that we would have war with Russia" and if it had not come, "we would have had it in two years' time under worse conditions" (ibid., 166–67).

13. Wolff, *Tagebücher*, 19 July 1917, 521–22. This was no post-hoc reconstruction of events. Just after Bethmann's statement that he feared war was inevitable, Wolff replied: "I know, I spoke to you then; you told me of your fear."

14. Quoted in Fritz Fischer, *Germany's Aims in the First World War* (New York: Norton, 1967), 51.

15. Quoted in Wolfgang J. Mommsen, *Imperial Germany, 1867–1918* (London: Arnold, 1995), 281, n. 67.

16. Quoted in ibid.

17. Riezler, *Tagebücher*, 184.

18. Geiss, *July 1914*, p. 89.

19. Geiss, *July 1914*, docs. 7 and 15.

20. Ibid., doc. 33.

21. The Austrian prime minister, Karl von Stürgkh, had remarked a day before that Vienna ran "the risk that by a policy of hesitation and weakness it could later on no longer be so certain of Germany's unqualified support." And Emperor Franz Joseph, as Berchtold records, on 9 July approved of a strong policy against Serbia, noting that he was "anxious that weak behavior would discredit our position vis-à-vis Germany." All quotations from Fritz Fischer, *War of Illusions* (New York: Norton, 1975), 480–81.

22. *DD*: doc. 19.

23. *DD*: doc. 49, 14 July.

24. *DD*: doc. 106; Fischer, *Germany's Aims*, 58.

25. Riezler, *Tagebücher*, 185. The word "liberation" likely refers to Riezler's prewar writings, where he argued that Germany had to "liberate itself from the nightmare of coalitions" against it (see Moses, *Politics of Illusion*, 33).

26. Riezler, *Tagebücher*, 186.

27. See John C. R. Röhl, "V. Admiral Von Müller and the Approach of War, 1911–1914," *Historical Journal* 12 (1969): 673, n. 105.

28. Fischer, *War of Illusions*, 483.

29. *DD*: doc. 74.

30. Quoted in Fischer, *War of Illusions*, 483.

31. Riezler, *Tagebücher*, 189–90.

32. Ibid., 189–91. On other secret preparations, see Wolff, *Tagebücher*, 153.

33. See D. C. B. Lieven, *Russia and the Origins of the First World War* (New York: St. Martin's, 1983), 140–45, and Luigi Albertini, *The Origins of the War of 1914*, 3 vols. (Oxford: Oxford University Press, 1952), 2:290–94.

34. Geiss, *July 1914*, doc. 71; *DD*: doc. 138.

35. *DD*: Appendix 4, doc. 2.

36. *DD*: doc. 257; Albertini, *Origins*, 2:455.

37. Quoted in Albertini, *Origins*, 2:460.

38. Inadvertent war theories require this notion in order to show that German leaders did not want war but could not prevent events from getting out of hand. Fischer requires it because he believes that Bethmann, counting on British neutrality, panicked when he saw that Britain would indeed oppose Germany.

39. They are thus often referred to as the "world-on-fire" telegrams. See Marc Trachtenberg, "The Meaning of Mobilization in 1914," *International Security* 15 (winter 1990/91): 120–51. Trachtenberg's position is similar to mine, in that he argues that the military did not usurp control, nor were preemptive motivations important (147–50). But Trachtenberg sees the telegrams as a genuine attempt by Bethmann to pull back from war, taken in response to Russian mobilization, not British warnings. When Bethmann failed, he did not lose control; rather, he "abdicated" it, allowing the military take over (142–43). Yet this leaves unexplained why Bethmann would simply give up when he still had time to negotiate. Trachtenberg's argument thus seems to rely ultimately on Bethmann's weak personality.

40. *DD*: doc. 3.

41. *DD*: doc. 72.

42. 25 July 1914, Wolff, *Tagebücher,* 64.

43. *DD*: doc. 456 (second part is drawn from Fischer's translation, *War of Illusions,* 492). See also *DD*: docs. 242, 291, 445.

44. *DD*: doc. 160.

45. *DD*: doc. 194.

46. See Riezler's entry on 23 July, recording Bethmann's view that the war will come through Russian mobilization. Once this occurred, "the whole nation will feel the danger and rise up": *Tagebücher,* 190.

47. *DD*: doc. 219.

48. See Albertini, *Origins,* 2:481–82. When the French ambassador, Jules Cambon, reminded him of his pledge later that week, Jagow admitted that he had made it; but stated that "the words … did not constitute a firm commitment on his part." *DDF,* vol. 11: doc. 380.

49. *DD*: doc. 236.

50. *DD*: doc. 238.

51. *DD*: doc. 237.

52. *DD*: docs. 258, 266, and 265.

53. See esp. Richard Ned Lebow, *Between Peace and War* (Baltimore: Johns Hopkins University Press, 1981), chap. 5.

54. Riezler, *Tagebücher,* 192.

55. *DD*: doc. 277.

56. Recall that Riezler had recorded that day Bethmann's belief that if Russia mobilized, "the whole nation will feel the danger and rise up" (n. 46).

57. *DD*: doc. 293 (kaiser's emphasis removed).

58. The proposal, in essentially the same form, was also put forward by England on 28 July.

59. *DD*: doc. 323.

60. *DD*: doc. 335. Wilhelm communicated with Vienna only through the chancellor, which allowed Bethmann to monitor and revise his messages.

61. *DD*: doc. 229.

62. *DD*: doc. 338.

63. It had been decided upon in secret by the czar and his advisers only at around 6:00 the night before, and Pourtalès had not yet been informed, nor had it been implemented.

64. *DD*: doc. 341 and 342.

65. Lieven, *Russia and the Origins,* 145–46; Albertini, *Origins,* 2:552–61.

66. *DD*: doc. 343.

67. See Geiss, ed., *Julikrise und Kreigsausbruch 1914,* vol. 2 (Hannover: Verlag für Literatur und Zeitgeschenen, 1964), doc. 676. See also Fischer, *War of Illusions,* 494; Albertini, *Origins,* 2: Chap.11.

68. *DD*: doc. 357. See *DD*: doc. 355 for a similar telegram received at 4:34 P.M.

69. *DD*: doc. 365.

70. See *DD*: doc. 377 and its n. 3.

71. *DD*: docs. 365A, 369, 370, and 376A.

72. *DD*: doc. 380.

73. From *DD:* doc. 359, sent to the czar at approximately 6:30 P.M. on 29 July; and doc. 335.

74. *DD*: doc. 332.

75. *DD*: doc. 387. There is also no question that the chancellor was responsible for these two telegrams: the original documents were in his own handwriting (see *DD*: doc. 383, n. 1; *DD*: doc. 387, n. 1).

76. *DD*: doc. 384.

77. See *DD*: doc. 357.

78. *DD*: doc. 384.

79. *DD*: doc. 385.

80. *DD*: doc. 342. Note that the passage reinforces the point that Bethmann knew that Russian mobilization was different, that it did not force Germany to preempt. See also Geiss, *Julikrise,* doc. 676, on Bethmann's 29 July conference with the generals, when he told them that he was "of the opinion that … the mobilization of Russia did not mean war."

81. *DD*: doc. 385.

82. *DD*: doc. 323.

83. At 10:15 P.M., 10:30 P.M., and 12:30 P.M.

84. *DD*: doc. 388.

85. *DD*: doc. 365 from Pourtalès, arriving at Berlin at 8:29 P.M., 29 July.

86. From *DD*: doc. 368. The missing fifth paragraph indicates that Grey believed that he could "secure for Austria every possible satisfaction." Because Bethmann did not send this to Austria, Vienna would not be encouraged to consult further with the English; all mediation would go through Berlin.

87. *DD*: doc. 395.

88. This interpretation may seem less plausible than the simpler explanation: that Bethmann truly wanted Austria to back down and agree to a deal with Russia. Yet while both interpretations are possible, the latter remains inconsistent with all of Bethmann's actions surrounding this telegram.

89. *DD*: doc. 365.

90. *DD*: doc. 396.

91. From his diary, quoted in Röhl, "Admiral Müller," 669. The Austrian naval attaché in Berlin wrote to Vienna the same day that "people here await all possible complications with the utmost calm and regard the moment as very favorable for a big settlement" (quoted in Fischer, *War of Illusions,* 487).

92. Jarausch, *Enigmatic Chancellor,* 169.

93. *DD:* doc. 456.

94. Riezler, *Tagebücher,* 193.

95. *DD:* doc. 407.

96. *DD:* doc. 408.

97. Geiss, *Julikrise,* doc. 1089.

98. *DD:* doc. 420; German White Book in *CDD:* exhibit 23.

99. This is not the only instance of tampering with times in the White Book to show Russia's responsibility. Compare Exhibits 20 and 21 of *CDD* to *DD:* docs. 335 and 332 respectively.

100. *DD:* doc. 422 in particular indicated that Russia was preparing along both the Austrian and German borders.

101. See Lieven, *Russia and the Origins,* chap. 5; Albertini, *Origins,* 3: chap. 1.

102. Why Berlin needed to provoke Petersburg first, and Paris second, is clear. Russia had the slowest mobilization schedule by far; hence, Germany, as the fastest mobilizer, could allow it to go first. France's mobilization, although not as quick as Germany's, was relatively efficient, so it had to be delayed until the last minute. This would allow Germany to claim that it was only responding to French mobilization, while still leaving the French army relatively unprepared for war. Berlin was playing a finely tuned game here: while trying to maximize the blame falling on Russia and France, which required others to mobilize first (or at least appear to have done so), Berlin had to ensure that their actual preparedness was low in order to increase the chance of victory. What is remarkable is how effectively the German leaders played this game, considering that the two objectives—blame and adversary preparedness—were pulling in different directions.

103. *DD:* docs. 433 and 465; see also 441.

104. *DD:* doc. 441.

105. Albertini, *Origins,* 2: 673.

106. Ibid., 3: 23–27.

107. *DD:* docs. 451 and 464.

108. *DD:* doc. 473.

109. From "Neue Dokumente zu Kriegsausbruch und Kriegsverlauf," documents collected by B. Schulte, *Militärgeschichtliche Mitteilungen* 25 (1979): 140. Wenninger continues: "From Vienna, still no answer to yesterday's telegram [presumably Moltke's to Conrad]. Again uncertainty, until we finally put this to bed."

110. Albertini (*Origins,* 3: 39–45) is the sole exception I could find, although he draws different conclusions.

111. Bethmann's alterations are shown in the footnotes of Kautsky's original publication of the documents *(DD).*

112. *DD:* doc. 490.

113. *DD:* doc. 491 (emphasis added).

114. *DD:* doc. 491, n. 4.

115. What if the French actually agreed to remain neutral? This would have destroyed the plan to attack France as an act of self-defense, while forcing Germany to turn against just Russia. Its western front would then be exposed to French attack. To avert this possibility, Bethmann attached to the telegram instructions that if France did declare

its neutrality, the ambassador was to "demand the turning over of the fortresses of Toul and Verdun as a pledge of neutrality," which Germany would occupy until the war with Russia was over (*DD*: doc. 491). This condition was so manifestly outrageous as to guarantee that Paris would reject neutrality and mobilize.

116. *DD*: doc. 492.
117. *DD*: doc. 492, n. 9.
118. *DD*: doc. 488 and its n. 6.
119. *DD*: doc. 479.
120. Albertini, *Origins,* 2: 671–74 and 3: 45–46.
121. *DD*: docs. 396 and 465.
122. Buchanan's paraphrase, in *My Mission to Russia,* vol. 1 (Boston: Little, Brown, 1923), 209.
123. Geiss, *Julikrise,* doc. 1000(d).
124. *DD*: doc. 542, n. 3.
125. *DD*: doc. 542. The ultimatum's demands were also clearly designed to be unacceptable to Russia (*DD*: doc. 490). Germany asked Russia to cancel not just general or partial mobilization, but all "measures." This was contrary to the 29 July promise that Germany would allow Russia to mobilize against Austria as long as it refrained from hostilities (*DD*: docs. 380 and 392). Moreover, given Russia's size, the demand was technically impossible to implement in twelve hours. Finally, the ultimatum offers no concessions despite Sazonov's previously conciliatory measures (*DD*: docs. 421 and 460; *BD*: vol. 11, doc. 340).
126. *DD*: doc. 542.
127. *DD*: doc. 542, n. 5.
128. *DD*: doc. 562.
129. Albertini, *Origins,* 3: 171.
130. One might think Jagow had read only the initial section of a partially decoded telegram which indicated the telegram's importance, but not its contents. Yet not only was the telegram short, but the key information about possible English and French neutrality appears in the first two sentences (*DD*: doc. 562).
131. *DD*: doc. 612.
132. Quoted in Albertini, *Origins,* 3: 177.
133. Ibid., 191–92.
134. Quoted in ibid., 195–96.
135. Quoted in ibid., 47.
136. Quoted in ibid., 47–48.
137. Quoted in ibid., 48.
138. Ibid., 48. Austrian civilian leaders were not so informed, for obvious reasons.
139. Quoted in ibid., 48.
140. Quoted in Röhl, "Germany," 27.
141. *DD*: doc. 629.
142. *DD*: doc. 662.
143. *DD*: docs. 667, 693, and 703.
144. *DD*: doc. 734.
145. Indeed, the British forces barely made it in time to help turn back the German tide.
146. Quoted in Fischer, *War of Illusions,* 505.

Chapter 4

WORLD WAR II: WHY DID WAR HAPPEN AGAIN?

4.1

THE 1930S AND THE ORIGINS OF THE SECOND WORLD WAR

Mark L. Haas

In this excerpt from a longer chapter, Mark L. Haas contrasts realist and identity (ideological) explanations of Nazi Germany's foreign policy decisions leading to World War II. He asks a basic counterfactual question: "in the absence of the impact of Nazi ideology on German leaders' perceptions of threat and consequent international choices, how different would German foreign policies in the 1930s have been?" He examines the details of conflicts at the foreign policy (decision-making) and systemic structural (ideological distances between groups in different countries) levels of analysis to show that a group of non-Nazi officers in the German army led by General Ludwig Beck opposed the war against France and Great Britain, even to the point of engaging in treasonous correspondence with London and Paris. This group saw the Soviet Union and communism as greater threats than western countries and liberalism, while Nazi ideology defined in terms of race saw both as equal threats. Hitler purged the non-Nazi officers, suggesting that "Germany's international decisions in the 1930s would have been very different if the Nazis had not been in power."

* * *

Source: Mark L. Haas, "The 1930s and the Origins of the Second World War," in *The Ideological Origins of Great Power Politics, 1789–1989* (Ithaca and London: Cornell University Press, 2005), 105–120. Bracketed editorial insertions are present in the original.

... Were Germany's leaders primarily driven to war for traditional security reasons or by the implications generated by Nazi beliefs? ...

* * *

The Foreign Policies of Nazi Germany, 1933–41

At first glance, it might appear that demonstrating the importance of ideological variables to Nazi Germany's foreign policies is a relatively easy exercise. Knowing what we do about Germany's horrific policies during the war, how else can we explain the Nazis' demonic conduct except by referring to their ideological beliefs?

In recent years, however, several influential books operating within the realist tradition have challenged the centrality of ideological variables to Germany's foreign policies in the 1930s. Most notably, Dale Copeland and John Mearsheimer claim that Nazi ideology was neither a necessary nor a sufficient condition for Germany to wage hegemonic war.[1] To these authors, power variables created very strong incentives that were pushing Germany to war regardless of its leaders' ideological beliefs. Because of its population advantages vis-à-vis the Western powers and its industrial and technological superiority in comparison to the Soviet Union, Germany in the 1930s had the potential to become the hegemon of the system. Copeland and Mearsheimer thus argue that Germany's leaders confronted incentives to wage major war in order to maximize their state's security. Moreover, these incentives were especially strong in the 1930s because the Soviet Union's industrial, and hence military, capacity was increasing at a fantastic rate.[2] When this fact is coupled with the USSR's resource advantages and huge population, it was highly likely that the Soviet Union in the near future would surpass Germany to become the dominant power on the continent. German leaders' decision to wage a major war when they did was therefore a preventive action against a rising power for the purpose of best ensuring Germany's position of dominance and thus its safety.

Although an analysis of power distributions and trends provides the best explanation for the timing of the Nazis' decision to initiate major war (i.e., while Germany was still substantially stronger than the Soviet Union), these variables fail to adequately explain Germany's motive for conflict: the belief that the other powers, particularly the USSR, were mortal enemies that needed to be defeated before they became too powerful. The mere *possibility* that states will use their power superiority to subjugate others in the future should not be a sufficient reason to impel leaders to engage in a preventive war in the present. Rational decision makers should base their actions, especially such risky and costly policies as preventive war, on the *probability* of particular outcomes occurring, not just their potentiality to occur. In terms of the 1930s, it is significant that Hitler and his supporters described a future conflict with the Soviet Union not as a mere possibility, but as a virtual inevitability.[3] Ideological—and not power—variables explain why the Nazis were so certain about the future course of German-Soviet relations.

Nazi leaders' ideological beliefs consisted of two primary organizing concepts: fierce anti-communism and dogmatic racism. The Nazis greatly amplified the aggressive effects of the latter beliefs by wedding them to a crude social Darwinist ethic. Life to Hitler, as he would repeat again and again, was a merciless struggle for existence among different "racial" (i.e., ethnic) groups. "In struggle," he asserted, "I see the destiny of all human beings; no one can escape the struggle if he does not want to be defeated."[4] Or as he stated in his book, *Mein Kampf,* "Those who want to live, let them fight, and those who do not want to fight in this world of eternal struggle do not deserve to live."[5] Jews were the primary, though by no means the only, object of the Nazis' racial enmity.

Hitler's ideological beliefs are often described as a domestic-level pathology that pushed him to aggress regardless of external considerations. There is obviously some truth to this description. However, because of the inherently relational dimension of Nazism's defining components (i.e., racism makes sense only by defining one's own race in relation to others, and anti-communism calls for a focus on communist beliefs and believers), this ideology should not be considered in strictly domestic-level terms. Instead, Hitler and his supporters repeatedly asserted that the ideological and "racial" distances separating states, and thus the nature of *other* regimes, were central to their policies. The greater the ideological and racial differences separating Hitler's Nazi "Aryans" from other groups, the more he feared and loathed them, and the reverse. Hence Hitler's undying enmity for "Jewish," Bolshevik Russia, and his obvious sympathy for fascist Italy. Looking only at the content of Nazi beliefs and not their impact on the ideological distances among regimes obscures these important differences. Examining the relational dimensions of Nazism thus allows us to better understand why the Nazis adopted the foreign policies they did while at no time excusing the pathological dimensions of their conduct.

The key question the remainder of this section seeks to answer is: How important was Nazism in pushing Germany's leaders to war? Or, to put it another way, in the absence of the impact of Nazi ideology on German leaders' perceptions of threat and consequent international choices, how different would Germany's foreign policies in the 1930s have been? I answer these questions primarily by examining the reasons for Germany's attack on the Soviet Union in 1941, which was an objective that remained the centerpiece of Hitler's foreign policies throughout the 1930s. Hitler was clear that any deviations from enmity with the USSR—most notably the Nazi-Soviet Pact of August 1939—were tactical decisions only that facilitated the realization of his ultimate goal: the destruction of the Soviet Union. As the Führer told Carl Burkhardt (the League of Nations commissioner in Danzig) in August 1939: "Everything I undertake is directed against the Russians; if the West is too stupid and blind to grasp this, then I shall be compelled to come to an agreement with the Russians, beat the West, and then after their defeat turn against the Soviet Union with all my forces."[6]

Although Germany and the Soviet Union shared similar totalitarian political institutions, on other key ideological issues the two states were polar opposites. Most notably, the Nazis' fierce hatred of communism and intense animosity to many of the prominent ethnic groups in the USSR clearly overwhelmed any institutional affinity between the two regimes. It is for this reason that both politicians and scholars of the day referred to Germany and the Soviet Union as dictatorships of the "right" and "left," respectively. Despite institutional similarities, the two states were at opposite ends of the ideological spectrum.

Hitler's statements repeatedly reflected this position. From the 1920s until the 1940s, both when he was in power and out, Hitler was clear that Germany's unavoidable conflict with the Soviet Union was primarily a product of the two states' huge ideological and racial differences. For example, in a February 1939 speech to the German army's field commanders, Hitler stated that the next war would be "purely a war of *Weltanschauungen,* that is, totally a people's war, a racial war."[7] Three months before Germany's attack on the Soviet Union, he told the Wehrmacht generals that the origins, objectives, and means of fighting the upcoming war were rooted in ideological differences between the two powers. According to the Führer: "This struggle is one of ideologies and racial differences and will have to be conducted with unprecedented, unmerciful, and unrelenting harshness.... The commissars are the bearers of ideologies directly opposed to National Socialism. Therefore the commissars will be liquidated."[8] In fact, the "main theme" of Hitler's reasoning for waging war on the Soviet Union, according to the Chief of the Armed Forces High Command, Wilhelm Keitel, was to engage "the decisive battle between two ideologies."[9] The Nazis believed that Germany's relations with a "Jewish," communist regime could only be a state of war. This view made the incentives for preventive hostilities against the USSR while Germany still had military superiority very powerful.

Supporting the claim that the huge ideological distance dividing Nazi Germany from communist Russia was critical to the Nazis' enmity toward this state is the fact that Hitler believed that the ideological differences dividing the Western democracies and the USSR would decrease the likelihood of these states coalescing into an effective alliance in time to prevent Germany's aggressive foreign policy aims. It is most likely this belief that pushed Hitler to try to establish in Western leaders' minds Germany's role as a "bulwark against communism."[10] Such a perception, the Führer obviously believed, would invariably lead to a confused understanding of his true aims by the Western democracies. This belief allowed Hitler to pursue his aggressive goals with more confidence in their success. The fact that Hitler and the Nazis believed that the ideological distances dividing states' leaders would play a significant role in shaping the foreign policies of Britain and France lends credence to the claim that this variable shaped Germany's foreign policies as well.

Ideological variables not only shaped Nazi leaders' estimates of other states' international intentions, but also their fears of domestic subversion, as the demonstration-effects mechanism predicts. The Nazis' conception of subversion was, however, different in emphasis from the way in which this fear manifested itself in other systems. Instead of being predominantly fearful, for example, of a particular regime type spreading throughout the system, Hitler and the Nazis were primarily terrified of *racial* subversion.[11] A foundational tenet of Hitler's political beliefs was that the superior Aryan race was destined to win the inter-racial struggle for existence that defined history. There was, however, an important caveat to this belief. To Hitler, the Aryans were destined for victory *only as long as they maintained their racial purity*.[12] Hitler believed that a policy of personal and political miscegenation (in which "inferior" races were allowed to possess political influence) had greatly weakened potentially powerful states in the past.[13] He was determined not to let this happen to Germany, though he recognized it as a distinct possibility.[14]

This understanding of threats to Germany's security had a direct impact on the Nazis' foreign policy choices. The desire to maintain the racial purity of the German nation necessitated a policy of racial purification at home—in which individuals of "inferior" races were either expelled from Germany or put in concentration camps—and a policy of racial extermination abroad. If "sub-human" peoples were exterminated or permanently subjugated, the possibility of German blood and political institutions being bastardized would be significantly mitigated, if not eliminated. With this understanding of the threats to Germany, both Hitler's need for war and his horrific policies during it are made more clear. The Führer feared the subversion of the German master race to the point where a war of annihilation against "inferior" races was the "logical" solution to this danger.[15] According to Keitel in a directive on behalf of Hitler on the eve of war with the USSR: "special tasks" (i.e., the murder of racial and ideological enemies) during the war would "result from the struggle which has to be carried out between two opposing political systems."[16] Realist theories cannot explain Germany's leaders' decision to wage a war of annihilation, especially when one considers its costliness in terms of both draining Germany's resources and alienating millions of potential sympathizers in eastern Europe who originally welcomed the German army as a liberating force from the Soviet Union.

Ideological differences among the great powers' leaders also contributed to the war by inhibiting effective understanding among them. Throughout the 1930s, many Western leaders assumed that Hitler had legitimate and limited aims, and that taking a strong deterrent stand against him would only provoke an unnecessary conflict. As a result of these beliefs, statesmen in France and especially in Britain attempted to placate the Führer by offering him various territorial and political concessions. Hitler, who understood life as an inevitable conflict in which war was both a necessary and ennobling activity, did not interpret British and French offers in the spirit in which they were made. Instead, he continually understood them to result from Western weakness.[17] Consequently, each concession made by Britain and France only solidified his conviction that these powers were decadent and that their leaders would never oppose him until it was too late. Thus, with each concession made to him, Hitler's willingness to risk major war grew. The worldviews of the Nazis and politicians in the Western democracies were simply too different to allow them to understand one another.

A final factor revealing the centrality of the Nazis' ideological beliefs to their foreign policy choices is that there is substantial evidence indicating that Germany's international decisions in the 1930s would have been very different if the Nazis had not been in power. Because officers in the German military continued to possess political influence throughout most of the 1930s, they were the most important group of non-Nazi decision makers in this period. If military leaders advocated similar foreign policies as Hitler and his supporters, *and* if they wanted conflict for traditional geopolitical reasons, then the uniqueness of an analysis based on ideological variables must be called into question.[18] Conversely, significant variation in foreign policy preferences between Nazis and non-Nazis would indicate the importance of ideological beliefs to policy formulation, especially in relation to realist arguments since power variables for all members of a particular state are identical.

In support of realist arguments, there was throughout the 1930s substantial foreign policy agreement on various important subjects between the Nazis and the traditional German military. Virtually all military officers concurred with the Nazis that the Versailles system that restricted Germany's sovereignty and power had to be destroyed; that the German-speaking peoples in Austria, Czechoslovakia, Poland, and Lithuania should be incorporated into Germany (by war, if necessary); and that Germany should engage in a massive rearmament program (the military's goals in this last area equaled Hitler's highly ambitious objectives for much of the 1930s).[19]

Beyond these objectives, however, substantial disagreement between the Nazis and many members of the traditional military continued to exist. There were a significant number of high-ranking individuals in the military and other security agencies who opposed core elements of Hitler's foreign policies to such a degree that these individuals became known in the historical literature as the "German resistance." Ideological differences between Nazis and the resisters were central to their foreign policy disagreements.

For representative expressions of the German resistance's foreign policy goals, I concentrate largely on the views of General Ludwig Beck, the Army Chief of Staff around whom, according to virtually all his contemporaries and scholars alike, the primary domestic opposition to Hitler focused. Other key military members of the resistance included Colonel Hans Oster (Chief of Staff and head of the Central Division of Abwehr, Germany's armed forces intelligence), Admiral Wilhelm Canaris (head of Abwehr), Colonel General Baron Werner von Fritsch (Army Commander-in-Chief), Lieutenant Colonel Helmuth Groscurth (Chief of an Abwehr division), Colonel General Erwin von Witzleben (Commander of the Berlin military district), and General Karl von Stülpnagel (Deputy Chief and Quartermaster General). The power of the German resistance centered around Beck is perhaps best revealed by the fact that Hitler in the late 1930s felt compelled to engage in deep purges of recalcitrant officers in order to realize his most ambitious international objectives.

Probably the most important foreign policy difference between the Nazis and the Beck group is that many of the latter opposed Germany going to war with France and especially Britain.[20] Not only did the resisters' support for a coup against Hitler reach its apogee in the months leading up to Germany's attack on France,[21] but some resisters engaged in treasonous correspondence with Britain and France to inform them of Hitler's battlefield plans in an attempt to prevent war with these states. These communications most powerfully illustrate the substantive (as opposed to merely tactical) nature of the differences between the Beck group and the Nazis.

The effects of ideological distances were central to the resisters' opposition to war with the Western democracies. Beck and most of his supporters viewed Britain and France as Germany's ideological allies against the greatest ideological threat in the system: the Soviet Union. Consequently, the Beck group believed that war among Germany, Britain, and France was a grave error because it would only weaken these states to the ultimate benefit of their primary enemy, the USSR.[22]

By claiming that most German resisters viewed Britain and France as ideological allies against the Soviet Union, I do not mean to imply that Beck, his supporters, and the key leaders in the Western democracies were dedicated to identical ideological objectives. Most members of the German resistance, especially in the military, were not liberals, but conservative nationalists. They remained committed to authoritarian political institutions, and believed that domestic order and respect for the armed forces should be of the highest social values.[23]

Despite these ideological differences with the Western democracies, the key point is that virtually all members of the German resistance viewed communism as a much greater ideological danger than liberalism. Beck and his allies therefore saw themselves as much closer ideologically to Western leaders (especially Western conservatives) than they were to Soviet elites.

Although the Nazis agreed with the Beck group that communism was a greater ideological danger than liberalism, this distinction was much more blurred for the Nazis than for the resisters. Beck and his allies repeatedly emphasized that Britain, France, and Germany were united by a "common European identity" that was based not only on mutual opposition to communism, but a common philosophical and moral heritage.[24] The German resisters to Hitler, as Klemons von Klemperer explains, were motivated by a vision of "the West" in which "law and humanity were to prevail."[25] This was a view that was absent from the fascists' ideology. To the Nazis, the Soviet Union was evil incarnate, but the Western powers were not far behind in terms of the Nazis' contempt for other political forms. As Hitler explained in *Mein Kampf*, "Democracy as practiced in Western Europe today is the forerunner of Marxism. In fact, the latter would not be conceivable without the former. Democracy is the breeding-ground in which the bacilli of the Marxist world pest can grow and spread. By the introduction of parliamentarianism, democracy produced an 'abortion of filth.' "[26]

The claims that Germany, Britain, and France should be allies against communist Russia, and thus that war among the former states would be deleterious to German interests, are themes that Beck and his allies would reiterate on a number of occasions, both publicly and privately. For example, in a 1937 meeting in Paris with the Chief of the French General Staff, General Maurice Gamelin, Beck told his French counterpart: "We do not wish to fight a war against France. You are convinced that you would emerge victorious. We think that we would be the victors.... But the real conclusion would be the destruction of Europe and our common civilization. The Bolsheviks would profit."[27] The historian Nicholas Reynolds, sums up Beck's views on this subject: "Beck obviously feared that Hitler's [aggressive policies] would ultimately lead to a second world war with disastrous consequences for Germany and Europe.... [No] matter who won ... it would offer unparalleled opportunities to Bolshevism. That was the lesson of 1918, and it obsessed Beck. For him it would be terrible if any European nation succumbed to communism.... Therefore Germany should try to achieve her goals without plunging Europe into another [great power] war," especially one between Germany, Britain, and France.[28]

In October 1939, Erich Kordt (head of the Foreign Office Ministerial Bureau) and Legation Counselor Hasso von Etzdorf formed a group advocating a coup against Hitler if the Führer ordered Germany to attack France. According to a memorandum written by this group, "Germany had never been closer to chaos and Bolshevism," and war between Germany and France would lead to further "expansionism of Bolshevism in Europe."[29] This document was warmly received by Beck and General Franz Haider (Chief of the General Staff), and it was subsequently shown as a basis for action against Hitler to General Walther von Brauchitsch (Commander-in-Chief of the Army), General Stülpnagel, Colonel Groscurth, and other members of the resistance.[30]

Beck explicitly expressed his opposition to Hitler's aggressive policies that were putting Germany on a collision course with France and Britain when he wrote in a memorandum in September 1939 after Germany's invasion of Poland: "We all want a large, strong, unified Germany with ... many independent and varied resources.... *This goal was to a large extent attained before the war began.* The material life of the German people was by and large adequate, if in need of some improvement. By no means does it necessitate a struggle for existence."[31] According to the historian Klaus-Jür-gen Müller, Beck's rejection of Nazi ideology created an "abyss" separating his primary foreign policy objectives from Hitler's. Whereas Hitler felt compelled to conquer the continent, "[Beck's] notion [of foreign policy expansion] was more that of an extension of German power in Central Europe by virtue of a position of influence and supremacy, not of annexations that went beyond the union with areas of German-speaking population."[32]

Because General Beck and his supporters believed Germany, Britain, and France to be ideological allies against the Soviet Union, the German resisters expected the Western powers to allow the creation of a strong German state so that it could be a more effective ally against the USSR.[33] These views are consistent with the predictions of the conflict-probability causal mechanism. The Beck group believed that disputes with the Western powers involving the Rhineland and the incorporation into Germany of Austria and the Sudetenland of Czechoslovakia would "sooner or later have been solved in Germany's favor" without the use of Hitler's aggressive tactics.[34] These were not unrealistic beliefs. Many French and especially British conservatives were willing to allow Germany to expand substantially its sphere of influence in eastern Europe in order to be a more effective "bulwark against communism," as long as this expansion was done peacefully and in a manner that was consistent with the principle of national self-determination.

One might argue that the Beck group's opposition to Hitler's most aggressive foreign policies was tactical only, that because Germany (in the resisters' minds) had not yet reached its greatest relative power advantage over its adversaries, it was rational to delay attack until that time. In support of this hypothesis is the fact that resisters frequently framed their opposition to Hitler's policies in terms of expediency and timing.[35]

Fear that Germany was not strong enough to win another world war no doubt contributed to military resisters' opposition to Hitler's core international objectives from 1938 through 1940. However, the depth of this opposition indicates that issues of timing were not the principal motivating factor of the Beck group.

In the first place, the fact that Hitler felt compelled both to purge extensively non-Nazis from the military and to eliminate the military's ability to affect policy suggests that the conflict between the Nazis and the military resisters went much deeper than issues of timing, but were instead a product of substantive policy differences. The greatest of Hitler's purges of the military occurred in February 1938 on the heels of the infamous Blomberg-Fritsch crisis (Field Marshal Werner von Blomberg was War Minister and Colonel General Baron Werner von Fritsch was Commander-in-Chief of the Army). Both these individuals were forced from their respective offices for scandalous reasons—Blomberg for marrying a former prostitute, Fritsch on trumped-up charges of homosexuality. Hitler used these scandals and the subsequent demoralization of the army to diminish significantly the power and influence of the military in favor of increased Nazi control.[36]

In the wake of the Blomberg-Fritsch crisis, sixteen (mostly senior) generals hostile to Nazism were forced to retire, and forty-six more were reassigned.[37] The independently minded ambassadors to Rome, Vienna, Beijing, and Tokyo were recalled. The obstinate Constantin von Neurath was replaced as foreign minister by the sycophantic Joachim von Ribbentrop. Hitler demanded that the army move closer to the National Socialist state in its ideology, that Beck be forced to resign in the near future, that new command structures for the military be implemented (including placing Hitler at the head of the armed forces), and that a clean sweep of the Army Personnel Office be made to better facilitate the placement of Nazi adherents.[38] These personnel and institutional changes not only removed from positions of power key opponents of Hitler's foreign policies, but no doubt coerced into silence many who retained their positions.

When all was said and done, the events of February 1938 marked the culmination of "Hitler's total success in gradually eliminating the army as a politically relevant factor, in eventually suppressing it completely and finally making it a simple, though thoroughly effective, instrument of his policies."[39] Although it is possible that Hitler felt the need to purge the army because of disagreements over the best time to engage in military hostilities as opposed to more substantive differences in foreign policy objectives, the extent of Hitler's purges and organizational changes belies such an interpretation.

The second, even more powerful, set of evidence that reveals the depths of non-Nazi resisters' substantive opposition to Hitler's foreign policies is that members of the Beck group, including military officers, engaged in a multitude of covert messages to Britain and France that were designed to thwart Hitler's most ambitious international goals. In these messages, the resisters informed British and French representatives of Germany's short- and long-run intentions, and even the details of military plans of attack in Czechoslovakia and the west.[40] The Beck group also pleaded with Britain and France in these messages to make a determined stand against Hitler in order to give Germany a foreign policy defeat that would provide significant aid to their coup plans (many resisters were even *discouraged* by Hitler's victory at Munich and the defeat of France in 1940 because these outcomes reduced the chances of forcing Hitler from power).[41]

That some of Germany's highest-ranking officials would engage in such treasonous correspondence for primarily reasons of expediency (i.e., that Germany had not yet reached its greatest power-political advantage over its rivals) seems very unlikely. It is an illogical position to assert that these individuals both conspired to have Germany suffer international defeat and risked plunging it into domestic turmoil in order to avoid these very pitfalls because Germany's relative military power had not yet peaked. Moreover, the nature of the resisters' treasonous correspondences with Britain and France reveal a level of trust (e.g., that these states would not take advantage of Germany's vulnerability during and after a coup) and a community of interests that cannot be explained with reference to expediency. Instead, these beliefs were a product of ideological affinities between the resisters and the Western democracies. It would have been unthinkable, for example, for the Beck group to send similar treasonous messages to Russia as long as it was a communist regime.

After Germany's defeat of France in 1940, however, there was a clear weakening of the German military's resistance to Hitler's foreign policies. After Hitler's seemingly endless string of foreign policy successes, there was

238 MARK L. HAAS

a noticeable bandwagon effect in which former resisters, including such notables as the Chief of the General Staff, General Franz Haider, abandoned their opposition to the Nazis' international objectives. In fact, most officers supported Hitler's decision to wage a war of extermination against the Soviet Union. Because members of the traditional military once again seemed to agree with Hitler's international goals, some have argued that this demonstrates the centrality of geopolitical concerns to Germany's foreign policies. Regardless of the ideological differences dividing Nazis and the traditional German military, most agreed with Hitler's campaign against the USSR.[42]

This argument has some merit, but it also has two significant weaknesses. First, although many in the military were willing to support Hitler's campaign against Russia *in 1941,* it is highly unlikely that without Hitler's constant pressure throughout the 1930s, including both substantial purges of the military and institutional reorganizations that limited the political power of the armed forces, Germany would have been in the situation it was in this year. The Nazis' particular vision of international relations, and especially their willingness to wage war against the Western democracies over the objections of the Beck group, were necessary preconditions for Germany to be in the position in 1941 to attack the USSR without the hazards of a two-front war. The incentives created by Germany's relative position in the international distribution of power were far from sufficient to arrive at this point.

Second, the evidence is clear that the German military leaders' fears and hostility toward the USSR, just as for the Nazis, were primarily a product of ideological variables. As indicated in the previous analysis, most members of the military, including those in the resistance, were fervently anti-communist. This ideological antipathy not only pushed German military leaders to view the Soviet Union as both a large subversive and power-political threat, but was, according to Müller, of "utmost importance" to these individuals' support of Hitler's eastern campaign. Bolshevism, to Germany's military officers, was "the very negation, the antithesis of all their political, social and moral values. Therefore, it had to be totally exterminated."[43]

Many leaders in the German military both described their motives for war with the Soviet Union as a result of the huge ideological differences dividing the two states, and supported the Nazis' policies during the war of exterminating undesirables based on ideological/racial criteria. The content of senior commanders' addresses, deployment directives, and battlefield orders supports this assertion.[44] For example, in May 1941 the High Command of the Wehrmacht issued a directive to its troops that stated that Bolshevism is the "deadly enemy of the National Socialist German nation. It is against this destructive ideology and its adherents that Germany is waging war."[45] In the same month, General Erich Hoepner, who was a resister to Hitler killed for his part in the coup of July 1944, wrote that Germany's war against the USSR was "the defense of European culture against ... Jewish Bolshevism. The objective of this battle must be the destruction of present-day Russia and it must therefore be conducted with unprecedented severity. Every military action must be guided in planning and execution by an iron will to exterminate the enemy mercilessly and totally. In particular, no adherents of the present Russian-Bolshevik system are to be spared."[46]

Consistent with these ideological objectives, from the beginning of the war the army leadership actively aided the SS in murdering hundreds of thousands of people based solely on ideological and racial criteria.[47] The Army High Command adopted these policies even though they proved to be militarily costly since Germany's brutality stiffened Russian soldiers' resistance to the German attack.[48]

This analysis indicates that it is likely that Nazis and non-Nazis in the military advocated similar policies toward the Soviet Union in 1941 not because geopolitical concerns impelled these decision makers to adopt certain policies regardless of ideological beliefs, but because these groups of leaders, regardless of other ideological differences, shared an important ideological conviction: hatred of communism. Put another way, although the contents of the ideological beliefs espoused by Nazis and members of the traditional German military were very different, the ideological distances dividing both groups' beliefs from Soviet principles were extremely large. To both Nazis and non-Nazis in the military, these ideological distances remained key determinants of their foreign policies throughout the 1930s and 1940s.

* * *

Notes

1. Dale C. Copeland, *The Origins of Major War: Hegemonic Rivalry and the Fear of Decline* (Ithaca: Cornell University Press, 2000), chap. 5; John J. Mearsheimer, *The Tragedy of Great Power Politics* (New York: W. W. Norton, 2001), chaps. 6, 8. See also Randall L. Schweller, *Deadly Imbalances: Tripolarity and Hitler's Strategy of World Conquest* (New York: Columbia University Press, 1998).

2. Paul Kennedy, *The Rise and Fall of the Great Powers: Economic Change and Military Conflict from 1500 to 2000* (New York: Random House, 1987), 323, 299, 330; Copeland, *Origins of Major War*, chap. 5.

3. Cf. Jeremy Noakes and Geoffrey Pridham, eds., *Nazism, 1919–1945: A History in Documents and Eyewitness Accounts,* vol. 2, *Foreign Policy, War and Racial Extermination* (New York: Schocken Books, 1988), doc. 185, p. 281; doc. 186, p. 288.

4. In William Carr, *Arms, Autarky, and Aggression: A Study in German Foreign Policy, 1933–1939* (London: Edward Arnold, 1972), 11.

5. Adolf Hitler, *Mein Kampf* (Boston: Houghton Mifflin, 1971), 289. These are themes that Hitler would repeat throughout his public and private writings, his speeches, and his private talks. For example, as Hitler explained to his senior army commanders in May 1939, Germany's relations with the other powers were not "a question of right or wrong but of to be or not to be for 80,000,000 people" (in Noakes and Pridham, *Nazism,* doc. 539, p. 738). See also doc. 541, p. 741; doc. 185, p. 181; P. M. H. Bell,

The Origins of the Second World War in Europe (London: Longman, 1986), 81; Hitler, *Mein Kampf,* vol. 1, chap. 11.

6. In Noakes and Pridham, *Nazism,* doc. 540, p. 739. Hitler expressed these points in a more emotional manner when he wrote to Benito Mussolini on the eve of Germany's attack on the Soviet Union: "[The "partnership" with the Soviet Union from 1939 to 1941 was] often very irksome to me, for in some way or other it seemed to me to be a break with my whole origin, my concepts and my former obligations. I am happy now to be relieved of these mental agonies" (in William L. Shirer, *The Rise and Fall of the Third Reich: A History of Nazi Germany* [New York: Simon and Schuster, 1960], 851).

7. In Jürgen Förster, "New Wine in Old Skins? The Wehrmacht and the War of 'Weltanschauungen,' 1941," in *The German Military in the Age of Total War,* ed. Wilhelm Deist (Dover, N.H.: Berg, 1985), 305; see also 306.

8. In Shirer, *Rise and Fall of the Third Reich,* 830. See also Schweller, *Deadly Imbalances,* 99; Jürgen Förster, "Barbarossa Revisited: Strategy and Ideology in the East," *Jewish Social Studies* 50, nos. 1, 2 (Winter-Spring 1988/92): 21. No doubt the *content* of Nazi ideology, especially the Social-Darwinist tenet that life is a brutal struggle for survival among ethnic groups, substantially contributed to the Nazis' animosity toward the other powers, including the USSR. Nevertheless, as evidenced by Hitler's explicit emphasis on ideological and racial differences to his choices, ideological distance remained central to the Nazis' acute perceptions of threat and aggressive international policies, especially toward the USSR.

9. In Shirer, *Rise and Fall of the Third Reich,* 846. The quotation is a summary of a "comprehensive political speech" by Hitler to his generals in June 1941.

10. Gerhard Weinberg, *The Foreign Policy of Hitler's Germany,* vol. 1: *Diplomatic Revolution in Europe, 1933–1936* (Chicago: University of Chicago Press, 1970), 310 (hereafter, *Foreign Policy of Hitler's Germany, 1933–1936*); Michael Jabara Carley, "'A Fearful Concatenation of Circumstances': The Anglo Soviet Rapprochement, 1934–6," *Contemporary European History* 5, no. 1 (March 1996): 44, 45.

11. The Nazis were also fearful of institutional subversion by those Aryan "traitors" who supported either liberalism or communism, but racial subversion is what obsessed Hitler.

12. Hitler, *Mein Kampf,* 285, 286, 289, 296, 297, 327, 328, 688.

13. This is clearly what Hitler believed had happened with Russia, the United States, and to some degree England (Hitler, *Mein Kampf,* esp. vol. 1, chap. 11; Gerhard Weinberg, "Hitler's Image of the United States," *American Historical Review* 69, no. 4 [July 1974]: 1010–1011; and Andreas Hillgruber, "England's Place in Hitler's Plans for World Domination," *Journal of Contemporary History* 9, no. 1 [January 1974]: 10, 21).

14. As Hitler put it in *Mein Kampf:* "The danger to which Russia succumbed [i.e., of "racial poisoning"] is always present for Germany" (661).

15. The differences between ideological content and ideological distance get somewhat blurry in this instance. The specific behavioral prescriptions of Nazism (ideological content) pushed its adherents to extreme forms of racism, but notions of racial and ideological differences (ideological distance) caused the Nazis to target for annihilation some groups and some states more than others.

16. In Shirer, *Rise and Fall of the Third Reich*, 832.

17. Weinberg, *Foreign Policy of Hitler's Germany, 1933–1936*, 206; Gerhard Weinberg, *The Foreign Policy of Hitler's Germany: Starting World War II, 1937–1939* (Chicago: University of Chicago Press, 1980), 141 (hereafter *Foreign Policy of Hitler's Germany, 1937–1939*).

18. Copeland, *Origins of Major War*, chap. 5.

19. Klaus-Jürgen Müller, *The Army, Politics, and Society in Germany, 1933–45* (Manchester: Manchester University Press, 1987); Copeland, *Origins of Major War*, chap. 5; Wilhelm Deist, *The Wehrmacht and German Rearmament* (Toronto: University of Toronto Press, 1981), esp. 91, 95, 108.

20. Robert O'Neill, "Fritsch, Beck, and the Führer," 33, and Klaus-Jürgen Müller, "Witzleben, Stülpnagel, and Speidel," 51–52, both in *Hitler's Generals*, ed. Correlli Barnett (London: Weidenfeld and Nicolson, 1989); Nicholas Reynolds, *Treason Was No Crime: Ludwig Beck, Chief of the German General Staff* (London: William Kimber, 1976), 113–115, 169, 177.

21. Müller, "Witzleben, Stülpnagel, and Speidel," 51–54.

22. Reynolds, *Treason Was No Crime*, 113–115; Harold C. Deutsch, *The Conspiracy against Hitler in the Twilight War* (Minneapolis: University of Minnesota Press, 1968), 205–207.

23. Klemons von Klemperer, *German Resistance against Hitler: The Search for Allies Abroad, 1938–1945* (Oxford: Clarendon Press, 1992), 10, 19, 23, 25; Reynolds, *Treason Was No Crime*, 33–34. Despite many military resisters' general commitment to authoritarianism, there was agreement among them that in the wake of a successful coup against Hitler, they would replace the Nazi regime with a conservative democracy (Shirer, *Rise and Fall of the Third Reich*, 375; von Klemperer, *German Resistance against Hitler*, 105–106). This preference provides additional evidence of ideological affinity between resisters and the Western democracies.

24. Reynolds, *Treason Was No Crime*, 200.

25. von Klemperer, *German Resistance against Hitler*, 29. See also 8, 9, 193, 196, 434, 437; Müller, *Army, Politics, and Society in Germany*, 80; Deutsch, *Conspiracy against Hitler in the Twilight War*, 206–207; Reynolds, *Treason Was No Crime*, 113.

26. In Werner Maser, *Hitler's Mein Kampf: An Analysis*, trans. R. H. Barry (London: Faber and Faber, 1970), 179. See also Weinberg, *Foreign Policy of Hitler's Germany, 1933–1936*, 4, 15–21; Carr, *Arms, Autarky, and Aggression*, 13. Despite Hitler's contempt for Britain's political system, he remained more sympathetic to this state than others due to perceptions of racial affinity between Anglo-Saxons and German "Aryans." Until almost the end of the war, Hitler believed that racial affinity and mutual antipathy to communism would push Britain to ally with Germany against the Soviet Union (Hillgruber, "England's Place in Hitler's Plans," 18–21; Schweller, *Deadly Imbalances*).

27. In Reynolds, *Treason Was No Crime*, 113.

28. Ibid., 115, 192. Consistent with these views, Beck and his allies were opposed to the Nazi-Soviet Pact (183, 189; see also Müller, *Army, Politics, and Society in Germany*, 119). The agreement not only increased the relative power of the Soviet Union, but made war between Germany and the Western powers more likely.

29. In Deutsch, *Conspiracy against Hitler in the Twilight War,* 206, Deutsch's summary of the memorandum.

30. Ibid., 207–208.

31. In Reynolds, *Treason Was No Crime,* 189–190 (emphasis added). See also 83–84; Deutsch, *Conspiracy against Hitler in the Twilight War,* 97–108.

32. Müller, *Army, Politics, and Society in Germany,* 79.

33. Reynolds, *Treason Was No Crime,* 119, 120, 192, 201, 202.

34. Ibid., 110. See also 108, 150; Harold C. Deutsch, *Hitler and His Generals: The Hidden Crisis, January-June 1938* (Minneapolis: University of Minnesota Press, 1974), 37, 72; Deutsch, *Conspiracy against Hitler in the Twilight War,* 207, 353.

35. Copeland, *Origins of Major War,* chap. 5.

36. General Alfred Jodl, a Nazi sympathizer, wrote in his diary at the time of the crisis that Hitler was planning major changes in both military organization and personnel in order to "at last bring the military to heel" (Shirer, *Rise and Fall of the Third Reich,* 316, Shirer's summary of Jodl's diary entry).

37. Matthew Cooper, *The German Army, 1933–1945: Its Political and Military Failure* (London: MacDonald and Jones, 1978), 77–78; Shirer, *Rise and Fall of the Third Reich,* 318–319.

38. Deutsch, *Hitler and His Generals,* 223–225. In addition to Hitler appointing himself as the head of the newly created Supreme Command of the Armed Forces (known by its German acronym, OKW), other structural changes initiated at this time included the end of the Army Commander-in-Chief's authority to direct all fighting services and the significant curtailment of access by military leaders to civilian authorities (see Cooper, *German Army,* 84–86, 190, 192, 248).

39. Müller, *Army, Politics, and Society in Germany,* 34, also 10, 34–37; Deutsch, *Hitler and His Generals,* 230, 267; Donald Cameron Watt, *How War Came: The Immediate Origins of the Second World War, 1938–1939* (New York: Pantheon Books, 1989), 24–25. In his attempt to show that the resisters' opposition to Hitler's foreign policies involved issues of timing only and not substantive aims, Copeland ignores the number of generals and other personnel either forced into retirement or reassigned in the wake of the Fritsch-Blomberg crisis, as well as the important institutional changes made at this time. Nor is there any mention in Copeland's analysis of the resisters' attempts to sabotage Hitler's policies through treasonous communications with the Western powers.

40. For example, in August 1939 Beck passed on to the Western powers minutes from a meeting between Hitler and his generals that detailed the Führer's plans for attack in Poland and his intentions to exterminate "undesirables" in this state. In 1940, Beck and other resisters told the Western powers that Hitler intended to violate the neutrality of Belgium and Holland in order to attack France. See Reynolds, *Treason Was No Crime,* 183–184, 206; Shirer, *Rise and Fall of the Third Reich,* 380–382.

41. Deutsch, *Conspiracy against Hitler in the Twilight War,* 106, 354; von Klemperer, *German Resistance against Hitler,* 89, 97, 109, 112, 219, 220; Reynolds, *Treason Was No Crime,* 211.

42. See especially Copeland, *Origins of Major War,* chap. 5.

43. Klaus-Jürgen Müller, "The Military, Politics, and Society in France and Germany," in *The Military in Politics and Society in France and Germany in the Twentieth*

Century, ed. Klaus-Jür-gen Müller (Oxford: Berg Publishers, 1995), 18–19; see also Förster, "Barbarossa Revisited."

44. Förster, "Barbarossa Revisited," 23.

45. In Jürgen Förster, "The German Army and the Ideological War against the Soviet Union," in *The Policies of Genocide: Jews and Soviet Prisoners of War in Nazi Germany,* ed. Gerhard Hirschfeld (London: Allen and Unwin, 1986), 20.

46. In Förster, "Barbarossa Revisited," 23.

47. Hirschfeld, ed., *Policies of Genocide,* esp. chaps. 1, 2, 5; Förster, "Barbarossa Revisited"; Peter Longerich, "From Mass Murder to the 'Final Solution': The Shooting of Jewish Civilians During the First Months of the Eastern Campaign within the Context of Nazi Jewish Genocide," in *From Peace to War: Germany, Soviet Russia, and the World, 1939–1941,* ed. Bernd Wegner (Oxford: Berghahn Books, 1997), 253–275.

48. Förster, "Barbarossa Revisited," 27.

4.2

SELECTIONS FROM *PRESIDENT ROOSEVELT AND THE COMING OF THE WAR, 1941: A STUDY IN APPEARANCES AND REALITIES*

Charles A. Beard

Charles A. Beard represents a revisionist or critical theory school of U.S. foreign policy. In these excerpts from his book *President Roosevelt and the Coming of the War, 1941,* he argues that Roosevelt took America to war in 1941 in violation of his pledges in the 1940 election and throughout 1941 to keep America out of the European war. While conventional wisdom subsequently justified that decision as necessary to save American democracy, Beard contends the decision actually destroyed American democracy. It extended unlimited powers to the presidency, undermined the Constitution, and set America on a course of global imperialism that substituted arbitrary for limited power. Why did this happen? Notice that as a critical theorist Beard indicts historical forces beyond the control of the people but that he also emphasizes several interconnected doctrines that exalted America as a great power (realist), gave America the moral right to lead the rest of the world (identity), and sanctioned the expansion of trade and commerce as the elixir of world peace (liberal). Can America change those doctrines? Not easily. For revisionist historians, these doctrines are merely the American version of deep-seated historical forces that keep producing imperial powers.

[From Chapter 1, "Moral Commitments for the Conduct of Foreign Affairs in 1941"]

President Roosevelt entered the year 1941 carrying moral responsibility for his covenants with the American people to keep this nation out of war—so to conduct foreign affairs as to avoid war. Those covenants, made in the election campaign of 1940, were of two kinds. The first were the pledges of the Democratic party to which he publicly subscribed while he was bidding for the suffrages of the people. The second were his personal promises to the people, supplementing the obligations of his party's platform.[1]

Source: Charles A. Beard, selections from "Moral Commitments for the Conduct of Foreign Affairs in 1941" (Chap. 1) and "Interpretations Tested by Consequences" (Chap. 18), in *President Roosevelt and the Coming of the War, 1941: A Study in Appearances and Realities* (New Haven: Yale University Press, 1948), 1, 8, 573–584, 590–598.

The antiwar covenants of the Democratic party, to which President Roosevelt had committed himself unreservedly during the campaign, were clear-cut....

* * *

If the processes of popular election and responsible government had any meaning or validity, the antiwar covenants with the American people, freely entered into by the Democratic party and President Roosevelt during the campaign of 1940, were specific commitments to be fulfilled after their victory at the polls in November. Those covenants were explicit mandates for the President in the conduct of foreign affairs in 1941. They were equally explicit mandates for the Democratic Senators and Representatives, who had indubitable control of Congress, in the enactment of legislation relative to all issues of peace and war.

Those covenants were no mere incidents or practical jokes of the campaign. They were, in fact, major promises of the campaign, extensively and definitely expounded in documents and speeches, and were binding in honor and good conscience after the election. In short, unless deceiving the people in matters of life and death is to be regarded as a proper feature of the democratic politics and popular decisions at the polls are to be treated as chimeras, President Roosevelt's peace pledges of 1940 were imperatives for him in 1941; and only by spurning the peace pledges of their party could Democratic Senators and Representatives dominant in Congress enact into law measures calculated to take the United States into war.

* * *

[From Chapter 18, "Interpretations Tested by Consequences"]

* * *

The Main Brief of Defense—Tested by Consequences

[To explain how America nevertheless went to war] a favorable interpretation has been and is still being offered by many American publicists in the following form. The great end which President Roosevelt discerned and chose justified the means which he employed. As a farsighted statesman he early discovered that unless the United States entered the war raging in Europe, Hitler would be victorious; and the United States, facing alone this monstrous totalitarian power, would become a victim of its merciless ideology and its despotic militarism. According to this interpretation, it was a question of democracy, the Four Freedoms, the noble principles of the Atlantic Charter, and world security on the one side; of totalitarianism, consummate despotism, and military subjugation on the other side. Since the American people were so smug in their conceit, so ignorant of foreign affairs, and so isolationist in sentiment that they could not themselves see the reality of this terrible threat to their own safety and a necessity to meet it by a resort to war, President Roosevelt had to dissemble in order to be reëlected in 1940 as against Wendell Willkie, then the antiwar candidate of the Republicans on an antiwar platform. Furthermore, as members of Congress, Democrats and Republicans alike, continued throughout the year, until December 7, their vigorous opposition to involvement in war, President Roosevelt, in conducting foreign affairs, had to maintain the appearance of a defensive policy until the Japanese attack on Pearl Harbor. But the means which President Roosevelt actually employed in the conduct of foreign affairs were justified by the great end which he, with peculiar clairvoyance, had early discerned and chosen for himself and his country.[2]

* * *

The interpretation that the end justified the means, like all other interpretations, depends upon the point of view of those who make or accept it; and though it be proclaimed as the settled truth, its validity is nonetheless open to tests of knowledge.[3] Even a cursory examination of the thesis raises questions of time and consequences, foreign and domestic.[4]

When did the end that justified the means actually come? With the surrender of Italy, Germany, and Japan? If not, when did it come or is it to come—in what span of time, short or long? By whom and according to what criteria is the question of time to be answered beyond all reasonable doubt?

If the time for the achievement of the end be postponed to some point in the indefinite future, the confirmation of the thesis must likewise be postponed indefinitely. In that case an effort to confirm it now becomes a matter of calculating probabilities, ponderable and imponderable. If, however, the results of the war—foreign and domestic—thus far known be taken into the reckoning, a question both logical and historical may be asked: Does it now appear probable that President Roosevelt did in fact so clearly discern the end—the consequences to flow from his actions in 1941—that he was in truth justified in his choice and use of means?

With regard to consequences in foreign affairs,[5] the noble principles of the Four Freedoms and the Atlantic Charter were, for practical purposes, discarded in the settlements which accompanied the progress, and followed the conclusion, of the war. To the validity of this statement the treatment of peoples in Estonia, Lithuania, Poland, Rumania, Yugoslavia, China, Indo-China, Indonesia, Italy, Germany, and other places of the earth bears witness. More significant still for the fortunes of the American Republic, out of the war came the triumph of another totalitarian regime no less despotic and ruthless than Hitler's system, namely, Russia, possessing more than twice the population of prewar Germany, endowed with immense natural resources, astride Europe and Asia, employing bands of Quislings as terroristic in methods as any Hitler ever assembled, and insistently effectuating a political and economic ideology equally inimical to the democracy, liberties, and institutions of the United States—Russia, one of the most ruthless Leviathans in the long history of military empires.

Since, as a consequence of the war called "necessary" to overthrow Hitler's despotism, another despotism was raised to a higher pitch of power, how can it be argued conclusively with reference to inescapable facts that the "end" justified the means employed to involve the United States in that war? If the very idea of neutrality with regard to Hitler was shameful in 1941, what is to be said of commitments made in the name of peace and international amity at Teheran and Yalta, where the avowed and endorsed principles of the Atlantic Charter for world affairs were shattered—in commitments which were subsequently misrepresented by President Roosevelt, publicly and privately?[6]

Nor more than two years after the nominal close of the war did the prospects of "reconstruction" in Germany and Japan promise the achievement of President Roosevelt's great end in any discernible time ahead.

In respect of domestic affairs, the consequences of the involvement in the war are scarcely less damaging to the thesis that the end justified the means. Among the many dangers long emphasized by advocates of war in the name of perpetual or durable peace, none was described in more frightening terms than the prospect that Hitler would be victorious in Europe and that the result of his victory would spell disaster for the United States. It would mean the transformation of the United States into a kind of armed camp for defense, with all the evils thereunto attached: a permanent conscript army, multiplied annual outlays for armaments, a huge national debt, and grinding taxes. The expansion of American economy, so necessary for domestic prosperity, would be blocked by the impossibility of "doing business with Hitler," that is, by barriers to American commerce in the form of state-fostered cartels and state-controlled economies in Europe. Moreover, the promotion of beneficent reforms at home, from which President Roosevelt had been compelled to turn in military preparations for defense, would be permanently barred. Only by victory over Hitler, it was claimed, could these frightful evils be avoided.

But judging by results of participation in the war, and the prospects of evident tendencies, were these dreadful evils obviated by the victory at arms? While the war was still raging, President Roosevelt recommended to Congress the adoption of conscription as a permanent policy for the United States—under the softer name of universal service; and his successor, President Truman, continued to urge that policy upon Congress even after large-scale fighting had nominally stopped. Furthermore, it was now claimed by former advocates of war that huge armed forces were necessary in "peacetime" to "secure the fruits of victory" and "win the peace"—by extirpating the spirit of tyranny in Germany and Japan and by restraining the expansion of Russian imperial power.

As for military expenditures, they were fixed in 1947 at many times the annual outlays of prewar years, despite the cuts made by the Republican Congress in President Truman's budget demands. To the people of the United States, the war bequeathed a national debt, augmented from about $60,000,000,000 in 1940 to approximately $279,000,000,000 in 1946, or about $2,000 for every man, woman, and child in the country. To meet the annual interest on the national debt it was necessary in 1947 for the government to raise about $5,000,000,000, or more than the total peacetime outlay of the government for all purposes in any year before 1933—the advent of the New Deal; and the tax rates of 1947 made the tax rates of any year before 1941 look positively trivial in comparison. So stupendous was the debt and so heavy the tax burden that only Communists, looking gleefully to repudiation and a general economic crash, could envisage the future with satisfaction. Nor was the outlook for doing business with Stalin save on his own terms, or for that matter with several other European governments, any brighter than doing business with Hitler in the prewar years had been in fact.

With regard to the Democratic party as the party offering beneficent and progressive reforms, the outcome of the war was little short of disastrous, at least immediately. Though entrenched in every department of the Federal Government and commanding the support of a bureaucracy numbering more than 3,000,000 officers and employees, enjoying all the economic perquisites therewith associated, the party was ousted from power in both houses of Congress by Republicans triumphant at the polls in the congressional elections of 1946.

Deprived of its "indispensable" leader through the death of President Roosevelt in 1945, the Democratic party broke immediately into belligerent factions, while internationalists quarreled over the proceedings, meaning, and utility of the United Nations. On the extreme right, gathered old-line Democrats bent on extinguishing all signs of the New Deal; on the extreme left, rallied the new-line "progressives," headed by Henry Wallace, pledged to innovations more radical, extensive, and costly than those of the New Deal; and in the middle a small number of reformers, claiming to be guardians of the true faith, established the Committee for Democratic Action, with which Mrs. Eleanor Roosevelt was affiliated. Hence, when the fortunes of the Democrats as the unified party of reform were considered, it was academic to raise the question whether the domestic consequences of the war for the new world order justified the means chosen by President Roosevelt to gain the end which he chose for himself and the United States.

Indeed, two years after the nominal close of the war for the end proclaimed, it was almost academic to discuss domestic affairs at all, for they were subordinate to overriding foreign commitments, known and secret, made by President Roosevelt and by his successor, President Harry Truman. In 1947, under President Truman's direction, the Government of the United States set out on an unlimited program of underwriting, by money and military "advice," poverty-stricken, feeble, and instable governments around the edges of the gigantic and aggressive Slavic Empire. Of necessity, if this program was to be more than a *brutum fulmen,* it had to be predicated upon present and ultimate support by the blood and treasure of the United States; and this meant keeping the human power and the economy of the United States geared to the potentials inherent in the undertaking.

In these circumstances, it was impossible for the Government or people of the United States to make any rational calculations as to economy, life, and work at home. Over young men and women trying to plan their future days and years hung the shadow of possible, in fact probable, calls to armed services. Congress could do no more than guess at the requirements of taxation and expenditures, domestic and foreign. Business enterprisers, with prospects of new war demands ahead, could lay out no programs for the production of civilian goods with any degree of assurance as to the future, immediate or remote. In short, with the Government of the United States committed under a so-called bipartisan foreign policy to supporting by money and other forms of power for an indefinite time an indefinite number of other governments around the globe, the domestic affairs of the American people became appendages to an aleatory expedition in the management of the world.

Judgment by Reference to the American Constitutional System

Nevertheless, if it is still contended that President Roosevelt was justified in his choice and use of means to accomplish his end, there remains to be faced the relation of the means, as actually employed, to the Constitution of the United States and all that it signifies in terms of limited government, consent of the governed, democratic processes, and political ethics. The issue of this relationship rises above political parties and political personalities. It is timeless in its reach for the American people, perhaps for the people of the whole world. In short and plain form this issue is: Given the precedents set by President Roosevelt in the choice and use of means, what is to be the future of representative government under the Constitution of the United States?

When the Constitution, with its provisions for popular government, its limitations and checks on personal and arbitrary government, and its safeguards for the rights of the people, is taken as the standpoint for reviewing the conduct of foreign affairs by President Roosevelt, a more permanent and concrete basis is established for judgment than is furnished by the theory that the end justified the means. According to that standard, the very conception of limited government, which is indubitably anchored in the Constitution, of necessity circumscribes the powers and the means which may be employed by every department of the Government of the United States.

It is true that the Constitution is flexible in many respects but as to the division and limitation of power its language is explicit.[7] Certainly it does not vest in the Congress or the President illimitable power secretly to determine the ends of the government in foreign or domestic affairs and secretly to choose and employ any means deemed desirable by either branch of the government to achieve those ends. The President, members of Congress, and all high officials take an oath to support and defend the Constitution; and unless legal commitments involve no moral commitments and oaths of office are to be belittled as empty formalities, the conduct of foreign affairs is subject to the Constitution, the laws, and the democratic prescriptions essential to the American system of government.

Yet, if the precedents set by President Roosevelt in conducting foreign affairs, as reported in the records of the Congressional Committee on Pearl Harbor and other documents, are to stand unimpeached and be accepted henceforth as valid in law and morals then:

The President of the United States in a campaign for re-election may publicly promise the people to keep the country out of war and, after victory at the polls, may set out secretly on a course designed or practically certain to bring war upon the country.

He may, to secure legislation in furtherance of his secret designs, misrepresent to Congress and the people both its purport and the policy he intends to pursue under its terms if and when such legislation is enacted.

He may, by employing legal casuists, secretly frame and, using the powers and patronage of his office, obtain from Congress a law conferring upon him in elusive language authority which Congress has no constitutional power to delegate to him.

He may, after securing such legislation, publicly announce that he will pursue, as previously professed, a policy contrary to war and yet at the same time secretly prepare plans for waging an undeclared "shooting war" that are in flat contradiction to his public professions.

He may hold secret conferences with the Premier of a foreign government and publicly declare that no new commitments have been made when, in fact, he has committed the United States to occupying, by the use of American armed forces, the territory of a third country and joining the Premier in parallel threats to another government.

He may make a secret agreement with a foreign power far more fateful in consequences to the United States than any alliance ever incorporated in a treaty to be submitted to the Senate for approval.

He may demand, and Congress may pliantly confer upon him, the power to designate at his discretion foreign governments as enemies of the United States and to commit hostile acts against them, at his pleasure, in violation of national statutes and the principles of international law hitherto accepted and insisted upon by the United States.

He may publicly represent to Congress and the people that acts of war have been committed against the United States, when in reality the said acts were secretly invited and even initiated by the armed forces of the United States under his secret direction.

He may, on the mere ground that Congress has made provisions for national defense, secretly determine any form of military and naval strategy and order the armed forces to engage in any acts of war which he deems appropriate to achieve the ends which he personally chooses.

He may, by employing his own subordinates as broadcasters and entering into secret relations with private agencies of propaganda, stir up a popular demand for some drastic action on his part which is not authorized by law, and then take that action, thus substituting the sanction of an unofficial plebiscite for the sanction of the Constitution and the laws enacted under it.

He may, after publicly announcing one foreign policy, secretly pursue the opposite and so conduct foreign and military affairs as to maneuver a designated foreign power into firing the first shot in an attack upon the United States and thus avoid the necessity of calling upon Congress in advance to exercise its constitutional power to deliberate upon a declaration of war.

He may, as a crowning act in the arrogation of authority to himself, without the consent of the Senate, make a commitment to the head of a foreign government which binds the United States to "police the world," at least for a given time, that is, in the eyes of other governments and peoples policed, to dominate the world; and the American people are thereby in honor bound to provide the military, naval, and economic forces necessary to pursue, with no assurance of success, this exacting business.

In short, if these precedents are to stand unimpeached and to provide sanctions for the continued conduct of American foreign affairs, the Constitution may be nullified by the President, officials, and officers who have taken the oath, and are under moral obligation, to uphold it. For limited government under supreme law they may substitute personal and arbitrary government—the first principle of the totalitarian system against which, it has been alleged, World War II was waged—while giving lip service to the principle of constitutional government.

* * *

The theory of limitless power in the Executive to conduct foreign affairs and initiate war at will, unhampered by popular objections and legislative control, is of course old in the history of empires and despotisms. It was long accepted and practiced by despotic monarchies. It was held and applied by Hitler and Mussolini. It is now the theory, as well as the practice, of totalitarian governments everywhere. But such governments have never been under the delusion that limitless power can be exercised over foreign affairs and war, while domestic affairs and domestic economy are left free and the authority of government over them is constitutionally limited.

Since the drafting of the Constitution, American statesmen of the first order have accepted the axiom that militarism and the exercise of arbitrary power over foreign affairs by the Executive are inveterate foes of republican institutions.[8] It was in part to meet the threatened establishment of a military dictatorship on the ruins of representative government that George Washington took leadership in the formation and ratification of the Constitution.[9] In No. 8 of *The Federalist,* Alexander Hamilton pointed out that any necessity which enhances the importance of the soldier "proportionably degrades the condition of the citizen. The military state becomes elevated above the civil."

But it is contended by some contemporary publicists, whose assurance is often more impressive than their knowledge of human government, that offense is the best defense, that unlimited striking power in the Executive is necessary to survival in an age of "power politics" and "atom bombs." Few of them, it is true, venture to say openly that the Constitution is obsolete and that such a centralization of authority should be, in fact, substituted for the system of limited government fortified by checks and balances. Yet the implication of their arguments is inexorable: constitutional and democratic government in the United States is at the end of its career.

If it be urged that the United Nations organization and American membership in it offer an escape from the dilemma so posed, many countervailing realities become obvious to reflective minds. If the violent differences of opinion among supporters of that organization as to its meaning and prospects furnish no caveats, events certainly do.

Neither the operations of the organization nor the procedures under the prolix and redundant asseverations of peace and human rights incorporated in its charter have indicated discernible alterations in the warlike, revolutionary, and ambitious propensities of politicians, governments, and nations. The ordinary conduct of international relations by separate diplomatic agencies and contests for prestige and supremacy among power-hungry politicians have continued despite the existence and nominal functioning of the United Nations organization. Whether the public and often vitriolic debates that occur in the so-called "town meeting of the world," especially with regard to controversial issues arising within and among nations, will produce more peaceful settlements and fewer wars than ordinary diplomatic processes is at best dubious. At any rate, the rights of independence, self-defense, and freedom from outside intervention in internal affairs are explicitly accorded by the charter to all member nations; and the pursuit of what are called "national interests" appears no less vigorous or intransigent than before the United Nations came into existence.

The crisis in constitutional government represented by the present foreign perils and the contest over Executive authority relative to the conduct of foreign affairs, including the war power, has not sprung entirely from physical objects such as atom bombs and rocket planes or from sources entirely outside the United States, beyond the control of the American people. In no small measure it has come from doctrines proclaimed by presidents and political leaders, strongly supported by subsidized propaganda and widely applauded by numerous American citizens since the opening of the twentieth century. Among these doctrines four are especially effective in creating moral and intellectual disorder at home and hostility toward the United States among the nations of the earth.

The first of these doctrines is the jubilant American cry that the United States is now a world power and must assume the obligations of a world power. Undoubtedly the United States is a great power *in* the world and has obligations as such. But the range of its *effective* power supportable by armed forces and economic resources is limited. The further away from its base on the American continent the Government of the United States seeks to exert power over the affairs and relations of other countries the weaker its efficiency becomes; and the further it oversteps the limits of its strength the more likely it is to lead this nation into disaster—a terrible defeat in a war in Europe or Asia beyond the conquering power of its soldiers, sailors, and airmen. If wrecks of overextended empires scattered through the centuries offer any instruction to the living present, it is that a quest for absolute power not only corrupts but in time destroys. A prudent recognition and calculation of the limits on power is a mandate for statesmen and nations that seek to survive in the struggles of "power politics." And, as there are limitations on power to control or obliterate other nations, so there are limitations on the obligation to serve them either morally, physically, or economically.

A second danger to the peace and the security of the United States is the doctrine which runs to the effect that the President of the United States has the constitutional and moral right to proclaim noble sentiments of politics, economics, and peace for the whole world and commit the United States to these sentiments by making speeches and signing pieces of paper on his own motion. The futility of this practice has been demonstrated again and again and again, as the history of the Open Door, the Fourteen Points, the Kellogg Pact, the Four Freedoms, and the Atlantic Charter attests.

But the hazards in it are usually overlooked. Such commitments, even if intended for popular consumption, are often accepted as real, meaningful, and enforceable by some foreigners who share the sentiments of good will, and as easy bargains by foreign governments in dire need of American blood and treasure. In the one case disappointed hopes provoke bitterness against the United States;[10] and in the other case ingratitude for favors received produces similar results. In both cases the United States is opened to the imputation of hypocrisy and in fact often deserves it, with a loss in self-respect and of moral standing among the nations.

*   *   *

Closely associated with the idea that the President is serving the United States and mankind when he emits grand programs for imposing international morality on recalcitrant nations by American power, alone or in conjunction with that of allies or associates, is another doctrine which helps to build up public support for Executive supremacy in foreign affairs and to make enemies abroad. This doctrine proudly announces that it is the duty of the United States to assume and maintain "the moral leadership of the world" in the interest of realizing American programs of world reform. Apart from the feasibility of establishing such moral leadership in fact, the assertion of it adds to the discord rather than the comity of nations.

To sensibility, the very idea is repulsive. As ladies and gentlemen who publicly proclaim their own virtues are suspected and resented by self-respecting persons, so the Government and people of the United States, by loudly proclaiming their moral leadership of the world, awaken suspicion and resentment in Great Britain, France, Russia, China, and other countries of the world; and, what may be worse in the long run, contemptuous laughter. Nor, in truth, can American democracy, culture, or ways of life be "sold" to the world over the radio or by any other means of communication.

Not less disturbing to the fostering of decency in international intercourse is an array of opinions pertaining to international commerce. Proponents of these opinions say, for example, international commerce ipso facto promotes peace; it will raise the low standards of life which are "causes" of wars; such commerce, if expanded, will make it unnecessary for "have-not" nations to wage war for economic purposes; lowering trade barriers to international commerce will assure the continuous expansion of the international trade that works for peace and prosperity at home and abroad; and, therefore, the Government of the United States, in its search for world peace, must employ the engines of pressure and money lending in order to insure peace through the establishment of universal prosperity. Separately or collectively, these ideas are supported by powerful economic interests in the United States and if pushed in application will aggravate domestic conflicts, lead to limitless spending of taxpayers' money,[11] and bring on collisions with the controlled or semicontrolled economies of foreign countries.

The dangers of evoking foreign antagonisms by the use of the powers of government to promote commerce with other nations were well understood by leading framers of the Constitution. Among the many fictions attacked by Alexander Hamilton were two popular ideas: (1) republics are necessarily pacific and (2) "the spirit of commerce has a tendency to soften the manners of men."[12]

With acumen, Hamilton asked: "Has commerce hitherto done anything more than change the objects of war? Is not the love of wealth as domineering and enterprising a passion as that of power or glory? Have there not been as many wars founded upon commercial motives since that has become the prevailing system of nations, as were before occasioned by the cupidity of territory or dominion? Has not the spirit commerce, in many instances, administered new incentives to the appetite, both for the one and for the other? Let experience, the least fallible guide of human opinions, be appealed to for an answer to these inquiries." While Washington, under whom Hamilton served in war and peace, favored the fostering of foreign commerce, he warned his fellow countrymen, in the Farewell Address, against forcing it.

It remained for the nineteenth century to produce a full-blown concept for using the engines of state to break and keep channels open for foreign trade and to create spheres of economic interest. Critics dubbed this concept "imperialism." Defenders finally accepted the term and clothed it in moral verbiage as a design for "doing good to them that sit in darkness," that is, have a low standard of life. Rejecting imperialism as motivated by greed and lacking in virtue, other promoters of foreign trade chose more gracious covering phrases but called for the use of government in the process on similar grounds of national and universal interest—raising the standards of life for everybody, everywhere, and giving four or more freedoms to the "common man" throughout the world.

In fact, this new internationalism of commerce does not, as often claimed, rise wholly above special economic interests into the pure empyrean of world welfare. If "greedy" and "purblind" manufacturers for the domestic market are to be found supporting high tariff rates on products that compete with their goods, exporters, importers, producers of raw materials, and manufacturers for the export market are likewise to be discovered using money, influence, and politics on their side.[13]

However that may be, delegating to the President the power to effect commercial treaties with other countries at will and to make loans to politicians temporarily at the head of their governments helps to augment Executive authority in the United States, and to give foreign peoples reasons or pretexts for suspecting the motives and impugning the character of the American Government, rightly or wrongly. At all events, using political engines and public funds in wholesale efforts to promote universal prosperity through free or freer international commerce so called, while in practice sowing the seeds of discord at home and abroad, approaches an impasse in thought and action.[14]

At this point in its history the American Republic has arrived under the theory that the President of the United States possesses limitless authority publicly to misrepresent and secretly to control foreign policy, foreign affairs, and the war power.

More than a hundred years ago, James Madison, Father of the Constitution, prophesied that the supreme test of American statesmanship would come about 1930.

Although not exactly in the form that Madison foresaw, the test is here, now—with no divinity hedging our Republic against Caesar.

Notes

1. For the record, see Beard, *American Foreign Policy in the Making, 1932–1940,* pp. 312 ff.
2. This is, in sum and substance, the official case as presented in the semiofficial work by Davis and Lindley, *How War Came*; Beard, *op. cit.,* pp. 25 ff.
3. For the use of the test of consequences, we have the very high authority of Sumner Welles. In his book, *The Time for Decision* (Harper, 1944), Mr. Welles says: "The wisdom of any foreign policy can generally be determined only by its results." CJC, Part 2, p. 509.
4. The proposition that President Roosevelt as a perceptive statesman foresaw, in advance of the American people, the great end to be attained and the necessity of America's entrance into war involves questions of chronology and history.

When, before December 7, 1941, did President Roosevelt and Secretary Hull decide that war for the United States was desirable and necessary, if they ever did before the Pearl Harbor attack? President Roosevelt's answer to that question of time is not yet forthcoming (see above, Chap. XIV). Secretary Hull, when it was put to him squarely by Senator Ferguson, parried it with the verbal skill of a trained diplomat (see above, pp. 563 f.). The majority of the Congressional Committee on Pearl Harbor eluded it by the use of the word "timely" (see above, p. 339). The conflict of the proposition with the official thesis on the coming of war, established by President Roosevelt on December 8, 1941, is obvious. According to that thesis, the President was seeking peace with Japan and the United States was precipitated into war by the surprise attack launched by the Japanese on December 7. Nor did the United States declare war on Germany and Italy at the request of President Roosevelt. On the morning of December 11, Germany and Italy declared war on the United States. The resolutions of Congress, December 11, 1941, said that a state of war had been "thrust upon" the United States by Germany and Italy and that this state of war "is hereby formally declared." If the state of war had been thrust upon the United States, were President Roosevelt and Secretary Hull merely victims, not makers, of history?

5. In respect of the alarming state of foreign affairs for the United States in February, 1947, testimony was given by a high-ranking authority, the Secretary of State, George C. Marshall, in an address at Princeton University, on the 22d of that month. On that occasion, Secretary Marshall said:

"As you all must recognize, we are living today in a most difficult period. The war years were critical, at times alarmingly so. But I think that the present period is, in many respects, even more critical [than during the war years]. The problems are different but no less vital to the national security than those during the days of active fighting. But the more serious aspect is the fact that we no longer display that intensity, that unity of purpose, with which we concentrated upon the war task and achieved the victory....

"We have had a cessation of hostilities, but we have no genuine peace. Here at home we are in a state of transition between a war and peace economy. In Europe and Asia fear and famine still prevail. Power relationships are in a state of flux. Order has yet to be brought out of confusion. Peace has yet to be secured. And how this is accomplished will depend very much upon the American people.

"Most of the other countries of the world find themselves exhausted economically, financially and physically. If the world is to get on its feet, if the productive facilities of the world are to be restored, if democratic processes in many countries are to resume their functioning, a strong lead and definite assistance from the United States will be necessary." *Congressional Record,* March 3, 1947 (Appendix).

6. For instance, as to Poland, see Jan Ciechanowski, *Defeat in Victory* (Doubleday, 1947).

7. For an authoritative exposition of this axiom of divided and limited power, see *The Federalist,* Nos. 47–51.

8. C. A. Beard, *The Republic* (Viking, 1943), pp. 212 ff.

9. *Ibid.,* pp. 22 ff.

10. A recent and classic example of such promises made by President Roosevelt under the head of world morality but also with some reference to the Polish-American vote

in coming elections and secretly broken at Teheran and Yalta, is provided by the former Polish Ambassador, Jan Ciechanowski, *op. cit., passim.*

11. It is well known that bankers and other private investors in the United States, having lost billions in the business of foreign "loans" after the conclusion of World War I, will not voluntarily finance such schemes of "trade promotion" and that, if the policy of promotion is pressed, these projects must be financed by agencies of the United States Government out of funds derived from taxing and borrowing.

12. *The Federalist,* No. 6.

13. A few years ago good Democrats were shocked and made loud outcries when a Republican Senator openly allowed the secretary of a manufacturers' association to help him write certain schedules in a pending tariff bill; but in 1947 good Democrats were deeply pained and highly indignant when a Republican member of the House of Representatives vociferously protested against permitting a rich cotton broker and exporter of cotton to serve as Undersecretary of State and engage in making "reciprocal" trade arrangements.

14. The extent to which government-controlled trade prevails, not only in Russia, where it is an absolute monopoly, but also in Great Britain, where a Socialist government is in power, and in other countries of western Europe, is well known to economic literates. The likelihood of a return to the "free trade" age of Richard Cobden and John Bright seems to be about as remote as a return to the ice age. At the Atlantic Conference in 1941, President Roosevelt and Undersecretary Welles took advantage of Prime Minister Churchill's dire need to press upon him the disruption of preferential trade within the British Empire, but Mr. Churchill was unable to commit the other members of the British Commonwealth and the subject was dismissed with a few vague words in the Atlantic Charter. See above, Chap. XV. Democratic sponsors of the bill for the large "loan" to Great Britain in 1946 defended it by broad and unfounded hints that breaking imperial preference would result from the passage of the bill. This is the use of the engines of government for commercial coercion.

Chapter 5

THE ORIGINS AND END OF
THE COLD WAR

5.1

THE LONG TELEGRAM

George Kennan

George Kennan, charge d'affaires at the U.S. Embassy in Moscow, wrote this famous "long telegram" in February 1946. It begins, like the telegram written by Nikolai Novikov, the Soviet ambassador in Washington (which was drafted eight months later and is reprinted in the following selection), with an analysis of the ideological motivations of the other country. But it concludes (unlike Novikov's, which emphasizes capitalist ideology) that what drives Soviet foreign policy ultimately is not ideology (identity) or disillusionment with international institutions (liberal) but a deep geopolitical insecurity reflecting Russia's repeated experience with invasions from the West (realist). Because communism is less important than geopolitics, Kennan urges a defensive strategy of containment that waits out the Soviet Union until it loses its ideological zeal and becomes again a normal nation with whom the United States can balance power in a prudent fashion, as called for by the realist perspective.

Source: George Kennan, ["The Long Telegram"], February 22, 1946, Harry S. Truman Administration File, Elsey Papers, available at the Harry S. Truman Library and Museum, http://www.truman library.org/whistlestop/study_collections/coldwar/documents/index.php?documentdate= 1946-02-22&documentid=6-6&studycollectionid=&pagenumber=1. The spellings, capitalization, and punctuation used in the original have been retained, as well as several uses of an asterisk set in parentheses, the significance of which is unclear.

258

Moscow via War
Dated February 22, 1946
Rec'd 3:52 p.m.

Secretary of State,
Washington.

511, February 22, 9 p.m.

Answer to Dept's 284, Feb 3 involves questions so intricate, so delicate, so strange to our form of thought, and so important to analysis of our international environment that I cannot compress answers into single brief message without yielding to what I feel would be dangerous degree of over-simplification. I hope, therefore, Dept will bear with me if I submit in answer to this question five parts, subjects of which will be roughly as follows:

(One) Basic features of post-war Soviet outlook.
(Two) Background of this outlook.
(Three) Its projection in practical policy on official level.
(Four) Its projection on unofficial level.
(Five) Practical deductions from standpoint of US policy.

I apologize in advance for this burdening of telegraphic channel; but questions involved are of such urgent importance, particularly in view of recent events, that our answers to them, if they deserve attention at all, seem to me to deserve it at once.

THERE FOLLOWS PART ONE: BASIC FEATURES OF POST WAR SOVIET OUTLOOK, AS PUT FORWARD BY OFFICIAL PROPAGANDA MACHINE, ARE AS FOLLOWS:

(A) USSR still lives in antagonistic "capitalist encirclement" with which in the long run there can be no permanent peaceful coexistence. As stated by Stalin in 1927 to a delegation of American workers:

"In course of further development of international revolution there will emerge two centers of world significance: a socialist center, drawing to itself the countries which tend toward socialism, and a capitalist center, drawing to itself the countries that incline toward capitalism. Battle between these two centers for command of world economy will decide fate of capitalism and of communism in entire world."

(B) Capitalist world is beset with internal conflicts, inherent in nature of capitalist society. These conflicts are insoluble by means of peaceful compromise. Greatest of them is that between England and US.

(C) Internal conflicts of capitalism inevitably generate wars. Wars thus generated may be of two kinds: intra-capitalist wars between two capitalist states, and wars of intervention against socialist world. Smart capitalists, vainly seeking escape from inner conflicts of capitalism, incline toward latter.

(D) Intervention against USSR, while it would be disastrous to those who undertook it, would cause renewed delay in progress of Soviet socialism and must therefore be forestalled at all costs.

(E) Conflicts between capitalist states, though likewise fraught with danger for USSR, nevertheless hold out great possibilities for advancement of socialist cause, particularly if USSR remains militarily powerful, ideologically monolithic and faithful to its present brilliant leadership.

(F) It must be borne in mind that capitalist world is not all bad. In addition to hopelessly reactionary and bourgeois elements, it includes (one) certain wholly enlightened and positive elements united in acceptable communistic parties and (two) certain other elements (now described for tactical reasons as progressive or democratic) whose reactions, aspirations and activities happen to be "objectively" favorable to interests of USSR. These last must be encouraged and utilized for Soviet purposes.

(G) Among negative elements of bourgeois-capitalist society, most dangerous of all are those whom Lenin called false friends of the people, namely moderate-socialist or social-democratic leaders (in other words, non-communist left wing). These are more dangerous than out-and-out reactionaries, for latter at least march under their true colors, whereas moderate left-wing leaders confuse people by employing devices of socialism to serve interests of reactionary capital.

So much for premises. To what deductions do they lead from standpoint of Soviet policy? To following:

(A) Everything must be done to advance relative strength of USSR as factor in international society. Conversely, no opportunity must be missed to reduce strength and influence, collectively as well as individually, of capitalist powers.

(B) Soviet efforts, and those of Russia's friends abroad, must be directed toward deepening and exploiting of differences and conflicts between capitalist powers. If these eventually deepen into an "imperialist" war, this war must be turned into revolutionary upheavals within the various capitalist countries.

(C) "Democratic-progressive" elements abroad are to be utilized to maximum to bring pressure to bear on capitalist governments along lines agreeable to Soviet interests.

(D) Relentless battle must be waged against socialist and social-democratic leaders abroad.

PART TWO: BACKGROUND OF OUTLOOK

Before examining ramifications of this party line in practice there are certain aspects of it to which I wish to draw attention.

First, it does not represent natural outlook of Russian people. Latter are, by and large, friendly to outside world, eager for experience of it, eager to measure against it talents they are conscious of possessing, eager above all to live in peace and enjoy fruits of their own labor. Party line only represents thesis which official propaganda machine puts forward with great skill and persistence to a public often remarkably resistant in the stronghold of its innermost thoughts. But party line is binding for outlook and conduct of people who make up apparatus of power—party, secret police and government—and it is exclusively with these that we have to deal.

Second, please note that premises on which this party line is based are for most part simply not true. Experience has shown that peaceful and mutually profitable coexistence of capitalist and socialist states is entirely possible. Basic internal conflicts in advanced countries are no longer primarily those arising out of capitalist ownership of means of production, but are ones arising from advanced urbanism and industrialism as such, which Russia has thus far been spared not by socialism but only by her own backwardness. Internal rivalries of capitalism do not always generate wars; and not all wars are attributable to this cause. To speak of possibility of intervention against USSR today, after elimination of Germany and Japan and after example of recent war, is sheerest nonsense. If not provoked by forces of intolerance and subversion "capitalist" world of today is quite capable of living at peace with itself and with Russia. Finally, no sane person has reason to doubt sincerity of moderate socialist leaders in western countries. Nor is it fair to deny success of their efforts to improve conditions for working population whenever, as in Scandinavia, they have been given chance to show what they could do.

Falseness of these premises, every one of which pre-dates recent war, was amply demonstrated by that conflict itself. Anglo-American differences did not turn out to be major differences of western world. Capitalist countries, other than those of Axis, showed no disposition to solve their differences by joining in crusade against USSR. Instead of imperialist war turning into civil wars and revolution, USSR found itself obliged to fight side by side with capitalist powers for an avowed community of aims.

Nevertheless, all these theses, however baseless and disproven, are being boldly put forward again today. What does this indicate? It indicates that Soviet party line is not based on any objective analysis of situation beyond Russia's borders; that it has, indeed, little to do with conditions outside of Russia; that it arises mainly from basic inner-Russian necessities which existed before recent war and exist today.

At bottom of Kremlin's neurotic view of world affairs is traditional and instinctive Russian sense of insecurity. Originally, this was insecurity of a peaceful agricultural people trying to live on vast exposed plain in neighborhood of fierce nomadic peoples. To this was added, as Russia came into contact with economically advanced west, fear of more competent, more powerful, more highly organized societies in that area. But this latter type of insecurity was one which afflicted rather Russian rulers than Russian people; for Russian rulers have invariably sensed that their rule was relatively archaic in form, fragile and artificial in its psychological foundation, unable to stand comparison or contact with political systems of western countries. For this reason they have always feared foreign penetration, feared direct contact between western world and their own, feared what would happen if Russians learned truth about world without or if foreigners learned truth about world within. And they have learned to seek security only in patient but deadly struggle for total destruction of rival power, never in compacts and compromises with it.

It was no coincidence that Marxism, which had smouldered ineffectively for half a century in Western Europe, caught hold and blazed for first time in Russia. Only in this land which had never known a friendly neighbor or indeed any tolerant equilibrium of separate powers, either internal or international, could a doctrine thrive which viewed economic conflicts of society as insoluble by peaceful means. After establishment of Bolshevist regime, Marxist dogma, rendered even more truculent and intolerant by Lenin's interpretation, became a perfect vehicle for sense of insecurity with which Bolsheviks, even more with previous Russian rulers, were afflicted. In this dogma, with its basic altruism of purpose, they found justification for their instinctive fear of outside world, for the dictatorship without which they did not know how to rule, for cruelties they did not dare not to inflict, for sacrifices they felt bound to demand. In the name of Marxism they sacrificed every single ethical value in their methods and tactics. Today they cannot dispense with it. It is fig leaf of their moral and intellectual respectability. Without it they would stand before history, at best, as only the last of that long succession of cruel and wasteful Russian rulers who have relentlessly forced country on to ever new heights of military power in order to guarantee external security of their internally weak regimes. This is why Soviet purposes must always be solemnly clothed in trappings of Marxism, and why no one should underrate importance of dogma in Soviet affairs. Thus Soviet leaders are driven necessities of their own past and present position to put forward a dogma which (*) outside world as evil, hostile and menacing, but as bearing within itself germs of creeping disease and destined to be wracked with growing internal convulsions until it is given final coup de grace by rising power of socialism and yields to new and better world. This thesis provides justification for that increase of military and police power of Russian state, for that isolation of Russian population from outside world, and for that fluid and constant pressure to extend limits of Russian police power which are together the natural and instinctive urges of Russian rulers. Basically this is only the steady advance of uneasy Russian nationalism, a centuries old movement in which conceptions of offense and defense are inextricably confused. But in new guise of international Marxism, with its honeyed promises to a desperate and war torn outside world, it is more dangerous and insidious than ever before.

It should not be thought from above that Soviet party line is necessarily disingenuous and insincere on part of all those who put it forward many of them are too ignorant of outside world and mentally too dependent to question (*) self-hypnotism, and who have no difficulty making themselves believe what they find it comforting and convenient to believe. Finally we have the unsolved mystery as to who, if anyone, in this great land actually receives accurate and unbiased information about outside world. In atmosphere of oriental secretiveness and conspiracy which pervades this government, possibilities for distorting or poisoning sources and currents of information are infinite. The very disrespect of Russians for objective truth—indeed, their disbelief in its existence—leads them to view all stated facts as instruments for furtherance of one ulterior purpose or another. There is good reason to suspect that this government is actually a conspiracy within a conspiracy; and I for one am reluctant to believe that Stalin himself receives anything like an objective picture of outside world. Here there is ample scope for the type of subtle intrigue at which Russians are past masters. Inability of foreign governments to place their case squarely before Russian policy makers—extent to which they are delivered up in their relations with Russia to good graces of obscure and unknown advisers whom they never see and cannot influence—this to my mind is most disquieting feature of diplomacy in Moscow, and one which western statesmen would do well to keep in mind if they would understand nature of difficulties encountered here.

PART THREE: PROJECTION OF SOVIET OUTLOOK IN PRACTICAL POLICY ON OFFICIAL LEVEL

We have now seen nature and background of Soviet program. What may we expect by way of its practical implementation?

Soviet policy, as Department implies in its query under reference, is conducted on two planes: (one) official plane represented by actions undertaken officially in name of Soviet Government; and (two) subterranean plane of actions undertaken by agencies for which Soviet Government does not admit responsibility.

Policy promulgated on both planes will be calculated to serve basic policies (A) to (D) outlined in part one. Actions taken on different planes will differ considerably, but will dovetail into each other in purpose, timing and effect.

On official plane we must look for following:

(A) Internal policy devoted to increasing in every way strength and prestige of Soviet state: intensive military-industrialization; maximum development of armed forces; great displays to impress outsiders; continued secretiveness about internal matters, designed to conceal weaknesses and to keep opponents in dark.

(B) Wherever it is considered timely and promising, efforts will be made to advance official limits of Soviet power. For the moment, these efforts are restricted to certain neighboring points conceived of here as being of immediate strategic necessity, such as Northern Iran, Turkey, possibly Bornholm. However, other points may at any time come into question, if and as concealed Soviet political power is extended to new areas. Thus a "friendly" Persian Government might be asked to grant Russia a port on Persian Gulf. Should Spain fall under communist control, question of Soviet base at Gibraltar Strait might be activated. But such claims will appear on official level only when unofficial preparation is complete.

(C) Russians will participate officially in international organizations where they see opportunity of extending Soviet power or of inhibiting or diluting power of others. Moscow sees in UNO not the mechanism for a permanent and stable world society founded on mutual interest and aims of all nations, but an arena in which aims just mentioned can be favorably pursued. As long as UNO is considered here to serve this purpose, Soviets will remain with it. But if at any time they come to conclusion that it is serving to embarass or frustrate their aims for power expansion and if they see better prospects for pursuit of these aims along other lines, they will not hesitate to abandon UNO. This would imply, however, that they felt themselves strong enough to split unity of other nations by their withdrawal, to render UNO ineffective as a threat to their aims or security, and to replace it with an international weapon more effective from their viewpoint. Thus Soviet attitude toward UNO will depend largely on loyalty of other nations to it, and on degree of vigor, decisiveness and cohesion with which these nations defend in UNO the peaceful and hopeful concept of international life, which that organization represents to our way of thinking. I reiterate, Moscow has no abstract devotion to UNO ideals. Its attitude to that organization will remain essentially pragmatic and tactical.

(D) Toward colonial areas and backward or dependent peoples, Soviet policy, even on official plane, will be directed toward weakening of power and influence and contacts of advanced western nations, on theory that in so far as this policy is successful, there will be created a vacuum which will favor communist-Soviet penetration. Soviet pressure for participation in trusteeship arrangements thus represents, in my opinion, a desire to be in a position to complicate and inhibit exertion of western influence at such points rather than to provide major channel for exerting of Soviet power. Latter motive is not lacking, but for this Soviets prefer to rely on other channels than official trusteeship arrangements. Thus we may expect to find Soviets asking for admission everywhere to trusteeship or similar arrangements and using levers thus acquired to weaken Western influence among such peoples.

(E) Russians will strive energetically to develop Soviet representation in, and official ties with, countries in which they sense strong possibilities of opposition to western centers of power. This applies to such widely separated points as Germany, Argentina, Middle Eastern countries, etc.

(F) In international economic matters, Soviet policy will really be dominated by pursuit of autarchy for Soviet Union and Soviet-dominated adjacent areas taken together. That, however, will be underlying policy. As far as official line is concerned, position is not yet clear. Soviet Government has shown strange reticence since termination hostilities on subject foreign trade. If large scale long term credits should be forthcoming, I believe Soviet Government may eventually again do lip service, as it did in nineteen-thirtys to desirability of building up international economic exchanges in general. Otherwise I think it possible Soviet foreign trade may be restricted largely to Soviets own security sphere, including occupied areas in Germany, and that a cold official shoulder may be turned to principle of general economic collaboration among nations.

(G) With respect to cultural collaboration, lip service will likewise be rendered to desirability of deepening cultural contacts between peoples, but this will not in practice be interpreted in any way which could weaken security position of Soviet peoples. Actual manifestations of Soviet policy in this respect will be restricted to arid channels of closely shepherded official visits and functions, with super-abundance of vodka and speeches and dearth of permanent effects.

(H) Beyond this, Soviet official relations will take what might be called "correct" course with individual foreign governments, with great stress being laid on prestige of Soviet Union and its representatives and with punctilious attention to protocol, as distinct from good manners.

PART FOUR: FOLLOWING MAY BE SAID AS TO WHAT WE MAY EXPECT BY WAY OF IMPLEMENTATION OF BASIC SOVIET POLICIES ON UNOFFICIAL, OR SUBTERRANEAN PLANE, i.e. ON PLANE FOR WHICH SOVIET GOVERNMENT ACCEPTS NO RESPONSIBILITY

Agencies utilized for promulgation of policies on this plane are following:

One. Inner central core of communist parties in other countries. While many of persons who compose this category may also appear and act in unrelated public capacities, they are in reality working closely together as an underground operating directorate of world communism, a concealed Comintern tightly coordinated and directed by Moscow. It is important to remember that this inner core is actually working on underground lines, despite legality of parties with which it is associated.

Two. Rank and file of communist parties. Note distinction is drawn between these and persons defined in paragraph one. This distinction has become much sharper in recent years. Whereas formerly foreign communist parties represented a curious (and from Moscow's standpoint often inconvenient) mixture of conspiracy and legitimate activity, now the conspiratorial element has been neatly concentrated in inner circle and ordered underground, while rank and file—no longer even taken into confidence about realities of movement—are thrust forward as bona fide internal partisans of certain political tendencies within their respective countries, genuinely innocent of conspiratorial connection with foreign states. Only in certain countries where communists are numerically strong do they now regularly appear and act as a body. As a rule they are used to penetrate, and to influence or dominate, as case may be, other organizations less likely to be suspected of being tools of Soviet Government, with a view to accomplishing their purposes through (*) organizations, rather than by direct action as a separate political party.

Three. A wide variety of national associations or bodies which can be dominated or influenced by such penetration. These include: labor unions, youth leagues, womens organizations, racial societies, religious societies, social organizations, cultural groups, liberal magazines, publishing houses, etc.

Four. International organizations which can be similarly penetrated through influence over various national components. Labor, youth and womens organizations are prominent among them. Particular, almost vital, importance is attached in this connection to international labor movement. In this, Moscow sees possibility of sidetracking western governments in world affairs and building up international lobby capable of compelling governments to take actions favorable to Soviet interests in various countries and of paralyzing actions disagreeable to USSR.

Five. Russian Orthodox Church, with its foreign branches, and through it the Eastern Orthodox Church in general.

Six. Pan-Slav movement and other movements (Azerbaijan, Armenian, Turcoman, etc.) based on racial groups within Soviet Union.

Seven. Governments or governing groups willing to lend themselves to Soviet purposes in one degree or another, such as present Bulgarian and Yugoslav governments, North Persian regime, Chinese Communists, etc. Not only propaganda machines but actual policies of these regimes can be placed extensively at disposal of USSR.

It may be expected that component parts of this far-flung apparatus will be utilized, in accordance with their individual suitability, as follows:

(A) To undermine general political and strategic potential of major western powers. Efforts will be made in such countries to disrupt national self confidence, to hamstring measures of national defense, to increase social and industrial unrest, to stimulate all forms of disunity. All persons with grievances, whether economic or racial, will be urged to seek redress not in mediation and compromise, but in defiant violent struggle for destruction of other elements of society. Here poor will be set against rich, black against white, young against old, newcomers against established residents, etc.

(B) On unofficial plane particularly violent efforts will be made to weaken power and influence of western powers of colonial, backward, or dependent peoples. On this level, no holds will be barred. Mistakes and weaknesses of western colonial administration will be mercilessly exposed and exploited. Liberal opinion in western countries will be mobilized to weaken colonial policies. Resentment among dependent peoples will be stimulated. And while latter are being encouraged to seek independence of western powers, Soviet dominated puppet political machines will be undergoing preparation to take over domestic power in respective colonial areas when independence is achieved.

(C) Where individual governments stand in path of Soviet purposes pressure will be brought for their removal from office. This can happen where governments directly oppose Soviet foreign policy aims (Turkey, Iran), where they seal their territories off against Communist penetration (Switzerland, Portugal), or where they compete too strongly, like Labor Government in England, for moral domination among elements which it is important for Communists to dominate. Sometimes, two of these elements are present in a single case. Then Communist opposition becomes particularly shrill and savage.

(D) In foreign countries Communists will, as a rule, work toward destruction of all forms of personal independence, economic, political or moral. Their system can handle only individuals who have been brought into complete dependence on higher power. Thus, persons who are financially independent—such as individual businessmen, estate owners, successful farmers, artisans and all those who exercise local leadership or have local prestige, such as popular local clergymen or political figures, are anathema. It is not by chance that even in USSR local officials are kept constantly on move from one job to another, to prevent their taking

(E) Everything possible will be done to set major western powers against each other. Anti-British talk will be plugged among Americans, anti-American talk among British. Continentals, including Germans, will be taught to abhor both Anglo-Saxon powers. Where suspicions exist, they will be fanned; where not, ignited. No effort will be spared to discredit and combat all efforts which threaten to lead to any sort of unity or cohesion among other (*) from which Russia might be excluded. Thus, all forms of international organization not amenable to communist penetration and control, whether it be the Catholic (*) international economic concerns, or the international fraternity of royalty and aristocracy, must expect to find themselves under fire from many, and often (*)

(F) In general, all Soviet efforts on unofficial international plane will be negative and destructive in character, designed to tear down sources of strength beyond reach of Soviet control. This is only in line with basic Soviet instinct that there can be no compromise with rival power and that constructive work can start only when communist power is dominant. But behind all this will be applied insistent, unceasing pressure for penetration and command of key positions in administration and especially in police apparatus of foreign countries. The Soviet regime is a police regime par excellence, reared in the dim half world of Tsarist police intrigue, accustomed to think primarily in terms of police power. This should never be lost sight of in gauging Soviet motives.

PART FIVE:

In summary, we have here a political force committed fanatically to the belief that with US there can be no permanent modus vivendi, that it is desirable and necessary that the internal harmony of our society be disrupted, our traditional way of life be destroyed, the international authority of our state be broken, if Soviet power is to be secure. This political force has complete power of disposition over energies of one of world's greatest peoples and resources of world's richest national territory, and is borne along by deep and powerful currents of Russian nationalism. In addition, it has an elaborate and far flung apparatus for exertion of its influence in other countries, an apparatus of amazing flexibility and versatility, managed by people whose experience and skill in underground methods are presumably without parallel in history. Finally, it is seemingly inaccessible to considerations of reality in its basic reactions. For it, the vast fund of objective fact about human society is not, as with us, the measure against which outlook is constantly being tested and re-formed, but a grab bag from which individual items are selected arbitrarily and tendenciously to bolster an outlook already preconceived. This is admittedly not a pleasant picture. Problem of how to cope with this force in undoubtedly greatest task our diplomacy has ever faced and probably greatest it will ever have to face. It should be point of departure from which our political general staff work at present juncture should proceed. It should be approached with same thoroughness and care as solution of major strategic problem in war, and if necessary, with no smaller outlay in planning effort. I cannot attempt to suggest all answers here. But I would like to record my conviction that problem is within our power to solve—and that without recourse to any general military conflict. And in support of this conviction there are certain observations of a more encouraging nature I should like to make:

(One) Soviet power, unlike that of Hitlerite Germany, is neither schematic nor adventuristic. It does not work by fixed plans. It does not take unnecessary risks. Impervious to logic of reason, and it is highly sensitive to logic of force. For this reason it can easily withdraw—and usually does—when strong resistance is encountered at any point. Thus, if the adversary has sufficient force and makes clear his readiness to use it, he rarely has to do so. If situations are properly handled there need be no prestige engaging showdowns.

(Two) Gauged against western world as a whole, Soviets are still by far the weaker force. Thus, their success will really depend on degree of cohesion, firmness and vigor which western world can muster. And this is factor which it is within our power to influence.

(Three) Success of Soviet system, as form of internal power, is not yet finally proven. It has yet to be demonstrated that it can survive supreme text of successive transfer of power from one individual or group to another. Lenin's death was first such transfer, and its effects wracked Soviet state for 15 years after Stalin's death or retirement will be second. But even this will not be final test. Soviet internal system will now be subjected, by virtue of recent territorial expansions, to series of additional strains which once proved severe tax on Tsardom. We here are convinced that never since termination of civil war have mass of Russian people been emotionally farther removed from doctrines of communist party than they are today. In Russia, party has now become a great and—for the moment—highly successful apparatus of dictatorial administration, but it has ceased to be a source of emotional inspiration. Thus, internal soundness and permanence of movement need not yet be regarded as assured.

(Four) All Soviet propaganda beyond Soviet security sphere is basically negative and destructive. It should therefore be relatively easy to combat it by any intelligent and really constructive program.

For these reasons I think we may approach calmly and with good heart problem of how to deal with Russia. As to how this approach should be made, I only wish to advance, by way of conclusion, following comments:

(One) Our first step must be to apprehend, and recognize for what it is, the nature of the movement with which we are dealing. We must study it with same courage, detachment, objectivity, and same determination not to be emotionally provoked or unseated by it, with which doctor studies unruly and unreasonable individual.

(Two) We must see that our public is educated to realities of Russian situation. I cannot over-emphasize importance of this. Press cannot do this alone. It must be done mainly by government, which is necessarily more experienced and better informed on practical problems involved. In this we need not be deterred by fglinness [ugliness] of picture. I am convinced that there would be far less hysterical anti-Sovietism in our country today if realities of this situation were better understood by our people. There is nothing as dangerous or as terrifying as the unknown. It may also be argued that to reveal more information on our difficulties with Russia would reflect unfavorably on Russian American relations. I feel that if there is any real risk here involved, it is one which we should have courage to face, and sooner the better. But I cannot see what we would be risking. Our stake in this country, even coming on heels of tremendous demonstrations of our friendship for Russian people, is remarkably small. We have here no investments to guard, no actual trade to lose, virtually no citizens to protect, few cultural contacts to preserve. Our only stake lies in what we hope rather than what we have; and I am convinced we have better chance of realizing those hopes if our public is enlightened and if our dealings with Russians are placed entirely on realistic and matter of fact basis.

(Three) Much depends on health and vigor of our own society. World communism is like malignant parasite which feeds only on diseased tissue. This is point at which domestic and foreign policies meet. Every courageous and incisive measure to solve internal problems of our own society, to improve self-confidence, discipline, morale and community spirit of our own people, is a diplomatic victory over Moscow worth a thousand diplomatic notes and joint communiques. If we cannot abandon fatalism and indifference in face of deficiencies of our own society, Moscow will profit—Moscow cannot help profiting by them in its foreign policies.

(Four) We must formulate and put forward for other nations a much more positive and constructive picture of sort of world we would like to see than we have put forward in past. It is not enough to urge people to develop political processes similar to our own. Many foreign peoples, in Europe at least, are tired and frightened by experiences of past, and are less interested in abstract freedom than in security. They are seeking guidance rather than responsibilities. We should be better able than Russians to give them this. And unless we do, Russians certainly will.

(Five) Finally we must have courage and self confidence to cling to our own methods and conceptions of human society. After all, the greatest danger that can befall us in coping with this problem of Soviet Communism, is that we shall allow ourselves to become like those with whom we are coping.

KENNAN

5.2

TELEGRAM FROM THE SOVIET AMBASSADOR TO THE UNITED STATES, TO THE SOVIET LEADERSHIP

Nikolai Novikov

Nikolai Novikov's telegram provides a fascinating counterpart to the long telegram by George Kennan (see preceding selection). It highlights the conflicting interpretations (perspectives) of world affairs by the United States and the Soviet Union in the crucial transition years from wartime allies in 1945 to Cold War adversaries in 1947. Notice that Novikov starts the telegram by referring to the "imperialist tendencies of American monopoly capital." He is reading U.S. intentions through the lens of Marxist-Leninism, an identity or even critical theory perspective in the sense that the United States cannot help the way it is acting. Unlike Kennan, he does not expect ideology to fade away slowly in favor of geopolitics. Rather, he concludes that, despite significant competition between the capitalist states of the United States and Great Britain, the United States will supplant British power in the Middle East and elsewhere and ultimately spread capitalism to achieve world domination unless the Soviet Union resists.

Reflecting the imperialistic tendency of American monopoly capital, US foreign policy has been characterized in the postwar period by a desire for *world domination*. [Emphasis here and from this point on indicates where V. M. Molotov underlined the original document.] This is the real meaning of repeated statements by President Truman and other representatives of American ruling circles that the US has a right to world leadership [*rukovodstvo*]. All the forces of American diplomacy, the Army, Navy, and Air Force, industry, and science have been placed at the service of this policy. With this objective in mind broad plans for expansion have been developed, to be realized both diplomatically and through the creation of a system of naval and air bases far from the US, an arms race, and the creation of newer and newer weapons.

Source: Nikolai Novikov, "Telegram from N. Novikov, Soviet Ambassador to the US, to the Soviet Leadership," September 27, 1946, available at: Woodrow Wilson International Center for Scholars, Cold War International History Project, Virtual Archive, http://www.wilsoncenter.org/index.cfm? topic_id=1409&fuseaction=va2.document&identifier=952E8C7F-423B-763D-D5662C42501C9BEA&sort=subject&item=UN. Bracketed editorial insertions are present in the Wilson Center document.

1. a) US foreign policy is being pursued right now *in a situation quite different* from that which existed in the prewar period.

This situation does not completely match the expectations of those reactionary circles who hoped during the Second World War that they would be able to remain apart from the main battles in Europe and Asia for a long time. Their expectation was that the United States of America, if it was not able to completely avoid participation in the war, would enter it only at the last moment when it might be able to influence its outcome without great effort, completely securing its own interests. It was intended thereby that the main rivals of the US would be crushed in this war or to weakened to a great degree and that due to this circumstance the US would *be the most powerful factor* in deciding the main issues of the postwar world. These expectations also were based on the assumption quite widespread in the US during the first period of the war that the Soviet Union, which had been attacked by German fascism in June 1941, would be weakened as a result of the war or even completely destroyed.

Reality has not borne out all the expectations of the American imperialists.

b) The two main aggressor powers, fascist Germany and militarist Japan, at the same time the main rivals of the US both in the economic and in foreign policy fields, were defeated as a result of the war. A third great power, Great Britain, having been dealt strong blows from the war, is now faced with enormous economic and political difficulties. The political foundations of the British Empire have been noticeably undermined, in some cases having taken on the nature of a crisis, for example in India, Palestine, and Egypt.

Europe came out of the war with a thoroughly shattered economy, and the economic devastation which resulted during the war cannot soon be repaired. All the countries of Europe and Asia are feeling an enormous need for consumer goods, industrial and transportation equipment, etc. Such a situation opens up a *vista* for American monopoly capital *of enormous deliveries of goods and the importation of capital* to these countries, which would allow it [American monopoly capital] to be introduced into their economies.

The realization of this opportunity would mean a serious strengthening of the economic position of the US throughout the entire world and would be one of the stages in the path toward establishing American world supremacy.

c) On the other hand, the expectations of those American circles have not been justified which were based on the Soviet Union being destroyed during the war or coming out of it so weakened that it was forced to bow to the US for economic aid. In this event it could have dictated such conditions which would provide the US with an opportunity to carry out its expansion in Europe and Asia without hindrance from the USSR.

In reality, in spite of all the economic difficulties of the postwar period associated with the enormous damage caused by the war and the German fascist occupation the Soviet Union continues to remain economically independent from the outside world and is restoring its economy by its own means.

In addition, *at the present time the USSR has a considerably stronger international position than in the prewar* period. Thanks to the historic victories of Soviet arms the Soviet armed forces are on the territory of Germany and other former enemy countries, a guarantee that these countries will not be used again to attack the USSR. As a result of their reorganization on democratic principles, in such former enemy countries as *Bulgaria, Finland, Hungary, and Romania* regimes have been created which have set themselves the task of strengthening and maintaining friendly relations with the Soviet Union. In the Slavic countries—Poland, Czechoslovakia, and Yugoslavia—liberated by the Red Army or with its help, democratic regimes have also been created and are consolidating which maintain relations with the Soviet Union on the basis of friendship and mutual aid agreements.

The enormous relative importance of the USSR in international affairs in general and in European affairs in particular, the independence of its foreign policy, and the economic and political aid which it gives neighboring countries, both allies and former enemies, is leading to a growth in the influence of the Soviet Union in these countries and a continuing strengthening in them of democratic trends.

Such a situation in eastern and southeastern Europe cannot fail to be viewed by the American imperialists as an obstacle in the path of an expansionist American foreign policy.

2. a) Right now US foreign policy is not being determined by those circles of the Democratic Party which (as when Roosevelt was alive) try to strengthen cooperation between the three great powers which composed the basis of the anti-Hitler coalition during the war. When President Truman, a politically unstable person with certain conservative tendencies, came to power followed by the appointment of Byrnes as Secretary of State it meant the *strengthening of the influence of the most reactionary circles of the Democratic Party on foreign policy.* The constantly increasing reactionary nature of US foreign policy, which as a consequence of this approached the policy advocated by the Republican Party, has created a foundation for close cooperation in this area between the extreme right wing of the Democratic Party and the Republican Party. This cooperation of the two parties, formalized in both houses of Congress in the form of an unofficial *bloc of reactionary Southern Democrats and the old guard of the Republicans* headed by Vandenberg and Taft, is especially clearly demonstrated in the fact that in their statements about foreign policy issues the leaders of both parties are essentially advocating the same policy. In Congress and at international conferences where as a rule prominent Republicans are represented in American delegations the latter actively support the foreign policy of the government, and often due to this the above [policy], moreover even in official statements of "bipartisan" foreign policy.

b) At the same time *the influence on foreign policy of the followers of the Roosevelt policy* of cooperation with *peaceloving powers* has been sharply reduced. The corresponding circles in the government, in Congress, and in the leadership of the Democratic Party are more and more being pushed to the background. The differences in the area of foreign policy which exist between Wallace and Pepper supporters on the one hand and the partisans of the reactionary "bilateral" policy on the other were recently displayed with great bitterness in Wallace's speech which led to his resignation as Secretary of Commerce. *Wallace's resignation signifies the victory of the reactionary forces of the Democratic Party* and the foreign policy which Byrnes is pursuing in cooperation with Vandenberg and Taft.

3. The increase in peacetime military potential and the organization of a large number of naval and air bases both in the US and beyond its borders are clear indicators of the US desire to establish world domination.

For the first time in the country's history in the summer of 1946 Congress adopted a law to *form a peacetime army not of volunteers but on the basis of universal military conscription.* The size of the Army, which is to reach 1 million men as of 1 July 1947, has been considerably increased. At the end of the war the size of the US Navy was reduced quite insignificantly compared to wartime. At the present time the US Navy occupies first place in the world, leaving the British Royal Navy far behind, not to mention other powers.

The colossal growth of expenditures for the Army and Navy, comprising $13 billion in the 1946–1947 budget (about 40% of the entire budget of $36 billion) and is more than 10 times the corresponding expenditures in the 1938 budget, when it did not even reach $1 billion.

These enormous budget sums are being spent along with the maintenance of a large Army, Navy, and Air Force and also the creation of a vast system of naval and air bases in the Atlantic and Pacific Oceans. According to available official plans, in the coming years *228 bases,* support bases, and radio stations are to be built *in the Atlantic Ocean* and 258 *in the Pacific Ocean.* The majority of these bases and support bases are located outside the United States. The following bases exist or are to be built on islands in the Atlantic Ocean: Newfoundland, Iceland, Cuba, Trinidad, Bermuda, the Bahamas, the Azores, and many others; in the Pacific: former Japanese mandated possessions—the Marianas, and the Caroline and Marshall Islands, Bonin, Ryukyu, the Philippines, the Galapagos Islands (which belong to Ecuador).

The situating of American bases on islands often 10–12,000 kilometers from US territory and located on the other side of the Atlantic and Pacific Oceans clearly shows *the aggressive nature of the strategic designs* of the US Army and Navy. The fact that the US Navy is studying the naval approaches to European shores in a concentrated manner is also confirmation of this. During 1946 US Navy ships visited Norway, Denmark, Sweden, Turkey, and Greece with this purpose in mind. In addition the US Navy constantly cruises the Mediterranean Sea.

All these facts clearly show that their armed forces are designed to play a decisive role in the realization of plans to establish American world domination.

4. a) One of the stages in the establishment of American world domination is their *agreement with Britain about a partial division of the world on the basis*

of mutual concessions. The main lines of the clandestine agreement between the US and Britain about the division of the world, as the facts indicate, are that they have agreed that the United States include Japan and China in the sphere of its influence in the Far East whereas for its part the US has agreed not to hinder Britain in solving the Indian problem or the strengthening of [British] influence in Thailand and Indonesia.

b) In connection with this division at the present time the US is dominant in China and Japan without any interference from Britain.

American policy *in China* strives for its complete economic and political subordination to control by American monopoly capital. In the pursuit of this policy the American government does not even stop at interference in the internal affairs of China. At the present time there are more than 50,000 American soldiers in China. In a number of cases US Marines have directly participated in combat operations against the people's liberation forces. The so-called "mediation" mission of General Marshall is only a cover for actual interference in the internal affairs of China.

How far the policy of the American government has gone with respect to China is witnessed by the fact that it is now trying to exercise control over its army. Recently the US government introduced a bill for congressional discussion concerning military aid to China which provides for the complete reorganization of the Chinese army, its training with the aid of American military instructors, and supply with American weapons and equipment. An American consulting mission of Army and Navy officers will be sent to China in order to implement this program.

China is gradually being turned into a base of the American armed forces. American air bases are situated throughout its entire territory. Their main ones are located in Beijing, Qingdao, Tianjin, Nanking, Shanghai, Chengdu, Chongqing, and Kunming. The main American Navy base in China is located in Qingdao. The headquarters of the 7th Fleet is also located there. In addition, more than 30,000 American Marines are concentrated in Qingdao and its outskirts. The measures taken by the American Army in northern China show that it is calculating on remaining there for a long time.

In Japan, control is in the hands of the Americans in spite of the presence of the small contingent of American troops there. Although British capital has substantial interests in the Japanese economy British foreign policy with respect to Japan is being pursued so as not to interfere with the Americans' penetration of the Japanese economy and the subordination to its influence. In the Far East Commission in Washington and in the Allied Council in Tokyo the British representatives as a rule are in solidarity with American representatives who pursue this policy.

The measures of the American occupation authorities in the area of domestic policy and directed at supporting reactionary classes and groups which the US is counting on using in the struggle against the Soviet Union also encounter a sympathetic attitude from Britain.

c) A similar policy is also being pursued in the United States with respect to the British sphere of influence in the Far East. The US recently halted its attempts which it had been making during the recent war to influence the solution of Indian problems. Now there are often cases when the mainstream American press, which more or less reliably reflects official American government policy, speaks favorably of the British policy in *India*. American foreign policy is also not hindering British troops from suppressing the national liberation movement in *Indonesia* together with the Dutch Army. In addition, even instances are known of assistance from the United States to this British imperialist policy by sending American weapons and supplies to the British and Dutch troops in Indonesia, the sending of Dutch Navy sailors from the US, etc.

5. a) If the *division of the world* in the Far East between the US and Britain can be considered a fait accompli then it cannot be said that a similar situation exists in the *Mediterranean* and the countries adjacent to it. The facts rather say that such an agreement in the Middle East and Mediterranean region has not yet been reached. The difficulty of an agreement between Britain and the US in this region is that British concessions to the United States in the Mediterranean would be fraught with serious consequences for the entire British Empire, for which it has exceptional strategic and economic importance. Britain would not be averse to using the American armed forces and influence in this region, directing them to the north against the Soviet Union. However, the United States is not interested in helping and supporting the British Empire in this point where it is vulnerable but in penetrating the Mediterranean and Middle East more thoroughly itself, which attracts them with its natural resources, primarily *oil*.

b) In recent years American capital has been being introduced into the economies of *Middle Eastern* countries quite intensively, particularly in the oil industry. At the present time there are American oil concessions in all the Middle East countries which have sources of oil (Iraq, Bahrain, Kuwait, Egypt, and Saudi Arabia). American capital, which first appeared in the Middle East oil industry only in 1927, now controls about 42% of the total proven reserves of the Middle East (less Iran). Of the total proven reserves of 26.8 billion barrels of oil 11 billion belong to US concessions. In striving to guarantee the further development of its concessions in individual countries, which are often the largest (as is the case in Saudi Arabia, for example), American oil companies are planning to build a trans-Arabian pipeline which is to pump oil from the American concession in Saudi Arabia and in other countries to the southeastern coast of the Mediterranean, ports in Palestine and Egypt.

In pursuing expansion in the Middle East American capital has British capital as its competition, which is stubbornly resisting this expansion. The fierce nature of the competition between them is the main factor which prevents Britain and the United States from achieving an agreement about the division of spheres of influence in the Middle East, which might only take place at the expense of direct British interests in this region.

Palestine, where the US has recently displayed great interest, creating many difficulties for Britain, can be cited as an example of the quite sharp differences in US and British policy in the Middle East as is occurring in the case of the demand of the US government to allow 100,000 European Jews into *Palestine.* American interest in Palestine, outwardly expressed in sympathy for the Zionist cause, actually only means that American capital is expecting to become rooted in the economy of Palestine by interfering in Palestinian affairs. The choice of a Palestinian port as one of the terminal points of the American oil pipeline explains a lot about American foreign policy on the issue of Palestine.

c) The lack of agreement between Britain and the US on the Middle East is also often displayed in the great *activity of the US Navy in the eastern Mediterranean,* which cannot fail to run counter to the main interests of the British Empire. This activity of the US Navy is undoubtedly also in connection with American oil and other economic interests in the Middle East.

However, it ought to be borne in mind that such facts as the visit of the American battleship Missouri to the Black Sea Straits, the visit of an American fleet to Greece, and the great interest which American diplomacy shows in the problem of the Straits have a dual meaning. On the one hand, it means that the US has decided to consolidate its position in the Mediterranean to support its interests in the countries of the Middle East and that it has chosen the Navy as the tool of this policy. On the other hand, these facts are a military and political demonstration against the Soviet Union. The strengthening of the US position in the Middle East and the creation of the conditions to base the US Navy at one or several places in the Mediterranean (Trieste, Palestine, Greece, Turkey) will therefore mean the appearance of a new threat to the security of the southern regions of the Soviet Union.

6. a) *The US attitude toward Britain* is determined by two circumstances. On the one hand, *the US views Britain as its greatest potential competitor* and, on the other, *Britain seems to view the United States as a possible ally.* The division of several regions of the world *into* American and British *spheres of influence* has created the possibility, if not to avoid competition between them, which is impossible, then at least of reducing it somewhat. At the same time such a division makes it easier for them to achieve economic and political cooperation.

b) Britain needs American credits to reorganize its economy which was ruined by the war and it has been forced to make significant concessions to get them. This is the *importance of the loan* which the US recently gave Britain. With the help of the loan Britain will be able to strengthen its economy. At the same time this loan opens the door for the penetration of American capital into the British Empire. The narrow scope within which trade in the countries of the so-called sterling bloc has been found in recent years has been expanded at the present time and gives the Americans an opportunity to trade with British dominions, India, and the other countries of the sterling bloc (Egypt, Iraq, and Palestine).

c) The political *support which the United States gives* Britain is quite often manifested in the international events of the postwar period. At recent international conferences the US and Britain have closely coordinated their policies, especially in those instances when it was necessary to oppose the policy of the Soviet Union. The US gives Britain moral and political aid in its reactionary policy in Greece, India, and Indonesia. Complete coordination of American and British policy can be observed with respect to the Slavic and other countries bordering the Soviet Union. The most important American and British demarches in these countries after the war have had a quite similar and parallel nature. American and British policy in the United Nations Security Council has the same features of coordination (especially in questions about Iran, Spain, Greece, the withdrawal of foreign troops from Syria and Lebanon, etc.).

d) US ruling circles evidently have a sympathetic attitude toward *the idea of a military alliance with Britain,* but at the present time the matter has still not reached the point of concluding an official alliance. Churchill's speech in Fulton [Missouri] calling for the conclusion of an Anglo-American military alliance in order to establish joint world domination was consequently not officially supported by Truman or Byrnes, although Truman indirectly sanctioned Churchill's call by his presence.

But if the US is not now seeking to conclude a military alliance with Britain then all the same in practice it supports the closest contact with it on military issues. The Joint Anglo-American staff in Washington still continues to exist in spite of the fact that it has been over a year since the war ended. Frequent personal contact between British and American military leaders also continues. The recent trip of Field Marshal Montgomery to America is one indication of this contact. It is characteristic that as a result of his meetings with American military leaders Montgomery said that *the British Army would be patterned after the American model.* Cooperation is also being conducted *between the navies of these two countries.* It is sufficient to mention in this connection the participation of the Royal Navy in the recent maneuvers of the American fleet in the Mediterranean and the participation of the US fleet in the North Sea this autumn.

e) In spite of the temporary achievement of agreements about very important issues, current relations between Britain and the United States are *quite conflictive* and cannot be long-term.

In many respects American economic aid holds a danger for Britain. Not to mention that by virtue of receiving the loan Britain will fall into a certain economic dependence on the US from which it will not be easy to free itself, it ought to be kept in mind that the conditions created by the loan for the penetration of American capital into the British Empire might entail serious political consequences. The countries in the British Empire or those dependent on it might reorient themselves to the United States under economic influence from powerful American capital, following the example of Canada in this respect, which is more and more escaping British influence and in the process orienting itself to the US. The strengthening of the American position in the Far East might stimulate a similar process in Australia and New Zealand. In the Arab countries of the Middle East which are trying to emancipate themselves from the British Empire there are also groups among the ruling classes which have no objection to trading with the United States. It is entirely possible that it is the Middle East that will become the *focal point of Anglo-American conflicts* where the agreements currently reached between the US and Britain will be destroyed.

7. a) *The "hard-line" policy with respect to the USSR* proclaimed by Byrnes after the rapprochement between reactionary Democrats and the Republicans is right now the main impediment in the way to cooperation between the great powers. It is mainly that in the postwar period the US has no longer been pursuing a policy of strengthening the cooperation of the Big Three (or Four) and, on the contrary, is trying to undermine the unity of these powers. The *goal* which is being set in the process is *to impose* the will of other countries on the Soviet Union. The attempt being made by several powers to undermine or completely *eliminate the veto principle* in the United Nations Security Council with the blessing of the United States is a move in this direction. This would give the United States an opportunity to create narrow groups and blocs among the great powers directed primarily against the Soviet Union and thereby split the united front of the United Nations. The renunciation of the veto by the great powers would turn the United Nations into an Anglo-American private domain in which the United States would have the leading role.

b) The current policy of the American government with respect to the USSR is also directed at limiting or displacing Soviet influence from neighboring countries. While implementing it the US is trying to take steps at various international conferences or directly in these very same countries which, on the one hand, manifest themselves in the support of reactionary forces in former enemy or allied countries bordering the USSR *with the object of creating obstacles to the processes of democratizing these countries* but, on the other, in *providing positions for the penetration of American capital into their economies.* Such a policy relies on weakening and disbanding [*razlozhit'*] the democratic governments in power there which are friendly to the USSR and then replacing them with new governments which would obediently carry out a policy dictated from the US. In this policy the US receives full support from British diplomacy.

c) One of the most important links of overall US policy directed at limiting the international role of the USSR in the postwar world is *policy with regard to Germany.* The US is taking steps in Germany with special persistence to strengthen reactionary forces in order to counteract democratic restructuring, accompanied by completely insufficient steps regarding demilitarization.

American occupation policy is not setting as its goal the elimination of the remnants of *German fascism* and the reorganization of German political life *on democratic principles* in order that Germany ceases to be an aggressive force. The US is not taking steps *to eliminate the monopolistic associations* of German industrialists on which German fascism relied in preparing aggression and waging war. An *agrarian* policy with the elimination of large landholders who were formerly a reliable bulwark of fascism is also not being pursued. Moreover, the US is providing for the possibility of ending the Allied occupation of German territory even before the main tasks of the occupation, consisting of the demilitarization and democratization of Germany, are finished. The preconditions would thereby be created for a revival of an imperialist Germany which the US is counting on using on its side in a future war. One cannot fail to see that such a policy has a clearly defined *anti-Soviet* focus and represents a serious danger to the cause of peace.

d) The numerous statements by American government, political, and military leaders about the Soviet Union and its foreign policy in an exceptionally hostile spirit are quite typical of the current attitude of American ruling circles toward the USSR. These statements are echoed in an ever more unbridled tone by the overwhelming majority of the American press. *Discussions about a "third war,"* meaning a war against the Soviet Union, even a direct call for this war with a threat to use the atomic bomb, this is the substance of statements about relations with the Soviet Union by reactionaries at public meetings and in the press. At the present time the advocacy of a war against the Soviet Union is not just the monopoly of the extreme right and the yellow American press which is represented by the Hearst and McCormick newspaper syndicates. This anti-Soviet campaign also includes such more "serious" and "respectable" publications of the conservative press like the New York Times and New York Herald Tribune. The numerous articles by Walter Lippmann in which he almost undisguisedly calls on the US to launch a strike on the Soviet Union in the most vulnerable places of the south and southeast of the USSR are characteristic of such publications of the conservative press.

The primary goal of this anti-Soviet campaign of American "public opinion" consists of exerting political pressure on the Soviet Union and forcing it to make concessions. Another, no less important goal of the campaign is a desire *to create an atmosphere of a fear of war* among the broad masses who are tired of war, which would make it easier for the government to take steps to maintain the great military potential in the US. It is in such an atmosphere that the law was passed in Congress about introducing peacetime military conscription, an enormous military budget was adopted, and plans are being developed to build a far-flung system of naval and air bases.

e) All these steps to preserve the great military potential are not an end in itself, of course. They are intended only *to prepare conditions to win world domination* in a new war being planned by the most warlike circles of American imperialism, the timeframe for which, needless to say, no one can determine right now.

It ought to be fully realized that American preparations for a future war are being conducted with the idea of *war against the Soviet Union,* which in the eyes of American imperialists is the chief obstacle in the American path to world domination. Such facts as the tactical training of the US Army for war with the USSR as a future enemy, the situating of American strategic bases in regions from which strikes can be launched on Soviet territory, the intensified training and reinforcement of Arctic regions as tactical approaches to the USSR, and attempts to pave the way in Germany and Japan to use them in a war against the USSR testify to this.

27.09.46 NOVIKOV

5.3

REAGAN, GORBACHEV, AND THE COMPLETION OF CONTAINMENT

John Lewis Gaddis

> In this excerpted article, Cold War historian John Lewis Gaddis analyzes Ronald Reagan's containment strategy and compares it to those of previous presidents. He emphasizes three points: (1) Reagan felt détente perpetuated rather than ended the Cold War, (2) Reagan exploited America's strengths and Soviet weaknesses, and (3) Reagan believed that a nuclear war could not be won but that freedom "will leave Marxism-Leninism on the ash-heap of history." Could you argue that Reagan's strategy emphasized ideational causes (identity) over détente (liberal) and material (realist) ones? Freedom would bury the Soviet Union, although détente diplomacy might delay this outcome and military competition might hasten it. Note, too, the stronger influence of the structural over individual level of analysis: Reagan's strategy "did not cause these things to happen. They resulted from structural tensions...."

* * *

II

* * *

The greatest uncertainty had to do with the man who took office on January 20, 1981. Reagan was the first major American politician—though not the last—to have begun his career as a film and television star. He had gained political prominence as a Barry Goldwater conservative, as governor of California from 1967 to 1975, and as a presidential contender during the 1968 and 1976 campaigns. He had been as critical of Republican as of Democratic approaches to containment, having almost derailed Ford's nomination in 1976 by condemning the alleged amorality of Kissinger's policies, but having also accused

Source: John Lewis Gaddis, "Reagan, Gorbachev, and the Completion of Containment," in *Strategies of Containment: A Critical Appraisal of American National Security Policy during the Cold War,* rev. ed. (New York: Oxford University Press, 2005), 342–373.

Carter, in 1980, of allowing moral concerns to inhibit the use of American power. Only one thing seemed obvious at the time of Reagan's inaugural: détente was dead, buried, and in the new administration at least not mourned. As the new President himself had admitted to a radio audience three years earlier, "I didn't exactly tear my hair and go into a panic at the possibility of losing détente."[1]

For years intellectuals, journalists, and political opponents derided Reagan as a telegenic lightweight, too simple-minded to know what containment had been about, much less to have had constructive ideas about how to ensure its success. It is true that Reagan relied more on instincts than on systematic study in shaping his positions: in this, he differed conspicuously from Carter. Derived from his Midwestern upbringing, his experiences in Hollywood, and an occasional tendency to conflate movies with reality, those instincts included an unshakable belief in democracy and capitalism, an abhorrence of communism, an impatience with compromise in what he regarded as a contest between good and evil, and—very significantly—a deep fear that the Cold War might end in a nuclear holocaust thereby confirming the Biblical prophecy of Armageddon.[2] This was, to say the least, an unorthodox preparation for the presidency. When combined with the fact that Reagan took office as the oldest elected chief executive—he turned seventy shortly after his inauguration—it seemed reasonable to expect an amiable geriatric who would for the most part follow the lead of his own advisers.

That expectation turned out to be wrong on several counts. First it overlooked the skill with which Reagan had managed his pre-presidential career: it was no small matter to have shifted the Republican Party to the right while centrist Republican presidents—Nixon and Ford—were occupying the White House.[3] Second, it failed to take into account Reagan's artful artlessness: his habit of *appearing* to know less than his critics did or *seeming* to be adrift even as he proceeded quietly towards destinations he himself had chosen.[4] Third, it neglected what Reagan himself had said in hundreds of radio scripts and speech drafts prepared between 1975 and 1980: these almost daily commentaries, composed in longhand on legal pads without the assistance of speechwriters, provided a more voluminous record of positions taken on national and international issues than had been available for any other modern presidential aspirant.[5] They put forward no comprehensive strategy for ending the Cold War. That would emerge only gradually, in response to what happened after Reagan entered the White House. These broadcasts and speeches did, however, contain most of the ideas that lay behind that strategy—and they establish that the ideas largely came from Reagan himself.

The one most obvious at the time was optimism: faith in the ability of the United States to compete successfully within the international system. One would have to go back to Roosevelt in 1933 to find a president who entered office with comparable self-confidence in the face of bleak prospects. Like F.D.R., Reagan believed that the nation was stronger than it realized, that time was on its side, and that these facts could be conveyed, through rhetoric, style, and bearing, to the American people. "[I]t is important every once and a while to remind ourselves of our accomplishments ... *lest* we let someone talk us into throwing out the baby with the bathwater," he told his radio audience in 1976. "[T]he system has never let us down—we've let the system down now & then because we're only human."[6]

It followed from this that the Soviet Union was weaker than it appeared to be, and that time was not on its side: Reagan had insisted as early as 1975 that communism was "a temporary aberration which will one day disappear from the earth because it is contrary to human nature."[7] This too was an unusual posture for an incoming president. The fundamental premise of containment had always been that the United States was acting *defensively* against an adversary that was on the offensive, and was likely to continue on that path for the foreseeable future. Now, just at the moment when the U.S.S.R. seemed to be pushing for superiority in strategic weaponry as well as influence on a global scale, Reagan rejected that premise, raising the prospect of regaining and indefinitely sustaining American preeminence.

He did so by assuming expandable resources on the part of the United States, a view consistent with NSC-68, which Reagan read and discussed on the air shortly after it was declassified in 1975. He concluded, as he later recalled, that "capitalism had given us a powerful weapon in our battle against Communism—*money.* The Russians could never win the arms race; we could outspend them forever."[8] Meanwhile, the Soviet Union was denying its people "all kinds of consumer products" in its quest for military supremacy. "We could have an unexpected ally," he noted in 1977, "if citizen Ivan is becoming discontented enough to start talking back."[9] After becoming president, Reagan quickly became convinced, on the basis of intelligence reports, that the Soviet economy "was a basket case, partly because of massive spending on armaments.... I wondered how we as a nation could use these cracks in the Soviet system to accelerate the process of collapse."[10]

The Soviet Union was also vulnerable, Reagan insisted, within the realm of ideas. Despite his support for the Committee on the Present Danger, founded by Paul Nitze in 1976 to warn of the Soviet military buildup,* Reagan had never accepted the assumption that armaments alone could make the U.S.S.R. an effective competitor with the United States. Moscow's failure to respect human rights, he maintained, was a serious weakness, even in a military superpower. Although Reagan had opposed the Helsinki Conference, which he regarded— shortsightedly—as having ratified Soviet control over Eastern Europe, by 1979 he was acknowledging that "something [is] going on behind the Iron Curtain that we've been ignoring and [that offers] hope for all mankind.... [A] little less

---

*The Committee on the Present Danger took its name from an earlier organization that had been formed in 1950 to lobby for the implementation of NSC-68. See Paul H. Nitze, with Ann M. Smith and Steven L. Rearden, *From Hiroshima to Glasnost: At the Center of Decision. A Memoir* (New York: 1989), pp. 353–54; also Jerry W. Sanders, *Peddlers of Crisis: The Committee on the Present Danger and the Politics of Containment* (Boston: 1983).

détente ... and more encouragement to the dissidents might be worth a lot of armored divisions."[11]

Mutual Assured Destruction, however, had to go. Unlike all previous presidents dating back to Kennedy, Reagan refused to accept the proposition that a nuclear balance of terror could ever lead to a stable international system: it was "the craziest thing I ever heard of."[12] The SALT process, geared as it was toward reinforcing MAD, was flawed because it did nothing to reverse reliance on nuclear weapons or to diminish the risks that their continued existence in such vast numbers entailed. "I have repeatedly stated that I would be willing to negotiate an honest, verifiable reduction in nuclear weapons ... to the point that neither of us represented a threat to the other," Reagan wrote in a 1980 speech draft. "I cannot, however, agree to a treaty—specifically the Salt II treaty, which, in effect, legitimizes a nuclear arms buildup."[13]

The problem with détente was not that it had encouraged negotiations with the U.S.S.R., but rather that it had done so without enlisting American strengths: the idea had been to "seek agreements just for the sake of having an agreement." The Russians had to understand that "we are ... building up our defense capability pending an agreement by both sides to limit various kinds of weapons." But "if we have the will & the determination to build a deterrent capability ... we can have real peace.... [T]he men in the Kremlin could in the face of such determination decide that true arms limitation makes sense."[14] In Reagan's view, then, *rejecting* détente was the way to reduce the danger of nuclear war and move toward a negotiated settlement of Cold War differences.

Such a settlement would require, however, a fundamental change in the nature of the Soviet Union itself. This had been the long-term objective of containment since Kennan first articulated that strategy; but as the nuclear danger had grown, the American interest in encouraging reform within the U.S.S.R. had receded—until the Carter administration made the promotion of human rights there one of its chief priorities.[15] Carter, however, had sought to do this while preserving détente, a futile endeavor because one could hardly challenge a state's internal makeup while simultaneously soliciting its cooperation within the international arena. For Reagan, reforming the Soviet Union required abandoning détente. "Our foreign policy should be to show by example the greatness of our system and the strength of American ideals," he wrote in August 1980. "[W]e would like nothing better than to see the Russian people living in freedom & dignity instead of being trapped in a backwash of history *as they are*."[16]

Reagan was, then, no lightweight. He came into office with a clear set of ideas, developed for the most part on his own, on how to salvage the strategy of containment by returning to the objective Kennan had set for it in 1947: "to increase enormously the strains under which Soviet policy must operate, to force upon the Kremlin a far greater degree of moderation and circumspection than it has had to observe in recent years, and in this way to promote tendencies which must eventually find their outlet in either the break-up or the gradual mellowing of Soviet power."[17] Reagan would do this, not by acknowledging the current Soviet regime's legitimacy but by challenging it; not by seeking parity in the arms race but by regaining superiority; not by compromising on the issue of human rights but by capitalizing on it as a weapon more powerful than anything that existed in the military arsenals of either side. "The Reagan I observed may have been no master of detail," Soviet Ambassador Dobrynin later observed, "but he had a clear sense of what he wanted."[18]

III

* * *

Reagan's objective was straightforward, if daunting: to prepare the way for a new kind of Soviet leader by pushing the old Soviet system to the breaking point. Kennan, Nitze, and other early strategists of containment had always held out the possibility that Moscow might someday acknowledge the failures of Marxism-Leninism and the futility of Russian imperialism—the two foundations upon which the Soviet state had been constructed.[19] But ... by the time Reagan took office early in 1981 the apparent strength and actual behavior of the U.S.S.R. made the prospect seem very distant indeed. It was not at all clear then that the Soviet economy was approaching bankruptcy, that Afghanistan would become Moscow's Vietnam, that the appearance of a Polish labor union called Solidarity portended the end of communism in Eastern Europe, or that the U.S.S.R. itself would disappear in just over a decade.

The strategy Reagan developed over the next several years did not cause these things to happen. They resulted from structural tensions that had been building within the Soviet Union and its satellites for many years. Even if Carter had been re-elected in 1980, they would at some point have produced a crisis. Whether it would have come as quickly or with such decisive results, though, is another matter. For however Carter's policies may have appeared from Moscow's perspective, no administration prior to Reagan's had deliberately sought to exploit those tensions with a view to destabilizing the Kremlin leadership and accelerating the decline of the regime it ran.

* * *

The first Reagan directive on national strategy, in contrast, called explicitly, in May 1982, for efforts to force "the U.S.S.R. to bear the brunt of its economic shortcomings, and to encourage long-term liberalizing and nationalist tendencies within the Soviet Union and allied countries."[20] Three weeks later, in a speech to the members of the British Parliament, Reagan elaborated on what he had in mind. Karl Marx had been right, he pointed out, in predicting "a great revolutionary crisis ... where the demands of the economic order are conflicting directly with those of the political order." This was happening, though, not in the capitalist world but in the Soviet Union, a country that "runs against the tide of history by denying human freedom and human dignity to its citizens." Nuclear superpower status provided no immunity from this great trend, for "[a]ny system is inherently unstable that has no peaceful means to legitimize its leaders." The West, therefore, should insist "that freedom is not the sole prerogative of a lucky few, but the inalienable and universal right of all human beings." What was needed was "a plan and a hope for the long term—the march of freedom and democracy that will leave Marxism-Leninism on the ash-heap of history."[21]*

No American president had ever before talked like this, and the effects were profoundly unsettling in Moscow. It had been difficult, Dobrynin later recalled, to imagine that anyone could be worse than Carter, "but it soon became clear that in ideology and propaganda Reagan [was] ... far more threatening."[22] The new administration sought, in the words of National Security Decision Directive 75, completed in January 1983, "[t]o contain and over time reverse Soviet expansionism by competing effectively on a sustained basis with the Soviet Union in all international arenas."[23] The contest would range from buildups in nuclear and conventional weaponry through new and openly discussed warfighting strategies, economic sanctions, the aggressive promotion of human rights, and overt and covert support for anti-Soviet resistance movements in Eastern Europe and Afghanistan as well as for opponents of Marxist regimes in Angola, Ethiopia, and Nicaragua. As Reagan's British Parliament speech made clear, the strategy would also include the vigorous employment of rhetoric as an instrument of psychological warfare, a trend which culminated in the President's March 1983 claim that the Soviet Union was "the focus of evil in the modern world."[24]

All of this came at a time when the domestic strains that had long been building within the U.S.S.R. had converged to produce a stagnant economy, environmental degradation, the beginnings of social unrest, and—remarkably for an advanced industrial society—declining life expectancy. Soviet military expenditures, meanwhile, were now consuming between 15 and 20 percent of gross domestic product; the comparable figure for the United States, through the last half of the 1970's, had averaged slightly under 5 percent.[25] The aging Kremlin leadership, burdened by both ideological and biological senescence, could only respond autistically to these developments, a trend that continued even after Brezhnev's death in November 1982, when the Politburo appointed successors, Yuri Andropov and Konstantin Chernenko, who were themselves approaching their deathbeds.[26] Reagan had, in this sense, picked a good time to push.

---

*The historian Richard Pipes, then serving on the National Security Council staff, played a significant role in shaping the drafting of these documents. (Richard Pipes, *Vixi: Memoirs of a Non-Belonger* [New Haven: 2003], pp. 197–200.)

Pushing, however, still carried risks. Reagan could hardly dismantle détente and exploit Soviet vulnerabilities without reviving fears of nuclear war. This is indeed what happened during the first two years of his administration, a period that seemed at the time—and still seems—the most dangerous one in Soviet-American relations since the Cuban missile crisis. Some of these fears resulted from the collapse of arms control negotiations, despite Reagan's willingness to abide by the numerical limits of the unratified SALT II treaty. Some arose from rhetorical excesses on the part of Reagan's subordinates, notably the official who immortalized himself by extending the assurance that with "enough shovels" to build backyard bomb shelters, it should be possible to survive a nuclear attack. Some grew out of protests in Europe against the forthcoming installation there of Pershing II and cruise missiles, NATO's response to the Soviet SS-20 deployment of the late 1970's. All of these fears were reflected in the campaign, within the United States, for a "freeze" on the production, testing, and deployment of Soviet and American nuclear weapons, in Jonathan Schell's best-selling 1982 book, *The Fate of the Earth,* a graphic account of the physical and biological consequences of nuclear war, and in the equally explicit ABC television production, *The Day After,* which riveted a national audience in the fall of 1983 with its portrayal of a nuclear attack on the United States.[27]

What hardly anyone realized at the time was that Reagan also feared a nuclear apocalypse—perhaps more deeply than most of his critics did. He had warned, as early as 1976, of "horrible missiles of destruction that can, in a matter of minutes, ... destroy virtually the civilized world we live in."[28] His rejection of Mutual Assured Destruction, and hence of the SALT process, stemmed from a long-standing conviction that relying on nuclear weapons to keep the peace was certain sooner or later to bring on a nuclear war. Détente itself, he believed, had frozen the nuclear danger in place, rather than doing anything to alleviate it. Soon after entering the White House, he began promoting initiatives to reduce that threat: these involved shifting SALT to START—from "strategic arms limitation talks" to "strategic arms reduction talks"—as well as endorsing the then radical idea of seeking an agreement with Moscow to phase out all intermediate-range nuclear missiles in Europe. But because the very concept of arms *control* as it had evolved over the past two decades had assumed that arms *reduction* was impossible, these Reagan proposals were widely regarded as efforts to kill rather than to advance progress toward eliminating the nuclear peril.[29] Then Reagan really shook up the arms control community, anti-nuclear protesters, the Russians, and most of his own advisers as well.

The Strategic Defense Initiative, which the President announced on March 23, 1983, shattered orthodoxies on all sides. By endorsing a program to defend the United States against long-range nuclear missile attacks, Reagan called into question the 1972 Soviet-American treaty banning strategic defenses, a fundamental pillar of the SALT I agreements. In doing so, he denied the basic premise of Mutual Assured Destruction, which was that vulnerability could produce safety. He thereby reversed an American position on arms control dating back to the Kennedy administration. He raised the prospect of extending the arms race into outer space, a region hitherto off limits to it. He exploited an overwhelming American superiority in computer technology, precisely the field in which the Soviet Union would find it most difficult to keep up. But he also linked SDI to the goal of *lowering* the nuclear danger: missile defense, he insisted, could in time make nuclear weapons "impotent and obsolete."[30]

Reagan did not invent the idea of strategic missile defense. The United States and the Soviet Union had made efforts to develop such systems prior to the SALT I agreements, and the Anti-Ballistic Missile Treaty had even allowed limited deployments.[31] Technical problems caused the Pentagon to abandon these, however, so that only the concept remained alive through the end of the 1970's, especially at the Lawrence Livermore Nuclear Laboratory, where Edward Teller, the father of the American H-bomb, had strongly endorsed it. But it was nowhere near the mainstream of policy until Reagan placed it there—very much to the consternation of aides and allies. "I was completely taken by surprise," Paul Nitze, the chief White House arms control negotiator, later acknowledged. "I had no idea," Secretary of State Shultz recalled, "that anything regarding strategic defense was on the president's agenda." Secretary of Defense Weinberger immediately scrambled "to ensure that the announcement did not fall on totally astonished NATO ears."[32]

From an operational perspective, SDI was as remote from reality in 1983 as Khrushchev's claims of strategic missile superiority had been in the 1950's. Reagan's interest in the concept had grown more out of incredulity that the United States lacked the means of defending itself against a Soviet attack—and perhaps also out of movies and science fiction—than from an informed assessment of what might be technologically feasible.[33] Two decades later a workable system seems almost as far away as it did then. As grand strategy, though, SDI was a striking demonstration of killing multiple birds with a single stone: in one speech Reagan managed simultaneously to pre-empt the nuclear freeze movement, to raise the prospect of not just reducing but eliminating the need for nuclear weapons, to reassert American technological preeminence, and, by challenging the Soviet Union in an arena in which it had no hope of being able to compete, to create the strongest possible incentive for Soviet leaders to reconsider the reasons for competition in the first place. To reinforce that argument, he later proposed—in a gesture so unorthodox that virtually no one apart from himself took it seriously—to *share* the technology of SDI with the nation against whose weapons it was to be developed.[34]

Reagan had never ruled out the possibility of negotiations with Moscow, as long as they could be geared toward ending, not perpetuating, the Cold War. He had written to Brezhnev as early as April 1981—while recovering from a nearly fatal assassination attempt—to express his hope for a "meaningful and constructive dialogue which will assist us in fulfilling our joint obligation to find lasting peace."[35] His May 1982 national strategy directive had predicted that although the next few years "will likely pose the greatest challenge to our survival and well-being since World War II, ... our response could result in a fundamentally different East-West relationship by the end of the decade."[36] He made it clear, in a quiet meeting with Secretary of State Shultz in February 1983—*before* the "evil empire" and SDI speeches—that he wanted to begin talking to the Russians, despite the reservations of his own staff.[37]* "Probably, people in the Soviet Union regard me as a crazy warmonger," he acknowledged shortly thereafter to Ambassador Dobrynin. "But I don't want a war between us, because I know it would bring countless disasters. We should make a fresh start."[38] He proposed, as a test of the possibilities, that the Soviet government facilitate the emigration, with no publicity, of a group of Pentecostals who had taken refuge in the American embassy in Moscow five years earlier and had not been allowed to leave. The release did occur, with minimal publicity, in July.[39]

None of this, however, reassured the new—but already mortally ill—Soviet leader, Yuri Andropov. He bitterly denounced SDI, claiming that the Americans were "devising one option after another in their search for best ways of unleashing nuclear war in the hope of winning it."[40] When the Soviet air force shot down a civilian South Korean airliner over Sakhalin on September 1, having mistaken it for an American reconnaissance plane, he insisted that the incident had been a "sophisticated provocation, organized by the US special services."[41] And after the West German Bundestag voted, in November, to go ahead with the deployment of Pershing II and cruise missiles, Andropov ordered his negotiators to break off arms control talks altogether, leaving Soviet-American relations at their lowest point in years.

These public positions were not nearly as ominous, though, as the conviction that had taken hold within Andropov's mind that the Reagan administration was planning a nuclear first-strike against the U.S.S.R. While still KGB chief in 1981, Andropov had instructed Soviet intelligence agencies to undertake a world-wide effort aimed at detecting evidence of such planning. When none was found, they fabricated it rather than question the assumption that had led to the order in the first place.[42] That operation was still under way in November 1983, as the United States and its NATO allies began a major military exercise known as "Able-Archer 83." Such maneuvers had taken place in the past, but these had a higher level of participation by top officials and new communications procedures, all carefully monitored in Moscow. Primed by Andropov to assume the worst, Soviet intelligence concluded that Able-Archer might be a ruse to cloak preparations for an actual attack—in which case Soviet war plans called for launching a pre-emptive nuclear strike against the United States.[43]

---

*NSDD-75, which Reagan approved in January 1983, set out as a major objective of American strategy "[t]o engage the Soviet Union in negotiations to attempt to reach agreements which protect and enhance U.S. interests and which are consistent with the principle of strict reciprocity and mutual interest. This is important when the Soviet Union is in the midst of a process of political succession." (NSDD-75, "U.S. Relations with the U.S.S.R.", January 17, 1963, p. 1.)

Fortunately, the Able-Archer crisis ended peacefully, but it badly shook Reagan, who had the nuclear danger very much on his mind in the fall of 1983. He had previewed *The Day After,* and shortly thereafter—having postponed it several times—he received his first full Pentagon briefing on American nuclear war plans: "[T]here were still some people at the Pentagon who claimed a nuclear war was 'winnable,'" he later wrote. "I thought they were crazy. Worse, it appeared there were also Soviet generals who thought in terms of winning a nuclear war."[44] After a British spy in Moscow, Oleg Gordievsky, confirmed how close to war the Able-Archer crisis had come, Reagan resolved to take a new approach. He chose, once again, to make a speech, on January 16, 1984, this time not for the purpose of rattling the Kremlin leadership, but rather to reassure it. The most important passage was unmistakably his own:

> Just suppose with me for a moment that an Ivan and an Anya could find themselves, say, in a waiting room, or sharing a shelter from the rain or a storm with a Jim and Sally, and that there was no language barrier to keep them from getting acquainted. Would they then deliberate the differences between their respective governments? Or would they find themselves comparing notes about their children and what each other did for a living? Before they parted company they would probably have touched on ambitions and hobbies and what they wanted for their children and the problems of making ends meet. And as they went their separate ways, maybe Anya would say to Ivan, "wasn't she nice, she also teaches music." Maybe Jim would be telling Sally what Ivan did or didn't like about his boss. They might even have decided that they were all going to get together for dinner some evening soon. Above all, they would have proven that people don't make wars.[45]

Within three weeks of this speech Andropov was dead. His feeble successor, Chernenko, maintained a hard line initially, but Reagan interpreted this as weakness: "maybe they are scared of us, and think we are a threat."[46]

In an effort to alleviate these anxieties, the President made a point, in September 1984, of inviting Soviet Foreign Minister Andrei Gromyko to a carefully prepared meeting at the White House. Three hours of arguments with "this frosty old Stalinist" convinced Reagan that he had achieved little: "If I scored any points, Gromyko didn't admit it to me. He was as hard as granite."[47] The President stuck to his strategy, though: his national security adviser, Robert McFarlane, assured Dobrynin in December that Reagan "believed that he had fulfilled the basic task of his presidency, which was to restore the potential of the American armed forces." Now it was time "to improve relations with the Soviet Union gradually and reach agreements on reducing nuclear arms."[48] When it became apparent that Weinberger and Casey were trying to get Shultz fired for seeking to reopen talks with the Russians, Reagan came down firmly on the Secretary of State's side: "George is carrying out my policy," he noted in his diary. "I'm going to meet with Cap and Bill and lay it out to them. Won't be fun, but it has to be done."[49]

Shultz's policy—following Reagan's lead—had one additional dimension, which was to wait for the Grim Reaper to complete his work in Moscow. "Sooner or later," he told the President in the summer of 1984, "the Soviets would have to face the hurdle of a generational turnover when the senior members of the Politburo retired or died and would be replaced by younger men who might have a significantly different outlook." These would be "post–World War II people. I suspect that ideology will be less of a living force for them, that they will believe more in technology and will look for policies that are genuinely effective.... It will pay dividends to treat them with civility, whatever our differences might be and to recognize the importance of their country."[50] Reagan needed no prompting to see the benefits of fresh leadership in the Kremlin. "How am I supposed to get anyplace with the Russians," he asked his wife, Nancy, after the news came of Chernenko's death on March 10, 1985, "if they keep dying on me?"[51]

IV

But they did not. The circumstances that produced Mikhail Gorbachev's appointment as General Secretary of the Communist Party of the Soviet Union on March 11 are, even now, not completely clear. What was apparent at the time, though, was that an important turning point had been reached. Gorbachev himself recalls telling his wife, Raisa, on the eve of his elevation, that "We can't go on living like this." He later acknowledged, as if to echo Reagan and Shultz: "The very system was dying away; its sluggish senile blood no longer contained any vital juices."[52]...

* * *

Gorbachev['s] ... presence there did not immediately improve Soviet-American relations: "Gorbachev will be as tough as any of their leaders," Reagan predicted in April 1985. "If he wasn't a confirmed ideologue, he never would have been chosen by the Politburo."[53] Soviet sources confirm, in turn, that Gorbachev was then, and remained for months to come, suspicious of Reagan.[54] But the new Kremlin leader—unlike his recent predecessors—was not so locked into ideology that he allowed it to close his eyes, ears, or mind. Exchanging messages with Brezhnev, Andropov, and Chernenko had been like conversing with robots, a frustrating experience for a president like Reagan who prided himself on his communications skills. Gorbachev, in contrast, was as unrobotic as it was possible to imagine, and Reagan was quick to sense the opportunity thereby provided. He had always intended for his strategy of confrontation to prepare the way for one of persuasion:* now the moment had come. The points of which

---

*NSDD-75 had concluded that "the U.S. must demonstrate credibly that its policy is not a blueprint for an open-ended, sterile confrontation with Moscow, but a serious search for a stable and constructive long-term basis for U.S.-Soviet relations." (NSDD-75, January 17, 1983, p. 9.)

he hoped to convince the skeptical but attentive Gorbachev boiled down to three:

First, *that the United States was sincere in seeking to lower the danger of nuclear war.* Reagan had long believed that "if I could ever get in a room alone with one of the top Soviet leaders, there was a chance the two of us could make some progress.... I have always placed a lot of faith in the simple power of human contact in solving problems."[55] It sounded naive, but when this finally happened—when Reagan actually did sit down across from Gorbachev, with only their interpreters present, at their first summit conference in Geneva on November 19, 1985—several interesting things occurred. One was that the meeting ran well beyond the time scheduled for it. Another was that an unscheduled meeting followed later in the day, at which the two leaders agreed to hold future summits in Washington and in Moscow. But the really big story, as Shultz recalled, was "that they had hit it off as human beings."[56] Despite vigorous disagreements on responsibility for the Cold War, human rights, regional conflicts, and especially SDI, Reagan found "something likeable about Gorbachev. There was warmth in his face and his style, not the coldness bordering on hatred I'd seen in most other senior Soviet leaders I'd met until then."[57] Gorbachev caught the mood as well: "something important happened to each of us on that day.... We both sensed that we must maintain contact and try to avoid a break."[58]

At one point during these conversations, Reagan suggested to Gorbachev that if there were no nuclear missiles, then there would be no need for defenses against them.[59] The President's desire to rid the world of all nuclear weapons—not just missiles—was nothing new: he had been talking about this for years, to the puzzlement of his aides, few of whom took him literally. Gorbachev did, though. In January 1986, no doubt with Reagan's Geneva comment in mind, he publicly proposed phasing out nuclear weapons and ballistic missiles by the year 2000. Most of Reagan's advisers dismissed this as a publicity stunt, and perhaps it was. But as one of Gorbachev's top aides noted at the time, the Soviet leader was "taking this 'risk' because, as he understands, it's no risk at all—because nobody would attack us even if we disarmed completely."[60] That was a big change from the fears that had beset Andropov and Chernenko: Reagan's reassurances at last were working. The President himself liked the Gorbachev proposal and wanted to go further: "Why wait until the end of the century for a world without nuclear weapons?" he asked Shultz. It was a good question, and it led the Secretary of State to conclude that, "utopian though his dream might be, the shared view of Reagan and Gorbachev on the desirability of eliminating nuclear weapons could move us toward the massive reductions in medium-range and strategic ballistic missiles that Reagan had proposed back in 1981 and 1982."[61]

The months that followed saw a top-level Soviet-American consensus begin to emerge in support of a proposition that, only a few years earlier, would have seemed improbable if not ludicrous: that it might indeed be possible to move, not just from the limitation to the reduction of strategic arms, but toward their *drastic* reduction, perhaps even *elimination*. It was Reagan who, by challenging the conventional wisdom of détente, the SALT process, and the concept of MAD that lay behind it, brought the United States around to this position. It was also he who persuaded Gorbachev—face-to-face in Geneva in front of a fireplace—that he meant what he said. And when Gorbachev claimed to share that vision, it was Reagan who reciprocated by assuming sincerity on the part of the Soviet leader, despite evidence to the contrary. Chance then intervened to reinforce this meeting of minds: the Chernobyl nuclear disaster of April 26, 1986, which contaminated large portions of Ukraine and Byelorussia, could hardly have been more effective in dramatizing a common nuclear danger. Reagan, by this time, did not need to be convinced. Gorbachev, however, was severely shaken by what had happened: what may have been opportunistic anti-nuclearism on his part now became much more serious.[62]

The next superpower summit, held at Reykjavik, Iceland, in October 1986, was the most astonishing one of the postwar era.[63] It had been hastily arranged to resolve a stalemate in negotiations on intermediate range missiles in Europe. To the surprise of Reagan and his advisers, though, Gorbachev arrived with far more sweeping proposals. Not only would he now accept Reagan's long-standing proposal to phase out such missiles altogether, he would also agree to a 50 percent cut in Soviet and American strategic weapons across the board, without insisting that British and French weapons be included in the count. This went well beyond any possibility of a publicity stunt, and the Americans responded quickly by offering to phase out all ballistic missiles within a decade in return for the right to deploy defenses against cruise missiles and bombers. Gorbachev countered by advancing his proposal for the abolition of all nuclear weapons to the year 1996. Reagan immediately jumped at this, and for a moment it appeared as though the leaders of the United States and the Soviet Union had agreed on a position that went beyond everyone's wildest dreams.*

It did not happen, though, because Gorbachev made his offer contingent upon banning the further development of SDI. Reagan, who saw SDI as necessary to ensure a safe transition to a non-nuclear world, refused to relinquish it. The summit broke up with angry words and anguished faces—but Gorbachev, collecting his wits prior to the inevitable press conference, resolved to "cool off

---

*The American record of the Reykjavik conference quotes Reagan as follows: "The President [said that] ten years from now he would be a very old man. He and Gorbachev would come to Iceland, and each of them would bring the last nuclear missile from each country with them. Then they would give a tremendous party for the whole world.... The President ... would be very old by then and Gorbachev would not recognize him. The President would say, 'Hello Mikhail.' And Gorbachev would say, 'Ron, is it you?' And then they would destroy the last missile." (Tom Simons notes, Reagan-Gorbachev meeting, October 12, 1986, Executive-Secretariat, NSC: Records, File 869075, Ronald Reagan Library. I am indebted to Matthew Ferraro for this document.)

and think it all over thoroughly.... [T]he merciless, often cynical and cheeky journalists ... standing in front of me seemed to represent mankind waiting for its fate to be decided. At this moment I realized the true meaning of Reykjavik and knew what further course we had to follow." The summit, he announced, "[i]n spite of all its drama ... is not a failure—it is a breakthrough, which allowed us for the first time to look over the horizon."[64] It was at Reykjavik, Dobrynin recalled, that "Gorbachev put away passion and decided that he could and would work with Reagan," that he was "a person capable of taking great decisions."[65] Reagan, who later admitted that "I was mad and showed it," also had second thoughts: "Despite a perception by some that the Reykjavik summit was a failure, I think history will show it was a major turning point in the quest for a safer and secure world."[66]

An agreement to phase out all nuclear weapons, had one been reached at Reykjavik, probably would not have held up. No one had thought through the implications for NATO strategy, which still relied upon nuclear "first-use" to counter Soviet conventional force superiority in Europe: "I felt as if there had been an earthquake beneath my feet," British Prime Minister Margaret Thatcher remembered.[67] Nor was it clear how such an agreement would affect the nuclear capabilities of France, China, India, or Israel, none of whose leaders were any more likely than Thatcher to accept, even as an aspiration, the idea of nuclear abolition. Still, the fact that the leaders of the United States and the Soviet Union had briefly done so was important. It paved the way for the Intermediate Nuclear Forces Treaty, signed at the third Reagan-Gorbachev summit in Washington in December 1987, which did bring about the dismantling and destruction of an entire category of weapons, under the watchful eyes of witnesses from both sides. It created the basis for deep cuts in ICBMs, SLBMs, and bombers that would, by the end of the century, significantly reduce the number of nuclear weapons Russians and Americans had targeted at one another.* And it led Gorbachev, on his return to Moscow, to report to the Politburo in words that acknowledged Reagan's persuasiveness:

> In Washington, probably for the first time we clearly realized how much the human factor means in international politics. Before ... we treated such personal contacts as simply meetings between representatives of opposed and irreconcilable systems. Reagan for us was merely the spokesman of the most conservative part of American capitalism and its military-industrial complex. But it turns out that politicians, including leaders of government if they are really responsible people, represent purely human concerns, interests, and the hopes of ordinary people—people who vote for them in elections and who

---

*In 1985, the Soviet Union was estimated to have over 40,000 nuclear weapons, and the United States approximately 24,000. By 2002, these numbers were down to approximately 11,000 each for Russia and the United States. (National Resources Defense Council, "US-U.S.S.R./Russian Nuclear Stockpile, 1945–2002," at http://www.nrdc.org/nuclear/nudb/dafigII.asp.)

associate their leaders' names and personal abilities with the country's image and patriotism.... In our age, it turns out, this has the biggest impact on political decisions.... And it was in Washington that we saw it so clearly for the first time.[68]

Gorbachev made a similar point when, on this visit, he met Kennan: "We in our country believe that a man may be the friend of another country and remain, at the same time, a loyal and devoted citizen of his own," the Soviet leader told the original strategist of containment. "[T]hat is the way we view you."[69]

The second point of which Reagan hoped to persuade Gorbachev was *that a command economy, when coupled with authoritarian politics, was a prescription for obsolescence in the modern world.* Reagan had argued this often in the past, most colorfully in May 1981, when he predicted that "[t]he West won't contain communism, it will transcend communism. It won't bother to ... denounce it, it will dismiss it as some bizarre chapter in human history whose last pages are even now being written."[70] But he left it to Shultz—who had taught economics at Stanford—to put the case to the new Kremlin leader. The Secretary of State was eager to do so, convinced that the generational shift in Moscow had opened the way for fresh thinking. What Gorbachev needed, he thought, was a tutorial on trends that "were already transforming the worlds of finance, manufacturing, politics, scientific research, diplomacy, indeed, everything." The conclusion would be that "[t]he Soviet Union would fall hopelessly and permanently behind the rest of the world in this new era unless it changed its economic and political system."[71]

Shultz began the seminar in Moscow in November 1985, just before the first Geneva summit. "Society is beginning to reorganize itself in profound ways," he told Gorbachev. "Closed and compartmented societies cannot take advantage of the information age. People must be free to express themselves, move around, emigrate and travel if they want to, challenge accepted ways without fear....The Soviet economy will have to be radically changed to adapt to the new era." Gorbachev responded surprisingly well to this, joking that Shultz should take over the Soviet planning ministry "because you have more ideas than they have." Shultz's observations on economics had attracted his interest, Gorbachev told Dobrynin afterward. "On that subject, he would willingly talk with Shultz in the future."[72]

What Shultz was arguing, in effect, was that Soviet power was becoming mono-dimensional in an increasingly multidimensional world. "The Soviet Union is a superpower only because it is a nuclear and ballistic missile superpower," he told his own advisers early in 1986.[73] It made sense, then, to reduce Soviet and American capabilities in that particular area—as both Reagan and Gorbachev seemed to want to do—because the United States and its allies were so far ahead of the Soviet Union in all other areas. It was also important, though, to be certain that Gorbachev understood the failures of the Soviet system in these other areas, together with the need to correct them. The only way he would be able to do that, Shultz believed, would be to "change the Soviet system. So we need to keep trying to influence Gorbachev in that direction."[74]

Shultz's seminar resumed on his next trip to Moscow, in April 1987. This time he had pie charts ready estimating the global distribution of gross domestic product and international trade through the year 2000, projections not at all to the advantage of the U.S.S.R. "What drives this growth?" he asked, professorially. "Science and technology," Gorbachev responded. "Yes," Shultz acknowledged, "but hitched to an incentive-based, market-oriented economic system.... There was a time when a government could control its scientific establishment and be basically successful. No longer." Shultz went on to point out that Marxism had always stressed the distinction between capital and labor. "But that dichotomy is becoming obsolete because we have entered a world in which the truly important capital is human capital, what people know, how freely they exchange information and knowledge, and the intellectually creative product that emerges." "We should have more of this kind of talk," Gorbachev acknowledged.[75]

It would be too much to claim that Shultz's tutorials planted the idea of *perestroika* in Gorbachev's mind: the Soviet economy faced such severe problems by the mid-1980's that there was no real alternative to fundamental restructuring. What Shultz did do was to explain why this was the case, and to point the way toward possible solutions. The Soviet leader himself was soon acknowledging the need "to get rid of the force of habit in our thinking" while recognizing "a world of fundamental social shifts, of an all-embracing scientific and technological revolution, ... of radical changes in information technology."[76] He admitted to Shultz, in April 1988, that he had thought a lot about "the charts you brought on what the world would look like in a few years," and had "consulted experts." If the trends projected in them continued, "our two countries have a lot of reason to cooperate."[77] A month later Reagan himself, with Gorbachev's approval, was standing beneath a huge bust of Lenin at Moscow State University, lecturing students on "a very different revolution that is taking place right now, quietly sweeping the globe without bloodshed or conflict.... It's been called the technological or information revolution, and as its emblem, one might take the tiny silicon chip, no bigger than a fingerprint."[78]

So just as Reagan had established common ground with Gorbachev on the dangers posed by nuclear weapons, Shultz managed something similar with respect to economic and technological issues. The idea, in both instances, was to bring the new Soviet leader around to the American way of thinking—and by doing so, to change the nature of the regime he led.

The Reagan administration's third objective was to persuade Gorbachev *that the Soviet Union had itself become, over the years, what it had originally sought to overthrow—an oppressive empire.* The principal instrument of persuasion here was the Reagan Doctrine: a plan to turn the forces of nationalism against the gains the Soviet Union had made in recent years in the "third world," and eventually against its sphere of influence in Eastern Europe itself. The idea echoed Kennan's predictions, from as early as 1947, that Stalin's determination to control communist parties beyond the boundaries of the U.S.S.R. might come across, in those regions, as a new form of imperialism which would, in time, generate local resistance.[79] Yugoslavia's defection from the Soviet bloc in 1948 and the rise of Sino-Soviet antagonism during the 1950's had proven him right; in the early 1970's Nixon and Kissinger capitalized on that latter development by playing the world's most populous communist state off against its most powerful communist state. They had remained pessimistic, however, about the possibility that nationalism might trump Marxism in Latin America, Africa, and Southeast Asia. They were slow to detect evidence, in the emergence of "Eurocommunism," that this had already begun to happen within the communist parties of Western Europe. And they saw few if any signs that resistance to Soviet authority in Eastern Europe might develop anytime soon: Kissinger himself went along reluctantly with the Helsinki Conference, and on balance preferred to stabilize rather than to try to upset the status quo in that part of the world. Political problems and economic stagnation would eventually bring about the collapse of the Soviet empire, he believed, but the way to hasten that process would be to delay a confrontation with the West, not to encourage one.[80]

By the end of the Carter administration the situation had changed. The expanding Soviet presence in southern and eastern Africa, the emergence of a Marxist regime in Nicaragua, the rise of Solidarity in Poland, and especially the invasion of Afghanistan suggested that the possibility might now exist to turn the tables on the Russians and begin portraying *them* as the new imperialists. Carter had created the basis for such an effort by authorizing overt and covert aid to anti-Soviet resistance movements in all of these regions; but since he had never given up the hope of reviving détente, he was wary of publicizing what he was doing.[81] The Reagan administration, which had fewer such inhibitions, expanded this assistance and by early 1983 the shape of a strategy was beginning to emerge. There were, NSDD-75 pointed out, "a number of important weaknesses and vulnerabilities within the Soviet empire which the U.S. should exploit," by seeking "wherever possible to encourage Soviet allies to distance themselves from Moscow in foreign policy and to move toward democratization domestically."[82]

Reagan's use of the term "evil empire," in March 1983, was the first public hint of this strategy: he had chosen the phrase, he admitted, "with malice aforethought; I wanted to remind the Soviets [that] we knew what they were up to."[83] In October of that year he authorized an American occupation of Grenada, a small Caribbean republic in which the Cubans and the Russians had been seeking to establish a sympathetic government.[84] By January 1985, Reagan was openly promising support to those "who are risking their lives—on every continent, from Afghanistan to Nicaragua—to defy Soviet-supported aggression and secure rights which have been ours from birth."[85] A month later Shultz elaborated publicly on what the Reagan Doctrine meant. "For many years," he noted, "we saw our adversaries act without restraint to back insurgencies around the world to spread communist dictatorships." In line with the "infamous" Brezhnev Doctrine, "any victory of communism was held to be irreversible." But in recent years, "Soviet activities and pretensions have run head-on into the democratic revolution. People are insisting on their right to independence, on their right to choose their government free of outside control." The United States had not created this phenomenon of "popular insurgencies *against* communist control." What was happening in Poland, Afghanistan, Cambodia, Nicaragua, Ethiopia, Angola, and even inside the Soviet Union itself was no different from what was taking place in South Africa, South Korea, the Philippines, and Chile: the citizens of those countries were simply seeking to determine their own futures. "The nature and extent of our support—whether moral support or something more—necessarily varies from case to case. But there should be no doubt about where our sympathies lie."[86]

The Reagan Doctrine was firmly in place, therefore, before Gorbachev took power. Once he had done so, Reagan and Shultz set out to convince him of its logic: that just as the tides of history were running against command economies, so they were also running against latter-day empires. The issue was an entirely pragmatic one, the President wrote to Gorbachev in February 1986: the war in Afghanistan "is unlikely to bring any benefit to the Soviet Union, so why is it continued?" Resistance there did not flow from the actions of the United States. "Even if we wished we do not have the power to induce thousands of people to take up arms against a well trained foreign army equipped with the most modern weapons." At the same time, though, "who can tell the people of another country they should not fight for their motherland, for their independence and for their national dignity?"[87]

Gorbachev, on Afghanistan, needed little convincing. He admitted to Reagan, at Geneva, that he had known nothing about the 1979 invasion until it had been announced on the radio. The President viewed this as confirmation that "it was a war he had no responsibility—and little enthusiasm—for."[88] The United States continued nevertheless to supply military assistance to the Afghan *mujahadeen,* including Stinger anti-aircraft missiles, which proved lethally effective against Soviet air operations. By September 1987, Gorbachev's new foreign minister, Eduard Shevardnadze, was assuring Shultz privately that the U.S.S.R. would soon leave Afghanistan, and that it would welcome American assistance in facilitating that process.[89] Shultz concluded from this that "the Brezhnev Doctrine was dead; the Reagan Doctrine was driving spikes into that coffin. The Soviets wanted to get out of Afghanistan, and I felt they were fading in other regional hot spots. I was hearing more and more about the possibility of change in at least some of the Warsaw Pact countries. I felt that a profound, historic shift was under way."[90]

And so it was—except that the shift had begun long before Shultz or anyone else in the Reagan administration had suspected. Recent research in Soviet archives suggests that the Brezhnev Doctrine from the beginning had been little more than a bluff. Brezhnev and his advisers had quietly concluded, after the invasion of Czechoslovakia in 1968, that the U.S.S.R. could never again use force to reassert its authority against an Eastern European satellite that was seeking either to reform or reject socialism. Moscow did succeed in convincing General Wojciech Jaruzelski to declare martial law in Poland in December 1981, thereby—for the moment at least—suppressing Solidarity. Had he refused to do so, however, the Soviet Union would almost certainly not have intervened, and its sphere of influence in Eastern Europe might have begun to unravel almost a decade earlier than it actually did.[91] Gorbachev himself attempted to signal an end to the Brezhnev Doctrine at his first meeting with Warsaw Pact leaders in September 1985, only to meet with incredulity: "I had the feeling that they were not taking [what I said] altogether seriously.... they probably thought that they would just wait and see."[92] When Reagan publicly challenged Moscow's control over East Germany, in a dramatic speech in West Berlin in June 1987—"Mr. Gorbachev, tear down this wall!"—the Kremlin's response was surprisingly restrained. Reagan, for his part, "never dreamed that in less than three years the wall would come down and a six-thousand-pound section of it would be sent to me for my presidential library."[93]

The final acknowledgment that the Brezhnev Doctrine was dead—and that the Reagan Doctrine had driven spikes into its coffin—came shortly after Reagan left office, when the year 1989 saw one Eastern European country after another throw out their Soviet-installed governments with no apparent objections, and certainly no resistance, from Moscow. It was a sign of how far things had come when Gorbachev's press spokesman, Gennadi Gerasimov, announced—with a degree of whimsy unprecedented for a Soviet official—that the Brezhnev Doctrine had been replaced with the Sinatra Doctrine: the Eastern Europeans were now "doing it their way."[94] Throughout these months of toppling dominoes, Gorbachev recalls, "not once did we contemplate the possibility of going back on the fundamental principles of the new political thinking—freedom of choice and non-interference in other countries' domestic affairs."[95] The irony is that Brezhnev himself, had he still been in power, would have had little choice but to do the same.

* * *

Notes

1. Reagan radio script, March 23, 1977, in Kiron K. Skinner, Annelise Anderson, and Martin Anderson, eds., *Reagan In His Own Hand* (New York: 2001), p. 118.
2. Lou Cannon, *President Reagan: The Role of a Lifetime* (New York: 1991), pp. 280–96, summarizes Reagan's instinct-based orthodoxies, their origins, and the extent to which they departed from established information-based Cold War orthodoxies.

3. See, on this point, Lee Edwards, *The Conservative Revolution: The Movement That Remade America* (New York: 1999), especially pp. 201–5.

4. For another president who operated in this way, see Fred I. Greenstein, *The Hidden-Hand Presidency: Eisenhower as Leader,* especially pp. 34–35, 53.

5. Skinner, ed., *Reagan In His Own Hand,* reprints several hundred hand-written commentaries on a wide range of domestic and foreign policy issues that Reagan prepared for his nationally syndicated radio program between 1975 and 1979. See also, on his speech-writing habits, Ronald Reagan, *An American Life* (New York 1990), p. 246.

6. Radio script, December 22, 1976, in *ibid.,* p. 12. See also scripts for May 25, 1977, October 10, 1978, November 28, 1978, and June 29, 1979, *ibid.,* pp. 85–86, 94–95, 146–47, 149–50. For the Roosevelt-Reagan analogy, see Cannon, *President Reagan,* pp. 109–11.

7. Radio script, May, 1975, in Skinner, ed., *Reagan In His Own Hand,* p. 12. For evidence of even earlier Reagan thinking along these lines, see Paul Lettow, *Ronald Reagan and His Quest to Abolish Nuclear Weapons* (New York: 2005), pp. 16, 27.

8. Reagan, *An American Life,* p. 267. For Reagan's commentaries on NSC-68, see his radio scripts of May 4, 1977, in Skinner, ed., *Reagan In His Own Hand,* pp. 109–13.

9. Radio script, May 25, 1977, in Skinner, ed., *Reagan In His Own Hand,* p. 147.

10. Reagan, *An American Life,* p. 238.

11. Radio script, June 29, 1979, in Skinner, ed., *Reagan In His Own Hand,* pp. 149–50. See also *ibid.,* pp. 129–34, 150–56.

12. Reagan, *An American Life,* p. 13. See also Lettow, *Ronald Reagan,* pp. 22–23.

13. Reagan's handwritten draft of a speech to the Veterans of Foreign Wars, Chicago, August 18, 1980, in Skinner, ed., *Reagan In His Own Hand,* especially p. 484; also Reagan, *An American Life,* pp. 257–58; Reagan's radio broadcast of December 12, 1978, in Skinner, ed., *Reagan In His Own Hand,* pp. 86–87; and Cannon, *President Reagan,* pp. 292–93, 305, 320, 751. I have benefited, as well, from reading Matthew Ferraro, "Going M.A.D.: Morality, Strategy, and Mutual Assured Destruction, 1957 to 1986," a senior essay prepared in the Yale University Department of History, 2004.

14. Reagan speech draft of August 18, 1980, in Skinner, ed., *Reagan In His Own Hand,* pp. 484–85.

15. For more on this point, see John Lewis Gaddis, *The United States and the End of the Cold War,* pp. 39–45.

16. Reagan speech draft of August 18, 1980, in Skinner, ed., *Reagan In His Own Hand,* p. 485. I have edited this passage slightly for clarity.

17. George F. Kennan, "The Sources of Soviet Conduct," p. 582.

18. Anatoly Dobrynin, *In Confidence,* p. 477.

19. Gaddis, *The United States and the End of the Cold War,* pp. 27–29.

20. NSDD 32, "U.S. National Security Strategy," May 20, 1982, http://www.fas.org/irp/offdocs/nsdd/nsdd-032.htm. See also, for background on this document, Lettow, *Ronald Reagan,* pp. 65–72.

21. Reagan address to members of the British Parliament, London, June 8, 1982, *Public Papers of the Presidents: 1982* [hereafter *RPP*] (Washington: 1983), pp. 744–47.

See also Reagan's speech at Notre Dame University, May 17, 1981, *RPP: 1982,* especially p. 434.

22. Dobrynin, *In Confidence,* p. 484.

23. NSDD 75, "U.S. Relations with the Soviet Union," January 17, 1983, http://www. fas.org/irp/offdocs/nsdd/nsdd-075.htm. For more on this document, see Richard Pipes, *Vixi: Memoirs of a Non-Belonger* (New Haven: 2003), pp. 188–202; and Lettow, *Ronald Reagan,* pp. 77–82.

24. Speech to the National Association of Evangelicals, Orlando, Florida, March 8, 1983, *RPP: 1983,* p. 364. For more on Reagan's rhetoric, see William K. Muir, Jr., "Ronald Reagan: The Primacy of Rhetoric," in Fred I. Greenstein, ed., *Leadership in the Modern Presidency* (Cambridge, Mass.: 1988), pp. 260–95.

25. Stephen Kotkin, *Armageddon Averted: The Soviet Collapse, 1970–2000* (New York: 2001), especially pp. 10–30, provides a good overview of the problems confronting the Soviet Union during this period; but see also Ronald Grigor Suny, *The Soviet Experiment: Russia, the U.S.S.R., and the Successor States* (New York: 1998), pp. 436–42. The figures on Soviet military spending come from Aaron Friedberg, *In the Shadow of the Garrison State: America's Anti-Statism and Its Cold War Grand Strategy* (Princeton: 2000), pp. 82–83. See also William E. Odom, *The Collapse of the Soviet Military* (New Haven: 1998), especially pp. 49–64....

26. Soviet leadership autism is well described in Dobrynin, *In Confidence,* pp. 472–76; and at considerably greater length in Georgi Arbatov, *The System: An Insider's Life in Soviet Politics* (New York: 1992), pp. 190–294.

27. See Spencer R. Weart, *Nuclear Fear: A History of Images* (Cambridge, Mass.: 1988), pp. 375–88; Beth A. Fischer, *The Reagan Reversal: Foreign Policy and the End of the Cold War* (Columbia, Mo.: 1997), pp. 115–20; and, for the administration's rhetorical excesses, Robert Scheer, *With Enough Shovels: Reagan, Bush, and Nuclear War* (New York: 1983).

28. Speech to the 1976 Republican National Convention, quoted in Cannon, *President Reagan,* p. 295. Cannon provides a brief account of Reagan's anti-nuclear views in *ibid.,* pp. 287–95. For a more recent and comprehensive treatment, see Lettow, *Ronald Reagan,* pp. 3–82.

29. Strobe Talbott, *Deadly Gambits,* pp. 80–81.

30. Radio-television address, March 23, 1983, *RPP: 1983,* pp. 442–43.

31. See above, p. 324n.

32. Paul Nitze *From Hiroshima to Glasnost,* p. 401; George P. Shultz, *Turmoil and Triumph: My Years as Secretary of State* (New York; 1993), p. 249; Caspar W. Weinberger, *Fighting for Peace: Seven Critical Years in the Pentagon* (New York: 1990), p. 306.

33. For the origins of Reagan's interest in SDI, see Cannon, *President Reagan,* pp. 292–93, 319; Lettow, *Ronald Reagan,* pp. 19–42; and Martin Anderson, *Revolution: The Reagan Legacy,* expanded and updated edition (Stanford: 1990), pp. 80–99.

34. Lettow, *Ronald Reagan,* pp. 120–21, 214–15; Mira Duric, *The Strategic Defense Initiative: US Policy and the Soviet Union* (Aldershot, England: 2003), pp. 24–25.

35. Reagan to Brezhnev, April 24, 1981, quoted in Reagan, *An American Life,* p. 273. See also, for Dobrynin's impression of Reagan's letter and Brezhnev's response, *In Confidence,* pp. 492–33.

36. NSDD 32, May 20, 1982, p. 3.

37. Shultz, *Turmoil and Triumph,* pp. 163–67. See also Don Oberdorfer, *From the Cold War to a New Era: The United States and the Soviet Union,* 1983–1991, updated edition (Baltimore: 1998), pp. 15–21.

38. Dobrynin, *In Confidence,* pp. 517–18.

39. *Ibid.,* pp. 518–21, 529–30; Shultz, *Turmoil and Triumph,* pp. 165–71.

40. Quoted in Duric, *The Strategic Defense Initiative,* p. 41.

41. Yuri Andropov statement, September 28, 1983, *Current Digest of the Soviet Press,* XXXV (October 26, 1983), 1.

42. Dobrynin, *In Confidence,* pp. 522–24; Christopher Andrew and Oleg Gordievsky, *KGB: The Inside Story of Its Foreign Operations from Lenin to Gorbachev* (New York: 1990), pp. 583–99.

43. For the Able-Archer crisis, see *ibid.,* pp. 599–601; also Fischer, *The Reagan Reversal,* pp. 122–31; Oberdorfer, *From the Cold War to a New Era,* pp. 65–68; and Robert M. Gates, *From the Shadows: The Ultimate Insider's Story of Five Presidents and How They Won the Cold War* (New York: 1996), pp. 266–73.

44. Reagan, *An American Life,* p. 586. See also pp. 588–89.

45. Reagan television address, January 16, 1984, *RPP: 1984,* p. 45. See also, on the preparation of this speech, Jack F. Matlock, Jr., *Autopsy on an Empire: The American Ambassador's Account of the Collapse of the Soviet Union* (New York: 1995), pp. 83–86.

46. Reagan, *An American Life,* p. 602.

47. *Ibid.,* p. 605.

48. Dobrynin, *In Confidence,* p. 563. See also, on this point, Barbara Farnham, "Reagan and the Gorbachev Revolution: Perceiving the End of Threat," *Political Science Quarterly,* CXVI (Summer, 2001), p. 233.

49. Reagan, *An American Life,* pp. 602–5.

50. Shultz, *Turmoil and Triumph,* p. 478.

51. Reagan, *An American Life,* p. 611.

52. Mikhail Gorbachev, *Memoirs* (New York 1995), pp. 165, 168. See also, on Gorbachev's appointment, Kotkin, *Armageddon Averted,* pp. 54–57.

53. Reagan, *An American Life,* p. 615.

54. William D. Jackson, "Soviet Reassessment of Ronald Reagan, 1985–1988," *Political Science Quarterly,* CXIII (Winter, 1998–99), 621–22; Vladislav M. Zubok, "Gorbachev and the End of the Cold War: Perspectives on History and Personality," *Cold War History,* II (January, 2002), 63. See also Anatoly Chernyaev, *My Six Years with Gorbachev,* translated and edited by Robert English and Elizabeth Tucker (University Park, Pennsylvania: 2000), p. 32, for an early indication of the extent to which Reagan's rhetoric placed Gorbachev and his advisers on the defensive.

55. Reagan, *An American Life,* p. 567.

56. Shultz, *Turmoil and Triumph,* pp. 600–2.

57. Reagan, *An American Life,* p. 635.

58. Gorbachev, *Memoirs,* p. 408. See also Dobrynin, *In Confidence,* pp. 592–93.

59. Shultz, *Turmoil and Triumph,* p. 700; Reagan, *An American Life,* p. 657.

60. Chernyaev diary, January 16, 1986, in Chernyaev, *My Six Years with Gorbachev,* pp. 45–46.

61. Shultz, *Turmoil and Triumph,* pp. 700–1. See also Matlock, *Autopsy on an Empire,* pp. 93–94; and Lettow, *Ronald Reagan,* pp. 137, 199–200.

62. Gorbachev, *Memoirs,* pp. 189–93. See also Chernyaev, *My Six Years with Gorbachev,* pp. 66–67; and Reagan, *An American Life,* pp. 676, 710.

63. My account here follows that in the Reagan, Shultz, and Gorbachev memoirs, as well as Oberdorfer, *From the Cold War to a New Era,* pp. 189–209; Jackson, "Soviet Reassessment of Reagan," pp. 629–34; Lettow, *Ronald Reagan,* pp. 223–31; Raymond L. Garthoff, *The Great Transition: American-Soviet Relations at the End of the Cold War* (Washington: 1994), pp. 285–291; and Jack F. Matlock, Jr., *Reagan and Gorbachev: How the Cold War Ended* (New York: 2004), pp. 215–37.

64. Gorbachev, *Memoirs,* p. 419.

65. Dobrynin, *In Confidence,* p. 610. See also the comments of Anatoly Chernyaev, in William C. Wohlforth, ed., *Witnesses to the End of the Cold War* (Baltimore: 1996), p. 109.

66. Reagan, *An American Life,* pp. 679, 683.

67. Margaret Thatcher, *The Downing Street Years* (New York: 1993), p. 471.

68. Gorbachev report to the Politburo, December 17, 1987, quoted in Chernyaev, *My Six Years with Gorbachev,* pp. 142–43.

69. Kennan diary, December 9, 1987, quoted in George F. Kennan, *Sketches from a Life* (New York: 1989), p. 351.

70. Speech at Notre Dame University, May 17, 1981, *RPP: 1981,* p. 434.

71. Shultz, *Turmoil and Triumph,* p. 586.

72. *Ibid.,* p. 591; Dobrynin, *In Confidence,* p. 583.

73. Shultz, *Turmoil and Triumph,* pp. 700–1. See also *ibid.,* pp. 716–17. For more on monodimensionality, see John Lewis Gaddis, *We Now Know: Rethinking Cold War History* (New: York 1997), pp. 283–84.

74. Shultz, *Turmoil and Triumph,* p. 711.

75. *Ibid.,* pp. 892–93; Oberdorfer, *From the Cold War to a New Era,* pp. 223–24. See also Chernyaev, *My Six Years with Gorbachev,* p. 142; and Fred I. Greenstein, "Ronald Reagan, Mikhail Gorbachev, and the End of the Cold War: What Difference Did They Make?" in Wohlforth, ed., *Witnesses to the End of the Cold War,* p. 217.

76. Mikhail Gorbachev, *Perestroika: New Thinking for Our Country and the World* (New York: 1987), p. 135.

77. Shultz, *Turmoil and Triumph,* p. 1098. See also, for Gorbachev's subsequent acknowledgment of the economic superiority of market capitalism, Mikhail Gorbachev and Zdenek Mlynar, *Conversations with Gorbachev: On Perestroika, the Prague Spring, and the Crossroads of Socialism,* translated by George Shriver (New York: 2002), p. 160.

78. Reagan speech at Moscow State University, May 31, 1988, *RPP: 1988,* p. 684.

79. See above, pp. 41–46.

80. For more on this, see pp. 287–88, 341–42, above; also Henry A. Kissinger, *Diplomacy* (New York: 1994), p. 714, and John Lewis Gaddis, "Rescuing Choice from Circumstance: The Statecraft of Henry Kissinger," in Gordon A. Craig and Francis L. Lowenheim, eds., *The Diplomats: 1939–1979* (Princeton: 1994), pp. 585–87. Kissinger's own account of the Helsinki Conference is in his *Years of Renewal* (New York: 1999), pp. 635–63.

81. Gates, *From the Shadows,* pp. 142–53, 161–69.

82. NSDD 75, "U.S. Relations with the U.S.S.R.," January 17, 1983, p. 4.

83. Reagan, *An American Life,* p. 569.

84. Shultz, *Turmoil and Triumph,* 323–45.

85. Reagan state of the union address, February 6, 1985, *RPP: 1985,* p. 136.

86. Speech to the Commonwealth Club of San Francisco, quoted in Shultz, *Turmoil and Triumph,* p. 525. Chernyaev describes the "panic" this speech caused in Moscow in *My Six Years with Gorbachev,* pp. 16–17. For more on the Reagan Doctrine, see Smith, *America's Mission,* pp. 297–304.

87. Reagan to Gorbachev, February 6, 1986, quoted in Reagan, *An American Life,* pp. 654–55.

88. Reagan, *An American Life,* p. 639. For Gorbachev's reservations about the war in Afghanistan, see also Chernyaev, *My Six Years with Gorbachev,* pp. 42–43, 89–90, 106.

89. Shultz, *Turmoil and Triumph,* p. 987.

90. *Ibid.,* p. 1003.

91. The evidence is laid out in detail in Ouimet, *The Rise and Fall of the Brezhnev Doctrine.*

92. Gorbachev, *Memoirs,* p. 465.

93. Reagan, *An American Life,* p. 683. Reagan's speech, delivered at the Brandenburg Gate on June 12, 1987, is in *RPP: 1987,* p. 686. For Gorbachev's response, see Garthoff, *The Great Transition,* pp. 316–18.

94. Bill Keller, "Gorbachev, in Finland, Disavows any Right of Regional Intervention," *New York Times,* October 26, 1989.

95. Gorbachev, *Memoirs,* p. 522.

5.4

DETERRENCE AND THE END OF THE COLD WAR

Richard Ned Lebow and Janice Gross Stein

> If you read this selection at the same time as the previous selection by John Lewis Gaddis, you will understand better why the subject of international relations is so complex and entertains not only multiple but even diametrically opposed interpretations of events. Richard Ned Lebow and Janice Gross Stein argue that Ronald Reagan's confidence in freedom, the U.S. military buildup, and Soviet economic bankruptcy, all factors emphasized by Gaddis, had little to do with ending the Cold War. Rather "the critical factor was the agenda of Soviet leaders." With his "New Thinking" Mikhail Gorbachev envisioned a more cooperative rather than competitive world and introduced reforms in the Soviet system (*glasnost* and *perestroika*) and in international diplomacy (eliminating nuclear arms) that eventually transformed the world "despite the Reagan buildup." Whether ideas (freedom and New Thinking), power (U.S. power and Soviet weakness), or institutions (deterrence and détente) ended the Cold War will be debated for a very long time, especially in light of new documents that are now being released from the Reagan era.

> I like many others knew that the USSR needed radical change. Khrushchev tried it, Kosygin tried it…. If I had not understood this, I would never have accepted the position of General Secretary. At the end of 1986, we feared that the process of reform was slowing down and that the same fate could befall our reforms as befell Khrushchev's.
>
> —Mikhail S. Gorbachev[1]

The final claim made for nuclear deterrence is that it helped to end the Cold War. As impeccable a liberal as *New York Times* columnist Tom Wicker reluctantly conceded that Star Wars and the massive military buildup in the Reagan administration had forced the Soviet Union to reorient its foreign and domestic policies.[2] The conventional wisdom has two components. American military capability and resolve allegedly convinced Soviet leaders that aggression anywhere would meet unyielding opposition. Forty years of arms competition also

Source: Richard Ned Lebow and Janice Gross Stein, "Deterrence and the End of the Cold War," in *We All Lost the Cold War* (Princeton, N.J.: Princeton University Press, 1994), 369–376.

brought the Soviet economy to the edge of collapse. The Reagan buildup and Star Wars, the argument goes, were the straws that broke the Soviet camel's back. Moscow could not match the increased level of American defense spending and accordingly chose to end the Cold War.

We cannot examine these propositions about the impact of deterrence on the end of the Cold War with the same quality of evidence we used to assess the role of deterrence in superpower relations during the Cold War. Nevertheless, the absence of a large body of documents, interviews, and memoirs has not discouraged columnists and scholars from rendering judgments about the end of the Cold War. Nor will it prevent policymakers from using these interpretations as guides to action in the future. It is therefore essential that the conventional wisdom does not go unexamined. The limited evidence that is now available is not consistent with these two propositions about the role of deterrence in ending the Cold War. Within the confines of the available evidence, we sketch the outlines of a very different interpretation.

The End of the Cold War

Soviet officials insist that Gorbachev's withdrawal of Soviet forces from Afghanistan, proposals for arms control, and domestic reforms took place *despite* the Reagan buildup. Mikhail Sergeevich Gorbachev came to power in March 1985 committed to liberalizing the domestic political process at home and improving relations with the West so that the Soviet Union could modernize its rigid economy. Within a month of assuming office, he announced his first unilateral initiative—a temporary freeze on the deployment of Soviet intermediate-range missiles in Europe—and in a series of subsequent proposals tried to signal his interest in arms control. President Reagan continued to speak of the Soviet Union as an "evil empire" and remained committed to his quest for a near-perfect ballistic-missile defense.

Gorbachev came to office imbued with a sense of the urgency of domestic reform and with a fundamentally different attitude toward the West. He was confident that the United States would not deliberately attack the Soviet Union and that the serious risk was an accidental or miscalculated exchange.[3] In conversations with his military advisors, he rejected any plans that were premised on a war with the United States. "During the period of stagnation," he observed, "we had assumed that such a war was possible, but when I became general secretary, I refused to consider any such plans."[4] Since he saw no threat of attack from the United States, Gorbachev was not "afraid" of any military programs put forward by the Reagan administration and did not feel forced to match them. Rather, he saw arms spending as an unnecessary and wasteful expenditure of scarce resources. Deep arms reductions were not only important to the reform and development of the Soviet economy, but also an imperative of the nuclear age.[5]

Rather than facilitating a change in Soviet foreign policy, Reagan's commitment to the Strategic Defense Initiative (SDI) complicated Gorbachev's task of persuading his own officials that arms control was in the Soviet interest. Conservatives, much of the military leadership, and captains of defense-related industries took SDI as further evidence of the hostile intentions of the United States and insisted on increased spending on offensive countermeasures. Gorbachev, Eduard Shevardnadze, Aleksandr Yakovlev, and many foreign-ministry officials did not feel threatened by Star Wars but were constrained and frustrated by the political impact of Reagan's policies at home.[6]

To break the impasse, Gorbachev used a two-pronged strategy. In successive summits he tried and finally convinced Reagan of his genuine interest in ending the arms race and restructuring East-West relations on a collaborative basis. When Reagan changed his estimate of Gorbachev, he also modified his assessment of the Soviet Union and became the leading dove of his administration. Gorbachev also worked hard to convince Western publics that he intended a radical departure from past Soviet policies. The withdrawal from Afghanistan, freeing of Soviet political prisoners, and liberalization of the Soviet political system evoked widespread sympathy and support in the West and generated strong public pressures on NATO governments to respond positively to his initiatives.

The first breakthrough—an agreement on intermediate nuclear forces (INF)—was the unintended result of the Reagan administration's need to placate American and European public opinion. American officials were deeply divided on the question of theater arms control and settled on the "double zero" proposal only because they thought that Moscow would reject the offer. The proposal required the Soviet Union, which had already deployed a new generation of nuclear delivery systems in Europe, to make deeper cuts in its arsenal than the United States, which had only just begun to field new weapons in Europe. Washington expected Gorbachev to reject the proposal and hoped thereby to make him appear responsible for the failure of arms control. They were astonished when he agreed in principle.[7] Soviet officials contend that Gorbachev accepted "double zero," not because of Soviet weakness, but in the expectation that it would trigger a reciprocal process of accommodation. President Gorbachev subsequently described the INF agreement as a watershed in Soviet-American relations. "Working on the treaty and the treaty itself," he said, "created trust and a network of personal links."[8] To Gorbachev, the absolute gain of accommodation was far more important than the relative distribution of military advantage in any particular arms-control agreement.[9]

Gorbachev's political persistence broke through Reagan's wall of mistrust. At their Reykjavik summit in October 1986, the two leaders talked seriously about eliminating all their ballistic missiles within ten years and significantly reducing their arsenals of nuclear weapons. No agreement was reached because Reagan was unwilling to limit SDI. The Reykjavik summit, as Gorbachev had hoped, nevertheless began a process of mutual reassurance and accommodation.[10] That process continued after an initially hesitant George Bush became a full-fledged partner. In hindsight, it is apparent that Gorbachev's initiatives began the process that brought the Cold War to an end.

Defense and the Economy

The conventional wisdom assumes that the Soviet Union was forced to match American defense spending and to end the Cold War when it could no longer compete. There is no evidence that Soviet defense spending rose or fell in response to American defense spending. Revised estimates by the CIA indicate that Soviet defense expenditures remained more or less constant throughout the 1980s. Neither the Carter-Reagan buildup nor Star Wars had any impact on gross spending levels. Their only demonstrable impact was to shift in marginal ways the allocation of defense rubles. After SDI, more funds were earmarked to developing countermeasures to ballistic defense.[11]

If American defense spending bankrupted the Soviet economy and led Gorbachev to end the Cold War, a sharp decline in defense spending should have occurred under Gorbachev. Despite his rejection of military competition with the United States, CIA statistics show that Soviet defense spending remained relatively constant as a proportion of Soviet gross national product during the first four years of Gorbachev's tenure. The Soviet gross national product declined precipitously in the late 1980s and early 1990s; Gorbachev's domestic reforms had a profoundly negative impact on the Soviet economy. Soviet defense spending was reduced only in 1989 and did not shrink as rapidly as the overall economy. In the current decade, Soviet, and then Russian defense spending has consumed a higher percentage of disposable national income than it did in the Brezhnev years.[12]

From Stalin through Gorbachev, annual Soviet defense spending consumed about 25% of Soviet disposable income. This was an extraordinary burden on the economy. Not all Soviet leaders were blind to its likely consequences. In the early 1970s, some officials recognized that the economy would ultimately stagnate if the military continued to consume such a disproportionate share of resources.[13] Brezhnev, however, was even more heavily dependent than Khrushchev on the support of a coalition in which defense and heavy industry were well represented. In defense, as in other budgetary outlays, allocations reflected the relative political power of different sectors of the economy. Within the different sectors, spending and investment were controlled by bureaucracies with strong vested interests. As a result, not only military but also civilian spending was frequently wasteful and inefficient. Logrolling among competing groups compounded the problem by increasing the aggregate level of spending.[14] Because Soviet defense spending under Brezhnev and Gorbachev was primarily a response to internal imperatives, it is not correlated with American defense spending. Nor is there any observable relationship between defense spending and changes in the political relationship between the superpowers, until the cuts in the American defense budget in 1991.

The proposition that American defense spending bankrupted the Soviet economy and forced an end to the Cold War is not sustained by the available evidence. The critical factor in the Soviet economic decline was the rigid "command economy" imposed by Stalin in the early 1930s. It offered little or no reward for individual or collective initiative, freed productive units from the competition normally imposed by the market, and centralized production and investment decisions in the hands of an unwieldy bureaucracy immune from market forces and consumer demands. The command economy predates the Cold War and was not a response to American deterrence.[15]

Why Soviet Foreign Policy Changed

To explain the dramatic reorientation of Soviet foreign policy, we need to look first at the domestic agendas of Soviet leaders. Khrushchev's and Gorbachev's efforts to transform East-West relations and Brezhnev's more limited attempt at détente were motivated in large part by their economic objectives.

Khrushchev sought an accommodation with the West to free manpower and resources for economic development. He hoped that success in reducing East-West tensions would enhance his domestic authority and make it more difficult for conservative forces to block his economic and political reforms. Gorbachev had a similar agenda and pursued a similar strategy. *Perestroika* required peaceful relations abroad to succeed at home. Accommodation with the West would permit a shift in resources from the military to productive investment; attract credits, investment, and technology from the West; and weaken the power of the conservatives opposed to Gorbachev and his reforms. Accommodation with the West was especially critical for Gorbachev because the Soviet economy had deteriorated sharply since the early 1970s and the brief détente between the United States and the Soviet Union. The impetus for domestic reform was structural; economic decline, or the threat of serious decline, motivated Gorbachev, like Khrushchev and Brezhnev, to implement domestic reforms and seek accommodation with the West.

The need to arrest economic decline and improve economic performance cannot by itself explain the scope of reforms or the kind of relationship Gorbachev tried to establish with the West. Only a few central Soviet leaders responded to economic imperatives by promoting a radical restructuring of the Soviet relationship with the West.[16] Almost all the fundamental components of Gorbachev's "new thinking" about security were politically contested.[17] Traditional thinkers powerfully placed within the defense ministry and the Soviet General Staff vigorously challenged the new concepts of security. Indeed, Gorbachev had to go outside the establishment to civilian and academic specialists on defense in the policy institutes in Moscow for new ideas about Soviet security.[18] Insofar as senior Soviet leaders and officials in the Gorbachev era disagreed fundamentally about the direction of Soviet foreign and defense policy, structural imperatives alone cannot adequately explain the change in Soviet thinking about security under Gorbachev.

Gorbachev differed significantly from Khrushchev and Brezhnev in his conception of security. Previous Soviet leaders had regarded the capitalist

West as the enemy and had feared military aggression against the Soviet Union or its allies. Like their Western counterparts, they measured security in terms of military and economic power; Soviet military prowess and socialist solidarity were necessary to deter attack and restrain the capitalist powers. Khrushchev and Brezhnev wanted to improve relations with the West, but they remained committed to their ideological view of a world divided into two hostile camps. Unlike Stalin, they recognized that nuclear weapons had made war between the superpowers irrational and unlikely, but they believed in the fundamental antagonism between the incompatible systems of capitalism and socialism.

Gorbachev and his closest advisors rejected the traditional Soviet approach to security. In their view, it had helped to create and sustain the Cold War and had placed a heavy burden on the Soviet economy. *Perestroichiks* were especially critical of the domestic consequences of postwar Soviet foreign policy; conflict with the West had been exploited by the Communist Party to justify its monopoly on power and suppression of dissent.[19]

Gorbachev's vision of Soviet security was cooperative rather than competitive. He and Eduard A. Shevardnadze repudiated the class basis of international relations that had dominated Soviet thinking about security since the Soviet state was created. They explicitly condemned as mistaken the thesis developed in the Khrushchev and Brezhnev years that peaceful coexistence was a specific form of the class struggle.[20] "New thinking" about security was based on five related propositions: the primacy of universal, "all-human" values over class conflict; the interdependence of all nations; the impossibility of achieving victory in nuclear or large-scale conventional war; the need to seek security in political and economic rather than military terms; and the belief that neither Soviet nor Western security could be achieved unilaterally.[21] Gorbachev called for the development of "a new security model" based on "a policy of compromise" among former adversaries.[22] National security was to be replaced by a "common, indivisible security, the same for all." The goal of the Soviet Union was to join a "common European house" that would foster security and prosperity through "a policy of cooperation based on mutual trust."[23]

Gorbachev, Shevardnadze, and other committed democrats believed in a complex, two-way relationship between domestic reform and foreign policy. Accommodation with the West would facilitate *perestroika*, but it was more than an instrument of reform and economic rejuvenation.[24] For the Soviet Union to join the family of nations, it had to become a democratic society with a demonstrable respect for the individual and collective rights of its citizens and allies. Granting independence to the countries of Eastern Europe was the international analogue to emptying the gulags, ending censorship in the media, and choosing members of the Supreme Soviet through free elections.

Gorbachev was able to pursue a more far-reaching and dramatic strategy of accommodation than his predecessors because of the evolution in the superpower relationship since the acute confrontations of the 1960s. He was much less fearful of Western intentions than Khrushchev and less concerned that the United States and its allies would exploit concessions as a sign of weakness. Khrushchev's fear of the West severely constrained his search for accommodation. He never considered, as did Gorbachev, that soft words and unilateral initiatives would evoke enough public sympathy and support so that Western governments would be pushed by their own domestic publics to reciprocate. Khrushchev did make some unilateral concessions; he reduced the size of the armed forces and proclaimed a short-lived moratorium on nuclear testing. When his actions were not reciprocated, the militant opposition at home forced him to revert to a confrontational policy. His inflammatory rhetoric in turn strengthened the forces in the West who opposed accommodation with the Soviet Union.

Gorbachev could not have succeeded in transforming East-West relations and ending the Cold War if the West had not become his willing partner. Unlike Khrushchev, whose quest for a German peace treaty frightened France and West Germany, Gorbachev met a receptive audience when he attempted to end the division of Europe. Disenchantment with the Cold War, opposition to the deployment of new weapons systems, and a widespread desire to end the division of Europe, given voice by well-organized peace movements, created a groundswell of support for exploring the possibilities of accommodation with the Soviet Union.

The Impact of American Policy

Throughout the Cold War, many leaders in the West argued that the internal structure and foreign-policy goals of the Soviet Union were ideologically determined and largely unaffected by the policies of other states. The West could only restrain Soviet aggression through a policy of strength. Many academic analysts rejected the argument that Soviet domestic and foreign policies were immutable. They maintained that Western policies made a difference, but disagreed among themselves about the nature of the interaction between Soviet and American foreign and domestic policies.

Some scholars contended that the links were reciprocal. Soviet "orthodoxy", which favored heavy industry, restricted individual freedoms, and a strong military, was strengthened by an international environment that appeared to confirm the enemy image of the capitalist West. Conciliatory Western policies could weaken the influence of Soviet militants and strengthen the hand of those officials who favored reform and accommodation with the West.[25] Other scholars subscribed only to the first of these propositions. Citing the Khrushchev experience, they agreed that a threatening international environment undermined reform and accommodation, but, drawing on the Brezhnev years, they denied the corollary that détente encouraged domestic liberalization.[26] The contrast between Gorbachev and Brezhnev led some specialists to argue that reform only came when the leadership confronted the prospect of domestic and foreign-policy disaster.[27]

The available evidence suggests a different proposition about the relationship between American and Soviet foreign policy. The critical factor was the agenda of Soviet leaders. American influence was limited when Soviet leaders were not seriously committed to internal reform. Confrontation then exacerbated Soviet-American tensions, but conciliation did not necessarily improve the relationship, nor did it encourage internal reforms. Jimmy Carter's efforts to transform Soviet-American relations had little effect because they came after Brezhnev had lost interest in domestic reform at home.

When the principal objective of Soviet leaders was economic reform and development, they were anxious to reach some kind of accommodation with the West. Gorbachev, like Khrushchev, was committed to domestic economic reform. Under these conditions, American policy, whether confrontational or conciliatory, had its greatest impact. Confrontation was most likely to provoke an aggressive response because it exacerbated the foreign-policy problems of Soviet leaders, undercut their domestic authority, and threatened their domestic economic goals. Conciliation was most likely to be reciprocated because Soviet leaders expected an improved relationship to enhance their authority at home, free scarce resources for development, and provide access to Western credits and technology.

If American policy did have an impact when Soviet leaders were committed to reform, then the strategy of deterrence likely prolonged the Cold War. The Cold War ended when Soviet leaders became committed to domestic reform and to a concept of common security that built on the reality of nuclear deterrence, and when Western leaders reassured and reciprocated. We cannot support these propositions with the kind of evidence we marshaled in support of our contention that the strategy of deterrence had complex but largely negative consequences for superpower relations during the Cold War. The same kind of detailed reconstruction of Soviet and American policy during the Gorbachev era will only be possible when documents, memoirs, and interviews of key participants become available. Until then, this alternative interpretation of the impact of the strategy of nuclear deterrence on the end of the Cold War may help to stimulate an important debate about the enduring lessons of the Cold War and its demise.

Notes

1. Interview, Mikhail S. Gorbachev, Toronto, 1 April 1993.
2. Tom Wicker, "Plenty of Credit," *New York Times,* 5 December 1989, p. A35, points to the irony that those who for years argued that a Communist-led Soviet Union could not be reformed, now claim credit for *perestroika* and the Soviet retreat from Eastern Europe.
3. Interview, Mikhail S. Gorbachev, Toronto, 1 April 1993.
4. Ibid.
5. Ibid. See also the comments by Soviet Foreign Minister Aleksandr Bessmertnykh and Anatoliy S. Chernyaev, advisor to President Gorbachev on foreign affairs, 1986–1991, "Retrospective on the End of the Cold War," Conference sponsored by the

John Foster Dulles Program for the Study of Leadership in International Affairs, Woodrow Wilson School, Princeton University, 25–27 February 1993.

6. Interview, Mikhail S. Gorbachev, Toronto, 1 April 1993, and comments by Aleksandr Bessmertnykh, "Retrospective on the End of the Cold War."

7. Thomas Risse-Kappen, *The Zero Option: INF, West Germany, and Arms Control* (Boulder, Colo.: Westview, 1988); Richard Eichenberg, "Dual Track and Double Trouble: The Two-Level Politics of INF," Peter Evans, Harold Jacobsen, and Robert Putnam, eds., *Double-Edged Diplomacy: International Bargaining and Domestic Politics* (Berkeley: University of California Press, in press); Fen Osler Hampson, Harald von Reikhoff, and John Roper, eds., *The Allies and Arms Control* (Baltimore: Johns Hopkins University Press, 1992); Don Oberdorfer, *The Turn: From the Cold War to a New Era, The United States and The Soviet Union, 1983–1990* (New York: Poseidon Press, 1991), pp. 169–74.

8. Interview, Mikhail S. Gorbachev, Toronto, 1 April 1993. See also the comments by Bessmertnykh, "Retrospective on the End of the Cold War."

9. Interviews, Fedor Burlatsky, Cambridge, 12 October 1987; Vadim Zagladin, Moscow, 18 May 1989; Oleg Grinevsky, Vienna and New York, 11 October and 10 November 1991.

10. The arms proposal that Gorbachev tabled at Reykjavik was the Soviet analogue to Reagan's "double zero" proposal. Oleg Grinevsky, interview, Stockholm, 25 April 1992, reports that before the summit, Gorbachev asked his chief arms-control advisors, Viktor Karpov, Yuli Kvitinsky, and Oleg Grinevsky to prepare proposals for arms control. Defense Minister Dmitri Yazov and Chief of the General Staff Sergei Akhromeyev learned about the preparation of new proposals and strongly opposed the initiative because they were convinced that any likely arms-control agreement would be unfavorable to the Soviet Union. They went to see Gorbachev and asked if he was seriously interested in deep cuts in the arsenals of both superpowers. When he responded affirmatively, they advised him that any proposal prepared by professional arms controllers would be overly conservative and require elaborate negotiations of definitions and verification. Yazov and Akhromeyev told a gullible Gorbachev of their abhorrence of nuclear weapons—they made conventional wars difficult, if not impossible to fight—and offered to prepare proposals for Reykjavik that would represent a serious step toward nuclear disarmament. Gorbachev immediately transferred responsibility for preparation of arms-control proposals for the summit to Yazov and Akhromeyev. They prepared the proposal that Gorbachev presented at Reykjavik, convinced that President Reagan and his advisors would reject it out of hand. Yazov and Akhromeyev were astonished when Reagan expressed serious interest.

11. Franklyn D. Holzman, "Politics and Guesswork: CIA and DIA Estimates of Soviet Military Spending," *International Security* 14 (Fall 1989), pp. 101–31; Central Intelligence Agency and Defense Intelligence Agency, "Beyond Perestroika: The Soviet Economy in Crisis," paper prepared for the Technology and National Security Subcommittee of the Joint Economic Committee, U.S. Congress, 14 May 1991.

12. The Soviet government reported that overall output declined by 2 percent in 1990 and by 8 percent in the first quarter of 1991. Big cuts in defense spending began in 1989, and the annual decline has been on the order of about 6 percent. Because the

economy is declining more rapidly than defense expenditure, defense as a percent of gross national product has increased. "Beyond Perestroika," pp. iv, 1, 11–12.

13. For criticism of the powerful role of the "defense lobby" under Brezhnev by younger officials and scholars, see Stephen F. Cohen and Katrina vanden Heuvel, *Voices of Glasnost: Interviews with Gorbachev's Reformers* (New York: Norton, 1989) and Georgi Arbatov, *The System: An Insider's Life in Soviet Politics* (New York: Random House, 1992).

14. For discussion of logrolling under Brezhnev, see Jack Snyder, *Myths of Empire* (Ithaca, N.Y.: Cornell University Press, 1991) and Richard Anderson, *Competitive Politics and Soviet Foreign Policy: Authority-Building and Bargaining in the Brezhnev Politburo,* Ph.D. diss., University of California, Berkeley, 1989.

15. The command economy cannot be attributed to the Nazi threat because Stalin promulgated the first five-year plan in 1929 and collectivized agriculture in the early 1930s, before Hitler's rise to power.

16. Analysts of Soviet politics, writing in late 1989, argued that "new thinking" was limited to a few central Soviet leaders and advisors. A. Lynch, *Gorbachev's International Outlook: Intellectual Origins and Political Consequences,* Institute for East-West Security Studies, Occasional Paper no. 9 (Boulder, Colo.: Westview, 1989), p. 53.

17. For an explanation of "new thinking" and the political debate it provoked, see Janice Gross Stein, "Cognitive Psychology and Political Learning: Gorbachev as an Uncommitted Thinker and Motivated Learner," in Richard Ned Lebow and Thomas Risse-Kappen, eds., *International Relations Theory and the Transformation of the International System,* forthcoming.

18. See Sarah E. Mendelson, "Internal Battles and External Wars: Politics, Learning, and the Soviet Withdrawal from Afghanistan," *World Politics* 45, 3 (April 1993), pp. 327–60; Jeff Checkel, "Ideas, Institutions, and the Gorbachev Foreign Policy Revolution," *World Politics* 45, 2 (January, 1993), pp. 271–300.

19. Interviews, Fedor Burlatsky, Cambridge, 12 October 1987; Vadim Zagladin, Moscow, 18 May 1989; Oleg Grinevsky, Vienna and New York, 11 October and 10 November 1991; Georgi Arbatov, Ithaca, N.Y., 15 November 1991; Anatoliy Dobrynin, Moscow, 17 December 1991.

20. See Mikhail Gorbachev, *Pravda,* 21 October 1986 and speech to the United Nations General Assembly, 7 December 1988, *Novosti,* no. 97, p. 13; and speech by Eduard A. Shevardnadze, in *Vestnik Ministerstva Inostrannykh Del USSR* 15, 15 August 1988, p. 33.

21. For Western discussion of "new thinking" in foreign policy, see David Holloway, "Gorbachev's New Thinking," *Foreign Affairs* 68 (Winter 1988–89), pp. 66–81; Robert Legvold, "The Revolution in Soviet Foreign Policy," *Foreign Affairs* 68, 1 (America and the World 1988/89), pp. 82–98; Stephen M. Meyer, "The Sources and Prospects of Gorbachev's New Political Thinking on Security," *International Security* 13, 2 (Fall 1988), pp. 124–63.

22. Mikhail Gorbachev, "Speech to the United Nations."

23. Mikhail Gorbachev, *Perestroika: New Thinking for Our Country and the World* (New York: Harper & Row, 1987), p. 187; Holloway, "Gorbachev's New Thinking."

24. By 1987, Gorbachev insisted that the unforgiving realities of the nuclear age demanded new concepts and new policies, independent of *perestroika* at home: "Some people say that the ambitious goals set forth by the policy of *perestroika* in our country have prompted the peace proposals we have lately made in the international arena. This is an oversimplification.... True, we need normal international conditions for our internal progress. But we want a world free of war, without arms races, nuclear weapons, and violence; not only because this is an optimal condition for our internal development." Gorbachev, *Perestroika,* p. 11.

25. Stephen F. Cohen, "Soviet Domestic Politics and Foreign Policy," in Robbin F. Laird and Erik P. Hoffman, eds., *Soviet Foreign Policy in a Changing World* (New York: Aldine, 1986), pp. 66–83; Jerry F. Hough, "Soviet Succession: Issues and Personalities," *Problems of Communism* 31 (September-October 1982), p. 20–40; Raymond L. Garthoff, *Détente and Confrontation: American-Soviet Relations from Nixon to Reagan* (Washington, D.C.: The Brookings Institution, 1985); Jack Snyder, "International Leverage on Soviet Domestic Change," *World Politics* 42 (October 1989), pp. 1–30.

26. Aleksandr Yanov, *The Drama of the Soviet 1960s: A Lost Reform* (Berkeley, Calif.: Institute of International Studies, 1984), pp. 97–98, 103–6; Timothy J. Colton, "The Changing Soviet Union and the World," in Laird and Hoffman, *Soviet Foreign Policy in a Changing World,* pp. 869–89.

27. This was also the original idea behind George Kennan's policy of containment; Richard Pipes, "Can the Soviet Union Reform?"; Laird and Hoffman, *Soviet Foreign Policy in a Changing World,* pp. 855–68; Harry Gelman, *The Brezhnev Politburo and the Decline of Detente* (Ithaca, N.Y.: Cornell University Press, 1984). For a good critique, see Matthew Evangelista, "Sources of Moderation in Soviet Security Policy," in Philip E. Tetlock, Jo L. Husbands, Robert Jervis, Paul C. Stern, and Charles Tilly, eds., *Behavior, Society, and Nuclear War,* II (New York: Oxford University Press, 1991) 2 vols., pp. 254–354. Evangelista argues against a mechanistic formulation of the relationship between Soviet and American foreign policies.

Chapter 6

FROM 11/9 TO 9/11: THE WORLD OF THE 1990S

6.1

THE END OF HISTORY?

Francis Fukuyama

> Francis Fukuyama explains the era introduced by the end of the Cold War as "the end of history," by which he means the triumph of the ideas of liberalism (the philosophy, not the perspective) over those of fascism and communism. Attacking materialist perspectives, such as Marxism, Fukuyama follows Hegel's notion that "consciousness … creates the material world." It "is cause and not effect." Moreover, the consciousness of modern liberalism is spreading and likely to prevail over future challenges such as religious fundamentalism and nationalism. Economic forces are not the cause of ideological and class conflicts, as foreseen by Marxist-Leninism, but, rather, the product of political ideas such as the "common marketization of world politics." Notice that identity factors drive not only military (realist) but also exchange or market (liberal perspective) outcomes. Notice too that the level of analysis is systemic, not individual or domestic. Even "if Gorbachev were ousted from the Kremlin," the outcome would be the same "because there is some larger process at work."

In watching the flow of events over the past decade or so, it is hard to avoid the feeling that something very fundamental has happened in world history. The past year has seen a flood of articles commemorating the end of the Cold War, and the fact that "peace" seems to be breaking out in many regions of the world. Most of these analyses lack any larger conceptual framework for distinguishing between what is essential and what is contingent or accidental in world

---

Source: Francis Fukuyama, "The End of History?" *National Interest* no. 16 (summer 1989): 107–114.

history, and are predictably superficial. If Mr. Gorbachev were ousted from the Kremlin or a new Ayatollah proclaimed the millennium from a desolate Middle Eastern capital, these same commentators would scramble to announce the rebirth of a new era of conflict.

And yet, all of these people sense dimly that there is some larger process at work, a process that gives coherence and order to the daily headlines. The twentieth century saw the developed world descend into a paroxysm of ideological violence, as liberalism contended first with the remnants of absolutism, then bolshevism and fascism, and finally an updated Marxism that threatened to lead to the ultimate apocalypse of nuclear war. But the century that began full of self-confidence in the ultimate triumph of Western liberal democracy seems at its close to be returning full circle to where it started: not to an "end of ideology" or a convergence between capitalism and socialism, as earlier predicted, but to an unabashed victory of economic and political liberalism.

The triumph of the West, of the Western *idea,* is evident first of all in the total exhaustion of viable systematic alternatives to Western liberalism. In the past decade, there have been unmistakable changes in the intellectual climate of the world's two largest communist countries, and the beginnings of significant reform movements in both. But this phenomenon extends beyond high politics and it can be seen also in the ineluctable spread of consumerist Western culture in such diverse contexts as the peasants' markets and color television sets now omnipresent throughout China, the cooperative restaurants and clothing stores opened in the past year in Moscow, the Beethoven piped into Japanese department stores, and the rock music enjoyed alike in Prague, Rangoon, and Tehran.

What we may be witnessing is not just the end of the Cold War, or the passing of a particular period of postwar history, but the end of history as such: that is, the end point of mankind's ideological evolution and the universalization of Western liberal democracy as the final form of human government. This is not to say that there will no longer be events to fill the pages of *Foreign Affairs'* yearly summaries of international relations, for the victory of liberalism has occurred primarily in the realm of ideas or consciousness and is as yet incomplete in the real or material world. But there are powerful reasons for believing that it is the ideal that will govern the material world *in the long run.* To understand how this is so, we must first consider some theoretical issues concerning the nature of historical change.

I

The notion of the end of history is not an original one. Its best known propagator was Karl Marx, who believed that the direction of historical development was a purposeful one determined by the interplay of material forces, and would come to an end only with the achievement of a communist utopia that would finally resolve all prior contradictions. But the concept of history as a dialectical process with a beginning, a middle, and an end was borrowed by Marx from his great German predecessor, Georg Wilhelm Friedrich Hegel.

For better or worse, much of Hegel's historicism has become part of our contemporary intellectual baggage. The notion that mankind has progressed through a series of primitive stages of consciousness on his path to the present, and that these stages corresponded to concrete forms of social organization, such as tribal, slave-owning, theocratic, and finally democratic-egalitarian societies, has become inseparable from the modern understanding of man. Hegel was the first philosopher to speak the language of modern social science, insofar as man for him was the product of his concrete historical and social environment and not, as earlier natural right theorists would have it, a collection of more or less fixed "natural" attributes. The mastery and transformation of man's natural environment through the application of science and technology was originally not a Marxist concept, but a Hegelian one. Unlike later historicists whose historical relativism degenerated into relativism tout court, however, Hegel believed that history culminated in an absolute moment—a moment in which a final, rational form of society and state became victorious.

* * *

II

For Hegel, the contradictions that drive history exist first of all in the realm of human consciousness, i.e. on the level of ideas[1] not the trivial election year proposals of American politicians, but ideas in the sense of large unifying world views that might best be understood under the rubric of ideology. Ideology in this sense is not restricted to the secular and explicit political doctrines we usually associate with the term, but can include religion, culture, and the complex of moral values underlying any society as well.

Hegel's view of the relationship between the ideal and the real or material worlds was an extremely complicated one, beginning with the fact that for him the distinction between the two was only apparent.[2] He did not believe that the real world conformed or could be made to conform to ideological preconceptions of philosophy professors in any simpleminded way, or that the "material" world could not impinge on the ideal. Indeed, Hegel the professor was temporarily thrown out of work as a result of a very material event, the Battle of Jena. But while Hegel's writing and thinking could be stopped by a bullet from the material world, the hand on the trigger of the gun was motivated in turn by the ideas of liberty and equality that had driven the French Revolution.

For Hegel, all human behavior in the material world, and hence all human history, is rooted in a prior state of consciousness—an idea similar to the one expressed by John Maynard Keynes when he said that the views of men of affairs were usually derived from defunct economists and academic scribblers of earlier generations. This consciousness may not be explicit and self-aware, as are modern political doctrines, but may rather take the form of religion or simple cultural or moral habits. And yet this realm of consciousness in the long run necessarily becomes manifest in the material world, indeed creates the material world in its own image. Consciousness is cause and not effect, and can develop autonomously from the material world; hence the real subtext underlying the apparent jumble of current events is the history of ideology.

Hegel's idealism has fared poorly at the hands of later thinkers. Marx reversed the priority of the real and the ideal completely, relegating the entire realm of consciousness—religion, art, culture, philosophy itself—to a "super-structure" that was determined entirely by the prevailing material mode of production. Yet another unfortunate legacy of Marxism is our tendency to retreat into materialist or utilitarian explanations of political or historical phenomena, and our disinclination to believe in the autonomous power of ideas. A recent example of this is Paul Kennedy's hugely successful *The Rise and Fall of the Great Powers,* which ascribes the decline of great powers to simple economic overextension. Obviously, this is true on some level: an empire whose economy is barely above the level of subsistence cannot bank-rupt its treasury indefinitely. But whether a highly productive modern indus-trial society chooses to spend 3 or 7 percent of its GNP on defense rather than consumption is entirely a matter of that society's political priorities, which are in turn determined in the realm of consciousness.

*   *   *

Failure to understand that the roots of economic behavior lie in the realm of consciousness and culture leads to the common mistake of attributing material causes to phenomena that are essentially ideal in nature. For example, it is commonplace in the West to interpret the reform movements first in China and most recently in the Soviet Union as the victory of the material over the ideal—that is, a recognition that ideological incentives could not replace material ones in stimulating a highly productive modern economy, and that if one wanted to prosper one had to appeal to baser forms of self-interest. But the deep defects of socialist economies were evident thirty or forty years ago to anyone who chose to look. Why was it that these countries moved away from central planning only in the 1980s? The answer must be found in the consciousness of the elites and leaders ruling them ... That change was in no way made inevitable by the material conditions in which either country found itself on the eve of the reform, but instead came about as the result of the victory of one idea over another.

*   *   *

III

Have we in fact reached the end of history? Are there, in other words, any fundamental "contradictions" in human life that cannot be resolved in the context of modern liberalism, that would be resolvable by an alternative political-economic structure? If we accept the idealist premises laid out above, we must seek an answer to this question in the realm of ideology and consciousness....

In the past century, there have been two major challenges to liberalism, those of fascism and of communism. The former[3] saw the political weakness, materialism, anomie, and lack of community of the West as fundamental contradictions in liberal societies that could only be resolved by a strong state that forged a new "people" on the basis of national exclusiveness. Fascism was destroyed as a living ideology by World War II. This was a defeat, of course, on a very material level, but it amounted to a defeat of the idea as well. What destroyed fascism as an idea was not universal moral revulsion against it, since plenty of people were willing to endorse the idea as long as it seemed the wave of the future, but its lack of success. After the war, it seemed to most people that German fascism as well as its other European and Asian variants were bound to self-destruct. There was no material reason why new fascist movements could not have sprung up again after the war in other locales, but for the fact that expansionist ultranationalism, with its promise of unending conflict leading to disastrous military defeat, had completely lost its appeal. The ruins of the Reich chancellery as well as the atomic bombs dropped on Hiroshima and Nagasaki killed this ideology on the level of consciousness as well as materially, and all of the pro-fascist movements spawned by the German and Japanese examples like the Peronist movement in Argentina or Subhas Chandra Bose's Indian National Army withered after the war.

The ideological challenge mounted by the other great alternative to liberalism, communism, was far more serious. Marx, speaking Hegel's language, asserted that liberal society contained a fundamental contradiction that could not be resolved within its context, that between capital and labor, and this contradiction has constituted the chief accusation against liberalism ever since. But surely, the class issue has actually been successfully resolved in the West.... This is not to say that there are not rich people and poor people in the United States, or that the gap between them has not grown in recent years. But the root causes of economic inequality do not have to do with the underlying legal and social structure of our society, which remains fundamentally egalitarian and moderately redistributionist, so much as with the cultural and social characteristics of the groups that make it up, which are in turn the historical legacy of premodern conditions. Thus black poverty in the United States is not the inherent product of liberalism, but is rather the "legacy of slavery and racism" which persisted long after the formal abolition of slavery.

As a result of the receding of the class issue, the appeal of communism in the developed Western world, it is safe to say, is lower today than any time since the end of the First World War. This can he measured in any number of ways: in the declining membership and electoral pull of the major European communist parties, and their overtly revisionist programs; in the corresponding electoral success of conservative parties from Britain and Germany to the United States and Japan, which are unabashedly pro-market and anti-statist; and in an intellectual climate whose most "advanced" members no longer believe that bourgeois society is something that ultimately needs to be overcome. This is not to say that the opinions of progressive intellectuals in Western countries are not deeply pathological in any number of ways. But those who believe that the future must inevitably be socialist tend to be very old, or very marginal to the real political discourse of their societies.

One may argue that the socialist alternative was never terribly plausible for the North Atlantic world, and was sustained for the last several decades primarily by its success outside of this region. But it is precisely in the non-European world that one is most struck by the occurrence of major ideological transformations. Surely the most remarkable changes have occurred in Asia. Due to the strength and adaptability of the indigenous cultures there, Asia became a battleground for a variety of imported Western ideologies early in this century. Liberalism in Asia was a very weak reed in the period after World War I; it is easy today to forget how gloomy Asia's political future looked as recently as ten or fifteen years ago. It is easy to forget as well how momentous the outcome of Asian ideological struggles seemed for world political development as a whole.

The first Asian alternative to liberalism to be decisively defeated was the fascist one represented by Imperial Japan. Japanese fascism (like its German version) was defeated by the force of American arms in the Pacific war, and liberal democracy was imposed on Japan by a victorious United States. Western capitalism and political liberalism when transplanted to Japan were adapted and transformed by the Japanese in such a way as to be scarcely recognizable.[4] Many Americans are now aware that Japanese industrial organization is very different from that prevailing in the United States or Europe, and it is questionable what relationship the factional maneuvering that takes place with the governing Liberal Democratic Party bears to democracy. Nonetheless, the very fact that the essential elements of economic and political liberalism have been so successfully grafted onto uniquely Japanese traditions and institutions guarantees their survival in the long run. More important is the contribution that Japan has made in turn to world history by following in the footsteps of the United States to create a truly universal consumer culture that has become both a symbol and an underpinning of the universal homogenous state. V. S. Naipaul traveling in Khomeini's Iran shortly after the revolution noted the omnipresent signs advertising the products of Sony, Hitachi, and JVC, whose appeal remained virtually irresistible and gave the lie to the regime's pretensions of restoring a state based on the rule of the *Shariah*. Desire for access to the consumer culture, created in large measure by Japan, has played a crucial role in fostering the spread of economic liberalism throughout Asia, and hence in promoting political liberalism as well.

The economic success of the other newly industrializing countries (NICs) in Asia following on the example of Japan is by now a familiar story. What is important from a Hegelian standpoint is that political liberalism has been following economic liberalism, more slowly than many had hoped but with seeming inevitability. Here again we see the victory of the idea of the universal homogenous state. South Korea had developed into a modern, urbanized society with an increasingly large and well-educated middle class that could not possibly be isolated from the larger democratic trends around them. Under these circumstances it seemed intolerable to a large part of this population that it should be ruled by an anachronistic military regime while Japan, only a decade or so ahead in economic terms, had parliamentary institutions for over forty years....

But the power of the liberal idea would seem much less impressive if it had not infected the largest and oldest culture in Asia, China. The simple existence of communist China created an alternative pole of ideological attraction, and as such constituted a threat to liberalism. But the past fifteen years have seen an almost total discrediting of Marxism-Leninism as an economic system. Beginning with the famous third plenum of the Tenth Central Committee in 1978, the Chinese Communist party set about decollectivizing agriculture for the 800 million Chinese who still lived in the countryside. The role of the state in agriculture was reduced to that of a tax collector, while production of consumer goods was sharply increased in order to give peasants a taste of the universal homogenous state and thereby an incentive to work. The reform doubled Chinese grain output in only five years, and in the process created for Deng Xiaoping a solid political base from which he was able to extend the reform to other parts of the economy. Economic statistics do not begin to describe the dynamism, initiative, and openness evident in China since the reform began.

China could not now be described in any way as a liberal democracy. At present, no more than 20 percent of its economy has been marketized, and most importantly it continues to be ruled by a self-appointed Communist party which has given no hint of wanting to devolve power. Deng has made none of Gorbachev's promises regarding democratization of the political system and there is no Chinese equivalent of *glasnost*. The Chinese leadership has in fact been much more circumspect in criticizing Mao and Maoism than Gorbachev with respect to Brezhnev and Stalin, and the regime continues to pay lip service to Marxism-Leninism as its ideological underpinning. But anyone familiar with the outlook and behavior of the new technocratic elite now governing China knows that Marxism and ideological principle have become virtually irrelevant as guides to policy, and that bourgeois consumerism has a real meaning in that country for the first time since the revolution. The various slowdowns in the pace of reform, the campaigns against "spiritual pollution" and crackdowns on political dissent are more properly seen as tactical adjustments made in the process of managing what is an extraordinarily difficult political transition. By ducking the question of political reform while putting the economy on a new footing, Deng has managed to avoid the breakdown of authority that has accompanied Gorbachev's *perestroika*. Yet the pull of the liberal idea continues to be very strong as economic power devolves and the economy becomes more open to the outside world. There are currently over 20,000 Chinese students studying in the U.S. and other Western countries, almost all of them the children of the Chinese elite. It is hard to believe that when they return home to run the country they will be content for China to be the only country in Asia unaffected by the larger democratizing trend. The student demonstrations in Beijing that broke out first in December 1986 and recurred recently on the occasion of Hu Yao-bang's death were only the beginning of what will inevitably be mounting pressure for change in the political system as well.

What is important about China from the standpoint of world history is not the present state of the reform or even its future prospects. The central issue is the fact that the People's Republic of China can no longer act as a beacon for illiberal forces around the world, whether they be guerrillas in some Asian jungle or middle class students in Paris. Maoism, rather than being the pattern for Asia's future, became an anachronism, and it was the mainland Chinese who in fact were decisively influenced by the prosperity and dynamism of their overseas co-ethnics—the ironic ultimate victory of Taiwan.

Important as these changes in China have been, however, it is developments in the Soviet Union—the original "homeland of the world proletariat"—that have put the final nail in the coffin of the Marxist-Leninist alternative to liberal democracy. It should be clear that in terms of formal institutions, not much has changed in the four years since Gorbachev has come to power: free markets and the cooperative movement represent only a small part of the Soviet economy, which remains centrally planned; the political system is still dominated by the Communist party, which has only begun to democratize internally and to share power with other groups; the regime continues to assert that it is seeking only to modernize socialism and that its ideological basis remains Marxism-Leninism; and, finally, Gorbachev faces a potentially powerful conservative opposition that could undo many of the changes that have taken place to date. Moreover, it is hard to be too sanguine about the chances for success of Gorbachev's proposed reforms, either in the sphere of economics or politics. But my purpose here is not to analyze events in the short-term, or to make predictions for policy purposes, but to look at underlying trends in the sphere of ideology and consciousness. And in that respect, it is clear that an astounding transformation has occurred.

Émigrés from the Soviet Union have been reporting for at least the last generation now that virtually nobody in that country truly believed in Marxism-Leninism any longer, and that this was nowhere more true than in the Soviet elite, which continued to mouth Marxist slogans out of sheer cynicism. The corruption and decadence of the late Brezhnev-era Soviet state seemed to matter little, however, for as long as the state itself refused to throw into question any of the fundamental principles underlying Soviet society, the system was capable of functioning adequately out of sheer inertia and could even muster some dynamism in the realm of foreign and defense policy. Marxism-Leninism was like a magical incantation which, however absurd and devoid of meaning, was the only common basis on which the elite could agree to rule Soviet society.

What has happened in the four years since Gorbachev's coming to power is a revolutionary assault on the most fundamental institutions and principles of Stalinism, and their replacement by other principles which do not amount to liberalism per se but whose only connecting thread is liberalism. This is most evident in the economic sphere, where the reform economists around Gorbachev have become steadily more radical in their support for free markets, to the point where some like Nikolai Shmelev do not mind being compared in public to Milton Friedman. There is a virtual consensus among the currently dominant school of Soviet economists now that central planning and the command system of allocation are the root cause of economic inefficiency, and that if the Soviet system is ever to heal itself, it must permit free and decentralized decision-making with respect to investment, labor, and prices. After a couple of initial years of ideological confusion, these principles have finally been incorporated into policy with the promulgation of new laws on enterprise autonomy, cooperatives, and finally in 1988 on lease arrangements and family farming. There are, of course, a number of fatal flaws in the current implementation of the reform, most notably the absence of a thoroughgoing price reform. But the problem is no longer a conceptual one: Gorbachev and his lieutenants seem to understand the economic logic of marketization well enough, but like the leaders of a Third World country facing the IMF, are afraid of the social consequences of ending consumer subsidies and other forms of dependence on the state sector.

In the political sphere, the proposed changes to the Soviet constitution, legal system, and party rules amount to much less than the establishment of a liberal state. Gorbachev has spoken of democratization primarily in the sphere of internal party affairs, and has shown little intention of ending the Communist party's monopoly of power; indeed, the political reform seeks to legitimize and therefore strengthen the CPSU'S rule.[5] Nonetheless, the general principles underlying many of the reforms—that the "people" should be truly responsible for their own affairs, that higher political bodies should be answerable to lower ones, and not vice versa, that the rule of law should prevail over arbitrary police actions, with separation of powers and an independent judiciary, that there should be legal protection for property rights, the need for open discussion of public issues and the right of public dissent, the empowering of the Soviets as a forum in which the whole Soviet people can participate, and of a political culture that is more tolerant and pluralistic—come from a source fundamentally alien to the USSR's Marxist-Leninist tradition, even if they are incompletely articulated and poorly implemented in practice.

Gorbachev's repeated assertions that he is doing no more than trying to restore the original meaning of Leninism are themselves a kind of Orwellian doublespeak. Gorbachev and his allies have consistently maintained that intraparty democracy was somehow the essence of Leninism, and that the various liberal practices of open debate, secret ballot elections, and rule of law were all part of the Leninist heritage, corrupted only later by Stalin. While almost anyone would look good compared to Stalin, drawing so sharp a line between Lenin and his successor is questionable. The essence of Lenin's democratic centralism was centralism, not democracy; that is, the absolutely rigid, monolithic, and disciplined dictatorship of a hierarchically organized vanguard Communist party, speaking in the name of the demos. All of Lenin's vicious polemics against Karl Kautsky, Rosa Luxemburg, and various other Menshevik and Social Democratic rivals, not to mention his contempt for "bourgeois legality" and freedoms, centered around his profound conviction that a revolution could not be successfully made by a democratically run organization.

Gorbachev's claim that he is seeking to return to the true Lenin is perfectly easy to understand: having fostered a thorough denunciation of Stalinism and Brezhnevism as the root of the USSR's present predicament, he needs some point in Soviet history on which to anchor the legitimacy of the CPSU'S continued rule. But Gorbachev's tactical requirements should not blind us to the fact that the democratizing and decentralizing principles which he has enunciated in both the economic and political spheres are highly subversive of some of the most fundamental precepts of both Marxism and Leninism. Indeed, if the bulk of the present economic reform proposals were put into effect, it is hard to know how the Soviet economy would be more socialist than those of other Western countries with large public sectors.

The Soviet Union could in no way be described as a liberal or democratic country now, nor do I think that it is terribly likely that perestroika will succeed such that the label will be thinkable any time in the near future. But at the end of history it is not necessary that all societies become successful liberal societies, merely that they end their ideological pretensions of representing different and higher forms of human society. And in this respect I believe that something very important has happened in the Soviet Union in the past few years: the criticisms of the Soviet system sanctioned by Gorbachev have been so thorough and devastating that there is very little chance of going back to either Stalinism or Brezhnevism in any simple way. Gorbachev has finally permitted people to say what they had privately understood for many years, namely, that the magical incantations of Marxism-Leninism were nonsense, that Soviet socialism was not superior to the West in any respect but was in fact a monumental failure. The conservative opposition in the USSR, consisting both of simple workers afraid of unemployment and inflation and of party officials fearful of losing their jobs and privileges, is outspoken and may be strong enough to force Gorbachev's ouster in the next few years. But what both groups desire is tradition, order, and authority; they manifest no deep commitment to Marxism-Leninism, except insofar as they have invested much of their own lives in it.[6] For authority to be restored in the Soviet Union after Gorbachev's demolition work, it must be on the basis of some new and vigorous ideology which has not yet appeared on the horizon.

If we admit for the moment that the fascist and communist challenges to liberalism are dead, are there any other ideological competitors left? Or put another way, are there contradictions in liberal society beyond that of class that are not resolvable? Two possibilities suggest themselves, those of religion and nationalism.

The rise of religious fundamentalism in recent years within the Christian, Jewish, and Muslim traditions has been widely noted. One is inclined to say that the revival of religion in some way attests to a broad unhappiness with the impersonality and spiritual vacuity of liberal consumerist societies. Yet while the emptiness at the core of liberalism is most certainly a defect in the ideology—indeed, a flaw that one does not need the perspective of religion to recognize[7]—it is not at all clear that it is remediable through politics. Modern liberalism itself was historically a consequence of the weakness of religiously-based societies which, failing to agree on the nature of the good life, could not provide even the minimal preconditions of peace and stability. In the contemporary world only Islam has offered a theocratic state as a political alternative to both liberalism and communism. But the doctrine has little appeal for non-Muslims, and it is hard to believe that the movement will take on any universal significance. Other less organized religious impulses have been successfully satisfied within the sphere of personal life that is permitted in liberal societies.

The other major "contradiction" potentially unresolvable by liberalism is the one posed by nationalism and other forms of racial and ethnic consciousness.... Two cataclysmic world wars in this century have been spawned by the nationalism of the developed world in various guises, and if those passions have been muted to a certain extent in postwar Europe, they are still extremely powerful in the Third World. Nationalism has been a threat to liberalism historically in Germany, and continues to be one in isolated parts of "post-historical" Europe like Northern Ireland.

But it is not clear that nationalism represents an irreconcilable contradiction in the heart of liberalism. In the first place, nationalism is not one single phenomenon but several, ranging from mild cultural nostalgia to the highly organized and elaborately articulated doctrine of National Socialism. Only systematic nationalisms of the latter sort can qualify as a formal ideology on the level of liberalism or communism. The vast majority of the world's nationalist movements do not have a political program beyond the negative desire of independence from some other group or people, and do not offer anything like a comprehensive agenda for socio-economic organization. As such, they are compatible with doctrines and ideologies that do offer such agendas. While they may constitute a source of conflict for liberal societies, this conflict does not arise from liberalism itself so much as from the fact that the liberalism in question is incomplete. Certainly a great deal of the world's ethnic and nationalist tension can be explained in terms of peoples who are forced to live in unrepresentative political systems that they have not chosen.

While it is impossible to rule out the sudden appearance of new ideologies or previously unrecognized contradictions in liberal societies, then, the present world seems to confirm that the fundamental principles of sociopolitical organization have not advanced terribly far since [the nineteenth century]. Many of the wars and revolutions fought since that time have been undertaken in the name of ideologies which claimed to be more advanced than liberalism, but whose pretensions were ultimately unmasked by history. In the meantime, they have helped to spread the universal homogenous state to the point where it could have a significant effect on the overall character of international relations.

IV

What are the implications of the end of history for international relations? Clearly, the vast bulk of the Third World remains very much mired in history, and will be a terrain of conflict for many years to come. But let us focus for the time being on the larger and more developed states of the world who after all account for the greater part of world politics. Russia and China are not likely to join the developed nations of the West as liberal societies any time in the foreseeable future, but suppose for a moment that Marxism-Leninism ceases to be a factor driving the foreign policies of these states—a prospect which, if not yet here, the last few years have made a real possibility. How will the overall characteristics of a de-ideologized world differ from those of the one with which we are familiar at such a hypothetical juncture?

The most common answer is—not very much. For there is a very widespread belief among many observers of international relations that underneath the skin of ideology is a hard core of great power national interest that guarantees a fairly high level of competition and conflict between nations. Indeed, according to one academically popular school of international relations theory, conflict inheres in the international system as such, and to understand the prospects for conflict one must look at the shape of the system—for example, whether it is bipolar or multipolar—rather than at the specific character of the nations and regimes that constitute it. This school in effect applies a Hobbesian view of politics to international relations, and assumes that aggression and insecurity are universal characteristics of human societies rather than the product of specific historical circumstances.

Believers in this line of thought take the relations that existed between the participants in the classical nineteenth century European balance of power as a model for what a de-ideologized contemporary world would look like. Charles Krauthammer, for example, recently explained that if as a result of Gorbachev's reforms the USSR is shorn of Marxist-Leninist ideology, its behavior will revert to that of nineteenth century imperial Russia.[8] While he finds this more reassuring than the threat posed by a communist Russia, he implies that there will still be a substantial degree of competition and conflict in the international system, just as there was say between Russia and Britain or Wilhelmine Germany in the last century. This is, of course, a convenient point of view for people who want to admit that something major is changing in the Soviet Union, but do not want to accept responsibility for recommending the radical policy redirection implicit in such a view. But is it true?

In fact, the notion that ideology is a superstructure imposed on a substratum of permanent great power interest is a highly questionable proposition. For the way in which any state defines its national interest is not universal but rests on some kind of prior ideological basis, just as we saw that economic behavior is determined by a prior state of consciousness. In this century, states have adopted highly articulated doctrines with explicit foreign policy agendas legitimizing expansionism, like Marxism-Leninism or National Socialism.

The expansionist and competitive behavior of nineteenth-century European states rested on no less ideal a basis; it just so happened that the ideology driving it was less explicit than the doctrines of the twentieth century. For one thing, most "liberal" European societies were illiberal insofar as they believed in the legitimacy of imperialism, that is, the right of one nation to rule over other nations without regard for the wishes of the ruled. The justifications for imperialism varied from nation to nation, from a crude belief in the legitimacy of force, particularly when applied to non-Europeans, to the White Man's Burden and Europe's Christianizing mission, to the desire to give people of color access to the culture of Rabelais and Moliere. But whatever the particular ideological basis, every "developed" country believed in the acceptability of higher civilizations ruling lower ones—including, incidentally, the United States with regard to the Philippines. This led to a drive for pure territorial aggrandizement in the latter half of the century and played no small role in causing the Great War.

The radical and deformed outgrowth of nineteenth-century imperialism was German fascism, an ideology which justified Germany's right not only to rule over non-European peoples, but over all non-German ones. But in retrospect it seems that Hitler represented a diseased bypath in the general course of European development, and since his fiery defeat, the legitimacy of any kind of territorial aggrandizement has been thoroughly discredited.[9] Since the Second World War, European nationalism has been defanged and shorn of any real relevance to foreign policy, with the consequence that the nineteenth-century model of great power behavior has become a serious anachronism. The most extreme form of nationalism that any Western European state has mustered since 1945 has been Gaullism, whose self-assertion has been confined largely to the realm of nuisance politics and culture. International life for the part of the world that has reached the end of history is far more preoccupied with economics than with politics or strategy.

The developed states of the West do maintain defense establishments and in the postwar period have competed vigorously for influence to meet a worldwide communist threat. This behavior has been driven, however, by an external threat from states that possess overtly expansionist ideologies, and would not exist in their absence. To take the "neo-realist" theory seriously, one would have to believe that "natural" competitive behavior would reassert itself among the OECD states were Russia and China to disappear from the face of the earth. That is, West Germany and France would arm themselves against each other as they did in the 1930s, Australia and New Zealand would send military advisers to block each others' advances in Africa, and the U.S.-Canadian border would become fortified. Such a prospect is, of course, ludicrous: minus Marxist-Leninist ideology, we are far more likely to see the "Common Marketization" of world politics than the disintegration of the EEC into nineteenth-century competitiveness. Indeed, as our experiences in dealing with Europe on matters such as terrorism or Libya prove, they are much further gone than we down the road that denies the legitimacy of the use of force in international politics, even in self-defense.

The automatic assumption that Russia shorn of its expansionist communist ideology should pick up where the czars left off just prior to the Bolshevik Revolution is therefore a curious one. It assumes that the evolution of human consciousness has stood still in the meantime, and that the Soviets, while picking up currently fashionable ideas in the realm of economics, will return to foreign policy views a century out of date in the rest of Europe. This is certainly not what happened to China after it began its reform process. Chinese competitiveness and expansionism on the world scene have virtually disappeared: Beijing no longer sponsors Maoist insurgencies or tries to cultivate influence in distant African countries as it did in the 1960s. This is not to say that there are not troublesome aspects to contemporary Chinese foreign policy, such as the reckless sale of ballistic missile technology in the Middle East; and the PRC continues to manifest traditional great power behavior in its sponsorship of the Khmer Rouge against Vietnam. But the former is explained by commercial motives and the latter is a vestige of earlier ideologically-based rivalries. The new China far more resembles Gaullist France than pre-World War I Germany.

The real question for the future, however, is the degree to which Soviet elites have assimilated the consciousness of the universal homogenous state that is post-Hitler Europe. From their writings and from my own personal contacts with them, there is no question in my mind that the liberal Soviet intelligentsia rallying around Gorbachev have arrived at the end-of-history view in a remarkably short time, due in no small measure to the contacts they have had since the Brezhnev era with the larger European civilization around them. "New political thinking," the general rubric for their views, describes a world dominated by economic concerns, in which there are no ideological grounds for major conflict between nations, and in which, consequently, the use of military force becomes less legitimate. As Foreign Minister Shevardnadze put it in mid-1988:

> The struggle between two opposing systems is no longer a determining tendency of the present-day era. At the modern stage, the ability to build up material wealth at an accelerated rate on the basis of front-ranking science and high-level techniques and technology, and to distribute it fairly, and through joint efforts to restore and protect the resources necessary for mankind's survival acquires decisive importance.[10]

The post-historical consciousness represented by "new thinking" is only one possible future for the Soviet Union, however. There has always been a very strong current of great Russian chauvinism in the Soviet Union, which has found freer expression since the advent of glasnost. It may be possible to return to traditional Marxism-Leninism for a while as a simple rallying point for those who want to restore the authority that Gorbachev has dissipated. But as in Poland, Marxism-Leninism is dead as a mobilizing ideology: under its banner people cannot be made to work harder, and its adherents have lost confidence in themselves. Unlike the propagators of traditional Marxism-Leninism, however, ultranationalists in the USSR believe in their Slavophile cause passionately, and one gets the sense that the fascist alternative is not one that has played itself out entirely there.

The Soviet Union, then, is at a fork in the road: it can start down the path that was staked out by Western Europe forty-five years ago, a path that most of Asia has followed, or it can realize its own uniqueness and remain stuck in history. The choice it makes will be highly important for us, given the Soviet Union's size and military strength, for that power will continue to preoccupy us and slow our realization that we have already emerged on the other side of history.

V

The passing of Marxism-Leninism first from China and then from the Soviet Union will mean its death as a living ideology of world historical significance. For while there may be some isolated true believers left in places like Managua, Pyongyang, or Cambridge, Massachusetts, the fact that there is not a single large state in which it is a going concern undermines completely its pretensions to being in the vanguard of human history. And the death of this ideology means the growing "Common Marketization" of international relations, and the diminution of the likelihood of large-scale conflict between states.

This does not by any means imply the end of international conflict per se. For the world at that point would be divided between a part that was historical and a part that was post-historical. Conflict between states still in history, and between those states and those at the end of history, would still be possible. There would still be a high and perhaps rising level of ethnic and nationalist violence, since those are impulses incompletely played out, even in parts of the post-historical world. Palestinians and Kurds, Sikhs and Tamils, Irish Catholics and Walloons, Armenians and Azeris, will continue to have their unresolved grievances. This implies that terrorism and wars of national liberation will continue to be an important item on the international agenda. But large-scale conflict must involve large states still caught in the grip of history, and they are what appear to be passing from the scene.

The end of history will be a very sad time. The struggle for recognition, the willingness to risk one's life for a purely abstract goal, the worldwide ideological struggle that called forth daring, courage, imagination, and idealism, will be replaced by economic calculation, the endless solving of technical problems, environmental concerns, and the satisfaction of sophisticated consumer demands. In the post-historical period there will be neither art nor philosophy, just the perpetual caretaking of the museum of human history. I can feel in myself, and see in others around me, a powerful nostalgia for the time when history existed. Such nostalgia, in fact, will continue to fuel competition and conflict even in the post-historical world for some time to come. Even though I recognize its inevitability, I have the most ambivalent feelings for the civilization that has been created in Europe since 1945, with its north Atlantic and Asian offshoots. Perhaps this very prospect of centuries of boredom at the end of history will serve to get history started once again.

Notes

1. This notion was expressed in the famous aphorism from the preface to the *Philosophy of History* to the effect that "everything that is rational is real, and everything that is real is rational."
2. Indeed, for Hegel the very dichotomy between the ideal and material worlds was itself only an apparent one that was ultimately overcome by the self-conscious subject; in his system, the material world is itself only an aspect of mind.
3. I am not using the term "fascism" here in its most precise sense, fully aware of the frequent misuse of this term to denounce anyone to the right of the user. "Fascism" here denotes any organized ultra nationalist movement with universalistic pretensions—not universalistic with regard to its nationalism, of course, since the latter is exclusive by definition, but with regard to the movement's belief in its right to rule other people. Hence Imperial Japan would qualify as fascist while former strongman Stoessner's Paraguay or Pinochet's Chile would not. Obviously fascist ideologies cannot be universalistic in the sense of Marxism or liberalism, but the structure of the doctrine can be transferred from country to country.
4. I use the example of Japan with some caution, since Kojève late in his life came to conclude that Japan, with its culture based on purely formal arts, proved that the universal homogenous state was not victorious and that history had perhaps not ended. See the long note at the end of the second edition of *Introduction à la Lecture de Hegel,* 462–3.
5. This is not true in Poland and Hungary, however, whose Communist parties have taken moves toward true power sharing and pluralism.
6. This is particularly true of the leading Soviet conservative, former Second Secretary Yegor Ligachev, who has publicly recognized many of the deep defects of the Brezhnev period.
7. I am thinking particularly of Rousseau and the Western philosophical tradition that flows from him that was highly critical of Lockean or Hobbesian liberalism, though one could criticize liberalism from the standpoint of classical political philosophy as well.
8. See his article, "Beyond the Cold War," *New Republic,* December 19, 1988.
9. It took European colonial powers like France several years after the war to admit the illegitimacy of their empires, but decolonialization was an inevitable consequence of the Allied victory which had been based on the promise of a restoration of democratic freedoms.
10. Vestnik Ministerstva Inostrannikh Del SSSR no. 15 (August 1988), 27–46. "New thinking" does of course serve a propagandistic purpose in persuading Western audiences of Soviet good intentions. But the fact that it is good propaganda does not mean that its formulators do not take many of its ideas seriously.

6.2

THE CLASH OF CIVILIZATIONS?

Samuel P. Huntington

> In this widely publicized article written in the early 1990s (and a book that followed), Samuel P. Huntington argues that the world after the end of the Cold War will remain divided—but now among civilizations rather than among states or political ideologies (such as liberalism and fascism). Unlike Francis Fukuyama (see the previous selection), he does not believe that ideology will unite the world. Huntington's analysis remains realist in the sense that there is no universal civilization and hence no single center of power in the world. Power remains decentralized. But the identity of the primary actors is shifting from national cultures, which dominated the study of international relations for the past five hundred years, to civilizations, which clashed repeatedly before the modern era (for example, Islam and Christianity). Differences in power constitute "one source of conflict," but differences in civilizations become "a second source." Power, a realist concept, is supplemented but not displaced by relative identities, an ideational concept.

I. The Next Pattern of Conflict

World politics is entering a new phase, and intellectuals have not hesitated to proliferate visions of what it will be—the end of history, the return of traditional rivalries between nation states, and the decline of the nation state from the conflicting pulls of tribalism and globalism, among others. Each of these visions catches aspects of the emerging reality. Yet they all miss a crucial, indeed a central, aspect of what global politics is likely to be in the coming years.

It is my hypothesis that the fundamental source of conflict in this new world will not be primarily ideological or primarily economic. The great divisions among humankind and the dominating source of conflict will be cultural. Nation states will remain the most powerful actors in world affairs, but the principal conflicts of global politics will occur between nations and groups of different civilizations. The clash of civilizations will be the battle lines of the future.

Conflict between civilizations will be the latest phase of the evolution of conflict in the modern world. For a century and a half after the emergence of the modern international system of the Peace of Westphalia, the conflicts of the

Source: Samuel P. Huntington, "The Clash of Civilizations?" *Foreign Affairs* 72, no. 3 (1993): 22–49.

Western world were largely among princes—emperors, absolute monarchs and constitutional monarchs attempting to expand their bureaucracies, their armies, their mercantilist economic strength and, most important, the territory they ruled. In the process they created nation states, and beginning with the French Revolution the principal lines of conflict were between nations rather than princes. In 1793, as R. R. Palmer put it, "The wars of kings were over; the wars of peoples had begun." This nineteenth-century pattern lasted until the end of World War I. Then, as a result of the Russian Revolution and the reaction against it, the conflict of nations yielded to the conflict of ideologies, first among communism, fascism-Nazism and liberal democracy, and then between communism and liberal democracy. During the Cold War, this latter conflict became embodied in the struggle between the two superpowers, neither of which was a nation state in the classical European sense and each of which defined its identity in terms of ideology.

These conflicts between princes, nation states and ideologies were primarily conflicts within Western civilization, "Western civil wars," as William Lind has labeled them. This was as true of the Cold War as it was of the world wars and the earlier wars of the seventeenth, eighteenth and nineteenth centuries. With the end of the Cold War, international politics moves out of its Western phase, and its center-piece becomes the interaction between the West and non-Western civilizations and among non-Western civilizations. In the politics of civilizations, the people and governments of non-Western civilizations no longer remain the objects of history as targets of Western colonialism but join the West as movers and shapers of history.

II. The Nature of Civilizations

* * *

What do we mean when we talk of a civilization? A civilization is a cultural entity. Villages, regions, ethnic groups, nationalities, religious groups, all have distinct cultures at different levels of cultural heterogeneity. The culture of a village in southern Italy may be different from that of a village in northern Italy, but both will share in a common Italian culture that distinguishes them from German villages. European communities, in turn, will share cultural features that distinguish them from Arab or Chinese communities. Arabs, Chinese and Westerners, however, are not part of any broader cultural entity. They constitute civilizations. A civilization is thus the highest cultural grouping of people and the broadest level of cultural identity people have short of that which distinguishes humans from other species. It is defined both by common objective elements, such as language, history, religion, customs, institutions, and by the subjective self-identification of people. People have levels of identity: a resident of Rome may define himself with varying degrees of intensity as a Roman, an Italian, a Catholic, a Christian, a European, a Westerner. The civilization to which he belongs is the broadest level of identification with which he intensely identifies. People can and do redefine their identities and, as a result, the composition and boundaries of civilizations change.

Civilizations may involve a large number of people, as with China ("a civilization pretending to be a state," as Lucian Pye put it), or a very small number of people, such as the Anglophone Caribbean. A civilization may include several nation states, as is the case with Western, Latin American and Arab civilizations, or only one, as is the case with Japanese civilization. Civilizations obviously blend and overlap, and may include subcivilizations. Western civilization has two major variants, European and North American, and Islam has its Arab, Turkic and Malay subdivisions. Civilizations are nonetheless meaningful entities, and while the lines between them are seldom sharp, they are real. Civilizations are dynamic; they rise and fall; they divide and merge. And, as any student of history knows, civilizations disappear and are buried in the sands of time.

Westerners tend to think of nation states as the principal actors in global affairs. They have been that, however, for only a few centuries. The broader reaches of human history have been the history of civilizations. In *A Study of History,* Arnold Toynbee identified 21 major civilizations; only six of them exist in the contemporary world.

III. Why Civilizations Will Clash

Civilization identity will be increasingly important in the future, and the world will be shaped in large measure by the interactions among seven or eight major civilizations. These include Western, Confucian, Japanese, Islamic, Hindu, Slavic-Orthodox, Latin American and possibly African civilization. The most important conflicts of the future will occur along the cultural fault lines separating these civilizations from one another.

Why will this be the case?

First, differences among civilizations are not only real; they are basic. Civilizations are differentiated from each other by history, language, culture, tradition and, most important, religion. The people of different civilizations have different views on the relations between God and man, the individual and the group, the citizen and the state, parents and children, husband and wife, as well as differing views of the relative importance of rights and responsibilities, liberty and authority, equality and hierarchy. These differences are the product of centuries. They will not soon disappear. They are far more fundamental than differences among political ideologies and political regimes. Differences do not necessarily mean conflict, and conflict does not necessarily mean violence. Over the centuries, however, differences among civilizations have generated the most prolonged and the most violent conflicts.

Second, the world is becoming a smaller place. The interactions between peoples of different civilizations are increasing; these increasing interactions intensify civilization consciousness and awareness of differences between civilizations and commonalities within civilizations. North African immigration to

France generates hostility among Frenchmen and at the same time increased receptivity to immigration by "good" European Catholic Poles. Americans react far more negatively to Japanese investment than to larger investments from Canada and European countries. Similarly, as Donald Horowitz has pointed out, "An Ibo may be … an Owerri Ibo or an Onitsha Ibo in what was the Eastern region of Nigeria. In Lagos, he is simply an Ibo. In London, he is a Nigerian. In New York, he is an African." The interactions among peoples of different civilizations enhance the civilization-consciousness of people that, in turn, invigorates differences and animosities stretching or thought to stretch back deep into history.

Third, the processes of economic modernization and social change throughout the world are separating people from longstanding local identities. They also weaken the nation state as a source of identity. In much of the world religion has moved in to fill this gap, often in the form of movements that are labeled "fundamentalist." Such movements are found in Western Christianity, Judaism, Buddhism and Hinduism, as well as in Islam. In most countries and most religions the people active in fundamentalist movements are young, college-educated, middle-class technicians, professionals and business persons. The "unsecularization of the world," George Weigel has remarked, "is one of the dominant social factors of life in the late twentieth century." The revival of religion, "la revanche de Dieu," as Gilles Kepel labeled it, provides a basis for identity and commitment that transcends national boundaries and unites civilizations.

Fourth, the growth of civilization-consciousness is enhanced by the dual role of the West. On the one hand, the West is at a peak of power. At the same time, however, and perhaps as a result, a return to the roots phenomenon is occurring among non-Western civilizations. Increasingly one hears references to trends toward a turning inward and "Asianization" in Japan, the end of the Nehru legacy and the "Hinduization" of India, the failure of Western ideas of socialism and nationalism and hence "re-Islamization" of the Middle East, and now a debate over Westernization versus Russianization in Boris Yeltsin's country. A West at the peak of its power confronts non-Wests that increasingly have the desire, the will and the resources to shape the world in non-Western ways.

In the past, the elites of non-Western societies were usually the people who were most involved with the West, had been educated at Oxford, the Sorbonne or Sandhurst, and had absorbed Western attitudes and values. At the same time, the populace in non-Western countries often remained deeply imbued with the indigenous culture. Now, however, these relationships are being reversed. A de-Westernization and indigenization of elites is occurring in many non-Western countries at the same time that Western, usually American, cultures, styles and habits become more popular among the mass of the people.

Fifth, cultural characteristics and differences are less mutable and hence less easily compromised and resolved than political and economic ones. In the former Soviet Union, communists can become democrats, the rich can become poor and the poor rich, but Russians cannot become Estonians and Azeris cannot become Armenians. In class and ideological conflicts, the key question was "Which side are you on?" and people could and did choose sides and change sides. In conflicts between civilizations, the question is "What are you?" That is a given that cannot be changed. And as we know, from Bosnia to the Caucasus to the Sudan, the wrong answer to that question can mean a bullet in the head. Even more than ethnicity, religion discriminates sharply and exclusively among people. A person can be half-French and half-Arab and simultaneously even a citizen of two countries. It is more difficult to be half-Catholic and half-Muslim.

Finally, economic regionalism is increasing. The proportions of total trade that are intraregional rose between 1980 and 1989 from 51 percent to 59 percent in Europe, 33 percent to 37 percent in East Asia, and 32 percent to 36 percent in North America. The importance of regional economic blocs is likely to continue to increase in the future. On the one hand, successful economic regionalism will reinforce civilization-consciousness. On the other hand, economic regionalism may succeed only when it is rooted in a common civilization. The European Community rests on the shared foundation of European culture and Western Christianity. The success of the North American Free Trade Area depends on the convergence now underway of Mexican, Canadian and American cultures. Japan, in contrast, faces difficulties in creating a comparable economic entity in East Asia because Japan is a society and civilization unique to itself. However strong the trade and investment links Japan may develop with other East Asian countries, its cultural differences with those countries inhibit and perhaps preclude its promoting regional economic integration like that in Europe and North America.

Common culture, in contrast, is clearly facilitating the rapid expansion of the economic relations between the People's Republic of China and Hong Kong, Taiwan, Singapore and the overseas Chinese communities in other Asian countries. With the Cold War over, cultural commonalities increasingly overcome ideological differences, and mainland China and Taiwan move closer together. If cultural commonality is a prerequisite for economic integration, the principal East Asian economic bloc of the future is likely to be centered on China. This bloc is, in fact, already coming into existence. As Murray Weidenbaum has observed,

> Despite the current Japanese dominance of the region, the Chinese-based economy of Asia is rapidly emerging as a new epicenter for industry, commerce and finance. This strategic area contains substantial amounts of technology and manufacturing capability (Taiwan), outstanding entrepreneurial, marketing and services acumen (Hong Kong), a fine communications network (Singapore), a tremendous pool of financial capital (all three), and very large endowments of land, resources and labor (mainland China).... From Guangzhou to Singapore, from Kuala Lumpur to Manila, this influential network—often based on extensions of the traditional clans—has been described as the backbone of the East Asian economy.[1]

Culture and religion also form the basis of the Economic Cooperation Organization, which brings together ten non-Arab Muslim countries: Iran, Pakistan, Turkey, Azerbaijan, Kazakhstan, Kyrgyzstan, Turkmenistan, Tadjikistan, Uzbekistan and Afghanistan. One impetus to the revival and expansion of this organization, founded originally in the 1960s by Turkey, Pakistan and Iran, is the realization by the leaders of several of these countries that they had no chance of admission to the European Community. Similarly, Caricom, the Central American Common Market and Mercosur rest on common cultural foundations. Efforts to build a broader Caribbean-Central American economic entity bridging the Anglo-Latin divide, however, have to date failed.

As people define their identity in ethnic and religious terms, they are likely to see an "us" versus "them" relation existing between themselves and people of different ethnicity or religion. The end of ideologically defined states in Eastern Europe and the former Soviet Union permits traditional ethnic identities and animosities to come to the fore. Differences in culture and religion create differences over policy issues, ranging from human rights to immigration to trade and commerce to the environment. Geographical propinquity gives rise to conflicting territorial claims from Bosnia to Mindanao. Most important, the efforts of the West to promote its values of democracy and liberalism to universal values, to maintain its military predominance and to advance its economic interests engender countering responses from other civilizations. Decreasingly able to mobilize support and form coalitions on the basis of ideology, governments and groups will increasingly attempt to mobilize support by appealing to common religion and civilization identity.

The clash of civilizations thus occurs at two levels. At the micro-level, adjacent groups along the fault lines between civilizations struggle, often violently, over the control of territory and each other. At the macro-level, states from different civilizations compete for relative military and economic power, struggle over the control of international institutions and third parties, and competitively promote their particular political and religious values.

IV. The Fault Lines Between Civilizations

The fault lines between civilizations are replacing the political and ideological boundaries of the Cold War as the flash points for crisis and bloodshed. The Cold War began when the Iron Curtain divided Europe politically and ideologically. The Cold War ended with the end of the Iron Curtain. As the ideological division of Europe has disappeared, the cultural division of Europe between Western Christianity, on the one hand, and Orthodox Christianity and Islam, on the other, has reemerged. The most significant dividing line in Europe, as William Wallace has suggested, may well be the eastern boundary of Western Christianity in the year 1500. This line runs along what are now the boundaries between Finland and Russia and between the Baltic states and Russia, cuts through Belarus and Ukraine separating the more Catholic western Ukraine from Orthodox eastern Ukraine, swings westward separating Transylvania from the rest of Romania, and then goes through Yugoslavia almost exactly along the line now separating Croatia and Slovenia from the rest of Yugoslavia. In the Balkans this line, of course, coincides with the historic boundary between the Hapsburg and Ottoman empires. The peoples to the north and west of this line are Protestant or Catholic; they shared the common experiences of European history—feudalism, the Renaissance, the Reformation, the Enlightenment, the French Revolution, the Industrial Revolution; they are generally economically better off than the peoples to the east; and they may now look forward to increasing involvement in a common European economy and to the consolidation of democratic political systems. The peoples to the east and south of this line are Orthodox or Muslim; they historically belonged to the Ottoman or Tsarist empires and were only lightly touched by the shaping events in the rest of Europe; they are generally less advanced economically; they seem much less likely to develop stable democratic political systems. The Velvet Curtain of culture has replaced the Iron Curtain of ideology as the most significant dividing line in Europe. As the events in Yugoslavia show, it is not only a line of difference; it is also at times a line of bloody conflict.

Conflict along the fault line between Western and Islamic civilizations has been going on for 1,300 years. After the founding of Islam, the Arab and Moorish surge west and north only ended at Tours in 732. From the eleventh to the thirteenth century the Crusaders attempted with temporary success to bring Christianity and Christian rule to the Holy Land. From the fourteenth to the seventeenth century, the Ottoman Turks reversed the balance, extended their sway over the Middle East and the Balkans, captured Constantinople, and twice laid siege to Vienna. In the nineteenth and early twentieth centuries at Ottoman power declined Britain, France, and Italy established Western control over most of North Africa and the Middle East.

After World War II, the West, in turn, began to retreat; the colonial empires disappeared; first Arab nationalism and then Islamic fundamentalism manifested themselves; the West became heavily dependent on the Persian Gulf countries for its energy; the oil-rich Muslim countries became money-rich and, when they wished to, weapons-rich. Several wars occurred between Arabs and Israel (created by the West). France fought a bloody and ruthless war in Algeria for most of the 1950s; British and French forces invaded Egypt in 1956; American forces returned to Lebanon, attacked Libya, and engaged in various military encounters with Iran; Arab and Islamic terrorists, supported by at least three Middle Eastern governments, employed the weapon of the weak and bombed Western planes and installations and seized Western hostages. This warfare between Arabs and the West culminated in 1990, when the United States sent a massive army to the Persian Gulf to defend some Arab countries against aggression by another. In its aftermath NATO planning is increasingly directed to potential threats and instability along its "southern tier."

This centuries-old military interaction between the West and Islam is unlikely to decline. It could become more virulent. The Gulf War left some Arabs feeling proud that Saddam Hussein had attacked Israel and stood up to the West. It also left many feeling humiliated and resentful of the West's military presence in the Persian Gulf, the West's overwhelming military dominance, and their apparent inability to shape their own destiny. Many Arab countries, in addition to the oil exporters, are reaching levels of economic and social development where autocratic forms of government become inappropriate and efforts to introduce democracy become stronger. Some openings in Arab political systems have already occurred. The principal beneficiaries of these openings have been Islamist movements. In the Arab world, in short, Western democracy strengthens anti-Western political forces. This may be a passing phenomenon, but it surely complicates relations between Islamic countries and the West.

Those relations are also complicated by demography. The spectacular population growth in Arab countries, particularly in North Africa, has led to increased migration to Western Europe. The movement within Western Europe toward minimizing internal boundaries has sharpened political sensitivities with respect to this development. In Italy, France and Germany, racism is increasingly open, and political reactions and violence against Arab and Turkish migrants have become more intense and more widespread since 1990.

On both sides the interaction between Islam and the West is seen as a clash of civilizations. The West's "next confrontation," observes M. J. Akbar, an Indian Muslim author, "is definitely going to come from the Muslim world. It is in the sweep of the Islamic nations from the Meghreb to Pakistan that the struggle for a new world order will begin." Bernard Lewis comes to a regular conclusion:

> We are facing a need and a movement far transcending the level of issues and policies and the governments that pursue them. This is no less than a clash of civilizations—the perhaps irrational but surely historic reaction of an ancient rival against our Judeo-Christian heritage, our secular present, and the world-wide expansion of both.[2]

Historically, the other great antagonistic interaction of Arab Islamic civilization has been with the pagan, animist, and now increasingly Christian black peoples to the south. In the past, this antagonism was epitomized in the image of Arab slave dealers and black slaves. It has been reflected in the on-going civil war in the Sudan between Arabs and blacks, the fighting in Chad between Libyan-supported insurgents and the government, the tensions between Orthodox Christians and Muslims in the Horn of Africa, and the political conflicts, recurring riots and communal violence between Muslims and Christians in Nigeria. The modernization of Africa and the spread of Christianity in Nigeria. The modernization of Africa and the spread of Christianity are likely to enhance the probability of violence along this fault line. Symptomatic of the intensification of this conflict was the Pope John Paul II's speech in Khartoum in February 1993 attacking the actions of the Sudan's Islamist government against the Christian minority there.

On the northern border of Islam, conflict has increasingly erupted between Orthodox and Muslim peoples, including the carnage of Bosnia and Sarajevo, the simmering violence between Serb and Albanian, the tenuous relation between Bulgarians and their Turkish minority, the violence between Ossetians and Ingush, the unremitting slaughter of each other by Armenians and Azeris, the tense relations between Russians and Muslims in Central Asia, and the deployment of Russian troops to protect Russian interests in the Caucasus and Central Asia. Religion reinforces the revival of ethnic identities and restimulates Russian fears about the security of their southern borders. This concern is well captured by Archie Roosevelt:

> Much of Russian history concerns the struggle between Slavs and the Turkish peoples on their borders, which dates back to the foundation of the Russian state more than a thousand years ago. In the Slavs' millennium-long confrontation with their eastern neighbors lies the key to an understanding not only of Russian history, but Russian character. To understand Russian realities today one has to have a concept of the great Turkic ethnic group that has preoccupied Russians through the centuries.[3]

The conflict of civilizations is deeply rooted elsewhere in Asia. The historic clash between Muslim and Hindu in the subcontinent manifests itself now not only in the rivalry between Pakistan and India but also in intensifying religious strife within India between increasingly militant Hindu groups and India's substantial Muslim minority. The destruction of the Ayodhya mosque in December 1992 brought to the fore the issue of whether India will remain a secular democratic state or become a Hindu one. In East Asia, China has outstanding territorial disputes with most of its neighbors. It has pursued a ruthless policy toward the Buddhist people of Tibet, and it is pursuing an increasingly ruthless policy toward its Turkic-Muslim minority. With the Cold War over, the underlying differences between China and the United States have reasserted themselves in areas such as human rights, trade and weapons proliferation. These differences are unlikely to moderate. A "new cold war," Deng Xaioping reportedly asserted in 1991, is under way between China and America.

The same phrase has been applied to the increasingly difficult relations between Japan and the United States. Here cultural difference exacerbates economic conflict. People on each side allege racism on the other, but at least on the American side the antipathies are not racial but cultural. The basic values, attitudes, behavioral patterns of the two societies could hardly be more different. The economic issues between the United States and Europe are no less serious than those between the United States and Japan, but they do not have the same political salience and emotional intensity because the differences between American culture and European culture are so much less than those between American civilization and Japanese civilization.

The interactions between civilizations vary greatly in the extent to which they are likely to be characterized by violence. Economic competition clearly predominates between the American and European subcivilizations of the West and between both of them and Japan. On the Eurasian continent, however, the proliferation of ethnic conflict, epitomized at the extreme in "ethnic cleansing," has not been totally random. It has been most frequent and most violent between groups belonging to different civilizations. In Eurasia the great historic fault lines between civilizations are once more aflame. This is particularly true along the boundaries of the crescent-shaped Islamic bloc of nations from the bulge of Africa to central Asia. Violence also occurs between Muslims, on the one hand, and Orthodox Serbs in the Balkans, Jews in Israel, Hindus in India, Buddhists in Burma and Catholics in the Philippines. Islam has bloody borders.

* * *

VI. The West Versus the Rest

The west is now at an extraordinary peak of power in relation to other civilizations. Its superpower opponent has disappeared from the map. Military conflict among Western states is unthinkable, and Western military power is unrivaled. Apart from Japan, the West faces no economic challenge. It dominates international economic institutions. Global political and security issues are effectively settled by a directorate of the United States, Britain and France, world economic issues by a directorate of the United States, Germany and Japan, all of which maintain extraordinarily close relations with each other to the exclusion of lesser and largely non-Western countries. Decisions made at the U.N. Security Council or in the International Monetary Fund that reflect the interests of the West are presented to the world as reflecting the desires of the world community. The very phrase "the world community" has become the euphemistic collective noun (replacing "the Free World") to give global legitimacy to actions reflecting the interests of the United States and other Western powers.[4] Through the IMF and other international economic institutions, the West promotes its economic interests and imposes on other nations the economic policies it thinks appropriate. In any poll of non-Western peoples, the IMF undoubtedly would win the support of finance ministers and a few others, but get an overwhelmingly unfavorable rating from just about everyone else, who would agree with Georgy Arbatov's characterization of IMF officials as "neo-Bolsheviks who love expropriating other people's money, imposing undemocratic and alien rules of economic and political conduct and stifling economic freedom."

Western domination of the U.N. Security Council and its decisions, tempered only by occasional abstention by China, produced U.N. legitimation of the West's use of force to drive Iraq out of Kuwait and its elimination of Iraq's sophisticated weapons and capacity to produce such weapons. It also produced the quite unprecedented action by the United States, Britain and France in getting the Security Council to demand that Libya hand over the Pan Am 103 bombing suspects and then to impose sanctions when Libya refused. After defeating the largest Arab army, the West did not hesitate to throw its weight around in the Arab world. The West in effect is using international institutions, military power and economic resources to run the world in ways that will maintain Western predominance, protect Western interests and promote Western political and economic values.

That at least is the way in which non-Westerners see the new world, and there is a significant element of truth in their view. Differences in power and struggles for military, economic and institutional power are thus one source of conflict between the West and other civilizations. Differences in culture, that is basic values and beliefs, are a second source of conflict. V. S. Naipaul has argued that Western civilization is the "universal civilization" that "fits all men." At a superficial level much of Western culture has indeed permeated the rest of the world. At a more basic level, however, Western concepts differ fundamentally from those prevalent in other civilizations. Western ideas of individualism, liberalism, constitutionalism, human rights, equality, liberty, the rule of law, democracy, free markets, the separation of church and state, often have little resonance in Islamic, Confucian, Japanese, Hindu, Buddhist or Orthodox cultures. Western efforts to propagate each ideas produce instead a reaction against "human rights imperialism" and a reaffirmation of indigenous values, as can be seen in the support for religious fundamentalism by the younger generation in non-Western cultures. The very notion that there could be a "universal civilization" is a Western idea, directly at odds with the particularism of most Asian societies and their emphasis on what distinguishes one people from another. Indeed, the author of a review of 100 comparative studies of values in different societies concluded that "the values that are most important in the West are least important worldwide."[5] In the political realm, of course, these differences are most manifest in the efforts of the United States and other Western powers to induce other peoples to adopt Western ideas concerning democracy and human rights. Modern democratic government originated in the West. When it has developed in non-Western societies it has usually been the product of Western colonialism or imposition.

The central axis of world politics in the future is likely to be, in Kishore Mahbubani's phrase, the conflict between "the West and the Rest" and the responses of non-Western civilizations to Western power and values.[6] Those responses generally take one or a combination of three forms. At one extreme, non-Western states can, like Burma and North Korea, attempt to pursue a course of isolation, to insulate their societies from penetration or "corruption" by the West, and, in effect, to opt out of participation in the Western-dominated global community. The costs of this course, however, are high, and few states have pursued it exclusively. A second alternative, the equivalent of "bandwagoning" in international relations theory, is to attempt to join the West and accept its values and institutions. The third alternative is to attempt to "balance" the West by developing economic and military power and cooperating with other non-Western societies against the West, while preserving indigenous values and institutions; in short, to modernize but not to Westernize.

* * *

VIII. The Confucian-Islamic Connection

The obstacles to non-Western countries joining the West vary considerably. They are least for Latin American and East European countries. They are greater for the Orthodox countries of the former Soviet Union. They are still greater for Muslim, Confucian, Hindu and Buddhist societies. Japan has established a unique position for itself as an associate member of the West: it is in the West in some respects but clearly not of the West in important dimensions. Those countries that for reason of culture and power do not wish to, or cannot, join the West compete with the West by developing their own economic, military and political power. They do this by promoting their internal development and by cooperating with other non-Western countries. The most prominent form of this cooperation is the Confucian-Islamic connection that has emerged to challenge Western interests, values and power.

Almost without exception, Western countries are reducing their military power; under Yeltsin's leadership so also is Russia. China, North Korea and several Middle Eastern states, however, are significantly expanding their military capabilities. They are doing this by the import of arms from Western and non-Western sources and by the development of indigenous arms industries. One result is the emergence of what Charles Krauthammer has called "Weapon States," and the Weapon States are not Western states. Another result is the redefinition of arms control, which is a Western concept and a Western goal. During the Cold War the primary purpose of arms control was to establish a stable military balance between the United States and its allies and the Soviet Union and its allies. In the post–Cold War world the primary objective of arms control is to prevent the development by non-Western societies of military capabilities that could threaten Western interests. The West attempts to do this through international agreements, economic pressure and controls on the transfer of arms and weapons technologies.

The conflict between the West and the Confucian-Islamic states focuses largely, although not exclusively, on nuclear, chemical and biological weapons, ballistic missiles and other sophisticated means for delivering them, and the guidance, intelligence and other electronic capabilities for achieving that goal. The West promotes nonproliferation as a universal norm and nonproliferation treaties and inspections as means of realizing that norm. It also threatens a variety of sanctions against those who promote the spread of sophisticated weapons and proposes some benefits for those who do not. The attention of the West focuses, naturally, on nations that are actually or potentially hostile to the West.

The non-Western nations, on the other hand, assert their right to acquire and to deploy whatever weapons they think necessary for their security. They also have absorbed, to the full, the truth of the response of the Indian defense minister when asked what lesson he learned from the Gulf War: "Don't fight the United States unless you have nuclear weapons." Nuclear weapons, chemical weapons and missiles are viewed, probably erroneously, as the potential equalizer of superior Western conventional power. China, of course, already has nuclear weapons; Pakistan and India have the capability to deploy them. North Korea, Iran, Iraq, Libya and Algeria appear to be attempting to acquire them. A top Iranian official has declared that all Muslim states should acquire nuclear weapons, and in 1988 the president of Iran reportedly issued a directive calling for development of "offensive and defensive chemical, biological and radiological weapons."

Centrally important to the development of counter-West military capabilities is the sustained expansion of China's military power and its means to create military power. Buoyed by spectacular economic development, China is rapidly increasing its military spending and vigorously moving forward with the modernization of its armed forces. It is purchasing weapons from the former Soviet states; it is developing long-range missiles; in 1992 it tested a one-megaton nuclear device. It is developing power-projection capabilities, acquiring aerial refueling technology, and trying to purchase an aircraft carrier. Its military buildup and assertion of sovereignty over the South China Sea are provoking a multilateral regional arms race in East Asia. China is also a major exporter of arms and weapons technology. It has exported materials to Libya and Iraq that could be used to manufacture nuclear weapons and nerve gas. It has helped Algeria build a reactor suitable for nuclear weapons research and production. China has sold to Iran nuclear technology that American officials believe could only be used to create weapons and apparently has shipped components of 300-mile-range missiles to Pakistan. North Korea has had a nuclear weapons program under way for some while and has sold advanced missiles and missile technology to Syria and Iran. The flow of weapons and weapons technology is generally from East Asia to the Middle East. There is, however, some movement in the reverse direction; China has received Stinger missiles from Pakistan.

A Confucian-Islamic military connection has thus come into being, designed to promote acquisition by its members of the weapons and weapons technologies needed to counter the military powers of the West. It may or may not last. At present, however, it is, as Dave McCurdy has said, "a renegades' mutual support pact, run by the proliferators and their backers." A new form of arms competition is thus occurring between Islamic-Confucian states and the West. In an old-fashioned arms race, each side developed its own arms to balance or to achieve superiority against the other side. In this new form of arms competition, one side is developing its arms and the other side is attempting not to balance but to limit and prevent that arms build-up while at the same time reducing its own military capabilities.

IX. Implications for the West

This article does not argue that civilization identities will replace all other identities, that nation states will disappear, that each civilization will become a single coherent political entity, that groups within a civilization will not conflict with and even fight each other. This paper does set forth the hypotheses that differences between civilizations are real and important; civilization-consciousness is increasing; conflict between civilizations will supplant ideological and other forms of conflict as the dominant global form of conflict; international relations, historically a game played out within Western civilization, will increasingly be de-Westernized and become a game in which non-Western civilizations are actors and not simply objects; successful political, security and economic international institutions are more likely to develop within civilizations than across civilizations; conflicts between groups in different civilizations will be more frequent, more sustained and more violent than conflicts between groups in the same civilization; violent conflicts between groups in different civilizations are the most likely and most dangerous source of escalation that could lead to global wars; the paramount axis of world politics will be the relations between "the West and the Rest"; the elites in some torn non-Western countries will try to make their countries part of the West, but in most cases face major obstacles to accomplishing this; a central focus of conflict for the immediate future will be between the West and several Islamic-Confucian states.

This is not to advocate the desirability of conflicts between civilizations. It is to set forth descriptive hypotheses as to what the future may be like. If these are plausible hypotheses, however, it is necessary to consider their implications for Western policy. These implications should be divided between short-term advantage and long-term accommodation. In the short term it is clearly in the interest of the West to promote greater cooperation and unity within its own civilization, particularly between its European and North American components; to incorporate into the West societies in Eastern Europe and Latin America whose cultures are close to those of the West; to promote and maintain cooperative relations with Russia and Japan; to prevent escalation of local inter-civilization conflicts into major inter-civilization wars; to limit the expansion of the military strength of Confucian and Islamic states; to moderate the reduction of counter military capabilities and maintain military superiority in East and Southwest Asia; to exploit differences and conflicts among Confucian and Islamic states; to support in other civilizations groups sympathetic to Western values and interests; to strengthen international institutions that reflect and legitimate Western interests and values and to promote the involvement of non-Western states in those institutions.

In the longer term other measures would be called for. Western civilization is both Western and modern. Non-Western civilizations have attempted to become modern without becoming Western. To date only Japan has fully succeeded in this quest. Non-Western civilization will continue to attempt to acquire the wealth, technology, skills, machines and weapons that are part of being modern. They will also attempt to reconcile this modernity with their traditional culture and values. Their economic and military strength relative to the West will increase. Hence the West will increasingly have to accommodate these non-Western modern civilizations whose power approaches that of the West but whose values and interests differ significantly from those of the West. This will require the West to maintain the economic and military power necessary to protect its interests in relation to these civilizations. It will also, however, require the West to develop a more profound understanding of the basic religious and philosophical assumptions underlying other civilizations and the ways in which people in those civilizations see their interests. It will require an effort to identify elements of commonality between Western and other civilizations. For the relevant future, there will be no universal civilization, but instead a world of different civilizations, each of which will have to learn to coexist with the others.

Notes

1. Murray Weidenbaum, *Greater China: The Next Economic Superpower?*, St. Louis: Washington University Center for the Study of American Business, Contemporary Issues, Series 57, February 1993, pp. 2–3.

2. Bernard Lewis, "The Roots of Muslim Rage," *The Atlantic Monthly,* vol. 266, September 1990, p. 60; *Time,* June 15, 1992, pp. 24–28.

3. Archie Roosevelt, *For Lust of Knowing,* Boston: Little, Brown, 1988, pp. 332–333.

4. Almost invariably Western leaders claim they are acting on behalf of "the world community." One minor lapse occurred during the run-up to the Gulf War. In an interview on "Good Morning America," Dec. 21, 1990, British Prime Minister John Major referred to the actions "the West" was taking against Saddam Hussein. He quickly corrected himself and subsequently referred to "the world community." He was, however, right when he erred.

5. Harry C. Triandis, *The New York Times,* Dec. 25, 1990, p. 41, and "Cross-Cultural Studies of Individualism and Collectivism," Nebraska Symposium on Motivation, vol. 37, 1989, pp. 41–133.

6. Kishore Mahbubani, "The West and the Rest," *The National Interest,* Summer 1992, pp. 3–13.

6.3

GREAT POWER POLITICS IN THE TWENTY-FIRST CENTURY

John J. Mearsheimer

John J. Mearsheimer, a preeminent realist scholar, makes the case that the world did not change much after the end of the Cold War. He systematically rejects liberal arguments that international institutions are replacing the state, force is no longer useful, and prosperity matters more than survival, as well as constructivist (identity) arguments that the democratic peace or Gorbachev's New Thinking reduces anarchy to "what states make of it." Power politics, he argues, is alive and well in both northeast Asia and Europe. If America leaves either region, even if relative power does not change much among the local powers, conflict in both regions will become more likely than it is today. And if relative power does shift in the region and a local power tries to achieve hegemony, the United States will be drawn back into the region to balance the hegemon. As an offensive realist, Mearsheimer sees states as striving for hegemony not balance, although global hegemony is made difficult by what he calls "the stopping power of water," meaning the difficulties of projecting power across massive oceans, even in modern times. However, while U.S. hegemony in the western hemisphere is apparently stable, potential hegemony in northeast Asia (currently multipolar) or Europe (currently bipolar) is not. Mearsheimer reflects the realist's ambivalence about whether hegemony or balance stabilizes.

A large body of opinion in the West holds that international politics underwent a fundamental transformation with the end of the Cold War. Cooperation, not security competition and conflict, is now the defining feature of relations among the great powers. Not surprisingly, the optimists who hold this view claim that realism no longer has much explanatory power. It is old thinking and is largely irrelevant to the new realities of world politics. Realists have gone the way of the dinosaurs; they just don't realize it. The best that might be said about theories such as offensive realism is that they are helpful for understanding how great powers interacted before 1990, but they are useless now and for the foreseeable future. Therefore, we need new theories to comprehend the world around us.

Source: John J. Mearsheimer, "Great Power Politics in the Twenty-first Century," in *The Tragedy of Great Power Politics* (New York: Norton, 2001), 360–386.

President Bill Clinton articulated this perspective throughout the 1990s. For example, he declared in 1992 that, "in a world where freedom not tyranny, is on the march, the cynical calculus of pure power politics simply does not compute. It is ill-suited to a new era." Five years later he sounded the same theme when defending the expansion of the North Atlantic Treaty Organization (NATO) to include some of the formerly communist Warsaw Pact states. Clinton argued that the charge that this expansion policy might isolate Russia was based on the belief "that the great power territorial politics of the 20th century will dominate the 21st century," which he rejected. Instead, he emphasized his belief that "enlightened self-interest, as well as shared values, will compel countries to define their greatness in more constructive ways ... and will compel us to cooperate in more constructive ways."[1]

The optimists' claim that security competition and war among the great powers has been burned out of the system is wrong. In fact, all of the major states around the globe still care deeply about the balance of power and are destined to compete for power among themselves for the foreseeable future. Consequently, realism will offer the most powerful explanations of international politics over the next century, and this will be true even if the debates among academic and policy elites are dominated by non-realist theories. In short, the real world remains a realist world.

States still fear each other and seek to gain power at each other's expense, because international anarchy—the driving force behind great-power behavior—did not change with the end of the Cold War, and there are few signs that such change is likely any time soon. States remain the principal actors in world politics and there is still no night watchman standing above them. For sure, the collapse of the Soviet Union caused a major shift in the global distribution of power. But it did not give rise to a change in the anarchic structure of the system, and without that kind of profound change, there is no reason to expect the great powers to behave much differently in the new century than they did in previous centuries.

Indeed, considerable evidence from the 1990s indicates that power politics has not disappeared from Europe and Northeast Asia, the regions in which there are two or more great powers, as well as possible great powers such as Germany and Japan. There is no question, however, that the competition for power over the past decade has been low-key. Still, there is potential for intense security competition among the great powers that might lead to a major war. Probably the best evidence of that possibility is the fact that the United States maintains about one hundred thousand troops each in Europe and in Northeast Asia for the explicit purpose of keeping the major states in each region at peace.

These relatively peaceful circumstances are largely the result of benign distributions of power in each region. Europe remains bipolar (Russia and the United States are the major powers), which is the most stable kind of power structure. Northeast Asia is multipolar (China, Russia, and the United States), a configuration more prone to instability; but fortunately there is no potential hegemon in that system. Furthermore, stability is enhanced in both regions by nuclear weapons, the continued presence of U.S. forces, and the relative weakness of China and Russia. These power structures in Europe and Northeast Asia are likely to change over the next two decades, however, leading to intensified security competition and possibly war among the great powers.

* * *

Persistent Anarchy

The structure of the international system, ... is defined by five assumptions about how the world is organized that have some basis in fact: 1) states are the key actors in world politics and they operate in an anarchic system, 2) great powers invariably have some offensive military capability, 3) states can never be certain whether other states have hostile intentions toward them, 4) great powers place a high premium on survival, and 5) states are rational actors who are reasonably effective at designing strategies that maximize their chances of survival.

These features of the international system appear to be intact as we begin the twenty-first century. The world still comprises states that operate in an anarchic setting. Neither the United Nations nor any other international institution has much coercive leverage over the great powers. Furthermore, virtually every state has at least some offensive military capability, and there is little evidence that world disarmament is in sight. On the contrary, the world arms trade is flourishing, and nuclear proliferation, not abolition, is likely to concern tomorrow's policymakers. In addition, great powers have yet to discover a way to divine each other's intentions. For example, nobody can predict with any degree of certainty what Chinese or German foreign policy goals will be in 2020. Moreover, there is no good evidence that survival is a less important goal for states today than it was before 1990. Nor is there much reason to believe that the ability of great powers to think strategically has declined since the Cold War ended.

* * *

Sovereignty at Bay

Some suggest that international institutions are growing in number and in their ability to push states to cooperate with each other.[2] Specifically, institutions can dampen security competition and promote world peace because they have the capability to get states to reject power-maximizing behavior and to refrain from calculating each important move according to how it affects their position in the balance of power. Institutions, so the argument goes, have an independent effect on state behavior that at least mitigates and possibly might put an end to anarchy.

The rhetoric about the growing strength of international institutions notwith-standing, there is little evidence that they can get great powers to act contrary to the dictates of realism.[3] I know of no study that provides evidence to support that claim. The United Nations is the only worldwide organization with any hope of wielding such power, but it could not even shut down the war in Bosnia between 1992 and 1995, much less push a great power around. Moreover, what little influence the United Nations (UN) holds over states is likely to wane even further in the new century, because its key decision-making body, the Security Council, is sure to grow in size. Creating a larger council, especially one with more permanent members who have a veto over UN policy, would make it virtually impossible to formulate and enforce policies designed to limit the actions of the great powers.

There is no institution with any real power in Asia. Although there are a handful of impressive institutions in Europe, such as NATO and the European Union, there is little evidence that they can compel member states to act against their strategic interests. What is most impressive about international institutions is how little independent effect they seem to have on great-power behavior.

Of course, states sometimes operate through institutions and benefit from doing so. However, the most powerful states in the system create and shape institutions so that they can maintain, if not increase, their own share of world power. Institutions are essentially "arenas for acting out power relationships."[4] When the United States decided it did not want Secretary-General Boutros Boutros-Ghali to head the UN for a second term, it forced him out, despite the fact that all the other members of the Security Council wanted him to stay on the job. The United States is the most powerful state in the world, and it usually gets its way on issues it judges important. If it does not, it ignores the institution and does what it deems to be in its own national interest.

Others argue that the state is being rendered impotent by globalization or by today's unprecedented levels of economic interdependence. In particular, great powers are said to be incapable of dealing with the mighty forces unleashed by global capitalism and are becoming marginal players in world politics.[5] "Where states were once the masters of markets, now it is the markets which, on many crucial issues, are the masters over the governments of states."[6] For some, the key actor in the market is the multinational corporation (MNC), which is seen as threatening to overwhelm the state.[7]

The fact is that the levels of economic transactions among states today, when compared with domestic economic dealings, are probably no greater than they were in the early twentieth century.[8] The international economy has been buffeting states for centuries, and they have proved remarkably resilient in the face of that pressure. Contemporary states are no exception in this regard; they are not being overwhelmed by market forces or MNCs but are making the adjustments necessary to ensure their survival.[9]

Another reason to doubt these claims about the state's impending demise is that there is no plausible alternative on the horizon. If the state disappears, presumably some new political entity would have to take its place, but it seems that nobody has identified that replacement. Even if the state disappeared, however, that would not necessarily mean the end of security competition and war. After all, Thucydides and Machiavelli wrote long before the birth of the state system. Realism merely requires anarchy; it does not matter what kind of political units make up the system. They could be states, city-states, cults, empires, tribes, gangs, feudal principalities, or whatever. Rhetoric aside, we are not moving toward a hierarchic international system, which would effectively mean some kind of world government. In fact, anarchy looks like it will be with us for a long time.

Finally, there is good reason to think that the state has a bright future. Nationalism is probably the most powerful political ideology in the world, and it glorifies the state.[10] Indeed, it is apparent that a large number of nations around the world want their own state, or rather nation-state, and they seem to have little interest in any alternative political arrangement. Consider, for example, how badly the Palestinians want their own state, and before 1948, how desperately the Jews wanted their own state. Now that the Jews have Israel it is unthinkable that they would give it up. If the Palestinians get their own state, they surely will go to great lengths to ensure its survival.

The usual rejoinder to this perspective is to argue that the recent history of the European Union contradicts it. The states of western Europe have largely abandoned nationalism and are well on their way toward achieving political unity, providing powerful evidence that the state system's days are numbered. Although the members of the European Union have certainly achieved substantial economic integration, there is little evidence that this path will lead to the creation of a superstate. In fact, both nationalism and the existing states in western Europe appear to be alive and well. Consider French thinking on the matter, as reflected in the comments of French president Jacques Chirac to the German Bundestag in June 2000: he said that he envisioned a "united Europe of states rather than a United States of Europe."[11] He went on to say, "Neither you nor we envisage the creation of a European superstate that would take the place of our nation states and end their role as actors on the international stage.... In the future, our nations will stay the first reference point for our people." But even if Chirac proves wrong and western Europe becomes a superstate, it would still be a state, albeit a powerful one, operating in a system of states.

Nothing is forever, but there is no good reason to think that the sovereign state's time has passed.

The Futility of Offense

Some suggest that great powers no longer have a meaningful offensive military capability against each other, because great-power war has become prohibitively costly. In essence, war is no longer a useful instrument of statecraft. John Mueller maintains that offense had become too costly for rational leaders even before the advent of nuclear weapons.[12] World War I was decisive proof, he argues, that conventional war among the great powers had degenerated to the point where it was essentially senseless slaughter. The main flaw in this line of argument is that great-power conventional wars do not have to be protracted and bloody affairs. Quick and decisive victories are possible, as Germany demonstrated against France in 1940—which means that great powers can still have a viable offensive capability against one another.

The more persuasive variant of this argument is that nuclear weapons make it almost impossible for great powers to attack each other. After all, it is difficult to imagine winning any kind of meaningful victory in an all-out nuclear war. This argument, too, falls apart on close inspection. There is no question that nuclear weapons significantly reduce the likelihood of great-power war, but ... war between nuclear-armed great powers is still a serious possibility. Remember that during the Cold War, the United States and its NATO allies were deeply worried about a Soviet conventional attack into Western Europe, and after 1979 about a Soviet invasion of Iran. The fact that both superpowers had massive nuclear arsenals apparently did not persuade either side that the other had no offensive military capability.

Certain Intentions

Democratic peace theory is built on the premises that democracies can be more certain of each other's intentions and that those intentions are generally benign; thus they do not fight among themselves.[13] If all the great powers were democracies, each could be certain that the others had friendly intentions, and thus they would have no need to compete for power or prepare for major war. Since democracy appears to be spreading across the globe, it is reasonable to think that the world will eventually become one giant zone of peace.

As challenges to realism go, democratic peace theory is among the strongest. Still, it has serious problems that ultimately make it unconvincing. The theory's proponents maintain that the available evidence shows that democracies do not fight other democracies. But other scholars who have examined the historical record dispute this claim. Perhaps the most telling evidence against the theory is Christopher Layne's careful analysis of four crises in which rival democracies almost went to war with each other.[14] When one looks at how the decision not to fight was reached in each case, the fact that both sides were democracies appears to have mattered little. There certainly is no evidence that the rival democracies had benign intentions toward each other. In fact, the outcome each time was largely determined by balance-of-power considerations.

Another reason to doubt democratic peace theory is the problem of backsliding. No democracy can be sure that another democracy will not someday become an authoritarian state, in which case the remaining democracy would no longer be safe and secure.[15] Prudence dictates that democracies prepare for that eventuality, which means striving to have as much power as possible just in case a friendly neighbor turns into the neighborhood bully. But even if one rejects these criticisms and embraces democratic peace theory, it is still unlikely that all the great powers in the system will become democratic and stay that way over the long term. It would only take a non-democratic China or Russia to keep power politics in play, and both of those states are likely to be non-democratic for at least part of the twenty-first century.[16]

Social constructivists provide another perspective on how to create a world of states with benign intentions that are readily recognizable by other states.[17] They maintain that the way states behave toward each other is not a function of how the material world is structured—as realists argue—but instead is largely determined by how individuals think and talk about international politics. This perspective is nicely captured by Alexander Wendt's famous claim that "anarchy is what states make of it."[18] Discourse, in short, is the motor that drives international politics. But unfortunately, say social constructivists, realism has been the dominant discourse for at least the past seven centuries, and realism tells states to distrust other states and to take advantage of them whenever possible. What is needed to create a more peaceful world is a replacement discourse that emphasizes trust and cooperation among states, rather than suspicion and hostility.

One reason to doubt this perspective is the simple fact that realism *has* dominated the international relations discourse for the past seven centuries or more. Such remarkable staying power over a lengthy period that has seen profound change in almost every other aspect of daily life strongly suggests that the basic structure of the international system—which has remained anarchic over that entire period—largely determines how states think and act toward each other. But even if we reject my materialist interpretation, what is going to cause the reigning discourse about world politics to change? What is the causal mechanism that will delegitimize realism after seven hundred years and put a better substitute in its place? What determines whether the replacement discourse will be benign or malign? What guarantee is there that realism will not rise from the dead and once again become the hegemonic discourse? The social constructivists provide no answers to these important questions, which makes it hard to believe that a marked change in our discourse about international politics is in the offing.[19]

Social constructivists sometimes argue that the end of the Cold War represents a significant triumph for their perspective and is evidence of a more promising future.[20] In particular, they maintain that in the 1980s a group of influential and dovish Western intellectuals convinced Soviet president Mikhail Gorbachev to eschew realist thinking and instead work to foster peaceful relations with the United States and his neighbors in Europe. The result was Soviet withdrawal from Eastern Europe and the end of the Cold War, a Soviet Union with an enlightened foreign policy, and fundamental change in the norms that underpin great-power politics.

Although Gorbachev surely played the key role in ending the Cold War, there are good reasons to doubt that his actions fundamentally transformed international politics.... [H]is decison to liquidate the Soviet empire in Eastern

Europe can be explained by realism. By the mid-1980s, it was clear that the Soviet Union was losing the Cold War and that it had little hope of catching up with the United States, which was in the midst of a massive arms buildup. In particular, the Soviet Union was suffering an economic and political crisis at home that made the costs of empire prohibitive and created powerful incentives to cooperate with the West to gain access to its technology.

Many empires collapsed and many states broke apart before 1989, and many of them sought to give dire necessity the appearance of virtue. But the basic nature of international politics remained unchanged. That pattern certainly appears to be holding up in the wake of the collapse of the Soviet Union. Consider that Gorbachev has been out of office and without much influence in Russia since the early 1990s, and there is little evidence that his "new thinking" about international politics carries much weight inside Russia today.[21] In fact, contemporary Russian leaders view the world largely in terms of power politics, … Moreover, Western leaders, as well as Russia's neighbors in eastern Europe, continue to fear that a resurgent Russia might be an expansionist state, which explains in part why NATO expanded eastward. In sum, it is not true that the collapse of the Soviet Union was unprecedented, that it violated realist conceptions, or that it is a harbinger of a new, post-realist international system.

Survival in the Global Commons

Realist thinking about survival gets challenged in two ways. Proponents of globalization often argue that states today are concerned more with achieving prosperity than with worrying about their survival.[22] Getting rich is the main goal of post-industrial states, maybe even the all-consuming goal. The basic logic here is that if all the great powers are prospering, none has any incentive to start a war, because conflict in today's interdependent world economy would redound to every state's disadvantage. Why torpedo a system that is making everyone rich? If war makes no sense, survival becomes a much less salient concern than realists would have you believe, and states can concentrate instead on accumulating wealth.

There are problems with this perspective, too.[23] In particular, there is always the possibility that a serious economic crisis in some important region, or in the world at large, will undermine the prosperity that this theory needs to work. For example, it is widely believed that Asia's "economic miracle" worked to dampen security competition in that region before 1997, but that the 1997–98 financial crisis in Asia helped foster a "new geopolitics."[24] It is also worth noting that although the United States led a successful effort to contain that financial crisis, it was a close call, and there is no guarantee that the next crisis will not spread across the globe. But even in the absence of a major economic crisis, one or more states might not prosper; such a state would have little to lose economically, and maybe even something to gain, by starting a war. A key reason that Iraqi dictator Saddam Hussein invaded Kuwait in August 1990 was that Kuwait was exceeding its oil production quotas (set by the Organization of

Petroleum Exporting Countries, or OPEC) and driving down Iraq's oil profits, which the Iraqi economy could ill-afford.[25]

There are two other reasons to doubt the claim that economic interdependence makes great-power war unlikely. States usually go to war against a single rival, and they aim to win a quick and decisive victory. Also, they invariably seek to discourage other states from joining with the other side in the fight. But a war against one or even two opponents is unlikely to do much damage to a state's economy, because typically only a tiny percentage of a state's wealth is tied up in economic intercourse with any other state. It is even possible ... that conquest will produce significant economic benefits.

Finally, an important historical case contradicts this perspective. As noted above, there was probably about as much economic interdependence in Europe between 1900 and 1914 as there is today. Those were also prosperous years for the European great powers. Yet World War I broke out in 1914. Thus a highly interdependent world economy does not make great-power war more or less likely. Great powers must be forever vigilant and never subordinate survival to any other goal, including prosperity.

Another challenge to the realist perspective on survival emphasizes that the dangers states face today come not from the traditional kind of military threats that realists worry about, but instead from non-traditional threats such as AIDS, environmental degradation, unbounded population growth, and global warming.[26] Problems of this magnitude, so the argument goes, can be solved only by the collective action of all the major states in the system. The selfish behavior associated with realism, on the other hand, will undermine efforts to neutralize these threats. States surely will recognize this fact and cooperate to find workable solutions.

This perspective raises two problems. Although these dangers are a cause for concern, there is little evidence that any of them is serious enough to threaten the survival of a great power. The gravity of these threats may change over time, but for now they are at most second-order problems.[27] Furthermore, if any of these threats becomes deadly serious, it is not clear that the great powers would respond by acting collectively. For example, there may be cases where the relevant states cooperate to deal with a particular environmental problem, but an impressive literature discusses how such problems might also lead to inter-state war.[28]

In sum, claims that the end of the Cold War ushered in sweeping changes in the structure of the international system are ultimately unpersuasive. On the contrary, international anarchy remains firmly intact, which means that there should not have been any significant changes in great-power behavior during the past decade.

Great-Power Behavior in the 1990s

The optimists' contention that international politics has undergone a great transformation applies mainly to relations among the great powers, who are no longer supposed to engage in security competition and fight wars with each other, or with minor powers in their region. Therefore, Europe and Northeast Asia, the areas that feature clusters of great powers, should be zones of peace, or what Karl Deutsch famously calls "pluralistic security communities."[29]

Optimists do not argue, however, that the threat of armed conflict has been eliminated from regions without great powers, such as 1) the South Asian sub-continent, where India and Pakistan are bitter enemies armed with nuclear weapons and caught up in a raging dispute over Kashmir; 2) the Persian Gulf, where Iraq and Iran are bent on acquiring nuclear weapons and show no signs of becoming status quo powers; or 3) Africa, where seven different states are fighting a war in the Democratic Republic of the Congo that some are calling "Africa's first world war."[30] Nor do optimists claim that great powers no longer fight wars with states in these troubled regions; thus, the American-led war against Iraq in early 1991 is not evidence against their position. In short, great powers are not yet out of the war business altogether, only in Europe and Northeast Asia.

There is no question that security competition among the great powers in Europe and Northeast Asia has been subdued during the 1990s, and with the possible exception of the 1996 dispute between China and the United States over Taiwan, there has been no hint of war between any of the great powers. Periods of relative peacefulness like this one, however, are not unprecedented in history. For example, there was little open conflict among the great powers in Europe from 1816 through 1852, or from 1871 through 1913. But this did not mean then, and it does not mean now, that the great powers stopped thinking and behaving according to realist logic. Indeed, there is substantial evidence that the major states in Europe and Northeast Asia still fear each other and continue to worry about how much relative power they control. Moreover, sitting below the surface in both regions is significant potential for intense security competition and possibly even war among the leading states.

Security Competition in Northeast Asia

In the large literature on security issues in Northeast Asia after the Cold War, almost every author recognizes that power politics is alive and well in the region, and that there are good reasons to worry about armed conflict involving the great powers.[31]

The American experience in the region since 1991 provides considerable evidence to support this pessimistic perspective. The United States came close to fighting a war against North Korea in June 1994 to prevent it from acquiring nuclear weapons.[32] War still might break out between North and South Korea, in which case the United States would automatically become involved, since it has 37,000 troops stationed in South Korea to help counter a North Korean invasion. If such a war happened, American and South Korean forces would probably trounce the invading North Korean army, creating an opportunity for them to strike north of the 38th parallel and unify the two Koreas.[33] This is what happened in 1950, prompting China, which shares a border with North Korea, to feel threatened and go to war against the United States. This could plausibly happen again if there is a second Korean war.

One might argue that the Korean problem is likely to go away soon, because relations are improving between the two Koreas, and there is actually a reasonable chance they will reunify in the decade ahead. Although future relations between North and South Korea are difficult to predict, both sides are still poised to fight a major war along the border separating them, which remains the most heavily armed strip of territory in the world. Moreover, there is hardly any evidence—at least at this point—that North Korea intends to surrender its independence and become part of a unified Korea. But even if reunification happens, there is no reason to think that it will enhance stability in Northeast Asia, because it will surely create pressures to remove American troops from Korea and will also revive competition among China, Japan, and Russia for influence in Korea.

Taiwan is another dangerous place where China and the United States could end up in a shooting war.[34] Taiwan appears determined to maintain its de facto independence from China, and possibly to gain de jure independence, while China seems equally determined to reincorporate Taiwan into China. In fact, China has left little doubt that it would go to war to prevent Taiwanese independence. The United States, however, is committed to help Taiwan defend itself if it is attacked by China, a scenario which could plausibly lead to American troops fighting with Taiwan against China. After all, between July 1995 and March 1996, China fired live missiles into the waters around Taiwan and conducted military exercises off the coast of its Fujian province, just across the strait from Taiwan. China rattled its saber because it thought that Taiwan was taking major steps toward independence. The United States responded by sending two aircraft-carrier battle groups into the waters around Taiwan. Fortunately, the crisis ended peacefully.

The Taiwan problem, however, shows no signs of going away. China is deploying large numbers of missiles (ballistic and cruise) in Fujian province, and it is procuring aircraft and naval ships from Russia that might some day make it risky for the United States to deploy naval forces in the region during a crisis. Furthermore, China issued a document in February 2000 in which it said that it was prepared to go to war before it would allow "the Taiwan issue to be postponed indefinitely."[35] Immediately thereafter, China and the United States exchanged thinly disguised nuclear threats.[36] Taiwan, for its part, is shopping for new weapons to counter China's growing arsenal, while remaining determined to maintain its independence from China. The United States could therefore get pulled into war with China over both Korea and Taiwan.

More needs to be said about China, the principal great-power rival of the United States in Northeast Asia. Many Americans may think that realism is outmoded thinking, but this is not how China's leaders view the world. According to one prominent Sinologist, China "may well be the high church of realpolitik in the post–Cold War world."[37] This is not surprising when you consider China's history over the past 150 years and its present threat environment. It shares borders, a number of which are still disputed, with thirteen different states. China fought over territory with India in 1962, the Soviet Union in 1969, and Vietnam in 1979. All of these borders are still contested. China also claims ownership of Taiwan, the Senkaku/Diaoyutai Islands, and various island groups in the South China Sea, many of which it does not now control.[38]

Furthermore, China tends to view both Japan and the United States as potential enemies. Chinese leaders maintain a deep-seated fear that Japan will become militaristic again, like it was before 1945. They also worry that the United States is bent on preventing China from becoming the dominant great power in Northeast Asia. "Many Chinese foreign- and defense-policy analysts," according to one scholar, "believe that U.S. alliances with Asian countries, particularly with Japan, pose a serious, long-term challenge, if not a threat, to China's national security, national unification, and modernization."[39]

It is worth noting that China's relations with Japan and the United States have gotten worse—not better—since the end of the Cold War.[40] All three states were aligned against the Soviet Union during the 1980s, and they had little cause to fear each other. Even Taiwan was not a major source of friction between China and the United States during the last decade of the Cold War. But times have changed for the worse since 1990, and now China fears Japan and the United States, who, in turn, worry about China. For example, in the immediate aftermath of the Cold War, Japan was confident that growing economic interdependence in Asia would allow it to maintain peaceful relations with China for the indefinite future.[41] By the mid-1990s, however, Japanese views about China had "hardened considerably," and showed evidence of "an anxious realism about China's strategic intentions."[42]

China certainly has not been quick to employ military force over the past decade, although it has demonstrated more than once that it is willing to employ the sword to achieve particular political goals. Besides the missile firings and military maneuvers during the Taiwan crisis, Chinese military forces in early 1995 seized Mischief Reef, one of the disputed Spratly Islands claimed by the Philippines. These incidents notwithstanding, the Chinese military has limited power-projection capability, and therefore it cannot be too aggressive toward other states in the region.[43] For example, China does not have the wherewithal to defeat and conquer Taiwan in a war. To rectify that problem, however, China has embarked on a major military modernization program. Indeed, China decided this year (2001) to increase its defense spending by 17.7 percent, which represents its largest expansion in real terms in the last two decades.[44]

Another indicator of security competition in Northeast Asia is the region's burgeoning arms race in missile technology.[45] North Korea has been developing and testing ballistic missiles throughout the 1990s, and in August 1998 it fired a missile over Japan. In response to the growing North Korean missile threat, South Korea is making moves to increase the range of its own ballistic missiles, while Japan and the United States are moving to build a "theater missile defense" (TMD) system to protect Japan as well as American forces stationed in the region. The United States is also determined to build a "national missile defense" (NMD) system to protect the American homeland from nuclear attacks by small powers such as North Korea. China, however, has made it clear that if Japan and the United States deploy missile defenses of any kind, it will markedly increase its arsenal of ballistic missiles so that it can overwhelm them.

Independent of these developments, China is deploying large numbers of missiles opposite Taiwan, which, not surprisingly, is now trying to acquire defensive systems from the United States. But if the United States aids Taiwan, especially if it helps Taiwan develop its own TMD system, China is sure to increase its arsenal of missiles, which would force the United States to upgrade its TMD system in the region, which would force China to build more missiles, and so on. How all this missile-building will play out over time is difficult to predict, but the key point is that an arms race centered on ballistic missiles is already underway in Asia and shows few signs of abating.

Finally, the fact that the United States maintains one hundred thousand troops in Northeast Asia contradicts the claim that the region is "primed for peace."[46] If that were so, those U.S. forces would be unnecessary and they could be sent home and demobilized, saving the American taxpayer an appreciable sum of money. Instead, they are kept in place to help pacify a potentially volatile region.

Joseph Nye, one of the main architects of post–Cold War American policy in Northeast Asia and a scholar with a well-established reputation as a liberal international-relations theorist (not a realist), made this point in an important 1995 article in *Foreign Affairs*.[47] "It has become fashionable," he notes, "to say that the world after the Cold War has moved beyond the age of power politics to the age of geoeconomics. Such clichés reflect narrow analysis. Politics and economics are connected. International economic systems rest upon international political order." He then makes the "pacifier" argument: "The U.S. presence [in Asia] is a force for stability, reducing the need for arms buildups and deterring the rise of hegemonic forces." Not only do "forward-deployed forces in Asia ensure broad regional stability," they also "contribute to the tremendous political and economic advances made by the nations of the region." In short, "the United States is the critical variable in the East Asia security equation."[48]

Security Competition in Europe

Europe might appear to be a better place than Northeast Asia to make the optimists' case, but on close inspection the evidence shows that security competition and the threat of great-power war remain facts of life in Europe, too. Consider the series of wars that have been fought in the Balkans in the 1990s, and that the United States and its European allies have twice been directly involved in the fighting. American airpower was used against Serb ground forces in Bosnia during the summer of 1995, helping to end the fighting in that embattled country. In the spring of 1999, NATO went to war against Serbia over Kosovo. It was a minor conflict for sure, but the fact remains that in the years since the Cold War ended, the United States has fought a war in Europe, not in Northeast Asia.

The evolution of Russian foreign policy during the 1990s provides further evidence that realism still has a lot to say about inter-state relations in Europe. After the Soviet Union collapsed, it was widely believed that Russia's new leaders would follow in Mikhail Gorbachev's footsteps and eschew the selfish pursuit of power, because they recognized that it made Russia less, not more, secure. Instead, they would work with the United States and its NATO allies to create a peaceful order that reached across all of Europe.

But this is not what has happened. NATO's actions in the Balkans and its expansion eastward have angered and scared the Russians, who now view the world clearly through realist lenses and do not even pay lip service to the idea of working with the West to build what Gorbachev called "a common European home."[49] Russia's hardheaded view of its external environment is reflected in "The National Security Concept of the Russian Federation," a seminal policy document that Russian president Vladimir Putin signed on January 10, 2000. "The formation of international relations," it states, "is accompanied by competition and also by the aspiration of a number of states to strengthen their influence on global politics, including by creating weapons of mass destruction. Military force and violence remain substantial aspects of international relations."[50]

Russia also made it clear in 1993 that it would initiate nuclear war if its territorial integrity was threatened, thus abandoning the Soviet Union's longstanding pledge not to be the first state to use nuclear weapons in a war.[51] Russia's military weakness, however, sharply limits what it can do outside of its borders to challenge the United States over issues such as NATO expansion and NATO policy in the Balkans. Nevertheless, Russia's actions in the breakaway republic of Chechnya make clear that it is willing to wage a brutal war if it thinks its vital interests are threatened.[52]

More evidence that great-power war remains a serious threat in Europe arises from the fact that the United States maintains one hundred thousand troops in the region, and its leaders often emphasize the importance of keeping NATO intact. If Europe is "primed for peace," as many claim, NATO would surely be disbanded and American forces would be sent home. Instead, they are kept in place. In fact, NATO has moved eastward and incorporated the Czech Republic, Hungary, and Poland into its ranks. Why? Because there is potential for dangerous security competition in Europe, and the United States is determined to keep the forces of trouble at bay. Otherwise why would it be spending tens of billions of dollars annually to maintain a large military presence in Europe?

There is considerable evidence that the pacifier argument is widely accepted among policymakers and scholars on both sides of the Atlantic. For example, President Clinton told the West Point graduating class of 1997, "Some say we no longer need NATO because there is no powerful threat to our security now. I say there is no powerful threat in part because NATO is there."[53] That same year, Secretary of State Madeleine Albright told the U.S. Senate at her confirmation hearing, "We have an interest in European security, because we wish to avoid the instability that drew five million Americans across the Atlantic to fight in two world wars."[54] It appears that many Europeans also believe in the pacifier argument. Between 1990 and 1994, Robert Art conducted more than one hundred interviews with European political-military elites. He found that most believed that "if the Americans removed their security blanket from Europe ... the Western European states could well return to the destructive power politics that they had just spent the last forty-five years trying to banish from their part of the continent."[55] Presumably that perspective is even more tightly held today, since the early 1990s was the heyday of optimism about the prospects for peace in Europe.

Finally, it is worth noting that Art, Michael Mandelbaum, and Stephen Van Evera, all prominent scholars who believe that Europe is primed for peace, favor keeping American troops there and maintaining a formidable NATO. Might it be that they are ultimately guided by pacifier logic, not their stated belief that great-power war is no longer a danger in Europe?[56]

Structure and Peace in the 1990s

There is no question that the presence of U.S. troops in Europe and Northeast Asia has played an important role in moderating security competition and promoting stability over the past decade. But periods of relative peace in those regions cannot be explained simply by the presence or absence of American forces. After all, there were no U.S. troops in Europe during the nineteenth century, yet there were long periods of relative peace. Moreover, even if the United States had committed military forces to Europe in the late 1930s, there still would have been intense security competition among the great powers, and Nazi Germany might have started a major war anyway.

To understand why the great powers were so tame in the 1990s, it is necessary to consider the overall distribution of power in each area, which means determining how much power is controlled by each major state in the region, as well as by the United States. In essence, we need to know whether the system is bipolar or multipolar, and if it is multipolar, whether it is unbalanced by the presence of a potential hegemon. Bipolar systems ... tend to be the most peaceful, whereas unbalanced multipolar systems are the most prone to conflict. Balanced multipolar systems fall somewhere in between.

Europe remains bipolar in the wake of the Cold War, with Russia and the United States as the region's principal rivals. There are three particular aspects of Europe's bipolarity that make it especially stable. First, both Russia and the United States are armed with nuclear weapons, which are a force for peace. Second, the United States behaves as an offshore balancer in Europe, acting primarily as a check on any local great power that tries to dominate the region. It has no hegemonic aspirations beyond the Western Hemisphere, which significantly reduces the threat it presents to the states of Europe.[57] Third, Russia, which is a local great power that might have territorial ambitions, is too weak militarily to cause serious trouble outside of its own borders.[58]

Northeast Asia, on the other hand, is now a balanced multipolar system; China, Russia, and the United States are the relevant great powers, and none has the markings of a potential hegemon. Balanced multipolarity tends to be less stable than bipolarity, but the same three factors that enhanced the prospects for peace in bipolar Europe do likewise in multipolar Northeast Asia. First, China, Russia, and the United States all have nuclear arsenals, which makes them less likely to initiate war with each other. Second, although the United States is clearly the most powerful actor in the region, it is an offshore balancer without territorial aspirations. Third, neither the Chinese nor the Russian military has much power-projection capability, making it difficult for them to behave aggressively toward other states in the area.

There are two possible objections to my description of how power is distributed in Europe and Northeast Asia. Some might argue that the post–Cold War world is unipolar, which is another way of saying that the United States is a global hegemon.[59] If true, there would be hardly any security competition in Europe and Northeast Asia, because there would be no great powers in those areas—by definition—to challenge the mighty United States. This is certainly the state of affairs in the Western Hemisphere, where the United States is the only great power, and it is not involved in security competition with any of its neighbors. Canada and Mexico, for example, pose no military threat whatsoever to the United States. Nor does Cuba, which is a minor political irritant, not a serious threat to American security.

But the international system is not unipolar.[60] Although the United States is a hegemon in the Western Hemisphere, it is not a global hegemon. Certainly the United States is the preponderant economic and military power in the world, but there are two other great powers in the international system: China and Russia. Neither can match American military might, but both have nuclear arsenals, the capability to contest and probably thwart a U.S. invasion of their homeland, and limited power-projection capability. They are not Canada and Mexico.

Furthermore, hardly any evidence indicates that the United States is about to take a stab at establishing global hegemony. It certainly is determined to remain the hegemon in the Western Hemisphere, but given the difficulty of projecting power across large bodies of water, the United States is not going to use its military for offensive purposes in either Europe or Northeast Asia. Indeed, America's allies worry mainly that U.S. troops will be sent home, not that they will be used for conquest. This lack of a hegemonic impulse outside the confines of the Western Hemisphere explains why no balancing coalition has formed against the United States since the Cold War ended.[61]

Others might argue that America's allies from the Cold War—the United Kingdom, France, Germany, Italy, and Japan—should count as great powers, an accounting that would produce markedly different power distributions in Europe and Northeast Asia. There is little doubt that these states, especially Germany and Japan, have the potential in terms of population and wealth to become great powers. They do not qualify for that ranking, however, because they depend in large part on the United States for their security; they are effectively semi-sovereign states, not great powers. In particular, Germany and Japan have no nuclear weapons of their own and instead rely on the American nuclear deterrent for protection.

In addition, America's allies have little maneuver room in their foreign policy, because of the presence of U.S. troops on their territory. The United States continues to occupy Western Europe and to dominate NATO decision-making, much the way it did during the Cold War, not only making war among its members unlikely, but also making it difficult for any of those states (especially Germany) to cause trouble with Russia.[62] Finally, the United States continues to maintain a formidable military presence in Japan, making it difficult for that potentially powerful state to engage in serious security competition with China.

In sum, a good deal of evidence indicates that power politics has not been stamped out of Europe and Northeast Asia, and that there is potential for serious trouble involving the great powers. Nevertheless, both regions have been largely free of intense security competition and great-power war during the 1990s. The taproot of that stability is the particular distribution of power that has emerged in each area since the Cold War ended and the Soviet Union collapsed. The question we must now ask is whether the structure of power in each of those regions is likely to remain intact over the next two decades.

* * *

Trouble Ahead

Predicting what the distribution of power will look like in Europe and Northeast Asia by 2020 involves two closely related tasks: 1) reckoning the power levels of the main actors located in each region, paying special attention to whether there is a potential hegemon among them; and 2) assessing the likelihood that the United States will remain militarily engaged in those regions, which depends largely on whether there is a potential hegemon among the local great powers that can be contained only with American help. It is difficult to predict the balance of power in a region, because it depends in good part on determining how fast each state's economy will grow, as well as its long-term political viability. Unfortunately, we do not have theories that can anticipate economic and political developments with high confidence. For example, it is hard to know how powerful the Chinese and Russian economies will be in 2020, or whether China will survive as a single political entity or break apart like the Soviet Union.

It is still possible, however, to make informed judgments about the architectures that are likely to emerge in Europe and Northeast Asia over the next twenty years. We can start with the conservative assumption that there will be no fundamental change in the *relative* wealth or political fortunes of the principal states in each region. In other words, the existing distribution of potential power remains essentially intact for the next two decades. Alternatively, we can assume significant change in state capabilities, focusing on the most weighty scenarios in each region, such as the complete collapse of Russian power or China's transformation into an economic superpower. The future of the American military presence in each region will depend on whether there is a potential hegemon.

I believe that the existing power structures in Europe and Northeast Asia are not sustainable through 2020. Two alternative futures loom on the horizon, both of which are likely to be less peaceful than the 1990s. If there is no significant change in the relative wealth or the political integrity of the key states located in each region, the United States is likely to bring its troops home, because they will not be needed to contain a potential hegemon. Removing American forces from either region, however, would change the structure of power in ways that would make conflict more likely than it is today. The structural change would be greater in Europe than in Northeast Asia, as would the likelihood of intensified security competition.

But if fundamental economic or political change occurs in either region and a potential hegemon emerges that the local powers cannot contain, U.S. troops are likely to remain in place or come back to the region to balance against that threat. Should that happen, an intense security competition would likely ensue between the potential hegemon and its rivals, including the United States. In short, either the United States will leave Europe or Northeast Asia because it does not have to contain an emerging peer competitor, in which case the region would becomes less stable, or the United States will stay engaged to contain a formidable rival in what is likely to be a dangerous situation. Either way, relations between the great powers are likely to become less peaceful than they were during the 1990s.

* * *

Notes

1. William J. Clinton, "American Foreign Policy and the Democratic Ideal," campaign speech, Pabst Theater, Milwaukee, WI, October 1, 1992; "In Clinton's Words: 'Building Lines of Partnership and Bridges to the Future,'" *New York Times,* July 10, 1997. Rhetoric aside, Clinton's foreign policy was largely consistent with the predictions of realism. See Stephen M. Walt, "Two Cheers for Clinton's Foreign Policy," *Foreign Affairs* 79, No. 2 (March–April 2000), pp. 63–79.

2. See the sources cited in Chapter 1, note 25. [David A. Baldwin, ed., *Neorealism and Neoliberalism: The Contemporary Debate* (New York: Columbia University Press, 1993); Robert O. Keohane, *After Hegemony: Cooperation and Discord in the World Political Economy* (Princeton, NJ: Princeton University Press, 1984); *International Organization* 36, No. 2 (Spring 1982, special issue on "International Regimes," ed. Stephen D. Krasner); Lisa L. Martin and Beth A. Simmons, "Theories and Empirical Studies of International Institutions," *International Organization* 52, No. 4 (Autumn 1998), pp. 729–57; and John G. Ruggie, *Constructing the World Polity: Essays on International Institutionalization* (New York: Routledge, 1998), chaps. 8–10.]

3. See Joseph Grieco, "Anarchy and the Limits of Cooperation: A Realist Critique of the Newest Liberal Institutionalism," *International Organization* 42, No. 3 (Summer 1988), pp. 485–507; Stephen D. Krasner, "Global Communications and National Power: Life on the Pareto Frontier," *World Politics* 43, No. 3 (April 1991), pp. 336–66; John J. Mearsheimer, "The False Promise of International Institutions," *International Security* 19, No. 3 (Winter 1994–95), pp. 5–49; John J. Mearsheimer, "A Realist Reply," *International Security* 20, No. 1 (Summer 1995), pp. 82–93; and Baldev Raj Nayer, "Regimes, Power, and International Aviation," *International Organization* 49, No. 1 (Winter 1995), pp. 139–70. It is worth noting that in a recent survey of the international institutions literature by two prominent institutionalists, little evidence is provided that institutions have caused states to alter their behavior in fundamental ways. See Lisa L. Martin and Beth A. Simmons, "Theories and Empirical Studies of International Institutions," *International Organization* 52, No. 4 (Autumn 1998), pp. 729–57.

4. Tony Evans and Peter Wilson, "Regime Theory and the English School of International Relations: A Comparison," *Millennium: Journal of International Studies* 21, No. 3 (Winter 1992), p. 330. Also see Lloyd Gruber, *Ruling the World: Power Politics and the Rise of Supranational Institutions* (Princeton, NJ: Princeton University Press, 2000).

5. Prominent examples of this perspective include Philip G. Cerny, "Globalization and the Changing Logic of Collective Action," *International Organization* 49, No. 4 (Autumn 1995), pp. 595–625; William Greider, *One World, Ready or Not: The Manic Logic of Global Capitalism* (New York: Simon and Schuster, 1997); Kenichi Ohmae, *The End of the Nation State: The Rise of Regional Economies* (New York: Free Press, 1996); Saskia Sassen, *Losing Control? Sovereignty in an Age of Globalization* (New York: Columbia University Press, 1995); and Walter B. Wriston, *The Twilight of Sovereignty: How the Information Revolution is Transforming Our World* (New York: Scribner's, 1992).

6. Susan Strange, *The Retreat of the State: The Diffusion of Power in the World Economy* (Cambridge: Cambridge University Press, 1996), p. 4.

7. See Richard J. Barnet and John Cavanagh, *Global Dreams: Imperial Corporations and the New World Order* (New York: Simon and Schuster, 1994); and David C. Korten, *When Corporations Rule the World* (West Hartford, CT: Kumarian Press, 1995). Similar claims about the dominating influence of multinational corporations were heard in the 1970s. See Raymond Vernon, *Sovereignty at Bay: The Multinational Spread of U.S. Enterprises* (New York: Basic Books, 1971). For the case against Vernon, see Robert Gilpin, *U.S. Power and the Multinational Corporation: The Political Economy of Foreign Direct Investment* (New York: Basic Books, 1975).

8. See Paul Hirst and Grahame Thompson, *Globalization in Question: The International Economy and the Possibilities of Governance,* 2d ed. (Cambridge: Polity Press, 1999); Janice E. Thomson and Stephen D. Krasner, "Global Transactions and the Consolidation of Sovereignty," in Ernst-Otto Czempiel and James N. Rosenau, eds., *Global Changes and Theoretical Challenges: Approaches to World Politics for the 1990s* (Lexington, MA: Lexington Books, 1989), pp. 195–219; and Robert Wade, "Globalization and Its Limits: Reports of the Death of the National Economy Are Greatly Exaggerated," in Suzanne Berger and Ronald Dore, eds., *National Diversity and Global Capitalism* (Ithaca, NY: Cornell University Press, 1996), pp. 60–88.

9. See Paul N. Doremus et al., *The Myth of the Global Corporation* (Princeton, NJ: Princeton University Press, 1998); Geoffrey Garrett, "Global Markets and National Politics: Collision Course or Virtuous Circle?" *International Organization* 52, No. 4 (Autumn 1998), pp. 787–824; Eric Helleiner, *States and the Reemergence of Global Finance: From Bretton Woods to the 1990s* (Ithaca, NY: Cornell University Press, 1994); Ethan B. Kapstein, *Governing the Global Economy: International Finance and the State* (Cambridge, MA: Harvard University Press, 1994); Stephen D. Krasner, *Sovereignty: Organized Hypocrisy* (Princeton, NJ: Princeton University Press, 1999); Steven K. Vogel, *Freer Markets, More Rules: Regulatory Reform in Advanced Industrial Countries* (Ithaca, NY: Cornell University Press, 1996); Linda Weiss, *The Myth of the Powerless State* (Ithaca, NY: Cornell University Press, 1998); and "The Future of the State," *Economist,* Special Supplement, September 20, 1997.

10. These points are clearly reflected in almost all the seminal works on nationalism. See, for example, Benedict Anderson, *Imagined Communities: Reflections on the Origins and Spread of Nationalism,* rev. ed. (London: Verso, 1991); Walker Connor, *Ethnonationalism* (Princeton, NJ: Princeton University Press, 1993); Ernest Gellner, *Nations and Nationalism* (Ithaca, NY: Cornell University Press, 1983); and Anthony D. Smith, *The Ethnic Origins of Nations* (New York: Blackwell, 1989).

11. All quotes in this paragraph are from Suzanne Daley, "French Leader, in Berlin, Urges a Fast Track to Unity in Europe," *New York Times,* June 28, 2000. Also see Suzanne Daley, "French Premier Opposes German Plan for Europe," *New York Times,* May 29, 2001; and William A. Hay, "Quiet Quake in Europe: The French and the Germans Divide," Foreign Policy Research Institute's *Watch on the West* 1, No. 9 (October 2000).

12. John Mueller, *Retreat from Doomsday: The Obsolescence of Major War* (New York: Basic Books, 1989). Also see Michael Mandelbaum, "Is Major War Obsolete?" *Survival* 40, No. 4 (Winter 1998–99), pp. 20–38.

13. See the works cited in Chapter 1, note 24. [Michael E. Brown, Sean M. Lynn-Jones, and Steven E. Miller, eds., *Debating the Democratic Peace* (Cambridge, MA: MIT Press, 1996), pts. I and III; Michael Doyle, "Liberalism and World Politics," *American Political Science Review* 80, No. 4 (December 1986), pp. 1151–69; Francis Fukuyama, "The End of History?" *The National Interest*, No. 16 (Summer 1989), pp. 3–18; John M. Owen IV, *Liberal Peace, Liberal War: American Politics and International Security* (Ithaca, NY: Cornell University Press, 1997); James L. Ray, *Democracy and International Conflict: An Evaluation of the Democratic Peace Proposition* (Columbia: University of South Carolina Press, 1995); and Bruce Russett, *Grasping the Democratic Peace: Principles for a Post–Cold War World* (Princeton, NJ: Princeton University Press, 1993).]

14. Christopher Layne, "Kant or Cant: The Myth of the Democratic Peace," *International Security* 19, No. 2 (Fall 1994), pp. 5–49. Other key works challenging democratic peace theory include Michael E. Brown, Sean M. Lynn-Jones, and Steven E. Miller, eds., *Debating the Democratic Peace* (Cambridge, MA: MIT Press, 1996), pts. 2–3; Miriam Fendius Elman, ed., *Paths to Peace: Is Democracy the Answer?* (Cambridge, MA: MIT Press, 1997); Miriam Fendius Elman, "The Never-Ending Story: Democracy and Peace," *International Studies Review* 1, No. 3 (Fall 1999), pp. 87–103; and Joanne Gowa, *Ballots and Bullets: The Elusive Democratic Peace* (Princeton, NJ: Princeton University Press, 1999).

15. For evidence of backsliding, see Samuel P. Huntington, *The Third Wave: Democratization in the Late Twentieth Century* (Norman: University of Oklahoma Press, 1991), chaps. 5–6; and Juan J. Linz and Alfred Stepan, eds., *The Breakdown of Democratic Regimes: Crisis, Breakdown, and Reequilibration* (Baltimore, MD: Johns Hopkins University Press, 1978).

16. Markus Fischer, in "The Liberal Peace: Ethical, Historical, and Philosophical Aspects," BCSIA Discussion Paper 2000–07 (Cambridge, MA: John F. Kennedy School of Government, Harvard University, April 2000), discusses the difficulty of creating and sustaining liberal democracy around the world.

17. The key work in this genre is Alexander Wendt, *Social Theory of International Politics* (Cambridge: Cambridge University Press, 1999). For other important social constructivist tracts, see the sources cited in Mearsheimer, "False Promise," p. 37 (n. 128). Also see Peter J. Katzenstein, ed., *The Culture of National Security: Norms and Identity in World Politics* (New York: Columbia University Press, 1996); John G. Ruggie, *Constructing the World Polity: Essays on International Institutionalization* (New York: Routledge, 1998); and John G. Ruggie, "What Makes the World Hang Together? Neo-Utilitarianism and the Social Constructivist Challenge," *International Organization* 52, No. 4 (Autumn 1998), pp. 855–85.

18. Alexander Wendt, "Anarchy Is What States Make of It: The Social Construction of Power Politics," *International Organization* 46, No. 2 (Spring 1992), pp. 391–425.

19. For further elaboration of my critique of social constructivism, see Mearsheimer, "False Promise," pp. 37–47; and Mearsheimer, "Realist Reply," pp. 90–92.

20. See the works cited in Chapter 6, note 86. [Jeffrey T. Checkel, *Ideas and International Political Change: Soviet/Russian Behavior and the End of the Cold War* (New Haven, CT: Yale University Press, 1997); Matthew Evangelista, *Unarmed Forces: The Transnational Movement to End the Cold War* (Ithaca, NY: Cornell University Press, 1999); Robert G. Herman, "Identity, Norms, and National Security: The Soviet Foreign Policy Revolution and the End of the Cold War," in Peter J. Katzenstein, ed., *The Culture of National Security: Norms and Identity in World Politics* (New York: Columbia University Press, 1996), pp. 271–316; and Richard Ned Lebow and Thomas W. Risse-Kappen, eds., *International Relations Theory and the End of the Cold War* (New York: Columbia University Press, 1995).]

21. For Gorbachev's views, see Mikhail Gorbachev, *Perestroika: New Thinking for Our Country and the World* (New York: Harper and Row, 1987).

22. See the sources listed in Chapter 1, note 23. [Norman Angell, *The Great Illusion: A Study of the Relation of Military Power in Nations to Their Economic and Social Advantage,* 3d rev. and enl. ed. (New York: G. P. Putnam's, 1912); Thomas L. Friedman, *The Lexus and the Olive Tree: Understanding Globalization* (New York: Farrar, Straus and Giroux, 1999); Edward D. Mansfield, *Power, Trade, and War* (Princeton, NJ: Princeton University Press, 1994); Susan M. McMillan, "Interdependence and Conflict," *Mershon International Studies Review* 41, Suppl. 1 (May 1997), pp 33–58; and Richard Rosecrance, *The Rise of the Trading State: Commerce and Conquest in the Modern World* (New York: Basic Books, 1986.)

23. See *inter alia* Katherine Barbieri, "Economic Interdependence: A Path to Peace or a Source of Interstate Conflict?" *Journal of Peace Research 33,* No. 1 (February 1996), pp. 29–49; Barry Buzan, "Economic Structure and International Security: The Limits of the Liberal Case," *International Organization* 38, No. 4 (Autumn 1984), pp. 597–624; Dale C. Copeland, "Economic Interdependence and War: A Theory of Trade Expectations," *International Security* 20, No. 4 (Spring 1996), pp. 5–41; Norrin M. Ripsman and Jean-Marc F. Blanchard, "Commercial Liberalism under Fire: Evidence from 1914 and 1936," *Security Studies* 6, No. 2 (Winter 1996–97), pp. 4–50; David M. Rowe, "World Economic Expansion and National Security in Pre–World War I Europe," *International Organization* 53, No. 2 (Spring 1999), pp. 195–231; and Kenneth N. Waltz, "The Myth of National Interdependence," in Charles P. Kindelberger, ed., *The International Corporation* (Cambridge, MA: MIT Press, 1970), pp. 205–23.

24. Paul Dibb, David D. Hale, and Peter Prince," Asia's Insecurity," *Survival* 41, No. 3 (Autumn 1999), pp. 5–20. Also see Robert A. Manning and James J. Przystup, "Asia's Transition Diplomacy: Hedging against Futureshock," *Survival* 41, No. 3 (Autumn 1999), pp. 43–67. For a discussion of the fragility of the contemporary world economy, see Robert Gilpin, *Global Capitalism: The World Economy in the 21st Century* (Princeton, NJ: Princeton University Press, 2000).

25. See "The Glaspie Transcript: Saddam Meets the U.S. Ambassador," in Micah L. Sifry and Christopher Cerf, eds., *The Gulf War Reader: History, Documents, Opinions* (New York: Times Books, 1991), pp. 122–33.

26. For examples of this perspective, see Hilary French, *Vanishing Borders: Protecting the Planet in the Age of Globalization* (New York: Norton, 2000); Carl Kaysen, Robert A. Pastor, and Laura W. Reed, eds., *Collective Responses to Regional*

Problems: The Case of Latin America and the Caribbean (Cambridge, MA: American Academy of Arts and Sciences, 1994); Ronnie D. Lipschutz and Ken Conca, eds., *The State and Social Power in Global Environmental Politics* (New York: Columbia University Press, 1993); Ronnie D. Lipschutz, "Reconstructing World Politics: The Emergence of Global Civil Society," *Millennium: Journal of International Studies* 21, No. 3 (Winter 1992), pp. 389–420; Jessica Tuchman Matthews, ed., *Preserving the Global Environment: The Challenge of Shared Leadership* (New York: Norton, 1991); Paul Wapner, *Environmental Activism and World Civic Politics* (Albany: State University of New York Press, 1996); and World Commission on Environment and Development, *Our Common Future* (Oxford: Oxford University Press, 1987).

27. See Julian L. Simon, ed., *The State of Humanity* (Cambridge, MA: Blackwell, 1995); and Julian L. Simon, *The Ultimate Resource 2* (Princeton, NJ: Princeton University Press, 1996).

28. See Nazli Choucri and Robert C. North, *Nations in Conflict: National Growth and International Violence* (San Francisco: W. H. Freeman, 1975); William H. Durham, *Scarcity and Survival in Central America: Ecological Origins of the Soccer War* (Stanford, CA: Stanford University Press, 1979); Peter H. Gleick, "Water and Conflict: Fresh Water Resources and International Security," *International Security* 18, No. 1 (Summer 1993), pp. 79–112; Thomas F. Homer-Dixon, *Environment, Scarcity, and Violence* (Princeton, NJ: Princeton University Press, 1999); and Arthur H. Westing, ed., *Global Resources and International Conflict: Environmental Factors in Strategic Policy and Action* (Oxford: Oxford University Press, 1986).

29. Karl W. Deutsch et al., *Political Community and the North Atlantic Area: International Organization in the Light of Historical Experience* (Princeton, NJ: Princeton University Press, 1957), pp. 5–9.

30. Ian Fisher and Norimitsu Onishi, "Many Armies Ravage Rich Land in the 'First World War' of Africa," *New York Times,* February 6, 2000.

31. See, for example, the many articles on Asian security published over the past decade in *Foreign Affairs, International Security,* and *Survival.* Some of the best pieces from *International Security* are published in Michael E. Brown, Sean M. Lynn-Jones, and Steven E. Miller, eds., *East Asian Security* (Cambridge, MA: MIT Press, 1996).

32. See Leon V. Sigal, *Disarming Strangers: Nuclear Diplomacy with North Korea* (Princeton, NJ: Princeton University Press, 1998); and Don Oberdorfer, *The Two Koreas: A Contemporary History* (New York: Basic Books, 1997), chaps. 11–13.

33. For the best net assessments of the military balance on the Korean Peninsula, see Nick Beldecos and Eric Heginbotham, "The Conventional Military Balance in Korea," *Breakthroughs* 4, No. 1 (Spring 1995), pp. 1–8; and Michael O'Hanlon, "Stopping a North Korean Invasion: Why Defending South Korea Is Easier Than the Pentagon Thinks," *International Security* 22, No. 4 (Spring 1998), pp. 135–70.

34. On the Taiwan problem, see Bernice Lee, *The Security Implications of the New Taiwan,* Adelphi Paper No. 331 (London: International Institute for Strategic Studies, October 1999); James R. Lilley and Chuck Downs, eds., *Crisis in the Taiwan Strait* (Washington, DC: National Defense University Press, 1997); Denny Roy, "Tension in the Taiwan Strait," *Survival* 42, No. 1 (Spring 2000), pp. 76–96; Andrew Scobell, "Show of Force: The PLA and the 1995–1996 Taiwan Strait

Crisis," discussion paper (Stanford, CA: Asia/Pacific Research Center, Stanford University, January 1999); and Suisheng Zhao, ed., *Across the Taiwan Strait: Mainland China, Taiwan, and the 1995–1996 Crisis* (New York: Routledge, 1999).

35. Taiwan Affairs Office and the Information Office of the State Council, People's Republic of China, "The One-China Principle and the Taiwan Issue," February 21, 2000.

36. In response to China's white paper, the U.S. undersecretary of defense warned China that it would face "incalculable consequences" if it attacked Taiwan. Steven Mufson and Helen Dewar, "Pentagon Issues Warning to China: U.S. Officials Criticize Beijing White Paper Backing Use of Force against Taiwan," *Washington Post,* February 23, 2000. Shortly thereafter, China's official military newspaper emphasized that China "is a country that has certain abilities of launching strategic counterattack and the capacity of launching a long-distance strike." Bill Gertz, "China Threatens U.S. with Missile Strike," *Washington Times,* February 29, 2000. China made a similar threat in January 1996. See Patrick E. Tyler, "China Threatens Taiwan, It Makes Sure U.S. Listens," *New York Times,* January 24, 1996.

37. Thomas J. Christensen, "Chinese Realpolitik," *Foreign Affairs* 75, No. 5 (September–October 1996), p. 37. Also see Alastair Iain Johnston, *Cultural Realism: Strategic Culture and Grand Strategy in Chinese History* (Princeton, NJ: Princeton University Press, 1995); and Andrew J. Nathan and Robert S. Ross, *The Great Wall and the Empty Fortress: China's Search for Security* (New York: Norton, 1997).

38. Mark J. Valencia, *China and the South China Sea Disputes,* Adelphi Paper No. 298 (London: International Institute for Strategic Studies, October 1995).

39. Yu Bin, "Containment by Stealth: Chinese Views of and Policies toward America's Alliances with Japan and Korea after the Cold War," discussion paper (Stanford, CA: Asia/Pacific Research Center, Stanford University, September 1999), p. 5. Also see Richard Bernstein and Ross H. Munro, "China I: The Coming Conflict with America," *Foreign Affairs* 76, No. 2 (March–April 1997), pp. 18–32; Thomas J. Christensen, "China, the U.S.–Japan Alliance, and the Security Dilemma in East Asia," *International Security* 23, No. 4 (Spring 1999), pp. 49–80; Christensen, "Chinese Realpolitik," pp. 37–52; Michael Pillsbury, *China Debates the Future Security Environment* (Washington, DC: National Defense University Press, 2000); David Shambaugh, "China's Military Views the World: Ambivalent Security," *International Security* 24, No. 3 (Winter 1999–2000), pp. 52–79; Allen S. Whiting, *China Eyes Japan* (Berkeley: University of California Press, 1989); and Jianwei Wang and Xinbo Wu, "Against Us or with Us? The Chinese Perspective of America's Alliances with Japan and Korea," discussion paper (Stanford, CA: Asia/Pacific Research Center, Stanford University, May 1998).

40. Bin, "Containment by Stealth," p. 7; and David Shambaugh, "Sino-American Strategic Relations: From Partners to Competitors," *Survival* 42, No. 1 (Spring 2000), pp. 97–115.

41. See Yoichi Funabashi, "Japan and the New World Order," *Foreign Affairs* 70, No. 5 (Winter 1991–92), pp. 58–74.

42. Michael J. Green, "The Forgotten Player," *National Interest,* No. 60 (Summer 2000), pp. 44–45. Also see Benjamin L. Self, "Japan's Changing China Policy," *Survival* 38, No. 2 (Summer 1996), pp. 35–58; and Gerald Segal, "The Coming

Confrontation between China and Japan?" *World Policy Journal* 10, No. 2 (Summer 1993), pp. 27–32.

43. On Chinese military weakness, see Bates Gill and Michael O'Hanlon, "China's Hollow Military," *National Interest,* No. 56 (Summer 1999), pp. 55–62; Robert S. Ross, "China II: Beijing as a Conservative Power," *Foreign Affairs* 76, No. 2 (March–April 1997), pp. 33–44; and Gerald Segal, "Does China Matter?" *Foreign Affairs* 78, No. 5 (September–October 1999), pp. 24–36. For a contrasting view, see James Lilley and Carl Ford, "China's Military: A Second Opinion," *National Interest,* No. 57 (Fall 1999), pp. 71–77. Thomas Christensen argues that China will have the capability to challenge American interests in Asia even if it remains a relatively weak military power. See Christensen, "Posing Problems without Catching Up: China's Rise and Challenges for U.S. Security Policy," *International Security* 25, No. 4 (Spring 2001), pp. 5–40.

44. See John Pomfret, "China Plans Major Boost in Defense Spending for Military," *Washington Post,* March 6, 2001. Also see James C. Mulvenon and Richard H. Yang, eds., *The People's Liberation Army in the Information Age* (Santa Monica, CA: RAND Corporation, 1999); Mark A. Stokes, *China's Strategic Modernization: Implications for the United States* (Carlisle Barracks, PA: Strategic Studies Institute, U.S. Army War College, 1999); and Michael Swaine, "Chinese Military Modernization and Asian Security," discussion paper (Stanford, CA: Asia/Pacific Research Center, Stanford University, August 1998).

45. Paul Bracken, *Fire in the East: The Rise of Asian Military Power and the Second Nuclear Age* (New York: HarperCollins, 1999). For more general discussions of the arms buildup in the region see Kent E. Calder, *Asia's Deadly Triangle: How Arms, Energy and Growth Threaten to Destabilize the Asia-Pacific* (London: Nicholas Brealey, 1997); and Tim Huxley and Susan Willett, *Arming East Asia,* Adelphi Paper No. 329 (London: International Institute of Strategic Studies, July 1999).

46. The phrase "primed for peace" was coined by Stephen Van Evera to describe post-Cold War Europe. See Stephen Van Evera, "Primed for Peace: Europe after the Cold War," *International Security* 15, No. 3 (Winter 1990–91), pp. 7–57.

47. Joseph S. Nye, Jr., "East Asian Security: The Case for Deep Engagement," *Foreign Affairs* 74, No. 4 (July–August 1995), pp. 90–102. The quotes in this paragraph are from pp. 90–91, 102. Also see Department of Defense, *United States Security Strategy for the East Asia–Pacific Region* (Washington, DC: U.S. Department of Defense February 1995); and Department of Defense, *The United States Security Strategy for the East Asia–Pacific Region: 1998* (Washington, DC: U.S. Department of Defense, November 1998). This perspective enjoys wide support on both sides of the Pacific. See, for example, United States Commission on National Security/21st Century, *New World Coming: American Security in the 21st Century,* Phase I Report (Washington, DC: U.S. Commission on National Security, September 15, 1999), p. 82. One notable exception is Chalmers Johnson and E. B. Keehn, "East Asian Security: The Pentagon's Ossified Strategy," *Foreign Affairs* 74, No. 4 (July–August 1995), pp. 103–14.

48. The argument that the United States can serve as a "pacifier" in regions such as Europe and Northeast Asia was first laid out in Josef Joffe, "Europe's American Pacifier," *Foreign Policy,* No. 54 (Spring 1984), pp. 64–82.

49. Gorbachev, *Perestroika*, pp. 194–95.

50. The document was originally published in *Nezavisimoye Voennoye Obozreniye* on January 14, 2000. For key translated excerpts, from which this quote is taken, see "Russia's National Security Concept," *Arms Control Today* 30, No. 1 (January–February 2000), pp. 15–20. For a discussion of the evolution of Russian thinking about security during the 1990s, see Celeste A. Wallander, "Wary of the West: Russian Security Policy at the Millennium," *Arms Control Today* 30, No. 2 (March 2000), pp. 7–12. It should be emphasized, however, that rhetoric aside, Russia has been acting like a traditional great power since the early 1990s. See the sources cited in Mearsheimer, "False Promise," p. 46 (n. 175, 176).

51. See Serge Schmemann, "Russia Drops Pledge of No First Use of Atom Arms," *New York Times,* November 4, 1993. NATO, which has always rejected a no-first-use policy regarding nuclear weapons, remains firmly wedded to that policy. For example, the "NATO Alliance Strategic Concept," which was approved by the North Atlantic Council on April 24, 1999, states that "the Alliance's conventional forces alone cannot ensure credible deterrence. Nuclear weapons make a unique contribution in rendering the risks of aggression against the Alliance incalculable and unacceptable. Thus they remain essential to preserve peace.... They demonstrate that aggression of any kind is not a rational option."

52. Russian public opinion polls from November 1999 show that 85 percent of the population believe that Russia must once again become a "great empire." Only 7 percent disagree. Michael Wines, "Russia Pines for a New Savior: Victory," *New York Times,* November 21, 1999, Sec. 4.

53. William J. Clinton, "Commencement Address," United States Military Academy, West Point, NY, May 31, 1997.

54. Madeleine Albright, prepared statement before the U.S. Senate Foreign Relations Committee, Washington, DC, January 8, 1997.

55. Robert J. Art, "Why Western Europe Needs the United States and NATO," *Political Science Quarterly* 111, No. 1 (Spring 1996), pp. 5–6. The views of Christoph Bertram, a former director of the International Institute for Strategic Studies in London and one of Germany's foremost strategic thinkers, are also instructive on this point. He wrote in 1995 that "to disband NATO now would throw Europe into deep insecurity.... It would be a strategic disaster." He goes on to say that "if the United States turned its back on Europe, NATO would collapse and the European Union would be strained to the point of disintegration. Germany would stand out as the dominant power in the West of the continent, and Russia as the disturbing power in the East. The United States would lose much of its international authority as well as the means to help prevent European instability from igniting international conflict once again." Bertram, *Europe in the Balance: Securing the Peace Won in the Cold War* (Washington, DC: Carnegie Endowment for International Peace, 1995), pp. 17–18, 85. Also see pp. 10–11.

56. Regarding their views on the obsolescence of great-power war in Europe, see Robert J. Art, "A Defensible Defense: America's Grand Strategy after the Cold War," *International Security* 15, No. 4 (Spring 1991), pp. 45–46; Mandelbaum, "Is Major War Obsolete?"; and Van Evera, "Primed for Peace." For evidence that they are influenced by the pacifier argument, see Art, "Why Western Europe," esp. pp. 4–9,

35–39; Michael Mandelbaum, *The Dawn of Peace in Europe* (New York: Twentieth Century Fund, 1996), esp. chaps. 1, 9; Van Evera, "Primed for Peace," pp. 16, 54–55; and Stephen Van Evera, "Why Europe Matters, Why the Third World Doesn't: American Grand Strategy after the Cold War," *Journal of Strategic Studies* 13, No. 2 (June 1990), pp. 9–11.

57. President Clinton put this point well when he noted that although there are good reasons to be critical of American foreign policy in the twentieth century, "no one suggests that we ever sought territorial advantage." President William J. Clinton, "Remarks to the American Society of Newspaper Editors Regarding the Situation in Kosovo," San Francisco, CA, April 15, 1999.

58. On the diminished state of the Russian military, see Alexei G. Arbatov, "Military Reform in Russia: Dilemmas, Obstacles, and Prospects," *International Security* 22, No. 4 (Spring 1998), pp. 83–134; Robert W. Duggleby, "The Disintegration of the Russian Armed Forces," *Journal of Slavic Studies* 11, No. 2 (June 1998), pp. 1–24; and Sergey Rogov, *Military Reform and the Defense Budget of the Russian Federation* (Alexandria, VA: Center for Naval Analyses, August 1997).

59. Charles Krauthammer, "The Unipolar Moment," *Foreign Affairs* 70, No. 1 (Winter 1990–91), pp. 23–33; Michael Mastanduno, "Preserving the Unipolar Moment: Realist Theories and U.S. Grand Strategies after the Cold War," *International Security* 21, No. 4 (Spring 1997), pp. 49–88; and William C. Wohlforth, "The Stability of a Unipolar World," *International Security* 24, No. 1 (Summer 1999), pp. 5–41.

60. For an interesting discussion of this point, see Samuel P. Huntington, "The Lonely Superpower," *Foreign Affairs* 78, No. 2 (March–April 1999), pp. 35–49. Also see Christopher Layne, "The Unipolar Illusion: Why New Great Powers Will Rise," *International Security* 17, No. 4 (Spring 1993), pp. 5–51; and Kenneth N. Waltz, "The Emerging Structure of International Politics," *International Security* 18, No. 2 (Fall 1993), pp. 44–79. Wohlforth, who makes the most compelling case for unipolarity, defines it as "a structure in which one state's capabilities are too great to be counterbalanced." Wohlforth, "Stability," p. 9. Although I agree with that definition, I take issue with his assessment that China and Russia do not have the wherewithal to stand up to the United States.

61. China and Russia have been on friendly terms in recent years, and both have made clear their displeasure with different aspects of American foreign policy. But they have not formed a serious balancing coalition against the United States, and few believe that they will do so in the future. See Jennifer Anderson, *The Limits of Sino-Russian Strategic Partnership,* Adelphi Paper No. 315 (London: International Institute for Strategic Studies, December 1997); Mark Burles, *Chinese Policy toward Russia and the Central Asian Republics* (Santa Monica, CA: RAND Corporation, 1999); and "Can a Bear Love a Dragon?" *Economist,* April 26, 1997, pp. 19–21. Also, there is a potential source of serious trouble between China and Russia: large-scale illegal immigration from China into Russia for the past decade, which could lead to ethnic conflict or territorial disputes. See David Hale, "Is Asia's High Growth Era Over?" *National Interest,* No. 47 (Spring 1997), p. 56; and Simon Winchester, "On the Edge of Empires: Black Dragon River," *National Geographic,* February 2000, pp. 7–33.

62. Many argue that it is difficult to imagine security competition, much less war, between France and Germany. The current happy situation, however, did not come about because those longtime rivals, who fought wars against each other in 1870–71, 1914–18, and 1940, suddenly learned to like and trust each other in 1945. The presence of a large American army in Western Europe since World War II has made it almost impossible for France and Germany to fight with each other and thus has eliminated the main cause of fear between them. In essence, hierarchy replaces anarchy in areas directly controlled by U.S. forces. Josef Joffe puts the point well: "Only the permanent intrusion of the United States into the affairs of the Continent changed the terms of state interaction to the point where West Europeans no longer had to conduct their business in the brooding shadow of violence. By promising to protect Western Europe against others and against itself, the United States swept aside the rules of the self-help game that had governed and regularly brought grief to Europe in centuries past." Joffe, "Europe's American Pacifier," p. 72.

Chapter 7

TERRORISM AND THE WORLD AFTER 9/11: RELIGIOUS, ETHNIC, AND NATIONAL CONFLICTS

7.1

FEMINIST PERSPECTIVES ON 9/11

J. Ann Tickner

> In this reflection on the 9/11 attacks, feminist scholar J. Ann Tickner explores the gendered images and definitions that project war as masculine and peace as feminine. 9/11, she fears, reinforced these stereotypes. She rejects both Occidentalist views in the Muslim world that regard the emancipation of women as leading to decadence and Orientalist views in the western world that portray women as religiously and culturally subordinate. For Tickner, gender is a socially constructed role, not a biological one. Seeking to recover lost voices, she calls for engagement between men and women and between Muslims and Westerners to discover the wide variety of possible gender roles for both men and women. "It is the degree of exclusion from economic and political participation," she emphasizes, "that fuels unrest and gender stereotyping." As critical theory, this feminist assessment of 9/11 portrays the problem as deepseated but surmountable through discourse and a broad process of consciousness-raising.

Gendered Images

Gendered images are everywhere, many of them threatening. Osama bin Laden taunts the West for becoming feminized; Francis Fukuyama is concerned about it too. In a 1998 article in *Foreign Affairs*, Fukuyama, although more positive than bin Laden about what they both see as the feminization of Western

Source: J. Ann Tickner, "Feminist Perspectives on 9/11," *International Studies Perspectives* 3, no. 4 (2002): 333–350.

culture, pointed to similar dangers. He counseled against putting women in charge of U.S. foreign policy and the military because of their inability to stand up to unspecified dangers (perhaps more specific since 9/11) from "those [non-democratic] parts of the world run by young, ambitious, unconstrained men," (Fukuyama, 1998:36, 38). Five years earlier, Samuel Huntington (1993) warned of a "clash of civilizations," an only slightly veiled reference to a demographically exploding Islam, a "fault line" between Western Christian societies that have progressed in terms of economic development and democratization, and the Muslim world where young men's frustrations are fuelled by the failure of these same phenomena.[1]

For others the danger is closer to home; the "real" fault lines are here in the United States. In a 1994 article that lauded Huntington's clash of civilizations thesis, James Kurth focused attention on the "real clash," an internal one. Extolling the rise of Western civilization and the Enlightenment, a secular society based on individualism, liberalism, constitutionalism, human rights, the rule of law, free markets, and the separation of church and state, which came of age at the beginning of the twentieth century, Kurth saw the Enlightenment in decline at the century's end. What he termed "post-industrialism" has moved women into the labor market and out of the home with negative consequences for children, particularly those reared in split family or single-parent households. The U.S. is, according to Kurth, threatened not only by feminism, which bears the responsibility for the liberation of women, but also by multiculturalism—the presence, and recognition, of large numbers of African-Americans, Latino Americans, and Asian Americans who, unlike earlier immigrant populations, remain unassimilated in terms of Western liberal ideas (Kurth, 1994:14).[2]

The fears of these scholars, and Fukuyama's solution—to keep strong men in charge—may seem more real today than when they were first articulated. And post-9/11 discourse has produced some strange bedfellows! As bin Laden goads America for its moral decadency and lack of manliness, Jerry Falwell and Pat Robertson blamed 9/11 on the ACLU, homosexuals, and feminists because they "make God mad" (Scheer, 2001a). The terrorists are those unconstrained young men, some of whom have managed to live among us rather than "out there" beyond the fault line. So, contra bin Laden, masculinity is back in vogue in the United States. Since 9/11, "the male hero has been a predominant cultural image, presenting a beefy front of strength to a nation seeking steadiness and emotional grounding. They are the new John Waynes ... men who charge up the stairs in a hundred pounds of gear, and tell everyone else where to go to be safe."[3] In spite of the Bush administration's appointment of the first female National Security Adviser, our TV screens after 9/11 were full of (mostly white) men in charge briefing us about "America's New War" both at home and abroad. We feel safer when "our men" are protecting us (against other men) and our way of life.

So where did all the women go? According to an analysis by the British newspaper *The Guardian,* women virtually disappeared from newspaper pages and

TV screens after 9/11.[4] Carol Gilligan notes that men's rising star all but eclipsed that of the many heroic women who rose to the occasion, be they firefighters or police officers.[5] Women were also amongst our combat forces deployed against Afghanistan where male warriors waving guns and shouting death to America looked menacing and unrestrained. If we did see women they were likely to be faceless Afghan women in the now familiar blue *burqa*. Their shadowy and passive presence seemed only to reinforce these gendered images I have drawn.[6]

Yet the picture is more complicated. Bin Laden taunts the West for its feminization but he also rails against its "crusaders," an image more likely to invoke mediaeval knights on horseback than modern-day "feminized" men about whom Fukuyama, as well as bin Laden, is concerned. And the masculinity of bin Laden's own foot soldiers has also come under scrutiny. Mohamed Atta, whose last will and testament banned women from his grave lest they pollute it, was "a polite shy boy who came of age in an Egypt torn between growing Western influence and the religious fundamentalism that gathered force in reaction, ... [he] had two sisters headed for careers as a professor and a doctor." Grumbling that his wife was raising him as a girl, his father is reputed to have "told him [Atta] I needed to hear the word 'doctor' in front of his name.... We told him your sisters are doctors ... and you are the man of the family."[7]

And, contra Fukuyama's and Kurth's fears about the feminized weakening of America, American women supported the war effort in overwhelming numbers while Afghan women beneath the burqa protested American bombing and exhorted their sisters to fight against gender oppression. World order scholar Richard Falk (2001) called the war the first just war since World War II,[8] and the U.S. Catholic bishops gave it qualified support on the same grounds (Cooperman, 2001) while realist John Mearsheimer (2001) counseled against it. Liberals, such as Laurence Tribe, condoned the use of military tribunals and the detention of more than 1,200 young men, none of whom (as of December 2001) had been charged in connection with the attacks.[9]

So, if the story is not a simple one where gender and other ideological lines are firmly drawn, what can a feminist analysis add to our understanding of 9/11 and its aftermath? ... [W]ar both reinforces gender stereotypes and shakes up gender expectations (Goldstein, 2002).... [G]ender is a powerful legitimator of war and national security; our acceptance of a "remasculinized" society during times of war and uncertainty rises considerably. And the power of gendered expectations and identifications have real consequences for women and for men, consequences that are frequently ignored by conventional accounts of war and civilizational clashes.

* * *

Defining Gender

... I define gender as a set of variable, but socially and culturally constructed relational characteristics. Those, such as power, autonomy, rationality, activity, and public are stereotypically associated with masculinity; their opposites, weakness, dependence, emotionality, passivity, and private are associated with femininity. There is evidence to suggest that both women and men assign a more positive value to the masculine characteristics which denote a culturally dominant ideal type, or "hegemonic" masculinity, to which few men actually conform; nevertheless, they do define what men ought to be.[10] It is important to note that gendered social relationships are relationships of power; it is through these hierarchical relationships that male power and female subordination are sustained, albeit in various degrees across time and place. Most feminists consider gendered relationships as social constructions because the specific content of these contrasted characteristics change over time and place; this allows for the possibility of female emancipation.

Gender distinctions can also be used to reinforce the power of dominant groups: minorities, and "outsiders," are frequently characterized by dominant groups as lacking in these hegemonic masculine characteristics. Gender is not, as is so often claimed, synonymous with women and feminine identities; it is also about men and masculine identities and, more important, about relations between men and women. Gender serves to legitimate certain activities and ways of thinking over others; it privileges certain societal tasks over others and assigns certain people, depending on their sex, to undertake them. The consequences for women (and for men) and for society more generally are significant. Nowhere are these gender lines more firmly drawn than in how societies view and conduct war.

Gendering War and Peace

George Patton's claim—that war gives purpose to life, evident in post-9/11 political discourse—is one that has been widely shared by both women and men. Whereas wars frequently energize societies and foster a communal and self-sacrificial spirit among women and men alike, war-fighting is an activity that has been undertaken almost exclusively by men.

In his book *War and Gender,* Joshua Goldstein questions why we have not been more curious about this fact. In an exhaustive cross-cultural investigation of wars throughout history, Goldstein finds no biological evidence for why men are almost always the fighters; instead, he attributes it to cultural socialization. "Cultures mold males into warriors by attaching to 'manhood' those qualities that make good warriors" (Goldstein, 2001:252).[11] The toughening up of boys is found across cultures and many cultures use gender to motivate participation in combat (Goldstein, 2001:406). Warriors require intense socialization in order to fight effectively (Goldstein, 2001:252).

While Goldstein finds it remarkable that this association between masculinity and war has received so little attention from scholars who write about war, war as a masculine activity has been central to feminist investigations (Stiehm, 1983; Elshtain, 1987; Enloe, 1993, 2000). Generally supporting Goldstein's claims about militarized masculinity, feminists have suggested that "military manhood," or a type of heroic masculinity that goes back to ancient Greece, attracts recruits and maintains self-esteem in institutions where obedience is the norm. The term "patriot" is frequently associated with service in military combat. The National Organization for Women's (NOW) support for women entering the U.S. military was based on the argument that, if women were barred from participation in the armed forces on an equal footing with men, they would remain second-class citizens denied the unique political responsibility of risking one's life for the state (Jones, 1990). The lack of ability to serve in combat has also acted as a handicap for women running for political office in the United States.

The notion that (young) males fight wars to protect vulnerable people, such as women and children who cannot be expected to protect themselves, has also been an important motivator for the recruitment of military forces. "Protection" has been an important myth that has sustained support for war by both men and women.[12] I use the term "myth" because the large number of civilian casualties in recent wars severely strains the credibility of female protection.

If war is a phenomenon we associate with men and "hegemonic" masculinity, peace is a term we stereotypically associate with women and some of the devalued feminine characteristics I outlined earlier. As Jean Elshtain (1987:230) has suggested, we are afraid to let go of war because we fear even more the prospects of a sterile peace. Peace is frequently seen as an ideal, and even uninteresting, state with little chance of success in the "real" world. Women have been linked to anti-war sentiment throughout history and most peace movements have been disproportionately populated by women. Indeed, many of these movements have drawn inspiration from maternal imagery to craft their strategies. Yet I believe that the association of women with peace renders both women and peace as idealistic, utopian, and unrealistic; it is profoundly disempowering for both. And as long as peace remains associated with women, this may reinforce militarized masculinity (Goldstein, 2001:413).

The association of men with the "realities" of war and women with an "idealistic" notion of peace reinforces the gender hierarchies I outlined earlier. The consequences of this gender hierarchy are real in that it reinforces men's legitimacy and helps sustain their continued dominance in world politics; it also serves to perpetuate the barriers that women face in gaining legitimacy in foreign and military policymaking, particularly in times of conflict. In most societies, women's under-representation in international security matters and the military cannot be explained by legal barriers alone. I shall now suggest some consequences of these gender stereotypes for our post-9/11 world.

Gendering 9/11
America Under Attack

"This is the warriors' time, the warriors, the martyrs—they're all men."[13] Those we fear today are angry young men wielding rifles and shouting death to America. Many of them were trained in madrassas—religious schools that teach little except an extreme version of Islam to boys and young men; many of them come from refugee camps where they live in poverty with few prospects in life. Frequently, they are also taught to hate women; in a situation where most of them feel powerless, the wielding of power over women can be a boost to self-esteem. Although Mohamed Atta's middle-class background does not fit this profile, this training must have alleviated his sense of inferiority with respect to the women in his own domestic life.

According to Ian Buruma and Avishai Margalit (2002), this newest form of "Occidentalism," evident in the teaching of madrassas, comes out of a long, warlike tradition of hatred of the West, a hatred that appeals to those who feel impotent, marginalized, and denigrated. Tracing its roots back to nineteenth-century Russia and mid-twentieth-century Japan, they suggest that the objects of hate associated with Occidentalism, all of which played a significant role in the attacks of September 11, are materialism, liberalism, capitalism, rationalism, and feminism. All these phenomena are epitomized in city life with its multiculturalism, wealth, sexual license, and artistic freedom which result in decadence and moral laxity. The twin towers, as powerful symbols of urban secular wealth, were an apt target for vengeance against these evils. Gender symbolism, and gender ambivalence borne out of misogyny, abounds in this discourse; the West is described as individualist, rational, and hard but, at the same time, decadent, effete, and addicted to personal safety at the expense of valuing the heroic self-sacrifice expected of "real men." Today's Occidentalists taunt the West with accusations of moral decadence in this world, yet promise sexual rewards for their men in heaven after their sacrificial death for the cause.

For Occidentalists, it is women's emancipation that leads to decadence. "Westoxification" denotes a plague from the West. Those most vulnerable are women, particularly middle-class women with a Western education; these women must be brought under control and conform to an idealized construct of womanhood (Moghadan, 1994:13). The proper role for women is to be breeders of heroic men. For the Taliban, Occidental sinfulness was present even in Kabul with "girls in school and women with uncovered faces populating and defiling the public domain" (Buruma and Margalit, 2002:5). The ideational and material consequences of this misogynist discourse was brought home to us through the post-9/11 media focus on the plight of women in Afghanistan. But we must remember that it is not only those "out there" who engage in oppositional thinking with its negative gender stereotyping.

America Strikes Back

America may have surprised these warriors with the determination of its response. Belying bin Laden's taunts and Fukuyama's fear that the U.S. is becoming feminized and thus less able to defend itself, the U.S. military response was swift and strong; it received high approval ratings from men and women alike.[14] From the start, policymakers framed the attack and the U.S. response as a war between good and evil—the message to the rest of the world was that you are either for us or against us—there is no middle position. Random attacks on innocent people, identified by their attackers as Muslim, immediately following 9/11, which the Bush administration went to lengths to denounce, manifested an unpleasant form of Orientalism.

Given the massive sense of insecurity generated by the first foreign terrorist attack on American civilians at home, there is something reassuring about "our men" protecting us from "other men."[15] However, even though the war exceeded all expectations in its swift destruction of the Taliban and al Qaeda networks, and despite increased attention to homeland security, the U.S. remains uncertain about its ability to deter future terrorist attacks.

In light of these continued fears, the U.S. Congress passed the USA Patriot Act, legislation that allows the Attorney General to detain aliens on mere suspicion and without a hearing. Prior to its passage, the U.S. had already detained more than 1,200 young men without charge; Arab men have been subject to ethnic, as well as gender, profiling under the excuse that we are "at war." These measures have received strong support from across the political spectrum. Criticism is seen as unpatriotic.[16] Equally disturbing is a political climate, typical of countries at war, that fosters intolerance of alternative points of view. Illustrations of this intolerance have been prevalent in media discussion as well as in political discourse.

In an article in the *New York Times,* Edward Rothstein (2001) articulated his hope that the attacks of September 11 might challenge the intellectual and ethical perspectives of postmodernism and postcolonialism thus leading to their rejection. Chastising adherents to these modes of thought for their extreme cultural relativism and rejection of objectivity and universalism, Rothstein expressed hope that, as it comes to be realized how closely the 9/11 attacks came to undermining the political and military authority of the U.S., these ways of thinking will come to be seen as "ethically perverse."

While the author did not mention feminism, feminists are frequently criticized on the same terms; women and feminists often get blamed in times of political, economic, and social uncertainty. Kurth's fear of feminists' destruction of the social fabric of society is one such example and the association of patriotism with "hegemonic" masculinity challenges women, minorities, and "aliens" to live up to this standard. It is the case that postcolonialists and feminists have questioned objectivity and universalism; but they do so because they claim these terms are frequently associated with ways of knowing that are not objective but based only on the lives of (usually privileged) men. Many feminists are sympathetic with postcolonialism, a body of knowledge that attempts to uncover the voices of those who have been colonized and oppressed. It is a form of knowledge-seeking that resonates with attempts to recover knowledge about women.

In a rather different piece, which acknowledged the recognition accorded to women of Afghanistan since 9/11, Sarah Wildman (2001) chastised American feminists on the grounds of irrelevance. Claiming that feminists have an unprecedented public platform because of the attention focused on women in Afghanistan,

Wildman accused them of squandering their opportunity by refusing to support the war. Equating what she called "feminist dogma" with pacifism, Wildman asserted that there is no logical reason to believe that nonviolent means always promote feminist ends. Wildman has fallen into the essentialist trap of equating feminism with peace which I discussed earlier; this has allowed her to dismiss feminist voices as irrelevant and unpatriotic. The feminists she selected to quote may have voiced reservations about the war, but feminism encompasses a wide range of opinions many of which include fighting for justice, particularly gender justice. And feminist voices are not all Western as is often assumed. In Afghanistan, women have been fighting a war that began well before September 11, a war against women.

Women Under Attack

After November 17, when Laura Bush used the president's weekly radio address to urge worldwide condemnation of the treatment of women in Afghanistan, a speech that coincided with a State Department report on the Taliban's war against women, their plight has been in the headlines in the U.S. (Stout, 2001). Although the war is not new, women in Afghanistan have not always been so oppressed. Prior to the Soviet invasion in 1979, women had been gaining rights; they had served in Parliament and in the professions and even as army generals. In 1970, 50 percent of students at Kabul University, 60 percent of teachers, and 40 percent of doctors in Afghanistan were women (Prosser, 2001). Frequently, however, steps forward precipitated a backlash from traditional and rural communities (Amiri, 2002). In 1989, Arab militants, working with the Afghan resistance to the Soviet Union based in Peshawar, Pakistan, issued a *fatwa,* or religious ruling, stating that Afghan women would be killed if they worked for humanitarian organizations. Subsequently Afghan women going to work were shot at and several were murdered. Soon after, another edict forbade Afghan women to "walk with pride" or walk in the middle of the street. This was followed by an edict in 1990, consistent with Occidentalism, that decreed that women should not be educated; if they were, the Islamic movement would be tainted and thus meet with failure.

According to Human Rights Watch (2001), and supported by the Revolutionary Association of the Women of Afghanistan (RAWA), the various parties that made up the United Front or Northern Alliance amassed a deplorable record of attacks on civilians during the civil war that took place in Afghanistan between 1992 and 1996, including the widespread rape of women. The Taliban came to power in 1996 promising to restore law and order and create a pure Islamic state that would guarantee the personal security of women and preserve the dignity of families (Mertus, 2000:56). At first, the restoration of order was seen as beneficial. But soon it was evident that the Taliban sought to erase women from public life and make them invisible in the name of "cleansing" Afghan society. Women were banned from employment, from education, and from going into public places without the accompaniment of a close male relative; they were required to be covered from head to toe in the familiar blue *burqa*. The Ministry for the Promotion of Virtue and the Prevention of Vice ruthlessly enforced these restrictions; in a mockery of female "protection," women were beaten publicly with leather batons containing metal studs for showing their hands or ankles, participating in home-based schooling, or violating any other of these restrictions.[17] For boys who have grown up and been socialized in the madrassas, the sight of a woman is the equivalent of seeing the foreign other, the incarnation of evil itself (Prosser, 2001:2). Given the ban on female employment, many women, particularly those without male relatives or supporters, were forced into begging and prostitution; restrictions on mobility meant that women and their children did not have access to health care.[18]

Since the war, many women and children who are family members of fleeing or killed foreign Taliban fighters have been stranded inside Afghanistan with nowhere to go to seek safety. And Afghanistan is the world's largest source of refugees; more than 2.5 million Afghans resided in Iran and Pakistan in refugee camps before the recent war began (Mertus, 2000:53). While all displaced people are vulnerable, displaced women are particularly subject to gender-based violence and abuse (Mertus, 2000:69). Evidence such as this offers a severe challenge to the myth that wars are fought for the protection of women and children.

Women Strike Back

Resistance in Afghanistan faced enormous hurdles as people struggled to meet daily needs and avoid physical harm, but it was ongoing and women were participating. The Revolutionary Association of the Women of Afghanistan (RAWA) was established in Kabul in 1977 as an independent organization of Afghan women fighting for human rights and social justice. RAWA's goal has been to increase the number of women in social and political activities and work for the establishment of a government based on democratic and secular values. After the Soviet occupation in 1979, RAWA became involved in the war of resistance. Its founding leader, Meena, who began RAWA's campaign against Soviet occupation ... was assassinated by agents of KHAD (the Afghan branch of the KGB) in 1987.

RAWA continued to work underground in Afghanistan and in the refugee camps of Pakistan to bring education and health care to women, and to mobilize them in defense of their rights.[19] RAWA activities in refugee camps have been described as training grounds for a different kind of fighter. Girls have received an education and, from these sites, women with hidden cameras were sent on dangerous missions into Afghanistan to document abuse. Even in the camps themselves, operations have remained secret since Taliban-style fundamentalism thrives there also (Tempest, 2001). Tahmeena Faryal (an alias she uses for protection), a member of RAWA who visited the United States in November 2001, was described as a "soldier of sorts"; she has documented her secret return to Afghanistan in 1999 under the *burqa* (Lopez, 2001). Faryal, with her goal of giving voice to the women and children of Afghanistan, claimed that no woman she met on her mission complained about the *burqa*; rather, they described the insult of their daily lives and the theft of their identities. In a society where everyday survival became, and has continued to be, an almost insurmountable task, fighting back has been severely constrained. Nevertheless, it is crucial that we see these women as agents as well as victims if we are to get beyond the gender stereotyping that we have witnessed since 9/11. I shall now suggest four lessons from this feminist analysis.

What Can We Learn from 9/11?

1. Biology Is Not Destiny, Even During Wars

Francis Fukuyama (1998) used his seemingly benign biological assertion that men are warlike and women peaceful to justify the need to channel men's aggression into activities in the political, economic, and military realms, thus diminishing opportunities for women. Yet Joshua Goldstein's study of gender and war suggests that biology is in fact less constraining than culture with respect to the roles men and women can play in war and peace (Goldstein, 2001:252). But if men are made not born, as Goldstein (2001:264) claims, could we envisage a new form of "hegemonic" masculinity less validated by a false biological association with war?

Since the "war against terrorism" began, our images of men and women, as warriors and victims, have become more rigid. Prior to September 11, we in the United States were becoming accustomed to less militarized models of masculinity. Heroes were men of global business conquering the world with briefcases rather than bullets: Bill Gates, a bourgeois hero who looks distinctly unwarrior-like amasses dollars not weapons.[20] Robert Connell (2000:26) has depicted this new type of "hegemonic masculinity" as embodied in business executives who operate in global markets as well as in the political and military leadership who support them.

Our new military heroes also are being defined in different ways: they come with a tough and tender image—"a new definition of manliness, forged from the depths of sorrow and loss."[21] Post-9/11 real men cried and tears were no longer a sign of weakness—"the ideal is that the warrior should be sad and tender, and because of that, the warrior can be very brave as well."[22]

Peace researcher Elise Boulding (2000) has suggested that men in the West are experiencing a great deal of pain due to the questioning of their traditional roles. In this transitional era, so worrying to Kurth and Fukuyama, women's gains are unsettling to many men and women, and men's role expectations are becoming more complicated. This pain may be one reason for the post-9/11 enthusiasm for old-fashioned masculinity and heroism. Nevertheless, as Boulding claims, men do not necessarily enjoy such assigned macho roles. She suggests that the Men's Movement is providing alternative roles for men; she hypothesizes that, with the diminishing of gender polarities, there are possibilities for a new model of partnership rather than domination.

Sympathetic with these new challenges to gender identities and assuming a strong social constructivist position, Robert Connell (2000:30) claims that the task is not to abolish gender but to reshape it—for example, to disconnect courage from violence and by making boys and men aware of the diversity of masculinities that already exist in the world. Democratic gender relations are those that move toward equality, nonviolence, and mutual respect; Connell claims that this reshaping requires constant engagement with women rather than separation which has been characteristic of contemporary men's movements.

While Connell outlines possibilities for shifting forms of masculinity freed from their association with war, Goldstein fears that rearing boys not to become warriors puts them at risk of being shamed by their peers. And Judith Stiehm (2000:224) has suggested that since women are biologically capable of doing everything men can do, masculinity is fragile and vulnerable; because men's superiority is socially rather than biologically defined, men need to assert and protect it. This makes shifting to new forms of masculinity a difficult task. And, as we know, it is generally harder for men to cross gender lines than it is for women.

Do new forms of masculinity in times of war depend on opening up spaces for new definitions of femininity? Clearly, women's increased visibility in public life, particularly in the military, is shaking up gender expectations. In the U.S. military, women are fighting and dying in the current conflict with much less attention than in the Gulf War where the presence of female soldiers in Saudi Arabia was one of the greatest provocations for bin Laden.[23] Yet feminists have been ambivalent about women as war-fighters—whether they should join men's wars in the name of equality or resist them in the name of women's special relationship with peace.

We must also ask what the presence of women in combat ranks does to men's sense of masculinity as a motivator for their war-fighting? Judith Stiehm (2000:224) argues for ending men's monopoly on the legitimate use of force, thus breaking the link between gender identity and the use of state force. She believes this would reduce the overall use of force; she sees peacekeeping as an activity that challenges the association of masculinity with war. Suspicious of the association of women with peace and of any possibility of "remaking human nature," Jean Elshtain (1987:352–353) suggests the notion of a "chastened patriot," a model that could be adopted by both women and men and one that would shed the excesses of nationalism and remain committed to, but detached from and reflective about, patriotic ties and loyalties.

Understanding gender as a social construction and the fluidity of gender identities allows us to see the possibilities of change while acknowledging the power of gendering distinctions to legitimate war as well as other practices that result in the subordination of women. It is not only the gendering of war and peace that constrains women's opportunities; frequently, women are oppressed in the name of culture and religion, a phenomenon that the recent war brought to our attention.

2. Women Bear the Burdens of Religion and Culture

Religious fundamentalists, both Christian and Islamic, used the 9/11 crisis to criticize women's advances: this tendency reflects a much more general phenomenon. As many feminists have pointed out, all fundamentalist religions are, to various degrees, bad for women. Historically, most religions have been as male-dominated as militaries. The connection between religious fanaticism, be it Christian, Judaic, or Islamic, and the suppression of women is almost universal. The patriarchal family, with its control of women, is usually central to fundamentalist movements and often seen as the panacea for social ills (Yuval-Davis, 1997:63). A paradox of fundamentalist movements is that often women collude with and seek comfort in them; and, in spite of their subservience in religious institutions, women constitute a majority of active members of most religions (Yuval-Davis, 1997:63).

Often, in the name of religion, women bear the brunt of identity politics which is frequently expressed in terms of control over their life choices. At the 1994 United Nations Conference on Population and Development in Cairo and at the U.N. Women's Conference in Beijing in 1995, the Vatican, and other conservative Catholic groups, joined with right-wing Muslim forces in their opposition to women's human and reproductive rights. In many Muslim societies, the majority of the population is not literate so religious knowledge is controlled by the ruling class who interpret texts for their own benefit and use it to control others. According to Zeiba Shorish-Shamley (2002), the Qur'an gives equal rights to men and women and women were leaders in early Islam—modest clothing was recommended so that when men and women met in public discussion, intellectuality rather than sexuality would be emphasized.

"When radical Muslim movements are on the rise, women are canaries in the mine" (Goodwin and Neuwirth, 2001). In the name of Islamic fundamentalism, the definition of collective identity is increasingly being tied to definitions of gender. According to Women Living Under Muslim Laws (WLUML), an international network of women, construction of the "Muslim woman" is integral to the construction of "Muslimness," explaining, in part, the emphasis on controlling all aspects of women's lives (WLUML, 1997:2–3). Ironically, the weakening of the patriarchal family structure may be a contributing cause of these movements (Moghadan, 1994:15). Azza Karam (2000:69 –70) sees the emergence of "neopatriarchy," a confluence of patriarchy and dependence that embodies the tension between internal patriarchal power structures and outside pressures of modernization. It is in the reinstatement of cultural values in response to pressures of globalization that women in the Arab world tend to be most affected. Defining "fundamentalism" as the use of religion to gain and mobilize political power, Women Living Under Muslim Laws argues that, with the ascendancy of identity politics, secular space shrinks with negative consequences for women (WLUML, 1997:3).[24] And, when women fight for their rights, they are frequently accused of betraying their culture and religion.

Although not reducible to each other, religion bears a close relationship to culture. Gender relations come to be seen as constituting the "essence" of cultures (Yuval-Davis, 1997:43). Women are often required to carry the burden of cultural representation: their "proper" behavior embodies lines that signify a collectivity's boundaries. Women are transmitters of group values and traditions; as agents of socialization of the young their place is in the home. For some this is an honor rather than a burden so all fundamentalist movements have women supporters as well as opponents (Moghadan, 1994:19).

Rina Amiri (2001) has claimed that the Western world has contributed to the perception that the current conflict is a battle between East and West by centering on the place of women in its depiction of Islam as repressive and backward. She has also suggested that a Western approach could damage a long-term vision for an indigenous model of a just society because a Western model can be contextually inappropriate for Afghan women and Islam traditionalists who are sympathetic to women but who will reject what is perceived as Western (Amiri, 2002).

Conversely, WLUML (1997:6) has claimed that well-meaning people, wanting to distance themselves from Islam hatred and the colonial past, epitomized in Orientalist thought, have frequently fallen into the trap of cultural relativism. Consistent with some of Rothstein's more negative assessments of postcolonialism, but in the name of cultural sensitivity, this can lead to endorsement of the right to seclude women.

Issues of culture and religion have been difficult ones for both Western and non-Western feminists. Western feminists have walked a fine line between supporting a "global sisterhood," and thus imposing Western definitions of female emancipation on other cultures, and trying to be culturally sensitive. Third Wave feminism of the 1990s introduced issues of class, race, and cultural variability into its analyses in order to get beyond essentialist generalizations about women that stem from Western middle-class women's experiences. As an alternative to the universalism/relativism dichotomy, Nira Yuval-Davis (1997:1) suggests what she calls "transversal politics," or the politics of mutual support—a form of coalition politics in which differences among women are recognized and given a voice.

In the Muslim world, women's struggles are frequently undermined by the idea of one homogeneous Muslim world, a deliberate myth fostered by both Occidentalism and Orientalism and promoted by interests within and outside (WLUML, 1997:1). In many cases, to be pro–women's rights means to be accused of being Western. Accusing women of being Westernized and, therefore, not representing an "authentic" women's voice allows for the dismissal of women's claims to justice. This has made it difficult for Muslim women to develop a discourse on their rights independent of a cultural debate between the Western and Muslim worlds.

Amiri urges moving beyond the stereotypical premise that Islam as a whole is anti-woman. She suggests that, while it is incumbent on the international community never to tolerate abuses against women in any part of the world, the West should ground its support in the positions of Muslim feminists. WLUML claims that women are frequently hampered by insufficient knowledge about their legal rights, their inability to distinguish between customs, law, and religion, and by their isolation. To this end, WLUML suggests that women pool information and create strategies across countries; they urge a respect for other voices while condemning bad practices.

All of these attempts to negotiate support for women—attempts that get beyond a false universalism based on Western norms and a type of cultural relativism that condones oppressive practices—depend on seeing women as agents rather than victims. "Moving toward gender equality is a political process—it requires new ways of thinking—in which the stereotyping of women and men gives way to a new philosophy that regards all people, irrespective of gender, as essential agents of change" (UNHDP, 1996:1).[25]

3. We Need Gender-Sensitive Conceptions of Development, Security, and Peace

The events of 9/11 brought the desperate circumstances of Afghanistan and its people to the world's attention. Afghanistan has been called a "failed state" harboring terrorists, a country whose infrastructure and government institutions have been destroyed by twenty years of war. Feminists have some important additional things to say about the kinds of underdevelopment and insecurity rife in that society today.

Jennifer Whitaker (2001) has suggested that there is a striking correlation between women's political and economic participation and more general advances in development. National standards of living improve—family income, education, nutrition, and life expectancy all rise and birthrates fall as women move toward equality. When women's influence increases, it strengthens the moderate center and increases economic stability and democratic order. In societies where women have social, political and economic power, there is a strong constituency for democracy and human rights.

These claims are supported by the United Nations Human Development Programme (UNHDP) which has developed indicators to measure gender inequality. The UNHDP asserts that countries with a low ranking in terms of its Gender Development Index (GDI) are among the poorest, with Afghanistan ranking at the bottom of countries measured (UNHDP, 1996).[26] Nevertheless, the UNHDP claims that gender equality does not depend on income level alone; it requires a firm political commitment, not enormous financial wealth (UNHDP, 1996:75–78). And changes are always evident: the report suggests that, between 1970 and 1992, the GDI values of all countries improved but at different rates. In many Arab states women's access to education and an increase in life expectancy brought up their values more than their increased access to income and employment (UNHDP, 1996:75–81); indeed, economic power has always been the most difficult for women to achieve.

More recently, the UNHDP has published a report on development in the Arab region which highlights the poor treatment of women as one of the major reasons for the region's lack of development. The report notes that women's participation in their countries' political and economic life is the lowest in the world.[27] The lower women's economic power, the more likely they are to be oppressed physically, politically, and ideologically (Godenzi, 2000). Although, technically, Islam gives women the right to keep their own income and property, cultural tradition maintains men as heads of households who control sources of wealth (Karam, 2000:72). Historically, this has been true in the West also. For this reason, feminists have claimed that extending the benefits of a liberal society to women has been problematic. Values, such as individualism and free markets, extolled by Kurth, have historically been based on a male norm of rational atomistic individuals maximizing welfare through market exchange. This model has depended on free, usually female, labor for reproductive and caring tasks (Tickner, 1992:73). Seeking equality in this type of world—whether Western or Islamic—has been problematic for women because it involves fitting into structures that are already gendered.

Just as feminists have helped us rethink the meanings of development and security, they can help us rethink the meaning of peace. Feminist definitions of peace have generally included the reduction of all forms of violence, including structural violence and oppressive gender hierarchies, as well as physical violence. And a variety of studies have shown that, contra Huntington and Fukuyama, countries with large cohorts of young men are not automatically warlike. Violence is more likely to occur in unstable societies that are politically and economically underdeveloped. It is the degree of exclusion from economic and political participation that fuels unrest and gender stereotyping.[28] Islamic movements have emerged in the context of a profound economic crisis in the Middle East (Moghadan, 1994:11).

WLUML (1997:9) defines peace as breaking down the deep divisions that war induces and preventing the internalization of hatred of "the other" fostered by discourses associated with Orientalism and Occidentalism and often expressed in gender terms. They cite a growing sense of insecurity that results from decision-making that shifts further away from people, and deepening poverty that widens the division between the haves and the have-nots. Frequently, women's struggles for peace and justice focus on a secure environment free from violence and economic deprivation. For example, Afghan women are more likely to talk about their desire for peace, health care, education, food, and shelter than about having to wear the *burqa* (Mertus, 2000:59). Peace involves a struggle for justice, including gender justice; to be successful it must be seen as a responsibility of both women and men.

4. Women's Gains from War May Not Last

Paradoxically, it is sometimes the case that wars are good for women. European and American women first received the vote after World War I and Japanese women did so after World War II. Frequently, women are mobilized into the paid economy during war thereby gaining more economic independence. Women have also been mobilized in times of struggle for national liberation and sometimes they have fought in liberation armies. Quite often these gains evaporate once the war is over; in the West, the years after both World Wars saw a return to the cult of domesticity and motherhood—a move that had to do with the need for women to step aside and let men resume the jobs they had left to go to war. And women who have fought alongside men in wars of national liberation, and who have been promised a greater role in post-liberation society, often find that these promises evaporate once the struggle is over. Few revolutionary movements directly address women's problems or attempt to solve these problems in post-revolution political and social constitutions and institutions (Tetrault, 1992:92).

When women fight for their rights, they generally get less support than when they are perceived as victims. This is because gender justice demands profound structural changes in almost all societies, changes that would threaten existing elites along with existing political, social, and economic structures. And, frequently, both international governmental and nongovernmental organizations (NGOs) find these types of radical changes too politically risky to support. For example, RAWA receives very little financial support from international NGOs, undoubtedly because its agenda is to empower women in ways that would demand very different political and social relations in Afghanistan.[29]

And what of the women of Afghanistan? Clearly, the war has brought them benefits and freedoms. The presence of women at the 2002 Loya Jirga called to pick the new government was a stark contrast with the Taliban years (Gall, 2002). But, in spite of the attention they have received, it is far from clear that women will play any significant role in the new government. Only two women were invited to the Bonn Conference and only two were given positions in the transitional government. One of the two, Sima Samar, the interim women's affairs minister, said recently that she feared for her safety. Under threat from Islamic conservatives, who do not believe that women should participate in public life, she has resigned as women's affairs minister and taken the less controversial post as head of the human rights commission (Gannon, 2002). Human Rights Watch has documented atrocities committed by members of the Northern Alliance in the early 1990s; RAWA has labeled them as misogynist and antidemocratic, yet they were our allies in the recent struggle and they have received rewards in the new government. There is concern that, without strong vigilance from the international community, Afghan women are unlikely to end up much better off than they were under the Taliban (Jefferson, 2001). Patriarchal culture does not vanish overnight and men are unlikely to give up the few privileges they may have in a difficult postwar period of reconstruction.

A spokesperson for the Feminist Majority recently suggested that never before has the women's movement had such an impact on American foreign policy as it is having today (McNamara, 2002). The Feminist Majority began its campaign, "Stop Gender Apartheid" in 1996, well before the plight of Afghan women was receiving much media attention: it played a key role in the Clinton administration's refusal to recognize the Taliban government. The Feminist Majority's optimism may be short-lived, however; it is unclear whether U.S. support for Afghan women will continue now the war against Afghanistan is over. Governments are generally reluctant to make women's human rights part of their foreign policies. There is less risk in portraying women as victims than in supporting their empowerment. The image of helpless victims behind the veil may be politically less risky than supporting articulate forceful advocates of women's rights. The Bush administration is quoted as having insisted that the campaign to highlight women in Afghanistan must be seen as a "justice issue" not a women's issue (Brant, 2001). And even if the Bush administration has put the plight of Afghan women on its foreign policy agenda, it has not been particularly progressive on other international women's issues. Twenty-two years after President Jimmy Carter sent the Covenant on the Elimination of Discrimination Against Women (CEDAW) to the U.S. Senate for ratification, the Senate Foreign Relations Committee is holding hearings on it, but the Bush administration is reneging on its initial support, making ratification unlikely. The U.S. is one of a very small minority of countries that has not ratified CEDAW (Kristof, 2002).

Conclusion

The "war against terrorism" has been described by American officials as a new kind of war, a war against a terrorist network, not against another state. In conclusion, one may wonder if there are other, more gendered ways in which this war is unlike the other wars Americans fought in the twentieth century. The prevalence of gendered images taken to be threatening or used to belittle one's opponents could surely be found in other such wars. But somehow these references seem more fundamental in the present case.

As quoted above, al Qaeda leaders have made a special point of criticizing Western gender relations. Gender relationships are an important aspect of what are taken by many fundamentalists to be key religious or civilizational differences. Even more surprising are the cases of "strange bedfellows" on different sides of the war making the same kinds of gendered arguments. Do not these features of the above analysis suggest that the 9/11 crisis reflects a globalization of gender politics, a clash of gendered orders usually hidden by the normalizing practices of unequal societies?

In times of uncertainty, fear of social change rises as does fear of feminist agendas. However, feminists are not advocating a "feminized society" as some of their critics have suggested but rather a society where gender differences are less polarized and gender structures are less hierarchical.

Notes

1. For a more elaborated version of this argument see Huntington (1996:20–32).
2. It should be noted that women's equality was not even thought of at the birth of the Enlightenment. For a discussion of women's unequal incorporation into the modern Western state see Pateman (1988). Males in the workforce have never received much criticism for neglecting their children. For ideas, similar to Kurth's, about the negative effects of cultural diversity see also Huntington (1996:304) and Fukuyama (2000). See also Fukuyama (1999) which also emphasizes the negative effects of 1960s women's liberation.
3. Peggy Noonan, quoted in Brown (2001).
4. *The Guardian,* September 20, 2001. Cited from http://www.guardian.co.uk/analysis/story/0,3604,554794,00.html.
5. Quoted in Brown (2001).
6. This gendered image of Afghanistan—men fighting and women invisible—was further reinforced by a comment by U.S. Secretary of Defense Donald Rumsfield on the PBS Lehrer Newshour on November 7, 2001, when he claimed that there were no people in Afghanistan who were not armed and fighting.
7. "A Portrait of the Terrorist: From Shy Child to Single-Minded Killer," *New York Times,* October 10, 2001, p. B9.
8. It should be noted that Falk, in an exchange with ten critics of his position, all but one of whom were men, subsequently retreated from his position saying he had been misled by the language of George Bush and Colin Powell which seemed initially to suggest a much more limited war than what actually evolved. See *The Nation,* November 26, 2001, p. 60.
9. *The Nation,* December 17, 2001, p. 4.
10. Women frequently describe themselves as possessing these masculine characteristics while still able to articulate what is stereotypically "feminine." There can be no hegemonic femininity since masculinity defines acceptable societal norms. The term "hegemonic masculinity" was first used by Connell (1987). Connell contrasts "hegemonic masculinity" with subordinated and devalued masculinities such as those associated with racial minorities and homosexuals.
11. This challenges Fukuyama's (1998) use of sociobiologically based arguments to support his claim about men's "innate" aggression. For further elaboration of sociobiological arguments of this type see Mesquida and Weiner (2001).
12. The Geneva Conventions extend special protections in wartime to women, mothers of small children, and children themselves. See Goldstein (2001:305).
13. Fouad Ajami, quoted in Croisette (2001).
14. On October 8, 2001, after the beginning of U.S. bombing, support for the war was running at 87 percent of both women and men (Goldstein, 2002).
15. To illustrate this more vividly, what would the reaction be to mostly female firefighters, police, and military personnel? Goldstein (2001) asserts that many women are biologically quite well suited to perform these protective tasks.
16. In light of my earlier discussion about patriotism, the naming of the USA Patriot Act was probably designed to forestall criticism.

17. It should be noted that men were also policed if their beards were not long enough or their dress not appropriate. However, men retained some control over their lives.

18. In 2000, life expectancy for Afghan women was 44 years and one in four children died before the age of 5 (Mertus, 2000:59). Of course, these deplorable statistics were as much due to years of warfare as to restrictions on women.

19. Information about RAWA may be found on their website at http://www.rawa.org.

20. For some recent IR feminist writings that take up the issue of masculinity see Zalewski and Parpart (1998) and Hooper (2001).

21. Robin Morgan, quoted in Brown (2001).

22. Tibetan Buddhist teacher Chogyam Trungpa, quoted in Wax (2001).

23. The *Los Angeles Times* (Perry, 2002) reported the death of seven U.S. Marines on a cargo plane in Pakistan on January 10, 2002, with only passing reference to the fact that one of them was a woman.

24. WLUML notes that the use of the term "fundamentalism" is a contested one within the organization. Some, but not all, find it the least objectionable term to name the phenomenon. RAWA also uses the term, at least when speaking to a Western audience. Writing in the context of the fate of Afghanistan, Robert Scheer (2001b) has suggested that President Bush must break with a popular American notion that religion is inherently a benign experience.

25. Although not the most recent, I cite the 1995 Annual Report because it contains the most extensive discussion of gender inequality of any of the Annual Reports.

26. *United Nations Human Development Report 1995,* the first annual report to use the GDI, ranked Afghanistan 130th out of 130 countries in terms of its GDI. In terms of its Human Development Index (HDI) Afghanistan was ranked 170th out of 174 countries. The UNHDP defines the HDI as the combination of a variety of quality-of-life indicators including life expectancy, education, and income. The GDI measures achievement in the same basic capabilities as the HDI but takes note of inequality in achievement between women and men.

27. A summary of the Arab Human Development Report 2002 may be found at http://www.economist.com/agenda/displaystory.cfm?storyid1212573.

28. Henrik Urdal, International Peace Research Institute, Oslo. Quoted in Sciolino (2001).

29. "About RAWA," http://www.rawa.org.

References

Amiri, R. (2001) "Muslim Women as Symbols—and Pawns." *New York Times,* Nov. 27, p. A21.

Amiri, R. (2002) "Afghanistan: Women in Government and Society." Panel discussion, U.S. Institute of Peace, Jan. 29. Cited from http://www.usip.org/oc/newsroom/es20020129.html.

Boulding, E. (2000) *Cultures of Peace: The Hidden Side of History.* Syracuse, NY: Syracuse University Press.

Brant, M. (2001) "The Bushies Unveil the Women's Issue." *Newsweek,* Nov. 26, p. 7.

Brown, P. L. (2001) "Heavy Lifting Required: The Return of Manly Men." *New York Times,* Oct. 28, sec. 4, p. 5.

Buruma, I., and A. Margalit (2002) "Occidentalism." *New York Review of Books,* vol. 49, no. 1, Jan. 17, pp. 4 –7.

Connell, R. W. (1987) *Gender and Power: Society, the Person and Sexual Identities.* Stanford, CA: Stanford University Press.

Connell, R. W. (2000) "Arms and the Man: Using the New Research on Masculinity to Understand Violence and Promote Peace in the Contemporary World." In *Male Roles, Masculinities and Violence: A Culture of Peace Perspective,* edited by I. Breines, R. W. Connell, and I. Eide, pp. 21–33. Paris: UNESCO.

Cooperman, A. (2001) "Roman Catholic Bishops Declare U.S. War Is Moral." *Washington Post,* Nov. 16, p. A37.

Croisette, B. (2001) "Living in a World Without Women." *New York Times,* Nov. 4, sec. 4, p. 1.

Elshtain, J. B. (1987) *Women and War.* New York: Basic Books.

Enloe, C. (1993) *The Morning After: Sexual Politics at the End of the Cold War.* Berkeley and Los Angeles: University of California Press.

Enloe, C. (2000) *Maneuvers: The International Politics of Militarizing Women's Lives.* Berkeley and Los Angeles: University of California Press.

Falk, R. (2001) "Ends and Means: Defining a Just War." *The Nation,* Oct. 29, pp. 11–15.

Fukuyama, F. (1998) Women and the Evolution of World Politics. *Foreign Affairs* 77(5):24–40.

Fukuyama, F. (1999) *The Great Disruption: Human Nature and the Reconstitution of Social Order.* New York: Free Press.

Fukuyama, F. (2000) "What Divides America." *Wall Street Journal,* Nov. 15, p. A26.

Gall, C. (2002) "Afghan Women in Political Spotlight." *New York Times,* June 26, p. A8.

Gannon, K. (2002) "Female Minister Driven From Her Post." *Boston Globe,* June 24, p. A8.

Godenzi, A. (2000) "Determinants of Culture: Men and Economic Power." In *Male Roles, Masculinities and Violence: A Culture of Peace Perspective,* edited by I. Brienes, R. W. Connell, and I. Eide, pp. 35–51. Paris: UNESCO.

Goldstein, J. (2001) *War and Gender.* Cambridge: Cambridge University Press.

Goldstein, J. (2002) "John Wayne and GI Jane." *The Christian Science Monitor,* Jan. 10, p. 11.

Goodwin, J., and J. Neuwirth (2001) "The Rifle and the Veil." *New York Times,* Oct. 1. Cited from http://www.rawa.org.

Hooper, C. (2001) *Manly States: Masculinities, International Relations, and Gender Politics.* New York: Columbia University Press.

Human Rights Watch (2001) "Poor Rights Record of Opposition Commanders." Oct. 6. Cited from RAWA website, http://www.rawa.org.

Huntington, S. (1993) The Clash of Civilizations? *Foreign Affairs* 72(3):22–49.

Huntington, S. (1996) *The Clash of Civilizations and the Remaking of World Order.* New York: Simon and Schuster.

Jefferson, L. (2001) "Out Go the Taliban, But Will Afghan Women Be Excluded Again?" *International Herald Tribune,* Nov. 16. Cited from http://www.hrw.org/editorials/2001.afghan-1116.htm.

Jones, K. (1990) "Dividing the Ranks: Women and the Draft." In *Women, Militarism, and War: Essays in History, Politics, and Social Theory,* edited by J. B. Elshtain and S. Tobias, pp. 125–136. Savage, MD: Rowman and Littlefield.

Judt, T. (2001) "America and the War." *New York Review of Books,* vol. 48, no. 10, Nov. 15.

Karam, A. (2000) "Democrats without Democracy: Challenges to Women in Politics in the Arab World." In *International Perspectives on Gender and Democratization,* edited by S. Rai, pp. 64–82. New York: St. Martin's Press.

Kristof, N. (2002) "Why Won't America Ratify? A Treaty Defends Women Against Men." *International Herald Tribune,* June 19, p. 6.

Kurth, J. (1994) "The Real Clash." *The National Interest,* no. 37(Fall):3–15.

Lopez, S. (2001) "Afghan Woman's Tale Rises From Bottomless Well of Sadness." *Los Angeles Times,* Nov. 14, p. B1.

McNamara, M. (2002) "With Shift to L.A., Feminist Majority Builds on Momentum." *Los Angeles Times,* Jan. 16, sec. E, p. 1.

Mearsheimer, J. (2001) "Guns Won't Win the Afghan War." *New York Times,* Nov. 4, sec. 4, p. 13.

Mertus, J. A. (2000) *War's Offensive on Women: The Humanitarian Challenge in Bosnia, Kosovo, and Afghanistan.* Bloomfield, CT: Kumarian Press.

Mesquida, C., and N. Weiner (2001) "Young Men and War." *PECS News,* Environmental Change and Security Project, Woodrow Wilson Center, Fall, pp. 2–3.

Moghadan, V. (1994) "Women and Identity Politics in Theoretical and Comparative Perspective." In *Identity Politics and Women: Cultural Reassertions and Feminisms in International Perspective,* edited by V. Moghadan, pp. 3–26. Boulder, CO: Westview Press.

Pateman, C. (1988) *The Sexual Contract.* Stanford, CA: Stanford University Press.

Perry, T. (2002) "Unspeakable Loss Shakes Marine Base." *Los Angeles Times,* Jan. 11, p. A16.

Prosser, S. E. (2001) "Taliban and Women—Oil and Water." Women in International Law (WILIG), Washington Steering Committee *Newsletter* 14(2):2–3.

Rothstein, E. (2001) "Attacks on U.S. Challenge the Perspectives of Postmodern True Believers," *New York Times,* Sept. 11, p. A17.

Scheer, R. (2001a) "Falwell Should Have Listened to the Feminists." *Los Angeles Times,* Sept. 25, p. 20.

Scheer, R. (2001b) "Secularism Unlocks the Door to Stability." *Los Angeles Times,* Dec. 18, p. B13.

Sciolino, E. (2001) "Radicalism: Is the Devil in the Demographics?" *New York Times,* Dec. 9, sec. 4, p. 1.

Shorish-Shamley, Z. (2002) "Afghanistan: Women in Government and Society." Panel discussion, U.S. Institute of Peace, Jan. 29. Cited from http://www.usip.org/oc/newsroom/es20020129.html. Stiehm, J. H. (1983) *Women and Men's Wars.* Oxford: Pergamon Press.

Stiehm, J. H. (2000) "Neither Male nor Female: Neither Victim nor Executioner." In *Male Roles, Masculinities and Violence: A Culture of Peace Perspective,* edited by I. Breines, R. W. Connell, and I. Eide, pp. 223–230. Paris: UNESCO.

Stout, D. (2001) "Mrs. Bush Cites Women's Plight Under Taliban." *New York Times,* Nov. 18, p. B4.

Tempest, R. (2001) "Training Camp of Another Kind." *Los Angeles Times,* Oct. 15, p. A1.

Tetrault, M. A. (1992) "Women and Revolution: A Framework for Analysis." In *Gendered States: Feminist (Re)Visions of International Relations Theory,* edited by V. S. Peterson, pp. 99 –121. Boulder, CO: Lynne Rienner.

Tickner, J. A. (1992) *Gender in International Relations: Feminist Perspectives on Achieving Global Security.* New York: Columbia University Press.

(UNHDP) United Nations Human Development Programme (1996) *Human Development Report 1995.* New York: Oxford University Press.

Wax, N. (2001) "Not To Worry. Real Men Can Cry." *New York Times,* Oct. 28, sec. 4, p. 5.

Whitaker, J. (2001) "Don't Betray the Women." *Washington Post,* Nov. 15, p. A47.

Wildman, S. (2001) "Arms Length: Why Don't Feminists Support the War?" *The New Republic,* Nov. 5, p. 23.

(WLUML) Women Living Under Muslim Laws (1997) "Plan of Action Dhaka 1997." Cited from http://www.wluml.org/English/publications/engpofa.htm.

Yuval-Davis, N. (1997) *Gender and Nation.* London: Sage.

Zalewski, M., and J. Parpart, eds. (1998) *The "Man" Question in International Relations.* Boulder, CO: Westview Press.

7.2

HOW BAIDA WANTED TO DIE

Alissa J. Rubin

> What drives a young Muslim woman with three children to strap on a
> heavy bomb vest and look for American, not Iraqi, soldiers to kill in a
> terrorist suicide assault? Perhaps the prospect of going to heaven; or
> revenge for the death of five brothers and a father at the hands of
> American soldiers and their Iraqi allies; or the chance to escape a life
> that mimics the early days of Islam and involves no education beyond
> the eighth grade, wife beating, and housing without electricity or
> other amenities. Baida is not a fictitious character. In her story, terror-
> ism acquires a human rage, stoked by foreign invaders (realist), his-
> torical grievances (liberal), and religious zealotry (identity) and enabled
> by anomie (individual level of analysis), lawlessness (domestic level of
> analysis), and globalization (systemic level of analysis). Where would
> you start to try to unwind this tragic story?

In Baquba, the Iraqi police detective flipped pointlessly through a file on his
desk; the daylight was too faint to read by and the electricity had long since gone
off. He seemed about to say something. Then a bomb exploded a few blocks
away, and his office shook. The radios on his desk crackled. He nodded to his
colleagues, and they ran into the hall to join police officers already rushing to
the bomb site. As he rose to follow them, the detective tried to reassure me.

"You will like Baida," Maj. Hosham al-Tamimi, then director of the National
Investigation and Information Bureau in the Diyala Police Command, said as he
nodded at the file before him. It was a curious thing to say about someone who
sought to kill people like him and like me. He added, almost pensively: "I like
Baida. She is"—he paused—"honest."

Baida is one of 16 female would-be suicide-bomber suspects or accomplices
who have been captured by the police in Diyala Province since the beginning of
2008; almost as many have blown themselves up. When I first met Baida in
February, she had already been in jail more than two months. She was in the
same cell with another would-be suicide bomber, Ranya, who was 15 when she
was caught on her way to a bombing, her vest already strapped on. Ranya's
mother was also in the jail because she was believed to be connected to those
involved in trying to organize Ranya's death.

Source: Alissa J. Rubin, "How Baida Wanted to Die," *New York Times Magazine,* August 16,
2009, available at: http://www.nytimes.com/2009/08/16/magazine/16suicide-t.html?_r=1.

Nowhere, it seems, have more women blown themselves up in so short a time as in Iraq, where there have been some 60 suicide bombings attempted or carried out by women, the majority of them in 2007–8, according to statistics gathered by the American military and the Iraqi police. (The numbers, for men as well as women, are lower this year, though the attacks continue.) At least a third of those bombers came from Diyala, mostly from the provincial capital, Baquba, 40 miles northeast of Baghdad, or from a small stretch of land that lies in the Diyala River valley. Thick with date-palm groves, small rivers and lush fields, Diyala appears to be an oasis in the desert. But over the last four years it has been home to some of Iraq's most violent terrorist factions. It was here and in Baghdad that the extremists' most lethal weapons were honed. One of those was suicide bombers who were women.

It is difficult to learn much about suicide bombers since there is rarely anything left of them. In Diyala, however, because there have been so many bombers who were women, the police have been driven to study the phenomenon, developing a nuanced and thoughtful picture of women who resolve to kill themselves. It was with the help of the police, who were willing to give me access to some of the would-be bombers, that I reported this piece. In particular, working with my interpreter, an Iraqi woman who was trained as a social worker, I was able to have long and even intimate conversations with two of the women in police custody. Police officers were able to corroborate much of what they said.

Each woman's story is unique, but their journeys to jihad do have commonalities. Many have lost close male relatives. Baida and Ranya lost both fathers and brothers. Many of the women live in isolated communities dominated by extremists, where radical understandings of Islam are the norm. In such places, women are often powerless to control much about their lives; they cannot choose whom they marry, how many children to have or whether they can go to school beyond the primary years. Becoming a suicide bomber is a choice of sorts that gives some women a sense of being special, with a distinguished destiny. But Major Hosham urged me not to generalize: "All the cases are different. Some are old; some are young; some are just criminals; some are believers. They have different reasons."

One thing stood out: The appearance in Diyala of suicide bombers who were women was entwined with the appearance of the Islamic State of Iraq—the local face of Al Qaeda in Mesopotamia, the umbrella name used in Iraq for homegrown Sunni extremist groups that have some foreign leadership. While many insurgent groups operate in Iraq, those with links to Al Qaeda in Mesopotamia are associated with suicide bombings. In Diyala, the Islamic State of Iraq was particularly strong. It was also brutal and organized. It orchestrated mass kidnappings, mass executions, beheadings and ambushes. No one was spared: women or children; Sunnis, Shiites or Kurds. Whole villages were forced to flee; others fell under extremist control. Many of the women who became bombers were from families immersed in jihadist culture.

"One of the differences between suicide bombers in Iraq and Palestine is that the Islamists have not been involved much" in recruiting women in Palestine, says Mohammed Hafez, an associate professor of national-security affairs at the Naval Postgraduate School in Monterey, Calif., who specializes in Islamic extremist movements and recently wrote a book on suicide bombings in Iraq. "The Islamists have been very involved in Iraq. Also, in general there is a debate in the Islamic world about whether to use women and children, but in Iraq they have no hesitation about using women."

The rise in the number of suicide bombers who were women in Iraq coincided with the expanding ability of the security forces to defeat bombers who were men. When, in 2006 and 2007, American and Iraqi forces began increasingly to use concrete barriers to insulate government buildings, markets and other gathering places from car bombs, the insurgents turned to women, who could use to advantage their traditional dress: a voluminous, floor-length black abaya, made of folds of flowing fabric. Tribal traditions and Arab notions of modesty make it unthinkable that the police or guards would search women. They could pass through even relatively robust security cordons as if they were invisible. They walked up the steps of government buildings, approached checkpoints and entered the offices and homes of people the militants wanted to assassinate.

Gradually, the police learned to look for telltale signs, Major Hosham told me. Women often wear double abayas to hide their suicide vests. And they apply heavy makeup, because they believe they are going to heaven and want to look their best.

Last September, the Iraqi government completed training for 27 police-women in Diyala. The effort came too late to save at least 130 people and probably more who have died in the province in suicide bombings carried out by women.

Major Hosham was right. I liked Baida immediately. She had an open face and pale skin, a medium build and an unassuming manner. She wore a traditional long black abaya whose only ornamental feature was a strip of black satin down the front. Her black veil was simple. A few strands of light brown hair strayed out, suggesting that while conservative she was not rigid. She seemed educated and told her story in a straightforward way. At times during our first meeting I would forget that we were in a cramped, dingy assistant detective's office with scuffed paint and bars on the windows.

She began in a soft voice: "My name is Baida Abdul Karim al-Shammari, and I am from New Baquba near the general hospital. I am one of eight children; five were killed. The police raided our home. It was a half-hour before dawn during Ramadan. The Americans were with them."

She added with a touch of pride: "My brothers were mujahideen. They made I.E.D.'s." The word "mujahideen" means holy fighters and, in the context of Iraq, they are fighters against the infidels, the Americans. I.E.D.'s are improvised explosive devices.

She told me she helped make such devices, going to the market to buy wire and other bomb parts and working at putting bombs together. Men are routinely paid for such work; women are generally paid too, but less. Baida was proud to be a volunteer. "I knew we were fighting against the Americans and they are the occupation," she told me. "We are doing it for God's sake. We are doing it as jihad."

Baida grew up shuttling between Baquba, which is the provincial capital of Diyala, and Husayba, a town on the Syrian border. She went to school through eighth grade, she told me, and had ideas of becoming an architect, but her mother wanted her to stay home. When Baida was 17, her mother died, and a few months later, at her father's behest, Baida married. Almost immediately she knew she had made a mistake. A week after her wedding, according to Baida, her husband threw a cup of cream at her head; soon, beatings became regular. She smiled sweetly and shrugged: "His hand got used to beating me."

For Baida, as for many Iraqi suicide bombers, violent insurgency was the family business. It was shortly after the American invasion that her brothers began to manufacture I.E.D.'s. One was killed when his handiwork exploded as he was concealing it. She had cousins who were also insurgents. While they were paid for their work, she said, she was herself motivated mainly by revenge. Later it would be revenge for the deaths of her father and four brothers in what she said was a joint American-Iraqi raid on their home, but at first it was more general. She told me she watched the Americans shoot a neighbor in 2005, and she replayed the image over and over in her mind: "I saw him running toward them, and then they shot him in the neck. I still see him. I still remember how he fell when the Americans shot him and I saw him clawing on the ground in the dust before his soul left his body. After that I began to help with making the improvised explosive devices."

Executing a successful suicide bombing is rarely a lone act. It requires preparing a suicide vest, teaching the would-be bomber how to use it and planning the mission. It means transporting the bomber close to the place where she will carry out the attack and in some cases setting up a camera nearby so that the event can be filmed. For women, who rarely drive in Iraq, except in Baghdad, it would be impossible to get to the bomb site without assistance. Most of the women who blew themselves up in Diyala were supported and trained by a network of extremists—often family members already active in the insurgency.

Baida told me she felt much more helpless after her father died. Until then, when she was unhappy with her husband, she would go to visit her family, although they had moved by then to Husayba, the Syrian border town. Sometimes she was so upset at home that she would call one of her brothers or cousins to come to Baquba and drive her to her father's. "You see, when my father was alive, he loved us a lot," she said wistfully. "So when I quarreled with my husband, I felt safe because I had my father."

After her brothers and father were killed, she began to work with some of her cousins; they were also fighters and even more radical Islamists than her brothers. One of them died in a suicide attack, but not before introducing her to a group, run from Syria, that was connected to the Islamic State of Iraq. A goal of the group was to prepare men and women for suicide missions. "Maybe I can introduce you to them," she said warmly. "You could go meet them since they are free."

Baida, having joined the group, initially did not plan to become a suicide bomber. She was drawn to it gradually as she became more deeply involved with the cell. Her cell members announced their readiness for a suicide mission in front of others in the group, making a public commitment, signaling they had crossed an invisible border and embraced the idea of a certain kind of death that would also bring membership in a holy community.

The group dynamic seemed designed to make participants feel as if they were freely choosing their destiny. That sense of freedom was an important component of their metamorphosis into suicide bombers. It was certainly important to Baida, who felt she controlled little in her life, to feel in control of her death. Her goal was to take revenge on her brothers' killers—American soldiers. When I brought up the reality that the vast majority of suicide bombings in Iraq kill ordinary Iraqis, she would only say that she thought killing Iraqis was haram, or forbidden.

"We had meetings of 11 people; some people came to the meeting with their faces covered," Baida told me. "There were three women in the group. Sometimes we were having discussions of Koran, sometimes we were meeting to see who is ready to do jihad. You could choose whether you wanted to do it. They wanted me to wear the explosive belt against the police, but I refused. I said, 'I will not do it against Iraqis.' I said: 'If I do it against the police I will go to hell because the police are Muslims. But if I do it against the Americans then I will go to heaven.'"

A few weeks later, when I met Baida again, she tried to explain to me the line dividing when it is halal (permitted) to kill a person and when it is forbidden. She said she followed the rules of her group, but her cousins had different rules: they would kill anybody. Was there a difference, I wondered, between killing American soldiers and killing American civilians, like reconstruction workers? No, she said: "I am willing to explode them, even civilians, because they are invaders and blasphemers and Jewish. I will explode them first because they are Jewish and because they feel free to take our lands."

My interpreter asked where she stood: Was it halal to kill her?

"We consider you a spy, working with them," Baida said.

Baida did not believe it was halal, however, to kill members of the Iraqi security forces if they were working on their own, only if they were in a convoy with the Americans.

She spoke with enthusiasm, her face animated, vividly alive. Unlike her prison companion Ranya—who claimed, implausibly, that she did not know that she was wearing a suicide belt—Baida was proud of her mission and determined to complete it.

Her choice of suicide was not entirely hers to make. The suicide vests the cell gave to participants were outfitted with remote detonators so that someone else could explode the would-be bomber if she somehow failed to do it herself. This was a relatively new aspect of suicide bombing in Iraq. A second person, with a second detonator, would go on the mission to ensure against changes of heart. "One day this woman, Shaima, said, 'I am ready.' I saw Shaima when they put the vest on her. It was very heavy. With Shaima, they exploded her, she did not explode herself. There were five or six killed."

By the time I met Baida she was eager to get on with her mission, waiting for the day when she would be released from jail and able to pick up her vest, which she said was being kept for her. (She has yet to be charged with any crime.) She appeared to have let go of most earthly ties. A mother of two boys and a girl, all under 8, she had not seen them since her arrest last year. When I asked if they missed her, she said, almost airily, "Allah will take care of them." She spoke as if much of her life was already in the past. When she mentioned her husband, whom she actively hated, she used the past tense. She was living for that moment that some might see as an ending but for her would be a moment of transformation.

"As soon as I get out I will explode myself against the invaders," she told me.

A few moments before we left, I asked when it would be convenient to come see her again. She said she was being moved soon to a psychiatric hospital in Baghdad, and she was afraid. I promised her we would visit her there and asked how we could get in touch. It turned out that she had smuggled a cellphone into the jail—or perhaps appealed to some guard not to take it from her. She never left the sim card in the phone; it was hidden in her underwear, she said. One time, the phone itself was discovered—she had hidden it in a ceiling-light fixture—and confiscated, but she still had the sim card and had somehow got access to another phone.

"They don't know," she said softly, nodding at the policemen in the room, who were staring at a music video. I felt a wave of unease. She was not a beginner.

The road to the Abu Sayda district in Diyala should cross a giant highway bridge, but it was bombed more than a year ago and has yet to be repaired. Cars snake single file into a deep gully, travel parallel to a line of towering girders and eventually crawl up the other side of the ravine. The district lies near a bend in the Diyala River, and many of the farms and villages are cut off on three sides by water, making it a haven for insurgents.

One of the district's villages is Makhisa, which was home to at least three women who became suicide bombers. A settlement on the edge of Makhisa was for many years the home of Baida's cellmate, Ranya Ibrahim. It had the dubious distinction of being the town favored by the notorious Al Qaeda in Mesopotamia leader Abu Musab al-Zarqawi. Police told me that he married a woman from Makhisa and sometimes stayed in the village until he was killed on June 7, 2006.

The town, set among thick date-palm and pomegranate orchards, consists of little more than a few streets lined with low slung, mostly rickety houses, many with simple palm-thatch porches. On the outskirts, one in every four vehicles is a wooden horse-drawn wagon. The animals pull canisters filled with gas used for cooking, transport wood and serve as an informal bus service for local women and children. The most recent suicide bombing near here occurred this spring. It killed at least 47 people, many of them Iranian Shiite pilgrims.

Until 2007, it was too dangerous for the Iraqi Army and the Iraqi police to enter the area. When they finally did, they found a strange community. "When we entered Makhisa we didn't find a TV because it's forbidden," Col. Khalid Mohammed al-Ameri, who was in the army under Saddam Hussein and has served all over the country, told me. "And no ice, no cigarettes and no tomatoes and cucumbers mixed together at the same shop."

The strictest Sunni extremists believe that people should not have anything that did not exist in the early days of Islam. Since there was no electricity in the seventh century, there could be neither refrigeration nor ice and no television. The aversion to mixing tomatoes and cucumbers is because cucumbers are viewed as a male vegetable and tomatoes are female, and mixing them in a box is seen as lascivious, Colonel Khalid said, shaking his head.

Ranya, like Baida, was from an insurgent family. There was her aunt Wijdan, who police say was a recruiter of women; her father, who the police believed was involved in making bombs for the insurgency; and a brother who was abducted and may also have been involved. A year after Ranya's father was kidnapped and killed by a Shiite militia, her mother acquiesced to Ranya's marriage in 2007 to a minor figure in the Islamic State of Iraq.

Less than a year after she was married, Ranya's husband brought her to a house in Baquba where two women he described as cousins outfitted her with a suicide vest: "They gave me something to eat and something to drink; it had a nice smell," she recalled. "Then they put the explosive belt on me, those two girls did. I remember there were red wires, but I didn't know what was inside it. They put it over my head." Baida later told me that, from her own conversations in jail with Ranya, it was clear that she knew exactly what she was doing and was proud of it.

After Ranya was outfitted with the vest, she told me, a woman in the house, named Um Fatima, took her shopping. They went to one of Baquba's bazaars and, as Um Fatima looked at pots and pans, Ranya drifted off.

"There was a moment, only a moment, when Ranya felt afraid of death," Major Hosham said. Ranya told me she just wanted to see her mother. You can imagine that moment: realizing that your life might be about to end and you aren't ready.

When Um Fatima saw that she had lost Ranya, she fled the market, throwing away the remote detonator she was planning to use if Ranya failed to explode herself, the police said. The police later found the detonator. Meanwhile Ranya, wearing her suicide vest, unsure where she was going, wandered Baquba's back alleys. As she approached a checkpoint manned by members of the Awakening, the American-backed neighborhood watch formed to fight Al Qaeda in Mesopotamia, they ordered her to stop, according to Lt. Kadhim Ahmed al-Tamimi, a detective involved in the case. The Awakening guards thought it suspicious that she was alone and wearing a big abaya. "When they were in doubt about whether she was a suicide bomber they asked a woman on the street to search her, the woman opened the abaya, and when she saw all the wires, she cried out and ran away," Lieutenant Kadhim said. A few hours later Ranya was in jail along with her mother. Ranya was convicted on Aug. 3 under Iraq's terrorism law and sentenced to seven and a half years in prison.

One day in March, an interpreter told me that Baida had called several times from the psychiatric hospital and wanted to see us again. I felt we had gained her confidence. Maybe she would open up more. We called and told her we would come the next morning.

The Rashad Psychiatric Hospital lies at the very end of the sprawling Shiite slum of Sadr City. On that particular day there was a dust storm, and it was hard to see more than a short distance. The sky was a brownishtan color, and we could taste the grit. The hospital, spread over extensive grounds, had been neglected for years: the grass was shoulder high in places, the plantings were scruffy and the wards were almost bare of furnishings. (Much of it had been looted immediately after the American invasion.) Some patients wandered about, talking to themselves. Some wore soiled clothes and looked as if they had not washed in months. As we approached Baida's ward, a woman, stark naked, came running out screaming; she was pursued by members of the hospital staff as well as by other patients and eventually was covered in a large blanket and brought back inside.

We met Baida in the office of the head nurse for the criminally insane. Baida told us she felt great affection for the head nurse, who was a dwarf, perfectly groomed in a white veil, her face meticulously made up. She would let Baida do anything, including keep her telephone in the hospital, Baida told us.

Baida looked tired and much less ebullient than when I saw her in jail. I could tell she found it difficult to live with people who were so strange. I had brought her a bag of fresh mandarin oranges. She accepted them with a weak smile and only asked: "When will you come back? Tomorrow?" I worried she needed the company of more normal people.

When we returned to the Times bureau, one of our other interpreters took me aside. A military interpreter before he switched to journalism, he was streetwise; a Shiite who lived in a Sunni neighborhood; a survivor. He told me Baida called the bureau many times in the last three weeks wanting to know when I would visit the hospital—a bad sign, he said. Our security adviser agreed. There are no sureties when dealing with insurgents, but one rule is not to tell them exactly when you will be in a particular place. If they know, they can plan an ambush or a kidnapping or detonate an I.E.D. under your car. "Don't go to see her again," the interpreter said.

For the next meeting with Baida, our security adviser set a time limit, estimating that as soon as we arrived at the hospital, she might hear we were there and make a phone call to her jihadist friends. Baida called us twice to see "exactly when you are coming." We lied, keeping it vague. Setting an ambush would be tricky at the hospital but manageable just outside the gate.

When we did finally go, we met with Baida alone, sitting together on a bed in the nurse's office because there were no chairs. I asked her gently, and as nonjudgmentally as I could, whether she wanted to kill me because I was a foreigner.

"Frankly, yes." Then she added, to soften it, "Not specifically you, because I know you."

Would she tell her extremist cousins or her friends about me? Would she give them my description and tell them enough that they could find me?

"I won't sacrifice my friendship," she said. A moment later she reversed herself. "But, if they insisted, yes, I would, yes. As a foreigner it is halal to kill you."

She continued: "If they kill Americans they will do a big huge banquet for dinner."

She smiled beatifically. As Major Hosham had said, "She is honest."

"Frankly, they called me when they knew I would meet a journalist and translator and they did their best to get your descriptions and the date you would come," she went on to say. "They asked me about the date many times. They know the way to the hospital. They would be waiting for you and would kill you. They said to me, 'If you will do that for us, we will help you escape from the hospital, even from prison.' They asked for other details: 'What were your names; what did you look like?'"

She seemed excited now at the thought of our capture. "They do not want to kill you, but to torture you and make lunch of your flesh. I could not do anything to help you."

She described seeing—she didn't say how—an American soldier the group had kidnapped. "They took out his eyes and burned his body," she said. "God keep you safe."

As she described the case, I realized it was one I knew. I covered the trial of three of the men involved in the murder. I asked her what year she saw this; she got it right, 2006. I felt nauseated. Members of what would become the Islamic State of Iraq kidnapped three young soldiers guarding a bridge. One was killed immediately, but the other two were slowly tortured to death. One had his eyes gouged out and his body was tied to the back of a truck and dragged along the roads.

"They showed it to the women because women have a soft heart so they must see it so that they get used to it," she said.

I looked at my watch; I worried we had stayed too long. I got up hurriedly, knocking my notebooks to the floor. I adjusted my veil, thanked her for her time, for teaching me about jihad and for making me understand how dangerous her world was.

Baida was smiling again. "If I had not seen you before and talked to you, I would kill you with my own hands," she said pleasantly. "Do not be deceived by my peaceful face. I have a heart of stone."

A few days later Baida was transferred back to the provincial jail in Baquba after doctors at Rashad hospital determined that she had no psychological disorder. (Baida said the doctors told her early on: "You have a brain like a computer. You shouldn't be here.") At this writing she is still in jail. For now, she tells whoever asks that she's prepared to go out and kill the enemy; but if she were to start saying that she no longer would do that, I imagine she would be released quite quickly. And I have no reason to doubt that she would then carry out her dream of blowing herself up.

7.3

WHAT CHINA WILL WANT: THE FUTURE INTENTIONS OF A RISING POWER

Jeffrey W. Legro

> Jeffrey W. Legro's article offers a superb illustration of how scholars use the three mainstream perspectives in international relations to elucidate complex historical and policy issues. Legro reviews the limits of the realist (power) and liberal (interdependence) perspectives as they apply to China's role in world affairs and the related U.S. policy responses of containment (realist) and engagement (liberal). He then offers an ideational (identity) perspective that emphasizes "national ideas" of prevailing and alternative groups in China influencing how China interprets global power shifts and economic interdependence. Although recognizing that outside countries have limited influence over this internal Chinese debate, he suggests that U.S. policy should reinforce domestic ideas that encourage China to be a satisfied power and penalize those that encourage revisionism. Notice the priority Legro gives to the domestic and foreign policy levels of analysis over systemic structural (power shifts) and process (interdependence) levels.

The "rising China" problem is not just about power, but purpose. China has consistently stressed that its development as a major power will be peaceful and non-obtrusive. Yet in the United States there is, as one U.S. Deputy Secretary of State put it, a "cauldron of anxiety" over China's future.[1] Expert testimony before the U.S.-China Economic and Security Review Commission, a body that monitors and reports to Congress on bilateral relations, has focused heavily on uncertainty over China's intentions.[2] In February 2007, Vice President Cheney cautioned that China's recent anti-satellite test and general military build-up were "not consistent with China's stated goal of a 'peaceful rise.'"[3] The stomachs of strategists are churning.

It is rare when a pressing policy issue connects so directly to a critical gap in the scholarly literature. Such is the case with the impact of the rise of China on world politics. Will growing power lead Beijing to challenge international norms, rules, and institutions—possibly generating dangerous conflict among major powers in East Asia if not elsewhere? Or might China's integration in the

Source: Jeffrey W. Legro, "What China Will Want: The Future Intentions of a Rising Power," *Perspectives on Politics* 5, no. 3 (2007): 515–534.

international economy, its growing middle class, and increasing participation in international institutions and exchanges lead to enduring satisfaction in the existing international order? Today China appears to be a "status quo" power.[4] Will it remain so?

Existing answers to this question lack the very thing needed: a general explanation of contingent change in the intentions of China.[5] The problem is not simply an issue of China's secrecy or repression of free expression since the problem of future intentions applies to democracies as well as dictatorships.[6] Even if we had access to the inner workings of the Chinese government today, it is unlikely that information would tell us about future aims. Even if China today has some secret plan for world hegemony or world harmony, those aims will be subject to change by China's very growth and the process by which it unfolds. Ironically even China's top leaders, despite their concentrated political power, cannot know with certainty what their country will want.

Indeed, that is what the two views dominating the debate on China argue, although they see different inevitable futures. The first focuses on China's *power* and claims that China's desire for revision will grow as China's relative capabilities increase despite what Beijing thinks today. In this view other countries must do all they can to contain a rising China because at some point China will wield its newfound power to challenge global order. The second view highlights China's growing *interdependence* and argues that such conflict can be avoided by continuing to engage China, which will build domestic interests in China that favor political liberalization and accommodation to the rules of the prevailing international system. Both answers tap into deep-seated forces shaping China, but both are flawed due to their linear projection of the future of Chinese policy towards international order—be it the conflictual revision expected by power theorists or the harmonious integration predicted by interdependence advocates.[7]

China's diplomatic future, however, is likely to be more contingent than either the power or interdependence positions allow. To highlight contingency requires that something be said about what the future depends on—no small problem with a country like China that is authoritarian and non-transparent on many issues. What policymakers most need, scholars have found difficult to study.[8] Clearly in the case of China both its relative power and its economic interdependence affect its foreign policy. The issue of course is how the two will do so over time.[9]

I argue that their influence depends on a third meshing gear—national ideas about how to achieve foreign policy goals. Such ideas perform three critical functions: they empower certain domestic interest groups over others, they generate expectations against which performance is assessed, and they either facilitate or impede the possibility for a new strategy to emerge. Specifically, when Chinese expectations about the benefits of integrating in the extant international order are defied by events with negative consequences, an opportunity exists for domestic critics to challenge that orthodoxy. Whether change actually occurs depends, however, on the distribution of replacement ideas that affects whether critics can coordinate on a feasible alternative world view.

This approach offers some twists on familiar thinking. Contrary to the power-centric view of China, the most dangerous scenario in the future is not the "rise" of China, but ruptures in China's economic growth. Opposed to the economic interdependence position, economic engagement need not lead to harmony. Countries that undertake rapid integration have generated considerable systemic conflict.[10] China itself has displayed wide variation in its approach, be it cooperate with, challenge, or separate itself from international society over the past two centuries. The point is not that power or economic liberalization is unimportant, but rather that those factors interact with dominant ideas in particular ways to shape enduring patterns of national behavior.

In terms of policy this means that neither a containment nor engagement policy is a reliable consistent choice. Indeed, the dominant view today among policymakers accepts this advice by advocating a "hedging" strategy that pursues both options simultaneously with the particular mix of strategy (conflictual vs. cooperative) dependent on Chinese behavior.[11]

The argument here offers a somewhat different and more proactive view: it suggests that managing a rising China will depend not on behavior per se but on the nature of the dominant ideas. When China espouses ideas and action that favor cooperative integration, it makes sense to do as much as possible to ensure that their internal supporters gain positive feedback and "I told you so" leverage vis-à-vis their domestic critics. Likewise, when China displays consistent revisionist tendencies, such ideas should be penalized—but only when influential opposition groups are promoting more attractive alternative ideas. Otherwise, no matter how loathsome any particular approach, if the alternative is even less desirable, dramatic pressure for rapid change is problematic. Therefore, it behooves the international community to be proactive (not just reactive to behavior) by nurturing groups and ideas in China that offer more benign replacements to the less desirable alternatives.

Naturally in all these areas, the potential for outside influence on a country of China's size and regime type has significant limits. Yet we know from the Soviet experience that even in authoritarian states, slow patient efforts to support reformers can have an impact.[12] The future of China will not be decided by the actions of others, but the actions of outside parties have influenced China's orientation in the past (e.g., Nixon and the opening of China) and may do so again in the future.

* * *

The Limits of Power and Interdependence

The debate over China is not about what China wants today, but what it might want tomorrow. The rise of China could lead to a fundamental reorientation of Chinese thinking and perhaps a challenge to world order, as those who focus on power predict. Or China could increasingly enmesh itself in and support the existing rules of international society, even undergoing political democratization, as most who emphasize China's growing interdependence foresee. Both offer an important vision, but both are half blind in ignoring the contingent nature of China's future intentions.

Power

Power theories expect a clear shift in a revisionist direction. As Robert Gilpin once put it, "As its relative power increases, a rising state attempts to change the rules governing the system."[13] John Mearsheimer concludes that China's growing capabilities will mean it "would not be a status quo power, but an aggressive state determined to achieve regional hegemony."[14] Denny Roy expects that "China's growth from a weak, developing state to a stronger, more prosperous state should result in a more assertive foreign policy ... bolder, more demanding, and less inclined to cooperate with the other major powers in the region."[15] The basic thrust of these analyses is that rising power leads to a growing geopolitical appetite and a likely change toward revisionism.

This view of China has two variations, the "patient hegemon" and the "innocent giant." In the first view, China is like Germany in the Weimar period, patiently biding its time until it is strong enough to reconfigure an oppressive international order. Hans Von Seeckt, the head of the outlawed (shadow) Germany army is reputed to have declared in the 1920s, "First we'll get strong, then we'll take back what we lost."[16] Deng supposedly advised, "Observe calmly; secure our position; cope with affairs calmly; hide our capacities and bide our time; be good at maintaining a low profile; and never claim leadership."[17] The implication, of course, is that after power is achieved different policies will follow. Lieutenant General Mi Zhenyu, Vice Commandant of the Academy of Military Sciences, put it more bluntly: "[As for the United States,] for a relatively long time it will be absolutely necessary that we quietly nurse our sense of vengeance.... We must conceal our abilities and bide our time."[18]

A second view of China is as an "innocent giant" that may not be revisionist right now, but is likely to shift in that direction as it gains power. China may genuinely believe its rise will be peaceful, but once it has gained enough resources, it is likely to want more and be willing to concede less and hence put up with less of the status quo. Sometimes such shifts will be provoked, not by China, but by the insecure actions of the declining hegemon, in this case the United States.[19]

Not only is revisionism likely according to power theorists, but so too is conflict. Power transitions are viewed as a quintessential source of war in the international arena.[20] This is especially the case when nations have histories that leave them aggrieved. Thus there is concern that China, like other countries that feel they have historically gotten the short end of the stick, are particularly prone to attempt to revise the international system.[21]

These power arguments correctly identify key elements shaping Chinese foreign policy and international relations. Chinese leaders pay close attention to power and geopolitics.[22] Indeed, to the extent that China is interested in joining international society, it should, by the very principles of the system, have an interest in balance of power politics. And China is certainly focused on increasing its own power and balancing U.S. power in Asia.[23] There are also good reasons to believe that Chinese aims and influence will grow in some respects as China's power grows. It would be a true anomaly if some portion of China's new-found wealth were not directed to increased and more modern military capabilities.

Likewise power transition theorists rightly point to the higher probability of international tensions when power transitions occur. It is easy to imagine that a more powerful China might use its capabilities in ways that raise hackles of those (e.g., the United States) used to calling the shots in Asia without such constraints.

The problem with this argument however is that power is not destiny. There are analytic and empirical anomalies that confound such a spare view. We might, for example, assume that states are concerned first and foremost with power, but that tells us nothing about how they think they can best achieve power—by challenging the world, cooperating with it, or ignoring it. Because international relations are complex and road testing grand strategies is difficult, states show lagged responses at best to external conditions. The possibility of effective adjustment to international demands is further impeded by the fact that "the state" is not a single actor but an aggregation of leaders with different constituencies, each with varying perceptions and preferences.[24] Aggregating those preferences into a coherent collective choice faces a variety of hurdles.[25] In short, grand strategy is filtered through domestic politics.

Empirically, states do not always expand their foreign policy as power increases (nor do they limit it as power declines). Historical anomalies are common.[26] In the First World War, America emerged as the dominant power in international relations, but its involvement and goals did not expand, but contracted in the interwar period. China in the Qing era did not alter its isolationist ideas to deal with the encroaching and threatening European powers even though the security situation indicated mounting dangers. And in terms of power trajectories, Britain and the United States did not go to war with each other at the turn of the twentieth century, even as the United States surpassed Britain as the dominant international power.[27] National strategy can rarely be understood by reference to external conditions alone.

Nor have ideas followed the balance of power in lockstep. China has been consistently weaker than the dominant powers of world politics since at least the late nineteenth century, yet its ideas have varied between separation in Qing China to integration in Republican and contemporary China to revisionism during Mao....[28] We might view China's power trajectory, not static position as being most important, but that trajectory has been rising (with fits and starts) since the communists seized control of the mainland. China's ideas, however, have made shifts between revisionism and integration.

And contrary to the "rising China" thesis—i.e., that foreign policy ambitions grow with relative power—China was most revisionist when it was at one of its weakest points in terms of relative power—i.e., after Mao came to power.

Scholars have attempted to modify the power view to take into consideration such anomalies. One notion is that states are shaped not just by raw power, but also by "intentions."[29] Power transition scholars have long noted that "national satisfaction with the status quo" is as important as transitions. In both instances these factors are viewed as distinct from, and not reducible to, power. They clearly imply that we cannot understand and predict what states will do without knowing how they think about appropriate action.[30] Yet they do not address the key issue of when such thinking is likely to change—or not.

Interdependence

A different response to Chinese power comes from those who believe that China's material improvement and social evolution through interdependence with the world give rise to domestic political forces that favor integration and support the existing system. This will occur through a number of mechanisms. First, government officials that take part in international diplomacy and negotiations over time come to define their interests in ways more consistent with the system.[31]

Second, China's increasing participation in the world economy is expected to give rise to domestic economic and political interests that press for even greater liberalization.[32] For example, as China modernizes, its middle class and its resources grow[33] ... —a trend that has historically been a force for political democratization.

Finally as China opens, the increase in travel and education abroad[34] ... the spread of free speech and ideas on the internet[35] ... and experiments with even limited voting and choice are expected to inspire a taste for liberty that feeds democratizing impulses that will more happily align China with international standards.

Overall, the more that China is economically and socially entwined with other major powers (e.g., the United States) the more it gains from the overall system and the more it has to lose in changing the system or engaging in major conflict.[36] We might also anticipate that as China participates in the system it will also change it, in consultation and agreement with other countries, more to its liking.

These related arguments that support engagement certainly capture an important influence on Beijing's thinking today. China has become captivated by the economic growth that has accrued from its openness to the international economy. Such interaction has generated more significant domestic political interests that favor opening. While the growth of the Chinese middle class is still nascent, there is some evidence to suggest increasing wealth may affect foreign policy opinions.[37] The People's Republic of China remains an authoritarian state yet Chinese citizens will also attest to the fact that their political situation today is vastly more liberal and open than it was in the pre-reform period and becoming more so.[38] And finally China realizes that it does have much at stake in the current system—with incentives to become more engaged.[39] This explanation usefully points us to the fact that world politics is enacted through domestic politics and what happens in China's foreign relations can affect those politics, potentially changing them dramatically over time.

The problem with these interdependence arguments is that they, like their power-centric debating opponents, are overly deterministic.[40] They assume that once China has been hooked up to the international system there is little chance it will ever change directions. Internationalist factions profiting or learning from integration are expected to snowball, pushing the country further in that direction. This view, however, also runs into analytical traps and historical anomalies.

Analytically, it has a difficult time accounting for how interests within societies "add up" to national policy choices.[41] For example, what number of internet users translates into a free speech society that prefers democracy? Right now the Chinese government is matching strides toward freedom of expression with its own control of the internet and press. Likewise it is difficult to determine how a growing middle class or expansion in China's international sectors will fit with political liberalization compatible with international society. Those who have benefited most from China's openness are either in, or linked to, the Communist party that rules China and provides for stability that attracts international investment.[42] Indeed, it may be that a democratic China—one where rural peasants and other disenfranchised groups have a say—would be distinctly opposed to the type of integration now occurring.[43]

Democratization is a precarious process—democratizing states are often prone to conflict under the pressures of new-found nationalism stoked by exaggerated expectations unrestrained by fledgling institutions. Contemporary Chinese nationalism threatens to be the Mr. Hyde to the Dr. Jekyll of the "reform and opening" policy that Deng initiated.[44] Economic interdependence may be a force that works against conflict, but it is not a failsafe—as seen in the interdependence of the early 1900s in Europe that ended in the Great War.

Nor does globalization—the shrinking of the globe and increased density of contacts within international society due to technological advances—guarantee Chinese integration. The potential interdependence of China in the System—in terms of the declining costs of transportation and communication and the relative openness of the world trade order—has been occurring for decades. Whether China took advantage of the potential gains of interdependence was at least in part a Chinese policy choice that needs to be explained.[45] For example, ... Chinese interdependence has not been driven simply by the march of technology, but instead by Chinese ideas (and those of others) about how much China should be engaged in the world. Thus, Chinese interdependence declined following the rise of Mao's revisionism and when China began to recalibrate after the disastrous Cultural Revolution, interdependence began to rise—especially after 1978.

The history of national economic modernization via engagement with the international arena is filled with stories of countries undertaking integration and then later moving in the opposite direction. Here we might think of Weimar Germany's shift under Hitler or Japan's shift from Taishō democracy to the Shōwa era or even the retreat of the United States in the interwar period. China itself reversed directions in moving from Qing China to Nationalist China and then reversed again in the transition to Communist China.

In sum, both power and economic interdependence may push strategy in particular directions but such moves have also been reversed even when power and interdependence conditions remain fairly constant. Similarly, sometimes states may stick to their plans even as conditions of power and interdependence alter significantly. Why?

The Meshing Gear: Collective Ideas

Neither power nor interdependence directly shaped Chinese grand strategy because such systemic factors are enacted through domestic politics and decision making. There are of course many types of domestic theories of politics. Here, however, I want to concentrate on the central (and misunderstood) role of enduring foreign policy ideas in domestic politics and subsequent national behavior.

There is a large and very insightful literature on how collective ideas (e.g., beliefs, norms, discourses, culture, etc.) "matter" in foreign policy.[46] What is usually missing in these arguments is *how ideas matter in their own transformation.* The literature is very good on how collective ideas might keep intentions fixed, but less clear on how they affect change. To suggest that ideas play a role in their own transformation is not to argue that outcomes are wholly caused by ideas. It is useful to distinguish the impact of ideas from other factors (e.g., strategic circumstances or economic pressures) and to make sense of how they might conjointly cause outcomes—i.e., how power and interdependence interact with ideas through predictable mechanisms to cause outcomes. The central emphasis in what follows is on the role of ideas (simply because it is the least understood) but the importance of power and transnational pressures will also be clear.

Foreign Policy Ideas and Intentions

States tend to formulate broad concepts—almost operational philosophies—that orient their international behavior. As large societies, nations require ideas that signify to their members what they stand for; as large organizations they require ideas to guide them in their interactions in the international arena. "Ideas," as I use the term here, are not mental constructs of individuals, but instead the collective beliefs of societies and organizations about how to act.

Examples of beliefs about "good policies" from the foreign policies of major powers include:

- "non-entanglement" in European politics (United States, 1776–1941)
- territorial expansion on the continent (Germany 1890–1945)
- isolation from extensive foreign interaction or presence (Japan 1640–1868)
- integration as a normal power (Soviet Union/Russia 1986–present)

They are embedded not only in some human brains, but most importantly in the collective memories, national symbols, government procedures, educations systems, and rhetoric of statecraft.[47]

Such views matter because they are a guide to national action and can shape what states want to achieve over time. Naturally state leaders strategically plan their actions but they often do so against a backdrop of certain dominant national ideas about what general behavior is appropriate. These ideas may be contested by some groups within societies but still serve as a guide for the collective "nation." Promoted by those who benefit and nurtured by habit, they grow roots. As organization theorists point out, particularly when groups have intangible goals such as "security" or "wealth" states will focus their efforts around doctrines of action rather than actual goals. Put differently, ideas become intentions.[48] In foreign affairs, such ideas are what Ernest May has called "axiomatic"—formulations derived from history that become accepted assumptions of policy.[49]

National ideas about international order are difficult to change for a number of reasons. First, they have constituencies that benefit from them and thus are energized to promote and defend them. Second, such dominant ideas become ingrained in public rhetoric and bureaucratic procedures that make them resilient like all traditions that are institutionally entrenched. Third, because of this effect they become normalized not just as means to achieve ends, but also as a standard of what the nation *should* do, or even what it is (i.e., identity).

Tokugawa Japan came to be defined by its policy of excluding foreigners and its leaders appealed to that tradition to sustain their position. Similarly, the United States was distinguished by its refusal to "get entangled" with the suspect traditional powers of Europe in the first 150 years of its existence and presidents paid homage to that norm (e.g., Harding in the 1920s) in order to bolster their popularity.[50] China in the nineteenth century in the face of foreign incursions attempted to hew to a traditional Qing Middle Kingdom mentality despite its waning authority.

It is therefore not surprising that continuity is the norm in foreign policy ideas. Those who want to challenge tradition face significant hurdles. It is often hard for individuals to know if others desire change and if they do, how much they will risk acting on such preferences. Lacking such information, they cannot be sure if their own desire and efforts for change (should they exist) will have any effect. They must mount a case for why the old ideas were defunct, which can involve considerable effort, and because it threatens tradition, invites social and political criticism.

Likewise the formation and institutionalization of new ideas breeds strife and uncertainty because particular orientations offer differing costs and benefits to domestic groups that can stalemate over which, if any, new direction is more desirable. Continuity, therefore, is a potent force. Yet as May points out, entrenched foreign policy concepts are nonetheless vulnerable to transformation "as history grows" and countries "see the past in a new light."[51] The interesting questions are when and how?

When Orthodoxy Disintegrates

Implicit in the above discussion is the fact that change is not a single phenomenon but involves two stages that must be explained: collapse of the old ideas and consolidation of the new. Both stages, I argue, are affected by pre-existing ideas.

In the *collapse* stage, pre-existing ideas affect how leaders justify policy and set a baseline of social expectations of what should result. Political opponents within countries then use those baselines to assess—and support or critique—existing policies, depending on events. When events contradict collective expectations *and* the consequences are starkly undesirable, change is more likely. Such situations facilitate change by giving ammunition to the opponents of the current orthodoxy, allowing them to rally support to their side while supporters of the current orthodoxy are put on the defensive. For example, the separatist approach of the Qing Empire was finally disrupted by the 1895 Japanese victory in the Sino-Japanese War. That event set off a race among outsiders to control China and encouraged forces within China to challenge tradition, including in foreign policy.[52]

In most other circumstances, continuity is likely. For example, continuity can be expected when deviations from existing ideas lead to undesired outcomes. When the United States intervened in World War I it violated its longstanding taboo against entanglement in Europe's politics. The results of World War I brought widespread disillusionment in the United States and the Americans embraced anew their tradition of "no-entanglement" in Europe. In such situations, defenders of the old ideas (as the American isolationists did) will be able to make political hay by claiming "told you so, we should never have strayed from our tried and true tradition." Intervention in World War I, they argued, had been a disastrous mistake.

Likewise continuity is even likely when dominant ideas are ignored yet desirable results occur. It is hard to gather momentum to change collective ideas when outcomes are agreeable. Consider, for example, the dearth of investigations of large stock market *increases* that no one expected versus the special commissions that always seem to form to examine unexpected stock market crashes. When outcomes are desirable, it is difficult to generate momentum to reorient bureaucracies and alter traditions. The delegitimation of an extant orthodoxy requires events that both contradict its logic *and* have undesired consequences. In such circumstances, individuals will be more motivated and more likely to challenge those ideas, believe others are of a like mind, and hence the possibilities for change are more significant....

Conditions of New Orthodoxy

Even when dominant ideas are delegitimated, however, change is not automatic. Consolidation, like collapse, faces hurdles that feed inertia. Individuals may agree that the old view has to go but may not be able to agree or coordinate on what new orthodoxy should be the guide. Such a dynamic has been charted in the study of revolution, but it also exists in foreign policy disputes and debates.[53] The consolidation of a new foreign policy approach depends not only on the collapse of the old ideas, but also on the distribution of replacement ideas, especially the existence of a prominent alternative. When there are no developed alternatives or when there are many equally strong alternatives, the result could be a return to the old thinking due to default in the first case and deadlock among factions in the second. For example, in Qing China in the nineteenth century, Sinocentric separation from the encroaching international society was so dominant that there were virtually no groups of any import with developed replacement ideas to guide China's foreign policy.[54]...

The sustainability of a new orthodoxy (when a prominent replacement does exist) over a longer period often hinges on some demonstration of its efficacy. Ideas that endure do so because they appear to generate desirable results. When those notions do not, revanchists often find fertile ground to argue for a return to the old ideas. This was the case in Weimar Germany when the results of Versailles undermined the liberal international policy of the fledgling Social Democratic government. Versailles also spawned the May Fourth Movement in China that helped discredit fledgling liberal democracy notions.[55] ...

This argument features ideas as a meshing gear—one that interacts with other factors and in doing so has its own influence. National strategies therefore are a product of multi-causal influence. Prior ideas play a role but of course do not unilaterally determine all aspects of new orthodoxies. Consider, for example, the role of the relative power of actors, which often shapes negative and positive feedback to prevailing ideas. Dominant concepts that ignore relative power can lead to disappointing results that contribute to their delegitimation. Consider the decline of the Qing-era tribute system and sinocentrism under the weight of superior European and Japanese capabilities that exposed their fragility in the late nineteenth century. Likewise, the number and nature of replacement ideas so central to consolidation is shaped by the political activity and resources of interest groups and individuals that promote them. Economic interdependence and the promises of growth inherent in it can indeed strengthen those in favor of such ideas.[56] Long-term efforts that encourage international exchange can facilitate the rise of replacement ideas in particular societies.[57] Thus the success of ideas can also be shaped by the degree a country is involved in the international economy.

Overall, then, the account of foreign policy change (and continuity) offered here is contingent. It depends on the interaction of the dominant foreign policy ideas of states with the results encountered, as well as the distribution of replacement ideas in a particular society and their initial success, if any. To stress contingency is not to forgo explanation.[58] We can posit that future intentions will depend on the degree to which the expectations of particular dominant ideas are defied by events, negative consequences result, and some socially viable replacement idea exists.

This general logic seems to have wide application in the history of great powers, and though there are differences, covers both democratic and authoritarian regimes.[59] What follows is a brief illustration of how some of the central dynamics captured by the logic might play out in the future of China's current "reform and opening" view on international order described above.

The Contingent Path of China's Future Intentions

The argument above highlights particular signposts as important for understanding what China might do with its growing power in the future. Most centrally, the longevity of China's integrationist orthodoxy will depend on the expectations it generates in the domestic arena and the results that are experienced (collapse considerations), as well as on the nature of the ideas that might replace integration (consolidation factors). I address each in turn.

Justifications and Expectations

Contemporary Chinese leaders justify and promote the dominant integration idea—i.e., "reform and opening"—in two different ways.

The first, and most important, justification of current policy is that integration within the existing international order provides the best means for national economic development.[60] China remains a government run by a communist party. Yet the legitimacy and popular support of the government does not rest on socialist ideology, but instead on economic performance. "Well-off Society" not "Workers Unite" is the national mantra. President Jiang Zemin's 2002 address to the 16th Party Congress put this claim starkly:

> It is essential for the Party to give top priority to development in governing and rejuvenating the country and open up new prospects for the modernization drive ... the progressiveness of the Party is concrete and historical, and it must be judged by whether the Party promotes the development of the advanced productive forces.[61]

The Fifth Plenary of the 16th Party Congress of the CPC in October 2005 called development "the overriding principle and the key to resolving all problems facing China."[62] The dominance of the integration orientation in contemporary Chinese foreign policy is largely based on economic considerations. Integration according to the reform and opening orthodoxy serves China's rapid development.

The second major justification for integration within the existing international order is that it enhances sovereignty—understood in terms of independence and territorial integrity. That is, integration should prevent the type of colonial subordination of the past and the infringement of China by outside powers. A defining point of history for the Communist Party (CPC) leadership is the "century of humiliation" China endured under the influence of imperialist powers (e.g., the West, Japan). One of the CPC's main claims to authority is that it liberated China from that outside influence.[63] Integration facilitates such a goal by providing access to institutional fora where global politics are decided that might affect China's autonomy. Such integration also provides the imprint of major power status, confirming that the country is no longer simply an object manipulated by more powerful Western countries or Japan, but an important actor itself.

The most concrete marker of sovereignty for China today is Taiwan. China expects that its participation in the extant institutions and conventions of world politics will help to fulfill a desire (seemingly widespread across the political spectrum) to unite the mainland and Taiwan. Such participation allows China to stymie efforts by Taiwan to claim sovereign international standing and to build its own international support.

These two themes, economic modernization and sovereignty, may look closely linked to the realist focus on power and autonomy. The key difference, however, is that Chinese leaders justify them not based on increasing China's security, but on bettering the living standard of Chinese citizens. Likewise, China's obsession with Taiwan and other territories is hard to understand from strictly a power perspective. Without knowing China's history and the centrality of Taiwan to CPC legitimacy gains, it is impossible to understand the role this issue can play in Chinese politics and security decision-making.

Economic development and sovereignty can of course also be in tension with one another, a fact that does much to explain the complexity of contemporary Chinese policies.[64] Integration can lead to deep inroads on issues of sovereignty. For example, membership in the World Trade Organization brings with it a number of significant implications for the Chinese social and political order, not the least of which is major turmoil in the massive Chinese agricultural sector and growing inequality within Chinese society.[65]

Anticipating Events That Favor Change

The durability of China's integrationist foreign policy, therefore, will depend on how results match social expectations related to economic growth and sovereignty. Events related to China's integration that represent significant setbacks to either of those issues would be occasions for China to rethink integration.

The first situation where the integrationist orthodoxy would be vulnerable involves troubles in China's economic modernization. From this viewpoint (and in contrast to the rise of China debate) the most likely scenario in which China will alter its integrationist mindset is not with the growth of Chinese power but, instead, major ruptures in that trajectory that could put the dominant "open-ness" view on a slippery defensive. A reasonable case can be made that a level-ing of Chinese economic growth is as likely in the future as is China's rise to supremacy.[66] Especially vis-à-vis current Chinese expectations, this would be a deeply disillusioning experience if China's government is somehow implicated. That is, in the absence of downturns that affect all countries or unforeseen crises, critics of the current orthodoxy will have incentive to use faltering Chinese economic prospects to rally political authority around a new approach to the international system. The motivating source in such a scenario will be the com-bination of surprising economic setbacks contrasted with optimistic expecta-tions generated by leaders seeking legitimacy.

The decline of economic growth would encourage previously silent groups that oppose integration. China's rapid development has led to daunting gaps between rich and poor.[67] Social protests and disturbances appear to have risen steadily in recent years, increasing from 8,700 in 1993 to 87,000 in 2005.[68] Involvement in the World Trade Organization (WTO) is putting significant pressures on poor farmers and peasants who cannot compete. As long as the economy is booming, some of these people can transfer to other types of jobs or the government can provide some form of subsidy.[69] Yet if growth falters in a way that makes the government seem complicit, this system looks brittle.

Second, events supported by the international community that China sees as neo-colonial or which move Taiwan towards independence could help to under-mine China's current integration orthodoxy. For example, the 1999 bombing of the Chinese embassy in Belgrade fueled nationalism and strengthened oppo-nents of opening.[70] Much, of course, will depend on the particular circum-stances and whether they make Beijing government seem complicit. Taiwanese efforts to establish formal independence cause deep concern in China—indeed the type that can set the stage for China to take aggressive efforts on an issue seen as priority even by "reformist" governments. Taiwanese independence efforts in 2004–2005 were met by a strong (and self-defeating) reaction from Hu Jintao and National People's Congress passing anti-secession legislation which authorized China to use force against Taiwan if it continued to push for independence.[71]

Replacements for "Reform and Opening"

If reform and opening does falter, what then? Presumably some sort of alter-native path. Anticipating such a new approach, however, depends on a key factor that is especially elusive in the Chinese case: the nature and distribution of replacement ideas about international society within China.[72] The outlines of three replacements are discernable in an admittedly opaque view.[73]

The first was identified by Jiang Zemin as a challenge to his own "reform and opening" emphasis in the years following the 1989 Tiananmen Square fiasco.[74] Jiang labeled this the threat from the "Right." For the government, the danger from the Right involves those who would attempt to pursue economic and political liberalization at an even more rapid pace at the expense of the Party and social stability. In recent years the CPC has been especially focused on this challenge and has gone to great effort to lure successful businessmen into the party and welcome the return of Chinese from abroad who might otherwise be a voice for more forceful political change. Think here of those who have bene-fited most from rapid integration but who are now chafing under CPC con-straints or believe China must take reforms to the next level (e.g., rule of law, education) at a faster pace—e.g., the new private businessmen or state-owned enterprise executives, artists or intellectuals, coastal city regions and their offi-cials, or even parts of the bureaucracy that have an interest in integration.

Jiang also identified a second group with alternative preferences for China's foreign policy. He called it "those with leftist tendencies" (distinct from the old Marxist variety) who critique reform—and international involvement—as con-tributing to social injustice and inequality. In the current context, this might include farmers, rural citizens, inland cities, and parts of the military or Com-munist party who have not shared equally in China's development and could rightly blame reform and opening or participation in the global order (think WTO) as the cause. In foreign policy such tendencies translate into social sup-port for halting and reversing China's integration in the current order. If the communiqué from the Fifth Plenary Session of the 16th Party Congress in October 2005 is an indicator, the challenge from the Left—and the inequality of growth—is of particular concern to the leadership of Hu Jintao who has emphasized the more egalitarian goal of "harmonious society" in contrast to Jiang's mantra of "well-off society."[75]

A third position would come from those who are critical of globalization and western values, but are not necessarily isolationist or anti-capitalist. These people might advocate a nationalist realpolitik policy that favors a more con-frontational strategy with the West, stability and central authority at home, while pursuing a soft line and integration in Asia. Think of this perhaps, as the platform for the resurgence of a modern day "Middle Kingdom" role where China would exercise increasing hegemony within Asia while perhaps distanc-ing itself from overall international order.[76]

Absent better information, it would appear that those who would emphasize withdrawal—either the new Left or realpolitikers—would occupy the rhetorical high ground should future events defy the "opening" justifications of the Chi-nese government with clear disappointing results. Both offer a greater difference with current dominant integration ideas (Rightists want even more integration) and would likely be in a better position to draw off the language of nationalism to make their case.[77] Chinese strategy will of course always be a mix of these different approaches; the issue is the direction of shift and the degree to which one orientation dominates.

To the extent that a factional account of Chinese politics is overdrawn (e.g., because the decision making dynamic is one of consensus, not groups fighting over control) then any change in foreign policy thinking will demand especially negative results and could take considerable time, just as it did in Qing China.[78] If there is a continued shared view that "isolation is the major factor explaining China's decline" and "opening fueled China's rise," then shifting significantly away from reform and opening would not happen quickly.[79] Although not so dominant as the separatist mentality of Qing China, integration today enjoys a privileged status against which replacement idea proponents may have a hard time making headway.

*   *   *

Notes

1. Zoellick 2005.
2. See, for example the hearings held from the summer of 2006 up to now. http://www.uscc.gov/hearings/hearingarchive.php.
3. Vice President's Remarks to the Australian-American Leadership Dialogue, Shangri-La Hotel Sydney, Australia, February 27, 2007. http://www.whitehouse.gov/news/releases/2007/02/20070223.html.
4. Johnston 2003.
5. Friedberg 2005 offers a typology and contingent analysis of future relations that lacks a general explanation to tell us whether events will move in one direction or another.
6. Copeland 2000a.
7. Friedberg 2005 documents that there is some variation in this dichotomy—some who focus on power do not see inevitable conflict and some liberals are more pessimistic.
8. For a study that explores the link between uncertainty about intentions and cooperative or conflictual strategies, see Edelstein 2000.
9. The classic synthesis of power and interdependence (without ideas) is Keohane and Nye, 1977.
10. See Snyder 1991 and Solingen 1998.
11. *The National Security Strategy of the United States of America* (March 2006) "seeks to encourage China to make the right strategic choices for its people, while we hedge against other possibilities." http://www.whitehouse.gov/nsc/nss/2006/. See also Carter and Perry 2007, 16–22; Council on Foreign Relations, *U.S.-China Relations: An Affirmative Agenda, A Responsible Course,* Independent Task Force Report 59 (April 2007).
12. Thomas 2001; Evangelista 1999.
13. Gilpin 1981, 187. See also Zakaria 1992.
14. Mearsheimer 2001, 402.
15. Roy 1994, 149–168, 159–160.
16. Geyer 1981, 107.
17. Hong Kong Jing bao, No. 172 (5 November 1991), 84–86, in FBIS-CHI, 6 November 1991, 28–30 as cited in Whiting 1995.
18. Quoted in Mosher 2001, ch. 1.
19. See Copeland 2000b.

20. E.g., see Organski and Kugler 1980; Gilpin 1981; Kim and Morrow 1992; Copeland 2000b. For different strategies of managing such a situation, see Schweller 1999.

21. Waldron 1995.

22. For an argument that China has a long strategic tradition of realpolitik thought, see Johnston 1995.

23. Pillsbury 2000; Qin 2001.

24. In the Chinese case see, Dittmer 1995, 1–39.

25. Gilbert 1987, 185–204.

26. For a variety of examples, see Walt 1987; Snyder 1991; Stein and Rosecrance 1993; Kupchan 1994.

27. Most power transitions occur without conflict. See De Soysa, Oneal, and Park 1997.

28. Relative power is given as a composite of the relative share of absolute total global data on six categories: energy consumption, iron & steel production, military expenditure, military personnel, total population, and urban population. See National Material Capabilities Study (v3.01) http://www.correlatesofwar.org and Singer et al. 1972, Singer 1987.

29. Walt 1987; Schweller 2006.

30. Lemke 2002. Ruggie 1982 speaks to the need to consider purpose as well as power.

31. Johnston 2001.

32. Frieden and Rogowski, 1996.

33. The index number of 100 for real disposable income in 1978 was equal to 343.4 RMB. See http://chinadataonline.org/member/yearbook/default.asp?StartYear1984& EndYear2006.

34. www.chinadataonline.org. For data prior to 1985, see *China Statistical Yearbook*, 633.

35. *Statistical Reports on the Development of Chinese Internet*, available at http://www. cnnic.net.cn/en/index/index.htm.

36. Rosecrance 1986; Russett and Oneal 2000.

37. Johnston 2004b, 603–628.

38. Zhao 2000, 11–12; Johnson 2003, 551–554.

39. Building on arguments offered by scholars, China's leaders such as General Secretary Hu Jintao and Premier Wen Jaibao have argued that China's modernization depends on peace and that China's "rise" would not lead to policies that pose threats or come at the expense of other countries. See Suettinger 2004. (http://www.chinaleadership-monitor.org/20044/rs.pdf) and Zheng 2005.

40. For a synthesis of the two that overcomes some of these problems, see Copeland 2003.

41. See Garrett and Lang 1996. It also applies to socialization arguments about China as well.

42. For an argument that China is unlikely to liberalize in any foreseeable time frame see Mann 2007.

43. Waldron 2004.

44. Mansfield and Snyder 1995; Snyder 2000; Gries 2004.

45. The Western powers of course had a say on this outcome as well. U.S. policy after Mao came to power was largely aimed at isolating China.

46. Berman 2001; Adler 2002.
47. See Anderson 1983; Halbwachs 1992; Kertzer 1988.
48. E.g., the mission statement for the United States Department of State is "*Create a more secure, democratic, and prosperous world for the benefit of the American people and the international community*"—see http://www.state.gov/m/rm/rls/dosstrat/2004/23503.htm. On the general organizational dynamic see Selznick, 1949, 69–70, 250–259; Selznick 1957, 16; Wilson 1989.
49. May 1962.
50. See Toby 1997, 323–364; Adler 1957.
51. May 1962, 667.
52. Gong 1984; Zhang 1991.
53. On consolidation in the literature on revolutions, see e.g., Goldstone 1991.
54. As the future revolutionary Sun Yatsen wrote to an official in 1893, "the reason why we have not achieved much (relative to other countries that had opened up); public opinion and entrenched ideas simply will not allow it." Mitter 2004, 32.
55. See Hunt 1996, 77ff.
56. This is the thrust of Frieden and Rogowski 1996 and ties in well with Copeland 2003.
57. See Keck and Sikkink 1998; Thomas 2001.
58. Friedberg 2005 rightly points out the difficulty of predicting the future when it depends on events that we cannot foresee. Nonetheless, it is possible to explicate the conditions and mechanisms through which events will produce different futures.
59. See Legro 2005.
60. Downs and Saunders 1998/99 argue that China has valued economic development ahead of nationalist goals.
61. *Jiang Zemin's Report to the 16th National Congress of the Chinese Communist Party*; Fewsmith 2003, 3. See too recent speeches by Hu Jintao, successor to Jiang, that offer similar themes, e.g., "President Hu Outlines Work Agenda for 2005," http://www.chinaembassy.org.il/eng/xwdt/t178046.htm.
62. Communiqué of the 15th CPC Central Committee Plenum, October 9–11, 2005. http://www.china.org.cn/english/features/45280.htm.
63. Lampton 2001, 251ff.; Zhao 2004. For an example of this view of history see China's October 2005 white paper "Building Political Democracy in China," especially Section I, "A Choice Suited to China's Conditions."
64. Wu 2001.
65. Riskin and Khan 2000; Lardy 2002; Eckholm 2002, 1; Kahn 2004a, 2004b.
66. Goldstein and Lardy 2004; Dollar 2005, 48–58.
67. Wang et al. 2007. www.132.203.59.36:81/Group/papers/papers/PMMA-2007-07.pdf.
68. Data based on figures released by China's Public Security Bureau. www.zonaeuropa.com/20061115_1.htm. See also Tanner 2004, 137–156.
69. Lin 2007.
70. See Zhen 2000; Gries 2004.
71. Cody 2005.
72. Seasoned China specialists note the difficulty assessing the nature and strength of competing coalitions, e.g., Christensen 2003, 4–6.

73. On different factions, see Swaine and Tellis 2000, 83–86; Johnston 2003; Yan 2001, 35; Deng and Gray 2001, 5–16. In general, see Dittmer 1995, 1–39; Nathan 1973, 33–66.

74. *Jiang Zemin's Report at the 14th National Congress of the Communist Party of China*, 1992.

75. "Chinese Communist Party Fifth Plenary Session Communiqué—Text," Xinhua News Agency Domestic Service, Beijing, October 11, 2005; Kahn 2005; Li 2005a, 2006.

76. Kang 2004, 165–81; Khoo and Smith 2005, 196–205.

77. E.g., the appeal to in-group/out-group biases—see Gries 2004.

78. Heer 2000; Li 2005a.

79. Yan 2001, 35.

References

Adler, Emanuel. 2002. Constructivism and international relations. In *Handbook of International Relations,* ed. Walter Carlsnaes, Thomas Risse, and Beth Simmons. London: Sage Publications.

Adler, Selig. 1957. *The Isolationist Impulse.* New York: Free Press.

Anderson, Benedict. 1983. *Imagined Communities: Reflections upon the Origin and Spread of Nationalism.* 2d ed. London: Verso.

Berman, Sheri. 2001. Ideas, norms, and culture in political analysis. *Comparative Politics* 33 (2): 231–50.

Carter, Ashton, and William Perry. 2007. China on the march. *National Interest* 88 (March/April), 16–22.

"Chinese Communist Party Fifth Plenary Session Communiqué—Text." 2005. Xinhua News Agency Domestic Service, Beijing, October 11.

Christensen, Thomas. 2003. The Party Transition: Will it bring a new maturity in Chinese security policy? *China Leadership Monitor 5,* Winter, http://www.china leadershipmonitor.org/20031/tc.html, 4–6.

———. 2006. Fostering stability or creating a monster? The rise of China and U.S. policy toward East Asia. *International Security* 31 (1): 81–126.

Cody, Edward. 2005. "China Sends Warning to Taiwan with Anti-Secession Law." *Washington Post,* March 8, A12.

Copeland, Dale. 2000a. The constructivist challenge to structural realism: A review essay. *International Security* 25 (2): 187–212.

———. 2000b. *Origins of Major War.* Ithaca: Cornell University Press.

———. 2003. Economic interdependence and the future of U.S.–Chinese relations. In *International Relations Theory and the Asia-Pacific,* ed. G. John Ikenberry and Michael Mastanduno. New York: Columbia University.

Council on Foreign Relations. 2007. *U.S.-China Relations: An Affirmative Agenda, A Responsible Course.* Independent Task Force Report 59 (April).

Deng, Yong, and Sherry Gray. 2001. Introduction: Growing pains—China debates its international future. *Journal of Contemporary China* 10 (26): 5–16.

De Soysa, Indra, John R. Oneal, and Yong-Hee Park. 1997. Testing power-transition theory using alternative measures of national capabilities. *Journal of Conflict Resolution* 41 (4): 509–28.

Dittmer, Lowell. 1995. Chinese informal politics. *China Journal* 34 (July): 1–34.

Dollar, David. 2005. China's economic problems (and ours). *Milken Institute Review* 7 (3): 48–58.

Downs, Erica Strecker, and Philip C. Saunders. 1998/99. Legitimacy and the limits of nationalism: China and the Diadyu Island. *International Security* 23 (3): 114–46.

Eckholm, Eric. 2002. "Leaner Factories, Fewer Workers Bring More Labor Unrest to China." *New York Times,* March 19.

Edelstein, David. 2000. Managing uncertainty: Beliefs about intentions and the rise of great powers. *Security Studies* 12 (1): 1–40.

Evangelista, Matthew. 1999. *Unarmed Forces: The Transnational Movement to End the Cold War.* Ithaca: Cornell University Press.

Fewsmith, Joseph. 2003. The Sixteenth National Party Congress: The succession that didn't happen. *China Quarterly* 173 (3): 1–16.

Friedberg, Aaron L. 2005. The future of U.S.-China relations: Is conflict inevitable? *International Security* 30 (2): 7–45.

Frieden, Jeffry A., and Ronald Rogowski. 1996. The impact of the international economy on national policies: An analytical overview. In *Internationalization and Domestic Politics,* ed. Robert O. Keohane and Helen V. Milner. New York: Cambridge University Press.

Garrett, Geoffrey, and Peter Lang. 1996. Internationalization, institutions, and political change. In *Internationalization and Domestic Politics,* ed. Robert O. Keohane and Helen Milner. New York: Cambridge University Press.

Geyer, Michael. 1981. Professionals and Junkers: German rearmament and politics in the Weimar Republic. In *Social Change and Political Development in Weimar Germany,* ed. Richard Bessel and E. J. Feuchtwanger. London: Croom Helm.

Gilbert, Margaret. 1987. Modeling collective beliefs. *Synthese* 73 (1): 185–204.

Gilpin, Robert. 1981. *War and Change in World Politics.* Princeton: Princeton University Press.

Goldstein, Morris, and Nicholas Lardy. 2004. "What Kind of Landing for the Chinese Economy?" Institute for International Economics, Policy Briefs in International Economics, PB04-7, November.

Goldstone, Jack A. 1991. *Revolution and Rebellion in the Early Modern World.* Berkeley: University of California Press.

Gong, Gerrit W. 1984. *The Standard of "Civilization" in International Society.* Oxford: Clarendon Press.

Gries, Peter Hays. 2004. *China's New Nationalism: Pride, Politics and Diplomacy.* Berkeley: University of California Press.

Halbwachs, Maurice. 1992. *On Collective Memory.* Ed. and trans. Lewis Coser. Chicago: University of Chicago Press.

Hao Yen-p'ing, and Erh-min Wang. 1978. Changing Chinese views of Western relations, 1840–1895. In *The Cambridge History of China,* vol. 2, ed. John K. Fairbank. Cambridge: Cambridge University Press.

Heer, Paul. 2000. A house united. *Foreign Affairs* 79 (4): 18–25.

Hunt, Michael. 1996. *Genesis of Chinese Communist Foreign Policy.* New York: Columbia University Press.

Jiang Zemin's Report at the 14th National Congress of the Communist Party of China, 1992. Reprinted in China Documents Annual, ed. Peter R. Mood, vol. 4. Gulf Breeze, FL: Academic International Press.

Jiang Zemin's Report at the 15th National Congress of the Communist Party of China, September 12, 1997. http://www.fas.org/news/china/1997/970912-prchtm.

Jiang Zemin's Report to the 16th National Congress of the Chinese Communist Party, November 8, 2002. http://www.china.org.cn/english/features/49007.htm.

Johnson, Ian. 2003. The death and life of China's civil society. *Perspectives on Politics* 1 (3): 551–54.

Johnston, Alastair Iain. 1995. *Cultural Realism: Strategic Culture and Grand Strategy in Chinese History.* Princeton: Princeton University Press.

———. 2001. Treating international institutions as social environments. *International Studies Quarterly* 45 (4): 487–515.

———. 2003. Is China a status quo power? *International Security* 27 (4): 5–56.

———. 2004a. Beijing's security behavior in the Asian-Pacific: Is China a dissatisfied power? In *Rethinking Security in East Asia: Identity, Power, and Efficiency,* ed. Allen Carlson, Peter Katzenstein, and J. J. Suh. Stanford: Stanford University Press.

———. 2004b. Chinese middle class attitudes towards international affairs: Nascent liberalization? *China Quarterly* 179: 603–28.

Kahn, Joseph. 2004a. "China's Elite Learn to Flaunt It While the New Landless Weep." *New York Times,* December 25, A1.

———. 2004b. "China's 'Haves' Stir the 'Have-nots' to Violence." *New York Times,* December 31.

———. 2005. "China Approves Plan to Ease Wealth Gap." *New York Times,* October 11.

———. 2007. "In China Talk of Democracy Is Simply That." *New York Times,* April 20.

Kang, David. 2004. Hierarchy, balancing, and empirical puzzles in Asian international relations. *International Security* 28 (3): 165–81.

Keck, Margaret, and Kathryn Sikkink. 1998. *Activists beyond Borders.* Ithaca: Cornell University Press.

Keohane, Robert, and Joseph S. Nye. 1977. *Power and Interdependence: World Politics in Transition.* Boston: Little, Brown.

Kertzer, David. 1988. *Ritual, Politics, and Power.* New Haven: Yale University Press.

Khoo, Nicholas, and Michael Smith. 2005. China engages Asia? Caveat lector: A response to David Shambaugh. *International Security* 30 (1): 196–205.

Kim, Woosang, and James D. Morrow. 1992. When do power shifts lead to war? *American Journal of Political Science* 36 (4): 896–922.

Kupchan, Charles A. 1994. *The Vulnerability of Empire.* Ithaca: Cornell University Press.

Lampton, David. 2001. *Same Bed, Different Dreams: Managing US-China Relations 1989–2000.* Berkeley and Los Angeles: University of California Press.

Lardy, Nicholas R. 2002. *Integrating China into the Global Economy.* Washington, DC: Brookings Institution.

Legro, Jeffrey W. 2005. *Rethinking the World: Great Power Strategies and International Order.* Ithaca: Cornell University Press.

Lemke, Douglas. 2002. *Regions of War and Peace.* Cambridge: Cambridge University Press.

Li Cheng. 2005a. Hu's policy shift and the Tuanpai's coming of age. *China Leadership Monitor,* 15 Summer. http://www.chinaleadershipmonitor.org/20053/lc.html.

———. 2005b. The new bipartisanship within the Chinese Communist Party. *Orbis* 49 (3): 387–400.

———. 2006. China's inner-party democracy: Toward a system of "one party, two factions." *China Brief* 6 (24), December 6, http://www.jamestown.org/china_brief/article.php?articleid 2373247

Lin, Joseph. 2007. In a fortnight—Beijing looking after the rural poor. *China Brief* 7 (5), March 8, http://?www.jamestown.org/china_brief/article.php?articleid 2373275.

Mann, James. 2007. *The China Fantasy.* New York: Viking.

Mansfield, Edward D., and Jack Snyder. 1995. Democratization and the danger of war. *International Security* 20 (1): 5–38.

May, Ernest R. 1962. The nature of foreign policy: The calculated versus the axiomatic. *Daedalus* 91 (4): 653–67.

Mearsheimer, John J. 2001. *The Tragedy of Great Power Politics.* New York: Norton.

Mitter, Rana. 2004. *A Bitter Revolution: China's Struggle with the Modern World.* New York: Oxford University Press.

Mosher, Steven. 2001. *Hegemon: China's Plan to Dominate Asia and the World.* San Francisco: Encounter Books.

Nathan, Andrew. 1973. A factionalism model for CCP politics. *China Quarterly* 53 (Jan./Mar.): 34–66.

Organski, A. F. K., and Jacek Kugler. 1980. *The War Ledger.* Chicago: University of Chicago Press.

Pillsbury, Michael. 2000. *China Debates the Future Security Environment.* Washington, DC: National Defense University Press.

Qin Yaqing. 2001. A response to Yong Deng: Power perception and the cultural lens. *Asian Affairs: An American Review* 28 (3): 155–58.

———. 2003. National identity, strategic culture and security interest: Three hypotheses on the interaction between China and international society. *SIIS Journal* 1, available at http://www.siis.org.cn/english/journal/en20031-2/qinyaqing.htm.

Riskin, Carl, and Azizur Rahman Khan. 2000. *Inequality and Poverty in China in the Age of Globalization.* New York: Oxford University Press.

Rosecrance, Richard. 1986. *The Rise of the Trading State.* New York: Basic Books.

Roy, Denny. 1994. Hegemon on the horizon? China's threat to East Asian security. *International Security* 19 (1) 149–168.

Ruggie, John Gerard. 1982. International regimes, transactions, and change: Embedded liberalism in the postwar economic order. *International Organization* 36 (2): 379–415.

Russett, Bruce, and John Oneal. 2000. *Triangulating Peace: Democracy, Interdependence, and International Organizations.* New York: Norton.

Schweller, Randall. 1999. Managing the rise of great powers: History and theory. In *Engaging China: The Management of a Rising Power,* ed. Alastair Iain Johnston and Robert Ross. New York: Routledge.

———. 2006. *Unanswered Threats: Political Constraints on the Balance of Power.* Princeton: Princeton University Press.

Selznick, Phillip. 1949. *TVA and the Grass Roots: A Study of Politics and Organization.* Berkeley: University of California Press.

———. 1957. *Leadership in Administration: A Sociological Interpretation.* New York: Harper & Row.

Singer, J. David. 1987. Reconstructing the Correlates of War Dataset on Material Capabilities of States, 1816–1985. *International Interactions* 14: 115–32.

Singer, J. David, Stuart Bremer, and John Stuckey. 1972. Capability distribution, uncertainty, and major power war, 1820–1965. In *Peace, War, and Numbers,* ed. Bruce Russett. Beverly Hills: Sage.

Snyder, Jack. 1991. *Myths of Empire.* Ithaca: Cornell University Press.

———. 2000. *From Voting to Violence: Democratization and Nationalist Conflict.* New York: Norton.

Solingen, Etel. 1998. *Regional Orders at Century's Dawn: Global and Domestic Influences on Grand Strategy.* Princeton, NJ: Princeton University Press.

State Statistical Bureau, People's Republic of China, Beijing. *China Statistical Yearbook 1996.* Beijing: China Statistical Publishing House.

Stein, Arthur, and Richard Rosecrance, eds. 1993. *The Domestic Bases of Grand Strategy.* Ithaca: Cornell University Press.

Suettinger, Robert L. 2004. The rise and descent of "peaceful rise." *China Leadership Monitor* 12, http://www.chinaleadershipmonitor.org/20044/rs.pdf.

Swaine, Michael, and Ashley Tellis. 2000. *Interpreting China's Grand Strategy: Past, Present, and Future.* Santa Monica: Rand Corporation.

Tanner, Murray Scot. 2004. China rethinks unrest. *Washington Quarterly* 27 (3): 137–56.

Thomas, Daniel C. 2001. *The Helsinki Effect: International Norms, Human Rights, and the Demise of Communism.* Princeton: Princeton University Press.

Toby, Ronald. 1997. Reopening the question of Sakoku: Diplomacy in the legitimation of the Tokugawa Bakufu. *Journal of Japanese Studies* 3 (2): 323–64.

Waldron, Arthur. 1995. Deterring China. *Commentary* 100 (4): 17–21.

———. 2004. How would democracy change China? *Orbis* 48 (2): 247–61.

Walt, Stephen. 1987. *The Origins of Alliance.* Ithaca: Cornell University Press.

Wang, Hongying. 2000. Multilateralism in Chinese foreign policy. In *China's International Relations in the 21st Century: Dynamics of Paradigm Shifts,* ed. Weixing Hu, Gerald Chan, and Daojiong Zha. Lanham: University Press of America.

Wang, Sangui, et al. 2007. "Inequality and Poverty in China during Reform." PMMA Working Paper 2007-07, March. www.132.203.59.36:81/Group/papers/papers/PMMA-2007-07.pdf.

Whiting, Allen. 1995. Chinese nationalism and foreign policy after Deng. *China Quarterly* 142 (June): 295–316.

Wilson, James Q. 1989. *Bureaucracy.* New York: Basic Books.

Wu, Xinbo. 2001. Four contradictions constraining China's foreign policy behavior. *Journal of Contemporary China* 10 (27): 293–301.

Yan, Xuetong. 2001. The rise of China in Chinese eyes. *Journal of Contemporary China* 10 (26): 33–39.

Zakaria, Fareed. 1992. Realism and domestic politics: A review essay. *International Security* 17 (1): 177–98.

Zhang, Yongjin. 1991. *China in the International System, 1918–1920*. London: Palgrave Macmillan.

Zhao, Suisheng. 2000. Introduction: China's democratization reconsidered. In *China and Democracy: Reconsidering the Prospects for a Democratic China*, ed. Suisheng Zhao. New York: Routledge.

———. 2004. *A Nation State by Construction: Dynamics of Modern Chinese Nationalism*. Stanford, CA: Stanford University Press.

Zhen, Yongnian. 2000. Nationalism, globalism, and China's international relations. In *China's International Relations in the 21st Century: Dynamics of Paradigm Shifts*, ed. Weixing Hu, Gerald Chan, and Daojiong Zha. Lanham: University Press of America.

Zheng, Bijian. 2005. China's "Peaceful Rise" to great power status. *Foreign Affairs* 84 (5): 18–24.

Zoellick, Robert B. 2005. "Whither China: From Membership to Responsibility?" Remarks to National Committee on U.S.-China Relations, New York, September 21, http://www.state.gov/s/d/rem/53682.htm.

7.4

US AND THEM: THE ENDURING POWER OF ETHNIC NATIONALISM

Jerry Z. Muller

with response:
SEPARATISM'S FINAL COUNTRY

Richard Rosecrance and Arthur Stein

> In these two articles, scholars debate the relative merits of separating
> peoples based on ethnic differences (ethnonationalism) versus mixing
> them based on cultural integration (civic nationalism). Americans
> instinctively prefer the integration model, but Jerry Z. Muller makes
> the case that modern Europe overcame centuries of ethnic warfare
> only by moving millions of people into more ethnically homogeneous
> units, allowing Czechoslovakia and the former Soviet Union to break
> up peacefully and the former Yugoslavia to follow suit, albeit more
> slowly, after bloody ethnic warfare in the 1990s. In their response to
> Muller's article, Richard Rosecrance and Arthur Stein dispute the sepa-
> ratist model, arguing that it is impractical in the modern age and
> belied by trends toward globalization and new forms of bigness in
> contemporary international affairs. Notice that different causal forces
> drive these two arguments—territory (realist) and emotional (identity)
> factors in the case of separatism versus assimilation and economic
> interdependence (liberal) in the case of integration models. Notice too
> that the primary levels of analysis are different—systemic structural
> and domestic in the case of the separatist argument versus systemic
> process and foreign policy in the case of the integration argument.

Us and Them: The Enduring Power of Ethnic Nationalism

by Jerry Z. Muller

Projecting their own experience onto the rest of the world, Americans generally belittle the role of ethnic nationalism in politics. After all, in the United
States people of varying ethnic origins live cheek by jowl in relative peace.

Sources: Jerry Z. Muller, "Us and Them: The Enduring Power of Ethnic Nationalism,"
Foreign Affairs 87, no. 2 (2008): 18–35; Richard Rosecrance and Arthur Stein, "Separatism's Final
Country," *Foreign Affairs* 87, no. 4 (2008): 141–145.

Within two or three generations of immigration, their ethnic identities are attenuated by cultural assimilation and intermarriage. Surely, things cannot be so different elsewhere.

Americans also find ethnonationalism discomfiting both intellectually and morally. Social scientists go to great lengths to demonstrate that it is a product not of nature but of culture, often deliberately constructed. And ethicists scorn value systems based on narrow group identities rather than cosmopolitanism.

*   *   *

The Politics of Identity

There are two major ways of thinking about national identity. One is that all people who live within a country's borders are part of the nation, regardless of their ethnic, racial, or religious origins. This liberal or civic nationalism is the conception with which contemporary Americans are most likely to identify. But the liberal view has competed with and often lost out to a different view, that of ethnonationalism. The core of the ethnonationalist idea is that nations are defined by a shared heritage, which usually includes a common language, a common faith, and a common ethnic ancestry.

The ethnonationalist view has traditionally dominated through much of Europe and has held its own even in the United States until recently. For substantial stretches of U.S. history, it was believed that only the people of English origin, or those who were Protestant, or white, or hailed from northern Europe were real Americans. It was only in 1965 that the reform of U.S. immigration law abolished the system of national-origin quotas that had been in place for several decades. This system had excluded Asians entirely and radically restricted immigration from southern and eastern Europe.

Ethnonationalism draws much of its emotive power from the notion that the members of a nation are part of an extended family, ultimately united by ties of blood. It is the subjective belief in the reality of a common "we" that counts. The markers that distinguish the in-group vary from case to case and time to time, and the subjective nature of the communal boundaries has led some to discount their practical significance. But as Walker Connor, an astute student of nationalism, has noted, "It is not what is, but what people believe is that has behavioral consequences." And the central tenets of ethnonationalist belief are that nations exist, that each nation ought to have its own state, and that each state should be made up of the members of a single nation.

The conventional narrative of European history asserts that nationalism was primarily liberal in the western part of the continent and that it became more ethnically oriented as one moved east. There is some truth to this, but it disguises a good deal as well. It is more accurate to say that when modern states began to form, political boundaries and ethnolinguistic boundaries largely coincided in the areas along Europe's Atlantic coast. Liberal nationalism, that is, was most apt to emerge in states that already possessed a high degree of ethnic homogeneity. Long before the nineteenth century, countries such as England, France, Portugal, Spain, and Sweden emerged as nation-states in polities where ethnic divisions had been softened by a long history of cultural and social homogenization.

In the center of the continent, populated by speakers of German and Italian, political structures were fragmented into hundreds of small units. But in the 1860s and 1870s, this fragmentation was resolved by the creation of Italy and Germany, so that almost all Italians lived in the former and a majority of Germans lived in the latter. Moving further east, the situation changed again. As late as 1914, most of central, eastern, and southeastern Europe was made up not of nation-states but of empires. The Hapsburg empire comprised what are now Austria, the Czech Republic, Hungary, and Slovakia and parts of what are now Bosnia, Croatia, Poland, Romania, Ukraine, and more. The Romanov empire stretched into Asia, including what is now Russia and what are now parts of Poland, Ukraine, and more. And the Ottoman Empire covered modern Turkey and parts of today's Bulgaria, Greece, Romania, and Serbia and extended through much of the Middle East and North Africa as well.

Each of these empires was composed of numerous ethnic groups, but they were not multinational in the sense of granting equal status to the many peoples that made up their populaces. The governing monarchy and landed nobility often differed in language and ethnic origin from the urbanized trading class, whose members in turn usually differed in language, ethnicity, and often religion from the peasantry. In the Hapsburg and Romanov empires, for example, merchants were usually Germans or Jews. In the Ottoman Empire, they were often Armenians, Greeks, or Jews. And in each empire, the peasantry was itself ethnically diverse.

Up through the nineteenth century, these societies were still largely agrarian: most people lived as peasants in the countryside, and few were literate. Political, social, and economic stratifications usually correlated with ethnicity, and people did not expect to change their positions in the system. Until the rise of modern nationalism, all of this seemed quite unproblematic. In this world, moreover, people of one religion, language, or culture were often dispersed across various countries and empires. There were ethnic Germans, for example, not only in the areas that became Germany but also scattered throughout the Hapsburg and Romanov empires. There were Greeks in Greece but also millions of them in the Ottoman Empire (not to mention hundreds of thousands of Muslim Turks in Greece). And there were Jews everywhere—but with no independent state of their own.

The Great Transformation

*   *   *

World War I led to the demise of the three great turn-of-the-century empires, unleashing an explosion of ethnonationalism in the process. In the Ottoman

Empire, mass deportations and murder during the war took the lives of a million members of the local Armenian minority in an early attempt at ethnic cleansing, if not genocide. In 1919, the Greek government invaded the area that would become Turkey, seeking to carve out a "greater Greece" stretching all the way to Constantinople. Meeting with initial success, the Greek forces looted and burned villages in an effort to drive out the region's ethnic Turks. But Turkish forces eventually regrouped and pushed the Greek army back, engaging in their own ethnic cleansing against local Greeks along the way. Then the process of population transfers was formalized in the 1923 Treaty of Lausanne: all ethnic Greeks were to go to Greece, all Greek Muslims to Turkey. In the end, Turkey expelled almost 1.5 million people, and Greece expelled almost 400,000.

Out of the breakup of the Hapsburg and Romanov empires emerged a multitude of new countries. Many conceived of themselves as ethnonational polities, in which the state existed to protect and promote the dominant ethnic group. Yet of central and eastern Europe's roughly 60 million people, 25 million continued to be part of ethnic minorities in the countries in which they lived. In most cases, the ethnic majority did not believe in trying to help minorities assimilate, nor were the minorities always eager to do so themselves. Nationalist governments openly discriminated in favor of the dominant community. Government activities were conducted solely in the language of the majority, and the civil service was reserved for those who spoke it.

In much of central and eastern Europe, Jews had long played an important role in trade and commerce. When they were given civil rights in the late nineteenth century, they tended to excel in professions requiring higher education, such as medicine and law, and soon Jews or people of Jewish descent made up almost half the doctors and lawyers in cities such as Budapest, Vienna, and Warsaw. By the 1930s, many governments adopted policies to try to check and reverse these advances, denying Jews credit and limiting their access to higher education. In other words, the National Socialists who came to power in Germany in 1933 and based their movement around a "Germanness" they defined in contrast to "Jewishness" were an extreme version of a more common ethnonationalist trend.

The politics of ethnonationalism took an even deadlier turn during World War II. The Nazi regime tried to reorder the ethnic map of the continent by force. Its most radical act was an attempt to rid Europe of Jews by killing them all—an attempt that largely succeeded. The Nazis also used ethnic German minorities in Czechoslovakia, Poland, and elsewhere to enforce Nazi domination, and many of the regimes allied with Germany engaged in their own campaigns against internal ethnic enemies. The Romanian regime, for example, murdered hundreds of thousands of Jews on its own, without orders from Germany, and the government of Croatia murdered not only its Jews but hundreds of thousands of Serbs and Romany as well.

Postwar But Not Postnational

One might have expected that the Nazi regime's deadly policies and crushing defeat would mark the end of the ethnonationalist era. But in fact they set the stage for another massive round of ethnonational transformation. The political settlement in central Europe after World War I had been achieved primarily by moving borders to align them with populations. After World War II, it was the populations that moved instead. Millions of people were expelled from their homes and countries, with at least the tacit support of the victorious Allies.

* * *

Between 1944 and 1945, five million ethnic Germans from the eastern parts of the German Reich fled westward to escape the conquering Red Army, which was energetically raping and massacring its way to Berlin. Then, between 1945 and 1947, the new postliberation regimes in Czechoslovakia, Hungary, Poland, and Yugoslavia expelled another seven million Germans in response to their collaboration with the Nazis. Together, these measures constituted the largest forced population movement in European history, with hundreds of thousands of people dying along the way.

The handful of Jews who survived the war and returned to their homes in eastern Europe met with so much anti-Semitism that most chose to leave for good. About 220,000 of them made their way into the American-occupied zone of Germany, from which most eventually went to Israel or the United States. Jews thus essentially vanished from central and eastern Europe, which had been the center of Jewish life since the sixteenth century.

Millions of refugees from other ethnic groups were also evicted from their homes and resettled after the war. This was due partly to the fact that the borders of the Soviet Union had moved westward, into what had once been Poland, while the borders of Poland also moved westward, into what had once been Germany. To make populations correspond to the new borders, 1.5 million Poles living in areas that were now part of the Soviet Union were deported to Poland, and 500,000 ethnic Ukrainians who had been living in Poland were sent to the Ukrainian Soviet Socialist Republic. Yet another exchange of populations took place between Czechoslovakia and Hungary, with Slovaks transferred out of Hungary and Magyars sent away from Czechoslovakia. A smaller number of Magyars also moved to Hungary from Yugoslavia, with Serbs and Croats moving in the opposite direction.

As a result of this massive process of ethnic unmixing, the ethnonationalist ideal was largely realized: for the most part, each nation in Europe had its own state, and each state was made up almost exclusively of a single ethnic nationality. During the Cold War, the few exceptions to this rule included Czechoslovakia, the Soviet Union, and Yugoslavia. But these countries' subsequent fate only demonstrated the ongoing vitality of ethnonationalism. After the fall of communism, East and West Germany were unified with remarkable rapidity, Czechoslovakia split peacefully into Czech and Slovak republics, and the Soviet Union broke apart into a variety of different national units. Since then, ethnic Russian minorities in many of the post-Soviet states have gradually immigrated to Russia, Magyars in Romania have moved to Hungary, and the few remaining ethnic Germans in Russia have largely gone to Germany. A million people of Jewish origin from the former Soviet Union have made their way to Israel. Yugoslavia saw the secession of Croatia and Slovenia and then descended into ethnonational wars over Bosnia and Kosovo.

The breakup of Yugoslavia was simply the last act of a long play. But the plot of that play—the disaggregation of peoples and the triumph of ethnonationalism in modern Europe—is rarely recognized, and so a story whose significance is comparable to the spread of democracy or capitalism remains largely unknown and unappreciated.

* * *

The Balance Sheet

Analysts of ethnic disaggregation typically focus on its destructive effects, which is understandable given the direct human suffering it has often entailed....

* * *

But if ethnonationalism has frequently led to tension and conflict, it has also proved to be a source of cohesion and stability. When French textbooks began with "Our ancestors the Gauls" or when Churchill spoke to wartime audiences of "this island race," they appealed to ethnonationalist sensibilities as a source of mutual trust and sacrifice. Liberal democracy and ethnic homogeneity are not only compatible; they can be complementary.

One could argue that Europe has been so harmonious since World War II not because of the failure of ethnic nationalism but because of its success, which removed some of the greatest sources of conflict both within and between countries. The fact that ethnic and state boundaries now largely coincide has meant that there are fewer disputes over borders or expatriate communities, leading to the most stable territorial configuration in European history.

These ethnically homogeneous polities have displayed a great deal of internal solidarity, moreover, facilitating government programs, including domestic transfer payments, of various kinds. When the Swedish Social Democrats were developing plans for Europe's most extensive welfare state during the interwar period, the political scientist Sheri Berman has noted, they conceived of and sold them as the construction of a folkhemmet, or "people's home."

Several decades of life in consolidated, ethnically homogeneous states may even have worked to sap ethnonationalism's own emotional power. Many

Europeans are now prepared, and even eager, to participate in transnational frameworks such as the EU, in part because their perceived need for collective self-determination has largely been satisfied.

New Ethnic Mixing

Along with the process of forced ethnic disaggregation over the last two centuries, there has also been a process of ethnic mixing brought about by voluntary emigration. The general pattern has been one of emigration from poor, stagnant areas to richer and more dynamic ones.

In Europe, this has meant primarily movement west and north, leading above all to France and the United Kingdom. This pattern has continued into the present: as a result of recent migration, for example, there are now half a million Poles in Great Britain and 200,000 in Ireland. Immigrants from one part of Europe who have moved to another and ended up staying there have tended to assimilate and, despite some grumbling about a supposed invasion of "Polish plumbers," have created few significant problems.

The most dramatic transformation of European ethnic balances in recent decades has come from the immigration of people of Asian, African, and Middle Eastern origin, and here the results have been mixed. Some of these groups have achieved remarkable success, such as the Indian Hindus who have come to the United Kingdom. But in Belgium, France, Germany, the Netherlands, Sweden, the United Kingdom, and elsewhere, on balance the educational and economic progress of Muslim immigrants has been more limited and their cultural alienation greater.

How much of the problem can be traced to discrimination, how much to the cultural patterns of the immigrants themselves, and how much to the policies of European governments is difficult to determine. But a number of factors, from official multiculturalism to generous welfare states to the ease of contact with ethnic homelands, seem to have made it possible to create ethnic islands where assimilation into the larger culture and economy is limited.

As a result, some of the traditional contours of European politics have been upended. The left, for example, has tended to embrace immigration in the name of egalitarianism and multiculturalism. But if there is indeed a link between ethnic homogeneity and a population's willingness to support generous income-redistribution programs, the encouragement of a more heterogeneous society may end up undermining the left's broader political agenda. And some of Europe's libertarian cultural propensities have already clashed with the cultural illiberalism of some of the new immigrant communities.

Should Muslim immigrants not assimilate and instead develop a strong communal identification along religious lines, one consequence might be a resurgence of traditional ethnonational identities in some states—or the development of a new European identity defined partly in contradistinction to Islam (with the widespread resistance to the extension of full EU membership to Turkey being a possible harbinger of such a shift).

Future Implications

Since ethnonationalism is a direct consequence of key elements of modernization, it is likely to gain ground in societies undergoing such a process. It is hardly surprising, therefore, that it remains among the most vital—and most disruptive—forces in many parts of the contemporary world.

More or less subtle forms of ethnonationalism, for example, are ubiquitous in immigration policy around the globe. Many countries—including Armenia, Bulgaria, Croatia, Finland, Germany, Hungary, Ireland, Israel, Serbia, and Turkey—provide automatic or rapid citizenship to the members of diasporas of their own dominant ethnic group, if desired. Chinese immigration law gives priority and benefits to overseas Chinese. Portugal and Spain have immigration policies that favor applicants from their former colonies in the New World. Still other states, such as Japan and Slovakia, provide official forms of identification to members of the dominant national ethnic group who are noncitizens that permit them to live and work in the country. Americans, accustomed by the U.S. government's official practices to regard differential treatment on the basis of ethnicity to be a violation of universalist norms, often consider such policies exceptional, if not abhorrent. Yet in a global context, it is the insistence on universalist criteria that seems provincial.

Increasing communal consciousness and shifting ethnic balances are bound to have a variety of consequences, both within and between states, in the years to come. As economic globalization brings more states into the global economy, for example, the first fruits of that process will often fall to those ethnic groups best positioned by history or culture to take advantage of the new opportunities for enrichment, deepening social cleavages rather than filling them in. Wealthier and higher-achieving regions might try to separate themselves from poorer and lower-achieving ones, and distinctive homogeneous areas might try to acquire sovereignty—courses of action that might provoke violent responses from defenders of the status quo.

Of course, there are multiethnic societies in which ethnic consciousness remains weak, and even a more strongly developed sense of ethnicity may lead to political claims short of sovereignty. Sometimes, demands for ethnic autonomy or self-determination can be met within an existing state. The claims of the Catalans in Spain, the Flemish in Belgium, and the Scots in the United Kingdom have been met in this manner, at least for now. But such arrangements remain precarious and are subject to recurrent renegotiation. In the developing world, accordingly, where states are more recent creations and where the borders often cut across ethnic boundaries, there is likely to be further ethnic disaggregation and communal conflict. And as scholars such as Chaim Kaufmann have noted, once ethnic antagonism has crossed a certain threshold of violence, maintaining the rival groups within a single polity becomes far more difficult.

This unfortunate reality creates dilemmas for advocates of humanitarian intervention in such conflicts, because making and keeping peace between groups that have come to hate and fear one another is likely to require costly ongoing military missions rather than relatively cheap temporary ones. When communal violence escalates to ethnic cleansing, moreover, the return of large numbers of refugees to their place of origin after a cease-fire has been reached is often impractical and even undesirable, for it merely sets the stage for a further round of conflict down the road.

Partition may thus be the most humane lasting solution to such intense communal conflicts. It inevitably creates new flows of refugees, but at least it deals with the problem at issue. The challenge for the international community in such cases is to separate communities in the most humane manner possible: by aiding in transport, assuring citizenship rights in the new homeland, and providing financial aid for resettlement and economic absorption. The bill for all of this will be huge, but it will rarely be greater than the material costs of interjecting and maintaining a foreign military presence large enough to pacify the rival ethnic combatants or the moral cost of doing nothing.

Contemporary social scientists who write about nationalism tend to stress the contingent elements of group identity—the extent to which national consciousness is culturally and politically manufactured by ideologists and politicians. They regularly invoke Benedict Anderson's concept of "imagined communities," as if demonstrating that nationalism is constructed will rob the concept of its power. It is true, of course, that ethnonational identity is never as natural or ineluctable as nationalists claim. Yet it would be a mistake to think that because nationalism is partly constructed it is therefore fragile or infinitely malleable. Ethnonationalism was not a chance detour in European history: it corresponds to some enduring propensities of the human spirit that are heightened by the process of modern state creation, it is a crucial source of both solidarity and enmity, and in one form or another, it will remain for many generations to come. One can only profit from facing it directly.

Separatism's Final Country

by Richard Rosecrance and Arthur Stein

Muller argues that ethnonationalism is the wave of the future and will result in more and more independent states, but this is not likely. One of the most destabilizing ideas throughout human history has been that every separately defined cultural unit should have its own state. Endless disruption and political introversion would follow an attempt to realize such a goal. Woodrow Wilson gave an impetus to further state creation when he argued for "national self-determination" as a means of preventing more nationalist conflict, which he believed was a cause of World War I.

The hope was that if the nations of the Austrian, Ottoman, and Russian empires could become independent states, they would not have to bring the great powers into their conflicts. But Wilson and his counterparts did not concede to each nation its own state. They grouped minorities together in Hungary, Italy, and Yugoslavia, and the Soviet Union ultimately emerged as a veritable empire of nationalities. Economists rightly questioned whether tiny states with small labor forces and limited resources could become viable, particularly given the tariffs that their goods would face in international trade.

More important, the nationalist prospect was and remains hopelessly impractical. In the world today, there are 6,800 different dialects or languages that might gain political recognition as independent linguistic groups. Does anyone seriously suggest that the 200 or so existing states should each, on average, be cut into 34 pieces? The doctrine of national self-determination reaches its reductio ad absurdum at this point.

Furthermore, the one-nation, one-state principle is unlikely to prevail for four good reasons. First, governments today are more responsive to their ethnic minority communities than were the imperial agglomerations of yesteryear, and they also have more resources at their disposal than their predecessors did. Many provinces populated by discontented ethnic groups are located in territories adjacent to national capitals, not overseas. And many governments in this era of globalization have annual budgets equivalent to nearly 50 percent of their GDPs, much of which is spent on social services. They can—and do—accommodate the economic needs of their states' differentiated units. They also respond to those units' linguistic requests. Basques, Bretons, Punjabis, Québecois, and Scots live quite well inside the bonds of multinational sovereignty and in some cases better than residents of other provinces with no claims of being a distinct nation.

Second, the achievement of separate sovereignty today depends on external recognition and support. Prospective new states cannot gain independence without military assistance and economic aid from abroad. International recognition, in turn, requires the aspiring nationalist movement to avoid international terrorism as a means of gaining attention. If a separatist group uses terrorism, it tends to be reviled and sidelined. If an ethnic group does not have enough support to win independence by peaceful electoral means inside its country, its resorting to terrorism only calls into question the legitimacy of its quest for independence.

Recognizing this, the Québecois abandoned the terrorist methods of the Quebec Liberation Front. Most Basques castigate Basque Homeland and Freedom (known by its Basque acronym ETA). Enlightened Europeans have withdrawn their support for the Chechen rebels. And the continued terrorist shelling of Israeli cities from a Hamas-dominated Gaza might undermine the previous international consensus in favor of a two-state solution to the Palestinian problem, or at least warrant an exceptional approach to Gaza.

With the possible exception of the Palestinians, the notion that any of these peoples would be better off in smaller and weaker independent states in a hostile neighborhood is unrealistic. Occasionally, dissidents make the case that if they were to leave the state unit, they would be taken into the comforting embrace of the European Union or the North American Free Trade Agreement, thereby gaining access to a large market. But that would depend a great deal on outsider support for their cause. The United Kingdom might not wish to see Scotland in the EU and would be in a position to veto its membership. The United States and Canada might not agree to let an independent Quebec join NAFTA. The belief that when a tiny nation is born it falls automatically into the loving hands of international midwives is questionable. The truth varies from case to case.

Third, although globalization initially stimulated ethnic discontent by creating inequality, it also provides the means for quieting discontents down the road within the fold of the state political system. Distributed economic growth is a palliative for political discontent. Indonesia, Malaysia, Singapore, and Thailand contain different ethnic groups that have largely profited from the intense economic resurgence of their states stimulated by globalization. Northern and southern Vietnam are culturally different, but both have benefited from the country's economic growth. Cambodia has a diverse population, but it has gained greatly from China's move to externalize some of its production.

Fourth, a discontented population may react to ethnic discrimination, but it also responds to economic need, and whatever its concerns, it does not always have to seek independence to alleviate them. It has another safety valve: emigration to another country. The state of Monterrey has not sought independence from Mexico; rather, many of its inhabitants have moved, legally or illegally, to the United States. The huge emigration from the Maghreb to France and Italy reflects a similar attitude and outcome; the dissatisfied populations of North Africa can find greater welfare in Europe. And when Poles move to France or the United Kingdom, they do not secede from the mother country but demonstrate greater satisfaction with French or British rule. Emigration is the overwhelming alternative to secession when the home government does not sufficiently mitigate economic disparities.

Even where the central government has used force to suppress secessionist movements, it has offered carrots at the same time that it has yielded sticks. The province of Aceh has been coaxed, even as it has been subjected to threats, to remain inside the Indonesian republic. Kashmir, facing a balance of restraints and incentives, is unlikely to emerge as an independent state in India. And the Tamil Tigers have lost the sympathy of the world by their slaughter of innocent Sinhalese.

The recent formation of an "independent" Kosovo, which has not yet been recognized by various key countries, does not foretell the similar arrival of other new states. It is unlikely that Abkhazia or South Ossetia, although largely autonomous in fact, will gain full and formal independence from Georgia or that the Albanian areas of Macedonia will secede. Rather, prospective secessionists, dissuaded by both central governments and the international community, are likely to hold back. Indeed, the most plausible future outcome is that both established states and their international supporters will generally act to prevent a proliferation of new states from entering the international system.

Much empirical work, which shows that a province's aspirations for sovereign status can be confined within a state if the province has access to monies from the central government and is represented in the governing elite, supports this conclusion. The Sikh party Akali Dal once sought Punjab's independence from India, but to little effect, partly because Punjabis are heavily represented in the Indian army and because fiscal transfers from New Delhi quieted dissidence in the region. The Québecois benefit from financing from Ottawa, elite connections, flows of private capital into Quebec, and the Canadian government's acceptance of bilingualism in the province. Chechnya remains poor, but if it seeks to remedy its relative neglect through a strategy of terrorism, it will undercut its own legitimacy. Lacking external support, and in the face of Russia's continued firmness, Chechnya has settled into a degree of political stability. In all three cases, the maintenance of the existing national boundaries seems likely, and so, too, does it seem likely in other cases.

The apostles of national self-determination would do well to consider a still more important trend: the return to bigness in the international system. This is happening not only because great powers such as China, India, and the United States are now taking on greater roles in world politics but also because international economics increasingly dwarfs politics. To keep up, states have to get bigger. The international market has always been larger than the domestic ones, but as long as international openness beckoned, even small powers could hope to prosper and attain some degree of economic influence. In the past decade, however, the tariff reductions proposed in the Doha Round of international trade negotiations have failed, industrial duties have not fallen, and agriculture has become even more highly protected than it was in the nineteenth century.

Globalization has clearly distributed economic boons to smaller countries, but these states still require greater political scale to fully realize globalization's benefits. To generate scale, states have negotiated bilateral and multilateral trade preferences with other states regionally and internationally, thereby gaining access to larger markets. The EU has decided to make up in the enlargement of its membership and a bigger free-trade area what it lacks in internal economic growth. The 27 countries of the EU currently have a combined GDP of over $14 trillion, besting the United States' $13 trillion, and the union's expansion is not over yet.

Europe never faced the limits on "manifest destiny" that confronted the United States—the shores of the Pacific Ocean. Charles de Gaulle was wrong when he heralded a "Europe from the Atlantic to the Urals": the EU has already expanded into the Caucasus. And with at least eight new members, it will proceed into Central Asia. As the borders of Europe approach Russia, even Moscow will seek de facto ties with the increasingly monolithic European giant.

In Asia, current tensions between China and Japan have not prevented proposals for a free-trade zone, a common currency, and an investment bank for the region. Chinese in Indonesia, Malaysia, the Philippines, Singapore, Taiwan, and Vietnam draw their adopted countries toward Beijing. China will not expand territorially (except titularly when Taiwan rejoins the mainland), but it will move to consolidate an economic network that will contain all the elements of production, except, perhaps, raw materials. Japan will adjust to China's primacy, and even South Korea will see the writing on the wall.

This will leave the United States in the uncomfortable position of experiencing unrealized growth and the possible failure of new customs unions in the Western Hemisphere. NAFTA may have been deepened, but a Free Trade Area of the Americas now seems beyond reach because of opposition from Argentina, Bolivia, Brazil, and Venezuela. U.S. politics has also turned, temporarily at least, against such ventures. South American nations have, in recent years, been far more responsive to China and Europe than to the United States. The U.S.-Central American Free Trade Agreement, now in the making, may be the only likely new string to the current U.S. bow.

Some economists contend that great size is not necessary in a fully open international economic system and that even small countries can sell their wares abroad under such conditions. But the international economic system is not open, and the future resides with broad customs unions, which substitute expanded regional markets for restricted international ones. China is seeking bilateral preferential trade arrangements with several other states, and so is the United States. Prospective secessionists will not prosper under such circumstances. They have to depend on international assistance, membership in trade pacts, and the acquiescence of their mother countries. They may have none of these, and they will fail if they use terrorism to advance their causes.

Under the present circumstances, secessionists will generally be better off remaining inside existing states, if only because the international system now advantages larger agglomerations of power. Economies of industrial scale are promoting economies of political size. In U.S. politics, the problem of outsourcing gets much political attention, but how is it possible to prevent that activity when national production and the national market are too small? Only larger political entities can keep production, research and development, and innovation within a single economic zone. Big is back.

Chapter 8

HISTORY OF GLOBALIZATION: MERCANTILISM, PAX BRITANNICA, AND PAX AMERICANA

8.1

DOMINANCE AND LEADERSHIP IN THE INTERNATIONAL ECONOMY: EXPLOITATION, PUBLIC GOODS, AND FREE RIDES

Charles P. Kindleberger

In this still often cited article from 1981, Charles P. Kindleberger makes the realist case that dominance (hegemony) or strong leadership is necessary to create and manage a stable world economy. The reason is that multiple and smaller powers free-ride on the system because they do not have enough power to provide the public goods of markets, capital, and currency. Thus they wait for other powers to provide them. Can you see the emphasis on explanations that stem from the distribution of power at the structural level of analysis? Countries are motivated and behave toward one another more on the basis of their position in the overall structure of power than on the basis of institutional relationships or ideas. As Kindleberger details in a larger book, Britain and the United States supplied the needed public goods during the prosperous global economies of 1870–1913 and 1945–1971, respectively. In 1981, fearing that America was in decline, he worries that the system will become unstable without a leader. As we now know, the United States remained the leader and became even more

Source: Charles P. Kindleberger, "Dominance and Leadership in the International Economy: Exploitation, Public Goods, and Free Rides," *International Studies Quarterly* 25, no. 2 (1981): 242–254.

preeminent after the end of the Cold War. But Kindleberger's concerns remain relevant for globalization today if and when China or other powers challenge American dominance.

* * *

Dominance was a concept introduced into economic discussion, especially French economic discussion, by Francois Perroux, professor of economics at the *Collège de France* and director of the *Institut Scientifique d'Economie Appliquée*. One country, firm, or person dominated another when the other had to take account of what the first entity did, but the first could equally ignore the second. It was a peculiarly French idea, with strong overtones of resentment at alleged domination by the United States in fields of foreign exchange, trade policy, multinational enterprise and the like.

Leadership may be thought of at first blush as persuading others to follow a given course of action which might not be in the follower's short-run interest if it were truly independent. As will be suggested below, it has strong elements of both arm-twisting and bribery. Without it, however, there may be an inadequate amount of public goods produced. This last is a relatively new concept in economics of great salience for political science.

A public good is one the consumption of which by an individual, household, or firm does not reduce the amount available for other potential consumers. The classical example of the pure public good is the lighthouse. By no means are all public goods pure, and one can conjure up complex mixed cases. Radio-directional signals for navigation require the consumer to have a radio-receiver: a private good to receive a public benefit. Roads can be so congested that the last car on it converts it from a public good to a public bad. General education is a mixture of public and private good. It increases the productivity and enjoyment of the individual, his capacities for citizenship, and his responsiveness to economic stimuli from others. The theory of clubs invokes goods which are consumable without being exhausted by a collectivity, but exclude others outside the group. One could go on. For present purposes, however, it is enough to note that within a single country, many public goods are provided by the government through a budget, most private goods by the market.

In the theory of representative democracy ... public goods are underproduced relative to private goods because of the fallacy of composition, or what some call the "free rider." The voter will get it anyhow; why then should one work and lobby, undertaking transactions costs which are expensive, if in any event one is going to get a full share? When no one pushes to vote expenditure on a public good, it may not be produced at all. Thus, vested interests whose benefits are sufficient to warrant exertion get a disproportionate share of the public goods they are interested in. This accords with the commonplace view that governments take better care of producers than of consumers, and accounts for the success of the military-industrial complex and the automobile-gasoline-highway lobby in having government spend money on public goods congruent with their interests. There need not be corruption. Choice among competing public goods is expensive, and the principle of the free ride means that those with only limited benefits from public goods do not get their full share. Public goods are underproduced. Note that this is quite different from the Galbraith view that private goods are overproduced because of the power of advertising. It assumes that producer and consumer are both rational.

* * *

This theory of representative democracy, however, needed a place for leadership.... Leaders work for something called "leadership surplus." They compete with other potential leaders for ascendancy, and once in office maximize their surplus or profit by providing collective goods against taxes, donations or purchases promised in the election process. A leader's personality may play a role, as he or she derives pleasure or utility simply by being head of the administrative office. In this instance, costs to the leader of exertion are matched by rewards of a nonpecuniary nature. Froelich et al. allow little room in their theories for the hereditary leader, or for leadership responsibilities, unless the last can be regarded as a negative surplus which is minimized through fulfillment of explicit or implicit commitments.

Leaders of course are subject to moral decay, as Lord Acton noted in saying, "Power corrupts, and absolute power corrupts absolutely." Responsibility can degenerate into exploitation....

* * *

...The essence of exploitation is that one party exerts power to produce a result more favorable to it than if that power had not been exerted. The typical illustration is a monopolist or monopsonist (monopoly buyer), which restricts his or her sales (purchases) to force buyer (seller) to pay a higher (accept a lower) price than would obtain in a perfectly competitive market in which all sellers and buyers were without power to affect the price.

When there are big rents, as economists call them, or a surplus that vastly exceeds what is necessary to get the work done, there is a strong possibility that the two sides to a transaction will each see itself as exploited when it may be only trying to provide leadership. The operation is regarded as a zero-sum game whereas most economists (and political scientists?) would regard it as a non-zero sum game from which both parties can benefit. Take the multinational corporation that discovers oil in a poor country. Is it leading or exploiting? The answer turns on the counterfactual, or what would have happened in other circumstances. And when both parties choose different counterfactuals, the room for disagreement is enormous. The corporation compares the existing situation with that before its discovery of oil, the country with circumstances in which one of its own citizens had discovered the oil and furnished the necessary technology to develop it. The company resents any and all taxes, until its counterfactual shifts to nationalization as a possibility. The country resents the company's profits. In these circumstances, extramarket power is likely to be applied by the country, whether as leadership, or exploitation of the company is difficult to determine.

* * *

For Adam Smith, within an economy public goods consisted of defense, law and order, and a minimum number of roads and bridges. To this list, John Stuart Mill added tranquility. Other economists noted that the government must provide the public good of money, to the extent that the economy did not rest on the pure gold standard without banking (which could be said to be privately produced) and rules for the conduct of enterprise. With Keynes, the list of public goods was enlarged to include stability of national income, sought through fiscal as well as monetary policy. Today we recognize other public goods, such as control over private negative externalities, as in pollution.

The analysis of public and private goods is also applicable to the international economy. For private goods, read national benefits, and for public, cosmopolitan goods, for the maintenance of the world economy. The question is how to distinguish domination and exploitation from responsibility in the provision of cosmopolitan goods in the world economy, and whether there are not occasions when the world suffers from the underproduction of the public good of stability, not because of greedy vested interests and domination or exploitation, but because of the principle of the free rider.

This was the theme of my book on the world depression of the 1930s. I argued that for the world economy to be stable, it needs a stabilizer, some country that would undertake to provide a market for distress goods, a steady if not countercyclical flow of capital, and a rediscount mechanism for providing liquidity when the monetary system is frozen in panic. Today I would add that the world leadership must also manage, in some degree, the structure of foreign-exchange rates and provide a degree of coordination of domestic monetary policies.

Britain, with frequent assistance from France, furnished coherence to the world economy along these lines during the nineteenth century and through the "belle époque." The United States did so from 1945 (or perhaps 1936) to 1968 (or 1963 or 1971). From 1919 to 1939, Britain could not, and the United States would not, act in the capacity of world leader. I find great difficulty in accepting the views of ... revisionists who maintain that the United States sought world dominance as early as World War I, or 1898. The beginnings of world power can be seen in the spread of New York finance abroad, to be sure, but in spite of Wilson, the leading political figures such as Hughes, Lodge, Harding,

Coolidge, Hoover, and the first-term Roosevelt were isolationists, ready to intrude on the world scene only briefly and wanting no part of Europe's or Asia's problems.

There is a legitimate debate, perhaps, between French and American positions, whether the United States sought domination or was only trying to provide the public good of world stability in the period after World War II.... At least through the period of the Marshall Plan, the American case that its purpose was leadership, even though domination was inadvertently involved, is not prima facie wrong. But whatever elements of domination were intended, I believed and believe that they had run out by 1960.

Part of the world's economic problem today is that the United States has resigned (or been discharged) as leader of the world economy, and there is no candidate willing and acceptable to take its place. We have not only the end to the domination role which I detected in 1960, but also faint signs of the end of United States leadership. The leadership persists perhaps in Middle East peacekeeping. It is hard to detect in matters of trade, aid, capital movements, monetary reform, and the like.

How should one distinguish exploitation from leadership? The issue is complex, and the answer not obvious. Management of the gold-exchange standard by Britain from 1870 to 1913 and by the United States from 1945 to 1971 can be viewed as provision of either the public good of international money, or the private good for itself of seignorage, which is the profit that comes to the seigneur, or sovereign power, from the issuance of money. Of course it can be both. Public goods are sometimes competitive with private good—as when there is a choice between taxing to build a lighthouse or a public park, and not taxing—and sometimes complementary: maintenance of Pax Britannica or Pax Americana provides peace for the world as well as the status quo for the provider. Or Prussia accepting a disproportionately small share of the revenues of Zollverein as against the smaller states and principalities it seduces into joining.

... [T]he leader of the alliance pays more than a pro rata share of the general benefits of the alliance because of the free rider principle. In return for its side-payment to Bavaria, Wurtenberg, Baden, and other small states, Prussia earned a leadership surplus in prestige and power from forging Imperial Germany. The difficulties of the European Economic Community may be traceable to lack of a leadership willing to bear the burdens of the group, or perhaps to the fact that the long-time leader, France, was interested in the private national goods of *gloire*, trade benefits for the *Communauté*, as well as the cosmopolitan good of the Community.

But my concern is with those instances where the abundance of free riders means that the public good is underproduced, and that there is neither domination nor self-abnegation in the interest of responsibility.

Take first the position of small countries. In international economics, we have the so-called "small-country assumption," which means that a country cannot affect its terms of trade (the prices at which it buys its imports and sells its exports), and if capital is mobile, the outside world determines its money supply and its interest rate. Small countries have no economic power. At the same time they have no responsibility for the economic system, nor any necessity to exert leadership. They seem to pose no problems for the international economy, and in a number of instances—Sweden, Canada, New Zealand, and so on—they can usually serve as examples through generous aid, or the provision of troops to the United Nations, and the like. But it is of some interest that on two occasions—1931 and again in 1971—it was the small countries, more or less simultaneously and in pursuit of their private interest, that pushed Britain first, and then the United States, off the gold standard.

* * *

The problem of middle-sized countries is a delicate one.... Big enough to do damage to the system, but not substantial enough to stabilize it, the question is whether middle-sized countries should run a large risk of private hurt in the interest of public stability, or seek to protect themselves at the expense of the system. I have a British friend who becomes indignant when he hears the rats criticized for leaving the sinking ship. "What," he asks, "do they want the rats to do? Stay on the bridge with the captain and salute?"

Countries powerful enough to take leadership responsibility may discharge it, may become corrupted into taking dominant advantage of it, may do the one and be perceived as doing the other, or may abdicate responsibility. It is also possible, as already indicated, that they will exercise leadership and do well out of it. But the system is essentially unstable, subject to entropy. Even if it is not perceived as domination, leadership is not regarded as legitimate. "What has he done for me lately?" is the apposite tag. And the country with, let us say, rising imports as it struggles to keep markets open, an overvalued exchange rate as it accepts the devaluations of others, an undue share of the burdens of NATO or of foreign aid, begins to concern itself with the free rides of others and talk of more equitable burden-sharing.

The need for a leader to assume the burden is nowhere better illustrated than in the reparations/war-debts/commercial-debts issue of the 1920s and 1930s. Britain's readiness to cancel reparations insofar as the United States relieved it of war debts is understandable in economic terms, as its war debts receivable and share of reparations receipts would just about equal war debts payable; but it could hardly gratify the United States, which had already given up a share of reparations and would lose on balance, or France, which was to be a net recipient of reparations over war debts payable to Britain and the United States. In addition, to keep commercial debts alive when it had few involved a loss for France and a benefit for Britain and the United States.

Lend-lease or the Marshall Plan were gestures more appropriate to leading. They are difficult to sustain over long years. The leader becomes corrupt, or is perceived as such; the leader becomes tired of free rides, or believes he or she is being bankrupted by excessive burdens, or both. The economic limit to the burden a country can sustain is of course much greater than the political limit, as is evident when one contemplates that the United States used half its income for war. The statement made frequently, for example, by Senator Robert Taft, that "my country could not afford" something—say the Marshall Plan—is to be translated into a more accurate form: "I do not want, or I believe voters in the United States do not want, to reduce the United States' standard of living by enough to carry a particular burden."

A system of world economy based on leadership is thus unstable over time in much the same way that a Pax Britannica, Pax Americana, balance-of-power system, or oligopoly is unstable. The threat may come from the outside in the presence of a thrusting aggressive competitor anxious for the prestige, and possibly the real income, of the dominant economy. Prussia in the second half of the nineteenth century is the prime example, but one could take England with its hatred of the Netherlands in the seventeenth century, or the France of Napoleon as examples. The leader can be overthrown by the refusal of followers to submit to what they have come to think of as exploitation.

But change can also come from within. The leader grows weary under burdens which grow as more and more free riders seek more luxurious free rides. The means of stabilizing the system are self-evident.

(1) Rely on long-run self-interest of the participants along the lines of Kant's Categorical Imperative, expecting them to renounce free riding and to act in ways that can be generalized to all participants. This is a counsel of perfection.
(2) Bind the members of the international community to rules of conduct, to which they agree, and which will restrain each member from free riding, and allocate burdens equitably, as a matter of international legal commitment. Not only will countries chisel on the commitments, but they will free ride the application of sanctions, as experience under the League of Nations and the United Nations amply demonstrated.
(3) Form a world government.

I choose not to discuss item 3, which sets limits to free rides within national states, on the ground that its idealistic and visionary character is self-evident. Free riding or escape from what was believed to be excessive burdens by a regional unit might have to take the form of secession, but there seems no doubt that in the present state of inadequate sense of world social and political cohesion, it would do so.

For as far ahead as today's social scientists can see, I think it is necessary to organize the international community—both related to policy and economy alike—on the basis of leadership. Entropy is inevitable. After breakdown, there follows a long, drawn-out, and dangerous process of establishing a new basis of legitimacy, under a new leader. Self-consciousness in the role does not appear to be a help, and will make many candidates, as today in the economic field (Germany, Japan and Switzerland), hesitant and shy. But leadership to provide the public good of stability, properly regarded, misunderstood as exploitation, or sniped at by free riders, seems a poor system, but like democracy, honesty, and stable marriages, is better than the available alternatives.

I should perhaps add that I have not discussed the possibilities of a compromise among these systems, where two or more countries take on the task of providing leadership together, thus adding to legitimacy, sharing the burdens, and reducing the danger that leadership is regarded cynically as a cloak for domination and exploitation. In 1931, the suggestion was widespread that France and the United States together make a big loan to Germany. The French insisted on political conditions, the United States was unwilling to throw good money after bad, although that is the crux of rediscounting in a crisis.

After World War II, Ernest Bevin suggested to William L. Clayton and Lewis W. Douglas that the "special relationship" be reinstituted by the Untied States undertaking a preliminary, antecedent Marshall Plan for the United Kingdom, following which both countries would undertake the economic recovery of the continent. The idea was never seriously considered, and Britain's decision in 1962 to apply for membership in the Common Market put "paid" to the special relationship.

For a time it looked as though the European Community itself would emerge as an economic and political entity capable of rivaling the United States for world economic leadership (outside the Socialist blocs), perhaps succeeding to first place as the United States faltered. In that event, domestic economic and political concerns in France, Britain, and Italy and the Ost-bloc policy of Germany have turned attention from world to national and regional concerns, and there appears to be no readiness in the Community to take on wider responsibilities.

A fourth idea is for the United States, Germany, and Japan to agree to a simple set of rules in the monetary field to give coherence to their policies and world stability. The idea is politically unattractive since it appears as an attack on the European Community—especially against France, on the one hand, and could be regarded as a division of the world into regional blocs on the other. In addition, there is no Japanese appetite for world responsibility.

I conclude that the danger we face is not too much power in the international economy, but too little, not an excess of domination, but a superfluity of would-be free riders, unwilling to mind the store, and waiting for a storekeeper to appear. No place, to quote President Truman, for the buck to stop. I say this without implication that there is any threat to the world economic system from outside. But without a stabilizer, the system in my judgment is unstable. It is perhaps too strong to say that a world of Denmarks is as unstable as a world of Prussias, but it poses the issue.

8.2

ECONOMIC INTERDEPENDENCE AND NATIONAL SECURITY IN HISTORICAL PERSPECTIVE

Robert Gilpin

> Robert Gilpin, a preeminent professor of political economy in the post-war era, explains the historical origins of the economic ideas and systems known as mercantilism, liberalism, nationalism, and Marxism. As he notes, each idea (identity) and period entail a unique conception of the relationship between economics and security (realist) and a unique set of trade, investment and monetary rules, and institutions (liberal) to organize the world economy. In mercantilist thinking, for example, realist factors (military competition) dictate market and ideological ones. In liberal thinking, market factors override power and ideological disparities. And in nationalist thinking, identity factors predominate. For critical theory, such as Marxism, historic mechanisms such as imperialist capitalism drive outcomes. From British laissez-faire, to German nationalism, to Soviet Marxism, and back to U.S. liberal markets, history elucidates the changing contours of global markets and gives us various ways of thinking about and critiquing contemporary globalization. Writing before the rise of constructivist perspectives, Gilpin was known as an insightful advocate of one of the other two mainstream theoretical perspectives on international affairs. Can you figure out which one?

* * *

Liberalism and mercantilism ... represent two different ways of organizing an interdependent world economy. Though they differ profoundly in theory, in reality they exist at opposite ends of a continuum. Whereas the one emphasizes the organization of a world economy through self-regulating markets, the other emphasizes state intervention and manipulation of market forces. Both doctrines depart from the non-market systems of reciprocity [VOLUME EDITOR'S NOTE: meaning barter], redistribution, and mobilization exchanges.

Source: Robert Gilpin, "Economic Interdependence and National Security in Historical Perspective," in *Economic Issues and National Security,* ed. Klaus Knorr and Frank N. Trager (Lawrence, Kans.: Regents Press of Kansas for the National Security Education Program of New York University, 1977), 19–66.

As economic doctrines, liberalism and mercantilism also differ from Marxism which in theory is a revival of redistribution and, as practiced in the Soviet bloc, is akin to mobilization exchange....

The Age of Mercantilism

... [M]ercantilism has generally had a "poor press," except in a few continental European countries.... [S]ubsequent critics, however, have [not] succeeded in destroying its appeal. Throughout the past two centuries, the mercantilist heresy has been revived in one form or another to attack economic orthodoxy. This fundamental tenacity of mercantilism at least suggests that it meets the economic and security needs of particular groups and nations regardless of its intrinsic merits as a scientific theory.

The common thread that runs through the several varieties of mercantilist thought and practice is the partial subordination of the economy to the perceived security and welfare needs of the state and society.[1] The measures and practices advocated by mercantilist writers and statesmen were those which would lead to the creation and maintenance of a strong nation-state and national economy. In effect, mercantilism can be described as the striving after security through economic means. As we shall see in a moment, under the conditions of the times, this meant the encouragement of trade and manufacture through protectionism and what we today would label monetarist policies.[2]

* * *

Mercantilism reflected and was a response to the political, economic, and military developments of the sixteenth, seventeenth, and eighteenth centuries. It represented the emergence of strong national states in constant competition; the rise of a middle class devoted at first to commerce and increasingly to manufacture; and the quickening of economic activities due to internal changes within Europe and the discovery of the New World. Of critical importance, however, were the evolution of a monetized market economy and the wide range of changes in the nature of warfare that have been characterized as the Military Revolution. It was not without good reason that mercantilists tended to identify a favorable balance of trade with national security. And concern about national security can be linked to the transformation in warfare. The beginning of transformation in warfare was the innovation of gunpowder and the rise of professional armies.[3] Other developments were also important, but these military innovations greatly enhanced the role of manufacturing as an element of national power. Increasingly, as mercantilists appreciated, manufacturing was beginning to displace agriculture as the basis of wealth and power.

With the rise of standing professional armies, warfare increasingly became an instrument of national policy. Armies became more costly and required new bureaucracies to support them. In this new environment of warfare, nation-states required large quantities of bullion to finance their newly formed professional armies and the balance of payments drain of foreign campaigns. The acquisition of money or bullion became the *sine qua non* of national power.

A related and paradoxical consequence of the Military Revolution in terms of national security was that the great European powers became decreasingly self-sufficient and increasingly dependent on the world economy. The rise of professional armies and the new technology of warfare required vital war materials, such as naval stores or saltpeter for gunpowder. These war materials could frequently be acquired only through trade or the export of bullion. Mercantilists appreciated that the international economy had become an important source of both the financial and material sinews of national power. The frequent and seemingly petty commercial wars of the mercantilist era were really conflicts over access to or control over the sources of treasure, markets, and raw materials upon which national security increasingly depended. This loss of self-sufficiency and new vulnerability contributed greatly to the insecurity of states.

The mercantile empires characteristic of this age were established by the northern European powers and reflected this new insecurity and dependence upon trade and markets for treasure and war materials. In contrast to the mobilization empires of the Assyrians or the Romans, they were primarily trading rather than tribute empires.[4] The European states regarded their colonial possessions as secure sources of raw materials—gold, furs, timber, sugar, tobacco, etc.—and as consumers of their expanding output of manufactured goods.[5] The purpose of the Navigation Acts and other acts governing trade was to "regulate colonial trade so that raw materials were produced for the mother country and manufactured goods were purchased from her."[6]

While several mercantile empires dominated the world economy, trade among the European states also increased. In truth, as Klaus Knorr has noted, prior to the Industrial Revolution, international economic integration was proceeding at a more rapid pace than national economic integration. It was primarily in the nineteenth century with improvements in land communications (particularly the railroad) and the advent of stronger nation-states that national integration caught up.[7]

Under mercantilism, then, the world economy was increasingly interdependent. This fact and its political significance were at the same time gaining recognition by theorists of international relations. Despite the outbreak of frequent commercial conflict, this era gave currency to the theme which became prominent in the nineteenth century that "peace is the natural effect of trade."[8] . . .

* * *

Alas! As we shall see, it hasn't turned out quite this way. The extension of markets and the growth of economic interdependence among societies have wrought high costs in the form of personal and national insecurity as well as immense benefits from an enlarged international division of labor.

The Rise of Liberalism[9]

Throughout the mercantilist era the major powers of Western Europe had fought for control of Asia and of the New World and had struggled over the European balance of power. One by one these contenders for empire and dominance had been eliminated until only France and Great Britain remained locked in combat. Although both were growing in wealth and power, after 1750 British power began a more rapid advance, due to the accelerating pace of the Industrial Revolution. Endowed with rich resources and an enterprising population, Great Britain was gaining an economic and technological lead which would take her to a commanding position over other nations following her victory in the Napoleonic Wars.

The defeat of Napoleon and the French ushered in a new era of international politics and economics which has been rightly identified as the *Pax Britannica*. Great Britain was supreme on the seas and controlled access to Asia and the New World for her European rivals. On the continent of Europe a balance had been established at the Congress of Vienna which kept the European powers in check. Until the unification of Germany and the rise of the United States in the latter part of the century, no nation or group of nations would be in a position to challenge British world hegemony.

The *Pax Britannica*, which was to provide the general structure of international relations until the collapse of the system under the impact of the First World War, transformed the conduct and general features of international economic relations. In place of the mercantilistic emphasis on the control and possession of colonies, the *Pax Britannica* at its height (1849-1880) emphasized an open, interdependent world economy based on free trade, non-discrimination, and equal treatment. Although Great Britain and several other European powers retained the remnants of colonial empires, the conquest of territory and colonies declined in importance. Behind the shield of British sea command, nations had relatively open and free access to the world's markets and sources of raw materials. In short, the *Pax Britannica* provided the political framework for the emergence of a liberal international economy.

* * *

The Revolution in the British Economy and Economic Thought

Underlying the development of an interdependent nineteenth-century world economy was Great Britain's redefinition of her national security interests based on the precepts of liberalism. The essence of the teaching of Adam Smith and of later free traders was that wealth from overseas trade was due to the exchange of goods and not to territorial possession. Economic growth, Smith had argued in *The Wealth of Nations* (1776), is primarily a function of the extent of the division of labor which, in turn, is dependent upon the scale of the market.

For an economy to grow, it must continually expand its territorial base and integrate a larger and larger market. Herein, Smith argued, lay the true security interests of Great Britain.

The free trade ideas of Smith, especially as they were developed by David Ricardo, became the ideology of the increasingly important British middle class. What this class and the liberal theoreticians appreciated was that the costs and disadvantages of empire and territorial control outweighed its benefits. By the end of the eighteenth century, they pointed out that ideals of imperial self-sufficiency and of exclusive economic spheres were impeding the natural flow of trade and handicapping growth. British supremacy and security, they argued, rested on her manufacturing and naval supremacy and not on the Empire. With only half the population of France, England was turning out two-thirds of the world's coal, half of its iron and cloth. Technologically more advanced than her competitors, Britain could capture world markets with cheaper goods. Why should Britain restrict her trade to a closed empire, when the whole world lay open and desired her goods? Her interest resided with universal free trade and the removal of all barriers to the exchange of goods. Through concentration on industrial efficiency, Great Britain could be the first power to create an empire of trade rather than one of colonies.

The objective of British foreign economic policy was to create complementary economic relations between industrial Britain and an overseas periphery which would supply cheap food and raw materials.[10] Through the migration of labor and the export of capital to developing lands (e.g., the United States, Canada, Australia, etc.), Britain could both acquire cheap imports and gain a market for her growing industrial exports. In this way, not only would the profit rate of capital remain high, but through the importation of cheap food and the concentration on her comparative advantage in industrial goods, Great Britain could out-compete the rest of the globe and thereby ensure her security.

Prior to the emergence of strong nationalistic sentiments in Europe and the rest of the world and before the rise of industrial competitors, Great Britain was able to extend her trade and influence without encountering much resistance. Throughout the early and middle portions of the nineteenth century, the primary mechanisms for integrating the periphery into the emerging world economy were largely economic in nature. Economic growth and industrialization at the British core stimulated a great volume of foreign trade and the spread of the network of international trade and investment to previously isolated areas.

The incorporation of the periphery into the world economy frequently meant imposition on these areas of numerous restrictions, such as extraterritoriality privileges for Western businessmen and denial of tariff autonomy. Where local rulers opposed the opening of trade and investment, or where they were unable to guarantee the security necessary for stable trading and investment relations, Great Britain (and subsequently other industrial powers) felt little reluctance to force them and to establish "law and order." The use of gunboat diplomacy, informal rule, and, where necessary, actual political control were frequent occurrences during the era of "free" trade. In the words of Lord Palmerston, the government's business is to "open and secure the roads for the merchant."[11] Kuznets wryly understates the point when he writes that "the greater power of the developed nations imposed upon the reluctant partners the opportunities of international trade and division of labor."[12] But, the primary nexus of the interdependent world economy created by Great Britain and the essential ingredients of British power were trade, investment, and the international monetary system.

* * *

The Revolt Against Liberalism: Economic Nationalism and Marxism

For the British in the nineteenth century, a liberal international economy was the natural order of things, founded on the laws of economics themselves: the laws of comparative advantage, of supply and demand, etc. While the market system was to Britain's own advantage, others also gained through trade and the maximization of global wealth. In an era of rapid economic growth, international economic relations ceased to be regarded as a zero sum game. Moreover, during these years of peace and prosperity, the identification of trade and peace achieved its foremost expression in the writings of the Manchester School. Trade, investment, and increasing ties of economic interdependence were held to be creating the preconditions of peace. Nations, it was said, could achieve security and welfare through trade and peaceful economic intercourse rather than through military conflict.

The defenders of economic liberalism, however, saw only one side of the picture. As spokesmen of the emergent middle class in England, they saw only its benefits. They overlooked the costs that a market system imposed, at least in the short run, on the welfare and security of other groups and classes within Great Britain and other societies. Nor were they sufficiently aware of the reaction of lesser developed economies to the impact of unregulated market forces. The evident costs of the free market system in the nineteenth century gave rise, therefore, to two major revolts against the British conception of a liberal economic order. One—the growth of economic nationalism—was, in effect, a revival of mercantilism, with its emphasis on the subordination of the market to the security objectives of the state. The other—Marxism and other forms of socialism—entailed a total rejection of the market exchange system in the interest of dispossessed classes and in effect advocated a return to the earlier emphasis on redistribution. Of the two, economic nationalism was by far the more serious challenge, at least in the nineteenth century.

Economic Nationalism

The intellectual origin of economic nationalism and the classic defense of economic protectionism was Alexander Hamilton's *Report on the Subject of*

Manufactures presented to the House of Representatives in December 1791.[13] Like the mercantilists before him, Hamilton's defense of protectionism was based on the so-called infant industry argument. But, he went further in contesting the basic assumption of liberalism: the static nature of comparative advantage. In doing so, Hamilton modernized the mercantilist thesis and, in effect, fostered a dynamic theory of economic development based on the superiority of manufacturing over agriculture.

The liberal theory of international trade as subsequently developed by David Ricardo was based on a static view of comparative advantage. Trade originated and was mutually profitable, because nations were endowed differently with respect to resources, labor, and other factors of production. Such factors were considered to be fixed attributes of individual countries. As Ricardo had demonstrated in his famous example, Portugal's advantage lay in the production of wine and Great Britain's in the production of cloth. Such an immutable international division of labor was determined by natural endowments and beyond the power of humans to change.

Contrary to both the earlier mercantilists and later liberals, Hamilton emphasized the transferability of factors between national economic systems. An economy's position in the international division of labor was not determined by unalterable endowments. The government, through national economic policies, could transform the nature of its economy and international economic position. For example, the encouragement of migration, especially of skilled labor, constituted "a much more powerful means of augmenting the fund of national industry than may at first sight appear."[14] In addition, the nation should encourage the importation of foreign capital and should establish a banking system to provide investment capital. In short, Hamilton's *Report* set against the classical liberal theory of static comparative advantage a dynamic theory of comparative advantage based on economic development.

Like the mercantilists before him, Hamilton identified national security with the development of manufactures and argued that the state had a principal role in guiding economic activities. Like them as well, he regarded economics as subordinate to the fundamental task of state-making. Although his ideas on protectionism were not to achieve full force until the victory of the rapidly industrializing North in the Civil War, his ideas were to exert a powerful influence at home and abroad. The developing nations today, with their emphasis on protectionism, industrialization, and state intervention, owe more than they may appreciate to Hamilton's conception of economic development.

Economic nationalism, both in the nineteenth century and today, is a response to the tendency of markets to concentrate wealth and power as well as to establish dependency relations between strong and weak economies. Although markets over time stimulate the diffusion of economic activities and industries, the tendency in the short run is for the concentration of wealth in the advanced economies to take place faster than the spread of economic activities in the developing economies. In order to protect its nascent industries and safeguard domestic interests against external market forces, the government of the developing economy tends to pursue protectionist and related nationalistic policies. As Harry Johnson and other liberal economists have noted, economic nationalism represents an alliance of producer interests and the state.[15] For these reasons, Hamilton's ideas favoring autarky continue to have a broad appeal among developing economies.

In the nineteenth century, Hamilton's ideas had their greatest impact on Germany. The ground had already been prepared there by Johann Fichte and Georg Hegel, who had enunciated the theme of economic nationalism in the early decades of the century.[16] The seeds of these ideas were planted by Friedrich List, who had spent a number of years in the United States and carried Hamilton's ideas back to Germany. Along with Wilhelm Roscher, Gustav Schmoller, and others, List helped found the German Historical School of economic analysis.[17] Their systematic and fierce attack on liberalism had a powerful influence on the development of Germany and on the world economy generally.

The thrust of List's argument in his influential *National System of Political Economy* was that liberalism was the economic policy of the strong.[18] The British, List argued, had used the power of the state to protect their own infant industries against foreign competition. But, once having achieved technological and industrial supremacy over their rivals, they had reversed themselves to become the champions of free trade. In advocating free trade, they were seeking to advance their own national economic interests in achieving unimpeded access to foreign markets. What we today would call an interdependent world economy List regarded as an expression of Britain's national interests. A true cosmopolitan world economy, he believed, would be possible only when other nations ranked equal with Great Britain in industrial power. In order to achieve this goal, the German economic nationalists advocated German unification and the erection of high tariff barriers to protect the development of German industry.

Following the unification and proclamation of the German Empire in January 1871, the ideas of the German Historical School became the official policy of Germany. In 1879, Bismarck negotiated the "compact of iron and rye" between the grain-growing Junkers east of the Elbe and the rising industrialists of the Rhineland. Tariff protection was extended both to grains and manufactures. The unification of Germany with its high tariff walls reversed the free trade movement and, as one writer has put it, "set every continental power on the search for security and self-sufficiency."[19] The sweep of economic nationalism across Europe meant that commercial policy became increasingly subordinate to diplomatic and balance of power considerations. The extension of these economic and political rivalries beyond the boundaries of Europe, in turn, led to the revival of intense imperialistic struggles. In effect, Europe had reverted to the mercantilistic conflicts characteristic of its earlier centuries.

In retrospect, the neo-mercantilists of the German Historical School may be seen as having identified a major security issue associated with the rise of a world market economy. Nineteenth-century liberals were quite right in emphasizing that never before in history had the world enjoyed a comparable era of peace and unprecedented prosperity. While England gained the most, others gained as well.

The expansion of trade, the flow of investment, and the efficiency of the international monetary system ushered in a period of economic growth which spread from England throughout the system. Perhaps never before or since has the cosmopolitan interest been so well joined to the national interest of the dominant power as under the *Pax Britannica*. But, while all may have gained, the neo-mercantilists emphasized that some gained more than others. In a world of competing states unequal gain is frequently more important than mutual gain. In order to increase their own relative gains, other nations seek to change the rules which tend to benefit the dominant industrial power(s). In the face of this neo-mercantilistic spirit which is never far from the surface, a liberal international economy cannot come into existence and be maintained unless it has behind it the most powerful state(s) in the system. A liberal economic system is not self-sustaining but is maintained only through the actions of the dominant power(s)—initiatives, bargaining, and sanctions. As Condliffe has put it, "[l]eadership in establishing the rule of law lay, ... as it always lies, in the hands of the great trading nations...."[20] As a consequence, as British power waned in the latter part of the century, so did the fortunes of a liberal world economy.

The Marxist and Socialist Critique of a Market System

Economic nationalism was not the only attack delivered against classical liberalism. A more fundamental critique was that of Marxism. Although the founders of this school of thought—Karl Marx and Friedrich Engels—wrote relatively little on international economics, they fully appreciated the political implications of the development of an interdependent world economy. But, in contrast to many modern scholars who hold this development as conducive to peaceful international relations, they regarded it as the prelude to world revolution.

* * *

For Marx and Engels, the rise and spread of an interdependent global market economy was progressive. Contrary to contemporary neo-Marxist denunciations of capitalistic imperialism, they believed that the extension of the market system was a step forward for humanity. The historic mission of the bourgeoisie and imperialism, they believed, was to smash the feudalistic and Asiatic mode of production which held back the modernization of what we would today call the Third World. In an essay, *The Future Results of British Rule in India (1853)*, which contemporary dependency theorists might read with profit, Marx argued that British imperialism was necessary for the modernization of India and that the establishment of a railroad system by the British was "the forerunner of modern industry."[21]

* * *

In brief, Marx believed the root cause of the underdevelopment of the Third World lay within these societies themselves, and that the outside "hammer" of western imperialism was necessary to smash social and cultural conditions inhibiting economic development.

Marx and Engels wrote in the belief that the maturing of capitalism in Europe and the drawing of the whole globe into the market economy had set the stage for the proletarian revolution and with it the end of the market exchange economy. That this development had not come to pass and that nationalism had proven to be a far more powerful force than proletarian internationalism were the primary concerns of Lenin's classic *Imperialism*.[22] Written during the First World War, *Imperialism* was both a polemic and a synthesis of socialist and communist critiques of a capitalist world economy.

The task which Lenin set for himself was to explain why economic nationalism had triumphed over proletarian internationalism. Why, in particular, had the socialist parties of the several European powers supported their respective bourgeoisies? Of equal importance, why had the impoverishment of the proletarian not taken place as Marx and Engels had predicted? The reason, he argued, was that capitalism had saved itself through overseas territorial imperialism. Through the export of surplus capital to their colonies, European nations had inhibited the operation of the law of the falling rate of profit. Moreover, super-profits from colonial exploitation had enabled the European capitalists to co-opt and deradicalize what Lenin called the labor aristocracy. In short, the tendency of profits to fall in a mature capital economy and the desire for secure outlets for surplus capital led inevitably to territorial imperialism.

Although Lenin's primary concern was the seizure of colonies by capitalist powers, Lenin recognized the existence of what today is called neo-colonialism: "The extraction of unequal gain from the domination of one society over another on the basis of power" rather than through formal territorial control.[23]

* * *

However, like Marx and unlike contemporary neo-Marxist theorists of imperialism and dependency theorists, Lenin regarded colonialism and neo-colonialism as progressive and necessary for the eventual modernization of lesser developed countries. The export of capital, technology, and know-how to colonies and dependencies, he argued, would "pave the way for the economic, and later, the political emancipation of the coloured races."[24] But, as we know from contemporary experience, both Marx and Lenin oversimplified the problems of economic development and of escape from dependency status.

The "Achilles Heel" of a capitalist international economy, Lenin argued, was what he called the law of uneven development. As capitalist economies mature, as capital accumulates, and as profit rates fall, the capitalist economies seize colonies and dependencies as investment outlets. In competition with one another, they divide up the colonial world in accordance with their relative strengths; the most advanced capitalist economy, namely Great Britain, appropriates the largest share of colonies. As other capitalist economies advance, they seek a redivision of colonies which inevitably leads to armed conflict among the rising and declining imperial powers. World War I, according to Lenin, was a war of territorial redivision between a declining Great Britain and rising continental capitalist powers. Such wars of redivision would continue until the industrializing colonies and dependencies revolted against the war-enfeebled capitalist powers.

In summary, Lenin argued that the inherent contradiction of capitalism was that it develops rather than exploits the world. The dominant capitalist economy plants the seeds of its own destruction in that it diffuses technology and industry, thereby undermining its own position. It raises up against itself foreign competitors which have lower wages and standards of living and can out-compete it in world markets. The intensification of the economic competition between the declining and rising capitalist powers leads to economic conflicts and imperial rivalries. Such was the fate of the British-centered liberal world economy of the nineteenth century. Today, he would undoubtedly argue, as the American economy is increasingly pressed by rising foreign competitors, a similar fate threatens the U.S.-centered twentieth-century liberal world economy.

* * *

Economic Interdependence and Security in the Interwar Period

The dominant motif of the interwar period was the spread of economic insecurity and national responses to the untoward effects of increasing economic interdependence. It was during this period that the United States redefined its own international economic and security interests. Like Great Britain in the early part of the nineteenth century, the United States came to regard its interests in terms of an open-world economy. As this change in national perception took place, the United States used its influence to reestablish a liberal interdependent world economy.

The First World War dealt a crippling blow to what in many respects was the Golden Age of an interdependent global market economy. The intensity and duration of the war revolutionized both domestic and international economies. The economic burden of the war had greatly weakened Great Britain and had forced her to liquidate much of her overseas investments. International markets had been disrupted and in many cases destroyed. The demands of the war effort on the major combatant had necessitated extensive government intervention in the economy; even in Great Britain the market economy gave way to a command economy. Outside of Europe, the demand for war material and the cutoff of European goods stimulated industrialization. In short, the war profoundly altered the role of the state in the economy and the international distribution of economic power.

Following the war, Great Britain sought to resume her role of economic leadership and to restore an interdependent market economy to working order. The international distribution of power had shifted decisively in favor of the United States, however, and it emerged from the war as a creditor nation and the foremost industrial power of the world. The United States was unwilling or unable to take over from the British the reins of international economic leadership, at least until late in the interwar period. The story of the interwar international economy, therefore, is essentially one of increasing American leadership in the face of steadily mounting challenges to the international economic order.

These challenges and the rise of the United States to world economic leadership constitute four major developments of the interwar period which profoundly altered the nature of global economic interdependence. As these developments continue to influence the evolution of the world economy, it is important to understand them.

The first major development was the Bolshevik Revolution and the subsequent withdrawal of the Soviet Union from the world market economy. In theory, as we have already suggested, Marxism rejects the market exchange system in favor of a redistributive exchange system. But in practice, and particularly following the victory of Stalin and the decision to emphasize rapid, heavy industrialization, the Soviet Union's economy can rightfully be characterized as a mobilization economy; the economy has been subordinated to the maximization of state power and self-sufficiency.

* * *

The communization of the Soviet Union meant a profound rupture and fragmentation of the interdependent world economy. This fissure was greatly extended following the Second World War; the Soviet ideals of aurarky and a command economy were expanded to include the economies of East Europe, which fell under the domination of the Red Army. The communization of China in 1948 meant a further extension of the mobilization exchange system. As a consequence, whereas the interdependent world economy of the nineteenth century incorporated most of the globe, the twentieth century has witnessed a major contraction. Economic interdependence has become nearly synonymous with the non-communist economies.

The second major transformation of the modern world economy has been the emergence of several major concentrations of economic power. In the nineteenth century, Britain, until the last two or three decades, stood alone as an economic power. Moreover, the units engaged in international commerce tended to be relatively small; they were either individual entrepreneurs or small firms. In the twentieth century, both aspects have changed. The world economy is composed not only of several powerful industrial economies but of large corporations whose resources dwarf those of the great majority of nation-states.

* * *

... [T]he world economy in the twentieth century has been transformed from an "international economy" to a "commerce of nations."[25] The presence of large concentrations of economic power in nations and corporations has made adjustments more difficult and less automatic. Moreover, the rise of welfare states committed to full employment has made nation-states less willing to subordinate their domestic economies to international discipline. Corporations which can exercise monopoly or monopsony power can easily resist market forces. As a consequence, the world economy has become increasingly characterized by bargaining and negotiations among large concentrations of state and corporate economic power.

The third major development of the interwar period was the rapid spread of economic nationalism. The origins of this economic nationalism are to be found in the war itself. Because of its totality and the demands imposed on the economy, one aspect after another of economic life was nationalized and brought into the service of the war effort. The role of the state in the economy was further enhanced in the post-war period by the disruptions caused by the war and its aftermath. Thus, whereas in the past balance of payments adjustment had been the major objective of economic policy, after the war price stability and full employment became major concerns of national policy. And with the rise of organized labor and mass movements of the Left and Right, national planning in the interest of internal stability became more important than external stability and adherence to international norms.

* * *

With the collapse of British leadership and the rise of powerful economies, economic nationalism took a still more virulent form in the 1930s with the rise of rival economic blocs and intensification of national insecurities. A decision which symbolized the final collapse of multilateral free trade was the British move in 1931 to go off the gold standard, which, along with the Ottawa Agreements of 1932, created the sterling area and the Commonwealth trading system (Imperial Preference). Although the intellectual origins of such a preference system composed of Britain and the Commonwealth nations are to be found in late nineteenth-century writers seeking an answer to the German and American trade challenge, the immediate cause for these decisions was the onset of the Depression, the contraction of world trade, and the breakdown of the multi-lateral system.

The fragmentation of the world economy into relatively isolated trading blocs and the retreat from global interdependence proceeded at a rapid pace. Already the United States had passed the high Smoot-Hawley Tariff (1930), and in 1933, on the eve of the London Economic Conference, President Franklin Roosevelt decided to leave the gold standard and thereby further isolate the United States from the world economy. But the two most ominous developments were taking place in Central Europe and the Far East, where Germany and Japan were organizing their own neighboring areas of strategic and economic importance under their respective hegemonies. Under the leadership of Adolph Hitler, defeated and revisionist Germany took advantage of the collapse of the Austro-Hungarian Empire and the divisions among her more powerful neighbors to create the greater Reich denied her by World War I. And in the Far East a rapidly industrializing Japan expanded into a crumbling China and sought to create a self-sufficient territorial base for Japanese industrial and military power.

* * *

The creation of exclusive economic blocs under the hegemony of the great industrial powers was one of the most significant international developments of the interwar period. It was a response to the breakdown of the international economic order and the global balance of power. With the collapse of the *Pax Britannica,* the competing industrial powers sought to enhance their security through the creation of exclusive spheres of economic influence; commercial relations became instruments of economic warfare. Through bilateral negotiations, competitive currency depreciation, and trade restrictions of various types, the large powers attempted to manipulate interdependence and to achieve economic and political advantages over each other and their weaker neighbors.

After the spread of economic nationalism, the fourth major development of the interwar period was the rise of the United States to a position of global economic leadership. Although America's meteoric rise to economic and industrial preeminence had begun in the latter part of the nineteenth century, it was only following the First World War that the United States really began to challenge British world leadership in trade, investment, and monetary affairs. As a consequence of the war, the American industrial plant had greatly expanded, and the nation had shifted from the status of debtor to creditor. A major force in world markets since the 1890s, American interest and concern over the international trading system expanded throughout the interwar period, with two major protectionist aberrations in 1930 and 1933. By the end of the Second World War, the United States had reached a point where it desired to see a major reformation of the world economy in a direction more in line with its own interests as the world's dominant economy.

The growth of American economic and industrial power was reflected in changing American attitudes and policies with regard to investment, trade, and the international monetary system. With respect to investment, at the same time that Great Britain had had to liquidate over $4 billion in overseas investment, the United States had become the major lending country of the world. American foreign investment, which had operated on a modest scale since the 1890s, now expanded rapidly....

* * *

Almost from the initial thrust of American business abroad, foreign direct investment, i.e., the establishment of foreign subsidiaries, has been an important mechanism to penetrate markets protected by tariffs, cartels, or other barriers; to gain control of valuable sources of raw materials; and to protect technological leads which American enterprise had established over foreign competitors. In the decades following the Second World War, the overseas expansion of what we today call multinational corporations would become a predominant feature of the interdependent world economy.

A second major change in America's world economic role was in trade. Traditionally a highly protectionist nation, America's industrial maturity and changing interests were reflected after World War I in the evolution of her tariff policy toward free trade. Although the Smoot-Hawley Tariff of 1930 and the 1933 decision to go off the gold standard were clear cases of backsliding, the passage of the Reciprocal Trade Agreements in 1934 signaled the conversion of the United States to free trade. Enacted as a solution to the Depression and reflecting America's industrial supremacy, the purpose of the Act was to negotiate mutual reductions in tariff barriers. As had been the case with Great Britain, with the maturing of its industrial strength and expanded productive capacity, the United States became the opponent of exclusive economic spheres and the proponent of the "open door" on a global scale.

* * *

In international monetary affairs a similar devolution of leadership from Great Britain to the United States was taking place. Whereas in the pre-war period, the City of London had, in effect, managed the international monetary system, during the interwar period, the system was initially divided into two spheres of influence. On the one hand, there was a loose sterling-dollar condominium under the joint management of London and New York, and, on the other, a European gold bloc, largely dominated by France.[26] While the Tripartite Agreement of 1936 foreshadowed the re-emergence of a global system and the supremacy of the dollar, the United States was not yet powerful enough to impose its will on the international monetary system. As a result, the centers of economic power were too divided to provide the central direction and coordination which had existed in the pre-war period.

* * *

The American-Centered World Economy

The United States emerged from the Second World War as the champion of a liberal international economy.[27] Like Britain in the nineteenth century, the United States hoped to create an international economy which would guarantee its economic and security interests. American economic interests on the whole lay with free trade and free investment. As the world's leading industrial power, the United States had no need for an exclusive imperial system. It looked to the whole world for its markets, outlets for investment, sources of raw materials. It demanded "equal treatment," though one can argue that in the case of the strong, equal treatment may mean unequal advantage.

But, in addition to these considerations of economic self-interest, the American desire for a return to an interdependent world economy was based on a redefinition of America's security interests. American leadership believed that economic nationalism and the competition for markets and resources had been at the root of the Second World War. The basis of American opposition to trade discrimination and bilateralism, therefore, was not merely that they harmed American economic interests, but President Roosevelt and other American leaders believed colonial empires, exclusive economic blocs, and "beggar-thy-neighbor" policies, exemplified particularly by the British empire, had been responsible for the Second World War. The Germans and the Japanese, for example, were excluded from colonial markets and sources of raw materials in the interwar years, and they were regarded as having been driven to create exclusive blocs of their own. The achievement of America's post-war goal of a lasting peace was impossible in the absence of free trade, security, and an open world. From the American perspective, a renewal of the competition between "have" and "have-not" states for exclusive economic spheres of trade, investment, and especially for raw materials would lead to a third world war. The American intention was to lessen the economic importance of political boundaries and enhance the security of all states by giving every state equal opportunity for access to markets and raw materials and thereby to defuse the issue that had led to the economic struggles of the 1930s. Economic interdependence and security would replace competition for exclusive economic spheres.

Under American leadership, economic interdependence in the contemporary world has had three distinguishing characteristics. In the first place (and this is perhaps the most significant innovation of the American post-war planners), international institutions were created to perform certain of the essential functions formerly lodged in the institutions of the City of London. Collectively known as the Bretton Woods System, after the conference held in 1944 to re-establish the international monetary system, these organizations provide the broader framework for multilateralism today. While it is not our intention to discuss these organizations, their history, or their functions here, the more important ones should be noted: the International Monetary Fund (IMF); the General Agreement on Tariffs and Trade (GATT); the International Bank for Reconstruction and Development (World Bank); the stillborn International Trade Organization; and, from an earlier era, the Bank for International Settlements.[28] In addition to the principles of free trade and free investment, the system governed itself through three key rules of the game: fixed exchange rates, currency convertibility, and the IMF as overseer of the international monetary system.[29] ...

In reality, however, and behind the facade of these institutions, the United States has run the international economy.[30] While American pressure played a large part in establishing the system, the major contribution of the United States was in providing its psychological underpinnings and in exercising leadership. Throughout the industrial non-communist world, with its memory of the disastrous experience of the interwar period, there was a general recognition of the need to eliminate discrimination. But the prevailing circumstances at the end of World War II made bilateralism, discrimination, and inconvertibility of currencies the most rational courses of action. No country could risk removing currency and trade restriction unless everyone else did so simultaneously; to do otherwise would have meant a hemorrhage of currency and commercial disaster.[31] "The restoration of an international system of trade and payments after the war was thus recognized at an early stage as a problem whose solution would require international negotiation and agreement rather than unilateral uncoordinated decisions by several scores of sovereign countries."[32] Together with Great Britain, the United States provided the necessary leadership and fostered an atmosphere of mutual confidence which would make the transition to multilateral free trade possible.[33]

Under the umbrella of these institutions, the market economies led by the United States have determined the rules of the game of international economic relations. Neither the Soviet bloc nor the nations of the so-called Third World, with their strong commitment to state intervention, have exercised much influence. The rules governing trade, investment, and monetary relations have been set by nations, corporations, and international organizations committed, at least in principle, to a market exchange system.

As a consequence of these institutional and policy initiatives, the second feature of economic interdependence over the past several decades has been the increased sensitivity of national economies to foreign trade flows, particularly the exchange of manufactures for manufactures.[34] Decreases in transportation costs, improved communications, and lower trade barriers have all operated to stimulate the exchange of goods. Moreover, the accumulation of capital and the international transmission of technical knowledge have caused a convergence in industrial structure. Comparative advantages have become more dynamic and less a consequence of national endowments. As a result, national economies are more intensely subjected to the insecurities of foreign competition and external disruptions.

The third and most controversial aspect of economic interdependence today has been the extensive integration of national economies by the large multinational corporations. These enterprises, most of which are American, have taken interdependence beyond the realm of trade, finance, and money to that of production itself. This internationalization of production has carried to its ultimate conclusion the logic of a market exchange system. The increased mobility of capital, technology, and managerial know-how associated with the multinational corporation has greatly benefited national economies. But the implantation of foreign-owned and managed enterprises in national economies has also threatened the core values of host societies. As a result, the threat of the multinational corporation to the economic, political, and cultural autonomy of states has led to a resurgence of economic nationalism on the part of host governments.[35]

* * *

Notes

1. See, for example, Eli Heckscher, *Mercantilism* (London: G. Allen and Unwin, 1935).
2. This point is made by John Maynard Keynes, *The General Theory of Employment Interest, and Money* (New York: Harcourt, Brace and World, 1936).
3. This discussion is based primarily on George Clark, *War and Society in the Seventeenth Century* (Cambridge: Cambridge University Press, 1958).
4. Strachey, *End of Empire.*
5. James Adams, *Epic of America* (Boston: Little, Brown, and Company, 1931), p. 73.
6. Edmund S. Morgan, *The Birth of the Republic 1763–1789* (Chicago: University of Chicago Press, 1956), pp. 8–9.
7. Klaus Knorr, *The Power of Nations: The Political Economy of International Relations* (New York: Basic Books, Inc., 1975), p. 210.
8. Baron de Montesquieu, *Spirit of the Laws,* trans. Thomas Nugent (New York: Harper Press, 1949), p. 316; first published in 1748.
9. The following discussion draws heavily upon my book, *U.S. Power and the Multinational Corporation: The Political Economy of Foreign Direct Investment* (New York: Basic Books, Inc., 1975).
10. For a more detailed analysis, see Gilpin, *U.S. Power.*
11. Quoted in Donald Gordon, *The Moment of Power: Britain's Imperial Epoch* (Englewood: Prentice-Hall, 1970), p. 87.

12. Simon Kuznets, *Modern Economic Growth* (New Haven: Yale University Press, 1966), p. 335.

13. Discussed in John Condliffe, *The Commerce of Nations* (New York: W. N. Norton, 1950) p. 240.

14. Ibid., p. 246.

15. Harry Johnson, *Economic Nationalism in Old and New States* (Chicago: University of Chicago Press, 1967).

16. On Fichte, see Knorr, *The Power of Nations,* p. 235.

17. List's classic defense of economic nationalism is *National System of Political Economy* (London: Longmans, Green and Co., 1928).

18. The views of this school are discussed by Condliffe, *Commerce of Nations,* Ch. 9.

19. Ibid., p. 233.

20. Ibid., p. 219.

21. Karl Marx, "The Future Results of British Rule in India," *Karl Marx on Colonialism and Modernization,* ed. Shlomo Avineri (Garden City, New York: Doubleday and Company, 1969), p. 136.

22. V. I. Lenin, *Imperialism, The Highest Stage of Capitalism* (New York: International Publishers, 1939).

23. Knorr, *The Power of Nations,* p. 57.

24. Lenin, *Imperialism,* p. 125.

25. Condliffe, *Commerce of Nations.*

26. Susan Strange, *Sterling and British Policy* (Oxford: Oxford University Press, 1971), p. 55.

27. An excellent analysis of this period is Richard Gardner, *Sterling-Dollar Diplomacy: Anglo-American Collaboration in the Reconstruction of Multilateral Trade* (Oxford: Clarendon Press, 1966), p. XLII.

28. Ibid., LVIII, pp. 42–44, 282, 313.

29. Ibid., p. 261.

30. Peter Kenen, *Giant Among Nations* (New York: Rand McNally, 1963), p. 87.

31. Ibid., p. 91.

32. Robert Triffin, *Europe and the Money Muddle* (New Haven: Yale University Press, 1957), p. 91.

33. Ibid., p. 93.

34. Richard Cooper, *The Economics of Interdependence: Economic Policy in the Atlantic Community* (New York: McGraw-Hill Book Company, 1968), p. 80.

35. See Gilpin, *U.S. Power,* Ch. 9.

Chapter 9

HOW GLOBALIZATION WORKS IN PRACTICE

9.1

THE "MAGIC" OF THE MARKET

Martin Wolf

> Martin Wolf, economic correspondent for the *Financial Times,* lays out the long historical view in favor of market mechanisms in the global economy. A significant world economy emerged only in the eighteenth century with the industrial revolution and the flowering of free markets and scientific and technological innovations. But market success was not a matter of "magic." Markets are cleverer than that, Wolf argues. They solve essential problems such as information, trust, competition, property rights, and externalities; create sophisticated institutions such as corporations, innovative systems, intellectual property rights, and financial markets; and rely on basic moral premises such as equality, freedom, and civic virtue. His account stresses interactive factors that are important from the liberal perspective and the individual, domestic, and process levels of analysis. But can you see how someone who gives more emphasis to national jobs (realist) and culture (identity) or worries more about the unequal and oppressive distribution of power operating from the structural level of analysis (critical theory) might disagree?

The enemies of globalization are opponents of the market economy. That is the heart of this debate. But what is such an economy? Where has it come from? How does it work, both within a country and across frontiers? It is impossible to assess the critique of globalization without trying to examine these fundamental questions....

Source: Martin Wolf, "The 'Magic' of the Market," in *Why Globalization Works* (New Haven and London: Yale University Press, 2005), 40–57.

Rise of the Market Economy

'Trade and market-regulated behaviour, though present from very early times, remained marginal and subordinate in civilized societies' until about a thousand years ago.[1] Thus did the American historian William McNeill describe the gathering revolution of the past millennium. Prior to that period, he argued, command systems were the principal way of mobilizing resources in complex societies.[2] Civilization—by which I mean large-scale hierarchical societies, with a complex internal division of labour—was the fruit of the agrarian revolution, which seems to have begun in the fertile crescent of West Asia some 10,000 years ago and arose not much later in the valleys of the Indus and the Yellow River.[3] The vast majority of people in these societies were tillers of the soil, feeding themselves and those in power over them, with their lives and livelihoods perennially vulnerable to the weather, disease and the stationary and roving bandits described by Mancur Olson.[4] Beyond the limits of complex civilizations were nomads of steppe and sand, mountain-dwellers and, remoter still, the hunter-gatherers. In the Americas a parallel evolution occurred, though some thousands of years later.[5]

Throughout the agrarian era of human history, commerce and trade, albeit significant, remained marginal activities.[6] The merchant and, still more, the moneylender were distrusted and despised. In many of the value systems of civilized society they came below the tillers of the soil, particularly in Confucian China.[7] Occupants of the highest social places were the ever-recurring figures of the warrior-ruler and the priest-scribe-bureaucrat. The power they held was also the most effective route to wealth. For the warrior-ruler, the two came naturally together. The highest position of all was held by those who combined the two aspects of authority in one—priest-kings, such as the Byzantine emperors, or, loftier still, god-kings, such as the pharaohs of ancient Egypt. The moral and mental machinery of contemporary revolutionaries harks back to those pre-modern times. The party-state of the communist era was a ruthless priest-kingdom. In contemporary North Korea, it even turns out to be a hereditary one.

Only when the commercial spirit—and its concomitant rationalistic approach to technological innovation and scientific inquiry—seized control of powerful states (as outlined in the previous chapter) did the market economy comprehensively transform ways of life. In the beginning its impact was fitful. In China, after a remarkable technological and commercial flowering under the Sung dynasty (960–1279), advance slowed sharply. It was on the western promontory of Eurasia that the commercial revolution broke through the crust of tradition and repression that lay over agrarian hierarchical societies. It gathered strength, albeit fitfully, over several centuries, before bursting into astonishing life in the nineteenth century.

From a technological view, the decisive shift was towards use of inanimate energy—wind, water and, most important, fossil fuels—from the old reliance on animate energy—human and animal power. What is called the industrial revolution is better named the energy revolution. Some economists refer to the growth of the past two centuries as 'Promethean', after the legendary titan who brought fire to man.[8] This distinguishes that form of growth from the 'Smithian', which works via the division of labour and economies of scale, as described in the *Wealth of Nations,* published in 1776. The arrival of Promethean growth was the most important event since the agrarian revolution. But adjusting to its onset has been painful. Never before have ways of life changed so much and so quickly. The agrarian revolution spread across the globe over thousands of years, not two centuries. In no more than six or seven generations, the Promethean revolution has brought in its train urbanization, industrialization, global economic integration, two world wars, the spread of democracy and a global commercial culture. The proportion of people working in British agriculture halved between 1780 and 1870. Not surprisingly, such upsetting changes have repeatedly brought a backlash by millenarians promising a perfect future and romantics longing for a more natural past.[9]

The liberating technological changes of Promethean growth did not emerge from nowhere. They reflected a new way of organizing the economic activities of society as a whole—a sophisticated market economy with secure protection of property rights. Unshackled from the constraints of tradition and driven by hope of gain, economic actors were tied by competition to the wheel of what the great Austrian economist Joseph Schumpeter called 'creative destruction'. To achieve success in their battles with their competitors, businesses have been driven to exploit and nurture the ever-burgeoning power of technology and science. Within a market economy the hope of gain and the fear of loss drive inventors and innovators to apply new ways of doing things or to produce new products.[10]

* * *

Growth during the Market Millennium

If the last thousand years have, as Professor McNeill argues, been the millennium of the market, what have been the consequences? The short answer is that the world has undergone an unprecedented transformation. According to the economic historian Angus Maddison, the population of the world rose twenty-two-fold over the last millennium, but world gross domestic product (at purchasing power parity) rose thirteen times as fast.[11]

This astonishing increase in population, output and incomes per head has no earlier parallels. The world's population barely increased in the first millennium, while the average standard of living in 1000 was also much the same as it had been a thousand years before, at a bare subsistence level. Today, however, very few countries have living standards close to the world average of a thousand years ago: Chad or Sierra Leone might be examples.

Moreover figures for economic growth in the second millennium understate the true increase in the standard of living. Life expectancy was twenty-four in England between 1300 and 1425. It had probably been much the same in the Roman Empire. By 1801–26, the English level had reached forty-one. By 1999 it had reached seventy-seven. Two centuries ago or more, nobody, however powerful and rich, had access to dentistry, medicine or sanitation worthy of the name. Nathan Rothschild, founder of the Rothschild dynasty in England, died in 1836 of an infected boil. Today, antibiotics would have cured him with ease. Anne, Queen of England, bore fifteen children, not one of whom survived to maturity. Even in 1900 one in ten children in the United States died before his or her first birthday. By the late 1990s the rate was down to seven in a thousand.

Growth accelerated enormously after 1820. But something important had already started to happen before then. World population rose nearly four-fold between 1000 and 1820. World GDP rose perhaps six-fold. This meant a 50 per cent rise in real incomes per head. This aggregate conceals very different performances by western Europe and the rest of the world. Between 1000 and 1820, European real incomes per head rose about three times. In the most successful market economies in Western Europe, the United Kingdom and the Netherlands, average incomes per head were about four times as high as they had been in 1000.[12] But, prior to the early nineteenth century, sustained rises in living standards were largely limited to western Europe and, from the seventeenth century onwards, the British colonies of North America.

In the period after 1820, the rate of global growth greatly accelerated. Between 1820 and 1998, world population rose almost six-fold, its GDP forty-nine-fold and its GDP per head almost nine-fold. Between 1820 and 1998, real GDP per head rose nineteen-fold in western Europe, the former British colonies of North America and Australasia. In Japan, which was relatively poor in 1820, standards of living had risen thirty-one-fold by 1998. In the rest of the world, real GDP per head rose only five-fold. Almost every economy is richer than it was two centuries ago, but some have done much better than others.

The historically unprecedented economic dynamism of the last two centuries and the divergence in performance across countries are the two most important features of the world we inhabit. The *dynamism* was the product of institutions, practices and attitudes that emerged in western Europe over an extended period. These cultural, social and political advantages combined with favourable resource endowments, particularly the proximity of coal and iron.[13]

The *divergence* was the result of the uneven spread of this form of rapid growth. In the course of the nineteenth century, rapid growth—what the Nobel-laureate Simon Kuznets called 'modern economic growth'—spread swiftly from Britain to the rest of western Europe and the former British colonies overseas. Incomes converged strongly among these countries.[14] Rapid growth also jumped from one end of Eurasia to the other once the United States forced Japan to open up its economy in the mid-nineteenth century. At the present stage in human history, all the successful economies are rooted in European or Sino-Japanese culture.[15]

In 1820, the richest country in the world had a real income per head about four and a half times as high as the poorest. The ratio was fifteen to one by 1913, twenty-six to one by 1950, forty-two to one by 1973, and seventy-one to one by 2000.[16] Not all is gloom. Africa's average real income per head is perhaps three times higher than it was a century or so ago. Asia's as a whole is up six-fold since 1820 and Latin America's nine-fold. In 1900 life expectancy was a mere twenty-six in today's developing world. It was sixty-four by 1999. This is much the same as the sixty-six achieved by today's advanced countries as recently as 1950.

Yet the overall picture of a world in which some countries have economies that grow more or less consistently while others do not is correct. A few countries have already caught up on the leaders of the nineteenth century, while some are growing very rapidly, including the world's biggest, China. India, the world's second biggest country, is also beginning to sustain reasonably rapid growth, at last. But many countries have been failing. As Lant Pritchett of the World Bank has noted, out of a sample of 108 developing countries for which data are available, 'sixteen developing countries had negative growth over the 1960–90 period.... Another 28 nations ... had growth rates of per capita GDP less than 0.5 per cent per annum ... and 40 developing nations ... had growth rates less than 1 per cent per annum.'[17] So what explains successful economies? The answer is that they have dynamic market economies. But what does this mean? That is the question to which we now turn.

How an Advanced Market Economy Works

Think for a moment about what our economy achieves. We can buy food produced all over the world, which is then bought, processed, distributed and sold though a long chain of wholesalers and retailers to satisfy our varying tastes. The food will be extraordinarily safe.[18] One can buy clothing made by workers in China, India, Italy or Mexico, in a staggering number of different fabrics and styles. For personal transport, one can choose from many varieties of motor car; for entertainment, one can select a DVD player and flat-screen television; for work, leisure or personal bureaucracy, one can buy a personal computer. An army of competing inventors, designers, producers and distributors try to meet all these and many other demands. A host of intermediaries takes money from households and supplies it to those who persuade them they can use it productively. In the process, they create an endless array of financial instruments, including bank deposits, bonds, equities and assorted derivatives, and package and repackage risk, allowing savers and investors to diversify and hedge their portfolios.

We take all this for granted. Yet it is extraordinary. What makes it far more extraordinary—and to many quite scary—is that nobody is in charge. Adam Smith's metaphor of the invisible hand remains as illuminating as ever.

Self-interest, co-ordinated through the market, motivates people to invent, produce and sell a vast array of goods, services and assets.

As a way of satisfying the material wants of mankind, self-interest exceeds the power of charity as the Amazon exceeds a rivulet. This is what Ronald Reagan called 'the magic of the market'. But 'the market process', as Friedrich Hayek called it, is not magic. It is far cleverer than that.

In his book *Reinventing the Bazaar,* John McMillan of the University of California, at Berkeley, indicates the nature of this institution by comparing an 'absolutely free market' to 'folk football'. But 'a real market is like American football, an ordered brawl'.[19] To a large extent, the rules governing markets evolve with markets themselves. The result today, in advanced economies, is a system of extraordinary complexity and efficiency.

Every society has some markets. Equally, in no society are markets ubiquitous. In contemporary advanced economies, three categories of transaction occur largely or entirely outside markets: those within households; those with the government and within it; and those inside corporations. Yet markets are significant institutions virtually everywhere. They emerge in prisons and concentration camps; they emerged in communist dictatorships even though the participants, condemned as 'speculators', were often shot out of hand; and in almost all developing countries they emerge as the informal sector where people trade outside the purview of foolish regulations and corrupt regulators.[20]

Yet many societies today and virtually all societies historically had only very limited markets. Those markets dealt only in immediately available goods and services. These transactions are self-enforcing: one buys a fruit or a carpet and pays for it. The constraint on development is the absence of markets for transactions that take a long time to reach fruition: borrowing, lending, investing and insuring. In such transactions trust and confidence matter a great deal. In many developing countries, these longer-term or complex transactions are limited to dealings with family or close friends, where misbehaviour carries credible sanctions.

If a sophisticated market economy is to work, it has to solve five problems: first, information must flow smoothly, giving people confidence in what they are buying; second, it must be reasonable to assume people will live up to their promises, even if these promises are to be executed decades into the future; third, competition must be fostered; fourth, property rights must be protected; and, finally, the worst side effects on third parties must be curtailed.[21]

The flow of reliable *information* and the ability to *trust* are the life-blood of markets. As James Q. Wilson, formerly professor at Harvard, puts it: 'trust must exist in a society for it to be a capitalist society because people who do not trust their neighbors, do not trust other groups, do not trust distant people, cannot trade with them; and, unable to trade with them, capitalism remains at the level of a bazaar economy'.[22] Sometimes, obtaining information on what is available is too expensive to allow any market to emerge. To this the rise of the information economy is providing some answers. At other times, the difficulty is 'asymmetric information'. If one thinks that the person one is dealing with not only knows more about what is being sold than one does oneself, but has an incentive to deceive one as well, the transaction may well not occur. Happily, there are solutions. People in business can provide guarantees or create reputations for honest dealing; they can invest in a brand that associates the company with the quality of what it sells; and they can employ more or less credible professionals (such as accountants) to certify the truth of what they are saying. Regulators can help by certifying the quality of a company's processes or products, their financial soundness or whatever else may be relevant. The law and other forms of recourse provide penalties for deceit or the breaking of contracts. Finally and perhaps most important, the values of a society can support honesty: if cheating and stealing are regarded as normal, a society will possess no more than a shallow and undeveloped market economy. If high levels of personal probity and honest dealing are encouraged, the market economy will work well.

Competition is essential to good performance. A private monopoly may be more efficient than a public one, largely because it has clearer objectives, but it is likely to be more exploitative and less innovative than competitive businesses. In principle, sound competition policy can remedy anti-competitive behaviour. Some actions—making price-fixing and other forms of cartel behaviour illegal, for example—are self-evident. But imposing competition by administrative or legal fiat can be tricky. There is often a temptation to use competition policy as a way of protecting competitors instead of competition or consumers.

Protection of *property* is the necessary condition for a sophisticated market economy. Indeed, it is the most important single condition. People need to be able to own things. What does ownership mean? It means, first, that people have a right to the residual income, over and above that committed to other parties—suppliers, lenders, employees and so forth. This gives them an incentive to use the asset productively or, if they cannot do so, to sell it to someone who can. Second, the owner also possesses residual control rights. Not only does the owner have the incentive to use the asset productively. He or she has the right to do so as well. In a sophisticated modern economy, such rights of ownership are complex. They rest in mere pieces of paper and may be exercised through chains of agents.[23]

The protection of property links to what economists call *externalities,* the production of 'goods' or 'bads' whose positive or negative value is not included in the calculations of those making the transactions themselves. They are in some way or another outside the market, usually because there is an incomplete specification of property rights. Where externalities exist, property rights may well need to be qualified. The right to make use of a river passing through one's land may exclude the right to take more than a certain proportion of the water it contains, or to pollute it. Sometimes, as the Nobel-laureate Ronald Coase has argued, such externalities can be addressed through bargaining among those affected.[24] Often, however, the costs of reaching and policing such bargains will be excessive or the costs (and benefits) may be distributed too widely for those affected to have an adequate incentive to coalesce to 'internalize' the externality. A solution will then have to be imposed by a coercive power—usually the state.[25]

Central Features of a Modern Market Economy

A modern market economy is therefore about as far from [a] jungle as can readily be imagined. The market is a complex and sophisticated piece of institutional machinery that has evolved over centuries on the basis of the broad principles of freedom of contract, secure property rights and a service-providing state. Four interconnected features of the modern market economy are of decisive importance, especially for any discussion of global economic integration. These are: the corporation; innovation and growth; intellectual property; and the role and functioning of financial markets. All depend on institutional arrangements underpinned by the state as creator and enforcer of the law. All are focal points for the criticisms of protesters against globalization. Yet, without them, we would not have the economic dynamism we take for granted. They are at the heart of a modern market economy.

Corporations[26]

The Nobel-laureate Kenneth Arrow has remarked that 'truly among man's innovations, the use of organization to accomplish his ends is among both his greatest and his earliest'.[27] The private corporation is the most extraordinary organizational innovation of the past two centuries. Today's economy would be unimaginable without its dynamism and flexibility. The corporation is a hybrid institution: it is hierarchical, but embedded in markets. Before the modern corporation, commerce was largely the province of individual merchants, while big hierarchical institutions, both civil and military, were the province of rulers.[28] Today, there exists an institution that combines the two. This required the merging of two distinct forms of social organization and value systems, that of the merchant and that of the administrator. Making such organizations entrepreneurial remains an abiding challenge.

The modern multi-unit business enterprise emerged in the 1840s, almost at the beginning of the era of Promethean growth. This was the point at which technological advance combined with an enlarging economy 'to make administrative co-ordination more productive and, therefore, more profitable than market co-ordination'.[29] The modern corporation also required the invention of limited liability, which occurred in 1856. Otherwise the immense capital needed would have remained unavailable.

Corporations are crucial to a modern economy. In the United States transactions in the market account for well under a third of total incomes.[30] Yet the corporation is not above or outside the market. Shifts in market conditions, including technology or trade, will alter the boundaries of corporations, force them to merge, impose fundamental changes in strategy or maybe bankrupt them. Companies are servants of market forces, not their overlords. If they do not meet the terms of market competition, they will disappear.

Why do companies exist? The simple reason, first proposed in a classic 1937 article by Ronald Coase, is that transaction costs can make hierarchical structures more efficient than market transactions.[31] For such an organization to work, it must be possible to form relationships of trust. As one might expect, therefore, large companies are far more prevalent in advanced countries with high levels of trust than in less developed ones: in the United States plants with fifty or more employees account for 80 per cent of manufacturing employment; in Indonesia, the proportion is only 15 per cent.[32]

The corporation is a wonderful institution. But it contains inherent drawbacks, the core of which are conflicts of interest. Control over the company's resources is vested in the hands of managers who may rationally pursue their interests at the expense of all others. Economists call this the 'principal-agent' problem. In the modern economy, where shares are held by fund managers, there is not just one set of principal-agent relations but a chain of them.[33] Asymmetric information and obstacles to collective action exacerbate the principal-agent problem. Corporate managers know more about what is going on in the business than anybody else and have an interest in keeping at least some of this information to themselves. It is hard to create incentives that ensure management acts in the interests of others. Equally, dispersed shareholders have a weak incentive to monitor management, because they would share the gains with others but bear much of the cost themselves.[34] The upshot is the vulnerability of the corporation to managerial incompetence, self-seeking, deceit or malfeasance.

In practice, there are six (interconnected) ways of reducing these risks. The first is market discipline: financial failure will ultimately find managers out, provided governments can be dissuaded from bailing failed companies out. The second is internal checks, with independent directors, requirements for voting by institutional shareholders and internal auditing. The third is private regulation, such as listing requirements of stock exchanges. The fourth is official regulation that covers the composition of boards, structure of businesses and reporting requirements. The fifth is transparency, including accounting standards and independent audits. The last is, once again, values of honest dealing.

Economists are very uncomfortable with the notion of morality. Yet it seems to have rather a clear meaning in the business context. It consists of acting honestly even when the opposite may be to one's advantage. Such morality is essential for all trustee relationships. Without it, costs of supervision and control become exorbitant. At the limit, a range of transactions and long-term relationships becomes impossible and society remains impoverished. Corporate managers are trustees. So are fund managers. The more they view themselves (and are viewed) as such, the less they are likely to exploit opportunities created by the conflicts of interest within the business.

Innovation[35]

Rising standards of living and their uneven spread have been, as noted above, the most remarkable features of a global market revolution. The source of this sustained growth has been technological innovation. Of that there is no doubt. In technological innovation modern market economies found the economist's free lunch. A brilliant book by William Baumol of New York University sheds light on this revolution.[36] He builds on the insights of the Austrian economist Joseph Schumpeter to expose the machine that drives capitalism. Professor Baumol argues that innovation rather than price competition is the central feature of the market process. Competition forces companies to invest in innovation. Otherwise, they risk falling behind and, ultimately, being driven out of their markets.

In Schumpeter's model of the capitalist economy, the engine of innovation was the extraordinary profits offered to the lone entrepreneur. Yet, as Baumol makes clear, the bulk of the innovation that drives economies occurs within existing companies. It is a routine aspect of their behaviour. Overall, such innovative activity will not be particularly profitable: some companies will be lucky; others will not. But the motivation is no longer the hope of exceptional profit. It is the certainty of failure if one is not in the race. Innovation then does not come from outside the market. It is hardwired into capitalism.

Intellectual Property

Given the role of innovation, intellectual property is not a marginal feature of the property-rights regime of a modern market economy, but its core. It is the most important example of property that only a powerful state can protect. The reason such action is needed is that ideas are public goods. Put plainly, this means that a person can enjoy the fruits of an idea without depriving anyone else of its benefits. But also, once divulged, they are available to everybody. Yet if ideas are freely available, nobody can make money out of creating them.

The solution has been intellectual property—patents, copyright and trademarks. For innovation, patents are the most important. But they are also a legally sanctioned restraint of trade.

Intellectual property protection requires striking a delicate balance. It is essential, but can easily go too far. There will be strong pressure from powerful and self-interested producer lobbies to make intellectual property protection too tight. Protection must also not be granted too freely. In the United States, that now seems to be happening, with protection granted to genes with unknown use and trivial business methods—such as 'one-click' purchasing on the Internet.[37] Over-liberal granting of intellectual property rights is a restraint on trade and should be viewed as such.

Financial Markets

Financial intermediation is as central a feature of a modern market economy as the corporation, innovation and intellectual property. It is its bloodstream, taking resources from people who do not need them or cannot use them and supplying them to people who do need them and can use them. Overwhelming evidence links the depth and sophistication of financial markets to levels of output per head. As a World Bank report on finance stated, 'there is now a solid body of research strongly suggesting that improvements in financial arrangements precede and contribute to economic performance. In other words, the widespread desire to see an effectively functioning financial system is warranted by its clear causal link to growth, macroeconomic stability, and poverty reduction'.[38] The Bank noted, for example, that developing countries with relatively deep financial markets in 1960 subsequently grew far faster than those with relatively shallow ones.

Financial systems perform four essential functions: they mobilize savings (for which outlets would otherwise be far more limited); they allocate capital (to finance productive investment and permit people to spend temporarily above their current incomes); they monitor managers (to ensure funds will be spent as promised); and they transform risk (by pooling risk and distributing it to those best able to bear it). These are vital functions. It is absolutely impossible to imagine a successful market economy without a dynamic, competitive and flexible financial system.

Yet market-driven financial arrangements, though irreplaceable, are liable to well-known difficulties.

First, financial markets suffer from inadequate supplies of information and obstacles to monitoring performance.

Second, financial markets are, partly for this reason, fragile. This is particularly true of banks. Their fragility comes from the fact that their liabilities are short term, in domestic or, occasionally, in foreign currency, usually payable at par and on demand, but their assets are long term, with values that are vulnerable to interest rate, credit and macroeconomic risks.

Third, financial markets are liable to wild swings in prices, both upwards and downwards, because of the instability of valuations of uncertain streams of income.

Fourth, financial markets tend towards herd behaviour. This is particularly true when ill-informed players believe they lack information available to others. When classes of assets are unfamiliar to a large number of investors, herding behaviour may be very powerful.

Fifth, financial markets may generate self-fulfilling expectations and so what economists call 'multiple equilibria'.

Financial markets are fragile because of the inherent challenge of orienting economic activity to an unknowable future. It would be quite wrong to conclude that the 'imperfections' underlying such fragility mean either that such markets should be abolished or that there exist some evident cures. Without financial intermediation, market economies would be unable to perform. As for eliminating market 'failures', one must remember that one can never do better than one's best. So-called imperfections are irrelevant, therefore, if the costs of eliminating them exceed the benefit of trying to do so.

*   *   *

Morality of Market Economies[39]

Intelligent critics are prepared to accept that a sophisticated market economy works far better than any other economic system. But they would proceed to complain that markets encourage immorality and have socially immoral consequences, not least gross inequality. These views, albeit common, are largely mistaken.

Inequality

All complex societies are unequal. In all societies people (generally men) seek power and authority over others. But, among sophisticated societies with an elaborate division of labour, societies with market economies have been the least unequal and the inequality they generate has been the least harmful. To many this may seem a shocking statement. It should not be.

Remember that in agrarian kingdoms or feudal societies, kings and lords had the power of life and death. The rich and powerful could seize the labour, the possessions and even the lives of subjects, serfs and slaves, at will. Perhaps the most unequal societies of all were the state-socialist and national-socialist regimes of the twentieth century. A Stalin or a Mao possessed absolute control over the resources of vast countries and their inhabitants. When, on a whim, Mao decided on the Great Leap Forward in the 1950s, 30 million people died. The irony is that such tyranny was justified by the alleged horrors of capitalist inequality. To eliminate market-driven inequality, all power was concentrated in the hands of the state, which then promptly and inevitably generated non-market-driven inequalities for the benefit of those who controlled it.

In all that matters—in the ability to lead one's own life and the legal rights one possesses—the modern liberal democracy is unprecedentedly equal. Virtually all citizens have access to a range of goods and services unavailable even to the wealthiest a century or even half a century ago. Wealthy people have more influence over the life of a democracy than do the majority of its citizens. But, compared to the power and influence that accrued to the wealthy in traditional societies, the power of today's wealthy is highly circumscribed. Politicians have more power and intellectuals more influence than men with big cheque books. Who has made more difference to the way Americans live their lives today, Ronald Reagan, Milton Friedman or Warren Buffett?

No rich man or corporation can ignore the law, as a number of corporate scoundrels discovered in 2002. Even Bill Gates, the world's richest man, discovered he could not ignore the low-paid lawyers of the Department of Justice when it went after Microsoft's alleged monopolistic abuses. A few centuries ago, the richest man in a European country could create a private army capable of defying the state. Today, Gates would exhaust his fortune in less than three months in trying to rival the spending of his country's defence department. In a competitive market economy subject to the rule of law, Gates or Warren Buffett can tyrannize over their bank balances, not over people. They can support politicians, not coerce them.[40] They can cajole customers, not compel them. They can give money to charity, not create armies. They can order their businesses, not buy their workers. Gates and Buffett are citizens, entrepreneurs, investors and philanthropists. They are neither tyrants nor overlords. A competitive market economy neither ends inequality nor eliminates the desire for power and prestige. It tames them instead.

Freedom, Democracy and the Permanent Opposition

A competitive market economy is a reflection—and a source—of freedom. It is also a necessary condition for democracy. In a society where political power determines the allocation of wealth, it is impossible to be independent without being powerful. But in a market society that combination is possible and this, in turn, provides a basis for competing political parties. As Vaclav Havel explained, 'a government that commands the economy will inevitably command the polity; given a commanding position it will distort or destroy the former and corrupt or oppress the latter'.[41]

Liberal democracies with market economies are, as Joseph Schumpeter argued in his classic book *Capitalism, Socialism and Democracy,* the only societies that create their own opposition. 'Capitalism created both a parvenu class of rich plutocrats and corporate climbers and a counter-culture of critical intellectuals and disaffected youth'.[42] It continues to do so today. Take a look at the campuses, the publications and the protesters in western democracies. Only in a market economy could books condemning society's rich and powerful be published and promoted with such success. Only in a market economy would the wealthy give large sums of money to universities that provide comfortable homes to those who despise the wealthy and the system that made them so. The market economy does not merely support its critics, it embraces them.

* * *

Morality

Markets also require, reward and reinforce valuable moral qualities: trustworthiness, reliability, effort, civility, self-reliance and self-restraint. These qualities are, critics argue, placed in the service of self-interest. Yet, since people are self-interested, this is neither surprising nor shocking. But people are not completely self-interested. Happily, a wealthy society allows people to be far less driven by material objectives than one in which the vast majority of people are on the threshold of subsistence. A prosperous market economy also generates a vast number of attractive activities for those who are not motivated by wealth alone. People can work for non-governmental organizations or charities. They can work in the public sector, as doctors, teachers or policemen. They can even live off the welfare state and devote their lives to campaigning against the iniquities of capitalism. It is only the wealth generated by successful market economies that has made a welfare state possible. Poor countries today and all societies historically lacked the means to provide economic security to their citizens. Moreover, if people do make a great deal of money, they can use it for any purpose they wish. They can give it all away—and some have.

Over the last two centuries in the advanced market economies, the value placed on eliminating pain and injustice and on human and, more recently, animal life and welfare has also hugely increased. This is partly because a liberal society places such heavy weight on individuals. It is partly because people, being richer and far more secure, can afford concern with deeper moral ends. It is partly because people are better informed about what goes on across the world. It is partly because premature death and pain have been so much reduced, making life seem far more precious. The savage punishments and casual injustices in the judicial systems, military services and educational institutions of two centuries ago are gone. It took militarists, extreme nationalists, communists and fascists— the anti-liberals—to bring these horrors back, indeed to glory in violence and cruelty. Now, with the passing of these creeds, advocacy of human and animal rights has gone global, ironically as part of the litany of anti-globalization.

Again, consider environmentalism. Business is supposedly indifferent to the environment. That, indeed, is one of the principal criticisms of a market economy. Yet we now know that the supposedly benevolent state-socialist economies were environmental catastrophes. The market economy has avoided these disasters for at least four reasons: first, it provides the means for independent critics of environmental abuses to flourish; second, it generates the prosperity that makes people concerned about the environment; third, it implies a separation between companies and the government that makes independent regulation possible; and, finally, companies are concerned about their reputations and will act to protect them, in response to campaigning against them. For these reasons, effective environmental pressure groups have emerged only in market democracies.

Conclusion

The liberal market economy is morally imperfect, because it reflects the tastes and desires of people, who are also imperfect. A market economy satisfies the desires of the majority more than the tastes of a refined minority. It rewards the hustler more than the sage. But it is also the basis of freedom and democracy. It encourages valuable moral virtues. It makes people richer and more concerned about environmental damage, pain and injustice. It makes the welfare state possible.

* * *

Notes

1. William H. McNeill, *The Pursuit of Power: Technology, Armed Force and Society since A.D. 1000* (Chicago: University of Chicago Press, 1982), p. 22.

2. Ibid., p. 21.

3. Jared Diamond, *Guns, Germs and Steel: The Fates of Human Societies* (New York and London: W. W. Norton, 1997) and Douglass C. North, *Structure and Change in Economic History* (New York: W. W. Norton, 1981) present interesting complementary accounts of the agrarian revolution. The former emphasizes the unique ecology of the areas where this revolution began, particularly the variety of domesticable plants and animals. The latter points to the economic incentives to shift from the hunter-gatherer to the tiller-hunter-gatherer and, finally, the tiller stage, as population grew. Intriguingly, warrior-rulers of agrarian societies viewed hunting as a mark of their superior status. It would be consistent with contemporary evolutionary psychology for the loss of hunting to have been felt as emasculating.

4. Stationary and roving bandits were the late Mancur Olson's felicitous description of the human parasites to whom peasants were vulnerable. Stationary bandits protected the peasantry from the bandits of the roving kind in return for taxation. They were monopolists of coercion. As such, they had an interest in promoting the productivity of their peasants, since they would also benefit from it. For the peasant, therefore, the shift from roving to stationary bandit was normally beneficial. Both sides would benefit, though the stationary bandit would benefit most. Sooner or later stationary bandits cemented their position by calling themselves emperor or king and claiming some form of divine claim to power. See Mancur Olson, *Power and Prosperity: Outgrowing Communist and Capitalist Dictatorships* (New York: Basic Books, 2000), chapter 1.

5. Jared Diamond suggests that the agrarian revolution came late to the Americas because of the North-South axis of the twin continents, the limited number of domesticable crops and animals and the difficulty of domesticating those that there were (maize, for example). The geographical axis made it harder to transfer crops bred for different latitudes. In the event, the late emergence of civilization in the Americas and their isolation from the decisive continent in human history, Eurasia, doomed the societies of the Americas to destruction by European greed and European diseases. See Diamond, *Guns, Germs and Steel*.

6. On this at least, the classic anti-liberal tract by Karl Polanyi is correct, though he certainly understates the significance of barter and exchange in human history. See Polanyi, *The Great Transformation: The Political and Economic Origins of Our Time* (Boston: Beacon Press, 1957 (first published 1944)), chapter 5.

7. On the historic status of merchants, see K. N. Chaudhuri, 'Reflections on the Organizing Principle of Premodern Trade', in James D. Tracy (ed.), *The Political Economy of Merchant Empires: State Power and World Trade 1350–1750* (Cambridge: Cambridge University Press, 1991), especially pp. 426–7.

8. See David Landes, *The Unbound Prometheus: Technological Change and Industrial Development in Western Europe from 1750 to the Present* (Cambridge: Cambridge University Press, 1969), and Deepak Lal and H. Myint, *The Political Economy of Poverty, Equity and Growth* (Oxford: Clarendon Press, 1996).

9. See David Landes, *The Wealth and Poverty of Nations: Why Some Are So Rich and Some So Poor* (London: Little Brown, 1998), p. 513.

10. In the literature on technology, the innovator is the person who makes an invention economically profitable. He or she brings inventions within the purview of the market.

11. Angus Maddison, *The World Economy: A Millennial Perspective* (Paris: Development Centre of the Organization for Economic Co-operation and Development, 2001), p. 28.

12. Maddison, *The World Economy*, pp. 46 and 42.

13. There has been much debate about why a Promethean take-off did not occur in the Islamic world. A large part of the reason must be environmental. Much of the Islamic world is in a desert zone, which limited agricultural productivity. There was virtually no possibility of using running water to power machinery. Water power was the precursor of steam in western Europe. Coal and iron were unavailable, while oil was discovered and exploited only in the twentieth century. The puzzle about the Islamic world is not that it lagged behind Europe up to the mid-twentieth century, but why it fell far behind east Asia in the second half of the twentieth century.

14. This point has often been noted. See, for example, the important article 'Divergence, Big Time', by the World Bank economist Lant Pritchett in the *Journal of Economic Perspectives*, Vol. 11, No. 3 (Summer 1997), pp. 4–6.

15. Economists loathe cultural explanations for economic success. Yet it is striking how limited the group of successful economies are from the cultural point of view. It is easy to understand that a literate agrarian civilization, with a tradition of large-scale commerce and rational bureaucracy, will find it easier to jump into modern economic growth than hunter-gatherers or a culture with no comparable traditions. Even so, this leaves the puzzle of the dire performance of almost all of the Islamic world and the mediocre performance of Latin America. The former was, not so long ago, among the world's most advanced civilizations and the latter was a European offshoot. India, long a laggard, now seems to be beginning its take off into sustained growth in real incomes per head.

16. The last ratio is from the World Bank's, *World Development Indicators 2002* (Washington DC: World Bank, 2002).

17. Pritchett, 'Divergence, Big Time', p. 14.

18. The food hysterias of recent years, particularly in Europe, belie this fact. But it is worth remembering that, to take just one example, cow's milk was an extremely dangerous drink before pasteurization. Tuberculosis was just one of the deadly threats it provided.

19. John McMillan, *Reinventing the Bazaar: A Natural History of Markets* (New York: W. W. Norton, 2002), p. 5.

20. Much of the best work on the informal sector is by the Peruvian Hernando De Soto. See *The Other Path: The Invisible Revolution in the Third World* (New York: Harper & Row, 1989).

21. McMillan, *Reinventing the Bazaar*, p. 135.

22. See James Q. Wilson, 'The Morality of Capitalism', John Bonython Lecture, 15 October 1997 (ww.cis.org.au/JBL/JBL97.htm), p. 3.

23. On the economic meaning of ownership, see Oliver Williamson, *The Economic Institutions of Capitalism* (New York: Free Press, 1985) and Oliver Hart, *Firms, Contracts and Financial Structure* (Oxford: Clarendon Press, 1995).

24. The classic article is Ronald Coase, 'The Problem of Social Cost', *Journal of Law and Economics,* Vol. 3 (October 1960), pp. 1–44.

25. See on this Olson, *Power and Prosperity,* chapter 3 and 4.

26. This discussion is partly based on two columns written for the *Financial Times*: 'A Manager's Real Responsibility', 30 January, 2002 and 'A Rescue Plan for Capitalism', 3 July 2002.

27. Kenneth Arrow, *Essays in the Theory of Risk-Bearing* (Chicago: Markham, 1971), p. 224.

28. The Dutch and British East Indies Companies were early examples of such hybrid institutions.

29. Alfred Chandler, *The Visible Hand* (Cambridge, Massachusetts: Harvard University Press, 1977).

30. McMillan, *Reinventing the Bazaar,* p. 169.

31. The classic article on the transaction-cost theory of the firm is Ronald Coase, 'The Nature of the Firm', *Economica,* Vol. 4, No. 6 (1937), pp. 386–405. A survey of contemporary developments is in Oliver Williamson, 'The New Institutional Economics: Taking Stock, Looking Ahead', *Journal of Economic Literature,* September 2000, pp. 595–613. The economic analysis of institutions in terms of transaction costs is among the most impressive developments in economics of the past few decades. Companies may emerge because of economies of scale and scope. But the reason why economies of scale dictate the creation of hierarchies is that a large investment in fixed capital demands a large, flexible and complex labour force, a steady stream of inputs and equally steady revenue from scales. Hierarchy, then, works much better than a series of spot markets. One cannot hire the labour force on a daily basis. Nor can one write down a contract that specifies all the requirements of employment.

32. McMillan, *Reinventing the Bazaar,* p. 175.

33. This assumes that ownership rights vest with shareholders. The argument for such shareholder control is that the shareholders are the people who bear the residual risk in the company, because they are the least protected by contracts. If it were possible to specify all contracts, shareholders would not be needed. But under these assumptions there would be no companies. As Professor McMillan remarks, 'ownership is society's way of handling the unexpected'. See *Reinventing the Bazaar,* p. 91. In countries that do not offer shareholders effective ownership rights, ownership of shares is likely to be more limited and returns are likely to be lower. But companies then need to be financed in some other way, because shareholders are at extreme risk of being expropriated, as has been the case in Japan.

34. The classic study of the logic of collective action, which argued that concentrated interests will be better served than widely shared ones because collective action has public good properties—that is, free-riders cannot be prevented from sharing in the benefits—is by Mancur Olson. See *The Logic of Collective Action* (Cambridge, Massachusetts: Harvard University Press, 1965).

35. This discussion is drawn from a column in the *Financial Times*: 'The Capitalist Growth Machine', 5 June, 2002.

36. William J. Baumol, *The Free-Market Innovation Machine: Analyzing the Growth Miracle of Capitalism* (Princeton: Princeton University Press, 2002).

37. *See Human Development Report 2001: Making New Technologies Work for Human Development* (New York: Oxford University Press, for the United Nations Development Program, 2001), pp. 103–4.

38. *Finance for Growth: Policy Choices in a Volatile World* (Washington, DC: World Bank, 2001), p.5.

39. A shorter version of this section was published as Martin Wolf, 'The Morality of the Market', *Foreign Policy,* September/October 2003, pp. 46–50.

40. Media moguls, such as Rupert Murdoch, are more powerful, though even their influence has its limits.

41. Wilson, 'The Morality of Capitalism', p. 2.

42. *Ibid.,* p. 5.

9.2

SELECTIONS FROM *HAS GLOBALIZATION GONE TOO FAR?*

Dani Rodrik

> In contrast to Martin Wolf (in the previous selection), Dani Rodrik, Harvard professor, critiques the role of free markets in the globalization process. Notice that he begins the book from which this excerpt is taken by arguing that the most serious challenge posed by globalization is not to create wealth but to make it "compatible with domestic social and political stability." He goes on to highlight three principal problems created by globalization: (1) it shifts advantage from unskilled to skilled workers, (2) it disrupts national norms and social institutions, and (3) it makes the role of governments in supporting the weak more difficult. To address these problems, governments, acting both nationally and internationally, have to balance open markets against social cohesion. Rodrik emphasizes social (identity) and relative (realist) rather than market (liberal) concerns about globalization. He doesn't neglect markets; they are still necessary. But he assesses them more from the domestic (social disintegration) than the international (economic integration) level of analysis and worries more about their drawbacks (social dislocation) than their benefits (higher standards of living) at the individual level of analysis.

[From Chapter 1, "Introduction"]

* * *

The process that has come to be called "globalization" is exposing a deep fault line between groups who have the skills and mobility to flourish in global markets and those who either don't have these advantages or perceive the expansion of unregulated markets as inimical to social stability and deeply held norms. The result is severe tension between the market and social groups such as workers, pensioners, and environmentalists, with governments stuck in the middle.[1]

Source: Dani Rodrik, "Introduction" (Chap. 1) and "Implications" (Chap. 5), in *Has Globalization Gone Too Far?* (Washington, D.C.: Institute for International Economics, 1997), 2–7, 77–81.

... [T]he most serious challenge for the world economy in the years ahead lies in making globalization compatible with domestic social and political stability—or to put it even more directly, in ensuring that international economic integration does not contribute to domestic social *dis*integration.

Attuned to the anxieties of their voters, politicians in the advanced industrial countries are well aware that all is not well with globalization. The Lyon summit of the Group of Seven, held in June 1996, gave the issue central billing: its communiqué was titled "Making a Success of Globalization for the Benefit of All." The communiqué opened with a discussion of globalization—its challenges as well as its benefits. The leaders recognized that globalization raises difficulties for certain groups, and they wrote:

> In an increasingly interdependent world we must all recognize that we have an interest in spreading the benefits of economic growth as widely as possible and in diminishing the risk either of excluding individuals or groups in our own economies or of excluding certain countries or regions from the benefits of globalization.

But how are these objectives to be met?

An adequate policy response requires an understanding of the sources of the tensions generated by globalization. Without such an understanding, the reactions are likely to be of two kinds. One is of the knee-jerk type, with proposed cures worse than the disease. Such certainly is the case with blanket protectionism à la Patrick Buchanan or the abolition of the WTO à la James Goldsmith. Indeed, much of what passes as analysis (followed by condemnation) of international trade is based on faulty logic and misleading empirics.[2] To paraphrase Paul Samuelson, there is no better proof that the principle of comparative advantage is the only proposition in economics that is at once true *and* nontrivial than the long history of misunderstanding that has attached to the consequences of trade. The problems, while real, are more subtle than the terminology that has come to dominate the debate, such as "low-wage competition," or "leveling the playing field," or "race to the bottom." Consequently, they require nuanced and imaginative solutions.

The other possible response, and the one that perhaps best characterizes the attitude of much of the economics and policy community, is to downplay the problem. Economists' standard approach to globalization is to emphasize the benefits of the free flow of goods, capital, and ideas and to overlook the social tensions that may result.[3] A common view is that the complaints of nongovernmental organizations or labor advocates represent nothing but old protectionist wine in new bottles. Recent research on trade and wages gives strength to this view: the available empirical evidence suggests that trade has played a somewhat minor role in generating the labor-market ills of the advanced industrial counties—that is, in increasing income inequality in the United States and unemployment in Europe.[4]

While I share the idea that much of the opposition to trade is based on faulty premises, I also believe that economists have tended to take an excessively narrow view of the issues. To understand the impact of globalization on domestic social arrangements, we have to go beyond the question of what trade does to the skill premium. And even if we focus more narrowly on labor-market outcomes, there are additional channels, which have not yet come under close empirical scrutiny, through which increased economic integration works to the disadvantage of labor, and particularly of unskilled labor. This book attempts to offer such a broadened perspective. As we shall see, this perspective leads to a less benign outlook than the one economists commonly adopt. One side benefit, therefore, is that it serves to reduce the yawning gap that separates the views of most economists from the gut instincts of many laypeople.

Sources of Tension

I focus on three sources of tension between the global market and social stability and offer a brief overview of them here.

First, reduced barriers to trade and investment accentuate the asymmetry between groups that can cross international borders (either directly or indirectly, say through outsourcing[5]) and those that cannot. In the first category are owners of capital, highly skilled workers, and many professionals, who are free to take their resources where they are most in demand. Unskilled and semiskilled workers and most middle managers belong in the second category. Putting the same point in more technical terms, globalization makes the demand for the services of individuals in the second category *more elastic*—that is, the services of large segments of the working population can be more easily substituted by the services of other people across national boundaries. Globalization therefore fundamentally transforms the employment relationship.

The fact that "workers" can be more easily substituted for each other across national boundaries undermines what many conceive to be a post-war social bargain between workers and employers, under which the former would receive a steady increase in wages and benefits in return for labor peace. This is because increased substitutability results in the following concrete consequences:

- Workers now have to pay a larger share of the cost of improvements in work conditions and benefits (that is, they bear a greater incidence of nonwage costs).
- They have to incur greater instability in earnings and hours worked in response to shocks to labor demand or labor productivity (that is, volatility and insecurity increase).
- Their bargaining power erodes, so they receive lower wages and benefits whenever bargaining is an element in setting the terms of employment.

These considerations have received insufficient attention in the recent academic literature on trade and wages, which has focused on the downward shift in demand for unskilled workers rather than the increase in the elasticity of that demand.

Second, globalization engenders conflicts within and between nations over domestic norms and the social institutions that embody them. As the technology for manufactured goods becomes standardized and diffused internationally, nations with very different sets of values, norms, institutions, and collective preferences begin to compete head on in markets for similar goods. And the spread of globalization creates opportunities for trade between countries at very different levels of development.

This is of no consequence under traditional multilateral trade policy of the WTO and the General Agreement on Tariffs and trade (GATT): the "process" or "technology" through which goods are produced is immaterial, and so are the social institutions of the trading partners. Differences in national practices are treated just like differences in factor endowments or any other determinant of comparative advantage. However, introspection and empirical evidence both reveal that most people attach values to processes as well as outcomes. This is reflected in the norms that shape and constrain the domestic environment in which goods and services are produced—for example, workplace practices, legal rules, and social safety nets.

Trade becomes contentious when it unleashes forces that undermine the norms implicit in domestic practices. Many residents of advanced industrial countries are uncomfortable with the weakening of domestic institutions through the forces of trade, as when, for example, child labor in Honduras displaces workers in South Carolina or when pension benefits are cut in Europe in response to the requirements of the Maastricht treaty. This sense of unease is one way of interpreting the demands for "fair trade." Much of the discussion surrounding the "new" issues in trade policy—that is, labor standards, environment, competition policy, corruption—can be cast in this light of procedural fairness.

We cannot understand what is happening in these new areas until we take individual preferences for processes and the social arrangements that embody them seriously. In particular, by doing so we can start to make sense of people's uneasiness about the consequences of international economic integration and avoid the trap of automatically branding all concerned groups as self-interested protectionists. Indeed, since trade policy almost always has redistributive consequences (among sectors, income groups, and individuals), one cannot produce a principled defense of free trade without confronting the question of the fairness and legitimacy of the practices that generate these consequences. By the same token, one should not expect broad popular support for trade when trade involves exchanges that clash with (and erode) prevailing domestic social arrangements.

Third, globalization has made it exceedingly difficult for governments to provide social insurance—one of their central functions and one that has helped maintain social cohesion and domestic political support for ongoing liberalization throughout the postwar period. In essence, governments have used their fiscal powers to insulate domestic groups from excessive market risks, particularly those having an external origin. In fact, there is a striking correlation between an economy's exposure to foreign trade and the size of its welfare state. It is in the most open countries, such as Sweden, Denmark, and the Netherlands, that spending on income transfers has expanded the most. This is not to say that the government is the sole, or the best, provider of social insurance. The extended family, religious groups, and local communities often play similar roles. My point is that it is a hallmark of the postwar period that governments in the advanced countries have been expected to provide such insurance.

At the present, however, international economic integration is taking place against the background of receding governments and diminished social obligations. The welfare state has been under attack for two decades. Moreover, the increasing mobility of capital has rendered an important segment of the tax base footloose, leaving governments with the unappetizing option of increasing tax rates disproportionately on labor income. Yet the need for social insurance for the vast majority of the population that remains internationally immobile has not diminished. If anything, this need has become greater as a consequence of increased integration. The question therefore is how the tension between globalization and the pressures for socialization of risk can be eased. If the tension is not managed intelligently and creatively, the danger is that the domestic consensus in favor of open markets will ultimately erode to the point where a generalized resurgence of protectionism becomes a serious possibility.

Each of these arguments points to an important weakness in the manner in which advanced societies are handling—or are equipped to handle—the consequences of globalization. Collectively, they point to what is perhaps the greatest risk of all, namely that the cumulative consequence of the tensions mentioned above will be the solidifying of a new set of class divisions—between those who prosper in the globalize economy and those who do not, between those who share its values and those who would rather not, and between those who can diversify away its risks and those who cannot. This is not a pleasing prospect, even for individuals on the winning side of the divide who have little empathy for the other side. Social disintegration is not a spectator sport—those on the sidelines also get splashed with mud from the field. Ultimately, the deepening of social fissures can harm all.

* * *

[From Chapter 5, "Implications"]
The Role of National Governments

Policymakers have to steer a difficult middle course between responding to the concerns discussed here and sheltering groups from foreign competition through protectionism. I can offer no hard-and-fast rules here, only some guiding principles.

Strike a Balance between Openness and Domestic Needs. ... [T]here is often a trade-off between maintaining open borders to trade and maintaining social cohesion. When the conflict arises—when new liberalization initiatives are under discussion, for example—it makes little sense to sacrifice social concerns completely for the sake of liberalization. Put differently, as policymakers sort out economic and social objectives, free trade policies are not automatically entitled to first priority.

Thanks to many rounds of multilateral trade liberalization, tariff and nontariff restrictions on goods and many services are now at extremely low levels in the industrial countries. Most major developing countries have also slashed their trade barriers, often unilaterally and in conformity with their own domestic reforms. Most economists would agree that efficiency benefits of further reductions in these existing barriers are unlikely to be large. Indeed the dirty little secret of international economics is that a tiny bit of protection reduces efficiency only a tiny bit. A logical implication is that the case for further liberalization in the traditional area of manufactured goods is rather weak.[6]

Moreover, there is a case for taking greater advantage of the World Trade Organization's existing escape clause, which allows countries to institute otherwise-illegal trade restrictions under specified conditions, as well as for broadening the scope of these multilateral safeguard actions. In recent years, trade policy in the United States and the European Union has gone in a rather different direction, with increased use of antidumping measures and limited recourse to escape clause actions. This is likely because WTO rules and domestic legislation make the petitioning industry's job much easier in antidumping cases: there are lower evidentiary hurdles than in escape clause actions,[7] no determinate time limit, and no requirements for compensation for affected trade partners, as the escape clause provides. Also, escape clause actions, unlike antidumping duties, require presidential approval in the United States. This is an undesirable situation because antidumping rules are, on the whole, consistent neither with economics principles nor with fairness. Tightening the rules on antidumping in conjunction with a reconsideration and reinvigoration of the escape clause mechanism would make a lot of sense.[8]

Do Not Neglect Social Insurance. Policymakers have to bear in mind the important role that the provision of social insurance, through social programs, has played historically in enabling multilateral liberalization and an explosion of world trade. As the welfare state is being pruned, there is a real danger that this contribution will be forgotten.

This does not mean that fiscal policy has to be profligate and budget deficits large. Nor does it mean a bigger government role. Enhanced levels of social insurance, for better labor-market outcomes, can be provided in most countries within existing levels of spending. This can be done, for example, by shifting the composition of income transfers from old-age insurance (i.e., social security) to labor-market insurance (i.e., unemployment compensation, trade adjustment assistance, training programs). Because pensions typically constitute the largest item of social spending in the advanced industrial countries, better targeting of this sort is highly compatible with responsible fiscal policies. Gearing social insurance more directly toward labor markets, without increasing the overall tax burden, would be one key step toward alleviating the insecurities associated with globalization.

There is a widespread feeling in many countries that, in the words of Tanzi and Schuknecht (1995, 17), "[s]ocial safety nets have ... been transformed into universal benefits with widespread free-riding behavior, and social insurance has frequently become an income support system with special interests making any effective reform very difficult." Further, "various government performance indicators suggest that the growth in spending after 1960 may not have brought about significantly improved economic performance or greater social progress" (1995, 30). However, ... social spending has had the important function of buying social peace. Without disagreeing about the need to eliminate waste and reform in the welfare state more broadly, I would argue that the need for social insurance does not decline but rather increases as global integration increases. So the message to reformers of the social welfare system is, don't throw the baby out with the bath water.[9]

Do Not Use "Competitiveness" as an Excuse for Domestic Reform. One of the reasons globalization gets a bad rap is that policymakers often fall into the trap of using "competitiveness" as an excuse for needed domestic reforms. Large fiscal deficits or lagging domestic productivity are problems that drag living standards down in may industrial countries and would do so even in closed economies. Indeed, the term "competitiveness" itself is largely meaningless when applied to whole economies, unless it is used to refer to things that already have a proper name—such as productivity, investment, and economic growth. Too often, however, the need to resolve fiscal or productivity problems is presented to the electorate as the consequence of global competitive pressures. This not only makes the required policies a harder sell—why should we adjust just for the sake of becoming better competitors against the Koreans or the Mexicans?—it also erodes the domestic support of international trade—if we have to do all these painful things because of trade, maybe trade isn't such a wonderful thing anyhow!

The French strikes of 1995 are a good case in point. What made the opposition to the proposed fiscal and pension reforms particularly salient was the perception that fundamental changes in the French way of life were being imposed for the sake of international economic integration. The French government presented the reforms as required by the Maastricht criteria, which they were. But presumably, the Maastricht criteria themselves reflected the policymakers' belief that a smaller welfare state would serve their economies better in the longer run. By and large, the French government did not make the case for reform on its own strengths. By using the Maastricht card, it turned the discussion into a debate on European economic integration. Hence the widespread public reaction, which extended beyond just those workers whose fates would be immediately affected.

The lesson for policymakers is, do not sell reforms that are good for the economy and the citizenry as reforms that are dictated by international economic integration.

Do Not Abuse "Fairness" Claims in Trade. The notion of fairness in trade is not as vacuous as many economists think. Consequently, nations have the right—and should be allowed—to restrict trade when it conflicts with *widely held* norms at home or undermines domestic social arrangements that enjoy *broad* support.

But there is much that is done in the name of "fair trade" that falls far short of this criterion. There are two sets of practices in particular that should be immediately suspect. One concerns complaints made against other nations when very similar practices abound at home. Antidumping proceedings are a clear example: standard business practices, such as pricing over the life of a product or pricing over the business cycle, can result in duties being imposed on an exporting firm. There is nothing "unfair" about these business practices, as is made abundantly clear by the fact that domestic firms engage in them as well.

The second category concerns cases in which other nations are unilaterally asked to change *their* domestic practices so as to equalize competitive conditions. Japan is frequently at the receiving end of such demands from the United States and the European Union. A more recent example concerns the declaration by the US Trade Representative that corruption in foreign countries will henceforth be considered as unfair trade. While considerations of fairness and legitimacy will guide a country's own social arrangements, even by restricting imports if need be, such considerations should not allow one country to impose its own institutions on others. Proponents of fair trade must bear this key distinction in mind. Thus, it is perfectly legitimate for the United States to make it illegal for domestic firms to engage in corrupt practices abroad (as was done with the Foreign Corrupt Practices Act of 1977). It is also legitimate to negotiate a multilateral set of principles with other countries in the Organization for Economic Cooperation and Development (OECD) with broadly similar norms. It may also be legitimate to restrict imports from a country whose labor practices broad segments of the domestic population deem offensive. But it is not acceptable to unilaterally threaten retaliation against other countries because their business practices do not comply with domestic standards at home *in order to force these countries to alter their own standards.*[10] Using claims of fairness to advance competitive aims is coercive and inherently contradictory. Trying to "export" norms by asking other countries to alter their social arrangements to match domestic ones is inappropriate for the same reason.

*   *   *

Notes

1. See also Kapstein (1996) and Vernon (forthcoming). Kapstein argues that a backlash from labor is likely unless policymakers take a more active role in managing their economies. Vernon argues that we might be at the threshold of a global reaction against the pervasive role of multinational enterprises.

2. Jagdish Bhagwati and Paul Krugman are two economists who have been tireless in exposing common fallacies in discussions on international trade. See in particular Bhagwati (1988) and Krugman (1996).

3. When I mention "economists" here, I am, of course, referring to mainstream economics, as represented by neoclassical economists (of which I count myself as one).

4. Cline (1997) provides an excellent review of the literature. See also Collins (1996).

5. Outsourcing refers to companies' practice of subcontracting part of the production process—typically the most labor-intensive and least skill-intensive parts—to firms in other countries with lower costs.

6. Of course, since trade barriers are still higher elsewhere than in the United States, multilateral liberalization would generate relatively greater trade opportunities for the United States. See Bergsten (1996) for an argument that emphasizes this "asymmetric" nature of the benefits.

7. In the United States, escape clause action requires demonstration of "serious injury" rather than "material injury," the latter being the lower threshold, which applies to antidumping, which can apply to any particular exporting country. Of course, an antidumping action requires a demonstration that there is dumping, but in practice US Commerce Department criteria for what constitutes "dumping" are not at all restrictive.

8. This was one of the options considered by Schott (1990).

9. Many economists would agree that the amount of resources needed to keep the most disadvantaged from falling through the cracks is actually not that big. Krugman (1996) cites a figure of 2 percent of GDP. In absolute terms, this is, of course, a lot of money, but it is less than half of what an average OECD country spends on servicing the public debt each year.

10. It may be that restricting imports will cause the exporting country to alter its practices, irrespective of whether that was the stated goal of the policy. But that does not make the distinction any less valid. The motives that drive trade policy in the advanced industrial countries are usually transparent. There is little doubt that the Foreign Corrupt Practices Act of 1977, for example, was motivated by domestic ethical considerations, while many US and European complaints against Japan and some developing countries are clearly driven by a desire to make "them" more like "us." How foreign trade partners choose to react to policies of the first kind (the "legitimate" actions, that is) is their own business.

References

Bergsten, C. Fred. 1996. "Globalizing Free Trade." *Foreign Affairs* 75, no. 3 (May/June): 105–20.

Bhagwati, Jagdish N. 1988. *Protectionism.* Cambridge, MA: MIT Press.

Cline, William R. 1997. *Trade and Wage Inequality*. Washington: Institute for International Economics. Forthcoming.

Collins, Susan, ed. 1996. *Imports, Exports, and the American Worker*. Washington: Brookings Institution.

Kapstein, Ethan. 1996. "Workers and the World Economy." *Foreign Affairs* 75, no. 3 (May/June): 16–37.

Krugman, Paul. 1996. *Pop Internationalism*. Cambridge, MA: MIT Press.

Schott, Jeffrey J. 1990. "The Global Trade Negotiations: What Can Be Achieved?" *Policy Analyses in International Economics* 29. Washington: Institute for International Economics.

Tanzi, Vito, and Ludger Schuknecht. 1995. *The Growth of Government and the Reform of the State in Industrial Countries*. IMF Working Paper WP/95/130. Washington: International Monetary Fund.

Vernon, Raymond. N.d. "In the Hurricane's Eye: Multinational Enterprises in the Next Century." Harvard University. Unpublished manuscript.

Chapter 10

TRADE, INVESTMENT, AND FINANCE: ENGINES OF GROWTH

10.1

THE ECONOMICS OF QWERTY

Paul Krugman

> In this clear and clever chapter from his book *Peddling Prosperity,* Paul Krugman explains the new strategic trade theory, the mathematics for which he won a Nobel Prize. Not all trade, he notes, is based on comparative advantage. Some is the product of who or what gets to the market first, as in the case of the typewriter keyboard sequence QWERTY. And who or what gets to markets first may reflect the popular appeal of different types of industries (identity factors) and the history or "path dependence" of individual product developments (liberal factors), as well as the distribution of material endowments (realist). Yet predicting a priori (ideas) which industries and hence which trade goods are strategic is more difficult than it seems. And it can be very costly, particularly if it becomes a way of rationalizing protectionism. So, most economists stick with free exchanges (liberal) as the best model to exploit comparative material endowments (realist) and determine by trial and error which industries (ideas), if any, may be strategic.

It is said that a true sage can see the universe in a grain of sand. Paul David is no sage, only a fine economic historian: the best he could do was see the nature of economic reality in the layout of a typewriter keyboard.

I am typing this chapter on a new, fast personal computer. The decal proudly proclaims, "Intel inside!", and indeed its 80486 chip allows it to carry out in a

Source: Paul Krugman, "The Economics of QWERTY," in *Peddling Prosperity: Economic Sense and Nonsense in the Age of Diminished Expectations* (New York: W. W. Norton, 1994), 221–244.

few minutes feats of computation that would have taken hours on a 1960s mainframe and that would have been simply out of the question in 1940. Yet the first line of my keyboard is the same as that on the clunky mechanical typewriter my mother used when she put my father through law school: QWERTYUIOP.

Why QWERTYUIOP? In the early 1980s, Paul David and his Stanford colleague Brian Arthur asked that question, and quickly realized that it led them into surprisingly deep waters. In a 1982 paper entitled "Clio[1] and the Economics of QWERTY," David made the QWERTY keyboard into a symbol for a new view about how the economy works, a view that had been quietly gaining ground even as conservative economic ideology was achieving its political triumph.

You can probably already guess the answer to the mystery of QWERTY. The standard keyboard layout of typewriters dates back to the nineteenth century. It is not the most efficient layout in terms of finger movement, but that was no disadvantage in the early days; indeed, given the tendency of keys to jam on early typewriters, there was some advantage to a layout that forced typists to work slowly. Eventually jamming keys became a thing of the past, and it would have made sense to shift to an alternative, more efficient design—but by then it was too late. Typists learned their trade on QWERTY keyboards, because that was what manufacturers produced; manufacturers made QWERTY typewriters, because those were what typists knew how to use. The standard keyboard, adopted more or less by accident, had become "locked in."

What Paul David, Brian Arthur, and a growing number of other economists began to recognize in the late seventies and early eighties was that stories like that of the typewriter keyboard are, in fact, pervasive in the economy. Some of the stories involve technology choices that bear an obvious resemblance to the QWERTY tale. For example, unless you are a fanatical movie buff who has invested in a laser-disk video player, your home VCR uses a tape cassette (VHS) system—not because VHS is a clearly better system, but because cassettes are what most video stores stock, which is in turn because most people have VHS systems in their homes. I write my books and articles in WordPerfect, not because I particularly like it, but because most of the editors I write for prefer to receive WordPerfect disks, since that's the word-processing software that most of their authors use.

Other stories sound a little different, but—as David and Arthur realized—they are at root the same. For example, where do you live if you work in the film industry? Probably in Los Angeles. Why? Because the other film industry people you need to work with are there. But they are there because they need to be near people like you. If you are an investment banker, you probably work in New York for pretty much the same reason.

What does all this have to do with economic policy? Maybe quite a lot. What conservatives believe in, above all, is the effectiveness of free markets as ways to organize economic activity. Leave people free to make their own, individual choices, say conservatives, and they will be far more productive and efficient than if you try to plan or direct their activities. And as Milton Friedman showed, "Free to choose" can be a powerful slogan. But what if the collective result of those free choices is to lock in a bad result? What if we end up stuck with an inferior technology, or with an industry in the middle of a congested metropolis when it might function better in a new location?

And what if another country manages, with a little timely government intervention, to "lock in" an advantage in some major industry—and thereby to lock us out?

No, the story of the QWERTY keyboard is not just a cute piece of trivia. Like the description of the pin factory with which Adam Smith began *The Wealth of Nations,* it is a parable that opens our eyes to a whole different way of thinking about economics.[2] That different way of thinking rejects the idea that markets invariably lead the economy to a unique best solution; instead, it asserts that the outcome of market competition often depends crucially on historical accident. (Paul David calls this "path dependence": where you end up depends on what happens along the way.) And this conclusion is fraught with political implications, because a sophisticated government may try to make sure that the accidents of history run the way it wants.

In this chapter we will trace how this new way of thinking emerged among professional economists during the very years of conservative political triumph....

* * *

Rethinking International Trade

Around 1978, several economists scattered around the world began to ask a seemingly naive question: Why is there international trade?

This may sound like a stupid question. The immediate answer is that countries trade because each country produces goods that other countries want. But on reflection this only pushes the question back a bit. *Why* do countries produce different goods?

Economists have long had a standard answer. Countries produce different goods because they are different from each other. These differences may involve natural resources—it's no mystery why Brazil exports coffee and Saudi Arabia exports oil—or such created differences in resources as differences in education or in the accumulated stock of capital per worker. In any case, countries have an incentive to specialize in producing the goods for which their resources and know-how best suit them, and to trade these goods for other goods produced elsewhere. The whole story goes under the name of the theory of "comparative advantage." Loosely, comparative advantage says that countries trade in order to benefit from their differences.

Of course that makes it sound trivial, when the idea of comparative advantage is anything but. In fact ... comparative advantage turns out to be an idea that many self-styled experts fail to understand. And there is no question that comparative advantage explains a lot of international trade.

By the late 1970s, however, a number of economists working on international trade were coming to suspect that there was an important part of world trade that could not be explained by comparative advantage. Both the *direction* and the *character* of international trade seemed to suggest that not all exports were like Brazilian coffee.

The Direction of Trade

Suppose that I told you that international trade involves a matching between complementary countries. Countries at the same level of development, with similar resources, can basically make the same set of goods equally well, so they have no strong reason to trade with each other. Instead, what each nation needs is to find other countries that have what it lacks and lack what it has. In particular, rich countries, with their abundant capital and temperate climates, will find their most important trading partners in the Third World, whose abundant labor can take over the labor-intensive aspects of manufacturing and whose tropical agriculture will supply coffee, tea, sugar, and other necessities.

Sounds plausible? It sounded plausible to nineteenth-century statesmen; they looked at the British Empire and saw it as a sound business arrangement. (And if they weren't British, they decided that their own countries needed a few colonies too.) As late as the 1940s, political leaders still tended to think of international trade as running largely in a North-South direction; the Greater East Asian Co-Prosperity Sphere that Japan tried to carve out during World War II was not contemplated as a union of similar economies.

Yet something funny happened after World War II. There was a great surge in world trade—not between complementary nations, between North and South, but among the advanced nations themselves. And this surge in trade among advanced nations took place even as those nations were becoming increasingly similar in their levels of technology, education, and capital.

In 1953, only about 38 percent of the exports of advanced countries went to other advanced nations—and if it had not been for the Marshall Plan, which allowed European nations to buy large quantities of American goods, the number would have been even smaller. By 1990, however, 76 percent of advanced country exports went to other advanced nations.

Familiarity breeds a false sense of understanding. Everyone knows that today's advanced industrial countries are similar in many ways. Hourly wage rates in Europe, the United States, and Japan are about the same. We all have highly educated work forces, working with technologies that are quickly diffused throughout the world. Our cities and ways of life become increasingly indistinguishable. Yet we take it for granted that there is a huge and ever-growing volume of trade among these increasingly similar societies. If we're all pretty much the same, why do we need to ship such huge volumes of goods back and forth across the oceans?

There is an old joke about how poor urban households used to make ends meet. "Oh, we make a living by taking in each other's washing," the women would explain. In effect, for a generation after World War II the advanced nations began taking in each other's washing on an unprecedented scale. Why?

The Content of Trade

A determined believer in the idea that trade always reflects underlying differences between countries might argue that the apparent similarity among advanced nations is only on the surface. At a deeper level, there may be differences that in the end determine trade flows. And she would surely be in part correct. But if these underlying differences are the main driving force behind trade among industrial countries, we ought to be able to "backcast" our way to the nature of those differences by looking at who exports what to whom.

The overwhelming conclusion from looking at the actual pattern of trade is, however, that exports from one industrial country to another *don't* give us much indication that they are based on any underlying national resource or characteristic.

Consider, for example, the strong U.S. presence in the world aircraft industry. Is there something about the U.S. mix of resources that makes Americans particularly adept at making aircraft? It is hard to argue that there is. Aircraft manufacture is a business in which the cost of capital is important, because investments in new generations of aircraft take so long to yield a return; but the U.S. cost of capital is no lower and often higher than the cost of capital in Japan or Europe. The aircraft industry requires highly skilled workers and engineers— but so does production of say, autos, in which the United States runs massive trade deficits.

The United States does, of course, have a large pool of workers and engineers with the very specific skills and knowledge required to design and build aircraft. But where did this pool of skills and knowledge come from? Was it innate in the U.S. character? Of course not. U.S. workers developed the skills they needed to build aircraft because there was a large demand for those skills in the United States, arising from our dominant position in the world aircraft industry.

But of course our dominance in aircraft is in large part due to the fact that we have such a large pool of people with the right skills and knowledge. And you know where that puts us: squarely in the land of QWERTY.

Now there is a special reason why the virtuous circle that sustains the U.S. aircraft industry got started: the huge base of demand for aircraft that arose from the needs of the U.S. military during World War II and the early years of the Cold War. The interesting thing, however, is that even though that special advantage is long gone, the dominant position of the U.S. aircraft industry endures (indeed, it would be complete, were it not for Europe's support of Airbus—which we will have to come to in a little while).

The point is that there are many industries like aircraft, industries in which an international competitive advantage can be self-reinforcing. And the presence of such industries explains why countries that are similar at a broad level do so much trade. American and German industry are nowadays very similar in their overall levels of technology and in the resources available to them. Time and chance have, however, caused the two countries to develop different competences at a more detailed level, with America leading in aircraft, semiconductors, computers, and Germany leading in luxury automobiles, cameras, machine tools. From a distance, the two economies look more and more alike; in close-up, we are sufficiently different to find reasons to engage in an ever-growing volume of international trade.

The New Trade Theory

Not every industry is like the aircraft industry. The ability of a country to grow wheat cheaply depends mostly on climate and soil. A big subsidy can turn a wheat importer into a wheat exporter, as European nations have done with their Common Agricultural Policy, but it cannot create an advantage where none existed: remove the subsidies and European wheat output would crash. In other words, comparative advantage is still alive and well, and still governs much of trade.

On the other hand, not every industry is like wheat. Between 1978 and 1985, a group of economists hammered out what has come to be known as the "new trade theory," a theory that says, in effect, that a lot of world trade is in goods like aircraft rather than goods like wheat.

The new trade theory picture of the world looks something like this: Each country has, at any given time, a set of broad resources—land, skilled labor, capital, climate, general technological competence. These resources define up to a point the industries in which the country can hope to be competitive on world markets. Japan is not going to make it in the world wheat market; Canada will not be a successful exporter of tropical fruit; Brazil is not ready to compete in supercomputers. But a country's resources do not fully determine what it produces, because the detailed pattern of advantage reflects the self-reinforcing virtuous circles, set in motion by the vagaries of history.

At a broad level, then, trade reflects resources. A country with a highly skilled labor force will, in general, export goods whose production requires a high ratio of skilled to unskilled labor, and import goods for which the reverse is true. But precisely which goods the country exports cannot be determined from its resources alone. That final determination rests in the realm of chance and history, in the land of QWERTY.

This may sound a little vague, and if the ideas of new trade theory had only been expressed in the general way, they would probably not have had much impact. What the new trade theorists did, however, was to package this vision of trade in extremely sharply focused mathematical models. These models served two purposes. First, they helped to pin down the concepts in a way that dispelled a fog of confusion that had previously surrounded these ideas. Second, they legitimized QWERTYish ideas for other economists, by showing that they could be expressed with the same degree of clarity as more traditional approaches.

It's all a nice example of intellectual progress. Still, does it matter? Does knowing that much of world trade is in goods like aircraft, not goods like wheat, change our opinions about economic policy?

Yes—maybe. And then again, maybe not.

Strategic Trade Policy

It's possible to study the economy the way an entomologist studies an ant colony: dispassionately, trying to understand how it works rather than trying to change it. Indeed, if you want to do good social science, you should try to cultivate a certain amount of detachment, so that you get into the habit of seeing how things are rather than how you would like them to be.

The new trade theory as I have described it so far sounds fairly entomological. It is a description of how the world economy is, not a prescription about what to do about it. That is not a condemnation; like medical researchers, economists who add to our understanding may make a greater contribution in the long run than those proposing immediate cures.

Nonetheless, the temptation to try to apply theory to policy is irresistible. Sooner or later, the new trade theory was going to be given a policy spin. And it was not going to be a spin that conservatives would like. As I have already hinted, in the world of QWERTY one cannot trust markets to get it right. So it was inevitable that the new trade theory would be used to provide a justification for a departure from the principles of laissez-faire.

What kind of departure? In 1982, the Canadian economist James Brander and his Australian co-author Barbara Spencer pointed out that some of the basic ideas of new trade theory could be used to rationalize a policy that has long been anathema to economists: aggressive support by a nation's government of the international competitive position of home firms. Their concept has come to be known under the name of *strategic trade policy*. It's a concept whose practical usefulness can be and has been sharply questioned, but it represents a dramatic demonstration of the ways that QWERTY can undermine a conservative faith in the perfection of markets.

The Brander-Spencer Model

The Brander-Spencer concept can perhaps best be explained with a stylized example. (This example also gives you an idea of the way in which highly simplified models can help clarify thinking.) So here it is: Imagine a world in which the technology will soon be available to produce some new product, say a new kind of passenger aircraft. And suppose that there are two firms in a position to develop that technology, one American, one European. Let's call the two firms Boeing and Airbus. (Any resemblance to real firms is purely intentional.)

How profitable will it be to enter this market? It is not enough to ask about cash flow over a short period of time. Typically, introducing a new technology requires heavy initial spending on R&D and capital, followed by a period in which the firm continues to lose money while it works its way down the learning curve. Only then will the firm start to make profits. On the other hand, one cannot simply count future profits one-to-one against current losses, because a dollar tomorrow is worth less than a dollar today. So one needs to "discount" expected future earnings. In principle, a firm can collapse the whole expected stream of cash flows from a project into a "present discounted value" that summarizes the project's desirability.

So let's suppose that Boeing and Airbus have done that. And each reaches the conclusion that if it enters the market alone, that entry will be highly profitable—but that if both firms enter, both will end up losing money. That is, they conclude that the economies of scale in the global market are so large relative to expected sales that only one firm can profitably enter.

* * *

What will happen? It is possible that through misjudgment both firms will enter. That's what happened to Lockheed and McDonnell-Douglas in the 1970s, when they both introduced three-engine widebody jets (the L1011 and DC-10 respectively), with devastating effects on both firms. But in general each firm will either try to forestall entry by the other, if possible by making a credible early commitment to enter the market, or drop out if it becomes convinced that the other firm will enter.

Economists refer to the efforts of firms to deter potential rivals as *strategic* competition. It is a source of seemingly perverse behavior. For example, a firm may invest in capacity that it doesn't need in order to convince possible rivals that they will face a price war if they challenge its position; or a company may charge a lower price than the market will bear as a way of signaling rivals that its costs are too low for them to challenge.

Going back to our example, let's suppose that, for whatever reason, Boeing has a head start in this race, and is able to commit to enter the market before Airbus. Then what should Airbus do? It will lose money if it enters, so it stays out ... and Boeing reaps the rewards.

Now, finally, we get to the Brander-Spencer point. Suppose that at an early stage in the competition, governments get into the picture. Suppose, in particular, that a group of European governments promise Airbus a subsidy of, say, 20 if it enters the market, regardless of what Boeing does....

... Now, whatever Boeing does, Airbus will find it profitable to enter. But this means that if Boeing enters, it will have to share the market; and lacking the Airbus subsidy, it will lose money. So Boeing doesn't enter and Airbus does.... In effect, the promised subsidy has given Airbus a *strategic* advantage that allows it to win the game. Thus the subsidy is a *strategic trade policy.*

* * *

This is only a hypothetical example, of course. But it suggests a broader principle: there are times when aggressive support of a domestic industry against its foreign competitors can be in the national interest. In this particular example, the policy involved supporting a single "national champion" in competition with a single foreign rival. Such examples of single combat are rare in world trade. But you can tell similar stories in which the combat is not between individual firms but between industries. If you really believe that we live in a QWERTY world, then there may be many cases in which a temporary policy of supporting an industry in international competition can create a virtuous circle of self-reinforcing, enduring competitive advantage—or, conversely, in which a foreign government, by supporting *its* industry, can either lock us out of a market or tip an established industry into a vicious circle of self-reinforcing decline.[3]

In other words, the strategic trade policy argument appears to open the door to a rigorous economic justification for international trade policies that are not only interventionist but involve an element of international confrontation.

And that is a potentially explosive conclusion, because it threatens to undermine one of the most dearly held dogmas of economists: their belief in free trade.

Strategic Trade vs. Free Trade

To understand why Tinkertoy examples like the one above created a major controversy among economists, you need to understand the special position that free trade holds in the profession's ideology and self-image.

International trade, more than any other area, is one in which the perceptions of the professors differ from those of the general public. When the public—and their elected representatives—look at international trade, they see it as a kind of competitive sport. America is trying to sell its goods on world markets; so are other countries like Japan, Germany, and China. To most people, the competition between countries looks a lot like the competition between companies; indeed, in many global industries a few American companies seem in effect to be acting as our national champions as they confront their European or Japanese rivals. And in competitive sports it's natural to root for the home team—especially if serious things like jobs are at stake.

If international trade basically means international competition, of course, it seems only common sense to do everything you can to help your side win. If import quotas that give our domestic industries the advantage of a protected home base or export subsidies that help them break into foreign markets help America compete, why not go ahead and use them?

Now, many people will concede that if every country follows such policies, the end result will be destructive, because world markets will end up fragmented. So they are willing to approve, grudgingly, of international agreements that limit import quotas or export subsidies. But free trade, to most people, looks like a good idea only if everybody practices it.

Economists who take the theory of comparative advantage seriously, how-ever, don't see the world this way at all. In their view, international trade is *not* a competitive sport. It is essentially a process of exchange, which is usually mutually beneficial. Interfering with this process hurts our economy, even if other countries do not retaliate (and of course hurts us even more if they do). An import quota, for example, may seem to create jobs; but the jobs gained in the protected industry are lost through the indirect effects of the quota in crowding out employment throughout the rest of the economy, leaving us with nothing but higher prices and reduced competition. An export subsidy normally costs the government and domestic consumers far more than it benefits producers in that industry....

The normal position of economists on international trade is therefore much stronger than the grudging "I'll play fair if everyone else will" that is the typical attitude of the man in the street. The economist advocates free trade *regardless of what other countries are doing*. The nineteenth-century French economist Bastiat once summed it up this way: Saying that our country should be protec-tionist because other countries do not practice free trade is like saying that we should block up our harbors because other countries have rocky coasts.

You might think that the conflict between what economists think and the rest of the world believes would give the professors pause. But it doesn't work that way. Because comparative advantage is a beautiful idea that it seems only economists understand, economists cling to the idea even more strongly, as a kind of badge that defines their professional identity and ratifies their intel-lectual superiority. In effect, the statements, "I understand the principle of comparative advantage," and, "I support free trade," have become part of the economist's credo.

This may sound sarcastic. Yet in fact the economists are mostly right in their attitude. The lay view of international trade as a conflict with winners and los-ers is deeply wrong-headed.... In many sectors of world trade, from wheat to sugar to steel to shoes, the conventional wisdom of economists is exactly right; with few exceptions, the policy entrepreneurs and politicians who criticize that conventional wisdom do so not because they have achieved a deeper under-standing but because they haven't even understood the simple things.

But here's the problem: the concept of strategic trade policy is a legiti-mate, well-reasoned theory of the kind that economists respect; yet it seems, at least on first sight, to yield conclusions that are similar to those of the non-economists....

So, is everything that economists thought they knew about international trade wrong? No, not really.

Limitations of the Strategic Trade Policy Argument

Brander and Spencer never claimed that they had offered a general argument for aggressive trade policies. What they provided was only an example of how such a policy *could* work. The important question, of course, is how realistic the example is—or, to put it differently, in how many cases will the conclusions be right? If the case for strategic trade policy applies to only a handful of industries, then the conventional view about free trade is still basically right.

What a number of economists argued, almost as soon as the idea of strategic trade began circulating, was that in most cases aggressive trade policies would simply backfire, for two main reasons.

First, they questioned the picture of international competition as a struggle between two national champions, with the winner assured of high profits. In most industries the choice is not so stark. Suppose that the competition is not between one firm from each country but between three or four firms from each. Then the payoff to winning the competition, at least in terms of profits, will not be all that large: even if our country wins, competition among domestic firms will tend to hold down prices and profits. So there won't really be a race to see who gets the global jackpot. Furthermore, any attempt to subsidize the domestic industry will be likely to encourage more domestic firms to enter, dissipating any potential gains in duplication of capacity.

Now this argument only applies to the profits that strategic trade policy may yield. There may be other benefits, particularly if there are external economies associated with the industry—that is, if entry of more firms lowers costs by supporting a wider network of suppliers, a larger pool of skilled labor, or a deeper knowledge base. Such benefits are, however, subtle and hard to evaluate, when the thing that made the strategic trade policy so attractive was precisely its seeming simplicity and concreteness.

Critics of the strategic trade policy idea were also quick to point out the crucial difficulty of deciding which industries to encourage. You can't promote all domestic industries; by subsidizing one, you help it bid capital and labor away from others. So a strategic trade policy on behalf of some industries is in effect a strategic policy *against* others. This immediately raises the question of whether governments are sophisticated or objective enough to do the job right.

Given these criticisms, how could economists tell how seriously they should take the strategic trade policy argument? The only answer seemed to be to get down to cases. But when it comes to deciding whether or not to pursue a strategic trade policy, looking at the facts is not as simple as it may seem. After all, just knowing an industry's history, or even knowing quite a lot about everything from technology to costs and market shares, does not automatically tell you anything useful about what policy is desirable. Inevitably, you want to ask "what if" questions—for example, if a subsidy of X percent is granted, will it deter foreign entry into sector Y, and will it lead another domestic firm to enter? You may think you know all about some industry; but when confronted with questions of this kind, you usually realize that you can only describe the industry, not predict what it will do.

Which is not to say that economists didn't try. During the 1980s, a number of efforts were made to produce simulations of industries that were potential targets of strategic trade policy. Nobody had much faith in these simulations—after doing several, I dubbed them Industrial Policy Exercises Calibrated to Actual Cases, so as to yield the acronym IPECACs. Still, they were the only game in town. And for what they were worth, they did not seem to suggest very much potential gain for countries that pursued aggressive trade policies.

Bold Ideas, Cautious Policy Recommendations

The rise of the economics of QWERTY felt like an intellectual revolution to those who participated in it; phrases like "paradigm shift" were used routinely. Yet when it came to actual policy applications, the professors were cautious.

There were at least three reasons for that caution. One is that while an acknowledgment of the importance of QWERTY refutes the near-religious faith of conservatives in free markets, it is not at all easy to decide which direction the government should pursue. We've already seen how subtle the issue of strategic trade policy becomes once one tries to deal with real-world complications. So unlike, say, the rational expectations school, the new economic theorists did not find that their theory translated readily into simple policy recommendations. That does not devalue the significance of the theory: it is unreasonable to expect each intellectual advance to be ready for immediate policy consumption. Nonetheless, the failure of QWERTY to yield easy policy conclusions has been a real disappointment.

And yet it may also have been, to some extent, a bit of a relief. While this should not be overstated, a certain timidity may have contributed to the quietness of the QWERTY revolution. Although most economists are not doctrinaire believers in laissez-faire, an acknowledgment of the power and effectiveness of the market as a mechanism is a central part of the professional identity even of liberal economists. So they are understandably reluctant to come out too brashly against letting markets have their own way, especially when it comes to the almost sacred principle of free trade.

But perhaps the most important reason that economists were diffident about making policy pronouncements based on their new theory was their fear that it would be used, not to make better policy, but to rationalize bad policies. Concepts such as strategic trade policy can all too easily be used to rationalize good old-fashioned protectionism.

But politicians will get their ideas somewhere. If professors will not provide them with the slogans they need to win votes—as they often won't—it's always possible to find someone else who will.

Notes

1. The Greek goddess of history.
2. There is no single accepted name for the new approach to economics. Brian Arthur, drawing an analogy with physics, calls it "positive feedback." Many economic theorists, with a precision that is useful but not worth trying to explain in this context, prefer to talk about "strategic complementarity." I think, however, that Paul David's QWERTY is the most evocative phrase, and I will generally use it in this chapter.

3. Clear-cut examples of vicious circles in international trade are hard to come by, because there are always special circumstances. Consider, however, the decline of the British aircraft industry—which is the flip side of the rise of the U.S. industry. Britain was once a leading aircraft producer. During World War II, the Spitfire fighter was technologically superior to anything Germany or for that matter the United States could put in the air, and the first commercial jet aircraft was actually British rather than American. Nor was it inevitable that British technology would fall behind; in spite of a lagging economy, Britain has managed to retain a strong position in a number of high-technology industries, including pharmaceuticals and even jet engines (manufactured by Rolls-Royce). The aircraft industry itself, however, shriveled up in the 1960s.

Why did Britain lose its aircraft capacity? As already suggested in the text, a likely culprit is the Pentagon. Huge orders by the U.S. military during the 1950s helped give American firms a decisive edge in jet technology. Once Britain had been driven out of the world aircraft market, it lacked the base of knowledge, suppliers, and skilled workers that would have allowed it to reenter.

10.2

GLOBAL IMBALANCES AND THE FINANCIAL CRISIS

Steven Dunaway

This article on global balance of payments deficits and surpluses is an excellent primer on how the world economy works. Today, the United States runs large balance of payments deficits and borrows from China, Japan, and oil-exporting states. The latter states, in turn, generate large balance of payments surpluses and lend to other countries. What if these financial flows slow down sharply? That's what happened in the global financial crisis of 2008. Governments rescued banks and other financial institutions by pouring in money—raising budget deficits and lowering interest rates. But longer-term solutions require that domestic macroeconomic and microeconomic policies that stimulate consumption in the United States and savings in China and other surplus countries be adjusted. Exchange rates, particularly the Chinese currency, must be allowed to rise. Trade markets must be kept open. And international financial institutions, such as the IMF, must do a better job of surveillance of government policies. Generally reflecting a liberal perspective on the world economy, this author is nevertheless aware of the power of national governments to resist adjustment (realist) and of the issue of whose ideas govern international economic transactions (identity).

* * *

Global Imbalances and the Crisis

Most explanations of the current economic and financial crisis focus on financial causes. The standard account runs along the following lines: relatively low interest rates worldwide for much of the 2000s drove investors to seek higher yields, and relative stability in financial markets, reflecting the low cost of funds and solid economic growth, led to significant underpricing of risk. Lending standards were weakened and leverage increased. The rise in leverage sharpened the exposure to liquidity risk for financial institutions as they depended increasingly on wholesale markets for funding and these funds became increasingly

Source: Steven Dunaway, "Global Imbalances and the Financial Crisis," Council Special Report no. 44, Council on Foreign Relations, New York and Washington, D.C, March 2009, 1–44.

short term. New, complex financial products obfuscated risks and contributed to serious mispricing. Risk controls failed and good old-fashioned fraud also created significant losses. All of this combined to precipitate unprecedented turmoil in global financial markets beginning in mid-2007.

But missing is a discussion of how the seeds of the crisis were sown by the economic policies in those major countries that fostered global imbalances and by the features of the international financial system that facilitated the growth of those imbalances. Substantial imbalances in savings and investment emerged after 2000, and were reflected in growing current account imbalances within major world economies. Rising U.S. deficits and increasing surpluses in emerging East Asian economies (especially China) and oil-exporting countries in the Middle East developed. In turn, the savings and investment imbalances gave rise to the so-called savings glut in developing countries and spawned sizable net flows of capital from developing to advanced countries, with the United States being the primary recipient of these flows. The savings glut helped to reduce world interest rates.[1] At the same time, the substantial rise in demand, especially by East Asian and Middle Eastern economies, for official reserve assets crowded out private demand for such high-quality, low-risk assets. Consequently, a scramble by private investors for other higher-yielding but relatively low-risk assets contributed to the financial excesses that finally culminated in the present turmoil in world financial markets.

* * *

The rise in global imbalances during the 2000s was driven by a combination of factors with mutually reinforcing effects. Significant changes took place in savings and investment behavior in major countries. In the United States, national savings declined as the fiscal position shifted from a surplus to a substantial deficit and as household savings fell, resulting in a dramatic rise in the current account deficit.... The decline in household savings in part reflected relatively low interest rates and increased availability of financing related to housing that sparked a boom in consumption and residential investment.

Consumption-fueled growth in the United States fostered economic recoveries in Japan and Europe on the back of higher exports. Particularly in Europe, corporate profits rose. But problems in the structures of these countries' economies—especially rigidities in product and labor markets—limited investment opportunities. The combination of high corporate savings and sluggish investment led to rising national savings and external surpluses....

Savings and investment imbalances and current account surpluses of developing countries also rose sharply.... In emerging economies in East Asia other than China, savings increased. More important, the increases in the external surpluses of these countries reflected a decline relative to GDP in investment—especially in structures—following the excesses in such investment that occurred in the buildup to the Asian financial crisis of 1997–98. External surpluses also reflected policy decisions in many of these countries to rebuild official reserves, which had been decimated during the financial crisis. The years after 2000 also showed a dramatic rise in the savings and investment imbalance in China. Despite a very strong investment performance, Chinese savings rose even more dramatically. The fiscal position (government savings) improved and corporate savings posted a sharp rise. In East Asia generally, external surpluses put upward pressure on exchange rates, but this pressure was mitigated by substantial sterilized currency intervention, delaying adjustment. After 2002, current account surpluses of Middle East oil-exporting countries began to rise as strong global demand and concerns about the security of oil supplies drove up prices.

The substantial savings by East Asian emerging economies and Middle East oil-exporting countries were reflected in large net capital outflows, which made their way to the United States.[2] With the desired level of savings in the world exceeding desired investment at the interest rates prevailing at the time, the glut of global savings drove down real rates of interest and set off a boom in asset prices.

At this point, the cycle began to feed on itself. With expanded availability of credit and lower interest rates, U.S. households used debt to sustain consumption and fuel a housing boom. Rising U.S. demand stimulated additional growth in the rest of the world, adding to current account surpluses, especially in East Asian emerging market economies. Among these countries, China's current account surplus skyrocketed and official reserves rose to record levels. Competitive pressures from China also created pressure on other East Asian countries to limit the appreciation of their currencies against the U.S. dollar, boosting external surpluses and reserve accumulation in these countries. The current account surpluses of oil-exporting countries in the Middle East also rose because increasing worldwide demand continued to push up oil prices. In turn, through net capital flows, developing countries' external surpluses were funneled back to the United States. This financing then helped fund a continuation of the consumption and housing boom and a steady rise in asset prices.

To a significant extent, the strong preference for U.S. dollar assets that emerged reflected the pivotal role the dollar plays as a reserve currency in the international financial system. Consequently, the United States was able to finance its growing external deficits relatively easily and delay needed adjustments in domestic savings and in its balance of payments.... However, there was also a net flow of private capital into the United States.... This reflected the sense that U.S. markets were better regulated, had better governance, and were more secure than markets in emerging economies. Moreover, in the first part of the 2000s economic growth was faster in the United States and returns on financial assets were perceived as being higher than in other advanced countries. As a result, a self-reinforcing effect set in. As capital inflows to the United States boosted asset prices and returns, additional flows of capital were stimulated.

Few analysts dispute the existence of the imbalances or their contribution to asset price inflation. But with the benefit of hindsight, many commentators have argued that the United States should have used monetary policy to blunt the effects of capital inflows, thereby averting the crisis. It is asserted that the Federal Reserve permitted loose monetary conditions to prevail for too long, allowing the buildup of too much liquidity in the financial system. The Fed is a convenient scapegoat, but what these commentaries suggest is that it could have used monetary policy alone to deal with global imbalances. They fail to recognize that monetary policy is a blunt instrument. With the inflows of capital, the yield curve in the United States was relatively flat through much of the 2000s, suggesting that a decision to hike short-term policy rates might not have fully fed through into long-term rates. Indeed, senior Fed officials had commented on the unusual difficulties being encountered in trying to use monetary policy to influence long-term interest rates. Then chairman Alan Greenspan often spoke of an interest rate conundrum,[3] and then deputy chairman Ben Bernanke offered the savings glut as an explanation for the low level of long-term interest rates that appeared hard for the Fed to control.

To be sure, the flat yield curve did not imply that the Fed could not bring about an increase in long-term interest rates. Monetary policy certainly could have been used to limit the effect of the inflows of capital to the United States and prevented some of the excesses that occurred. However, to be successful, there would have had to be a substantial tightening of monetary policy. Such aggressive use of monetary policy to deal with this problem would have inflicted a high cost on the U.S. economy and, in turn, the rest of the world. Granted, the costs inflicted by the current economic and financial crisis are quite high, but the relevant question is whether other policy alternatives would have been better placed than monetary policy in dealing with the situation at a much lower cost. Obviously, dealing more aggressively with global imbalances would have been the best policy response.

* * *

[VOLUME EDITOR'S NOTE: The selections below (extending to the next subheading) appear earlier in the published report and are presented here out of their original order to follow rather than precede a discussion of the problem of global imbalances.]

Since the Bretton Woods system was established after World War II, three of its features have worked at times to delay adjustment in current account imbalances. One is that a country that issues reserve assets can finance current account deficits for an extended period. The second is that a country facing upward pressure on the value of its currency can manage its exchange rate to resist such pressure and delay adjustment in its balance of payments for an extended period. A third feature that can provide incentives to delay adjustment emerged as a consequence of the shift to flexible exchange rates that began in the 1970s. For countries with floating exchange rates, a depreciating currency can provide a sheltering effect that can diminish pressures for structural adjustment. Rather than simply cushioning one-off shocks, as proponents of floating rates envisage, currency depreciation can also enable policymakers to ignore enduring structural challenges.

* * *

Normally, a current account imbalance triggers forces that encourage adjustment and maintain the imbalance at a sustainable level. Countries with deficits face increasing pressures in obtaining financing. This fosters adjustment through upward pressure on domestic interest rates, downward pressure on the real exchange rate, and slowing domestic economic activity. Surplus countries face similar pressures in the opposite direction, with rising economic activity and appreciation of the real exchange rate the main forces that prompt balance-of-payments adjustment. That global imbalances have grown and remain unchecked points to features of the international financial system that have worked to delay adjustment.

One such feature, which has existed since the Bretton Woods system was established, is the role played by countries that provide reserve assets. This is an important feature that gives needed scope for reserve assets in the system to expand as the world economy and international trade grow. But it can also enable a country that provides reserve assets to delay adjustment when its external position becomes unsustainable because of macroeconomic policies or economic shocks. Such a country can finance a deficit in its external position rather easily for some time by issuing assets in its domestic currency.

Accordingly, the United States, which is the primary provider of reserve assets to the system, has been able to finance current account deficits for long periods. After 2001, rising U.S. current account deficits largely reflected expansionary fiscal policy in the United States and booming consumption growth.[4] Financing was in large part provided by foreign governments. The cost to the United States for this financing was relatively low because of the premium foreign governments were willing to pay to obtain presumably risk-free U.S. government securities. One distinct advantage the United States has is the breadth and liquidity of its government securities markets. This is a particularly important consideration for investments by countries in official reserve assets. The definition of a reserve asset stresses that such an asset should be highly liquid and that the volatility of its value should be low.[5] However, ultimately there is a limit to the willingness of other countries to hold U.S. assets. This limit depends on how close other potential reserve assets are to being substitutes for U.S. dollar assets.[6] But until the limit is reached, the availability of cheap foreign financing allows the United States to put off painful measures to boost national savings.... [B]etween 1990 and the onset of the financial crisis in 2007, the United States was able to double its national debt in dollar terms without being penalized by a diminishing appetite for the debt. On the contrary, investors accepted lower yields on U.S. government securities.

Recall that the second feature of the international system is that countries with balance-of-payments surpluses that manage their exchange rates can resist upward pressure on their currencies for an extended period. Similarly, deficit countries facing downward pressure on their exchange rates can defend the rate and finance their deficits only as long as they have official reserves or are willing to use their reserve assets.[7] Countries facing upward pressure on their rates, however, have no such reserve constraint, given that the rest of the world is demanding their currencies. They can hold their exchange rates by intervening in the market and selling their own currencies. They can then attempt to "sterilize" this exchange market intervention through domestic monetary policy actions. The intention is to avoid a rise in inflation that would otherwise induce a real appreciation of their currencies.

There are limits, however, to how long sterilized intervention will work. In particular, the cost of such intervention in terms of higher domestic interest rates will eventually take its toll on the finances of the central bank and have consequences for the real economy, but these adverse effects may go unnoticed for quite some time. To diminish some of these consequences, sterilized intervention can be supported by capital controls and administrative controls over domestic financial markets (e.g., moral suasion or window guidance to control credit growth).[8] Although the effectiveness of capital and administrative controls will diminish over time, such measures can succeed for a while.[9]

Imposing capital and administrative controls is not without cost, given the distortions they create and the repression of the financial system that tends to occur. Moreover, maintaining an undervalued exchange rate imposes large costs on the real economy. The distortion in the value of the exchange rate will create serious misallocations of resources in the export- and import-substituting sectors of the economy. The longer an undervaluation of the currency is maintained, the greater the misallocations created and the more difficult the readjustment the economy must undergo to unwind the distortion.

Among the emerging economies in East Asia, China most exploited this flaw in the international financial system during the 2000s. To maintain an increasingly undervalued exchange rate, particularly because productivity growth in China exceeded that in the rest of the world, China had to amass a stunning amount of official reserves, with nearly $1.5 trillion of these reserves accumulating in the three and a half years after the country's exchange rate regime was changed in July 2005. China's exchange rate policy also influenced those of other East Asian countries in that they sought to limit appreciation of their currencies in response to competitive pressure from China, and these countries probably built official reserves to levels higher than they ever intended.

China's investment-driven growth model, with its heavy reliance on exports, has delivered rapid growth and development. As a result, the government is reluctant to do more than make gradual changes to it. But maintaining an undervalued exchange rate imposes growing costs on the economy. In particular, it creates serious overallocations of resources to export- and import-substituting industries. This will have to be sorted out; the more the adjustment is delayed, the greater the distortion becomes and the more costly the process. Moreover, when the inevitable currency appreciation comes, the country will encounter a substantial loss on the foreign exchange reserves it has accumulated while trying to keep its currency cheap. The longer the country accumulates excess reserves, the more costly these portfolio losses are.

Maintaining an undervalued exchange rate also stunts the development of China's financial sector. Efforts to get its banking system to operate on a sound commercial basis are undermined by the government's heavy reliance on window guidance to control credit expansion and establish lending priorities. Window guidance has been an important part of China's sterilization efforts in response to concerns that upward pressure on domestic interest rates would induce increasing inflows of foreign money as capital controls have become more porous. In addition, currency undervaluation makes foreign financing look more attractive than domestic financing. The resulting spur to foreign borrowing further stunts the domestic financial sector. The buildup in foreign liabilities by Chinese enterprises may go unreported as companies seek to avoid capital controls, but it could eventually make the country vulnerable to a financial shock. However, these problems do not occur immediately or are not apparent, so it is easy for policymakers to discount them.

Another feature of the international financial system that may encourage delay in external adjustment arises as an inadvertent consequence of the shift to floating exchange rates. A depreciating currency can, as mentioned earlier, provide a sheltering effect and thus slow adjustment to adverse economic shocks arising from structural changes.[10] Specifically, currency depreciation can reduce pressure on a country's external position, providing an opportunity to more gradually make policy changes—especially reforms in the structure of a country's economy—that may be needed to deal with the consequences of such a shock. Because currency depreciation initially has a positive effect on economic growth, the tendency is to overlook the longer-term negative consequences. Moreover, slower initial adjustment can also contribute to depreciation pressures on a country's exchange rate that can persist for some time, providing additional incentive to delay adjustment.

Liberalization of trade during the 1990s and the rise of newly industrializing countries, particularly China, was a major competitive shock to advanced economies. It had especially strong effects on European economies, with their rigid product and labor markets, though Japan was also affected. Depreciating currencies in the late 1990s took the pressure off Europe and Japan to push structural reforms. In Europe in particular, labor market reforms were badly needed but politically difficult to implement. However, by delaying reform, European countries set themselves up for a sharp slowdown in growth when the euro began to appreciate in the 2000s. The impact of that appreciation was initially offset because strong demand from the Middle East and China boosted exports of the major European economies, principally Germany and France, but this demand evaporated when the Middle East and China slowed. Now facing a major recession, European countries are suffering the consequence of their earlier decision to delay needed reforms. Economic recovery in the euro area may well be slow.

The False Hope of Decoupling

In the past couple of years, a view has emerged that the problem of global imbalances would diminish over time as growth in the rest of the world—particularly in Europe and East Asia—was seen to decouple from growth in the United States. In conjunction, it was also argued that other countries—especially China—were stepping up to become engines to sustain world growth. It was therefore argued that global imbalances could be self-correcting and that there was time for more gradual changes in economic policies in the major countries. That the recession in the United States has had a more severe than expected impact on the rest of the world has exposed these propositions as myths and dashed hopes that a permanent correction in global imbalances could be achieved without a severe disruption in world growth. Now there is a clear need for policy actions to deal with the problem, and global imbalances should no longer be considered a medium-term problem that can be dealt with gradually.

* * *

The United States finds itself in a somewhat ironic position. For years, economists have called for actions to boost national savings in order to reduce the current account deficit. Now, substantial fiscal stimulus is needed to save the U.S. economy from a sharp downward spiral. But it has to be implemented with an eye to the need to consolidate the U.S. fiscal position over the medium term. To maximize its effect, a premium should be placed on spending that provides a direct stimulus to the economy without permanently raising expenditures.

Beyond the questions of stimulus design, the United States will have to increase national savings in the medium term, and the most efficient way to do so is to raise government savings. Efforts will have to include reforming the tax system. Reforms of spending programs can provide some savings, but given large and growing demands, spending constraints will not achieve the needed increase in government savings. In the end, there will have to be tax increases. One option is to restore the top marginal income tax rates of the 1990s when the cuts enacted during the Bush administration expire in 2010. A substantial amount of revenue could thus be raised without creating significant disincentives for work and investment, judging by the high rates of growth during the 1990s. Simplifying both the personal and corporate income tax code could also boost efficiency, improve equity, and at the same time raise revenue.[11]

In Europe and Japan, medium- and longer-term demands on government resources present challenges but should not block near-term fiscal action. The short-term to medium-term trade-off in these countries is similar to that in the

United States. Significant fiscal stimulus now could prevent an economic recession from turning into a depression. Accordingly, for the European countries, substantial flexibility should be used in adherence to the objectives in the Stability and Growth Pact. It is also important for the euro-area countries that looser monetary policy supports fiscal stimulus.

Stimulus in the short term will help soften the downturns in Europe and Japan, but structural reforms in labor and product markets are needed to reinforce these efforts and lay the basis for more balanced and sustainable growth over the medium term. To break out of the cycle of relatively slow growth and heavy dependence on exports, Europe and Japan must boost competition in product markets by removing barriers to entry and by improving business opportunities. Labor market reform is particularly critical in Europe. It must enhance competitiveness by increasing labor flexibility and mobility, reducing employment protection, and better aligning wages with labor market supply and demand. In both Europe and Japan, it is also essential to boost labor force participation to offset the effects of aging.

Europe and Japan will be tempted to put off structural reforms out of concerns to preserve employment. But both have delayed structural reform for too long. Each time these economies face shocks, they put off adjustment. The tendency to delay reforms out of concern for short-term employment is becoming self-reinforcing and, in particular, is condemning Europe to slower and slower growth. Near-term losses in employment resulting from labor and product market reforms are likely to be more than made up because such reforms will foster more rapid growth when economic recovery takes hold.

East Asian emerging economies also have room to provide fiscal stimulus to help offset the impact of the global slowdown, and they should move ahead quickly. How China responds is particularly important to the world economy. China has already announced a large fiscal package and has taken steps to ease monetary and credit conditions. However, some of China's actions may serve simply to reinforce the country's dependence on investment-driven growth and exports. The government has taken steps to sustain export growth, including increasing value-added tax (VAT) rebates for many categories of exports and by effectively repegging China's renminbi to the U.S. dollar.[12] Such efforts to sustain export growth are likely to cause difficulties in other East Asian economies and could provoke protectionist responses in advanced countries.

The Chinese authorities must deliver a stimulus that promotes domestic consumption. The government needs to continue improving critical social services, especially education, health care, and pensions. Reducing the uncertainties surrounding the provision of these services will substantially diminish households' strong precautionary savings motive and give households the confidence to raise consumption. These are areas where significant short-term stimulus could be provided. Nevertheless, although the Chinese authorities have acknowledged the need to bolster social services, economic stimulus plans thus far appear to be predominantly oriented toward sustaining investment and export growth.

The Chinese authorities are aware that significant changes in policies are imperative to sustaining rapid growth over the medium term. They have publicly stated that the economy needs to be rebalanced away from its heavy dependence on investment and exports toward consumption.[13] To do so requires removing price distortions and other policy changes to eliminate inefficiencies and incentives favoring investment over consumption. Distortions exist in such areas as energy, other utilities, and land, but a major problem is the low cost of capital. Capital costs need to be raised significantly, and that cannot be done without permitting more flexibility and a more rapid rate of appreciation of the exchange rate. The ceiling imposed on interest rates paid on savings deposits is a major factor behind the low cost of capital, keeping the bank lending rate low and holding down the opportunity cost for enterprises' use of their retained earnings for investment. This ceiling needs to be lifted. In turn, a higher cost of capital and a stronger currency will help curb investment in the export- and import-substituting sectors. Real household incomes would be boosted by a rise in both the exchange rate and bank deposit rates. Consumption would rise, particularly because, with a strong precautionary motive for savings, a greater proportion of an increase in household interest income from a rise in deposit rates is more likely to be spent than saved.

Financial market reform is also needed to improve the intermediation of savings in China. Lifting the cap on deposit rates would not only help push up the cost of capital, it would also increase competition in the banking sector and provide incentives for banks to expand credit to new customers. Greater access to credit would reduce the incentives of both firms and households to hold large savings. Bond and equity markets must be developed to provide alternative sources of financing for firms and a much broader array of assets for households to invest in. Small and medium-sized firms have had to rely largely on retained earnings or the assets of their owners to finance investment. Consumers also have had limited access to credit. Better credit access and higher-yielding assets to invest in would reduce household savings and raise household incomes over time, boosting consumption.

Better IMF Surveillance

An important part of dealing with global imbalances (and trying to diminish the prospect of a similar situation arising again) entails finding ways to mitigate the potential effects of the features in the international financial system that can permit countries to delay adjustment to external imbalances. There are no easy or hard-and-fast solutions to these problems.

The U.S. dollar's status as a reserve currency is not likely to change in the near future. Even in the midst of the current financial crisis, money is pouring into the United States, which is seen as a safe haven despite the fact that the crisis originated in U.S. financial markets. U.S. Treasury securities remain the world's premier risk-free asset. Accordingly, the United States is likely to remain the dominant provider of reserve assets, and when the global economy recovers from the current downturn, a steady underlying demand for foreign official holdings of U.S. dollar assets will continue. And just as the United States will be able to use this advantage to put off adjustment, so countries facing upward pressure on their currencies will be able to delay adjustments in their external surpluses. Likewise, it is not feasible to diminish the sheltering effect that exchange rate depreciation may have and how it may delay adjustment to structural shocks in countries with floating exchange rates. Nor would it be desirable, because floating rates undoubtedly make countries more resilient to temporary shocks and serve to stabilize the system overall.

Bilateral pressure has not been effective in inducing countries—especially the major countries—to make necessary policy adjustments. Such pressure is often seen as being motivated by self-interest and therefore biased. Ad hoc groups of countries have been no more successful. The same question concerning motives can apply, and there are usually members of the group that are reluctant to firmly judge the behavior of one country, lest their own policies attract scrutiny.

The designers of the international financial system recognized the need for an impartial body to enforce the rules of the system, to flexibly respond to its potential flaws, and to change the system as the global economy evolves. This is a primary goal of the International Monetary Fund. In particular, the IMF's articles of agreement require the organization to promote the smooth functioning of the international financial system by conducting surveillance of the economic policies of member countries. As mentioned earlier, however, the IMF cannot compel member countries to change their economic policies; it can only urge them to make needed changes. The persistence of global imbalances suggests that the IMF has failed in the execution of its surveillance mandate, especially with regard to its larger, systemically important members, which have been the main players in the global imbalances saga.[14]

One approach advocated to improve IMF performance is to make the rules governing surveillance more specific, particularly with regard to exchange rate policy. The articles of agreement establish the obligations of IMF member countries and the general principles on which the institution's surveillance function is based. Rules for applying these principles are specified in decisions by the IMF's executive board, and the application of these decisions is laid out in guidance notes from IMF management to the institution's staff. It is argued that these decisions and guidance notes should be more specific in identifying policy actions, the value and behavior of exchange rates, the size of external imbalances, and other relevant variables that would make it more straightforward and automatic to determine whether member countries are violating their obligations.

Although in principle this approach may sound good, in practice it is difficult to implement. Countries' economic situations are not always black and white, and their policy actions may not be easily judged as conforming to, or violating, their IMF obligations beyond a reasonable doubt. Moreover, possible indicators of inappropriate policy actions may be subject to considerable variance in interpretation, and their measurement may also be imprecise. It is difficult, for example, to measure the value of a country's equilibrium real effective exchange rate to determine whether its currency is significantly over- or undervalued. Attempts to apply specific rules will likely result in numerous exceptions being made to ensure that countries are not unfairly held for violating IMF obligations. The larger the number of exceptional cases (and the number will be large as countries strongly argue why they should be exceptions), the more questionable it will be that anything is gained by embracing more specific rules for surveillance.

There is more to be gained from steps to strengthen the way the IMF operates under its current guidelines. The surveillance process at the IMF involves the staff, management, and the executive board. The staff conducts the IMF's surveillance, but the framework for surveillance is proposed by management and approved by the executive board. The IMF's managing director and the deputy managing directors provide guidance on the conduct of surveillance to staff, both formally and informally. The executive board ultimately determines the results of the surveillance process. The board is considered to be the IMF, and it alone can speak officially for the institution. Accordingly, all Article IV consultation reports must be reviewed by the executive board, and the board makes a formal, public statement on the IMF's assessment of each member country's economic policies at the conclusion of the surveillance process.

The failure of the IMF to exercise firm surveillance reflects to an important extent the influence of the executive board and management. The board is a relatively large body with a disproportionate representation of advanced countries. It strives for consensus, and so does not generally take strong positions in its assessments of countries' economic policies. In particular, this tends to be the case in dealings with the IMF's major member countries, which are well represented on the board. Consequently, public messages resulting from IMF surveillance tend to be muted and unclear, and opportunities to exert pressure in favor of needed policy changes are lost.

IMF management has been characterized by rapid turnover in recent years, especially at the top. This has not been conducive to the IMF being able to articulate strong, coherent assessments of major countries' policies. Moreover, management-led reforms to the surveillance process (partly aimed at establishing more specific rules) and debate over the guidance for the implementation of these reforms have served more as a distraction over the past few years than as an enhancement to IMF surveillance.

Significant improvements in the IMF's surveillance could be achieved by limiting the executive board's role in the surveillance process and by making IMF management more effective. The board should no longer be involved directly in surveillance reviews. Its responsibility should be limited to approving the overall framework for surveillance (consistent with the articles of agreement) and holding IMF management responsible for the effective execution of surveillance. To carry out its responsibilities effectively, IMF management, including the managing director and the deputy managing directors, needs to be selected in an open process solely on the basis of the candidates' qualifications and competence. The current selection process is relatively closed and tends to be dominated by political considerations. [15]

A question naturally arises as to whether earlier adoption of these reforms in IMF governance would have changed the course of events that led to the current crisis. It is difficult to argue convincingly that the crisis would have been averted, but improving the IMF's surveillance efforts could have made a material difference to its severity and duration. Although governments are not in the habit of publicly recognizing the salutary effect of IMF pressure, there have been many occasions when IMF surveillance has helped change countries' economic policies for the better. The Canadian authorities have acknowledged the important role IMF surveillance played in policy decisions of the mid-1990s that resulted in the elimination of fiscal deficits, as have the U.S. authorities in regard to support for its fiscal consolidation in the second half of the 1990s and the Chinese in regard to the restructuring and recapitalization of China's largest state-owned banks since 2003.

Given this track record, tougher surveillance of the major countries could have fostered policy changes that would have slowed the growth in global imbalances. The United States could have been pressed more forcefully on the need to increase national savings and reduce its cyclically adjusted fiscal deficit. This could have strengthened the hand of those arguing for policy changes. For Europe, greater emphasis could have been placed on the significant losses in competitiveness that euro-area economies experienced during the 2000s as the euro appreciated, which would have reinforced the argument for liberalization of labor and product markets. Such changes could have been easier to achieve in more prosperous times. Similarly, prosperous times could have provided a better opportunity for changes in economic policies in China. In particular, earlier and stronger pressure might have helped build a consensus for a significantly faster change in China's exchange rate and had a measurable impact on China's external imbalance. That the annual IMF surveillance consultation with China has not in fact taken place since 2006 points to missed opportunities to influence the country's economic policies.

In the end, whether IMF surveillance would have materially altered the current crisis depends on how the surveillance would have been conducted had the reforms suggested here been adopted. This is a matter of speculation. But improving surveillance is at least an important first step toward strengthening the global system. There is no reason not to attempt it.

* * *

Notes

1. Ben S. Bernanke, "The Global Savings Glut and the U.S. Current Account Deficit," *Homer Jones Lecture,* April 14, 2005, and "Global Imbalances: Recent Developments and Prospects," *Bundesbank Lecture,* September 11, 2007.

2. See Brad W. Setser, *Sovereign Wealth and Sovereign Power: The Strategic Consequences of American Indebtedness,* Council Special Report No. 37 (New York: Council on Foreign Relations Press, 2008).

3. See "Testimony of Chairman Alan Greenspan," *The Federal Reserve Board's Semiannual Monetary Policy Report to the Congress,* delivered before the Committee on Banking, Housing, and Urban Affairs, U.S. Senate, February 16, 2005.

4. The factors driving the rise in deficits after 2001 were sharply different from those that had contributed to sizable U.S. current account deficits in the second half of the 1990s. At that time, changes in information technology and their application in productive processes raised returns on investment in the United States and prompted substantial inflows of private capital.

5. *Balance of Payments Manual,* 5th ed. (rev.), International Monetary Fund.

6. In the Bretton Woods system, gold was a substitute for the U.S. dollar as a reserve asset. The system basically collapsed when demands for gold in exchange for dollars rose sharply, especially because the French government was less willing to hold dollar assets and the United States was reluctant to continue selling its gold stock at the price at which the dollar was pegged to gold.

7. Using foreign exchange controls can extend the period, but the resulting impact on the real economy can be rather harsh, and such actions directed at current account transactions can invite retaliation by other countries.

8. The so-called iron trinity argument suggests that by instituting capital controls, a country trying to peg its exchange rate is able to pursue an independent monetary policy.

9. Capital controls can be seen as being equivalent to a tax on international capital movements. When potential returns are high enough, investors will be willing to incur additional costs to evade the controls; the higher the potential return, the greater the incentive for investors to evade.

10. See, for example, Richard G. Harris, *The New Economy and the Exchange Rate Regime,* Center for International Economic Studies, Adelaide University, March 2001.

11. As an example of improving equity while raising revenue, the elimination of the inheritance tax could be made permanent, but equity in the tax system would be improved and revenue would be raised if the markup basis for pricing of inherited equities were changed. Currently, inherited stock is valued at the price when inherited instead of at the original purchase price. Hence, capital gains taxes on these securities can be avoided by people who inherit stocks but not by those who purchase and later sell stock for a gain. Eliminating the markup and valuing inherited stock at the original purchase price would put all stock transactions on the same basis for tax purposes.

12. Since mid-July 2008, the value of the Chinese renminbi against the U.S. dollar has been largely unchanged, after the currency appreciated roughly 7 percent in the first half of the year.

13. Chinese premier Wen Jiabao in his address to the National People's Congress in March 2007 said that "the biggest problem in China's economy is that growth is unstable, unbalanced, uncoordinated, and unsustainable."

14. Speakers at the October 2008 Per Jacobsson Roundtable on the Role and Governance of the IMF were particularly vocal on the failures in surveillance. Former IMF chief economist Raghuram Rajan summed up the panel's assessment with the statement: "What I think we are missing in these moments is the presence of a strong international, independent voice which stands for the world economy and fights for the world economy. And it is a loss that the Fund is not performing that role."

15. Similar recommendations are made in a report on governance of the IMF issued by the IMF's Independent Evaluation Office (*Governance of the International Monetary Fund: An Evaluation,* Report of the Independent Evaluation Office of the IMF, 2008). In response to that report, the IMF's managing director appointed a committee of eminent persons to review IMF governance and make recommendation for changes. The committee's report is expected to be delivered in spring 2009.

Chapter 11

MIRACLE AND MISSED OPPORTUNITY: DEVELOPMENT IN ASIA AND LATIN AMERICA

11.1

FROM MIRACLE TO CRISIS TO RECOVERY: LESSONS FROM FOUR DECADES OF EAST ASIAN EXPERIENCE

Joseph E. Stiglitz

Joseph E. Stiglitz, a Noble Prize–wining economist, criticizes market explanations for Asia's postwar "economic miracle," especially in the context of the Asian financial crisis of the late 1990s. Market advocates attribute Asian growth to greater efficiency and higher savings and blame the financial crisis in the 1990s on crony bank lending, lack of equity markets, and distorting industrial policies. Stiglitz, by contrast, attributes the growth to government policies that closed the knowledge gap, forced higher savings, used bank lending to avoid equity market crises, and targeted efficient industrial and export growth. The financial crisis resulted, he concludes, from western-advocated market reforms to reduce government's role. No one denies the empirical fact of higher growth in Asia—but analysts disagree about whether markets (liberal) or governments (realist/identity) are the primary causes. Such is the world of multiple causes and differing perspectives that weight those causes differently.

There has been much debate about whether there was or was not an East Asia miracle, and if there was, what contributed to it, and whether there are lessons that are applicable to other regions. By the same token, there has been much

Source: Joseph E. Stiglitz, "From Miracle to Crisis to Recovery: Lessons from Four Decades of East Asian Experience," in *Rethinking the East Asian Miracle,* ed. Joseph E. Stiglitz and Shahid Yusuf (New York: Oxford University Press, 2001), 509–526. © The International Bank for Reconstruction and Development/The World Bank.

debate about what caused the East Asian crisis, what lessons should be drawn from that experience, and what insights the crisis itself sheds on the economic developments of the preceding three decades. As countries have recovered from the crisis—some more quickly than others—the debate has not diminished. Some have viewed the quick recovery as evidence of these countries' long-standing strengths, others as bearing testimony to the wisdom of the reforms that had been urged upon them in the midst of the crisis....

* * *

Was There a Miracle?

... [T]he debate as to whether what happened in East Asia deserves the appellation of a miracle is just a matter of semantics: whether we call it a miracle or not, the fact of the matter is that the increases in living standards were virtually unprecedented. Only a tiny number of other countries have succeeded in achieving comparable rates of saving on a voluntary basis, over an extended period of time, and even countries with considerably lower savings rates have found it difficult to invest comparable amounts (relative to gross domestic product) efficiently, with high and sustained incremental output capital ratios. A large part of the *real* debate on East Asia's development prowess revolves around explaining these high savings rates and the relative efficiency of investment.

There is another aspect of the miracle that has received all too little attention but plays a role in the sequel: capitalism has always been plagued by fluctuations, including financial panics. What is remarkable about East Asia is not that it experienced a crisis in 1997, but that it had experienced so few crises over the preceding three decades—two of the countries had not had one year of downturn and two had had one year of recession, a better record than any of the supposedly advanced and well-managed Organisation for Economic Co-operation and Development (OECD) countries. This experience naturally raises several questions: Were there features of the "miracle" that led both to growth and to relative stability? Did the crisis of 1997 represent a manifestation of weaknesses that had long been latent, a change in the world, with a failure of the region to make concomitant adaptations, or an abandonment—partly under the influence of outsiders—of long-standing policies? I will argue below that while there are elements of all three explanations, the last almost surely was pivotal.

The Total Factor Productivity Debate

Whether one can explain increases in East Asian incomes largely as a result of changes in inputs turns on technical issues.... These have not been, and are not likely to be, ever cleanly sorted out: in effect, there is a problem of underidentification. Some now claim that "all" one has to do in order to attain rapid growth is to reach East Asian levels of savings and ensure that the funds are well invested. According to this view, there was little evidence of a "miracle" in the sense that the pace of total factor productivity (TFP) increase was not large at all. In fact ... TFP made no contribution to the growth of the newly industrializing East Asian economies.... The East Asian countries still lag far behind the major industrial countries in terms of TFP.

However, I remain skeptical as to the robustness of the results generated by growth accounting.... [S]light (and plausible) changes in how human capital is measured can lead to markedly different results. The difficulties of aggregating capital are well known. Moreover, the standard Solow methodology for measuring TFP (based on the residual method) assumes that factors get paid their marginal product (as they would in fully competitive markets). But there is overwhelming evidence that, especially in many of the markets in East Asian countries, competition is far from perfect. Governments intervene in wage setting. This is important: because of the high rate of increase in capital, *if* a large weight is assigned to capital in measuring inputs, then, not surprisingly, the amount of TFP is low....

The unreliability of the Solow methodology has long been recognized: it is as if the distance between Newark and New York were to be determined by using a 12-inch rule to measure the distance between New York and Los Angeles and Newark and Los Angeles, and subtracting the difference. The errors in measurement of each of the components are likely to determine the outcome.

... [The argument] that the freedom of markets in Hong Kong, China, can explain the relatively rapid increase in its total factor productivity illustrates how the Solow technique can yield erroneous results. Not only is it the case that the measurement of total factor productivity increases can be unreliable, as we have just suggested, but the interpretation of the residual, what is left over after measuring inputs, is highly ambiguous. Assume that one could feel confident that Hong Kong's residual was greater than that of Singapore. Is it because of better economic policies? Or is it because Hong Kong was the entrepôt for the mainland of China, and as the mainland's economy grew, so did the demand for Hong Kong's services? In this interpretation ... Hong Kong's success actually was a result of the growth of perhaps the least free-market regime of the region.

In a sense, the total factor productivity debate is much ado about nothing. There has been a narrowing of the technology gap—and there is every reason to believe that this will continue. Those who argue for little TFP are not denying the decrease in the technology gap, but only that the technological gains were "purchased." But the key policy issue facing all developing countries remains: how to close the knowledge gap. It may be reassuring to know that technology can be acquired at a price. But money alone will not do the trick, or else many other countries would have narrowed the technology gap as well. At the very least, we have to allow for the possibility that governments in some Asian countries provided the preconditions, through a variety of channels, most notably their support for technical education. While the closing of the knowledge gap *may* have been a by-product of the high levels of investment, the successful countries made deliberate efforts to enhance the transfer of technology, including foreign direct investment.

Savings

Similar issues surround many of the other components of the "miracle." Several governments deliberately promoted savings. In Japan, postal savings banks made it easier (and more secure) for those in the rural sector to save, while in Singapore the National Provident Fund, in effect, imposed a 42 percent savings rate on workers. There is a debate: Can the high savings rate be "simply" explained by characteristics of the economy, such as the high growth rate? If increases in consumption lag behind increases in income, then a high growth rate will be associated with a high savings rate. There may then be multiple equililibria in the short run—one with high savings and high growth, the other with low savings and low growth. But that leaves unanswered the key question: Why did East Asia gravitate toward one equilibrium, the rest of the world the other? Government action may have been a key determinant. Indeed, as in other multiple equilibria models, government actions, which move the economy from one equilibrium to another, can be self-sustaining; once the economy has moved to the new equilibrium, the intervention is no longer needed. Thus it may be the case that after Singapore succeeded in moving to the high growth/high savings equilibrium, there was no longer any need to "force" savings, and the government interventions made little further difference to total savings.

Financial Markets

When financial depth is measured by the ratio of money to gross domestic product, financial markets appear deeper in East Asia than in most of the rest of the developing world. To be sure, security markets emerged slowly, but broad-based equities markets require strong legal protections for minority shareholders—of a kind that relatively few industrial countries have succeeded in providing. Moreover, asymmetries of information imply that even in industrial countries, a very small percentage of new investment is financed by equity issues, in spite of their greater virtues in risk diversification. It is thus not surprising that East Asia relied heavily on bank-financed debt. There was always a risk with debt finance: with high, fixed obligations, an economic downturn could lead to firms facing cash constraints. But the countries of the region (especially the Republic of Korea) addressed the problem through a system of *flexible bank finance,* which had distinct advantages over securitized debt instruments. Bank finance is *information intensive,* entailing, in principle, close monitoring of the borrower. So long as the firm's net worth remains sufficiently positive, a cash flow shortage need not be a problem: the bank can roll over loans and make good on any shortfalls, *provided the bank itself is in a position to make loans.* Thus, it is largely when there are macroeconomic problems, which make it difficult or unattractive for banks to lend, that the high leverage becomes problematic. But one can argue that government has a responsibility not only to maintain macrostability, but to mitigate the consequences of any residual volatility. It can do this in several ways: for example, regulatory forbearance (on capital adequacy standards) or capital injections into the banking system. In East Asia, the rationale for government interventions was even stronger: given the state of development of the capital market, there was, as we have noted, less reliance on equity than in more developed countries. Hence, there was a need for alternative mechanisms for societal risk sharing—to compensate for the market failure. The government "bailouts" *in the face of macroeconomic instability* were a form of risk sharing (in effect, converting the debt into partial equity), with limited adverse incentive effects....

A number of East Asian governments played a large role both in helping create financial institutions and in maintaining their capacity to lend. Historically, financial institutions in most countries have lent largely for trade credit and collateralized real estate. Development lending (long-term investment lending) by banks is limited. But in countries such as Korea, the government helped create a number of banks and encouraged them (through a variety of mechanisms) to go beyond these traditional lending avenues. *Financial restraint* (as opposed to financial repression) led to faster economic growth as well as the growth of the banking sector. By limiting competition and lowering deposit rates, governments in some East Asian countries increased the profitability of banking, and thus both the net worth and the franchise value. Some of the benefits were passed on to borrowers in the form of lower lending rates. The lower rates at which both firms and financial institutions had access to funds enhanced bank and corporate equity—especially important in an environment where directly raising new equity was difficult. The higher level of bank and corporate equity enabled firms to undertake riskier—and higher-return—investments. Moreover, since the marginal propensity to save of corporations was higher than that of individuals, and the interest elasticity of household savings was very low, the effective transfer of funds from the household to the corporate and banking sector led to higher national savings, again enhancing economic growth.

As noted above, given the almost inevitable limitations on equity markets as a source of finance, growth could have been sustained only by a high debt policy. The alternative would have been to limit expansion to what could be financed by retained earnings. East Asian countries thus faced two challenges: finding alternative ways of enhancing equity and managing the risks associated with high debt.

The financial restraint described in the previous paragraph represented the most important way that governments helped strengthen the equity bases of firms. To be sure, some of the governments recognized the importance of the legal reforms that would facilitate the creation of a deeper equity market; at the same time they realized that even in the most advanced of the industrial countries, well-established firms financed only a small percentage of their investment by new equity issues.

Accordingly, much of the burden of risk management was placed on the banking system, which, often under government pressure, rolled over loans in the face of macroeconomic shocks. However, in such cases the government often tacitly or explicitly underwrote the risks incurred. This risk absorption mechanism, while it allows countries like Korea to weather some of the macroeconomic shocks (like the oil price increases of the 1970s) far better than other countries, was put under stress in the 1990s from several sources. First, the countries of the region liberalized their capital markets quickly, under pressure from the International Monetary Fund (IMF) and the U.S. Treasury (and the decision to seek OECD membership), before the appropriate regulatory structures were in place. The pressure for rapid liberalization also meant that the gradualist strategy of the early 1990s was set aside. With the focus on rapid liberalization, and insufficient attention to the details, what appeared in hindsight as mistakes were almost inevitable.

While the reduced extent of government involvement in banking—presumably with less policy (and "connected") lending—should have strengthened the banking system, liberalization increased the scope for risk taking (for example, by eliminating the restrictions on speculative real estate lending that had been a hallmark of Thailand's policies in the miracle period) and the incentives for doing so (greater competition reduced the franchise value, and therefore the incentive for prudential behavior) at the same time that it increased the risks that the banking systems were exposed to. Compounding these problems was the fact that just at the time that *better* regulation was required, government regulators found it virtually impossible to keep their best and brightest, who were lured away by higher salaries offered by the private sector. Finally, the strictures against the risk-sharing mechanisms that had been customary under the earlier regime in some countries meant that firms had to fend for themselves to a greater degree—though their financial structures did not have time to adapt.

The criticism from the West compounded these problems, and not only in contributing to the massive flight of capital. It was not clear to what extent cronyism had played a role or to what extent cronyism Asian-style was different from cronyism American-style. Certainly, the publicly orchestrated, privately financed bailout of LTCM (Long-Term Capital Management), where CEOs seemed to use their corporate positions to bail out their private positions, raised questions about crony capitalism, corporate governance, *and* financial regulation even in the most advanced of the industrial countries. The fact that the *marginal* lenders in Korea were Western banks suggested bad judgment might be playing a more important role in bank lending policy than hidden government influence. Nonetheless, Korea took to heart the criticism of the government/banking/industrial nexus of the *chaebol,* and these concerns played a key role in the restructuring of the Korean economy, and indeed, are likely to play an important role in the rebalancing of political power as well.

These reforms are likely to lead an economic system that, while it exposes the country to greater risks, is better able to manage risks than the one that it replaced, and one that is likely to suffer less from political influence in resource allocation. Whether they will lead to an economic system better able to manage risks than the one that prevailed before liberalization is a moot question; the process of integration into the global economy has advanced to the point where it would have been hard, at best, to adapt that system to today's world. But it is also surely the case that the reforms, including the limitations on debt-equity ratios (as a result of both government pressure and the recognition of the huge risks that the high volatility in interest rates that mark IMF micromanagement strategies impose on highly levered companies) will imply that future long-term growth rates will almost surely be lower than they otherwise would have been.

Industrial Policy and the Role of Government

Those who put their faith in the market tend to downplay the role of government during the miracle period, particularly in the northeast Asian countries—but they can, at times, elevate its role when it comes to the crisis of 1997–98. Evidently, according to this view, during the period of success, markets drove the efficient allocation of resources, and more recently, it is government that has been the source of the problem. But again, the evidence is to the contrary: over time, the role of government in resource allocation has diminished in the 1990s, not increased.

* * *

It is clear that the government intervened in the allocation of resources. For instance, some governments promoted exports by making credits more available to successful exporters and by directing credit to selected sectors. Where such policy was subject to strict rules, the corruption and distortions associated with more ad hoc policies was avoided or at least kept relatively limited. It is also clear that the sectors that were supported grew and, in many cases, have become the foundations of these countries' economies as they enter the new millennium.

Part of the success of the leading East Asian economies relates to the closing of the technology/knowledge gap. Of this, there can be little doubt. The externalities and public goods aspects of knowledge provide a theoretical rationale for a role of government. In other countries that have implemented successful growth strategies, governments have pursued active policies promoting the production and dissemination of knowledge and technology, going well beyond just the protection of intellectual property through patent and copyright laws. In the United States, the increases in productivity in agriculture in the 19th century were promoted by the land grant colleges, with their research and extension services. The U.S. telecommunications industry was promoted by government, by establishing the first telegraph line, between Baltimore and

Washington, in 1842, and, more recently, by creating the Internet. Moreover, industrialization occurred within the United States behind the protection afforded by industrial tariffs. Would the countries in the East Asian region have succeeded in closing the knowledge and technology gap had they limited themselves simply to education? Possibly, but there is little historical precedent for such an achievement.

Still, the subject of industrial policy remains highly controversial. The controversy surrounds two questions—the counterfactual and the aggregative *quantitative* significance of these interventions, that is, what would have happened otherwise, did they work and did they make much difference? The more extreme critics argue that, by and large, they were distortive and thereby counterproductive. A few failures such as Japan's attempt to "rationalize" the automobile industry and inhibit the entry of Honda into car production, are cited time and time again. In my view, some of the criticism is misplaced. These arguments suggest that these countries would have grown even faster but for the interventions—possible, but not very probable. Today, as Korea has joined the OECD and become a major player in some of the key electronics industries, one hears less criticism of Korea's high-technology strategy.

The more subtle criticism is that while there was considerable fanfare surrounding the industrial policies, they really were not of much quantitative significance. To be sure, they affected *particular* industries; but did they make much difference *in the aggregate*? ... The controversy remains unresolved: How much credence can be put in the admittedly flawed econometric techniques that sometimes seem to suggest that these interventions played a limited role, versus the broader analysis, which links these policies to the sectors that are playing key roles in the economies in the region today?

To understand the central features that contributed to the rapid growth in the region one can look across countries for *common* policies. That is, the countries in the region shared some policies in common, while they differed in others. Most have high savings rates, though the *particular* policies they used to achieve that high savings rate differed. They have differed in their attitudes toward foreign direct investment. While foreign direct investment was at the center of Singapore's and Malaysia's strategies, Korea and Japan relied on investment by their own firms.

The fact that almost *all* of the economies in the region had industrial policies (with the exception of Hong Kong, which benefited from the industrial policies of its neighbor, mainland China) *suggests* that such policies were an important part of their growth strategies, whether or not the highly imperfect econometric techniques for quantifying such impacts succeeded in verifying such claims.

One of the principal ways that industrial policies were pursued was through interventions in financial markets. As I have noted, government both encouraged some forms of lending (for exports, to small and medium-size enterprises, to particular sectors) and, at times, in a few countries, discouraged other forms of lending (for speculative investment in real estate). These interventions in the capital market too have been widely criticized, both for their potential for corruption and for their distortions in resource allocation. But again, the relevant question concerns the counterfactual. One can argue that the interventions were helping to address market failures that are endemic in capital markets. Again, other successful "market" economies, like the United States, have massively intervened in the capital market—quite recently, more than a quarter of all loans in the United States either were intermediated by government or government-sponsored enterprises or had government guarantees. Governments, like any human institution, are fallible, and so one should not expect *perfection* in resource allocation. The question is, given the imperfections, would growth have been higher had governments intervened far less in their financial markets? This question is even harder to answer than the previous one, since in every country, governments intervene in financial markets, if only to ensure the safety and soundness of the financial system and to protect consumers against fraud.

In retrospect, perhaps the criticism that should have been leveled is that the government did not take strong enough actions, not that it intervened too much: it deregulated the financial sector when it should have been asking what was the *appropriate* set of regulations, and it did not do enough to ensure good corporate governance, which would have been necessary to create an effective stock market.

A third area of contention is the role of cooperation between business and government, ... The coordination provided by Japan, Inc., or Malaysia, Inc., was at one time, widely lauded. In effect, it was argued that market prices do not convey all the relevant information. However, even while it was lauded, many warned of the risks: cooperation could become capture and lead to corruption. It is hard to assess the *relative* importance of corruption—both relative to what occurs in other countries and relative to the benefits that accrued from cooperation. There is corruption in every society. Campaign contributions lead to corporate welfare, including special tax benefits for housing, large subsidies for agriculture, and a host of other tax expenditures and direct subsidies. Were the distortions in Korea, say, larger than those in the United States? There is no way of ascertaining the answer to that question. And were the costs of the distortions greater than the benefits that accrued from the cooperation? The fact of the matter is that we simply do not have tools with which we can answer these questions with any degree of certitude.

This poses both easy and hard policy questions. It is easy enough to say that the government should do everything it can to reduce corruption, and that government interventions should be designed in such a way as to mitigate the risk of corruption. It is easy enough to explain why corruption has adverse effects on economic growth. It is harder to design and implement corruption-resistant strategies. It is even harder to assess with any precision the impact of the particular level and forms of corruption on the growth of the economy.

Reducing the scope for rent seeking is clearly one aspect of corruption-resistant policies. But in many countries, reforms intended to reduce rent seeking, in particular, privatizations, have themselves been highly corrupted. In the light of *market* and *government* failures, there are two alternative strategies: to focus one and ignore the other or to try to address the weaknesses in each, viewing the public and private sectors as *complementary*. Singapore illustrates nicely the advantages of the latter approach. It undertook great efforts in reducing public corruption and, by most accounts, succeeded remarkably well. In doing so, it employed, in part, what have now become standard efficiency wage/incentive approaches. It relied heavily on the private sector but did not shy away from an active government role, not only in social policy but also in industrial policy. It developed a highly effective financial regulatory system, earning its marks when it excluded BCCI (the Bank of Credit and Commerce International), which succeeded in duping the United States' regulatory authorities. And partly because of the soundness and credibility of its financial system—based on effective regulation—it has become a regional financial center.

Concluding Remarks

Whether one calls it a miracle or not, the increases in income and reductions in poverty in East Asia were real and impressive. They showed that development is possible and that rapid development could be associated with egalitarian policies that greatly reduced poverty. And the contrasting experiences in the rest of the world showed not only that development was not inevitable but indeed that there seemed something very unusual about what had occurred in East Asia, the most populous region of the world. The crisis has tarnished that record only slightly and, if anything, together with the strong recovery in several of the countries, may have reinforced the conclusion that there is something very special about these countries. At the same time, the rapid growth in India over the past decade (especially if one looks at *particular* states within India) shows that East Asia has no monopoly on growth. India's success suggests that other countries too can achieve rapid economic growth and, at the very least, reinforces the need to understand the ingredients that contribute to success.

At one level, the problem of interpreting the miracle, crisis, and recovery is that we have an underidentified system: we do not have the controlled experiments that would allow us to assess what would have happened *but for*. If, say, the governments had simply had good micromanagement but not liberalized markets earlier, would growth have been even faster, and would the crisis not have occurred? We have a wealth of countries in other regions that followed different policies. On the basis of this juxtaposing their experience with that of East Asia, we can offer a few suggestions for the future.

All of the countries in the East Asian region will need to reexamine their *risk management* strategies: as their economies have become increasingly open, they are more exposed to the vagaries of international markets.... [C]urrency and term mismatching poses severe risks to banks in the management of their portfolios. East Asian countries will need to determine how to reduce their exposure, how to reduce their overall sensitivity to the risks that remain, and how to insulate the most vulnerable elements of their population. Some of these changes will likely result in a slowing down of growth, while some of the changes will enhance their ability to grow more rapidly, by becoming more integrated into the global economy. For instance, Korea's rapid growth has been based on a high debt policy. Without debt finance, firms would have had to rely on retained earnings, and growth would inevitably have been slower. Lowering debt equity ratios *may* thus lead to lower growth. But institutional reforms may lead to a strengthened equity market—although I must repeat that even in the most advanced industrial countries, relatively little new investment is financed through equity issues, and few countries have managed to create equity markets with dispersed ownership. But the reforms under way in Korea may strengthen equity markets, and so the country will be in a better position to both sustain growth momentum and manage shocks at the same time.

The weakness of safety nets is not a surprise, given that prior to the recent crisis the countries in the region had faced few economic downturns. But even in this area, some of the countries have shown an impressive level of institutional creativity: Singapore's provident fund has integrated the various social insurance programs and, in a relatively short span of time, improved housing, health, and income security.

The countries of the region face enormous challenges going forward. They have fundamental strengths on which to build, but they will have to adapt in numerous ways to the changing global environment and the changes in their own economies. The role of government will have to be redefined. Just as before they were misled by the chimera of deregulation—they should have asked instead what is the *right* regulatory structure for their current situation—so too in the future, they will have to resist accepting without question the current mantras of the global marketplace of ideas. There will have to be *strengthened* regulation of securities markets and an improved overall legal environment, especially in areas such as corporate governance and bankruptcy. The legal structures will have to comport with international standards, yet be adapted to their own special situations; wholesale borrowing will not work. The countries have moved toward democracy; democratic institutions and processes will need to be strengthened. Progress on all these fronts in most of the countries has already been impressive. Transparency is being increased, with Thailand even incorporating a right-to-know within its constitution.

Each of the countries faces its own individual challenges: Thailand needs to strengthen its secondary and tertiary education; in Korea, there is widespread support for reducing the role of the *chaebol*; in Indonesia, the difficult and delicate process of decentralization will have to be addressed. But while each of the countries faces different challenges, most of the countries are well poised to take advantage of many of the opportunities that are afforded by globalization and the new economy: the government-led strategies of closing the technology gap and investing heavily in human capital have placed several of the countries in a position not only to avail themselves of the new technologies, but even to become leaders in their exploitation.

Gazing through our cloudy crystal ball into the future, we can see prospects for continued robust growth—probably at a somewhat more muted pace, but still fast enough to continue the process of closing the gap between the countries in the region and the more advanced industrial countries. There are reasons for expecting a slowdown:

- Diminishing returns eventually set in. There are diminishing returns not only to capital but to investments in knowledge as well. It is almost surely easier to close the gap in knowledge (by a given amount) when the gap is moderate than when the gap is small.
- The export-oriented strategy may encounter difficulties, as such policies become widely imitated, and the world becomes saturated with the goods that represented the traditional comparative advantage of East Asian economies, and more broadly, as they become larger relative to the rest of the world. This can be a problem especially for China. Clearly, East Asia will again have to develop new sources of dynamic comparative advantage—just as the countries in the region have repeatedly adjusted over the past four decades.
- The larger countries will face concern about growing regional inequalities. These concerns will drive strategies that focus more attention on these regions. The successes achieved in some areas imply that it may be possible to sustain high growth rates even as the benefits are broadened out, but many of the poorer regions face severe geographical disadvantages.
- Even with new safeguards, the increased openness to volatile foreign capital flows will make it difficult to manage the economies with debt-driven growth. But even with substantial legal reforms, such as those related to corporate governance, it will be difficult to channel efficiently the high savings into the corporate sector through equity markets. Thus, firms will have to rely more on retained earnings, and this will slow down growth.

The growth slowdown itself will present a challenge: Many economic structures have become adapted to high-growth scenarios, and the moderation of growth will, accordingly, require potentially serious adjustments.

But beyond these economic challenges are the broader challenges: increases in gross domestic product are a means to an end, not an end in itself. Elsewhere I have spoken of the broader mandate for democratic, equitable, sustainable development and traced out some of the implications for the countries in the region in the coming decades. Here, I emphasize two aspects: First, the development of the region has been accompanied by enormous urbanization. The cities that have expanded need to be made more livable—with better public transportation systems, improved environments, and public amenities, such as parks. Second, the success of the region has been based in part on building on existing social capital, reaching broad social consensus, maintaining reasonable levels of social cohesion, and fostering a broader sense of community. In some cases, doing so has not been easy: the societies are highly ethnically fractionated. The most successful governments have realized the importance of these *social* policies (including egalitarian income distribution and education policies), not only as ends in themselves but even as *necessary* for long-term economic growth. The challenge going forward is to maintain these traditional values as the process of globalization and market development continues; there will be strong forces leading to greater inequality and undermining traditional cultural norms.

11.2

AN EMPTY REVOLUTION: THE UNFILLED PROMISES OF HUGO CHÁVEZ

Francisco Rodríguez

In this article, Francisco Rodríguez writes about something in which he has been directly involved—Venezuelan politics and economic development. We should be alert because he is biased. But perspectives already alert us to bias in all political scholarship and debate. President Hugo Chávez of Venezuela offers a left-wing state-driven economic alternative to the right-wing free-market policies of the Washington consensus, and Rodriguez subjects Chávez's program to the same test of facts and evidence that critics of the Washington consensus apply. He finds Chávez's program wanting not only in economic terms but also in political terms as Venezuela drifts toward authoritarianism. The debate between state-driven (realist) and market-driven (liberal) economic policies goes on, always within the context of different cultures and political ideologies (identity).

On December 2, [2007], when Venezuelans delivered President Hugo Chávez his first electoral defeat in nine years, most analysts were taken by surprise. According to official results, 50.7 percent of voters rejected Chávez's proposed constitutional reform, which would have expanded executive power, gotten rid of presidential term limits, and paved the way for the construction of a "socialist" economy. It was a major reversal for a president who just a year earlier had won a second six-year term with 62.8 percent of the vote, and commentators scrambled to piece together an explanation. They pointed to idiosyncratic factors, such as the birth of a new student movement and the defection of powerful groups from Chávez's coalition. But few went so far as to challenge the conventional wisdom about how Chávez has managed to stay in power for so long.

Although opinions differ on whether Chávez's rule should be characterized as authoritarian or democratic, just about everyone appears to agree that, in contrast to his predecessors, Chávez has made the welfare of the Venezuelan poor his top priority. His government, the thinking goes, has provided subsidized food to low-income families, redistributed land and wealth, and poured money from Venezuela's booming oil industry into health and education programs. It should

---

Source: Francisco Rodríguez, "An Empty Revolution: The Unfilled Promises of Hugo Chávez," *Foreign Affairs* 87, no. 2 (2008): 49–62.

not be surprising, then, that in a country where politics was long dominated by rich elites, he has earned the lasting support of the Venezuelan poor.

That story line may be compelling to many who are rightly outraged by Latin America's deep social and economic inequalities. Unfortunately, it is wrong. Neither official statistics nor independent estimates show any evidence that Chávez has reoriented state priorities to benefit the poor. Most health and human development indicators have shown no significant improvement beyond that which is normal in the midst of an oil boom. Indeed, some have deteriorated worryingly, and official estimates indicate that income inequality has increased. The "Chávez is good for the poor" hypothesis is inconsistent with the facts.

My skepticism of this notion began during my tenure as chief economist of the Venezuelan National Assembly. In September 2000, I left American academia to take over a research team with functions broadly similar to those of the U.S. Congressional Budget Office. I had high expectations for Chávez's government and was excited at the possibility of working in an administration that promised to focus on fighting poverty and inequality. But I quickly discovered how large the gap was between the government's rhetoric and the reality of its political priorities.

Soon after joining the National Assembly, I clashed with the administration over underfunding of the Consolidated Social Fund (known by its Spanish acronym FUS), which had been created by Chávez to coordinate the distribution of resources to antipoverty programs. The law establishing the fund included a special provision to ensure that it would benefit from rising oil revenues. But when oil revenues started to go up, the Finance Ministry ignored the provision, allocating to the fund in the 2001 budget only $295 million—15 percent less than the previous year and less than a third of the legally mandated $1.1 billion. When my office pointed out this inconsistency, the Finance Ministry came up with the creative accounting gimmick of rearranging the law so that programs not coordinated by the FUS would nevertheless appear to be receiving resources from it. The effect was to direct resources away from the poor even as oil profits were surging. (Hard-liners in the government, incensed by my office's criticisms, immediately called for my ouster. When the last moderates, who understood the need for an independent research team to evaluate policies, left the Chávez camp in 2004, the government finally disbanded our office.)

Chávez's political success does not stem from the achievements of his social programs or from his effectiveness at redistributing wealth. Rather, through a combination of luck and manipulation of the political system, Chávez has faced elections at times of strong economic growth, currently driven by an oil boom bigger than any since the 1970s. Like voters everywhere, Venezuelans tend to vote their pocketbooks, and until recently, this has meant voting for Chávez. But now, his mismanagement of the economy and failure to live up to his pro-poor rhetoric have finally started to catch up with him. With inflation accelerating, basic foodstuffs increasingly scarce, and pervasive chronic failures in the provision of basic public services, Venezuelans are starting to glimpse the consequences of Chávez's economic policies—and they do not like what they see.

Fake Left

From the moment he reached office in 1999, Chávez presented his economic and social policies as a left-wing alternative to the so-called Washington consensus and a major departure from the free-market reforms of previous administrations. Although the differences were in fact fairly moderate at first, the pace of change accelerated significantly after the political and economic crisis of 2002–3, which saw a failed coup attempt and a two-month-long national strike. Since then, the Venezuelan economy has undergone a transformation.

The change can be broadly characterized as having four basic dimensions. First, the size of the state has increased dramatically. Government expenditures, which represented only 18.8 percent of GDP in 1999, now account for 29.4 percent of GDP, and the government has nationalized key sectors, such as electricity and telecommunications. Second, the setting of prices and wages has become highly regulated through a web of restrictions in place since 2002 ranging from rigid price and exchange controls to a ban on laying off workers. Third, there has been a significant deterioration in the security of property rights, as the government has moved to expropriate landholdings and private firms on an ad hoc basis, appealing to both political and economic motives. Fourth, the government has carried out a complete overhaul of social policy, replacing existing programs with a set of high-profile initiatives—known as the misiones, or missions—aimed at specific problems, such as illiteracy or poor health provision, in poor neighborhoods.

Views differ on how desirable the consequences of many of these reforms are, but a broad consensus appears to have emerged around the idea that they have at least brought about a significant redistribution of the country's wealth to its poor majority. The claim that Chávez has brought tangible benefits to the Venezuelan poor has indeed by now become commonplace, even among his critics. In a letter addressed to President George W. Bush on the eve of the 2006 Venezuelan presidential elections, Jesse Jackson, Cornel West, Dolores Huerta, and Tom Hayden wrote, "Since 1999, the citizens of Venezuela have repeatedly voted for a government that—unlike others in the past—would share their country's oil wealth with millions of poor Venezuelans." The Nobel laureate economist Joseph Stiglitz has noted, "Venezuelan President Hugo Chávez seems to have succeeded in bringing education and health services to the barrios of Caracas, which previously had seen little of the benefits of that country's rich endowment of oil." Even The Economist has written that "Chávez's brand of revolution has delivered some social gains."

One would expect such a consensus to be backed up by an impressive array of evidence. But in fact, there is remarkably little data supporting the claim that the Chávez administration has acted any differently from previous Venezuelan governments—or, for that matter, from those of other developing and Latin American nations—in redistributing the gains from economic growth to the poor. One oft-cited statistic is the decline in poverty from a peak of 54 percent at the height of the national strike in 2003 to 27.5 percent in the first half of 2007. Although this decline may appear impressive, it is also known that poverty reduction is strongly associated with economic growth and that Venezuela's per capita GDP grew by nearly 50 percent during the same time period—thanks in great part to a tripling of oil prices. The real question is thus not whether poverty has fallen but whether the Chávez government has been particularly effective at converting this period of economic growth into poverty reduction. One way to evaluate this is by calculating the reduction in poverty for every percentage point increase in per capita income—in economists' lingo, the income elasticity of poverty reduction. This calculation shows an average reduction of one percentage point in poverty for every percentage point in per capita GDP growth during this recovery, a ratio that compares unfavorably with those of many other developing countries, for which studies tend to put the figure at around two percentage points. Similarly, one would expect pro-poor growth to be accompanied by a marked decrease in income inequality. But according to the Venezuelan Central Bank, inequality has actually increased during the Chávez administration, with the Gini coefficient (a measure of economic inequality, with zero indicating perfect equality and one indicating perfect inequality) increasing from 0.44 to 0.48 between 2000 and 2005.

Poverty and inequality statistics, of course, tell only part of the story. There are many aspects of the well-being of the poor not captured by measures of money income, and this is where Chávez's supporters claim that the government has made the most progress—through its misiones, which have concentrated on the direct provision of health, education, and other basic public services to poor communities. But again, official statistics show no signs of a substantial improvement in the well-being of ordinary Venezuelans, and in many cases there have been worrying deteriorations. The percentage of underweight babies, for example, increased from 8.4 percent to 9.1 percent between 1999 and 2006. During the same period, the percentage of households without access to running water rose from 7.2 percent to 9.4 percent, and the percentage of families living in dwellings with earthen floors multiplied almost threefold, from 2.5 percent to 6.8 percent. In Venezuela, one can see the misiones everywhere: in government posters lining the streets of Caracas, in the ubiquitous red shirts issued to program participants and worn by government supporters at Chávez rallies, in the bloated government budget allocations. The only place where one will be hard-pressed to find them is in the human development statistics.

Remarkably, given Chávez's rhetoric and reputation, official figures show no significant change in the priority given to social spending during his administration. The average share of the budget devoted to health, education, and housing under Chávez in his first eight years in office was 25.12 percent, essentially identical to the average share (25.08 percent) in the previous eight years. And it is lower today than it was in 1992, the last year in office of the "neoliberal" administration of Carlos Andrés Pérez—the leader whom Chávez, then a lieutenant colonel in the Venezuelan army, tried to overthrow in a coup, purportedly on behalf of Venezuela's neglected poor majority.

In a number of recent studies, I have worked with colleagues to look more systematically at the results of Chávez's health and education misiones. Our findings confirm that Chávez has in fact done little for the poor. For example, his government often claims that the influx of Cuban doctors under the Barrio Adentro health program is responsible for a decline in infant mortality in Venezuela. In fact, a careful analysis of trends in infant and neonatal mortality shows that the rate of decline is not significantly different from that of the pre-Chávez period, nor from the rate of decline in other Latin American countries. Since 1999, the infant mortality rate in Venezuela has declined at an annual rate of 3.4 percent, essentially identical to the 3.3 percent rate at which it had declined during the previous nine-year period and lower than the rates of decline for the same period in Argentina (5.5 percent), Chile (5.3 percent), and Mexico (5.2 percent).

Even more disappointing are the results of the government's Robinson literacy program. On October 28, 2005, Chávez declared Venezuela "illiteracy-free territory." His national literacy campaign, he announced, had taught 1.5 million people how to read and write, and the education minister stated that residual illiteracy stood at less than 0.1 percent of the population. The achievement received considerable international recognition and was taken at face value by many specialists as well as by casual observers. A recent article in the San Francisco Chronicle, for example, reported that "illiteracy, formerly at 10 percent of the population, has been completely eliminated." Spanish President José Luis Rodríguez Zapatero and UNESCO's general director, Koïchiro Matsuura, sent the Venezuelan government public letters of congratulation for the achievement. (After Matsuura's statement, the Chávez administration claimed that its eradication of illiteracy had been "UNESCO-verified.")

But along with Daniel Ortega of Venezuela's IESA business school, I looked at trends in illiteracy rates based on responses to the Venezuelan National Institute of Statistics' household surveys. (A full presentation of our study will appear in the October 2008 issue of the journal Economic Development and Cultural Change.) In contrast to the government's claim, we found that there were more than one million illiterate Venezuelans by the end of 2005, barely down from the 1.1 million illiterate persons recorded in the first half of 2003, before the start of the Robinson program. Even this small reduction, moreover, is accounted for by demographic trends rather than the program itself. In a battery of statistical tests, we found little evidence that the program had had any statistically distinguishable effect on Venezuelan illiteracy. We also found numerous inconsistencies in the government's story. For example, it claims to have employed 210,410 trainers in the anti-illiteracy effort (approximately two percent of the Venezuelan labor force), but there is no evidence in the public employment data that these people were ever hired or evidence in the government budget statistics that they were ever paid.

The Economic Consequences of Mr. Chávez

In fact, even as the conventional wisdom has taken hold outside of Venezuela, most Venezuelans, according to opinion surveys, have long been aware that Chávez's social policies are inadequate and ineffective. To be sure, Venezuelans would like the government's programs—particularly the sale of subsidized food—to remain in place, but that is a far cry from believing that they have reasonably addressed the nation's poverty problem. A survey taken by the Venezuelan polling firm Alfredo Keller y Asociados in September 2007 showed that only 22 percent of Venezuelans think poverty has improved under Chávez, while 50 percent think it has worsened and 27 percent think it has stayed the same.

At the same time, however, Venezuelan voters have given Chávez credit for the nation's strong economic growth. In polls, an overwhelming majority have expressed support for Chávez's stewardship of the economy and reported that their personal situation was improving. This is, of course, not surprising: with its economy buoyed by surging oil profits, Venezuela had enjoyed three consecutive years of double-digit growth by 2006.

But by late 2007, Chávez's economic model had begun to unravel. For the first time since early 2004, a majority of voters claimed that both their personal situation and the country's situation had worsened during the preceding year. Scarcities in basic foodstuffs, such as milk, black beans, and sardines, were chronic, and the difference between the official and the black-market exchange rate reached 215 percent. When the Central Bank board received its November price report indicating that monthly inflation had risen to 4.4 percent (equivalent to an annual rate of 67.7 percent), it decided to delay publication of the report until after the vote on the constitutional reform was held.

This growing economic crisis is the predictable result of the gross mismanagement of the economy by Chávez's economic team. During the past five years, the Venezuelan government has pursued strongly expansionary fiscal and economic policies, increasing real spending by 137 percent and real liquidity by 218 percent. This splurge has outstripped even the expansion in oil revenues: the Chávez administration has managed the admirable feat of running a budget deficit in the midst of an oil boom.

Such expansionary policies were appropriate during the deep recession that Venezuela faced in the aftermath of the political and economic crisis of 2002–3. But by continuing the expansion after the recession ended, the government generated an inflationary crisis. The problem has been compounded by efforts to address the resulting imbalances with an increasingly complex web of price and exchange controls coupled with routine threats of expropriation directed at producers and shopkeepers as a warning not to raise prices. Not surprisingly, the response has been a steep drop in food production and widening food scarcity.

A sensible solution to Venezuela's overexpansion would require reining in spending and the growth of the money supply. But such a solution is anathema to Chávez, who has repeatedly equated any call for spending reductions with neoliberal dogma. Instead, the government has tried to deal with inflation by expanding the supply of foreign currency to domestic firms and consumers and increasing government subsidies. The result is a highly distorted economy in which the government effectively subsidizes two-thirds of the cost of imports and foreign travel for the wealthy while the poor cannot find basic food items on store shelves. The astounding growth of imports, which have nearly tripled since 2002 (imports of such luxury items as Hummers and 15-year-old Scotch have grown even more dramatically), is now threatening to erase the nation's current account surplus.

What is most distressing is how predictable all of this was. Indeed, Chávez-nomics is far from unprecedented: the gross contours of this story follow the disastrous experiences of many Latin American countries during the 1970s and 1980s. The economists Rudiger Dornbusch and Sebastian Edwards have characterized such policies as "the macroeconomics of populism." Drawing on the economic experiences of administrations as politically diverse as Juan Perón's in Argentina, Salvador Allende's in Chile, and Alan García's in Peru, they found stark similarities in economic policies and in the resulting economic evolution. Populist macroeconomics is invariably characterized by the use of expansionary fiscal and economic policies and an overvalued currency with the intention of accelerating growth and redistribution. These policies are commonly implemented in the context of a disregard for fiscal and foreign exchange constraints and are accompanied by attempts to control inflationary pressures through price and exchange controls. The result is by now well known to Latin American economists: the emergence of production bottlenecks, the accumulation of severe fiscal and balance-of-payments problems, galloping inflation, and plummeting real wages.

Chávez's behavior is typical of such populist economic experiments. The initial successes tend to embolden policymakers, who increasingly believe that they were right in dismissing the recommendations of most economists. Rational policy formulation becomes increasingly difficult, as leaders become convinced that conventional economic constraints do not apply to them. Corrective measures only start to be taken when the economy has veered out of control. But by then it is far too late.

My experience dealing with the Chávez government confirmed this pattern. In February 2002, for example, I had the opportunity of speaking with Chávez at length about the state of the Venezuelan economy. At that point, the economy had entered into a recession as a result of an unsustainable fiscal expansion carried out during Chávez's first three years in office. Moderates within the government had arranged the meeting with the hope that it would spur changes in the management of the public finances. As a colleague and I explained to Chávez, there was no way to avoid a deepening of the country's macroeconomic crisis without a credible effort to raise revenue and rationalize expenditures. The president listened with interest, taking notes and asking questions over three hours of conversation, and ended our meeting with a request that we speak with his cabinet ministers and schedule future meetings. But as we proceeded to meet with officials, the economic crisis was spilling over into the political arena, with the opposition calling for street demonstrations in response to Chávez's declining poll numbers. Soon, workers at the state oil company, PDVSA, joined the protests.

In the ensuing debate within the government over how to handle the political crisis, the old-guard leftists persuaded Chávez to take a hard line. He dismissed 17,000 workers at PDVSA and sidelined moderates within his government. When I received a call informing me that our future meetings with Chávez had been canceled, I knew that the hard-liners had gained the upper hand. Chávez's handling of the economy and the political crisis had significant costs. Chávez deftly used the mistakes of the opposition (calling for a national strike and attempting a coup) to deflect blame for the recession. But in fact, real GDP contracted by 4.4 percent and the currency had lost more than 40 percent of its value in the first quarter of 2002, before the start of the first PDVSA strike on April 9. As early as January of that year, the Central Bank had already lost more than $7 billion in a futile attempt to defend the currency. In other words, the economic crisis had started well before the political crisis—a fact that would be forgotten in the aftermath of the political tumult that followed.

The government's response to the crisis has had further consequences for the Venezuelan economy. The takeover of PDVSA by Chávez loyalists and the subordination of the firm's decisions to the government's political imperatives have resulted in a dramatic decline in Venezuela's oil-production capacity. Production has been steadily declining since the government consolidated its control of the industry in late 2004. According to OPEC statistics, Venezuela currently produces only three-quarters of its quota of 3.3 million barrels a day. Chávez's government has thus not only squandered Venezuela's largest oil boom since the 1970s; it has also killed the goose that lays the golden egg. Despite rising oil prices, PDVSA is increasingly strained by the combination of rising production costs, caused by the loss of technical capacity and the demands of a growing web of political patronage, and the need to finance numerous projects for the rest of the region, ranging from the rebuilding of Cuban refineries to the provision of cheap fuel to Sandinista-controlled mayoralties in Nicaragua. As a result, the capacity of oil revenues to ease the government's fiscal constraints is becoming more and more limited.

Plowing the Sea

Simón Bolívar, Venezuela's independence leader and Chávez's hero, once said that in order to evaluate revolutions and revolutionaries, one needs to observe them close up but judge them at a distance. Having had the opportunity to do both with Chávez, I have seen to what extent he has failed to live up to his own promises and Venezuelans' expectations. Now, voters are making the same realization—a realization that will ultimately lead to Chávez's demise. The problems of ensuring a peaceful political transition will be compounded by the fact that over the past nine years Venezuela has become an increasingly violent society. This violence is not only reflected in skyrocketing crime rates; it also affects the way Venezuelans resolve their political conflicts. Whether Chávez is responsible for this or not is beside the point. What is vital is for Venezuelans to find a way to prevent the coming economic crisis from igniting violent political conflict. As Chávez's popularity begins to wane, the opposition will feel increasingly emboldened to take up initiatives to weaken Chávez's movement. The government may become increasingly authoritarian as it starts to understand the very high costs it will pay if it loses power. Unless a framework is forged through which the government and the opposition can reach a settlement, there is a significant risk that one or both sides will resort to force.

* * *

Chapter 12

FOREIGN AID AND DOMESTIC GOVERNANCE: DEVELOPMENT IN AFRICA AND THE MIDDLE EAST

12.1

TOWARDS THE RISE OF WOMEN IN THE ARAB WORLD: CONCEPTS AND PROBLEMATIC ISSUES

United Nations Development Programme, Regional Bureau for Arab States

The Arab Human Development Report provides an honest assessment by Arab leaders and specialists themselves of the problems and controversies that beset the region. The fourth and most recent (as of summer 2009) report, issued in 2005, from which this excerpt is taken, assesses the discrimination against women in the Arab world. It weighs the external pressures from outside (systemic level of analysis) and the political, economic, and cultural legacies from inside (domestic level of analysis) affecting the treatment of women. In line with earlier reports, it underlines what it calls "rights-based societal reforms," affording women full opportunities not only to essential services such as health and education but also to participation in all aspects of society as women see fit. Stressing changes in thinking as well as institutions and material circumstances, the report adopts a perspective that stresses identity and is both proud and critical of Arab culture.

* * *

Source: United Nations Development Programme, Regional Bureau for Arab States (RBAS), *The Arab Human Development Report 2005* (New York: United Nations Publications, 2006), 5–24.

Concepts

The Report considers that, as human beings, women and men have an innate and equal right to achieve a life of material and moral dignity, the ultimate goal of human development. It thus views the rise of women in the joint framework of human rights and human development. In terms of human rights, the advancement of women is to be achieved as part of society's advancement to freedom, in its most comprehensive definition. This definition includes not only civil and political rights, the mainstays of citizenship, but freedom from ignorance, disease, want, fear and all else that diminishes human dignity.

In terms of human development, the rise of women entails:

- Complete equality of opportunity between women and men in the acquisition and employment of human capabilities;
- Guaranteed rights of citizenship for all women on an equal footing with men;
- Acknowledgement of, and respect for differences between the sexes. Women are different from men, but that in no way implies they are deficient. Under no conditions is it acceptable to use gender differences to support theories of inequality between the sexes or any form of sexual discrimination.

Historically, various women's nongovernmental organisations have focused on different objectives. Some have concentrated on promoting women's equal rights and the elimination of discrimination embedded in Arab laws, whether these concern personal status issues or social guarantees. Others have targeted charitable development activities, providing loans and income-generating projects for women or services in health, education and other sectors. Relatively few however, have focused on women's empowerment as the collective goal and undertaking of society as a whole.

The Question of the "Internal" and the "External"

The spread of the concept of "women's empowerment" in the Arab region has excited the rancour of certain socio-political forces. They have tended to see it as "imposed" by the West and not emerging from either the realities or needs of Arab societies, which are based on the entrenched role of the family as society's basic building block. This has driven some to resist development plans that adopt the gender perspective and to resist the governments and the women's organisations which work in accordance with it.

An enforced anatomic separation between what is deemed local and what is deemed foreign is no longer possible in this age. What we call "foreign" culture actually thrives within Arab societies—particularly in terms of values and modes of behaviour—owing to the increasing globalisation of Arab societies. Nor is such a separation beneficial for the aspiration for progress in the Arab world—which is an authentic aspiration—and which has continued, since the beginning of the Arab Renaissance, to be positively influenced by the best human accomplishments of the prevailing Western civilisation.

To be more precise, there is a largely beneficial collaboration between the struggle for women's emancipation in Arab countries as a liberating dynamic in society, and women's movements around the world, including those in the West. The efforts of international organisations are particularly important here, especially the agreements, resolutions, mechanisms and international activities aimed at protecting women's rights and equal treatment.

However, the crassness of the call from outside for reform, sometimes imposed by force, has elicited a negative reaction among some segments of society. This reaction, directed against a dominant Western-imposed women's empowerment agenda, is considered by such segments to be a simultaneous violation of Arab culture and of national independence.

The Report maintains that the rise of women, in both intellectual and practical terms, remains an essential axis of the Arab project for a human renaissance. The advancement of women—viewed both as struggle against despotism on the inside and appropriation from the outside—is part of the construction of a renaissance that will bring about freedom, pride and vigour for all Arabs, men and women on an equal footing.

Despotic Authority and the Rise of Women. Paradoxically, repressive regimes, for their own reasons, have encouraged women's rights in ways that might not have been possible if matters had been left to the natural progress of society, given its imposed and inherited constraints. The mechanisms of political oppression have even served at times to accelerate the rise of women. But the Report notes that this imperious, top-down style of "progress," however enlightened, inevitably encounters objections and resistance from the popular base. It argues that a shift to free and well-governed societies in Arab countries would be quite capable of realising those historic breakthroughs required for women to advance, while also attracting broad social support that will guarantee the movement popular strength and sustainability.

The Undervaluation of Women's Participation in Economic Activity. Arab society does not acknowledge the true extent of women's participation in social and economic activities and in the production of the components of human well being, and it does not reward them adequately for such participation. Since most women work without pay for their families, their contributions are not recognised as economic activity.

This historical prejudice is reflected in the undervaluing of women's contributions to different types of human activity in general, and to economic activity in particular.

A proper evaluation of women's contribution to producing the elements of human welfare requires a creative theoretical foundation that goes beyond the national accounts' system, restricted as it is to market exchange and the cash valuation of goods and services. This can be done by using a broad definition of human welfare that is commensurate with the concept of human development. From a procedural perspective, this will require diligence in developing research and statistical tools that aim to measure accurately women's contribution to the production of human welfare and the construction of human development. This is a field that remains open to research.

The State of Women in the Arab World

The state of women in Arab countries results from, and contributes to a number of cultural, social, economic and political factors which interact to affect levels of human development. Some factors are problematic in nature and thus call for a close analysis of various components of Arab society.

The Report examines the situation of women in the region by tracing a basic axis of human development: the acquisition and utilisation of human capabilities and resulting levels of well being. It probes levels of health and education in particular. It also assesses experiences in the advancement of women by reviewing two factors crucial for the success of such a movement: the extent of Arab society's desire for such progress and the forms of social action adopted to pursue it.

Acquiring Capabilities: The Denial of Opportunities to Women

Health. Women in Arab countries, especially the least developed countries, suffer unacceptably high rates of risk of morbidity and mortality connected with pregnancy and reproductive functions. The maternal mortality rate in Arab countries averages 270 deaths per 100,000 live births. This rises to over 1,000 deaths in the poorest Arab countries (Mauritania and Somalia) and falls to levels such as 7 for every 100,000 births in Qatar.

Women lose a larger number of years to disease, and this appears to be unconnected to standards of living, risk factors, and deaths linked to pregnancy or childbirth, indicating that this relatively greater loss is attributable to general life styles that discriminate against women.

The Arab region remains one of those relatively least affected by HIV/AIDS at present. Despite this, women and girls are increasingly infected by the disease and now represent half the total number of people carrying the virus in the Arab world. Women are at greater risk of catching the virus and contracting the disease: the probability of infection among females from 15 to 24 years of age is double that of males in the same age group.

Education. Despite the tremendous spread of girls' education in Arab countries, women continue to suffer more than men do from a lack of opportunities to acquire knowledge. This occurs despite the fact that girls excel in knowledge pursuits, outstripping boys in competitive academic performance.

In terms of basic indicators, the Arab region has one of the highest rates of female illiteracy (as much as one half, compared to only one third among males). It also displays one of the lowest rates of enrolment at the various levels of education. This is in spite of the success of some Arab states, most notably those in the Gulf, in increasing the percentage of girl's enrolment and narrowing the gap between the sexes at the three levels of education.

The relatively greater denial of educational opportunities to girls contrasts with Arab public opinion. The Report's field study indicates that the majority of people believe that girls have a right to education on an equal footing with men.

Female enrolment in university education has risen, yet women are still concentrated in fields such as literature, the humanities and the social sciences where they constitute the majority. These are the subjects in least demand by employers. By contrast, enrolment rates for females in fields that lead to jobs, such as engineering and science, are noticeably lower. Again, this trend runs counter to Arab public opinion which favours letting women students choose their fields of specialisation.

International data indicate that girls in the Arab region perform better in school than boys. Drop out rates for girls are lower than those for boys in all the countries for which data are available. Notwithstanding this, discrimination against women in Arab countries continues to limit their access to knowledge despite the mass of statistical and other evidence indicating that Arab girls are the better learners, especially on the first rungs of the educational ladder.

The share of girls among top scoring students in all Arab countries where data is available is over 50 percent. Since, on average, girls account for fewer than half those enrolled in education, this achievement underlines their academic ascendancy. Such achievement is all the more remarkable given the unhelpful societal and familial environment that some face arising from the myth that a girl is destined for the house and that education and work are basically male domains.

The Report thus stresses that Arab countries stand to reap extraordinary benefits from giving men and women equal opportunities to acquire and utilise knowledge for the advancement of society. What deprive the region of these gains are its harmful and discriminatory practices that hold back women.

The Use of Human Capabilities
Economic Activities

Slow growth in the region predisposes economies towards low demand for female labour. In addition, the traditional view that the man is the breadwinner blocks the employment of women and contributes to an increase in women's unemployment relative to men. Women thus encounter significant obstacles outside family life that reduce their potential. Most limiting of these are the terms and conditions of work: women do not enjoy equality with men in job opportunities, conditions or wages let alone in promotion to decision-making positions.

Starting from a low base, between 1990 and 2003, the Arab region witnessed a greater increase in women's share in economic activity than all other regions of the world: the increase for Arab women was 19 per cent compared to 3 per cent for the world as a whole. Despite this, Arab women's economic participation remains the lowest in the world: not more than 33.3 per cent of women fifteen years and older in contrast to the world average of 55.6 per cent. Furthermore, their participation does not exceed 42 per cent that of men, again the lowest rate in the world compared to a global average of 69 per cent.

Except in low-income economies where women work primarily in agriculture under conditions of poverty, they tend to find jobs in the services sector, which in the Arab world is characterised by low productivity and low remuneration. Women thus commonly experience low returns on work.

The causes of Arab women's weak economic participation include but are not confined to the prevailing male culture where some employers prefer to employ men, the scarcity of jobs in general, employment and wage discrimination between the sexes, and high reproductive rates. Laws hindering women, including those designed for their "protection," such as personal status and labour legislation, also restrict women's freedom by requiring a father's or a husband's permission to work, travel or borrow from financial institutions. Additionally, women's job opportunities have been undercut by weak support services and structural adjustment programmes.

Dependency ratios in the Arab region remain the highest in the world, with each worker supporting more than two non-working people, compared to less than one in East Asia and the Pacific. The principal reason for this is the low rate of participation by women. The situation becomes even graver when this high level of family maintenance occurs in combination with an absence of pension plans and of a National Insurance network covering all worker cohorts.

With the increasing expansion of the informal sector, where worker coverage is low, family support becomes a tremendous burden for the small number of those working. The strains on women in providing care for children and the sick, elderly, disabled and handicapped without sufficient social support also continue to grow.

The failure to use human capital, especially highly educated women, curbs economic development and squanders important energies and investments, which might otherwise contribute to greater economic development for all.

Arab Women in the Political Sphere

In the Report's field survey, Arab public opinion clearly endorses the right of women to participate in political activity and to hold the highest executive positions. Yet these are areas from which women are often excluded.

In most Arab countries (with the exception of the Gulf States) women obtained the right to vote and be candidates in parliamentary elections in the fifties and sixties of the past century. Lebanon was the first Arab country to grant women these two rights, in 1952.

Later, the adoption of quota systems increased women's parliamentary participation in Jordan and Morocco. Despite these favourable changes, the proportion of women representatives in Arab parliaments remains the lowest in the world at under 10 per cent.

Arab women have shared in executive power in some Arab countries since the middle of the last century. The first woman minister was appointed in Iraq in 1959, in Egypt in 1956 and in Algeria in 1962. The number of Arab countries that appoint women as ministers has increased in the last three years to the extent that women now participate in all governments except that of Saudi Arabia. Such appointments do not however reflect a general trend towards women's empowerment. Women in power are often selected from the ranks of the elite or appointed from the ruling party as window dressing for the ruling regimes.

Outstanding Achievements of Arab Women

Certain Arab women have realized outstanding achievements in various fields including those in which women do not receive training on an equal footing with men, such as athletics and the natural and precise sciences.

Literary Creativity. Women writers have proved that they can write and are capable of equalling and, at times, surpassing their male colleagues.

Artistic Creativity, with the Cinema as an Example. Arab women have played an outstanding role in the effective foundation of the cinema.

Social Sciences. The works of pioneering feminists such as Nawal al-Sa'dawi and Fatima Mernissi evince a joy in the discovery of unknown "continents" in the history, heritage, beliefs and renaissance of the Arab world. Though such writers set up a sharp and divisive dualism based on male/female antagonism, the following generation transcended the issue and its writings reveal a more balanced scholarly tone without the loss of a feminist orientation.

Natural and Exact Sciences. Despite severe barriers to women's entry into scientific fields, a galaxy of Arab women has made stellar contributions to the natural and exact sciences. Indeed, when Arab women scientists and technicians have been given an opportunity to use their abilities at the international level, they have succeeded in producing exceptional results.

Athletics. In the last six Olympic Games (1984–2004), six women from the Arab world, five from the Maghreb and one from Syria, carried off one of the three top prizes in track and field events. Two-thirds of these are gold medal winners, a relatively high figure given that only a quarter of male Arab Olympic medallists won gold.

Business. The region's movement towards free market economies, together with growing advocacy for the empowerment of women in Arab countries, have combined to increase the contributions of women entrepreneurs in Arab economies and to augment their influence in private sector business organisations. It has given rise to their own business organisations, even in those Arab countries most conservative on women's issues.

Levels of Well Being

No clear scientific indicator exists for the feminisation of poverty defined as lack of income. However, women apparently suffer higher levels of "human poverty" as measured in terms of deprivation of the three dimensions of the human development index, namely, health, knowledge and income.

Specifically, women suffer from a noticeable impairment of personal liberty.

The Spread of Poverty and the Disempowerment of Women

The Report indicates that the spread of income poverty generally leads to women's disenfranchisement in the areas of parliamentary participation, professional and technical employment, and control of economic resources. Human poverty results in the wide disempowerment of women and the exclusion of women from upper-level legislative, administrative and organisational jobs as well as from the professional and technical arenas.

The Impairment of Personal Liberty

The forms of violence practised against Arab women confirm that Arab legislators and governments, together with Arab social movements, face a large task in achieving security and development in its comprehensive sense. The mere discussion of violence against women arouses strong resistance in some Arab countries.

The most important step to oppose violence in the Arab world is to fight against its concealment, to remove the cloak of silence surrounding it and to expose it wherever it occurs, whether in public or in private. Continued silence on the subject will incur a heavy cost for individuals, society, and even the state. It is equally important to place forms of violence that many women affected have come to accept as natural in the category of unacceptable behaviour.

Such forms of violence range from honour killings, in which a woman is killed on the pretext of protecting family honour, to domestic violence, which is found and condemned in many areas of the world. Additionally, the high incidence of female circumcision in some Arab countries leads to serious health complications for women.

Women living in difficult circumstances, especially those in areas of conflict or under occupation, suffer additional difficulties. Women living in desert and marginal regions and in informal settlements are often unaware of their rights and of the services available to them. Often, they do not possess the papers, such as birth certificates, that would permit them to receive such services. Many of them endure violence in some form.

Foreign female domestic workers in Arab countries are often victimised. Labour laws do not protect their work, they endure unspecified working hours, and they are denied freedom of movement and residence. Some female workers in this sector are also exposed to physical and mental violence from their employers, including sexual assault.

Fortunately, Arab public opinion as indicated by the Report's field survey overwhelmingly condemns violence against women of any form.

The Arab Women's Movement: Struggles and Experiences

The most influential factor in the history of the women's movement may have been its involvement in the struggle for liberation from imperialism before it embarked on the struggle for women's liberation within Arab societies.

The first generation of women's associations (formed at around the end of the nineteenth century) was focused on charitable work. They emerged amid the wealthy classes and their standard was carried by aristocratic women, or women from ruling families.

The colonial period impacted the women's movement by dislocating the structure of occupied Islamic countries. Traditional Arab economic, social, cultural and moral frameworks were shaken. It thus became necessary to marshal national sentiment and consciousness in order to conduct national struggles of liberation as the overriding priority. As a result, social development, and the rise of women as a part of it, remained hostage to the drive for national independence, falling much lower on the list of priorities.

The 1940s and 1950s were rich for the moulding of women's discourse. Political parties started to form women's associations under their own banners, thereby bringing men into the women's movement. Thus, immediately following the Second World War, another set of women's associations emerged throughout the Arab world.

The Arab women's movement went through a host of transformations during the colonial period as a result of social changes. The Report cites the spread of education among females; the entry of many women into the higher professions as doctors, university faculty, engineers and lawyers; the accession by some women to positions of power in the leadership of political parties and governments; the development of a well rooted consciousness of the situation in which women were living; and an increase in societal sympathy for women's issues.

Governments attempted to bring women's associations together into "unions," in line with a common phenomenon in the Arab world, namely, the confinement of women within a framework monitored and directed by the male power structure. Some scholars describe this as the feminisation of the ruling discourse.

This trend coincided during the last three decades with another significant development, the rise of Islamic movements and the spreading influence of proselytisers urging a return to the Islam of the "venerable forebears" (Salafism). These movements held women responsible for the difficulties that society was undergoing. They based their attacks on the idea that equality in public life would, by its nature, reduce men's opportunities in the job market and that the man was the master of the family and the woman his dependent.

Starting with the 1975 UN Conference in Mexico and under the influence of international organisations working for the rise of women, new instances of the so-called "feminisation of the state" began to emerge.

A number of Arab regimes saw in the Islamic groups a means to weaken left-ist and labour forces. This led to the growth of the Islamic revivalist movement, whose concerns extended to all spheres of public and private life and whose discourse attracted broad segments of youth, especially young women.

In response, a call emerged for the restriction of Islam to the realm of personal belief and spiritual value. Some groups were obliged to modify their stance, asking that the door to independent religious thinking (ijtihad) be opened on questions connected with women in the belief that enlightened readings of the regulatory Qur'anic verses would establish a new discourse on women nourished by the Islamic heritage. The second half of the 1970s saw the founding of women's organisations independent of official political organisations. Debate centered on the inadequacy of, and loopholes in, the Personal Status Code in terms of achiev-ing equality, notwithstanding its pioneering nature compared with family legisla-tion in many other Arab countries. Attention also concentrated on forms of violence inflicted upon women and on how this violence was reflected in their status in society.

The women's movement saw a qualitative upswing in the 1980s in the estab-lishment and extension of associations. Politically active associations emerged, linked to parties. The eighties were also a crucial period in the transformation of the women's movements, especially in the Maghreb countries. It is no coincidence that the names of the new women's associations included words such as "demo-cratic," "progressive," and "rights." Their independence and courage distin-guished these movements as they trod a path strewn with obstacles, under siege from, and beset by the ruling regimes.

The new generation of women's associations is distinguished by its qualita-tive closeness to the topic of women and women's issues. It considers these as central questions no less important than those of democracy, development, and human rights.

The international discourse on women has been a significant influence on the Arab women's movement and a driving force in the latter's perseverance and reformulation of its goals. The new consciousness was reinforced at interna-tional conferences, chiefly those convened under the auspices of the United Nations. The new approach aimed to dislodge traditional views still clinging to the women's question. Thus, personal status laws were the most important priority among these goals, followed by the enactment of legislation guarantee-ing the equality of women and men in political and economic life. Women's associations were also active in urging Arab governments to implement the international agreements that they had approved, especially the Convention on the Elimination of All Forms of Discrimination against Women (CEDAW).

The 1990s are considered to have been difficult years for Arab society, filled with contradictions, tribulations, and successive, bitter disappointments. The Report observes that it lies beyond the power and resources of the women's movements to affect such an entangled politico-social situation by themselves, which confirms that the fight for women's freedom is the fight of Arab societies as a whole.

Evaluating Achievements for Women

The participation of women in national movements helped women to articulate their case and enhanced their legitimacy in society's eyes. Nevertheless, and despite some palpable gains by women, the postponement of the resolution of their social and political demands had regrettable consequences after independence (Algeria is an excellent example of this). For, in most cases, the new nationalist governments pretended to forget or ignored some or most of these demands, especially those related to the Personal Status Codes. In general, and with the exception of the modifications made to the personal status laws in Tunisia, unequal relations of power within the family survived.

The impact of women's movements in Arab countries has varied from one country to another. Their principal achievement may have been to increase awareness among women of the lesser status accorded to them and the need to work to change it. By concentrating public scrutiny on Personal Status Laws, the movement has impelled Arab states to take tangible steps to improve family law and legislation on marriage and divorce in general.

The Tunisian Experience. Tunisia remains a model among the Arab states in terms of women's emancipation. Half a century has passed since the issuing of its Personal Status Code, through which Tunisian law gave legal effect to the principle of women's equality with men. The changes to family law instituted by President Habib Bourguiba soon after independence sprang from a reformist movement that viewed the rise of women positively on the social, economic and political levels. Likewise, it is important to note that the laws of the Personal Status Code sprang from an initiative undertaken by two schools of Islamic jurisprudence, the Maliki and the Hanafi.

However, progressive changes in family laws have coincided with restrictions on the freedom of action of activist women and with state monopolisation and monitoring of the movement's discourse. This leaves only a limited field for women's initiatives and demands. The tendency to transform the rise of women into a political tool that may be used to enhance the image of the state abroad, even at the expense of women, has become very clear.

The Moroccan Experience. The Moroccan women's movement has become acutely conscious that amendments to the legal code are the key to women's ownership of their own issues. Its struggle in that area was crowned by the new Family Code, issued in 2004.

Looking at experiences in other Arab countries, at the present time, Egyptian women have only managed to win the right, granted in 2000, to initiate divorce proceedings (khul'), after waiving certain financial rights entailed in other forms of divorce. They have also won the right to travel without their husbands' permission and to obtain Egyptian nationality for their children by a foreign husband.

Jordan has raised the legal age for marriage to eighteen years for both spouses and granted women the right to obtain a passport without their husbands' permission.

In Algeria, the Family Law still remains in force. However, there are positive signs in the difference between the form the latter took in 1984 and the modifications issued in 2005.

The Report concludes that re-evaluating the position of Arab women today is a sine qua non for a stronger civil society, one that demands a conviction that overrules pretexts for inaction that reject all forms of women's development as part of the culture of "the Other".

The Societal Context of the State of Women
Culture

The Report considers social patterns that contribute to shaping the position of women in Arab societies today. It focuses on three central sources of influence: religious heritage, popular culture and Arab intellectual, artistic and media production.

Religious Heritage: Gender Bias in Juristic Interpretations. In Arab Islamic history, religious culture is not built on sacred texts of indisputable authority, but, rather, on differing interpretations of the content, substance, forms and views of multiple writings and sayings in the collective memory of society. It is also based on customs and traditions that have been consolidated to preserve a specific order for the family and society.

General principles of interpretation enable us to infer the broad outlines of a social system that responds to the objectives accepted by the Islamic community in order to live a life of interdependence and consensus, while recognising the equality of all human beings, males and females. On the other hand, juristic interpretations, crystallised in some schools of Islamic jurisprudence, contributed to the establishment of a number of norms approving the principle of discrimination between the sexes.

The strictness of legislation in Islamic jurisprudence conceals other matters that originate in Arab Islamic society itself, particularly since jurists deliberately read the canonical provisions through the lens of custom. They believed that any other kind of readings would disrupt the continuity of the social order in its reinforcement of social cohesion, which, in their view, was congruent with "the order of nature".

Men have always been given priority and preference in jurisprudential studies related to women. This predisposition entrenched itself as a result of reading the Qur'an with a bias in men's favour. Nonetheless, enlightened legal interpretations did exist.

Because the dynamics of transformation in contemporary Arab societies are different from those in Arab societies at the time when the schools of jurisprudence were established, earlier endeavours are no longer appropriate to either the nature or pace of current social transformations. Rather, it is a right to try to open the gates of interpretation anew and to seek further understanding of the spirit of the Qur'anic text in order to produce jurisprudential texts based on values of equality. Such texts will seek to embody a jurisprudence of women that goes beyond the linguistic and historical equation of what is feminine with what is natural (pregnancy, childbirth, breast feeding, upbringing and cooking). They will contribute to the promotion of feminine cultural values and transform them into a general attitude.

The Arab Woman in Popular Proverbs

Arab popular culture projects contradictory images of women, girls and wives at different stages of their lives. Proverbs dealing with women are repeated in most Arab social classes and generally provide clear examples of the perception of women as inferior, indicating that popular awareness is isolated from the fundamental transformations taking place in Arab societies. The proverbs create several myths about the conditions and state of women, which often conflict with women's actual circumstances.

Hundreds of popular proverbs project an attitude akin to that which led to the burying of girls alive. In order to justify their retrograde spirit, these proverbs use moral and other arguments expressed in the language of tales and myths. Some also rely on psychology. In their various forms, these proverbs serve to underline the inferior social and moral position of women in society. Some go even further, considering a woman to have only half a mind, half a creed, and half an inheritance, and to be worth only half a male. Their general drift is to limit women's biological and domestic life and denigrate their worth and independence.

Yet several popular traditions and texts render another image of woman, a woman who is intelligent, articulate and, indeed, something of an enchantress but in the positive sense of the word.

* * *

Social Structures
Tribalism and Patriarchy

Arab tribal society understood very well the structural and functional importance of women to its existence. It viewed honour, respect and protection as a unity linking any one of its members with the whole and thus also the women with the whole, This made any interference with the status of women a matter touching the very heart of her kinfolk's security and standing.

Islam brought with it the concept of the umma (the Islamic community) as an expression of collective identity to replace that of the tribe. However, the Arab tribes, primarily the Bedouin but also the urban-rural tribes, preserved their authoritarian structures unchanged.

Although Islam established the notion of individual responsibility for both men and women, and emphasised respect for both sexes and their rights, the socio-cultural and economic-political formation of the conquests imposed limits on these broad vistas that the new religion had opened for women.

The emergence of the modern authoritarian system played a large role in curtailing the growth of civil institutions. Though European capitalism brought with it new values relating to the state, politics and society, these did not originate in local conditions. Hence the cycle through which the foundations of a law-based state and an independent civil society resistant to oppression might have been established was never completed.

Initially, the all-encompassing Arab state contributed to a greater participation by women in the public sphere, professional fields and social services, as well as to the relative protection of motherhood and childhood. But in the end, bureaucratic rigidity, the expropriation of different social and civic initiatives and the system of the local dignitary (a man, of course) as the sole intermediary between authority and society held women's rights hostage to the nature and vicissitudes of power. The symbiotic relationship between state authority and patriarchy saw to it that these early achievements soon became opportunities for personal gain. The position of women thus continued to deteriorate with the retreat of citizenship rights and the return of organic patriarchal rights as the final means of self-defence of a society forbidden to engage in the various forms of civic activity.

Relations within the family have continued to be governed by the father's authority over his children and the husband's over his wife, under the sway of the patriarchal order. Changes to which this authoritarian family framework has since been subjected cannot be considered far-reaching. Nor have they appreciably affected the functional nature of the relationship between the sexes. While they have had an effect on some forms of discrimination between men and women, they have not effected a qualitative change in the nature of the relationships between them except in limited circles. Male control at the economic, social, cultural, legal and political levels remains the abiding legacy of patriarchy.

The belief that women must be controlled remains, of course, subject to variation across different countries, social classes, standards of living and general consciousness. It shows itself particularly among the poor whose marginal position in society affords them less legal and social protection and leaves them exposed to the dominant patriarchal culture.

Yet despite lacking political freedoms, women have been able to manoeuvre under traditional social conditions to defend their rights by establishing charitable, medical or literary women's or family organisations. They have formed delegations to demand their rights, benefiting from the social space allowed them in some countries that nevertheless restrict their ideological space. Some resourceful women activists have taken advantage of this narrow latitude to establish civil society groups for women's rights, ironically creating social change out of the very structures that have restrained it.

In some societies, the qualitative accumulation of small victories by women has caused patriarchal hegemony to retreat, to varying degrees. And women often rise to the challenge of coping with harsh changes and have proven to be the protectors of social existence in exceptionally tough situations as is the case with women under siege and sanctions in Iraq, and under the multi-faceted violence afflicting Sudan, Lebanon, Iraq, and Palestine. In this sense, social structures have not prevented women, in different degrees and forms, from becoming active players in the historical transition that some Arab countries are undergoing.

The Family and the Status of Women

The family continues to be the first social institution that reproduces patriarchal relationships, values and pressures through gender discrimination. Such pressures on women increase in violence at times of crisis when a woman becomes subject to surveillance. The man's right of disposal over her body, his watch over it, his use of it, his concealment, denial and punishment of it all become more blatant. This violence in turn comes into play to intensify the feminisation of poverty, political misery, dependency, domination and alienation.

To date, personal status laws constitute the most emblematic and profound embodiment of this problem. Matrimony is the first and foremost form of the relationship between women and men whether in the conscious or unconscious mind, in religion or society, in terms of the permissible or prohibited and the sacred or the desecrated. These laws may well represent the most pronounced embodiment of the relationship between Arab patriarchy and the forbidden and the taboo. Key laws relating to gender discrimination find refuge in that relationship, allowing family laws to become the lair protecting culture, traditions and customs, religious as well as popular.

Elements of modernity have reached into Arab traditional culture, within and across countries. Nevertheless, large social sectors still remain closer to tradition than to innovation. A girl pays a heavy price for asserting her independence in milieus where individualisation in both the human rights and economic senses is weak.

Yet the Arab family is too complex to be summed up in one generalised and absolute characterisation; nor should society succumb to a negative stereotype of fatherhood. Such one-sided images lead individuals to surrender to authority figures and give credence to the notion that rebelling against authoritarianism or changing the status quo is impossible. Additionally, the assertion that women are repressed denies value to their lives, implying that these are wasted. Under the shadow of any harsh environment, a woman can yet take possession of her freedom by taking decisions that will give her unexpected happiness. This freedom is the source of the inspiration for change.

Socialisation and Education

School systems under authoritarian rule rarely give sufficient encouragement to initiative, discovery or the development of creative and critical faculties or personal aptitudes. Despite the inroads Arab women have made in political, social and economic fields, the gap between such progress and the stereotypical images of women in school curricula is enormous. Those images invariably confine a woman to the roles of mother, homemaker and housekeeper.

As a result, pedagogy specialists have demanded that some curricula be modified, and that new guidelines and concepts be formulated for content that rescues girls from the superficial setting to which they are still confined. They have also called on Arab women to participate in drawing up educational policies, a task from which they have been almost completely excluded. Female participation in the setting of school subjects was estimated at less than 8 per cent in a random sampling of Arab curricula.

Legal Structures

Many laws in the Arab countries discriminate against women. Constitutional provisions for the protection of women's rights exist in nearly all countries but are often flouted, contradicted by other legislation or not enforced. The Report illustrates a range of discriminatory provisions and practices that reveal the bias of the Arab legislator against women.

Attitudes Towards the Convention on the Elimination of All Forms of Discrimination Against Women

Most Arab states have signed and ratified CEDAW and are thus bound by its provisions, reservations excepted. Those reservations entered by Arab states (and they are many) give cause for concern; they put in doubt the will to abide by the provisions of CEDAW. Particularly worrying are their reservations with regard to Article 2, which establishes the principle of equality of men and women: reservations to this crucial article effectively render the ratifications meaningless.

Arab states based their reservations to the provisions of the Convention on one of two grounds: that the articles concerned contradicted national legislation or that they conflicted with the provisions of Shari'a (Islamic Law). On occasion this reservation was intended generally so as to absolve the state of its commitment to any provision of the Convention that it considered conflicted with Shari'a. In certain cases, a state would provide no justification for its reservation.

In a number of Arab states, and at the urging of civil society and some national institutions, legislative reviews are under way to reconsider the state's stand on reservations. This positive move deserves to be encouraged, along with greater efforts to raise awareness of the Convention in public and legislative circles and law enforcement agencies.

Constitutional Conditions

Equality in the Law. Most Arab constitutions contain provisions affirming the principle of equality in general and the principle of equality between men and women in particular. Some contain specific provisions for equality of men and women in, for example, employment in public office, political rights, and rights and duties. Some also contain provisions stipulating the right to equal opportunity; affirming the state's obligation to preserve the family, to protect motherhood and children, and to guarantee a proper balance between women's duties towards their families and their work in society; and prohibiting the employment of women in certain types of industries or at specified times of day.

Much to their credit, Arab legislators, and constitutional lawmakers in particular, have respected the principle of gender differences and have made provision for regulating the effects of these differences legislatively. Unfortunately, in many areas of law, legislators have leaned so heavily towards the principle of gender differences that they have codified gender discrimination, thereby violating the principle of equality, which is sanctified in religious canons and rendered an international obligation under international treaties.

Women's Political and Public Rights. National legislation in many Arab states contains provisions guaranteeing women's political rights and stipulating the principle of equality of men and women in the exercise of the right to participate in electoral processes and to stand for public office.

Nevertheless, despite these constitutional and legislative guarantees of women's right to political participation, the actual extent of this participation is still meagre.

The paltry representation of women in parliament in the Arab Mashriq (eastern Arab world) should impel states of this region to seriously consider emulating the example of the Arab Maghreb (North Africa), where most states have adopted quota systems to ensure a significant representation of women in their parliaments.

Parliamentary Quota Systems for Women. Even when laws provide for gender equality in political participation, such formal equality has been of little aid to women in a cultural and social environment inimical to women's acquisition and free exercise of their political rights. Affirmative legislative intervention to allocate a quota of parliamentary seats for women would help society to make amends for its historical injustice against women. Such action would also make up for lost time in giving effect to the principle of equal opportunity enshrined in many Arab constitutions. The Report firmly supports such steps.

Incrimination and Punishment. Negative discrimination between men and women can be found in the penal codes of some Arab states. For example, in some Arab penal codes, in the crime of adultery, men are held guilty only if the act takes place in the marital home. Women are guilty regardless of where the act takes place.

Arab legislators have made inroads towards eliminating gender bias in Arab penal codes, but their approach remains ad hoc and piecemeal. Attention must be given to developing a more intensive and comprehensive approach.

Personal Status Laws. Arab personal status laws, with regard to Muslims and non-Muslims alike, are witness to legally sanctioned gender bias. This stems from the fact that personal status statutes are primarily derived from theological interpretations and judgements. The latter originate in the remote past when gender discrimination permeated society and have acquired a sanctity and absoluteness in that confused area where the immutable tenets of religious creed interact with social history.

Nonetheless, evidence from the report's public opinion survey indicates that the Arab public is moving towards a more liberal perspective on personal status issues, such as asserting women's right to choose a spouse.

The Lack of Codification in Some States. Arab personal status laws remain conservative and resistant to change because a number of Arab States are reluctant to develop a national personal status code. Instead, they leave matters entirely to the judiciary, which is heavily influenced by the conservative nature of classical Islamic jurisprudence (fiqh). Some Arab states, such as Egypt, Lebanon, Qatar and Bahrain lack a unified personal status code entirely, whereas others have unified personal status codes for Muslims.

Personal status regulations for non-Muslims are derived from the canons of their respective religious sects or denominations. For the most part, these regulations sharply curtail the right of both spouses to divorce and, in some cases, prohibit it altogether.

In general, personal status law in the Maghreb is more progressive and less discriminatory than that in the Mashriq.

Nationality. In general, in Arab legislation, native nationality is determined by paternal descent. If a father is a citizen of a particular Arab country, his children acquire his nationality automatically. The children of a female national only acquire their mother's nationality if the father's identity is unknown or if he is stateless.

Recently Arab lawmakers have been working to counter the inhumane consequences of Arab states' long-held refusal to grant nationality to the children of female citizens married to foreigners (Egypt, Algeria, Lebanon).

Away from Official Law

The social environment is a crucial factor in discrimination against women, regardless of what the law may say. Because of what is commonly considered appropriate or inappropriate behaviour for a dutiful, decent and virtuous wife, recourse by a woman to the courts to demand her rights, or those of her children, is widely frowned upon as a form of public indecency. As a result, many women refrain from pursuing their family rights through official legal processes. Instead, matrimonial disputes in many Arab societies are resolved either within the family or through the unofficial channels of tribal arbitration. As these mechanisms evolved in the context of a male-dominated culture and male-oriented values, their biased outcomes are often a foregone conclusion.

Awareness of Gender Equality among Arab Legal Practitioners

Arab tribal culture, which sanctions discrimination against women, has strongly influenced juristic interpretations that establish the inferiority of women to men. Otherwise put, the male-dominated culture has been a crucial factor in shaping juristic judgements and endowing them with religious sanctity.

Some Arab legislators evince hostility towards gender equality, despite the provisions of their national constitutions and the international conventions to which their states are party. Frequently, the application of the principle of gender equality founders on the reservations of Arab judiciaries, a resistance fuelled by the growth of fundamentalist trends and their increasing impact on the legal consciousness of Arab judges. The depth of male chauvinism among members of the judiciary in some Arab states can be seen in their opposition to the appointment of female judges.

Discrimination by the legal community against women is also evident in the way judges use their discretionary authority to deliver lighter or harsher sentences in cases where a woman is one of the litigants. Many interpreters of legislation echo this discriminatory tendency when faced with the principle of equality before the law. In contrast to such views there exists a body of enlightened Islamic jurisprudence that interprets such texts in their context and inclines to the espousal of the principle of gender equality. However, the first—conservative—school of thought still finds a sympathetic ear in practice and still appeals to the man on the street because of the support it receives from conservative clerics.

* * *

A Strategic Vision: Two Wings for the Rise of Women
Key Features

The rise of Arab women must go beyond a merely symbolic makeover that permits a few distinguished Arab women to ascend to positions of leadership in State institutions. Rather, it must extend to the empowerment of the broad masses of Arab women in their entirety.

In human development terms, the rise of Arab women requires, first, that all Arab women be afforded full opportunities to acquire essential capabilities firstly and essentially in health. As a primary requirement, all Arab girls and women must also be able to acquire knowledge on an equal footing with boys and men.

Second, full opportunities must be given to Arab women to participate as they see fit in all types of human activity outside the family on an equal footing with their male counterparts.

It is also essential that the appropriate social value be given to women's role in the family as an indispensable contribution to the establishment of a sound social structure capable of supporting a project for the renaissance of the Arab world. From that follows the pivotal importance of the reform of education in Arab countries in order to ensure that all girls are guaranteed opportunities to acquire knowledge and to utilise it, within and outside the family.

In line with the calls in previous Reports for comprehensive, rights-based societal reforms, the rise of Arab women entails:

- Total respect for the rights of citizenship of all Arab women.
- The protection of women's rights in the area of personal affairs and family relations.
- Guarantees of total respect for women's personal rights and freedoms and in particular their lifelong protection from physical and mental abuse.

The achievement of these rights requires extensive legal and institutional changes aimed at bringing national legislation in line with CEDAW.

The Report also calls for the temporary adoption of the principle of affirmative action in expanding the participation of Arab women to all fields of human activity according to the particular circumstances of each society. This will allow the dismantling of the centuries-old structures of discrimination against women.

The Report envisages these societal reforms as one wing of the bird symbolising the rise of women in the Arab world.

The second wing is the emergence of a widespread and effective movement of struggle in Arab civil society. This movement will involve Arab women and their male supporters in carefully targeted societal reform on the one hand, and, on the other, empower all Arab women to enjoy the fruits of changes that serve the rise of both women and the region as a whole.

The First Wing: Societal Reform for the Rise of Women

This will address attitudinal shifts and the reform of cultural frameworks. In particular, it will modernise religious interpretation and jurisprudence through the widespread adoption of the enlightened readings of ijtihad. The latter must escape the thrall of existing religious institutions and personages to become the right and duty of every Muslim of learning, woman or man, who has the capacity to engage in the study of her or his religion.

Efforts to overcome attitudinal obstacles will extend to new syllabi and techniques in social education that promote equal treatment between the sexes. They will associate the media in educating the public to understand the significance of CEDAW. Efforts to overcome structural obstacles will include deep-seated political and legislative reforms in the areas indicated in this Report. The latter relate particularly to the functions of the judiciary at all levels, and all political, administrative, local, academic and other leadership functions.

In particular, a culture of equal treatment and respect for human rights should be encouraged among men in the judiciary and all those responsible for enforcing the rule of law.

The first wing will also address the issue of social justice, aiming to reduce the spread of income poverty by supporting economic growth, and achieving greater justice in income distribution. It will simultaneously seek to reverse the spread of human poverty, which refers to the denial to people of opportunities to acquire and effectively exercise their essential capabilities. Among the most important mechanisms for the attainment of social justice is expenditure on education, health and social safety nets.

A final priority under this wing is to confront reductions in women's personal liberties. This calls for inculcating an understanding that violence against women in all forms is a degradation of their humanity. It extends to the enactment of laws that criminalise violence against women and the provision by states and civil society of safe sanctuaries for women victims of violence.

The Second Wing: A Societal Movement Fit to Bring about the Rise of Women

The Report maintains that the rise of women cannot be separated from a wide and effective movement in Arab civil society aimed at achieving human development for all. Such a movement will be the means by which Arab women may empower themselves and their male supporters. It will have two levels. The first is national and will involve all levels of society in every Arab country. The second is regional: it will be founded on trans-border networks for the co-ordination and support of regional efforts to achieve a comprehensive Arab movement for the rise of Arab women, benefiting from modern information and communications technology. The movement will give birth to active civil society organisations in the Arab world linked to politically neutral international and UN organisations working for women's advancement.

This movement will begin by focusing on two sets of priorities:

1. Eliminating Women's Legacy of Deprivation in Health and in Knowledge through Education: Health. This requires guaranteeing that all women enjoy good health, in the positive and comprehensive sense. Thus, the general trend to ensure positive health for all, which is an integral part of human development, extends automatically to the provision of special care for the needs of the weak in general and of women in particular. Implementation of the Report's recommendations for the elimination of poverty, and especially human poverty, are relevant here.

Ending the Denial of Education to Girls and Women. Ending once and for all the denial to girls and women of their human right to education over a period of, say, ten years is an indispensable requirement. The movement will be called upon to embark on a serious programme, with official and civic dimensions, as well as regional and national ones, over a finite decade, which would ensure all girls and women a complete basic education. The goal will be to achieve, by 2015, the eradication of Arab female illiteracy, and to ensure that every Arab girl completes twelve years of basic schooling.

2. Eliminating Stubborn Obstacles to Women's Use of Their Capabilities as They See Fit. Priorities in this focus area include:

- Accelerating the rate of economic growth to enable the creation of employment opportunities on a large scale. The significant increase in the price of oil over the last few years constitutes a revenue source that may enable Arab economies to develop and diversity their productive infrastructure.
- Resisting the cultural obstacles facing women's employment of their full capacities in all areas of human development as freely chosen by them.
- Guaranteeing in Arab constitutions, legislation and implementation mechanisms equality of employment opportunities for all regardless of gender.
- Guaranteeing women's enjoyment of appropriate working conditions consistent with human dignity, and when necessary, providing some aspects of positive discrimination, protective of their family roles, without making them pay for this preferential treatment, by decreasing their work privileges vis-à-vis men.
- Building the mechanisms of an efficient and modern labour market both at the regional and national level, equally open to both women and men.

Conclusion

This Report argues that the rise of women is in fact a prerequisite for an Arab renaissance, inseparably and causally linked to the fate of the Arab world and its achievement of human development.

Despite Arab women's equal rights under international law, their demonstrated talents and achievements in different spheres of human activity and their priceless contributions to their families and society, many are not encouraged to develop and use their capabilities on an equal footing with men. In public life, cultural, legal, social, economic and political factors impede women's equal access to education, health, job opportunities, citizenship rights and representation. In private life, traditional patterns of upbringing and discriminatory family and personal status laws perpetuate inequality and subordination. At a time when the Arab world needs to build and tap the capabilities of all its peoples, fully half its human potential is often stifled or neglected.

In the short run, time-bound affirmative action to expand women's participation in society and dismantle centuries-old discrimination is both legitimate and imperative. However, the comprehensive advancement of Arab women requires accelerating and expanding past achievements through a collective renaissance project: a historic transformation that encompasses all of Arab society and aims to secure the citizenship rights of all Arabs, women and men equally.

The authors hope that the transformation they call for will be carried out under their preferred future scenario by taking the path of a vibrant human renaissance (izdihar) based on a peaceful process of negotiation for redistributing power and building good governance. Guaranteeing Arab societies the key freedoms of opinion, expression and assembly will facilitate the emergence of a dynamic, effective civil society as the vanguard of such a peaceful process that will avoid the impending disaster whose dark clouds are gathering in more than one key Arab country at this time.

12.2

IS AFRICA'S ECONOMY AT A
TURNING POINT?

Jorge Arbache, Delfin S. Go, and John Page

This excerpt from a World Bank study reviews the progress of African countries over the past two decades. You might be thinking, why should I read such a technical and boring account? Well, one reason is that you can't help African countries much with your heart until you understand African economies more with your head. When you are ignorant of the technical features of economic development, whatever you do risks being undone by broader mechanisms such as macroeconomic policies, exchange rates, good versus corrupt governance, domestic prices, aid flows, oil and trade transactions, business practices, infrastructure, and education. If you introduce micro-lending into a country to help women sell vegetables and don't know that monetary policy in that country is so loose that inflation and high interest rates will offset the benefits of the loans, you haven't helped anyone. Or if you help rural farmers become more efficient producing their food crops but are unaware that the government controls all food purchases and pays low prices to feed urban elites, you have helped the government and urban populations obtain more abundant food supplies at even cheaper prices, not raised the returns going to rural farmers.

Introduction

There is something decidedly different and new about the economic landscape of Sub-Saharan Africa (Africa or the region hereafter). After stagnating for much of 45 years, economic performance in Africa is markedly improving. In recent years, for example, GDP growth in SSA is accelerating to its strongest point at about 6 percent a year while inflation registered below two-digit level, its lowest point. The much improved economic performance is confirmed by several recent assessments.[1]

Although the current economic growth is still short-lived relative to Africa's long history of growth crisis and is certainly nowhere close to the standard of East Asia, it is nonetheless noteworthy and a cause for guarded optimism.

Source: Jorge Arbache, Delfin S. Go, and John Page, "Is Africa's Economy at a Turning Point?" in *Africa at a Turning Point? Growth, Aid, and External Shocks,* ed. Delfin S. Go and John Page (Washington, D.C.: The International Bank for Reconstruction and Development/The World Bank, 2008), 13–85.

The performance at least calls for a closer examination. Several interesting questions can immediately be raised: Is Africa finally overcoming the challenges of growth and poverty to claim the 21st century, as posed, for example, by Gelb et al. (2000), Collier (2007), and Ndulu et al. (2007)? In particular, is there indeed a turning point? How widespread are the recent gains among the 47 countries in the region? What are the key factors underlying the recent improvements in Africa's economic performance? Why have the recent oil price increases not dampened its growth performance? Is the growth robust and supported by improvements in the economic fundamentals? What major risks and challenges remain? Will Africa attain the Millennium Development Goals by 2015?

* * *

The Recent Acceleration of Growth in Africa

Is the growth failure in Sub-Saharan Africa finally reversing? An upward shift in the recent growth rates suggests that a trend break may have taken place around the mid-1990s.[2] Annual GDP growth was a sluggish 2.9 percent in the 1980s and 1.7 percent during 1990–94. Since 1994, however, the pace of economic expansion has approached the threshold of moderate growth of 5 percent a year. Even if the record is measured more conservatively with regard to per capita income, the shift is perceptible: relative to its prolonged stagnation or contraction, per capita income grew by 1.6 percent a year in the late 1990s and by 2.1 percent to 3.0 percent a year since 2000. Despite the recent oil price shock, growth has remained good. From 2004 to 2006, the annual growth in GDP and per capita income, when weighted by each country's GDP, approaches 6 and 4 percent, respectively. Although improvement in aggregate output does not necessarily indicate broad economic development of the region, the current growth episode has nonetheless lasted 12 years altogether, a period that is neither trivial nor brief.

* * *

How Widespread Is the Current Growth Acceleration?

The recent economic expansion seems to be registering across an increasing number of countries. The number of countries with economic declines dropped from 15 to 18 in the early 1990s to about 2 to 5 countries in recent years. Only one country has significant economic contraction—Zimbabwe.[3] In contrast, about 40–45 countries have positive growth, and 14–19 countries are growing by more than 5 percent a year.

During 2000–06, about 26 countries had GDP growth exceeding 4 percent a year, while as many as 14 countries exceeded 5.5 percent. Countries with at least 4 percent GDP growth now constitute a sizable portion of Sub-Saharan Africa—about 70 percent of the region's total population and 80 percent of the region's GDP. As a group, these countries have been growing consistently at nearly 7 percent a year, whether considered in the more recent period or a longer period since the mid-1990s.... There are some exceptions near the cut-off point: the performance of São Tomé and Principe, Sierra Leone, South Africa, and Zambia has improved in performance during the more recent period (2004–06), whereas that of Malawi and, to a smaller extent, Cameroon and Mauritius has deteriorated.

*   *   *

Large Countries. Nigeria and South Africa are the two largest economies in Sub-Saharan Africa, accounting for almost half the regional GDP and one-fourth the population. Their slow growths in the past have tended to pull down any regional growth averages, especially if GDP weights were used. However, the growth performance of Nigeria and South Africa has improved significantly since 2000. During 2004–06 in particular, their GDP growth reached about 6.2 and 5.0 percent a year, respectively. The rest of Sub-Saharan Africa continued to do better at 6.5 percent a year during 2004–06. The weighted average (about 6 percent) for the whole region is better than its simple average (about 5 percent) for the same period, which suggests that large countries in general are doing well.

Oil Exporting Countries. Higher oil prices since 2000 now directly benefit eight countries where net oil exports make up 30 percent or more of total exports: Angola, Cameroon, Chad, Republic of Congo, Equatorial Guinea, Gabon, Nigeria, and Sudan. Côte d'Ivoire is also producing oil, but its net exports of oil are still low. Angola and Nigeria are the largest oil exporters, accounting for about 20 percent and 53 percent, respectively, of Africa's total oil exports. As a group, the oil exporters represent about 25 and 29 percent of Africa's GDP and population, respectively. Moreover, fuel now makes up about 40 percent of Africa's total merchandise exports.

Partly as a result of the recent higher oil prices, real GDP growth in oil-exporting countries accelerated to about 8.4 percent a year during 2000–06. This growth represents the strongest economic expansion among the possible country groupings. Growth during the 1990s was also significant at 5.9 percent a year.

Oil Importing Countries by Endowment and Location. Although growth in oil-importing countries lagged behind the regional average, it has also been improving, reaching 4.7 percent during 2004–06. This group is large and diverse, encompassing the majority of African countries and a wide range of characteristics. For digging deeper, the classification of countries by endowment and location ... is useful. Countries are grouped in a nonoverlapping way as non-oil resource-intensive countries, coastal, and landlocked countries.[4]

The six *non-oil resource-intensive countries* represent roughly 4.9 percent of Africa's GDP and 4.2 percent of its population.[5] Like the oil exporters, the group also did very well relative to its own past performance: 5.1 percent during 2000–06 or 5.7 percent since 2000.

The 19 *coastal countries* account for about 53 percent of the regional GDP and 32 percent of the total population.[6] This group has been growing by 3.4 percent a year since 2000—a rate that has further improved to 4.4 percent a year during 2004–06.

The 13 *landlocked countries* were traditionally the laggards in growth.[7] Although they represent as much as 32 percent of the total population in the region, they take up only 17 percent of the regional income. Annual growth in GDP since 2000 has averaged only 3 percent but has improved to 4.2 percent recently. The individual records are mixed. Although the group includes noted growth failures such as the Central African Republic and Zimbabwe, it nonetheless has several bright spots: Burkina Faso, Ethiopia, Mali, Rwanda, and Uganda.

Oil Importing Countries by Income and Fragile States. An alternative classification of the oil-importing countries is by income level and fragile states—that is, low- and middle-income countries plus fragile states....

The eight *middle-income countries* correspond to less than 8 percent of the region's total population but to 40 percent of regional income.[8] South Africa alone represents 6.3 percent of the population and 35 percent of Africa's GDP. The individual performances in this group have been mixed: whereas South Africa's performance has been improving in recent periods, that of others (such as the Seychelles, Swaziland, and to some extent Mauritius) has slowed down. Zimbabwe, which used to be in this group, is now a fragile low-income country. As a result of the mixed performance of several countries, average growth for the group has fallen slightly from the 1980s and 1990s. However, growth during 2004–06 has again rebounded to about 4 percent a year.

Fifteen countries may be classified as *low income* and non-oil exporting.[9] They are home to 45 percent of the total population but only 25 percent of the total income in the region. However, the recent performance of the group is heartening: growth has been steadily improving, from 2.1 percent a year in the 1980s to 3.5 percent in the 1990s and 4.9 percent since 2000. In recent years, growth has been approaching 5.6 percent annually. The top performers in this group include Ghana, Mozambique, Senegal, and Tanzania plus the bright spots mentioned for landlocked countries: Burkina Faso, Ethiopia, Mali, Rwanda, and Uganda.

Fragile states without significant oil resources—14 countries—still account for 18 percent of the total population and 10 percent of total income in the region.[10] For the most part, GDP growth in this group is stuck at less than 2.5 percent, but it improved to 3.2 percent during 2004–06. The challenges faced by this group are many and daunting, as has been portrayed persuasively by sources such as Collier (2007) and the World Bank (2007b, 2007c). Even so, there are hopeful signs; a few countries have managed to turn around at least their output growth: The Gambia, Liberia, São Tomé and Principe, and Sierra Leone.

* * *

Good Luck or Good Policy: How Robust Is the Recent Growth?

Today's Africa is clearly different from the Africa of the early 1990s, when it was coming out of the declines after the first two oil price shocks, the debt problems, and stagnation of the adjustment years. Thanks to the recent acceleration of growth, there is definitely a higher economic base to work with. But how sustainable is that growth? Are the main contributing factors good luck or good policy? As the growth diagnostics so far indicate, the answer hinges not only on policy and governance but also on economic fundamentals, such as factor accumulation and productivity as well as trade and export diversification—and the significance of the changes in these fundamentals....

Commodity Prices and Terms-of-Trade. External circumstances have certainly been favorable since the mid-1990s: the global economy has been expanding at 3.2 percent a year, global trade expanded by 40 percent a year, and the share of FDI in the world GDP nearly doubled from 1.15 percent in 1995 to more than 2.23 percent in 2005. As a result of greater demand, commodity prices, including oil prices, have been pushed to new high levels. Hence, the better economic performance in the recent period is certainly partly due to the higher export prices of many African countries. Higher oil prices now benefit about 8–10 oil-exporting countries in Sub-Saharan Africa. Non-oil commodity prices have also risen significantly. Of the 40 commodity prices monitored regularly, only cotton prices declined from the high prices of the 2003 drought year. Hence, gains from higher export prices for commodities such as gold, aluminum, copper, and nickel more than offset the losses from higher oil import bills in several oil-importing countries, such as Burundi, Ghana, Guinea, Mali, Mozambique, Rwanda, Uganda, Zambia, and Zimbabwe. Overall, compared with the previous major oil price cycle during 1973–1980, the aggregate terms of trade for Sub-Saharan African countries have fared much more favorably in the current oil price cycle, relative to their respective starting points.[11]

For oil-importing countries, the weakening of the U.S. dollar has also meant that the oil price in euros or local currency has not risen as much. For Sub-Saharan Africa in particular, the real price increases of oil were in fact significantly lower than the recent nominal price increases quoted in dollars, after adjusting for exchange rate movements and domestic inflation. Since 2000, the nominal price of oil has tripled, whereas the real price has doubled. Although the nominal price was approaching $100 a barrel toward the end of 2007, the real oil price for oil importers in Africa was only 2.6 percent higher than in 2006.

Nonetheless, although economic performance remains strong in many African countries, several non-resource-rich countries will have to be monitored because their terms-of-trade losses were exacerbated by unfavorable changes in both oil and import prices. These countries include Benin, Burkina Faso, Cape Verde, Comoros, Eritrea, Ethiopia, The Gambia, Kenya, Lesotho, Madagascar, Mauritius, Niger, Senegal, the Seychelles, and Togo. In most cases, the additional negative shock came from prices of staple imports, such as wheat, rice, and vegetable oils. Eritrea, for example, had an estimated negative terms-of-trade impact of greater than 5 percent of GDP from higher food prices, while Lesotho, Mauritania, Senegal, and Togo had an estimated negative terms-of-trade impact in excess of 2 percent of GDP because of changes in food prices.

Effects of External Shocks on Growth and Poverty. The importance of terms-of-trade shocks in Sub-Saharan Africa has been evolving. Historical data suggest that external shocks are important determinants of growth in Africa.... [A]id may mitigate the negative consequences of external shocks. However, ... positive external shocks are strongly correlated only with short-term economic expansions, not with sustained growth episodes.... [Oil prices] are not particularly important for output volatility in the typical African country, but only among those countries that are net oil exporters. Without compensating developments, such as higher export prices, exogenous flows, or adjustment policies, however, the marginal impact of an oil price shock can be quite significant....

Aid Flows and Debt Relief. Moreover, new commitments to scale up foreign aid from industrial countries have already led to greater external resources and debt relief for poor countries. Recent aid commitments and actual disbursements (inclusive of debt relief) have already recovered to the high points of the early 1990s. Moreover, additional and significant debt relief became a reality when the World Bank and IMF approved the financing and implementation of the Multilateral Debt Relief Initiative (MDRI) starting on July 1, 2006. Sixteen countries in Sub-Saharan Africa, together accounting for 23 percent of the regional income but 43 percent of the total population, have now reached the completion point for significant debt relief under the enhanced Heavily Indebted Poor Country Initiative and have qualified for further assistance from the MDRI. Benefiting from debt relief, MDRI countries did very well recently and grew by over 5.3 percent during 2000–06.[12]

Nonetheless, the promises made at the Gleneagles summit to scale up aid have yet to materialize. In particular, aid still has to go much beyond the high points of the 1990s to double by 2010, as pledged by donors....

* * *

Better Leadership. However, the current acceleration of growth is not all due to luck; better policy seems to be taking place in Sub-Saharan Africa. Africa today enjoys better economic prospects because its leaders have undertaken major reforms during the past 10 years and are taking increasing control of their economic destiny. African governments are making regional initiatives in conflict resolution and are taking action to improve governance under the African Union and the New Partnership for Africa's Development initiatives. These initiatives are designed to

- Push African countries to be assertive about ownership and to assume leadership and accountability for their development programs.

- Improve the reputation of the region through certification of good practices in governance for a critical mass of African countries under the African Peer Review mechanism.
- Increase regional connectivity to improve capacity to trade within the region and with the outside world.
- Enhance the capacity of a rationalized system of regional bodies to provide regional public goods, such as cross-country transportation and power sharing, coordination in managing pandemics, and protection of regional commons such as the Nile and the Great Lakes.

Overall Policy and Institutional Environment. Although there is no perfect or leading indicator of the overall quality of policy and institutional environment, the World Bank's CPIA provides a consistent framework for assessing country performance on 16 items, which are grouped into four wide-ranging clusters: economic management, structural policies, policies for social inclusion and equity, and public sector management and institutions.

The average CPIA scores for African countries have been rising. The average CPIA score in 1995 was 2.8. By 2006, it had risen to 3.2. The number of African countries with scores equal to or greater than the threshold of 3.5 for international good performance had also risen, from 5 countries in 1997 to 17 in 2006.

Economic performance among African countries is highly correlated with the quality of policy. Countries with CPIA scores of greater than or equal to 3.5 by 2006 tend to have higher growth and lower inflation than those with scores lower than 3.5 (excluding Zimbabwe). The low-income countries (excluding middle-income and oil-exporting countries) with good policy and institutional environment are in fact doing very well: growth averaged 5.1 percent and inflation was 6.9 percent.

Macroeconomic Management. The most striking improvement in policy is observed for macroeconomic stabilization. Inflation among African countries has come down dramatically since 1995. The number of countries able to keep inflation below 10 percent a year increased from 11–26 in the early 1990s to about 31–35 since 2000. From the 1980s to the present, there were as many as 10 different African countries with hyperinflation (greater than 50 percent) at one point or another. The extreme values can run over thousands of percentage points. The countries with hyperinflation have included Angola, the Democratic Republic of Congo, Guinea, Guinea-Bissau, Mozambique, São Tomé and Principe, Sierra Leone, Sudan, Uganda, Zambia, and Zimbabwe.

In recent years, all these countries except Zimbabwe have been able to contain inflation drastically. The regional average has fallen below 10 percent since 2002.[13] This performance is all the more remarkable in view of the significant increase in oil prices that started in 1999.

Another indicator of macroeconomic stabilization, the overall fiscal balance, also improved.[14] The average fiscal deficit as a percentage of GDP in African countries declined from 5.7 percent during the 1980s and 1990s to 2.9 percent during 2000–06. Fiscal policy in oil-exporting countries has also improved. Unlike the unchecked wasteful spending in the past, windfalls from oil revenue are increasingly being saved. At the start of the current oil price shock, fiscal deficits were increasingly reduced, and by 2004–06, the overall fiscal surplus averaged about 8 percent for the group.…

Adjustment to Higher Oil Prices. For the past seven to eight years, most oil-importing countries in Africa have already been slowly adjusting to the new and higher trend of oil prices, and their ability to continue the adjustment will be the key to future growth, especially if higher oil prices persist. Since 2003, the majority of African countries have allowed frequent and full passthrough of higher oil prices to domestic prices. The passthrough is less pronounced in oil-exporting countries. A few countries, such as Côte d'Ivoire and Ethiopia, have at one point or another suspended the use of formulas in favor of less frequent and ad hoc adjustments. Many countries have also tried to protect the poor by limiting price increases and taxation of kerosene. For 14 African countries for which data are available, petroleum subsidies increased from 0.75 percent of GDP in 2003 to 1 percent in 2005. On average, petroleum taxes are important sources of revenue and constitute close to 2 percent of GDP in indirect taxes.

In a recent Energy Sector Management Assistance Program (ESMAP)[15] study of 31 developing countries, the amount of passthrough in gasoline and diesel was found to be positively correlated with a country's terms of trade and inflation (GDP deflator) and negatively correlated with a country's oil vulnerability, overall fiscal position, and per capita income or growth; interestingly, it is also negatively correlated with whether a country is an oil producer or exporter. The debt-to-GDP ratio affects gasoline pricing negatively but not diesel pricing. The 31 developing countries in the sample showed less passthrough of oil cost when compared with industrial countries, particularly with respect to diesel. However, the results for 11 African countries confirmed that African countries have not been delaying adjustment to their fuel prices, even when compared with developed countries; hence, the risks of an unsustained fiscal position appear to be less than in past episodes of oil price shocks. Overall, diesel prices tended to be protected from increases to protect the poor—although such increases are implemented relatively less often in African countries. Outside of a few instances in which market mechanisms were directly suspended, African governments have been actively intervening in the fuel markets in other ways to help the poor or consumers: by adjusting taxes and subsidies, regulating margins, mandating conservation measures and cash transfers, and so forth.[16]

Exchange Rate Regimes. Unlike the past, countries with flexible exchange regimes now account for about 76 percent of Africa's GDP and 68 percent of the region's population. In recent years, and during the current oil price shock, these countries have also tended to grow better than the regional average and better than countries with fixed exchange rates. In franc zone countries, a strong currency tied to the euro is bringing about concerns regarding real exchange rate appreciation and its impact on export competitiveness.

Reduction of Policy Mistakes across Countries. Hence, though external circumstances have been favorable, there is also strong evidence that African countries have increasingly learned to avert economic mistakes and have avoided bad leadership, conflict, corruption, and macroeconomic instability. Such reduction of policy mistakes is central to preventing growth collapses—a key point from the growth analysis described earlier.

... The likelihood of growth decelerations has clearly declined by half across the board for different types of countries to about 12–14 percent, which is the average for Africa during 1995–2005. In addition, the probability of major conflict has declined the most: from 17 to 6 percent. Likewise, the likelihood of growth acceleration has improved for different types of countries. That said, oil exporters and resource-rich countries have experienced more growth accelerations than all other country subsets—well above the mean for the entire period or all countries during same recent period. This finding suggests that better commodity prices and terms of trade were still significant factors; for the recent period at least, possessing mineral resources has not been a curse to growth.

Economic Fundamentals before and after 1995. If growth is robust, economic fundamentals should have become stronger in the past decade....

Progress among all African countries was observed in the means of several economic fundamentals for all economic episodes, but the record was not uniform. Savings were higher than in the previous decade. Although aggregate investments did not change significantly, private investment and FDI went up. In particular, FDI increased by threefold in the period 1995–2005, to 5 percent from 1.5 percent in the previous decade. Nonetheless, neither the magnitudes of savings and investments as a percentage of GDP nor their changes were large, relative to levels in other successful sustained-growth economies (such as those in South and East Asia).

Trade as a share of GDP increased significantly (by about 8 percent) with exports and imports increasing by 4 percent each. The small change in the current account balance was not statistically significant, remaining close to about 6 percent. The real exchange rate appreciated substantially to an index of 103.5 from 138.0 in 1985–94, most likely as a result of favorable commodity prices since 2000. This trend raises concerns that the export competitiveness of nonprimary exports will continue to be an issue. On average, the terms of trade became slightly less favorable in the more recent decade, also reflecting the offsetting patterns before and after 2000. Average inflation was cut by half, but the change was not statistically significant because of large variations in the consumer price indexes of individual countries. The present value of public debt increased significantly, but it is likely that these data do not reflect fully the debt relief in more recent years. Government consumption decreased by about 2 percent of GDP to 15.5 percent from 17.2 percent, while no significant difference was observed for private consumption.

... For non-resource-rich countries, improvements were also observed for FDI, trade, exports, and imports in the full sample, but they were slightly more muted when compared with the results for all countries. The means for the real exchange rate, terms of trade, public debt, and government were significantly different in the two decades and more or less followed the same pattern as for all countries. In contrast, the means for savings and private investments in non-resource-rich countries were not significantly different in the two periods. The reduction in inflation remains insignificant because of great variation.

The results are somewhat more favorable for the resource-rich countries. Savings and aggregate investments in resource-rich countries experienced substantial increases (by about 5 percent of GDP) in 1995–2005. FDI showed an impressive jump to 8.2 percent of GDP from 1.8 percent, confirming that most FDI flows to Africa are concentrated in the mineral sectors. No significant change was observed for private investment. Mineral wealth did not lead to a higher level of private and public consumption, suggesting that windfall revenue was increasingly saved. However, public debt still increased. Trade, particularly exports, increased more than imports, but not enough to turn the current accounts into surplus. The real exchange rate appreciated, as expected, but as for other countries, the terms of trade became less favorable. Inflation did not improve, and the level was high on average for 1995–2005.

Important compositional effects were at work, affecting the differences of means for the subset of countries experiencing growth accelerations. Savings for all African countries undergoing growth accelerations, for instance, fell significantly, from 21 percent in 1985–94 to 13 percent in 1995–2005. Two factors were at work. Because the probability of a growth acceleration was higher during 1995–2005, the number of observations was larger (for example, 201 country-years for savings), pulling in a wider variety of country circumstances, including economies with low savings rates. In contrast, the probability of a growth acceleration was much lower for 1985–94, and the number of observations was therefore few (for example, 84 country-years for savings). However, the countries that did grow during this more difficult period had substantially better economic indicators than those experiencing normal or bad times. In addition to savings, compositional effects for all countries were also observed in aggregate investment, trade, exports, imports, and terms of trade. This factor was less important for FDI, the real exchange rate, public consumption, and public debt.

In general, there were more significant compositional effects for non-resource-rich countries than for resource-rich countries during growth accelerations. The effect was common only for savings. In non-resource-rich countries, these compositional effects were also observed for aggregate investment, private sector investment, trade, exports, and imports. One area in which the non-resource-rich countries did much better during growth accelerations was inflation: not only was the level much lower in the second period, but also the means in the two periods were significantly different.

Overall, there is therefore modest evidence of improvements in economic fundamentals, in particular for resource-rich countries. The data are, however, somewhat mixed, and the robustness of Africa's growth remains fragile.

* * *

Key Areas of Actions to Sustain Growth

The avoidance of economic collapses will continue to depend on good policy, leadership, and aid. To sustain an accelerating growth, however, the region will have to tackle several barriers and constraints to greater productivity and investment. Addressing these barriers will require both continuing reforms and greater external assistance.

... Research shows that efficient African enterprises can compete with Chinese and Indian firms in factory floor costs. They become less competitive, though, because of higher indirect business costs, including infrastructure. In China, indirect costs are about 8 percent of total costs, but in African countries they are 18–35 percent.

Building the African private sector will be crucial both for growth and for fostering a national consensus for growth-oriented policies. Improving the investment climate and enhancing the capacity of African entrepreneurs to invest and engage in business are central to this effort.

Africa remains a high-cost, high-risk place to do business. Overall, the cost of doing business in Africa is 20–40 percent above that for other developing regions, including the costs associated with bureaucracy, corruption, risk, and essential business services. During 2006/07, the average rank of African countries was 136 in the Doing Business indicators, but four middle-income countries rank in the top third: Mauritius, 32; South Africa, 35; Namibia, 43; and Botswana, 51. Value-chain analysis ... also indicated several choke points in the supply chain for African firms: high cost of import logistics and time, low speed to market delivery, high cost of export logistics, and high incidence of rejects.

The picture is somewhat brighter for additional reforms, albeit still uneven. Forty-six sub-Saharan countries introduced at least one business environment reform in 2006/07, and Ghana and Kenya were among the top 10 reformers (Tanzania was also on the list in 2005/06). Kenya rose from 82 to 72, and Ghana from 109 to 87. But all others had ranks of 90 or higher. Nonetheless, several countries saw improvements: Mozambique went from 140 to 134, Madagascar from 160 to 149, and Burkina Faso from 161 to 165. In 2005/06, the region came in third behind Eastern Europe and Central Asia and Organisation for Economic Co-operation and Development countries with regard to countries that made at least one positive reform.

Improving the performance of Africa's financial systems is also high on the agenda for enterprise development. Firms in Africa identify financing constraints as even more severe than lack of infrastructure in limiting their business development.

Closing the Infrastructure Gap

An export push requires an infrastructure push in Africa, because many of the bottlenecks pertain to lack of infrastructure. Sub-Saharan Africa lags at least 20 percentage points behind the average for International Development Association countries on almost all major infrastructure measures.[17] In addition, quality of service is low, supplies are unreliable, and disruptions are frequent and unpredictable—all pushing up production costs, a critical impediment for investors. There are also large inequities in access to household infrastructure services, with coverage rates in rural areas lagging those in urban areas. The region's unmet infrastructure needs are estimated at $22 billion a year (5 percent of GDP), plus another $17 billion for operations and maintenance. Recent progress is encouraging. Except roads, indicators of infrastructure access rose between the 1990s and 2000s. The Africa Partnership Forum reported steady improvements in effectively using existing infrastructure and in increasing public investments. Countries are also undertaking regulatory and policy reforms, especially for water, telecommunications, and transport. Twenty of the largest African countries have or are formulating reform agendas for water and sanitation.

Compared with other regions, Africa has been slow to mobilize the private sector for the provision and financing of infrastructure. The Infrastructure Consortium reports that private sector interest has gradually spread. There is an upward trend in private sector provision and management of infrastructure, which stood at $6 billion in 2006, up from $4 billion in 2004. Most private flows (84 percent) go to telecommunications and energy. Concessions have now been awarded to operate and rehabilitate many African ports and railways and some power distribution enterprises, but financial commitments by the concessionaire companies are often small. The small commitments reflect both the value of the management improvements that the concessionaire is expected to bring and the limited scale and profitability of the enterprises taken over. An important facilitator in some cases has been the insurance instruments developed over the past 15 years by such bodies as the U.S. Overseas Private Investment Corporation and the Multilateral Investment Guarantee Agency and by the World Bank's Partial Risk Guarantee offerings.

There has been significant progress in information and communication technology. Access to communications services has increased dramatically over the past three years, with the proportion of the population (excluding South Africa) living under the mobile telephone footprint rising from 3 percent in 1999 to 50 percent in 2006. This increase has been matched by an equally rapid increase in the use of communications services. By the end of 2006, there were 123 million mobile subscribers. Average penetration rates in the region doubled between 2004 and 2006 to reach 16 percent.

Integrating the Region's Economies

The small size of African economies and the fact that many countries are landlocked call for regional approaches to common problems: infrastructure in trade corridors; common institutional and legal frameworks (customs adminis-tration, competition policy, regulation of common property resources, such as fisheries); and transborder solutions to regional health issues.

African leaders have become more aware of the benefits of regional approaches, especially in matters related to trade and infrastructure. The New Partnership for Africa's Development has adopted regional integration as one of its core objectives, and the African Union is leading efforts to rationalize regional economic communities. Most countries in Africa are party to multiple treaties or conventions addressing joint development and management of shared water resources (including navigation and fisheries), hydropower, trade corridors, irrigation, and flood control. Progress has been most notable in regional infrastructure, particularly regional power pools (in West Africa and southern Africa) and in launching customs unions (in West Africa, East Africa, and southern Africa). Progress on regional infrastructure is slowed by the tech-nical complexity of multicountry projects and the time required for decisions by multiple governments. There is less progress in creating regional approaches to education and in systematically addressing regional health issues.

Making Agriculture More Productive

Sustained growth that reduces rural poverty will require that more countries achieve 5 percent annual growth in agricultural value added. Although growth in agricultural value added has been strong since 2000, averaging 4.6 percent in 2004, too little of it has come from higher productivity or yields.[18] Although land productivity is increasing in 38 of 46 countries, only 6 have a rate of increase of 5 percent or more.[19] Labor productivity is increasing in 29 countries, with 10 achieving increases of 3 percent a year or higher.[20]

Productivity growth will require an expansion of irrigated areas, as well as better performance of rain-fed agriculture. But less than 4 percent of cultivated land is irrigated. Because of the long lead time before investments are completed and operational, this proportion changed little in recent years. Improvements in management of soil fertility have been slow, as has been the adoption of better seeds. Spending for agricultural research and technology remains low, although it is starting to increase along with overall spending on agricultural programs in the region. On a positive note, there has been an increase in the use of water management techniques (water harvesting, reduced tillage).

Using Natural Resource Rents Well

Resource-based rents are widespread and growing because of new discoveries and favorable prices. During the 1990s, 65 percent of all FDI was concentrated in oil, gas, and mining. Between 2000 and 2010, $200 billion in oil revenue will accrue to African governments. The 2004 oil windfall alone on average resulted in a 26 percent increase in government revenue in oil-exporting countries.

However, in Africa, mineral-dependent countries tend to do worse in social indicators than non-mineral countries at the same income level, including having higher poverty rates, greater income inequality, less spending on health care, higher prevalence of child malnutrition, and lower literacy and school enrollments. But mineral-exporting economies can achieve shared growth. Indonesia, and Malaysia have all used natural resource wealth to provide a basis for a more diversified economy in which the poor have been able to participate and contribute to the process of growth.

Elements of a strategy for mineral revenue management include the following:

- Promote transparency in accounting for revenues by adopting the EITI.
- Establish fiscal rules, including setting savings rules and maintaining fiscal discipline in decentralized fiscal systems.
- Strengthen public financial management and the Medium Term Expenditure Framework.
- Monitor and evaluate outcomes.

Increasing Regional and Global Support

Developing and implementing regional strategies for increasing connectivity to the world and within Africa are crucial. Cross-country infrastructure projects are particularly important, but so too are institutional reforms, such as common customs procedures, that lower transactions costs. Complementary action by the global development community to reduce barriers to trade and to scale up aid to enhance the region's capacity to trade is also required.

Sharing the Benefits of Growth

Growth alone will not be enough to reach the Millennium Development Goals (MDGs) for Africa. At the same time that Africa's governments are pursuing a new growth strategy—and with the same vigor—they will also need to focus on delivering more and better services for human development.

Many MDGs Will Not Be Met

Despite the recent good performance, Africa's GDP per capita is still 50 percent of the level of East Asia, and the growth rate is far short of the 7 percent needed if poverty is to be halved by 2015. The mean income/expenditure of the poor, those earning less than one PPP dollar a day, is much lower in Africa than in East Asia or South Asia. Africa is far behind all other regions in terms of the UN human development index. It will also remain behind on most MDGs; if current trends continue, it will not meet the 2015 targets. In 1990, 47 percent of Africans lived in poverty. In 2004, 41 percent did, and with present trends, 37 percent will in 2015.

Although Sub-Saharan Africa is one of two regions not expected to reach most of the MDGs by 2015 (the other is South Asia), there is substantial variation among countries in both the level of attainment of the goals and the pace of progress. Mauritius has met four goals. Botswana has met three and will likely meet one more. And South Africa has met three. Among other countries, 9 will meet two goals, and 13 will meet at least one. But despite better progress—especially in education, malaria, and HIV/AIDS—23 African countries are unlikely to meet any of the MDGs. Scaling up the efforts on MDGs presents several challenges in low-income country and a recent paper by Lofgren and Diaz-Bonilla (2008) examines the trade-offs and scenarios in the case of Ethiopia.

Sharing the Benefits of Public Services Will Be Key

Africa has the lowest and most unequal access to essential services. In the 1960s and into the 1970s, many African countries widened access to essential social services and saw significant improvements in many social indicators. However, this progress did not prove sustainable. Africa has the lowest access to all essential services. Service delivery is costly for African governments because of long distances and sparsely populated areas.

The rural populations have extremely limited access to services of decent quality, including education, health care, safe drinking water, paved roads, and telecommunications. They also lack access to factors of production, such as means of transportation, fertilizer, and improved seeds.

Women in Africa provide more than half the region's labor but lack equal access to education and factors of production. Gender differentials in the areas of labor force participation and labor productivity are constraints to economic growth. A study in Kenya, for example, concluded that giving women farmers the same level of agricultural inputs and education as men could increase their yields by more than 20 percent.

Service Delivery Must Reach the Poor, Rural Populations, and Women

African rural populations and the poor have a distinct disadvantage in their access to services. To build and sustain service delivery, African countries will need to do the following:

- Improve social sector policies.
- Strengthen financial management and costing.
- Decentralize service delivery, capacity building, and training.
- Integrate sectors into multisectoral budgetary programming to underpin the implementation of the national poverty reduction strategy.

Since 1999 ... many African governments have consciously started to invest more in pro-poor service delivery, especially in the areas of health, education, HIV/AIDS, rural development (roads), agriculture, and water.

So, Is Africa at a Turning Point?

Based on the records, the verdict is guarded. There is indeed an acceleration of growth in Sub-Saharan Africa, but its sustainability is fragile. African countries in general are increasingly able to avoid mistakes and economic collapses, but increasing and sustaining growth are a difficult challenge. In the short to medium term, much depends on the continuation of favorable terms of trade, aid, and debt relief, as well as good policy. In the medium to long term, it is essential to raise the economic fundamentals, which are still lagging. Particularly needed are higher exports, more private sector growth, greater productivity of investment, higher foreign investment and remittances from migrant workers, greater regional efforts at tackling the infrastructure gaps, and improved agriculture. These economic fundamentals can be raised through continuing reforms and improved governance. In the long term, there is no substitute for improving human development and sharing the benefits of growth.

Predictions of Africa's imminent recovery or demise have proved wrong on numerous occasions in the past 40 years. Some of its economies have been badly managed and have declined, whereas others have prospered. But the energy, imagination, and entrepreneurship of its people have overcome both limited opportunities and bad policies to place the region at a position in this new century where better governments and better policies can make a difference. Shared growth can become a reality in Africa.

Notes

1. These assessments include AfDB and OECD (2007); AFRCE (various years); EIU (2007); IMF (2007a, 2007b); and World Bank (2007a, 2007b, 2007d). AFRCE briefs, from which much of this paper is derived, are biannual economic briefs prepared by the Chief Economist Office of the Africa Region at the World Bank. The briefs cover recent economic growth in Sub-Saharan Africa, issues about the scaling up of foreign aid, and the effect of external shocks....

2. The statistical significance of this hypothesis is tested in the growth analysis in the next section.

3. This assessment does not include Somalia, where no good data are available, and the numbers for Sudan may not fully cover its southern regions. Both current and past data face the same limitations.

4. Strictly speaking, oil-exporting and oil-importing countries may belong to two or more subgroups simultaneously. For purposes of describing the performance, however, the classification is not overlapping, so that the subgroups add up to 100 percent. Collier (2007) and Collier and O'Connell (2006) also argue that oil and non-oil resource endowments are dominant characteristics relative to the others.

5. These countries are Botswana, Guinea, Namibia, São Tomé and Principe, Sierra Leone, and Zambia.

6. These countries are Benin, Cape Verde, Comoros, Côte d'Ivoire, Eritrea, The Gambia, Ghana, Guinea-Bissau, Kenya, Liberia, Madagascar, Mauritania, Mauritius, Mozambique, Senegal, the Seychelles, South Africa, Tanzania, and Togo.

7. These countries are Burkina Faso, Burundi, the Central African Republic, the Democratic Republic of Congo, Ethiopia, Lesotho, Malawi, Mali, Niger, Rwanda, Swaziland, Uganda, and Zimbabwe.

8. These countries are Botswana, Cape Verde, Lesotho, Mauritius, Namibia, the Seychelles, South Africa, and Swaziland.

9. These countries are Benin, Burkina Faso, Ethiopia, Ghana, Kenya, Madagascar, Malawi, Mali, Mozambique, Niger, Rwanda, Senegal, Tanzania, Uganda, and Zambia.

10. These countries are Burundi, the Central African Republic, Comoros, the Democratic Republic of Congo, Côte d'Ivoire, Eritrea, The Gambia, Guinea, Guinea-Bissau, Liberia, São Tomé and Principe, Sierra Leone, Togo, and Zimbabwe.

11. The recovery of terms of trade in non-oil-exporting developing countries since the late 1990s is, however, still below the peaks of the early 1980s. Data are from the World Bank's World Economic Indicators.

12. So far, MDRI countries include Benin, Burkina Faso, Cameroon, Ethiopia, Ghana, Madagascar, Malawi, Mali, Mozambique, Niger, Rwanda, Senegal, Sierra Leone, Tanzania, Uganda, and Zambia.

13. Excluding the hyperinflation in Angola and Zimbabwe. In Angola's case, inflation fell over 300 percent in 2000 to about 13 percent in 2006.

14. Low-income countries in Africa are generally constrained from borrowing in international capital markets. As a result, the current account balance, the other significant macrobalance, is not a policy-dependent variable or a good indicator of macroeconomic management. Imports in these countries tend to adjust to export revenues and aid inflows.

15. See Bacon and Kojima (2006). ESMAP is a global technical assistance partnership that has been administered by the World Bank and sponsored by bilateral official donors since 1983.

16. See Bacon and Kojima (2006) for various case studies of African countries.

17. An important exception is the penetration of fixed-line and mobile telephones, where Sub-Saharan Africa leads low-income countries by as much as 13 percent. The largest gaps are for rural roads (29 percentage points) and electricity (21 percentage points).

18. Growth in Angola, Burkina Faso, Cape Verde, the Republic of Congo, Eritrea, Ethiopia, Ghana, Mauritius, Mozambique, Nigeria, and Tanzania has been through an expansion of cropped area.

19. This rate is the five-year moving average based on 2001–05.

20. This rate is the five-year moving average based on 2000–04.

References

AfDB and OECD (African Development Bank and Organisation for Economic Co-operation and Development). 2007. *African Economic Outlook*. Paris: OECD.

AFRCE (Office of the Chief Economist, Africa Region). Various years. "Biannual Economic Briefs." World Bank, Washington, DC.

Bacon, Robert, and Masami Kojima. 2006. "Coping with Higher Oil Prices." Report of the Energy Sector Management Assistance Programme, World Bank, Washington, DC.

Collier, Paul. 2007. *The Bottom Billion*. Oxford, U.K.: Oxford University Press.

Collier, Paul, and Stephen A. O'Connell. 2006. "Opportunities and Choices." Draft chapter 2 of the synthesis volume of the African Economic Research Consortium's

Explaining African Economic Growth project. Nairobi, African Economic Research Consortium.

EIU (Economist Intelligence Unit). 2007. *Sub-Saharan Africa: Regional Overview.* London: EIU.

Gelb, Alan, Ali A. G. Ali, Tesfaye Dinka, Ibrahim Elbadwi, Charles Saludo, and Gene Tidrick. 2000. *Can Africa Claim the 21st Century?* Washington, DC: World Bank.

IMF (International Monetary Fund). 2007a. "Sub-Saharan Africa Regional Economic Outlook: Fall 2007." SM/07/319, IMF, Washington, DC.

———. 2007b. *World Economic Outlook: Spillovers and Cycles in the Global Economy.* Washington, DC: IMF.

Lofgren, Hans and Carolina Diaz-Bonilla. 2008. "Foreign Aid, Taxes, and Government Productivity: Alternative Scenarios for Ethiopia's Millennium Development Goal Strategy." In *Africa at a Turning Point? Growth, Aid, and External Shocks,* ed. Delfin S. Go and John Page. Africa Development Essays Series, The World Bank. (forthcoming).

Ndulu, Benno J., Lopamudra Chakroborti, Lebohang Lijane, Vijaya Ramachandran, and Jerome Wolgin. 2007. *Challenges of Africa Growth: Opportunities, Constraints, and Strategic Directions.* Washington, DC: World Bank.

World Bank. 2007a. *Global Economic Prospects 2007: Managing the Next Wave of Globalization.* Washington, DC: World Bank.

———. 2007b. *Global Monitoring Report 2007: Millennium Development Goals and Confronting the Challenges of Gender Equality and Fragile States.* Washington, DC: World Bank.

———. 2007c. "Operational Approaches and Financing in Fragile States." IDA 15, International Development Agency, World Bank, Washington, DC.

———. 2007d. "The World Bank Group's Africa Action Plan: Progress in Implementation." Report M2007-0112, World Bank, Washington, DC.

12.3

THE MAKING, AND UNMAKING,
OF A CHILD SOLDIER

Ishmael Beah

It is tough enough to be a poor child in a developing country. Now consider being dragooned into a civil war that destroys your family, friends, country, and childhood. It's impossible for any of us in the United States today to imagine such an experience. Yet that's the story told in this article by a young African boy living in Sierra Leone, one day poor but happy with his family and village friends and the next day drugged and enraged, slaughtering other children just like himself in a violent and senseless conflict. Civil war, ostensibly over diamond resources, consumed Sierra Leone from 1991 to 2002 killing thousands and displacing 2 million people, or one-third of the population. Ishmael, a boy soldier, experienced this upheaval, you might say, "on the ground floor." The torment he endured and no doubt still endures, even after recovery, oozes out of every word of his story. If you think this kind of suffering is now over, consider the violence that children and adults still live with daily in places such as eastern Congo, the Nigerian delta, Somalia, and other African countries.

Sometimes I feel that living in New York City, having a good family and friends, and just being alive is a dream, that perhaps this second life of mine isn't really happening. Whenever I speak at the United Nations, Unicef or elsewhere to raise awareness of the continual and rampant recruitment of children in wars around the world, I come to realize that I still do not fully understand how I could have possibly survived the civil war in my country, Sierra Leone.

Most of my friends, after meeting the woman whom I think of as my new mother, a Brooklyn-born white Jewish-American, assume that I was either adopted at a very young age or that my mother married an African man. They would never imagine that I was 17 when I came to live with her and that I had been a child soldier and participated in one of the most brutal wars in recent history.

Source: "The Making, and Unmaking, of a Child Soldier" by Ishmael Beah appeared in the *New York Times Magazine,* January 14, 2007, and was adapted by the author from his book, *A Long Way Gone: Memoirs of a Boy Soldier* (New York: Farrar, Straus and Giroux, 2007).

In early 1993, when I was 12, I was separated from my family as the Sierra Leone civil war, which began two years earlier, came into my life. The rebel army, known as the Revolutionary United Front (R.U.F.), attacked my town in the southern part of the country. I ran away, along paths and roads that were littered with dead bodies, some mutilated in ways so horrible that looking at them left a permanent scar on my memory. I ran for days, weeks and months, and I couldn't believe that the simple and precious world I had known, where nights were celebrated with storytelling and dancing and mornings greeted with the singing of birds and cock crows, was now a place where only guns spoke and sometimes it seemed even the sun hesitated to shine. After I discovered that my parents and two brothers had been killed, I felt even more lost and worthless in a world that had become pregnant with fear and suspicion as neighbor turned against neighbor and child against parent. Surviving each passing minute was nothing short of a miracle.

After almost a year of running, I, along with some friends I met along the way, arrived at an army base in the southeastern region. We thought we were now safe; little did we know what lay ahead.

1994: The First Battle

I have never been so afraid to go anywhere in my life as I was that first day. As we walked into the arms of the forest, tears began to form in my eyes, but I struggled to hide them and gripped my gun for comfort. We exhaled quietly, afraid that our own breathing could cause our deaths. The lieutenant led the line that I was in. He raised his fist in the air, and we stopped moving. Then he slowly brought it down, and we sat on one heel, our eyes surveying the forest. We began to move swiftly among the bushes until we came to the edge of a swamp, where we formed an ambush, aiming our guns into the bog. We lay flat on our stomachs and waited. I was lying next to my friend Josiah. At 11, he was even younger than I was. Musa, a friend my age, 13, was also nearby. I looked around to see if I could catch their eyes, but they were concentrating on the invisible target in the swamp. The tops of my eyes began to ache, and the pain slowly rose up to my head. My ears became warm, and tears were running down my cheeks, even though I wasn't crying. The veins on my arms stood out, and I could feel them pulsating as if they had begun to breathe of their own accord. We waited in the quiet, as hunters do. The silence tormented me.

The short trees in the swamp began to shake as the rebels made their way through them. They weren't yet visible, but the lieutenant had passed the word down through a whisper that was relayed like a row of falling dominos: "Fire on my command." As we watched, a group of men dressed in civilian clothes emerged from under the tiny bushes. They waved their hands, and more fighters came out. Some were boys, as young as we were. They sat together in line, waving their hands, discussing a strategy. My lieutenant ordered a rocket-propelled grenade (RPG) to be fired, but the commander of the rebels heard it as it whooshed its way out of the forest. "Retreat!" he called out to his men, and the grenade's blast got only a few rebels, whose split bodies flew in the air. The explosion was followed by an exchange of gunfire from both sides.

I lay there with my gun pointed in front of me, unable to shoot. My index finger became numb. I felt as if the forest had turned upside down and I was going to fall off, so I clutched the base of a tree with one hand. I couldn't think, but I could hear the sounds of the guns far away in the distance and the cries of people dying in pain. A splash of blood hit my face. In my reverie I had opened my mouth a bit, so I tasted some of the blood. As I spat it out and wiped it off my face, I saw the soldier it had come from. Blood poured out of the bullet holes in him like water rushing through newly opened tributaries. His eyes were wide open; he still held his gun. My eyes were fixed on him when I heard Josiah screaming for his mother in the most painfully piercing voice I had ever heard. It vibrated inside my head to the point that I felt my brain had shaken loose from its anchor.

I searched for Josiah. An RPG had tossed his tiny body off the ground, and he had landed on a tree stump. He wiggled his legs as his cry gradually came to an end. There was blood everywhere. It seemed as if bullets were falling into the forest from all angles. I crawled to Josiah and looked into his eyes. There were tears in them, and his lips were shaking, but he couldn't speak. As I watched him, the water in his eyes was replaced with blood that quickly turned his brown eyes red. He reached for my shoulder as if to pull himself up. But midway, he stopped moving. The gunshots faded in my head, and it was as if my heart had stopped and the whole world had come to a standstill. I covered his eyes with my fingers and lifted him from the tree stump. His back-bone had been shattered. I placed him flat on the ground and picked up my gun. I didn't realize that I had stood up to take Josiah off the tree stump. I felt someone tugging at my foot. It was the corporal; he was saying something that I couldn't understand. His mouth moved, and he looked terrified. He pulled me down, and as I hit the ground, I felt my brain shaking in my skull again, and my deafness gave way.

"Get down," he was screaming. "Shoot," he said, as he crawled away from me to resume his position. As I looked to where he lay, my eyes caught Musa, whose head was covered with blood. His hands looked too relaxed. I turned toward the swamp, where there were gunmen running, trying to cross over. My face, my hands, my shirt and my gun were drenched in blood. I raised my gun and pulled the trigger, and I killed a man. Suddenly all the death I had seen since the day I was touched by war began flashing in my head. Every time I stopped shooting to change magazines and saw my two lifeless friends, I angrily pointed my gun into the swamp and killed more people. I shot everything that moved, until we were ordered to retreat because we needed another plan.

We took the guns and ammunition off the bodies of my friends and left them there in the forest, which had taken on a life of its own, as if it had trapped the souls that had departed from the dead. The branches of the trees seemed to be holding hands and bowing their heads in prayer. In the swamp, crabs had already begun feasting on the eyes of the dead. Limbs and fragmented skulls lay on top of the bog, and the water in the swamp was stagnant with blood. I was not afraid of these lifeless bodies. I despised them and kicked them to flip them and take their guns. I found a G3 and some ammunition. I noticed that most of the dead gunmen and boys wore lots of jewelry on their necks and wrists.

We arrived in the village, our base, with nightfall and sat against the walls of houses. It was quiet, and perhaps afraid of the silence, we began cleaning the blood off our guns, oiling their chambers, and shooting them into the air to test their effectiveness. I went for supper that night but was unable to eat. I only drank water and felt nothing. I lay on my back in the tent with my AK-47 on my chest and the G3 I had taken from a dead rebel leaning on the peg of the tent. Nothing happened in my head. It was a void, and I stared at the roof of the tent until I was miraculously able to doze off. I had a dream that I was picking up Josiah from the tree stump and a gunman stood on top of me. He placed his gun against my forehead. I immediately woke up from my dream and began shooting inside the tent, until the 30 rounds in the magazine were finished. The corporal and the lieutenant came in afterward and took me outside. I was sweating, and they threw water on my face and gave me a few white capsules. They were the same capsules that we'd all been given before we had gone into battle, and to this day, I do not know what they contained. I stayed up all night and couldn't sleep for days. We went out two more times that week, and I had no problem shooting my gun.

Rebel Raids

After that first week of going out on raids to kill people we deemed our rebel enemies or sympathizers of the rebels, our initiation was complete. We stayed put at the base, and we boys took turns guarding posts around the village. We smoked marijuana and sniffed "brown brown," cocaine mixed with gunpowder, which was always spread out on a table near the ammunition hut, and of course I took more of the white capsules, as I had become addicted to them. The first time I took all these drugs at the same time, I began to perspire so much that I took off all my clothes. My body shook, my sight became blurred and I lost my hearing for several minutes. I walked around the village restlessly. But after several doses of these drugs, all I felt was numbness to everything and so much energy that I couldn't sleep for weeks. We watched war movies at night, Rambo "First Blood," "Rambo, First Blood, Part II," "Commando" and so on, with the aid of a generator or a car battery. We all wanted to be like Rambo; we couldn't wait to implement his techniques.

When we ran out of supplies, we raided rebel camps in towns, villages and forests. "We have good news from our informants" the lieutenant would announce. "We are moving out in five minutes to kill some rebels and take their supplies, which really belong to us." He often made speeches about how we were defending our country, how honorable we were. At these times, I would stand holding my gun and feeling special because I was part of something that took me seriously and I was not running from anyone anymore. The lieutenant's face evinced confidence; his smiles disappeared before they were completed. We would tie our heads with the green cloths that distinguished us from the rebels, and we boys would lead the way. There were no maps and no questions asked. We were simply told to follow the path until we received instructions on what to do next. We walked for long hours and stopped only to eat sardines and corned beef with gari, sniff brown brown and take more white capsules. The combination of these drugs made us fierce. The idea of death didn't cross my mind, and killing had become as easy as drinking water. After that first killing, my mind had stopped making remorseful records, or so it seemed.

Before we got to a rebel camp, we would deviate from the path and walk in the forest. Once the camp was in sight, we would surround it and wait for the lieutenant's command. The rebels roamed about; some sat against walls, dozing off, and others, boys as young as we, stood at guard posts passing around marijuana. Whenever I looked at rebels during raids, my entire body shook with fury; they were the people who had shot my friends and family. So when the lieutenant gave orders, I shot as many as I could, but I didn't feel better. After every gunfight, we would enter the rebel camp, killing those we had wounded. We would then search the houses and gather gallons of gasoline, enormous amounts of marijuana and cocaine, bales of clothes, watches, rice, salt, gari and many other things. We rounded up any civilians—men, women, boys and young girls—hiding in the huts and houses and made them carry our loot back to the base. We shot them if they tried to run away.

On one of these raids, we captured a few rebels after a long gunfight and a lot of civilian casualties. We undressed the prisoners and tied their arms behind their backs until their chests were tight as drums. "Where did you get all this ammunition from?" the corporal asked one of the prisoners, a man with an almost dreadlocked beard. He spat in the corporal's face, and the corporal immediately shot him in the head at close range. He fell to the ground, and blood slowly leaked out of his head. We cheered in admiration of the corporal's action and saluted him as he walked by. Suddenly, a rebel hiding in the bushes shot one of our boys. We dispersed around the village in search of the shooter. When the young muscular rebel was captured, the lieutenant slit his neck with his bayonet. The rebel ran before he fell to the ground and stopped moving. We cheered again, raising our guns in the air, shouting and whistling.

During that time, a lot of things were done with no reason or explanation. Sometimes we were asked to leave for war in the middle of a movie. We would come back hours later after killing many people and continue the movie as if we had just returned from intermission. We were always either on the front lines, watching a war movie or doing drugs. There was no time to be alone or to think. When we conversed with one another, we talked only about the movies and how impressed we were with the way either the lieutenant, the corporal or one of us had killed someone. It was as if nothing else existed.

The villages that we captured and turned into our bases as we went along and the forests that we slept in became my home. My squad was my family, my gun was my provider and protector and my rule was to kill or be killed. The extent of my thoughts didn't go much beyond that. We had been fighting for more than two years, and killing had become a daily activity. I felt no pity for anyone. My childhood had gone by without my knowing, and it seemed as if my heart had frozen. I knew that day and night came and went because of the presence of the moon and the sun, but I had no idea whether it was a Sunday or a Friday.

Taken from the Front

In my head my life was normal. But everything began to change in January 1996. I was 15.

One morning that month, a truck came to the village where we were based. Four men dressed in clean blue jeans and white T-shirts that said "Unicef" in big blue letters jumped out. They were shown to the lieutenant's house. It seemed as if he had been expecting them. As they sat talking on the veranda, we watched them from under the mango tree, where we sat cleaning our guns. Soon all the boys were told to line up for the lieutenant who selected a few of us and asked the adult soldiers to take away our guns and ammunition. A bunch of boys, including my friend Alhaji and me, were ushered to the truck. I stared back at the veranda where the lieutenant now stood, looking in the other direction, toward the forest, his hands crossed behind his back. I still didn't know exactly what was going on, but I was beginning to get angry and anxious. Why had the lieutenant decided to give us up to these civilians? We thought that we were part of the war until the end.

We were on the road for hours. I had gotten used to always moving and hadn't sat in one place idly for a long time. It was night when the truck stopped at a center, where there were other boys whose appearances, red eyes and somber faces resembled ours. Alhaji and I looked at this group, and he asked the boys who they were. A boy who was sitting on the stoop angrily said: "We fought for the R.U.F.; the army is the enemy. We fought for freedom, and the army killed my family and destroyed my village. I will kill any of those army bastards every time I get a chance to do so." The boy took off his shirt to fight, and on his arm was the R.U.F. brand. Mambu, one of the boys on our side, shouted, "They are rebels," and reached for his bayonet, which he had hidden in his army shorts; most of us had hidden either a knife or a grenade before our guns were taken from us. Before Mambu could grab his weapon, the R.U.F. boy punched him in the face. He fell, and when he got up, his nose was bleeding. The rebel boys drew out the few bayonets they had in their shorts and rushed toward us. It was war all over again. Perhaps the naïve men who had taken us to the center thought that removing us from the war would lessen our hatred for the R.U.F. It hadn't crossed their minds that a change of environment wouldn't immediately make us normal boys; we were dangerous, brainwashed to kill.

One boy grabbed my neck from behind. He was squeezing for the kill, and I couldn't use my bayonet effectively, so I elbowed him with all my might until he let go. He was holding his stomach when I turned around and stabbed him in his foot. The bayonet stuck, so I pulled it out with force. He fell, and I began kicking him in the face. As I went to deliver the final blow with my bayonet, someone came from behind me and sliced my hand with his knife. It was a rebel boy, and he was about to kick me down when he fell on his face. Alhaji had stabbed him in the back. He pulled the knife out, and we started kicking the boy until he stopped moving. I wasn't sure whether he was unconscious or dead. I didn't care. No one screamed or cried during the fight. After all, we had been doing such things for years and were all still on drugs.

We continued to stab and slice one another until a bunch of MPs came running through the gate toward the fight. The MPs fired a few rounds into the air to get us to stop, but we were still fighting, so they had to part us by force. They placed some of us at gunpoint and kicked others apart. Six people were killed: two on our side and four on the rebel side.

As MPs stood guard to make sure we didn't start another fight, we, the army boys, went to the kitchen to look for food. We ate and chatted about the fight. Mambu told us that he had plucked an eye out of the head of one of the R.U.F. boys, and that the boy ran to punch him, but he couldn't see, so he ran into the wall, banging his head hard and fainting. We laughed and picked up Mambu, raising him in the air. We needed the violence to cheer us after a whole day of boring travel and contemplation about why our superiors had let us go.

That night we were moved to a rehabilitation center called Benin Home. Benin Home was run by a local NGO called Children Associated With the War, in Kissy neighborhood, on the eastern outskirts of Freetown, the capital. This time, the MPs made sure to search us thoroughly before we entered. The blood of our victims and enemies was fresh on our arms and clothes. My lieutenant's words still echoed in my head: "From now on, we kill any rebel we see, no prisoners." I smiled a bit, happy that we had taken care of the rebel boys, but I also began to wonder again: Why had we been taken here? I walked up and down on the veranda, restless in my new environment. My head began to hurt.

Relearning Boyhood

It was infuriating to be told what to do by civilians. Their voices, even when they called us for breakfast, enraged me so much that I would punch the wall, my locker or anything nearby. A few days earlier, we could have decided whether they would live or die.

We refused to do anything that we were asked to do, except eat. At the end of every meal, the staff members and nurses came to talk to us about attending the scheduled medical checkups and the one-on-one counseling sessions that we hated at the minihospital that was part of Benin Home. As soon as the live-in staff, mostly men, started telling us what to do, we would throw bowls, spoons, food and benches at them. We would chase them out of the dining hall and beat them. One afternoon, after we had chased off several staff members, we placed a bucket over the cook's head and pushed him around the kitchen until he burned his hand on a boiling pot and agreed to put more milk in our tea. During that same week, the drugs were wearing off. I craved cocaine and marijuana so badly that I would roll a plain sheet of paper and smoke it. Sometimes I searched the pockets of my army shorts, which I still wore, for crumbs of marijuana or cocaine. We broke into the minihospital and stole some painkillers—white tablets and off-white—and red and yellow capsules. We emptied the capsules, ground the tablets and mixed them together. But the mixture didn't give us the effect we wanted. We got more upset day by day and, as a result, resorted to more violence. We began to fight one another day and night. We would fight for hours for no reason at all. At first the staff would intervene, but after a while they just let us go. They couldn't really stop us, and perhaps they thought that we would get this out of our systems. During these fights, we destroyed most of the furniture and threw the mattresses out in the yard. We would stop to wipe the blood off our lips, arms and legs only when the bell rang for mealtime.

It had been more than a month, and some of us had almost gone through the withdrawal stage, even though there were still instances of vomiting and collapsing at unexpected moments. These outbreaks ended, for most of us, at the end of the second month. But we now had time to think; the fastened mantle of our war memories slowly began to open. We resorted to more violence to avoid summoning thoughts of our recent lives.

Whenever I turned on the faucet, all I could see was blood gushing out. I would stare at it until it looked like water before drinking or taking a shower. Boys sometimes ran out of the hall screaming, "The rebels are coming." Other times, the younger ones sat weeping and telling us that nearby rocks were their dead families.

It took several months before I began to relearn how to sleep without the aid of medicine. But even when I was finally able to fall asleep, I would start awake less than an hour later. I would dream that a faceless gunman had tied me up and begun to slit my throat with the zigzag edge of his bayonet. I would feel the pain that the knife inflicted as the man sawed my neck. I'd wake up sweating and throwing punches in the air. I would run outside to the middle of the soccer field, sit on a stone and rock back and forth, my arms wrapped around my legs. I would try desperately to think about my childhood, but I couldn't. The fighting memories seemed to have formed a barrier that I had to break in order to think about any moment before the war. On those mornings, I would feel one of the staff members wrap a blanket around me, saying: "This isn't your fault, you know. It really isn't. You'll get through this." He would then pull me up and walk me back to the hall.

Past and Present

One day after I'd been in Benin Home for more than three months, I was sent to the minihospital for a checkup. The nurse on duty was named Esther. I had met her once before when I was sent to the minihospital after cutting my hand punching a window. Esther wore a white uniform and a white hat. Her white teeth contrasted with her dark, shiny skin, and when she smiled, her face glowed. She was tall and had big brown eyes that were kind and inviting. She must have been about 30, which I thought was too old.

That day, before Esther examined me, she gave me a present, a Walkman and a Run-DMC tape. I used to listen to rap music a lot before the war and loved it because of its poetic use of words. I put the headphones on and didn't mind being examined because the song had taken hold of me, and I listened closely to every word. But when she began examining my legs and saw the nasty scars on my left shin, she took my headphones off and asked, "How did you get these scars?"

"Bullet wounds," I casually replied.

Her face filled with sorrow, and her voice was shaking when she spoke: "You have to tell me what happened so I can prescribe treatment." At first I was reluctant, but she said she would be able to treat me effectively only if I told her what happened, especially about how my bullet wounds were treated. So I told her the whole story not because I really wanted to but because I thought that if I told her some of the truth of my war years, she would be afraid of me and would cease asking questions. She listened attentively when I began to talk:

During the second dry season of my war years, we were low on food and ammunition. So as usual, we decided to attack another village, which was a three-day walk away. We left our base that evening, stopping once a day to eat, drink and take drugs. Each of us had two guns, one strapped to our backs, the other held in our hands. On the evening of the third day, the village was in sight.

Surrounding it, we waited for the lieutenant's command. As we lay in ambush, we began to realize that the place was empty. We were beginning to suspect that something was amiss when a shot was fired from behind us. It was clear now: we were being ambushed. We ended up in a fight that lasted more than 24 hours. We lost several men and boys. When we finally seemed to have captured the village, we began to look around for anything we could find. I was filling my backpack with ammunition from a hut when bullets began to rain on the village again. I was hit three times in my left shin. The first two bullets went in and out, and the last one stayed inside. I couldn't walk, so I lay on the ground and released an entire round of the magazine into the bush where the bullets had come from. I remember feeling a tingle in my spine, but I was too drugged to really feel the pain, even though my leg had begun to swell. The sergeant doctor in my squad dragged me into one of the houses and tried to remove the bullet. Each time he raised his hands from my wound, I saw my blood all over his fingers. My eyes began to grow heavy, and I fainted.

I do not know what happened, but when I woke the next day, I felt as if I had nails hammered into the bones of my shin and my veins were being chiseled. I felt so much pain that I was unable to cry out loud; tears just fell from my eyes. The ceiling of the thatched-roof house where I was lying on a bed was blurry. My eyes struggled to become familiar with my surroundings. The gunfire had ceased and the village was quiet, so I assumed that the attackers had been successfully driven away. I felt a brief relief for that, but the pain in my leg returned. I tucked my lips in, closed my heavy eyelids and held tight to the edges of the wooden bed. I heard the footsteps of people entering the house. They stood by my bed, and as soon as they began to speak, I recognized their voices.

"The boy is suffering, and we have no medicine here to lessen his pain. Everything is at our former base." The sergeant doctor sighed and continued. "It will take six days to send someone to get the medicine and return. He will die from the pain by then."

"We have to send him to the former base, then," I heard my lieutenant saying. "We need those provisions from that base, anyway. Do all you can to make sure that the boy stays alive," he said and walked out. "Yes, sir," the sergeant doctor said. I slowly opened my eyes, and this time I could see clearly. I looked at his sweaty face and tried to smile a little. After having heard what they said, I swore to myself that I would fight hard and do anything for my squad after my leg was healed.

"We will get you some help," the sergeant doctor said gently, sitting by my bed and examining my leg. "Just be strong, young man,"

"Yes, sir," I said, and tried to raise my hand to salute him, but he tenderly brought my arm down.

Two soldiers came into the house, took me off the bed, placed me in a hammock and carried me outside. The treetops of the village began to spin around as they carried me out. The journey felt as if it took a month. I fainted and awoke many times, and each time I opened my eyes, it seemed as if the voices of those who carried me were fading into the distance.

Finally we got to the base, and the sergeant doctor, who had come along, went to work on me. I was injected with something. I was given cocaine, which I frantically demanded. The doctor started operating on me before the drugs took effect. The other soldiers held my hands and stuffed a cloth into my mouth. The doctor stuck a crooked-looking scissorslike tool inside my wound and fished for the bullet. I could feel the edge of the metal inside me. My entire body was racked with pain.

Just when I thought I had had enough, the doctor abruptly pulled the bullet out. A piercing pain rushed up my spine from my waist to the back of my neck. I fainted.

When I regained consciousness, it was the morning of the next day, and the drugs had kicked in. I reached my hands down to my leg and felt the bandage before I stood up and limped outside, where some soldiers and the sergeant were sitting. "Where is my weapon?" I asked them. The sergeant handed me my G3, and I began cleaning it. I shot a couple of rounds sitting against a wall, ignoring the bandage on my leg and everyone else. I smoked marijuana, ate and snorted cocaine and brown brown. That was all I did for a few days before we went back to the new base we had captured. When we left, we threw kerosene on the thatched-roof houses, lighted them with matches and fired a couple of RPGs into the walls. We always destroyed the bases we abandoned so that rebel squads wouldn't be able to use them. Two soldiers carried me in the hammock, but this time I had my gun, and I looked left and right as we traveled the forest path.

At the new base, I stayed put for three weeks. Then one day, we heard that a rebel group was on its way to attack our village. I tightened the bandage around my shin, picked up my gun and followed my squad to ambush them. We killed most of the attackers and captured a few whom we brought back to base. "These are the men responsible for the bullet holes in your leg. It's time to make sure they never shoot at you or your comrades." The lieutenant pointed at the prisoners. I was not sure if one of the captives was the shooter, but any captive would do at that time. They were all lined up, six of them, with their hands tied. I shot them in their shins and watched them suffer for an entire day before finally deciding to shoot them in the head so that they would stop crying. Before I shot each man, I looked at him and saw how his eyes gave up hope and steadied before I pulled the trigger. I found their somber eyes irritating.

When I finished telling Esther the story, she had tears in her eyes, and she couldn't decide whether to rub my head, a traditional gesture indicating that things would be well, or hug me. In the end she did neither but said: "None of what happened was your fault. You were just a little boy, and anytime you want to tell me anything, I am here to listen." She stared at me, trying to catch my eye so she could assure me of what she had just said. I became angry and regretted that I had told someone, a civilian, about my experience. I hated the "It is not your fault" line that all the staff members said every time anyone spoke about the war.

I got up, and as I started walking out of the hospital, Esther said, "I will arrange a full checkup for you." She paused and then continued: "Let me keep the Walkman. You don't want the others to envy you and steal it. I will be here every day, so you can come and listen to it anytime." I threw the Walkman at her and left, putting my fingers in my ears so I couldn't hear her say, "It is not your fault."

After that, whenever Esther would see me around, she'd smile and ask me how I was doing. At first I detested her intrusions. But slowly I came to appreciate them, even looked forward to them. It was like this at the center; most boys found a staff member whom they eventually began to trust. Mine was Esther.

Over the next few months, I started to visit Esther occasionally at the mini-hospital, which was just across the dirt road from the dorm that I shared with more than 35 boys. During that time, Esther got me to tell her some of my dreams. She would just listen and sit quietly with me. If she wanted to say anything, she would first ask, "Would you like me to say something about your dream?" Mostly I would say no and ask for the Walkman.

One day Esther gave me a Bob Marley tape and a really nice notebook and pen and suggested that I use them to write the lyrics of the songs and that we could learn them together. After that I visited Esther at the minihospital every day, to show her what I had written. I would sing her the parts of songs I had memorized. Memorizing lyrics left me little time to think about what happened in the war. As I grew comfortable with Esther, I talked to her mainly about Bob Marley's lyrics and Run-DMC's too. She mostly listened.

One night, close to my fifth month at the center, I fell asleep while reading the lyrics of a song. I startled awake after having a dream that involved lots of people stabbing and shooting one another, and I felt all their pain. The room I stood in filled with their blood. In the dream, I then went outside to sit at dinner with my father, mother and two brothers. They didn't seem to notice that I was covered with blood.

It was the first time I dreamed of my family since I started running away from the war. The next afternoon I went to see Esther, and she could tell that something was bothering me. "Do you want to lie down?" she asked, almost whispering.

"I had this dream last night," I said looking away. "I don't know what to make of it."

She came and sat next to me and asked, "Would you like to tell me about it?" I didn't reply.

"Or just talk about it out loud and pretend I am not here. I won't say anything. Only if you ask me." She sat quietly beside me. The quietness lasted for a while, and for some reason I began to tell her my dream.

At first she just listened to me, and then gradually she started asking questions to make me talk about the lives I had lived before and during the war. "None of these things are your fault," she said, as she had repeated sternly at the end of every conversation. Even though I had heard that phrase from every staff member—and had always hated it—I began that day to believe it. That didn't make me immune to the guilt that I felt for what I had done. But it somehow lightened my burdensome memories and gave me strength to think about things. The more I spoke about my experiences to Esther, the more I began to cringe at the gruesome details, even though I didn't let her know that. I still didn't completely trust her. I only liked talking to her because I felt that she didn't judge me for what I had been a part of; she looked at me with the inviting eyes and welcoming smile that said I was still a child.

One day during my fifth month at Benin Home, I was sitting on a rock behind the classrooms when Esther came by. She sat next to me without uttering a word. She had my lyrics notebook in her hand. "I feel as if there is nothing left for me to be alive for," I said slowly. "I have no family, it is just me. No one will be able to tell stories about my childhood." I sniffled a bit.

Esther put her arms around me and pulled me closer to her. She shook me to get my full attention before she started. "Think of me as your family, your sister."

"But I didn't have a sister," I replied.

"Well, now you do," she said. "You see, this is the beauty of starting a new family. You can have different kinds of family members." She looked at me directly, waiting for me to say something.

"O.K., you can be my sister—temporarily." I emphasized the last word.

"That is fine with me. So will you come to see your temporary sister tomorrow, please?" She covered her face as if she would be sad if I said no.

"O.K., O.K., no need to be sad," I said, and we both laughed a bit.

Rejoining the Civilian World

Soon after, a group of visitors from the European Union, the United Nations, Unicef and several NGOs arrived at the center in a convoy of cars. At the request of the staff, we boys had prepared a talent show for them. I read a monologue from "Julius Caesar" and performed a short hip-hop play about the redemption of a former child soldier that I had written with Esther's encouragement. After that event, the head of the center asked me to be the spokesman for Benin Home and to speak about my experiences.

I was at the beginning of my seventh month at Benin Home when one of the field agents, Leslie, came to tell me that he was responsible for "repatriating" me—the term used to describe the process of reuniting ex-child soldiers with their former communities. My family was dead, but I knew that my father had a brother whom I had never met who lived somewhere in Freetown. Leslie said he would try to find him, and if he couldn't, he'd find me a foster family to live with.

One Saturday afternoon about two weeks later, as I chatted with Esther at the minihospital, Leslie walked in, smiling widely. "What is the good news?" Esther asked. Leslie examined my curious face, then walked back to the door and opened it. A tall man walked in.

"This is your uncle," Leslie proudly announced.

The man walked over to where I was sitting. He bent over and embraced me long and hard. My arms hung loose at my sides.

What if he is just some man pretending to be my uncle? I thought. The man let go of me. He was crying, which is when I began to believe that he was really my family, because men in Sierra Leone rarely cried.

He crouched on his heels next to me and began: "I am sorry I never came to see you all those years. I wish I had met you before today. But we can't go back now. We just have to start from here. I am sorry for your losses." He looked at Leslie and continued: "After you are done here, you can come and live with me and my family. You are my son. I don't have much, but I will give you a place to sleep, food and my love." He put his arms around me.

No one had called me "son" in a very long time. I didn't know what to say. Everyone, it seemed, was waiting for my response. I turned to my uncle, smiled at him and said: "Thank you for coming to see me. I really appreciate that you have offered me to stay with you. But I don't even know you." I put my head down.

"As I said, we cannot go back," he replied, rubbing my head and laughing a little. "But we can start from here. I am your family, and that is enough for us to begin liking each other."

I got up and hugged my uncle, and he embraced me harder than he had the first time and kissed me on my forehead. We briefly stood in silence before he began to speak again. "I will visit you every weekend. And if it is O.K., I would like you to come home with me at some point, to see where I live and to meet my wife and children—your family." My uncle's voice trembled; he was trying to hold back sobs. He rubbed my head with one hand and shook Leslie's hand with the other.

As my uncle promised, he came to visit every weekend. We would take long walks together, and they gave me a chance to get to know him. He told me about what my father was like when he was a child, and I told him about my childhood. I needed to talk about those good times before the war. But the more I heard and talked about my father, the more I missed my mother and brothers too.

About a month or so later at Benin Home, Leslie told me it was time for me to go live with my uncle. I was happy, but I was also worried about living with a family. I had been on my own for years and had taken care of myself without any guidance from anyone. If I distanced myself from the family, I was afraid that I might look ungrateful to my uncle, who didn't have to take me in; I was worried about what would happen when my nightmares took hold of me. How was I going to explain my sadness, which I was unable to hide when it took over my face, to my new family, especially the children?

I lay in my bed night after night staring at the ceiling and thinking, Why have I survived the war? Why was I the last person in my immediate family to be alive? I went to see Esther every day, though, and would say hello, ask how she was and then get lost in my own head thinking about what life was going to be like after the center. At night, I sat quietly on the veranda with my friends. I wouldn't notice when they left the bench that we all sat on.

When the day of my repatriation finally came, I walked to the minihospital building where I was to wait, my heart beating very fast. My friends Alhaji and Mambu and a boy named Mohamed were sitting on the front steps, and Esther emerged, smiling. Leslie sat in a nearby van waiting to take me to my new home.

"I have to go," I said to everyone, my voice shaking. I extended my hand to Mohamed, but instead of shaking it, he leapt up and hugged me. Mambu embraced me while Mohamed was still holding me. He squeezed me hard, as if he knew it was goodbye forever. (After I left the center, Mambu's family refused to take him in, and he ended up back on the front lines.) At the end of the hug, Alhaji shook hands with me. We squeezed each other's hands and stared into each other's eyes, remembering all that we had been through. I never saw him again, since he continually moved from one foster home to another. Esther stepped forward, her eyes watery. She hugged me tighter than she ever had.

I didn't return her hug very well, as I was busy trying to hold back my tears. After she let go, she gave me a piece of paper. "This is my address," she said. "Come by anytime."

I went to Esther's home several weeks after that. But my timing wasn't good. She was on her way to work. She hugged me, and this time I squeezed back; this made her laugh after we stood apart. She looked me straight in the eyes. "Come and see me next weekend so we can have more time to catch up, O.K.?" she said. She was wearing her white uniform and was on her way to take on other traumatized children. It must be tough living with so many war stories. I was living with just one, mine, and it was difficult. Why does she do it? Why do they all do it? I thought as we went our separate ways. It was the last time I saw her. I loved her but never told her.

Chapter 13

GLOBAL INEQUALITY, IMPERIALISM, AND INJUSTICE: A CRITICAL THEORY PERSPECTIVE

13.1

CARMEN MIRANDA ON MY MIND: INTERNATIONAL POLITICS OF THE BANANA

Cynthia Enloe

In this probing feminist critique, Cynthia Enloe dissects the destructive and discriminatory culture imposed on Latin America and other developing countries by U.S. multinational corporations and the western media to produce and advertise bananas and other plantation crops for consumption in affluent countries. Notice in this critical theory approach how subtle and deep-seated the oppression is. It's not just the control of land and labor to produce crops that corporations exercise but the manipulation of local culture, the exploitation of feminine stereotypes, the "masculinization" of plantation life, the fostering of prostitution, the neglect of women and children left behind as men leave to work on plantations, the assignment of least-skilled work to women, the marginalization of women in household statistics that conceal gross inequality, and so on. What should be done about it? She describes the progress made by some women's groups to advocate land reform and other improvements but warns that patriarchal power is too great to unseat by single measures. What's needed is a change of consciousness that will be achieved only when women and their contributions become more visible. One purpose of critical theory is to become that voice for marginalized peoples.

Source: Cynthia Enloe, "Carmen Miranda on My Mind: International Politics of the Banana," in *Bananas, Beaches, and Bases: Making Feminist Sense of International Politics* (Berkeley: University of California Press, 1989), 124–150.

When she appeared on screen, the tempo quickened. Dressed in her outrageous costumes, topped by hats featuring bananas and other tropical fruits, Carmen Miranda sang and danced her way to Hollywood stardom. While she was best known for her feisty comic performances, she also played a part in a serious political drama: the realignment of American power in the Western hemisphere. Carmen Miranda's movies helped make Latin America safe for American banana companies at a time when US imperialism was coming under wider regional criticism.

Between 1880 and 1930 the United States colonized or invaded Hawaii, the Philippines, Puerto Rico, the Dominican Republic, Cuba and Nicaragua. Each was strategically valuable for its plantation crops. The British, French and Dutch had their plantation colonies producing rubber, tea, coffee, palm oil, coconuts, tobacco, sisal, cotton, jute, rice and, of course, the monarch of plantation crops, sugar. Bananas, sugar, coffee, pineapples—each had become an international commodity that Americans, too, were willing to kill for. But by the time Franklin Roosevelt came into office, sending in the marines was beginning to lose it political value; it was alienating too many potential regional allies. New, less direct means had to be found to guarantee American control of Latin America.

Carmen Miranda was born in Lisbon in 1909, but emigrated as a child to Brazil, where her father established a wholesale fruit business. Despite her parents' hopes that their convent-educated daughter would grow up to be a respectable young woman, she secretly auditioned for and won a regular spot on a Rio de Janeiro radio station. She became a hit and soon was an attraction on the local nightclub circuit. By 1939 Carmen Miranda had recorded over 300 singles, appeared in four Brazilian films and was being referred to by her compatriots as a national institution. It was at this point in her career that Broadway theatrical producer Lee Schubert saw Carmen Miranda perform and offered her a contract to move north. When she stepped off the boat in New York on May 4, 1939, Schubert had the press corps already primed to greet his new 'Brazilian bombshell'. With her outrageous headgear and limited but flamboyant English (she spoke French and Spanish as well as Portuguese), she was on her way to being turned into the 1940s American stereotype of the Latin American woman. In response to reporters' questions, Miranda replied, 'Money, money, money ... hot dog. I say yes, no, and I say money, money, money and I say turkey sandwich and I say grape juice.'[1]

The world's fair was attracting throngs to the Sunken Meadow fairgrounds just outside New York City in the summer of 1939, but Carmen Miranda still managed to make Schubert's show, *Streets of Paris,* a commercial success. *Life* magazine's reviewer noted:

Partly because their unusual melody and heavy accented rhythms are unlike anything ever heard in a Manhattan revue before, partly because there is not a clue to their meaning except the gay rolling of Carmen Miranda's insinuating eyes, these songs, and Miranda herself, are the outstanding hit of the show.[2]

In 1940 Hollywood studio directors were boarding the Latin America band-wagon. Men like Darryl Zanuck, head of Twentieth Century Fox, had long cultivated friendships with politicians in Washington. It was one way of overcoming the barriers of anti-Semitism confronting many of the film industry's moguls. Thus when President Franklin Roosevelt launched his Latin American 'Good Neighbor' policy, the men who ran Hollywood were willing to help the government's campaign to replace a militaristic, imperial approach to US-Latin America diplomacy with a more 'cooperative' strategy. Roosevelt and his advisers were convinced that gunboat diplomacy was arousing too much opposition among precisely those Latin American governments which American businessmen would have to cultivate if the country was to pull itself out of the Depression. Tourism and investment were promoted in glossy brochures. Pan-American Airways flew holiday-makers to Havana and Managua; construction of the Pan-American Highway was started. Nicaragua's Anastasio Somoza was invited to the world's fair to celebrate regional democracy and progress. Latin American movie stars replaced the marines as the guarantors of regional harmony.[3]

Darryl Zanuck enticed Carmen Miranda away from Broadway to be his studio's contribution to the 'Good Neighbor' policy. She appeared in the 1940 film *Down Argentine Way,* starring Betty Grable and Don Ameche, singing 'South American Way'. Her film career soared during World War II, when Washington officials believed that it was diplomatically vital to keep Latin American regimes friendly to the United States. Propaganda and censorship agencies urged the entertainment industry to promote Latin actors and popularize Latin music.

Carmen Miranda was confined to light roles, treated by the studios as a comic or character actor, never a romantic lead. Perhaps her most lavish film was Busby Berkeley's *The Gang's All Here* (1943), whose set was adorned with giant bananas and strawberries. She mastered English, but was careful to maintain in her performances a heavily accented pronunciation, which suggested feminine *naïveté.* For many Americans, during the 1940s Carmen Miranda became a guide to Latin culture. While Hollywood's Latin American male was stereotypically a loyal but none-too-bright sidekick, like Donald Duck's parrot pal José Carioca, Miranda personified a culture full of zest and charm, unclouded by intense emotion or political ambivalence. Like the bananas she wore on her head, Miranda was exotic yet mildly amusing.

'Carmen Miranda is the chief export of Brazil. Next comes coffee.' So recalls Uruguayan historian Eduardo Galeano.[4] Brazilians themselves were proud of Miranda's Hollywood success. When she died suddenly of a heart attack in 1955, her body and effects were shipped back to Rio to be memorialized in a Carmen Miranda museum. Brazilian President Kubitschek declared a national day of mourning.

'I'm Chiquita Banana and I've Come to Say'

The banana has a history, a gendered history. The fruit has its origins in Southeast Asia and was carried westward by traders. By the fifteenth century it had become a basic food for Africans living on the Guinean coast. When Portuguese and Spanish slave-traders began raiding the coast for Africans to serve as forced labor on colonial estates, they chose bananas as the food to ship with them; it was local and cheap. These were red bananas, a variety still popular in the West Indies and Africa. The yellow banana so familiar today to consumers in Europe, Japan, the Persian Gulf and North America wasn't developed as a distinct variety until the nineteenth century. Then it was imagined to be food fit not for slaves, but for the palates of the wealthy. The first record of bunches of bananas being brought to New York from Havana was in 1804. But it was when the yellow banana was served as an exotic delicacy in the homes of affluent Bostonians in 1875 that it took off as an international commodity. In 1876 the banana was featured at the United States Centennial Exhibition in Philadelphia. The yellow banana symbolized America's new global reach.[5]

Notions of masculinity and femininity have been used to shape the international political economy of the banana. Banana plantations were developed in Central America, Latin America, the Caribbean, Africa and the Philippines as a result of alliances between men of different but complementary interests: businessmen and male officials of the importing countries on the one hand, and male landowners and government officials of the exporting countries on the other. To clear the land and harvest the bananas they decided they needed a male workforce, sustained at a distance by women as prostitutes, mothers and wives. However company executives' manly pride was invested not so much in their extensive plantations as in the sophisticated equipment and technology they developed to transport the fragile tropical fruit to far-away markets: railroads, wire services and fleets of refrigerator ships. Even today company officials take special satisfaction in describing their giant cold-storage ships circling the globe, directed by a sophisticated international communications network, all to ensure that bananas that leave Costa Rica or the Philippines by the green tonnage will arrive in New York or Liverpool undamaged and unspoiled, ready for the ripening factory.[6] The companies envisaged their customers to be women: mothers and housewives concerned about their families' nutrition and looking for a reliable product. The most successful way of bonding housewives' loyalty to a particular company was to create a fantasized market woman.

The United Fruit Company, the largest grower and marketer of bananas, made its contribution to America's 'Good Neighbor' culture. In 1943 the company opened a Middle American Information Bureau to encourage 'mutual knowledge and mutual understanding'. The bureau wrote and distributed materials which emphasized the value of Central American products such as hardwoods, coffee, spices and fruits to the US war effort. It targeted school children and housewives: those who ate bananas and those who bought them. *Nicaragua in Story and Pictures* was a company-designed school text celebrating the progress brought to Nicaragua by foreign-financed railroads and imported tractors. 'Fifty Questions on Middle America for North American Women' and 'Middle

America and a Woman's World' explained to the North American housewife, United Fruit's chief customer, how the Japanese invasion of Malaysia made imported foods from Nicaragua and Costa Rica all the more important to her wartime security.[7]

United Fruit's biggest contribution to American culture, however, was 'Chiquita Banana'. In 1944, when Carmen Miranda was packing movie houses and American troops were landing on Europe's beaches, United Fruit advertising executives created a half-banana, half-woman cartoon character destined to rival Donald Duck. Dressed as a Miranda-esque market woman, this feminized banana sang her calypso song from coast to coast. Chiquita Banana helped to establish a twentieth-century art form, the singing commercial. One could hear her singing the praises of the banana on the radio 376 times daily.

* * *

United Fruit sales strategists set out to do the impossible—to create in housewives a brand-name loyalty for a generic fruit. They wanted women to think 'Chiquita' when they went to the grocery store to buy bananas. Roosevelt's 'Good Neighbor' policy and Carmen Miranda's Hollywood success had set the stage; animated cartoons and the commercial jingle did the rest. Between the woman consumer and the fruit there now was only a corporation with the friendly face of a bouncy Latin American market woman. Forty years later United Fruit Company has become United Brands; its principal subsidiary is Chiquita Brands, bringing us not only bananas, but melons, grapefruits and tropical juices.

Today virtually every affluent, industrialized country imports bananas from mainly poor, still agrarian countries. Each consumer society gets its bananas from two or three large agribusiness corporations which either have large plantations of their own or monopolize the marketing system through which small growers sell their fruit. Since United Fruit's advertising coup in 1944, its competitors have followed suit, designing stickers for their own bananas. This allows a shopper to go into any grocery store in Europe, North America or Japan and check at a glance the state of international banana politics: just look for the sticker with its corporate logo and the country of origin. In London one might peel off a Geest sticker that says 'WINBAN' (the Windward Island nations of St. Lucia, St. Vincent or Dominica) or look for the Fyffes sticker (Fyffes is United Brands' European subsidiary) that gives the country of origin as Surinam. In Detroit or Toronto a shopper would be more likely to find a Chiquita, Del Monte or Dole sticker, with Costa Rica, Ecuador, or Colombia written below the logo in small print, while in Tokyo Sumitomo's Banambo sticker would identify bananas produced in the Philippines.

After a century of banana big business, Americans remain the largest consumers of bananas, eating some 2 million tons of the fruit each year. But with the opening of the Philippines to banana companies, especially under the debt-ridden Marcos regime, hungry for foreign investment, consumers in Japan and the Persian Gulf have become the latest targets for advertising campaigns.

* * *

Women in Banana Republics

It is always worth asking, 'Where are the women?' Answering the question reveals the dependence of most political and economic systems not just on women, but on certain kinds of relations between women and men. A great deal has been written about countries derisively labeled 'banana republics'. They are described as countries whose land and soul are in the clutches of a foreign company, supported by the might of its own government. A banana republic's sovereignty has been so thoroughly compromised that it is the butt of jokes, not respect. It has a government, but it is staffed by people who line their own pockets by doing the bidding of the overseas corporation and its political allies. Because it is impossible for such compromised rulers to win the support of their own citizens, many of whom are exploited on the corporation's plantations, the government depends on guns and jails, not ballots and national pride.

The quintessential banana republics were those Central American countries which came to be dominated by the United Fruit Company's monoculture, the US marines and their hand-picked dictators. Their regimes have been backed by American presidents, mocked by Woody Allen, and overthrown by nationalist guerrillas.

Yet these political systems, and the international relationships which underpin them, have been discussed as if women scarcely existed. The principal actors on all sides have been portrayed by conventional commentators as men, and as if their being male was insignificant. Thus the ways in which their shared masculinity allowed agribusiness entrepreneurs to form alliances with men in their own diplomatic corps and with men in Nicaraguan or Honduran society have been left unexamined. Enjoying Cuban cigars together after dinner while wives and mistresses powder their noses has been the stuff of smug cartoons but not of political curiosity. Similarly, a banana republic's militarized ethos has been taken for granted, without an investigation of how militarism feeds on masculinist values to sustain it. Marines, diplomats, corporate managers and military dictators may mostly be male, but they tend to need the feminine 'other' to maintain their self-assurance.

One of the conditions that has pushed women off the banana republic stage has been the masculinization of the banana plantation. Banana-company executives imagined that most of the jobs on their large plantations could be done only by men. Banana plantations were carved out of wooden acres. Clearing the brush required workers who could use a machete, live in rude barracks, and who, once the plantation's trees were bearing fruit, could chop down the heavy bunches and carry them to central loading areas and from there to the docks, to be loaded by the ton on to refrigerator ships. This was men's work.

Not all plantation work has been masculinized. Generally, crops that call for the use of machetes—tools that can also be used as weapons—are produced with large inputs of male labor: bananas, sugar, palm oil. Producers of crops that require a lot of weeding, tapping and picking hire large numbers of women, sometimes comprising a majority of workers: tea, coffee, rubber.

Nor is the gendered labor formula on any plantation fixed. Plantation managers who once relied heavily on male workers may decide to bring in more women if the men become too costly; if their union becomes too threatening; if the international market for the crop declines necessitating cost-cutting measures such as hiring more part-time workers; if new technology allows some physically demanding tasks to be done by workers with less strength. Today both sugar and rubber are being produced by plantation companies using more women workers than they did a generation ago.[8] What has remained constant, however, is the presumption of international corporations that their position in the world market depends on manipulations of masculinity and femininity. Gender is injected into every Brooke Bond or Lipton tea leaf, every Unilever or Lonrho palm-oil nut, every bucket of Dunlop or Michelin latex, every stalk of Tate & Lyle sugar cane.

Like all plantation managers, banana company executives considered race as well as gender when employing what they thought would be the most skilled and compliant workforce. Thus although the majority of banana workers were men, race was used to divide them. On United Brands' plantations in Costa Rica and Panama, for instance, managers recruited Amerindian men from the Guaymi and Kuna communities, as well as West Indian Black men and hispanicized Ladino men. They placed them in different, unequally paid jobs, Ladino men at the top (below white male managers), Amerindian men at the bottom. Amerindian men were assigned to menial jobs such as chopping grass and overgrown bush, thus ensuring that Ladino men's negative stereotypes of Amerindians—*cholos,* unskilled, uncultured natives—would be perpetuated. The stereotypes were valuable to the company because they forestalled potential alliances between Ladino, Black and Amerindian men over common grievances.[9]

Manager: It's easier to work with *cholos.* They're not as smart and don't speak good Spanish. They can't argue back at you even when they're right … Hell, you can make a *cholo* do anything.

Ladino foreman: My workers are [not] *cholos.* … It's different here. Sure I can grab them [Ladino and Black male workers] and make them work faster; but the consequences will catch up with me tomorrow. We're not *cholos* here … you understand?

Guaymi worker: They used to have up to 200 of us crammed into shacks eating boiled bananas out of empty kerosene cans.[10]

To say, therefore, that a banana plantation is masculinized is not to say that masculinity, even when combined with social class, is sufficient to forge political unity. On the other hand, the presumption that a banana plantation is a man's world does affect the politics of any movement attempting to improve workers' conditions, or to transform the power relationships that comprise a 'banana republic'.

A banana plantation's politics are deeply affected not just by the fact that the majority of its workers—and virtually all of its managers and owners—are men, but by the *meaning* that has been attached to that masculinization. Even male banana workers employed by a foreign company that, in alliance with local élites, had turned their country into a proverbial banana republic, could feel some pride. For they were unquestionably performing men's work. They knew how to wield a machete; they knew how to lift great weights; they worked outside in close coordination with trains and ships. Whether a smallholder or a plantation employee, a banana man was a *man*.

* * *

In the 1920s when banana workers began to organize and to conduct strikes that even the US government and local élites had to pay attention to, their demands reached beyond working conditions to political structures. These workers' protests took on strong nationalist overtones: the local regime and foreign troops were as much the target of their protests as the plantation companies. But so long as banana plantation work was imagined to be men's work, and so long as the banana workers' unions were organized as if they were men's organizations, the nationalist cause would be masculinized. A banana republic might fall, but patriarchy remained in place.

Women Weed, Women Clean

The banana plantation has never been as exclusively male as popular imagery suggests. It takes women's paid and unpaid labor to bring the golden fruit to the world's breakfast tables.

A banana plantation is closest to a male enclave at the beginning, when the principal task is bulldozing and clearing the land for planting. But even at this stage women are depended upon by the companies—and their male employees—to play their roles. As in the male-dominated mining industry from Chile to South Africa and Indonesia, companies can recruit men to live away from home only if someone back home takes care of their families and maintains their land. The 'feminization of agriculture'—that is, leaving small-scale farming to women, typically without giving them training, equipment or extra finance—has always been part and parcel of the masculinization of mining and banana plantations.[11] The male labor force has to make private arrangements with wives, mothers or sisters to assure them of a place to return to when their contracts expire, when they get fed up with supervisors' contemptuous treatment or when they are laid off because world prices have plummeted. Behind every all-male banana plantation stand scores of women performing unpaid domestic and productive labor. Company executives, union spokesmen and export-driven government officials have all preferred not to take this into account when working out their bargaining positions. International agencies such as the International Monetary Fund scarcely give a thought to women as wives and subsistence farmers when they press indebted governments to open up more land to plantation companies in order to correct their trade imbalances and pay off foreign bankers.

Once the banana trees have been planted, women are likely to become residents and workers on the plantations. Plantation managers, like their diplomatic and military counterparts, have found marriage both a political asset and a liability. On the one hand, having young male workers without wives and children has advantages: the men are in their physical prime, they are likely to view life as an adventure and be willing to tolerate harsh working and living conditions. On the other hand, young unattached men are more volatile and are willing to take risks if angered precisely because they will not jeopardize anyone's security aside from their own. This makes the married male worker seem more stable to a calculating plantation manager. He may demand more from the company in the form of rudimentary amenities for his wife and children, but he is more likely to toe the company line for their sake.[12]

Women are most likely to be employed by the banana companies if the plantation cannot recruit men from a low-status ethnic group, like Amerindians in Central America, to do the least prestigious and lowest-paid jobs. In all sorts of agribusiness, women tend to be given the most tedious, least 'skilled' jobs, those that are most seasonal, the least likely to offer year-round employment and those company benefits awarded to full-time employees. Weeding and cleaning are the quintessential 'women's' jobs in agriculture, both in socialist and capitalist countries.[13]

Bananas today are washed, weighed and packed in factories on the plantations before being transported to the docks for shipment overseas. Inside these packing houses one finds the women on the modern banana plantation. They remove the bunches of fruit from the thick stems, an operation that has to be done carefully (one might say skillfully) so that the bananas are not damaged. They wash the bananas in a chemical solution, a hazardous job. They select the rejects, which can amount to up to half the bananas picked in the fields. Companies often dump rejected bananas in nearby streams, causing pollution which kills local fish. Women weigh the fruit and finally attach the company's tell-tale sticker on each bunch. They are paid piece-rates and foremen expect them to work at high speed. In between harvests they may have little work to do and not receive any pay. At harvest time they are expected to be available for long stretches, sometimes around the clock, to meet the company's tight shipping schedule.[14]

Tess is a Filipino woman who works for TADECO, a subsidiary of United Brands, Philippines. She works on a plantation on the country's southern island, Mindanao. A decade-long war has been fought in the area between government troops and indigenous Muslim groups protesting against the leasing of large tracts of land either to multinational pineapple and banana companies or to wealthy Filipino landowners, who then work out lucrative contracts with those corporations. Tess herself is a Christian Filipina. She, like thousands of other women and men, migrated, with government encouragement, to Mindanao from other islands in search of work once the bottom fell out of the once-dominant sugar industry. She works with other young women in the plantation's packing plant, preparing bananas to be shipped to Japan by Japanese and American import companies. She is paid approximately $1 a day. With an additional living allowance, Tess can make about $45 a month; she sends a third of this home to her family in the Visayas.

Tess uses a chemical solution to wash the company's bananas. There is a large, reddish splotch on her leg where some of the chemical spilled accidentally. At the end of a day spent standing for hours at a time, Tess goes 'home' to a bunkhouse she shares with 100 other women, twenty-four to a room, sleeping in eight sets of three-tiered bunks.[15]

Many women working on banana plantations are young and single, and, in the Philippines, often have secondary-school or even college educations. They may be the daughters of male employees, or they may be recruited from outside. They are subjected to sexual harassment in the packing plants and can be fired if found to be pregnant. The life of a banana washer is dull and isolated: 'We have no choice than to stay here. First, the company is quite far from the highway and if we ... spend our fare what else would be left for our food?'[16]

Large banana companies—Geest in Britain, United Brands, Del Monte and Dole in the United States and Japan's Sumitomo—also require workers at the other end of the food chain, in the countries where they market their bananas. The docks, the trucks and the ripening plants reveal how company managers shape the sexual division of labor. Stevedors in every country are thought of as doing a classic 'man's' job, though again ethnic politics may determine which men will unload the bananas from the company's ships. Today in Japan, where immigrant labor is being increasingly relied upon to do the low-status, low-paid jobs, Filipino men do the heavy work of transferring bananas from ships to trucks. The job has become so closely associated with the fruit that to be long-shoreman in Japan is to be a 'banana'. Women are hired in all the consumer countries to weigh and sort at the ripening plant before the fruit heads for the supermarket. Food processing is as feminized—as dependent on ideas about femininity—as nursing, secretarial work and sewing.

Women are hired by the banana companies to do low-paid, often seasonal jobs that offer little chance of training and promotion; some involve the hazards of chemical pollution and sexual harassment. But many women still seek these jobs because they seem better than the alternatives: dependence on fathers or husbands (if they are employed), life on the dole (if work is not available), work in the entertainment industry around a military base, subsistence farming with few resources, emigration.

Many women are heads of households and take exploitative jobs in order to support their children; other women see their employment as part of being dutiful daughters, sending part of their meager earnings back to parents, who may be losing farm land to agribusinesses. Neither women nor men working on any plantation—banana, tea, rubber, sugar, pineapple, palm oil, coffee—are simply 'workers'. They are wives, husbands, daughters, sons, mothers, fathers, lovers; and each role has its own politics. The politics of being a daughter, a mother or a wife allows First World and Third World governments to rely on international plantation companies, which in turn are able to recruit and control women workers and win the consumer loyalty of women buyers. 'Daughter', 'mother', and 'wife' are ideas on which the international political system today depends.

Brothels and Bananas

Bananas have long been the object of sexual jokes and pranks. One food company recently complained when an AIDS education campaign used a banana to demonstrate how a man should put on a condom. But the banana industry—not the banana itself—is far more seriously sexualized. Sexual harassment helps to control women working the plantation factories; prostitution has been permitted in order to control the still largely male plantation workforce.

* * *

Plantations are self-contained worlds. Workers, managers and the crops they cultivate live together side by side, but regulated by strict hierarchies, the more blatant because they are carved into the landscape. Male managers and their wives live in comfortable houses with gardens and kitchens maintained by local employees and have access to their own clubs with well-stocked bars and refreshing swimming pools. Foremen and their families have their own more modest housing compound and privileges. Workers live in spartan accommodation that often lacks minimal sanitary facilities. Some plantations are better equipped than others. Head offices like to talk about the clinics and schools they provide. They rarely talk about the isolation, or the paralyzing debts accumulated by employees at the company store. Some companies have had to provide basic necessities for workers in order to obtain land rights and tax concessions from local governments. Caribbean critics of their countries' past dependency on monoculture have coined the term 'plantation economy': foreign agribusiness giants have so dominated an entire society that it is reduced to a community permeated by dependency and paternalistic control.[17]

Plantations that depend on a predominately male workforce operate much like military bases. Women's sexual availability just outside the gates (thus supposedly beyond the plantation manager's control) has been offered as one of the rewards for enduring the isolated, harsh conditions of plantation life.

Few commentators on 'plantation economies' have thought to ask about the ways that sexuality has been used to control male workers. One who has is historian Ann Laura Stoler. When investigating life on Dutch-owned sisal, tea, rubber and palm-oil plantations in colonial Indonesia she asked about sexual politics.[18] Stoler found that prostitution was integral to the way managers recruited and controlled male workers from several different ethnic groups. There were many more men than women on these estates. Women were hired at half the rates paid to men, not enough to meet daily necessities. Most were single Javanese women, hired on contract and living far away from home. To make ends meet many of these women provided sexual services to Chinese male workers living in the plantation barracks. Some young women were pushed into prostitution by being sexually harassed by foremen in the packing plants. White plantation supervisors enjoyed the privilege of selecting their sexual partners from the most recent female arrivals.

Prostitution became the norm on many plantations by design, not simply by chance. There are records revealing that managers debated the advantages and disadvantages of prostitution for their company. The debates have a familiar ring; they echo debates about military prostitution. Some Dutch commentators were alarmed at the high incidence of venereal disease among plantation workers and blamed the prostitutes. Others noted that white supervisors were assaulted by male Javanese workers who believed their daughters were being lured into prostitution. But the prevailing view was that it would be too difficult to recruit male workers for plantation work if they were not provided with female sexual services. Furthermore, in the eyes of many plantation managers, prostitution was a lesser evil than homosexual relations between male workers deprived of female companionship. Finally, devoting a sizeable portion of their wages to prostitution left many male workers further in debt and thus made it harder for them to abandon estate work when their current contracts expired.

Around some United Brands plantations in Central America brothels are commonplace. They are situated just outside the company gates. While the men on banana plantations are Amerindian, Black and Ladino, the women working in the brothels are overwhelmingly Ladino. Information is limited, but most women servicing banana workers seem to have done other sorts of work before becoming prostitutes, and many are the sole supporters of their children. Racism and sexism are woven together in Central America's banana plantation brothels, as is so often the case in prostitution politics. Ladino prostitutes told one researcher that they preferred Amerindian customers because, they said, these men were too shy to fully undress and got their intercourse over with quickly. This was not necessarily meant as a compliment to Amerindian masculinity and may have reinforced negative stereotypes among Ladino and Black male workers.[19]

Patriarchal Land Reform

Not all bananas are grown on plantations owned or leased by large corporations. Many people in Africa, Asia, the Caribbean and Latin America eat bananas that are grown in their own yards or by small-scale independent farmers, a large proportion of them women, and sold by market women—Carmen Miranda's and Chiquita's inspiration—in provincial towns. Even some of the bananas reaching the supermarkets of industrialized countries—for instance, many Philippines bananas shipped to Japan—are cultivated by smallholders. Geest, one of Britain's largest food companies, buys its bananas from smallholders in the Windward Islands: St. Lucia, Dominica, Grenada and St. Vincent.[20]

In 1985 Britons consumed nearly 2 billion bananas; over half of them were Windward Island bananas imported and marketed by Geest. Charles Geest, one of two Dutch brothers who founded the company, was listed in 1989 as one of 200 Britons personally worth over £30 million.[21] But Geest operates quite differently to Dole, United Brands or other large-scale plantation companies. Its suppliers may have as much as twelve acres of land or as little as half an acre of land. These smallholders sell their bananas to the local Banana Growers Association, which in turn sells them to Geest. As the sole purchaser of Windward bananas and as the operator of the shipping company, the ripening plants and the wholesale network, Geest is able to impose quality standards, rules and a pricing formula that determine how its Caribbean suppliers must operate. Critics in the Caribbean and Britain charge that Geest makes unfair profits and controls local farmers without having to assume direct responsibility.

It is all too easy to carry out an analysis of Geest without asking where the women are. The question seems unnecessary if one assumes that once the plantation system is removed and a crop is grown by smallholders on their own land, women and men within a household will work together as equals. The only political question then worth pursuing is whether the smallholders are dealt with fairly by the international marketing firm and the governments which link the farmers and the ultimate consumers.

But scratch the surface of small-scale farming and a more complex reality appears. In Dominica a survey of 120 banana farms ranging from one to five acres in size revealed that 82 per cent were owned by men; only 18 per cent were owned by women. This, despite the fact that on virtually every farm it took both women's and men's labor to nurture and harvest bananas that met Geest's high standards. In neighboring St. Lucia 95 per cent of the small farms surveyed were owned by the men of the household, only 5 per cent by the women. In St. Vincent the same pattern was repeated: men owned 70 per cent, women owned 30 per cent.[22]

The Banana Growers Association and Geest's managers are overwhelmingly male. They deal with small-scale owners who are mostly male. 'The smallholder and his wife' is the phrase commonly heard in international development circles. The phrase is not just sloppy semantics. It permits development agencies and local agricultural ministries to imagine that the person in the rural household to whom technical training, new seeds or agricultural credit should be given is the adult man. The unspoken corollary is that what is progress for a husband will turn into progress for his wife.

* * *

'The farmer and his wife' disguises the reality of the world's food production. Most technical agencies agree that women produce at least half of the world's food. In Africa they produce between 60 per cent and 80 per cent. It is the politics of land *ownership* that obscures this reality. If one is talking about food production, not land ownership, it might be more accurate to refer to 'the farmer and her husband'.

More seriously, 'the farmer and his wife' not only obscures the gendered politics of land ownership; it also makes invisible the ways in which women organize their daily lives to sustain families and still produce bananas on their smallholdings. The use of 'the household' as the unit for measuring the success or failure of any project or policy is radically flawed. It presumes—without testing that presumption against reality—that the relationships within any house are equal, that emotional, sexual and economic relationships between men and women and sons and daughters are naturally harmonious, without tension, without intimidation of coercion. This was the presumption used in Britain, France, Canada and the United States to deny women the right to vote: why would a woman need a vote of her own when her father, husband or brother would 'naturally' cast his ballot with her best interest in mind? What was a naïve assumption in the suffrage debate is an unfounded argument in the politics of the banana.[23]

Feminists in Third World countries who have made land reform a political cause have insisted that dismantling large plantations—whether locally or foreign-owned—must not be seen as sufficient to ensure that women gain the power and resources they need to shape rural development so that women as well as men benefit. If land reform is implemented without a critical examination of *which* small farmers will receive the precious land title, land reform can serve to perpetuate patriarchal inequities in the countryside.

In several countries where plantation agriculture has been dominant, women's groups are challenging relations between men and women that shape the way food is produced. In Kenya, where both high-ranking government officials and foreign agribusinesses have profited from the opening of more land to large-scale plantations, Kikuyu women working in a Del Monte pineapple packing plant went on strike in 1987 to protest at working conditions.[24] Honduran peasant organizations with strong women leaders have created autonomous women peasants' groups to permit women to develop political skills. Honduras depends on bananas for over 30 per cent of its export earnings, and the government is closely allied militarily to the United States; the organized peasant women take part in land seizures and call on the government to revise its modest land distribution law so that women other than widows can gain direct title to land.[25] A small group of Honduran women, who have to support their children on $2 a day earned by picking melons and cantaloupes for a multinational, joined the Honduran Federation of Peasant Women (FEHMUC) and began thinking about ways to generate income for themselves. They learned carpentry skills and made the broomsticks and bookshelves. With the money she earned one woman bought the village's first sewing machine, while another woman saved enough to send her daughter to secondary school.[26]

On rubber plantations in Malaysia, the world's largest exporter of rubber, most workers are Indian Malaysians, descendants of workers brought from India at the turn of the century to supply cheap labor for Britain's colonial estates. Women started to work on rubber plantations decades ago, but with the decline in world rubber prices, plantation owners have been turning more and more to women to tap their trees. They are hired as casual labor and thus are less costly than full-time male employees. Britain's legacy of ethnic divide-and-rule and Malaysia's anti-union laws have made bridge-building between Malay, Chinese and Indian women difficult. In addition, the rubber workers' union has been run by Indian Malaysian men. Despite the formidable obstacles, one Malaysian working-women's organization has begun performing dramas on rubber plantations to highlight the dangers for women tappers of the widely used pesticide paraquat. Some plantation women have gone blind from accidental spraying of paraquat, but with rubber prices falling and tappers earning as little as $35 per month, women workers have little time or energy to read, and newspapers cost money that must be spent on food and clothing. So the combination of dramatic performances and sending press clippings to be shared is the Malaysian women activists' strategy for making a small dent in the gender structure on which the rubber industry depends.[27] In using drama to give rural women a new sense of their worth and their political capabilities, the Malaysian women are paralleling Sistren, a Jamaican feminist theater group, whose members are tackling the complex problems flowing from the decline of Jamaica's one-time sugar-dependent economy.[28]

In Nicaragua coffee and banana plantations that have been collectivized have not radically altered the sexual division of labor—there is still 'men's work' and 'women's work' outside and especially inside the rural home. But more Nicaraguan women are beginning to do field jobs, not just packaging, on the banana estates. In coffee cultivation, where women in the past were expected to plant and transplant seedlings, women are starting to use flame throwers in the clearing of hillsides. Later in the coffee-growing cycle women are beginning to join men in what used to be a 'men's job', the pruning of coffee trees. These small steps toward redefining the division of labor have led to an unexpected change in sexual politics. When only men worked together, they forged friendships that spilled over into their after-work socializing. Nicaraguan women on one coffee estate describe how men used to go off together to town to drink and visit brothels. Working buddies became brothel buddies. But, according to these women, now that men are more likely to work alongside women when they clear the land or prune the trees, they form friendships with those women and are less inclined to see drinking and going to prostitutes as the only after-work recreation.[29]

Developing a politics of land reform and agricultural labor that does not reproduce patriarchal relationships between rural women and men is not something that happens automatically. It does not derive necessarily from either a class-conscious or a nationalist politics of food. Where unequal and unfair relations between rural women and men have been seriously challenged, it has usually required women's own analysis and autonomous organizing. Both have been seen by some male land-reform activists either as a waste of time or as a threat to peasant unity. In 1985, as rural Filipinos were mobilizing to overthrow the Marcos regime, some activist peasant women decided that if land reform, a principal demand of the anti-Marcos movement, was to benefit women as well as men, women would have to organize autonomously. They created RICE (not an acronym). Eighteen months later, with Marcos replaced by Corazon Aquino, RICE had grown to 100 members and had affiliated with Gabriela, the umbrella women's group. RICE members also affiliated with the National Peasant Movement, popularly known as the KMP. Although the KMP is perhaps the most visible advocate of genuine land reform, the women in RICE saw it as a male-dominated organization. In villages where KMP was formed before RICE became active, KMP has remained dominated by male peasants. But where a branch of RICE brought together local women for discussions before KMP organized villagers, KMP's local councils have had more women participants and have accorded serious attention to matters of concern to women. One such issue is husbands' refusal to acknowledge the economic contributions made by their wives.

* * *

RICE was not the name these women peasants gave themselves. But they soon adopted this English name in the hope that it would sound less threatening to local military commanders. It has been difficult for RICE to criticize the KMP's male domination in part because the army and military-supported vigilante groups have continued to torture and murder KMP activists.

Bananas, like anything else, can be militarized. In the Philippines, as in Honduras and Colombia, banana-plantation union activists have been assassinated by troops loyal to a government that sees multinational agribusiness as good for the economy. The current land system has been maintained in part by intimidation and force.[30] But militarization not only bolsters the plantation system and undermines land-reform movements in general; it also makes any woman's criticism of a progressive movement's male leaders and masculinized agenda appear illegitimate, even dangerous. How can a woman dare to criticize a fellow peasant activist when he is the target of military harassment? An army which uses coercion to maintain the rural status quo makes it hard to shake a nationalist land-reform movement free from its patriarchal base.

Women peasant activists in Honduras and the Philippines have themselves become the objects of an American counter-insurgency doctrine called 'Low-Intensity Conflict'. LIC employs a sprawling definition of 'insurgency' to justify harassment, intimidation and local disruption, and relies on vigilante groups as well as uniformed troops. Its implementation in the Philippines and Central America has made it politically hazardous for rural women to challenge rural men. It has also undermined rural women's independent efforts. To a national-security official who views 'development' through the prism of low-intensity conflict, day-care centers and food cooperatives—projects rural women believe are integral to real land reform—are subversive; they are thus legitimate targets for counter-insurgency operations. In 1987 RICE had twelve groups on Mindanao; a year later only five had survived.[31]

Conclusion

Today's affluent consumers are increasingly conscious of the nutritional content of their daily food. Walk into any supermarket and you see the aisles crowded with customers reading the fine print on labels. As affluent consumers' tastes change, the international agribusinesses prick up their ears. So do the bankers, foreign advisors and politicians who work with them to shape international food policies. If the banana was the 'new food' of 1880s America and 1920s Japan, broccoli, radicchio and winter strawberries are the 'new foods' of the 1990s. This affects not only what women buy and cook in Saucilito and in Hampstead; it affects what women and men produce for plantation companies in Kenya, Malaysia, Guatemala and Jamaica.

It may be tempting to imagine plantations as part of an 'old-fashioned' way of life. They seem to symbolize the bad old days of slavery and colonialism. They conjure up the American ante-bellum South or the British empire according to Somerset Maugham. In reality plantations are as modern (or 'post-modern') as the home computer or toxic waste. Large plantation companies such as Castle and Cook (owner of Dole and Standard Fruit), Unilever (owner of both Liptons and Brooke Bond), Del Monte (recently purchased by R. J. Reynolds as part of its buyout of RJR Nabisco) and United Brands, are some of the largest multinational companies in the world today, wielding influence over their own as well as foreign governments.

Furthermore, plantation company executives don't stand still. When the political climate where they are operating becomes chilly—with the passage of land-reform laws or the successful unionization of agricultural workers—they try to persuade new governments to open up lands for plantation crops. When Honduran banana workers used strikes to compel their government to deny recognition to a company-controlled union, their employer, United Brands, began to look more favorably on the Philippines. Similarly, as 1992 looms in

Europe, Del Monte has taken steps to persuade the government of Cameroon to open its lands to banana cultivation. Del Monte's Cameroon bananas will be marketed in Europe with the benefit of EEC trade concessions given to former European colonies. Other companies switch to new crops when the market begins to decline in once-profitable products. Thus nowadays the Chiquita label is turning up on melons. Britain's Brooke Bond, once synonymous with tea and still known by the woman tea-picker on its label, has moved into the flower business. Brooke Bond has convinced senior Kenyan government officials that it is in their interest to open extensive flower plantations. Carnations-for-export have become part of the international political economy.[32]

Similarly, Coca Cola, world-famous for its soft drinks, has become one of the world's largest growers of citrus fruits. Its executives have persuaded the government of Belize, still hosting British troops but increasingly pressed to further American interests, to allow it to develop thousands of acres for exported oranges. Palm oil was seen in the 1970s and early 1980s by many export-sensitive governments and their foreign bankers as an attractive substitute for less stable plantation crops such as rubber; now oil-palm plantations are being threatened by Americans' aversion to cholesterol. Companies such as Unilever may rethink their investments in Zaïre, Malaysia and Ecuador if Europeans follow the Americans in insisting that food-processing companies eliminate saturated fats from their cereals, cookie batter and other foods. In Guatemala and Chile, nervous governments and their military commanders are looking to grape and broccoli farming to pacify their rural populations and stabilize their currencies. General Pinochet has given governmental assistance to large-scale fruit estates owned by supporters of his regime so that they and fruit exports have become a principal prop for his government at a time when popular opposition has become alarmingly bold. Military counter-insurgency strategists in Guatemala are pinning their hopes on the opening of large broccoli, cauliflower and cabbage estates to pacify alienated highland Indians.[33]

These plantation companies and the importing and exporting governments that rely on them for tax revenues and political support each make gendered calculations. They appeal to women as food purchasers and as food preparers. If Carmen Miranda helped smooth the way for a more subtle form of American regional influence, 'Chiquita Banana' helped create consumer loyalty for a product that yielded huge profits for an American corporation; the real market women of Latin America were marginalized by a potent combination of 'Good Neighbor' diplomacy and agribusiness advertising.[34] On the other hand, while women consumers often have a difficult time acquiring accurate nutritional information, acting together they have helped open up the files of food corporations. Women who today buy more fresh broccoli than canned peas are not merely passive creatures in an advertising agency's scenario.

As women consumers—in Third World as well as First World countries—try to reorganize the politics of food, women food-industry workers—in the First

World as well as the Third World—try to reorganize the politics of land and labor. Plantation companies and the governments who need them have depended on the control of women in order to profitably produce every one of their agricultural products. This has been especially obvious in those sectors where plantation managers have defined most of the tasks as 'women's work': tea, coffee and to a lesser extent rubber. The dependence on women has been harder to recognize in sectors where work has been masculinized: bananas, palm oil, and to a lesser extent sugar. But in *both* masculinized and feminized plantation agriculture women have been crucial to the success of the company and its governmental allies. For even where women do not supply the bulk of the paid labor, they perform certain crucial jobs—as seasonal weeders, as processing-plant workers—and they supply cheap, part-time labor, to be called on when the world price drops for the company's product. Women also provide a plantation's male workers with unpaid food cultivation, child care and sexual satisfaction. Women plantation workers and women farmers share a politics of invisibility. A woman agriculturalist is transformed by writers, policy-makers and economists into 'the farmer's wife'. This transformation is a political process that is being challenged by women farmers not only in Third World countries, but also in West Germany, France, Spain and the United States.[35]

All too often the international politics of bananas (and sugar, rubber and broccoli) are discussed as if they were formulated only in bankers' board rooms or union leaders' meetings. Because both of these settings have been so male-dominated, the dependence of food politics on women and on ideas about masculinity and femininity has been ignored. This in turn has meant that even genuine non-feminist attempts to reform agrarian politics—in the name of nationalism or development—have failed to change patriarchal relationships. The politics of bananas and broccoli cannot be fully transformed until both women and men are made visible, as consumers, producers, managers and policy-makers.

Notes

1. James Robert Parish, *The Fox Girls,* New Rochell, NY, Arlington House, 1972, pp. 499–528.
2. Ibid., p. 504.
3. George Black, *The Good Neighbor: How the United States Wrote the History of Central America and the Caribbean,* New York, Pantheon, 1988, pp. 68–71. See also Neal Gabler, *An Empire of Their own: How the Jews Invented Hollywood,* New York, Crown, 1988.
4. Eduardo Galeano, *Century of the Wind,* New York, Pantheon, 1988, p. 131. For Galeano's description of Hollywood's Latin American male stereotype in the 1940s, see p. 122.
5. Claire Shaver Houghton, *Green Immigrants: The Plants that Transformed America,* New York and London, Harcourt Brace Jovanovich, 1978, pp. 30–5. Also, *People Like Bananas,* Boston, United Fruit Company, 1968.

6. *People Like Bananas,* op. cit. Chiquita Brands, a subsidiary of United Brands (formerly United Fruit), publishes a newsletter, *Chiquita Quarterly,* which makes regular mention of the company's shipping fleet, the world's largest refrigerated shipping fleet, 12 per cent of the world's total.

7. Black, op. cit., pp. 77–8. For a critical assessment of American banana companies' political role in Central America, see Stephen Schlesinger, *Bitter Fruit: The Untold Story of the American Coup in Guatemala,* New York, Doubleday, 1982.

8. Books and articles analyzing the gendered character of plantation agriculture include Angela Davis, 'Reflections on the Black Women's Role in the Community of Slaves', *The Black Scholar,* no. 3, December, 1971; Rhoda Reddock, 'Women and the Slave Plantation Economy in the Caribbean', in S. Jay Kleinberg, editor, *Retrieving Women's History,* Oxford and New York, Berg, 1988, pp. 105–32. Jacqueline Jones, *Labor of Love, Labor of Sorrow: Black Women, Work and the Family from Slavery to the Present,* New York, Vintage, 1986; Elizabeth Fox-Genovese, *Within the Plantation Household: Black and White Women of the Old South,* Chapel Hill, NC: University of North Carolina, 1988; Ronald Takaki, *Pau Hana: Plantation Life and Labor in Hawaii,* Honolulu, University of Hawaii Press, 1983; Belinda Coote, *The Hunger Crop: Poverty and the Sugar Industry,* Oxford, Oxfam, 1987; Shaista Shameen, 'Gender, Class and Race Dynamics: Indian Women in Sugar Production in Fiji', *The Journal of Pacific Studies,* special issue, 'Women and Work in the Pacific', vol. 13, 1987, pp. 10–35; Sidney Mintz, *Worker in the Cane: A Puerto Rican Life History,* New Haven, Yale University Press, 1960; Laurel Herbener Bossen, *The Redivision of Labor: Women and Economic Choice in Four Guatemalan Communities,* Albany, SUNY Press, 1984; Noeleen Heyzer, *Working Women in South-East Asia,* Milton Keynes and Philadelphia, Open University Press, 1986; Ravinda K. Jain, *South Indians on the Plantation Frontier in Malaya,* New Haven, Yale University Press, 1970; Ann Laura Stoler, *Capitalism and Confrontation in Sumatra's Plantation Belt, 1870–1979,* New Haven, Yale University Press, 1985; Rachel Kurian, *Women Workers in the Sri Lanka Plantation Belt,* Geneva, International Labor Organization, 1982; Rachel Kurian, 'Ethnicity, Patriarchy and Labor Control: Tamil Women in Plantation Production', Institute of Social Sciences, The Hague, 1986; Dan Jones, *Tea and Justice: British Tea Companies and the Tea Workers of Bangladesh,* London, Bangladesh International Action Group, 1986; Maitrayee Mukhopadhyay, *Silver Shackles: Women and Development in India,* Oxford, Oxfam, 1984; Stella Hillier and Lynne Gerlach, *Whose Paradise? Tea and the Plantation Tamils in Sri Lanka,* London, Minority Rights Group, 1987.

9. Philippe Bourgois, *Ethnic Diversity on a Corporate Plantation,* Cambridge, MA, Cultural Survival, 1986.

10. Ibid., pp. 10–11.

11. On the feminization of agriculture and its developmental consequences, see Esther Boserup, *Women's Roles in Economic Development,* London, George Allen & Unwin, 1970; Barbara Rogers, *The Domestication of Women: Discrimination in Developing Societies,* London, Kogan Page, 1980. For a perceptive examination of the gender and ethnic hierarchies that support a multinational mining company's operations in Indonesia, see Kathryn M. Robinson, *Stepchildren of Progress,* Albany, State University of New York Press, 1986.

12. Philippe Bourgois, Department of Anthropology, Washington University, St. Louis, in correspondence with the author, October 2, 1986.

13. See Susan Bridger, *Women in the Soviet Countryside,* Cambridge and New York, Cambridge University Press, 1987; Sharon L. Wolchik and Alfred G. Meyer, editors, *Women, State and Party in Eastern Europe,* Durham, Duke University Press, 1988.

14. Elizabeth U. Eviota, 'The Articulation of Gender and Class in the Philippines', in Eleanor Leacock and Helen I. Safa and contributors, *Women's Work,* South Hadley, MA, Bergin & Garvey, 1986, p. 199. Also correspondence with Philippe Bourgois, October 2, 1986. On women working in the food-processing business, see Lourdes Arizpe and Josephina Aranda, 'Women Workers in the Strawberry Agribusiness in Mexico', in Leacock and Safa, op. cit., pp. 174–93; Vicki Ruiz, *Cannery Women, Cannery Lives,* Albuquerque, NM, University of New Mexico Press, 1987; Patricia Zavella, *Women's Work and Chicano Families,* Ithaca, NY, Cornell University Press, 1987.

15. Sr. Mary Soledad Perpinan, 'Women and Transnational Corporations: The Philippines Experience', reprinted in Daniel Schirmer and Stephen R. Shalom, editors, *The Philippines Reader,* Boston, South End Press, 1987, p. 243.

16. Quoted in the slide-show, 'Bananas', produced by a progressive Filipino organization in the early 1980s. For a description of women workers' lives on Dole's pineapple plantations in the Philippines, see 'Women of Dole', originally published in *Womenews,* vol. 3, no. 1, January–March, 1986, reprinted in *Philippine Women,* NY, Women's International Resources Exchange, 1987. On Castle and Cook's banana and pineapple operations in the Philippines, see Dorothy Friesen, *Critical Choices: A Journey with the Filipino People,* Grand Rapids, MI, William B. Eerdmans Publishing Co., 1988. For an assessment of policies needed to ensure redistribution of plantation land—much of it leased from large Filipino landowners, not owned outright by the foreign companies—see Yujio Hayami, Lourdes S. Adriano and Agnes R. Quisumbing, *Agribusiness and Agrarian Reform: A View from the Banana and Pineapple Plantations,* Quezon City, Center for Policy and Development Studies, University of the Philippines, 1988.

17. Clive Thomas, *Plantations, Peasants and the State,* Los Angeles, Center for Afro-American Studies, UCLA, 1984.

18. Ann Laura Stoler, op. cit., pp. 30–34.

19. Correspondence with Philippe Bourgois, October 2, 1986.

20. Information on Geest comes from: *Geest Gold: Bananas and Dependency in the Eastern Caribbean,* London, Latin American Bureau, and New York, Monthly Review Press, 1987; *Whose Gold: Geest and the Banana Trade,* London, Latin America Bureau, 1987. For information on women's and men's relationships in Zaïre's banana farming, see Catherine Newbury, 'From Bananas to Cassava', typescript, Department of Political Science, University of North Carolina, Chapel Hill, NC, 1985.

21. 'Britain's Rich', *Sunday Times* colour supplement, April 2, 1989, p. 41.

22. *Geest Gold,* op. cit., pp. 45–6. See also Pat Ellis, editor, *Women of the Caribbean,* London, Zed Books, and Atlantic Highlands, NJ, Humanities Press, 1986; *Daughters of the Nightmare: Women in the Caribbean,* London, Change, International Reports on Women, 1983.

23. Gita Sen and Caren Grown, *Development, Crises and Alternative Visions: Third World Women's Perspectives*, New York, Monthly Review Press, 1987; Troth Wells and Foo Gaik Sim, *Till They Have Faces: Women as Consumers*, Penang and Rome, International Organization of Consumers' Unions, Regional Office for Asia and ISIS International, 1987; Ng Sock Nye, 'Status of Rural Women', in Evelyn Hong, editor, *Malaysian Women: Problems and Issues*, Penang, Consumers' Association of Penang, 1983, pp. 38–48; Lucy E. Creevey, editor, *Women Farmers in Africa*, Syracuse, Syracuse University Press, 1986; Barbara Rogers, op. cit.; Georgina Ashworth, *Of Conjuring and Caring: Women in Development*, London, Change, International Reports on Women, 1984; Peggy Antrobus, 'Feminist Issues in Development', *Reports*, World Education, Boston, Fall, 1987, pp. 5–8; Bina Agarwal, *Structures of Patriarchy, the State, the Community and the Household*, New Delhi, Kali for Women, London, Zed Books, 1988.

24. Elizabeth Odour, a Kenyan environmental expert, has noted the problems of plantation expansion for her country's environment, making the connection between women's concerns and environmental issues: conversation with the author, Clark University, Worcester, MA, December, 1988.

25. Elvia Alvarado, with Medea Benjamin, *Don't Be Afraid, Gringo,* San Francisco, Food First, 1987.

26. 'Bananas, Broomsticks and Bookshelves', *Pueblo to People,* holiday issue, 1988, pp. 22–23.

27. 'Organizing Malaysian Women Workers', *Voices Rising: A Bulletin about Women and Popular Education,* International Council for Adult Education, Toronto, May/June, 1987, p. 19.

28. Sistren, with Honor Ford Smith, *Lionheart Gal: Life Stories of Jamaican Women,* London, The Women's Press, 1986.

29. Chuck Klein Hans and Julia Lesage, editors, 'Life and Work at El Crucero: Interviews with Nicaraguan Coffee Workers', *Radical America*, vol. 9, no. 5, 1985, pp. 48–9.

30. 'Banana Ban: Colombia Killings', *New Internationalist,* special issue on international debt, November 1988, p. 27. The plantation companies involved are Del Monte, United Brands and Standard Fruit (owned by Castle and Cook, which also owns Dole).

31. Judith Sutphen, ' "Low Intensity Conflict" in the Philippines,' *Sojourner,* November, 1988, p. 22. I have tried to develop a feminist approach to Low Intensity Conflict doctrine in the new edition of *Does Khaki Become You?,* London and Winchester, MA, Pandora Press, 1988. For more on Filipino feminist thinking about Low Intensity Conflict and agrarian reform, contact the Women's Resource and Research Center, Maryknoll College Foundation, Quezon City, Philippines.

32. Denise Stanley, 'Banana Workers End Walkout over Company-sponsored Union', *Guardian* (US), December 2, 1988; 'Del Monte: Fresh Fruit Sales Climbing', *Boston Globe,* June 26, 1988. On Brooke Bond's flower business in Kenya, see John Clark, *For Richer or Poorer,* Oxford, Oxfam, 1986.

33. I am grateful to Ximena Bunster for information on Chile's fruit industry; to Shari Geistfeld for information on Unilever's oil-palm operations in Zaïre; to Jennifer Schirmer and Mimi Stephens for information on Guatemalan military thinking

about broccoli cultivation; Mimi Stephens, *The Impact of Militarized Development on Indigenous Culture in Guatemala and USAID's Role in It,* master's thesis, International Development Program, Clark University, Worcester, MA, 1988. For more on Unilever, see *New Internationalist,* special issue on Unilever, issue no. 172, June, 1987; *Unilever's World,* a report by the Counter-Information Service, London, 1975. On Coca Cola's Belize plantations, see *Rainforest Action Network,* San Francisco, February, 1987 and May, 1987.

34. For an insightful analysis of Latin American market women, see Ximena Bunster and Elsa Chaney, *Sellers and Servants: Working Women in Lima, Peru,* South Hadley, MA, Bergin & Garvey, 1988.

35. 'Women in Agriculture', special issue of *Women in Europe,* Women's Information Service, Commission of the European Community, Brussels, October, 1988. In 1988 there were an estimated 62,000 women running farms in the EEC, 8.2 per cent of the total. There were 566,000 women farmers working full-time on EEC farms; another 322,000 worked part-time on farms. Still, European women farmers lack training, tax benefits and pensions.

13.2

DEPENDENT CAPITALIST DEVELOPMENT IN LATIN AMERICA

Fernando Henrique Cardoso

In this influential article in 1972, Fernando Henrique Cardoso, president of Brazil in 1995–2003, extends Lenin's analysis of capitalist imperialism to explain why industrial development in Latin America leads to dependency—not equality—in the world economy. Lenin said capitalist countries would develop the agricultural and raw material markets of developing countries but reserve manufacturing markets for their own exports. Now, Cardoso acknowledges, capitalist countries assist the development of local manufacturing markets through a combination of international, local government, and private bourgeois capital, a policy advocated by Latin American elites and known as "import substitution." But this strategy does not lead to real development; rather, it leads to international "dependency" and national "authoritarianism." Local elites join the monopoly of global bourgeoisie interests, while the masses of society become further alienated. Cardoso calls for a political strategy to awaken the awareness of the masses and resist national dependency and widening social inequalities.

The theory of imperialist capitalism, as is well known, has so far attained its most significant treatment in Lenin's works. This is not only because Lenin attempts to explain transformations of the capitalist economies that occurred during the last decade of the 19th century and the first decade of the 20th, but mainly because of the political and historical implications contained in his interpretations. In fact, the descriptive arguments of Lenin's theory of imperialism were borrowed from Hobson's analysis. Other writers had already presented evidence of the international expansion of the capitalist economies and nations. Nevertheless, Lenin, inspired by Marx's views, was able to bring together evidence to the effect that economic expansion is meaningless if we do not take into consideration the *political* and *historical* aspects with which economic factors are intimately related. From Lenin's perspective, imperialism is a new form of the capitalist mode of production. This new form cannot be considered as a *different* mode of economic organization, in so far as capital accumulation based on private ownership of the means of production and exploitation of the

Source: Fernando Henrique Cardoso, "Dependent Capitalist Development in Latin America," *New Left Review* 74 (July–August 1972): 83–95.

labour force remain the basic features of the system. But its significance is that of a new *stage* of capitalism. The historical 'momentum' was a new one, with all the political consequences of that type of transformation: within the dominant capitalist classes, new sectors tried to impose their interests and ideologies; the State, the Army and all basic social and political institutions were redefined in order to assure expansion abroad. At the same time new types of liberation and social struggles came onto the historical scene—the colonial liberation movements and the fight against 'trade unionism', the latter a struggle against an initial form of working class compromise with the bourgeoisie made possible by the exploitation of the colonial world.

From that broad picture of a new historical stage of capitalist development Lenin inferred new political tasks, tactics and strategies for socialist revolution.

Lenin's Characterization of Imperialism

The main points of Lenin's characterization of imperialism that are essential to the present discussion can be summarized as follows:

a) the capitalist economy in its 'advanced stages' involves a concentration of capital and production (points that were well established by Marx in *Capital*) in such a way that the competitive market is replaced in its basic branches by a monopolistic one.

b) this trend was historically accomplished through internal differentiation of capitalist functions, leading not only to the formation of a financial stratum among entrepreneurs but to the marked prominence of the banking system in the capitalist mode of production. Furthermore, the fusion of industrial capital with financial capital under the control of the latter turned out to be the decisive feature of the political and economic relations within capitalist classes, with all the practical consequences that such a system of relations has in terms of state organization, politics and ideology.

c) capitalism thus reached its 'ultimate stage of development' both internally and externally. Internally, control of the productive system by financiers turned the productive forces and the capital accumulation process toward the search for new possibilities for investment. The problem of 'capital realization' became in this way an imperative necessity to permit the continuing of capitalist expansion. In addition there were internal limits that impeded the continuous reinvestment of new capital (impoverishment of the masses, a faster rate of capital growth than that of the internal market, and so on). *External outlets* had to be found to ensure the continuity of capitalist advance and accumulation.

d) the increased and increasing speed of the development of productive forces under monopolistic control also pushed the advanced capitalist countries toward the political control of foreign lands. The search for control over *raw materials* is yet another reason why capitalism in its monopolistic stage becomes expansionist.

In short, Lenin's explanations of why advanced capitalist economies were impelled toward the control of backward lands, was based on two main factors. One stressed movements of capital, the other outlined the productive process. Both were not only linked to each other but also related to the global transformation of the capitalist system that had led to the control of the productive system by financiers. It is not difficult to see that such modifications deeply affected state organization and functions as well as the relationships among nations, since a main thrust of capitalist development in the stage of imperialism was toward the territorial division of the world among the leading capitalist countries. This process guaranteed capital flows from the over-capitalized economies to backward countries and assured provision of raw materials in return.

Imperialism and Dependent Economies

From that perspective, the consequence of imperialism with respect to dependent economies and nations (or colonies) was the integration of the latter into the international market. Inequality among nations and economies resulted from imperialism's development to the extent that import of raw materials and export of manufactured goods were the bases of the imperialist-colonial relationship. The reproduction and amplification of inequality between advanced economies and dependent economies developed as a by-product of the very process of capitalist growth.

Certainly, Lenin was aware of particular types of interconnections, as in Argentina and other economies dependent on Great Britain, where local bourgeoisies controlled sectors of the productive system creating more complex patterns of exploitation. The same was true with respect to the political aspects of dependency in those countries where the state tried to defend the national bourgeoisie against imperialist pressures.

Nevertheless, from the theoretical point of view, as a mode of exploitation, imperialism should tend to restrict the economic growth of backward countries to mineral and agricultural sectors in order to assure raw materials for the advanced capitalist nations in their drive for further industrialization. For the same reasons the indigenous labour force could be kept at low wage and salary levels. By that means the dominant central economies were assured of cheap raw material prices. Consequently, in colonized or dependent nations, internal markets did not have any special strategic significance.

Of course, in terms of 'capital realization', selling products abroad had importance. But even so, the main imperialistic tie in terms of direct capital investment was oriented toward the concession of loans to the dependent State or to private local entrepreneurs. In both cases, however, political and financial guarantees were assured by the State or the administration of the receiver country.

In short, imperialist profit was based on unequal trade and financial exploitation. The latter could be measured by the increasing indebtedness of exploited economies to the central economies. The former was evidenced through the different types of products exchanged, i.e., raw materials for manufactured goods. This process of exploitation of the indigenous labour force thus insured an unevenness in both types of economies. Moreover, technological advances in the industrial sectors of central economies provided a high level of exploitation, increasing the relative surplus value extracted through a continuously advancing technology of production (leading in turn to unevenness of the rate of organic composition of capital), while in the dominated economies the direct over-exploitation of labour prevailed in the productive system.

Politically, this type of economic expansion thus reinforced colonial links, through wars, repression and subjugation of peoples that previously were not only marginal to the international market, but were culturally independent and structurally did not have links with the Western world. Such were the African and Asian regions where nations, in spite of previous commercial-capitalist expansion, remained largely untouched in terms of their productive systems.

Latin America from the beginning was somewhat different in its links to the imperialist process. It is true that this process of colonialistic penetration obtained with respect to some countries (mainly the Caribbean nations). Yet throughout most of Latin America, the imperialistic upsurge occurred by way of a more complex process, through which Latin American countries kept their political independence, but slowly shifted from subordination to an earlier British influence to American predominance.

Ownership of the productive system was the site of the main differences. Some Latin American economies, even after imperialist predominance, were able to cope with the new situation by maintaining proprietorship of the local export economy in the hands of native bourgeoisies. Thus in some countries (such as Argentina, Brazil, Uruguay, Colombia, Chile), the export sector remained at least to some extent controlled by the local bourgeoisie and the links of dependence were based more on trade and financial relations than directly on the productive sectors. In some countries the internal financial system was itself mainly dominated by internal bankers, and financial dependence was based on international loans contracted, as noted above, by the State or under State guarantees.[1]

In spite of numerous political and economic variations, Lenin's basic picture remained valid: the internal market of Latin American countries grew in a limited way during the period of the first imperialist expansion; the industrial sector was not significantly expanded; external financial dependence grew enormously; raw materials including foodstuffs constituted the basis of export economies.

At the same time not only were the majority of Latin American countries unable to keep control of the export sector, but some of the countries that had previously retained dominance of raw materials or food production, now lost that capacity (as in the Chilean mineral economy).

New Patterns of Capital Accumulation

In spite of the accuracy of Lenin's insights as measured against historical events during the first half of the century in many parts of the world, some important recent changes have deeply affected the pattern of relationship between imperialist and dependent nations. These changes demand a reappraisal of emergent structures and their main tendencies. Even if these modifications are not so deep as the shift that enabled Lenin to characterize a new stage of capitalism during the period of imperialist expansion, they are marked enough to warrant a major modification of the established analyses of capitalism and imperialism. Nevertheless, contemporary international capitalist expansion and control of dependent economies undoubtedly prove that this new pattern of economic relationships among nations remains imperialist. However, the main points of Lenin's characterization of imperialism and capitalism are no longer fully adequate to describe and explain the present forms of capital accumulation and external expansion.

* * *

New Forms of Economic Dependency

... [F]oreign investment in the new nations and in Latin America is moving rapidly away from oil, raw materials and agriculture and in the direction of the industrial sectors. Even where the bulk of assets continues to remain in the traditional sectors of imperialist investment, the rate of expansion of the industrial sector is rapid. This is true not only for Latin America but also for Africa and Asia.

The point is not only that multinational corporations are investing in the industrial sectors of dominated economies, instead of in the traditional agricultural and mineral sectors. Beyond that, even [within] 'traditional' sectors of dependent economies, they are operating in technically and organizationally advanced modes, sometimes accepting local participation in their enterprises. Of course, these transformations do not mean that previous types of imperialistic investment, i.e., in oil or metals, are disappearing, even in the case of the most industrialized dependent economies, i.e., Argentina, Brazil and Mexico in Latin America. However, the dominant traits of imperialism in those countries, as the process of industrialization continues, cannot be adequately described and interpreted on the basis of frames of reference that posit the exchange of raw material for industrialized goods as the main feature of trade, and suppose virtually complete external ownership of the dependent economies' means of production.

Even the mineral sector (such as manganese in Brazil, copper in Chile during Frei's government, or petro-chemicals in various countries) is now being submitted to new patterns of economic ownership. The distinguishing feature of these new forms is the joint venture enterprise, comprising local state capital, private national capital and monopoly international investment (under foreign control in the last analysis).

As a consequence, in some dependent economies—among these, the so called 'developing countries' of Latin America—foreign investment no longer remains a simple zero-sum game of exploitation as was the pattern in classical imperialism. Strictly speaking—if we consider the purely economic indicators—it is not difficult to show that *development* and *monopoly penetration* in the industrial sectors of dependent economies are not incompatible. The idea that there occurs a kind of development of underdevelopment, apart from the play on words, is not helpful. In fact, *dependency, monopoly capitalism* and *development* are not contradictory terms: there occurs a kind of *dependent capitalist development* in the sectors of the Third World integrated into the new forms of monopolistic expansion.

As a result in countries like Argentina, Brazil, Mexico, South Africa, India, and some others, there is an internal structural fragmentation, connecting the most 'advanced' parts of their economies to the international capitalist system. Separate although subordinated to these advanced sectors, the backward economic and social sectors of the dependent countries then play the role of 'internal colonies'. The gap between both will probably increase, creating a new type of dualism, quite different from the imaginary one sustained by some non-Marxist authors. The new structural 'duality' corresponds to a kind of internal differentiation of the same unity. It results directly, of course, from capitalist expansion and is functional to that expansion, in so as far as it helps to keep wages at a low level and diminishes political pressures inside the 'modern' sector, since the social and economic position of those who belong to the latter is always better in comparative terms.

If this is true, to what extent is it possible to sustain the idea of *development* in tandem with dependence? The answer cannot be immediate. First of all I am suggesting that the present trend of imperialist investment allows some degree of local participation in the process of economic production. Let us indicate a crucial feature in which present and past forms of capitalism differ. During the previous type of imperialism, the market for goods produced in dependent economies by foreign enterprise was mostly, if not fully, the market of the advanced economies: oil, copper, coffee, iron bauxite, manganese, etc., were produced to be sold and consumed in the advanced capitalist countries. This explains why the internal market of dependent economies was irrelevant for the imperialist economies, excepting the modest portion of import goods consumed by the upper class in the dominated society.

Today for G.M. or Volkswagen, or General Electric, or Sears Roebuck, the Latin American market, if not the particular market in each country where those corporations are producing in Latin America, is the immediate goal in terms of profit. So, at least to some extent, a certain type of foreign investment needs some kind of internal prosperity. There are and there will be some parts of dependent societies, tied to the corporate system, internally and abroad, through shared interests.

On the other hand, and in spite of internal economic development, countries tied to international capitalism by that type of linkage remain economically dependent, insofar as the production of the means of production (technology) are concentrated in advanced capitalist economies (mainly in the US).

In terms of the Marxist scheme of capital reproduction, this means that sector I (the production of means of production)—the strategic part of the reproductive scheme—is virtually non-existent in dependent economies. Thus, from a broad perspective, the realization of capital accumulation *demands* a productive complementarity which does not exist within the country. In Lenin's interpretation the imperialist economies needed external expansion for the realization of capital accumulation. Conversely, within the dependent economies capital returns to the metropole in order to complete the cycle of capitalist reproduction. That is the reason why 'technology' is so important. Its 'material' aspect is less impressive than its significance as a form of maintenance of control and as a necessary step in the process of capital accumulation. Through technological advantage, corporations make secure their key roles in the global system of capital accumulation. Some degree of local prosperity is possible insofar as consumption goods locally produced by foreign investments can induce some dynamic effects in the dependent economies. But at the same time, the global process of capitalist development determines an interconnection between the sector of production of consumption goods and the capital goods sector, reproducing in this way the links of dependency.

One of the main factors which explained imperialist expansion in Lenin's theory was the search for capitalist investment. Now since foreign capital goes to the industrial sector of dependent economies in search of external markets, some considerable changes have occurred. First, in comparison with expanding assets of foreign corporations, the net amount of foreign capital actually invested in the dependent economies is decreasing: local savings and the reinvestment of profits realized in local markets provides resources for the growth of foreign assets with limited external flow of new capital. This is intimately related to the previously discussed process of expansion of the local market and it is also related to the mounting of 'joint ventures' linking local capitalists and foreign enterprise.

Secondly, but no less important, statistics demonstrate that dependent economies during the period of monopolistic imperialist expansion are *exporting* capital to the dominant economies.

As a reaction against that process, some dependent countries have tried to limit exportable profits. Nevertheless, international corporations had the foresight to sense that the principal way to send returns abroad is through the payment of licenses, patents, royalties and related items. These institutional devices, together with the increasing indebtedness of the exploited nations vis-à-vis international agencies and banks (in fact controlled by the big imperialist countries), have altered the main forms of exploitation.

It is not the purpose of this presentation to discuss all the consequences of this for a monopoly capitalist economy. However, some repercussions of the new pattern of imperialism on the US and other central economies are obvious. If a real problem of capital realization exists under monopoly capitalism, the new form of dependency will increase the necessity to find new fields of application for the capital accumulated in the metropolitan economies. Witness the push toward more 'technical obsolescence' administered by corporations. Military expenditures are another means of finding new outlets for capital.

* * *

The idea that the growth of capitalism depends on Third World exploitation requires some further elaboration. In fact, the main trends of the last decade show that Latin American participation in both the expansion of international trade and investment is decreasing. If we accept the distinction between two sectors of international trade—the Centre and the Periphery—one finds that the trade rate of growth was 7.9 per cent per year in the central economies and 4.8 per cent in the peripheral ones. As a consequence, exports of the peripheral economies which reached a peak in 1948 (32 per cent of the international trade) decreased to 26 per cent in 1958 and to 21 per cent in 1968 (below the 28 per cent of the pre-war period). In the Latin American case this participation decreased from 12 per cent in 1948 to 6 per cent in 1968.[2] The same is happening with respect to the importance that the periphery has for US investments. The periphery absorbed 55 per cent of the total US direct investment in 1950 and only 40 per cent in 1968. Latin American participation in this process fell in the same period from 39 percent to 20 percent.

Of course, these data do not show the increase of 'loans and aid' which—as was stressed before—has been of increasing importance in economic imperialism. However, the fact that the interrelations among the most advanced economies are growing cannot be utilized as an argument to infer the 'end of imperialism'. On the contrary, the more appropriate inference is that the relations between advanced capitalist countries and dependent nations lead rather to a 'marginalization' of the latter within the global system of economic development.

Some Political Consequences

The new forms of dependency will undoubtedly give rise to novel political and social adaptations and reactions inside the dependent countries. If my analysis is correct, the above mentioned process of fragmentation of interests will probably lead to an internal differentiation that in very schematic terms can be suggested as follows. Part of the 'national bourgeoisie', (the principal one in terms of economic power—agrarian, commercial, industrial or financial) is the direct beneficiary, as a junior partner, of the foreign interest. I refer not only to the direct associates, but also to economic groups that benefit from the eventual atmosphere of prosperity derived from dependent development (as is easily demonstrated in Brazil or Mexico). The process goes further and not only part of the 'middle class' (intellectuals, state bureaucracies, armies, etc.) are involved in the new system, but even part of the working class. Those employed by the 'internationalized' sector structurally belong to it.

Of course, structural dependence does not mean immediate political co-option. Effective political integration of groups and persons depends on the political processes, movements, goals and alternatives that they face.

Nevertheless, as the process of internationalization of dependent nations progresses, it becomes difficult to perceive the political process in terms of a struggle between the Nation and the anti-Nation, the latter conceived as the Foreign Power of Imperialism. The anti-Nation will be inside the 'Nation'—so to speak, among the local people in different social strata. Furthermore, to perceive that, in these terms, the Nation is an occupied one, is not an easy process: there are very few 'others' in cultural and national terms physically representing the presence of 'the enemy'.

* * *

Some more general remarks can be summarized thus:

a) Analysis which is based on the naive assumption that imperialism unifies the interests and reactions of dominated nations is a clear oversimplification of what is really occurring. It does not take into consideration the internal fragmentation of these countries and the attraction that development exerts in different social strata, and not only on the upper-classes.

b) The term 'development of underdevelopment' summarizes another mistake. In fact, the assumption of a structural 'lack of dynamism' in dependent economies because of imperialism misinterprets the actual forms of economic imperialism and presents an imprecise political understanding of the situation. It is necessary to understand that in specific situations it is possible to expect *development* and *dependency*.

It would be wrong to generalize these processes to the entire Third World. They only occur when corporations reorganize the international division of labour and include parts of dependent economies in their plans of productive investment.

* * *

Now, I am assuming that there are different forms of dependency in Latin America and that in some of them, development produces a shift in internal power, displacing the old oligarchical power groups and reinforcing more 'modern' types of political control. In that sense, the present dictatorships in Latin America, even when militarily based, do not express, by virtue of pure structural constraints, a traditional and 'anti-developmentalist' (I mean anti-modern capitalism) form of domination.

It is hardly necessary to repeat that from the left's point of view there are strong arguments to maintain its denunciation of both new forms of imperialism or dependency and political authoritarianism. But clearly, new political analyses are needed to explain the bureaucratic-technocratic form of authoritarian state which serves the interests of the internationalized bourgeoisie and their allies.

In this context, and in order to avoid a mechanistic approach, a correct orientation of the struggles against capitalist imperialism demands special attention to cultural problems and the different forms of alienation.

If the capitalist pattern of development in industrialized dependent countries pushes toward internal fragmentation and inequalities, values related to national integrity and social participation might be transformed into instruments of political struggle. To permit the State and bourgeois groups to command the banner of nationalism—conceived not only in terms of sovereignty but also of internal cohesion and progressive social integration—would be a mistake with deep consequences. I am not supporting the idea that the strategic (or revolutionary) side of dependent industrialized societies is the 'marginalized sector'. But denunciation of marginalization as a consequence of capitalist growth, and the organization of unstructured masses, are indispensable tasks of analysis and practical politics.

For this reason it is not very realistic to expect the national bourgeoisie to lead resistance against external penetration. Consequently, denunciation of the dependency perspective cannot rest on values associated with bourgeois nationalism. National integrity as cited above means primarily popular integration in the nation and the need to struggle against the particular form of development promoted by the large corporations.

In the same way that trade unionism may become a danger for workers in advanced capitalist societies, development is a real ideological pole of attraction for middle class *and workers'* sectors in Latin American countries. The answer to that attractive effect cannot be a purely ideological denial of economic progress, when it occurs. A reply must be based on values and political objectives that enlarge the awareness of the masses with respect to social inequalities and national dependency.

Notes

1. See, F. H. Cardoso, and E. Faletto, *Dependencia y Desarrollo en America Latina,* Mexico, 1972.
2. These data and analyses can be found in Anibal Pinto and Jan Knakel's interesting paper 'El sistema centro-periferia 20 años después', ECLA, 3rd version, 11–11–71, pp. 14 and following.

Chapter 14

WORLD ENVIRONMENT: POPULATION, POLLUTION, AND PANDEMICS

14.1

SELECTION FROM *AN INCONVENIENT TRUTH*

Al Gore

> No one has done more to publicize the dangers of global warming than former senator and vice president Al Gore. In this introduction from his best-selling book, *An Inconvenient Truth,* Gore demonstrates for all of us how personal and passionate our policy concerns can be. Even when we study nature or inanimate objects, we are concerned about nature's consequences for us or the consequences we might impose on nature. A large body of scientific opinion supports Gore's contention that human activity is the principal cause of global warming. But as he says in this essay, "this is not ultimately about any scientific discussion or political dialogue. It is about who we are as human beings." Dealing with global warming and overriding the "procrastinators and deniers" is "a moral, ethical and spiritual challenge." How would you assess the relative influence of material, institutional (interactive), and ideological factors in Gore's perspective?

Some experiences are so intense while they are happening that time seems to stop altogether. When it begins again and our lives resume their normal course, those intense experiences remain vivid, refusing to stay in the past, remaining always and forever with us.

Seventeen years ago my youngest child was badly—almost fatally—injured. This is a story I have told before, but its meaning for me continues to change and to deepen.

Source: Al Gore, "Introduction," in *An Inconvenient Truth: The Planetary Emergency of Global Warming and What We Can Do About It* (New York: Rodale, 2006).

That is also true of the story I have tried to tell for many years about the global environment. It was during that interlude 17 years ago when I started writing my first book, *Earth in the Balance*. It was because of my son's accident and the way it abruptly interrupted the flow of my days and hours that I began to rethink everything, especially what my priorities had been. Thankfully, my son has long since recovered completely. But it was during that traumatic period that I made at least two enduring changes: I vowed always to put my family first, and I also vowed to make the climate crisis the top priority of my professional life.

Unfortunately, in the intervening years, time has not stood still for the global environment. The pace of destruction has worsened and the urgent need for a response has grown more acute.

The fundamental outline of the climate crisis story is much the same now as it was then. The relationship between human civilization and the Earth has been utterly transformed by a combination of factors, including the population explosion, the technological revolution, and a willingness to ignore the future consequences of our present actions. The underlying reality is that we are colliding with the planet's ecological system, and its most vulnerable components are crumbling as a result.

I have learned much more about this issue over the years. I have read and listened to the world's leading scientists, who have offered increasingly dire warnings. I have watched with growing concern as the crisis gathers strength even more rapidly than anyone expected.

In every corner of the globe—on land and in water, in melting ice and disappearing snow, during heat waves and droughts, in the eyes of hurricanes and in the tears of refugees—the world is witnessing mounting and undeniable evidence that nature's cycles are profoundly changing.

I have learned that, beyond death and taxes, there is at least one absolutely indisputable fact: Not only does human-caused global warming exist, but it is also growing more and more dangerous, and at a pace that has now made it a planetary emergency.

Part of what I have learned over the last 14 years has resulted from changes in my personal circumstances as well. Since 1992 much has happened in my life. Our children have all grown up, and our two oldest daughters have married. Tipper and I now have two grandchildren. Both of my parents have died, as has Tipper's mother.

And less than a year after *Earth in the Balance* was published, I was elected vice president—ultimately serving for eight years. I had the opportunity, as a member of the Clinton-Gore administration, to pursue an ambitious agenda of new policies addressing the climate crisis.

At that time I discovered, firsthand, how fiercely Congress would resist the changes we were urging them to make, and I watched with growing dismay as the opposition got much, much worse after the takeover of Congress in 1994 by the Republican party and its newly aggressive conservative leaders.

I organized and held countless events to spread public awareness about the climate crisis, and to build more public support for congressional action. I also learned numerous lessons about the significant changes in recent decades in the nature and quality of America's "conversation of democracy." Specifically, that entertainment values have transformed what we used to call news, and individuals with independent voices are routinely shut out of the public discourse.

In 1997 I helped achieve a breakthrough at the negotiations in Kyoto, Japan, where the world drafted a groundbreaking treaty whose goal is to control global warming pollution. But then I came home and faced an uphill battle to gain support for the treaty in the U.S. Senate.

In 2000 I ran for president. It was a long and hard-fought campaign that was ended by a 5–4 decision in the Supreme Court to halt the counting of votes in the key state of Florida. This was a hard blow.

I then watched George W. Bush get sworn in as president. In his very first week in office, President Bush reversed a campaign pledge to regulate CO_2 emissions—a pledge that had helped persuade many voters that he was genuinely concerned about matters relating to the environment.

Soon after the election, it became clear that the Bush-Cheney administration was determined to block any policies designed to help limit global-warming pollution. They launched an all-out effort to roll back, weaken, and—wherever possible—completely eliminate existing laws and regulations. Indeed, they even abandoned Bush's pre-election rhetoric about global warming, announcing that, in the president's opinion, global warming wasn't a problem at all.

As the new administration was getting underway, I had to begin making decisions about what I would do in my own life. After all, I was now out of a job. This certainly wasn't an easy time, but it did offer me the chance to make a fresh start—to step back and think about where I should direct my energies.

I began teaching courses at two colleges in Tennessee, and, along with Tipper, published two books about the American family. We moved to Nashville and bought a house less than an hour's drive from our farm in Carthage. I entered the business world and eventually started two new companies. I became an adviser to two already established major high-tech businesses.

I am tremendously excited about these ventures, and feel fortunate to have found ways to make a living while simultaneously moving the world—at least a little—in the right direction.

With my partner Joel Hyatt I started Current TV, a news and information cable and satellite network for young people in their twenties, based on an idea that is, in our present-day society, revolutionary: that viewers themselves can make the programs and in the process participate in the public forum of American democracy. With my partner David Blood I also started Generation Investment Management, a firm devoted to proving that the environment and other sustainability factors can be fully integrated into the mainstream investment process in a way that enhances profitability for our clients, while encouraging businesses to operate more sustainably.

At first, I thought I might run for president again, but over the last several years I have discovered that there are other ways to serve, and that I am really enjoying them.

I am also determined to continue to make speeches on public policy, and—as I have at almost every crossroads moment in my life—to make the global environment my central focus.

Since my childhood summers on our family's farm in Tennessee, when I first learned from my father about taking care of the land, I have been deeply interested in learning more about threats to the environment. I grew up half in the city and half in the country, and the half I loved most was on our farm. Since my mother read to my sister and me from Rachel Carson's classic book, *Silent Spring,* and especially since I was first introduced to the idea of global warming by my college professor Roger Revelle, I have always tried to deepen my own understanding of the human impact on nature, and in my public service I have tried to implement policies that would ameliorate—and eventually eliminate—that harmful impact.

During the Clinton-Gore years we accomplished a lot in terms of environmental issues, even though, with the hostile Republican Congress, we fell short of all that was needed. Since the change in administrations, I have watched with growing concern as our forward progress has been almost completely reversed.

After the 2000 election, one of the things I decided to do was to start giving my slide show on global warming again. I had first put it together at the same time I began writing *Earth in the Balance,* and over the years I have added to it and steadily improved it to the point where I think it makes a compelling case, at least for most audiences, that humans are the cause of most of the global warming that is taking place, and that unless we take quick action the consequences for our planetary home could become irreversible.

For the last six years, I have been traveling around the world, sharing the information I have compiled with anyone who would listen. I have traveled to colleges, to small towns and big cities. More and more, I have begun to feel that I am changing minds, but it is a slow process.

In the spring of 2005, I gave my slide show to a large gathering in Los Angeles organized and hosted by environmental activist (and film producer) Laurie David. Afterward, she and another producer, Lawrence Bender, suggested that I ought to consider making a movie out of my presentation. I was skeptical about the idea because I couldn't see how my slide show would translate to film. But they later came to another slide show and brought Jeff Skoll, founder and CEO of Participant Productions, who expressed interest in backing the project. They also introduced me to a highly talented film veteran, Davis Guggenheim, who expressed interest in directing it. Later, Scott Burns joined the production team and Lesley Chilcott became the coproducer and legendary "trail boss."

My principal concern in all this was that the translation of the slide show into a film not sacrifice the central role of science for entertainment's sake. But the more I talked with this extraordinary group, and felt their deep commitment to exactly the same goals I was pursuing, the more convinced I became that the movie was a good idea. If I wanted to reach the maximum number of people quickly, and not just continue talking to a few hundred people a night, a movie was the way to do it. That film, also titled *An Inconvenient Truth,* has now been made, and I am really excited about it.

But the idea for a book on the climate crisis actually came first. It was Tipper who first suggested that I put together a new kind of book with pictures and graphics to make the whole message easier to follow, combining many elements from my slide show with all of the new original material I have compiled over the last few years.

Tipper and I are, by the way, giving 100% of whatever profits come to us from the book—and from the movie—to a nonprofit, bipartisan effort to move public opinion in the United States to support bold action to confront global warming.

After more than thirty years as a student of the climate crisis, I have a lot to share. I have tried to tell this story in a way that will interest all kinds of readers. My hope is that those who read the book and see the film will begin to feel, as I have for a long time, that global warming is not just about science and that it is not just a political issue. It is really a moral issue.

Although it is true that politics at times must play a crucial role in solving this problem, this is the kind of challenge that ought to completely transcend partisanship. So whether you are a Democrat or a Republican, whether you voted for me or not, I very much hope that you will sense that my goal is to share with you both my passion for the Earth and my deep sense of concern for its fate. It is impossible to feel one without the other when you know all the facts.

I also want to convey my strong feeling that what we are facing is not just a cause for alarm, it is paradoxically also a cause for hope. As many know, the Chinese expression for "crisis" consists of two characters side by side ... The first is the symbol for "danger," the second the symbol for "opportunity."

The climate crisis is, indeed, extremely dangerous. In fact it is a true planetary emergency. Two thousand scientists, in a hundred countries, working for more than 20 years in the most elaborate and well-organized scientific collaboration in the history of humankind, have forged an exceptionally strong consensus that all the nations on Earth must work together to solve the crisis of global warming.

The voluminous evidence now strongly suggests that unless we act boldly and quickly to deal with the underlying causes of global warming, our world will undergo a string of terrible catastrophes, including more and stronger storms like Hurricane Katrina, in both the Atlantic and the Pacific.

We are melting the North Polar ice cap and virtually all of the mountain glaciers in the world. We are destabilizing the massive mound of ice on Greenland and the equally enormous mass of ice propped up on top of islands in West Antarctica, threatening a worldwide increase in sea levels of as much as 20 feet.

The list of what is now endangered due to global warming also includes the continued stable configuration of ocean and wind currents that has been in place since before the first cities were built almost 10,000 years ago.

We are dumping so much carbon dioxide into the Earth's environment that we have literally changed the relationship between the Earth and the Sun. So much of that CO_2 is being absorbed into the oceans that if we continue at the current rate we will increase the saturation of calcium carbonate to levels that will prevent formation of corals and interfere with the making of shells by any sea creature.

Global warming, along with the cutting and burning of forests and other critical habitats, is causing the loss of living species at a level comparable to the extinction event that wiped out the dinosaurs 65 million years ago. That event was believed to have been caused by a giant asteroid. This time it is not an asteroid colliding with the Earth and wreaking havoc; it is us.

Last year, the national academies of science in the 11 most influential nations came together to jointly call on every nation to "acknowledge that the threat of climate change is clear and increasing" and declare that the "scientific understanding of climate changes is now sufficiently clear to justify nations taking prompt action."

So the message is unmistakably clear. This crisis means "danger!"

Why do our leaders seem not to hear such a clear warning? Is it simply that it is inconvenient for them to hear the truth?

If the truth is unwelcome, it may seem easier just to ignore it.

But we know from bitter experience that the consequences of doing so can be dire.

For example, when we were first warned that the levees were about to break in New Orleans because of Hurricane Katrina, those warnings were ignored. Later, a bipartisan group of members of Congress chaired by Representative Tom Davis (R-VA), chairman of the House Government Reform Committee, said in an official report, "The White House failed to act on the massive amounts of information at its disposal," and that a "blinding lack of situational awareness and disjointed decision-making needlessly compounded and prolonged Katrina's horror."

Today, we are hearing and seeing dire warnings of the worst potential catastrophe in the history of human civilization: a global climate crisis that is deepening and rapidly becoming more dangerous than anything we have ever faced.

And yet these clear warnings are also being met with a "blinding lack of situational awareness"—in this case, by the Congress, as well as the president.

As Martin Luther King Jr. said in a speech not long before his assassination:

We are now faced with the fact, my friends, that tomorrow is today. We are confronted with the fierce urgency of now. In this unfolding conundrum of life and history, there is such a thing as being too late.

Procrastination is still the thief of time. Life often leaves us standing bare, naked, and dejected with a lost opportunity. The tide in the affairs of men does not remain at flood—it ebbs. We may cry out desperately for time to pause in her passage, but time is adamant to every plea and rushes on. Over the bleached bones and jumbled residues of numerous civilizations are written the pathetic words 'Too late.' There is an invisible book of life that faithfully records our vigilance in our neglect. Omar Khayyam is right: 'The moving finger writes, and having writ moves on.'

But along with the danger we face from global warming, this crisis also brings unprecedented opportunities.

What are the opportunities such a crisis also offers? They include not just new jobs and new profits, though there will be plenty of both, we can build clean engines, we can harness the Sun and the wind; we can stop wasting energy; we can use our planet's plentiful coal resources without heating the planet.

The procrastinators and deniers would have us believe this will be expensive. But in recent years, dozens of companies have cut emissions of heat-trapping gases while saving money. Some of the world's largest companies are moving aggressively to capture the enormous economic opportunities offered by a clean energy future.

But there's something even more precious to be gained if we do the right thing.

The climate crisis also offers us the chance to experience what very few generations in history have had the privilege of knowing: *a generational mission*; the exhilaration of a compelling *moral purpose*; a shared and unifying *cause*; the thrill of being forced by circumstances to put aside the pettiness and conflict that so often stifle the restless human need for transcendence; *the opportunity to rise*.

When we do rise, it will fill our spirits and bind us together. Those who are now suffocating in cynicism and despair will be able to breathe freely. Those who are now suffering from a loss of meaning in their lives will find hope.

When we rise, we will experience an epiphany as we discover that this crisis is not really about politics at all. It is a moral and spiritual challenge.

At stake is the survival of our civilization and the habitability of the Earth. Or, as one eminent scientist put it, the pending question is whether the combination of an opposable thumb and a neocortex is a viable combination on this planet.

The understanding we will gain—about who we really are—will give us the moral capacity to take on other related challenges that are also desperately in need of being redefined as moral imperatives with practical solutions: HIV/AIDS and other pandemics that are ravaging so many; global poverty; the ongoing redistribution of wealth globally from the poor to the wealthy; the ongoing genocide in Darfur; the ongoing famine in Niger and elsewhere; chronic civil wars; the destruction of ocean fisheries; families that don't function; communities that don't commune; the erosion of democracy in America; and the refeudalization of the public forum.

Consider what happened during the crisis of global fascism. At first, even the truth about Hitler was inconvenient. Many in the west hoped the danger would simply go away. They ignored clear warnings and compromised with evil, and waited, hoping for the best.

After the appeasement at Munich, Churchill said: "This is only the first sip, the first foretaste of a bitter cup which will be proffered to us year by year—unless by supreme recovery of moral health and martial vigor, we rise again and take our stand for freedom."

But when England and then America and our allies ultimately rose to meet the threat, together we won two wars simultaneously in Europe and the Pacific.

By the end of that terrible war, we had gained the moral authority and vision to create the Marshall Plan—and convinced taxpayers to pay for it! We had gained the spiritual capacity and wisdom to rebuild Japan and Europe and launch the renewal of the very nations we had just defeated in war, in the process laying the foundation for 50 years of peace and prosperity.

This too is a moral moment, a crossroads. This is not ultimately about any scientific discussion or political dialogue. It is about who we are as human beings. It is about our capacity to transcend our own limitations, to rise to this new occasion. To see with our hearts, as well as our heads, the response that is now called for. This is a moral, ethical and spiritual challenge.

We should not fear this challenge. We should welcome it. We must not wait. In the words of Dr. King, "Tomorrow is today."

I began this introduction with a description of an experience 17 years ago that, for me, stopped time. During that painful period I gained an ability I hadn't had before to feel the preciousness of our connection to our children and the solemnity of our obligation to safeguard their future and protect the Earth we are bequeathing to them.

Imagine with me now that once again, time has stopped—for all of us—and before it starts again, we have the chance to use our moral imaginations and to project ourselves across the expanse of time, 17 years into the future, and share a brief conversation with our children and grandchildren as they are living their lives in the year 2023.

Will they feel bitterness toward us because we failed in our obligation to care for the Earth that is their home and ours? Will the Earth have been irreversibly scarred by us?

Imagine now that they are asking us: "What were you thinking? Didn't you care about our future? Were you really so self-absorbed that you couldn't—or wouldn't—stop the destruction of Earth's environment?"

What would our answer be?

We can answer their questions now by our actions, not merely with our promises. In the process, we can choose a future for which our children will thank us.

14.2

IS HUMANITY LOSING THE GLOBAL WARMING DEBATE?

S. Fred Singer and Dennis T. Avery

Does science give definitive answers to public policy controversies such as global warming? Most scientists who warn about global warming say that it does. In this brief summary of a larger book, S. Fred Singer and Dennis T. Avery question the conventional wisdom. Global warming is taking place, they agree. But that's not the issue. The issue is why. The authors argue that Earth has been alternately warming and cooling every 1,500 years for the last 400,000 years or more. The reason has to do with the sun's activity, not greenhouse gases produced by industrial development. If Singer and Avery are right, the world may divert billions, perhaps trillions of dollars to develop alternative energy resources that might otherwise be invested today to modernize poor countries. Can natural science no less than social science get all the causal arrows right to predict events, and even if it can, who should decide how the costs and consequences of such events are to be distributed among the various peoples of the world?

The Earth is warming but physical evidence from around the world tells us that human-emitted CO_2 (carbon dioxide) has played only a minor role in it. Instead, the mild warming seems to be part of a natural 1,500-year climate cycle (plus or minus 500 years) that goes back at least one million years.

The cycle has been too long and too moderate for primitive peoples lacking thermometers to recount in their oral histories. But written evidence of climatic change does exist. The Romans had recorded a warming from about 200 B.C. to A.D. 600, registered mainly in the northward advance of grape growing in both Italy and Britain. Histories from both Europe and Asia tell us there was a Medieval Warming that lasted from about 900 to 1300; this period was also known as the Medieval Climate Optimum because of its mild winters, stable seasons, and lack of severe storms. Human histories also record the Little Ice Age, which lasted from about 1300 to 1850. But people thought each of these climatic shifts was a distinct event and not part of a continuing pattern.

Source: S. Fred Singer and Dennis T. Avery, "Is Humanity Losing the Global Warming Debate?" in Unstoppable Global Warming: Every 1,500 Years (Lanham, Md.: Rowman & Littlefield, 2007), 1–19.

This began to change in 1984 when Willi Dansgaard of Denmark and Hans Oeschger of Switzerland published their analysis of the oxygen isotopes in the first ice cores extracted from Greenland.[1] These cores provided 250,000 years of the Earth's climate history in one set of "documents." The scientists compared the ratio of "heavy" oxygen-18 isotopes to the "lighter" oxygen-16 isotopes, which indicated the temperature at the time the snow had fallen. They expected to find evidence of the known 90,000-year ice ages and the mild interglacial periods recorded in the ice, and they did. However, they did not expect to find anything in between. To their surprise, they found a clear cycle—moderate, albeit abrupt—occurring about every 2,550 years running persistently through both. (This period would soon be reassessed at 1,500 years, plus or minus 500 years.)

By the mid-1980s, however, the First World had already convinced itself of the Greenhouse Theory and believed that puny human industries had grown powerful enough to change the planet's climate. There was little media interest in the frozen findings of obscure, parka-clad Ph.D.s in far-off Greenland.

A wealth of other evidence has emerged since 1984, however, corroborating Dansgaard and Oeschger's natural 1,500-year climate cycle:

- An ice core from the Antarctic's Vostok Glacier—at the other end of the world from Iceland—was brought up in 1987 and showed the same 1,500-year climate cycle throughout its 400,000-year length.
- The ice-core findings correlate with known advances and retreats in the glaciers of the Arctic, Europe, Asia, North America, Latin America, New Zealand, and the Antarctic.
- The 1,500-year cycle has been revealed in seabed sediment cores brought up from the floors of such far-flung waters as the North Atlantic Ocean and the Sargasso Sea, the South Atlantic Ocean and the Arabian Sea.
- Cave stalagmites from Ireland and Germany in the Northern Hemisphere to South Africa and New Zealand in the Southern Hemisphere show evidence of the Modern Warming, the Little Ice Age, the Medieval Warming, the Dark Ages, the Roman Warming, and the unnamed cold period before the Roman Warming.
- Fossilized pollen from across North America shows nine complete reorganizations of our trees and plants in the last 14,000 years, or one every 1,650 years.
- In both Europe and South America, archaeologists have evidence that prehistoric humans moved their homes and farms up mountainsides during the warming centuries and retreated back down during the cold ones.

The Earth continually warms and cools. The cycle is undeniable, ancient, often abrupt, and global. It is also unstoppable. Isotopes in the ice and sediment cores, ancient tree rings, and stalagmites tell us it is linked to small changes in the irradiance of the sun.

The temperature change is moderate. Temperatures at the latitude of New York and Paris moved about 2 degrees Celsius above the long-term mean during warmings, with increases of 3 degrees or more in the polar latitudes. During the cold phases of the cycle, temperatures dropped by similar amounts below the mean. Temperatures change little in lands at the equator, but rainfall often does.

The cycle shifts have occurred roughly on schedule whether CO_2 levels were high or low. Based on this 1,500-year cycle, the Earth is about 150 years into a moderate Modern Warming that will last for centuries longer. It will essentially restore the fine climate of the Medieval Climate Optimum.

The climate has been most stable during the warming phases. The "little ice ages" have been beset by more floods, droughts, famines, and storminess. Yet, despite all of this evidence, millions of well-educated people, many scientists, many respected organizations—even the national governments of major First World nations—are telling us that the Earth's current warming phase is caused by human-emitted CO_2 and deadly dangerous. They ask society to renounce most of its use of fossil fuel-generated energy and accept radical reductions in food production, health technologies, and standards of living to "save the planet."

We have missed the predictive power of the 1,500-year climate cycle.

Will the fear of dangerous global warming lead society to accept draconian restrictions on the use of fertilizers, cars, and air conditioners?

Will people give up the scientific and technological advances that have added thirty years to life expectancies all over the globe in the last century?

Massive human sacrifices would be required to meet the CO_2 stabilization goals of the Kyoto Protocol. The treaty's "introductory offer" is a tiny 5 percent reduction in fossil fuel emissions from 1990 levels, but that would do almost nothing to forestall greenhouse warming of the planet. Saving the planet from man-made global warming was supposed to wait on Kyoto's yet-unspecified second stage, scheduled to begin in 2012.

In 1995, one U.S. environmentalist assessed the outlook: "According to the [United Nations] Intergovernmental Panel on Climate Change, an immediate 60 to 80 percent reduction in emissions is necessary just to stabilize atmospheric concentrations of CO_2—the minimum scientifically defensible goal for any climate strategy. Less-developed nations, with their relatively low emissions, will inevitably increase their use of fossil fuels as they industrialize and their populations expand. Thus heavily polluting regions like the [United States] will have to reduce their emissions even more [than 60 to 80 percent] for the world as a whole to meet this goal."[2]

Humans use eighty million tons per year of nitrogen fertilizer to nourish their crops. The nitrogen is taken from the air (which is 78 percent N_2) through an industrial process generally fueled by natural gas. In 1900, before industrial nitrogen fertilizer, the world could support only 1.5 billion people, at a far lower standard of living, and was clearing huge tracts of forest to get more cropland.

Suppose the world went all-organic in its farming, gave up the man-made fertilizer, and cleared half of the world's remaining forests for more low-yield crops. It's reasonable to expect that half the world's wildlife species would be lost in the land clearing and one-fourth of the world's people would succumb to malnutrition. What if research then confirmed that the climate was warming due to the natural cycle instead of CO_2? Is that a no-regrets climate insurance policy?

What if the Kyoto treaty or some similar arrangement prevented the Third World from moving away from using wood for heating and cooking? How much additional forest would then be sacrificed for firewood in the developing countries over the next fifty years?

The stakes in the global warming debate are huge. Humanity and wildlife may both be losing the debate.

Does a 1,500-Year Climate Cycle Rule Our Earth?

Greenhouse warming advocates say:

Nineteen ninety-nine was the most violent year in the modern history of weather. So was 1998. So was 1997. And 1996.... A nine-hundred-year-long cooling trend has been suddenly and decisively reversed in the past fifty years.... Scientists predicted that the Earth will shortly be warmer than it has been in millions of years. A climatological nightmare is upon us. It is almost certainly the most dangerous thing that has ever happened in our history.[3]

Climate extremes would trigger meteorological chaos—raging hurricanes such as we have never seen, capable of killing millions of people; uncommonly long, record-breaking heat waves; and profound drought that could drive Africa and the entire Indian subcontinent over the edge into mass starvation.[4]

From sweltering heat to rising sea levels, global warming's effects have already begun.... We know where most heat-trapping gases come from: power plants and vehicles. And we know how to limit their emissions.[5]

Such policies like cutting energy use by more than 50 percent can contribute powerfully to the material salvation of the planet from mankind's greed and indifference.[6]

No matter if the science of global warming is all phony ... climate change [provides] the greatest opportunity to bring about justice and equality in the world.[7]

Reality-based skeptics say:

The study, appearing in the March 21 issue of the journal *Science*, analyzed ancient tree rings from 14 sites on three continents in the northern hemisphere and concluded that temperatures in an era known as the Medieval Warm Period some 800 to 1,000 years ago closely matched the warming trend of the 20th century.[8]

I want to encourage the committee to be suspicious of media reports in which weather extremes are given as proof of human-induced climate change. Weather extremes occur somewhere all the time. For example, in the year 2000 in the 48 coterminous states, the U.S. experienced the coldest combined November and December in 106 years.... The intensity and frequency of hurricanes have not increased. The intensity and frequency of tornados have not increased.... Droughts and wet spells have not statistically increased or decreased.[9]

Hurricanes, brutal cold fronts and heat waves, ice storms and tornadoes, cycles of flood and drought, and earthquakes and volcanic eruptions are not unforeseeable interruptions of normality. Rather, these extremes are the way that the planet we live on does its business. Hurricanes, in some parts of the world, provide a third of the average annual rainfall. What we call "climate" is really an average of extremes of heat and cold, precipitation and drought.... [A]ll the evidence from paleoclimatology and geology suggests that over the long haul, the extremes we face will be substantially greater than even the strongest in our brief historical record.[10]

[T]he number of major [Chinese] floods averaged fewer than four per century in the warm period of the ninth through eleventh centuries, while the average number was more than double that figure in the fourteenth through seventeenth centuries of the Mini Ice Age.[11]

* * *

The Earth has recently been warming. This is beyond doubt. It has warmed slowly and erratically—for a total of about 0.8 degrees Celsius—since 1850. It had one surge of warming from 1850 to 1870 and another from 1920 to 1940. However, when we correct the thermometer records for the effects of growing urban heat islands and widespread intensification of land use, and for the recently documented cooling of the Antarctic continent over the past thirty years, overall world temperatures today are only modestly warmer than they were in 1940, despite a major increase in human CO_2 emissions.

The real question is not whether the Earth is warming but why and by how much.

We have a large faction of intensely interested persons who say the warming is man-made, and dangerous. They say it is driven by releases of greenhouse gases such as CO_2 from power plants and autos, and methane from rice paddies and cattle herds. The activists tell us that modern society will destroy the planet; that unless we radically change human energy production and consumption, the globe will become too warm for farming and the survival of wild species. They warn that the polar ice caps could melt, raising sea levels and flooding many of the world's most important cities and farming regions.

However, they don't have much evidence to support their position—only (1) the fact that the Earth is warming, (2) a theory that doesn't explain the warming of the past 150 years very well, and (3) some unverified computer models. Moreover, their credibility is seriously weakened by the fact that many of them have long believed modern technology should be discarded whether the Earth is warming too fast or not at all.

Many scientists—though by no means all—agree that increased CO_2 emissions could be dangerous. However, polls of climate-qualified scientists show that many doubt the scary predictions of the global computer models. [There are] many hundreds of researchers, authors, and coauthors whose work testifies to the 1,500-year cycle. There is no "scientific consensus," as global warming advocates often claim. Nor is consensus important to science. Galileo may have been the only man of his day who believed the Earth revolved around the sun, but he was right! Science is the process of developing theories and *testing them against observations* until they are proven true or false.

If we can find proof, not just that the Earth is warming, but that it is warming to dangerous levels due to human-emitted greenhouse gases, public policy will then have to evaluate such potential remedies as banning autos and air conditioners. So far, we have no such evidence.

If the warming is natural and unstoppable, then public policy must focus instead on adaptations—such as more efficient air conditioning and building dikes around low-lying areas like Bangladesh. We have the warming. Now we must ascertain its cause.

The Story of the 1,500-Year Climate Cycle

Carefully retrieved ice cores now reveal 900,000 years of the planet's climate changes. The information in the ice layers is being supplemented by such scientific breakthroughs as solar-monitoring satellites and mass spectrometer measurements of oxygen and carbon isotopes. These are allowing the Earth itself to tell us about its own climate history.

The ice cores say the newly understood 1,500-year cycle has dominated Earth's climate during the 11,000 years since the last ice age. Moreover, its fingerprints are being found all over the world, stretching through previous ice ages and interglacials.

We'll cover the evidence that past climate cycles such as the Medieval Warming and the Little Ice Age were truly global, not just Europe-only events as some man-made warming advocates have suggested. Our search for evidence will carry us from European castles to Chinese orange groves to Japanese cherry blossom viewings, from Saharan lakes to Andean glaciers and a South African cave.

No single climate proxy is totally equal to having thermometer records from the Middle Ages or ancient Rome. Tree rings reflect not only temperature and sunlight but also other factors that affect the tree, including rainfall, the number of competing trees, tree insects, and diseases. Borehole temperature signals become fainter as they go deeper.

Individually, each piece of proxy evidence could be questioned. That's why we'll examine a broad array of them, widespread in their geography, and almost dizzying in their variety.

We'll examine lots of tree rings, ice cores, and seabed sediments because they're the most important long-record proxies and among the most accurate, if properly treated. We'll also look at peat bogs full of antique organic residues; stalagmites from caves where varying amounts of moisture and minerals from the surface have dripped for century after century; coral reefs whose tiny creators have left behind clues to the sea temperatures while they were working; and ancient iron dust that betrays huge droughts.

We'll check out the reasons why many people today fear global warming. This fear of warm weather comes in dramatic contrast to our forebears—who loved warming climates and hated the mini-ice ages.

After all, it was during the cooling Dark Ages that the Roman and Mayan empires collapsed, after they had thrived during a warming that was hotter than it is today. And, it was during the cold of the Little Ice Age that Europe had its worst-ever floods and famines.

Earth's Climate Link to the Sun

Humans have known about a link between Earth's climate cycles and solar variability for more than four hundred years because of sunspot variations. Most dramatically, the Maunder Sunspot Minimum occurred from 1640 to 1710, when there were virtually no sunspots at all for some seventy years. That marked the sun's weakest recent moment—and that was the very coldest point in the Little Ice Age. Observers have also known that sunspot cycles that lasted longer than the average eleven years (the variation is eight to fourteen years) produce warmer temperatures on Earth. What our ancestors didn't know was how the solar-Earth climate link functioned.

Until the age of satellites, we didn't even know that tiny cycles of variation in the sun's irradiance existed. Until recently, scientists spoke of the "solar constant." Now, measuring from outside the clouds and gases of the Earth's atmosphere, we find that the sun's intensity varies by fractions of a percentage point.

Until 2001, the global warming debate was what a lawyer would call a "he-said/she-said" controversy. The science for man-made global warming looked weak. The science for solar-driven climate cycles on Earth looked more plausible, but was inconclusive.

But on 16 November 2001, the journal *Science* published a report on elegant research, done by unimpeachable scientists, giving us the Earth's climate history for the past 32,000 years—along with our climate's linkage to the sun. The late Gerard Bond and a team from the Columbia University's Lamont-Doherty Earth Observatory published "Persistent Solar Influence on North Atlantic Climate during the Holocene."[12]

Science's Richard Kerr wrote:

> Paleo-oceanographer Gerard Bond and his colleagues report that the climate of the northern North Atlantic has warmed and cooled nine times in the past 12,000 years in step with the waxing and waning of the sun.
>
> "It really looks like the sun has mattered to climate," says glaciologist Richard Alley of Pennsylvania State University.... "The Bond et al., data are sufficiently convincing that [solar variability] is now the leading hypothesis to explain the roughly 1,500-year oscillation of the climate seen since the last ice age, including the Little Ice Age of the 17th century," says Alley.[13]

Bond's sun-climate correlation rests on a rare combination of long, continuous, and highly detailed records of both climate change and solar activity. The climate record is Bond's well-known and laborious accounting of the microscopic bits of rock dropped by melting icebergs onto the floor of the northern North Atlantic over thousands of years.

Bond and his team found that the amounts of debris increased in abundance every 1,500 years (give or take 500) as the ice was carried farther out into a temporarily colder Atlantic. During the last Ice Age's coldest spells, huge amounts of ice were carried clear across the Atlantic's polar region and south as far as Ireland.

Bond's linkages to solar activity are the carbon-14 isotopes in tree rings and beryllium-10 isotopes in the Greenland ice cores. The carbon and beryllium isotopes are linked to solar activity through the intensity of solar-modulated cosmic rays, and are produced when cosmic rays strike the upper atmosphere. (Oxygen isotopes found in ice cores reveal past temperatures.)

The startling element of Bond's results is the close correlation found when the global temperatures and solar-strength records are laid next to each other.

How Does the Sun Change Our Climate?

How does a tiny change in the sun's irradiance make a big difference in the Earth's climate? First of all, we know that the linkage exists and is powerful, which puts the solar cycle far ahead of the Greenhouse Theory.

We now have strong, new scientific evidence of how the linkage works. The key amplifier is cosmic rays. The sun sends out a "solar wind" that protects the Earth from some of the cosmic rays bombarding the rest of the universe. When the sun is weak, however, more of the cosmic rays get through to the Earth's atmosphere. There, they ionize air molecules and create cloud nuclei. These nuclei then produce low, wet clouds that reflect solar radiation back into outer space. This cools the Earth.

Researchers using neutron chambers to measure the cosmic rays have recently found that changes in Earth's cosmic ray levels are correlated with the number and size of such cooling clouds.

The second amplifier is ozone chemistry in the atmosphere. When the sun is more active, more of its ultraviolet rays hit the Earth's atmosphere, shattering more oxygen (O_2) molecules—some of which reform into ozone (O_3). The additional ozone molecules absorb more of the near-UV radiation from the sun, increasing temperatures in the atmosphere. Computer models indicate that a 0.1 percent change in the sun's radiation could cause a 2 percent change in the Earth's ozone concentration, affecting atmospheric heat and circulation.

Intergovernmental Panel on Climate Change Charges Man-Made Warming

What about the claim of the United Nations' Intergovernmental Panel on Climate Change (IPCC): that they've found a "human fingerprint" in the current global warming?

That statement was inserted in the executive summary of the IPCC's 1996 report for political, not scientific, reasons. Then the "science volume" was edited to take out five different statements—all of which had been approved by the panel's scientific consultants—specifically saying no such "human fingerprint" had been found.

The author of the IPCC science chapter, a U.S. government employee, publicly admitted making the scientifically indefensible "back room" changes. He was under pressure from top U.S. government officials to do so.[14]

The Failures of the Greenhouse Theory

Let's quickly review the shortcomings of the Greenhouse Theory for explaining known realities.

First, and most obvious, CO_2 changes do not account for the highly variable climate we know the Earth has recently had, including the Roman Warming, the Dark Ages, the Medieval Warming, and the Little Ice Age. However, these variations fit into the 1,500-year cycle very well.

Second, the Greenhouse Theory does not explain recent temperature changes. Most of the current warming occurred *before 1940,* before there was much human-generated CO_2 in the air. After 1940, temperatures declined until 1975 or so, despite a huge surge in industrial CO_2 during that period. These events run *counter* to the CO_2 theory, but they are in accord with the 1,500-year cycle.

Third, the early and supposedly most powerful increases in atmospheric CO_2 have not produced the frightening planetary overheating that the theory and climate models told us to expect. We must discount *future* increments of CO_2 in the atmosphere, because each increment of CO_2 increase produces less warming than the unit before it. The amounts of CO_2 already added to the atmosphere must already have "used up" much—and perhaps most—of CO_2's forcing capability.

Fourth, we must discount the "official" temperature record to reflect the increased size and intensity of today's urban heat islands, where most of the official thermometers are located. We must take account of the changes in rural land use (forests cleared for farming and pastures, more intensive row-crop and irrigated farming) that affect soil moisture and temperatures. When meteorological experts reconstructed U.S. official temperatures "without cities and crops"—using more accurate data from satellites and high-altitude weather balloons—*about half of the recent "official" warming disappeared.*

Fifth, the Earth's surface thermometers have recently warmed faster than the temperature readings in the lower atmosphere up to 30,000 feet. Yet the Greenhouse Theory says that CO_2 will warm the lower atmosphere first, and then the atmospheric heat will radiate to the Earth's surface. *This is not happening.*

[Research] shows the very moderate trend in the satellite readings over the past two decades, totaling 0.125 degrees Celsius per decade. [VOLUME EDITOR'S NOTE: Data presented in Figure 1.1 ("Satellite Temperature Record, 1979–2004," p. 11) in the original essay have been omitted here. See the original source for this figure.] The short-term temperature spike in 1998 was one of the strongest El Niño events in recent centuries, but its effect quickly dissipated, as always happens with El Niños.

A reconstruction of weather-balloon temperature readings at two meters above the Earth's surface (1979–1996) shows a trend increase of only 0.015 degree Celsius per decade.[15] Nor can we project even that slow increase over the coming centuries, since the 1,500-year cycles have often achieved half of their total warming in their first few decades, followed by erratic warmings and coolings like those we've recorded since 1920.

Sixth, CO_2 for at least 240,000 years has been a *lagging indicator* of global warming, not a causal factor. Within the last 15 years, the ice cores have revealed that temperatures and CO_2 levels have tracked closely together during the warmings after each of Earth's last three ice age glaciations. However, the CO_2 changes have lagged about 800 years behind the temperature changes. *Global warming has produced more CO_2, rather than more CO_2 producing global warming.* This accords with the reality that the oceans hold the vast majority of the planet's carbon, and the laws of physics let cold oceans hold more CO_2 gas than warm oceans.

Seventh, the Greenhouse Theory predicts that CO_2-driven warming of the Earth's surface will start, and be strongest, in the North and South Polar regions. *This is not happening either.* A broadly scattered set of meteorological stations and ocean buoys show that temperature readings in the Arctic, Greenland, and the seas around them are colder today than in the 1930s. Alaska has been warming, but researchers say this is due to the recent warming of the Pacific Decadal Oscillation (PDO), not a broader Arctic warming pattern. The twenty to thirty year cycle of the PDO seems to have recently reversed again, so Alaska may now cool with the rest of the Arctic.

In the Antarctic, only the thin finger of the Antarctic Peninsula, which juts up toward Argentina (and the equator) has been warming. Temperatures over the other 98 percent of the Antarctic continent have been declining slowly since the 1960s, according to a broad array of Antarctic surface stations and satellite measurements.

Eighth, the scary predictions of planetary overheating require that the warming effect of additional CO_2 be amplified by increased water vapor in the atmosphere. Warming will indeed lift more moisture from the oceans into the air. But what if the moister, warmer air increases the efficiency of rainfall, and leaves the upper atmosphere as dry, or even dryer, than it was before? We have absolutely no evidence to demonstrate that the upper atmosphere is retaining more water vapor to amplify the CO_2.

To the contrary, a team of researchers from NASA and MIT recently discovered a huge vertical heat vent in the Earth's atmosphere. It apparently increases the efficiency of rainfall when sea surface temperatures rise above 28° C. This effect seems to be big enough to vent all the heat the models predict would be generated by a doubling of CO_2.[16]

In 2001, NASA issued a press release about the heat vent discovery and the failure of the climate models to duplicate it but it attracted little media attention.[17]

The Inherent Dangers of the Kyoto Protocol

Early in my career, I served as a missionary in Africa. I lived upcountry with people who did not have access to useful energy.... I watched as women walked in the early morning to the forest edge, often several miles away, to chop wet green wood for fuel.... They became beasts of burden as they carried the wood on their backs on the return trip home.... Burning wood and dung inside the homes for cooking and heat created a dangerously polluted indoor atmosphere for the family. I always thought that if each home could be fitted with an electric light bulb and a microwave oven electrified by a coal-fired power plant, several good things would happen. The women would be freed to work on other, more productive, pursuits. The indoor air would be much cleaner so health would improve. Food could be prepared more safely. There would be light for reading and advancement. Information through television or radio would be received. And the forest with its beautiful ecosystem could be saved.[18]

The Kyoto Protocol will likely cost at least $150 billion a year, and possibly much more. UNICEF estimates that just $70–80 billion a year could give all Third World inhabitants access to the basics like health, education, water and sanitation.[19]

The Kyoto Protocol would probably double First World energy costs before 2012, and might quadruple them after that year. Kyoto would thus impair or even cancel out the enormous beneficial effects of technology in people's lives.

The myths of "free" wind and solar power continue to fascinate journalists and activists. Kyoto proponents assert that "renewable" energy sources will not only be adequate for the needs of modern society, but the shift from fossil fuels to solar and wind will "create jobs." This is like claiming that repairing a broken window makes us richer; instead, it just gets us back to where we had been. A shift to renewable fuels would certainly create jobs, but it would also require time and talents that could have produced additional well-being.

Energy experts note that wind and solar power are not very reliable; they are only generated when the wind is right or the sun is shining, and they are difficult to store. Backup nonrenewable power plants are needed in "spinning reserve" so the traffic lights and hospital operating theaters don't go dark. Despite decades of heavy subsidies, solar and wind power provide only about 0.5 percent of current U.S. electricity, and almost none of our transport energy.

Solar and wind are still four to ten times as expensive as fossil and nuclear energy sources. Shifting to "renewables" would also force us to convert hundreds of millions of forest and wildlands acres to windmill farms, solar panel arrays, biofuel crops, and the like.

In fact, a team of energy experts from various academic, government, and private sector research units said in a 2002 "Science Compass" article for the journal *Science,* that it would be a Herculean task to replace the fossil energy supplies any time soon.[20]

The biggest problem is that the world's current 12 trillion watt-hours of energy used per year (85 percent of it fossil-fueled) will need to be expanded to 22–42 trillion over the next fifty years in order to accommodate the world's growing population and provide economic growth for developing countries.

Energy experts say that even nuclear power will not be enough, due to a shortage of uranium ore. We will need safe nuclear breeder reactors and, ultimately, fusion power. That means developing very expensive energy technology we don't yet have.

Modern technology has also been humanity's strongest environmental conservation tool. For thousands of years, humans lived by preying on wildlife. Then we invented farming, and took most of the world's good land away from Nature for crops and pastures. Only in the past half-century has most of the world adopted the high-yield farming that permits more food to be grown per farming acre. That high-yield farming has forestalled the need to plow down millions more square miles of forests. Without the nitrogen captured from the air by fertilizer factories powered by natural gas, we'd have to clear the world's remaining forests for low-yield crops—tomorrow.

The rural half of India's population is scouring its forests daily for scarce firewood, and cutting trees it doesn't replant. India's demand for firewood is likely to double again by 2020.

Most of the Third World is already in the most polluting phase of industrial development, with grimy cities burning huge amounts of coal and smelting lots of iron for heavy machinery. The Third World needs economic growth, not another Great Depression, to move up to the cleaner industries and technologies used by the First World.

World Bank researchers have now concluded that, while the early stages of economic growth are harmful to the environment, the later stages of economic growth are environmentally constructive. Incomes above $5,000 to $8,000 per capita, where Brazil and Malaysia are today, trigger more investments in air and water cleanup and high-yield farming. They also bring massive reductions in industrial emissions, and the creation of more parks and wildlife preserves that are actually policed to protect the wildlife.[21]

Bjorn Lomborg, author of *The Skeptical Environmentalist,* recently convened a panel of leading economists to propose the most effective ways the world could use $50 billion to benefit humankind. The panel was cosponsored by the Danish government and *The Economist.* This "Copenhagen Consensus" recommended that the money be spent, first, on combatting new cases of AIDS ($27 billion); second, on reducing iron deficiency anemia in women and children through food supplements ($12 billion); third, on controlling the malaria ($13 billion) that afflicts 300 million people and kills 2.7 million annually. (The malaria control will necessarily involve the indoor use of DDT as a mosquito insecticide.) The Copenhagen panel's fourth spending priority was on agricultural research to sustainably raise crop yields and ease the competition for land between people and wildlife.

The Copenhagen Consensus ranked the Kyoto Protocol sixteenth out of seventeen proposed ways to use the money. The panelists said Kyoto's costs would outweigh its benefits—even though they assumed significant warming driven by CO_2. If they had been aware of the physical evidence endorsing the 1,500-year climate cycle, they might have ranked Kyoto even lower.

"The panel's findings are a reproach to many European leaders and to left-wing environmentalists, health activists, and anti-globalists, whose sloganeering has dominated much of the discussion of global welfare issues," wrote syndicated columnist James Glassman. "This report—sober, nonpartisan, and compassionate, with an emphasis on sound science and economic cost-benefit analysis—makes the noisy radicals look foolish."[22]

We don't necessarily subscribe to the rankings of the Copenhagen Consensus but agree that the Kyoto Protocol should be near the bottom.

Why Fear Global Warming?

History, science, and our own instincts tell us that cold is more frightening than warmth. It is a psychological mystery why comfortable First World residents, armed for the first time in all of history's warmings with air conditioning, have chosen to fear "global warming."

Of course, the advocates of man-made warming have attempted to bolster a scientifically weak case with a number of essentially baseless scary scenarios.

Rising Sea Levels Will Flood Cities and Cropland, and Submerge Islands

Judging from measurements made on corals, sea levels have been rising steadily since the peak of the last Ice Age about 18,000 years ago. The total rise since then has been four hundred feet. The sea levels rose fastest during the Holocene Climate Optimum, when the major ice sheets covering Eurasia and North America melted away. For the last 5,000 years or so, the rate of rise has been about seven inches per century. Tide gauge data from the past century show a rise of about six inches—even after the strong warming between period 1920 and 1940.

When the climate warms, ocean waters expand and glaciers melt, so sea levels rise. But a warmer ocean evaporates more water, some of which ends up as snow and ice on Greenland and on the Antarctic continent, and that makes sea levels fall. More warming and more evaporation are adding ice to the Antarctic ice cap. Thus, there is no reason to expect any big acceleration of sea level increase in the twenty-first century. Researchers say it would take another 7,000 years to melt the West Antarctic Ice Sheet—a small fraction of all the ice—and we're almost sure to get another ice age before then.

More than a Million of the World's Wild Species Will Go Extinct in the Next Century

We know that species can adapt to abrupt global warming because the climate shifts in the 1,500-year cycle have often been abrupt. Moreover, the world's species have already survived at least six hundred such warmings and coolings in the past million years.

The major effect of global warming will be more biodiversity in our forests, as most trees, plants, birds, and animals extend their ranges. This is already happening. Some biologists claim that a further warming of 0.8 degrees Celsius will destroy thousands of species. However, the Earth warmed much more than that during the Holocene Climate Optimum, which occurred 8,000 to 5,000 years ago, and *no known species were driven extinct* by the temperature increase.

There Will Be More Hunger and Famine as Fields Become Too Hot to Grow Crops

High-tech farming, not climate, has governed the world's overall food production since the seventeenth century. There will be little temperature change in the tropics, where food production is still inadequate. The northern plains in Canada and in Russia will become warmer, and will produce more food. Modern society can help make tropical farming high-tech, or transport more food from Siberia to people with new nonfarm jobs in India or Nigeria. Any famines will be humanity's fault, not the fault of the climate.

There Will Be More Storms and Worse Storms with Global Warming

There has been no increase in the frequency or severity of hurricanes, blizzards, cyclones, tornadoes, or any other kind of storms during the warming of the past 150 years. That makes sense, because storms are driven by the temperature differential between the equator and the polar regions. Since greenhouse warming should boost the temperatures at the poles much more than at the equator, warming will reduce the differential and moderate the storms. History and paleontology tell us the warmings have experienced better, more stable weather than the coolings.

Global Warming Will Trigger Abrupt Global Cooling

The warming activists claim that increased meltwater due to higher temperatures could overwhelm the Great Atlantic Conveyor, the huge ocean current that distributes heat from the equator to the poles. The Gulf Stream would then shut down, and we would all be covered in ice before you can say "carbon dioxide." It happened once before—but then the world had trillions of additional tons of ice in Canadian and Siberian ice sheets for the warming to melt. The climate models—surprise!—tell us that it won't happen during the Modern Warming, because the Earth doesn't have enough ice left.

Human Death Tolls Will Rise with the Heat, Insects, and Disease of Global Warming

Freezing weather kills far more people than hot weather, and there'll be less freezing winter weather during the Modern Warming. As for mosquito-borne diseases, window screens and insecticides wiped out most of the world's malaria and yellow fever, not cold weather. The world's biggest malaria outbreak was in Russia in the 1920s.

Coral Reefs Will Die Out with Warming

Many coral reefs have "bleached" (lost the algae that live in symbiotic partnership with them) when sea temperatures rose. But they also bleach when temperatures fall. That's because the corals partner with the algae varieties best adapted to their current temperature. When the water warms, they eject their cold-water partners and welcome warmer-weather friends, and vice versa. That's how they have survived for millions of climate-varied years.

Fear the Next Ice Age

The climate event that deserves real concern is the next Big Ice Age. That is inevitably approaching, though it may still be thousands of years away. When it comes, temperatures may plummet 15 degrees Celsius, with the high latitudes getting up to 40 degrees colder. Humanity and food production will be forced closer to the equator, as huge ice sheets expand in Canada, Scandinavia, Russia, and Argentina. Even Ohio and Indiana may gradually be encased in mile-thick ice, while California and the Great Plains could suffer century-long drought.

Keeping warm will become the critical issue, both night and day. Getting enough food for eight or nine billion people from the relatively small amount of arable land left unfrozen will be a potentially desperate effort. The broad, fertile plains of Alberta and the Ukraine will become sub-Arctic wastes. Wildlife species will be extremely challenged, even though they've survived such cold before—because this time there will be more humans competing for the ice-free land.

That's when human knowledge and high-tech farming will be truly needed.

In contrast, none of the scary scenarios posited by today's global warming advocates took place during the Earth's past warm periods.

Why have humans chosen to panic about the planet returning to what is very probably the finest climate the planet has known in all its millions of years? Is it simply guilt because climate alarmists told us we humans were causing the change?

If so, then it becomes all the more important to check their evidence.

Notes

1. W. Dansgaard et al., "North Atlantic Climatic Oscillations Revealed by Deep Greenland Ice Cores," in *Climate Processes and Climate Sensitivity,* ed. F. E. Hansen and T. Takahashi (Washington, D.C.: American Geophysical Union, 1984), Geophysical Monograph 29, 288–98.

2. John C. Ryan, "Greenhouse Gases on the Rise in the Northwest," Northwest Environment Watch, 1995, <www.northwestwatch.org> (12 February 2004).

3. Art Bell and Whitley Strieber, *The Coming Global Superstorm* (New York: Pocket Books, 2000), 10–11.

4. Former U.S. Senate Majority Leader George Mitchell (D-Maine), *World on Fire: Saving an Endangered Earth* (New York: Scribner, 1991), 70–71.

5. Natural Resources Defense Council, www.nrdc.org/globalWarming/ (27 May 2003).

6. Sir John Houghton, Chairman, Scientific Assessment Working Group, United Nations Intergovernmental Panel on Climate Change, letter to the World Council of Churches, 1996.

7. Christine Stewart, then Canadian Minister of the Environment, before the editors and reporters of the *Calgary Herald,* 1998, and quoted by Terence Corcoran, "Global Warming: The Real Agenda," *Financial Post,* 26 December 1998, from the *Calgary Herald,* 14 December 1998.

8. Paul Recer, "Study of Tree Rings Shows Earth Has Normal Cycles of Warmth, Cooling," Associated Press, 22 March 2002.

9. John Christy, Professor of Atmospheric Science, University of Alabama–Huntsville and a lead author for the UN Intergovernmental Panel on Climate Change, speaking before the House of Representatives committee, 13 May 2003.

10. William H. Hooke, policy director, American Meteorological Society, "Avoiding a Catastrophe of Human Error," *Washington Post,* 5 January 2005.

11. Thomas Gale Moore, "Why Global Warming Would Be Good for You," *The Public Interest* (Winter 1995): 83–99.

12. Gerard Bond et al., "Persistent Solar Influence on North Atlantic Climate during the Holocene," *Science* 294 (16 November 2001): 2130–136.

13. Richard Kerr, "A Variable Sun Paces Millennial Climate," *Science* 294 (16 November 2001): 1431–433.

14. Frederick Seitz, former president, National Academy of Sciences, "A Major Decep-
tion on Global Warming," *Wall Street Journal,* 12 June 1996, editorial page. S. Fred
Singer, *Climate Policy from Rio to Kyoto: A Political Issue for 2000 and Beyond*
(Palo Alto, CA: Hoover Institution, Stanford University, 2000), 19.

15. D. H. Douglass, B. Pearson, and S. F. Singer, "Disparity of Tropospheric and
Surface Temperature Trends: New Evidence," *Geophysical Research Letters* 31:
L13207.doi:10.1029/2004/GL020212 (2004).

16. Richard Lindzen, Ming-Dah Chou, and Arthur Hou, "Does the Earth Have an
Adaptive Infrared Iris?" *Bulletin of the American Meteorological Society* 82 (2001):
417–32.

17. "Natural 'Heat Vent' in Pacific Cloud Cover Could Diminish Greenhouse
Warming," press release, NASA Goddard Space Flight Center, 28 February 2001.

18. John Christy, climatologist, University of Alabama–Huntsville.

19. Bjorn Lomborg, *The Skeptical Environmentalist* (London: Cambridge University
Press, 2001), 322.

20. M. I. Hoffert et al., "Science Compass: Advanced Technology Paths to Global
Climate Stability: Energy for a Greenhouse Planet," *Science* 298 (2002): 981–87.

21. *International Trade and the Environment,* World Bank Discussion Paper 159,
Patrick Low, ed. (January 1992); also, G. Grossman and A. Kreuger, "Economic
Growth and the Environment," *The Quarterly Journal of Economics* 370 (1995):
353–77.

22. James Glassman, "How to Save the World," *Washington Times,* 9 June 2004,
A16.

Chapter 15

GLOBAL CIVIL SOCIETY: NONSTATE ACTORS AND BASIC HUMAN RIGHTS

15.1

SELECTION FROM *A NEW WORLD ORDER*

Anne-Marie Slaughter

> Anne-Marie Slaughter, professor and dean of the Woodrow Wilson School at Princeton University (and in 2009 the director of policy planning in the State Department), offers a way of thinking about the world in terms of decentralized policy networks rather than world government or interstate relations. A "disaggregated world order" responds to the need for global governance without threatening national sovereignty or risking unaccountable international institutions. But what ensures that these networks are "inclusive, tolerant, respectful and decentralized" and not coercive like terrorist networks? She offers a set of norms: open participation, cultural pluralism, affirmative cooperation, checks and balances, and subsidiarity. Can you tell why her account, which relies less on institutional authority (liberal) and assumes that norms will trump power (realist), might be called constructivist (identity) and why she emphasizes the interactive (system process) level of analysis over world government (systemic structure) or national sovereignty (domestic)?

Terrorists, arms dealers, money launderers, drug dealers, traffickers in women and children, and the modern pirates of intellectual property all operate through global networks.[1] So, increasingly, do governments. Networks of government officials—police investigators, financial regulators, even judges and legislators—increasingly exchange information and coordinate activity to combat global

---

Source: Anne-Marie Slaughter, "Introduction," in *A New World Order* (Princeton, N.J.: Princeton University Press, 2004), 1–35.

crime and address common problems on a global scale. These government networks are a key feature of world order in the twenty-first century, but they are underappreciated, undersupported, and underused to address the central problems of global governance.

Consider the examples just in the wake of September 11. The Bush administration immediately set about assembling an ad hoc coalition of states to aid in the war on terrorism. Public attention focused on military cooperation, but the networks of financial regulators working to identify and freeze terrorist assets, of law enforcement officials sharing vital information on terrorist suspects, and of intelligence operatives working to preempt the next attack have been equally important. Indeed ... the domestic agencies responsible for customs, food safety, and regulation of all kinds must extend their reach abroad, through reorganization and much closer cooperation with their foreign counterparts.[2] And after the United States concluded that it did not have authority under international law to interdict a shipment of missiles from North Korea to Yemen, it turned to national law enforcement authorities to coordinate the extraterritorial enforcement of their national criminal laws.[3] Networked threats require a networked response.

Turning to the global economy, networks of finance ministers and central bankers have been critical players in responding to national and regional financial crises. The G-8 is as much a network of finance ministers as of heads of state; it is the finance ministers who make key decisions on how to respond to calls for debt relief for the most highly indebted countries. The finance ministers and central bankers hold separate news conferences to announce policy responses to crises such as the East Asian financial crisis in 1997 and the Russian crisis in 1998.[4] The G-20, a network specifically created to help prevent future crises, is led by the Indian finance minister and is composed of the finance ministers of twenty developed and developing countries. More broadly, the International Organization of Securities Commissioners (IOSCO) emerged in 1984. It was followed in the 1990s by the creation of the International Association of Insurance Supervisors and a network of all three of these organizations and other national and international officials responsible for financial stability around the world called the Financial Stability Forum.[5]

Beyond national security and the global economy, networks of national officials are working to improve environmental policy across borders. Within the North American Free Trade Agreement (NAFTA), U.S., Mexican, and Canadian environmental agencies have created an environmental enforcement network, which has enhanced the effectiveness of environmental regulation in all three states, particularly in Mexico. Globally, the Environmental Protection Agency (EPA) and its Dutch equivalent have founded the International Network for Environmental Compliance and Enforcement (INECE), which offers technical assistance to environmental agencies around the world, holds global conferences at which environmental regulators learn and exchange information, and sponsors a website with training videos and other information.

Nor are regulators the only ones networking. National judges are exchanging decisions with one another through conferences, judicial organizations, and the Internet. Constitutional judges increasingly cite one another's decisions on issues from free speech to privacy rights. Indeed, Justice Anthony Kennedy of the U.S. Supreme Court cited a decision by the European Court of Justice (ECJ) in an important 2003 opinion overturning a Texas antisodomy law. Bankruptcy judges in different countries negotiate minitreaties to resolve complicated international cases; judges in transnational commercial disputes have begun to see themselves as part of a global judicial system. National judges are also interacting directly with their supranational counterparts on trade and human rights issues.

Finally, even legislators, the most naturally parochial government officials due to their direct ties to territorially rooted constituents, are reaching across borders. International parliamentary organizations have been traditionally well meaning though ineffective, but today national parliamentarians are meeting to adopt and publicize common positions on the death penalty, human rights, and environmental issues. They support one another in legislative initiatives and offer training programs and technical assistance.[6]

Each of these networks has specific aims and activities, depending on its subject area, membership, and history, but taken together, they also perform certain common functions. They expand regulatory reach, allowing national government officials to keep up with corporations, civic organizations, and criminals. They build trust and establish relationships among their participants that then create incentives to establish a good reputation and avoid a bad one. These are the conditions essential for long-term cooperation. They exchange regular information about their own activities and develop databases of best practices, or, in the judicial case, different approaches to common legal issues. They offer technical assistance and professional socialization to members from less developed nations, whether regulators, judges, or legislators.

In a world of global markets, global travel, and global information networks, of weapons of mass destruction and looming environmental disasters of global magnitude, governments must have global reach. In a world in which their ability to use their hard power is often limited, governments must be able to exploit the uses of soft power: the power of persuasion and information.[7] Similarly, in a world in which a major set of obstacles to effective global regulation is a simple inability on the part of many developing countries to translate paper rules into changes in actual behavior, governments must be able not only to negotiate treaties but also to create the capacity to comply with them.

Understood as a form of global governance, government networks meet these needs. As commercial and civic organizations have already discovered, their networked form is ideal for providing the speed and flexibility necessary to function effectively in an information age. But unlike amorphous "global policy networks" championed by UN Secretary General Kofi Annan, in which it is never clear who is exercising power on behalf of whom, these are networks composed of national government officials, either appointed by elected officials or directly elected themselves. Best of all, they can perform many of the functions of a world government—legislation, administration, and adjudication—without the form.

Understood as a foreign policy option, a world of government networks, working alongside and even within traditional international organizations, should be particularly attractive to the United States. The United States has taken the lead in insisting that many international problems have domestic roots and that they be addressed at that level—within nations rather than simply between them—but it is also coming to understand the vital need to address those problems multilaterally rather than unilaterally, for reasons of legitimacy, burden sharing, and effectiveness.... [G]overnment networks could provide multilateral support for domestic government institutions in failed, weak, or transitional states. They could play an instrumental role in rebuilding a country like Iraq and in supporting and reforming government institutions in other countries that seek to avoid dictatorship and self-destruction.

Further, government networks cast a different light on U.S. power, one that is likely to engender less resentment worldwide. They engage U.S. officials of all kinds with their foreign counterparts in settings in which they have much to teach but also to learn and in which other countries can often provide powerful alternative models. In many regulatory areas, such as competition policy, environmental policy, and corporate governance, the European Union attracts as many imitators as the United States. In constitutional rights, many judges around the world have long followed U.S. Supreme Court decisions but are now looking to the South African or the Canadian constitutional courts instead.

Where a U.S. regulatory, judicial, or legislative approach is dominant, it is likely to be powerful through attraction rather than coercion—exactly the kind of soft power that Joseph Nye has been exhorting the United States to use.[8] This attraction flows from expertise, integrity, competence, creativity, and generosity with time and ideas—all characteristics that U.S. regulators, judges, and legislators have exhibited with their foreign counterparts. And where the United States is not dominant, its officials can show that they are in fact willing to listen to and learn from others, something that the rest of the world seems increasingly to doubt.

Yet to see these networks as they exist, much less to imagine what they could become, requires a deeper conceptual shift. Stop imagining the international system as a system of states—unitary entities like billiard balls or black boxes—subject to rules created by international institutions that are apart from, "above" these states. Start thinking about a world of governments, with all the different institutions that perform the basic functions of governments—legislation, adjudication, implementation—interacting both with each other domestically and also with their foreign and supranational counterparts. States still exist in this world; indeed, they are crucial actors. But they are "disaggregated." They relate to each other not only through the Foreign Office, but also through regulatory, judicial, and legislative channels.

... Seeing the world through the lenses of disaggregated rather than unitary states allows leaders, policymakers, analysts, or simply concerned citizens to see features of the global political system that were previously hidden. Government networks suddenly pop up everywhere, from the Financial Action Task Force (FATF), a network of finance ministers and other financial regulators taking charge of pursuing money launderers and financers of terrorism, to the Free Trade Commission, a network of trade ministers charged with interpreting NAFTA, to a network of ministers in charge of border controls working to create a new regime of safe borders in the wake of September 11. At the same time, it is possible to disaggregate international organizations as well, to see "vertical networks" between national regulators and judges and their supranational counterparts. Examples include relations between national European courts and the ECJ or between national U.S., Mexican, and Canadian courts and NAFTA arbitral tribunals.

Equally important, these different lenses make it possible to imagine a genuinely new set of possibilities for a future world order. The building blocks of this order would not be states but parts of states: courts, regulatory agencies, ministries, legislatures. The government officials within these various institutions would participate in many different types of networks, creating links across national borders and between national and supranational institutions. The result could be a world that looks like the globe hoisted by Atlas at Rockefeller Center, crisscrossed by an increasingly dense web of networks.

This world would still include traditional international organizations, such as the United Nations and the World Trade Organization (WTO), although many of these organizations would be likely to become hosts for and sources of government networks. It would still feature states interacting as unitary states on important issues, particularly in security matters. And it would certainly still be a world in which military and economic power mattered; government networks are not likely to substitute for either armies or treasuries.

At the same time, however, a world of government networks would be a more effective and potentially more just world order than either what we have today or a world government in which a set of global institutions perched above nation-states enforced global rules. In a networked world order, primary political authority would remain at the national level except in those cases in which national governments had explicitly delegated their authority to supranational institutions. National government officials would be increasingly enmeshed in networks of personal and institutional relations. They would each be operating both in the domestic and the international arenas, exercising their national authority to implement their transgovernmental and international obligations and representing the interests of their country while working with their foreign and supranational counterparts to disseminate and distill information, cooperate in enforcing national and international laws, harmonizing national laws and regulations, and addressing common problems.

1. The Globalization Paradox: Needing More Government and Fearing It

Peoples and their governments around the world need global institutions to solve collective problems that can only be addressed on a global scale. They must be able to make and enforce global rules on a variety of subjects and through a variety of means. Further, it has become commonplace to claim that the international institutions created in the late 1940s, after a very different war and facing a host of different threats from those we face today, are outdated and inadequate to meet contemporary challenges. They must be reformed or even reinvented; new ones must be created.

Yet world government is both infeasible and undesirable. The size and scope of such a government presents an unavoidable and dangerous threat to individual liberty. Further, the diversity of the peoples to be governed makes it almost impossible to conceive of a global demos. No form of democracy within the current global repertoire seems capable of overcoming these obstacles.

This is the globalization paradox. We need more government on a global and a regional scale, but we don't want the centralization of decision-making power and coercive authority so far from the people actually to be governed. It is the paradox identified in the European Union by Renaud Dehousse and by Robert Keohane in his millennial presidential address to the American Political Science Association. The European Union has pioneered "regulation by networks," which Dehousse describes as the response to a basic dilemma in EU governance: "On the one hand, increased uniformity is certainly needed; on the other hand, greater centralization is politically inconceivable, and probably undesirable.[9] The EU alternative is the "transnational option"—the use of an organized network of national officials to ensure "that the actors in charge of the implementation of Community policies behave in a similar manner."[10]

Worldwide, Keohane argues that globalization "creates potential gains from cooperation" if institutions can be created to harness those gains;[11] however, institutions themselves are potentially oppressive.[12] The result is "the Governance Dilemma: although institutions are essential for human life, they are also dangerous."[13] The challenge facing political scientists and policymakers at the dawn of the twenty-first century is discovering how well-structured institutions could enable the world to have "a rebirth of freedom."[14]

Addressing the paradox at the global level is further complicated by the additional concern of accountability. In the 1990s the conventional reaction to the problem of "world government" was instead to champion "global governance," a much looser and less threatening concept of collective organization and regulation without coercion. A major element of global governance, in turn, has been the rise of global policy networks, celebrated for their ability to bring together all public and private actors on issues critical to the global public interest.[15]

Global policy networks, in turn, grow out of various "reinventing government" projects, both academic and practical. These projects focus on the many ways in which private actors now can and do perform government functions, from providing expertise to monitoring compliance with regulations to negotiating the substance of those regulations, both domestically and internationally. The problem, however, is ensuring that these private actors uphold the public trust.

*   *   *

The governance dilemma thus becomes a tri-lemma: we need global rules without centralized power but with government actors who can be held to account through a variety of political mechanisms. These government actors can and should interact with a wide range of nongovernmental organizations (NGOs), but their role in governance bears distinct and different responsibilities. They must represent all their different constituencies, at least in a democracy; corporate and civic actors may be driven by profits and passions, respectively. "Governance" must not become a cover for the blurring of these lines, even if it is both possible and necessary for these various actors to work together on common problems.

In this context, a world order based on government networks, working alongside and even in place of more traditional international institutions, holds great potential. The existence of networks of national officials is not itself new. In 1972 Francis Bator testified before Congress: "it is a central fact of foreign relations that business is carried on by the separate departments with their counterpart bureaucracies abroad, through a variety of informal as well as formal connections."[16] Two years later, in an important article that informed their later study of complex interdependence, Robert Keohane and Joseph Nye distinguished "transgovernmental" activity from the broader category of transnational activity. They defined transgovernmental relations as "sets of direct interactions among sub-units of different governments that are not controlled or closely guided by the policies of the cabinets or chief executives of those governments."[17] Moreover, government networks established for limited purposes such as postal and telecommunications have existed for almost a century.

What is new is the scale, scope, and type of transgovernmental ties. Links between government officials from two, four, or even a dozen countries have become sufficiently dense as to warrant their own organization—witness IOSCO or INECE. Government networks have developed their own identity and autonomy in specific issue areas, such as the G-7 or the G-20. They perform a wider array of functions than in the past, from collecting and distilling information on global or regional best practices to actively offering technical assistance to poorer and less experienced members. And they have spread far beyond regulators to judges and legislators.

More broadly, government networks have become recognized and semiformalized ways of doing business within loose international groupings like the Commonwealth and the Asian-Pacific Economic Cooperation (APEC). At the same time, they have become the signature form of governance for the European Union, which is itself pioneering a new form of regional collective governance that is likely to prove far more relevant to global governance than the experience of traditional federal states. Most important, they are driven by many of the multiple factors that drive the hydra-headed phenomenon of globalization itself, leading to the simple need for national officials of all kinds to communicate and negotiate across borders to do business they could once accomplish solely at home.

*   *   *

Government networks can help address the governance tri-lemma, offering a flexible and relatively fast way to conduct the business of global governance, coordinating and even harmonizing national government action while initiating and monitoring different solutions to global problems. Yet they are decentralized and dispersed, incapable of exercising centralized coercive authority. Further, they are government actors. They can interact with a wide range of NGOs, civic and corporate, but their responsibilities and constituencies are far broader. These constituencies should be able to devise ways to hold them accountable, at least to the same extent that they are accountable for their purely domestic activity.

2. The Disaggregated State

Participants in the decade-long public and academic discussion of globalization have routinely focused on two major shifts: from national to global and from government to governance. They have paid far less attention to the third shift, from the unitary state to the disaggregated state.

The disaggregated state sounds vaguely Frankenstinian—a shambling, headless bureaucratic monster. In fact, it is nothing so sinister. It is simply the rising need for and capacity of different domestic government institutions to engage in activities beyond their borders, often with their foreign counterparts. It is regulators pursuing the subjects of their regulations across borders; judges negotiating minitreaties with their foreign brethren to resolve complex transnational cases; and legislators consulting on the best ways to frame and pass legislation affecting human rights or the environment.

The significance of the concept of the disaggregated state only becomes fully apparent in contrast to the unitary state, a concept that has long dominated international legal and political analysis. International lawyers and international relations theorists have always known that the entities they describe and analyze as "states" interacting with one another are in fact much more complex entities, but the fiction of a unitary will and capacity for action has worked well enough for purposes of description and prediction of outcomes in the international system. In U.S. constitutional law, for instance, the Supreme Court and the president have often had recourse to James Madison's famous pronouncement in the Federalist papers: "If we are to be one nation in any respect, it clearly ought to be in respect to other nations."[18] And in international law, the foundational premise of state sovereignty traditionally assumed that members of the international system have no right to pierce the veil of statehood.

In an international legal system premised on unitary states, the paradigmatic form of international cooperation is the multilateral international convention, negotiated over many years in various international watering holes, signed and ratified with attendant flourish and formality, and given continuing life through the efforts of an international secretariat whose members prod and assist ongoing rounds of negotiation aimed at securing compliance with obligations already undertaken and at expanding the scope and precision of existing rules.[19] The "states" participating in these negotiations are presumed to speak with one voice—a voice represented by either the head of state or the foreign minister. Any differences between the different parts of a particular government are to be worked out domestically; the analytical lens of the unitary state obscures the very existence of these different government institutions.

The result is the willful adoption of analytical blinders, allowing us to see the "international system" only in the terms that we ourselves have imposed. Compare our approach to domestic government: we know it to be an aggregate of different institutions. We call it "the government," but we can simultaneously distinguish the activities of the courts, Congress, regulatory agencies, and the White House itself. We do not choose to screen out everything except what the president does or says, or what Congress does or says, or what the Supreme Court does or says. But effectively, in the international system, we do.

Looking at the international system through the lens of unitary states leads us to focus on traditional international organizations and institutions created by and composed of formal state delegations. Conversely, however, thinking about states the way we think about domestic governments—as aggregations of distinct institutions with separate roles and capacities—provides a lens that allows us to see a new international landscape. Government networks pop up everywhere.

Horizontal government networks—links between counterpart national officials across borders—are easiest to spot. Far less frequent, but potentially very important, are vertical government networks, those between national government officials and their supranational counterparts. The prerequisite for a vertical government network is the relatively rare decision by states to delegate their sovereignty to an institution above them with real power—a court or a regulatory commission. That institution can then be the genuine counterpart existence of a national government institution. Where these vertical networks exist, as in the relations between national courts and the ECJ in the European Union, they enable the supranational institution to be maximally effective.

* * *

3. A New World Order

Appreciating the extent and nature of existing government networks, both horizontal and vertical, makes it possible to envision a genuinely new world order. "World order," for these purposes, describes a system of global governance that institutionalizes cooperation and sufficiently contains conflict such that all nations and their peoples may achieve greater peace and prosperity, improve their stewardship of the earth, and reach minimum standards of human dignity. The concept of a "new world order" has been used and over-used to refer to everything from George H. W. Bush's vision of a post–Cold War world to the post-9/11 geopolitical landscape. Nevertheless, I use it to describe a different conceptual framework for the actual infrastructure of world order—an order based on an intricate three-dimensional web of links between disaggregated state institutions.

Recall Atlas and his globe at Rockefeller Center. A disaggregated world order would be a world latticed by countless government networks. These would include horizontal networks and vertical networks; networks for collecting and sharing information of all kinds, for policy coordination, for enforcement cooperation, for technical assistance and training, perhaps ultimately for rule making. They would be bilateral, plurilateral, regional, or global. Taken together, they would provide the skeleton or infrastructure for global governance.

* * *

4. A Just New World Order

"World order" is not value-neutral; any actual world order will reflect the values of its architects and members. Most of these values will not be specific to particular structures or institutions operating in different issue areas. Sustainable development, for instance, is a goal or a value that may drive global environmental policy. Whether it is pursued through traditional international organizations or through a combination of horizontal and vertical government networks should not affect the goal itself.

In other circumstances, however, the choice of form may implicate substance. Some observers see government networks as promoting global technocracy—secret governance by unelected regulators and judges. Others fear that the informality and flexibility of networks is a deliberate device to make an end run around the formal constraints—representation rules, voting rules, and elaborate negotiating procedures—imposed on global governance by traditional international organizations. Absent these constraints, critics charge, powerful nations run roughshod over weaker ones. Still others, however, worry more that weak nations will be excluded from powerful government networks altogether. At the domestic level, critics charge harmonization networks with distorting domestic political processes and judicial networks through the introduction of polluting or diluting national legal traditions. Still others picture government networks as vehicles for special interests—shadowy decision-making forums to which those who are "connected" or "in the know" have access.

In response to these criticisms, I propose a set of potential solutions:

- A conceptual move to recognize all government officials as performing both a domestic and an international function. Such recognition would mean that national constituents would automatically hold them accountable for their activities both within and across borders.
- An effort to make government networks as visible as possible. Creating a common website and linking the individual websites of participants in a government network will have the paradoxical effect of making a government network real by making it virtual.
- Increasing the number and activities of legislative networks, both to monitor the activity of regulatory networks and to launch initiatives of their own.
- Using government networks as the spine of broader policy networks, including international organizations, NGOs, corporations, and other interested actors, thereby guaranteeing wider participation in government network activities but also retaining an accountable core of government officials.
- A grab-bag of domestic political measures designed to enhance the accountability of government networks, depending on the extent to which a particular polity perceives a problem and what it decides to do about it.

None of these measures addresses the question of how members of government networks should treat each other, however, as fellow participants in, and constituents of, a world order. National and supranational officials participating in a full-fledged disaggregated world order would be accountable not only to specific national constituencies, but also to a hypothetical global polity. They would be responsible for defining and implementing "global public policy."[20] It is impossible to define the substance of that policy in the abstract. But the officials responsible should be guided by general "constitutional" norms in their relations with one another. In this context, I propose five basic principles designed to ensure an inclusive, tolerant, respectful, and decentralized world order. They include the horizontal norms of global deliberative equality, legitimate difference, and positive comity, and the vertical norms of checks and balances and subsidiarity.

Global Deliberative Equality

A global order of networks among government officials and institutions cannot work without efforts to maximize the possibilities of participation both by individuals and groups at the level of national and transnational society and by nations of all kinds at the level of the state. Absent such a principle, networks become a euphemism for clubs and a symbol of elitism and exclusion.

Global deliberative equality, building on ideas developed by Michael Ignatieff, is a principle of maximum inclusion, to the extent feasible, by all relevant and affected parties in processes of transgovernmental deliberation.

Legitimate Difference

The principle of "legitimate difference" is a principle of pluralism. In contrast to the imagined uniformity that would be imposed by a central authority under an imagined and feared world government, a disaggregated world order begins from the premise of multiple ways of organizing societies and polities at the national level. Ministers, heads of state, courts, legislators, even bureaucrats all reflect national differences, flowing from distinct histories, cultural traditions, demographic and geographic necessities, and the contingencies of national fortune. Each must be prepared to recognize the validity of each other's approach, as long as all accept a core of common fundamental principles.

Positive Comity

In contrast to the traditional principle of comity as a negative principle of deference to the interests of other nations, positive comity is a principle of affirmative cooperation. As a principle of governance for transnational regulatory cooperation, it requires regulatory agencies, courts, and even legislators to substitute consultation and active assistance for unilateral action and noninterference.

Checks and Balances

All participating government institutions, national and supranational, must interact with each other in accordance with a global concept of checks and balances, whereby the distribution of power is always fluid on both the horizontal and particularly the vertical axes. The clearest example is the way in which the national courts of the European Union maintain a shifting balance of power with the ECJ, within the framework of a "cooperative relationship."

Subsidiarity

Just as the principle of checks and balances borrows from the U.S. Constitution, as translated originally from Montesquieu, the principle of subsidiarity borrows from the ideals and experiences of the European Union. It is a principle of locating governance at the lowest possible level—that closest to the individuals and groups affected by the rules and decisions adopted and enforced. Whether this level is local, regional, national, or supranational is an empirical question, dictated by considerations of practicability rather than a preordained distribution of power.

The choice and formulation of any such principles is inevitably personal and partial. The point here is that some set of constitutional principles must operate at a metalevel across all types of government networks, specifying basic ground rules for how the members of these networks treat each other and what the basic division of labor is between them. The principles I put forward reflect values of equality, tolerance, autonomy, interdependence, liberty, and self-government. These values underlie my personal conception of a just world order based on government networks, even though some of the advantages of networked governance, such as flexibility and speed, are likely to be weakened if my principles were adopted. Ultimately, however, the process both of identifying specific values and translating them into principles must be a collective one. I thus hope that the principles offered here and any competing versions will become a matter for debate among scholars, policymakers, and ultimately voters.

The disaggregation of the state is a phenomenon. Government networks are a technology of governance that are probably both cause and effect of this phenomenon. The types of power they exercise are both old and new, but are critical to their ultimate impact, as is a better understanding of the conditions most favorable to their operation. But the norms and principles that would guide their operation in a deliberately constructed disaggregated world order would be a matter of conscious public choice. They will ultimately determine whether a disaggregated world order is a world order worth having.

* * *

Notes

1. Naím, "Five Wars of Globalization," 29.
2. Flynn, "America The Vulnerable," 60.
3. Sanger, "The World: When Laws Don't Apply; Cracking Down on the Terror-Arms Trade," *New York Times,* 15 June 2003, Sect. 4, 4.
4. Chote, "A World in the Woods," *Financial Times,* 2 November 1998, 20.
5. The Financial Stability Forum was initiated by the finance ministers and central bank governors of the Group of Seven (G-7) industrial countries in February 1999, following a report on international cooperation and coordination in the area of financial market supervision and surveillance by the president of the Deutsche Bundesbank. In addition to representatives from the Basel Committee, IOSCO, and the International Association of Insurance Supervisors (IAIS), its members include senior representatives from national authorities responsible for financial stability in significant international financial centers; international financial institutions such as the Bank for International Settlements (BIS), the IMF, the Organization of Economic Cooperation and Development (OECD), and the World Bank; and committees of central bank experts. "A Guide to Committees, Groups and Clubs," on the International Monetary Fund homepage (cited 7 July 2003); available from http://imf.org/external/np/exr/facts/groups.htm#FSF.
6. American readers may be skeptical of these reports due to the widespread and completely false statistic about how few members of Congress have a passport. In fact, 93 percent of all members hold passports and average two trips abroad a year.

Indeed, 20 percent claim to speak a foreign language. Eric Schmitt and Elizabeth Becker, "Insular Congress Appears to be Myth," *New York Times,* 4 November 2000, sect. A, 9. What is true is that some members fear that their constituents will identify trips to meet their counterparts abroad with "junkets," but that is a matter of public education.

7. Nye, *Paradox of American Power,* 9.
8. Ibid., xvi.
9. Dehousse, "Regulation by Networks in the European Community," 259.
10. Ibid., 254.
11. Robert O. Keohane, "Governance in a Partially Globalized World," presidential address, annual meeting of the American Political Science Association, 2000, *American Political Science Review* 95 (March 2001): 1.
12. Ibid., 5.
13. Ibid., 1.
14. Ibid., 12, quoting Abraham Lincoln, "The Gettysburg Address," 19 November 1863.
15. Annan, *We the Peoples,* 70; see also Reinicke and Deng, *Critical Choices* and Reinicke, "The Other World Wide Web."
16. Testimony of Francis Bator before the Subcommittee on Foreign Economic Policy, Committee on Foreign Affairs, House of Representatives, 25 July 1972. *U.S. Foreign Economic Policy: Implications for the Organization of the Executive Branch,* 110–11, quoted in Robert O. Keohane and Joseph S. Nye, Jr., "Transgovernmental Relations and International Organizations," 39, 42.
17. Keohane and Nye, "Transgovernmental Relations," 43. They included in their definition the increased communication between governmental agencies and business carried on by separate departments with their counterpart bureaucracies abroad. Ibid., 41–42. By contrast, a meeting of heads-of-state at which new initiatives are taken was still the paradigm of the state-centric (inter-state) model. Ibid., 43–44.
18. Cooke, *The Federalist,* No. 42.
19. See, e.g., the process of international rule-making described in Chayes and Chayes, *The New Sovereignty.*
20. See Reinecke, "Global Public Policy," 137. Reinecke argues that public policy issues, traditionally confined within state borders, must be addressed at a global level.

Bibliography

Annan, Kofi A. *We the Peoples: The Role of the United Nations in the 21st Century.* New York: United Nations, Department of Public Information, 2000.

Chayes, Abram, and Antonia H. Chayes. *The New Sovereignty: Compliance with International Regulatory Agreements.* Cambridge, Mass.: Harvard University Press, 1995.

Cooke, Jacob E., ed., *The Federalist,* No. 42 (James Madison). Middletown, Conn.: Wesleyan University Press, 1961.

Dehousse, Renaud. "Regulation by Networks in the European Community: The Role of European Agencies." *Journal of European Public Policy* 4 (1997): 246–61.

Flynn, Stephen E. "America The Vulnerable." *Foreign Affairs* 81 (2002): 60–74.

Keohane, Robert O., and Joseph S. Nye, Jr. "Transgovernmental Relations and International Organizations." *World Politics* 27 (1974): 39.

Naím, Moise. "Five Wars of Globalization." *Foreign Policy* (January/February 2003): 29–36.

Nye, Joseph S., Jr. *The Paradox of American Power: Why the World's Only Superpower Can't Go It Alone.* New York: Oxford University Press, 2002.

Reinicke, Wolfgang H. "Global Public Policy." *Foreign Affairs* 76 (1997): 137.

Reinicke, Wolfgang H., and Francis Deng, *Critical Choices: The United Nations, Networks, and the Future of Global Governance.* Ottawa: International Development Research Centre, 2000.

15.2

TRANSITIONAL JUSTICE: CRIMINAL COURTS AND ALTERNATIVES

David P. Forsythe

David P. Forsythe describes the development since World War II of international courts to try individuals for war and other crimes. Bringing individuals rather than states to court in international affairs is relatively new and, especially in the middle of ongoing conflicts, rather tricky. Does it prolong such conflicts because leaders in local conflicts are reluctant to surrender for fear of being taken to court, or does it lead to expedient settlements that grant immunity for war crimes to expedite peace? Forsythe contrasts realist views, which prefer to keep international courts under national control, and liberal views, which prefer to subject national courts to international rules and institutions.

After gross violations of human rights, what is one to do? This is the subject of transitional justice.... Should one prosecute individuals in international courts, or in hybrid or special courts, or in national courts? Should one avoid courts and rely on truth commissions, or bar violators from public office, or just move on to concentrate on building a rights protective state in the future rather than looking back via criminal prosecution? ...

* * *

Historical Background to 1991: Few Trials, Small Impact

The history of criminal prosecution—both international and national—related to international events is reasonably well known ...

While there was some discussion of criminal prosecution of German leaders after World War I, movement in that direction was aborted.[1] It was only after World War II that the first international criminal proceedings transpired, with well-known defects.[2] For a time allied leaders leaned toward summary execution of high German policy makers, but eventually concluded a treaty creating the Nuremberg tribunal. The stated objectives were lofty enough, but the taint of victor's justice was pervasive. At Nuremberg (and Tokyo) only the losing

Source: David P. Forsythe, "Transitional Justice: Criminal Courts and Alternatives," in *Human Rights in International Relations,* 2nd ed. (Cambridge, UK: Cambridge University Press, 2006), 89–120.

leaders were tried, even though allied leaders had engaged in such acts as attacking cities through conventional, incendiary, and atomic bombings, thus failing to distinguish between combatants and civilians—a cardinal principle of international humanitarian law (viz., that part of the law of war oriented to the protection of victims of war, especially the 1949 Geneva Conventions). Soviet military personnel committed perhaps 100,000 rapes in Berlin after the defeat of the Nazis. Rapes were systematic practice, yet no commanding officers, much less lower ranking soldiers, were ever held accountable. The Soviet Union then sat in judgement of Germans at Nuremberg.[3]

* * *

Twenty-two German leaders were prosecuted at Nuremberg in the first round of trials, nineteen of whom were convicted, with twelve of these being executed. Other individual German cases occurred, in both international and national courts. Similar proceedings were held at Tokyo for Japanese leaders, through fiat of the US military command.[4] A pronounced defect of especially the Tokyo tribunal was the total ignoring of gender crimes, despite a broad policy of sexual slavery carried out by Japanese officials.[5]

* * *

In numerous situations between the end of World War II and the end of the Cold War international criminal proceedings were not practical. As in the Korean War, most international armed conflicts ended inconclusively, and certainly without unconditional surrender, thus preventing the trial of those not in custody who were suspected of violations of international law. Those wars like the 1991 Persian Gulf War that ended in decisive military defeat still did not result in unconditional surrender and the victors gaining control over the losers. The George H. W. Bush Administration made the judgment, among other considerations, that pursuit of prosecution for Iraqi war crimes was not worth the continued death, injury, and destruction that would have been involved in the attempted capture of the Iraqi leadership. This was a reasoned policy, not devoid of moral considerations. It was almost universally accepted at that time as the proper policy. Later the US House of Representatives voted overwhelmingly in favor of Iraqi trials for war crimes. But based on congressional reactions to American casualties in both Lebanon in the 1980s and Somalia in the 1990s, that body would have been among the first to heatedly criticize a costly ground war designed to apprehend the Iraqi leadership had such been launched by the senior Bush or his successor. By 2005, a majority of the American public gave the George W. Bush Administration very low marks for its Iraqi policy. Even though that Administration could point to the capture and forthcoming trial of Saddam Hussein (and others), the public was primarily concerned with American casualties and lack of a clear exit strategy.

In other situations international tribunals could have been organized but for the strength of nationalism. Decisive outcomes produced by such as the Soviet intervention in Hungary or the US intervention in Grenada did not result in international trials since the victors did not want an international tribunal to closely examine embarrassing aspects of the use of force. Clearly the preferred value was not impartial application of human rights, humanitarian law, or criminal justice but rather protection of the national record and safeguarding unfettered decision making in the future.

Some war crimes usually occur during any use of force. This was made clear, *inter alia,* by eventual disclosure that Israelis had massacred a number of Egyptian prisoners of war during the 1956 Middle East War.[6] Either by design, in the context of what is judged to be pressing military necessity, or by loss of control, even personnel of democracies commit war crimes.

As for crimes against humanity, before the 1990s only the French and Israelis held national trials involving this concept. Britain, France, the Soviet Union, and the United States were willing enough to apply this concept *ex post facto* to Nazi Germany and Imperial Japan, but of these only France developed the concept (slightly) in its own national law. French and Israeli cases were exceedingly few in number, and, with the exception of the Eichmann trial in Jerusalem, pursued with considerable domestic political difficulties. This was especially so in France, as charges against French citizens for aiding in the Holocaust through crimes against humanity resurrected a painful episode in French history. Officials of the Vichy government administered half of France during World War II. Some of its French officials displayed a vicious anti-Semitism.

As for genocide, until the mid-1990s and events in Bosnia and Rwanda, no procedurally correct national trials were held entailing this concept, only procedurally suspect trials in places like Equatorial Guinea. Germany, being the temporary home of a number of refugees from the fighting in the former Yugoslavia, found itself the site of at least one national trial pertaining to both war crimes and genocide in the 1990s.[7] Rwandan national courts were to pursue this subject in numerous cases.

By far the most numerous national trials for gross violations of human rights connected to international events concern war crimes, although they are not always technically called that when prosecuted under national military law. For the most part these trials involve western liberal democracies applying the laws of war to their own military personnel. Very rarely, a country such as Denmark, Switzerland or Germany will hold a war crimes trial concerning a foreigner, usually pertaining to events in the former Yugoslavia. National war crimes trials have not been without problems. As noted above, the military personnel even of democracies do commit war crimes, for those democracies that have used force abroad have not lacked for courts martial for violations of the laws of war. This, for example, the Americans discovered at My Lai and other places in Vietnam, the Israelis discovered in Arab territory occupied since 1967, and the Canadians and Italians discovered in Somalia during the 1990s.

Even when such national trials are held in liberal democracies, it has not always proved easy to apply the full force of national military law (which is derived from international law). No US senior officers were ever held responsible for the massacre at My Lai. Moreover, President Nixon felt compelled by public opinion to reduce the punishment for Lt. Calley who was held responsible for the deaths of between twenty and seventy "Oriental" civilians at My Lai. At the time of writing US officials have moved only against low ranking soldiers for prisoner abuse connected to Washington's "war on terrorism." The Israeli authorities have been quite lenient in punishing their military personnel for violations of various human rights and humanitarian norms in disputed territory. The Canadians have found it difficult to come to full terms with the actions of some of their troops in Somalia. Only the Italians moved rapidly and vigorously against some of their soldiers who had abused Somalis. Rome concluded that the incidents in question were the result of a few "bad apples" and not part of a systematic or structural problem.

More than anything else this national record suggests the continuing power of nationalism, rather than any carefully reasoned and morally compelling argument about national criminal justice associated with war. That is to say that no compelling political or moral argument explains why the US military justice system mostly failed in its handling of the My Lai massacre.[8] ... A defensive and emotional nationalism has frequently overwhelmed aspects of proper criminal justice. If this is true in national trials, it indicates much difficulty for the prospects of international criminal justice. If national governments have trouble prosecuting their own, particularly those who authorized or allowed the wrong doing, how much more difficult it will be for them to turn over their own for trial by others. Serbia and America are not so different in this regard.

* * *

International Criminal Justice since 1991

After the Cold War and the demise of European communism, international relations saw the creation of two UN ad hoc criminal courts, several special hybrid criminal courts, and for the first time in history a standing—which is to say permanent—International Criminal Court. There were also important national developments in criminal justice, linked to international human rights and humanitarian law. Paradoxically, this movement toward increased international criminal justice only intensified the debate about other forms of transitional justice—and whether some forms of justice might be preferred that downplayed criminal justice in favour of social or political justice.

The ICTY

At first glance, the creation of the International Criminal Tribunal for the former Yugoslavia (ICTY) in 1993 by the UN Security Council seemed to usher in a new age in international criminal justice.[9] The Security Council voted to create a balanced and mostly procedurally correct international tribunal while the fighting and atrocities still raged, and legally required all UN member states to cooperate with the tribunal by invoking Chapter VII of the Charter. Those who committed war crimes, crimes against humanity, and genocide in that particular situation were to be prosecuted. The emphasis was on commanders who authorized or allowed the crimes.

* * *

From the creation of the tribunal in 1993 to the conclusion of the Dayton agreement in 1995, many policy makers and observers found fault with the very existence of the ICTY for possibly impeding diplomatic peacemaking.[10] The logic was clear enough. Would one prolong the fighting, with accompanying atrocities, by requiring that the principal fighting parties make a just peace— after which their responsible officials would be subjected to criminal justice? Would they not prefer to fight on, rather than cooperate in a peace agreement that would make their arrest and trial more likely?

This classic dilemma between peace and justice, between stability and punishment, became pronounced with the creation of the new court. Thus particularly the British during the John Major government played a hypocritical double game, voting for the tribunal but operating behind the scenes to hamper its work. London preferred the diplomatic to the juridical track, arguing in private that diplomacy was a better path to peace and human security. Public posturing aside, this was a pragmatic liberal strategy, hopeful of ending atrocities via diplomacy, but not one that gave more than cosmetic support to adjudication. Even Scheffer, before he entered the State Department, perhaps with El Salvador or South Africa in mind where criminal justice had been bypassed or minimized, wrote that "Despite the hard hits human rights standards take in these [unspecified] cases and the risk of never breaking the cycle of retribution and violence, the choice of 'peace over justice' is sometimes the most effective means of reconciliation."[11] It can be a serious matter to question the wisdom of international criminal justice, and whether its pursuit reflects judicial romanticism.

Even Judge Goldstone, the first prosecutor for the ICTY, noted that truth commissions had certain advantages over criminal trials as far as establishing facts in a form broadly understandable and thus in providing education and catharsis. He advocated both trials and truth commissions.[12]

The Dayton agreement showed that at least superficially or on paper one could have both relative peace and some criminal justice—one could end most of the combat and reduce much of the multifaceted victimization of individuals while at least promising criminal justice for those who had engaged in war crimes, crimes against humanity, and genocide.[13] However, one could secure the cooperation of Slobodan Milosevic, and the Serb-dominated Yugoslavian army that he controlled, only by an evident deal at Dayton exempting him from prosecution—at least for a time. At that time there was no public indictment against Milosevic who, more than any other single individual, was responsible for the break up of former Yugoslavia and no doubt the Serbian strategy of ethnic cleansing. As far as we know from the public record and the logic of the situation, in Milosevic's case one had to trade away in 1995 criminal justice for diplomatic peacemaking, although lawyers for the ICTY argued that they simply did not have a good legal case against him. It seemed to be a fact that Western states did not make a serious effort to go after certain individuals like Milosevic, Radko Mladic, and Radovan Karadic until later—when the Dayton agreement was more secure.

The same dilemma resurfaced regarding Kosovo. Milosevic was both the arsonist and the fire fighter in that situation, as in Bosnia earlier. He undertook repressive policies and forced expulsions in Kosovo, a province in new Yugoslavia, that inflamed discontent among the ethnic Albanians who made up 90 per cent of the local population. But the West had to deal with him, since he possessed the authority and power to restrain the Yugoslav forces (of Serbian ethnicity) who were engaged in hostilities in the province. How could one solicit his cooperation in reducing human rights and humanitarian violations if one threatened him with criminal justice? The US Congress, on record earlier as in favor of prosecuting Iraqi war criminals, voted to urge the Clinton Administration to offer Milosevic a deal—sanctuary in a friendly country in return for his abdication of power within new Yugoslavia. The prosecutor's office of the ICTY finally indicted Milosevic and several of his high-ranking colleagues in Belgrade for ordering criminal acts in Kosovo, but this was after hope was lost for a negotiated deal with Milosevic, à la Bosnia, to end the atrocities in Kosovo.

Immediately after Dayton, the fear of doing more harm than good via criminal justice resurfaced in still other forms. One fear was that pursuit of indicted suspects would cause the fragile commitment to the Dayton accord to collapse. In early 1996 certain Bosnian Serb military officers wandered into areas controlled by the Bosnian Muslims by error and were arrested on suspicion of war crimes. Bosnian Serb parties then refused to cooperate with talks on continued military disengagement called for under the peace agreements and supervised by IFOR (the NATO implementation force). A political crisis resulted, entailing high-level mediation by US diplomats. The Serbian officers were eventually returned to Serbia rather than transferred to The Hague for trial. It was a vivid if small demonstration of how pursuit of legal justice could endanger the broader political agreements that had ended both the combat and related human rights violations.

A similar fear was that pursuit of criminal justice in Bosnia would produce another Somalia. In that East African country in 1993, the attempt to arrest one of the warlords, General Aideed, leading as it did to the deaths of eighteen US soldiers and the wounding of many more, produced an early US withdrawal from that country and more generally a US reluctance to support other

UN-approved deployments of force in places like Rwanda the following year. The goal of national reconciliation with liberal democracy was never achieved by the international community in Somalia, arguably at least in part because of the defection of the USA from the international effort in 1994. The companion fear in Bosnia was that similar US casualties would force a premature withdrawal of NATO forces (via IFOR and SFOR—the latter being the stabilization force) and a collapse of the effort to make the Dayton agreement work. European contributors to NATO deployments made it clear that if the USA pulled out, they would also.

After a passive policy of non-arrests by NATO forces during 1993–1995, some arrests were made after 1995. But for considerable time NATO did not seek to arrest the Serbian leaders who had devised and commanded the policies of ethnic cleansing of Muslims in Bosnia. They were well connected and well protected. In Washington especially, it was feared that a costly shoot-out would undermine the shaky congressional tolerance of American military personnel on the ground in the Balkans. It was only later, when the Dayton agreement seemed more secure, as enforced by a sizable contingent of first NATO and then EU troops on the ground, that a more vigorous pursuit of Milosevic, Mladic, and Karadic took place. Eventually, particularly because of US financial pressure, a newly elected Serbian government detained Milosevic in spring of 2001 and transferred him to The Hague for trial in the ICTY. Thus in 1995 the USA negotiated with Milosevic at Dayton, but by 2001 the USA was demanding his arrest and trial. Either policy could be justified, taking into account the broader political context of the Balkans.

What we see with regard to the ICTY is an early tension between pragmatic liberalism and international criminal justice, a tension that was resolved only with the negotiated Dayton peace agreement for Bosnia, plus NATO intervention regarding Kosovo. It was only after these political events that there was serious pursuit of various Serbian leaders in order to hold them personally accountable for certain crimes. What we also see in the example of the ICTY is the creation of the court for essentially realist reasons, but then the transformation of the Court into a serious enterprise of criminal justice largely through the office of its Prosecutor, supported by many non-governmental organizations and a few states.

* * *

The Rwandan Court

The reasons for the creation of a second *ad hoc* UN criminal court were similar to the first. States on the Security Council, principally the United States, did not want to incur the costs of a decisive intervention in Rwanda in 1994 to stop the long standing conflict between Hutu and Tutsi communities which resulted in a genocide with perhaps 500,000–800,000 deaths.[14] They saw no vital self interests in such action. Somalia in 1993 had shown that international intervention in a situation where persons of ill will engaged in brutal and inhumane power struggles could be a dangerous venture. The USA and others were eventually willing to pay billions of dollars for the care of those fleeing genocide in Rwanda. But loss of western life, even in a professional and volunteer military establishment, was another matter. This was certainly true of Belgium, a former colonial power in Rwanda, which, when faced with ten deaths in its peacekeeping unit there, was in favour of the withdrawal, not the expansion, of those forces. Feeling nevertheless the impulse to do something, states on the Council created a second criminal court with similar jurisdiction and authority. Thus, as in former Yugoslavia, it was not consistent attention to moral norms and legal rules that drove the Security Council to action. Rather, it was a search for a tolerable expedient that resulted in attention to criminal justice. The best that can be said for the USA and the Security Council was that evident unease at the absence of moral and legal consistency across roughly similar cases produced at least some action on the question of prosecution for atrocities via ethnic/tribal slaughter in Rwanda.

As was true for the ICTY, so for the ICTR, it fell to the prosecutor's office, supporting NGOs, and a few concerned states to turn a venture based on guilt and public relations into something more substantive. The prosecutor's position proved problematic. The initial shared prosecutor showed more interest in former Yugoslavia than in Rwanda, and a later prosecutor, del Ponte, developed major frictions with the Rwanda government (Tutsi controlled) that had triumphed in the fighting of 1994. So eventually a separate prosecutor was established for the ICTR in 2003.

The court has been hamstrung by petty corruption, mismanagement, lack of adequate support, and not so veiled hostility on the part of more than one Rwandan.[15] Despite all this, by fall of 2004 the Court had rendered 17 final judgments involving 23 persons.[16] Several high officials had been convicted, including a prime minister and a mayor. The ICTR produced the first conviction for genocide ever recorded in a proper court of law. This was the Akayesu case, in which, in the view of the trial chamber, the major of the Taba Commune "had reason to know and in fact knew that sexual violence was taking place ... and that women were being taken away ... and sexually violated."[17] In this same judgment, rape of women was seen as part of genocide and crimes against humanity.

Ironically, high Hutu officials convicted of genocide and/or crimes against humanity in the ICTR received only a maximum sentence of life imprisonment, whereas lower Hutu officials or citizens convicted in Rwanda national courts—mostly staffed by Tutsi—could receive the death penalty (after being held in squalid conditions, and convicted in a proceeding lacking full due process).

Beyond punishment of individuals and development of legal concepts, the ICTR merits further discussion. First, it was highly unlikely that an international tribunal prosecuting Hutus during a time of Tutsi control of Rwanda could interject a decisive break in the cycle of ethnic violence that had long characterized that country. True, Hutus had planned, organized, and executed the wave of killing in 1994. But consider the parallels with former Yugoslavia. By most accounts, Serbs had committed the greatest number of atrocities during 1992–1995, even though Croats and Bosnian Muslims did not have clean hands. And Serbs had certainly persecuted ethnic Albanians in Kosovo. But when the prosecutor brought indictments mostly against Serbs, many in this latter ethnic group claimed bias by the ICTY.[18] Thus the pattern of indictments and convictions did little to break down group allegiance and group hostility. In similar fashion, it was unlikely that many Rwandan Hutus would be led to re-evaluate their prejudices by trials focusing only on Hutus, especially when earlier waves of Tutsi violence had not been met with international prosecution.[19] So one might punish leading Hutu criminals, but using the tribunal to break the cycle of ethnic violence was a tougher nut to crack. It was fairly clear, unfortunately, that the ICTR had not contributed to regional stability.

Second, during the life of the ICTR, ethnic violence continued on a large scale in the Great Lakes region of Africa with only relative decline compared with 1994. There was mounting evidence that Tutsis had massacred Hutus in eastern Zaire during the struggle for control of that country. That is precisely why the late President Kabila in the new Congo, who owed his position to Tutsi support, among other factors, consistently tried to block a United Nations investigation into the reported massacre. Tutsi and Hutu continued to fight in both the Democratic Republic of the Congo and Burundi, as well as in Rwanda. Murder and torture continued to be practiced by both sides. Could one realistically expect one international court, with a lack of respect and support from either ethnic group, to make any great difference in the evolution of events?

So for both the ICTY and the ICTR, punishment and legal development were one thing; personal closure and reconciliation were something else. By late 2004, the ICTR, operating on an annual budget of about $235 million, has been asked to close up shop by 2008, excepting appeals. Like the ICTY, the ICTR made some contribution to the new ICC.

The International Criminal Court

On July 17 1998 a Diplomatic Conference meeting in Rome, relying heavily on the experience of the ICTY and ICTR, approved the statute of a permanent criminal court to be loosely associated with the United Nations. The statute consists of 128 articles and is longer than the UN Charter.[20] Subject matter jurisdiction covers genocide, crimes against humanity, war crimes—and aggression (crimes against peace) when international law presents a sufficiently precise definition, which was not the case in July 1998. Judges are elected by the states that are parties to the statute; these judges sit in their individual capacity and not as state representatives. An independent prosecutor is attached to the court. The final vote was 120 in favor, 7 opposed (the USA, Israel, China, Iraq, Sudan, Yemen, Libya), and the rest abstaining.

The court operates, as of July 1, 2002, sixty ratifications being obtained, on the basis of complementarity. This means that the court does not function unless a state in question is unable or unwilling to investigate and, if warranted, prosecute for one of the covered crimes. Thus, whereas the ICTY and ICTR had primary jurisdiction and could supersede state action, the ICC only has complementary jurisdiction. It is a backup system, designed to encourage states to exercise their primary jurisdiction and authority in responsible ways. The prosecutor can go forward with a case if the state where the crime has been committed is a party to the statute, or is the state of the defendant. But the prosecutor must obtain approval of a pre-trial chamber of the court, whose decision to approve prosecution is subject to appeal to another chamber. This is designed to prevent political or other improper action by the prosecutor, who is also elected by state parties to the statute. The UN Security Council can also refer cases to the court, or can delay proceedings for up to a year, renewable. This latter provision is to allow for diplomacy to trump prosecution—to allow pragmatic liberalism to trump criminal justice.

In the final analysis the ICC court was the product of a group of "like-minded" states, led periodically by Canada, and a swarm of NGOs. They, as in Ottawa a year earlier with regard to a treaty banning anti-personnel landmines, decided to move ahead despite belated but clear opposition from the USA. Ironically, part of the momentum for a standing criminal court had come from the latter. But in Rome the USA made very clear that it did not intend to have its nationals appear before the tribunal. According to Scheffer, Ambassador at Large for War Crimes Issues:

> There is a reality, and the reality is that the United States is a global military power and presence. Other countries are not. We are. Our military forces are often called upon to engage overseas in conflict situations, for purposes of humanitarian intervention, to rescue hostages, to bring out American citizens from threatening environments, to deal with terrorists. We have to be extremely careful that this proposal [for a standing court] does not limit the capacity of our armed forces to legitimately operate internationally. We have to be careful that it does not open up opportunities for endless frivolous complaints to be lodged against the United States as a global military power.[21]

This was largely a smokescreen argument. The rule of complementarity meant that if US personnel should be charged with international crime, a proper investigation by the USA and, if warranted, prosecution would keep the new court from functioning. A prosecutor who wanted to bring charges against the USA would need to secure approval from the pre-trial chamber, whose approval could be appealed to a different chamber. By simple majority vote, the UN Security Council could delay proceedings, renewable, against the USA. Yet the Clinton Administration was unyielding in opposition. This was largely in deference to the Pentagon, and to the ultra-nationalists in the Congress. Senator Jesse

Helms, the Chair of the Senate Foreign Relations Committee, declared the treaty dead on arrival should it ever be submitted to the Senate.

For a country that saw itself as a leader for human rights, and that had led the effort to create two *ad hoc* criminal tribunals with jurisdiction over others, its posture at Rome was not a policy designed to appeal to the rest of the world. The double standards were too evident....

The George W. Bush Administration "unsigned" the Clinton signature on the Rome statute, sought through bilateral diplomacy to persuade or coerce other states into exempting US personnel from the coverage of the ICC, delayed UN peacekeeping deployments until the Security Council exempted any participating US personnel from any review by the ICC, and in almost every way imaginable tried to undermine the ICC. In 2005, however, the USA abstained on a UN Security Council resolution that authorized the ICC prosecutor to open investigations about possibly indicting certain Sudanese leaders for atrocities in the Darfur region of that country.

For its part the Congress passed the so-called American Service Members Protection Act, which among other provisions authorized in advance US military action to free any US national detained abroad in connection to ICC proceedings. President George W. Bush signed it, despite considerable foreign criticism.

The real reasons for such a US assault on the ICC were not hard to discern. After the September 11, 2001 attacks on New York and Washington by Al-Qaeda, high US officials authorized the abuse of certain enemy detainees held under US authority at various places.[22] Some of this coercive interrogation violated not only international humanitarian law but also the UN Convention against Torture. Hence behind the rhetoric about rogue prosecutors and politicized trials lay the reality that Washington officials might choose realist policies resulting in torture and/or degrading treatment of prisoners and other violations of human rights and humanitarian norms. Some of these actions would almost assuredly result in serious violations of these international norms and so constitute war crimes if not crimes against humanity. (Systematic torture of civilians might qualify as a crime against humanity.) It was also reasonably clear that during time of war, real or metaphorical, the US Congress would not exercise close oversight of Presidential claims to be acting properly in the name of national security. US courts would likely prove slow to get involved. Thus it might well be the case that the USA would prove unwilling or unable to seriously investigate charges of wrong doing and if necessary prosecute under the Rome statute. This was indeed the factual situation between early 2002 and late 2005 with regard to high level authorization of abuse of enemy prisoners in the "war on terrorism." Such a situation could logically lead a responsible prosecutor for the ICC to consider serious war crimes proceedings against a US official under the principle of complementarity.

It was for this same reason that Israel voted against the Rome Statute and refused to ratify or accede to it. It had used coercive interrogation against Palestinian and other detainees, which violated international humanitarian and human rights law.[23] Interestingly, other democracies like Britain and France, which had used coercive interrogation in the past in places like Algeria, Cyprus, Aden, and Northern Ireland,[24] voted for the Rome Statute and ratified it. So did Canada and Italy, whose troops had misbehaved in Somalia in the early 1990s.

Stripped of misleading rhetoric, Washington's position toward the ICC was that international relations was still a dangerous game meriting realist rather than liberal policies. To protect the security of the USA, Washington might have to authorize torture, degrading treatment, and other policies that violated international human rights and humanitarian law. Rather than being brutally truthful about its perception of the need to play dirty in a dangerous world, Washington preferred to talk about rogue prosecutors and politicized trials. What it really wanted was international criminal justice for Slobodan Milosevic but not for Donald Rumsfeld.[25] In Washington's eyes, Milosevic had engaged in ethnic cleansing and worse, while Rumsfeld was defending US security and advancing freedom in the world.[26]

* * *

Hybrid Courts

After atrocities in Kosovo, East Timor, Sierra Leone, and Cambodia, courts were created that might be called special, hybrid, or transnational.[27] In Kosovo in 1999, the UN field mission (UNMIK), operating under Security Council resolutions, created a hybrid court with local and international judges, applying a mixture of local and international law. The focus was mostly war crimes. Particularly the Serb population preferred this court to any court that would be dominated by the local majority of ethnic Albanians. The respect earned by this court was impressive in the context of continuing Serb-Albanian frictions. But the jurisprudence of this hybrid court did not mesh well with the ICTY, since the former did not use the cases of the latter as precedent.

In East Timor in 2000, the UN field mission there (UNTAET), again under UN Security Council mandate, created another hybrid court since the local legal infrastructure was non-existent. Panels of three judges contained two international and one local judge. The focus was on serious violations of international humanitarian law. A rather large number of indictments by the special prosecutor did not lead to rapid trials, as both neighboring Indonesia and the new authorities in East Timor showed considerable hesitance about cooperating on criminal justice matters. Indonesian authorities had much to hide about their brutal attempt to hang on to East Timor, while the new authorities in the latter were wary of antagonizing their powerful neighbour. From the latter's view, criminal justice might interfere with building a stable, rights protective state respected by Indonesia. When an Indonesian commander (General Wiranto) was indicted, East Timor said it would not cooperate in the case.

In Sierra Leone in 2002, the government that emerged from a brutal internal armed conflict signed an agreement with the United Nations to create a special criminal court. Local authorities wanted some hand in trials, but not total responsibility. This court operates outside of, and has legal primacy over, local courts. Again, there are two international judges and one local judge in each case, and they use a mixture of local and international law. Indictments have been issued against pro-government individuals as well as against rebel commanders. Among those indicted was Charles Taylor, the former President of neighboring Liberia, but at the time of writing he had been given asylum and immunity in Nigeria. From Nigeria's view, this was the price for getting him out of Liberia and reducing the fighting and atrocities there. Among rulings of this special court was a judgment that the recruitment of child soldiers constituted a war crime. In Sierra Leone there was also a truth commission to establish past facts, completely apart from considerations of criminal justice.[28]

Finally in this brief review, long and tortuous negotiations finally in 2004 produced a special criminal court in Cambodia, long after the agrarian communists known as the Khmers Rouges had killed about two million persons during 1975–1979. The government of Hun Sen, who himself had been a low level member of the Khmers Rouges, was ambivalent about criminal justice, but finally agreed to panels entailing two local and one international judge. This arrangement, against the background of a very weak local judicial system, prompted criticism by international human rights advocacy groups, as well as from the UN Secretary General. But certain circles of opinion thought that imperfect legal justice was better than no legal justice, particularly since the senior Khmers Rouges leadership was rapidly dying off.

One reason for having the ICC is to reduce the "transaction costs" so evident in the creation of the two UN ad hoc courts and these hybrid courts. It takes much time to negotiate the composition, jurisdiction, authority, and rules of the court—and sometimes the details of the additional prosecutor's office. Moreover, these hybrid courts do not produce a uniform jurisprudence, as their rules of procedure and substantive judgments do not always follow similar tracks.

National Courts

It should not be forgotten that most international law, to the extent that it is adjudicated at all, is treated in national courts. That being so, it is impossible here to review over 190 national legal systems and their treatment of major violations of international human rights and humanitarian law. Two points began to deal with the tip of this large iceberg.

First, after atrocities, particularly during and after war, real or metaphorical, it is often difficult for national courts to provide independent and impartial due process, leading to substantive judgments widely regarded as legitimate forms of criminal justice. After the fall of communism in Poland, for example, the subsequent trial of General Jaruzelski turned into a comical show trial, with numerous irregularities. At one point in his trial the presiding official said that "The hearings will continue, and the accusations will be formulated later."[29] Victor's justice is often easy to identify.

Against this background, the new criminal court created by the Interim Government in Iraq after the fall of the Saddam Hussein regime raised questions about proper criminal justice. Given the political instability of that situation after the US-led invasion and occupation, the newness and transitory nature of the ruling authorities, the weakness of the embryonic Iraqi judicial system—if there was a real system, the lack of due process already evident in the interrogation of defendants, and so on, it was hardly surprising that the UN Secretary-General and many international human rights advocacy groups were critical of the process. Even the 2004 announcement of the planned start of trials for leading Hussein lieutenants seemed more like a pre-election ploy designed to secure Iraqi Shia support for the Interim Government (but much Iraqi Sunni disaffection) than a non-partisan and independent legal step. Yet the USA, highly influential in such matters, was so opposed to the ICC and many international forms of criminal justice that it and its Iraqi allies pushed ahead with national legal measures that were sure to remain controversial. In Iraq it might have been better to proceed with a hybrid court, with some international judges and international standards of due process, in order to enhance independence, impartiality, and ultimately legitimacy.

Moreover, often remnants of the previous regime remain powerful for a time, as in Chile or Argentina, blocking serious national criminal justice based on due process.

Second, the principle of universal jurisdiction has had something of a renaissance, stimulated by the Pinochet case. But states like Britain and Belgium found the subject perplexing.

The concept of universal jurisdiction attaches to certain crimes like torture, genocide, and crimes against humanity—and also to serious violations of the Geneva Conventions of August 12, 1949 pertaining to victims of war.[30] Thus the principle of universal jurisdiction permits national authorities to pursue foreign as well as domestic suspects. Certain crimes are seen as so heinous that prosecution is allowed regardless of the place of the crime or the nationality of the defendant. In general, however, states remain reluctant to exercise extensive universal jurisdiction. They remain reluctant to open Pandora's box by establishing themselves as a global judge that would complicate relations with other states by legally judging their citizens.

In 1998, Spanish legal authorities presented British authorities with a request to extradite the visiting former Chilean dictator to Spain, to stand trial for genocide, terrorism, and torture. Britain arrested Pinochet, and in complicated and confusing rulings finally decided that the former head of state was indeed extradictable, since Britain had ratified, and incorporated into British law, the UN Torture Convention. This treaty recognized that universal jurisdiction was appropriate in the case of charges of torture.

While the British ruling technically was a matter of interpreting British law, it held among other things that Pinochet's status as former head of state offered him no immunity from Spanish charges. Indeed, Slobodan Milosevic had been indicted by the prosecutor of the ICTY while he was a sitting high Serbian official. And Charles Taylor had been indicted by the special court in Sierra Leone despite his being a high former official of Liberia. Moreover, the British ruling made clear that it made no difference that the victims of Pinochet's alleged abuses were Spanish or otherwise. For heinous crimes like torture, the nationality of the victims or the defendant is not a relevant factor.

It is true that under intense pressure from former Prime Minister Margaret Thatcher and other British arch conservatives, who were admirers of the staunch anti-communist Pinochet, British executive authorities released Pinochet to Chile on grounds of alleged poor health. Thus he was in fact not extradited to Spain to face charges. But the importance of the Pinochet ruling was that he legally could have been extradited to Spain, that as a legal matter claims to sovereign immunity did not trump valid attention to gross violations of human rights, and that other high officials in other situations might indeed have to face accountability for deeds done in office. There were other ripple effects from the British ruling in Chile, Argentina, and other places.[31]

As for Belgium, in 1993 its parliament passed a broad law opening the door to many suits in Belgian courts based on universal jurisdiction.[32] While the legislative history of this Belgian statute showed an intent to allow cases in Belgium stemming originally from Rwanda, very quickly enterprising lawyers filed cases against a variety of public officials including Ariel Sharon of Israel, Yasir Arafat of the Palestinian authority, George H. W. Bush of the USA, and so on. The Belgian executive was certainly not happy about that country being involved in so many controversial matters, and so successfully worked for a much narrower statute requiring some Belgian connection to charges. The USA brought heavy pressure on Belgium, including discussing the relocation of NATO headquarters from Brussels, to alter the broad assertion of Belgian judicial authority.

In both the British and Belgian examples above, it is clear that many executive branch officials are highly reluctant to see criminal justice proceedings interfere with good relations with other states. And the activation of the principle of universal jurisdiction, by an investigative judge like Baltasar Garzon of Spain, can certainly generate frictions that many national authorities, especially in Foreign Offices, would prefer to avoid. Noting this situation is not an argument for amnesty, immunity, or tolerance for heinous crimes like torture, genocide, crimes against humanity, or major breaches of international humanitarian law. It is only to note that political difficulties often arise in exercising universal jurisdiction in contemporary international relations.

* * *

Alternatives to Criminal Justice

A large number of human rights activists, like Aryeh Neier, argue for consistent implementation of criminal justice and decry any amnesty or immunity offered to those who have committed atrocities.[33] But our discussion above of criminal justice in places like Bosnia, Somalia, Rwanda, Sierra Leone, Poland, Iraq, etc. has already suggested that criminal justice might interfere with, or fail to make a contribution to, other desirable goals such as peace, stability, reconciliation, consolidation of liberal democracy, or full closure for affected individuals.

Criminal justice is not the only way to advance human rights, and the human rights discourse is not the only way to advance human dignity in international relations. Well considered diplomatic/political steps also have their role to play in advancing a liberal international order beneficial to individuals.[34]

No less than Nelson Mandela, supported by others with impeccable liberal and human rights credentials like Bishop Desmond Tutu, thought that in the Republic of South Africa after the apartheid era, the best way to build a multi-racial rights-protective society there was to avoid criminal justice as much as possible. They opted for a truth and reconciliation commission with apologies and reparations as the preferred course of action. If those responsible for political violence, on both the government and rebel sides, would acknowledge what they had done and express remorse, trials would be avoided and reparations paid to victims or their families. After all, trials focus on the past and often stir up animosities. Complicated rules of evidence can sometimes make it difficult to get the truth out in a clear and simple way. Truth commissions may be better than courts at getting to the "macro-truth"—the big social and political picture of why atrocities took place.[35] Since criminal courts focus on individual responsibility for particular acts, the larger context with its group responsibility may escape examination in judicial proceedings and remain in place to impede "social repair."[36]

Certainly the relatives of some victims of white minority rule in South Africa are not happy that the perpetrators of foul deeds have gone unpunished. A full accounting of the pluses and minuses of the South African T&R Commission is still in progress. But the South African model for dealing with transitional justice, which downplays criminal justice, is an interesting one—especially since the new South Africa features all-race elections and the protection of many human rights.[37]

In other places like El Salvador after protracted civil war, again trials were avoided. Leading suspects in criminal behaviour were eased out of public office and sometimes eased out of the country altogether. Two commissions made their reports. In this case, as in some other cases like Chile and Argentina, the continuing power of the supporters of the old regime made full and fair criminal justice exceedingly difficult in the short run. El Salvador is another country that has made progress toward stable liberal democracy without a prominent role for criminal justice after atrocities.[38] Still other countries like Spain and Portugal moved from dictatorships to stable liberal democracy without either criminal trials for past political behaviour or even truth commissions. But not all countries can be like Spain and Portugal and join regional organizations like the Council of Europe and the European Union that strongly insist on liberal democracy in member states.

What is now the Czech Republic implemented a policy of barring former high communist officials from public office after the fall of communism in that country. Yet controversy and hard feelings were still evident in 2005. A former judge in the communist era, not a party member but one who had supported the old regime with repressive rulings, was elevated to the Constitutional Court, as confirmed by the democratic Senate. This provoked outrage on the part of some, but not on the part of others who felt the democratic state needed experienced judges.[39]

Through an act of Congress, the USA apologized for, and paid reparations for, the internment of Japanese-Americans during World War II. Since that time there has been considerable debate in the USA over an apology and reparations to African-Americans for slavery and racial discrimination in that country.[40]

Democracy was at least encouraged in Haiti by offering the high officials of the Cedras regime a pleasant amnesty abroad, a diplomatic move by the USA and others that managed to restore an elected President Aristide there without major bloodshed. Likewise, George W. Bush offered Saddam Hussein safe passage out of Iraq in 2003. In this latter case, more than 2,000 American lives, and no doubt tens of thousands of Iraqi lives, along with much injury and destruction, would have been saved had Saddam accepted the offer of asylum. True, criminal trials would not have been held for him and his equally despicable colleagues. But what price to human life and dignity will those trials eventually entail? Avoiding war is also a liberal value.

In Uganda, the government sought the aid of the International Criminal Court in order to prosecute leaders of the vicious rebel movement known as The Lord's Resistance Army. Yet a number of traditional Ugandans preferred traditional rituals emphasizing forgiveness, rather than criminal prosecution.[41]

* * *

Notes

1. James F. Willis, *Prologue to Nuremberg: The Politics and Diplomacy of Punishing War Criminals of the First World War* (Westport: Greenwood, 1982).
2. A vast bibliography is recorded in Telford Taylor, *The Anatomy of the Nuremberg Tribunal: A Personal Memoir* (New York: Knopf, 1992).
3. Anonymous, *A Woman in Berlin* (Boston: Henry Holt, 2005).
4. Arnold Brackman, *The Other Nuremberg: The Untold Story of the Tokyo War Crimes Trials* (New York: Morrow, 1987). Compare Richard Minear, *Victor's Justice: The Tokyo War Crimes Trial* (Princeton: Princeton University Press, 1971).
5. For a concise review see Kelly D. Askin, "A Decade of the Development of Gender Crimes in International Courts and Tribunals: 1993 to 2003," in *Human Rights Brief,* American University, Center for Human Rights and Humanitarian Law, 11, 3 (Spring 2004), 16–19.
6. Barton Gellman, "Confronting History," *Washington Post,* National Weekly Edition, August 28–September 3, 1995, 12; Serge Schmemann, "After a General

Tells of Killing POWs in 1956, Israelis Argue Over Ethics of War," *New York Times,* August 21, 1995, Al.

7. In re Jorgic (http://www.domovina.net/calenddar.html), regarding the Bosnian Serb convicted in Germany for atrocities committed in Bosnia during 1992–1993.

8. Joseph Goldstein, Burke Marshall, and Jack Schwartz, eds., *The My Lai Massacre and Its Cover-Up: Beyond the Reach of Law?* (New York: The Free Press, 1976).

9. A useful compilation of documents about the creation of the ICTY can be found in Virginia Morris and Michael Scharf, *An Insider's Guide to the International Criminal Tribunal for the Former Yugoslavia* (Irvington-on-Hudson: Transnational Publishers, 1995).

10. See further Anthony D'Amato, "Peace v. Accountability in Bosnia," *American Journal of International Law,* 88, 3 (July 1994), 500–506. And Anonymous, "Human Rights in Peace Negotiations," *Human Rights Quarterly,* 18, 2 (May 1966), 249–258.

11. David Scheffer, "International Judicial Intervention," *Foreign Policy,* 102 (Spring 1996), 37.

12. "Ethnic Reconciliation Needs the Help of a Truth Commission," *International Herald Tribune,* October 24, 1998, 6. See also Goldstone, "Bringing War Criminals to Justice during an Ongoing War," in Jonathan Moore, ed., *Hard Choices: Moral Dilemmas in Humanitarian Intervention* (Lanham, MD: Rowman and Littlefield, 1998), 195–210. Given the difficulty of educating the public via technical trials, Mark Osiel proposes liberal show trials in *Mass Atrocity, Collective Memory, and the Law* (New Brunswick: Transaction Publishers, 1997). But liberal show trials are inherently contradictory, as Samantha Power notes in the *New Republic,* March 2, 1998, 32–38.

13. See further Richard Holbrooke, *To End A War* (New York: Random House, 1998). Holbrooke was the key mediator at Dayton.

14. The difference between Hutus and Tutsis had been codified by Belgium when colonial power and was originally more a class than biological or blood distinction. By the time of Rwandan independence the distinction had been solidified, and it had great political significance—as those identifying as Hutu made up a large majority of the country, controlling the outcome of elections. By 1994 the Hutu community was divided between militants advocating Hutu power to the detriment of Tutsi, and moderates interested in power sharing. By contrast to the perhaps 800,000 killed in Rwanda in 1994, eighteen US soldiers were killed in one day in Mogadishu, among a total of some thirty-five US military deaths in Somalia in the early 1990s overall. This is a modest cost for a "great power" or superpower in relative terms. The USA suffered nine deaths in one military air crash off South Africa in September 1997, but the media did not emphasize it and commentators did not call for a change of policy there. See further Edward N. Luttwak, "Where Are the Great Powers?" *Foreign Affairs,* 73, 4 (July/August 1994), 23–29.

15. For a brief summary see Paul Lewis, "UN Report Comes Down Hard on Rwandan Genocide Tribunal," *New York Times,* February 13, 1997, A9.

16. Even early on, those so inclined had made a positive assessment of the ICTR. See Payam Akhavan, "Justice and Reconciliation in the Great Lakes Region of Africa: The Contribution of the International Criminal Tribunal for Rwanda," *Duke Journal of Comparative & International Law,* 7 (1997), 325–348.

17. Prosecutor v. Akayesu, Judgment, Case No. 96-4-T (September 2, 1998).

18. For a critique of the pattern of indictments by the office of the independent prosecutor, see Cedric Thornberry, "Saving the War Crimes Tribunal," *Foreign Policy,* 104 (Fall 1996), 72–86.

19. See further Leo J. DeSouza, "Assigning Blame in Rwanda," *Washington Monthly,* 29, 9 (September 1997), 40–43.

20. This section draws on my editorial comment in *The Netherlands Quarterly of Human Rights,* 16, 3 (September 1998), 259–260.

21. *New York Times,* August 13, 1997, A8.

22. See further David P. Forsythe, *The Humanitarians: The International Committee of the Red Cross* (Cambridge: Cambridge University Press, 2005); Mark Danner, *Torture and Truth: America, Abu Ghraib, and the War on Terror* (New York: New York Review of Books, Inc., 2003); Seymour Hersh, *Chain of Command: The Road from 9/11 to Abu Ghraib* (New York: Harper Collins, 2004).

23. Forsythe, ibid.

24. See Kirsten Sellars, *The Rise and Rise of Human Rights* (Phoenix Mill, UK: Sutton Publishing, 2002).

25. Secretary of Defense Rumsfeld had authorized abusive treatment of certain prisoners at Guantanamo and perhaps in Afghanistan and Iraq. There are two schools of thought about all this in the US security community. The first is that coercive interrogation, principally based on sensory deprivation, can produce useful information. The second is that abuse is only guaranteed to produce pain, not reliable information, since a person under duress will say anything to stop the pain. It is not clear which school of thought is correct. Parts of the US security community are opposed to torture, and parts are not. See Forsythe, *The Humanitarians.*

26. Mixed in with Washington's realist calculations was American exceptionalism, a version of romantic or chauvinistic nationalism, that saw the USA as a shining city on a hill. American exceptionalism also rejected muscular multilateralism in which US independence would be restricted by an international court. See further David P. Forsythe, "The US and International Criminal Justice," *Human Rights Quarterly,* 24, 4 (Fall 2002), 974–991.

27. For further information, with the exception of Cambodia, see Laura A. Dickinson, "The Promise of Hybrid Courts," *American Journal of International Law,* 97, 2 (April 2003), 295–310.

28. See further William A. Schabas, "The Relationship Between Truth Commissions and International Courts: The Case of Sierra Leone," *Human Rights Quarterly,* 25, 4 (November 2003), 1035–1066.

29. Tina Rosenberg, *The Haunted Land: Facing Europe's Ghosts After Communism* (New York: Vintage Books, 1996), 254. She argues that criminal trials were inappropriate for the violations of human rights committed under European communism. In passing she suggests that trials were more appropriate in Latin America for human rights violations under military regimes. But it was precisely in Latin America that the military remained strong, and a threat to democracy, after the end of formal military rule. See also David Pion-Berlin, "To Prosecute or Pardon: Human Rights Decisions in the Latin American Southern Cone," *Human Rights*

Quarterly, 15, 1 (Winter 1993), 105–130, who tries to explain different policies in Argentina, Chile, and Uruguay regarding investigations and trials for human rights violations. See further the special issue "Accountability for International Crime and Serious Violations of Fundamental Human Rights," *Law and Contemporary Problems,* 59, 4 (Autumn 1996). Most of the authors are lawyers who predictably endorse legal proceedings and oppose impunity. But see the articles by Stephan Landsman, Naomi Roht-Arriaza, and Neil J. Kritz.

30. Darren Hawkins, "Universal Jurisdiction for Human Rights: From Legal Principle to Limited Reality," *Global Governance,* 9, 3 (July–Sept., 2003), 347–366. And Stephen Macedo, ed., *Universal Jurisdiction: National Courts and the Prosecution of Serious Crimes under International Law* (Philadelphia: University of Pennsylvania Press, 2004).

31. Stacie Jonas, "The Ripple Effect of the Pinochet Case," *Human Rights Brief,* 36–38. See also Richard Falk, "Assessing the Pinochet Litigation," in Macedo, *Universal Jurisdiction* 97–120. At the time of writing, Spanish courts were trying an Argentine for acts in the Dirty War carried out by the Argentine Junta against a variety of victims in that country. Finding the defendant within Spain, Spanish legal authorities moved against him in an exercise of universal jurisdiction.

32. Richard Bernstein, "Belgium Rethinks Its Prosecutorial Zeal," *New York Times,* April 1, 2003, A8.

33. Aryeh Neier, "The New Double Standard," *Foreign Policy,* 105 (Winter 1996–1997), 91–101. See further Aryeh Neier's book extolling the virtues of criminal justice: *War Crimes: Brutality, Genocide, Terror, and the Struggle for Justice* (New York: Times Books, 1998).

34. See further Jeffrey E. Garten, "Comment: The Need for Pragmatism," *Foreign Policy,* 105 (Winter 1996–1997), 103–106. This is a rebuttal to the Neier argument for consistent implementation of criminal justice.

35. See Audrey R. Chapman and Patrick Ball, "The Truth of Truth Commissions: Comparative Lessons from Haiti, South Africa, and Guatemala," *Human Rights Quarterly,* 23, 1 (February 2001), 1–43.

36. Laurel E. Fletcher and Harvey M. Weinstein, "Violence and Social Repair: Rethinking the Contribution of Justice to Reconciliation," *Human Rights Quarterly,* 24, 3 (August 2002), 573–639.

37. Priscilla B. Hayner, *Unspeakable Truths: Facing the Challenge of Truth Commissions* (New York: Routledge, 2002). She places the South African experience in the context of some 20 other truth commissions dealing with human rights, concluding that there is no one way to create a model truth commission. She also deals with the relationship between such commissions and criminal justice. See further the substantive book review of the Hayner volume by Juan E. Mendez and Javier Mariezcurrena in *Human Rights Quarterly,* 25, 1 (February 2003), 237–256.

38. We note in passing that not all relatives of victims were satisfied with the absence of criminal justice related to the past civil war. Some Salvadorans have pursued legal action in US courts under provisions allowing civil suits for aliens claiming violation of international law. Under the US 1879 Alien Tort Statute, these Salvadorans sought monetary compensation from former Salvadoran security officials

now residing in the USA. So while avoidance of public criminal justice was part of the political deal to end fighting and atrocities in El Salvador, some civil litigation went forward in US courts. For a journalistic summary, see David Gonzalez, "Victim Links Retired General to Torture in El Salvador War," *New York Times,* June 25, 2002.

39. Matt Reynolds, "A Top Judicial Posting Stirs Anger in Prague," *International Herald Tribune,* August 22, 2005.

40. See further Mark Gibney and Erik Roxstrom, "The Status of State Apologies," *Human Rights Quarterly,* 23, 4 (November 2001), 911–939. And Max du Plessis, "Historical Injustice and International Law: An Exploratory Discussion of Reparation for Slavery," *Human Rights Quarterly,* 25, 3 (August 2003), 624–659.

41. Mark Lacey, "Victims of Uganda Atrocities Follow a Path of Forgiveness," *New York Times,* April 18, 2005, A1.

Chapter 16

GLOBAL GOVERNANCE: INTERNATIONAL AND REGIONAL INSTITUTIONS

16.1

THE CHALLENGES OF GLOBAL GOVERNANCE

Margaret P. Karns and Karen A. Mingst

Margaret P. Karns and Karen A. Mingst describe the world of global governance not as "a top-down, hierarchical structure of authority" but as "the collection of government-related activities, rules, and mechanisms, formal and informal, existing at a variety of levels in the world today." This includes NGOs and IGOs as well as international law, norms, regimes, civil society, conferences, and multinational corporations, among other actors. The existence of this larger sphere of governance represents a "power shift" from state actors but also raises key questions about the legitimacy, accountability, and effectiveness of new global actors and mechanisms.

September 11, 2001, brought home to Americans and to people around the world the threat posed by global networks of terrorists. A variety of other problems pose similarly complex challenges. These include HIV/AIDS and other diseases; weapons of mass destruction—nuclear, chemical, and biological; the continuing conflicts in the Middle East and the Balkans, as well as tensions between India and Pakistan; global financial markets and the increasingly globalized economy; the Internet; the persistence of poverty; environmental threats such as climate change and collapse of global fisheries; ethnic conflicts; and failed states.

Source: Margaret P. Karns and Karen A. Mingst, "The Challenges of Global Governance," in *International Organizations: The Politics and Processes of Global Governance* (Boulder, Colo., and London: Lynne Rienner, 2004), 3–33.

None of these problems can be managed by sovereign states acting alone, even by the sole superpower, the United States. All require cooperation of some sort among governments and the increasing number of nonstate actors in the world; many require the active participation of ordinary citizens; some demand the establishment of new, international mechanisms for monitoring or the negotiation of new international rules; and most require the refinement of means for securing states' compliance.

In short, there is a wide variety of international policy problems that require governance. Sometimes the need is truly global in scope as with terrorism, financial markets, HIV/AIDS and other public health threats, climate change, and weapons of mass destruction. In other cases, the governance problem is specific to a region of the world or group of countries, as with the need to manage a major river system such as the Danube, Rhine, or Mekong that flows through several countries, or a regional sea such as the Mediterranean. But what do we mean by governance and is the need for global governance increasing?

What Is Global Governance?

In 1995 the Commission on Global Governance, an independent group of prominent international figures, formed to consider what reforms in modes of international cooperation were called for by global changes, and published a report on their five years of deliberations. The group included leaders such as Oscar Arias, president of Costa Rica; Barber Conable, president of the World Bank and former U.S. congressman; Olara Otunnu, former foreign minister of Uganda; and Maurice Strong, former Canadian businessman and first executive director of the United Nations Environment Programme (UNEP). The commission defined governance as "the sum of the many ways individuals and institutions, public and private, manage their common affairs. It is a continuing process through which conflicting or diverse interests may be accommodated and cooperative action may be taken. It includes formal ... as well as informal arrangements that people and institutions have agreed to or perceive to be in their interest" (Commission on Global Governance 1995: 2).

How does governance relate to government? While clearly related, they are not identical. As James Rosenau (1992: 4) put it,

> Both refer to purposive behavior, to goal-oriented activities, to systems of rule; but government suggests activities that are backed by formal authority, by police powers to insure the implementation of duly constituted policies, whereas governance refers to activities backed by shared goals that may or may not derive from legal and formally prescribed responsibilities and that do not necessarily rely on police powers to overcome defiance and attain compliance. Governance, in other words, is a more encompassing phenomenon than government. It embraces governmental institutions, but it also subsumes informal, nongovernmental mechanisms whereby those persons and organizations within its purview move ahead, satisfy their needs, and fulfill their wants.

Thus, global governance is not global government; it is not a single world order; it is not a top-down, hierarchical structure of authority. It is the collection of governance-related activities, rules, and mechanisms, formal and informal, existing at a variety of levels in the world today. We refer to these as the "pieces of global governance."

The Pieces of Global Governance

The pieces of global governance are the cooperative problem-solving arrangements and activities that states and other actors have put into place to deal with various issues and problems. They include international rules or laws, norms or "soft law," and structures such as formal international intergovernmental organizations (IGOs) as well as improvised arrangements that provide decisionmaking processes, information gathering and analytical functions, dispute settlement procedures, and operational capabilities for managing technical and development assistance programs, relief aid, and force deployments. In some instances the rules, norms, and structures are linked together in what some scholars refer to as international regimes to govern a particular problem such as nuclear weapons proliferation, whaling, trade, food aid, transportation, ozone, or telecommunications....

International Law

The scope of what is generally known as public international law has expanded tremendously since the 1960s. Although the Statute of the International Court of Justice recognizes five sources of international law (treaties or conventions, customary practice, the writings of legal scholars, judicial decisions, and general principles of law), much of the growth has been in treaty law. Between 1951 and 1995, 3,666 new multilateral treaties were concluded (Ku 2001). They include the Vienna Convention on Treaties, environmental conventions such as those for ozone, climate change, and whaling, law of the sea, humanitarian law (the Geneva conventions), human rights law, trade law, arms control agreements, and intellectual property law. By far the largest number of new multilateral agreements deals with economic issues. Treaty-based law has been particularly valued because the process of negotiation now involves all affected countries. Nonetheless, customary practice persists as an important source of new law, particularly because of the long time it takes to negotiate and bring into effect agreements involving large numbers of countries.

For purposes of global governance, one major limitation of public international law is that it applies only to states, except for war crimes and crimes against humanity. At present, except within the European Union (EU), multilateral agreements cannot be used directly to bind individuals, multinational corporations, nongovernmental organizations (NGOs), paramilitary forces, terrorists, or international criminals. They can, however, establish norms that states are expected to observe and, where possible, enforce against these nonstate actors.

Another problem in the eyes of many is the absence of international enforcement mechanisms and the role of self-interest in shaping states' decisions about whether or not to accept treaties and other forms of international rules. International law has traditionally left states to use "self-help" means to secure compliance. In reality, the United Nations Charter and European Union treaties, for example, provide enforcement mechanisms, yet the threat of sanctions is not a key motivator for compliance with international rules. Abram Chayes and Antonia Chayes (1995), instead, cite efficiency, interests, and norms as key factors and lack of capability or treaty ambiguity as principal sources of noncompliance. States often value a reputation for law-abiding behavior and desire the benefits of reciprocity (the "golden rule" of "doing unto others as you would have them do unto you"); they are generally inclined to comply with international law. Peer pressure from other states and domestic or transnational pressures from NGOs may induce compliance. For weaker and developing states, failure to comply can be a consequence of inadequate local expertise and governmental capacity to do what is required for compliance. In short, the "force" of international law often comes from the "felt need to coordinate activities ... and to ensure stable and predictive patterns of behavior" and the reality is "imperfect, varied, and changing implementation and compliance," with many factors affecting the extent to which states meet legal commitments (Jacobson and Weiss 1995: 122).

International Norms or "Soft Law"

Many international legal conventions set forth what are not in fact binding obligations for states, but rather norms or standards of behavior, sometimes referred to as "soft law." Some human rights and labor rights, the concept of the global commons applied to the high seas, outer space, and polar regions, as well as the concept of sustainable development are all examples of such "soft law." In environmental law, an initial framework convention often sets forth norms and principles that states agree on, such as those for ozone depletion, loss of biodiversity, and global climate change. As scientific understanding of the problem improves and technology provides possible substitutes for ozone-depleting chemicals, for example, or carbon dioxide-producing energy sources, leading states, key corporations, and other interested actors may later come to agreement on specific, binding steps to be taken. Protocols are used to supplement the initial framework convention, and they are considered to form the "hard" law dealing with the issue.

Intergovernmental Organizations (IGOs)

IGOs are organizations whose members include at least three states, that have activities in several states, and whose members are held together by a formal intergovernmental agreement. In 2003/04, the *Yearbook of International Organizations* identified about 238 IGOs. These organizations range in size from three members (North American Free Trade Agreement [NAFTA]) to more than 190 members (Universal Postal Union [UPU]). Members may come from primarily one geographic region (Organization of American States [OAS]) or from all geographic regions (World Bank). Although some IGOs are designed to achieve a single purpose (Organization of Petroleum Exporting Countries [OPEC]), others have been developed for multiple tasks (United Nations [UN]). Most IGOs are not global in membership, but regional where a commonality of interest motivates states to cooperate on issues directly affecting them. Among the universe of IGOs, most are small in membership and designed to address specific functions. Most have been formed since World War II, and among the different regions, Europe has the densest concentration of IGOs ...

IGOs are recognized subjects of international law with separate standing from their member states. In a 1949 advisory opinion, *Reparations for Injuries Suffered in the Service of the United Nations,* the International Court of Justice (ICJ) concluded,

> The Organization [the United Nations] was intended to exercise and enjoy, and is in fact exercising and enjoying, functions and rights which can only be explained on the basis of international personality and the capacity to operate upon an international plane. It is at present the supreme type of international organization, and it could not carry out the intentions of its founders if it was devoid of international personality.

IGOs serve many diverse functions, including collecting information and monitoring trends (United Nations Environment Programme [UNEP]), delivering services and aid (United Nations High Commissioner for Refugees [UNHCR]), providing forums for intergovernmental bargaining (European Union [EU]), and settling disputes (International Court of Justice and World Trade Organization [WTO]). IGOs are instrumental in forming stable habits of cooperation through regular meetings, information gathering and analysis, and dispute settlement as well as operational activities....

Yet how IGOs serve their various functions varies across organizations. Organizations differ in membership. They vary by the scope of the subject and rules. They differ in the amount of resources available and by level and degree of bureaucratization.

Why do states join such organizations? Why do they choose to act and to cooperate through formal IGOs? Kenneth Abbott and Duncan Snidal (1998: 4–5) answer these questions by suggesting that "IOs [intergovernmental organizations] allow for the centralization of collective activities through a concrete and stable organizational structure and a supportive administrative apparatus. These increase the efficiency of collective activities and enhance the organization's ability to affect the understandings, environment, and interests of states." Thus, states join to participate in a stable negotiating forum, permitting rapid reactions in times of crisis. They join IGOs to negotiate and implement agreements that reflect self- and community interests. They participate to provide mechanisms for dispute resolution. They join to take advantage of centralized organization in the implementation of collective tasks. By participating, they agree to shape international debate on important issues and forge critical norms of behavior. Yet states still maintain their sovereignty and varying degrees of independence of action.

IGOs not only create opportunities for their member states, but they also exercise influence and impose constraints on their member states' policies and processes. IGOs affect member states by setting international and, hence, national agendas and forcing governments to take positions on issues. They subject states' behavior to surveillance through information sharing. They encourage the development of specialized decisionmaking and implementation processes to facilitate and coordinate IGO participation. They embody or facilitate the creation of principles, norms, and rules of behavior with which states must align their policies if they wish to benefit from reciprocity....

The "power" of IGOs is limited in terms of their ability to enforce decisions, except in specific cases such as the EU, which has supranational authority over member states in many policy domains. Most IGO actions are, in fact, recommendations. Their effectiveness lies in actors' willingness to make and comply with commitments. Their suasion is largely moral. Peer pressure can be powerful, however, in pushing states to act in ways that others wish, and IGOs are prime arenas for exercising peer pressure and moral suasion.

Most countries, nevertheless, perceive that there are benefits to being participants in IGOs and international regimes even if they are targets of criticism and condemnation in international forums over long periods, or not receiving as many benefits as they might hope. South Africa never withdrew from the UN over the long years when it was repeatedly condemned for its policies of apartheid. Iraq did not withdraw from the UN in protest over more than a decade of stringent sanctions. China spent fourteen years negotiating the terms of its entry into the international trade system and undertaking changes in laws and policies required to bring itself into compliance with WTO rules. Ten countries joined the EU in 2004, despite the extensive and costly changes required.

Although the earliest IGOs were established in the nineteenth century, there was a veritable explosion of IGOs in the twentieth century.... Major power wars (especially World Wars I and II), economic development, technological innovation, and the growth of the state system, especially with decolonization in the 1950s and 1960s, provided impetus for creating many IGOs. Since the 1960s, there has also been a growing phenomenon of IGOs creating other IGOs. One study noted that IGO birthrates "correlate positively with the number of states in the international system," but found death rates of IGOs low (Cupitt et al. 1997: 16). Of thirty-four IGOs functioning in 1914, eighteen were still operational at the end of the twentieth century. The Cold War's end brought the death of the Warsaw Treaty Organization and the Council of Mutual Economic Assistance, both Soviet bloc institutions. The creation of the UN in 1945 led to the demise of the League of Nations....

Nongovernmental Organizations

NGOs are private voluntary organizations whose members are individuals or associations that come together to achieve a common purpose. Some organizations are formed to advocate a particular cause such as human rights, peace, or environmental protection. Others are established to provide services such as disaster relief, humanitarian aid in war-torn societies, or development assistance. Some are in reality government-organized groups (dubbed GONGOs). There is a key distinction between not-for-profit groups (the vast majority) and for-profit corporations. NGOs are increasingly active today at all levels of human society and governance, from local or grassroots communities to national and international politics. National-level groups are often called interest or pressure groups, and many of them are now linked to counterpart groups in other countries through transnational networks or federations. International NGOs, like IGOs, may draw their members from one region or several regions, and they may have very specific functions or be multifunctional.

The estimates of numbers of NGOs vary enormously. The *Yearbook of International Organizations* identifies over 6,500 nongovernmental organizations that have an international dimension either in terms of membership or commitment to conduct activities in several states. Exclusively national NGOs number in the millions. Many large international NGOs (INGOs) are transnational federations involving formal, long-term links among national groups. Examples include the International Federation of Red Cross and Red Crescent Societies, Oxfam, CARE, Médecins Sans Frontières (Doctors Without Borders), World Wildlife Fund, Transparency International (the leading NGO fighting corruption worldwide), Human Rights Watch, Amnesty International, and Save the Children. An example of an INGO that is not a federation of country chapters would be Greenpeace, which claims 4.1 million members worldwide.

NGOs' governance functions parallel many functions provided by IGOs. They create and mobilize global networks, gathering information on local conditions and mobilizing pressures both within states and transnationally. In fact, they have become key sources of information and technical expertise on a wide variety of international issues from the environment to human rights. They participate at least indirectly in IGO-sponsored conferences, raising new issues, submitting documents, and disseminating their expertise. In some instances, such as with the Convention to Ban Landmines, they may be direct contributors of treaty language. They educate delegates, expand policy options, and bring parties together in third-party venues. They play increasingly important governance roles in monitoring implementation of human rights norms and environmental regulations. They enhance public participation, mobilizing individuals and groups to undertake political action, developing networks, monitoring the actions taken and government and corporate behavior.

As a result of global trends to privatize activities previously controlled by governments, NGOs are playing an ever-increasing role. Services once provided by governments or IGOs are being contracted out to private, nongovernmental organizations. They deliver disaster relief; run refugee camps; provide micro-credit loans to poor women and men in countries such as Bangladesh; administer development programs; attempt to contain the international spread of disease; and work to clean up the environment. They also have promoted corporate codes of conduct such as the Valdez Principles (a set of environmental principles) and consumer labeling such as "rugmark" (for carpets made with child labor)....

International Regimes

Scholars have developed the concept of international regimes to understand governance for a given issue area such as nuclear weapons proliferation, whaling, European transboundary air pollution, food aid, trade, telecommunications, and transportation, where principles, norms, rules, and decisionmaking procedures are linked to one another. Where an international regime exists, participating states and other international actors recognize the existence of certain obligations and feel compelled to honor them. Because this is "governance without government," they comply because they accept the legitimacy of the rules and underlying norms, and the validity of the decisionmaking procedures. They expect other states and actors also to comply and to utilize dispute settlement procedures to resolve conflicts. Key characteristics of international regimes are their association with a specific issue area and the links among the constituent elements.

International regimes encompass rules and norms, as well as the practices of actors that show both how their expectations converge and their acceptance of and compliance with rules. IGO decisionmaking procedures, bureaucracy, budget, headquarters building, and legal personality may be required (or established) within a given issue area, but by themselves, individual IGOs do not constitute a regime. Some issues such as nuclear accidents that trigger widespread nuclear fallout do not need a formal organization that functions regardless of whether there is an accident. Ad hoc arrangements for decisionmaking and action when an accident occurs can be coupled with rules and norms. Nuclear weapons proliferation, however, benefits from the inspection machinery and safeguards systems of the International Atomic Energy Agency (IAEA), as well as the Nuclear Non-Proliferation Treaty, the Comprehensive Test Ban Treaty, and IAEA's technical assistance programs to non-nuclear weapon countries for developing peaceful uses of nuclear energy.

Ad Hoc Arrangements

In situations where an existing IGO does not provide a suitable forum for dealing with a particular problem and a new IGO is not needed, states and other actors may create an ad hoc arrangement. The pattern can be best illustrated with three examples. The Group of 7 (G-7), for example, began in an ad hoc fashion in the mid-1970s when summit meetings of governmental leaders were not yet common practice and major changes in international economic relations suggested the value of periodic, informal gatherings. These later evolved into a regular arrangement, but not a formal IGO.

When Canadian Prime Minister Lloyd Axworthy decided to negotiate a convention banning antipersonnel landmines in 1996, none of the existing IGO structures such as the UN Conference on Disarmament and the UN General Assembly seemed appropriate for achieving this goal in a short period of time. Instead, Axworthy convened a special conference in Ottawa in December 1997 for the sole purpose of securing agreement on a total ban by the largest possible number of countries. In the mid-1990s, ethnic cleansing in the former Yugoslavia and genocide in Rwanda prompted the UN Security Council to create ad hoc war crimes tribunals to bring those responsible to justice. This gave impetus to the creation of a permanent International Criminal Court.

Global Conferences

During the 1990s, the United Nations convened nine global conferences on economic and social matters, following a similar series in the 1970s and 1980s. Some were designated world summits rather than global conferences because they included meetings of heads of state and government. NGO participation in parallel conferences grew exponentially. Each successive conference exhorted the UN itself and member states to give priority to another set of issues such as environmental protection and sustainable development, women's rights, the rights of the girl child, human settlements, food supply, or the elimination of poverty. As one observer has asked, are these "media events or genuine diplomacy?" (Fomerand 1996) What purposes do they serve? How do they fit into the pieces of global governance?

Conferences like the Summit for Children (1990), the Earth Summit in Rio (1992), or the Fourth World Conference on Women in Beijing (1995) have become an important part of the global political processes for addressing interdependence issues, for seeking ways to improve the lives and well-being of humans, and for strengthening other pieces of governance. They also serve to raise awareness of interdependence issues; galvanize the creation, dissemination, and sharing of knowledge; create new norms and new international law; create new structures; and define global political priorities. Cumulatively, the global conferences have also bolstered understanding of the linkages among issues of environmental protection, equal rights (especially for women), elimination of poverty, improved access to economic resources, sharing of knowledge and technology, and participation of local communities.

Global conferences have spawned complex multilateral diplomacy with NGOs, scientific experts, corporations, and interested individuals trying to influence conference outcomes. They have raised important issues of who gets to participate and in what ways. Often the results are disappointing those most concerned about the issues because they may represent the least common denominator of agreement among the large number of participants, of whom only states, however, actually have a formal say.

Private Governance

Private governance is a growing, but little studied phenomenon. Although the very meaning of the term is controversial, it involves authoritative decision-making in areas that once were part of national legal frameworks, the government, the sovereign state, or the public sector (Hall and Biersteker 2002: 203). Examples include international accounting standards; the private bond-rating agencies such as Moody's Investors Service, whose rules can shape government actions through the threatened drop in a country's rating; International Chamber of Commerce rules and actions; private industry governance such as the Worldwide Responsible Apparel Manufacturing Principles and the Forest Stewardship Council, or labor standards within a single multinational firm such as Nike or Ford.

Cyberspace is governed by hybrid institutions, which presently involves a strong dose of private authority. Private firms are attempting to establish enforceable intellectual property rules for music, software, and published materials available on the Internet. Visa and MasterCard have created the Secure Electronic Transaction Protocol to enable bank card transactions to be made securely via the Internet. As Debora Spar (1999: 47) notes about this new electronic environment,

> International organizations lack the power to police cyberspace; national governments lack the authority; and the slow pace of interstate agreement is no match for the rapid-fire rate of technological change. If rules are to emerge along the Internet, private entities will have to create them ... [including] University consortia and library groups ... industry associations such as the Electronic Frontier Foundation and the Business Software Alliance.

Private authorities are neither inherently good nor bad. "What is evident, though," Spar (48) says, "is that private entities will play an ever-increasing role in the development and management of electronic interaction.... They will assume quasi-governmental functions in many instances, regulating activity in their particular spheres through a combination of formal and informal rules, administrative and technical means." ...

An interesting hybrid of public and private governance is illustrated by the World Commission on Dams, composed of representatives from government, private industry, and NGOs. Its function is to establish guidelines for decision-making on large dam construction.

These various pieces of global governance are not well organized. They vary in scope, effectiveness, and durability....

* * *

Actors in Global Governance

* * *

Multinational Corporations (MNCs)

MNCs are a particular form of nongovernmental actor organized to conduct for-profit business transactions and operations across the borders of three or more states. Multinational corporations can take many different forms, from licensing local industries to providing foreign suppliers, contract manufacturing, turnkey projects, manufacturing, and assembly operations. What they share in common is that they are companies based in one state with affiliated branches or subsidiaries and activities in other states. They have the ability to invest capital and thus to create jobs, influence political actors, offer incentives to host governments, lobby for changes in state laws, and threaten to move jobs and investment elsewhere should the conditions not be conducive to profitable business.

Since the 1970s, MNCs have been increasingly recognized as significant international actors, controlling resources far greater than those of many states. The world's largest MNCs account for four-fifths of world industrial output. In the 1990s, foreign direct investment grew rapidly, although it was still highly concentrated and distributed unevenly in Europe, the United States, Latin America (particularly Brazil and Mexico), and East and Southeast Asia (especially China). As actors in global governance, MNCs have "profoundly altered the structure and functioning of the global economy" (Gilpin 2001: 290). By choosing where to invest or not to invest, MNCs shape the economic development opportunities of individual communities, countries, and entire regions such as Africa, where little foreign investment takes place compared to East Asia. By moving production from communities such as Peoria, Illinois, or Dayton, Ohio, to Mexico or Malaysia, MNCs' activities can benefit or hurt both developed and developing countries.

Globalization of markets and production in industries such as automobiles challenges corporate leaders and managers to govern these complex structures and challenges states and local governments experiencing a keen loss of connection and control to these larger corporate networks. Corporate choices about investment have changed the landscape of development assistance. Far more funding for development today comes from private investment capital than from bilateral, government-to-government aid, or multilateral aid through the UN and other IGOs. In short, MNCs' activities have raised a number of governance questions: How can MNCs' activities best be regulated—through new forms of international rules or through private mechanisms? How can they be mobilized for economic development in collaboration with international agencies and NGOs? How can less developed countries be assured that powerful MNCs will not interfere in their domestic affairs, challenge their sovereignty, destroy their resources and environment, and relegate them to permanent dependency? MNCs are particularly important actors in addressing trade, labor, and environmental issues. Their participation has been critical, for example, in efforts to address ozone depletion and global warming. They are also targets of NGO activism ...

UN Secretary-General Kofi Annan has been a champion of new mechanisms to regulate corporate behavior and to engage MNCs as positive contributors to global governance. In 1999, Annan broke new ground for the UN by convening a meeting with world business leaders and exhorting them to embrace the UN Global Compact whose nine principles cover human rights, labor, and the environment. Companies that participate must submit online updates of their progress for NGOs to scrutinize, thus involving NGOs in policing MNC compliance....

* * *

An Increasing Need for Global Governance?

* * *

Emergent Transnational Civil Society

Contributing to the Cold War's end and benefiting from both increased democratization and accelerating globalization is the growth of civil society within many countries and transnationally. First, a word about definition. There is a common tendency to equate NGOs with civil society, but the latter is really a broader concept, encompassing all organizations and associations that exist outside of the state and the market (i.e., government and business). It includes not just advocacy groups but also associations of professionals such as doctors, lawyers, and scientists, along with labor unions, chambers of commerce, religious groups, ethnic associations, cultural groups, sporting associations, and political parties. The key distinction between NGOs and civil society groups is their links to citizens. Many NGOs are elite-run groups with tenuous links to citizens on whose behalf they claim to act. Especially in developing and newly democratizing countries, grassroots and national NGOs may depend on international funding. Like NGOs, civil society is neither inherently good nor bad. People work together to advance both nefarious and worthy ends.

The spread of democracy to many corners of the globe has bolstered the growth of civil societies in countries where restrictions on citizens' groups have been lifted. Civil society groups communicate with each other domestically and cross-nationally, creating new coalitions from the local to the global. These "networks of knowledge and action" (Lipschutz 1992: 390) are unconstrained by geographic borders and largely beyond states' control. Transnational civil society groups permeate numerous issue areas, including the environment, human rights, technology, economic development, and security. Their demands for representation in processes of global governance contribute to the increased need to reform existing international institutions and to find new ways to incorporate actors other than states in governance.

*   *   *

The Politics and Effectiveness of Global Governance

The politics of global governance reflects "struggles over wealth, power, and knowledge" in the world (C. Murphy 2000: 798). Thus, U.S. power and preferences shaped, and continue to shape, many of the pieces of global governance, especially the liberal international economic system, and ensures that U.S. interests (and often European as well) are accommodated in many regimes.

Power: Who Gets What?

Power and influence in global governance, however, does not belong just to powerful states or coalitions of states. Susan Strange (1996: 54), along with others, has noted that "TNCs have come to play a significant role in who-gets-what in the world system." Jessica Mathews (1997), writing about the proliferation of NGOs, refers to a "power shift" to draw attention to their growing influence. The question of how to provide representation in multilateral decisionmaking or some more systematic means of input for key nonstate actors is an important one.

South African Peter Vale (1995), however, argues that economic liberalism and the increased influence of multilateral institutions have only intensified "market-driven poverty" for the vast majority of Africans, Eastern Europeans, and others whose states are failing. The widening inequality between rich and poor, the failure to address growing environmental crises, concerns about labor conditions in many areas of the world, and other shortfalls of contemporary global governance have provoked a lively debate about the politics of global governance and, in particular, the "who gets what" and "who benefits" questions. For many, contemporary pieces of global governance are "Too geographically unbalanced, dominated by the largest economies ... Most small and poor developing countries are excluded, as are people's organizations ... The structures and processes for global policy-making are not representative ... There are no mechanisms for making ethical standards and human rights binding for corporations and individuals, not just governments" (UNDP 1999: 8). For some, then, the politics of global governance is about U.S. power and dominant coalitions. For others, it is about not only who gets included in decisionmaking, but also who gets excluded (and at what price). We borrow from Ronnie Lipschutz (1997: 83) a useful set of questions regarding governance: "Who rules? Whose rules? What rules? What kind of rules? At what level? In what form? Who decides? On what basis?" And, who benefits? Answers to these questions will emerge ... but first we examine three critical challenges: legitimacy, accountability, and effectiveness.

Legitimacy

In the earlier discussion of international law, we touched briefly on the question of why states comply. This question goes to the heart of a fundamental characteristic of power, governance, and rules more generally: namely, how the characteristic of legitimacy leads actors to obey rules without coercion. Thomas Franck in *The Power of Legitimacy Among Nations* (1990: 24) defines legitimacy as "a property of a rule or rulemaking institution which itself exerts a pull toward compliance on those addressed normatively because those addressed believe that the rule or institution has come into being and operates in accordance with generally accepted principles of right process." Some would add that a rule must also be perceived as just to be considered legitimate. As Franck notes, the "compliance pull" of rules and institutions varies widely, meaning that legitimacy "must be a matter of degree" (26). One way this distinction has been expressed internationally is through the concepts of hard and soft law discussed earlier.

A key aspect of legitimacy in the international system is membership in the international community whose system of multilateral, reciprocal interactions helps to validate its members, institutions, and rules. International institutions like the UN, for example, are perceived as legitimate to the extent that they are created and function according to certain principles of right process such as one-state, one-vote. The UN Security Council's legitimacy as the core institution in the international system imbued with authority to authorize the use of force derives from the widespread acceptance of that role, but ... that legitimacy is also under challenge. As political theorists have long noted, flags and rituals are important symbols of legitimate authority. Thus, when peacekeeping forces wear UN blue helmets, they symbolize the international community's desire to preserve a ceasefire in hostilities. Since their coercive power is severely limited, it is their token presence that induces states and other actors to comply. As Franck (1990: 205) explains, "It is because states constitute a community that legitimacy has the power to influence their conduct."

With many nonstate actors and an increasingly vocal civil society demanding a voice, the question of who participates in global governance touches on a fundamental issue of legitimacy. If IGOs' decisionmaking processes exclude civil society or marginalize the voice of small, poor states, does that undermine the legitimacy and viability of these institutions? ...

Accountability

As a result of the diffusion of domestic democratic norms into the international arena, international institutions also have faced growing demands for greater accountability, gender balance in staffing, and transparency. Some of these demands come from NGOs and civil society groups; others from democratic governments. As Keohane and Nye (2000: 27) note, "International bureaucrats are more remote than national bureaucracies. The chain of connection to elections is more indirect." Even if delegates to international conferences and IGO meetings come from democratic governments and are instructed by and accountable to elected officials, the conferences and meetings may well be closed to the public and operate more like private clubs. The World Bank, World Trade Organization, and IMF have particularly been charged with operating in secrecy. Likewise, there is an active debate over the "democratic deficit" in EU institutions.

Critical to insuring accountability and effectiveness is transparency. Abram Chayes and Antonia Chayes (1995: 22) argue that transparency—"the generation and dissemination of information about the requirements of the regime and the parties' performance under it—is an almost universal element of management strategy ... [that] influences strategic interactions among parties ... in the direction of compliance." In some cases, the lack of transparency has been a key to the efficacy of some institutions, usually highly specialized ones such as trade and telecommunications, ensuring that participating governmental ministers could reach decisions absent outside political pressures. But the concerns about legitimacy, accountability, and transparency are not limited to IGOs; they apply equally to many NGOs. A fundamental problem for multilateral cooperation and global governance in the future, then, is how to increase transparency and accountability without undermining the very conditions that made dealmaking possible.

Effectiveness: Measuring Success and Failure

A third critical challenge involves the effectiveness of governance and the success or failure of different approaches to addressing needs and problems. As Simmons and de Jonge Oudraat (2001: 13–14) note, "Effectiveness goes beyond formal compliance; parties may come into compliance with agreements effortlessly for a time and without undertaking any measures that change behavior or contribute to solving the problem. Agreements themselves may not be ambitious enough to provide more than temporary or cosmetic relief of global problems." The key question is: "What works?" "The complexity of international issues, their overlapping nature, and the turmoil of the arena in which they surface defy tidy theorizing about effective management." There are many points of view and interests to be reconciled, shifting politics, and uncertainties about the efficacies of different policy alternatives.

In assessing effectiveness, several key questions may be asked. Who does what to translate agreements into action, including incorporating norms into domestic laws? Which techniques or mechanisms work best to get targeted actors to change their behavior? And what reactions are there to noncompliance? Who provides incentives or technical assistance to get developing countries to comply with environmental rules? Which actors employ diplomacy or public shaming, impose economic sanctions, or employ military force to punish failure to comply? And what is the outcome? How are people actually affected by the pieces of global governance? The task of assessing effectiveness is one of the central challenges in public policymaking, whether at local, national, regional, or global levels of politics and governance.

The challenges of global governance, then, include a variety of international policy problems and issues that require governance. Many pieces are not necessarily global in scope. Rather, what we see is a multilevel and often very diffuse system of pieces of governance with many different actors playing key roles alongside states. The need for more pieces of governance is clearly rising with globalization and other developments; the processes are complex; the politics, even in a world with a single superpower, is an ongoing struggle to control "who gets what"; and the issues of legitimacy, accountability, and effectiveness require constant attention.

References

Abbott, Kenneth W., and Duncan Snidal. (1998) "Why States Act Through Formal International Organizations." *Journal of Conflict Resolution* 42:1 (February): 3–32.

Chayes, Abram, and Antonia Handler Chayes. (1995) *The New Sovereignty: Compliance with International Regulatory Agreements*. Cambridge: Harvard University Press.

Commission on Global Governance. (1995) *Our Global Neighbourhood: Report of the Commission on Global Governance*. Oxford, UK: Oxford University Press.

Cupitt, Richard, Rodney Whitlock, and Lynn Williams Whitlock. (1997) "The (Im)morality of International Governmental Organizations." In *The Politics of Global Governance: International Organizations in an Interdependent World,* edited by Paul F. Diehl. Boulder, CO: Lynne Rienner Publishers, pp. 7–23.

Fomerand, Jacques. (1996) "UN Conferences: Media Events or Genuine Diplomacy?" *Global Governance* 2:3 (Sept.–Dec.): 361–375.

Franck, Thomas M. (1990) *The Power of Legitimacy Among Nations*. New York: Oxford University Press.

Gilpin, Robert. (2001) *Global Political Economy: Understanding the International Economic Order*. Princeton: Princeton University Press.

Hall, Rodney Bruce, and Thomas J. Biersteker, eds. (2002) *The Emergence of Private Authority in Global Governance*. New York: Cambridge University Press.

Jacobson, Harold K., and Edith Brown Weiss. (1995) "Strengthening Compliance with International Environmental Accords: Preliminary Observations from a Collaborative Project." *Global Governance* 1:2 (May–August): 119–148.

Keohane, Robert O., and Joseph S. Nye, Jr. (2000) "Introduction." In *Governance in a Globalizing World,* edited by Joseph S. Nye, Jr. and John D. Donahue. Washington: Brookings Institution Press, pp. 1–41.

Ku, Charlotte. (2001) *Global Governance and the Changing Face of International Law*. The John W. Holmes Memorial Lecture. ACUNS Reports and Papers No. 2.

Lipschutz, Ronnie D. (1992) "Reconstructing World Politics: The Emergence of Global Civil Society." *Millennium* 21:3: 389–420.

———. (1997) "From Place to Planet: Local Knowledge and Global Environmental Governance." *Global Governance* 3:1 (Jan.–April): 83–102.

Mathews, Jessica T. (1997) "Power Shift." *Foreign Affairs* 76:1 (Jan.–Feb.): 50–66.

Murphy, Craig. (2000) "Global Governance: Poorly Done and Poorly Understood." *International Affairs* 75:4: 789–803.

Rosenau, James N. (1992) "Governance, Order and Change in World Politics." In *Governance Without Government: Order and Change in World Politics,* edited by James N. Rosenau and E. O. Czempiel. Cambridge: Cambridge University Press, pp. 1–29.

Simmons, P. J., and Chantal de Jonge Oudraat. (2001) "Managing Global Issues: An Introduction." In *Managing Global Issues: Lessons Learned,* edited by P. J. Simmons and Chantal de Jonge Oudraat. Washington: Carnegie Endowment for International Peace, pp. 3–24.

Spar, Debora L. (1999) "Lost in (Cyber) Space: The Private Rules of Online Commerce." In *Private Authority and International Affairs,* edited by A. Claire Cutler, Virginia Haufler, and Tony Porter. Albany: State University of New York Press, pp. 31–51.

Strange, Susan. (1996) *The Retreat of the State: The Diffusion of Power in the World Economy.* Cambridge: Cambridge University Press.

United Nations Development Program. (1999) *Human Development Report 1999. Globalization with a Human Face.* New York: United Nations.

Vale, Peter. (1995) "Engaging the World's Marginalized and Promoting Global Change: Challenges for the United Nations at 50." *Harvard International Law Journal* 36:2: 283–294.

16.2

REGIONAL ORDERS

Peter J. Katzenstein

> In this passage from his book *A World of Regions*, Peter J. Katzenstein weaves together the interplay of power, institutions, and identity in explaining Asian and European regionalism. American power or the "American imperium" shadows the foundation and openness of the two regions, multilateral in Europe and bilateral in Asia. But European and Asian institutions and identities flesh out the content of the two regions. Asia is characterized by "ethnic capitalism," a Japanese version strong on insular institutions and strategies and a Chinese version strong on overseas Chinese networks and family ties. Europe, by contrast, features a more highly institutionalized form of capitalism, permeated by a European sense of political constitutionalism and legal order. Notice the constructivist methodology in this account, the seamless causal web of power, institutions, and ideas rather than the primary causal influence of any one of these variables and the interaction of multiple levels of analysis. Still, would he bother to focus on regions if he did not feel that national and regional institutions and cultures were more important than global ones?

The United States plays the central role in a world of regions. Gone are the clearly demarcated, rival blocs of East and West. Since the end of the cold war, the collapse of socialism has made anachronistic the distinction between a first and a second world. And even before the disintegration of the Soviet Union, the third world had ceased to exist as a cohesive force in world politics. The distinction between an industrialized North and a nonindustrialized South became outdated with the rapid industrialization of numerous poor countries, while the gap in income and wealth within and between North and South has widened. The American imperium is now the hub in a wheel with many regional spokes. In short, world politics has undergone a huge shift from bloc bipolarity to an American-centered regionalism.

Actions that the United States took in the late 1940s were crucial in bringing about the regional institutional orders that have characterized Asia and Europe for the last half century. Markets and law were the two key institutions through

Source: Peter J. Katzenstein, "Regional Orders," in *A World of Regions: Asia and Europe in the American Imperium* (Ithaca, N.Y.: Cornell University Press, 2005), 43–75.

which Asian and European regions organized. In Asia, regionalism has been shaped by the powerful impact of ethnic capitalism in markets that are typically organized through networks. In Europe, law and judicial institutions are embedded in a variety of political institutions that link countries together in a European polity. Drawing this sharp distinction is not to deny the existence of important networks in Europe and of developmental states in Asia. But the comparison of Europe and Asia highlights two important facts. European networks are embedded in a legal context that profoundly shapes their operations; Asian states seek to ride markets that are evolving in broader networks. The fact that similar institutions, in part emanating from U.S. influence, can be found in both regions takes nothing away from the more important idea that I develop here: the distinctive institutions that shape Europe and Asia differ greatly.

Regional Politics, Present at the Creation

Throughout the twentieth century, state power and purpose have shaped the ups and downs of regionalism. When the United States failed to back the League of Nations and the principle of universalism it stood for, Nazi Germany and the Japanese military developed different versions of closed regionalism, in the form of Europe's "New Order" and Asia's "Co-Prosperity Sphere." At the end of World War II, globalism and regionalism offered again two contrasting blueprints for world politics. U.S. Secretary of State Cordell Hull stood for universalism; British prime minister Winston Churchill championed regionalism. This split is preserved in the United Nations Charter: Article 24 charges the Security Council to preserve world peace and international security, whereas Article 52 emphasizes the importance of regional organizations. Soon after 1945, anti-Communist coalition politics came to define regional politics in both Europe and Asia. Reflecting a hierarchical view of the world that had strong civilizational and at times racial connotations, U.S. policy engaged Europe multilaterally and Asia bilaterally, with consequences that proved to be far reaching for the evolution of European and Asian regionalism.[1]

* * *

Ethnic Capitalism in Asian Market Networks

China and Japan are important centers of the new Asian regionalism, but in ways that differ from the regionalism of Japan's Co-Prosperity Sphere of the 1930s and 1940s. The old regionalism emphasized autarky, the new one relies on open networks. East Asia's regional networks are linked tightly to the world at large. The region's leading dozen metropolitan areas account for about 80 to 90 percent of its international activities.[2] Currently, Asian regionalism takes two different forms. Japanese capitalism is the result of indigenous economic developments and a conscious political strategy, orchestrated jointly by government and business elites. At the regional level, by contrast, Chinese capitalism lacks both an integrated, indigenous political economy and a coherent political strategy. It is almost unlimited in its flexibility.[3]

Japan

Japan's economic insularity is partly a function of the relatively small number of Japanese living in Asia. More than one million overseas Chinese lived in Southeast Asia in the first half of the nineteenth century, a population that doubled between 1900 and the early 1930s.[4] There were about eight to ten million ethnic Chinese in Southeast Asia in 1945, about 5–6 percent of the total population.[5] Because of the long tradition of isolationism under the Tokugawa shogunate (1603–1868), corresponding figures for Japanese nationals were much smaller. The spontaneous movement to Southeast Asia of marginal groups in Japanese society, "prostitutes, pimps, and subsequently, shop owners, clerks, and plantation workers," increased in the early decades of the twentieth century from only 2,800 in 1907 to 36,600 in 1936.[6] Local consulates, local bosses, local Japanese associations, and eventually the spread of Japan's uniform education system beyond national borders, all served to "re-Nipponize" Japanese colonial communities throughout Southeast Asia. At the same time, overseas Japanese relied on Chinese business networks to become competitive, especially in retail trade.[7] In 1945, the Japanese population in Southeast Asia dropped to the vanishing point. Japan's postwar relations with Asia were built on these historical connections and the many legacies of its military occupation, especially of Southeast Asia.

In recent decades, Japan's approach to Asia has been shaped by Kaname Akamatsu's flying geese theory of industrial growth and senescence.[8] Akamatsu's work on industrial change was based on a conception of Asian markets in which governments were directly involved in the flow of trade, investment, and aid. Saburo Okita, deeply influenced by Akamatsu, became head of the research division of Japan's Economic Planning Agency in 1955. Following Akamatsu's basic insight, Okita's plan for expanding Japanese exports focused on the unavoidable and hoped-for economic development of Asian economies. If Japan assisted that development, it would dispel historical animosities, divert attention from dangerous and wasteful political quarrels in Asia, enhance regional growth prospects, and create a more stable international environment that would be especially profitable for Japan's highly competitive capital goods sector.

This understanding of development provided a strong intellectual foundation for Japan's Asia policy. Kiyoshi Kojima, Akamatsu's most distinguished and influential student, pursued in the 1960s the idea of creating a regional system in the Pacific area, one that would support regional economic integration through which Japan and its Asian neighbors would be indelibly linked. The "Pacific free trade area" that Kojima proposed in 1965 included the United States, Canada, Australia, and New Zealand. It was to be linked to an integrated region encompassing the Southeast Asian economies. Thus Japan would be connected to the advanced U.S. economy, on whose markets its exports depended, as well as to backward Southeast Asia, destined to absorb Japan's sunset industries.

Throughout the 1960s, the Japanese government proposed different schemes for the regional integration of Asia.[9] Informed by the same broad conception of Asia-Pacific as a region at the center of Japan's diplomacy in the 1980s and 1990s, these schemes were stymied by the other Asian states' deep suspicions regarding Japan. In reaction to the failures of the 1960s, Japan favored subsequently an informal and soft form of economic regionalism in Asia.[10] The Japanese government supported looser, nongovernmental institutions that either diffused Japanese influence through broad memberships or operated without Japanese participation.

The Pacific Basin Economic Council was the first such grouping. Created in 1968, it initially included businessmen from the five Pacific Rim countries and subsequently opened to many other Asian states. The "second-track" meetings that started in 1969 became a powerful lobby for integrating business in a broad Pacific area. A decade later, Foreign Minister Okita and Prime Minister Masayoshi Ohira, together with Australian prime minister Malcolm Fraser, convened a meeting that led to a nongovernmental international seminar (the Pacific Economic Cooperation Conference). It furthered a broad, market-based approach to Asia-Pacific. PECC embodied a regional idea requiring economic rather than political language. It reinforced rather than undermined national sovereignty. And it put economic development and the future ahead of political atonement for past transgressions. In contrast to the failed initiatives of the 1960s, these nongovernmental institutions emphasized personal networking and the exchange of information over political negotiations and binding decisions.

The sharp appreciation of the yen in 1985 started a surge of Japanese direct foreign investment and aid, setting the stage for a dramatic regional extension of Japanese firms and the emergence of vertical networks of subcontractors and affiliated firms. These groups moved quickly to recreate their accustomed supplier chains abroad, first in textiles and electronics, later in automobiles. Multinational corporations now control an unprecedented share of foreign trade in Asia. These chains link myriad hierarchically organized subcontractors and producers of components in complex, multitiered arrangements that are either producer- or buyer-driven. Japanese foreign investment creates production chains and methods of technology transfer that have a deep impact on the trajectory of economic sectors, individual countries, and the entire Asian region.

Japan's growing economic enmeshment in northeast and Southeast Asia helped create an integrated Asian regional economy. It also reinforced a triangular trade structure in which Japanese exports and investments resulted in a rapid expansion of exports to Western markets, primarily the United States. Backed by a surge in foreign investment, trade, and the largest aid disbursements in the region, the Japanese government also sought to influence business and government abroad by exporting, with minor modifications and more or less successfully, its prized system of administrative guidance.[11] In the fall of 1990, Japan's Ministry of International Trade and Industry (MITI) set up organizations in various Asian countries to facilitate periodic meetings between local businessmen, Japanese investors, government officials, and MITI bureaucrats. These offices, it was hoped, would offer "local guidance."[12] Japanese aid programs also exported the Japanese practice of bid rigging (*dango*), common in Japan's domestic public work programs. In the words of David Arase, Japan's request-based approach to foreign aid allows "for graft and corruption while giving the Japanese government deniability."[13]

This regionwide Japanese system of political and economic power is especially adept at maximizing technological efficiencies, thus fortifying its economic and political leadership over an Asia that is developing in Japan's embrace. In Walter Hatch and Kozo Yamamura's view, increasing technological disparities translated in the 1980s and early 1990s into economic and political domination.[14] Asian regionalism is in this view little more than an international extension of Japan's approach to economic development. That approach has become institutionalized since the mid-1980s in far-flung regional production networks, supported by a broad array of trade, aid, and investment policies. This regional extension of Japanese practices is remarkably coherent across different domains of policy. It is, however, guided by no secret master plan. Rather, Japan's regionalization extends the useful life of domestic arrangements and practices that in the 1990s proved to be increasingly unworkable at home.[15]

Overseas Chinese

Chinese business in Asia-Pacific has witnessed vast changes since 1945, in particular the rise of developmental states and the growing importance of foreign multinationals. Chinese networks became important intermediaries connecting bureaucrats, the military, and politicians, on the one hand, and foreign firms, on the other—both in the phase of import-substitution during the 1950s and 1960s, and in the phase of export-led industrialization since then. The core of Chinese business has remained family-controlled, but surrounding layers of equity-holding and political control were taken over by members of the indigenous elite. In the late 1980s, the overseas Chinese economy in Southeast Asia, Taiwan, and Hong Kong reportedly ranked fourth in the world in terms of its "economic size."[16]

"Overseas Chinese" are people of ethnic Chinese descent living outside mainland China. Before the twentieth century, overseas Chinese lacked a homogeneous identity: hometowns, dialects, blood relationships, and guild associations were far stronger than the sense of being Chinese. Eventually, a diaspora identity began to spread as a result of the revolutionary upheavals on the mainland. As a social category, however, "overseas Chinese" unduly minimizes the wide diversity of the Chinese experience in different parts of Southeast Asia.

It is thus not surprising that the cultural characteristic typifying the Chinese business diaspora is its enormous flexibility.[17] As the Chinese state crumbled in the nineteenth and early twentieth centuries, Chinese capitalism spread throughout Southeast Asia, creating networks that overcame political divisions and state boundaries. As the Chinese political order declined and collapsed, the main network nodes were safe havens on the Chinese coast, such as Shanghai, Canton, and other treaty ports, as well as overseas in Southeast Asia, Hawaii, and the American West Coast.[18] Chinese regional networks covered finance, trade, and production.

The entrepreneur Gordon Wu suggests that the business organization of the overseas Chinese is like a tray of sand. The grains are families, not individuals, and they are held together by blood, trust, and obligation, not law, government, or national solidarity.[19] Enterprise groups are family-centered, and the carriers of Chinese capitalism typically are heads of households. In Taiwan, for example, irrespective of their size and independence, family firms predominate over large conglomerates.[20] In these firms "there is very little delegation of responsibility, even to the sons ... if the old man says go right, you go right."[21] Social ties are not simply a matter of blood and marriage but rely on social norms that govern specific relationships marked by submission, trust, loyalty, and predictability. Interpreted by the participants in both personal and instrumental terms, these social norms permeate the economic institutions of Chinese society, embed economic activity, and produce distinctive forms of allocative efficiency.

A survey of more than 150 overseas Chinese entrepreneurs in the early 1990s confirmed that, to their way of thinking, only family members can really be trusted.[22] Keeping strict control within the family typically constrains size and growth, especially of high-tech firms. Because of the strength of kinship, wealthy businessmen often invest in extensive networks of small firms covering numerous economic sectors or sector segments. Hence, economies of scale are achieved not from the acquisition of individual firms but from networks that connect small firms.[23] Statistically speaking, in terms of employment, Taiwanese business groups, not firms, are five to six times smaller than Japanese business groups, and they hold a less central position in the national economy.[24] Yet Chinese not Japanese tycoons dominate most of the economic life of Southeast Asia and Hong Kong. Chinese capitalism, Gary Hamilton argues, "is a nonpolitically based form of capitalism that is very flexible and readily adaptable to external economic opportunities."[25]

Chinese networks do not simply serve economic purposes. They are also social systems.[26] Formal overseas Chinese mutual aid associations are based on clan, province, or dialect (including Cantonese, Hakka, Hokkien, Chiu Chow). "These associations act like banks through which members can borrow money, trade information, recruit workers, and receive business introductions." And in the many situations where markets are underdeveloped and law is unpredictable, these networks are the preferred vehicle for complex business transactions that enforce the handshake deals on which much Chinese business is based.[27]

Local, regional, and occupational groups and relational kinship systems, not the state, promoted the standardization and predictability that are necessary for the growth of economic transactions.

The existence of powerful overseas Chinese business networks left the government of the People's Republic of China with a difficult issue. The 1953 census listed the overseas Chinese as part of China's population, and the 1954 Constitution of the People's Republic of China provided for representation of all overseas Chinese in the National People's Congress. Soon thereafter, however, the PRC government abandoned the doctrine of *ius sanguinis* and left the choice of national citizenship to individual overseas Chinese. A bitter conflict with Indonesia over the discriminatory regulations with which Jakarta had targeted ethnic Chinese eventually pushed the government of the PRC to adopt a pragmatic policy in the late 1950s, altered only during the early years of the Cultural Revolution. That policy sacrificed the security interests of overseas Chinese to the foreign policy interests of the PRC.

Growing affluence and national policies of economic discrimination have caused the overwhelming majority of overseas Chinese to accept citizenship in their new homelands, claim equal rights there, and hope for nondiscriminatory policies. Within the first three decades after the Communist takeover of China, more than 80 percent of overseas Chinese had adopted the nationality of their Southeast Asian countries of residence.[28] The connotations of the term "Chinese" became more cultural than political, and "overseas Chinese" now denotes ethnic Chinese of Southeast Asian birth and nationality.[29] Today, more than 95 percent of overseas Chinese in Southeast Asia were born there.[30] Virtually all are firmly settled, if not fully assimilated, in Southeast Asian polities. Their control over economic resources in each of the major Southeast Asian countries is impressively large. Although estimates vary, ethnic Chinese are reported to control up to 80 percent of the corporate sector in Malaysia, Indonesia, and Thailand, and about 40 percent in the Philippines.[31]

Since the 1980s the Chinese government has been very interested in strengthening economic relations with the overseas Chinese through active encouragement of foreign investments, remittances, and tourism. Government policy is now fully supportive of what Barry Naughton calls the "China Circle" that connects Hong Kong, Taiwan, and overseas Chinese throughout Southeast Asia with the Chinese mainland.[32] Since the mid-1980s, about four-fifths of contracted and two-thirds of realized foreign investments in the PRC is estimated to have come from business networks in this China Circle.[33] After Asia's 1997 financial crisis, closer tie-ups between overseas and mainland Chinese are constituting the next phase in the spread of Asian business networks. The importance of these networks for the political economy of Asia-Pacific is by all accounts far greater than that of formal institutions such as APEC. Equally important, the evolution of Chinese capitalism cannot be understood as a domestic phenomenon. It is inherently international and linked closely to the dynamics of the global economy.[34]

A web of entrepreneurial relationships thus has reintegrated "Greater China" since the late 1980s. Ethnic and familial ties help establish regional business networks that are "informal though pervasive, with local variations but essentially stateless, stitched together by capital flows, joint ventures, marriages, political expediency and common culture and business ethic."[35] What is distinctive about Chinese business networks, compared to those in Europe or the United States, is the vast distances they cover, the large amount of interpersonal trust they embody, and the lack of formal institutionalization they exhibit. Through mutual shareholding and other mechanisms, overseas Chinese firms have cooperated and thus strengthened one another. These firms have been linked to small- and medium-sized enterprises in retail and wholesale that have acted as intermediary agencies. In the 1990s, large Chinese family firms began to engage financial markets on a worldwide scale and to diversify, moving away from their dependence on Chinese banks.[36]

Japanese and Chinese Networks

Asian regionalism is institutionalized in different business networks, with national Japanese and ethnic Chinese identities playing an important role. The benefits of cultural affinities and old familial and business ties in overcoming problems of trust and reliability offer some advantages to a Chinese mode of organizing that contrasts with the dynamic technological efficiencies created in more hierarchical Japanese networks. While Chinese networks are excellent for rent-seeking behavior and quick returns on capital, Japan controls the flow of aid and technologies and provides producers in other countries with capital and intermediate inputs.[37] South Korea and Taiwan, though closing the development gap quickly, specialize in somewhat less sophisticated goods and remain dependent on Japanese imports for key technologies and intermediate products. Thus, they have taken their place between Japan and Southeast Asia, which currently provides raw materials and markets and is upgrading industrial platforms for assembly and increasingly indigenous production.

The overlay of Japanese and Chinese business networks is evident in the case of Thailand. On the basis of his field research, Mitchell Sedgwick concluded:

> Japanese multinationals in Thailand have reproduced an atomization of labor and strong centralization of decision-making authority.... Beyond internal plant dynamics, however, the strict centralization is also reflected in the position of subsidiaries vis-à-vis headquarters. Subsidiaries in Thailand are part of a tightly controlled and rigorously hierarchical organizational structure extending down from Japan.[38]

Thailand's Chinese-dominated business community, in contrast, has taken different forms over time; but in the last three decades, younger Chinese entrepreneurs have responded to the internationalization of the Thai economy by running their businesses along traditional Chinese lines and maintaining close contacts with the Chinese business communities in Hong Kong, Singapore, Taiwan, and China. Thailand illustrates that rapid corporate growth can result from the horizontal and open networks of the overseas Chinese as much as the vertical and closed ones typical of Japan.[39]

These Japanese and Chinese variants of Asian regionalism take the form of ethnonationalist business networks and subregional zones, but their historical sources differ greatly. Japanese capitalism flowered between 1870 and 1930 in an era of state- and empire-building; Chinese capitalism, developing at the same time, bears the marks of imperial and state collapse.[40] Since the mid-nineteenth century, the population of overseas Japanese has been dwarfed by the Chinese diaspora; and Chinese business networks are more extensive and have deeper historical roots than do their Japanese counterparts. Japanese officials have built up Japanese networks in full awareness of the severe limitations that Japanese firms face in Asia. Different historical origins thus have shaped the character of China's and Japan's economic extensions into Asia.

This general pattern is evident in specific industrial sectors. Japanese networks of firms rely substantially on known Japanese suppliers with comparable technical capacities. Overseas Chinese firms work through networks that draw on the increasing technical specialization of small- and medium-sized firms scattered throughout Asia. Japanese networks are closed, vertical, Japan-centered, and long term. Chinese networks are open, horizontal, flexible, and ephemeral.[41] In vertical organizations, groups are controlled by shareholding ownership, whereas horizontal networks favor family ownership and partnerships. Within a group, vertical networks control through cross-shareholding and mutual domination; horizontal ones manage through multiple positions held by core personnel. Vertical systems organize between group networks with cross-shareholding; horizontal ones favor loans and joint ventures by individuals and firms. In the former, subcontract relations are structured or semiformal; in the latter, they are informal and highly flexible. Growth patterns are differentiated by bank financing in vertical systems, and informal financing and reinvestment in horizontal ones.[42]

Japanese and Chinese patterns of organization are both distinct and complementary. The new crop of Chinese tycoons in Southeast Asia often cooperates with Japanese business, for example, in the Siam Motor Group in Thailand, the Astra Company and Rodamas Group in Indonesia, the Yuchenco Group in the Philippines, and the Kuok Brothers in Malaysia.[43] Of 138 joint ventures between Japanese and Indonesian firms in 1974, 70 percent of the Indonesian partners were local Chinese.[44] Frequently, Japanese firms find it very difficult to work without Chinese middlemen. Furthermore, foreign trade between China and Japan is expanding very rapidly. In 2003 the weekly air traffic of about ten thousand people between Japan and China exceeded the total number for all of 1992. When Hawaii is excluded, Japanese buy more package tours to China than to the United States. And as Japanese business is now convinced that China is the most important market to pull the Japanese economy out of its long stagnation, foreign investment is booming. There are forty-six hundred joint ventures in the Shanghai region alone; in 2003, two or three new Japanese businesses opened in and around the city every day.[45]

In sum, Asian markets do not consist of a series of unconnected and atomized individual transactions. "Interlinked commodity chains," writes Gary Hamilton, "simultaneously are embedded in the social and political institutions of locales and are extremely sensitive to such global conditions as price and currency fluctuations."[46] At the regional level, these social and market links typically follow ethnic Chinese or national Japanese lines. Both types of business network avoid formal institutionalization, as Japanese conglomerates structures and Chinese family firms bring about economic integration without formal political institutions. In the 1990s, regionalism and regionalization in Asia was porous to developments in the world economy; its economic form was network-like; and its political shape was multicephalic.

Law and Politics in a European Polity

"Return to Europe" is the political metaphor that dominates the study of regional integration and enlargement in Europe since the end of World War II, and especially since the end of the cold war. Examples are legion: Germany after 1945; Spain, Portugal, and Greece in the 1980s; the central and eastern European states since 1990. What is the "Europe" to which these states wish to return? Postwar European regionalism rested on a liberal view that was both antifascist and anticommunist. The onset of the cold war quickly began to narrow the Pan-European vision to a West European one. With the end of the cold war, and in the interest of strengthening and broadening this liberal community, the European Union reaffirmed its commitment to overcoming Europe's division between East and West at its Strasbourg summit in December 1989.

European regionalism differs greatly in its institutional form from Asia's. This is mostly due to the European Union. The values of liberal democracy define the membership rules. The rule of law, private property in a market economy, the rights of democratic participation, and respect for minority rights and social pluralism all are part of the liberal human rights that are central to the European Union. They are embedded in a system of multilateral arrangements of states committed to a peaceful resolution of all conflicts. Since 1957, these values have been cast in legal language and are specified in various treaties that European governments have signed and ratified. They were restated succinctly by the European Council in its 1993 Copenhagen meeting.

With the passing of time, regional integration in Europe has changed from a system of bargaining between governments to a polity in which, among others, governments and other institutions also bargain. Governance in Europe is driven by functional needs, has a large bureaucratic component, and occurs at multiple levels that link subnational, national, and European institutions. Groups, parties, and government bureaucracies are drawn into a polity that is acquiring legitimacy while remaining contested. This process is leading neither to unification through the creation of a European superstate nor to fragmentation into a plethora of nationalistic states.

The European polity suffers from persistent decisional inefficiencies that come from this in-between status. They are rooted in a growing gap between "positive" and "negative" integration, between far-reaching, legally mandated eliminations of economic and social borders on the one hand and, at best, cautious and uneven advances in regulating merging European markets on the other. Central in that enterprise are formal institutions—the Council of the European Union, formerly the Council of Ministers; the European Commission; the European Parliament; the European Court of Justice—that share powers with national governments and with one another.[47]

The European Union has evolved into a distinctive polity that fuses executive and legislative powers in different institutions operating at the European level, as well as between the European and the national levels. The Council of Ministers and twenty-two different functional councils of ministers deal, respectively, with foreign policy and a broad array of specialized issues. Although these councils have many executive prerogatives and are sites for the creation of transgovernmental coalitions, they are also the most important legislative bodies of the European Union. In the execution of policy, furthermore, they are linked closely to national bureaucracies. Addressing often highly technical issues, these councils interact with committees of the European Parliament and interest groups operating at national and, increasingly, European levels. As the councils work mostly by consensus, their operations are typically shrouded in secrecy. They illustrate how power in the European Union is spread among different centers of power and across different levels of governance.

With its twenty members meeting as a cabinet, the Commission acts in concert with the Council of Ministers. It supervises the roughly thirteen thousand civil servants who work in Brussels. It also initiates most of the European Union's important legislation. Issued largely by the Commission in the form of regulations and decisions, the total legislative output of the European Union since 1957 reportedly approaches one hundred thousand pages. About half of the new laws adopted in EU member states are drafted in Brussels, especially those dealing with issues of the environment, public health, consumer protection, and internal security; pensions, welfare benefits, and education are still primarily subject to national legislation. Furthermore, although it lacks enforcement powers, the Commission supervises the implementation of EU laws by member states. It often relies on the expertise of national bureaucracies, both in the development of new policies and in the implementation of existing ones. Because it seeks to lessen its dependence on national governments, the Commission is a voracious consumer of the information provided by nongovernmental sources. In its operation, the Commission thus merges both legislative and executive as well as supranational and national powers.

Elected directly since 1979, the members of the European Parliament caucus along ideological rather than national lines. But despite the provision for limited co-decision, the European Parliament's power has remained largely advisory. It can delay actions, and it has the right to impeach members of the Commission. But its veto power is restricted to less than half of the EU budget. For example, the European Parliament has no significant budgetary control over agricultural spending, the largest single budget item. Because of the absence of a European public, elections to the European Parliament are often plebiscites on unrelated national issues rather than focused on the substance of the European polity. Institutional changes introduced in the mid-1980s have, however, enhanced the European Parliament's power. The result has been an intensification of bargaining prior to the introduction of Council or Commission proposals. In the eyes of the German, but not of the French or British, governments, these reforms fall far short of remedying the European Union's democratic deficit. In the future, that deficit is likely to narrow due to the forging of stronger links between the European Parliament and national legislatures. Parliamentary practice thus bridges different arenas of power and levels of government.

The emergence of a wide range of institutions at the European level is noteworthy, but the feature that most clearly distinguishes Europe from Asia is its far-reaching process of *legal* integration. The European Court is known for its activism, as its judicial identity shields it from political interference. At the national level, in contrast, courts and executives explicitly contest the institutional prerogative of who defines the balance of power among government institutions, as well as the pace, scope, and manner of an integrating European polity. The Commission's right to sue member states (Article 169), the right of member states to sue one another (Article 170), and the Court's right to review the legality of all actions taken by the EU Council and the Commission (Article 173) aim at securing compliance with the obligations of the Treaty of Rome, which established the EEC in 1957. But the prime task of the Court is to enforce a uniform interpretation and application of European law (Article 177). Furthermore, as part of its evolving practices, the Court monitors national laws for possible incompatibilities with the treaty. In this role, the Court rules on cases in which individual citizens sue national legislatures and executives. Finally, as specified in Article 177, the Court rules on general issues involving the validity of European Union law. That the Court does not decide these issues directly is an indication of the strong link between the supranational and national levels of governments. Rather, the Court issues "preliminary rulings" and thus seeks to guide lower courts in their judgments. There are reasonable grounds for disagreement on whether the Court's decentralized method of enforcement is a source of weakness, or strength, or both. But it is evident that the Court's activism occurs in the context of the actions taken by national courts.

The evolution of European law has been marked by the constitutionalization of the EC treaties by the European Court of Justice and national courts. This process combined institution building with legal interpretation. The term "constitutionalization" describes the process by which a set of treaties evolved "from a set of legal arrangements binding upon sovereign states, into a vertically-integrated legal regime conferring judicially enforceable rights and obligation on all legal persons and entities, public and private, within EC territory.[48] Constitutionalization results both from the European Court's judicial activism and from an incessant judicial dialogue between the Court and national courts.

The process of constitutionalization occurred in two waves.[49] In the first period (1962–79), the European Court of Justice succeeded in securing both the principle of the supremacy of European over national law and its direct effect on all legal subjects in the European Community. In the second period (1983–90), the process of legal integration gave national judges enhanced means for guaranteeing the effective application of EC law. In 1983, for example, the Court established the principle of indirect effect, which compels national judges to interpret existing national law to conform to EC law. It extended the principle of indirect effect in a 1992 ruling: in situations where directives have not been adopted, or have been adopted incorrectly, national judges must interpret and apply national law in conformity with European law: "The doctrine empowers national judges to rewrite national legislation—an exercise called 'principled construction'—in order to render EC law applicable in the absence of implementing measures."[50] In 1990, a high point in Europe's legal integration, the Court established the doctrine of government liability. Under this doctrine, a national court can hold a member state liable for the damage it may have caused by not having properly implemented or applied an EU directive.

Over time, the European Court of Justice has pushed legal integration much further than member states initially had contemplated, and also beyond economic or political integration.[51] Legal integration results from the institutionally linked decision streams of a variety of actors, including litigants, lawyers, and judges. The process by which national courts have accepted the supremacy and the direct effect of European law is highly variable and path-dependent. Rather than looking at legal developments at different levels, Thijmen Koopmans, a judge on the Court of Justice during the 1980s, argues that it is "more rewarding, intellectually, and also more interesting, to look at it as one global process: that of the progressive construction of one many-sided legal edifice."[52]

The competition among national courts, and between courts and other political actors, normally promotes, though at times retards, Europe's legal integration. Between the mid-1980s and mid-1990s, in particular, the European Court of Justice attempted to strengthen a decentralized system of enforcing European law. This development created conditions in which lower and higher national courts compete in the use they make of European law. "It is the difference in lower and higher court interests which provides a motor for legal integration to proceed," writes Karen Alter.[53] Lower courts tend to use European law to achieve desired legal outcomes. Higher courts tend, instead, to restrain the expansion of European legal orders into national ones. Generally speaking, lower courts have moved higher courts to a position where the latter must accept the supremacy and direct effects of European law.[54]

Legal integration, however, is not a one-way street. The judicial process in different states can also lead to a retardation of legal integration. In famous decisions in 1974 (Solange I) and 1993 (Maastricht), the German Constitutional Court significantly constrained the process of European legal integration.[55] And short of outright legal obstruction, the ambiguities of national compliance with new European law are unavoidable. They derive from the application of new legal rules in national settings with deep-rooted legal traditions and often very different interpretations of the social meaning of legal rules. Lack of state capacity or clarity about priorities and obfuscation of responsibilities and opportunities creates "contained compliance" as a distinctive trait of the European Union's legal order.[56]

Legal integration occurs also through dialogue. That dialogue has two parts: the creation of new doctrine, such as the primacy and direct effects of EU law; and the acceptance of this new jurisprudence by national courts and national politicians. The European Court of Justice has typically created this jurisprudence in cases brought by national courts. Although all national judiciaries insist on a national constitutional basis for the supremacy of European law, national courts now apply the decisions of the Court even when national politicians and administrators object.[57] The constitutionalization of the EC treaties and the process of legal integration thus rest crucially on how national courts interpret, apply, and challenge European law, and how the national reception of that law influences subsequent decisions of the European Court of Justice. At the intersection of law and politics, Europe's legal integration is a process in which judges and other political actors navigate within the institutional order of a European polity.

These EU developments suggest an image of politics under law rather than of law contingent on politics.[58] In a prescient summary, an early student of European law, Stuart Scheingold, concluded in 1971 that "a rather flexible process of litigation is taking shape within a consensual framework of modified national choice."[59] Instead of focusing attention on the advantages or disadvantages of intergovernmentalism or supranationalism, the Europeanization of law underlines instead the dynamics of legal integration in a multitiered European polity—one that combines traditional, hierarchical, and centralized elements of state power with nontraditional, nonhierarchical, and plural systems of governance.

These legal and political aspects of European unification are hardly the only dimensions of Europeanization. Other dimensions also help define Europe as an evolving, multitiered polity.[60] Two are especially noteworthy here. First, Europe seeks to export its own political models, distinctive institutions and practices, which it hopes will affect the conduct of world politics. "Europeanization" refers to a different calibration of the requirements of economic efficiency with social justice, resistance to treating culture as a commodity, stronger opposition to the death penalty, more self-conscious commitment to environmental causes, and insistence on the primacy of international law and multilateral international organizations in world affairs. Second, through the process of enlargement, Europeanization has an even stronger effect on the domestic institutions and practices of member states and, especially, the accession countries in southern and eastern Europe. Europeanization processes are quite marked on the economic and social issues that are at the center of capitalist welfare states. But European regulations also cover moral and cultural issues that stretch well into the sphere of social morality.[61] In the competition for legitimacy in world affairs, Europeanization often takes precedence over the exercise of coercive military power in the pursuit of narrow national security interests.

Institutionalization in Europe is a pervasive phenomenon affecting many dimensions of social and political life. Yet, compared to Asia, it is the constitutionalization of the European treaty system, more than the adoption of a European constitution, that is the distinctive trait of the evolving European polity. Consensus decision making occurs in a multitiered political system that fuses and separates power and is always open to serious conflicts of interest, pitting national governments against one another. Joseph Weiler draws our attention to the principle of constitutional *tolerance*. Very different European states are committed to coming together in an ever closer union. They are connected through a growing number of ties that invite, more than oblige, the submission of national power to the decisions of a political community—one in which other states, not a democratic public, exercise authority. "European federalism," concludes Weiler, "is constructed with a top-to-bottom hierarchy of norms, but with a bottom-to-top hierarchy of authority and real power."[62] These intersecting political processes direct our attention to Europe as a problem-solving, deliberative polity that complements the alternative political logics of state sovereignty and societal associability.[63]

U.S. policy has had a lot to do with the core differences in Europe's and Asia's regional orders. After 1945 multilateralism was an institutional innovation that U.S. policymakers pursued vigorously in Europe but not in Asia. Washington helped set the two regions on different institutional trajectories, leading to ethnic capitalism in Asian markets and law embedded in various European political arrangements. These differences are consequential both for the American imperium, which seeks to manage a world of regions, and for Germany and Japan, which play leading roles in two of the world's most important regions.

Notes

1. The following section draws on Hemmer and Katzenstein 2002.
2. Rohlen 2002, 8–9.
3. This section is adapted from Katzenstein 2000.
4. Hui 1995, 41, 143.
5. Hui 1995, 143–44.
6. Shiraishi and Shiraishi 1993, 7.
7. Hui 1995, 175–76.
8. Akamatsu 1961.

9. Katzenstein 1997a, 16–18.
10. Lincoln 1992, 13.
11. Hatch 2002, 187–94.
12. Lincoln 1993, 125, 127–28, 145–46, 178, 192.
13. Arase 1995, 161.
14. Hatch and Yamamura 1996, 97–129.
15. Hatch 2000.
16. Kao 1993, 24. Hui 1995, 16–17.
17. Hui 1995, 25; see also 287–88.
18. Hamilton 1996, 336.
19. Brick 1992, 5.
20. Hamilton and Kao 1990, 142, 147–48.
21. Quoted in Ridding and Kynge 1997, 13.
22. Kao 1993.
23. Hamilton 1996, 334–35.
24. Hamilton and Kao 1990, 140, 142.
25. Hamilton 1996, 335.
26. Esman 1986, 149.
27. Weidenbaum and Hughes 1996, 51–52.
28. Hui 1995, 191. Gambe 1997, 19–22.
29. Hui 1995, 172, 191, 194.
30. Hicks and Mackie 1994, 48.
31. Hui 1995, 254–58.
32. Naughton 1997.
33. Berger and Lester 1997, 5. Esman 1986, 150–53. Hui 1995, 259–68.
34. Hamilton 1996, 331. Hui 1995, 13–14, 219.
35. Sender 1991, 29.
36. Yeung 2003.
37. Hatch and Yamamura 1996, 96.
38. Sedgwick 1994, 8.
39. Hamilton and Walters 1995, 94, 99–100.
40. Hamilton 1996, 332–33, 336.
41. Hamilton, Orrù, and Biggart 1987, 100. Hamilton and Feenstra 1997, 67–73.
42. Orrù, Biggart, and Hamilton 1997.
43. Hui 1995, 189.
44. Hui 1995, 189. Brick 1992, 3–4.
45. Pilling and McGregor 2004.
46. Hamilton 1999, 52.
47. The following paragraphs draw on Katzenstein 1997b, 33–36.
48. Stone Sweet 1998, 306.
49. Stone Sweet 1998, 306–8.
50. Stone Sweet 1998, 307.
51. Stone Sweet and Brunell 1998, 67–68. Mattli and Slaughter 1998, 254.
52. Koopmans 1991, 506.
53. Alter 1998a, 242.
54. Alter 1998a, 243, 249–50; 1996. Stone Sweet 2000, 153–93; 1998, 324–25.

55. Alter 1998b. Mattli and Slaughter 1998, 270–71, 274–75.
56. Conant 2002, 52.
57. Alter 1998a, 227–28, 231. Witte 1998, 292–93. Stone Sweet 1998, 312–23.
58. Armstrong 1998, 163.
59. Scheingold 1971, 14.
60. Olsen 2002.
61. Kurzer 2001.
62. Weiler 2000, 244, 240.
63. Cohen and Sabel 2003.

Bibliography

Akamtsu, Kaname. 1961. "A Theory of Unbalanced Growth in the World Economy." *Weltwirtschaftliches Archiv* 86, no. 2: 196–217.

Alter, Karen. 1996. "The European Court's Political Power." *West European Politics* 19, no. 3: 458–87.

———. 1998a. "Explaining National Court Acceptance of European Court Jurisprudence: A Critical Evaluation of Theories of Legal Integration." In Anne-Marie Slaughter, Alec Stone Sweet, and J. H. H. Weiler, eds., *The European Court and National Courts—Doctrine and Jurisprudence,* pp. 227–52. Oxford: Oxford University Press.

———. 1998b. "Who Are the Masters of the Treaty? European Governments and the European Court of Justice." *International Organization* 52, no. 1 (Winter): 121–48.

Arase, David. 1995. *Buying Power: The Political Economy of Japan's Foreign Aid.* Boulder: Lynne Rienner.

Armstrong, Kenneth A. 1998. "Legal Integration: Theorizing the Legal Dimension of European Integration." *Journal of Common Market Studies* 36, no. 2 (June): 155–74.

Berger, Suzanne, and Richard K. Lester, eds. 1997. *Made by Hong Kong.* Hong Kong: Oxford University Press.

Brick, Andrew B. 1992. "The Emergence of Greater China: The Diaspora Ascendant." *The Heritage Lectures* No. 411. Washington, D.C.: The Heritage Foundation.

Cohen, Joshua, and Charles F. Sabel. 2003. "Sovereignty and Solidarity: EU and US." In Jonathan Zeitlin and David M. Trubek, eds., *Governing Work and Welfare in a New Economy: European and American Experiments,* pp. 345–75. Oxford: Oxford University Press.

Conant, Lisa. 2002. *Justice Contained: Law and Politics in the European Union.* Ithaca: Cornell University Press.

Esman, Milton. 1986. "The Chinese Diaspora in Southeast Asia." In Gabriel Sheffer, ed., *Modern Diasporas in International Politics,* pp. 130–63. New York: St. Martin's.

Gambe, Annabelle. 1997. "Competitive Collaboration: Western Liberal and Overseas Chinese Ethnic Entrepreneurship in Southeast Asia." *Forschungsberichte aus dem ISW* 22 (November).

Hamilton, Gary G. 1996. "Overseas Chinese Capitalism." In Tu Wei-ming, ed., *Confucian Traditions in East Asian Modernity: Moral Education and Economic Culture in Japan and the Four Mini-Dragons,* pp. 328–42. Cambridge: Harvard University Press.

———. 1999. "Asian Business Networks in Transition: or, What Alan Greenspan Does Not Know about the Asian Business Crisis." In T. J. Pempel, ed., *The Politics of the Asian Economic Crisis,* pp. 45–61. Ithaca: Cornell University Press.

Hamilton, Gary G., and Robert C. Feenstra. 1997. "Varieties of Hierarchies and Markets: An Introduction." In Marco Orrù, Nicole Woolsey Biggart, and Gary G. Hamilton, eds., *The Economic Organization of East Asian Capitalism,* pp. 55–94. Thousand Oaks, Calif.: Sage.

Hamilton, Gary G., and Cheng-Su Kao. 1990. "The Institutional Foundations of Chinese Business." *Comparative Social Research* 12: 135–51.

Hamilton, Gary G., Marco Orrù, and Nicole Woolsey Biggart. 1987. "Enterprise Groups in East Asia: An Organizational Analysis." *Shoken Keizai* 161 (September): 78–106.

Hamilton, Gary G., and Tony Walters. 1995. "Chinese Capitalism in Thailand: Embedded Networks and Industrial Structure." In Edward K. Y. Chen and Peter Drysdale, eds., *Corporate Links and Foreign Direct Investment in Asia and the Pacific,* pp. 87–111. New York: Harper Educational.

Hatch, Walter. 2000. "Rearguard Regionalization: Preserving Core Coalitions in the Japanese Political Economy." PhD diss., University of Washington, Seattle.

———. 2002. "Regionalizing the State: Japanese Administrative and Financial Guidance for Asia." *Social Science Japan Journal* 5, no. 2: 179–97.

Hatch, Walter, and Kozo Yamamura. 1996. *Asia in Japan's Embrace: Building a Regional Production Alliance.* New York: Cambridge University Press.

Hemmer, Christopher, and Peter J. Katzenstein. 2002. "Why Is There No NATO in Asia? Collective Identity, Regionalism, and the Origins of Multilateralism." *International Organization* 56, no. 3 (Summer): 575–608.

Hicks, George, and J. A. C. Mackie. 1994. "Overseas Chinese: A Question of Identity." *Far Eastern Economic Review*: 46–48.

Hui, Po-Keung. 1995. "Overseas Chinese Business Networks: East Asian Economic Development in Historical Perspective." PhD diss., State University of New York, Binghamton.

Kao, John. 1993. "The Worldwide Web of Chinese Business." *Harvard Business Review* 71 (March–April): 24–36.

Katzenstein, Peter J. 1997a. "Introduction: Asian Regionalism in Comparative Perspective." In P. J. Katzenstein and T. Shiraishi, eds., *Network Power: Japan and Asia,* pp. 1–44. Ithaca: Cornell University Press.

———. 1997b. "United Germany in an Integrating Europe." In P. J. Katzenstein, ed., *Tamed Power: Germany in Europe,* pp. 1–48. Ithaca: Cornell University Press.

———. 2000. "Varieties of Asian Regionalisms." In P. J. Katzenstein, N. Hamilton-Hart, K. Kato, and M. Yue, *Asian Regionalism,* pp. 1–34. Ithaca: Cornell University, Center for International Studies, East Asia Program.

Koopmans, Thijmen. 1991. "The Birth of European Law at the Cross Roads of Legal Traditions." *American Journal of Comparative Law* 39, no. 3 (Summer): 493–507.

Kurzer, Paulette. 2001. *Markets and Moral Regulation: Cultural Change in the European Union.* Cambridge: Cambridge University Press.

Lincoln, Edward J. 1992. *Japan's Rapidly Emerging Strategy toward Asia.* Paris: OECD, Research Program on Globalisation and Regionalization.

————. 1993. *Japan's New Global Role*. Washington, D.C.: Brookings Institution.

Mattli, Walter, and Anne-Marie Slaughter. 1998. "The Role of National Courts in the Process of European Integration: Accounting for Judicial Preferences and Constraints." In Anne-Marie Slaughter, Alec Stone Sweet, and J. H. H. Weiler, eds., *The European Court and National Courts—Doctrine and Jurisprudence*, pp. 253–76. Oxford: Oxford University Press.

Naughton, Barry, ed. 1997. *The China Circle: Economics and Technology in the PRC, Taiwan, and Hong Kong*. Washington, D.C.: Brookings Institution.

Olsen, Johan P. 2002. "The Many Faces of Europeanization." *Journal of Common Market Studies* 40, no. 5: 921–52.

Orrù, Marco, Gary G. Hamilton, and Mariko Suzuki. 1997. "Patterns of Interfirm Control in Japanese Business." In Marco Orrù, Nicole Woolsey Biggart, and Gary G. Hamilton, eds., *The Economic Organization of East Asian Capitalism*, pp. 188–214. Thousand Oaks, Calif.: Sage.

Orrù, Marco, Nicole Woolsey Biggart, and Gary G. Hamilton, eds. 1996. *The Economic Organization of East Asian Capitalism*, pp. 55–94. Thousand Oaks, Calif.: Sage.

Pilling, David, and Richard McGregor. 2004. "Crossing the Divide: How Booming Business and Closer Cultural Ties Are Bringing Two Asian Giants Together." *Financial Times* (March 30): 13.

Ridding, John, and James Kynge. 1997. "Empires Can Strike Back." *Financial Times* (November 5): 13.

Rohlen, Thomas P. 2002. *Cosmopolitan Cities and Nation States: Open Economics, Urban Dynamics, and Government in East Asia*. Stanford: Stanford University, Asia/Pacific Center.

Scheingold, Stuart. 1971. *The Law in Political Integration: The Evolution and Integrative Implications of Regional Legal Processes in the European Community*. Occasional Papers in International Affairs, No. 21 (June). Cambridge: Harvard University, Center for International Affairs.

Sedgwick, Mitchell W. 1994. "Does the Japanese Management Miracle Travel in Asia? Managerial Technology Transfer at Japanese Multinationals in Thailand." Paper presented at the Workshop on Multinationals and East Asian Integration, at MIT Japan Program, Cambridge, November 18–19.

Sender, Henny. 1991. "Inside the Overseas Chinese Networks." *Institutional Investor* 25, no. 10 (September): 29–43.

Shiraishi, Saya, and Takashi Shiraishi. 1993. "The Japanese in Colonial Southeast Asia: An Overview." In Shiraishi and Shiraishi, eds., *The Japanese in Colonial Southeast Asia*, pp. 5–20. Ithaca: Cornell University, Southeast Asia Program.

Stone Sweet, Alec. 1998. "Constitutional Dialogues in the European Community." In Anne-Marie Slaughter, Alec Stone Sweet, and J. H. H. Weiler, eds., *The European Court and National Courts—Doctrine and Jurisprudence*, pp. 305–30. Oxford: Oxford University Press.

————. 2000. *Governing with Judges: Constitutional Politics in Europe*. Oxford: Oxford University Press.

Stone Sweet, Alec, and Thomas L. Brunell. 1998. "The European Court and the National Courts: A Statistical Analysis of Preliminary References, 1961–95." *Journal of European Public Policy* 5, no. 1 (March): 66–97.

Weidenbaum, Murray, and Samuel Hughes. 1996. *The Bamboo Network: How Expatriate Chinese Entrepreneurs Are Creating a New Economic Superpower in Asia.* New York: Free Press.

Weiler, John H. H. 2000. "Federalism and Constitutionalism: Europe's Sonderweg." *Jean Monnet Working Paper No. 10.* New York: New York University Law School, Jean Monnet Center for International and Regional Economic Law and Justice.

Witte, Bruno de. 1998. "Sovereignty and European Integration: The Weight of Legal Tradition." In Anne-Marie Slaughter, Alec Stone Sweet, and J. H. H. Weiler, eds., *The European Court and National Courts—Doctrine and Jurisprudence,* pp. 277–304. Oxford: Oxford University Press.

Yeung, Henry Wai-chung. 2003. "Financing Chinese Capitalism: Principal Banks, Economic Crisis, and Chinese Family Firms in Singapore." Paper presented at the conference "Cultural Approaches to Asian Financial Markets," Cornell Law School, Ithaca, April 26.

Conclusion

APPLYING PERSPECTIVES AND LEVELS OF ANALYSIS: THE CASE OF THE DEMOCRATIC PEACE

C.1

THE KANTIAN PEACE IN THE TWENTY-FIRST CENTURY

Bruce Russett and John R. Oneal

> Professors Bruce Russett and John R. Oneal have devoted their professional lives to studying the validity and causes of the democratic peace. In this excerpt from one of their latest books, they summarize the evidence that, as the eighteenth-century German philosopher Immanuel Kant foresaw, democracies (republics) behave more peacefully in international relations than nondemocracies. The causes of this behavior appear to stem from three factors: their democratic systems, their economic interdependence, and their common membership in international organizations. Notice the focus here on identity (democracy) and liberal (trade and international organizations) factors from the domestic and systemic process levels of analysis. National power (realism) is relatively deemphasized. Indeed, if democracy spreads, the democratic peace eventually replaces the military balance of power. Factors from the critical theory perspective and structural level of analysis, such as the deep-seated imperialism of U.S. and western democracy, are also relatively underplayed.

In 1795, Immanuel Kant contended that international peace could be established on a foundation of three elements: republican constitutions, "cosmopolitan

Source: Bruce Russett and John R. Oneal, "The Kantian Peace in the Twenty-First Century," in *Triangulating Peace: Democracy, Interdependence, and International Organizations* (New York: W. W. Norton, 2001), 271–305.

law" embodied in free trade and economic interdependence, and international law and organizations. Kant's vision is remarkable for several reasons. There were very few democracies in the world in the late 1700s and no international organizations as we now know them. There was trade, of course, but most countries followed mercantilist principles, subordinating the economy to the interests of the state and seeking economic independence when possible. Kant's interest in the problem of war is in itself noteworthy, because he believed that peace—a "perpetual peace," not just a lull in the fighting between wars—was possible. Most people then, as many do now, thought that war was inherent in human nature, but Kant proposed that a stable, long-lasting peace could be achieved. He believed the world would eventually become weary of war and that democracy, interdependence, and international organizations could constrain states from resorting to military force. Kant and the other classical liberals were not idealists. They accepted that not all wars could be eliminated but believed the frequency of violence between states could be substantially reduced. Nor did they think that peace depended upon a great moral conversion. Peace was possible not because people everywhere would finally begin to love their neighbors as themselves, but because emerging institutions made war contrary to people's self-interest.

* * *

The Evidence for a Kantian Peace

Kant began his theorizing with attention to democracy. It is in many ways the linchpin of his analysis. He was confident that democracies would be more peaceful than autocracies for a simple reason: in a democracy, those who would bear the costs of a war are the ones who decide whether it shall be fought. As Kant put it in *Perpetual Peace* ([1795] 1970, 100):

> If ... consent of the citizens is required to decide whether or not war is to be declared, it is very natural that they will have great hesitation in embarking on so dangerous an enterprise. For this would mean calling down on themselves all the miseries of war, such as doing the fighting themselves, supplying the costs of the war from their own resources, painfully making good the ensuing devastation, and, as the crowning evil, having to take upon themselves a burden of debt which will embitter peace itself and which can never be paid off on account of the constant threat of new wars.

It is evident from this passage that Kant did not believe that the citizens of democratic states were necessarily more moral than other people, just that they had greater control over the policies of their country and would make careful, self-interested calculations in deciding whether to fight. He was confident that many wars that otherwise would occur would not withstand the careful scrutiny of citizens in a democracy.

On the other hand, when a state is not democratic,

it is the simplest thing in the world to go to war. For the head of state is not a fellow citizen, but the owner of the state, and a war will not force him to make the slightest sacrifice so far as his banquets, hunts, pleasure palaces and court festivals are concerned. He can thus decide on war, without any significant reason, as a kind of amusement, and unconcernedly leave it to the diplomatic corps (who are always ready for such purposes) to justify the war for the sake of propriety. (Kant [1795] 1970, 100)

* * *

Kant emphasized the importance of the sovereignty of the people in reducing the incidence of war. Citizens in a democratic state can influence governmental policy directly, through public opinion, or indirectly, through their representatives. The regular occurrence of elections is obviously important in this process. It is the mechanism that forces government to consider the will of the people. A division of responsibility in the declaration and prosecution of war is also beneficial. That is why the U.S. Constitution gives Congress the power to declare war and the authority to fund the military. It is also why Congress in 1973, following the Vietnam War, passed the War Powers Act. This law was intended to strengthen congressional influence over the president when military means short of war are being considered.

The existence of a loyal but independent political opposition not only limits the ability of a democratic government to wage a capricious, ill-advised war, it also enhances the ability of the state to signal that it is really willing to use force when important interests are truly threatened. When the opposition expresses a widespread popular belief that fundamental interests are at stake, its support for any threat to use the military means that the government cannot then easily retreat. Democratic leaders will not lightly risk the political consequences of backing down or fighting a losing battle, and they cannot override the wishes of the people once a line in the sand has been drawn. The existence of a vocal opposition thus reduces the danger of war by miscalculation. If, however, the opposition rallies against the use of force, any threat by the government loses credibility in the eyes of the opposing country—it is apt to be only a bluff (Schultz 2000). The limited ability of a president or prime minister to determine policy not only constrains him or her from using military force, it also makes a commitment to maintain the peace more credible, because this policy, too, once adopted by popular sanction and the action of diverse governmental bodies, is not easily reversed.

In addition to structural or institutional constraints, recent theories call attention to the cultural basis for the democratic peace and to the ability of democracies to commit themselves to international agreements. A culture that emphasizes the nonviolent resolution of domestic conflict encourages a state to employ such methods in its external relations, and indeed, there is empirical evidence that governments that use force against their own people are more likely to use the military against their neighbors (Rummel 1997). All these forces for peace operate most effectively in relations between democratic states. Kant did not believe that democracies would never fight, only that they would avoid unnecessary conflict. In their relations with nondemocratic states willing to use force, democracies, too, will resort to the older, more terrible logic of realism.

... Even controlling for the pacifying effects of interdependence and joint memberships in intergovernmental organizations, we found that two democracies are 33 percent less likely than the average dyad to become involved in a militarized dispute. This is a conservative estimate of the pacific benefits of democracy, because we have also shown that democracies are more likely to trade with one another and to join the same international organizations. Democracy has, therefore, important indirect benefits through these other Kantian elements. We have also seen that the risk of conflict declines as the proportion of democracies in the international system increases. As their number grows, democracies seem able to influence international norms and institutions, thereby affecting the probability that force will be used even by states that are not themselves particularly democratic. This influence is also plausible because democracies are more likely to win their wars than autocracies are. Consequently, autocracies must be concerned about the security implications of weakening themselves in war, whether the war is with democracies or other autocracies. They must become increasingly careful as the number of democracies in the system grows. This systemic influence is another indirect benefit of democracy for peace.

* * *

Democracies act according to realist principles in their dealings with autocracies, but they are no more likely to fight with an autocracy than is another autocratic state. This is important. It means that a newly established democracy will be at peace with its democratic neighbors, and being democratic will not make it more prone to fight autocratic neighbors than if it had remained nondemocratic.... [T]he process of democratization does not generally increase the likelihood of conflict, as some have feared. It is the *level* of democracy that influences the likelihood of conflict, not how recently these political institutions were established. Thus, if policies designed to promote democracy around the world lead promptly to the consolidation of democratic institutions and practices, there is no reason, even in the short term, to expect an increase in the frequency of violence between countries.

Interest in the pacific benefits of economic interdependence preceded even Kant's treatise on perpetual peace. In the early seventeenth century, the French philosopher Emeric Cruce argued that wars arose from international misunderstandings and the domination of society by the warrior class but that both causes of interstate violence could be ameliorated by commerce: trade and investment create common interests for commercial partners; increase the prosperity and political power of the peaceful, productive members of society; and encourage mutual understanding. Though over the years many philosophers, historians, economists, and politicians have expressed confidence in the conflict-reducing consequences of international commerce, the British liberals deserve particular credit for developing and promoting this argument. David Ricardo, for example, wrote in 1817:

> Under a system of perfectly free (international) commerce, each country naturally devotes its capital and labour to such employments as are most beneficial to each. This pursuit of individual advantage is admirably connected with the universal good of the whole. By stimulating industry, by rewarding ingenuity, and by using most efficaciously the peculiar powers bestowed by nature, it distributes labour most effectively and most economically while, by increasing the general mass of production, it diffuses general benefit, and binds together, by one common tie of interest and intercourse, the universal society of nations. (Quoted in Cole 1999, 185)

As with democracy, the pacific benefits of interdependence do not depend on people everywhere becoming convinced that war is immoral. Instead, the classical liberals emphasized that the "pursuit of individual advantage," as Ricardo put it, leads to actions that link individuals and nations by interdependent ties of mutual benefit. Interdependence increases the prospects for peace because individuals can generally be expected to pursue their interests rationally, and it is not in the interest of one state to fight another with which it has important economic relations.

While liberals emphasize the role of reason and self-interest in explaining the pacific benefits of interdependence, the constructivist school of international relations calls attention to the collateral benefits of commerce for people's understanding of one another. Trade and foreign investment serve as media for communication between nations on a broad range of matters beyond their specific commercial relations, thereby exposing people to the ideas and perspectives of others on a range of issues. These communications, too, are apt to be important channels for averting interstate conflict. As interdependence grows, it contributes to the creation of a security community (Deutsch et al. 1957), in which shared values make a resort to force unimaginable.... [T]rade also encourages the development of international law and organizations. This occurs for the same reason that such institutions arise in domestic societies: they are needed to regulate and manage commercial relations. In a variety of ways, then, international trade and investment are expected to increase the likelihood of peace.

While Crucé advocated free trade as a means to promote peace long before any state had become truly democratic, contemporary social scientists ... have been relatively slow to appreciate the important role that interstate commerce, too, can play. Much of the explanation for this can be traced to the effect of

World War I on the liberal view. Just before that war, Sir Norman Angell published a book called *The Great Illusion* (1911). He argued that the most important states of Europe had become so interdependent that war could no longer serve their economic interests. Angell's book was well received, especially because many feared there might be a war between England and Germany. Indeed, the two countries were engaged in a dangerous naval arms race. *The Great Illusion* was translated into seventeen languages and sold over a million copies. Many came to believe that Angell had proven that war was impossible. He had not, as the events of 1914–18 soon demonstrated. Although the states of Europe were more interdependent than they had ever been, a terrible war still erupted. It was not a limited war of the type Europe had experienced on several occasions since the defeat of Napoleon in 1815; it was the "Great War."

Angell did *not* argue that interdependence made war impossible. It was not war that was the great illusion. Rather, it was the belief, then common, that war could serve national economic interests: that a state, by successful military action, could secure new sources of raw materials or access to new markets, or could seize territory from a bordering state and incorporate its wealth. The tremendous financial cost of World War I—not to mention the loss of ten million lives—and the collapse of the international economy in the Great Depression proved that Angell had not been mistaken. It *is* an illusion to believe that when states are interdependent, force can be used without incurring economic loss: the more interdependent the states, the greater the cost of military conflict. That was what Angell had tried to say. He published *The Great Illusion* to educate Europeans regarding the nature of their interdependence. Angell hoped to show that war in the modern world was unprofitable and, thereby, to avert the war that so many feared. For his efforts, Angell was awarded the Nobel Peace Prize for 1933.[1]

Our analyses show that Kant, Ricardo, Angell, and the other classical liberals were correct. The use of military force does adversely affect states' commercial relations.... [M]ilitary disputes reduce the level of bilateral trade. Interstate conflict does have economic costs. Some of the gains of trade are lost even at low levels of violence. The logical consequence is that states will try to avoid conflict when their commercial relations are economically important.... [T]wo states with a relatively high level of bilateral trade are 33 percent less likely to become involved in a dispute than are states with an average level of interdependence, all other things being equal.... [T]his benefit is not limited to states of roughly equal size. Asymmetry in the economic importance of trade, as is characteristic of the commercial relations of a large and a small country, does not reduce the benefits of trade or provoke military conflict, as many have feared. Furthermore, states that are open to the global economy are more peaceful than average, even controlling for the level of their bilateral interdependence. A state that trades a lot with any country or group of countries—that is open economically—is constrained from using force, even against states with which its commercial ties are limited. Indeed, ... the total trade-to-GDP ratio has nearly as large a beneficial effect on the prospects for peace as the bilateral trade-to-GDP ratio does.

* * *

Finally, we considered the consequences of shared memberships in inter-governmental organizations on the risk that two states will become involved in a militarized dispute. States that are in close and frequent contact, like indivi-duals, inevitably disagree on what should be done, who should bear costs incurred in mutually beneficial enterprises, or what is the fair division of joint gains. They experience conflict in the broadest meaning of that word. This is true of the United States and Canada, the United States and Japan or Europe, and among the states of the European Union. What is needed are nonviolent means of resolving conflict when it does arise. Kant suggested that a loose federation of sovereign (but interdependent) states could aid in preserving the peace.

The literature on the contribution of particular international organizations to world peace is vast, but there are few social scientific studies of how IGOs in general affect interstate relations. Do dense networks of intergovernmental organizations reduce the incidence of interstate violence? Many international relations scholars believe that international organizations are relatively unim-portant because they lack the means of enforcing their decisions. Whatever authority IGOs have, they argue, is simply derivative of the power of their members. In fact, few international organizations can force compliance with their directives or with international law by coercive means; nevertheless, they frequently perform many other functions associated with governments. They may encourage cooperation by facilitating consultation and coordina-tion among their members. They may create norms that make noncompliance with their decisions politically difficult. More centralized IGOs can impose various economic sanctions: allow states to impose countervailing tariffs, freeze assets, refuse to grant loans, prohibit commercial aviation or shipping, for instance....

Our analyses indicate that a dense network of IGOs does reduce the incidence of conflict. A pair of states that shares membership in a substantial number of international organizations is 24 percent less likely than average to have a dispute, holding other influences constant. Other research ... shows that the pacific benefits of intergovernmental organizations are smaller than those of democracy or economic interdependence. And the estimated effect of IGOs is more dependent on the precise form of the test. It is important to note, however, that evidence for the constraining effect of IGOs is strongest for what we have called the politically relevant dyads—contiguous pairs of states and pairs that include at least one major power—and that these dyads account for the great majority of interstate disputes. It may be, too, that the constructive role played by IGOs is captured in some statistical analyses by the measures of democracy and trade. We know that democracies and economically interdependent states

are involved together in more IGOs: cooperation seems to grow naturally out of the affinity liberal states have for one another. The pacific benefits of international organizations may be largely derivative of these more fundamental liberal factors. This does not mean IGOs are unimportant. If they were, liberal states would not create and join them, but the contribution of intergovernmental organizations to maintaining the peace in some tests may largely be subsumed by the measures of democracy and interdependence.

The summary of our findings thus far understates the pacific contribution of the Kantian system because we have emphasized the independent contributions of each of its three elements. In the real world, one Kantian influence does not usually increase while the others are held constant. Rather, as Kant anticipated, democracies tend to be interdependent and members of the same IGOs. There are also important feedback loops connecting trade and international organizations. And it may be that economically important trade opens up societies to external influences, making it hard to sustain autocratic rule. This last possible link is outside the scope of our current research, but it does seem consistent with the experiences of Eastern Europe and even China. Good things do often go together. It is important, therefore, to recall that the likelihood of a dispute drops by 71 percent if all the Kantian influences are increased simultaneously. This clearly shows that, as Kant was bold to say, peace is possible.

In our view, peace is not only possible, it is becoming more and more likely. The prognosis for the future of international relations is good because democracy is likely to spread and interdependence to increase. The reasons are simple: people prefer self-government to authoritarian rule, and they would rather enjoy the prosperity that comes from interdependence than remain isolated and poor. But if these long-term influences are to have the opportunity to have their beneficial effects, the West and other members of the Kantian system will need to deal successfully with the challenge posed by the inevitable recovery of Russia and the continued growth of China. These countries will have to be integrated into the Kantian system....

* * *

The False Hope of Hegemony

* * *

There are good reasons for optimism. We have seen that the three Kantian elements substantially reduce the danger of war, and we can reasonably expect that the number of democracies and their economic interdependence will increase. People naturally desire to be free, to govern themselves in order that they may enjoy liberty. As a consequence, democracy will be preferred to authoritarianism. People also desire prosperity. They would rather be rich than poor. The collapse of the Soviet bloc is evidence that this entails capitalism in some form (Fukuyama 1992). Free markets lead to specialization according to comparative advantage and international trade, a tendency that seems bound to increase as the costs of communication and transportation continue to decline. In turn, the growth of democracy and interdependence encourages the rise of international organizations and law to facilitate interstate relations.

Peace does not depend, therefore, on people being transformed into angels, but on constructing a system of incentives whereby even self-seeking devils would be well behaved "so long as they possess understanding" (Kant [1795] 1970, 112). For Kant, a philosopher of the Enlightenment, the causal sequence leading to perpetual peace was evidence of an ordered universe and, perhaps, of providential design. Yet he did not think that the process was determined or the outcome certain (Bohman and Lutz-Bachmann 1997; Williams and Booth 1999). Reason will not inevitably prevail because individuals do not always act in ways that are consistent with their long-term interests. Human affairs are not governed by mechanistic laws like those that regulate the tides: People must learn from experience, including the experience of war, and choose to change their behavior. The outcome is not certain, but there is hope because

> states find themselves compelled to promote the noble cause of peace, though not exactly from motives of morality.... Nature guarantees perpetual peace by the actual mechanism of human inclinations. And while the likelihood of its being attained is not sufficient to enable us to *prophesy* the future theoretically, it is enough for practical purposes. It makes it our duty to work our way towards this goal, which is more than an empty chimera. (Kant [1795] 1970, 114; italics in original)

For the foreseeable future, military force will remain an important tool for preventing and rebuffing aggression. Some states remain outside the Kantian system and can be dangerous. But force no longer needs to be the chief means of maintaining peace—nor, because of the risks created by modern weapons, can it continue to be. Deterrence is unnecessary in most situations because international politics is not an unending violent struggle. Assuming that everyone is a potential enemy is a mistake, and a poor guide to action. It risks becoming a self-fulfilling prophecy that is ultimately self-defeating.

A different kind of world can be nurtured, one in which most conflicts of interests are not managed primarily by the threat of violence. Democracy and free enterprise already govern much of the global polity and economy. Those—whether Asian authoritarians, religious fundamentalists, or Western postmodernists—who reject one or the other do so in tones more defensive than confident. The Kantian conditions for peace should be enhanced by Western economic and political assistance to countries willing to liberalize their political and economic systems. It is important to help them achieve a high level of democracy smoothly and rapidly. This is cheaper than building the arms necessary for survival in a world governed by realist principles.... [T]ransitions to democracy do not make international conflict more likely, and ... the pacific benefits of international commerce are not confined to states of similar size: neither democratization nor asymmetric interdependence increases the likelihood of interstate violence. The benefits of liberalism need not be confined, therefore, to the powerful. Nor should the powerful seek to impose liberalism on others.[2]

Extending the Kantian system will require cooperation. Multilateralism will be crucial. The United States has a major role to play, but if it is to lead effectively, it cannot do so through the unilateral exercise of power. It will have to appeal to shared beliefs and perceptions about what actions are legitimate. The less the disparity in capabilities between the leading state and others, the more the leading state must articulate and respect the common principles that unite them. In many cases, the specific means by which these principles are to be advanced is subject to debate; nevertheless, agreement is often possible, as the recent interventions in Iraq, Somalia, Haiti, Bosnia, and Kosovo indicate. Power provides an opportunity for leadership, but it also creates the danger of oppression. It behooves the United States to be constrained by other states' perceptions of what is just and proper. Multilateralists understand that. In 1990, President George Bush used that understanding to assemble, under UN auspices, the coalition that fought the Gulf War.

If multilateralism is to be effective, international organizations will have to play an important role. The United Nations in particular deserves support. Other countries must believe, however, that the UN and other international institutions serve their interests as well as those of the United States. Those institutions need to be enhanced, not gutted. In the longer term, the composition and procedures of key organizations, such as the UN Security Council, will have to be critically and imaginatively reconsidered and constructive reforms undertaken (Hurd 1999; Russett 1997). The United States will be in a stronger position to lead if it supports the United Nations. Its leadership and its ability to promote democracy in other countries will suffer if it behaves undemocratically with its allies and in international organizations.

The United States has undermined its moral authority in recent years by refusing to sign or to ratify a long list of multilateral treaties, covering just about the full spectrum of international issues. These include the Comprehensive Test Ban Treaty, the Land Mines Convention, the Law of the Sea Convention, the International Convention on the Rights of the Child, the treaty to establish a permanent International Criminal Court, and the Kyoto Protocol on global warming. None of these agreements is flawless, and they should be improved, but most other countries have ratified them or will do so. The war over Kosovo should have been brought to the UN Security Council at an early stage for its approval. Washington is still grudging about fulfilling its legal obligations to pay its United Nations dues, threatens to abrogate the Anti-Ballistic Missile Treaty if Russia will not accept a U.S. system of missile defense, and moves ever more overtly toward making nuclear threats to deter the use of biological and chemical weapons, thereby violating its pledge in support of the Nuclear

Non-Proliferation Treaty. Watching all this, even some of America's friends perceive the United States as a state that invokes international law to bind others but ignores it when it seems in its immediate self-interest to do so.

A country with only 4 percent of the world's population cannot indefinitely act unilaterally with impunity. If the world is to escape the sword hanging over it, the United States will need not just the approval but the active support of the allies that stood with it during the cold war as well as of those that can be brought into the Kantian community in the future. Some Americans might prefer a different kind of world. Isolationists want to avoid exercising power abroad, but they are not always ready to live with the consequences of inaction. Unilateralists are prepared to use military force in pursuit of important national interests without much concern for international support and to expand the military budget while cutting support for international institutions. But the unipolar character of our world is inevitably transitory. It does provide, however, an opportunity to create a more peaceful world, one based not so much on military force as on the principles of democracy, interdependence, and international cooperation. Kant would say it is a moral imperative.

Notes

1. Our discussion of Angell benefited from reading Miller 1986.
2. Accepted principles of sovereignty prohibit fighting a war for the purpose of changing another state's form of government. Kant ([1797] 1970, 168–70) accepted war to resist blatant aggression, never to punish or subjugate. In a just postwar settlement, however, he thought the victor might require a defeated aggressor to adopt a republican constitution so as to discourage its warlike inclinations. See Orend 1998.

References

Angell, Norman. 1911. *The Great Illusion: A Study of the Relation of Military Power in Nations to Their Economic and Social Advantage.* New York: Putnam.

Bohman, James, and Matthias Lutz-Bachmann, eds. 1997. *Perpetual Peace: Essays on Kant's Cosmopolitan Ideal.* Cambridge, MA: MIT Press.

Cole, Matthew A. 1999. Examining the Environmental Case against Free Trade. *Journal of World Trade* 33: 183–96.

Deutsch, Karl W., Sidney Burrell, Robert Kahn, Maurice Lee, Martin Lichterman, Raymond Lindgren, Francis Loewenheim, and Richard Van Wagenen. 1957. *Political Community and the North Atlantic Area.* Princeton, NJ: Princeton University Press.

Fukuyama, Francis. 1992. *The End of History and the Last Man.* New York: Free Press.

Hurd, Ian. 1999. Legitimacy and Authority in International Politics. *International Organization* 53 (2): 379–408.

Kant, Immanuel. [1795] 1970. *Perpetual Peace: A Philosophical Sketch.* Reprinted in *Kant's Political Writings,* edited by Hans Reiss. Cambridge: Cambridge University Press.

————. [1797] 1970. The Metaphysics of Morals. Reprinted in *Kant's Political Writings,* edited by Hans Reiss. Cambridge: Cambridge University Press.

Miller, J. D. B. 1986. *Norman Angell and the Futility of War: Peace and the Public Mind.* Basingstoke, Hampshire: Macmillan.

Orend, Brian. 1998. Kant on International Law and Armed Conflict. *Canadian Journal of Law and Jurisprudence* 11 (2): 329–81.

Rummel, R. J. 1997. *Power Kills: Democracy as a Method of Non-Violence.* New Brunswick, NJ: Transaction.

Russett, Bruce, ed. 1997. *The Once and Future Security Council.* New York: St. Martin's.

Schultz, Kenneth. 2000. *Democracy and Bargaining in International Crises.* Cambridge: Cambridge University Press.

Williams, Howard, and Ken Booth. 1999. Kant: Theorist beyond Limits. In *Classical Theories of International Relations,* edited by Ian Clark and Iver Neumann, New York: St. Martins.

CREDITS

Introduction: Why We Disagree about International Relations

I.1 Excerpted from Hans J. Morgenthau, "The Dilemma of Scientific Man," in *Scientific Man vs. Power Politics* (Chicago: University of Chicago Press, 1946), 1–10. © 1946 by The University of Chicago. All rights reserved. Reprinted by permission of the University of Chicago Press.

I.2 Excerpted from Peter J. Katzenstein and Nobuo Okawara, "Japan, Asian-Pacific Security, and the Case for Analytical Eclecticism," *International Security* 26, no. 3 (2001–2002): 153–185. © 2001 by the President and Fellows of Harvard College and the Massachusetts Institute of Technology. Reprinted by permission of MIT Press Journals.

Chapter 1: How to Think about International Relations: Perspectives and Levels of Analysis

1.1 Excerpted from E. H. Carr and Michael Cox, "The Realist Critique," in *The Twenty Years' Crisis, 1919–1939: An Introduction to the Study of International Relations* (Basingstoke, UK: Palgrave, 2001 [1940]), 62–83. © 1981 E. H. Carr. Reprinted by permission of Palgrave Macmillan.

1.2 Excerpted from Robert O. Keohane and Joseph S. Nye, "Realism and Complex Interdependence," in *Power and Interdependence: World Politics in Transition* (Boston: Little, Brown, 1977), 23–37. © 2001 by Robert O. Keohane and Joseph S. Nye. Reprinted by permission of Addison-Wesley Educational Publishers, Inc.

1.3 Excerpted from Alexander Wendt, "Anarchy Is What States Make of It: The Social Construction of Power Politics," *International Organization* 46, 2 (1992): 391–425. © 1992 by the World Peace Foundation and the Massachusetts Institute of Technology. Reprinted by permission of MIT Press Journals.

1.4 From Milja Kurki, "Karl Marx," in *Critical Theorists and International Relations*, ed. Jenny Edkins and Nick Vaughan-Williams (London and New York: Routledge, 2009), 246–250. © 2009 Milja Kurki. Reproduced by permission of Taylor & Francis Books UK.

1.5 From Leo Panitch, "Thoroughly Modern Marx: Lights. Camera. Action. *Das Kapital*. Now," *Foreign Policy* no. 172 (May–June 2009): 140–145. Copyright 2009 by *Foreign Policy*. Reproduced with permission of *Foreign Policy* via the Copyright Clearance Center.

1.6 From J. David Singer, "The Level-of-Analysis Problem in International Relations," *The International System: Theoretical Essays,* special issue of *World Politics* 14, no. 1 (1961): 77–92. © Trustees of Princeton University. Reprinted by permission of Cambridge University Press.

Chapter 2: Perspectives on World History: Change and Continuity

2.1 Excerpted from Paul Schroeder, "Historical Reality vs. Neo-realist Theory," *International Security* 19, no. 1 (1994): 108–148. © 1994 by the President and Fellows of Harvard College and the Massachusetts Institute of Technology. Reproduced with permission of MIT Press Journals via the Copyright Clearance Center.

2.2 Excerpted from Stuart J. Kaufman, "The Fragmentation and Consolidation of International Systems," *International Organization* 51, no. 2 (1997): 173–208. © 1997 by the IO Foundation and the Massachusetts Institute of Technology. Reprinted by permission of MIT Press Journals.

2.3 Excerpted from Martha Finnemore, "Intervention and International Order," in *The Purpose of Intervention: Changing Beliefs about the Use of Force* (Ithaca and London: Cornell University Press, 2003), 85–140. Copyright © 2003 by Cornell University. Used by permission of the publisher, Cornell University Press.

Chapter 3: World War I: World on Fire

3.1 Excerpted from Marc Trachtenberg, "The Coming of the First World War: A Reassessment," in *History and Strategy* (Princeton, N.J.: Princeton University Press, 1991), 47–99. © 1991 Princeton University Press. Reprinted by permission of Princeton University Press.

3.2 Excerpted from Dale C. Copeland, "The July Crisis and the Outbreak of World War I," in *The Origins of Major War* (Ithaca: Cornell University Press, 2000), 79–117. Copyright © 2000 by Cornell University. Used by permission of the publisher, Cornell University Press.

Chapter 4: World War II: Why Did War Happen Again?

4.1 Excerpted from Mark L. Haas, "The 1930s and the Origins of the Second World War," in *The Ideological Origins of Great Power Politics, 1789–1989* (Ithaca and London: Cornell University Press, 2005), 105–120. Copyright © 2005 by Cornell University. Used by permission of the publisher, Cornell University Press.

4.2 Excerpted from Chapters 1 and 5 in Charles A. Beard, *President Roosevelt and the Coming of the War, 1941: A Study in Appearances and Realities* (New Haven: Yale University Press, 1948), 1, 8, 573–584, 590–598. Reprinted by permission of Transaction Publishers.

Chapter 5: The Origins and End of the Cold War

5.1 George Kennan, "The Long Telegram," February 22, 1946. Reproduced from the Harry S. Truman Administration File, Elsey Papers, at the Harry S. Truman Library and Museum, accessed at http://www.trumanlibrary.org/whistlestop/study_collections/cold

war/documents/index.php?documentdate=1946-02-22&documentid=6-6&studycollec
tionid=&pagenumber=1.

5.2 Nikolai Novikov, "Telegram from N. Novikov, Soviet Ambassador to the U.S., to the Soviet Leadership," September 27, 1946. Reproduced from the Woodrow Wilson International Center for Scholars, Cold War International History Project, Virtual Archive, www.cwihp.org. Reprinted by permission of the Woodrow Wilson International Center for Scholars.

5.3 Excerpted from John Lewis Gaddis, "Reagan, Gorbachev, and the Completion of Containment," in *Strategies of Containment: A Critical Appraisal of American National Security Policy during the Cold War,* rev. ed. (New York: Oxford University Press, 2005), 342–373. Copyright © 1982, 2005 by Oxford University Press, Inc. Reprinted by permission of Oxford University Press.

5.4 From Richard Ned Lebow and Janice Gross Stein, "Deterrence and the End of the Cold War," in *We All Lost the Cold War* (Princeton, N.J.: Princeton University Press, 1994), 369–376. © 1994 Princeton University Press. Reprinted by permission of Princeton University Press.

Chapter 6: From 11/9 to 9/11: The World of the 1990s

6.1 Excerpted from Francis Fukuyama, "The End of History?" *National Interest* no. 16 (summer 1989): 107–114. Copyright © 1989 by Francis Fukuyama for *The National Interest.* Reprinted by permission of International Creative Management, Inc.

6.2 Excerpted from Samuel P. Huntington, "The Clash of Civilizations?" *Foreign Affairs* 72, no. 3 (1993): 22–49. Reprinted by permission of *Foreign Affairs.* Copyright 1993 by the Council on Foreign Relations, Inc. www.ForeignAffairs.com.

6.3 Excerpted from John J. Mearsheimer, "Great Power Politics in the Twenty-first Century," in *The Tragedy of Great Power Politics* (New York: W. W. Norton, 2001), 360–386. Copyright © 2001 by John J. Mearsheimer. Used by permission of W. W. Norton & Company, Inc.

Chapter 7: Terrorism and the World after 9/11: Religious, Ethnic, and National Conflicts

7.1 Excerpted from J. Ann Tickner, "Feminist Perspectives on 9/11," *International Studies Perspectives* 3 (2002): 333–350. © 2002 International Studies Association. Reprinted by permission of Wiley-Blackwell.

7.2 From Alissa J. Rubin, "How Baida Wanted to Die," *New York Times Magazine,* August 16, 2009. © 2009 *The New York Times.* All rights reserved. Used by permission and protected by the Copyright Laws of the United States. The printing, copying, redistribution, or retransmission of the Material without express written permission is prohibited.

7.3 Excerpted from Jeffrey W. Legro, "What China Will Want: The Future Intentions of a Rising Power," *Perspectives on Politics* 5, no. 3 (2007): 515–534. Copyright 2007 by the American Political Science Association. Reprinted with the permission of Cambridge University Press.

7.4 Excerpted from Jerry Z. Muller, "Us and Them: The Enduring Power of Ethnic Nationalism," *Foreign Affairs* 87, no. 2 (2008): 18–35. Reprinted by permission of *Foreign Affairs*. Copyright 2008 by the Council on Foreign Relations, Inc. www.Foreign Affairs.com.

7.4 (response to Muller) From Richard Rosecrance and Arthur Stein, "Separatism's Final Country," *Foreign Affairs* 87, no. 4 (2008): 141–145. Reprinted by permission of *Foreign Affairs*. Copyright 2008 by the Council on Foreign Relations, Inc. www.Foreign Affairs.com.

Chapter 8: History of Globalization: Mercantilism, Pax Britannica, and Pax Americana

8.1 Excerpted from Charles P. Kindleberger, "Dominance and Leadership in the International Economy: Exploitation, Public Goods, and Free Rides," *International Studies Quarterly* 25, no. 2 (1981): 242–254. © 1981 by the International Studies Association. Reprinted by permission of Wiley-Blackwell.

8.2 Excerpted from Robert Gilpin, "Economic Interdependence and National Security in Historical Perspective," in *Economic Issues and National Security,* ed. Klaus Knorr and Frank N. Trager (Lawrence, Kans.: Regents Press of Kansas for the National Security Education Program of New York University, 1977), 19–66. Copyright 1977 by Rosanna Ramey. Reproduced with permission of Rosanna Ramey via the Copyright Clearance Center.

Chapter 9: How Globalization Works in Practice

9.1 Excerpted from Martin Wolf, "The 'Magic' of the Market," in *Why Globalization Works* (New Haven and London: Yale University Press, 2005), 40–57. Copyright © 2004 Martin Wolf. Reprinted by permission of Yale University Press.

9.2 Excerpted from Chapters 1 and 5 in Dani Rodrik, *Has Globalization Gone Too Far?* (Washington, D.C.: Institute for International Economics, 1997), 2–7, 77–81. © 1997 by the Peterson Institute for International Economics. Reproduced with permission of the Peterson Institute for International Economics via the Copyright Clearance Center.

Chapter 10: Trade, Investment, and Finance: Engines of Growth

10.1 Excerpted from Paul Krugman, "The Economics of QWERTY," in *Peddling Prosperity: Economic Sense and Nonsense in the Age of Diminished Expectations* (New York: W. W. Norton, 1994), 221–244. Copyright © 1994 by Paul Krugman. Used by permission of W. W. Norton & Company, Inc.

10.2 Excerpted from Steven Dunaway, "Global Imbalances and the Financial Crisis," Council Special Report no. 44 (New York and Washington, D.C.: Council on Foreign Relations, March 2009), 1–44. Copyright © 2009 by the Council on Foreign Relations Press. Reprinted with permission.

Chapter 11: Miracle and Missed Opportunity: Development in Asia and Latin America

11.1 Excerpted from Joseph E. Stiglitz, "From Miracle to Crisis to Recovery: Lessons from Four Decades of East Asian Experience," in *Rethinking the East Asian Miracle,* ed. Joseph E. Stiglitz and Shahid Yusuf (New York: Oxford University Press, 2001), 509–526. © 2001 The International Bank for Reconstruction and Development/The World Bank. Reprinted by permission of The World Bank, Office of the Publisher.

11.2 Excerpted from Francisco Rodríguez, "An Empty Revolution: The Unfilled Promises of Hugo Chávez," *Foreign Affairs* 87, no. 2 (2008): 49–62. Reprinted by permission of *Foreign Affairs*. Copyright 2008 by the Council on Foreign Relations, Inc. www.Foreign Affairs.com.

Chapter 12: Foreign Aid and Domestic Governance: Development in Africa and the Middle East

12.1 Excerpted from United Nations Development Programme, Regional Bureau for Arab States (RBAS), "Towards the Rise of Women in the Arab World," in *The Arab Human Development Report 2005* (New York: United Nations Publications, 2006), 5–24. © 2006 by the United Nations Development Programme, Regional Bureau for Arab States. Reprinted by permission of the Regional Bureau for Arab States.

12.2 Excerpted from Jorge Arbache, Delfin S. Go, and John Page, "Is Africa's Economy at a Turning Point?" in *Africa at a Turning Point? Growth, Aid, and External Shocks,* ed. Delfin S. Go and John Page (Washington, D.C.: The International Bank for Reconstruction and Development/The World Pank, 2008), 13–85. © 2008 The International Bank for Reconstruction and Development/The World Bank. Reprinted by permission of The World Bank, Office of the Publisher.

12.3 "The Making, and Unmaking, of a Child Soldier" by Ishmael Beah appeared in the *New York Times Magazine,* January 14, 2007, and was adapted by the author from his book, *A Long Way Gone: Memoirs of a Boy Soldier* by Ishmael Beah. Copyright © 2007 by Ishmael Beah. Reprinted by permission of Farrar, Straus and Giroux, LLC.

Chapter 13: Global Inequality, Imperialism, and Injustice: A Critical Theory Perspective

13.1 Excerpted from Cynthia Enloe, "Carmen Miranda on My Mind: International Politics of the Banana," in *Bananas, Beaches, and Bases: Making Feminist Sense of International Politics* (Berkeley: University of California Press, 1989), 124–150. Copyright 1989 by Cynthia H. Enloe. Reproduced with permission of Cynthia H. Enloe via the Copyright Clearance Center.

13.2 Excerpted from Fernando Henrique Cardoso, "Dependent Capitalist Development in Latin America," *New Left Review* 74 (July–August 1972): 83–95. Reprinted by permission of *New Left Review*, London, UK.

Chapter 14: World Environment: Population, Pollution, and Pandemics

14.1 Reprinted from "Introduction" in Al Gore, *An Inconvenient Truth: The Planetary Emergency of Global Warming and What We Can Do About It* (New York: Rodale, 2006). Copyright © 2006 by Al Gore. Permission granted by Rodale, Inc., Emmaus, PA 18098.

14.2 From S. Fred Singer and Dennis T. Avery, "Is Humanity Losing the Global Warming Debate?" in *Unstoppable Global Warming: Every 1,500 Years* (Lanham, Md.: Rowman

& Littlefield, 2007), 1–19. Copyright © 2007 by S. Fred Singer and Dennis T. Avery. Reprinted by permission of Roman & Littlefield.

Chapter 15: Global Civil Society: Nonstate Actors and Basic Human Rights

15.1 Excerpted from "Introduction" in Anne-Marie Slaughter, *A New World Order* (Princeton, N.J.: Princeton University Press, 2004), 1–35. © 2004 by Princeton University Press. Reprinted by permission of Princeton University Press.

15.2 Excerpted from David P. Forsythe, "Transitional Justice: Criminal Courts and Alternatives," in *Human Rights in International Relations,* 2nd ed. (Cambridge, UK: Cambridge University Press, 2006), 89–120. © David P. Forsythe 2006. Reprinted with the permission of Cambridge University Press.

Chapter 16: Global Governance: International and Regional Institutions

16.1: Excerpted from Margaret P. Karns and Karen A. Mingst, "The Challenges of Global Governance," in *International Organizations: The Politics and Processes of Global Governance* (Boulder, Colo., and London: Lynne Rienner, 2004), 3–33. Copyright © 2004 by Lynne Rienner Publishers, Inc. Used with permission of the publisher.

16.2 Excerpted from Peter J. Katzenstein, "Regional Orders," in *A World of Regions: Asia and Europe in the American Imperium* (Ithaca, N.Y.: Cornell University Press, 2005), 43–75. Copyright © 2005 by Cornell University. Used by permission of the publisher, Cornell University Press.

Conclusion: Applying Perspectives and Levels of Analysis: The Case of the Democratic Peace

C.1 Excerpted from Bruce Russett and John R. Oneal, "The Kantian Peace in the Twenty-First Century," in *Triangulating Peace: Democracy, Interdependence, and International Organizations* (New York: W. W. Norton, 2001), 271–305. Copyright © 2001 by W. W. Norton & Company, Inc. Used by permission of W. W. Norton & Company, Inc.